BIBLIOTHECA AMERICANA

Catalogue of the John Carter Brown Library

IN BROWN UNIVERSITY

BOOKS PRINTED 1675-1700

Brown University Press   Providence   1973

International Standard Book Number: 0-87057-140-0

Library of Congress Catalog Card Number: 73-7120

Brown University Press, Providence, Rhode Island 02912

© 1973 by Brown University. All rights reserved

Published 1973

Printed in the United States of America

By Connecticut Printers, Inc.

On Mohawk Vellum

Bound by Stanhope Bindery

CONTENTS

Preface	vii
Introduction	xi
The Printed Catalogues	xi
Cataloguing Principles	xii
Catalogue Descriptions	xiii
Headings	xiii
Titles and Imprints	xiii
Collation	xiv
Notes	xvi
Reference Citations	xvi
Call Numbers and Accession Numbers	xvii
Analytical Entries	xvii
Supplemental Files in the Library	xvii
Books Cited in the Catalogue	xix
Abbreviations	xxxi
The Catalogue	1
Index	433

PREFACE

The John Carter Brown Library collects anything printed during the colonial period that reflects what happened as a result of the discovery and settlement of the New World. This collecting policy long ago carried the Library beyond the obvious Americana prized by collectors. Our many fields of interest have never been treated as separate entities; on the contrary, each new item--whether book, map, or print--is closely integrated with the rest of the collection, so that the history of America can be seen as a whole whether it is viewed from Europe, North America, or South America. As the collection has developed, new aspects of the fields of Americana have been recognized, and their significance has often been explored by scholars. This catalogue of books printed during the years 1675-1700 shows how the Library is implementing its collecting policy.

According to John Carter Brown, his first "American book" was purchased about 1830. At first Mr. Brown concentrated on New England theological works, but by 1846 his interests included the period of early discovery and exploration, and later, colonization of North America and the colonial wars of the eighteenth century. However, his collecting showed that he early recognized the broad implications of the concept "Americana," and every apparent extension of our collecting activities has been based upon directions indicated by a book or books that John Carter Brown himself purchased. His son John Nicholas Brown expanded the collection, notably in the fields of Spanish America and the history of cartography and geography.

In 1904, when the Library came to Brown University, a terminal imprint date of 1800 was formally adopted. The first librarian, George Parker Winship, moved into such new fields as early cosmography, the West Indies, and trade and commerce. His successor, Lawrence C. Wroth, continued growth in the directions indicated by his predecessors and made the Library outstanding in such fields as colonization tracts, the history of cartography, and American prints. Furthermore, he added a new dimension when he began to deal with the intellectual questions raised by the concept "America" in such fields as philosophy, the history of religion, the history of science, and areas that today are called political science, economics, and anthropology. In 1964, a new collecting policy was established consistent with these broadly based activities; it adopted the "colonial period" instead of the terminal date of 1800. The step-by-step growth of the Library can be traced in its Annual Reports, 1901-1966 (reprinted in 1972). We see our collection as a challenge to explore the meaning of the discovery of America, an event whose full implications are not yet understood.

To make its collections as widely known as possible and to further the study of early books about America, the Library has from time to time published printed catalogues. This volume, with the third printed catalogue of the Library, issued 1919-1931, and the Short-Title List of Additions--Books Printed 1471-1700, completes the record of books printed before 1701 that were in the Library on 1 July 1971. Together they are a lineal descendant of bibliographical tools for the study of early Americana that stretch back over two and a half centuries. When John Carter Brown began collecting, the only available guide was Bishop White Kennett's Bibliothecæ Americanæ Primordia: An Attempt towards Laying the Foundation of an American Library (1713), and Mr. Brown's interleaved and heavily annotated copy played an important role in the early years. Although White Kennett's definition of what was an American book was liberal, he listed only 717 items printed before 1701.

A welcome advance in early American bibliography was the publication in 1837 of Henri Ternaux-Compans's Bibliothèque américaine: ou Catalogue des ouvrages relatifs à l'Amérique qui ont paru depuis sa découverte jusqu'à l'an 1700 (1,153 items). Ternaux-Compans's work was the standard by which John Carter Brown measured his own progress, again indicated by his interleaved and annotated copy. And between 1846 and 1859 Mr. Brown took that measure when he purchased from Henry Stevens in London a substantial part of Ternaux-Compans's collection. By the beginning of the second half of the nineteenth century, Mr. Brown was a major collector in the field, a fact that was clear when in 1865 and 1866 he printed the first two volumes of his Bibliotheca Americana: A Catalogue of Books Relating to North and South America, covering the years 1493-1700. The remarkable total of 2,242 items in the two volumes of the second printed catalogue (printed in 1875 and 1882) was a 30 per cent increase over the previous edition and a clear indication that new ground in Americana had been broken. Since that time, continued effort by the Library has brought the number to 6,715 items for the years 1460-1700.

Half of the books described in this volume originated in England, and one quarter in Spain; French, Dutch, German, Portuguese, Italian, and Scandinavian books make up the remainder. That English books predominate can be explained on two counts. In the first place, John Carter Brown began his collection with English books--as did most other Anglo-American collectors. However, there is an explanation based on the events of the period. Almost half of the books deal with religion, and of this half, 56 per cent are Protestant works from England and its colonies, and 42 per cent are Roman Catholic works from Spain and its colonies; religious issues were comparatively stable in the Spanish colonies but not in the British. During the twenty-five years covered by this catalogue, the brief reign of James II and the Glorious Revolution directly affected colonial affairs. Among the effects was the establishment of the two Quaker colonies in Pennsylvania and West Jersey, and half of the English works recorded here are Quaker tracts. There is also a large group of Congregational writings--in which, not surprisingly, the Mather family occupies a prominent place.

The nonreligious books fall into eight different categories, the largest of which (18 per cent) consists of the usual Americana of the period: books and pamphlets dealing with the settlement and development of individual colonies. During this period, Great Britain was actively colonizing, and thus over half of these books are English. From Pennsylvania there are thirteen of the sixteen promotion tracts, and from Jersey all of the "Scottish Proprietor's Tracts"--including two that were hitherto unrecorded. Events in New England produced two groups of publications: twenty-two tracts inspired by Sir Edmund Andros's attempt to create the Dominion of New Eng-

Preface

land (fifteen are included in the catalogue) and fifteen tracts inspired by King Philip's War (all are included). Britain was actively colonizing the West Indies, too, and a substantial number of the books and pamphlets that resulted appear in this catalogue. Finally, ninety-six broadsides and tracts written during the abortive attempt to establish a Scottish colony on the Isthmus of Panama (Darien) at the end of the seventeenth century constitute the largest single group of British colonization material in this volume. Books and pamphlets about the colony continued to appear until 1715, and it is regrettable that those printed after 1700 must be excluded.

The next category in order of size consists of histories of discovery, exploration, and settlement and of the reprinted accounts of earlier voyages. In this literature French books account for 33 per cent of the total (including twenty-two editions of Hennepin's accounts of La Salle's exploration of the Mississippi). Perhaps the most complex problem in this volume was the bibliographical description of Melchisédech Thévenot's collections of voyages, which appeared over a period of thirty-three years in separate parts and were issued as bound volumes in baffling combinations: following the practice begun in the second and third printed catalogues with the De Bry and Hulsius voyages, an exhaustive study of the Thévenot publications has been provided. The next largest group of histories is the Spanish (just over 25 per cent). The fact that France and Spain, two Roman Catholic countries, produced 60 per cent of the items may reflect the stability of their colonial empires as compared with the still-expanding Protestant areas. The same explanation can probably be offered for the distribution in the next category--colonial laws. Here Spain and France account for 66 per cent of the publications.

The next categories do not occupy a large place on these pages, yet they represent some of the dynamic forces that were at work in the years 1675-1700. They are geography and cartography (seventy-one items), trade and commerce (sixty-eight items), and maritime history (sixty-two items, including twenty-four books on pirates and piracy). Over 50 per cent of these books are British or Dutch. The history of science is represented by seventy books, with natural history and astronomy predominating. The American Indian is dealt with in fifty publications, with Indian languages the leading subject.

This catalogue contains only about half of the works recorded in standard bibliographies of Americana for the period it covers; however, a third of the titles are new to the field. As the Library continues to grow, it will always be interested in acquiring recognized Americana that it does not have. But it is the works that give new dimension to the concept of America that we take the greatest pleasure in adding to our collection.

Finally, it should be emphasized that this printed record of the John Carter Brown Library holdings records a small part of the whole. Our collections for the eighteenth and early nineteenth centuries are at least eight times larger than those for the fifteenth through the seventeenth centuries, and the later periods are growing the fastest. Plans are being made for the publication of the catalogue for this later material.

This catalogue could not have been compiled without the work of those who found, selected, and acquired the books now in the Library, and the many staff members who have contributed to its preparation since 1957. Its foundations were laid out by the present Librarian in 1957. Most of the basic procedures were worked out and some of the cataloguing was done by William F. E. Morley,

PREFACE

who was succeeded by Samuel J. Hough. Since 1965, Donald L. Farren has had general responsibility for the various phases of production. Most of the cataloguing was done by Miss Ilse E. Kramer, who also compiled the index. The typing is chiefly the work of Mrs. John F. Garin. Mrs. Gary E. Daughn did most of the layout and mounting, and Woodley L. Wright photographed the pages.

Librarians of many other institutions have generously aided by contributing information. Lewis Stark of the New York Public Library and Frederick R. Goff of the Library of Congress have been especially helpful.

Thomas R. Adams
Librarian

INTRODUCTION

This volume describes books, pamphlets, broadsides, and atlases printed from 1675 through 1700. Manuscripts, prints, drawings, separate maps not in atlases, newspapers, and facsimiles are excluded, but they are represented in card files in the Library. Like earlier printed catalogues of the Library, this volume is arranged chronologically by date of imprint and is indexed by author and title. Three printed catalogues preceded this volume, each recording the books in the Library at the time of its publication and covering a shorter period than its predecessor. An outline of the history of the printed catalogues of the Library explains how this publication fits into the pattern of the preceding catalogues.

THE PRINTED CATALOGUES

First Catalogue

The first printed catalogue, Bibliotheca Americana: A Catalogue of Books Relating to North and South America in the Library of John Carter Brown of Providence, R.I., covered the period from 1493 (the date of the earliest book then in the Library) through 1800. It was edited by John Russell Bartlett and published in three parts in four volumes between 1865 and 1871. It listed 5,635 numbered items:

Part I: 1493-1600. Published 1865, 302 items

Part II: 1601-1700. Published 1866, 1,160 items

Part III, Vol. 1: 1701-1771. Published 1870, 1,809 items

Part III, Vol. 2: 1772-1800. Published 1871, 2,364 items (numbered 1,810-4,173 in continuation of Vol. 1)

Part III of the first printed catalogue was reissued by the Kraus Reprint Corporation in 1963.

Second Catalogue

The second printed catalogue was also issued under the title Bibliotheca Americana: A Catalogue of Books Relating to North and South America.... (A few presentation copies of Part I were issued under the title Bibliographical Notices of Rare and Curious Books Relating to America....) It brought coverage of the Library holdings up to date for the period 1482-1700. The catalogue was edited by John Russell Bartlett, the young John Nicholas Brown assisting him in the second part, and had numerous illustrations and critical and expository notes. It was published in two parts (issued in 1875 and 1882) and listed 2,242 numbered items:

Part I: 1482-1600. Published 1875, 600 items

Part II: 1601-1700. Published 1882, 1,642 items

Third Catalogue

The third printed catalogue, Bibliotheca Americana: Catalogue of the John Carter

INTRODUCTION

Brown Library in Brown University, Providence, Rhode Island, again brought the record of the Library holdings up to date, but only through 1674. It was prepared under the direction of Worthington C. Ford--except for the third volume, done under Lawrence C. Wroth--and differed from the earlier catalogues in that the bibliographical descriptions were more detailed and precise. It was published in three volumes in five parts and listed 3,737 unnumbered items:

- Volume I, Part I: to 1569. Published 1919, 820 items
- Volume I, Part II: 1570-1599. Published 1921, 512 items
- Volume II, Part I: 1600-1634. Published 1922, 748 items
- Volume II, Part II: 1634-1658. Published 1923, 818 items
- Volume III: 1659-1674. Published 1931, 839 items

The third printed catalogue was reissued by the Kraus Reprint Corporation between 1961 and 1965.

Present Volume and List of Additions

The present volume, beginning where the last volume of the third catalogue ended, covers the years 1675-1700 in 1,852 items. The Short-Title List of Additions published simultaneously with this volume lists books not represented in any of the printed catalogues of the Library and covers the years 1471-1700 in 1,126 unnumbered items. Both the cataloguing of the Library and the page layout of the present volume proceeded chronologically, and each year of imprint was finished in turn. But the Library acquired some books after work on their year of imprint was finished, and thus the Short-Title List of Additions includes some books printed between 1675 and 1700. Because of production requirements, however, no books that were acquired after June 1971 could be included in the present volume or the Short-Title List of Additions. Collectively, therefore, the third printed catalogue, the present volume, and the Short-Title List of Additions include all books printed before 1701 that were in the Library on the production cutoff date.

The present volume is an outgrowth of a decision made in 1959 to replace a shelving system and a card inventory that were no longer adequate for the operation of the Library with a new shelving system and a card catalogue with fuller descriptions. Because work proceeded chronologically, starting where the third printed catalogue had ended, it was possible to use the new cataloguing as copy for a card file and also for a continuation of the printed catalogue.

The traditions of the printed catalogues and the fact that they are used outside the Library as standard references required certain qualitative standards in the cataloguing. But in order to save space in the card format, certain limitations were placed on the information given and the way it was presented. A comparison of this volume with the third printed catalogue shows that the quasi-facsimile reproduction of title-pages has been simplified; the signing of the sheets of a book is usually not recorded; less information is given about the particular copy of a book catalogued (modern bindings are not described unless they are exceptional, and provenances, although recorded in the Library, are not recorded here); and a highly abbreviated style is used for notes. This volume, however, was not compiled directly from photographs of the cards (which would have increased the size of the catalogue and made it less readable) but from information taken from them.

CATALOGUING PRINCIPLES

Implicit in the choice of what to present in this volume is the belief that the books described are important both as material objects and because of the text they contain.

[xii]

Introduction

The cataloguing is intended to be compatible with current standard library practice and to bring out the special bibliographical and subject importance of the books in the Library. The principles underlying the catalogue descriptions are:

1. The cataloguing must describe a physically complete copy. It is not, therefore, necessarily based only on copies in the Library: when questions arise from examining a book in the Library or comparing it with descriptions of other copies, other collections are consulted, either by correspondence or by visit. Thus the cataloguing gathers information about copies of books in and outside the Library. If this information is important for the description of a book, it is recorded in the catalogue description when it is practicable to do so. Otherwise the information is recorded at the Library in the Bibliographical File. (See below, Supplemental Files in the Library.) If the John Carter Brown Library copy is imperfect, the fact is noted in the catalogue description. Whenever possible a facsimile of the imperfect part is obtained from another copy.

2. The cataloguing must avoid critical and interpretive commentary, which is more apt to encapsulate temporary bibliographical and historical fashions than adequately depict the various aspects of interest and importance of a book. The cataloguing uses title-page transcriptions, listings of contents, and reference citations to suggest the interest and importance of the books, especially the American interest (which is broadly conceived, as explained in the Preface).

CATALOGUE DESCRIPTIONS

Headings

The headings used in the catalogue and in the index are based on current library practice in the United States as established by the Library of Congress and the American Library Association. Statements of fact implied in headings (such as attributions of authorship, birth and death dates) have been independently verified.

Titles and Imprints

The title-page, a book's advertisement of itself, is generously transcribed with the aim of describing a book in terms taken from the book itself. Along with the title proper, certain other information is transcribed from the title-page whenever practicable (otherwise it is recorded in a note): the subject matter and scope of the book, the names (with some accompanying biographical information) of persons responsible for the form in which the text appears (e.g., authors, editors, translators); the relation of a particular book to earlier or concurrent (not later) appearances of the same text (shown by edition statements, for instance), and the relation of a book to other texts (when a book is part of a pamphlet exchange, for instance).

The imprint, essential to an understanding of a book, is transcribed in a separate paragraph completely and without change of the word order as it appears in the book. When a licensing statement or price line accompanies the imprint, it is included with the transcription of the imprint in the catalogue description.

Facts stated in an imprint, especially place and date of publication, are verified if there is reason to doubt them. When a book lacks a statement of place or date of publication in an imprint, this information is supplied as specifically as possible in cataloguing. When no specific place or date can reasonably be assigned, an approximation is given (for place, a country rather than a city; for date, a decade or approximate year rather than a specific year).

An imprint is taken for a catalogue description from wherever it appears as such in a book--on a title-page or at the end of the

Introduction

text. Brackets are not placed around the imprint statement in a catalogue description if the statement has been transcribed from anywhere in the book, but the source of the imprint is noted if it is not the title-page.

Normally a date of imprint is recorded as it appears in the imprint of a book regardless of whether it is reckoned according to Old Style or New Style. English and Scottish government documents require an exception to this practice because they are arranged in the catalogue according to New Style dates but their imprint dates are reckoned according to Old Style. If the imprint date of such a document in Old Style differs from its year of issue reckoned according to New Style, the year in New Style has been added in brackets to the imprint statement of the catalogue description.

Method of Transcription. Matter to be transcribed from a book is recorded according to a limited quasi-facsimile method. The first letter of a word is capitalized in transcription if that letter in the book is a capital. All other letters are transcribed as lower case. The wording of the book is followed exactly, with omissions indicated by dots of ellision. Punctuation, accentuation, and other diacritical marks are given as they appear in the book, to the extent they can be reproduced by a typewriter. Fraktur is transcribed in roman and is not noted in the catalogue description. The "e" sometimes placed over a vowel in Germanic languages is transcribed as an umlaut. Printed braces and brackets are reproduced by hand-drawn angle brackets. The indication sic has been used sparingly in view of the wide variation in spelling and punctuation during the period covered by this catalogue.

Brackets surround matter supplied by the cataloguer to distinguish it from matter transcribed. As explained above, brackets are not placed around an imprint if it is transcribed from any place in the book.

Collation

Paging and illustrations are described according to ALA Catalog Rules, Chicago, American Library Association, 1941 (preliminary edition), somewhat modified in practice at the Library. The 1941 rules, although never adopted generally by libraries, are useful for describing a diversified collection of rare books. They provide a practicable method--one short of full descriptive bibliography yet precise--for recording paging and illustrations in an extremely concise form.

Although the cataloguing principles call for a description of a physically complete copy, for certain atlases there can be no such standard of completeness. These atlases, although conceived of as entities by the issuer, consist of separately printed maps and other plates. The contents of a specific copy was determined by which state of a map or plate was available at a particular time from the issuer; moreover, the purchaser might often choose the particular maps or plates to be included in his copy. Descriptions of such atlases are necessarily more completely based on the contents of the Library copy than is the case with other books. But internal evidence, like printed registers of maps or contemporary manuscript indexes, is taken into account. (For an example of this, see Le Neptune François, 1693, and its continuations.) Maps fortuitously bound together are treated in the Library as separate maps and are not within the scope of this catalogue.

Pagination. Every printed page of a book is accounted for whether the book is in one volume or several. The term page (p.) is used in counting matter printed on both sides of each of a group of leaves. If the pages do not have printed numeration, the count is given within brackets. The term leaf (ℓ.) is used in counting matter printed on only one side of each of a group of leaves lacking printed numeration. The term leaf is also used in counting matter at the end of a book

[xiv]

Introduction

that is printed partly on both sides and partly on one side only of leaves lacking printed numeration. The term numbered leaf (numb. ℓ.) is used in counting matter with printed numeration that numerates by leaf rather than by page; it does not distinguish between leaves printed on one side or on both. The term preliminary leaf (p. ℓ.) is used in counting matter without printed numeration that precedes the main text of a book; it does not distinguish between leaves printed on one side or on both. In this catalogue an engraved title-page is considered a preliminary leaf and is counted in the paging statement, not in the illustration statement. (A note is also made to record an engraved title-page.)

When the page or leaf numbering of a book begins with 1 and is continuous, only the last number of the sequence is recorded. When a paging sequence does not begin with 1, both the beginning number and the last number are recorded. When the over-all numeration sequence in a book is interrupted and erroneously resumed so that the final number given in the book is erroneous, accurate shorter sequences are given in the collation. Errors in the printed numeration of a book that do not affect the accuracy of the final number of a sequence are ignored in the collation; but if errors in paging are useful for identifying recorded bibliographical variants, they are mentioned in a note. When the final number of a paging sequence is misprinted, that number is recorded in the collation and is followed in parentheses by the correct number. Any paging sequence recorded in a collation, whether taken from numeration printed in a book or counted by the cataloguer, runs normally with odd numbers on the rectos of leaves and even numbers on the versos unless an exception is noted. Blank leaves are not counted in the collation. (Blank leaves that are integral to a printed gathering of a book are noted when present in a copy catalogued, but their absence is not noted.)

Illustrations. Inserted illustrations, independent of any text gathering printed for a book but intended to be issued with the book, are recorded in the following terms: plate (pl.), covering both engravings and woodcuts without distinction; frontispiece (front.); portrait (port.); map; chart; plan; diagram (diagr.); table (tab.); and, as the occasion requires, genealogical table (geneal. tab.), coat of arms, music. Because the presence of this matter in a book is not otherwise brought out in the collation, the number of items of each type is specified when any type has more than one item.

Full-page illustrations on pages counted in a paging statement are recorded in the terms used for inserted illustrations and are also specified by number. They are recorded immediately following the paging statement and are preceded by the term included (incl.), meaning that they are included in the paging. Inserted illustrations in the same book are recorded in a separate illustration statement.

Illustrations occupying part of a page of text are recorded by the expression illus. and are not further specified unless they form an important feature of a book that would otherwise not be brought out.

Illustrations are further specified, as the occasion requires, as: colored (col.); engraved (engr.); double, occupying space equivalent to two facing pages (but the term double-page is used for maps); or folded (fold.), that is, not of double-page size, but folded to permit insertion in a book.

As explained above, an engraved title-page is not counted as a part of the illustration statement, but as a preliminary leaf in the paging statement.

Size. The size of each copy of a book catalogued is recorded to the nearest half centimeter. For bound books, the binding is measured rather than the leaves. (Size is given as information important in the operation of the Library rather than as descriptive bibliographical data.) For normal books, only height is recorded. For oblong books and for broadsides, height, followed by width, is recorded.

Format. Format is recorded in terms of the folding of the printed sheet, expressed in the following abbreviations:

fol.	folio
4º	quarto
8º	octavo
12º	duodecimo
1º	full-sheet broadside
1/2º	half-sheet broadside

Broadsides are specified as such in the collation. The term broadside is used for an unfolded single sheet or part of a sheet issued separately and printed on only one side.

Signatures. The signatures of a book are given only to clarify a collation that otherwise would be ambiguous or to distinguish recorded variants.

Notes

Notes provide information that cannot be adequately or effectively expressed in other sections of the catalogue description:

Authorship and contents

Persons responsible for the form in which a text appears (if not mentioned in the title transcription)

Textual contents important for an understanding of the scope and subject of a book, especially its American interest (if not mentioned in the title transcription)

Errata lists
Booksellers' advertisements

Material characteristics

Any feature of a perfect copy of a book not expressed by the collation

The source of a title or imprint transcription if not taken from the title-page of a book or from the caption and imprint at the foot of a broadside

Cancels observed in a book or recorded in the bibliographical literature treating it

A picture or design printed from an engraved plate, woodcut, or metal cut that appears on the title-page of a book. These are recorded by the expression cut on t.-p. and may be briefly described or identified by a reference. A design printed on a title-page from individual pieces of type is not noted.

Textual history and bibliographical relations

Place and date of the first publication of the text and the original title when different in the book catalogued. If the book catalogued is the first printing of the text, nothing is noted about publishing history.

Other issues and states of a book within the same edition, distinguished either by citing such features as paging errors, press figures, typographical variation, or by reference to a bibliographical publication

The latest date stated anywhere in a book (before which it could not have been issued)

A book to which the book catalogued is a supplement or reply

Characteristics of the copy catalogued

Errors in binding up the parts
Imperfections (missing, damaged, or illegible parts)
The presence of integral blank leaves
A binding contemporary with the publication date
An extra binding
Contemporary manuscript annotations
Other books bound in the same volume

Reference Citations

See Books Cited in the Catalogue for a list of the references cited in the catalogue descriptions.

The citations have been used to indicate which books appeared in an earlier printed

INTRODUCTION

catalogue of the Library; to refer to commentary on books in the annual reports of the Library; to refer to more detailed descriptions of books; and to place books in context among imprints of a place, among the works of an author, and within the literature of a subject. Whenever possible, a reference that indicates the subject of a book has been cited in preference to adding a note to the catalogue description. When a catalogue cited describes a copy of a book now in the Library, this is noted with the citation. (Noting this incidentally records provenance, but provenances are systematically recorded in one of the supplemental files in the Library mentioned below.)

Call Numbers and Accession Numbers

These are in the left margins of the catalogue descriptions. The accession numbers incorporate the dates individual copies were acquired by the Library.

Analytical Entries

A full, separate description is given in this catalogue of any section of a book that has a special title-page complete with imprint and whose paging and signatures are in sequences separate from the rest of the book. The section is also treated in the catalogue description of the larger entity to which it belongs. That this kind of section was intended to be issued as a part of a larger entity may be evident from a statement on a general title-page or from a common list of errata or of contents, but it is clear from their distinctive bibliographical characteristics that they could also have been issued separately. The catalogue entries are intended to clarify the relationship of the quasi-independent section and the book to which it belongs. For an example, see the treatment of Richard Blome's The present state of Algiers (1678) in relation to his A description of the island of Jamaica ... published ... together with the present state of Algiers (1678).

SUPPLEMENTAL FILES IN THE LIBRARY

The Bibliographical File contains any information encountered since the foundation of the Library about its books that cannot be recorded in this catalogue or in the other files mentioned below. It includes records of research, correspondence (often including facsimiles of parts of books) from and to individuals and institutions about copies of books located both in and outside the Library, cuttings from dealers' and auction catalogues, and facsimiles of parts of books that are imperfect in the Library copy. This file records the authority for statements made in the catalogue descriptions. It is arranged by the accession numbers of individual copies.

The Dictionary Card Catalogue of Books contains, in addition to the main and added entries indexed in this catalogue, subject cataloguing and information organized under form headings that bring together almanacs, atlases, booksellers' advertisements, colonization tracts, etc.

The Imprint File groups books according to the place in which they were printed.

The Provenance File groups books according to their previous owners.

The Dedicatees File groups books according to personal or institutional dedicatees.

The Engravers File contains names of engravers of title-pages.

For other catalogues and files in the Library treating portions of the collections not covered by this catalogue, see the handbook of the Library, Opportunities for Research in the John Carter Brown Library.

Donald L. Farren
Chief of Cataloguing

BOOKS CITED IN THE CATALOGUE

Actes royaux — Paris--Bibliothèque nationale--Département des imprimés. *Catalogue général des livres imprimés de la Bibliothèque nationale. Actes royaux.* Paris, 1910-60.

Aldis — Aldis, Harry G. *A list of books printed in Scotland before 1700.* [Edinburgh] 1904.

Andrade — Andrade, José María. *Catalogue de la riche bibliothèque de D. José Maria Andrade.* Leipzig, Paris, 1869.

Andrade, V de P — Andrade, Vicente de P. *Ensayo bibliográfico mexicano del siglo XVII.* 2.ed. Mexico, 1899-1900.

Arents — Arents, George. *Tobacco; its history illustrated by the books, manuscripts, and engravings in the library of George Arents, Jr. Together with ... notes by Jerome E. Brooks.* New York, 1937-52.

Arents (Adds.) — New York--Public Library--Arents Tobacco Collection. *Tobacco; a catalogue of the books, manuscripts and engravings acquired since 1942 in the Arents Tobacco Collection at the New York Public Library.* New York, 1958-

Armao — Armao, Ermanno. *Vincenzo Coronelli.* Firenze, 1944.

Arocena — Arocena, Luis A. "Noticia bibliográfica," in his *Antonio de Solís, cronista indiano.* Buenos Aires [1963]

Asher — Asher, G. M. *A bibliographical and historical essay on the Dutch books and pamphlets relating to New-Netherland, and to the Dutch West-India Company and to its possessions in Brazil, Angola, etc., as also on the maps, charts, etc., of New-Netherland.* Amsterdam, 1854-67.

Ayer-Captivities — Newberry Library, Chicago, Ill.--Edward E. Ayer Collection. *Narratives of captivity among the Indians of North America; a list of books and manuscripts on this subject in the Edward E. Ayer Collection of the Newberry Library.* Chicago [1912] *Supplement.* Chicago, 1928.

Books Cited in the Catalogue

BLH	Simón Díaz, José. Bibliografía de la literatura hispánica. Madrid, 1950-
BPL (Defoe)	Boston--Public Library. A catalog of the Defoe collection. Boston, 1966.
Backer	Backer, Augustin de. Bibliothèque de la Compagnie de Jésus. Nouv. éd. par Carlos Sommervogel. Bruxelles, Paris, 1890-1900; Paris, 1909-32.
Baer (Md.)	Baer, Elizabeth. Seventeenth century Maryland; a bibliography. Baltimore, 1949.
Baginsky	Baginsky, Paul Ben. "German works relating to America, 1493-1800; a list compiled from the collections of the New York Public Library," in New York Public Library. Bulletin, v.42-44, 1938-40.
Beristain	Beristain y Souza, José Mariano. Biblioteca hispano americana setentrional. 2.ed. Amecaneca, Mexico, 1883; Santiago de Chile, 1897.
Besterman(4)	Besterman, Theodore. A world bibliography of bibliographies and of bibliographical catalogues, calendars, abstracts, digests, indexes, and the like. 4th ed. Lausanne [1965-66]
Bibliografía Colombina	Academia de la Historia, Madrid. Bibliografía colombina; enumeración de libros y documentos concernientes á Cristobal Colón y sus viajes. Madrid, 1892.
Bibliotheca belgica	Marques typographiques des imprimeurs et libraires qui ont exercé dans les Pays-Bas, et marques typographiques des imprimeurs et libraires belges établis à l'étranger. Gand, La Haye, 1891-1923. (Bibliotheca belgica; bibliographie générale des Pays-Bas, fondée par Ferd. van der Haeghen, 2.sér., t. 18-19)
Bibl. Lindesiana	[Crawford, James Ludovic Lindsay, 26th earl of] Bibliotheca Lindesiana, vol. I-IV; catalogue of the printed books. [Aberdeen] 1910.
Bissainthe	Bissainthe, Max. Dictionnaire de bibliographie haïtienne. Washington, 1951.
Borba de Moraes	Moraes, Rubens Borba de. Bibliographia brasiliana. Amsterdam [1958]
Brinley	Brinley, George. Catalogue of the American library. Hartford, 1878-93.
Bristol	Bristol, Roger Patrell. Supplement to Charles Evans' American bibliography. Charlottesville [1970]

Books Cited in the Catalogue

Brunet	Brunet, Jacques-Charles. Manuel du libraire et de l'amateur de livres. Paris, 1860-65. Supplément. Paris, 1878-80.
Brushfield	Brushfield, T. N. A bibliography of Sir Walter Raleigh. Exeter, 1908.
Bygdén	Bygdén, Anders Leonard. Svenskt anonym- och pseudonym-lexikon. Upsala, 1898-1915.
CP	Roden, Robert F. "A bibliographical list of the issues of the Cambridge press," in his The Cambridge press, 1638-1692. New York, 1905.
Cal.S.P.Col.	Great Britain--Public Record Office. Calendar of state papers, Colonial series. London, 1860-
Camus: Thévenot	Camus, A. G. Mémoire sur la collection des grands et petits voyages, et sur la collection des voyages de Melchisédech Thévenot. 2.ptie. Paris, 1802.
Chavanne	Chavanne, Josef, Alois Karpf, and Franz, Ritter von Le Monnier. The literature on the polar-regions of the earth. Vienna, 1878.
Church	Church, E. D. A catalogue of books relating to the discovery and early history of North and South America forming a part of the library of E. D. Church. Compiled and annotated by George Watson Cole. New York, 1907.
Church(Eng.Lit.)	Church, E. D. A catalogue of books, consisting of English literature and miscellanea, ... forming a part of the library of E. D. Church. Compiled and annotated by George Watson Cole. New York, 1909.
Cioranescu(17)	Cioranescu, Alexandre. Bibliographie de la littérature française du dix-septième siècle. Paris, 1965-66.
Colmeiro	Colmeiro, Manuel. Biblioteca de los economistas españoles de los siglos XVI, XVII, XVIII. [Madrid, 1900] (In Academia de Ciencias Morales y Políticas, Madrid. Memorias, t.1, 3.ed.)
Cordier	Cordier, Henri. Bibliotheca sinica. 2.éd. Paris, 1904-08.
Crane and Kaye	Crane, R.S., and F. B. Kaye. A census of British newspapers and periodicals 1620-1800. Chapel Hill, N.C., 1927.
Cundall(Jam.)	Cundall, Frank. Bibliographia Jamaicensis; a list of Jamaica books and pamphlets, magazine articles, newspapers, and maps. Kingston, Jamaica [1902]

Cundall(Jam. Press)	Cundall, Frank. "The press and printers of Jamaica prior to 1820," in American Antiquarian Society, Worcester, Mass. Proceedings, v. 26, 1916.
Cundall(Jam. Supp.)	Cundall, Frank. Supplement to Bibliographia Jamaicensis. Kingston, Jamaica, 1908.
Cundall(WI)	Cundall, Frank. Bibliography of the West Indies (excluding Jamaica). Kingston, Jamaica, 1909.
Darlow and Moule	British and Foreign Bible Society--Library. Historical catalogue of the printed editions of Holy Scripture in the library of the British and Foreign Bible Society. Compiled by T. H. Darlow and H. F. Moule. London, 1903-11.
Davenport	Davenport, Frances Gardiner. European treaties bearing on the history of the United States and its dependencies. Washington, 1917-37.
De Puy	De Puy, Henry F. A bibliography of the English colonial treaties with the American Indians. New York, 1917.
Dexter(Cong.)	Dexter, Henry Martyn. "Collections toward a bibliography of Congregationalism," in his The Congregationalism of the last three hundred years, as seen in its literature. New York, 1880.
Dionne	Dionne, N.-E. Inventaire chronologique... Québec, 1905-09.
Eames(N.E.Cat.)	Eames, Wilberforce. Early New England catechisms. Worcester, Mass. 1898.
Eames(N.Y.)	Eames, Wilberforce. The first year of printing in New York, May 1693 to April 1694. New York, 1928.
Evans	Evans, Charles. American bibliography; a chronological dictionary of all books, pamphlets and periodical publications printed in the United States of America from the genesis of printing in 1639 down to and including the year 1820 [i.e. 1800]. Chicago, 1903-34; Worcester, Mass., 1955-59.
Faribault	Faribault, G. B. Catalogue d'ouvrages sur l'histoire de l'Amérique, et en particulier sur celle du Canada, de la Louisiane, de l'Acadie, et autres lieux, ci-devant connus sous le nom de Nouvelle-France. Québec, 1837.

Books Cited in the Catalogue

Ford(Mass.Brds.)	[Ford, Worthington Chauncey] Broadsides, ballads, &c. printed in Massachusetts, 1639-1800. Boston, 1922.
Ford(Mass.Laws)	Ford, Worthington Chauncey, and Albert Matthews. A bibliography of the laws of the Massachusetts Bay, 1641-1776. Cambridge, Mass., 1907.
Fulton(Boyle)	Fulton, J. F. A bibliography of Robert Boyle. Oxford, 1932-[33]
González (1952)	González de Cossío, Francisco. La imprenta en Mexico (1553-1820); 510 adiciones a la obra de José Toribio Medina. Mexico, 1952.
Graesse	Graesse, Jean George Théodore. Trésor de livres rares et précieux; ou, Nouveau dictionnaire bibliographique. Dresden, 1859-69.
Green(John Foster)	Green, Samuel Abbott. "Bibliographical list of titles printed by Foster," in his John Foster, the earliest American engraver and the first Boston printer. Boston, 1909.
Hanke (Las Casas)	Hanke, Lewis. Bartolomé de las Casas, 1474-1566; bibliografía crítica y cuerpo de materiales. Santiago de Chile, 1954.
Harrisse(BAV)	[Harrisse, Henry] Bibliotheca Americana vetustissima; a description of works relating to America published between the years 1492 and 1551. New York, 1866.
Harrisse(Colomb): Mémorial	Harrisse, Henry. "Dossiers et pièces judiciaires," in his Christophe Colomb; son origine, sa vie, ses voyages, sa famille, & ses descendants. Paris, 1884.
Harrisse(NF)	[Harrisse, Henry] Notes pour servir à l'histoire, à la bibliographie et à la cartographie de la Nouvelle-France et des pays adjacents 1545-1700. Paris, 1872.
Hatin	Hatin, Eugène. Bibliographie historique et critique de la presse périodique française. Paris, 1866.
Henríquez Ureña	Henríquez Ureña, Pedro. "Bibliografía de Sor Juana Inés de la Cruz," in Revue hispanique, v.40, 1917.
Hildeburn	Hildeburn, Charles R. A century of printing; the issues of the press in Pennsylvania, 1685-1784. Philadelphia, 1885-86.
Hildeburn (NY)	Hildeburn, Charles R. A list of the issues of the press in New York, 1693-1752. Philadelphia, 1889.

Books Cited in the Catalogue

Holmes(C.)	Holmes, Thomas James. Cotton Mather; a bibliography of his works. Cambridge, Mass., 1940.
Holmes(I.)	Holmes, Thomas James. Increase Mather; a bibliography of his works. Cleveland, Ohio, 1931.
Holmes(M.)	Holmes, Thomas James. The minor Mathers; a list of their works. Cambridge, Mass., 1940.
Hunt Bot. Cat.	Hunt, Rachel McMasters Miller. Catalogue of botanical books in the collection of Rachel McMasters Miller Hunt. Pittsburgh, 1958-61.
Huth Catalogue	Huth, Henry. The Huth library; a catalogue of the printed books, manuscripts, autograph letters, and engravings, collected by Henry Huth. London, 1880.
Icazbalceta (Apuntes)	García Icazbalceta, Joaquín. Apuntes para un catálogo de escritores en lenguas indígenas de América. Mexico, 1866.
Icazbalceta-Carlo	García Icazbalceta, Joaquín. Bibliografía mexicana del siglo XVI. Nueva ed., por Agustín Millares Carlo. Mexico, 1954.
Innocencio	Silva, Innocencio Francisco da. Diccionario bibliografico português. Lisboa, 1858-1923.
JCB(1)	Brown, John Carter. Bibliotheca Americana; a catalogue of books relating to North and South America in the library of John Carter Brown of Providence, R. I. With notes by John Russell Bartlett. Providence, 1865-71. Three parts.
JCB(2)	Brown, John Carter. Bibliotheca Americana; a catalogue of books relating to North and South America in the library of the late John Carter Brown of Providence, R.I. With notes by John Russell Bartlett. Providence, 1875-82. Two parts.
JCB(3)	Brown University--John Carter Brown Library. Bibliotheca Americana; catalogue of the John Carter Brown Library in Brown University, Providence, Rhode Island. Providence, 1919-31. Three parts.
JCBAR	Brown University--John Carter Brown Library. Annual report, 1901- Providence.
Jones(1938)	Jones, Herschel V. Americana collection of Herschel V. Jones; a check-list, 1473-1926. Compiled by Wilberforce Eames. New York, 1938.

Books Cited in the Catalogue

Kane(Promotion)	Kane, Hope Frances. "Notes on early Pennsylvania promotion literature," in Pennsylvania magazine of history and biography, April, 1939.
Karpinski	Karpinski, Louis C. Bibliography of mathematical works printed in America through 1850. Ann Arbor, 1940.
Knuttel	Hague--Koninklijke Bibliotheek. Catalogus van de pamfletten-verzameling berustende in de Koninklijke Bibliotheek. Bewerkt...door W.P.C. Knuttel. 'sGravenhage, 1889-1920.
Koeman	Koeman, Cornelis. Atlantes Neerlandici; bibliography of terrestrial, maritime, and celestial atlases and pilot books, published in the Netherlands up to 1880. Amsterdam, 1967-71.
Kress	Harvard University--Graduate School of Business Administration--Baker Library--Kress Library of Business and Economics. Catalogue... Boston, 1940-
Leclerc(1867)	Leclerc, Charles. Bibliotheca Americana. Paris, 1867.
Leclerc(1878)	Leclerc, Charles. Bibliotheca Americana. Paris, 1878. Supplément. no. 1-2. Paris, 1881-87.
Leite	Leite, Serafim. "Suplemento biobibliográfico," in his História da Companhia de Jesus no Brasil. Lisboa, Rio de Janeiro, 1938-50.
Lenox: Thévenot	Lenox Library, New York. Contributions to a catalogue of the Lenox Library, no. III: the voyages of Thévenot. New York, 1879.
McAlpin	New York--Union Theological Seminary--Library. Catalogue of the McAlpin collection of British history and theology. Compiled and edited by Charles Ripley Gillett. New York, 1927-30.
McCoy(Hand-list)	McCoy, J. C. Canadiana and French Americana in the library of J. C. McCoy; a hand-list of printed books. Grasse, 1931.
Macdonald(Dryden)	Macdonald, Hugh. John Dryden; a bibliography of early editions and of Drydeniana. Oxford, 1939.
McKerrow(Devices)	McKerrow, Ronald B. Printers' & publishers' devices in England & Scotland 1485-1640. London, 1913.
Maffei	Maffei, Eugenio, and Ramón Rúa Figueroa. Apuntes para una biblioteca española de libros, folletos y artículos, impresos y manuscritos, relativos al conocimiento y explotación de las riquezas minerales y á las ciencias auxiliares. Madrid, 1871-72.

Books Cited in the Catalogue

Medina(BHA)	Medina, José Toribio. Biblioteca hispano-americana (1493-1810). Santiago de Chile, 1898-1907.
Medina(Chile)	Medina, José Toribio. Biblioteca hispano-chilena (1523-1817). Santiago de Chile, 1897-99.
Medina(Filipinas)	Medina, José Toribio. Bibliografía española de las islas Filipinas (1523-1810). Santiago de Chile, 1897-[98]
Medina(Lima)	Medina, José Toribio. La imprenta en Lima (1584-1824). Santiago de Chile, 1904-07.
Medina(Manila)	Medina, José Toribio. La imprenta en Manila desde sus orígenes hasta 1810. Santiago de Chile, 1896.
Medina(Mexico)	Medina, José Toribio. La imprenta en México (1539-1821). Santiago de Chile, 1907-12.
Medina(Puebla)	Medina, José Toribio. La imprenta en la Puebla de los Angeles (1640-1821). Santiago de Chile, 1908.
Melzi	Melzi, Gaetano. Dizionario di opere anonime e pseudonime di scrittori italiani. Milano, 1848-59.
Meulman	Meulman, Isaac. Catalogus van de tractaten, pamfletten, enz. over de geschiedenis van Nederland, aanwezig in de bibliotheek van Isaac Meulman. Bewerkt door J. K. van der Wulp. Amsterdam, 1866-68.
Muller(1872)	Muller, Frederik. Catalogue of books, maps, plates on America. Amsterdam, 1872-75.
NYPL(Va.1907)	New York--Public Library. "List of works in the New York Public Library relating to Virginia," in its Bulletin, February-April, 1907.
Navarrete	Navarrete, Martín Fernández de. Biblioteca marítima española. Madrid, 1851.
Palau(1)	Palau y Dulcet, Antonio. Manual del librero hispano-americano. Barcelona, 1923-27.
Palau(2)	Palau y Dulcet, Antonio. Manual del librero hispano-americano. 2.ed. Barcelona, 1948-
Palmer	Palmer, Philip Motley. German works on America, 1492-1800. Berkeley, 1952. (University of California publications in modern philology, v.36, no.10)

Books Cited in the Catalogue

Paltsits(Hennepin)	Paltsits, Victor Hugo. "Bibliography of the works of Father Louis Hennepin," in Hennepin, Louis. *A new discovery of a vast country in America... Introduction, notes, and index by Reuben Gold Thwaites.* Chicago, 1903.
Parenti	Parenti, Marino. *Dizionario dei luoghi di stampa falsi, inventati o supposti in opere di autori e traduttori italiani.* Firenze, 1951.
Park	Park, Helen. "A list of architectural books available in America before the Revolution," in *Journal of the Society of Architectural Historians,* v.20, 1961.
Peeters-Fontainas (1965)	Peeters-Fontainas, Jean. *Bibliographie des impressions espagnoles des Pays-Bas méridionaux.* Niewkoop, 1965.
Pforzheimer	Pforzheimer, Carl. *The Carl H. Pforzheimer library, English literature, 1475-1700.* New York, 1940.
Phillips(Atlases)	U.S.--Library of Congress--Map Division. *A list of geographical atlases in the Library of Congress... Compiled under the direction of Philip Lee Phillips.* Washington, 1909-
Phillips(Maps)	U.S.--Library of Congress--Map Division. *A list of maps of America in the Library of Congress... By P. Lee Phillips.* Washington, 1901.
Pilling	Pilling, James Constantine. *Proof-sheets of a bibliography of the languages of the North American Indians.* Washington, 1885.
Pilling(Algonquian)	Pilling, James Constantine. *Bibliography of the Algonquian languages.* Washington, 1891.
Poggendorff	Poggendorff, Johann Christian. *J. C. Poggendorff's biographisch-literarisches Handwörterbuch.* Leipzig, 1863.
Pritzel	Pritzel, G. A. *Thesaurus literaturae botanicae.* Leipzig, 1872-[77]
Rahir	Rahir, Edouard. *Catalogue d'une collection unique de volumes imprimés par les Elzevier et divers typographes hollandais du XVIIe siècle.* Paris, 1896.
Retana	Retana, W. E. *Aparato bibliográfico de la historia general de Filipinas.* Madrid, 1906.
Rodrigues	Rodrigues, J. C. *Bibliotheca brasiliense; catalogo annotado dos livros sobre o Brasil e de alguns autographos e manuscriptos pertencentes a J. C. Rodrigues.* Rio de Janeiro, 1907.

Books Cited in the Catalogue

Rodrigues (Dom. Hol.)	Rodrigues, José Honório. Historiografia e bibliografia do domínio holandês no Brasil. Rio de Janeiro, 1949.
Sabin	Sabin, Joseph. Bibliotheca Americana; a dictionary of books relating to America, from its discovery to the present time. Begun by Joseph Sabin, continued by Wilberforce Eames, and completed by R.W.G. Vail for the Bibliographical Society of America. New York, 1868-1936.
Santiago Vela	Santiago Vela, Gregorio de. Ensayo de una biblioteca ibero-americana de la Orden de San Agustín. Madrid, 1913-31.
Scheepvaart Mus.	Amsterdam--Nederlandsch Historisch Scheepvaart Museum--Bibliotheek. Catalogus. Amsterdam, 1960.
Schoenrich Document	Schoenrich, Otto. "Appendix: Court Documents," in his The legacy of Christopher Columbus. Glendale, California, 1949-50.
Scott	Scott, John. A bibliography of printed documents and books relating to the Darien Company. Edinburgh, 1904. Additions and corrections. By George P. Johnston. Edinburgh, 1906.
Smith(Anti-Quak.)	Smith, Joseph. Bibliotheca anti-quakeriana; or, A catalogue of books adverse to the Society of Friends. London, 1873.
Smith(Friends)	Smith, Joseph. A descriptive catalogue of Friends' books, or books written by members of the Society of Friends, commonly called Quakers. London, 1867.
Steele	[Crawford, James Ludovic Lindsay, 26th earl of] Bibliotheca Lindesiana, vol. V-VI; a bibliography of royal proclamations of the Tudor and Stuart sovereigns and of others published under authority, 1485-1714. With an historical essay ... by Robert Steele. Oxford, 1910.
Streit	Streit, Robert. Bibliotheca missionum. Münster [etc.], 1916-
Swem	Swem, Earl G. A bibliography of Virginia, pt.1. Richmond, 1916. (Bulletin of the Virginia State Library, v.8, nos. 2/3/4)
TC	The Term catalogues, 1668-1709 A.D., with a number for Easter term, 1711 A.D. ... Edited ... by Edward Arber. London, 1903-06.
TPL	Toronto--Public Libraries. A bibliography of Canadiana; being items in the Public Library of Toronto, Canada, relating to the early history and development of Canada. Edited by Frances M. Staton and Marie Tremaine. Toronto, 1934. Supplement. 1st- 1959-

Books Cited in the Catalogue

Taylor(Mathematical practitioners: Tudor & Stuart)	Taylor, E.G.R. "Works on the mathematical arts and practices, with descriptive notes," in her The mathematical practitioners of Tudor & Stuart England. Cambridge, 1954.
Ter Meulen-Diermanse	Meulen, Jacob ter, and P.J.J. Diermanse. Bibliographie des écrits imprimés de Hugo Grotius. La Haye, 1950.
Torrence	Virginia--State Library, Richmond--Dept. of Bibliography. A trial bibliography of colonial Virginia; special report of the Department of Bibliography, William Clayton-Torrence, bibliographer. Richmond, 1908-10. (In Virginia--State Library, Richmond. 5th-6th Annual report)
Tiele	Tiele, P. A. Nederlandsche bibliographie van land- en volkenkunde. Amsterdam, 1884.
Tiele-Muller	Muller, Frederik. Mémoire bibliographique sur les journaux des navigateurs Néerlandais... en la possession de Frederik Muller... Rédigé par P. A. Tiele. Amsterdam, 1867.
Tower	Pennsylvania--Historical Society--Library. The Charlemagne Tower collection of American colonial laws. [Philadelphia] 1890.
Tremaine(Arctic)	Arctic bibliography. [Vol. 1- edited by Marie Tremaine] Montreal, 1953-
Ugarte	Ugarte, Salvador. Catálogo de obras escritas en lenguas indígenas de Mexico o que tratan de ellas. Mexico, 1949.
Vail	Vail, R. W. G. "A bibliography of North American frontier literature, 1542-1800," in his The voice of the old frontier. Philadelphia, 1949.
Vargas Ugarte	Vargas Ugarte, Rubén. Impresos peruanos. Lima [1949]-57. (His Biblioteca peruana, t. 6-12)
Vekené	Vekené, Emile van der. Bibliographie der Inquisition. Hildesheim, 1963.
Viñaza	Viñaza, conde de la. Bibliografía española de lenguas indígenas de América. Madrid, 1892.
Vindel	Vindel, Francisco. Manual gráfico-descriptivo del bibliófilo hispano-americano (1475-1850). Madrid [etc.] 1930-34.

Books Cited in the Catalogue

Vindel(Escudos)   Vindel, Francisco. Escudos y marcas de impresores y libreros en España durante los siglos XV a XIX (1485-1850). Barcelona, 1942.

Wagner   Wagner, Henry R. The Spanish Southwest, 1542-1794. Albuquerque, N.M., 1937.

Waring   Waring, Edward John. Bibliotheca therapeutica; or, Bibliography of therapeutics, chiefly in reference to articles of the materia medica. London, 1878-79.

Wegelin(Poetry)   Wegelin, Oscar. Early American poetry; a compilation of the titles of volumes of verse and broadsides by writers born or residing in North America north of the Mexican border. 2d ed. New York, 1930.

Wing   Wing, Donald. Short-title catalogue of books printed in England, Scotland, Ireland, Wales, and British America, and of English books printed in other countries, 1641-1700. New York, 1945-51.

Wroth & Annan   Wroth, Lawrence C., and Gertrude L. Annan. Acts of the French royal administration concerning Canada, Guiana, the West Indies and Louisiana, prior to 1791; a list. New York, 1930.

Wroth(Md.)   Wroth, Lawrence C. "Maryland imprints; an annotated bibliography of books, broadsides and newspapers printed in Maryland from 1689 to 1776," in his A history of printing in colonial Maryland, 1686-1776. [Baltimore] 1922.

Zegarra   Zegarra, Félix Cipriano C. "Santa Rosa de Lima (Isabel Flórez y Oliva); estudio bibliográfico," in Lima--Junta Para Celebrar el Tercer Centenario del Nacimiento de Santa Rosa. Concurso literario en honor de Santa Rosa de Lima. Lima, 1886.

ABBREVIATIONS

col., colored
diagr(s)., diagram(s)
ed., edited; editor
enl., enlarged
fol., folio
fold., folded
front(s)., frontispiece(s)
geneal., genealogical
illus., illustration(s); illustrated
incl., including
ℓ., leaf; leaves
n, note
numb. ℓ., numbered leaf;
   numbered leaves
p., page(s)
p.ℓ., preliminary leaf;
   preliminary leaves
pl., plate
port(s)., portrait(s)

pt(s)., part(s)
ptie., partie
pub., published
r (superscript), recto
rev., revised
t., tome, tomo
t.-p., title-page
tab., table
tr., translator
transl., translated; translation
v (superscript), verso
v. or vol(s)., volume(s)

1°, full sheet broadside
$1/2^o$, half-sheet broadside
fol., folio
4°, quarto
8°, octavo
12°, duodecimo

CATALOGUE
of the
JOHN CARTER BROWN LIBRARY

1675

C675
A354h
    Alcoforado, Francisco, fl. 1418-1420.
      An Historical Relation Of the First Discovery Of The Isle Of Madera. Written Originally in Portugueze by Don Francisco Alcafarado... Who was one of the First Discoverers, thence translated into French, and now made English. ...
    London, Printed for William Cademan at the sign of the of the [sic] Popes-Head at the Entrance into the New Exchange in the Strand. 1675.
      1 p.ℓ., 37 p. 21cm. 4°
      Transl. from Relation historique de la découverte de l'isle de Madere, Paris, 1671. First appeared as "Descobrimento da ilha da Madeira. Anno 1420" in Francisco Manuel de Mello. Epanaphoros de varia historia portugueza, Lisbon, 1660.
      Imperfect: last leaf wanting; supplied in pen and ink facsimile.
      JCB(2)2:1115; Sabin680; WingA888.

01643, 1853

DA68
C697
    Ames, William, d. 1662.
      Een Declaratie, Verklaringe, of Aanwysinge Van de Getuyge Gods, In's Menschen inwendige deelen. In 't Engels geschreven door Willem Ames. En nu in 't Nederduyts obergeset.
    Tot Rotterdam, Gedrukt by Pieter van Wynbrugge, in de Leeuwe-straat. En zijn ook te bekomen tot Amsterdam, by Iacob Claus, op de Achter-burgwal, in de vergulde drie-hoek. Anno 1675.
      1 p.ℓ., 10 p. 20cm. 4° (No.[28] as issued, in Collectio, Of Versamelinge. [Amsterdam, ca. 1680])
      Cut on t.-p.
      Transl. from: A declaration of the witness of God. [London] 1656.
      Cf. Smith(Friends)1:26.

03269, 1866

DA68
C697
    Ames, William, d. 1662.
      Een geklank uyt Sion, Den Heyligen Bergh, Die den Heere op den top van alle Bergen is vast stellende, en bevestigende.... Door... William Ames, ... Uyt het Engels Overgeset.
    Tot Rotterdam, Gedrukt by Pieter van Wijnbrugge, in de Leeuwe-straat. En zijn ook te bekomen tot Amsterdam, by Iacob Claus, op de Achter-burgwal, in de vergulde Drie-hoek. Anno 1675.
      1 p.ℓ., 13 p. 30cm. 4° (No.[29] as issued, in Collectio, Of Versamelinge. [Amsterdam, ca. 1680]) Transl. from: A sound out of Sion. London, 1773.
      Smith(Friends)1:28.

03270, 1866

BA675
B389f
    Becerra Tanco, Luis, 1602-1672.
      Felicidad De Mexico En El Principio, Y Milagroso Origen, que tubo el Santuario de la Virgen Maria N. Señora De Gvadalvpe, Extramuros: En la Apparicion admirable de esta Soberana Señora, y de su prodigiosa Imagen Sacada à luz, y añadida por el Bachiller Lvis Bezerra Tanco, Presbytero, difunto; para esta segunda impression, que ha procurado el Doctor D. Antonio de Gama...
    Con Licencia. En Mexico, por la Viuda de Bernardo Calderon Año de 1675.
      11 p.ℓ., 31 numb. ℓ. fold. plate. 20.5cm. 4°
      Errata, ℓ. 31^v.
      First pub. under title: Origen milagroso del Santuario de Nuestra Señora de Guadalupe. Mexico, 1666.
      License dated (6th p.ℓ.^{v}) 25 June 1675.
      Medina(Mexico)1121; Palau(2)26230; cf. Sabin 4216.

04379, before 1902

D675
B853b
    A Brief and True Narration Of the Late VVars Risen In New-England: Occasioned by the Quarrelsom disposition, and Perfidious Carriage Of The Barbarous, Savage and Heathenish Natives There.
    London Printed for J.S. 1675.

[1]

8 p. 18cm. 4º
Dated (p. 3): Boston September 7th. 1675.
"King Philip's War Narratives" quarto no. 1.
cf. Church 639n.
JCB(2)2:1134; Sabin52616; Vail(Front.)163; WingB4534.

0508, 1846

C675
-B862n
Brito Freire, Francisco de, fl. 1655-1675.
Nova Lusitania, Historia da Guerra Brasilica A Purissima Alma E Savdosa Memoria Do Serenissimo Principe Dom Theodosio Principe De Portvgal, E Principe Do Brasil. Por Francisco De Brito Freyre. Decada Primeira.
Lisboa Na Officina De Joam Galram. Anno 1675.
9 p. ℓ., 460, [39] p., 4 ℓ., 64 p. 34.5cm. fol.
Added t.-p., engr.; signed: Berain Sculp.
Preliminary matter includes poetry.
With, as issued, his Viage Da Armada Da Companhia Do Commercio. [Lisboa, 1675] with special t.-p. and separate paging and signatures.
JCB(2)2:1120; Sabin8130; Borba de Moraes 1:277.

03608, before 1866

C675
-B862n
Brito Freire, Francisco de, fl. 1655-1675.
Viage Da Armada Da Companhia Do Commercio, E Frotas Do Estado Do Brasil. A Cargo Do General Francisco De Brito Freyre. Impressa Por Mandado De El Rey Nosso Senhor. Anno 1655.
[Lisboa, Joam Galram, 1675]
4 p. ℓ., 64 p. 34.5cm. fol. (Issued as a part of his Nova Lusitania. Lisbon, 1675.)
Cut (royal arms) on t.-p.
Order to print (3d p. ℓ.) dated: Lisboa em 13. de Abrie de 1657.
First pub. under title: Relação da Viagem. Lisboa, 1657.
JCB(2)2:783; Sabin8131; Borba de Moraes1:277.

03609, before 1866

J675
C238v
Capell, Rudolf, 1635-1684.
Vorstellungen Des Norden/Oder Bericht von einigen Nordländern/und absonderlich von dem so genandten Grünlande/aus Schreibern/welche zu unterschiedenen Zeiten gelebet/auff guter Freunde begehren zusammen gezogen und dargereichet/auch endlich umb ferner zu Betrachten/ zu ändern und zu mehren aus D. Capel P. P. Bibliothec auszgefertiget.
Hamburg/In Verlegung Joh. Naumanns und Georg Wolffen/Buchhändeler. Im Jahr Christi 1675.

2 p. ℓ., 212 p. 20cm. 4º
Title vignette (printer's or publisher's device).
Part 1 deals with arctic discoveries and attempts to find a northwest passage; part 2 concerns explorations to Greenland.
JCB(2)2:1116; Sabin10735; Palmer303.

01516, 1847

DA68
C697
Crisp, Stephen, 1628-1692.
Een Geklanck des Alarms, Geblaezen binnen de Landt-paelen van het Geestelijcke AEgypten, dat in Babylon gehoort; ... In de Engelsche Tale geschreven ... door ... Stephen Crisp. En nu op nieuws overgeset. Den tweeden Druck.
t'Amsterdam, by Jacob Claus, op d'oudezijts achter Burghwal, in de vergulde Drie-hoeck. 1675.
36 p. 20cm. 4º (No.[18], as issued, in Collectio, Of Versamelinge. [Amsterdam, ca. 1680])
Transl. from: An Alarum sounded. [London] 1671. Dutch transl. first pub. 1671.
Cf. Smith(Friends)1:469; cf. Knuttel 9920.

03259, 1866

DA68
C697
[Crisp, Stephen] 1628-1692.
Een naauw-keurigh ondersoek, En Ernstige berispinge van de Proceduren, van de Bvrgermeesteren en Raadt der Stad Embden, Tegens het onnoosele Volk Gods, genaamt Quakers. [Amsterdam, 1675]
16 p. 20cm. 4º (No. [21] as issued, in Collectio, Of Versamelinge. [Amsterdam, ca. 1680])
Caption title; imprint at end.
Dated (p. 16): In Amsterdam, den 18/28 September 1675.
Smith(Friends)1:476.

03262, 1866

B675
-E74g
Escalona y Agüero, Gaspar de, d. 1659.
Gazophilativm Regivm Pervbicvm. Opvs Sane Pvlcrvm, A Plerisqve Petitvm, Et ab omnibus, in vniuersum, desideratum, non sine magno labore, & experientia digestum, provideque, & accurate illustratum. In Qvo Omnes Materiæ Spectantes, Ad Administrationem calculationem, & conservationem, iurium regalium Regni Peruani latissimè, discutiuntur, & plene manu per tractantur. Editvm A D. Gaspare De Escalona Agvero. ...
Año 1675. Cvm Facvltate Matriti. Ex Typographia Antonij Gonzalez Reyes. Sumptibus Gabrielis de Leon Bibliopolæ.
10 p. ℓ., 199, 302, [3], [53] p. 29cm. fol.
Title in red and black; publisher's device of Gabriel de Leon on t.-p.
Errata, verso of 6th p. ℓ.
All except first Part is in Spanish; Latin and

Spanish parts separately paged.
    First pub. under title: <u>Arcae Limensis. Gazophilativm Regivm Pervbicvm</u>. Madrid 1647.
    Bound in 18th or early 19th century red morocco; inlaid, gold-tooled, with arms of Lord Stuart de Rothesay on front and back covers.
    Contents.—De Administratione Maiori, Et Vniversali Regii Patrimonii Spectante Ad Mvnvs Proregivm Pervbicvm.—Gazofilacio Real De El Reyno Del Perv.—Ordenanzas Generales, dadas por su Magestad à oficiales Reales, para la administracion, recaudacion, y cobro de su hazienda, buen regimiento, instruccion, y custodia de sus caxas.

B675   ————Another copy. 30.5cm.
-E74g   JCB(2)2:1114; Palau(2)80776; Sabin520, 22820;
cop.2   Brunet1:115-6; Streit2:2099.

04381, 1887
01904, before 1854

C585   An Exact Narrative Of The Tryals Of The
E96t   Pyrats: And All the Proceedings at the late
11A   Goal-Delivery of the Admiralty, Held in the Old-Bayly, on Thursday and Saturday, the 7th and 9th of Jan. 167$\frac{4}{5}$. Where Eight Persons were Condemned to dye. Viz. Capt. George Cusack, alias Dixon, alias Smith. [and others] ... For taking, and Robbing Two Ships, viz. the Robert, near the Fly: And the Anne on the Dogger-Sands; With several others. And many other Circumstances there very Remarkable: The like Court having not been held for many years before.
    [London] Printed [for Jonathan Edwin] in the Year, 1675.
    25-31 p. 20cm. 4º (Issued as a part of <u>The Grand Pyrate</u>, London, 1676.)

11352-11A, 1918

B675   Fernández de Belo, Benito, fl. 1654-1675.
F363b   Breve Aritmetica, Por El Mas Svcinto Modo, Qve hasta oy se ha visto: Trata en las quentas que se pueden ofrecer para formar Campos, y Esquadrones. Compuesta Por D. Benito Fernandez De Belo...
    Con Licencia En Mexico, por la Viuda de Bernardo Calderon, Año de 1675.
    4 p.ℓ., 11 numb. ℓ. illus., fold. diagr. 19cm. 4º
    Preliminary matter includes poetry.
    Dedication dated (2d p.ℓ.) 27 Jan 1675.
    Karpinski 34; Palau(2)88090; cf. Medina (Mexico)1125.

10705, 1915

DA675   Fox, George, 1624-1691.
F791   Cain Against Abel, Representing New-England's Church-Hirarchy [sic], In Opposition to Her Christian Protestant Dissenters. By George Fox.
    [London?] Printed in the Year 1675.
    48 p. 19.5cm. 4º
    Signed (p. 40): This 20th of the 11th Moneth, 1675. G. F.
    Pages 41-48 are in reply to an order against Quakers of the Massachusetts General Court, 3 Nov. 1675.
    JCB(2)2:1119; Sabin25346; WingF1754; Smith(Friends)1:674.

03606, before 1866

DA675   Fox, George, 1624-1691.
F791c   Christian Liberty Commended, and Persecution Condemned. ... In a Letter to the Magistrates and Ministers of the City of Dantzick. By G. Fox:
    [London?], Printed in the Year, 1675.
    1 p.ℓ., 17,[1] p. 20cm. 4º
    Signed (p. 17): Swarthmore this 3. of the 9. Month, 1675. G. F.
    In this copy there is a blank ℓ. at beginning and at end.
    Smith(Friends)1:674; WingF1760.

11457, 1918

DA675   Fox, George, 1624-1691.
F791f   For All The Bishops and Priests In Christendom, To Measure themselves by the Scriptures of Truth, ... By George Fox. ...
    [London? 1675]
    67 p. 19cm. (20cm. in case) 4º
    Signed: Worcester-Prison, the 11th Moneth, 1664 [sic., i.e. 1674/5] George Fox.
    Smith(Friends)1:673; WingF1819.

11455 1918

DA675   Fox, George, 1624-1691.
F791p   Primitive Ordination And Succession, Of Bishops, Deacons, Pastors and Teachers in the Church of Christ. By George Fox. ...
    [London?], Printed in the Year 1675.
    50 p. 17.5cm. (18.5cm. in case) 4º
    Signed: Swarthmore, the 10th of the 9th Month, 1675. G. F.
    Smith(Friends)1:674; WingF1885.

11453, 1918

DA675   Fox, George, 1624-1691.
F791t   To all that would Know the Way To The Kingdom, Whether they be in Forms, without Forms, or got above all Forms. ... Given forth by G. Fox.
    [London?], Printed in the Year 1675.
    15 p. 20.5cm. 4º
    First pub. [London] 1653; this, however, has the revisions of the 1655 ed.
    Smith(Friends)1:646; WingF1947.

11456, 1918

EB   France--Laws, statutes, etc., 1643-1715
-F8155   (Louis XIV)   9 Feb 1675
1675   Edit Du Roy, Portant revocation de la
1   Compagnie des Indes Occidentales, & union
au Domaine de la Couronne des Terres, Isles,
Païs & Droits de la dite Compagnie, avec permission à tous les Sujets de Sa Majesté d'y
trafiquer, &c. Donné à Saint Germain en Lays
au mois de Decembre 1674. Registré en Parlement & Chambre des Comptes, les dix-huit
Janvier & neuf Février 1675.

A Paris. Chez la Veuve Saugrain & Pierre
Prault, à l'entrée du Quay de Gêvres, au Paradis. [1675]

8 p. 27cm. 4°

Caption title; imprint at end.

JCB(2)2:1118; Wroth&Annan156-7; Harrisse
(NF)140.

04356, 1873

+Z   Goos, Pieter, 1616-1675.
-G659   De Zee-Atlas/Ofte Water-Wereld, Waer in
1675   vertoont werden alle de Zee-Kusten Van het
bekende des Aerd-Bodems. Seer dienstigh voor
alle Heeren en Kooplieden, Als oock voor alle
Schippers en Stuurlieden.

Gesneden, gedruckt en uytgegeven t'Amsteldam, By de Weduwe van pieter Goos, in de Zee-Spiegel, 1675.

9 p.ℓ., 40 double-page maps (col.). 56cm. fol.

Title and imprint within engr. ornamental border (col.).

First pub. Amsterdam, 1666.

Register (9th p.ℓ.ᵛ) does not include map [33].
Register includes "De geheele Werelt-kaert" and
"Paskaert van Yslant, tot de Straet Davis," not
present in this copy; "Wereld-kaert" probably
originally present. This copy probably issued
without dedication.

Cf. Phillips(Atlases)473, 474, 5690.

Contents:
[1] Pascaart van Europa, Als mede een gedeelt vande cust van Africa. ...
[2] Pascaart van de Noort Zee Verthoonende in zich alle de Custen en havens daer rontom gelegen. ... 1669. Gesneden bÿ Geraerd Coeck.
[3] Pas-Caart van de Oost Zee Verthoonende Alle de ghelegentheydt tusschen 't Eylandt Rugen ende Wÿborg. ... 1669. Gesneden bÿ Gerard Coeck.
[4] Pascaarte vande Zuyder-Zee, Texel, ende Vlie-stroom, als mede 't Amelander-gat. ... 1666.
[5] Pascaart van de Noord Zee, Van Texel, tot de Hoofden Nieulyex uijtgegeven ...
[6] Cust van Hollant tusschen de Maes ende Texel.
[7] De Texel Stroom met de gaten vant Marsdiep. [Inset:] Caarte vande Reede end Haven van Medenblick ... —Caarte van De Mase, Ende het Goereesche gat.
[8] De Cust van Zeelandt, Begrypende in sich de gaten, als vande Wielingen, ter Veere, Ziericzee, Brouwershaven, Goeree, en de Maes.
[9] Paskaert Van de Zeeusche en Vlaemsche Kusten, tonende alle drooghten, diepten, en ondiepten, tusschen 't eylandt Schouwen en de Hoofden, curieuselyck beschreven door Dirck Davidsz.
[10] [Continuation of no. [9], untitled]
[11] Pascaarte van Engelant Van t' Voorlandt tot aen Blakeney waer in te sien is de mont vande Teemse.
[Inset:] Rivier van Londen.
[12] Pas-Caart vant Canaal Vertoonende in't Gheheel Engelandt, Schotlandt, Yrlandt, en een gedeelte van Vrancrÿck. ... 1669. Gesneden bÿ Gerard Coeck.
[13] Het Canaal tusschen Engeland en Vrancrijck. ...
[14] Paskaarte om Achter Yrlandt om te Zeÿlen van Hitlant tot aen Heÿssat Nieuwlycx Vytgegeven ... 1669.
[15] Paskaerte van't in comen Van't Canaal, hoemen dat sal aen doen, als men uyt de West comt. ...
[16] Paskaerte Vande Bocht van Vranckrijck Biscajen en Galissen tusschen Heysant en C. de Finisterre.
[17] Pas-Caart van Hispangien, Vertoonende de Custen van Granade, Andaluzie, Algarve, Portugael, Galissien, en Biscaien, met een gedeelte van Vranckrÿck; streckende van Hey sant tot de Straet van Gibralter. Verbetert door A. en I. de Bree. ... 1669.
[18] Paskaerte Van't Westelyckste Der Middelandsche Zee. ...
[19] Paskaerte Van't Oostelyckste Der Middelandsche Zee. ...
[20] De Cust van Barbaria, Gualata, Arguyn, en Geneheo, van Capo S. Vincente tot Capo Verde.
[21] de Cust van Barbaryen van out Mamora tot Capo Blanco.—De Cust van Barbaryen van Capo Blanco Tot Capo de Geer.—De Reede van Punte del Gada int Eylandt S. Michiels [with inset:] De zuydhoec vant Eylandt Fayal.—De Reede voor de Stadt Angra int eylandt Tercera.—De Eylanden van Madera en Porto Santo.
[22] Caarte Voor een gedeelte der Canarise Eylanden als Canaria, Tenerifa, Forteventura, etc.
[Inset:] De tyhavens, Porto de Naos en Porto de Cavallos aen de Zuydoostzyde van Lãcerota.
[23] Pas-Caart van Guinea en de Custen daer aen gelegen Van Cabo verde tot Cabo de Bona Esperanca.
[24] Pas-Kaarte van de Zuyd-west-kust van Africa; van Cabo Negro tot beoosten Cabo

de Bona Esperança. Niiwlyks besgreven en uyt-gegeven...
[Insets:] Cabo de Bona Esperanca.—Vlees bay.
[25] Pascaerte Van't Westelycke Deel van Oost Indien, Van Cabo de Bona Esperanca, tot C. Comorin. ...
[26] Paskaerte Zynde t'Oosterdeel Van Oost Indien, met alle de Eylanden daer ontrendt geleegen van C. Comorin tot aen Iapan.
[27] Noordoost Cust Van Asia Van Iapan tot Nova Zemla.
[28] De Zee Custen van Ruslant, Laplant, Finmarcken, Spitsbergen en Nova Zemla. ...
[Inset:] De Reviere Dwina, Ofte De Reviere van Archangel Soo het Nieuwe als 't Oude diep.
[29] De Custen van Noorwegen, Finmarcken, Laplandt, Spitsbergen, Ian Mayen Eylandt, Yslandt, als mede Hitlandt, en een gedeelte van Schotlandt. ...
[30] Paskaert Zÿnde de Noordelijckste Zeekusten Van America Van Groenland door de Straet Davis en de Straet Hudson tot Terra Neuf.
[31] Pascaerte vande Vlaemsche, Soute, en Caribesche Eylanden, als mede Terra Nova, en de Custen van Nova Francia, Nova Anglia, Nieu Nederlandt, Venezuela, Nueva Andalusia, Guiana, en een gedeelte, van Brazil. Abraham Deur fecit.
[32] Pas caerte van Nieu Nederlandt en de Engelsche Virginies Van Cabo Cod tot Cabo Canrick.
[33] Paskaerte Van de Zuÿdt en Noordt Revier in Nieu Nederlant Streckende van Cabo Hinloopen tot Rechkewach.
[34] Pascaerte Van Westindien De Vaste Kusten En de Eylanden.
[Inset:] Het Canael tusschen Havana aen Cuba en de Tortugas en Martyres aen Cabo de la Florida in Groot besteck.
[35] Pascaert Vande Caribes Eylanden. ...
[36] Paskaart van Brasil Van Rio de los Amazones, tot Rio de la Plata.
[37] Paskaarte van Het Zuydelijckste van America Van Rio de la Plata, tot Caap de Hoorn, ende inde Zuyd Zee, tot B. de Koquimbo. Nieuwlÿck Vÿtgegeven Anno 1666.
[38] Pascaerte Van Nova Hispania Chili, Perv, en Guatimala... 1666.
[39] Paskaerte Van Nova Granada. en t'Eylandt California. ... 1666.
[40] Pascaerte Vande Zvyd-Zee tussche California, en Ilhas de Ladrones... 1666.

8843, 1912

DA68 Green, Thomas, 1634-1699.
C697   Korte Antwoordt, Op het Antichristisch Mandaet Van de Regeerders van Embden. Dat van haerlieden, tegens het onnosele Volck Gods, (gemeenelijck Quakers genaemt) is gemaeckt en gepubliceert. ... Geschreven uyt Amsterdam, door Thomas Green En John Croock.
t'Amsterdam, gedruckt in 't Jaer 1675.
15p. 20cm. 4° (No. [43] as issued, in Collectio, Of Versamelinge. [Amsterdam, ca. 1680])
Smith(Friends)1:489 & 866.

03284, 1866

DA68 [Hendricks, Elizabeth] Quaker, Amsterdam, fl.
C697   1672-1683.
Een Algemeene Send-Brief aen de Vrienden der Waerheyt, In Hollandt, Vrieslandt, Duitslandt en elders, ...
Tot Amsterdam, Gedruckt by Christoffel Cunradus, Boeck-drucker / 1675.
8p. 20cm. 4° (No. [50] as issued, in Collectio, Of Versamelinge. [Amsterdam, ca. 1680])
Signed: In Amsterdam den 22 der eerste Maent, 1675. Elizabet Hendriks.
Smith(Friends)1:936.

03291, 1866

FC650 Hollandtze Mercurius, Behelssende, De
H737   voornaemste voorvallen in Europa Binnen
25   het Jaer 1674. tot 1675. Het Vijf-entwintigste Deel. ...
Gedruckt tot Haerlem, by Pieter Casteleyn, Boeckdrucker op de Marckt, in de Keysers Kroon. Anno 1675. Met Privilegie.
3 p.ℓ., 270 p. 20cm. 4° (Bound in [vol. 5] of Hollandse Mercurius)
Added t.-p., engraved: Hollandtse Mercurius. Anno 1674 by Pieter Casteleyn. tot Haarlem met Privilegie.
"Extract van Privilegie" (3d p.ℓ.) dated: 17. Deçember...1668.
Preface (3d p.ℓ.) dated: Haerlem den 9. April, 1675.
JCB(3)2:410; Sabin32523.

8487Y, 1912

FC650 Den Hollandtze Mercurius, Brengende, Het
H737   verhael der aenmerckelijckste zaken in
5   Christenryck voor-gevallen, Binnen het geheele Jaer 1654. Zijnde het Vijfde Deel. ...
Gedruckt tot Haerlem, by Pieter Casteleyn, Boeckdrucker op de Marckt, in de Keysers Kroon. Anno 1675. Met Privilegie.
4 p.ℓ., 116, [2] p. 20cm. 4° (Bound in [vol. 1] of Hollandse Mercurius)
Added t.-p., engraved: Hollantsche Mercurius. Tot Haerlem by Pieter Casteleyn, op de Marckt.

	"Extract van Privilegie" (2d p. ℓ.) dated: 17. December... 1668. Preliminary matter includes poetry signed: C. Gravesteyn, Franc⁰ Snellinx, and T.A.V. First pub. Haerlem, 1655. In this copy there is a blank leaf at end. JCB(3)2:410; Sabin32523.
8487E, 1912	
DA675 H768w	Homwood, Nicholas, d. 1676. A Word Of Counsel: Or A Warning to All Young-Convinced Friends, and Others whom it may concern; that are called forth to bear a Testimony for the Lord in the Case of Tythe. Which may also serve for Answer to a late Pamphlet, entituled, The Lawfulness of Tythes by W. J. as it concerns the Quakers Conscience in the Case; ... Nicholas Homwood. ... [London] Printed in the Year 1675. 8 p. Signed: From the Kings-Bench Prison in the 9th Moneth, 1675. ... Nicholas Homwood. A reply to: [William Jeffery], The lawfulnes of Tethes. London, 1675. Includes poetry, p. 8. Smith(Friends)1:969; WingH2579.
04629, before 1915	
DA675 H784f	[Hookes, Ellis] d. 1681. For The King And both Houses of Parliament. Being A brief and general Account of the late and present sufferings of many of the Peaceable Subjects called Quakers, upon the late Act against Conventicles; for no other Cause but Meeting together to Worship God according to their perswasions and Consciences. ... [London] Printed in the Year, 1675. 19 p., 18.5cm. 4⁰ A collection of "Original Accounts sent out of the Countreys..." signed (p. 19) by Ellis Hookes. Smith(Friends)1:971, 2:673; WingH2661.
16506, 1934	
DA675 H978f	[Hutchinson, Thomas] fl. 1675. Forced Uniformity Neither Christian nor Prudent. Presented To those in Authority whom it may concern. [London, 1675] 8 p. 18.5cm. 4⁰ Caption title; imprint from Wing. Signed: Tho. Hutchinson. 17th of the 2d Month, 1675.

	This copy closely trimmed at top and bottom with some loss of text. Smith(Friends)1:1026; WingH3836.
16514, 1934	
BA675 I12a	Ibarra, Miguel de. Annvæ Relectiones Ac Canonicæ Ivris Explicationes In Dvas Partes Divisæ. In quibus varia capita Magistri Gratiani Decreti Scholasticâ methodo expenduntur, & Sapientissimorum Doctorum tutiores doctrine afferuntur: vtriusque Iuris incumbentibus valdè vtiles. Perlecte secundúm Statutorum ordinem in Regali Mexicana Academia à Doctore D. Michaele De Ybarra ... Pars Prima. Anno 1675. Svperiorvm Permissv. Mexic[i] apud Viduam Bernardi Calderon, in via Sancti Augustini 29 p. ℓ., 76 numb. ℓ., 78-329 numb. ℓ., 16 ℓ. 18.5cm. 4⁰ Title in red and black. Preliminary matter includes poetry. Eulogy dated (20th p. ℓ.ᵛ) 4 Feb. 1675. No more published. Marginal annotations in ms. Bound in contemporary vellum. Palau(2)117613; Medina(Mexico)1130.
67-272	
DA675 J33m	Janeway, James, 1636?-1674. Mr. James Janeway's Legacy To His Friends: Containing Twenty Seven Famous Instances of Gods Providences in and about Sea-Dangers and Deliverances; with the Names of Several that were Eye-witnesses to many of them. Whereunto is Added a Sermon on the same Subject. ... London, Printed for Dorman Newman, at the Kings Armes in the Poultry, 1675. 4 p. ℓ., 87 p., 1 ℓ., 89-133 p. front.(port.) 15cm. 8⁰ "The Epistle To The Reader" (2d-4th p. ℓ.) signed: John Ryther. Wapping 14 Apr. 1674. First pub. London, 1674. Bound in contemporary calf. With, as issued, John Ryther, Sea-Dangers And Deliverances Improved. London, 1674, with special t.-p. but continuous paging and signatures. JCB(2)2:1122; WingJ474.
29640, 1944	

[6]

D675
J84n
Josselyn, John, fl. 1630-1675.
New-Englands Rarities Discovered: In Birds, Beasts, Fishes, Serpents, and Plants of that Country, Together with The Physical and Chyrurgical Remedies wherewith the Natives constantly use to Cure their Distempers, Wounds, and Sores. Also A Perfect Description of an Indian Squa, in all her Bravery; with a Poem not improperly conferr'd upon her. By John Josselyn, Gent. The Second Addition. [sic] Illustrated with Cuts.
London, Printed for C. Widdowes at the Green Dragon in St. Pauls Church-yard, 1675.
2 p.ℓ., 114, [3] p. A⁸ (±A2) B-G⁸ H⁶ illus., fold. pl. 15cm. 8º
First pub. London, 1672; these are the same sheets with cancel t.-p.
Bookseller's advertisement, p.[1-2] at end.
In this copy H6 bearing printer's device is bound before A2 (t.-p.) in place of blank A1 (wanting).
JCB(2)2:1123; Wing J1094.

03603, before 1866

DA675
K28i
Keith, George, 1639?-1716.
Immediate Revelation, (Or, Jesus Christ The Eternal Son of God, Revealed in Man, Revealing the Knowledge of God, and the things of his Kingdom, Immediately) Not Ceased, ... The Second Edition: With an Appendix, containing an Answer to some farther Objections. ... By George Keith.
[London] Printed in the Year, 1675.
4 p.ℓ., 259p., 2 ℓ. 20cm. 8º
"Errata": 1st p.ℓ.
First pub. [Aberdeen] 1668.
Signed (p. 215): The 7th. of the 4th. Month, 1668. G.K.
"Postscript" (p. 216-224) signed: Writ in the time of my Imprisonment, in the Tolbooth of Aberdeen, in Scotland, ...The 3d. of the 6th. Month, 1668. G. Keith.
"An Appendix": p. 225-259.
Smith(Friends)2:18-19; WingK176.

8386, 1912

G675
K85b
Kort Berättelse om Wäst Indien eller America, Som elliest kallas Nya Werlden.
[Wisingsborg, Johannes Kankel] Anno MDCLXXV.
1 p.ℓ., 42 p. 20cm. 4º
Transl. by Ambrosius Nidelberg.
Treats of Bermuda and Virginia only in North America; otherwise concerned with South America.
JCB(2)2:1124; Sabin38244; Bygdén 1:834.

1391, 1906

E675
L217h
La Martinière, Pierre Martin de, 1634-1690.
Herrn Martiniere Neue Reise In die Nordischen Landschafften. Das ist: Eine Beschreibung Der Sitten/ Gebräuche/ Aberglauben/ Gebäuden/ und Kleidung der Norweger/ Lappländer/ Killopen/ Borandianer/ Siberianer/ Samojeden/ Zemblaner und Eissländer/ Sampt einem Bedencken über den Irrthum unser Erdbeschreiber/ wo nemlich Grönland und Nova Zembla liegen/ und wie weit sie sich erstrecken. Aus dem Englischen ins Deutsche übersetzet Durch Johann Langen.
Hamburg/ In Verlegung Johann Naumans und Georg Wolffs/ Buchhändler. Gedruckt zu Glückstadt bey Melchior Rochen/ Im Iahr 1675.
4 p.ℓ., 80 p. 20cm. 4º
Cut (printer's device) on t.-p.; reproduced JCB(2)2:1128.
Transl. from: A New Voyage Into The Northern Countries. London, 1674; 1st pub. as Voyage Des Septentrionaux. Paris, 1671.

J675
S317j
—— —— Another copy. Bound as no. 2 of 4 items.
JCB(2)2:1128; Sabin38715; Palmer349.

03605, before 1866
04653, 1860

BA675
L879h
[Losa, Francisco de] 1536-1624.
The Holy Life Of Gregory Lopez, A Spanish Hermite In The West-Indies. Done out of Spanish. The Second Edition. ...
[London] Printed in the Year, 1675.
28 p.ℓ., 232 p. 15.5cm. 8º
Errata: 28th p.ℓ.
Transl. from: La Vida Que Hizo El Siervo De Dios Gregorio Lopez. Mexico, 1613. Another English transl., by Alonzo Remon, was pub.: Paris, 1638. (cf. BM)
JCB(1)2:813; JCB(2)2:1125; Sabin42584; WingL3080; cf. Palau (2)142535.

0509, 1846

DA68
C697
Marshall, Charles, 1637-1698.
Een Boodschap Van Den Heere, De Godt des Hemels, aen alle Menschen. ... Uyt Engeland geschreven door Charles Marshal. En uyt het Engels vertaalt, door Benjamin Furly. Wyders noch eenige aanmerkinge voor Galenus Abrahamsz en zijne Aanhangers. Met eenige Vragen ende Antwoorden wegens's Menschen bekeeringe.

[Rotterdam] Zijn Gedruckt en te Koop by Pieter van Wijnbrugge, in de Leeuwestraat. 1675.
15p. 20cm. 4° (No. [53] as issued, in Collectio, Of Versamelinge. [Amsterdam, ca. 1680])
"Een boodschap" (p. 3-6) and "Een aensprake" (p. 7-8) both signed: Charles Marchal. Geschreven uyt Harwits, den I van de 5/7 Maent, genaemt July, 1674; "Eenige van de waardige en wichtige Aanmerkingen, die Galenus Abrahamsz" (p. 9-10) signed: John Higgins; "Eenige Vragen en Antwoorden aangaande's menschen bekeeringe, en de tederheyt, of gevoeligheyt des gemoeds. Door Isaack Pennington in d'Engelse tale geschreven, en aldus vertaalt." (p. 12-15) signed I.P.
Smith(Friends)2:144.

03294, 1866

J675 M377f Martens, Friedrich, fl. 1675.
Friderich Martens vom Hamburg Spitzbergische oder Groenlandische Reise Beschreibung gethan im Jahr 1671. Aus eigner Erfahrunge beschrieben/ die dazu erforderte Figuren nach dem Leben selbst abgerissen/ (so hierbey in Kupffer zu sehen und jetzo durch den Druck mitgetheilet.
Hamburg/ Auff Gottfried Schultzens Kosten gedruckt/ Im Jahr 1675.
4 p.ℓ., 132, [3] p. 16 plates (incl. 6 fold.) 20cm. 4°
Cut on t.-p.
Errata, last p.

J675 S317j ———— Another copy. In this copy plates precede last ℓ. and plates A with B and C with D not cut apart. Bound as No. 3 of 4 items.
JCB(2)2:1127; Sabin44834; Palmer356; Muller(1872)670.

03604, before 1866
04654, 1860

DB -M4143 1675 1 Massachusetts (Colony)--Laws, statutes, etc.
The General Laws And Liberties Of The Massachusets Colony In New-England, Revised and Reprinted, By Order of the General Court holden at Boston, May 15th, 1672. Edward Rawson, Secr. ...
Cambridge in New-England, Printed by Samuel Green, for John Usher of Boston, and to be sold by Richard Chiswel, at the Rose and Crown in St. Paul's Church-yard, London, 1675.
1 p.ℓ., 161, 162-170, [27] p., 1 ℓ. 29cm. fol.
Pagination 162-170 begins on a recto.
Errata (10 lines): p.170.
Same sheets as the 1672 edition except for p. 168-70, t.-p., and bookseller's list on final leaf, all of which were possibly printed in London.
cf. Albert Matthews, Note on the 1672 edition and the 1675 volume of the Massachusetts General Laws. (Col. Soc. of Mass. Pubs., 19: 9-21. Reprinted 1917)
"Sold also by Richard Chiswel" (booklist): final leaf.
First pub. under title: The Book Of The General Lauues And Libertyes. Cambridge, 1648, rev. and enl. Cambridge, 1660.
...Several Laws... 15th. of May 1672 (6 p.) inserted between t.-p. and p. 1 of The General Laws.
JCB(1)2:818; JCB(2)2:1129; Evans200; Ford(Mass. Laws)10; Tower135; cf. Sabin45743; WingM1004.

0790, 1846

D. Math I. 37 1 Mather, Increase, 1639-1723.
A Discourse Concerning the Subject of Baptisme Wherein the present Controversies, that are agitated in the New English Churches are from Scripture and Reason modestly enquired into By Increase Mather, Teacher of a Church in Boston in New-England. ...
Cambridge Printed by Samuel Green 1675.
2 p.ℓ., 76 p. 21cm. 4°
"To the Reader" dated (2d p.ℓ.v): Boston. N.E. 1. of 2 M. 1675.
Errata, p. 76.
Catchwords on p. 16: "I. nA", and p. 52: "ie [?]"
Brinley967(this copy).

D. Math I. 37 2 ———— Another copy. Catchwords corrected on p. 16 to: "I. An" and on p. 52 to: "And".
JCB(2)2:1130; Holmes(I)37; Church633; Evans207; Sabin46661; WingM1200.

04687, 1878
04060, 1870

D. Math I. 54 Mather, Increase, 1639-1723.
The First Principles of New-England, Concerning The Subject of Baptisme & Communion of Churches. Collected partly out of the Printed Books, but chiefly out of the Original Manuscripts of the First and chiefe Fathers in the New-English Churches; With the Judgment of Sundry Learned Divines of the Congregational Way in England, Concerning the said Questions. Published for the Benefit of those who are of the Rising Generation in New-England. By Increase Mather, Teacher of a Church in Boston in New-England...
Cambridge Printed by Samuel Green, 1675.
4 p.ℓ., 40, 7 p. 19.5cm. 4°
Errata: verso of 4th p.ℓ.
"To the Reader" (2nd-4th p.ℓ.) signed: Increase Mather. From my Study in Boston N.E. 1. of 3d Moneth, 1671.

"Postscript" (p. 1-7, 2d count) comprises a letter to Mather from John Allin, and another from Jonathan Mitchel dated: Cambridg. December. 26. 1667, both concerning baptism.
Inscribed by the author "For the Rev'd & much honor'd Dr John Owen."
JCB(1)2:815; JCB(2)2:1131; Holmes(I.)54; cf. Church 634; Evans 208; Sabin 46683; Wing M1211

0596, 1846

D. Math Mather, Increase, 1639-1723.
I.174A   The Wicked mans Portion. Or A Sermon (Preached at the Lecture in Boston in New-England the 18th day of the I Moneth 1674. when two men were executed, who had murthered their Master.) Wherein is shewed That excesse in wickedness doth bring untimely Death. By Increase Mather, Teacher of a Church of Christ. ...
Boston, Printed by John Foster. 1675.
2 p. ℓ., 25 p. 20cm. 4°
Errata, (5 lines): p. 25.
"To The Reader" (2d p. ℓ.) signed: Increase Mather. Boston, N.E. 15. of 2 Moneth, 1675.
Preached prior to the execution of Nicholas Feaver and Robert Driver.
Holmes(I)174A; Evans 210; Sabin 46758; Church 635; Wing M1260; Green(John Foster) 60-62.

15486, 1929

BA675   Molina, Alonso de, d. 1585.
M722d   Doctrina Christiana, Y Cathecismo, En Lengua Mexicana. Nuevamente Emendada, Dispuesta, y Añadida; para el vso, y enseñança de los Naturales. Compuesta Por el P. Fr. Alonso De Molina, de la Orden del Glorioso Padre San Francisco.
Año de 1675. Con Licencia. En Mexico, Por la Viuda de Bernardo Calderon.
[32] p. 15cm. ¶^{4} B^{12} 8°
Cut on t.-p.
Earlier editions of this may be the Doctrina christiana breve traduzida en lengua Mexicana, Mexico, 1546, and the Doctrina breve en lengua Mexicana, Mexico, 1571, cited in Icazbalceta-Carlo 10, 66, but no surviving copies are known. The fragment cited in Icazbalceta-Wagner 10 is a different version.
Medina(Mexico)1132; Pilling 2610; Viñaza 206; Andrade, VdeP:665; Palau(2)174347; Icazbalceta (Apuntes)133; Sabin 49875; cf. Icazbalceta-Carlo 10.

04689, Before 1902

F675   Nederlandsche West-Indische Compagnie.
N371a   Articul-Brief Van de Generale Nederlandtsche Geoctroyeerde West-Indische Compagnie, Ter Vergaderinge van de Thienen der selver Compagnie gearresteert, ende by de Hoogh Mogende Heeren Staten Generael der Vereenighde Nederlanden op den twaelfden April 1675 geapprobeert ende geconfirmeert.
In 's Gravenhage, By Jacobus Scheltus, Ordinaris Drucker van de Hoogh Mogende Heeren Staten Generael der Vereenighde Nederlanden. Anno 1675.
40 p. 21cm. 4°
Cut on t.-p.
Muller(1872)415; Sabin 2154a

32291, 1958

F675   Netherlands (United Provinces, 1581-1795)--Staten
N469c   Generaal.
Conditien, De welcke by d'Ed. Mog. Heeren Staten van Hollandt ende West-Vrieslandt, toegestaan werden aen een yeder, die genegentheydt mochten hebben, om een aensienlijcke Colonie uyt te setten op een seer bequame ende wel-gelegene Plaetse, op de vaste Kuste van America, die daer toe vast-gestelt, ende aan-gewesen sal worden.
[The Hague, 1675]
[8] p. 19cm. 4°
Caption-title.
Dated at end 20 July 1675.
Conditions proposed to emigrants for establishing a Dutch colony on the coast of America (Guiana).
JCB(2)2:1117; Knuttel 11288; Muller(1872)706 (this copy); Sabin 15185.

04691, Before 1882

DA675   [Penn, William] 1644-1718.
P412c   The Continued Cry Of The Oppressed For Justice, Being A farther Account of the late Unjust and Cruel Proceedings of Unreasonable Men against the Persons and Estates of many of the People call'd Quakers, only for their peaceable Meetings to worship God. Presented to the Serious Consideration of the King and both Houses of Parliament. With a Postscript of the Nature Difference and Limits of Civil and Ecclesiastical Authority, and the inconsistency of such Severities with both. Recommmended [sic] and submitted to the Perusal of Cæsar's True Friends. By the Author of England's Present Interest, &c...
[London] Printed in the Year 1675.
34 p. 17cm. (18cm. in case) 4°
Errata: p. 34.
Smith(Friends)2:294; Wing P1270.

11512, 1918

1675   CATALOGUE OF THE JOHN CARTER BROWN LIBRARY

DA675   [Penn, William] 1644-1718.
P412e   England's Present Interest Discover'd With Honour to the Prince, And Safety to the People. ... Presented and Submitted to the Consideration of Superiours. ...
          [London] Printed in the Year 1675.
          2 p. ℓ., 6, [32], 7-30 p. [ ]¹ A⁴ a-d⁴ B-C⁴ D³ E¹   19cm.   4°
          Errata: p.30
          Signed (p.28): William Penn.
          Bound as no. 1 with 1 other item.
          Sabin59693; Smith(Friends)2:293; WingP1279.
04692, 1918

DA675   Penn, William, 1644-1718.
P412e   England's Present Interest Discover'd With Honour to the Prince, And Safety to the People. ... Presented and Submitted to the Consideration of Superiours, By William Penn. ...
          [London] Printed in the Year 1675.
          2 p. ℓ., 62 p.   19cm.
          Signed (p. 60): William Penn.
          First pub. same year without author's name on t.-p.
          Bound as no. 2 with 1 other item.
          Smith(Friends)2:293; Church637; WingP1280.
11511. 1918

DA675   [Penn, William] 1644-1718.
P412t   A Treatise Of Oaths, Containing Several Weighty Reasons why the People call'd Quakers refuse to Swear:... Presented to the King and Great Council of England, Assembled in Parliament. ...
          [London?] Printed Anno 1675.
          1 p. ℓ., 4, 166 p.   18.5cm.   4°
          Signed: William Penn, Richard Richardson.
          Smith(Friends)2:293; WingP1388.
11346, 1918

DA68   Penn, William, 1644-1718.
C697   De Waarheyt Ontdekt, en Verhoogt: In een kort, maar echter zeker getuygenisse ... Door Willem Pen, de Jonge. ... Uyt het Engels overgeset. ...
          Gedrukt voor Iacob Claus, Boek-verkooper op de Achter-burgwal, inde vergulde drie-hoek, tot Amsterdam. Anno 1675.
          6p. ℓ., 72[i.e. 27], [1]p. 20cm. 4° (No. [14], as issued, in Collectio, of Versamelinge. [Amsterdam, ca. 1680])
          Transl. from Truth exalted, London, 1668.
          "Voor-Reden" (p. ℓ. 1-6) and "Na-Reden" (p. 24-27) by Benjamin Furley.
          Bookseller's advertisement, p. 27-end.
          Errata, last p.
          Smith(Friends)2:283; Knuttel 11364.
03255, 1866

D675   The Present State Of New-England, With Respect
-P942s1   to the Indian VVar. Wherein is an Account of the true Reason thereof, (as far as can be Judged by Men.) Together with most of the Remarkable Passages that have happened from the 20th of June, till the 10th of November, 1675. Faithfully Composed by a Merchant of Boston, and Communicated to his Friend in London. Licensed Decemb. 13, 1675. Roger L'Estrange.
          London, Printed for Dorman Newman, at the Kings-Arms in the Poultry, and at the Ship and Anchor at the Brig-foot on Southwark side. 1675.
          19 p.   29cm.   fol.
          "King Philip's War Narratives" folio no. 1. cf. Church636n.
          A Continuation Of the State of New-England. London, 1676, signed N. S. (Nathaniel Saltonstall?), is a continuation by the same author.
          Woodcut title vignette (royal arms)
          "New-England" in title is all in capitals.
          Isaiah, chap. 23, verse 1-3, in the Massachuset language from John Eliot's Bible: p. 11.
          Contains two orders of Councils held at Boston, Aug. 30 and Sept. 17, 1675.
          Church636(this copy); Sabin65324; Pilling 3113; Vail(Front)168; WingS120A.
11888, 1919

D675   The Present State Of New-England, With Respect
-P942s2   to the Indian War. Wherein is an Account of the true Reason thereof, (as far as can be Judged by Men.) Together with most of the Remarkable Passages that have happened from the 20th of June, till the 10th of November, 1675. Faithfully Composed by a Merchant of Boston, and Communicated to his Friend in London.
          Licensed Decemb. 13. 1675. Roger L'Estrange. London. Printed for Dorman Newman, at the Kings-Arms in the Poultry, and at the Ship and Anchor at the Bridg-foot on Southwark side. 1675.
          81 [i.e. 19] p.   29cm.   fol.
          "King Philip's War Narratives" folio no. 1. cf. Church636n.
          A Continuation Of the State of New-England. London, 1676, signed N. S. (Nathaniel Saltonstall?), is a continuation by the same author.

Woodcut title vignette (royal arms)
First pub. with same imprint and "New-England" in title all in capitals; here the name is in capital and lower-case letters.
Isaiah, chap. 23, verse 1-3, in the Massachuset language from John Eliot's Bible: p. 11.
Contains two orders of Councils held at Boston, Aug. 30 and Sept. 17, 1675.
JCB(2)2:1133; Vail(Front.)169; WingS120B.

0511, 1846

DA675 Q1c
Quakerism Canvassed: Robin Barclay baffled in the defending of his Theses against your Students at Aberdene, ... Or, A most true and faithful accompt of a Dispute betwixt some Students of Divinity at Aberdene, and the Quakers in and about the place, holden in Alexander Harper his Closs (or Yard) April 14. 1675. years, ... Together with the Quakers pretended true and faithful accompt of the same Dispute examined. As also, A further Confutation of the Quakers Principles, ... Published by <Al. Shirreff. John Leslie. Paul Gellie.> M. A. ...
[Edinburgh, Andrew Anderson] Printed in the Year, 1675.
6 p. ℓ., 236 (i.e. 136) p. 20.5cm. 4°
Last leaf printed [Aberdeen, John Forbes]
Errata, last page; also ms. corrections passim, which "We our selves have corrected...in most, if not all the Copies" (last page).
A reply to Robert Barclay, A true and faithful accompt of...a dispute betwixt some students... of the University of Aberdeen, and...the Quakers. London, 1675.
In this copy last leaf is torn with slight loss of text; available in facsim.
Smith(Anti-Quak)395; WingQ9; Aldis2063.

1319, 1906

D675 R163r
Raleigh, Sir Walter, 1552?-1618.
Remains Of Sʳ· Walter Raleigh; Viz. Maxims of State. Advice to his Son: his Sons advice to his Father. His Sceptick. Observations concerning the causes of the Magnificency and Opulency of Cities. Sir Walter Raleigh's Observations touching Trade and Commerce with the Hollander... His Letters to divers Persons of Quality. The Prerogative of Parliaments in England,...
London, Printed for Henry Mortlock, at the Phœnix in St. Paul's Churchyard, and at the White Hart in Westminster-Hall. 1675.
5 p. ℓ., 396 p. illus. (port.) 12.5cm. 12°
First pub. under title: Sir Walter Raleigh's sceptick. London 1651. The contents vary in the different editions.

Three parts have each a special t.-p. with same imprint.
"These Books...printed for Henry Mortlock..." (p. ℓ. 4-5).
JCB(2)2:1135; Sabin67581; Brushfield219i; WingR184.

03607, before 1866

H675 R317f
Redi, Francesco, 1626-1698.
... Epistola Ad Aliquas Oppositiones factas in suas Observationes circa Viperas: Scripta ad D. Alexandrum Morum, & D. Abbatem Bourdelot, Dominum de Condé & de S. Leger. Ex Italica in Latinam translata.
[Amstelodami, Sumptibus Andreæ Frisii. 1675.
72 p. 14.5cm. 12° (Issued as a part of his ...Experimenta circa res diversas naturales. Amstelodami, 1675)
At head of title: Francisci Redi, Nobilis Aretini.
Transl. from: Lettera...sopra alcune opposizioni fatte alle Sue Osservazioni intorno alle vipere. Firenze, 1670.
"...Observationes, Circa illas Guttulas & Fila ex vitro..." (half-title): p. [53]-72.
Brunet4:1175.

3033, 1907

H675 R317f
Redi, Francesco, 1626-1698.
... Experimenta circa res diversas naturales, speciatim illas, Quæ ex Indiis adferuntur. Ex Italico Latinitate donata.
Amstelodami, Sumptibus Andreæ Frisii. MDCLXXV.
2 p. ℓ., 193, [194-208], 111, [112-120], 70, 52, [6] p. illus. (2 engr.), 17 plates (incl. 14 fold.) 14.5cm. 12°
Added t.-p., engr.: Francisci Redi Experimenta Naturalia Sumpt. And. Frisii. Signed: C. Decktr. f.
At head of title: Francisci Redi, Nobilis Aretini.
Cut (printer's device) on t.-p.
Transl. from Esperienze intorno a diverse cose naturali, 1st pub. Florence, 1671.
With, as issued, his ...Observationes de viperis and his ...Epistola ad aliquas oppositiones factas in suas observationes circa viperas, with special half-titles, separate paging and signatures, and Lachmund, F., De ave diomedea dissertatio, Amsterdam, 1674, with special t.-p. and separate paging and signatures.
Bound in contemporary vellum.
In this copy there is a blank ℓ. at end.
Sabin68517; Arents333.

3033, 1907

H675　　　Redi, Francesco, 1626-1698.
R317f　　　...Observationes De Viperis. Scriptæ
Literis Ad Generosissimum Dominum Lauren-
tium Magalotti, Magni Ducis Hetruriæ Came-
rarium Ex Italica in Latinam translatæ.
[Amstelodami, Sumptibus Andreæ Frisii.
MDCLXXV.]
111, [112-120] p. 14.5cm. 12º (Issued as
a part of his ...Experimenta circa res diver-
sas naturales, Amsterdam, 1675)
At head of title: Francisci Redi, Nobilis
Aretini.
Transl. from: Osservazioni intorno alle
vipere, Florence, 1664.
Brunet4:1174.
3033, 1907

B675　　　Rocha, Diego Andrés, 1607-1688.
R672c　　Carta Al Exc.mo Señor. Don Baltasar De La
Cueva, Conde del Castellar, Marques de Malagon,
Virrey, Gouernador, y Capitan General de los
Reynos del Peru, Tierrafirme, y Chile. Por El
Doctor Don Diego Andres Rocha, Alcalde del
Crimen de la Real Audiencia de los Reyes. En
Que Se tratan algunos discursos tocantes a la
Milicia Christiana.
Con licencia. En Lima, Año de 1675.
66 numb. ℓ., 1 ℓ. 20.5cm. 4º
Bound in contemporary vellum.
Sabin72288;　　　Medina(Lima)495; Palau
(2):271822.
5495, 1909

DA675　　Rutherford, Samuel, 1600?-1661.
R974ℓ　　Mr Rutherfoord's Letters, The Third Edition
Now divided in three Parts. The First Contain-
ing those which were written from Aberdeen,...
The Second and Third Containing some, which
were written from Anwoth,...and others...
from St. Andrews, London, &c. Published...
By a well-wisher to the work, and People of God
...
[London] Printed in the Year cIɔ Iɔ cLxxv.
4 p. ℓ., 1-144, 129-144, 129-235, 268-464,
65-272 p. *⁴, B-E⁸, 1F⁸ F-2F⁸ 2²2F⁸ 2G-2S⁸.
17cm. 8º
First pub. under title: Joshua Redivivus, or,
Mr. Rutherfoord's Letters. [Amsterdam] 1664.
"The Postscript, By another Author," (i.e.,
Robert Macquare): p. 256-272.
cf. Smith(Anti-Quak)385-6; WingR2385
6681, 1910

DA675　　Ryther, John, 1634?-1681.
J33m　　Sea-Dangers And Deliverances Improved.
In A Sermon Preached By John Ryther, Minister
of the Gospel. ...
London, Printed for Dorman Newman, 1674.
[i.e. 1675]
1 p. ℓ., 89-133 p. 15cm. 8º (Issued as a
part of James Janeway, Mr. James Janeway's
Legacy, London, 1675).
JCB(2)2:1122.
29640, 1944

J675　　　Scheffer, Johannes, 1621-1679.
S317j　　　Joannis Schefferi von Strassburg Lappland/,
Das ist: Neue und wahrhafftige Beschreibung von
Lappland und dessen Einwohnern/ worin viel
bisshero unbekandte Sachen von der Lappen An-
kunfft/ Aberglauben/ Zauberkünsten/ Nahrung/
Kleidern/ Geschäfften/ wie auch von den Thieren
und Metallen so es in ihrem Lande giebet/ er-
zählet/ und mit unterschiedlichen Figuren für-
gestellet worden.
Franckfurt am Mäyn und Leipzig. In Verle-
gung Martin Hallervorden/ Buchhändlern zu
Königsberg in Preussen. Gedruckt bey Johann
Andreä. Im Jahr 1675.
8 p. ℓ., 424 p. illus. 20cm. 4º
Woodcut title vignette.
Added t.-p., engraved: Ioannis Schefferi
Argentoratensis Lapponia Cum Privileg: Reg:
Majest: Sveciæ Francofurti et Lipsiæ Impensis
Christiani Wolffii Bibliop. Aº. 1674.
First pub. under title: Lapponia; id est re-
gionis Lapponum...Francofurti, 1673.
Bound as no. 1 of 4 items.
Tremaine(Arctic)25926; Kress1389
04652, 1860

F675　　　Schouten, Joost, fl. 1636.
S376s　　　Sanfärdig Beskrijffning / Om Konungarijket
Siam, Thess Regering / Macht / Religion, Seder/
Handel och Wandel / så ock andre tänckärdige
Saaker / Aff Holländiske Compagniets, uthi detta
Ost-Indianiske Konungarijket tillordnade Direc-
teur Jobst Schovten, Uthi Holländska Språket åhr
MDCXXXVJ. författat: Och sedermehra åhr
1663. theruthaff på Tyskan förwändt och tryckt
uthi Nürnberg: Men nu på innewarande åhr för-
swenskat. Tryckt på Wijsingzborg / Aff Hans
Hög-Greffl: Nådes Herr Rijkz Drotzetens
Booketryckare Johann Kankel. Anno MDCLXXV.
1 p. ℓ., 60 p. 20cm. 4º
Transl. by Ambrosius Nidelberg.
Printed at the private press of Count Peder
Brahe.
First pub. under title: Notitie vande situatie,
regeeringe, macht... 's Gravenhage, 1638.
In this copy there is a blank ℓ. at end.
Bygdén2:408; Scheepvaart Mus.240; Tiele980n.
1392, 1906

+Z
-S467
1675

Seller, John, fl. 1658-1698.
Atlas Maritimus, Or The Sea-Atlas; Being A Book of Maritime Charts. Describing The Sea-Coasts, Capes, Headlands, Sands, Shoals, Rocks and Dangers. The Bays, Roads, Harbors, Rivers and Ports, in most of the known Parts of the World. Collected From the latest and best Discoveries that have been made: by divers able and experienced Navigators of our English Nation. Accommodated with a Hydrographical Description of the whole World; Shewing the chief Cities, Towns, and Places of Trade and Commerce; with the Nature of the Commodities and Merchandizes of each Country; very useful for Merchants, and all other Persons concerned in Maritime Affairs. By John Seller, Hydrographer to the King. Cum Privilegio Regis.
London, Printed by John Darby, for the Author, and are to be sold at his Shop at the Hermitage in Wapping, M.DC.LXXV.
1 p.ℓ., [2] p., 34 double-page maps (col.) 53cm. fol.
Cut (royal arms) on t.-p.
"The Preface" dated (p. [2]) 25 April 1675.
First pub. London, ca. 1670.
Cf. Phillips(Atlases)4154; WingS2464.
Contents:

[1] The Right Ascensions and Declinations of the Principal Fixed Starrs in both Hemisphears to ye year 1678.
[2] [Continuation of no. 2, untitled]
[3] A Mapp of the two Hemispheres of the Heavens By John Seller...
[4] A Mapp of the Regions & Countreyes vnder and about the North Pole by Iohn Seller...
[5] A Generall Chart of the Northerne Navigation Discribed by John Seller... Francis Lamb Sculp.
[6] A Chart of the North Sea By John Seller... James Clark engra:.
[7] A Chart of the Seacoasts of England Flanders & Holland...By John Seller...Ja: Clark Sculpsit.
[8] A Description of the Coast of Flanders From the Island Walcheren to Calice. Ia: Clerk Sculp:
[9] A Chart of the Sea-coast of Zealand...Ia: Clark Sculp.
[10] The Coast of Holland From the Maes to the Texel.
[11] A Chart of the Baltick Sea With the North Bodom & Lading Described by Iohn Seller...
[Insets:] The North Bodom. - The Meer or Lading.
[12] A Chart of the two Channels goeing into the Baltique Sea one Through Catte Gat and the Sound And the other Through the Belt By John Seller...
[Inset:] Coppenhaven...
[13] A Chart of the Sea Coasts of Russia Lapland Finmarke NovaZemla and Greenland Described by Iohn Seller... [Steph Board Sculp] [imperfect: lower right corner torn off].
[14] A Large Description of the two Chanells in the River Dwina goeing up to the City of Archangel by John Seller.
[15] A Chart of the Seacoasts from the Landsend of England to Cape Bona Esperanca By John Seller...
[16] A Chart of ye Narrow Seas Newly Corrected by Iohn Seller...
[17] the Coasts of England & France from the Start, to the Isles of Silly,...
[18] The Coasts of England & France from Arundel to the Start...
[19] The Coasts of England and France from Dover to the Isle of Wight...
[20] A Chart of the Channel By John Seller...
[21] A Chart of the Sea-Coasts of England and Ireland By Jo: Seller...
[22] A Chart Of the Bay of Biscaia By John Seller...Ia:Clerk Sculpsit
[23] A Chart of Spaine Perticulerly Discribing the Coasts of Biscaia Gallissia Portugal Andaluzia Granada &c by Ioh: Seller... [Insets:] Bourdeaux. - Island of Cales. - Lisbona.
[24] The Royall Citty of Tangier in Africa. By John Seller...Io. Oliver Fecit. -[Inset:] The Bay of Tangier.
[25] A Mapp Containing The Island & Kingdome Of Sicily, With A Part Of Naples, & Other Adjacent Coasts Including The Tyrrhenean Sea, Where Most Of Things Betwixt Spaine & France & Their Alyes Are Acted,... London A^O. 1676. W: Hollar fecit, 1676. - [Insets:] Prospect of the Straights of Sicily, vulgarly calld Faro Di Messina, from the North. -Messina. -Faro di Messina.
[26] A Mapp of The Citie and Port of Tripoli In Barbary, By Iohn Seller...A^O 1675. W. Hollar fecit 1675. - [Inset:] A Prospect of the City of Tripoli in Barbary.
[27] A Chart of the Levant or Eastermost part of the Mediterranean Sea By Iohn Seller...
[28] A Chart of the Coasts of Barbarie Gualata Arguyn & Genehoa from C Vincent to C Verd Described by John Seller...
[29] A Chart of Guinea Describeing the Seacoast from Cape de Verde to Cape Bona Esperanca by John Seller
[30] A New Mapp of the Jsland of Saint Hellena By John Seller...Io. Oliver. Fe.
[31] A Chart of the Western part of the East Indies. With all the Aejacent Islands. from Cape Bona Esperanca to Cape Comorin By Iohn Seller...F. Lamb Sculp.
[32] A Chart of the Tartarian Sea from Novazemla to Iapan By John Seller...
[33] A General Chart of the West India's By

John Seller... -
[Inset:] Straits of Magellan.
[34] A Chart of the Seacoasts of New-England New-Jarsey Virginia Maryland and Carolina From C. Cod to C. Hatteras By John Seller... Iames Clerk Sculpsit

9773, 1914

D675
S495h
[Settle, Dionyse] fl. 1577.
...Historia Navigationis Martini Forbisseri Angli Prætoris sive Capitanei, A. C. 1577. Majo, Junio, Julio, Augusto & Septembri mensibus, Jussu Reginæ Elisabethæ, Ex Angliâ, in Septemtrionis & Occidentis tractum susceptæ, ephemeridis sive diariimore conscripta & stilo, triennioq; post, ex gallico in latinum sermonem, a Joh. Thoma Freigio translata, & Noribergæ, antè A. 94. cum præfatione utili, observationib9 aliquot & appendice edita, denuò prodit, è museo D. Capelli P.P.
Hamburgi, Sumptibus Joh. Naumanni & Georgi Wolffii, Anno 1675.
1 p. ℓ., [15], 37 p. front. 19.5cm. 4°
Cut (printer's device) on t.-p.
At head of title: I. N. J.
Pagination 1-37 begins on a verso.
Latin transl. 1st pub. under title De Martini Forbisseri Angli Navigatione, Nuremberg, 1580; transl. from La navigation du capitaine Martin Forbisher, [Geneva] 1578, which had been transl. by Nicolas Pithou from the English original pub. under title A true reporte of the laste voyage, London, 1577.
JCB(2)2:1121; Church638; Sabin79346.

01534, 1846

JA675
-T167s
Tanner, Mathias, 1630-1692.
Societas Jesu Usque Ad Sanguinis Et Vitæ Profusionem Militans, In Europa, Africa, Asia, Et America, Contra Gentiles, Mahometanos, Judæos, Hæreticos, Impios, Pro Deo, Fide, Ecclesia, Pietate. Sive Vita, Et Mors Eorum, Qui Ex Societate Jesu in causa Fidei, & Virtutis propugnatæ, violentâ morte toto Orbe sublati sunt. Auctore R. Patre Mathia Tanner e Societate Jesu, SS. Theologiæ Doctore.
Pragæ, Typis Universitatis Carolo-Ferdinandeæ, in Collegio Societatis Jesu ad S. Clementem, per Joannem Nicolaum Hampel Factorem. Anno M. DC. LXXV.
9 p. ℓ., 548, [4] p. illus. (engr.; section titles). 30cm. fol.
"Errata itâ corrige": last page.
"Societas Jesu Americana" p. 433-548.
Added t.-p. engr. Illus., incl. engr. titles signed C. Screta del., M. Küsell f.
JCB(2)2:1136; Sabin94332; Backer7:1860; Streit 1:652.

04362, 1873

DA675
H457q
[Thompson, Thomas] pseud.?
The Quakers Quibbles, In Three Parts. First set forth in an Expostulatory Epistle to Will. Penn, Concerning the late Meeting held in Barbycan between the Baptists and the Quakers. Also The Pretended Prophet, Lod, Muggleton, and the Quakers Compared. The Second Part, In Reply to a Quibbling Answer of G. Whiteheads, Entituled, The Quakers Plainness, ... The Third Part, Being a Continuation of their Quibbles, ... With some Remarks on G. W's. Slight Sheet, ... By the same Indifferent Pen.
London, Printed for F. Smith at the Elephant and Castle, in Cornhill. 1675.
1 p. ℓ., 5-38, [1] p., 4 ℓ., 101, [1] p., 5 ℓ., 99, [1] p. 17cm. 8°
Letter to the printer (p. [39]) signed: Thomas Tompson, but George Whitehead (t.-p. of The Timorous Reviler Slighted. [London, 1675]) and Smith(Anti-Quak)222, both suspect Henry Hedworth of authorship. For author's denial that he is Hedworth see Part 3, p. 48, 57-66.
With, as issued, his The Second Part Of The Quakers Quibbles. London, 1675; and his The Third Part Of The Quakers Quibbles. London, 1675, each with special t.-p. and separate paging and signatures.
Part 1 first pub. London, 1675.
JCB(2)2:1137; Smith(Anti-Quak)423-4; Sabin 95527; WingT1013.

03848A, 1868

DA675
H457q
[Thompson, Thomas] pseud.?
The Second Part Of The Quakers Quibbles, Set forth In a Reply to a Quibbling pretended Answer of G. Whiteheads, Intituled the Quakers Plainness &c. ... Also the Comparison betwixt the pretended Prophet Muggleton and the Quakers Justified; to be True, Rational, and necessary; Whereunto is added an Advertisement to Mr. W. Penn, George Whitehead, and the Quakers. ... By the same indifferent Penn. ...
London, Printed for F. Smith at the Elephant and Castle in Cornhil near the Royal-Exchange, 1675.
4 p. ℓ., 101, [1] p. 17cm. 8° (Issued as a part of his The Quakers Quibbles. London, 1675)
"Errata": 5th p. ℓ.
Preface signed (5th p. ℓ.): Thomas Thompson, but George Whitehead (t.-p. of The Timorous Reviler Slighted. [London, 1674]) and Smith (Anti-Quak)222, both suspect Henry Hedworth of authorship. For author's denial that he is Hedworth see Part 3, p. 48, 57-66.
Letter to the printer signed (p. [102]: T. T. Jan. I. 7 4/5.
A reply, in part, to George Whitehead, The

	Quaker's Plainness. [London] 1674. JCB(2)2:1137; Smith(Anti-Quak)423-4; Sabin 95527; WingT1013.
03848B, 1868	

DA675 H457q	[Thompson, Thomas] pseud. ? The Third Part Of The Quakers Quibbles. Being A Continuation of their Quibbles, ... Whereunto is Added Remarks on G. W's. Slight Sheet, given forth by him as a Reprehension (for want of an Answer) to the Second Part of the Quakers Quibbles. ... By the same Indifferent Pen. ... London, Printed for F. Smith at the Elephant and Castle in Cornhil, near the Royal Exchange. 1675. 5 p.ℓ., 99, [1] p. 17cm. 8° (Issued as a part of his The Quakers Quibbles. London, 1675) Errata, p. [100] Preface signed (5th p.ℓ.): Thomas Thompson, but George Whitehead (t.-p. of The Timorous Reviler Slighted. [London, 1674]) and Smith (Anti-Quak)222, both suspect Henry Hedworth of authorship. For author's denial that he is Hedworth see Part 3, p. 48, 57-66. Sam. Fisher Transpos'd (poetry): p. 45. A reply, in part, to George Whitehead, The Timorous Reviler Slighted. [London, 1674] JCB(2)2:1137; Smith (Anti-Quak)423-4; Sabin 95527; WingT1013.
03848C, 1868	

D675 W553n	[Wharton, Edward] d. 1678. New-England's Present Sufferings, Under Their Cruel Neighbouring Indians. Represented In two Letters, lately Written from Boston to London. London. Printed [by Benjamin Clark] in the Yeer 1675. 7, [1] p. 19.5cm. 4° First letter (p. 1 [i.e. 3]-5) begins: ... Boston the 4th of the 11th Month, 1675. Second letter (p. 5-7) begins: Boston, the 10th of the 8th. Month, 1675. Both letters signed: E. W. "King Philip's War Narratives" quarto no. 2. cf. Church639n. JCB(2)2:1138; Church639; Sabin103100; Smith (Friends)2:878; Vail (Front.)170; WingW1536.
03832, 1868	

B672 Z36t	Zaragoza, Joseph, 1627-1679. Esphera En Comvn Celeste, Y Terraqvea. Avtor El M.R.P. Ioseph Zaragoza, de la Compañia de Iesvs. ... Consagrada A La Excelentissima señora Condesa de Villa Vmbrosa, ... Primera Impression, Año de 1675. Con Licencia. En Madrid: Por Iuan Martin del Barrio. 4 p.ℓ., 256, [8] p. illus., 12 fold. diagrs. 20cm. 4° License dated (3d p.ℓ.ᵛ) 20 Jan. 1675. Errata, 4th p.ℓ.ᵛ First pub. Madrid, 1674. Bound as no. 4 of 5 items. Backer8:1466; Palau(1)7:249.
04701, 1920	

B672 Z36t	Zaragoza, Joseph, 1627-1679. Fabrica, Y Vso De Varios Instrumentos Mathematicos, Con Que Siruio Al Rey N.S. D. Carlos Segundo, En El Dia De Sus Catorze Años, El Excelentissimo Señor D. Ivan Francisco Delacerda Duque De Medina-Celi, ...Por El Rmo. P. Ioseph Zaragoza De la Compañia de Iesus, ... En Madrid: Por Antonio Francisco de Zafra, dia 5. de Nouiembre de 1675. Con licencia de los Superiores. 1 p.ℓ., 222 p. illus., 7 fold. diagrs. 20cm. 4° First pub. Madrid, 1674. Bound as no. 5 of 5 items. Backer8:1467; Palau(1)7:249.
12665, 1920	

1676

B69 G643v 15	Agurto y Loaysa, Joseph de, fl. 1676-1688. Villancicos, Qve Se Cantaron En La Santa Iglesia Metropolitana de Mexico. En Los Maitines De La Pvrissima Concepcion de Nuestra Señora. A devocion de vn afecto al Misterio. Año de 1676. Compuestos en Metro musico, por el B.ʳ Ioseph de Agurto, y Loaysa, Maestro Compositor de dicha Santa Iglesia. Con licencia En Mexico. Por la Viuda de Bernardo Calderon, en la calle de San Augustin. [1676].

B676
B228a
    Barba, Alvaro Alonso, b. 1569.
        1 p.l., [6] p. 20cm. 4°
        Woodcut title vignette (the Virgin surrounded by angels with harps; initialed in corners: S., O., V., BC.)
        Bound, in contemporary vellum, as no. 15 with 42 other items.
28915, 1941

B676
B228a
    Barba, Alvaro Alonso, b. 1569.
        Albaro Alonso Barba, Eines Spanischen Priesters und hocherfahrnen Naturkündigers Berg-Büchlein/Darinnen Von der Metallen und Mineralien Generalia und Ursprung/ wie auch von derselben Natur Eigenschafft/ Mannigfaltigkeit/ Scheidung und Fein-machung/ imgleichen allerhand Edelgesteinen/ ihre Generation etc. aussführlich und nutzbarlich gehandelt wird. Anfangs in Spanischer Sprache beschrie-ben/ und in zwey Theile getheilet. ...In Teutsch übersetzet Von I. L. M. C. Mit Chur Sachsischer Freyheit nicht nach zudrucken.
        Hamburg/ Auf Gottfried Schultzens Kosten/ 1676.
        2 p.l., 128 p., 1l., 129-204, [4] p. plate. 17cm. 8°
        Transl. (by Johann Lange, Medicinae Candidato) from: Arte De Los Metales, first pub. Madrid, 1640.
        With, as issued, his Das Andere Buch von der Kunst der Metallen. Hamburg, 1676, with special t.-p. but continuous paging and signatures.
        Palau(2):23634; Maffei 177; Sabin3255b.
30684A, 1950

B676
B228a
    Barba, Alvaro Alonso, b. 1569.
        Das Andere Buch von der Kunst der Metallen/ Worinnen der gemeine Weg das Silber durch Qvecksilber fein zu machen gelehret wird/nebst etlichen neuen Regulen solches desto besser ins Werck zu setzen. Anfangs im Jahr 1640. in Spanischer Sprach beschrieben von Albaro Alonso Barba, Kunstmeistern Priestern der Gemeine in der St. Bernhards Kirchen in der Königl. Stadt Potosi in dem Konigreich Peru in West-Indien; Numehro aber den Liebhabern zu gefallen ins Teutsch überbracht von I. L. M. C.
        Hamburg/Auff Gottfried Schultzens Kosten/ gedruckt im Jahr 1676.
        1 p.l., 129-204, [4] p. plate. 17cm. 8° (Issued as a part of his... Berg-Büchlein.

Hamburg, 1676)
        Transl. (by Johann Lange, Medicinae Candidato) from: Arte De Los Metales, first pub. Madrid, 1640.
30684B, 1950

DA676
B244t
    Barclay, Robert, 1648-1690.
        Roberti Barclaii Theologiæ Verè Christianæ Apologia. ...
        Typis excusa, M. DC. LXXVI. Pro Jacob Claus, Bibliopola, habitante Amstelodami, op de oudezijds achter-burgwal, in de vergulde Drie-hoek. Veneunt præterea, Londini, Roterodami, Francofurti, }apud{ Benjamin Clark, in George-Court, Lumbard-street. Isaacum Næranum, op het Steyger. Henricum Betkıum. Et in quibusdam aliis locis.
        12 p.l., 374, [25] p. 23.5cm. 4°.
        Errata: p. [24-5] at end.
        Half-title: Theologiæ Verè Christianæ Apologia, Carolo Secundo, Magnæ Britanniæ, &c. Regi, à Roberto Barclaio, Scoto-Britanno, oblata.
        Dedication (3d-6th p.l.) signed: Robertus Barclaius. Ab Uria ... Novembris, Anno 1675.
        Marginal rules in ms.
        With this is bound his Epistola Amatoria, Nec Non Consultoria Ad Legatos Magnatum Europæ. Rotterdam, 1678.
        Smith(Friends)1:182; McAlpin3:720; WingB736.
64-214, 1964

DA676
B359c
    Bayly, William, d. 1675.
        A Collection Of The Several Wrightings Of That True Prophet, Faithful Servant of God and Sufferer for the Testimony of Jesus, William Bayly, Who finished his Testimony, and laid down his Head in Peace with the Lord, the First Day of the Fourth Moneth, in the Year 1675...
        [London] Printed in the Year, 1676.
        34 p.l., 29 numb. l., 31-38, 35-58, 65-176 p. 1 l., 187-495, [8] p., 1 l., 664 [i. e. 499]-604, [4], [605]-748 p. [a]^1 b^4 c^2 *-**^{4} (*1+[ ]^2) (A)^4 (B)^2 (C)-(D)^4 A-G^4 [1]-[4]^4 H-Y^4 Aa-Zz^4 Aaa-Qqq^4] [^{4} Rrr-Zzz^4 Aaaa-Gggg^4 (Gggg^{2+}⌐^{2}) Hhhh-Zzzz^4 Aaaaa^4 Bbbbb^2 19cm. (20cm. in case) 4°
        **1 marked [ ]; Y3 and Y4 signed Z1 and Z2.
        Imperfect: 9-10th p.l. and p. 745-48 wanting; supplied in facsimile (attached to Bibliographical Sheet)
        Smith(Friends)1:220; McAlpin3:721; Wing B1517.
31130, 1952

F676 B741*l* [Bos, Lambert van den] 1610-1698.
Leeven en Daden Der Doorluchtighste Zee-Helden En Ontdeckers van Landen, Deser Eeuwen. Beginnende met Christoffel Colombus, Vinder van de Nieuwe Wereldt. En eyndigende met den Roemruchtigen Admirael M. A. de Ruyter, Ridd. &c. Vertoonende veel vreemde Voorvallen, dappere Verrichtingen, stoutmoedige Bestieringen, en swaere Zee-slagen, &c. Naeukeurigh, uyt veele geloofwaerdige Schriften, en Authentijcke Stucken, by een gebracht, en befchreven, Door V. D. B.
t'Amsterdam, By Jan Claesz. ten Hoorn, en Jan Bouman, Boeckverkoopers. Anno 1676. Met Privilegie voor 15. Jaren.
4 p.*l*., 350 p., 1 *l*., 303,[304-310] p. 31 plates (incl. 6 fold., 9 ports.) 21cm. 4°.
Added t.-p., engraved: Leeven, en Daden, der Doorlughtige Zee-Helden. J-Padebrugge scu. ...
In 2 parts with separate half-title and paging but continuous signatures.
Cut on t.-p.
The life of Ruyter in part 2 includes an account of the English conquest of New Netherland and the subsequent treaty (p. 197-9), and Ruyter's account of the recapture of New Amsterdam (p. 284).
JCB(2)2:1149; Muller(1872)126; Scheepvaart Mus.842; Sabin6439.
02950, 1861

BA626 V722s [Buendía, José] 1644-1727.
Sudor, Y Lagrimas De Maria Santissima En Su Santa Imagen De La Misericordia. Reconocidas A 29. De Setiembre dia del Arcangel S. Miguel año de 1675. Veneradas En La Capilla De Loreto de la Iglesia de la Compañia de Jesvs en el Prefidio, y Puerto del Callao. Segun consta del processo juridico hecho ante el Juez Ordinario de orden del Ilustrissimo y Reuerendissimo Señor D. Fr. Juan de Almoguera Arçobispo de Lima del Consejo de su Magestad. Que Escribe Y Consagra A La Exc.^ma Senora D. Teresa Maria Arias De Saavedra, ... Virreyna del Peru, Tierrafirme, y Chile, &c. La Noble Congregacion De La SS. Virgen de Loreto del Puerto del Callao.
Con licencia. En Lima. En casa de Iuan de Queuedo 1676.
8 p.*l*., [29] p. 20cm. 4°
License (4th p.*l*.) dated 3 July 1676.
Bound as no. 5 of 6 items.
Medina(Lima)498; Backer2:337; Palau(2) 36674.
5465, 1909

Church of England--Book of Common Prayer.
The Book Of Common Prayer, And Administration of the Sacraments, And Other Rites and Ceremonies of the Church. According to the Use of the Church of England; Together with the Psalter or Psalms Of David, Pointed as they are to be sung or said in Churches.
London, Printed by the Assigns of John Bill and Christopher Barker, Printers to the Kings most Excellent Majesty. 1676. Cum Privilegio.
[320] p. 17.5cm. A-U⁸. 8°
Includes at end the "three Forms of Prayer and Service" ordered annexed to the Book of Common Prayer by a royal command printed on last p. dated 2 May [1662].
In this copy *l*. bearing Psalms 55-59 mutilated.
With this is bound Sternhold and Hopkins' Psalms, London, 1677 (WingB2526).
JCBAR39:43; WingB3646.
28447, 1939

B676 C719h Colón, Fernando, 1488-1539
Historie Del Signor D. Fernando Colombo: Nelle quali s'hà particolare, & vera relatione della vita, e de'fatti dell' Ammiraglio. D. Christoforo Colombo Suo Padre: E dello scoprimento, ch'egli fece dell'Indie Occidentali, dette Mondo Nuouo, hora possedute dal Serenissimo Rè Catolico. Nuouamente di lingua Spagnuola tradotte nell'Italiana dal Sign Alfonso Vlloa.
In Venetia, M.DC.LXXVI. Presso Gio: Pietro Brigonci. Con Licenza de'Superiori, e Priuilegio.
24 p.*l*., 489,[490-498]p. 14.5cm. 12°
Title vignette (decorated scene of Venice).
Half-title: Viaggi Del Signor Christoforo Colombo.
First pub. Venice, 1571.
"Scrittura di Frà Roman [i.e. Ramón Pane] delle antichità de gl'Indiani...": p. 250-87.
In this copy there is a blank *l*. at end.
JCB(2)2:1141; Sabin14675; Streit2:2108; Palau (2)57211; Leclerc(1867)363.
01790, 1854

D676 -C762s A Continuation Of the State of New-England; Being a Farther Account of the Indian Warr, And of the Engagement betwixt the Joynt Forces of the United English Collonies and the Indians, on the 19th. of December 1675. With the true Number of the Slain and Wounded, and the Transactions of the English Army since the said Fight.

With all other Passages that have there Hapned from the 10th. of November, 1675. to the 8th. of February 1675/6. Together with an Account of the intended Rebellion of the Negroes in the Barbadoes. Licensed March 27. 1676. Henry Oldenburg.
London, Printed by T. M. for Dorman Newman, at the Kings Armes in the Poultry, 1676.
20 p. 29cm. fol.
"King Philip's War Narratives" folio no. 2. cf. Church 636n.
Errata: p. [2]
Woodcut title vignette (royal arms)
Includes: two letters from Boston dated respectively February 9, 1675 (O.S.) concerning the Great Swamp Fight, and February 8, 1675/6, signed: N.S. (Nathaniel Saltonstall?); the account of Barbadoes is dated November 30, 1675, and signed: G.W.
A continuation of: The Present State Of New-England, first pub. London, 1675, and by the same writer.
JCB(2)2:1153; Church645; Sabin52623; Vail (Front.)171; WingC5971.

0512, 1846

BA676 Córdoba y Salinas, Diego de, 1591-1654.
C796l   Leben/ Tugenden/vnnd Wunderwerck/ dess Apostels von Peru. Nemblich Dess seeligen Vatters F. Francisci Solani Auss dem H. Seraphischen Orden der Minderen Brüder der Regularischen Observantz/erwöhlten Patrons zu Lima/... Durch P. F. Didacum von Cordoua, auss der Statt Lima gebürtig/Apostolischen Predigern/und General Chronisten der Provintzen von Peru/ auss dem Orden dess heiligen Vatters Francisci. Vermehrt In der anderen Anno 1643. zu Madrit in Truck gegebnen Hispanischen Edition, durch P. F. Alphonsum von Mendieta, eben auss disem Orden/... Anietzo aber Von der Hispanischen-in die Teutsche Sprach übersetzt/durch Johann Georg von Werndle zu Adelsriedt/&c. ... im Jahr Christi 1676. Cum Licentia Superiorum, & Privilegio.
München/Getruckt und Verlegt durch Johann Jäcklin Churfl. Hoffbuechtrucker/Im Jahr 1676.
8 p. ℓ., 774, 779-795, [796-810] p. front. (port.) 20.5cm. 4°.
Errata: final page.
First pub. under title: Vida, Virtudes, y Milagros del nuevo Apostol del Peru. Lima, 1630, rev. and enl. (by Alonso de Mendieta) Madrid, 1643.
Approbation dated (4th p. ℓ.ᵛ) 20 Feb 1676.
JCB(2)2:1142;   Streit2:2112; Medina (BHA)1608;   Palmer309; Palau(2)61943.

01626, 1847

K676   [Courland, James, Duke of] 1632-1682.
C861b   Briefve Deduction Par laquelle il est clairement monstré que L'Isle de Tobago, Sise en L'Amerique. Appartient A Monseigneur le Duc en Livonie de Courlande & Semgalle. Et que la possession que Mʳˢ. les Lambsons pretendent sur la dite Isle, n'a aucun fondement. Imprimé l'an de grace 1668. A Mittaw, Chez Michel Karnali.
[France? Holland? 1676?]
22 p. 19.5cm. 4°
Pages 1-16 1st printed Mittaw [i.e. Jelgava, Latvia] 1668; what follows brings events down to October, 1676.
Title-page in French and Dutch; text in French and Dutch in parallel columns.
Title in Dutch: Korte Deductie By dewelcke klaerlijck werdt betoont dat het Eyland van Tobago, Gelegen in America...Gedruckt in 't Jaer onses Heeren, 1668. in Mittaw, tot Michiel Carnali.
JCB(2)2:1000; Sabin7932

02305, 1850

DA68   Crisp, Stephen, 1628-1692.
C697   Een Sendt-Brief, Om gelesen te worden in alle Vergaderingen van de Vrienden der Waarheyt, In de Steden van Holland, ... Geschreven door Steven Crisp. Uyt het Engels Overgeset.
Tot Rotterdam, Gedrukt by Pieter van Wijnbrugge, in de Leeuwe-straat: En zijn ook te bekomen by Iacob Claus, in de vergulde Drie-hoek, op d'Achterburghwal, tot Amsterdam. Anno 1676.
1p. ℓ., 6p. 20cm. 4° (No. [20], as issued, in Collectio, of Versamelinge. [Amsterdam, ca. 1680])
Cut on t.-p.
Dated at end: Colchester, den 31. der 1 Maant, 1676.
Smith(Friends)1:476.

03261, 1866

E676   Duval, Pierre, 1618-1683.
D983l   Le Monde ou La Géographie Vniuerselle contenant Les Descriptions, les cartes, et le Blason, des principaux Païs du Monde. Par P. DuVal d'Abbeville Geogr. Ord. du Roy.
A Paris Chez l'Auteur proche du Palais, sur le Quay de l'Orloge, au coin de la ruë de Harlay.
Auec Priuilege de sa Majesté, pour 20 Ans. M.DC. LXXVI.
2v.: 6 p. ℓ., 312 p. incl. double table.

11 col. plates (coats of arms), 49 double maps; 2 p.ℓ., 313-603 p. 28 col. plates (coats of arms), 1 double table, 31 double maps. 15.5cm. 12º

Engraved t.-p. on two leaves.

Added t.-p., engraved: La Geographie Vniuerselle qui fait voit l'Estat present des 4 Parties Du Monde, ... A Paris... 1676.

Vol. 2 has different t.-p., engraved on two leaves: L'Europe IIe Partie de La Geographie Vniuerselle, En plusieurs Cartes.

First pub. Paris, 1658.
"L'Amerique": p. 15-90.
Imperfect: p. 135-140 wanting.
Bound in contemporary paper boards.

13111, 1921

D676 F247
A farther Brief and True Narration Of The Late VVars Risen in New-England, Occasioned by the Quarrelsome Disposition and Perfidious Carriage of the Barbarous and Savage Indian Natives there. With an Account of the Fight, the 19th of December last, 1675.
London, February 17th, 167 5/6. Licensed, Henry Oldenburg. London, Printed by J.D. for M.K. and are to be Sold by the Booksellers, 1676.
12 p. 20.5cm. 4º

Caption: Boston December 28th, 1675.
"King Philip's War Narratives", quarto, no. 6 (cf. Church 639n).

"To our Brethren and Friends the Inhabitants of the Colony of the Massachusets" (p. 6-8) ends: Dated in Boston, the 7th of December, Anno Christi, 1675. ... By the Council, Edward Rawson, Secret.

List of English casualties in the Great Swamp Fight: p. 11.

A continuation of: <u>A Brief and True Narration Of the Late VVars. London, 1675.</u>

In this copy top of p. 12 torn, affecting one line of text.
Sabin 52638; Vail(Front.)172; Wing F529.

3902, 1907

DA676 F317t
[Fell, Lydia (Erbury)], fl. 1676.
A Testimony and Warning Given forth in the love of Truth, and is for the Governour, Magistrates & People inhabiting on the Island of Barbadoes; which is a Call to turn to the Lord.
[London? 1676]
7 p. 18.5cm. 4º

Caption title; imprint from Wing.
Signed: Lydia Fell.
Sabin 24012; Smith(Friends)1:597; Wing F625.

10768, 1915

B676 -F363t
Fernández Navarrete, Domingo, Abp. of St. Domingo, d. 1689.
Tratados Historicos, Politicos, Ethicos, Y Religiosos De La Monarchia De China. Descripcion Breve De Aqvel Imperio, Y Exemplos Raros De Emperadores, Y Magistrados Del. Con Narracion Difvsa De Varios Svcessos, Y Cosas Singulares De Otros Reynos, Y Diferentes Navegaciones. Añadense Los Decretos Pontificios, Y Proposiciones Calificadas En Roma Para La Mission Chinica; y vna Bula de N. M. S. P. Clemente X. en fauor de los Missionarios. Por El P. Maestro Fr. Domingo Fernandez Navarrete ...
Año 1676. Con Privilegio: En Madrid: En la Imprenta Real. Por Iuan García Infançon. A costa de Florian Anisson, Mercader de Libros.
10 p.ℓ., 518, [25] p. 30cm. fol.
Title in red and black; cut on t.-p.
Errata, 9th p.ℓ.
"Suma de la Tassa" dated (9th p.ℓ.) 20 June 1676.
A 2d vol., Madrid, 1679, was probably suppressed (cf. Medina and Streit); an incomplete copy is in the British Museum.
Medina(BHA)1611; Streit 5: 2440; Sabin 52095; Palau(2)89431.

63-209

D676 F992a
A Further Account Of New Jersey, In an Abstract of Letters Lately Writ from thence, By several Inhabitants there Resident.
[London] Printed in the Year 1676.
1 p.ℓ., 13 p. 20.5cm. 4º
"Scottish Proprietors' Tracts", no. 1. (Church 649n).
Letters from Quakers in East and West Jersey.
Contents.—[letter 1] (p. 1-3), signed: Richard Hartshorne. New Jersie, Midleton 12, of the 9th Month 1675.—[letter 2] (p. 4-5), addressed "For my Dear Bro. Richard Craven in Limehouse", signed: Martha S. New Jersey the 22. of 9th. Month, 1675.—[letter 3] (p. 6-7), signed: Robert Wade. Delarware River the place called Upland, the 2d. of the 2d. Month 1676.—[letter 4] (p. 8-9), to John Sunison, signed: Ester Huckens. New Jersie Delaware, April the 4th. 1676.—[letter 5] (p. 10-11), signed: Robert

Wade. The 17th. day of the 4th. Month 1676.—[letter 6] (p. 12-13), signed: Roger Pederick. From Delaware River the 14th. day of the 14th. [sic] Month 1676.
 Church649; Sabin30710; Smith(Friends)1:922; Vail(Front.)173; WingH1007.

11820, 1919

E708   Gage, Thomas, 1603?-1656.
D563r   Nouvelle Relation, Contenant Les Voyages
cop.1   De Thomas Gage dans la Nouvelle Espagne, ses diverses avantures; & son retour par la Province de Nicaragua, jusques à la Havane. Avec La Description De La Ville de Mexique telle qu'elle estoit autrefois, & comme elle est à present. Ensemble Vne Description exacte des Terres & Provinces que possedent les Espagnols en toute l' Amerique, de la forme de leur gouvernement Ecclesiastique & Politique, de leur Commerce, de leurs Mœurs, & de celles des Criolles, des Metifs, des Mulatres, des Indiens, & des Negres. Et un Traité de la Langue Poconchi ou Pocomane. ... Le tout traduit de l' Anglois, par le sieur De Beaulieu Huës O Neil [pseud?]. Premiere [-Qvatrième] Partie.
 A Paris, Chez Gervais Clouzier, au Palais, sur les degrez en montant pour aller à la Sainte Chapelle au Voyageur. M. DC. LXXVI. Avec Privilege Dv Roy.
 4 pts. in 2 v.: pt.1, 13 p.ℓ., 246, [4] p.; pt. 2, 4 p.ℓ., 240 p.; pt.3, 4 p.ℓ., 297, [298-302] p.; pt.4, 4 p.ℓ., 153, [154-159] p. 15.5cm. 12°
 Transl. from: A new survey of the West-Indies, 1st pub. London, 1648, under title: The English-American his travail by sea and land; or, A new survey ...
 Translation has been attributed to Adrien Baillet.
 Title-page of pt.1 is a cancel; some copies have an integral, general t.-p.: Novvelle Relation Des Indes Occidentales, Contenant Les Voyages de Thomas Gage ... A Paris, Chez Gervais Clouzier, ... M. DC. LXXVI. ...
 "Achevé d'imprimer pour la premiere fois le vingtième Janvier 1676." (pt.1, p. [4] at end; pt.2, 4th p.ℓ.v), "... le 2. Juin 1676." (pt.3, p. [301-302]; pt.4, p. [158-159]).
 Imperfect: pts. 3-4 wanting; data supplied from Boston Public Library copy.
 Bound in contemporary calf with: Dièreville, Relation, Rouen, 1708.
 JCB(2)2:1144; Sabin26303; Leclerc(1878)222; Streit 2:2113; Pilling1364a.

0824, 5 rev 1846

C585   The Grand Pyrate: Or, the Life and Death Of
E96t   Capt. George Cusack The great Sea-Robber.
11   With An Accompt of all his notorious Robberies both at Sea and Land. Together With his Tryal, Condemnation, and Execution. Taken by an Impartial Hand.
 Licensed Novemb. 19. 1675. Roger L'Estrange.
London, Printed for Jonathan Edwin at the Sign of the Three Roses in Ludgate-street. MDCLXXVI.
 31 p. 20cm. 4°
 Includes (p. 16-18) a letter from Richard Wharton in Boston reporting Cusack's activities.
 With, as issued, An exact narrative of the tryals of the pyrats... , [London] 1675, with separate t.-p. and continuous paging and signatures.
 Bound as no. 11 of 19 items in vol. with binder's title: Tracts 1681-1701.
 WingG1505; Sabin18078.

11352-11, 1918 rev

D676   Great Newes From The Barbadoes. Or, A
G786n   True and Faithful Account Of The Grand Conspiracy Of The Negroes against the English. And The Happy Discovery of the same. With The number of those that were burned alive, Beheaded, and otherwise Executed for their Horrid Crimes. With a short Discription of that Plantation.
 With Allowance. London, Printed for L. Curtis in Goat-Court upon Ludgate-Hill, 1676.
 14 p. 17.5cm. 4°
 JCB(2)2:1140; Sabin3270; Cundall(WI)9.

03613, before 1866

DA676   [Groome, Samuel] d. 1683.
G876g   A Glass For the People of New-England, In Which They may see themselves and Spirits, and if not too late, Repent and Turn from their Abominable Ways and Cursed Contrivances: That so the Lord God may turn away his Wrath, which he will bring upon them (if they Repent not) for their Blasphemies against himself, and for all the Murders and Cruelties done to his tender People, ever since they usurped Authority to Banish, Hang, Whip, and Cut Off Ears, and Spoil the Goods of Dissenters from them in Religious Matters, while themselves disown Infallibility in those things. By S. G. ...
 [London] Printed in the Year, 1676.
 43 p. 19.5cm. 4°.
 Errata: p. 43.
 A secretly-printed Quaker account of persecution by the Massachusetts General Court against Quakers and others including Anne Hutchinson.
 Includes extracts from "a Book called, The

Elders Tenents in the Bay": p. 24-28; "Queries by another Hand for the New-England Priests and Elders to Answer", by George Fox: p. 29-33; and "The Copy of a Letter [dated in Boston, "15th of the 4th Moneth", 1667] which was delivered into the Hands of R. Bellingham, late Governour of Boston...", and addenda, by John Tyso: p. 34-43.
Addendum dated (p. 43) in London, "the 28th of the 5th Moneth, 1676".
JCB(2)2:1145; Sabin 28926; Smith(Friends) 1:875; Dexter(Cong.)2091; Wing G2065.

02135, before 1859

DA68 C697
Hendricks, Pieter, Quaker, Amsterdam, fl. 1661-1687.
Noch een Goede, Getrouwe, en Ernstige Vermaninge, Mitsgaders goeden raad Aan Burgermeesteren en Regeerders der Stadt Embden. ... Door Pieter Henriksz.
Gedrukt voor Jacob Claus, Boek-verkooper in de vergulde Drie-hoek, op de achter Burg-wal, tot Amsterdam. 1676.
1p.ℓ., 8p. 20cm. 4° (No. [48] as issued, in Collectio, Of Versamelinge. [Amsterdam, ca. 1680])
Signed: In Amsterdam den 23 der sevende Maant, 1676. P.H.
In this copy there is a blank ℓ. at end.
Smith(Friends)1:935.

03289, 1866

FC650 H737 26
Hollandtze Mercurius, Verhalende, De voornaemste geschiedenissen, voor-gevallen binnen Europa, In het Jaer 1675. tot 1676. Het Ses-en-twintighste Deel. ...
Gedruckt tot Haerlem, by Pieter Casteleyn, Boeckdrucker op de Marckt, in de Keysers Kroon. Anno 1676 Met Privilegie.
4 p.ℓ., 270, [2] p. 20cm. 4° (Bound in [vol. 6.] of Hollandse Mercurius)
Errata: p. [272]
Added t.-p., engraved (2d p.ℓ.): Hollantse Mercurius. By Pieter Casteleyn Anno 1676. Met Privilegie.
"Extract van Privilegie" (4th p.ℓ.) dated: 17. December...1668.
JCB(3)2:410; Sabin 32523.

8487Z, 1912

DA676 -H859
Howgill, Francis, 1618-1668.
The Dawnings Of The Gospel-Day, And Its Light and Glory Discovered: By... Francis Howgil, ...
[London] Printed in the Year 1676.
16 p.ℓ., 252, 255-326, 329-736, [5] p. 30cm. fol.
The works of Francis Howgill, edited by Ellis Hookes.
Preliminary matter includes testimonials of George Fox, Richard Pinder, and in verse Edward Guy, Thomas Langhorn, and Thomas Carlton.
Dated (2d p.ℓ.): London the 3d Day of the 5th Moneth, 1676.
Bound in contemporary calf.
Smith(Friends)1:997; Wing H3157.

4394, 1908

D677 H876n1
Hubbard, William, 1621-1704.
The Happiness of a People In the Wisdome of their Rulers Directing And in the Obedience of their Brethren Attending Unto what Israel ougho [sic] to do: Recommended In A Sermon Before the Honourable Governour and Council, and the Respected Deputies of the Mattachusets Colony in New-England. Preached at Boston, May 3d. 1676. being the day of Election there. By William Hubbard Minister of Ipswich. ...
Boston, Printed by John Foster. 1676.
4p.ℓ., 63p. 19cm. 4° (Issued as a part of his A Narrative Of The Troubles With The Indians. Boston, 1677)
Errata: 4th p.ℓ.ᵛ.

D677 H876n2
—— ——Another copy. (Issued as a part of another issue of his A Narrative Of The Troubles With The Indians. Boston, 1677)
JCB(1)2:837; JCB(2)2:1147; Sabin 33444; Evans 214; Church 641; Wing H3209; Green(John Foster) 69-70.

15485, 1929
04610, 1854

E676 J37j
Jarrige, Pierre, 1604-1670.
Les Iesvites Mis sur L'Echafavd, Pour plusieurs Crimes Capitaux qu'ils ont commis dans la Province de Guienne. Avec La Response Avx Calomnies De Iaqves Beavfés Par le Sieur Pierre Iarrige, Cy devant Iesuite, Profés du quatriéme Vœu, & Predicateur.
[Germany? Holland?] Iouxte la Copie imprimée à Leiden, 1676.
12 p.ℓ., 259 p. 14.5cm. 12°.
First pub. Leiden, 1648. On the evidence of paper and typography this was most likely issued in Germany, but possibly in Holland.
'Guienne' on the t.-p., which has been mistaken for Guiana, was an old province of France (until 1790) with its capital and parlement at Bordeaux, the principal locale of this work. The author was converted to Calvinism.
"La Response", p. [117]-259, is a reply to: Jacques Beaufez, Les impietés et sacrileges de

Pierre Iarrige. Tulle, 1648.
Imperfect: p. 217-240 (signature k) wanting.
JCB(2)2:1148; Sabin35792; Backer4:753; Graesse3:454.

04956, before 1882

DA676 K28i
Keith, George, 1639?-1716.
Immediate Revelation, (Or, Jesus Christ The Eternal Son of God, Revealed in Man, Revealing the Knowledge of God, and the things of his Kingdom, Immediately) Not Ceased, ... The Second Edition: With an Appendix, containing an Answer to some farther Objections. ... By George Keith.
[London] Printed in the Year, 1676.
6 p.ℓ., 259 p. 18.5cm. 8°
"Errata": 4th p.ℓ.
This is the same setting of type as 1675 ed. with date altered. First pub. Aberdeen, 1668.
Signed (p. 215): The 7th. of the 4th. Month, 1668. G. K.
"Postcript" (p. 216-224) signed: Writ in the time of my Imprisonment, in the Tolbooth of Aberdeen, in Scotland, ... The 3d. of the 6th. Month, 1668. G. Keith.
"An Appendix": p. 225-259.
Smith(Friends) 2:18-19; WingK177.

6426, 1910

J678 C238n
Kurtze Erzehlung Von dem Anfange und Fortgange Der Schiffahrt/ biss auff diese unsere Zeit. Aus der Holländischen in die hochdeutsche Sprache gebracht.
Hamburg/ In Verlegung Johan Naumans und Georg Wolffs/ Buchhändlere für S. Johans Kirchen. Im Jahr Christi 1676.
[213]-236 p. 20cm. 4° (Issued as a part of R. Capell, Norden/ Oder Zu Wasser und Lande. Hamburg, 1678)

02544C, 1851

E676 L217v
La Martinière, Pierre Martin de, 1634-1690.
Voyage Des Pays Septentrionavx. Dans lequel se void [sic] les mœurs, maniere de vivre, & superstitions des Norweguiens, Lappons, Kiloppes, Borandiens, Syberiens, Samojedes, Zembliens, Islandois. Par le sieur De La Martiniere, Seconde Edition, reveuë & augmentée de nouveau.
A Paris, Chez Louis Vendosme, Libraire au Palais dans la Salle Royalle, au Sacrifice d'Abraham. 1676. Avec Privilege Dv Roy.
6 p.ℓ., 322, [2] p. illus. (incl. map). 16cm. 12°
Added t.-p., engraved: Voyage Des Païs Septentrionavx Par le S.r D. LM. A Paris Chez Louis Vandosme proche Monseig.r le Premier President. G. Ladame f. (from same plate as 1671 edition)
A revision of the 1st ed., Paris, 1671.
"Extraict du Privilege" dated (last p.) 28 Aug. 1671.
The last chapter refers to Greenland.
Contemporary calf, rebacked.
Sabin38711.

32625, 1960

D. Math I.16A
Mather, Increase, 1639-1723.
A Brief History Of The VVarr With the Indians in Nevv-England, (From June 24, 1675. when the first English-man was murdered by the Indians, to August 12. 1676. when Philip, alias Metacomet, the principal Author and Beginner of the Warr, was slain.) Wherein the Grounds, Beginning, and Progress of the Warr, is summarily expressed. Together With A Serious Exhortation to the Inhabitants of that Land, By Increase Mather, Teacher of a Church of Christ, in Boston in New-England. ...
Boston, Printed and Sold by John Foster over against the Sign of the Dove. 1676.
3 p.ℓ., 51, 8 p., 1 ℓ., [2], 26 p. 18.5cm. 4°
This copy closely trimmed at bottom with slight effect on text.
Errata, p. 8 (2d count) and p. 26 (3d count)
"King Philip's War Narratives" quarto no. 3. cf. Church 639n.
With, as issued, his An Earnest Exhortation To the Inhabitants of New-England. Boston, 1676, with special t.-p. and separate paging and signatures.
JCB(1)2:827; JCBAR35:8-10; Evans220; Sabin 46640; Holmes(I) 16A; Vail(Front.) 174; Church 642; WingM1187; Green(John Foster) 65-66.

16717A, 1935

D. Math I.16B1
Mather, Increase, 1639-1723.
A Brief History Of The VVar, With The Indians In New-England. From June 24, 1675. (when the first Englishman was Murdered by the Indians) to August 12, 1676. when Philip, alias Metacomet, the principal Author and Beginner of the War, was slain. Wherein the Grounds, Beginning, and Progress of the War, is summarily expressed. Together with a serious Exhortation to the Inhabitants of that Land. By Increase Mather, Teacher of a Church of Christ, in Boston in New-England. ...
London, Printed for Richard Chiswell, at the Rose and Crown in St. Pauls Church-Yard, according to the Original Copy Printed in New-England. 1676.
4 p.ℓ., 51, 8 p. a⁴ A-G⁴ H² (G3 missigned H) 21cm. 4°
In this copy: "Increase Mather. Engrd. for the New Eng. Histl. & Genl. Regr." inserted before half-title.
"King Philip's War Narratives" quarto no. 3. Cf. Church 639n.

D. Math
I.16B2
——— With G3 unsigned.
JCB(2)2:1150; WingM1188; Holmes(I)16B; Sabin46641; Vail(Front.)175.
04605, before 1874 rev
01905, 1854 rev

D. Math
I.16A
Mather, Increase, 1639-1723.
An Earnest Exhortation To the Inhabitants of New-England, To hearken to the voice of God in his late and present Dispensations As ever they desire to escape another Judgement, seven times greater then any thing which as yet hath been. By Increase Mather; Teacher of a Church in Boston in New-England. ...
Boston Printed by John Foster: And are to be Sold over against the Dove. 1676.
2 p.ℓ., 26p. 18.5cm. 4° (Issued as a part of his A Brief History Of The VVarr With the Indians in Nevv-England. Boston, 1676)
Errata, at end.
"To The Reader" (2d p.ℓ.) signed: Increase Mather. Boston N.E. 26. of 5 m. 1676.
"King Philip's War Narratives" quarto no. 3. cf. Church 639n.
This copy closely trimmed at bottom with slight effect on text.
Evans221; Sabin46677; Holmes(I)50; Church 644; WingM1205; Green(John Foster)66-67.
16717B, 1935

C676
M527e
Mello, Francisco Manuel de, 1608-1666.
Epanaphoras De Varia Historia Portvgveza. Ao Excellentissimo Senhor Dom Ioaõ Da Sylva Marquez De Gouvea, Conde De Portalegre, Presidẽte do Dezembargo do Paço, do Cõselho de Estado, & Guerra, Mordomo Mòr da Casa Real, &c. Em Cinco Relaçoens De sucessos pertencentes a este Reyno. Que Contem Negocios Publicos, Politicos, Tragicos, Amorosos, Belicos, Triunfantes. Por Dom Francisco Manvel.
Lisboa. Com todas as licenças necessarias. A despesa d' Antonio Craesbeeck de Mello, Impressor de S. Alteza. Anno 1676.
2 p.ℓ., 244, 246-257, 259-339, 440-624, [1] p. 20cm. 4°
First pub. Lisbon, 1660.

Half-title (1st p.ℓ.): The Wars Of New-England.
First pub. Boston, 1676. In this edition the "serious Exhortation" of the t.-p. has been omitted.

"Taixão esto livro... 12. de Dezẽbro de 675" (2d p.ℓ.ᵛ).
Pages 173-174 mutilated; available in facsim.
Bound in contemporary calf.
Borba de Moraes 2:51; Palau(2)160459.
67-77, 1966

BA676
M777p
Montemayor y Córdova de Cuenca, Juan Francisco de, 1620-1685.
Pastor Bonus: Dominus Iesvs: Sacerdos In Æternvm, Christus, secundum ordinem Melchisedech; Exemplum dedit Crucem suam, baiulantibus, illius vestigia sequentibus. Præsvli Sanctissimo Divo Nicolao, Myræ Archiepiscopo Ipsi Ex Corde Addictvs Servvs D. D. Ioannes Franciscus à Montemaior, & Cordova, de Cuenca: ... Svperiorum Licentia, & ipsius Sancti Officij remissione.
Mexici ex typographia Francisci Rodriguez Lupercio 1676.
17 p.ℓ., 67, 81, 56, 56-75 numb. ℓ., [20] p. front. 15cm. (16cm. in case) 8°
Errata, 16th p.ℓ.
"Ivdicivm" dated (4 p.ℓ.ᵛ) 8 Apr. 1676.
Imperfect: front. wanting.
Bound in contemporary vellum.
Sabin50108; Medina(Mexico)1141; Palau(2) 178031.
04889, about 1910

D676
M937k
[Moxon, Joseph] 1627-1691.
Ein kurtzer Discours von Der Schiff-Fahrt bey dem Nord-Pol Nach Japan/ China/ und so weiter. Durch drey Erfahrunge dargethan und erwiesen/ nebenst Beantwortungen aller Einwürffe/ welche wieder die Fahrt auff diesen Weg können eingewendet worden. ... Sampt einer Land-Charte so alle Länder nechst dem Polo anweiset. Aus dem Englischen ins Hochdeutsche übersetzet.
Hamburg/ In Verlegung Johan Naumans und Georg Wolffs/ Buchhändlere für S. Johans Kirchen. Im Jahr Christi 1676.
[7] p. incl. illus.(map). map. 20cm. 4°
Transl. from: A Brief Discourse Of A Passage By The North-Pole. London, 1674.
Imperfect: engraved polar map on separate sheet wanting.

J678
C238n
——— Another copy. (Issued as a part of R. Capell, Norden/ Oder Zu Wasser und Lande. Hamburg, 1678)
JCB(2)2:1156.
04639, before 1874
02544B, 1851

F676 Netherlands(United Provinces, 1581-1795)--
N469e   Staten Generaal.
        Extracten uyt het Register der Resolutien van
    de Hoogh Mog. Heeren Staten Generael der Ver-
    eenighde Nederlanden, waer by de Geoctroyeerde
    West-Indische Compagnie geauthoriseert werdt te
    ontfangen het Convoy, Veyl ende Last-geldt van
    de Schepen ende Goederen naer haer District-
    gaende, ende van daer komende, volgens haer
    respective datums.
        [Netherlands, ('s Gravenhage?) 1676].
        8 p. 20cm. (21cm. in case) 4º.
        Caption title.
        The 5 Extracts, taken from the Register of
    the Staten Generaal concerning the Dutch West
    India Company, are dated in 1675: 19 July (sig-
    ned: H. Fagel), 9 and 12 August (both signed:
    J. Spronssen), 20 November (unsigned); and in
    1676: 26 September (unsigned).
32313, 1958

F676 Netherlands(United Provinces, 1581-1795)--Staten
N469v   Generaal.
        Een Vertoogh van de considerabele Colonie, By
    de Edele Groot Mog. Heeren Staten van Hollandt
    ende West-Vrieslandt, uytgeset op de vaste Kust
    van America. 1. De favorabele conditien, by
    haer Edele Groot Mog. vergunt aen hondert Per-
    soonen, die haer eerst als Principalenin de
    Associatie sullen inlaten. 2. Een onderricht-
    tinge van de goede gelegentheden van die Landen,
    ... 3. Met een korte oplossinge van de swarig-
    heden by eenige voorgewent.
        In 's Graven-hage, By Jacobus Scheltus, Ordina-
    ris Drucker van de Edele Groot Mog. Heeren
    Staten van Hollandt ende West-Vrieslandt, woo-
    nende op 't Binnen-Hoff, Anno 1676.
        70 p. 19.5cm. 4º.
        An account of the colony developed by the Staten
    Generaal on the South American coast, later
    called Surinam or Dutch Guiana.
        JCB(1)2:829; JCB(2) 2:1143; Sabin99310;Muller
    (1872)709; Knuttel 11388.
03615, about 1849

D676   A New and Further Narrative Of the State of
-N532f   New-England, Being A Continued Account of the
    Bloudy Indian-War, From March till August,
    1676. Giving a Perfect Relation of the Several
    Devastations, Engagements, and Transactions
    there; As also the Great Successes Lately ob-
    tained against the Barbarous Indians, The Re-
    ducing of King Philip, and the Killing of one of
    the Queens, &c. Together with a Catalogue of
    the Losses in the whole, sustained on either
    Side, since the said War began, as near as
    can be be collected. Licensed October 13.
    Roger L'Estrange.
        London, Printed by J.B. for Dorman Newman
    at the Kings Arms in the Poultry, 1676.
        1 p. ℓ., 14 p. 29cm. fol.
        "King Philip's War Narratives" folio No. 3,
    cf. Church 636n.
        Woodcut title vignette (royal arms)
        Consists of a letter dated in Boston, 22 July
    1676, and signed: N.[athaniel?] S.[altonstall?]
        A continuation of: A Continuation Of the State
    of New-England. London, 1676, both by the
    same writer.
        JCB(2)2:1154; Church646; Sabin52445; Vail
    (Front.)176; WingS120.
0513, 1846

D676   News From New-England, Being A True and
N558   last Account of the present Bloody Wars
    carried on betwixt the Infidels, Natives,
    and the English Christians, and Converted
    Indians of New-England, declaring the many
    Dreadful Battles Fought betwixt them: As
    also the many Towns and Villages burnt by
    the merciless Heathens. And also the true
    Number of all the Christians slain since
    the beginning of that War, as it was sent
    over by a Factor of New-England to a Mer-
    chant in London. Licensed Aug. I. Roger
    L'Estrange.
        London, Printed for J. Coniers at the Sign
    of the Black-Raven in Duck-Lane, 1676.
        1 p. ℓ., 6 p. 18cm. 4º
        "King Philip's War Narratives" quarto no. 4.
    cf. Church639n.
        First issued, with "Licensed by Roger
    L'Estrange" on t.-p. and without final para-
    graph: London, 1676.
        JCB(1)2:840; JCB(2)2:1151; Sabin55061; Dexter
    (Cong.)2090; Vail(Front.)177; Church647;
    WingN983.
0515, 1846

DA676 Penn, William, 1644-1718.
P412s   The Skirmisher Defeated And Truth Defended;
    Being an Answer to a Pamphlet, Entituled, A
    Skirmish made upon Quakerism. By William
    Penn. ...
        [London] Printed in the Year, 1676.
        1 p. ℓ., 41 p. 18.5cm. 4º.
        A reply to: [John Cheyney] A Skirmish made
    upon Quakerism. London, 1676.
        Smith(Friends)2:295; WingP1364.
11349, 1917

F676
P469b
Pertinente Beschrijvinge Van Guiana. Gelegen aen de vaste Kust van America. Waer in korte elijck verhaelt wordt / het aenmerckelijckste dat in en omtrent het Landt van Guiana valt / als de Limiten, het Klimaet en de stoffen der Landen / de Mineralen, Edele Gesteenten, Vruchten Dieren, ende overvloedigheyt der Vissen, nevens der selver Inwoonderen aldaer. Hier is bygevoeght Der Participanten uytschot ende profijten, die daer uyt te volgen staen. Als oock de Conditien van mijn Heeren de Staten van Hollandt en West-Vrieslandt, voor die gene die nae Guiana begeeren te varen. t'Amsterdam, By Jan Claesz. ten Hoorn, Boeckverkoper tegen over 't Oude Heeren Logement. 1676.

12, 55 p. fold. map. 21cm. 4°.

Title vignette, engraved ("de Kust van Guiana")

"Aen den Leezer" (p. 3-4 following t.-p.), signed N.N., acknowledges the pamphlet's dependence on the writings of De Laet, Otte Kay, and David Pietersz. de Vries, and on an anonymous tract called Nieuwe Colonie.

"Conditien, de welcke by de Ed Groot Mog. Heeren Staten van Hollandt ... " (p. 5-12), signed Simon van Beaumont, was 1st pub. [The Hague, 1675].

A description of the Dutch colony of Guiana, with encouragement to investors and emigrants.

Sabin29186; Knuttel 11389; Muller(1872)711.

9427, 1913

D676
-P942s
The Present State Of New-England, With Respect to the Indian War. Wherein is an Account of the true Reason thereof, (as far as can be Judged by Men.) Together with most of the Remarkable Passages that have happened from the 20th of June, till the 10th of November, 1675. Faithfully Composed by a Merchant of Boston, and Communicated to his Friend in London. Licensed Decemb. 13. 1675. Roger L'Estrange. London. Printed for Dorman Newman, at the Kings-Arms in the Poultry, and at the Ship and Anchor at the Bridg-foot on Southwark side. 1676.

19 p. 27cm. fol.

"King Philip's War Narratives" folio no.1. cf. Church636n.

A Continuation Of the State of New-England. London, 1676, signed N.S. (Nathaniel Saltonstall?), is a continuation by the same author.

Cut (royal arms: Steele 85) on t.-p.

First pub. with same imprint and "New-England" in title all in capitals; here the name is in capital and lower-case letters.

Isaiah, chap. 23, verse 1-3, in the Massachuset language from John Eliot's Bible: p. 11.

Contains two orders of Councils held at Boston, Aug. 30 and Sept. 17 respectively, 1675, both signed: Edward Rawson, Secr.

Sabin65324; WingSl20C.

29188, 1942

+Z
-R733
1676
Roggeveen, Arent, d. 1679.
Le Premier Tóme De la Tourbe Ardante, illuminant toute la region des Indes Occidentales, Commençant depuis Rio Amazones, Jusqu'a la partië Septentrionále de Terranova. Décrit par Arent Roggeveen.

A Amsterdam, Taileé, Imprimé, & Mis en lumiere par Pierre Goos, en Compagnie de l' Autheur. 1676. Avec Privelege pour 15. an.

1 p.ℓ., 67, [1] p. illus. (incl. map), 33 double-page maps. 45.5cm. fol.

Title and imprint within engr. ornamental border.

First pub. under title Het eerste deel van het brandende veen, Amstedam [1675]. No more pub.

This copy has text in Spanish.

Register (last p.) does not include maps [7A], [24A], [31].

JCB(2)2:1158; Sabin72764-5; cf. Phillips2694-5; cf. Tiele929.

Contents:
[1A] Generaele Kaert Van West Indien Vande Linie Æquinoctiacl tot Benoorde Terra Neuf.
1. De Zeekusten van Westindien, strcckende Van Rio d'Amesones, tot Rio Wya.
2. Paskaert vande Cust Van Westindien Streckende van Rio Wia tot Rio Soronama.
3. Paskaert vande Cust Van Westindien Tusschen Rio Soronama En Rio Demerary Beschreven door Arent Roggeveen.
4. De Cust van Westindien, Tusschen Rio Demerary, en Rio d'Oronoque. Beschreven Door Arent Roggeveen.
5. Paskaerte vande Rivier Oronoque van Moco tot St Thome, en een gedeelte van Golfo de Paria. Beschreven door A. Roggeveen.
6. Paskaerte van 'T Eylandt Trinidad En de Eijlanden daer ontrent gelegen, mitsgaders de Vaste Cust van Cabo Salines tot Commonagod Bay. Beschreven door Arent Roggeveen.
7. Pascaert vande Cust Van Westindien Tusschen Baija Commonagod en Golfo de Venecuela Beschreven door Arent Roggeveen.
[7A] 't Eijlandt Cvracao ende de Afbeeldinghe van t Fort Amsterdam groot besteck. K. Eispenius f. 1676.
[Inset:] 't Fort Amsterdam en t'inkoomen van Baia St Anna int groot gelegen opt Eijlant Curacao.
8. De Cust van Westindien Tusschen Golfo Venecuela en St Martha Beschreven Door

Arent Roggeveen.

9. Paskaerte vande Cust Van West-Indien Tusschen S.t Martha en Ilha Cares Beschreven door Arent Roggeveen.
10. De Cust van Westindien, Tusschen I. Cares, en C. de Tijburon. Beschreven door A. Roggeveen.
11. De Cust van Westindien, Van Cabo de Tijburon, tot Punta S.t Blaes. Beschreven door Arent Roggeveen.
12. De Cust van Westindien, Tusschen Punta S.t Blaes, en Punta d Naes. Beschreven Door Arent Roggeveen.
13. Paskaert vande Cust Van Westindien, Van Punta de Naes, tot Rio Desaguadera. Beschreven door Arent Roggeveen.
14. Paskaerte vande Cust Van Westindien Van R. Desaguadera tot C. de Honduras Beschreven door Arent Roggeveen.
15. De Cust van Westindien, Van C. Honduras, tot C. Serra. Beschreven door Roggeveen.
16. De Cust van Westindien, Van La Desconoscida, tot C. Escondido. Beschreven door Arent Roggeveen.
17. Pascaerte Van't Canael de Bahama, En de Eijlanden gelegen benoorden Cuba. Beschreven door Roggeveen.
18. Pascaerte Vande Caribes Eijlanden, Van 't Eijlant Granadillos, tot 't Eijlant Anguilla. Beschreven door Arent Roggeveen.
19. Pascaerte van 't Eijlant S.t Iuan de Puerto Rico En de andere resterende Caribes Eijlanden van Anguilla tot Spagnola. [Inset:] Afbeeldinghe vande Haven en Stadt Puerto Rico ...
20. Pascaerte van 't Eijlant Spagnola En alle de andere Eijlanden Daer aen gelegen Beschreven door A. Roggeveen.
21. Pascaerte van de Noordcust van Spagnola Tusschen de Baij van Mansaniella tot de reede van 't eijlandt Tortugas Beschreven door A. Roggeveen.
22. Pascaerte van De West Cust van Spagnola, Tusschen Cabo S.t Nicolaes, en Ilha de Vaca. Beschreven door Arent Roggeveen.
23. Pascaerte van de Eijlanden Cuba en Iamaica En de andere Eijlanden daer ontrent gelegen Beschreven door Arent Roggeveen.
24. Paskaert vande Noord Cust Van Cuba, streckende van Bahia de Matancas tot Bahia Honda. Beschreven door Arent Roggeveen.
[24A] Mappa de la Isla de Santa Catalina. [full-page map]: p. [60].
25. Caerte vande Cust van Florida tot de Verginis Streckende van Cabo de Canaveral tot Baya de la Madalena.
26. Pascaerte vande Virginies Van Baija de la Madelena tot de Zuijdt Revier.
27. Pascaerte van Nieu Nederland Streckende vande Zuijdt Revier tot de Noordt Revier en 't Lange Eijland.
28. Pascaerte van Nieu Nederland Streckende vande Noordt Revier tot Hendrick Christiaens Eijlandt.
29. Pascaert van Nieu Nederland Van Hendrick Christiaens Eijland tot Staten hoeck of Cabo Cod.
30. Pascaert van 't Eijland la Bermuda of Sommer Ilands en de andere Eijlanden daer bij geleeghen.
[31] Pascaerte van Terra Nova Nova Francia Nievw Engeland En de Groote Revier van Canada.

03849, 1868

F676 R733v

Roggeveen, Arent, d. 1679.
Voorlooper Op 't Octroy, Van de Hoog. Mog. Heeren Staten Generael, Verleent aen Arent Roggeveen en sijn Medestanders, Over de Australisse Zee ofte beter geseght het onbekende gedeelte des Werelts, gelegen tusschen de Meridiaen der Strate Magalanes Westwaert, tot de Meridiaen van Nova Gunea, soo Noordtwaert als Zuydtwaert. Midtsgaders, De Articulen waer naer een yder die eenige somme gelts inteeckent hem sal hebben te reguleren; beneffens een Kaerte van 't selfde District. Beschreven door den voornoemden A. Roggeveen.
Tot Middelburgh, Gedruckt by Pieter van Goetthem, Ordinaris Drucker van de Ed. Mo. Heeren Staten van Zeelandt. 1676.
2 p.l., 24 p. fold. map. 18.5cm. 4°.
Includes a letter from the Dutch West India Company to the Staten Generaal, dated at Amsterdam, 16 December, 1675, and 2 Extracts from the Register of the Staten Generaal dated 21 December 1675 and 22 September 1676.
Reviews discoveries in the South Seas, and plans for further explorations by Roggeveen and his partners in the Dutch West India Company under patent from the Staten Generaal. Cut on t.-p.
JCB(2)2:1157; Sabin72766; Knuttel 11391; Muller(1872)1994(this copy); Tiele930.

04890, about 1872

F676 -S376w

Schouten, Wouter, 1638-1704.
Wouter Schoutens Oost-Indische Voyagie; Vervattende veel voorname voorvallen en ongemeene vreemde Geschiedenissen/bloedige Zee-en Landt gevechten tegen de Portugeesen en Makassaren; ... Mitsgaders Een curieuse Beschrijving der voornaemste Landen, Eylanden, Koninckrijcken en Steden in Oost-Indien; ... Als oock Sijn seer gevaerlijcke Wederom-Reyse naer 't Vaderlandt/

daer in een bysondere harde ontmoetinge met d'Engelsche Oorloghs-Vloot/soo in Bergen Noorwegen/als in de Noord-Zee. Verçiert met seer konstige Koopere Platen, soo van de voornaemste Steden, als andere aenmerckelijcke saken; door den Schrijver in Indien self geteeckent.

t'Amsterdam, By Jacob Meurs, op de Keysers-Graft; en Johannes van Someren, in de Kalverstraet, 1676. Met Privilegie.

6 p.ℓ., 328, 253, [254-276] p. front. (port), illus., 43 plates (incl. 20 double) 28.5cm. 4°

"Druckfouten": last 2 pages.

Added t.-p., engraved (1st p.ℓ.): Aanmercklijke Voyagie Gedaan door Wouter Schouten Naar Oost-Indien 1676. t'Amsterdam By Jacob van Meurs en Johannes van Someren Boeckverkoopers in Compagnie ...

Title vignette (Printer's device)

State ordinance (verso of t.-p.) dated: 23 September, 1675.

In 3 Books; Book 3 has separate paging and signatures.

Contemporary sprinkled calf.

The voyage was made from 1658 to 1665 in the service of the Netherlands East India Company with Schouten as physician.

Muller(1872)2238(this copy); Tiele990; Scheepvaart Mus. 174.

04896, 1872

+Z
-S467
1676

Seller, John, fl. 1658-1698.

Atlas Terrestris: Or A Book of Mapps, of all the Empires, Monarchies, Kingdomes, Regions, Dominions, Principalities, and Countreys in the Whole World Accomodated with a Brief Description, of the nature and Quality of each particular Countrey. By Iohn Seller Hydrographer to the Kings most excellent Majestie. Cum privilegio. And are to be sold at his Shopps, in Wapping at the Hermitage: And in Exchange-Alley near the Royall-Exchange in London.

[London, 1676?]

1 p.ℓ., 4 p., 1 double-page map (col.), 4 p., 14 double-page maps (col.), [4] p., 1 double-page map (col.), 4 p., 28 double-page maps (col.), [4] p., 6 double-page maps (col.), [4] p., 6 double-page maps (col.), [4] p., 11 double-page maps (col.). 52cm. fol.

Engr. t.-p. (col.); at head of title: Englands Famous Discoverers.

On the evidence of Map 16, which notes events of 1672-73, and the preceding [4] p. of text on the same events ("A Relation of the French Conquests in the Netherlands...", Term. Cat. I:151, probably inserted as topical information), this atlas was issued not long after 1673; Seller's address (t.-p., etc.) "in Exchange-Alley" suggests publication before 1679, by which date he was in "Popes Head Alley". The map of the West Indies, and of Brazil, are published at Wapping only, Seller's address during 1676-77 (cf. Plomer, Dictionary...1668-1725).

The 4-page texts inserted between the maps are titled respectively: A Description Of The World, and of the Moon, and of the three Systems of Ptolemy, Tycho, and Copernicus; A Geographical Description of the Earth, And first of Europe; A Relation of the French Conquests in the Netherlands, in the Years 1672, and 1673; A Description Of The Seventeen Provinces...; A Geographical Description of Asia; A Geographical Description of Africa; A Geographical Description of America.

Bound in contemporary calf.

Cf. Phillips(Atlases)529; WingS2466.

[1] Novissima Totius Terrarum Orbis Tabula. Auctore Joh:Seller Hydrographo Regio. [Insets of the moon, & solar systems]
[2] Europa delineata et recens edita per Nicolaum Visscher.
[3] Totius Regnorum Hispania et Portugallia Descriptio auct: F. de Wit. Gedruckt tot Amsterdam by Frederick de Wit ...
[4] Tabula Portugalliæ et Algarbia. denno Edita a F. de Wit ...
[5] Gallia Vulgo La France, Ex Officina Nicolai Visscher.
[6] Tabula Italiæ Corsicæ, Sardaniæ, et adjacentium Regnorum. Amstelredami, Apud Fredericum de Wit.
[7] Hellas seu Grecia Vniuersa Hugo Allardt Excudit Voor aen inde Kaluerstraet inde Werreldt Caart.
[8] Insula Candia Ejusque Fortificatio edita per F. de Wit. [Insets:] Canea.-Candia.-Spina Longa.-Retimo.-Thine.-Suda.
[9] Totius Regni Hungariæ, Maximæque Partis Danubii Fluminis, ... Novissima Delineatio, per Nicolaum Visscher.
[10] Tabula Germaniæ emendata recens per Nicolaum Joh Piscatorum ... Claes Ianssen Visscher Excudebat.
[11] Carta Noua accurata del Passagio et strada dalli Paesi Bassi per via de Allemagna per Italia et per via di Paesi suizeri à Geneua, Lione et Roma... dato in luce da Cornelio Dancherts di Amsterdam l'anno 1651. 'tAmsterdam by Frederick de Wit ...
[12] Totius Fluminis Rheni Novissima Descriptio ex Officina F. de Wit. Gedruckt tot Amsterdam by Frederick de Wit ... [2 strips on 1 plate]
[13] Austria Archiducatus Auctore Wolfgango Lazio. Amstelodami. Ioannes Ianssonius excudit.
[14] Silesiæ Ducatus Accurata et vera delin-

eatio ... Amstelodami Sumptibus Ioannis Ianssonii.

[15] Moraviæ Nova Et Post Omnes Priores Accuratissima Delineatio. auctore I. A. Comenio. Noviter edita, à Nicolao Iohannide Piscatore. Anno Domini 1664. AGoos sculpsit [Insets:] Polna.-Olmuts.-Brin.-Znaim.

[16] A Mapp of the French Conquests In The Netherlands in the Yeares 1672 & 1673 ... By Iohn Seller...

[17] Novissima et accuratissima XVII Provinciarum Germaniæ Inferior Delineatio Ex Officina Iohannis Selleri Regis Hydrographi. Londini.

[18] Fœderatæ Belgicæ Tabula In multis locis emendata et in lucem edita à F. de Wit. tot Amsterdam by Frederick de Wit ...

[19] Ducatus Lutzenburgici Tabula Nuperrime In Lucem Edita Per Fredericum De Wit. t'Amsterdam by Frederick de Wit ...

[20] Tabula Ducatus Limburch. Et Comitatus Valckenburch. In Lucem Edita A F. De Wit. Gedruckt 't Amsterdam by Frederick de Wit ...

[21] Comitatus Namurci Tabula In Lucem Edita À Frederico De Wit. Gedruckt tAmsterdam by Frederick de Wit ...

[22] Comitatus Hannoniæ Et Episcopatus Cambresis Descriptio, Auctore F. De Wit. Gedruckt t Amsterdam by Frederick de Wit ...

[23] Tabula Comitatus Artesiæ emendata A. Frederico De Wit. Gedruckt tot Amsterdam by Frederick de Wit ...

[24] Comitatus Flandriæ Tabula, In Lucem Edita A Frederico De Wit Amsterodami. Gedruckt t Amsterdam by Frederick de Wit ... Abraham Deur fecit.

[25] Tabula Ducatus Brabantiæ ... emendata à F. De Wit. 1666. t' Amsterdam gedruckt by Frederick de Wit ...

[26] Marchionatus Sacri Imperii Et Dominii Mechelini Tabula Auctore F. De Wit. Gedruckt tot Amsterdam by Frederick de Wit ...

[27] Comitatus Zelandiæ Tabula emendata a Frederico De Wit amstelodami.

[28] Belgii Regii Accuratissima Tabula Pluribus Locis Recens Emen: A F. De Wit. Gedruckt tot Amsterdam by Frederick de Wit ...

[29] Comitatus Hollandiæ Tabula Pluribus Locis Recens Emendata A Frederico De Wit. Gedruckt 't Amsterdam by Frederick De Wit ... [Inset:] De resterende Eylanden van Hollant ...

[30] Dominii Ultraiectini Tabula Auctore Frederico De Wit Amsterodami. tot Amsterdam by Frederick de Wit ...

[31] Ducatus Geldriæ, Et Comitatus Zutphaniæ, Tabula Auctore F. De Wit. Gedruckt 't Amsterdam by Fredrick de Wit ... Gesneden by Abram Deur.

[32] Comitatus Zutphaniæ Et Fluminis Isulæ Nova Delineatio Auctore F. De Wit. 't Amsterdam by Fredrick de Wit ...

[33] Transisalania Provincia Vulgo Over-Yssel Auctore N. Ten Have Emendata A F. De Wit. 't Amsterdam by Frederick de Wit ...

[34] Tabula Comitatus Frisiæ Auctore B: Schotano á Sterringa in Lucem edita a Frederico de Wit Amstelodami. Gedruckt 't Amsterdam by Frederick de Wit ... [Inset:] ... Vriese Eylanden ...

[35] Tabulæ Dominii Groeningæ Quæ Et Complectitur Maximam Partem Drentiæ Emendata A F. De Wit. ... tot Amsterdam. [Inset:] ... Groeninger Landt.

[36] Nova totius Westphaliæ Descriptio emendata a F. de Wit, Gedruckt tot Amsterdam by Frederick de Wit ...

[37] Electoratus Brandenburgi, Mekelenburgi, Et maximæ Partis Pomeraniæ novissima Tabula. Nicolaus Visscher Excudebat.

[38] Regni Daniæ, Novissima et Accuratissima Tabula Per Nicolaum Visscher.

[39] Tabula Regnorum Sueciæ et Norvegiæ. Amstelodami Apud Frederick de Wit. T Shuilier Sc.

[40] A New Mapp of the Estates of the Crown of Poland. ... By Rob:t Morden. Sold by Robert Morden. ... Iohn Seller ... and by Arther Tuckur. ...

[41] Tabula Prussiæ Eximiâ Curâ Conscripta Per Casparum Henneberch Erlichensem et denuo edita, per Nicolaum Iohannidem Piscatorem AGoos Sculpsit Anno 1656. [Inset:] Konigsberg.

[42] Nova Totius Livoniæ accurata Descriptio. Apud Joan Janssonium.

[43] Magni Ducatus Lithuaniæ ... Sumptibus Ioannis Ianssonii. [Insets of the Dneiper River]

[44] Tabula Russia Vulgo Moscovia t amsterdam Gedruckt by Fredrick de wit ... T. Shuilier fecit.

[45] Asiæ Nova Delineatio Auctore N. Visscher.

[46] Tabula Tartariæ et majoris partis Regni Chinæ. edita a F. de Wit. Gedruckt t' Amsterdam by Frederick de Wit ...

[47] Imperii Sinarum Nova Descriptio. Auctore, Joh van Loon.

[48] Tabula Indiæ Orientalis. Emendata a F. de Wit. Joannes Shuilier fecit 1662.

[49] Nova Persiæ Armeniæ Natoliæ et Arabiæ Descriptio per F. de Wit. t'Amsterdam by Frederick de Wit ...

[50] Terra Sancta, Siue Promissionis, olim Palestina recens delineata, et in lucem edita per Fredericum De Wit. Gedruckt tot Amsterdam by Frederick de Wit ...

[51] Africæ Accurata Tabula ex officina Nic. Visscher.
[52] Aethiopia Superior vel Interior; vulgo Abissinorum siue Presbiteri Ioannis Imperium.
[53] Aegypti Recentior Descriptio: ...
[54] Nova Barbariæ Descriptio Amstelodami Apud Joannem Janssonium.
[55] A Chart of the Coasts of Barbarie ... from C. Vincent to C Verd Described by John Seller Regis Hydrographus.
[56] A Chart of Guinea Describeing the Seacoast from Cape de Verde to Cape Bona Esperanca by John Seller.
[57] Novissima et Accuratissima Totius Americæ Descriptio. per N. Visscher.
[58] America Septentrionalis. Amstelodami, Excudit Ioannes Ianssonius.
[59] A Chart of the North Part of America. Describing the sea Coast of Groenland Davies Streights Baffins Bay Hudsons Streights Buttons Bay And James Bay. by John Seller. Hydrographer ... London. [Inset:] A Polar Projection describing ye Northermost Parts of the World Jo S.
[60] A Chart of The West Indies From Cape Cod. to the River Oronoque. By John Seller. Hydrographer ... London.
[61] Virginiæ partis australis, et Floridæ partis orientalis, ... Nova Descriptio.
[62] Novissima et Accuratissima Insulæ Jamaicæ. Descriptio per Johannem Sellerum. Hydrographum Regium Londini Made and Sold by Iohn Seller ... London. [Inset:] A Catalogue of the severall Precincts, ...
[63] Guiana siue Amazonum Regio Amstelodami, Ioannes Ianssonius excudit.
[64] Nova Hispania, Et Nova Galicia.
[65] Peru Amstelodami, Apud Ioannem Ianssonium.
[66] A Chart of the Sea Coast of Brazil. From Cape S.t Augustine. to the Straights of Magellan, ... Made and Sold by John Selle[r]. Hidrographer to the King, at the Hermitage in Wapping. [Dedication by Seller to] ... Capt. John Narborough. ... 1670 ...
[67] A New Mapp of Magellan Straights Discovered by Capt John Narbrough. ... Made and sold by John Thornton ... & by James Atkinson ... [Inset, on reduced scale:] Patagonum Regio [and] Terra Del Fuogo.

9771, 1914

B676 -S689d Solorzano Pereira, Juan de, 1575-1655.
D. Ioan De Solorzano Pereyra, Cavallero Del Orden De Sant-Iago, Del Consejo De Sv Magestad En El Svpremo De Castilla, Y De Las Indias, Ivnta De Gverra Dellas, Y De La De Minas. Obras Posthvmas. Recopilacion De Varios Tratados; Memoriales, Y Papeles, Escritos Algvnos En Cavsas Fiscales, Y Llenos Todos De Mvcha Enseñanza, Y Ervdicion. Dedicanse Al Ilvstrissimo Señor D. Lvis De Exea Y Talayero, Ivsticia De Aragon.
Con licencia En Zaragoça, por los Herederos de Diego Dormer, Impressores de la Ciudad; con Privilegio en los Reinos de Castilla, y a su costa. [1676]
12 p. ℓ., 712 p. 28.5cm. fol.
Title in red and black.
Half-title: D. Ioan De Solorzano Pereyra Obras Posthvmas.
Dedication (3d-6th p. ℓ.) signed "Iosef Dormer" and dated: Zaragoça y Deziembre à 2. de 1676.
Also issued in the same place and year under title: ... Obras varias. Recopilación de diversos tratados ...
Compilation of 8 works, each of which has special t.-p. (except where caption title is indicated in Contents) but continuous paging and signatures.
Contents:—... Diligens et accurata de parricidii crimine disputatio, 1st pub. Salamanca, 1606 (9th p. ℓ.-p. 172).—Decem conclusionum manus, 1st pub. Salamanca, 1609 (p. 173-210).—Memorial o discurso informativo ... de los derechos ... que se deven dar ... a los consejeros honorarios ... , 1st pub. Madrid, 1642 (p. 211-350).—Memorial y discurso de las razones que se ofrecen para que el ... Consejo de las Indias deva preceder ... al que llaman de Flanders, 1st pub. Madrid, 1629 (p. 351-397).—caption title: "Papel político con lugares de buenas letras" (p. 398-410). —... Con los bienes y herederos del governador D. Francisco Vanegas, 1st pub. Madrid, 1660 (p. 411-490).—Discurso y alegación en derecho sobre la culpa que resulta contra el general don Juan de Benavides Baçan y almirante don Juan de Leoz ... en razón de aver desamparado la flota de su cargo ... el año de 1628, 1st pub. Madrid, 1631 (p. 491-686).—caption title: "Discurso político sobre aver los alcaldes de la chancillería de Valladolid herrado en la cara a unos gitanes" (p. 687-692).
Discurso... sobre la culpa concerns the loss of the Spanish silver fleet to the Dutch under Peter Heyn at Matanzas Bay, Cuba, in 1628.
Medina(BHA)1617n; Palau(1)6:532; Sabin 86542.

63-150, 1962

DA68 C697 [Sonnemans, Arent] d. 1683.
Eenige Aanmerkingen voor den Philosopherenden Boer, Met eenige Vragen aan den zelven. Voorge-

stelt door die gene, diemen spots-gewijse noemt Quakers.

Tot Rotterdam. Gedrukt by Pieter van Wijnbrugge, in de Leeuwestraat: En zijn ook te bekomen by Iacob Claus, in de vergulde Drie-hoek, op d'Achterburghwal, tot Amsterdam. Anno 1676.

1 p. l., 13 p. 20cm. 4° (No. [58] as issued, in Collectio, Of Versamelinge. [Amsterdam, ca. 1680]) Cut on t.-p.

Authorship attributed jointly to Arent Sonnemans and Benjamin Furly (cf. William I. Hull, Benjamin Furly (Swarthmore, 1941) p. 36-40)

A reply to: [Barend Joosten Stol], Den Philosopherenden Boer. [Rotterdam], 1676.

"Verklaring van de Stellingen" (p. 3-4) by Frans Kuyper, also issued separately, Rotterdam, 1676.

Knuttel 11475; Smith(Friends)2:451.

03299, 1866

+Z -S742 1676

Speed, John, 1552?-1629.

A Prospect Of The Most Famous Parts Of The World, Viz. Asia, Africa, Europe, America, ... By John Speed. To which are added in this New Edition, The Empire of the Great Mogul, with the rest of the East-Indies. < Palestine, or the Holy-Land, The Empire of Russia. As Also The Descriptions of His Majesty's Dominions abroad; with a Map fairly Engraven to each Description. Viz. <New-England, New-York, Carolina, Florida, Virginia, Mary-Land,> Jamaica, Barbadoes.

London; Printed for Thomas Basset at the George in Fleet-street, and Richard Chiswel at the Rose and Crown in St. Paul's Church-yard, MDCLXXVI. ...

1 p. l., 56 numb. l., [11] p. incl. 28 double-page maps. 46cm. fol. (Issued as a part of his The theatre of the empire of Great-Britain, London, 1676.)

Text with leaf numbering on reverse of maps.
"Advertisement" (corrigenda): last p.
First pub. London, 1631.
Sabin89228n.

Contents:

[1] A New And Accurat Map Of The World Drawne according to ye truest Descriptions latest Discoueries & best Obseruations y^t haue beene made by English or Strangers. 1651 ... [hemispheres]

[2] Asia with the Islands adioyning described, ... [and] newly augmented by I. S: Ano. Dom: 1626. ... Sculptum apud Abrahamum Goos. [Insets:] Candy.-Goa.-Damascus.-Ierusalem.-Ormus.-Bantam.-Aden.-Macao.

[3] Africæ, described, ... [and] newly done into English by I. S. ... Abraham Goos Sculpsit. [Insets:] Tanger.-Ceuta.-Alger.-Tunis.-Alexandria.-Alcair.-Mozambique.-Canaria.

[4] Europ, and the cheife Cities contayned therein, described; ... By Jo: Speed Ano. Dom: 1626. ... Sculptum apud Abrahamum Goos. [Insets:] London.-Paris.-Rome.-Constantinople.-Venice.-Prague.-Amsterdam.-Lisbone.

[5] America with those known parts in that unknowne worlde ... Discribed and inlarged by I. S. Ano. 1626 ... Abraham Goos Amstelodam Ensis Sculpsit. [Insets:] Havan porte.-S:Domingo.-Cartagena.-Mexico.-Cusco.-Il. of Mocha in Chili.-R. Ianeiro.-Olinda.-The Northernely part of America

[6] Ελλας Greece Reuised by John Speed ...

[7] A New Mappe Of The Romane Empire newly described by Iohn Speede ... [Insets:] Rome.-Genua.-Ierusalem.-Venice.-Constantinople.-Alexandria.

[8] A. Newe Mape Of Germany Newly Augmented by Iohn Speed. Ano. Dom:1626. ... [Insets:] Heidelberg.-Francfurt am Main.-Wien.-Prag.-Coln.-Nurnberg.-Strasburg.-Augsburg.

[9] Bohemia Newly described by Iohn Speed Anno Dom: 1626 ... [Insets:] Czalas.-Comethau.-Corte of the Emparer.-Praga.-Polm.-Schlani.-Laun.

[10] France revised and augmented, ... by John Speede ... [Insets:] Angiers.-Poictiers.-Orleans.-Paris.-Roan.-Rochelle.-Bordeaux.-Calis.

[11] A New Mape Of Y^e XVII Provinces Of Low Germanie, mended a new in manie places. by I. Speed. ... [Insets:] Amsterdam.-Antwerpen.-Ghendt.-Middelburg.-Groeningen.-Zutphen.-Vtrecht.-Atrecht.

[12] Spaine Newly described with many adictions, ... by John Speed. 1626 ... [Insets:] Madrid.-Sevilla.-Lixbona.-Valladolid.-Granada.-Toledo.-Barcelona.-Burgos.-Cadiz.

[13] Italia Newly augmented by. I. Speede. ... [Insets:] Verone.-Naple.-Venice.-Rome.-Genua.-Florence.

[14] The Mape Of Hungari newly augmented by. Iohn Speede Ano Dom: 1626. ... Sculptum apud Abrahamum Goos. [Insets:] Presburch.-Ofen.-Comorra.-Raab.

[15] The Kingdome Of Denmarke ... Evert Symons Z. Hamers Veldt Sculp. [Inset:] Coppenhagen.-Elsenor.-Lantskroon.-Ripen.-Sleswyck.-Hamburgh.

[16] A Newe Mape of Poland Done into English by I. Speede ... Dirck Gryp Sculp. [Insets:] Cracovia.-Dantzick.-Posna.-Crossen.-Sandomiria.-Breslaw.

[17] The Kingdome Of Persia ... described by Iohn Speede ... Abraham Goos Sculpsit. [Insets:] Spaha.-Ormus.-Tarvis.-Gilan.

[18] The Turkish Empire. Newly Augmented by Iohn Speed. 1626... [Insets:] Famagusta.-Damascus.-Alcairo.-Ierusalem.-Constantinople.-Rhode.-Alexandria.-Ormus.

[19] the Kingdome Of China newly augmented by I.S. 1626... [Insets:] Macao.-Quinzay.

[20] A Newe Mape Of Tartary augmented by John Speede... Dirck Gryp Sculp. [Insets:] Astracan.-Samarchand.-Cambalu.-The House of Nova Zemla.

[21] Mappa Æstivarum Insularum alias Bermudas dictarum, ... A Mapp of the Sommer Ilands once called the Bermudas... Abraham Goos Amstelodamensis Sculpsit.

[22] A Map Of Virginia And Maryland. ... F. Lamb Sculp.

[23] A Map of New England And New York ... F. Lamb Sculp.

[24] A Map Of Jamaica ... Barbados.

[25] A New Description Of Carolina. ... Francis Lamb Sculp.

[26] A New Map of East India. ... F. Lamb Sculp.

[27] A Map Of Russia ... F. Lamb Sculp. [Insets:] The Famous And Imperiall City Of Moscow.-Russche Narva.-Archangel.-The Emperours Court.

[28] Canaan. Begun by Mr. John More continued and finished by John Speede. Anno Domini 1651. ... [Inset:] Ierusalem.

04941B, 1896-7

+Z -S742 1676

Speed, John, 1552?-1629.
The Theatre of the Empire Of Great-Britain, Presenting an Exact Geography of the Kingdom of England, Scotland, Ireland, and the Isles adjoyning: ... With a Chronology of the Civil-wars in England, Wales and Ireland. Together With A Prospect Of the most Famous Parts of the World, Viz. Asia, Africa, Europe, America. ... By John Speed. In this New Edition are added; In the Theatre of Great-Britain. The Principal Roads, ... The Market Towns ... A Continuation of all the Battels fought in England, Scotland, Wales and Ireland; with all the Sea-Fights to this present time. The Arms of all the Dukes and Earls. ... The Descriptions of His Majesty's Dominions abroad; with a Map fairly engraven to each Description, Viz. New-England, New-York, Carolina, Florida, Virginia, Mary-Land, Jamaica, Barbadoes. In the Prospect of the World. The Empire of the Great Mogul, with the rest of the East-Indies.><Palestine, or the Holy-Land, The Empire of Russia.

London; Printed for Thomas Basset at the George in Fleet-street, and Richard Chiswel at the Rose and Crown in St. Paul's Church-yard, MDCLXXVI.

5 pts. in 1 v.: 9 p.ℓ., 94 numb. ℓ., [95]-98 p., 99-126 numb. ℓ., 2 ℓ., 5-8 p., 10 ℓ., [127]-[130] p., 131-132 numb. ℓ., [133]-[136] p., 137-146 numb. ℓ., 1 ℓ., 56 numb. ℓ., [11] p. Engr. fold + [A]² B-3U² (***)² ***2² [a-e]² 3X-3Y² []² 4A-4E² []¹ 2A-2E² 4F-4H² incl. 96 double-page maps. coat of arms. 46cm. fol.

Title in red and black.
Added t.-p., engr. (signed R: White sculp.).
License dated (3d p.ℓ.ᵛ) 2 Aug. 1675.
"Advertisement" (corrigenda): last p.
Text with leaf numbering on reverse of maps.
The Theatre, in 4 books with special t.-p.'s for bks. 2-4, 1st pub. London, 1611. His A prospect of the most famous parts of the world, London, 1676, with, as issued (with special t.-p., separate paging and signatures) 1st pub. London, 1631.
Cf. Phillips(Atlases)5949; Sabin89228n; Wing S4886.
Contents (maps):

[1] The Kingdome Of Great Britaine And Ireland by I. Speed...
[Insets:] London. - Edynburgh.-The Iles Of Orknay.

[2] Britain As It Was Devided in the tyme of the Englishe-Saxons especially during their Heptarchy. ...

[3] The Kingdome Of England Described by Christopher Saxton augmented by John Speed... Abraham Goos Amsteloda mensis Sculpsit Anno 1646.

[4] Kent With Her Cities And Earles Described and oberued. ...
[Insets:] Canterbury.-Rochester.

[5] Sussex ... Described by Iohn Norden. Augmented by Iohn Speede... Jodocus Hondius cælavit Anno Domini 1616 [altered on plate to 1666]. [Inset:] Chichester.

[6] Surrey ... Described by the travills of John Norden Augmēted and performed by Iohn Speede ... Jodocus Hondius. cælavit. Anno 1610.
[Insets:] Richmont.-Nonesuch [Castles]

[7] Hantshire described and devided. Jodocus Hondius cælavit.
[Inset:] Winchester.

[8] Wight Island. Described by William White Gent. Augmented and published by Iohn Speed ...
[Insets:] Newport.-Southhampton.

[9] Dorsetshyre ... 1662. ... Jodocus Hondius Cælavit Cum privilegio.
[Inset:] Dorchester.

[10] Devonshire With Excester Described ...

[31]

[Inset:] Excester.
- [11] Cornwall Described by the travills of John Norden augmented and published by I. Speed. ... Iodocus Hondius Cælavit Anno Domini 1610. [Inset:] Launceston Or Ancient Dunhevet.
- [12] Somerset-Shire Described: ... by I. S. ... Anno 1610. [Inset:] Bathe.
- [13] Wilshire. ... Jodocus Hondius cælavit Anno 1610. [Insets:] Salesbury.-Stone Henge.
- [14] Barkshire Described ... [Inset:] Windsor [Castle]
- [15] Midle-Sex ... Described by Iohn Norden. Augmēted by I. Speed ... Jodocus Hondius cælavit Cum Privilegio Anno 1610.
- [16] Essex ... 1662. ... Jodocus Hondius cælavit. [Inset:] Colchester.
- [17] Suffolke described ... 1610. ... [Inset:] Ipswiche.
- [18] Norfolk A Countie Florishing & Populous ... Described by Christopher Saxton augmented by I. Speed ... J. Goddard ju: fe. [Inset:] Norwiche.
- [19] Cambridgshire described ... 1610. [Inset:] Cambridge.
- [20] Hartford Shire Described ... Jodocus Hondius cælavit. [Insets:] Hartforde.-Verolanium.
- [21] Bedford Shire And The Situation Of Bedford described ... Jodocus Hondius Cælavit Anno Domini 1610. ... [Inset:] Bedforde.
- [22] Buckingham Both Shyre, and Shire towne describ. Anno 1666. ... [Insets:] Buckingham.-Redding.
- [23] Oxfordshire described, ... 1605. ... Anno. 1610. [Inset:] [Oxford]
- [24] Glocestershire contriued.... by I. S. Anno Domini 1610. ... [Insets:] Glocester.-Bristow.
- [25] Herefordshire described ... [Inset:] Hereford.
- [26] Worcester Shire ... Described by Christopher Saxton, Augmēt: and published by Iohn Speede ... 1610 Jodocus Hondius cælavit. [Inset:] Worcester.
- [27] The Counti Of Warwick ... 1610. ... Jodocus Hondius cælavit. [Insets:] Warwicke.-Coventree.
- [28] Northampton Shire ... Jodocus Hondius Cælavit Anno 1610. [Insets:] Northampton.-Peterborow.
- [29] Huntington ... Jodocus Hondius Cælavit Anno Domini 1662. [Insets:] Huntington.-Ely.
- [30] Rutlandshire ... [Insets:] Oukham.-Stanford.
- [31] Leicester ... Jodocus Hondius cælavit Cum Privilegio [Inset:] Leicester.
- [32] The Countie And Citie Of Lyncolne Described ... Jodocus Hondius cælavit Anno Domini 1610 ... [Inset:] Lincolne.
- [33] The Countie Of Nottingham described ... Jodocus Hondius cælavit ... 1610 ... [Inset:] Nottingham.
- [34] Darbieshire described Anno 1666 ... Jodocus Hondius cælavit. [Insets:] Darbye.-Buxton [Spa].
- [35] Stafford Countie And Towne ... described ... [Insets:] Stafford.-Lichfield.
- [36] Shropshyre Described ... [Inset:] Shrowesbury.
- [37] The Countye Palatine Of Chester ... [Inset:] Chester.
- [38] The Countie Pallatine Of Lancaster Described ... 1610 ... Jodocus Hondius cælavit Anno Domini 1610. [Inset:] Lancaster.
- [39] York Shire ...
- [40] The West Ridinge Of Yorkeshyre ... 1610 ... [Inset:] Yorke.
- [41] The North And East Ridins Of Yorkshire ... [Insets:] Hull.-Richmond.
- [42] The Bishoprick And Citie Of Durham ... [Inset:] Durham.
- [43] The Countie Westmorland ... Described ... [Inset:] Kendale.
- [44] Cumberland ... Described ... [Inset:] Carlile.
- [45] Northumberland. ... [Insets:] Barwick.-Newe-Castle. Described by William Mathew.
- [46] The Isle Of Man Exactly desribed, ... By Tho Durham Ano. 1595. Performed By Iohn Speed Anno 1610 ...
- [47] Holy Iland.-Garnsey.-Farne.-Iarsey. Jodocus Hondius Cælavit ... 1610.

Book 2:
- [1] Wales ...[Insets:] Bangor.-Beaumaris.-Carnarvan.-Harlieg.-Cardigan.-Penbrok.-Carmarthen.-S.t Davids.-Landafe.-Cardife.-Brecknok.-Radnor.-Montgomery.-Flint.-Denbigh.-S.t Assaph.
- [2] Penbrokshyre described ... by John Speed ... Jodocus Hondius cælavit. [Insets:] Penbroke.-Saint Davids.
- [3] Caermarden ... 1662 ... Jodocus Hondius cælavit ... [Inset:] Caermarden.
- [4] Glamorgan Shyre ... Jodocus Hondius Cælavit ... 1610. [Insets:] Cardyfe.-Landaffe.
- [5] The Countye Of Monmouth ... Described Ann 1610 ... [Inset:] Monmouth.
- [6] Breknoke ... 1610 ... [Inset:] Breknoke.
- [7] The Countie Of Radnor Described ... 1610 ... Jodocus Hondius Cælavit [Inset:] Radnor.

[8] Cardigan Shyre Described ... by I. S. Anno 1610. Jodocus Hondius Cælavit ... [Inset:] Cardigan.
[9] Montgomery Shire. Described by Christopher Saxton Augmented and published by Iohn Speed ... [Inset:] Montgomery.
[10] Merioneth Shire Described 1610 ... [Inset:] Harlech.
[11] Denbigh Shire ... Jodocus Hondius Cælavit. [Inset:] Denbigh.
[12] Flint-Shire ... [Insets:] Saint Asaph.-Flint.-St Winffrids Well.
[13] Caernarvon ... 1610 ... [Insets:] Caernarvon.-Bangor.
[14] Anglesey Antiently called Mona. Described 1610 ... Jodocus Hondius Cælavit ... [Inset:] Beaumaris.
[15] The Invasions Of England And Ireland ... By I. Speed ... Corn Danckertsz: Sculpsit.

Book 3:
[1] The Kingdome Of Scotland ... [Inset:] The Yles of Orknay.

Book 4:
[1] The Kingdome Of Irland ... Newly described. ... Jodocus Hondius cælavit.
[2] The Province Of Mounster by I. Speed. ... Jodocus Hondius Cælavit. [Insets:] Lymericke.-Corcke.
[3] The Countie Of Leinster ... by I. Speed. ... Iodocus Hondius cælavit ... 1610. [Inset:] Dubline.
[4] The Province Of Connaugh ... Described by I. Speed ... 1610. [Inset:] Galwaye.
[5] The Province Ulster described. ... [Inset:] Enis Kelling Fort.

A prospect of the ... world ...
See contents under his Prospect, London, 1676.

04941A, 1896-7

D676 [Tompson, Benjamin] 1642-1714
T662n New-Englands Tears For Her Present Miseries: Or, A Late and True Relation of the Calamities of New-England Since April last past. With an Account of the Battel between the English and Indians upon Seaconk Plain: And of the Indians Burning and Destroying of Marlbury, Rehoboth, Chelmsford, Sudbury, and Providence. With the Death of Antononies the Grand Indian Sachem; And a Relation of a Fortification begun by Women upon Boston Neck. Together with an Elegy on the Death of John Winthrop Esq; late Governour of Connecticott, and Fellow of the Royal Society. Written by an Inhabitant of Boston in New England to his Friend in London. With Allowance.
London Printed for N. S. 1676.
1 p. ℓ., 14 p. 19.5cm. 4º
"King Philip's War Narratives" quarto no. 5b. cf. Church 639n.
Also pub. as a supplement to New Englands Crisis. Boston, 1676. cf. Samuel A. Green, Benjamin Tompson. Boston, 1895. (Mass. Hist. Soc. Procs., ser. 2, 10:263-84)
Caption title: A Narrative Of New Englands Present Calamities. 15 April 1676.
A collection of poetry.
JCB(2)2:1152; Sabin 96156; Vail(Front.)180; Wing T1867; Wegelin (Poetry)395.

0510, 1846

D676 [Trott, Perient], fl. 1658-1676, comp.
T858t A True Relation of the just and unjust Proceedings of the Somer-Islands-Company: In relation to 20 Shares of Land that Perient Trott bought of the R.^{t} Honble the late Robert Earl of Warwick the 22th of February 1658. And the great Justice shewed by the Said Earl of Warwick in the sale of the said Lands. And the great Justice shewed by the R.^{t} Honble the Earl of Shaftsbury. And the like Justice done by the R.^{t} Honble the Earl of Danby Lord high Treasurer of England. And the Justice done by the Councill in Somer-Islands. Printed for the better Information of all Men in England, and in the Somer-Islands, and of all unbiassed persons in the World.
[London] Anno MDCL XXVI.
3 p. ℓ., 64 p. 21cm. 4º.
Cut (arms of London) on t.-p.
Collection of documents in support of Trott's case against Charles, 4th earl of Warwick, concerning land titles in Bermuda.
In this copy there is a blank ℓ. following t.-p.

D676 —— ——Another copy. 23.5cm.
T858t Imperfect: 2d p. ℓ. wanting.
cop. 2 Bound in contemporary sheep, rebacked.
JCB(2)2:1159; Sabin 97142; Wing T2306.

03611, before 1866
04898, before 1923

D676 A True Account Of the Most Considerable Occur-
-T866a rences That have hapned in the Warre Between The English and the Indians In New-England, From the Fifth of May, 1676, to the Fourth of August last; as also of the Successes it hath pleased God to give the English against them:

As it hath been communicated by Letters to a Friend in London. The most Exact Account yet Printed. ... Licensed, October 11. 1676. Roger L'Estrange.
London, Printed for Benjamin Billingsley at the Printing-Press in Cornhill, 1676.
1 p.l., 6 [i.e. 10] p. 29cm. fol.
"King Philip's War Narratives" folio no. 4 cf. Church636n.
JCB(1)2:842; JCB(2)2:1155; Church648; Sabin 97085; Vail(Front.)181; WingT2385.

0514, 1846

B676
V181e
Valle, Gonzalo del, d. 1682.
Espejo De Varios Colores, En Cvyos Chrystales, Veran Los Oradores sagrados, la hermosura en las virtudes, para alentar á las almas à buscarlas, y la fealdad de los vicios, para que los huyan, y aborrescan. Da Este Espejo El Material de la doctrina en Capitulos, que contienen las principales ferias de el Adviento, y la Quaresma, Passion, Semana Sāta, Actos de amor de Dios, Examen de conciencia, Exequias funerales, y Animas: por que es Espejo vniversal para todos. Lo Saca A Luz, Para Qve Se miren en él, el Maestro Fr Gonzalo de el Ualle, Provincial de la Provincia de el Sātissimo Nombre de Iesus de la Nueva España, ...
Con licencia en Mexico: por Francisco Rodriguez Lupercio. Año de 1676.
11 p.l., 106 numb. l., [8] p., 107-224 numb. l., [6] p. 20.5cm. (21.5cm. in case) 4°
License dated (5th p.l.v) 26 Aug. 1675.
Bound in contemporary vellum.
Medina(Mexico)1150; Palau(1)7:108; Andrade, V de P:673; Santiago Vela8:84:1.

4919, 1908

B676
V181p
Valle, Gonzalo del, d. 1682.
Palestra De Varios Sermones De Mysterios De Christo Señor Nuestro: algunos de su Santissima Madre; y de algunos Ilustres Santos de la Iglesia. Donde Los sagrados Oradores tendràn motivos de trabesear y pelear con sus ingenios, y estudiar mas excelentes demostraciones, delinear mas gloriosos triumphos à las virtudes, y hazañas de los Santos. Fabricados vàn los Sermones (contra el estilo, que observo en mi Parayso, Adviento, Y Quaresma)

por dar algun alivio à la juventud, que comiença, à los haraganes pereçosos, y à los de edad provecta, que se cansan: Los Escrivia El M. Fray Gonzalo Del Valle, hijo de la Angelical Provincia de la Andaluzia, del Orden de mi P. S. Augustin, Provincial de esta gravissima del Sanctissimo Nombre de Jesvs de la Nueva-España. A Quien La Dedica.
Con Licencia En Mexico, por la Viuda de Bernardo Calderon, en la calle de S Augustin, año de 1676.
11 p.l., 198 numb. l., [10] p. 20.5cm. (21.5cm. in case) 4°.
Errata: 9th p.l.
"Licencia" (6th p.l.) dated: 8 de Agosto de 1675.
Bound in contemporary vellum.
Medina(Mexico)1149; Palau(1)7:108; Santiago Vela8:85:3.

4918, 1908

D676
W564t
Wheeler, Thomas, 1620?-1686.
A Thankefull Remembrance Of Gods Mercy To several Persons at Quabaug or Brookfield: Partly in a Collection of Providences about them, and Gracious Appearances for them: And partly in a Sermon Preached by Mr. Edward Bulkley, Pastor of the Church of Christ at Concord, upon a day of Thanksgiving, kept by divers for their Wonderfull Deliverance there. Published by Capt. Thomas VVheeler.
Cambridge, Printed and Sold by Samuel Green 1676.
3 p.l., 10 (i.e. 14), 32 p. 18cm. 4°
"King Philip's War Narratives" quarto no. 7. cf. Church 639n.
"A True Narrative Of the Lords Providences ...", p. 1-10 (i.e. 14).
"The Sernon [sic]", p. 1-32.
JCB(2)2:1160 and 1139 (former imperfect copy); Evans226; Sabin103200; Vail(Front.) 182; WingW1600; CP176.

03612, before 1866

DA676
W726g
[Williams, Roger] 1604?-1683.
George Fox Digg'd out of his Burrovves, Or an Offer of Disputation On fourteen Proposalls made this last Summer 1672 (so call'd) unto G. Fox then present on Rode-Island in New-England, by R. W. As also how (G. Fox slily

[34]

departing) the Disputation went on being managed three days at Newport on Rode-Island, and one day at Providence, between John Stubs, John Burnet, and William Edmundson on the one part, and R. W. on the other. In which many Quotations out of G. Fox & Ed. Burrowes Book in Folie are alleadged. With An Apendix Of some scores of G. F. his simple lame Answers to his Opposites in that Book, quoted and replyed to By R. W. of Providence in N. E.
    Boston Printed by John Foster, 1676.
    4 p.ℓ., 208, 119 p. 20.5cm. 4°
    "To The Kings Majesty Charles the IId:" Signed (2d p.ℓ.): Providence in N-England, March 10th. 167$\frac{5}{6}$: ... Roger Williams.
    A reply to Fox's The Great Mistery Of The Great Whore Unfolded, London, 1659. Occasioned by Fox's visit to Newport and the public debate that followed.
    T.-p. of a variant issue of the same year reads: G. Fox Digg'd. ...
    JCB(1)2:828; JCB(2)2:1161; Evans228; Sabin 104337; Smith(Anti-Quak)451-52; Dexter(Cong.) 2080; Wing W2764; Green(John Foster)67-69.

03610, 1868

1677

B69 G643v 16
    Agurto y Loaysa, Joseph de, fl. 1676-1688.
    Villancicos, Qve Se Cantaron En La Santa Iglesia Metropolitana De Mexico. En honor de Maria Santissima Madre de Dios en su Assumpcion triumphante, Año de 1677. ... Compuestos en Metro musico, por el B^r. Ioseph de Agurto, y Loaysa Maestro Compositor de dicha Santa Iglesia.
    Con licencia. En Mexico, por la Viuda de Bernardo Calderon, en la calle de San Agustin [1677].
    [8] p. 20cm. 4°
    Woodcut title vignette (the Virgin surrounded by angels).
    Bound, in contemporary vellum, as no. 16 with 42 other items.
    cf. Medina(Mexico)1152; Palau(2)1:4026.

28916, 1941

DA68 C697
    Ames, William, d. 1662.
    Een Getuygenis van den Wegh des Lévens, ... In't Engels geschréven, door ... William Ames.
    Wyders noch een Tractátje Hoe de zonde versterkt, en hoeze óverwonnen word.
    Gedrukt voor Jacob Claus, Boek-verkooper: wónende op d'Achterburgwal, in de vergulde Drie-hoek, tot Amsterdam. 1677.
    36p. 20cm. 4° (No. [30] as issued, in Collectio, Of Versamelinge. [Amsterdam, ca. 1680])
    "Tractatie" (unsigned): p. 23-36.
    Smith(Friends)1:30.

03271, 1866

D677 -B516s
    Bermuda Company.
    Some of the By-Laws made by the Governour and Company of the City of London, for the Plantation of the Summer-Islands. Humbly offered to the Consideration of Parliament.
    [London, 1677]
    4 p. 30cm. fol.
    Caption title.
    Apparently printed for the committee of the House of Commons which in March 1676/77 examined a petition from some members of the Bermuda Company which complained that the regulations, here contained, concerning shipping of tobacco, etc., were contrary to the company's charter.
    Sabin86698.

64-184

DA676 C562b
    Bible--O.T.--Psalms--English--Paraphrases--1677--Sternhold and Hopkins.
    The Whole Book Of Psalms; Collected into English Metre By Thomas Sternhold, John Hopkins, And others. Set forth and allowed to be Sung in all Churches, of all the People together, before and after Morning and Evening Prayer; and also before and after Sermons: And moreover in Private Houses, for their godly solace and comfort, laying apart all ungodly Songs and Ballads, which tend onely to the nourishing of Vice, and corrupting of Youth. ...
    London, Printed by A.[ndrew] C.[lark] for the Company of Stationers. 1677.
    104 p. 17.5cm. A-F^8 G^4. 8°
    Bound with The Book Of Common Prayer. London, 1676. (Wing B3646).
    Wing B2526.

28448, 1939

F677 B954c	[Burg, Pieter van der] fl. 1653-1671. Curieuse Beschrijving Van de Gelegentheid, Zeden, Godsdienst, en Ommegang, van verscheyden Oost-Indische Gewesten En machtige Landschappen. En inzonderheid van Golkonda en Pegu. Als mede een pertinente aanwijzing, hoemen door heel Indien, alle plaatsen op zijn tijd moet bevaren. Alles uyt de eygen ondervinding, in veel jaaren aangeteekent en by een vergadert door de Heer P. V. D. B. Niet alleen voor allerhande slach van Liefhebbers, maar bezonderlijk voor alle gemeene en Gezachhebbende Oost-Indischvaarders, en voor alle Heeren Bewindhebberen en Participanten, van de Hoog-gemelde Oost-Indische Compagnie, zeer dienstig om gelezen te werden. Tot Rotterdam. By Isaak Næranus; Boekverkooper. M. DC. LXXVII. 2 p.ℓ., 170, [2] p. 20.5cm. 4º Cut on t.-p. With this is bound: Berkel, A. van. Amerikaansche voyagien, Amsterdam, 1695. Muller(1872)92(this copy); Tiele215. 02521A, 1851	E677 D231a	Dassié, F fl. 1677. L'Architecture Navale, Contenant La Maniere De Construire les Navires, Galeres & Chaloupes, & la Definition de plusieurs autres especes de Vaisseaux. Avec Les Tables des Longitudes, Latitudes & Marées, Cours & distances des principaux Ports des quatre parties du Monde; une Description des Dangers, Ecueils, & l'explication des Termes de la Marine. Le tout enrichy de Figures. Par le Sr. Dassié, C. R. A Paris, Chez Jean De La Caille, ruë S. Jacques, à la Prudence. M. DC. LXXVII. Avec Privilege Du Roy. 8, [5] p., 1 ℓ., 285, [286-288] p., 1 ℓ., 209 [210-212] p. illus. (tables), fold. table, 8 diagrs. (incl. 5 fold.) 24cm. 4º Cut (engr. printer's device) on t.-p. Errata, last ℓ. of prelims. "Achevé d'imprimer pour la premiere fois le 25. Novembre 1676." (p. 8, 1st count). In this copy p. 113-114 bound (as printed) between p. 200-201. Bound in contemporary calf with, as issued, his Routier des Indes orientales et occidentales, Paris, 1677, with special t.-p. and separate paging and signatures. Brunet(Sup.)1:348; Leclerc(1878)163n. 30958A, 1951
BA677 C363ℓ	Catholic Church--Liturgy and ritual--Special offices--Felipe de Jesús, Saint. Lectiones Tertii Nocturni Recitandæ In Festo Vnivs Martyris Non Pontificis, Ex Octavario Romano, Festorum á Sacra Ritum Congregatione aprobato. Et Recitari debent in hac Civitate Mexicana In Festo Sancti Philippi A Iesv. Die v. Februarii. [Mexico, 1677?] [2 p.] 14cm. 8º Woodcut on verso. In this copy lower outer edge mutilated with slight loss of text. 5761B, 1909	E677 D231d	Dassié, F fl. 1677. Description Generale Des Costes De L'Amerique, Havres, Isles, Caps, Golfes, Bancs, Ecueils, Basses, profondeurs, vents & courans d'eau. Des Peuples qui les Habitent, du temperamment de l'air, de la qualité des Terres & du Commerce. Utile à tous Navigateurs, Hydrographes & Geographes, le tout recueilly des Autheurs les plus modernes, & des Memories des Pilotes, François, Espagnols & Portugais. Par le Sieur Dassié … A Rouen, Chez Bonaventure Le Brun, Imprimeur dans la Cour du Palais. M. DC. LXXVII. Avec Permission. 8 p.ℓ., 342, 345-421 p. 15.5cm. 12º JCB(2)2:1162; Sabin18654; Leclerc(1878) 163; Baer(Md.)87. 03616, before 1866
BA677 C363o	Catholic Church--Liturgy and ritual--Special offices--Fernando III, Saint. Officivm In Festo B. Ferdinandi Tertij Regis Castellæ, Et Legionis, Cognomento Sancti. Omnia de Communi Confess. non Pont. præter Orationem, & Lectiones proprias pro Secundo Nocturno. Svperiorum Permissv. Mexici, apud Viduam Bernardi Calderon. 1677. [8] p. 14cm. (15cm in case) 8º. Cut (papal arms) on t.-p. Promulgation dated (p. [8]) 18 May 1675. 5761A, 1909	E677 D231a	Dassié, F. fl. 1677. Le Routier Des Indes Orientales Et Occidentales: Traitant Des Saisons propres à y faire Voyage: Une description des Anchrages, Pro-

fondeurs de plusieurs Havres & Ports de Mer. Avec vingt-six differentes Navigations. Par le Sieur Dassié, C. R.
A Paris, Chez Jean De La Caille, ruë Saint Iacques, à la Prudence. M. DC. LXXVII. Avec Privilege Dv Roy.
1 p.ℓ., 209, [210-212] p. 24cm. 4⁰ (Issued as a part of his L'Architecture Navale. Paris, 1677)
Cut on t.-p.
Bound in contemporary calf.
Sabin18656; Leclerc(1878)2521.

30958B, 1951

Fisher, Samuel, 1605-1665.
Rusticus ad academicos
[London?] 1677 [i.e. 1679].
See entry under 1679

DA677
F612i
Fletcher, Giles, 1549?-1611.
Israel Redux: Or The Restauration of Israel, Exhibited in Two short Treatises. The First contains an Essay upon some probable grounds, that the present Tartars near the Caspian Sea, are the Posterity of the ten Tribes of Israel. By Giles Fletcher LL. D. The Second, a dissertation concerning their ancient and successive state, with some Scripture Evidences of their future Conversion, and Establishment in their own Land. By S. L. ...
London, Printed by S. Streater, for John Hancock at the three Bibles in Popes-head Alley in Cornhill. 1677.
3 p.ℓ., 131 p., 1 ℓ., 124 p. 14.5cm. 12⁰
"Preface" signed: Samuel Lee. August 7. 1667.
"A Dissertation concerning the Place and State Of The dispersed Tribes Of Israel" by S.[amuel] L.[ee]: p. 29-131.
With, as issued, [Samuel Lee] Ἐπείσαγμα, Or A Superaddition to the former Dissertation. London, 1677, with special t.-p. and separate paging, but continuous signatures.
Bound as no. 1 of 3 items.
WingF1333; WingL898.

4390, 1908

B677
=F843r
Frasso, Pedro, fl. 1675.
De Regio Patronatv, Ac Aliis Nonnvllis Regaliis, Regibvs Catholicis, In Indiarvm Occidentalivm Imperio, Pertinentibvs. Qvæstiones Aliqvæ Desvmptae, Et Dispvtatae, In Qvinqvaginta Capita Partitæ. Avctore D. Petro Frasso, ...
Matriti. Ex Typographia Imperiali, apud Iosephum Fernandez à Buendia. Ann. M. DC. LXXVII. [-M. DC. LXXIX.] Cvm Privilegio Regis.
2 v.: 31 p.ℓ., 395, [108] p. port.; 41 p.ℓ., 34 p., 35-37 numb. ℓ., 37-458, [129] p. port. 34cm. fol.
Titles in red and black.
Added title-pages, engr.: Tractatvs De Regio Patronatv... Signed, v.1: Gregorius Fosman faciebat Matriti Anno. 1677; v. 2: ... 1679.
Errata, v.1, 19th p. ℓ.ʳ, v. 2, 17th p. ℓ.ʳ.
Preliminary matter, v. 2, includes poetry.
"Tassa" dated (v.1, 19th p. ℓ.ʳ) 6 May 1677 and (v.2, 17th p. ℓ.ʳ) 21 Oct. 1679.
Palau(2)94684; Medina(BHA)3:1626; Streit 1:660.

5496, 1909

D677
G133n
Gage, Thomas, 1603?-1656.
A New Survey of the West-Indies: Or, The English American his Travel by Sea and Land: Containing A Journal of Three thousand and Three hundred Miles within the main Land of America: Wherein is set forth His Voyage from Spain to S. John de Ulhua; and thence to Xalappa, to Tlaxcalla, the City of Angels, and forward to Mexico: With the Description of that great City, ... Likewise His Journey from Mexico, through the Provinces of Guaxaca, Chiapa, Guatemala, Vera Paz, Truxillo, Comayagua, with his abode XII. years about Guatemala, especiall[y] in the Indian Towns of Mixco, Pinola, Petapa, Amatitlan. ... With his Return through the Province of Nicaragua and Costa Rica, to Nicoya, Panama, Porto bello, Cartagena and Havana, ... Also A new and exact Discovery of the Spanish Navigation to those Parts: And of their Dominions, Government, Religion, Forts, Castles, Ports, Havens, Commodities, Fashions, Behavior of

Spaniards, Priests and Friers, Black-moors, Mulatto's, Mestiso's, Indians; and of their Feasts and Solemnities. With a Grammar, or some few Rudiments of the Indian Tongue, called Poconchi or Pocoman. The third Edition enlarged by the Author, with a new and accurate Map. By Thomas Gage.
 London: Printed by A. Clark, and are to be sold by John Martyn, Robert Horn and Walter Kettilby. 1677.
 4 p.ℓ., 383, 386-577 [i.e. 477], [18] p. fold. map. 19.5cm. 8º.
 "Some brief and short Rules for the better learning of the Indian tongue, called Pochonchi... commonly used about Guatemala...": p. 465-577 [i.e. 477].
 First pub. under title: The English-American his Travail by Sea and Land. London, 1648; the dedication to Lord Fairfax of earlier editions is here addressed "To the Reader" (2d-4th p.ℓ.), and Chaloner's poem and chap. 22 (on the author's journey to Rome) are omitted.
 In this copy "An Accurate Map of the West Indies...Emanl. Bowen Sculpt." London, E. Cave [1739]: fold., tipped in at end.
 JCB(2)2:1165; Sabin26300; Palau(2)96481; Streit 2:2125; Cundall(WI)1978n; WingG114; Pilling1365.
0884, 1846

D DePuy 1
 Great Britain--Treaties, etc., 1660-1685 (Charles II).
 Articles Of Peace Between The Most Serene and Mighty Prince Charles II. By the Grace of God, King of England, Scotland, France and Ireland, Defender of the Faith, &c. And Several Indian Kings and Queens, &c. Concluded the 29th day of May, 1677. Published by his Majesties Command.
 London, Printed by John Bill, Christopher Barker, Thomas Newcomb and Henry Hills, Printers to the Kings Most Excellent Majesty. 1677.
 18 p. 19.5cm. 4º
 JCBAR28:8-11; Sabin2145; Church657; Jones (1928)133; De Puy 1; Torrence83; WingC2909.
15098, 1928

D677 -H163p
 Hale, Sir Matthew, 1609-1676.
 The Primitive Origination Of Mankind, Considered And Examined According to The Light of Nature. Written By the Honourable Sir Matthew Hale Knight: Late Chief Justice of His Majesties Court of King's Bench.
 London, Printed by William Godbid, for William Shrowsbery at the Sign of the Bible in Duke-Lane. cIɔ Iɔc LXXVII.
 5 p.ℓ., 380 p. front. (port.) 31cm. fol.
 Cut on t.-p.
 WingH258; McAlpin3:748.
32761, 1960

D677 -H537s
 [Herbert, Sir Thomas] 1606-1682.
 Some Years Travels Into Divers Parts Of Africa, And Asia the Great. Describing More particularly the Empires of Persia and Industan: Interwoven with such remarkable Occurrences as hapned in those parts during these later Times. As also, many other rich and Famous Kingdoms in the Oriental India, with the Isles adjacent. Severally relating their Religion, Language, Customs and Habit: As also proper Observations concerning them. In this Fourth Impression are added (by the Author now living) as well many Additions throughout the whole Work, as also several Sculptures, never before Printed. ...
 London, Printed by R. Everingham, for R. Scot, T. Basset, J. Wright, and R. Chiswell. 1677.
 4 p.ℓ., 399, [18] p., 1 ℓ. illus. (incl. maps), 3 plates (incl. 1 fold.). 32cm. fol.
 Added t.-p., engr.: ... The third Edition ... London... 1677.
 First pub. London, 1634, under title: A Relation of some yeares travaile.
 "America..." (p. 394-397) includes claim for Madog ab Owain Gwynedd as 1st discoverer of America, 12th cent.
 Preliminary matter includes poetry by Charles Herbert, Arthur Johnston, Martin Belwood, Walter Quin, and Thomas Fairfax.
 JCB(2)2:1166; Sabin31471; WingH1536.
03617, before 1866

FC650 H737 27
 Hollandtze Mercurius, Behelssende, De voornaemste Voorvallen Binnen Europa, In het Jaer 1676. tot 1677. Het Seven-en-twintigste Deel. ...
 Gedruckt tot Haerlem, by de Erfgenamen van Pieter Casteleyn, op de Marckt, in de Keysers Kroon. Anno 1677. Met Privilege.
 2 p.ℓ., 245, [246-247] p. 20cm. 4º (Bound in [vol.6] of Hollandse Mercurius).
 Added t.-p., engraved: Anno 1676. Hollantsche Mercurius. Gedruckt tot Haerlem bij de Erfgenamen van Pieter Casteleijn. op de Marckt Anno 1677. met Privilegie.

"Extract van Privilegie" (2d p. ℓ.) dated 17 Dec. 1668.
JCB(3)2:410; Sabin32523.
8487AA, 1912

D677
H876n1
Hubbard, William, 1621-1704.
A Narrative Of The Troubles With The Indians In New-England, from the first planting thereof in the year 1607. to this present year 1677. But chiefly of the late Troubles in the two last years, 1675. and 1676. To which is added a Discourse about the Warre with the Pequods In the year 1637. By W. Hubbard, Minister of Ipswich. ... Pnblished [sic] by authority.
Boston; Printed by John Foster, in the year 1677.
7 p. ℓ., 132, [8], 7-12, 88 p., 1 ℓ., [6], 63 p. fold. map. 19cm. (21cm. in case) 4°
Errata: 7th p. ℓ.^{v} and p. 88, 2d count.
"King Philip's War Narratives" quarto no. 8. cf. Church 639n.
Dedication (3d-4th p. ℓ.) signed: VVilliam Hubbard. From my Study 16th. 12th. 1676. Licence (1st p. ℓ.) dated: Boston, March 29, 1677.
"To the Reverend Mr. William Hubbard on his most exact History of New-Englands Troubles" (poem, 6th p. ℓ.) signed: J. S. [John Sherman?]
"Upon The elaborate Survey of New-Englands Passions from the Natives By the impartial Pen of that worthy Divine Mr. William Hubbard" (poem, 6-7th p. ℓ.) signed: B. [enjamin] T. [ompson]
Lines 15-16 of t.-p.: ... in|Brooks of Arnon. Of 17 variations noted by R. G. Adams, "William Hubbard's 'Narrative', 1677" (in BSA Papers, 33:35), this variant has 12 first readings and 5 second readings, and the 'White Hills' map.
Bound in contemporary calf by John Ratcliff.
With, as issued, his The Happiness of a People. Boston, 1676, with special t.-p. and separate paging and signatures.
In this copy there is a blank ℓ. following p. 7-12, 2d count.
JCB(2)2:1168; JCBAR30:29; Sabin33445; Evans231; Vail(Front.)184; Church650; WingH3210; Green(John Foster)73-79.
15484, 1929

D677
H876n2
Hubbard, William, 1621-1704.
A Narrative Of The Troubles With The Indians In New-England, from the first planting thereof in the year 1607, to this present year 1677. But chiefly of the late Troubles in the two last years, 1675. and 1676. To which is added a Discourse about the Warre with the Pequods In the year 1637. By W. Hubbard, Minister of Ipswich. ... Pnblished [sic] by Authority.
Boston; Printed by John Foster, in the year 1677.
7 p. ℓ., 132, [8], 7-12, 88 p., 1 ℓ., [6], 63 p. fold. map. 20cm. 4°
Errata: 7th p. ℓ.^{v} and p. 88, 2d count.
"King Philip's War Narratives" quarto no. 8. cf. Church639n.
Dedication (3d-4th p. ℓ.) signed: VVilliam Hubbard. From my Study 16th. 12th. 1676. Licence (1st p. ℓ.) dated: Boston, March 29, 1677.
"To the Reverend Mr. William Hubbard on his most exact History of New-Englands Troubles " (poem, 6th p. ℓ.) signed: J. S. [John Sherman?]
"Upon The elaborate Survey of New-Englands Passions from the Natives By the impartial Pen of that worthy Divine Mr. William Hubbard" (poem, 6-7th p. ℓ.) signed: B. [enjamin] T. [ompson]
Lines 15-16 of t.-p.: ... in| the Brooks of Arnon. Of 17 variations noted by R. G. Adams, "William Hubbard's 'Narrative', 1677" (in BSA Papers, 33:35), this variant has 7 first readings and 10 second readings.
Imperfect: 1st p. ℓ. (license) and map wanting
With, as issued, his The Happiness of a People. Boston, 1676, with special t.-p. and separate paging and signatures.
In this copy there is a blank ℓ. following p. 7-12, 2d count.
JCB(2)2:1168; JCBAR30:29; Sabin33445; Evans231; Vail(Front.)184; Church650; WingH3210; Green(John Foster)73-79.
01906, 1854

D677
H876p1
Hubbard, William, 1621-1704.
The Present State Of New-England. Being A Narrative Of the Troubles with the Indians In New-England, from the first planting thereof in the year 1607, to this present year 1677: But chiefly of the late Troubles in the two last years 1675, and 1676. To which is added a Discourse about the War with the Pequods in the year 1637. By W. Hubbard Minister of Ipswich. ...
London: Printed for Tho. Parkhurst at the Bible and Three Crowns in Cheapside, near Mercers-Chappel, and at the Bible on London-Bridg. 1677.
7 p. ℓ., 131, [132-144], 88 p. fold. map. 20.5cm. 4°
"King Philip's War Narratives" quarto no. 8. cf. Church639n.
License (1st p. ℓ.^{v}) dated in London, 27 June 1677.
"To the Revernd [sic] Mr. William Hubbard on his most exact History of New-Englands Troubles" (poem, 6th p. ℓ.) signed: J. S. [John Sherman?]
"Upon the elaborate Survey of New-Englands Passions from the Natives, By the impartial Pen of that worthy Divine Mr. William Hubbard" (poem, 7th p. ℓ.) signed: B. [enjamin] T. [ompson]
License leaf (with   2 lines of type ornaments)

reads "Juue"; p. 120 numbered 118. cf. R.G. Adams, "William Hubbard's 'Narrative', 1677" (in BSA Papers, 33:36)
 In this copy there is a blank ℓ. at beginning.
 Imperfect: map wanting.
 Bound in contemporary calf.
 JCB(2)2:1167; Sabin33446; Vail(Front.)185; Church651; WingH3212.

04611, before 1874

D677 Hubbard, William, 1621-1704.
H876p2 The Present State Of New-England. Being A Narrative Of the Troubles with the Indians In New-England, from the first planting thereof in the year 1607, to this present year 1677: But chiefly of the late Troubles in the two last years 1675, and 1676. To which is added a Discourse about the War with the Pequods in the year 1637. By W. Hubbard Minister of Ipswich. ...
 London: Printed for Tho.Parkhurst at the Bible and Three Crowns in Cheapside, near Mercers-Chappel, and at the Bible on London-Bridg. 1677.
 7 p.ℓ., 131, [132-144], 88p. fold. map. 20cm. 4⁰
 "King Philip's War Narratives" quarto no. 8. cf. Church 639n.
 License (1st p.ℓ.ᵛ) dated in London, 27 June 1677.
 "To the Revernd [sic] Mr. William Hubbard on his most exact History of New-Englands Troubles" (poem, 6th p.ℓ.) signed: J.S. [John Sherman?]
 "Upon the elaborate Survey of New-Englands Passions from the Natives, By the impartial Pen of that worthy Divine Mr. William Hubbard" (poem, 7th p.ℓ.) signed: B.[enjamin] T.[ompson]
 License leaf (with line of type ornaments and rule) reads "Juue"; p.120 numbered 118; has the 'Wine Hills' map. cf. R.G. Adams, "William Hubbard's 'Narrative', 1677" (in BSA Papers 33:36)
 JCB(2)2:1167; Sabin33446; Vail(Front.)185; Church651; WingH3212.

01907, 1854

D677 [Hutchinson, Richard] fl. 1676.
-H977w The Warr In New-England Visibly ended. King Philip that barbarous Indian now Beheaded, and most of his Bloudy Adherents submitted to Mercy, the Rest fled far up into the Countrey, which hath given the Inhabitants Encouragement to prepare for their Settlement. Being a True and Perfect Account brought in by Caleb More Master of a Vessel newly Arrived from Rhode-Island. And Published for general Satisfaction. Licensed November 4. Roger L'Estrange.
 London, Printed by J. B. for Francis Smith at the Elephant and Castle in Cornhill. 1677.
 1 p.ℓ., 2 p. 27.5cm. fol.
 "King Philip's War Narratives" folio no. 5. cf. Church636n.
 Signed: R.H.
 Woodcut title vignette (royal arms)
 JCB(1)2:847; JCB(2)2:1170; Church652; Sabin 101454; Vail(Front.)189; WingH3835.

0516, 1846?

B69 Juana Inés de la Cruz, sister, 1651-1695.
G643v Villancicos, Qve Se Cantaron En La Santa
32 Iglesia Cathedral de Mexico, à los Maytines del Gloriosissimo Principe de la Iglesia, el Señor San Pedro. ... Año de 1677. ...
 Con Licencia. En Mexico, por la Uiuda de Bernardo Calderon. [1677]
 [8]p. 20cm. 4⁰.
 Caption title; imprint at end.
 Woodcut title vignette (bust of St. Peter).
 Bound in contemporary vellum, as no. 32 with 42 other items.
 Medina(Mexico) 1157.

28932, 1941

DA677 Keith, George, 1639?-1716.
K28w The Way Cast up, And the Stumbling-blocks removed from before the feet of those, who are seeking the way to Zion, with their faces thitherward. Containing An Answer to a Postscript, Printed at the end of Samuel Rutherford's Letters, third Edition, by a namelesse Author, ... By George Keith, Prisoner in the Tolbooth of Aberdeen, ...
 [Netherlands] Printed in the Year 1677.
 12 p.ℓ., 215 p. 16.5cm. 8⁰.
 Imprint at end.
 Preface (2d-12th p.ℓ.) and postscript (p. 203-215) by Alexander Skein. Preface dated "the 20 of the 12 moneth, called February. 16$\frac{76}{77}$."
 McAlpin3:750-1; Smith(Friends)2:21; WingK233.

7553, 1910

DA677 [Lee, Samuel,] 1625-1691.
F612i Ecclesia Gemens: Or, Two Discourses On the mournful State of the Church, with a Prospect of her Dawning Glory. Exhibited in a View of two Scriptures, ...
 London, Printed for John Hancock, at the

	three Bibles in Popes-head Alley in Cornhill. 1677. 2 p.ℓ., 92 p. 14.5cm. 12⁰ Dedication (2d p.ℓ.) signed: S.[amuel] L.[ee]. Dated (p. 45) 20 July 1673. Bound as no. 3 of 3 items. McAlpin(3)751; WingL894.
4393, 1908	

DA677 L481e	[Lee, Samuel] 1625-1691. Ἐλεοθρίαμβος. Or the Triumph of Mercy In the Chariot of Praise. A Treatise Of Preventing secret and unexpected Mercies with some mixt Reflexions. ... London, Printed for John Hancock, at the three Bibles in Popes-head Alley in Cornhill, 1677. [10], 200, [6] p. 14cm. 12⁰ "Epistle dedicatory" signed (5th p.ℓ.): Febr. 8. 1676. Samuel Lee. "Some Passages to be inserted in page 26. which through a casualty did happen to be misplaced" p. 198-200. "Books printed for and are to be sold by John Hancock, at the Sign of the three Bibles in Popes Head Alley in Cornhill": last 3 ℓ.
DA677 F612i	——— Another copy. Bound as no. 2 of 3 items. McAlpin(3)751; WingL895.
04958, after 1882 4392, 1908	Title transliterated: Eleothriambos

DA677 F612i	[Lee, Samuel] 1625-1691. Ἐπείσαγμα, Or A Superaddition to the former Dissertation. Containing a Discourse of the grand Charter of the Donation of the Land of Canaan to Israel. Together with a short Natural History of the Animals, Vegetables, and Minerals, found in that Country, and of its present Fertility. ... London, Printed Anno Domini 1677. 1 p.ℓ., 124 p. illus. 14.5cm. 12⁰ (Issued as a part of Giles Fletcher, Israel Redux ... , London, 1677).
4391, 1908	Title transliterated: Epeisagma

E677 M379v	[Martin, Claude] 1619-1696. La Vie De La Venerable Mere Marie De L'Incarnation Premiere Superieure Des Ursulines De La Nouvelle France. Tirée de ses Lettres & de ses Ecrits. ...

A Paris, Chez Loüis [sic] Billaine, au second pillier de la grande Salle du Palais, au grand Cesar. M. DC. LXXVII. Avec Approbation Et Privilege.
18 p.ℓ., 520, 523-757, [758-763] p. front. (port.). 25cm. 4⁰
"... composée par le R. P. Dom Claude Martin Religieux Benedictin de la Congregation saint Maur ..." (18th p.ℓ.ᵛ).
"Achevé d'Imprimer. le 15 Octobre 1676." (p. 757).
"Livres François de devotion à l'Ordre ... se trouveront dans la méme Boutique, au second pillier de la Grand-Salle du Palais. 1676." (p. 757).
Errata, last page.
Bound in contemporary calf.
JCBAR52:38-39; Sabin44861; Streit 2:2698; Faribault 437; McCoy(Hand-list) 59 (this copy); Harrisse(NF)143.

31051, 1952

D. Math I.110A	Mather, Increase, 1639-1723. An Historical Discourse Concerning the Prevalency Of Prayer Wherein is shewed that New-Englands late Deliverance from the Rage of the Heathen, is an eminent Answer of Prayer. By Increase Mather Teacher of a Church in Boston in New-England. ... Boston, Printed and sold by John Foster. 1677. 2 p.ℓ., 19 p. 17.5cm. 4⁰ (Issued as a part of his <u>A Relation Of the Troubles Which have hapned in New-England</u>. Boston, 1677). "To the Reader" (2d p.ℓ.) signed: Increase Mather. Boston, N-E. August. 16, 1677. JCB(2)2:1169; Evans238(2d title); Sabin46692; Holmes(I)63A; Church653; WingM1220; Green (John Foster) 72-73.
0517B, 1846	

D. Math I.110A	Mather, Increase, 1639-1723. A Relation Of the Troubles which have hapned in New-England, By reason of the Indians there. From the Year 1614. to the Year 1675. Wherein the frequent Conspiracyes of the Indians to cutt off the English, and the wonderfull providence of God, in disappointing their devices, is declared. Together with an Historical Discourse concerning the Prevalency of Prayer shewing that New Englands late deliverance from the Rage of the Heathen is an eminent Answer of Prayer. By Increase Mather Teacher of a Church in Boston in New-England. ... Boston, Printed and sold by John Foster, 1677. 3 p.ℓ., 76 p., 1 ℓ., [2], 19 p. 17.5cm. 4⁰ Errata, 3d p.ℓ.

"King Philip's War Narratives" quarto no. 9. cf. Church639n.

"To the Reader"(2d-3d p. ℓ.) signed: Increase Mather. Boston N.E. Sept. 14, 1677

"Some Grounds of the War against the Peqnots [sic]" and "A Brief History Of the War with the Pequot Indians in New-England; Anno 1637" (p. 24-43) constitute Mather's editing of part of John Mason's ms., first pub. as A Brief History Of The Pequot War. Boston, 1736, erroneously ascribed to John Allyn. cf. Holmes.

The narrative of "an old Planter" (p. 17-20) is Mather's version of Phinehas Pratt's ms. A Decliration Of The Afaires Of The Einglish People; cf. Mass. Hist. Soc. Colls., ser.4, v.4, p. 474-91.

Closely trimmed at top with some loss of text.

With, as issued, his An Historical Discourse Concerning the Prevalency Of Prayer. Boston, 1677, with special t.-p. and separate paging and signatures.

D. Math I.110A cop.2
────── Another copy. 19cm. (20cm. in case)
Imperfect: p. 27-76 only.
Brinley copy (Sale Cat. no. 950).
JCB(1)2:844=JCB(2)2:1185; Evans238; Sabin46727; Holmes(I)110A(2d state); Vail(Front.)186; Church 654; WingM1243; Green(John Foster)80-81.

0517A, 1846
04810, 1879

bBB M6113 1677 1
Mexico(Viceroyalty)--Laws, statutes, etc., 1673-1680 (Enríquez de Ribera).
El M.D. Fr. Payo De Ribera, del Orden de San Augustin, Arçobispo de Mexico, del Consejo de su Magestad, su Virrey Lugar-Theniente, Governador, y Capitan General desta Nueva-España, y Presidente de la Real Audiencia de ella, &c. Por Quanto en conformidad de parecer del Real Acuerdo, ...
[Mexico, 1677]
[2] p. 31x21cm. fol.
Title from beginning of text.
Grain regulations.
Dated in Mexico, 4 May 1677.
Manuscript additions: signature of the viceroy, and others; direction to the Province of Tula.
Papel sellado dated 1676-77.

7007, 1910

bBB M6113 1677 1
Mexico(Viceroyalty)--Laws, statutes, etc., 1673-1680 (Enríquez de Ribera)
El M.D. Fr. Payo De Ribera, del Orden de San Augustin, Arçobispo de Mexico, del Consejo de su Magestad, su Virrey Lugar-Theniente, Governador, y Capitan General desta Nueva-Espana, y Presidente de la Real Audiencia de ella, &c. Por Quanto los dueños de panaderia desta Ciudad, ...
[Mexico, 1677]
Broadside. 31x21cm. fol.
Title from beginning of text.
Concerns an order of 4 May 1677 regulating grain trade.
Dated in Mexico, 17 May 1677.
Manuscript additions: signature of the viceroy, and others; direction to the Province of Tula; certificate of the province (on verso).
Papel sellado dated 1676-77.

7008, 1910

DA677 M679d
Mitchel, Jonathan, 1624-1668.
A Discourse Of The Glory To which God hath called Believers By Jesus Christ. Delivered in some Sermons out of the I Pet. 5 Chap. 10 Ver. Together with an annexed Letter. Both, by that Eminent and Worthy Minister of the Gospel, Mr. Jonathan Mitchil, late Pastor to the Church at Cambridge in New-England.
London, Printed for Nathaniel Ponder at the Peacock in the Poultry. Anno Dom. 1677.
7 p.ℓ., 263, 21 p. 15.5cm. 8⁰
"To The Reader" signed: June 29 1667. John Collins.
"A Letter written by the Author to his Friend in New-England" (21 p. at end) signed: From Harrard [sic] Colledge in Cambridge, May 19. 1649 ... J.M.
Sabin49655; WingM2289.

5087, 1909

J677 S591v
[Müller, Wilhelm Johann] fl. 1654-1669.
Africanische Reissbeschreibung/in die Landschaft Fetu. Auf der Guineischen Gold-Cüst gelegen/Samt deroselben beschaffenheit/auch der Einwohneren Sitten/Religion und Gebräuchen. Auss eigener Neun-Jähriger Erfahrung/im Dienst der Königlich-Dännemärckish-Africanischen Compagnie/kurz beschriben/und auf begehren in Truck übergeben. Von Jans Jacob Zur-Eich [i.e. Wilhelm Johann Müller] Burgern und Schlossern in Zürich. In Verlegung Johann Wilhelm Simlers/Und Johann Rudolff Rhanen. Getrukt zu Zürich/Bey Michael Schauffelbergers seligen Erbin/Durch Johannes Bachmann/ 1677.
91-174 p. 2 plates. 18cm. 8⁰ (Issued as a part of Spöri, F.C., Americanische Reissbeschreibung, Zürich, 1677, itself issued as

a part of Simler, J.W., ed. Vier loblicher Statt Zürich verbürgerter Reiss beschreibungen [Zürich, 1677-1678]).
JCB(2)2:1175; Sabin99534; cf. Palmer405.
01598C, 1847 rev

F677　Nylandt, Petrus, fl. 1669-1686.
N995v　Den Verstandigen Hovenier, Over de twaelf Maenden van 't Jaer. Zijnde het II.Deel van het Vermakelyck Landt-Leven. ... Beschreven door P. Nyland, der Medicijnen Doctor. Nooit voor desen soo gedruckt.
t'Amsterdam, By de Weduw. van Michiel de Groot, en Gijsbert de Groot, Boeckverkoper tusschen de twee Haerlemmer-sluysen. [1677] Met Privilegie voor 15 Jaren.
4 p.ℓ., 84 p, [4] p. illus., 20cm. 4°
Added t.-p., engraved: De Verstandigen Hovenier. t Amsterdam by Michiel De Groot, op de Niewendyck...
"Extract uyt de Privilegie." (verso 1st p.ℓ.) dated: 30 Juny 1677.
First pub. as part II of Het Vermakelijck Landt-Leven, Amsterdam, 1669.
Woodcut title vignette.
With this is bound, in contemporary vellum, his Het Schouw-Toneel Der Aertsche Schepselen, Amsterdam, 1672.
12484-1, 1920

B677　Ortiz de Zúñiga, Diego, 1633-1680.
-O77a　Annales Eclesiasticos, Y Secvlares De La Mvy Noble, Y Mvy Leal Civdad De Sevilla, Metropoli De La Andalvzia, Qve Contienen Svs Mas Principales Memorias. Desde El Año De 1246. En Qve Emprendio conquistarla del poder de los Moros, el gloriosissimo Rey S. Fernando Tercero de Castilla, y Leon, hasta el de 1671. en que la Catolica Iglesia le concedió el culto, y titulo de Bienauenturado. Formados Por D. Diego Ortiz De Zvñiga, ...
Año 1677. Con Privilegio. En Madrid: En la Imprenta Real. Por Iuan Garcia Infançon. Acosta de Florian Anisson, Mercader de Libros.
12 p.ℓ., 375, 378-669, 700-817, [818-830] p., 1 ℓ. illus. 31cm. fol.
Title in red and black.
Cut (coat of arms) on t.-p.
Added t.-p. engraved: Annales Eclesiasticos ... Marcus Orozco Presby^{er} Delinea^t et. Sculp^t M^{ti} 1677.
Tax statement dated (8th p.ℓ.) 29 Apr. 1677.
Errata, 8th p.ℓ.
Contains biographical information concerning Columbus, Las Casas, Cortés, Ponce de León and other figures who went to the New World.

Bound in contemporary vellum.
Sabin57716; Palau(2)206132; Vindel 2019; Streit2:2127.
30500, 1949

DA677　Penn, William, 1644-1718.
P412t　To The Churches of Jesus Throughout the World. Gathered and setled in his Eternal Light, Power, and Spirit, to be One Holy Flock, Family, and Household to the Lord, who hath Redeemed them from among all the Kindreds of the Earth. ... William Penn.
[London] Printed in the Year, 1677.
1 p.ℓ., 13 p. 19.5cm. 4°.
Signed (p. 13): Franckfort, the 22th of the 6th Moneth, 1677. W.P.
Smith(Friends)2:295; McAlpin3:755; WingP1387.
11513, 1918

D677　Raleigh, Sir Walter, 1552?-1618.
=R163h　The History Of The World, In Five Books. ... By Sir Walter Ralegh, Knight. Whereunto is added in this Edition, the Life and Tryal of the Author.
London, Printed for Robert White, T. Basset, J. Wright, R. Chiswell, G. Dawes and T. Sawbridge. 1677.
3 p.ℓ., 44, 51-54, [43], 376, 393-480, 569-660, 557-708, 737-885, [46] p. incl. illus., tables. front. (port.), 6 double maps, 2 double plans. 39cm. fol.
Errata: p. 54 1st count.
Title in red and black.
Added t.-p., engraved (allegorical): The History Of The World ... 1676. Ren: Elstrack Sculpsit.
First pub. London, 1614.
"The Life Of Sir Walter Raleigh" (p. 1-54, 1st count) is by John Shirley.
Bound in contemporary calf, rebacked.
Sabin67560; Brushfield223J and 3; Wing R167.
28729, 1941

E677　Relation De La Bataille De Tabago.
R382b　[Paris? 1677?]
9 p. 23cm. 4°
Caption title.
Concerns the Battle of February-March, 1677.
In this copy there is a blank ℓ. at end.
Sabin69263; Leclerc(1875)2599.
1184, 1906

J677
R533
	Richshoffer, Ambrosius, b. 1612.
	    Ambrosij Richsshoffers, Brassilianisch-und West Indianische Reisse Beschreibung
	      Strassburg Beij Jossias Städeln, A⁰ 1677.
	      182, [5] p. front. (port.), 2 fold. maps, 2 fold. plates. 16cm. 8⁰
	      Errata on last p.
	      Title and portrait of the author engraved by J. C. Sartorius.
	      Commendatory verses at end by Johann Joachim Böckenhoffer and Johann Heinrich Rapp.
	      JCB(2)2:1174; Baginsky196; Borba De Moraes 2:208; Church656; Palmer379; Rodrigues(Dom. Hol.)415; Sabin71219.

01579, 1847

D671
B792t
	[Royal Society of London]
	    Philosophical Transactions: Giving Some Accompt Of The Present Undertakings, Studies and Labours Of The Ingenious In Many Considerable Parts Of The World. Vol. XI. For the Year MDCLXXVI.
	      London, Printed by T.R. for John Martyn, Printer to the Royal Society; at the Bell in St. Pauls Church-yard. [1677]
	      2 p.ℓ., 551-814, [4] p. illus. (tables, diagr.), 5 fold. diagrs. 22cm. 4⁰
	      Issued in parts numbered 123-132 and dated 25 Mar. 1676-26 Feb. 1676/7; nos. issued monthly (except no. 128 covering Aug./Sept. and no. 129 Oct./Nov.). Each no. has caption title and (except no. 132) imprint at end; imprint no. 125-131 dated 1676.
	      Dedication (2d p.ℓ.) signed by the editor and Secretary of the Society, Henry Oldenburg.
	      Imprimatur dated (1st p.ℓ.ᵛ) 1 Mar. 1676/7.
	      Errata, p. 598, 622, 646, 750, 774.
	      Includes: "An Account of Virginia, its Scituation, Temperature, Productions, Inhabitants, and their manner of planting and ordering Tobacco, &c." by Thomas Glover (p. 623-636); "An extract of a Letter &c. from Dublin May the 10th. 1676." with American references (p. 647-653); and "An Extract of some Observations, to be met with in the Journal des Scavans [t. 6, 2 Mar. 1676]; concerning the Lake of Mexico ..." (p. 758).
	      In this copy p.ℓ. bound preceding no. 132.
	      Bound in contemporary calf, rebacked, as the 2d of 4 items.

9677, 1914

D677
S558ℓ
	[Shirley, John] 1648-1679.
	    The Life Of the Valiant & Learned Sir Walter Raleigh, Knight. With His Tryal At Winchester.
	      London, Printed by J. D. for Benj. Shirley, and Richard Tonson, under the Dial of St. Dunstans Church in Fleetstreet, and under Grays-Inn Gate next Grays-Inn Lane, 1677.
	      243, [1] p. 17.5cm. 8⁰
	      First published in Raleigh's The History of the World, London, 1677.
	      Imprimatur dated (1st p.ℓ.ᵛ) 30 Aug. 1676.
	      Bookseller's advertisement, last p.
	      Imperfect: 1st p.ℓ. wanting; available in facsim.
	      JCB(2)2:1171; Sabin67567; Brushfield 3; Wing S3495.

0597, 1846

J677
S591v
	Simler, Johann Wilhelm, fl. 1677, ed.
	    Vier Loblicher Statt Zürich verbürgerter Reiss beschreibungen: geschehen in 1. Das Gelobte-Land. 2. Die Insul Jamaica. 3. Die Caribes Inslen, und Neüw Engel Land, in America. 4. Die Landtschafft Fetü in Africa.
	      in verlegung Joh. Wilhelm Simlers und Joh. Rudolff Rahnen.
	      [Getrukt zu Zürich/Bey Michael Schauffelbergers seligen Erbin/Durch Johannes Bachmann/1677-78]
	      9 p.ℓ., 192, 174 p. front. (port.), 2 plates, fold. plan. 18cm. 8⁰
	      Engraved t.-p., signed: Conrad Meÿer fecit A⁰ 1677.
	      Contents. 1. Amman, J.J., Reiss in das gelobte Land, Zürich, 1678, with special t.-p. 2. Zeller, J.J., "Neue Beschreibung der Insul Jamaica," with paging and signatures continuous with the preceding. 3. Spöri, F.C., Americanische Reiss-beschreibung nach den Caribes Insseln und Neu-Engelland, Zürich, 1677, with special t.-p., separate paging and signatures. 4. [Müller, W.J.] Africanische Reissbeschreibung in die Landschaft Fetu, Zürich, 1677, with special t.-p. but paging and signatures continuous with the preceding.
	      JCB(2)2:1175, 1173; Sabin99534: Palmer405.

01598A-C, 1847 rev

BB -S7333 1677	Spain--Laws, statutes, etc. Svmarios De La Recopilacion General De Las Leyes, Ordenanças, Provisiones, Cedvlas, Instrvcciones, Y Cartas Acordadas, q̃ por los Reyes Catolicos de Castilla se han promulgado, expedido, y despachado, para las Indias Occidentales, Islas, y Tierra-Firme del mar Occeano: desde el año de mil y quatrocientos y noventa y dos, que se descubrieron, hasta el presente, de mil y seiscientos y veinte y ocho. Al Rey Nvestro Señor Don Felipe Qvarto En su

Real, y Supremo Consejo de las Indias. Por El Licenciado Don Rodrigo De Aguiar y Acuña, del mismo Consejo.
   Con Licencia, En Mexico. Impressos por Francisco Rodriguez Lupericio. Año de M. DC. LXXVII.
   8 p. ℓ., 385 numb. ℓ. 29cm. fol.
   Spanish coat of arms engraved below title.
   Cut (royal arms) on t.-p.
   First pub. Madrid, 1628. Reprinted under supervision of Juan Francisco de Montemayor y Córdova de Cuenca.
   License dated (8th p. ℓ.ᵛ) 26 Apr. 1677.
   Bound in contemporary vellum.
   Sabin525; Medina(Mexico)1151; Palau(2)3496.
04959, 1895

BA677
T337p
Tesoro Pervano, De Vn Mineral Rico, Labrado En Vn Ingenio Famoso, Ensayado, Y Tenido Por De Bvena Ley, Por Varios Maestros Del Reyno Del Perv, Y Sacado A Lvz En Este De España. En Diez Y Ocho Sermones, Predicados A Diversos Assvmptos. Dirigido A La Avgvstissima, Y Soberana Reyna De Cielos, Y Tierra Nvestra Señora Del Bven Consejo.
   Con Licencia: En Zaragoza, por los herederos de Iuan de Ybar Ano de 1677.
   4 p. ℓ., 89, 100-318, 315-326, 315-363, [364-384] p. 20.5cm. 4º
   Imprimatur dated (3d p. ℓ.ᵛ) 16 Mar. 1677.
   Errata, 4th p. ℓ.ʳ.
   In this copy t.-p. torn, lower-right corner, affecting imprint.
   Medina(BHA)1635; Sabin94900; Palau(1)7:25.
5497, 1909

J677
S591v
Spörri, Felix Christian, fl. 1677.
   Americanische Reiss-beschreibung Nach den Caribes Insslen/Und Neu Engelland. Verrichtet und aufgesezt durch Felix-Christian Spöri/ Schnitt-und Wund-Artzet von Zürich. In Verlegung Johann Wilhelm Simlers/Johann Rudolff Rhanen.
   Getrukt zu Zürich/Bey Michael Schauffelbergers sel. Erbin/Durch Johannes Backmann/ 1677.
   174 p. 2 plates. 18cm. 8º (Issued as a part of Simler, J.W., ed., <u>Vier loblicher Statt Zürich verbürgerter Reiss beschreibungen,</u> [Zürich, 1677-1678]).
   With, as issued, p. 91-174, [Müller, W.J.] <u>Africanische Reissbeschreibung,</u> Zürich, 1677, with special t.-p., but continuous paging and signatures.
   JCB(2)2:1173; Sabin89554A, cf. Palmer405.
01598B, 1847 rev

D677
-T865r
A True Relation Of the late Action between the French and Dutch At Tobago In The West-Indies. Giving an Account of what happened there upon the Assault made by the Count D'Estrees, Both By Sea and Land, For the Gaining of the said Place. With an Account of the Losses on both Sides, by a diligent Hand.
   London, Printed for D. W. in the Year 1677.
   4 p. 28cm. fol.
   JCBAR60:28; Sabin97143; WingT2974.
32653, 1960

D677
S897v
Strange News From Virginia; Being a full and true Account Of The Life and Death Of Nathanael Bacon Esquire, Who was the only Cause and Original of all the late Troubles in that Country. With a full Relation of all the Accidents which have happened in the late War there between the Christians and Indians.
   London, Printed for William Harris, next door to the Turn-Stile without Moor-gate. 1677.
   8 p. 19.5cm. 4º.
   Sabin2679, 92716; Church657A; Vail 188; Torrence84; WingS5911.
3903, 1907

J677
W162s
Waldenfels, Christoph Philippus von, fl. 1662.
   Selectæ Antiquitatis Libri XII. De Gestis primævis, item de Origine Gentium Nationumque migrationibus, atqua præcipuis Nostratium dilocationibus, Ex Sacræ Scripturæ, aliorumque gravissimorum Autorum monumentis collecti; Indice quoque sufficiente adimpleti à Christophoro Philippo de Waldenfels.
   Norimbergæ, Sumtibus Wolgangi Mauritii Endteri, & Johannis Andreæ Endteri Hæredum. Anno M.DC.LXXVII.
   8 p. ℓ., 480, [46] p. 21cm. 4º
   Title in red and black.
   Cut (printer's device) on t.-p.
   "Annotata, quæ ita restituenda." (last p.)
   In this copy there is a blank ℓ. at end.
32229, 1958 rev

DA677 [Willsford, John] fl. 1673-1681.
W741g   A General Testimony To the Everlasting Truth of God; Partly intended for the Iuhabitants [sic] of Nether-Broughton in the County of Leicester. Wherein there is some short Relation of the Manner of my Convincement; and also, some few of the Sufferings which were inflicted upon me by some of the said Inhabitants for my faithful Testimony, which I bare for God and his blessed Truth. Wi[t]h Copies of two Letters sent to the Spiritual or Ec.clesiastical Court (so called) in Leicester ... And the Court's Answer, whereby their Cruelty may be seen, and also how willing they are to keep men in Prison, ... With a Postscript ... By J. W. a Sufferer in Leicester-County-Goal, ...
  [London?] Printed in the Year, 1677.
  19 p. 18.5cm. 4⁰.
  Preface "Friends and Neighbours" signed: Leicester-County-Goal, the 6th of the 12th Moneth, 1676. Your Friend, John Wilsford.
  Wing W2871; Smith(Friends)2:944.

16509, 1934

DA677 Wilson, John, 1588-1667.
W749s   A Seasonable VVatch-VVord Unto Christians Against the Dreams & Dreamers Of this Generation: Delivered in a Sermon November 16th. 1665. And being the last Lecture, which was Preached By that Reverend, Faithful and Eminent Man of God Mr. John Wilson. Sometime Pastor of the Church of Christ in Boston in New-England. ...
  Cambridge: Printed by S. Green & S. Green. 1677.
  2 p.l., 10 p. 18.5cm. 4⁰
  Preface, "Christian Reader", signed: Boston 23. 5. 1677. Thomas Thacher.
  Evans243; Sabin104654; Wing W2897; Dexter (Cong.)2094; CP178.

2012, 1906

Voormaals in den Járe 1674. gedrukt. En nu op nieuws Tot Rotterdam Gedrukt, by Jan Pietersz Groenwout, Boekverkooper, wonende op het Speuy. 1678.
  16 p. 20cm. 4⁰ (No. [31] as issued, in Collectio, Of Versamelinge. [Amsterdam, ca. 1680])
  Cut on t.-p.
  Transl. from: Good Counsell and advice. London, 1661, with Stephen Crisp's letter added.
  Bookseller's advertisement, p. 2.
  "Een Sendbrief" (p. 13-16) signed: Steven Crisp. Geschréven in Colchester, den 30 der 8 Maant, 1674.
  Smith(Friends)1:26.

03272, 1866

J677 Amman, Johann Jacob, 1586-1658.
S591v   Reiss in das Gelobte Land/Hrn. Hans Jacob Ammans sel. genant der Thalwyler Schärer. Von Wien auss Oestereich/durch Ungariam/ Serviam/Bulgariam und Thraciam/auf Constantinopel: Fehrner durch Natoliam/Cappadociam/Ciliciam/Syriam und Judæam/auf Jerusalem? Von dannen durch die Wüste und Aegypten gen Allexandriam/folgends über das Mittländische Meer in Siciliam und durch Italiam auf Zürich/in die Eidgnosschaft. In dreyen Theilen/samt deren Landen und Stätten gelegenheiten/Einwohnern/Policeyen/ Sitten und Gebräuchen/auch andern denkwürdigen Sachen und Begebenheiten? Mit nach [sic] dreyen andern Reissbeschreibungen vermehret/und schönen Kupfern gezieret. In Verlegung Joh. Wilhelm Simlers/und Joh. Rudolff Rhanen.
  Getrukt zu Zürich/Bey Michael Schauffelbergers seligen Erbin/Durch Johannes Bachmann/1678.
  8 p.l., 192 p. front. (port.), fold. plan. 18cm. 8⁰ (Issued as a part of Simler, J.W., ed., Vier loblicher Statt Zürich verbürgerter Reiss beschreibungen [Zürich, 1677-1678]).
  First pub. Zürich, 1618.
  "Neue Beschreibung Der Insul Jamaica" by Johann Jakob Zeller and Heinrich Huser: p. 171-192.
  JCB(2)2:1175;   Sabin1339; cf. Palmer405.

01598A, 1847 rev

1678

DA68 Ames, William, d. 1662.
C697   Goeden raadt En Vermaninge Aan alle Vrienden der Waarheyd; ... Geschréven door Willem Ames. Met noch een Brief aan dezelve, Door Steven Crisp.

DA678 Barclay, Robert, 1648-1690.
B244a   An Apology For the True Christian Divinity, As the same is held forth, and preached by the people, Called, in Scorn, Quakers; Being a full explanation and vindication of their Principles and Doctrines, ... Presented to the King. Written and published in Latine, for the information of Strangers, by Robert Barclay. And

now put into our own language, for the benefit of his countrey-men. ...
[Rotterdam] Printed in the Year 1678.
12 p.ℓ., 412, [27] p. 18.5cm. 4º.
Dedication (2d-6th p.ℓ.) signed: Robert Barclay. From Ury, the place of my Pilgrimage, in my native countrey of Scotland, the 25 of the Moneth, called November, in the Year 1675.
First pub. under title: Theologiæ Verè Christianæ Apologia, Amsterdam, 1676.
With this is bound in contemporary calf: his Apology for the true Christian divinity vindicated, [Rotterdam] 1679.
Smith(Friends)1:179-180;McAlpin3:760; Wing B720.

6537, 1910

DA676
B244t
Barclay, Robert, 1648-1690.
Epistola Amatoria, Nec Non Consultoria Ad Legatos Magnatum Europæ, Jam de pace Christianorum, quantum cujusque eorum intersit, consultandi gratiâ Noviomagi congressos. Quâ certa præsentis belli causa indicatur, verumque pro firma constantique pace remedium declaratur à Roberto Barclaio. Pacis Christianismi amante, ejusdemque alloborante. ...
Roterodami, Excudebat Iohannes Pietersz Groenwout, Typographus, secus amnem Belgico idiomate het Speuy nuncupatum, habitans. Anno 1678.
14 p. 23.5cm. 4º.
Signed: Robertus Barclaius. Hoc mihi Uriæ in Scotiâ, ... 22 die Mensis dicti Novembris, 1677.
Letter to the delegates at the Nijmegen peace negotiations to end the third Dutch war.
Marginal rules in ms.
Bound with his Theologiæ Verè Christianæ Apologia ... Amsterdam, 1676.
Smith(Friends)1:185.

64-215, 1964

D678
B653d
Blome, Richard, d. 1705.
A Description Of the Island of Jamaica; With the other Isles and Territories in America, to which the English are Related, viz. Barbadoes, St. Christophers, Nievis, or Mevis, Antego, St. Vincent. Dominica, Montserrat, Anguilla, Barbada, Bermudes, Carolina, Virginia, Maryland, New-York, New-England, New-Found-Land. Published by Richard Blome.

Together With the Present State of Algiers.
London, Printed by J.B. for Dorman Newman, at the Kings-Arms in the Poultrey. 1678.
3 p.ℓ., 88 p., 1 ℓ., 17 p., 2 ℓ. front. (port.) 4 fold. maps. 19cm. 8º
With, as issued, his The present state of of Algiers, in the year, 1678, London, 1678, with special t.-p. and separate paging, but continuous signatures.
First pub. London, 1672.
JCB(2)2:1177; Sabin5967; Leclerc1418; Cundall(Jam.)267; WingB3209.

01909A, 1854

D678
B653d
[Blome, Richard, d. 1705]
The present State Of Algiers, In the Year, 1678. Also, A List of the Ships then belonging to that Port.
London, Printed, in the Year, 1678.
1 p.ℓ., 17 p., 2 ℓ. 19cm. 8º (Issued as part of his Description of the Island of Jamaica ... London, 1678.)
Title-page on verso of p.ℓ.
"A list of the Ships in Algiers in the Year, 1678": 1st ℓ at end.
"A list of the Ships brought in and destroyed by the Algier Corsayres": 2d ℓ. at end.

01909B, 1854

D678
B812s
[Bradstreet, Anne (Dudley)] 1612?-1672.
Several Poems Compiled with great variety of Wit and Learning, full of Delight; Wherein especially is contained a compleat Discourse, and Description of The Four Elements, Constitutions, Ages of Man, Seasons of the Year. Together with an exact Epitome of the three first Monarchyes Viz. The Assyrian, Persian, Grecian. And beginning of the Romane Common-wealth to the end of their last King: With diverse other pleasant & serious Poems, By a Gentlewoman in New-England. The second Edition, corrected by the Author, and enlarged by an Addition of several other Poems found amongst her Papers after her Death.
Boston, Printed by John Foster, 1678.
7 p.ℓ., 255 p. 14.5cm. 8º
First pub. London, 1650, under title: The Tenth Muse.
This ed. probably edited by John Rogers, although John Norton also has been suggested.

[47]

'Kind Reader" (2d p. ℓ.) and "To my dear Sister, the Author of these Poems." (3d-4th p. ℓ.) by John Woodbridge. Commendatory verse by Nathaniel Ward (3d p. ℓ.); Benjamin Woodbridge (5th p. ℓ.); C.B. and N.H. (5th p. ℓ.); C.B. and H.S. (6th p. ℓ.). "Upon Mrs. Anne Bradstreet Her Poems, &c. by John Rogers (6-7th p. ℓ.). "A Funeral Elogy" by John Norton" p. 252-255.

Leaf of errata was also issued; available in facsim.

JCB(2)2:1178; Evans 244; Sabin 7297; Wegelin (Poetry) 29; Green (John Foster) p. 91-95; Wing B4166.

0518, 1949 rev

DA678
B878q

Brown, John, 1610?-1679.
Quakerisme The path-way to Paganisme Or A Vieu of the Quakers Religion; Being An Examination of the Theses and Apologie of Robert Barclay, one of their number, published lately in latine, to discover to the World, what that is, which they hold and owne for the only true Christian Religion. By John Brown Minister of the Gospel.

[Rotterdam] Printed for John Cairns, and other Booksellers in Edinburgh Anno cIɔ Iɔc LXXVIII.
10 p. ℓ., 565, [566-568] p. 20cm. 4°
A reply to Robert Barclay, Theologiae verè Christianae Apologia, Amsterdam, 1676.
"A Postscript." (p. 554-563) signed R.[obert] M.[ac] Q.[uare].
Bound in contemporary calf, rebacked.
Wing B5033; Smith (Anti-Quak) 89; McAlpin 3: 762.

68-75

J678
C238n

Capell, Rudolf, 1635-1684.
Norden/ Oder Zu Wasser und Lande im Eise und Snee/ mit Verlust Blutes und Gutes zu Wege gebrachte/ und fleissig beschriebene Erfahrung und Vorstellung des Norden/ Ausz Denen/ welche zu unterschiedenen Zeiten gelebet/ viel im Norden versuchet/ viel auch umbsonst angefangen und angewandt haben: Auff guter Freunde Begehren zusammen gebracht dargereichet/ und ferner zu betrachten und zu vermehren/ von Rudolff Capel/ der H. Schrifft D. und Historiarum P.P. aussgefärtiget.

Hamburg/ Bey Johann Nanmann. und Stockholm Bey Gottfried Liebezeit/ Im 1678sten Jahre der Christen.
25 p. ℓ., 236, [7], [24] p. incl. illus. (map), map.)(⁴ A-E⁴ A⁴(-A1) B-2D⁴ a-c⁴)(⁴)1(-)3(⁴ 20cm. 4°
A reissue of the sheets of his Vorstellungen Des Norden. Hamburg, 1675, with new preliminary material (25 p. ℓ.) and.-[1] Kurtze Erzehlung von dem Anfange und Fortgange Der Schiffahrt. Hamburg, 1676, with special t.-p., separate signatures and continuous paging (213-236). -[2] J. Moxon, Ein kurtzer Discours von Der Schiff-Fahrt bey dem Nord-Pol. Hamburg, 1676, with special t.-p., separate paging and signatures. ([7] p. at end). -[3] "Alphabetisch Register" and "Einhalt und Verbesserung" ([24] p. at end).
In this copy Moxon's work has been incorrectly bound following p. 212. There is an extra copy of the engraved polar map inserted.
JCB(1)2:858; JCB(2)2:1179; Sabin 10736; Palmer 303.

02544A, 1851

E678
C483c

[Charonier, Gaspar Joseph] d. 1719.
Clarissimo Et Excellentissimo Viro, D. D. Joan. Bapt. Colbert, Marchioni De Seignelay, D'Alegre, Blainville, &c. Regi Ab Intimis Consiliis, Secretis, Et Mandatis, Regiorum Ordinum Quæstori, Gratulatio De Multiplici, Ex Quo Ille Rem Maritimam administrat, reportata in Utroque Mari victoria, à Classibus Ludovici Magni. Ex occasione captæ nuper in America Insulæ Tabacci, A Comite D'Estrées.

Lugduni. Excudebat, Rolinus Glaize, Typographus. M.DC.LXXVIII.
1 p. ℓ., 13 p. 23cm. 4°
Cut on t.-p.
Signed at end: Lugduni III. Kalendes Apriles M.DC.LXXXVIII. ... Gasp. Josephvs Charonier. Societ. Jesu.
In verse.
JCB(2)2:1180; Backer 2:1084.

0792, 1846 rev

B678
C719h

Colón, Fernando, 1488-1539
Historie Del Signor D. Fernando Colombo. Nelle quali s'ha particolare, & vera relatione della vita, e de'fatti dell' Ammiraglio. D. Christoforo Colombo Suo Padre.

E dello scoprimento, ch'egli fece dell'indie Occidentali, dette Mondo Nuouo, hora possedute dal Serenissimo Rè Catolico. Nuouamente di lingua Spagnuola tradotte nell' Italiana dal Sign. Alfonso Vlloa. Dedicato. Al illustriss. Sign. Marc'antonio Colalto Conte di San Michiele.
  In Venetia, M.DC.LXXVIII. Appresso Iseppo Prodocimo. Con Licenza de'Sup. e Priuilegio.
    24 p.ℓ., 489, [490-500] p. 14.5cm. 12°
    Cut(coronet) on t.-p.
    "Dalla Stampatia. Li 19. Maggio 1678.": 4th p.ℓ.
    First pub. Venice, 1571.
    "Scrittura di Frà Roman [i.e. Ramón Pane] delle antichità de gl'Indiani...": p. 250-87.
    In this copy there are 2 blank ℓ. at end.
    JCB(2)2:1181; Sabin14675; Streit2:2133; Palau(2)57212; Leclerc(1878)141.

04714, before 1874

DA68 Crisp, Stephen, 1628-1692.
C697   Noch een Ernstige Uermaeninge Aen de Burgermeesteren en Raedt der Stadt Embden. ... Van ... Steven Crisp.
    t'Amsterdam, Gedruckt voor Jacob Claus, Boeckverkooper. Anno 1678.
      7p. 20cm. 4° (No. [22] as issued, in Collectio, Of Versamelinge. [Amsterdam, ca. 1680])
      Signed at "Amsterdam den 26. der 6. Maent, genoemt Augusti, 1678".
      Smith(Friends)1:476.

03263, 1866

D678   [Crouch, Nathaniel] 1632?-1725?
C952m   Miracles Of Art and Nature: Or, A Brief Description of the several varieties of Birds, Beasts, Fishes, Plants, and Fruits of other Countreys. Together with several other Remarkable Things in the World. By R.[obert] B.[urton] Gent.[pseud.]
    London, Printed for William Bowtel at the Sign of the Golden Key near Miter-Court in Fleet-Street, 1678.
      3 p.ℓ., 120 p. 14.5cm. 8°
      "Chapters" on America, Peru, Quivira, Cuba, Chile, Paria, Nova Albion, Nova Hispania, Brasil, Florida.
      JCB(2)2:1186; WingC7345.

04341, 1866-1882

D678   [Derby, Charles Stanley, 8th earl of] 1628-1672.
D427j   The Jesuites Policy To Suppress Monarchy, Proving out of their own Writings That The Protestant Religion Is A Sure Foundation And Principle Of A True Christian. Written by a Person of Honor.
    London, Printed for William Cademan, at the Pope's Head in the Lower Walk of the New-Exchange, 1678.
      4 p.ℓ., 27 p. 23.5cm. 4°
      Chiefly a compilation; includes the Bull of Alexander VI dated 4 May 1493 dividing the New World between Spain and Portugal and extracts from Thomas Gage's A new survey of the West Indies, 1st pub. 1648.
      First pub. London, 1669, under this title and under title: The Protestant religion is a sure foundation.
      Sabin90296; McAlpin3:781; WingD1088.

13253, 1922 rev

DA678 Eliot, John, 1604-1690.
E42h   The Harmony of the Gospels, In The Holy History Of The Humiliation and Sufferings Of Jesus Christ, From His Incarnation To His Death and Burial. Published by John Eliot, Teacher of the Church in Roxbury. ...
    Boston; Printed by John Foster, in the Year 1678.
      2 p.ℓ., 131 p. 20.5cm. 4°
      Errata, 2d p.ℓ.ᵛ.
      Preliminary leaves mutilated; completed in pen and ink facsim.
      JCB(2)2:1183; Evans246; Sabin22153; McAlpin3:767; WingE512; Green (John Foster)89; Brinley763 (this copy).

04973, 1878

F678   Exquemelin, Alexandre Olivier.
E96a   De Americaensche Zee-Roovers. Behelsende een pertinente en waerachtige Beschrijving van alle de voornaemste Roveryen, en onmenschelijke wreedheden, die de Engelse en Franse Rovers, tegens de Spanjaerden in America. gepleeght hebben. ... Beschreven door A. O. Exquemelin. ...
    t'Amsterdam, By Jan ten Hoorn, Boeckverkoper/over 't Oude Heeren Logement. Anno 1678.
      4 p.ℓ., 64, 69-186, [2] p. 6 plates (incl. 2 fold.), 4 ports., 2 fold. maps. 19cm. 4°
      Added t.-p., engr.
      "Voorreden" (3d-4th p.ℓ.) signed: Amsterdam uyt myn Boeckwinckel den 1 September 1678. U E. Dienstw. Jan Claesz. ten Hoorn.

DA678 [Fox, George] 1624-1691.
F791a   An Answer To several New Laws and Orders Made by the Rulers of Boston In New-England The Tenth Day of the Eighth Moneth, 1677. By G. F.
    [London] Printed in the Year 1678.
    7 p. 18.5cm. 4°
    Signed: The 18th of the 8th Moneth, 1678. G. F.
    WingF1744; Sabin25345; Smith(Friends)1:677.
1190, 1906

DA68   [Fox, George] 1624-1691, supposed author.
C697   Antwoort Op twee Vrágen. Waar uyt niet alleen die géne, die de voorseyde Vragen schriftelijk heest óvergelévert, ...
    Gedrukt voor Jan Pietersz Groenwout, wónende op het Speuy, tot Rotterdam. En zijn ook te bekómen tot Amsterdam, by Iacob Claus, op de Achterburgwal, in de vergulde Drie-hoek. 1678.
    1p. ℓ., 6p. 20cm. 4° (No. [60] as issued, in Collectio, Of Versamelinge. [Amsterdam, ca. 1680])
    Cut on t.-p.
    Signed: Aldus beantwoort door die Christenen, die men Spots-gewyse Quakers noemt. In Amsterdam, in de maant October 1677.
    Authorship: Cf. William I. Hull, The Rise of Quakerism in Amsterdam (Swarthmore, 1938) p. 265.
03301, 1866

DA678 [Fox, George] 1624-1691.
F791   Christliches Sendschreiben An Johannes III. König in Pohlen/ Groszfürst zu Littauen/ Reussen und Preussen/ &c. &c. Wie auch an den Raht der Stadt Dantzig abgefertiget. Worinnen von der Freyheit des Gewissens gehandelt wird.
    Amsterdam/ Gedruckt vor Jacob Claus, Buchhändlern. 1678.
    8 p. 21cm. (25.5cm. in case) 4°
    Signed: London 12. Novembr. 1677. George Fox [and 9 others]
    Smith(Friends)1:696.
62-34

"Catalogus ... Jan ten Hoorn" p. [1-2] at end. JCB(2)2:1182; Church658; Sabin23468; Medina (BHA)1714; Palau(2)85729.
03618, 1849

DA68   Fox, George, 1624-1691.
C697   Eenige Vragen Om óverwogen te worden by den Paus van Rómen, En die géne, Die men Papisten noemt. In d'Engelse Tále geschréven door George Fox. En daar uyt óvergeset.
    Tot Rotterdam, Gedrukt voor Jan Pietersz Groenwout, Boekverkooper, wónende op het Speuy. 1678.
    8p. 20cm. 4° (No. [9], as issued, in Collectio, of Versamelinge. [Amsterdam, ca. 1680])
    Cut on t.-p.
    Cf. Smith(Friends)1:696.
03250, 1866

DA678 [Fox, George] 1624-1691.
F791e   An Epistle To Friends By G. F.
    [London, 1678]
    11p. 18.5cm. 4°
    Caption title; imprint from Wing.
    Signed: Swarthmore, in Lancashire, the 30th of the 11th Moneth, 1678. G. F.
    Smith(Friends)1:677; WingF1810.
11458, 1918

DA678 Fox, George, 1624-1691.
F791n   A New-England-Fire-Brand Quenched, Being Something in Answer Unto A Lying, Slanderous Book, Entituled; George Fox Digged out of his Burrows, &c. Printed at Boston in the Year 1676. of one Roger Williams of Providence in New-England. ... Of a Dispute ... debated ... At Providence and Newport in Rode-Island, in the Year 1672. Where his Proposals are turn'd upon his own Head, and there and here he was and is sufficiently Confuted. In Two Parts. As Also, Something in Answer to R. W.'s Appendix, &c. ... By George Fox and John Burnyeat.
    [London] Printed in the Year MDCLXXVIII.
    2 v.: 14 p. ℓ., 233 p.; 1 p. ℓ., 255, [1] p. 19.5cm. 4°
    Errata, v. 2, last p.
    With, as issued, his A New-England-fire-brand quenched. The Second part, Boston, 1678, with special t.-p. and separate paging and signatures.
    Part 2 signed (p. 207): The 5th. Month, 1677. G. F. J. B.
    Church660; Sabin25363; WingF1864&F1866.
1254-5, 1906

DA678 Fox, George, 1624-1691.
F791n   A New-England-Fire-brand Quenched. The
2   Second Part. Being Something in Answer to Roger
        Williams... By George Fox and John Burnyeat.
        [London] In the Year MDCLXXVIII.
        1 p.l., 255, [1] p. 19.5cm. 4º (Issued as a
        part of his A New-England-fire-brand quenched.
        [London] 1678.
        A reply to Roger Williams, George Fox digg'd
        out of his burrows, Boston, 1676.

DA679 ——— ———Another copy. (Issued as a part of his
F791n   A New-England- fire-brand quenched.
        [London] 1679.)
1255, 1906
02115, before 1859 rev

DA68 Fox, George, 1624-1691.
C697   Een Sentbrief Aangaande Het Wáre Vasten, Bid-
        den, en de Wáre Eere. ... In de Engelse Tále
        geschréven Door George Fox, En daar uyt óver-
        geset.
        Tot Rotterdam, Gedrukt voor Jan Pietersz Groen-
        wout, Boekverkooper, wónende op het Speuy. 1678.
        1p.l., 14p. 20cm. 4º (No. [8], as issued, in
        Collectio, of Versamelinge. [Amsterdam, ca. 1680])
        Signed: George Fox. Geschréven in Fréderikstad,
        in de 7 de Maant 1677.
        Knuttel 11649; cf. Smith(Friends)1:677, 696.
03249, 1866

DA678 [Fox, George] 1624-1691.
F791s   Something in Answer To A Letter (Which I have
        seen) Of John Leverat Governour of Boston, To
        William Coddington Governour of Rode-Island,
        Dated, 1677. Wherein he mentions my Name, and
        also wherein John Leverat justifies Roger William's
        Book of Lyes.
        [London, 1678?]
        11p. 18cm. 4º
        Caption title; imprint from Wing.
        Signed (p. 7 and 9): G. F.
        Condemns Gov. Leverett for supporting Roger
        Williams' book George Fox Digg'd out of his
        Burrovves (Boston, 1676), and for his persecution of
        Margaret Brewster and other Quakers.
        JCB(1)2:845; JCB(2)2:1164; Sabin25355; Smith
        (Friends)1:677; WingF1912.
02866, 1861

DA68 Fox, George, 1624-1691.
C697   Spiegel Voor de Jóden ... Door George Fox, in de
        Engelse tále, geschréven, en in den Járe 1674. tot
        Londen gedrukt. Ennu, ook tot dienst van de Ioodse
        Nátie in dése Landen, óvergeset, Door J.[an] C.[laus]
        Tot Rotterdam, Gedrukt by Ian Pietersz Groenwout,
        Boekverkooper: wónende op't Speuy. En zijn ook te
        bekómen tot Amsterdam by Iacob Claus, Boekver-
        kooper, in de nieuwe Lély-straat, óver de drie ge-
        kroonde Kas-rieten. 1678.
        30 p. 20cm. 4º (No. [11] as Issued, in Collectio,
        Of Versamelinge. [Amsterdam, ca. 1680]).
        Transl. from: A looking-glass for the Jews.
        [London] 1674, by Jan Claus.
        In this copy there is a blank l. at end.
        Smith(Friends)1:673.
03252, 1866

DB   Gt. Brit.--Sovereigns, etc., 1660-1685
-G7888   (Charles II).   28 Jan. 1678
1678   His Majesties Gracious Speech To both
1   Houses of Parliament, On Munday the 28th
        of January, 1677/8 [O.S.]. Published by his
        Majesties Command.
        London, Printed by John Bill, Christopher
        Barker, Thomas Newcomb and Henry Hills,
        Printers to the Kings most Excellent Majesty.
        1677/8.
        8 p. 27.5cm (28.5cm. in case). fol.
        Cut (royal arms) on t.-p. (Steele 88).
        A statement of Charles' activities concern-
        ing the Netherlands and France, and the mar-
        riage of his niece Princess Mary to William
        of Orange; with the recital of royal expendi-
        tures is mentioned (p. 6) that for suppressing
        Bacon's Rebellion.
        WingC3060.
10753, 1915

DB   Gt. Brit.--Sovereigns, etc., 1660-1685
G7888   (Charles II)   28 Jan. 1678
1678   ... La Harangve Qve Le Roy De La
2   Grand' Bretagne A Faite Avx Devx Chambres
        du Parlement d'Angleterre, le 7 Février
        1678 [N.S.].
        A Paris, du Bureau d'Adresse, aux Galler-
        ies du Louvre, le 23 Fevrier 1678.
        133-140 p. 23.5cm. 4º ([Extraordinaires
        du Mercure de France] no. 18.)
        Caption title; imprint on p. 140.
        At head of title: N. 18.

Transl. from: His Majesties Gracious Speech To both Houses of Parliament, On Monday the 18th of January, 1677/8 [O.S.] London, 1678.

A statement of Charles' activities concerning the Netherlands and France, and the marriage of his niece Princess Mary to William of Orange; with the recital of royal expenditures is mentioned (p. 138) that for suppressing Bacon's Rebellion.

1166, 1906

DA68 C697
Hendricks, Pieter, Quaker, Amsterdam, fl. 1661-1687.

Een tédere Groetenisse Van opregte en ongeveynsde Liefde, Aan de Kudde Christi, ... Geschréven door Pieter Hendriksz. Gedrukt voor den Autheur, By Ian Pietersz Groenwout, Boekverkooper, wónende op het Speuy, tot Rotterdam. En zijn ook te bekómen tot Amsterdam by Iacob Claus, Boekverkooper in de nieuwe Lélystraat, óver de drie gekroonde Kas-rieten. Anno 1678.

8 p. 20cm. 4º (No. [49] as issued, in Collectio, Of Versamelinge. [Amsterdam, ca. 1680])

Cut on t.-p.
Signed: Amsterdam den 25 der 4 Maand, 1678. Hollandse Stijl. P. Hendriksz.
Smith(Friends)1:935.

03290, 1866

FC650 H737 13
Hollandse Mercurius, Behelsende De aldergedenckwaerdigste Voorvallen in Europa, Ende de gantsche Wereldt, In't Jaer 1662. Dertiende Deel.

Tot Haerlem, Gedruckt by Abraham Casteleyn, Stadts Drucker, op de Marckt, in de Blye Druck, Anno 1678. Met Privilegie.

3 p. ℓ., 182, [2] p. plate. 20cm. 4º Bound in [vol. 2] of Hollandse Mercurius)

Added t.-p., engr.
"Extract van Privilegie" (2d p. ℓ.) dated: 17 December...1668.
First pub. Haerlem, 1663.
Imperfect: added t.-p. and plate wanting; available in facsim.
JCB(3)2:410; Sabin32523.

8487M, 1912

FC650 H737 2
Hollandse Mercurius, Brengende Het Verhael der Aenmerckelijckste Saecken, Voor-gevallen in het Jaer 1651. tot Januario 1652. In Christenryck, Zijnde het Tweede Deel.

Tot Haerlem. Gedruckt by Abraham Casteleyn, Stadts Drucker, op de Marckt, in de Blye Druck. Anno 1678. Met Privilegie.

4 p. ℓ., 103, [1] p. 20cm. 4º (Bound in [vol. 1] of Hollandse Mercurius)

Added t.-p., engraved: Hollantse Mercurius.
"Extract van Privilegie" (3d p. ℓ.) dated 1668.
Preface (4th p. ℓ.) dated: In Haerlem den 20 April 1652.
First pub. Haerlem, [1652]
JCB(3)2:410; Sabin32523.

8487B, 1912

DA678 K28w1
Keith, George, 1639?-1716.

The Way To the City of God described, or A Plaine Declaration How any man may, within the day of Visitation given him of God, pass out of the unrighteous, into the righteous state: As also, how he may go forward, in the Way of Holyness and righteousness, and so be fitted for the Kingdom of God, and the beholding and enjoying thereof. ... Written by George Keith, in the Year 1669, In the time of his being a close Prisoner in the Tolbooth at Edinburgh. Whereunto is added, The way to discern the convictions, motions, &c. of the Spirit of God, and divine Principle in us, from those of a man's own natural Reason, &c. Written in the time of his confinement in Aberdeen, in the Year 1676. With a Preface to the whole, written this Year.

[Netherlands] 1678.

10 p. ℓ., 178 p. 16.5cm. 8º.
Errata: p. 178.
"Friendly Reader" (2d-8th p. ℓ.) Signed: In the Prison of Aberdeen, the 15 of the 4 moneth, 1678 George Keith.
Smith(Friends)2:21; WingK235.

8387, 1912

DA678 K28w2
Keith, George, 1639?-1716.

The Way To the City of God Described, Or, A Plain Declaration How any man may within the day of Visitation given him of God, pass out of the Unrighteous, into the Righteous state: As also, how he may go forward, in the Way of Holiness and Righteousness, and so be fitted for the Kingdom of God, and the beholding and enjoying thereof. ... Written by George Keith, in the Year 1669. In the time of his being a close Prisoner in the Tolbooth at Edinburgh. Whereunto is added, The way to discern the Convictions, Motions, &c. of the Spirit of God, and Divine Principle in us, from those of a man's own Natural Reason, &c. Written in the time of his Confinement in Aberdeen, in the Year 1676. With a Preface to the whole, written this Year.

[London] Printed in the Year, 1678.

8 p.ℓ., 96, 99-181, [182-186] p. 15.5cm. 8°
Errata, p. [182]
First pub. the same year in the Netherlands.
"Friendly Reader" (2d-8th p.ℓ.) Signed: "In the Prison of Aberdeen, the 15 of the 4 month, 1678. George Keith."
McAlpin3:772-3; Smith(Friends)2:21; WingK235.

8388, 1912

E678 [La Peyrère, Isaac de] 1594-1676.
L31ln   Nauwkeurige Beschrijvingh Van Groenland Aen Heer De La Mothe Le Vayer; Verdeelt in twee Boecken/ 't Eerste van't Oud (nu verloorne) Groenlandt, Gelegentheyd; Vindinghswijs; Besettingh met Inwooners; Beschrijvingh; Vrughtbaerheyd; Gewassen/ Dieren/ Zeewonderen/ &c. 't Tweede van't Nieuw (door't soecken van't Oud' gevondene) Groenland, Beschrijving; eygenschap der Wilde/ en veel andere seer aenmercklijke saken. Nevens 't kort begrijp der seldsaeme Reysen, gedaen om Oud-Groenland weer te vinden door M. Forbeisser uyt Engelland, in't Jaer 1577. Door Gotzke Lindenauw uyt Deenemarcken, in de Jaeren 1605. en 1606. Door Karsten Richards, in't Jaer 1601. Door't Groenlandsch Geselschap te Koppenhagen, in't Jaer 1636. Met aenhangingh van't Dagh-verhael der wonderlijke Bejegeningen des Deenschen Hoofdmans Johan Munck, in't soecken van een wegh tusschen Groenland en America nae Oost-Indien: Gelijck oock van den korten Inhoud en Seldsaeme gevallen der Hollandsche en Zeeuwsche Scheeps-uytrustingh nae Nova Zembla, gedaen ten selven eynde: Der ontmoetingen van seven persoonen/ noch seven/ en noch andere seven/ gebleven op Spitsbergen, om aldaer t' overwinteren/ e.s.v. Vertaeld, en met veelerley Historische Byvoeghselen doorgaens vergroot, door S. de V.

t'Amsterdam, by Jan Claesz. ten Hoorn, Boeckverkooper tegen over 't Oude Heeren Logement. 1678.

4 p.ℓ., 128 p. 2 fold. maps with border illus. 21cm. 4°
Added t.-p., engraved: Naeuw Keurige Beschryvingh van Oud en Nieuw Groen-Land.
Transl. from: Relation du Groenland. Paris, 1647, with additions and appendices (by Simon de Vries) on Greenland, Spitzbergen, Nova Zembla and the Northeast Passage. The last section concludes with 5 pages of verse.
JCB(1)2:856; JCB(2)2:1184; Sabin38973; Muller (1872)676.

01610, 1847

BA678 López, Gregorio, 1542-1596.
L864v   Vida, Y Escritos Del Venerable Varon Gregorio Lopez. Dispvesta Por Diligemcia [sic] Del Maestro Fr. Gregorio De Argaiz, Para Los Devotos, Y Doctos. Dedicalos Al Glorioso Arcangel San Gabriel.

Con Privilegio. En Madrid: Por Antonio Francisco de Zafra. Año de 1678. Acosta de Leon, Mercader de Libros.

16 p.ℓ., 121, [5] p. 21cm. 4°
Preliminary matter dated (2d p.ℓ.ᵛ) 2 May 1678.
Consists of his "Tratado del Apocalipsi", p. 1-121, edited by Gregorio de Argaiz. Not a biography of López by Argaiz.
Imperfect: last ℓ. wanting.

BA674 ——— ———Another copy. 21cm.
L879v   Bound in contemporary vellum with: Francisco de Losa, Vida que el siervo de Dios Gregorio Lopez... , Madrid, 1674.
cop.1
JCB(2)2:1176; Medina(BHA)1638; Streit 2: 2131; Palau(2)16074; Sabin1944; BLH5:4160.

02644, 1851
04647, about 1910 rev

EC   Mercure Galant Mars
M557g   A Paris, Av Palais. [1678]
1678   12 p.ℓ., 383, [1] p. 4 plates (incl. 3 fold.:
[3]   music). 3 maps. 14.5cm. 12°
Cut (coat of arms) on t.-p.
Edited by Jean Donneau de Vizé.
Printed by C. Blageart.

"A Paris, Chez Guillaume De Luyne, ... Charles De Sercy, ... Estienne Loyson, ... Claude   , ... Jean Guignard, ... Theodore Girard, ... La Veuve Olivier De Varennes, ... Charles Osmont, ... M. D. [C]. LXXVIII. Avec Privilege Dv Roy." (verso t.-p.).
"Achevê d'imprimer pour la premiere foit le 31, Mars 1678." (last p.).
Includes poetry.
In this copy t.-p. mutilated.
Hatin 24.

67-207

FC650 H737 28
De nieuwe Hollantse Mercurius, Verhalende van Oorlog en Vrede, 't Geen in en omtrent de Vereenigde Nederlanden, en by gevolge In geheel Europa, In't Iaer 1677 is voorgevallen. Het Acht-en-twintigste Deel.
Tot Haerlem, Gedruckt by Abraham Casteleyn, Stadts-drucker, op de Marckt, in de Blye Druck. Anno 1678.
4 p.l., 264, [4]p. 4 plates (1 fold.), 5 maps. 20cm. 4° (Bound in [vol. 6] of Hollandse Mercurius)
Added t.-p., engraved: Hollantse Mercurius Tot Haerlem by Abraham Casteleyn Stadts drucker Op de Marckt Anno 1678.
Preface (3d p.l.) signed: A. Casteleyn.
"Op den nieuwen Hollandtschen Mercurius, Van den Jaere 1677" (4th p.l.) signed: G. Brandt.
JCB(3)2:410; Sabin 32523.

8487BB, 1912

E678 N934d
Nouvelles De L'Amerique, Ou Le Mercure Ameriquain. Ou sont contenües trois Histoires veritables arrivées de nostre temps.
à Cologne, [i.e. Holland] Chés Jean L'Ingenu, à la Verité. MDCLXXVIII.
248 p. 13.5cm. 12°
Cut (armillary sphere) on t.-p.
First pub. Rouen, 1678.
A pirated edition: see E. Weller, Die falschen und fingierten Druckorte.
A collection of three romantic tales about pirates.
Contents.–Histoire de Don Diego de Rivera.–Histoire de Mont-Val.–Le Destin De L'Homme, Ou Les Avantures de Don Bartelimi de la Cueba, Portugais.
JCB(1)2:863; Sabin 56094.

04214, before 1866

D678 N948a
[Nowell, Samuel] 1634-1688.
Abraham in Arms; Or The first Religious General With His Army Engaging in A VVar For which he had wisely prepared, and by which, not only an eminent Victory Was obtained, but A Blessing gained also. Delivered in an Artillery-Election-Sermon, June, 3. 1678. By S. N.
Boston; Printed by John Foster, 1678.
2 p.l., 19 p. 19cm. 4°.
"To the Reader" signed: Samuel Nowell.
JCBAR 51:21-24;   Evans 256; Sabin 56206; Wing N1440; Green (John Foster) 81-83.

30844, 1951

BA678 N972s
Núñez De Miranda, Antonio, 1618-1695.
Sermon De Santa Teresa De Iesvs. En La Fiesta Qve Sv Mvy Observante Convento de San Joseph, de Carmelitas Descalças de esta Corte celebrò por authentica declaracion del Milagro de la prodigiosa reintegracion de sus Panecitos. Domingo 23. de Enero, deste Año de 1678. Predicolo En Presencia Del Ilvstris.^{mo} Y Excelentis.^{mo} Señor M. D. Fr. Payo De Ribera, Arçobispo de Mexico, del Consejo de su Magestad, Virrey, Governador, y Capitan General de esta Nueva-España, y Presidente de la Real Audiencia de ella. El P. Antonio Nuñez De Miranda, Rector del Colegio Maximo de S. Pedro y S. Pablo de la Compañia de Jesus de Mexico, Prefecto de la Congregacion de la Purisima, y Calificador del Santo Officio de la Inquisicion de esta Nueva-España. Solicitò sacarlo à luz, para mayor gloria de Dios, y devocion de la Santa Madre, y segura noticia del Milagro, y su declaracion el Br. D. Ivan De La Barrera, Presbytero, y Capellan de Coro, de esta Santa Iglesia Metropolitana.
Con Licencia En Mexico. Por la Viuda de Bernardo Calderon, en la calle de San Augustin. [1678]
3 p.l., 11 numb. l. 18.5cm. 4°.
License dated (3d p.l.^{v}) 18 Apr. 1678.
Outer margins closely trimmed, affecting marginal notes.
Medina (Mexico) 1175; Palau (2) 197337.

4920, 1908

B678 P397i
Peña Montenegro, Alonso de la, bp., d. 1688.
Itinerario Para Parochos De Indios, En Que Se Tratan Las Materias mas particulares, tocantes a ellos, para su buena Administracion:

[54]

Compuesto Por El Ilustrissimo, Y Reverendissimo Señor Doctor Don Alonso De La Peña Montenegro, Obispo Del Obispado De San Francisco del Quito, del Consejo de su Magestad, Colegial que fue del Colegio mayor de la Universidad de Santiago, &c. Nueva Edicion Purgada De Muchos Yerros.

En Leon De Francia, A Costa De Joan-Ant. Huguetan, y Compañia. M. DC. LXXVIII. Con Licencia.

    32 p. ℓ., 848, [111] p. 23.5cm. 4º.
    Title in red and black.
    First pub. Madrid, 1668.
    Engraved vignette on t.-p.
    JCB(2)2:1187; Medina(BHA):1649; Sabin59624; Palau(2)217533.

03789, 1868

DA678
P412b

[Penn, William] 1644-1718.
A Brief Answer To A False and Foolish Libell, Called, The Quakers Opinions, For their sakes that Writ it and Read it. By W.P. ...
[London] Printed in the Year 1678.
    26 p. 19cm. 4º
    Signed (p. 26): William Penn.
    The Quakers Opinions to which this is a reply has not been identified.
    Smith(Friends)2:296; McAlpin3:779; Sabin 59683; WingP1259.

11514, 1918

B678
Q8s

Quiros, Pedro de, 1646-1714.
Sermones Varios. Predicados Por El Padre Pedro De Qviros, De La Compañia de Iesus, en el Reyno del Perù. Dirigidos Al Santissimo Padre Francisco Xavier, Hijo, y Compañero de San Ignacio de Loyola, Apostol de la India.
    Con Privilegio. En Madrid. Por Ioseph Fernandez de Buendia. Año 1678. A costa de Iuan Garcia Infançon, Impressor de Libros.
    8 p. ℓ., 176, [14] p. 20.5cm. (21.5cm. in case) 4º
    Cut (Jesuit monogram) on t.-p.
    Errata, 8th p. ℓ.
    Privilege (6th p. ℓ.ᵛ) dated 10 Nov. 1677.
    Bound in contemporary vellum.
    Sabin67352; Medina(BHA)1653; Palau(2)245616; Backer6:1354.

5498, 1909

E678
R382p

...Relation De La Prise Des Isles de Gorée au Cap-Vert & de Tabago, dans l'Amérique, sur les Hollandois, par l'Escadre des Vaisseaux du Roy, commandée par le Comte d'Estrées, Vice-Amiral de France. Avec les Particularitez de la Prise du Fort d'Orange, & de la rüine des Habitations appartenant aux Hollandois, sur la riviére d'Oüyapogue, par le Chevalier de Lézi Gouverneur de la Cayenne.
A Paris, du Bureau d'Adresse, aux Galleries du Louvre, le 25 Fevrier 1678. Avec Privilége.
    141-151 p. 22cm. 4º [Extraordinaires du Mercure de France, no. 19.]
    Caption title; imprint on p. 151.
    At head of title: N. 19.
    Concerns the fleet of d'Estrées during October-December, 1677.
    Sabin69271.

9525, 1913

J678
S317h

Scheffer, Johannes, 1621-1679.
Histoire De La Laponie, Sa Description, L'Origine, Les Moeurs, La Maniere De Vivre De Ses Habitans, leur Religion, leur Magie, & les choses rares du Païs. Avec plusieurs Additions & Augmentations fort curieuses, qui jusques-icy n'ont pas esté imprimées. Traduites du Latin de Monsieur Scheffer. Par L.P.A.L. Geographe ordinaire de sa Majesté.
    A Paris, Chez la Veuve Olivier De Varennes, au Palais, dans la Salle royale, au Vase d'or. M. DC. LXXVIII. Avec Privilege du Roy.
    8 p. ℓ., 408 p. illus., 21 plates, double map. 25cm. 4º
    Transl. by Augustin Lubin. 1st pub. under title: Lapponia; id est regionis Lapponum, Frankfurt, 1673.
    Added t.-p., engr.
    Dedication (3d-5th p. ℓ.) signed: Jeanne Cailloüé De Varennes.
    Errata, 7th p. ℓ.
    "Achevé d'imprimer pour la premiere fois le cinquiéme jour de Mars 1678."
    Tremaine(Arctic)25926.

04676, 1962

F678
S453g

Seer gedenckwaerdige Vojagien, Van Johan Sanderson, Hendrick Timberly, en Capt. Johan Smith, Door Europa, Asia en America. Nevens een pertinente Beschrijvinge van 't Heylige Landt, En voornamelijck van het Oudt en Nieuw Jerusalem en Tempel Salomons. Als

oock de schrickelijcke Belegeringen/Elendigen Hongersnoot/en verscheyde verwoestingen der selver Stadt/volgens de Prophecye van onsen Saligmaker Jesus Christus, En hoedanigh Jerusalem van de hedendaeghse Reysigers bevonden wordt. Met kopere Platen verçiert.
 t'Amsterdam, by Jochem van Dyck, Boeckverkooper op den Dam/bezijden 't Stadthuys/1678.
 6 p.ℓ., 158 p. 4 fold. plates. 20cm. 4º
 Added t.-p., engraved: Gedenckwaerdige Zee en Landt Voyagie... t'Amsterdam bij Jochem van Dyck Boeckverkooper op den Dam. Aº 1678.
 Cut on t.-p.
 Foreword and dedication signed: Jochem van Dyck.
 A publisher's translation and adaption of sections of Purchas his Pilgrime, London, 1625, with dates omitted in order to give it a timely flavor. Nothing on America; section on Smith deals with his old world adventures only. Also contains C. Furer's description of the Holy Land plus another account which is not in Purchas.
 Sabin 78871; Tiele 955; Scheepvart Mus. 134.

11544, 1918

1679

DA679   Adams, William, 1650-1685.
A197n   The Necessity Of The pouring out of the Spirit from on High Upon A Sinning Apostatizing People, set under Judgment, in order to their merciful Deliverance and Salvation. As it was Delivered in part, upon 21.9.1678. being a general Fast throughout the united Colonies of N.E. By William Adams, Pastor of the Church of Christ in Dedham. ...
 Boston; Printed by John Foster, for William Avery, near the sign of the blew Anchor. 1679.
 4 p.ℓ., 48 p. 19cm. 4º.
 Errata: verso of 4th p.ℓ.
 "To the Reader," signed by Samuel Torrey and Josiah Flint (2d-4th p.ℓ.)
 Evans 259; Sabin 348; Wing A499.

4970, 1908

D679   Allen, James, 1632-1710.
A427n   New-Englands choicest Blessing And the Mercy most to be desired by all that wish well to this People. Cleared in a Sermon Preached before the Court of Election At Boston on May 28. 1679. By James Allen, Teacher to the first gathered Church therein.
 Boston, Printed by John Foster, 1679.
 2 p.ℓ., 14 p. 19cm. 4º
 "Errata": p.14.
 Brinley copy(Sale cat. no. 695).
 JCB(2)1189; Evans 260; Sabin 827; Church 662; Wing A1028; Green(John Foster)104.

04216, before 1882

D679   Allen, James, 1632-1710.
A427s   Serious Advice to delivered Ones from Sickness, or any other Dangers threatning Death, how they ought to carry it, that their Mercyes may be continued, and After Misery prevented. Or The Healed Ones Prophulacticon Or Healthfull Diet. Delivered in several Sermons On John 5.14. By James Allin, Teacher to the most antient Church of Christ in Boston.
 Boston, Printed by John Foster, and sold by Edmund Ranger. 1679.
 2 p.ℓ., 30 (i.e. 31) p. [A]-D⁴, E². 19cm. 4º
 Another edition with imprint: Boston, Printed by John Foster, in the year 1679.
 "To the Reader" (2d p.ℓ.) Signed: James Allin. Boston, May 16, 1679.
 Imperfect: ℓ. D4-E2 wanting; available in facsim.
 Evans 262; Sabin 829; Wing A1031; Green (John Foster) p.106.

10026, 1914

B679   Avila, Alonso de, fl. 1679.
A958s   Sermon, Qve Predicó El P. Fr. Alonso De Avila Predicador del Convento de N.P.S. Francisco de Mexico, A La Apparicion Milagrosa De Nvestra Señora Del Pilar De Zaragoza, celebrada en el octavo dia de la Fiesta de N.P.S. Francisco, en su Convento de Mexico, á 12. de Octubre de 1678. años ...
 Con Licencia de los Superiores. [Mexico,] Por Francisco Rodriguez Lupercio. Año 1679.
 5 p.ℓ., [21] p. 19.5cm. 4º
 Imperfect: lower half of t.-p. wanting; data supplied from Medina (Mexico).
 "Censura" dated (3d p.ℓ.ᵛ) 2 May 1679.
 Medina(Mexico)1182.

1031, 1905

DA678 Barclay, Robert, 1648-1690.
B244a Robert Barclay's Apology For the true Christian Divinity Vindicated From John Brown's Examination and pretended confutation thereof, in his book, called, Quakerisme The Path-Way to Paganisme. In which Vindication I.B. his many gross perversions and abuses are discovered, and his furious and violent Railings and Revilings soberly rebuked, By R. B. VVhereunto is added A Christian and Friendly Expostulation with Robert MacQuare, touching his Postscript to the said book of J. B. written to him by Lillias Skein, wife of Alexander Skein, and delivered some moneths since at his house in Rotterdam. ...
[Rotterdam] Printed in the Year. 1679. And are to be sold by Benjamin Clerk, Stationer, in Georgeyard Lumberstreet, At London.
4 p.ℓ., 205, [206-208] p. 18.5cm. 4º
Errata: 1st p.ℓ.
"An Expostulatory Epistle, directed to Robert Macquare." (p. 196-205.) Signed: Newtyle, the 8 of the fourth moneth, 1678. Lillias Skein.
A reply to: John Brown, Quakerisme, The Path-Way to Paganisme, Edinburgh [i.e. Rotterdam] 1678.
Bound in contemporary calf with his An Apology For the True Christian Religion [Rotterdam] 1678.
Smith(Friends)1:186; McAlpin3:789-790; WingB724.
6538, 1910

D679 [Blount, Charles] 1654-1693.
-H313s An Appeal from the Country to the City, for the preservation of His Majesties Person, Liberty, Property, and the Protestant Religion.
[London, Benjamin Harris, 1679]
8 p. 31cm. fol.
Caption title.
Signed (p. 8): Junius Brutus.
An anti-Catholic tract associated with the Popish Plot.
Bound as no. 2 of 8 items.
WingB3300.
7081, 1910

BA679 Bravo, Fernando, fl. 1679.
C334s Oracion Evangelica Panegyrica De La Beatificacion de N. Glorioso Padre S. Francisco Solano. Predicola En La Santa Iglesia Cathedral Desta Civdad De Lima El R. P. Fr. Fernando Bravo ... Domingo 23. De Abril deste año de 1679.
Con Licencia. En Lima, Por Lvis De Lyra Año de 1679.
1 p.ℓ., [24]-[30] numb. ℓ. 19.5cm. 4º
(Issued as a part of Gregorio Casasola, Solemnidad Festiva, Lima, 1679.)
64-74A

D679 A Brief Narrative And Deduction of the several
-B853 Remarkable Cases of Sir William Courten, and Sir Paul Pyndar, Knights; and William Courten late of London Esquire, Deceased: Their Heirs, Executors, Administrators and Assigns, together with their Surviving Partners and Adventurers with them to the East-Indies, China and Japan, and divers other parts of Asia, Europe, Africa and America: Faithfully represented to both Houses of Parliament. Reduced under four Principal Heads, viz. I. The Discovery and Plantation of Barbadoes. II. Their Undertakings, and Expeditions to the East-India, China and Japan. III. The Denyal of Justice upon their civil Actions depending in Holland and Zealand. IV. Their Loanes and Supplyes for the Service of the Crown, upon the Collection of Fines and Compositions out of the Popish Recusants Estates, &c. Recollected out of the Original Writings and Records, for publick Satisfaction.
London, Printed in the Year 1679.
2 p.ℓ., 12 p. 29.5cm. fol.
"Epistle" signed (2d p.ℓ.): Edward Graves, ... George Carew [and 10 others].
"A Brief State of the Allome-Works" (p. 10-11).
Bound with 2 ℓ. extracted from [George Carew] Fraud & Oppression detected and arraigned. [London] 1676.
Sabin7880 & 17178; WingG1605.
4366, 1908

BA679 Casasola, Gregorio, fl. 1679.
C334s Solemnidad Festiva, Aplavsos Pvblicos, Aclamaciones Ostentosas, Qve Hizo Esta Nobilissima Civdad De Los Reyes Lima, A La Pvblicacion Del Breve De La Beatificacion Del Bienaventvrado S. Francisco Solano del Orden Seraphico de la regular observancia desta Santa Prouincia de los Doze Apostoles del Peru. Dedicada Al Mismo Santo. En Cuya Dedicatoria Se Recopilan las mas heroicas obras de su vida, y los mas singulares milagros, que por

su intercession, y meritos obrò la diuina omnipotencia, mientras buelue a las prensas su vida. Escrita Por El P. Lector Ivbilado Fr. Gregorio Casasola Limense, hijo de la misma Provincia. ...

Con Licencia. Impresso En Lima; por Luis de Lyra. Año de 1679.

5 p. l., 23 numb. l., 1 l., [24]-[30] numb. l. 19.5cm. 4º

License dated (3d p. l.ᵛ) 15 July 1679.
With, as issued, Fernando Bravo. Oracion Evangelica Panegyrica De La Beatificacion de ... Francisco Solano. Lima, 1679, with special t.-p., but continuous paging and signatures.
Bound in contemporary vellum.
Palau(2)47103; Medina(Lima)509.

64-74, 1963

BA679
D352a

Delgado y Buenrostro, Antonio, fl.1676-1696.
Accion De Gracias A Nuestra Señora la Virgen Maria Concebida En Gracia Trasuntada En su Florida Milagrosa Imagen de Guadalupe. Aparecida En la Imperial Corte, y Ciudad de Mexico. Por el feliz viaje, que hizo de la nueva España á la Isla de Cuba, el Ilustrissimo Señor Doctor D. Garcia de Palacios, Obispo suyo, y de la Havana, en cuya Iglesia Mayor se celebrò. Y Predico El Licenciado Don Antonio Delgado y Buenrostro, Capellan, y Secretario de su Señoria Ilustrissima, que le assistió, descubierto el Santissimo Sacramento, en 16. de Abril Dominica secunda post Pascha, año 1679.

En Sevilla, Por Thomas Lopez de Haro, en las siete Rebueltas junto à la Imagen. [1679?].

4 p. l., 24 p. 19.5cm. 4º
Cut on t.-p.
License dated (3d p. l.) 18 Sept. 1679.
Medina(BHA)1690.

10863, 1913

B679
-E56t

Enríquez de Ribera, Payo, abp., viceroy of Mexico, 1612-1684.
Tratado En Que Se Defienden Nueve Proposiciones, En quienes la V. M. Ana De La Cruz, Religiosa en el observantissimo Convento de Santa Clara de la Ciudad de Montilla dexò propuestas las gracias, ... Escribele El M. D. Fr. Payo de Ribera, Religioso del Orden del Gran P. San Augustin, Obispo de Goatemala, (aora Arçobispo de Mexico) y hermano dichosamente de la nombrada U. M. Ana de la Cruz.

Año de 1679. Impresso En Mexico: Por la Viuda de Bernardo Calderon, en la calle de S. Augustin.

46 p. l., 82 numb. l. 29.5cm. fol.
"Censura" dated (17th p. l.) 10 Sept. 1679.
Medina(Mexico)1191; Palau(1)6:275; Santiago Vela6:516-526:13; BLH5:2285.

5499, 1909

BA679
E74b

Escalante, Thomas, d. 1708.
Breve Noticia De La Vida Exemplar Y Dichosa Mverte Del Venerable Padre Bartholome Castaño. de la Compañia de Jesvs, Qve Dio A Los Svperiores de las Casas, y Colegios desta Provincia de Nueva-España el P. Francisco Ximenez siendo Preposito de la Casa Professa desta Ciudad de Mexico en Carta. Dispvesta Por el P. Thomas de Escalante de la misma Compañia.

Con Licencia, En Mexico, por Juan de Ribera, en el Pedradillo. 1679.

6 p. l., 46 numb. l. port. 21cm. 4º
Cut (Jesuit device) on t.-p.
"Protesta" dated (6th p. l.) 18 Sept. 1679.
Bound in contemporary vellum.
Medina(Mexico)1183; Palau(2)80729; Wagner52; Streit2:2136; Backer3:425.

12889, 1921

DA679
-F536t

Fisher, Samuel, 1605-1665.
An Additional Appendix To the Book Entituled, Rusticus ad Academicos, Or The Country correcting the Clergy. ...

[London?] Printed for the Service of Truth. [1679]

p. [735]-788. 29.5cm. fol. (Issued as part of his The Testimony of Truth Exalted [London?] 1679.)
First pub. London, 1660.
Includes (p. 775-788) "Christs Light Springing ... Lux Christi Emergens, ..." English and Latin in parallel columns.
Smith(Friends)1:615.

11383B, 1918

DA679
-F536t

Fisher, Samuel, 1605-1665.
... The Bishop busied Beside the business. Or That Eminent Overseer, Dr. John Gauden, Bishop of Exeter, so Eminently Overseen, as

to wound his Own Cause well-nigh to Death with his Own Weapon, in his late so Super-eminently-applauded Appearance For the ⟨Liberty / Legitimacy⟩ of ⟨Tender Consciences. / Solemn Swearings.⟩ Entituled, A Discourse concerning Publick Oaths, and the Lawfulness of Swearing in Judicial Proceedings, in order to answer the Scruples of the Quakers. ... By ⟨Samuel Fisher ...

[London?] Printed for the Service of Truth. [1679]

42, [45]-92, 95-98 p. 29.5cm. fol. (Issued as part of his The Testimony of Truth Exalted [London?] 1679.)

 Title also in   Greek at head of title.

 First pub. [London] 1662.

 A reply to the bp. of Exeter, John Gauden's A Discourse Concerning Public Oaths, London, 1662.

 Smith(Friends)1:617.

11383F, 1918

DA679 Fisher, Samuel, 1605-1665.
-F536t   One Antidote More Against That Provoking Sin Of Swearing By Reason of which this Land now Mourneth. Given forth from under the Burden of the Oppressed Seed of God, by way of Reply both to Henry Den's Epistle about the Lawfulness, Antiquity and Universality of an Oath, and his Answers to the Quakers Objections against it, Recommended (by him) to all the Prisons in this City and Nation, to such as chuse Restraint, rather than the Violation of their Consciences. And also to Jeremiah Ives his Printed Plea for Swearing, Entituled, The Great Case of Conscience Opened, &c. about the Lawfulness or Unlawfulness of Swearing. ... By Samuel Fisher. ...

[London?] Printed for the Service of Truth [1679]

p. [789]-832. 29.5cm. fol. (Issued as part of his The Testimony of Truth Exalted [London?] 1679.)

 First pub. London [1661]

 A reply to Jeremiah Ives' The Great Case of Conscience Opened, London, 1660, and to an unidentified Epistle by Henry Den.

 Smith(Friends)1:615.

11383C, 1918

DA679 Fisher, Samuel, 1605-1665.
-F536t   Rusticus ad Academicos In Exercitationibus Expostulatoriis, Apologeticis Quatuor. The Rustick's Alarm to the Rabbies: Or, The Country Correcting the University and Clergy, and (not without good Cause) Contesting for the Truth, Against the Nursing Mothers and their Children. In Four Apological and Expostulatory Exercitations; Wherein is contained as well ⟨A General Account to All Enquirers, As A General Answer to All Opposers⟩ Of the most truly Catholick, and most truly Christ-like Christians, called Quakers, and of the True Divinity of their Doctrine. By way of Entire Entercourse held in special with Four of the Clergy's Chieftains, viz. John Owen D.D. late Dean of Christ's Church Coll. Oxon. Thomas Danson M.A. once Fellow of Magd. Coll. Oxon, since one of the Seers for the Town of Sandwich in Kent. John Tombs B.D. once of Bewdly, since of Lemster. Rich. Baxter Minister at Kederminster, another Eminent Master in this English Israel. ... By Samuel Fisher. Who sometimes went astray, as a Lost Sheep among the many Shepherds, but is now returned to the Great Shepherd and Overseer of the Soul. ...

[London?] Printed in the Year 1677. [i.e. 1679]

p. [27]-84, [89]-692, 695-733.

29.5cm. fol. (Issued as part of his The Testimony of Truth Exalted [London?] 1679.)

 First pub. London, 1660.

 Smith(Friends)1:615.

11383A, 1918

DA679 Fisher, Samuel, 1605-1665.
-F536t   Supplementum Sublatum. John Tombes His Supplement Or, Second Book About Swearing Disproved, and made Void; and his Abusing the Scripture plainly Manifested Against which the Truth of Christ's Words is Vindicated and Maintained. In a few words briefly returned to him from Samuel Fisher.

[London? 1679]

p. [833]-838. 29.5cm. fol. (Issued as part of his The Testimony of Truth Exalted [London?] 1679.)

 First pub. [London? 1660?]

 A reply to John Tombes A Supplement to the Serious Consideration of the Oath, London [1660]

 Smith(Friends)1:616.

11383D, 1918

DA679
-F536t
Fisher, Samuel, 1605-1665.
The Testimony Of Truth Exalted, By The Collected Labours Of That Worthy Man, Good Scribe, and Faithful Minister of Jesus Christ, Samuel Fisher. Who died a Prisoner for the Testimony of Jesus, and Word of God, Anno 1665. ...
[London?] Printed in the Year, MDCLXXIX.
6 p.ℓ., 84, [89]-692, 695-856, 42, [45]-92, 95-98, [16] p. A^{2}b-c^{2}B-C^{4}D^{6}E-Q^{4}R-8T^2 8U1 [8X]-90^2 [9P1] (a)-(z)^{2}A-D^2.
A collection of his writings, some of which are given a special half-title.
Edited by Ellis Hookes.
Preliminary matter includes "The Epistle To The Reader." signed "London the Eighth day, of the Twelfth Month, 1678. Ellis Hookes." and 3 different "Testimonies Concerning Samuel Fisher" signed by Luke Howard, Hallelujah Fisher, and William Penn.
In this copy p. 153-156 supplied from another copy.
Contents:
"The Scorned Quaker's True and Honest Account" (p. 1-20) and "The Burden Of The Word of the Lord" (p. 21-26). Both were 1st pub. [London] 1656.
With special half-titles: Rusticus ad academicos, p. [27]-733, An additional appendix to ... Rusticus ad academicos, p. [775]-788, One antidote more, p. [789]-832, Supplementum sublatum, p. [833]-838, ... Velata quaedam revelata, p. [839]-856, and ... The bishop busied, p. [1]-98, 2d count.
Smith(Friends)1:617; WingF1058; McAlpin 3:801

1383, 1918

DA679
-F536t
Fisher, Samuel, 1605-1665.
... Velata Quædam Revelata. Some Certain Hidden or Vailed Spiritual Verities Revealed, &c. Upon Occasion of Various very Prying, and Critical Queries ... Propounded to George Fox and Samuel Fisher. And after that (with a Complaint for want of, and stricter Urgency for an Answer) re-propounded to Edward Burroughs. By two Persons, choosing rather to notifie themselves to us no other way then by these two unwonted (if not self-assumed) Titles, viz. Livinus Theodorus, and Sabina Noriah. Which Truth (as these inspired by the Spirit of God) are here expired in Love to the Souls of Men. From out of a Hole in the Gate-House at Westminster, through an Earthen Vessel there Imprisoned for the Testimony of Jesus, known among men by the Name of Samuel Fisher.
[London? 1679]
p. [839]-856. 29.5cm. fol. (Issued as part of his The Testimony of Truth Exalted, [London?] 1679.)
Title also in Greek at head of title.
First pub. London, 1661.
Smith(Friends)1:616.

11383E, 1918

DA679
F791c
[Fox, George] 1624-1691.
Cæsar's Due Rendred unto Him according to his Image and Superscription; ... Also, The Blind Zeal of such Discovered, as profess God & the Scriptures, who think they do God good Service in the Killing of his Servants, ... And likewise such, who are the true Christian-Protestants and Reformed Church, according to the Practice of the Apostles and Primitive Church, and who are not; ... By G. F.
[London], Printed in the Year 1679.
35p. 19cm. 4°
Signed: This 24th of the 3d Moneth, 1679. G. F.
"For The Magistrates and Rulers of New-England" (p. 3-7), and other references to New England persecution of Quakers.
Smith(Friends)1:679; WingF1753.

29, 1902

DA679
F791d
[Fox, George] 1624-1691.
A Demonstration To The Christians in Name Without The Nature of it, How they Hinder the Conversion of the Jews. ...
[London] Printed in the Year 1679.
25 (i.e. 27] p. 17.5cm. 4°
Signed: The 28th of the 2d Moneth, 1679. ... G. F.
Smith(Friends)1:678; WingF1793.

04570, 1918

DA68
C697
Fox, George, 1624-1691.
Een getuygenisse Aan alle Menschen, Zoo wel van hoogen, als van lágen stand. ... In 't Engels geschréven door George Fox. En daar uyt óvergeset. Gedrukt by Ian Pietersz Groenwout, Boekverkooper: wónende op het Speuy, tot Rotterdam. En zijn méde te bekómen tot Amsterdam, by Iácob Claus, Boekverkooper: wónende in de nieuwe Lély-straat, óver de drie gekroonde Kas-rieten: die ook bevraagt kan worden in de Heere-straat, in de vergulde Vijf-hoek. Anno 1679.

[60]

20p. 20cm. 4º (No. [10], as issued, in Collectio, of Versamelinge. [Amsterdam, ca. 1680])
"Geschréven in Amsterdam, den 18. September, 1677. G. F.": p. 20.
cf. Smith(Friends)1:696.

03251, 1866

DA679 Fox, George, 1624-1691.
F791m   The Man Christ Jesus The Head of the Church And True Mediator, In Opposition to the Papist Head Their Pope: ... By George Fox.
[London] Printed in the Year 1679.
31p. 18cm. 4º
Signed (p. 29): The 10th Moneth 1678. G. F.
Smith(Friends)1:678; WingF1860.

11460, 1918

DA679 Fox, George, 1624-1691.
F791n   A New-England-Fire-Brand Quenched, Being an Answer Unto A Slanderous Book, Entituled; George Fox Digged out of his Burrows, &c. Printed at Boston in the Year 1676. by Roger Williams of Providence in New-England. ... Of a Dispute... debated ... At Providence and Newport in Rode-Island, in the Year 1672. In which his Cavils are Refuted, & his Reflections Reproved. In Two Parts. As Also, An Answer to R. W's Appendix, &c. ... By George Fox and John Burnyeat.
[London] Printed in the Year M DC LXXIX.
2 pts. in 1 v.: 14 p. ℓ., 233 p.; 1 ℓ., 255, [1] p. 19.5cm. 4º
With, as issued, his A New-England-fire-brand quenched, The second part, Boston, 1678, with special t.-p. and separate paging and signatures.
First pub. [London] 1678. These sheets were reissued with cancel general t.-p. dated 1679, pt. 2 retaining its t.-p. dated 1678.
Errata, pt. 2, last p.
Pt. 2 signed (p. 207): The 5th. Moneth, 1677. G. F. J. B.
Imperfect: v.1, t.-p. wanting; supplied in pen and ink facsim.
JCB(2)2:1191; Sabin25364; Smith(Friends)1:678; WingF1865; Dexter(Cong.)2116.

02115, before 1859

DA679 [Fox, George] 1624-1691.
F791s   Something in Answer to a Law Lately made at the first Sessions of the General Court held at Boston in New-England May the 28th, 1679. And published by their Order, Edw, Rawson Secretary The Title of the Law, viz. Meeting-Houses not to be Erected without Licence, &c.
[London, 1679]
20p. 18.5cm. 4º
Caption title.
Signed (p.18): The 19th of the 7th Moneth, 1679. G. F.
Deals with New England persecution of Quakers.
Sabin25354; Smith(Friends)1:679; WingF1911.

04591, Before 1900

DA68 Fox, George, d. 1661.
C697   Een Eedele Salutatie, ende een Getrouwe Groetinge Aen U Charles Stuart, Dewelke nu zijt Geproclameert Konink van Engelandt, Schotlandt, Vrankrijk ende Ierlandt. ... Een Copy hier van wiert overgelevert in Schrift door Richard Hubberthorn in des Koninks-handt in Whitehal, den vierden dagh van de vierde Maent, 1660. ... Den tweeden druk.
Gedrukt tot Harlingen, voor Reiner Jansen, 1679.
19 p. 20cm. 4º (No. [5], as issued, in Collectio, of Versamelinge. [Amsterdam, ca. 1680])
Cut on t.-p.
Transl. from: A Noble Salutation. London, 1660. Dutch transl. first pub. 1660.
Cf. Smith(Friends)1:700.

03246, 1866

D679 Harris, Benjamin, fl. 1673-1716, defendant.
-H313s   A Short But Just Account Of The Tryal Of Benjamin Harris, Upon An Information Brought against him For Printing and Vending a late Seditious Book called An Appeal from the Country To the City, For the Preservation of His Majesties Person, Liberty, Property, And The Protestant Religion.

[London, Benjamin Harris] Printed in the Year 1679.
8 p. 31cm. fol.
Concerns his publication of Charles Blount's An appeal from the country to the city [London, 1679]
Bound as no. 1 of 8 items.
WingS3565.
7080, 1910

DA68 C697
Hendricks, Elizabeth, Quaker, Amsterdam, fl. 1672-1683.
Een Brief Van toegenégentheyd en Vriendelijke Vermaninge, Aan alle Vrienden der Waarheyd, In Holland, ... Geschréven door Elisabeth Henrix.
Gedrukt by Ian Pietersz Groenwout, Boekverkooper: wónende op het Speuy, tot Rotterdam. En zijn mede te bekómen tot Amsterdam, by Iácob Claus, Boekverkooper: woonende in de nieuwe Lély-straat, óver de drie gekroonde Kas-rieten: die ook bevraagt kan worden in de Heere-straat, in de vergulde Vijfhoek. Anno 1679.
7 p. 20cm. 4⁰ (No. [51] as issued, in Collectio, Of Versamelinge. [Amsterdam, ca. 1680])
Cut on t.-p.
Signed: In Amsterdam, den 4 der 4 Maand. 1678. Elisabeth Henrix.
Cf. Smith(Friends)1:936.
03292, 1866

DA679 H631
Hicks, Thomas, fl. 1657-1690.
Three Dialogues Between A Christian and a Quaker: Wherein Is Faithfully Represented, some of the Chief and most Concerning Opinions Of The Quakers, ... Unto which is now annexed the Quakers appeal Answered; being a full Relation of a Dispute betwixt William Pen and the Author. ... by Thomas Hicks.
London, Printed, and are to be sold by Peter Parker, at the Leg and Star in Cornhil, against the Royal Exchange, 1679.
1 p.ℓ., 1 ℓ., 94 p., 1 ℓ., [6], 88 p., 1 ℓ., [6], 88 p., 1 ℓ., [10], 32, [4] p. 17cm. 8⁰
Publisher's collection consisting of: his, A Dialogue Between A Christian and a Quaker ... The Second Edition, London, 1673; his, A Continuation of the Dialogue, London, 1673; his, The Quaker Condemned out of his own Mouth ..., London, 1674; and The Quakers Appeal Answer'd, London, 1674. Each has special t.-p. and separate paging and signatures.
Smith(Anti-Quak.)226; WingH1927.
11534, 1918

D728 B799s
Hobbes, Thomas, 1588-1679.
Behemoth; Or An Epitome Of The Civil Wars Of England, From 1640, to 1660. By Thomas Hobs of Malmsbury.
London, Printed Anno Dom. 1679.
1 p.ℓ., 214 p. 15.5cm. (21.5cm. in case) 12⁰
First pub. the same year in London as The History of the Civil Wars.
"John C. Brown's Dec. 20th 1808" inscribed on t.-p.
The first book in the John Carter Brown Library known to have been owned by John Carter Brown.
In slip case with two other books signed by members of the Brown family as children.
WingH2213.
0201, 1808

FC650 H737 29
Hollantse Mercurius, Verhalende van Oorlog en Vrede, 't Geen in en omtrent de Vereenigde Nederlanden, En elders in Europa, In het Jaer 1678 Is voorgevallen. Het Negen-en-twintigste Deel. Voorsien met kopere Platen.
Tot Haerlem, Gedruckt by Abraham Casteleyn, Stadts Drucker, op de Marckt, in de Blye Druck. Anno 1679.
3 p.ℓ., 290, [5]p. 2 plates, 6 maps. 20cm. 4⁰ (Bound in [vol. 7] of Hollandse Mercurius)
Added t.-p., engraved: Anno Pacis 1678. Hollantsche Mercurius tot Haerlem Bij Abraham Casteleijn.
Preface (3d p.ℓ.) signed: A. Casteleyn.
Imperfect: p. 119-120 wanting; available in facsim.
JCB(3)2:420; Sabin32523.
8487CC, 1912

FC650 H737 14
Hollantse Mercurius, Vervatende De voornaemste Geschiedenissen, Voorgevallen in het gantsche Jaer 1663, in Christenryck. Het Veertiende Deel.
Tot Haerlem, Gedruckt by Abraham Casteleyn, Stadts Drucker, op de Marckt, in de Blye Druck, Anno 1679. Met Privilegie.
3 p.ℓ., 171, [1] p. fold. plate. 20cm. 4⁰ (Bound in [vol. 3] of Hollandse Mercurius)
Added t.-p., engraved: Hollantse Marcurius Tot Haerlem by Pieter Casteleyn Anno 1664.
First pub. Haerlem, 1664.
Preface (3d p.ℓ.) dated: Haerlem, den 28 Martij 1664.
JCB(3)2:410; Sabin32523.
8487N, 1912

E679 [La Peyrère, Isaac de] 1594-1676.
L217a Ausführliche Beschreibung des theils bewohnt-
theils unbewohnt-so gennannten Grönlands/ in
zwey Theile abgetheilt: Deren erster handelt von
des Alt-(nunmehro verlohrnen) Grönlands Gele-
genheit, Erfindung/ Inwohnern/ Fruchtbarkeit/
Gewächsen/ Thieren und Meerwundern. Der
andere: von dem Neuen (durch Suchung des alten/
gefundenen) Grönland/ Eigenschafft der Wilden/
und viel andern merckwürdigen Dingen mehr.
Nebenst Einem kurtzem Begriff der seltsamen
Reisen/ so M. Forbeisser/ Gotzke Lindenau/
Christian Richard/ und die Koppenhagen-Grön-
ländische Gesellschafft/ alt Grönland wieder zu
finden/ in unterschiedlichen Jahren gethan. Mit
Anfügung des Tagbuchs eines die Durchfahrt
zwischen Grönland und America suchenden Dä-
nischen Schiffes: wie auch des kurtzen Inhalts
und seltsamen Zufälle der Holl-und Seellän-
dischen Schiffsausrüstung nach Nova Zembla zu
eben dem Ende vorgenommen: Samt Erzehlung
der wunderbaren Zufälle/ so dreymal Sieben
Personen/ welche den Winter über auf den Spitzbergen und der Mauritiusbay sich aufgehalten/
begegnet/ und wie elendiglich sie umkommen
sind. Beschrieben/ und mit verschiedenen His-
torischen Anhängen durchgehends erklärt und
erweitert durch S von V.
 Nürnberg/ in Verlegung Christof Riegels/ 1679.
 4 p.ℓ., 131 p. 2 fold. maps with border illus.
20cm. 4°
 Added t.-p., engraved: Neueste Beschreibung
Von Alt und Neu Groen-Land.
 Transl. from: Nauwkeurige Beschrijvingh
Van Groenland. Amsterdam, 1678; 1st pub. under title: Relation du Groenland. Paris, 1647.
 JCB(2)2:1192; Sabin38974; Palmer350; Baginsky
202; Muller(1872)677.
03620, before 1866

D679 [Marvell, Andrew] 1621-1678.
-H313s Advice to a Painter, &c.
 [London, 1679?]
 4 p. 31cm. fol.
 Caption title.
 In verse; concerns the Popish Plot.
 Bound as no. 5 of 8 items.
 WingM864.
7084, 1910

D657 Maryland(Colony)--Charters.
G259p The Charter Of Maryland.
 [London, ca. 1679]
 23 p. 17.5cm. 4°
 Caption title.

 Cut (royal arms, Steele 84) at head of title.
 First pub. [London, 1635]
 Cf. Wroth, L.C., "The Maryland coloniza-
tion tracts" in Essays offered to Herbert Putnam,
New Haven, 1929, p. 539 ff., and Wyllie, J.C.,
"The first Maryland tract" in Essays honoring
Lawrence C. Wroth, Portland, Me., 1951,
p. 475 ff.
 JCB(3)2:473; WingM896; Baer(Md.)80.
02127, before 1859 rev

D.Math Mather, Increase, 1639-1723.
I.19A² A Call from Heaven To the Present and Succeeding Generations Or A Discourse Wherin is
shewed, I. That the Children of Godly Parents
are under special Advantages and Encouragements to seek the Lord. II. The exceeding
danger of Apostasie, especially as to those that
are the Children and Posterity of such as have
been eminent for God in their Generation. III.
That Young Men ought to Remember God their
Creator. By Increase Mather, Teacher of a
Church in Boston in New-England. ...
 Boston, Printed by John Foster, 1679.
 4 p.ℓ., 114, 29 p. 14cm. (15cm. in case)
 "To the Reader." dated (4th p.ℓ. verso)
Boston. 3.m. 16.d. 1679.
 Includes "A Call To The Rising Generation."
p. 1-32.
 With, as issued, his A Discourse Concerning
the Danger of Apostasy, Boston, 1679, with
special t.-p. but continuous paging and signa-
tures, and his Pray for the Rising Generation,
Boston, 1679, with special t.-p. and separate
paging and signatures.
 In this copy there is a blank leaf following
Discourse.
 Bound in contemporary calf.
 Errata, 12 lines, 4th p.ℓ. verso.
 Evans274; Sabin46645; Holmes(I)19A²; Wing
M1190; Green (John Foster)97-98.
15478, 1929

D.Math Mather, Increase, 1639-1723.
I.19A² A Discourse Concerning the Danger of Apostasy, Especially as to those that are the Children
and Posterity of such as have been eminent for
God in their Generation. Delivered in a Sermon,
preached in the Audience of the general Assembly of the Massachusets Colony, at Boston in
New-England, May 23. 1677. being the day of
Election there. By Increase Mather, Teacher of
a Church in Boston in New-England. ...
 Boston, Printed in the Year, 1679.

1679   CATALOGUE OF THE JOHN CARTER BROWN LIBRARY

           p. [33]-114. 14cm. 8° (Issued as a part of his A Call from Heaven, Boston, 1679.).
           Includes Sermon on "Eccles. XII. I. Remember now thy Creator in the dayes of thy Youth." p. 95-114.
           WingM1199; Green(John Foster)98-99.
15478A, 1929

D. Math.   [Mather, Increase] 1639-1723.
I. 80A   The Necessity Of Reformation With the Expedients subservient thereunto, asserted; in Answer to two Questions I. What are the Evils that have provoked the Lord to bring his Judgments on New-England? II. What is to be done that so those Evils may be Reformed? Agreed upon by the Elders and Messengers Of the Churches assembled in the Synod At Boston in New-England, Sept. 10. 1679. ...
           Boston; Printed by John Foster. In the Year, 1679.
           4 p.ℓ., 15 p. 19.5cm. 4°.
           License dated (1st p.ℓ.ᵛ) 15 Oct. 1679.

D. Math   —— —— Another copy. 19cm. Note on 1st
I. 80A   p.ℓ. in contemporary hand: For members of
cop. 2   Synod & Selectmen in all so per Deputy   for Watertowne.
           JCB(1)2:870; JCB(2)2:1193; Evans263; Sabin 46710; Holmes(I)80-A; WingM1232; Green(John Foster)100-103.
02779, 1859
04177, after 1882

D. Math   Mather, Increase, 1639-1723.
I. 19A²   Pray for the Rising Generation. Or A Sermon Wherein Godly Parents are encouraged to Pray and Believe for their Children. Preached the third day of the fifth Moneth, 1678, which day was set apart by the second Church in Boston in New-England, humbly to seek unto God by Fasting and Prayer, for a Spirit of Converting Grace to be poured out upon the Children, and Rising Generation in New-England. The second Impression. By Increase Mather, Teacher of that Church. ...
           Boston, Printed by John Foster, 1679.
           29 p. 14cm. 8° (Issued as a part of his A Call from Heaven, Boston, 1679.)
           First pub. Cambridge, Mass., 1678.
           "To the Reader." dated (p. [4]): Boston, August 22. 1678.
           Sabin46721; Holmes(I)89B; WingM1239; Green (John Foster)105.
15479, 1929

BA679   Mispilıvar, Bernardo de, fl. 1679.
M678s   Sagrado Arbitrio, Commvtacion De Comedias De Corpvs, En Vna Octava Solemne Al Santissimo Sacramento. Rendimiento Penitente. Para Aplacar Las Iras Divinas, En Vn Temblor Grande manifestadas, pacificar la Monarquia, e imprecar prosperidades a N. Rey. y Señor Carlos Segundo. Que Predico El Dia Octavo De La Solemnidad, y proprio del Glorioso Precursor San Juan Bautista El R. P. Fr. Bernardo De Mispiliuar, Cathedratico de Prima, y Regente mayor de estudios en el Colegio de nuestro Padre S. Pedro Nolasco. ...
           Impresso En Lima, Por Lvis de Lyra. Año de 1679.
           8 p.ℓ., 12 numb. ℓ. 19.5cm. 4°
           Outer margins closely trimmed, affecting some marginal glosses.
           License dated (3d p.ℓ.) 21 Aug. 1679.
           Medina(Lima)510.
5500, 1909

Z   Ortelius, Abraham, 1527-1598.
O77   Theatro Del Mondo Di Abraamo Ortelio. Nel
1679   quale si dà notitia distinta di tutte le Prouincie, Regni, & Paesi del Mondo. ...
           In Venetia, M. DC. LXXIX. Presso Stefano Curti. Con Licenza de' Superiori, e Priuilegio.
           255 p. 4 fold maps. 15cm. 8°
           Cut on t.-p.
           An abridged transl., edited by Pietro Maria Marchetti, of Theatrum Orbis Terrarum, 1st pub. Brescia, 1598.
           The section on America occupies p. 20-21.
           Phillipps489.
12768, 1920

BA679   Ortiz, Lorenzo, 1632-1698.
-O77o   Origen, Y Institvto De La Compañia De Iesvs. En La Vida De San Ignacio De Loyola, Sv Padre, Y Fvndador, Qve Ofrece A Las Seis Mvy Religiosas, Y Apostolicas Prouincias de la Compañia de Iesvs de las Indias Occidentales, Qve Comprehende La Assistencia General en Roma, por la Corona de Castilla El Hermano Lorenzo Ortiz, Religioso de la mesma Compañia Iesvs.
           Con licencia, impresso en Seuilla, en el Colegio de San Hermenegildo de la Compañia de Iesvs. En este año de 1679. Vendése en calle de Genoua, en casa de Iuã Saluador Perez, Mercader de Libros.

[64]

67-341
    8 p. l., 197 numb. l., [2] p. 30cm. fol.
    License (3d p. l.ᵛ) dated 3 November 1678.
    Bound in contemporary vellum.
    Sabin 57720; Backer 5:1964; Palau(2) 205682.

DA679
P412a
  Penn, William, 1644-1718.
    An Address To Protestants Upon The Present Conjuncture. In II. Parts. By a Protestant, William Penn.
    [London] Printed in the Year 1679.
    5 p. l., 3-240, 141-148 p. 19cm. 4°
    Errata, last p.
    First pub. [London] 1678.
    In this copy l. bearing p. 3-4 misbound before 2d-5th p. l.
    JCB(2)2:1194; Sabin 59675; Smith(Friends)2:296; McAlpin 3:816; Wing P1248.
03619, 1866

D679
-H313s
  [Penn, William] 1644-1718.
    Englands Great Interest In The Choice of this New Parliament, Dedicated to all her Freeholders and Electors.
    [London, 1679]
    4 p. 31cm. fol.
    Caption title.
    Signed (p. 4): Philanglus.
    While Penn presses for firm discovery and punishment of the Popish Plot, his main concern is the preservation of civil liberties.
    Bound as no. 6 of 8 items.
    Smith(Friends)2:297; Wing P1278.
7085, 1910

E679
P998v
[R]
  Pyrard, François, ca. 1570-1621.
    Voyage De François Pyrard, De Laval, Contenant Sa Navigation Aux Indes Orientales, Maldives, Moluques, & au Bresil: & les divers accidens qui luy sont arrivez en ce Voyage pendant son sejour de dix ans dans ces Païs. Avec Vne Description Exacte Des Moevrs, Loix, Façons de faire, Police & Gouvernement; du Trafic & Commerce qui s'y fait; des Animaux, Arbres, Fruits, & autres singularitez qui s'y rencontrent. Divisé En Trois Parties. Nouvelle edition, reveuë, corrigée & augmentée de divers Traitez & Relations curieuses. Avec des Observations Geographiques sur le present Voyage, qui contiennent entr' autres, l'Estat present des Indes, ce que les Europeens y possedent, les diverses Routes dont ils se servent pour y arriver, & autres matieres. Par le Sieur Du Val, Geographe ordinaire du Roy.
    A Paris, Chez Louis Billaine, en la grande Salle du Palais. M. DC. LXXIX.
    5 p. l., 192, 197-327, 218, 144, [23] p. fold. map. 24cm. 4°
    First pub. as Discours Du Voyage... , Paris, 1611.
    "Discovrs Des Voyages Avx Pays éloignez, ... Par M. N. N.": p. 49-58 (3d count)
    "Description Exacte De La Coste d'Afrique": p. 59-72 (3d count)
    "Observations Geographiques Svr Le Voyage De François Pyrard. Par P. Dv Val": p. 73-114 (3d count)
    "Observations Geographiques Svr La Seconde Partie Dv Voyage De François Pyrard. Par P. Dv Val": p. 115-144 (3d count)
    Bound in contemporary vellum.
    JCB(2)2:1195; Sabin 66882; Borba de Moraes 2:169.
03621, before 1866

C679
R217c
  Raphael de Jesus, 1614-1693.
    Castrioto Lvsitano Parte I. Entrepresa, E Restavraçaõ de Pernambuco; & das Capitanias Confinantes. Varios, E Bellicos Svccessos Entre Portuguezes, E Belgas. Acontecidos Pello Discurso De Vinte E Quatro Annos, E tirados de noticias, relaçoẽs, & memorias certas. Compostos Em Forma De Historia pello Muyto Reverendo Padre Prégador Géral Fr. Raphael de Iesus Natural da muyto Nobre, & sempre Leal Villa de Guimaraẽs. Religioso Da Ordem Do Principe Dos Patriarchas S. Bento. Professo Na Sua Reformada Congregaçam De Portugal, & nella D. Abbade do Insigne Mosteyro de S. Bento de Lisboa este presente anno de 1679. Offerecidos A Ioaõ Fernandes Vieira Castrioto Lvsitano E Por Elle Dedicados Ao Serenissimo Principe D. Pedro Nosso Senhor. Regente Da Lusitana Monarchia.
    Lisboa. Com as licenças necessarias. Na Impressaõ de Antonio Craesbeeck de Mello Impressor de Sua Alteza Anno. 1679.
    9 p. l., 701, [702-748] p. front. (port.). 29.5cm. fol.
    License dated (3d p. l.) 26 Apr. 1678.
    No more published.
    JCB(2)2:1196; Sabin 67912; Palau(2):246112; Rodrigues 2025; Leclerc(1878):1639; Borba de Moraes 1:361.
01629, 1847

E679
S265p
Savary, Jacques, 1622-1690.
  Le Parfait Negociant Ou Instruction Generale Pour Ce Qui Regarde Le Commerce des Marchandises de France, & des Pays Estrangers. ... Avec des Formulaires de Lettres & Billets de Change, d'Inventaire, & de toutes sortes de Societez. Et L'Application Des Ordonnances & Arrests rendus sur toutes les Questions les plus difficiles qui arrivent entre les Marchands, Negocians & Banquiers, sur toutes sortes de matieres concernant le Commerce des Lettres, & Billets de Change. Par le Sieur Jacques Savary. Seconde Edition. Reveüe, corrigée, & augmentée par l'Auteur de plusieurs questions sur le fait du Commerce des Lettres & Billets de Change, & des Faillites. Du Banco de Venise, & du Commerce des Soyes de Messine. Avec un Traité du Commerce qui se fait par la Mer Mediterranée dans toutes les Echelles du Levant; Sçavoir, à Smirne, à Alexandrette & Alep, à Seide à Chipre, à Echelle neuve; à Angora & Beibazar villes de Perse; à Constantinople, à Alexandrie, à Rossette, au Caire, & au Bastion de France. Premiere [-Seconde] Partie.
  A Paris, Chez Louis Billaine, dans la grande Salle du Palais, au grand Cesar. M. DC. LXXIX. Avec Privilege Du Roy.
  2 pt. in 1 v.: 32 p.ℓ., 335 p.; 4 p.ℓ., 422, 443-484 p. 23.5 cm. 4°
  First pub. Paris, 1675.
  Certificate dated (pt. 1, 32d p.ℓ.ᵛ) 14 Apr. 1679.
  Chapters 9 and 10 of pt. 2 deal with French discoveries and commerce in America.
  Original sheep.
16458, 1933

D679
-S435
Scroggs, Sir William, 1623?-1683.
  The Lord Chief Justice Scroggs His Speech In The Kings-Bench The first day of this present Michaelmas Term 1679. Occasioned by the many Libellous Pamphlets which are publisht against Law, to the Scandal of the Government, and Publick Justice. Together With what was Declared at the same Time on the same Occasion, in open Court, by Mr. Justice Jones, and Mr. Justice Dolbin.
  London, Printed for Robert Pawlet at the Bible in Chancery-Lane. 1679.
  2 p.ℓ., 8 p. 31cm. fol.
  Privilege dated (2d p.ℓ.ᵛ) 23 Oct. 1679.
  Bookseller's advertisement, p. 8.
  Wing S2122.
12018, 1919

DA68
C697
Spiegel Voor de Stad van Embden. Die voormaals, in den tijd der reformátie... vermaart geweest is als een herberge der verdrévene, en der gevluchte om der Consciëntie, Maar Die nu getoont wordt, dat zy, ... tégenwoordig geworden is een wreede, en onbarmhertige Vervolgster van d'... Quakers. Bestaande In een oprecht verhaal hoe de Magistraat van die Stad, 't zédert den Járe 1674 ... met dat Volk ... gehandelt hebben, en als nog handelen. Uitgegéven door I. R. vander VVerf, I. Arentsz, B. v. Tongeren, en P. Henrixsz. Met Een Antwoort op het Antichristise - Mandaat by die van Embden, tégens de voorseyde Christenen gepubliceert. Door G. Fox. ...
  Gedrukt by Ian Pietersz Groenwout, Boekverkooper: wónende op het Speuy, tot Rotterdam. En zijn méde te bekómen tot Amsterdam, by Iacob Claus, Boekverkooper: woonende in de nieuwe Lely-straat, óver de drie gekroonde Kas-rieten: die ook bevraagt kan worden in de Heere-straat, in de vergulde Vijf-hoek. 1679.
  4 p.ℓ. 73 p. 20cm. 4° (No. [12] as issued, in Collectio, of Versamelinge [Amsterdam, ca. 1680]).
  Dated (p. 73): In Amsterdam den 1 maand 4 dag 1679.
  Errata, p. 73.
  In this copy there is a blank ℓ. at end.
  Knuttel 11698.
03253, 1866 rev

DA68
C697
Stephenson, Marmaduke, d. 1660.
  Een Roep, Van de Doot, tot het Leeven, ... Beschreeven door Marmaduke Stephenson; Dewelke (met een ander waerde dienstknegt des Heeren / genaemt William Robinson) heeft (na dit schrijven) tot der Doot geleden / om getuigenis te dragen voor deselve waerheit / onder de Belijders van Bostons Jurisdictie / in nieu Engelandt (in America) Met een waare Copy van twee Brieven / welke sy-lieden geschreeven hebben / aen het volk des Heeren / een weinig voor haere dood. Mede een Copy van een Brief, so als die tot onse handen quam, van een Vriend in nieu-Engeland; welk verhaalt, van de manier haarder Mar-telizatie, met eenige van haar woorden, die sy-lieden aan de Regeer-ders, en het volk, een weinig voor haar doot, schreven, en spraaken. Een Copy van Konink Karel ordre, aen de Gouverneurs in nieu-Engelandt, om haer het dooden en mishandelen tegens de Quakers te beletten. Nog een Copy van een ordre waer door aeldaer de Quakers zijn vry in los gelaten. ...
  [Amsterdam] Gedrukt voor Reyner Jansen, Anno 1679.

2 p. ℓ., 30 p. 20cm. 4° (No. [52] as issued, in Collectio, Of Versamelinge. [Amsterdam, ca. 1680])
Cut (fleur-de-lis) on t.-p.
Transl., perhaps by Reinier Jansen, from: A call from death to life. London, 1660, with additional documents and letter, p. 25-30.
Preface signed: John Whitehead [and 4 others]
In this copy there is a blank ℓ. at end.
JCB(2)2:1199; Sabin91320.

03293, 1866

D679 T773d Trapham, Thomas, d. 1692?
A Discourse Of The State of Health In The Island Of Jamaica. With a provision therefore Calculated from the Air, the Place, and the Water: The Customs and Manners of Living, &c. Licensed, Aug. 1. 1678. R. L'Estrange. ... By Thomas Trapham, M.D.Coll.Med.Lond. Soc.Hon.
London, Printed for R. Boulter at the Turks Head in Cornhil over against the Royal Exchange 1679.
8 p. ℓ., 149, [150-153] p. 16.5cm. 8°
"The Epistle Dedicatory" signed: At Port-Royal in Jamaica.
JCB(1)2:869; JCB(2)2:1200; Sabin96473; Wing T2030; Cundall(Jam.)455; Cundall(Jam.Supp.) 350.

0793, 1846

B679 V336e Velez de Guevara, Juan, fl. 1679.
Octavas A La Aparicion De La Imagen Milagrosa De La Virgen Santissima De Gvadalvpe, Qve Afectuoso Escrivio El Capitan Don Ivan Velez De Gveuara, Y Dedica, Al Sᵒʳ D. Ivan Migvel De Agvrto, Y Salzedo Cavallero de la Orden de Alcantara del Consejo de su Magestad, su Oydor en la Real Audiencia de la Ciudad de Mexico, ...
Con Licencia. En Mexico, Por Frācisco Rodriguez Lupercio, Mercader de libros en la Puente de Palacio, Año de 1679.
2 p. ℓ., [12] p. 14.5cm. 8°
Cf. Beristain3:259.

05077, before 1902

CA679 V665s 1-2 Vieira, Antonio, 1608-1697.
Sermoens Do P. Antonio Vieira, Da Companhia De Iesu, Prégador de Sua Alteza. Primeyra Parte. ...
Em Lisboa. Na Officina de Ioam Da Costa. M.DC.LXXIX. Com todas as licenças, & Privilegio Real.
12 p. ℓ., 1118 col., [108] p. 21cm. 4°
Cut (Jesuit trigram floriated) on t.-p.
Text in 2 columns to a page.
Privilege dated (12th p. ℓ.ᵛ) 30 Sept. 1679.
"Lista Dos Sermoens, que andaõ impressos com nome do Author em varias linguas, para que se conheça quaes saõ proprios, & legitimos, & quaes alheyos, & suppostos": 6th p. ℓ.ᵛ-9th p. ℓ.
Errata, 11th p. ℓ.ᵛ
Contains 15 sermons preached in Lisbon, 1645, 1647, 1652, 1655, 1669, Rome, 1670, 1672-1674, and São Luiz, Brazil, 1657.
According to Leite "Deste volume, com a mesma data de 1679, há duas edições diferentes, reconhecíveis pelo tipo e variantes."
With this is bound his Sermoens ... segunda parte, Lisbon, 1682.
Rodrigues2503; Backer8:659; Leite9:194; Innocencio1:289.

68-192.1 rev

1680

D682 -B658c Blome, Richard, d. 1705.
A Geographical Description Of The World, Taken from the Works Of the Famous Monsieur Sanson, Late Geographer to the present French King. To which are Added, About an hundred Geographical and Hydrographical Tables, of the Kingdoms, Countreys, and Isles in the World, with their Chief Cities and Sea-Ports; drawn from the Maps of the said Monsieur Sanson, and according to the Method of the said Description. Illustrated with Maps. The Second Part. By Richard Blome.
[London, Samuel Roycraft] Printed in the Year, 1680.
1 p. ℓ., 493 p. illus. (tables), 24 fold. maps. (Issued as a part of his Cosmography and geography in two parts, London, 1682). 34cm. fol.
An altered and expanded version of his Geographical description of the four parts of the world, 1st pub. London, 1670.
Compiled and translated by Blome in great part from works of Nicolas Sanson.
Bound in contemporary calf.
WingV102; Sabin76720; Baer(Md.)101.

67-357

BA680   Castañeda, Antonio de, fl. 1679.
C346o   Oracion Panegirica Á La Solemne Fiesta del
            Triunfo Naual de Maria Santissima, y su
            Rosario, colocacion de su Soberana Imagen en
            su nueua Capilla, que erigio, y celebrô la
            deuocion del Capitan Manuel de la Chica
            Naruaez en el conuento de Predicadores de la
            villa de San Miguel de Ybarra, haziendo el
            oficio N. M. R. P. Fr. Juan Freile Ministro Pro-
            uincial de la Seraphica Orden en la Prouincia
            de Quito. Año de 1679. Dedicala Al Devoto
            Celebrante el R. P. Fr. Antonio de Castañeda
            Predicador, y Suprior [sic] del Conuento de
            Predicadores de la Ciudad de Quito.
                 Con Licencia; Impresso En Lima, por Luis
            de Lyra. Año de 1680.
                 4 p. l., 11 p. 20.5cm. 4°
                 License dated (verso 3d p. l.) 3 April 1680.
                 Medina(Lima)511.
5501, 1909

BA673   Catholic Church--Liturgy and ritual--Of-
C363o   ficium Beatissimae Virginis Mariae de
            Mercede Redemptionis Captivorum.
            Officivm Beatissimæ Virginis Mariæ De
            Mercede Redemptionis Captivorum. ...
                 Cum Licentia. Angelopoli: Apud Viduā
            Joannis á Borgia, anno 1680.
                 [8] p. 19cm. (20cm. in case) 4°
                 Cut (Our Lady of Ransom) on t.-p.
                 Promulgation (p. [8]) dated 18 Jan. 1680.
                 Bound with: Catholic Church--Liturgy and
            ritual--Special offices. Omnia officia
            sanctorum noviter concessa. Mexico, 1673.
                 JCB(3)3:264, 265n.
5164-16, 1909

BA680   Catholic Church--Liturgy and ritual--Special
C363o   offices--Margaret of Scotland, Saint.
                 Officivm S. Margaritæ Scotorvm Reginæ.
            Semidvplex. A Sacr. Rit. Congregat. recogni-
            tum, & approbatum. De mandato SS. D. N.
            Innocentii Papæ XI. in Breviario Romano apponen.
            Et ab omnibus vtriusque sexus Christi fidelibus,
            qui ad horas Canonicas tenentur, ad libitum
            recitandum. Die viij Iulij.
                 Superiorum permissu. Mexici: Ex Typo-
            graphia Viduæ Bernardi Calderon, Anno
            M. DC. LXXX.
                 1 p. l., [6] p. 14.5cm. 8°
                 "Et facta de prædictis Sanctissimo relatione
            Sanctitas sua annuit die prima Februarij 1679."
            (p. [6]).
5761¹, 1909

DA68   Collectio, Of Versamelinge, van eenige van de
C697   Tractaten, Boeken, en Brieven, Die geschreven
            sijn door verscheyde Vrienden der Waarheyt,
            Die van de Weereld, spots-gewijse, genoemt
            worden Quakers. ...
                 [Amsterdam, ca. 1680]
                 1 v. 20cm. 4°
                 Bound in contemporary vellum.
                 Collective t.-p. for publisher's collection of
            sixty separately-paged Quaker tracts in Dutch,
            pub. in the Netherlands from 1660 to 1680. Many
            of these are transl. from English by Benjamin
            Furly and Stephen Crisp. See W. I. Hull, Benjamin
            Furly, Swarthmore, Pa., 1941, p. 42.
                 JCB(2)2:1017; Smith(Friends)1:800.
03241, 1866

DA680   Congregational Churches in Massachusetts--
C749c   Boston Synod, 1680.
                 A Confession Of Faith Owned and consented
            unto by the Elders and Messengers of the
            Churches Assembled at Boston in New-England,
            May 12. 1680. Being the second Session of that
            Synod. ...
                 Boston; Printed by John Foster. 1680.
                 3 p. l., 65 p., 1 l., [21], 64, [3] p. 14.5cm.
            8°
                 "A Preface" (2d - 3d p. l.) by Increase
            Mather
                 With as issued: A Platform of Church
            Discipline ... agreed upon ... at Cambridge ...
            8th. moneth, Anno 1649, Boston, 1680, with
            special t.-p., separate paging, but continuous
            signatures.
                 Sabin15449; Evans280; Holmes(I)92A; WingC5792.
05018, before 1914

DA680   Congregational Churches in Massachusetts--
C749c   Cambridge Synod, 1648.
                 A Platform Of Church-Discipline Gathered out
            of The Word Of God; And Agreed upon by the
            Elders and Messengers of the Churches Assem-
            bled in the Synod. At Cambridge in N. E. To
            be presented to the Churches & General Court
            for their Consideration and Acceptance in the
            Lord, the 8th. Moneth, Anno. 1649. ...
                 Boston: Printed by John Foster. 1680.
                 1 p. l., [21], 64, [3] p. 14.5cm. 8° (Issued
            as a part of A Confession Of Faith Owned ... at
            Boston ... May 12. 1680. Boston 1680.)
                 First pub. Cambridge, Mass., 1649.
                 Known as the Cambridge Platform; written by
            Richard Mather with the preface by John Cotton.
                 Sabin63334; Evans282; Holmes(M)51E; Wing
            P2400.
05018A, before 1914

BA680 D352o	Delgado y Buenrostro, Antonio, fl. 1676-1696. Oracion Evangelica En Tierno Recuerdo De Christo N. Señor Açotado A La Colvmna, Anualmente Declamado En El Mvy Observante Monasterio de señoras Religiosas del Maximo Doctor de la Iglesia S. Geronimo, de la Puebla de los Angeles, el Viernes de la Viña, tercero de Quaresma. Dixola El Licenciado Don Antonio Delgado y Buenrostro, Capellan, y Secretario del Ilustrissimo, y Reuerendissimo señor Doct. D. Juan Garcia de Palacios, Obispo de la Hauana, año de 1673. Consagrala Al señor Lic. D. Joseph de Yllana Viera de la Cueua, Capellan de dicho Monasterio; y à las señoras Religiosas dèl, que declaman afectuosas este deuotissimo Passo. Con Licencia. En Seuilla por Juan Cabeças, año de 1680. 4 p.l., [12] p. 20.5cm. 4º License dated (verso 4th p.l.) 23 Feb 1680. Palau(2)4:70113; Medina(BHA)1694.	DA680 F791e	Fox, George, 1624-1691. An Exhortation To all them that Profess Themselves Christians, And Say, The Scripture is their Rule for their Life, Doctrine and Practice. By George Fox. ... [London] Printed in the Year 1680. 19 p. 19.5cm. 4º Signed (p. 17): The 18th of the 9th Moneth, 1679. G. Fox. Smith(Friends)1:680; Wing F1816.
62-615		11462, 1918	
D680 -F224i	Faria, Francisco de, fl. 1680. The Information Of Francisco de Faria, Delivered at the Bar of the House Of Commons, Munday the First day of November, in the year of our Lord, 1680. Perused and Signed to be Printed, according to the Order of the House of Commons, By Me William Williams, Speaker. London, Printed by the Assigns of John Bill, Thomas Newcomb, and Henry Hills, Printers to the Kings most Excellent Majesty, 1680. 2 p.l., 12 p. 31cm. fol. Cut (royal arms, Steele 95) on t.-p. License dated (verso 1st p.l.): Novemb. 10th 1680. Faria, identified here as "born in America," gave evidence of the Popish Plot. Wing F425.	JA680 F819t	Franciscans. Tabvla Geographica Totivs Seraphici Ordidinis [sic] FF. Minorvm S. Francisci, Sub Generali Ministro Reverendissimo Patre in Christo P. F. Josepho Ximenez de Samaniego...Exceptis RR. PP. Capvccinis Conventualibus, Tertiariis & Monialibus quibuscunque, extra præfati Generalis Ministri gubernium ac sigillum, sub S.P. N. Francisci invocatione, directione vel Institutione quomodocunque Deo servientibus... Cum Licentia Superiorum Monachij, Typis Lucæ Straub, 1680. 1 p.l., 59 p. 12.5cm. 12º "De Missionibus ad Indias Occidentales": p. 53-56. JCB(2)2:1213; Streit 1:681.
64-144		03625, before 1866	
DA680 F791	Fox, George, 1624-1691. Concerning the Living God of Truth And The World's God, In whom there is No Truth. ... With some Queries for all to consider of, in the latter-end of this Book; and other remarkable things, which are too large to mention in the Title-Page. By George Fox. London, Printed for Benjamin Clark in George-Yard in Lumbard-street, 1680. 47 p. 19.5cm. (21cm. in case) 4º Signed at end: The 6th Moneth, 1679. By George Fox. Smith(Friends)1:679; Wing F1775.	E680 =F849w	[Fréart de Chambray, Roland] d. 1676? The Whole Body Of Antient and Modern Architecture: Comprehending What has been said of it by these Ten Principal Authors who have written upon the Five Orders, Viz. Palladio and Scamozzi, Serlio and Vignola, D. Barbaro and Cataneo, L.B. Alberti and Viola, Buliant and De Lorme, Compared with one another. Also an Account of Architects and Architecture, in an Historical, and Etymological Explanation of certain Terms particularly used by Architects. With Leon Baptista Alberti's Treatise of Statues. The three Greek Orders, Dorique, Ionique, and Corinthian, comprise the First Part of this Treatise. And the two Latine, Tuscan and Composita the Latter. Published for the Benefit of Builders, Limners, and Painters. By John Evelyn Esq; Fellow of the Royal Society. Adorned with Fifty one Copper Plates. London, Printed for J. P. Sold by C. Wilkinson, T. Dring, C. Harper, R. Tonson, and J. Tonson. MDCLXXX. 12 p.l., 159,[1] p. incl. plates. 35.5cm. fol.
62-36			

A transl. by John Evelyn of Parallèle de l'-
Architecture Antique avec la moderne, Paris,
1650. First English transl. issued London,
1664, as A Paralell of Ancient Architecture.
"Amico optimo & Charissimo Johanni Evelyno
Armig. ... Jo. Beale S. P. D. In Architectur-
am ab ipso Anglicè redditam & Graphicè
exornatam." 9th p.ℓ. recto.
Added t.-p., engr.: A Paralell of Architecture...
By Roland Fréart. Sr De Chambray with a por-
trait of Monseiur de Noyers, Baron of Dangu.
Errata, p. 159.
Bookseller's advertisement, p. [1] at end.
WingC1924; cf. Park15.

30042, 1947

D680 Gadbury, John, 1627-1704.
G123e Ephemerides Of The Celestial Motions And
Aspects, Eclipses of the Luminaries, &c. For
XX Years. Beginning anno 1682. and ending an.
1701 ... Accommodated to the Meridian of the
Honourable City of London; and for the service
and benefit of all the Sons of Urania, now made
publick: By John Gadbury, Student in Physick
and Astrology.
London, Printed by J. Macock, for the Company of Stationers, MDCLXXX.
2 p.ℓ., [60], [520] p. incl. tables. 19.5cm.
(20.5cm. in case) 4° A⁴ a-g⁴ B-3U⁴.
Divided into sections of data concerning each
particular year. The sections are continuously
signed but each has a special t.-p. with imprint
dated 1679 and title statement reading. An
Ephemeris Of The Celestial Motions And Aspects
For the Year of Our Lord ... Respecting the
Meridian of London.
Imperfect: 1st 4 ℓ. and last 13 ℓ. wanting;
available in facsim.
Manuscript annotations, some by William
Bradford, the printer.
Bound in contemporary calf; front cover wanting.
WingA1737.

29737, 1945 rev

DA680 Godwin, Morgan, fl. 1685.
G592n The Negro's & Indians Advocate, Suing for
their Admission into the Church: Or A Per-
suasive to the Instructing and Baptizing of the
Negro's and Indians in our Plantations. ... To
which is added, A brief Account of Religion in
Virginia. By Morgan Godwyn, Sometime St. of
Ch. Ch. Oxon. ...
London, Printed for the Author, by J.[ohn]
D.[arby] and are to be Sold by most Booksellers.
1680.
7 p.ℓ., 174 p. 18cm. 8°
"Errata": verso of 7th p.ℓ.
In this copy the first leaf and the last are
blank and genuine.
"The State of Religion in Virginia, as it was
some time before the late Rebellion, repre-
sented in a Letter to Sir W.[illiam] B.[erkeley]
then Governour thereof.": p. 167-174.
Bound in contemporary calf, rebacked.
JCB(2)1202; Sabin27677; Church663; WingG971;
Torrence85.

0216, 1827

BA680 Gonzales de Olmeda, Balthasar, fl. 1679.
G643s Sermon, Qve Predico En La Santa Iglesia
Cathedral De La Civdad De Anteqvera Valle De
Oaxaca El Bʳ. Balthasar Gonzales De Olmedo,
Cura Beneficiado por su Magestad de la Ciudad
de Tehuacan, ... El Dia 29. De Jvnio Del año
de 1679. à la celebridad del Glorioso Apostol
Principe de la Iglesia N.P. San Pedro. Dedicalo
Al Ilvstrissimo, Y Reverendissimo Señor Doctor
D. Nicolas Del Pverto, ... Obispo de dicha
Santa Iglesia Cathedral.
Con Licencia En Mexico Por Juan de Ribera,
Mercader de Libros en el Empedradillo. 1680.
4 p.ℓ., 10 numb. ℓ. 20.5cm. 4°
Dedication dated (verso 2d p.ℓ.): 18 Jan 1680.
Palau(2)105622; Medina(Mexico)1209.

1032, 1905

H680 [Gudenfridi, Giovanni Batista]
G922r Replica Alla Risposta Dimostrativa Del Sig.
Dottor Caualier Francesco Felini Ristretta in
vna Lettera All'Illvstriss. Et Eccell. Sig.
Niccolo D'Oria Principe D'Angri Dvca D'Evoli
Sig. Di Seggio.
In Firenze Alla Condotta. MDCLXXX. Con
lic. de'Sup.
116, [2] p. 15.5cm. (16.5cm. in case) 8°
Half-title: Differenza Tra'Il Cibo, E'L
Cioccolate Esposta All'Illvstriss. Et Eccell.
Sig. Niccolo D'Oria Principe D'Angri &c.
Da Gio: Batista Gvdenfridi.
With endorsements (p. 115-116) by Sebastiano
Bado, Giovanni Batista Antonelli, and Giovanni
Zamboni.
License dated (p. [1] at end) 22 Oct. 1680.
In this copy there is a blank ℓ. at end.
Bound in contemporary paper boards.

69-112

E680 Guillet de Saint-George, Georges, 1625?-1705.
G958a Les Arts De L'Homme D'Epée, Ou Le Dictionaire Du Gentilhomme Divisé en trois parties, Dont la Premiére contient L' Art De Monter à Cheval. La Seconde L'Art Militaire. Et la Troisiéme L'Art De La Navigation. Dédié à Monseigneur le Dauphin. Par le Sieur de Guillet. Suivant la Copie de Paris.
A La Haye, Chez Adrian Moetjens, Marchand Libraire à la Cour, au dessous de la Galerie, 1680.
6 p.l., 512 p. 2 fold. plates, 1 fold. plan. 15cm. 12º
First pub. Paris, 1678.
Bound in contemporary vellum.

32587, 1960

HA680 Hansen, Leonhard, d. 1685.
-H249v Vita Mirabilis Mors Pretiosa Sanctitas Thavmatvrga Inclytae Virginis S. Rosæ Pervanæ Ex Tertio Ordine S. P. Dominici, pridem ex autenticis approbatorum Processuum documentis excerpta & collecta Per P. Magistrvm F. Leonardvm Hansen... Editio Tertia Ac Novissima Ab Autore recognita, mendis expurgata, notisq; marginalibus & numeris ad commodiorem usum interstincta. Denique Clementis X. Pont. Max. solemni Bulla Canonizationis integrè sub finem adnexa.
Romae, Typis Nicolai Angeli Tinassij. MDCLXXX. Svperiorvm Permissv.
3 p.l., 321, [322-324] p. 31.5cm. fol.
First pub. Romae, 1664.
Cut (Dominican coat of arms) on t.-p.
JCB(2)2:1203; Sabin30251; Medina(BHA)1699; Palau(2)112197; Zegarra268.

03628, before 1866

E680 Histoire Ameriqvaine. Novuelle Comiqve &
H673a Tragicomique.
Imprimé à Roüen [Chez François Vaultier] & se vend. A Paris, Chez I. Baptiste Loyson, au Palais, à la Croix d'Or, devant la Ste Chapelle. M. DC. LXXX.
1 p.l., 3-267, [1] p. 13.5cm. 12º
Cut on t.-p.
First pub. under title: Nouvelles de l'Amérique, ou le Mercure Ameriquain. Rouen, 1678. These are the same sheets with cancel t.-p.
Privilege (last p.) granted to "François Vaultier le jeune, Imprimeur & Marchand Libraire en cette Ville de Roüen" dated 4 Aug. 1678.
A collection of three romantic tales about pirates.

Contents.—Histoire de Don Diego de Rivera.—Histoire de Mont-Val.—Le destin de l'Homme, ou les avantures de Don Bartelimi de la Cueba, Portugais.
Bound in contemporary calf.
cf. Sabin56094.

62-321 rev

FC650 Hollantse Mercurius, Verhalende van Oorlog en
H737   Vrede, 't Geen in en omtrent de Vereenigde
30   Nederlanden, En elders in Europa, In het Jaer 1679 Is voorgevallen. Het Dertigste Deel.
Tot Haerlem, Gedruckt by Abraham Casteleyn, Stadts Drucker, op de Marckt, in de Blye Druck, Anno 1680.
3 p.l., 282 [2]p. plate. 20cm. 4º (Bound in [vol. 7] of Hollandse Mercurius)
Added t.-p., engraved: Hollantse Mercurius Ao. 1679. By Abraham Casteleyn Tot Haerlem
JCB(3)2:410; Sabin32523.

8487DD, 1912

DA68   [Isaaksz, Herman] Quaker, fl. 1680.
C697   Vertoog Aan Den Baron de Kinski, Drossaart van Meurs, Als ook aan die van de Regeeringe, En aan De Ingesetenen van de Stad Krevel, ...
[Rotterdam] Gedrukt in't Jaar 1680. En zijn te bekomen tot Rotterdam, by Ian Pietersz Groenwout, Boekverkooper op't Speuy. Als méde tot Amsterdam, by Iacob Claus, Boekverkooper: die bevraagt kan worden in de Heere-straat, in de vergulde Vijf-hoek.
8p. 20cm. 4º (No. [59] as issued, in Collectio, Of Versamelinge. [Amsterdam, ca. 1680])
Cut. on t.-p.
Signed: Herman Isaaksz. Henrik Iansz. Geschréven in Holland, den 22sten der 2 Maand 1680. Hollandse Stijl.
"De brieven en korte verantwoordingen" (p. 8), a list of Quaker titles, concludes: Alle welke geschriften by Jacob Claus, en by Jan Pietersz Groenwout, beyde hier voor gemelt/te bekomen zijn.

03300, 1866

DA680 Keith, George, 1639?-1716.
K28r   The Rector Corrected: Or, The Rector of Arrow, Shooting His Arrow Beside the Mark. In Answer to Thomas Wilson's Book, called, The Quakers False Interpretations of Holy Scripture. In which Answer it is manifested, that T. W's. Interpretations of the Scripture

[71]

1680

(so far as he opposeth the Truth, testified unto by us) are False; and that the Sense given by Us, of all these Scriptures mentioned, is true. By George Keith.
    London, Printed in the Year 1680.
    2 p.l., 1-30, 29-230 p. 15cm. 8°
    A reply to: Thomas Wilson. Quaker's False Interpretation of Holy Scripture. London, 1678.
    It was intended to cancel the leaf bearing p. 27-28 and to substitute two cancelling leaves bearing p. 27-28 and p. 29-30 (1st count). In this copy are bound both the original leaf and, following it, the two cancelling leaves.
    Also issued with an errata slip pasted on p. 230, not found in this copy.
    Smith(Friends)2:22; McAlpin4:22; WingK198.
6539, 1910

J680
M377v1
    Martens, Friedrich, fl. 1675.
    Viaggio Di Spizberga O' Gronlanda Fatto da Federico Martens Amburghese l'Anno 1671. Oue si descriuono que' remotissimi Paesi del Settentrione sotto gli 81. gradi, ne' quali soggiorna il Sole per lo spazio di trè Mesi intieri, Con vna copiosa Relazione di quell'aggiacciato Clima, e de gli Vccelli, Quadrupedi, Pesci, e Piante rare, che vi nascono, colla descrizione delle Balene, e lor Pesca. Portato nuouamente dalla lingua Alemana nell' Italiana dal Sig. Iacopo Rautenfels Gentiluomo Curlandese. Al Molt' Illustre, e Molto Reu. Sig. Il Signor D. Domenico Bertvzzini.
    In Bologna, per Giacomo Monti. 1680. Con licenza de' Superiori.
    264 p. illus., 2 fold. plates. 14.5cm. 12°
    Half title, 1st p.l.
    Contemporary boards.
    Transl. from: Spitzbergische oder Groenlandische Reise. Hamburg, 1675.

J680
M377v1
cop.2
    ———— Another copy. 14cm.
    Sabin44838.
12795, 1920
04678, 1857

J680
M377v2
    Martens, Friedrich, fl. 1675.
    Viaggio Di Spizberga O' Grolanda Fatto da Federico Martens Amburghese l'Anno 1671. Oue si descriuono que' remotissimi paesi del Settentrione sotto gli 81. gradi, ne' quali soggiorna il Sale per lo spazio di trè Mesi intieri. Con vna copiosa relatione di quell' aggiacciato Clima e de gli vccelli, Quadrupedi, Pesci, e Piante rare, che vi nascono, colla descritione delle Balene, e lor Pesca. Portato nuouamente dalla lingua Alemana nell' Italiana dal Sig. Iacopo Rautenfens Gentilhuomo Curlandese. Consacrato All'Illustriss. & Eccellentiss. Sig. Antonio Da' Canal Nobile Veneto.
    In Venetia, M.D.C. LXXX. Per Iseppo Prodocimo. Con Licenza de' Superiori, e Priuilegio.
    264 p. 15cm. 12°
    "Dalle mie stampe li 12 Decembre 1680": 3d p.l.^{v}
    Transl. of: Spitzbergische oder Groenlandische Reise. Hamburg, 1675; reprinted from the Bologna edition of the same year.
    JCB(2)2:1205; Sabin44837.
03624, before 1866

D.Math
I.44
    Mather, Increase, 1639-1723.
    The Divine Right Of Infant-Baptisme Asserted and Proved from Scripture And Antiquity. By Increase Mather, Teacher of a Church of Christ in Boston in New-England. ...
    Boston, Printed by John Foster, in the Year 1680.
    4 p.l., 27 p. 18cm. 4°
    Errata, 2 lines, p. 27.
    "To the Reader."(p.l. 2-4) signed: Cambridge, Febru. 21. 1679/80. Urian Oakes.
    JCB(2)2:1206; Sabin46670; Evans292; Holmes(I) 44; WingM1203; Green(John Foster)112-114. Church664.
04061, 1870

D.Math
I.112
    Mather, Increase, 1639-1723.
    Returning unto God the great concernment of a Covenant People. Or A Sermon Preached to the second Church in Boston in New-England, March 17. $\frac{79}{80}$. when that Church did solemnly and explicitly Renew their Covenant with God, and one with another. By Increase Mather Teacher of that Church. ...
    Boston, Printed by John Foster. 1680.
    3 p.l., 19, [2] p. 18.5cm. 4°
    "The Covenant which was unanimously consented unto, is as   followeth." (last 2 p.)
    It was adopted at the "Reforming Synod," which met in Boston Sept. 10, 1679 and May 12, 1680.
    "To the second Church of Christ in Boston in New-England." dated (verso 3d p.l.): April 19. 1680.
    In this copy the page number of p. 19 is not printed; apparently Dexter's entry records this variation.

Title-page mutilated and repaired; title and imprint from facsim. in Holmes.
JCB(2)2:1207; Evans293; Sabin46730; Holmes(I)112; WingM1245; Green(John Foster)115-117; Church665; McAlpin4:27; Dexter(Cong.)2137.
05129, before 1882

Z
M834
1680
Morden, Robert, d. 1703.
Geography Rectified: Or, A Description Of The World... Illustrated with above Sixty New Maps. The whole work performed according to the more Accurate discoveries of Modern Authors. By Robert Morden.
London, Printed for Robert Morden and Thomas Cockeril. At the Atlas in Cornhill, and at the three Legs in the Poultrey over against the Stocks-Market. 1680.
7 p.ℓ., 204, 241-288, 285-364, 363-418 p. A⁴ (A1+1) a² B-2C⁴ 22C² 3A-3Z⁴. illus. (64 maps) 20cm. 4°
Title in red and black is an insert.
Maps engr. in text.
Errata, p. 204.
In this copy the leaves in 3Y are bound out of order.
The section on America occupies p. 361-418.
Bound in contemporary calf.
Sabin50535; WingM2619; Phillips(Atlases)4265.
11645, 1918

HA680
N661v
Nicoselli, Anastasio.
Vita Del Beato Toribio Alfonso Mogrobesio Arciuescouo di Lima Raccolta Da Anastagio Nicoselli. Dedicata Alla Santita Di N. Signore Innocenzo XI.
In Roma, Per Nicolò Angelo Tinassi. M.DC.LXXX. Con Licenza De' Svperiori.
6 p.ℓ., 344 p. 22.5cm. 4°
Cut (papal arms, engr.) on t.-p.
Transl. and abridged chiefly from: Herrera, Cipriano de, Mirabilis vita et mirabiliora acta dei Vener. servi Toribio Alfonso Mogrobesio, Rome, 1670.
First pub. Rome, 1679, under title: Compendio della vita...
Dedication (2d-3d p.ℓ.) by Giovanni Francesco de Valladolid.
Palau(2)190501; Streit3:2148.
69-315

bB680
R382v
Relacion Verdadera, En Qve Se dà quenta del horrible Huracăn que sobrevino à la Isla, y Puerto de Santo Domingo de los Españoles el dia quinze de Agosto de 1680... Padeciendo la mayor derrota veinte y cinco Navios de Frăcia, que alli avia, con muerte de los mas de sus Cabos, Soldados, y Marineros que los ocupavan: Con otras particularidades que verà el Curioso.
Con Licencia En Madrid: Por Lucas Antonio de Bedmar, en la Calle de los Preciados. [1680?]
[4] p. 29.5cm. fol.
Medina(BHA) 6802.
13507, 1923

DA680
R382v
A Relation Of The Labour, Travail And Suffering Of that faithful Servant of the Lord Alice Curwen. Who departed this Life the 7th Day of the 6th Moneth, 1679. and resteth in Peace with the Lord. ...
[London?] Printed in the Year 1680.
10 p.ℓ., 55 p. 19cm. 4°
Testimonies by Anne Martindall, Thomas Curwen, Alice Cobb and R.T.: p.ℓ. 2-10. The Relation of the trip through New England, New Jersey, New York and then to Barbados consists of a series of letters from and to Alice and Thomas Curwen.
Sabin18073; Smith(Friends)1:504; WingM857.
05122, before 1902

BA669
-L864u
Riofrío, Bernardo de, d. 1700.
Centonicvm Virgilianvm Monimentvm Mirabilis Apparitionis Pvrissimae Virginis Mariae De Gvadalvpe Extramvros Civitatis Mexicanae: Avthore Lic.ᵗᵒ D. Bernardo De Riofrio Michoacanensis Ecclesiae Canonico Doctorali: Ad Illustrissimum, Reverendissimum, & Excellentissimum Principem, M.D.D.Fr.Payvm De Ribera Enriqvez, Archiepiscopatus Mexicani Antistitem...
Mexici, apud Viduam Bernardi Calderon. Anno 1680.
7 p.ℓ., 5 numb. ℓ. pl. 30cm. fol.
License dated (verso 3d p.ℓ.) 11 Nov. 1680.
Preliminary matter (poetry) by Bartolomeo Rosales and Diego de Ribera.
Bound with: López de Avilés, José. Ueridicvm Admodvm Anagramma, Epigramma Obseqviosvm. Mexici, 1669.
Medina(Mexico)1214; Palau(1)6:284; Sabin71481.
12903B, 1921

DA680 R731c	Rogers, William, fl. 1680. 　The Christian-Quaker, Distinguished from the Apostate & Innovator. In Five Parts. Wherein, Religious Differences amongst the People termed in Derision, Quakers are treated on. George Fox, one (at least, if not the chief) reputed Author thereof, is detected. Doctrines of Truth owned by the Children of Light, (and cleared from Objections) are laid down, according to Holy Scriptures, and Revelation of the Spirit. By William Rogers, on behalf of himself and other Friends in Truth concerned. ... 　London, Printed in the Year, 1680. 　7 sections in 1 v.: preface, 22 p.ℓ., 32, [3] p.; pt. 1, 3 p.ℓ., 96 p.; pt. 2, 2 p.ℓ., 92 p.; pt. 3, 112, 129-136, 121-140 p.; pt. 4, 108 p.; pt. 5, 92 p.; index, 26 p. 20cm. 4° 　Each part has special t.-p., separate paging and signatures. "... though the five parts of this Treatise, are now bound up together; yet 'twas once designed, that they should also be published in single parts..." (22d p. ℓ.ᵛ). 　Preface dated (22d p. ℓ.ᵛ): Bristol the first day of the eighth Month 1680. 　Errata, preface p. [1-3]. 　In this copy there is a blank ℓ. at beginning. 　Bound in contemporary sheep, rebacked. 　Smith(Friends)2:509; WingR1858. 11473, 1918		London, Printed in the Year, 1680. 　3 p.ℓ., 96 p. 20cm. 4° (Issued as a part of his The Christian-Quaker, Distinguished from the Apostate & Innovator. London, 1680.) 11473A, 1918
		DA680 R731c	Rogers, William, fl. 1680. 　The Fourth Part Of The Christian-Quaker Distinguished from the Apostate & Innovator. Wherein A Relation is given of several Proceedings, (since George Fox's Wife caused a Paper, dated the 21ᵗʰ· of the 11ᵗʰ· Mᵒⁿ· 1672. to be Read against John Story, in a Quarterly-Meeting in Westmoreland: Therein signifying, that he judged the Power of God, as it broke forth in Hymns, or Spiritual Songs.) And is chiefly to discover, That George Fox hath Erroneously concerned himself in the Divisions amongst the People called Quakers. Which therefore may serve for A Warning To The Children of Light, that their Dependency may not be on G. F. ... By William Rogers. ... 　[London] Printed in the Year, 1680. 　108 p. 20cm. 4° (Issued as a part of his The Christian-Quaker, Distinguished from the Apostate & Innovator. London, 1680.) 11473D, 1918
DA680 R731c	Rogers, William, fl. 1680. 　The Fifth Part Of The Christian-Quaker, Distinguish'd From the Apostate & Innovator. Being An Additional Discovery (to the First and Fourth Parts of the Christian-Quaker, &c.) That George Fox hath been acted by an Erroneous Spirit, ... By William Rogers. ... 　London, Printed in the Year, 1680. 　92 p. 20cm. 4° (Issued as a part of his The Christian-Quaker, Distinguished from The Apostate & Innovator. London, 1680.) 11473E, 1918	DA680 R731c	Rogers, William, fl. 1680. 　The Second Part Of The Christian-Quaker, Distinguished from the Apostate & Innovator ... Also, An Appendix, detecting Charles Marshal and sixty five more, as Unrighteous Judges, in a Case pretended to relate to John Story, and John Wilkinson, two antient and honourable Labourers in the Gospel of Christ. By William Rogers, on behalf of himself and other Friends in Truth concerned. ... 　London, Printed in the Year, 1680. 　2 p.ℓ., 92 p. 20cm. 4° (Issued as a part of his The Christian-Quaker, Distinguished from the Apostate & Innovator. London, 1680.) 11473B, 1918
DA680 R731c	Rogers, William, fl. 1680. 　The First Part Of The Christian-Quaker, Distinguished from the Apostate & Innovator. ... To Which Is Added, A Paper Touching the Scattered of Israel, given forth in the Year 1661, by Edward Burrough Minister of the Everlasting Gospel, ... Also, A Particular Discovery of that Bait, by Which George Fox hath been Tempted And Ensnared, ... By William Rogers on Behalf of himself and other Friends in Truth concerned. ...		
		DA680 R731c	Rogers, William, fl. 1680. 　The Third Part Of The Christian-Quaker, Distinguished from the Apostate & Innovator ... And ... an Answer to a part of Robert Barclay's Book of Governmeut [sic] is Cited. To which is added, A Testimony given forth in Print, in the

Year 1660. by Isaac Penington the younger; being part of a Discourse, Intituled, The Authority and Government which Christ excluded out of his Church. Also, an Epistle written by Robert Barclay, as an Explanatory Post-script to his Book of Government; ... To which is added a Letter Written (as is pretended) by W. R. but Published by R. B. together with a Paper termed, The Judgment of the Brethren, in a Discourse had between R. B. and W. R. with Observations and Answer thereto. By William Rogers, on behalf of himself and other Friends in Truth concerned. ...
[London] Printed in the Year, 1680.
112, 129-136, 121-140 p. 20cm. 4°
(Issued as a part of his The Christian-Quaker, Distinguished from the Apostate & Innovator. London, 1680.)
"The Innovations And Scripture-Misapplications of R.B. Detected.... Given forth in the Year 1676. By William Rogers..." (with half-title, p. 15-88), a reply to Robert Barclay's The Anarchy of the Ranters...[London?], 1676.
Includes "a Testimony Publish't in Print by Isaac Penington the younger, in the year, One Thousand six hundred and sixty, Being a part of a Discourse, Entituled, The Authority and Government which Christ excluded out of his Church, &c." (p. 88-98), and an "Explanatory Postscript", 1679, by Robert Barclay to his The Anarchy of the Ranters. (p. 98-99).
11473C, 1918

bB68- Señor mio. Mañana Martes 10. del corriente
S478m ...
[Lima, 168-?]
Broadside. 20 x 14cm. 4°
Title from beginning of text.
Invitation to the viceroy to attend the public defense of the thesis of Antonio Calvo Domonte in the College of San Martín, Lima.
With this copy a blank, conjugate leaf is present.
06642

DA680 Shepard, Thomas, 1605-1649.
S547s The Sincere Convert: Discovering the small number of True Believers, And the great difficulty of Saving Conversion. ... Whereto is now added The Saint's Jewel, shewing how to apply the Promises; and The Soul's Invitation unto Jesus Christ. By Tho. Sheppard, sometimes of Emanuel Colledge in Cambridge. ...
London, Printed by M. Flesher for Robert Horn at the South Entrance of the Royal Exchange. 1680.

8 p.ℓ., 223, [1] p. 17cm. 8°
First pub. London, 1640.
The Saint's Jewel has special t.-p. but continuous paging and signatures, p. [185]-223.
"Several Books, Bills, Bonds, &c. hereafter mentioned, sold by Robert Horne..." p. [224]
"To the Christian Reader" p. ℓ. 2-4, signed: W. Greenhill.
JCB(2)2:1208; Sabin80234; WingS3131.
03627, before 1860

BA680 Sigüenza y Góngora, Carlos de, 1645-1700.
S579g Glorias De Queretaro En La Nueva Congregacion Eclesiastica de Maria Santissima de Guadalupe, con que se ilustra: Y En El Sumptuoso Templo, Que dedicò à su obsequio D. Juan Cavallero, Y Ocio Presbytero, Comissario de Corte del Tribunal del Santo Oficio de la Inquisicion. Escrivelas D. Carlos de Siguenza, y Gongora Natural de Mexico, Cathedratico proprietario de Mathematicas en la Real Universidad de esta Corte.
En Mexico: Por la Viuda de Bernardo Calderon. IXI DC LXXX [i.e. 1680].
6 p. ℓ., 80 p., 12 ℓ. 19cm. 4°
Cut (winged horse) on t.-p., incl. motto: Itvr Sic Ad Astra.
License dated (verso 6th p. ℓ.) 20 Aug. 1680.
Errata (verso 6th p. ℓ.)
Includes his "Primavera Indiana Poema..." 12 ℓ. at end with special half-title; 1st pub. Mexico, 1668.
Imperfect: half-title wanting.
In this copy the half-title of his Theatro de virtudes politicos, Mexico, 1680, is bound in as the final leaf.
JCB(2)2:1210, 1212; Palau(1)6:515; Medina (Mexico)1215; Sabin80973.
0794, 1846

B680 Sigüenza y Góngora, Carlos de, 1645-1700.
S579t Theatro De Virtvdes Politicas, Qve Constituyen á vn Principe: advertidas en los Monarchas antiguos del Mexicano Imperio, con cuyas efigies se hermoseó el Arco Trivmphal, Que la muy Noble, muy Leal, Imperial Ciudad De Mexico Erigiò para el digno recivimiento en ella del Excelentissimo Señor Virrey Conde De Paredes, Marqves De La Lagvna, &c. Ideòlo entonces, y ahora lo describe D. Carlos de Siguenza, y Gongora Cathedratico proprietario de Mathematicas en su Real Vniversidad.
En Mexico: Por la Viuda de Bernardo Calderon. ∞DC LXXX. [i.e. 1680]

4 p.ℓ., 88 p. 19cm. 4°
Cut (winged horse) on t.-p., incl. motto: Sic Itvr Ad Astra.
Imperfect: half-title wanting; bound with the Library's copy of his Glorias de Querétaro, Mexico, 1680.
JCB(2)2:1211; Palau(2)312966; Medina(Mexico) 1216; Sabin80985.

0795, 1846

bBB
S7336
1680
1

Spain--Sovereigns, etc., 1665-1700 (Charles II)
28 Feb 1679
El Rey. Mvy Reuerendo in Christo Padre Arçobispo de la Iglesia Metropolitana de la ciudad de los Reyes en las Prouincias del Peru, de mi Consejo, Virrey Gouernador, y Capitan General dellas en interin. Los grandes gastos ...
[Lima, 1680]
[2] p. 31.5cm. fol.
Title from caption and beginning of text.
Solicits donations in Peru to defray expenses of the sovereign's marriage.
Dated in Madrid, 28 Feb 1679.
Manuscript certificate dated in Lima, 1 July 1680.
With this copy a blank, conjugate leaf is present.
Papel sellado dated 1679, 1680, and 1681.

28196, 1938

B680
T228a

Tauste, Francisco de, d. 1698.
Arte, Y Bocabvlario De La Lengva De Los Indios Chaymas, Cvmanagotos, Cores, Parias, Y Otros Diversos De La Provincia De Cvmana, O Nveva Andalvcia. Con Vn Tratado A Lo Vltimo de la Doctrina Christiana, y Catecismo de los Misterios de nuestra Santa Fè, traducido de Castellano en la dicha Lengua Indiana. Compvesto, Y Sacado A Lvz Por El Reuerendo Padre Fray Francisco de Tauste ...
En Madrid, En la Imprenta de Bernardo de Villa-Diego, Impressor de Su Magestad, Año de M.DC.LXXX. Con Licencia De Los Svperiores.
8 p.ℓ., 187 p. 20cm. 4°
"Licencia Del Svpremo Consejo de las Indias" (6th p.ℓ.ᵛ): dated 31 May 1680.
Errata, 8th p.ℓ.ʳ.
Title-page torn in lower outer corner affecting title and part of the imprint; available in facsim.
JCB(2)2:1214; Sabin94424; Medina(BHA)1710; Viñaza 208.

0519, 1846

G680
T522t

Thorsteins saga Vikingssonar.
Thorstens Viikings-Sons Saga På Gammal Göthska Af ett Åldrigt Manuscripto afskrefwen och uthsatt på wårt nu wanlige språk sampt medh några nödige anteckningar förbettrad af Regni Sveoniæ Antiqvario Jacobo J. Reenhielm.
Upsalæ Excudit Henricus Curio S.R.M. & Academiæ Vpsal. Bibliopola MDCLXXX.
2 p.ℓ., 140, [20], 130, [2] p. illus. 16.5cm. 8°
Errata: verso 2d p.ℓ.
Title wormed affecting imprint slightly.
Woodcut title vignette (a Viking).
Parallel texts in Icelandic and Swedish.
Dedication signed: Upsala Anno 1680. Jacob J. Reenhielm (recto 2d p.ℓ.); Icelandic-Latin glossary (p. [141-158]); commendatory matter by Iohannes Loccenius, Ol. Rudbeck, Olavs Werelivs, and Ionas Rvgman (p. [159-160]); Notes in Latin (p. 1-130. 2d count); "Auctores Citati" (p. [131-132], 2d count).
Bound in contemporary vellum; spine title: Thorstens Saga.
See Hermannsson, Halldór, Icelandic books of the seventeenth century, Ithaca, New York, p. 118-119.

31278, 1953

DA680
T751e

[Townsend, Theophila] fl. 1676-1690.
An Epistle of Love To Friends in the Womens Meetings in London, &c. To be read among them in the fear of God.
[London? ca. 1680].
8 p. 18cm. 4°
Caption title.
"A Testimony out of the Old Testament and New of the Lord..." (p. 6-8) signed: G. F. [i.e., George Fox].
Smith(Friends)1:680 and 2:752; WingT1987A.

11451, 1918

D680
V132p

The Vain Prodigal Life, And Tragical Penitent Death Of Thomas Hellier Born at Whitchurch near Lyme in Dorset-Shire: Who for Murdering his Master, Mistress, and a Maid, was Executed according to Law at Westover in Charles City, in the Country of Virginia, neer the Plantation called Hard Labour, where he perpetrated the said Murders. He Suffer'd on Munday the 5th of August, 1678. And was after Hanged up in Chains at Windmill-Point on James River. ...
London: Printed for Sam. Crouch, at the Princes Arms, a corner-shop of Popes-head-alley in Cornhil. 1680.
2 p.ℓ., 40 p. 19.5cm. 4°

Hellier's life story and confession to the murder of his master, "Cutbeard Williams," and others was narrated to "one Mr. [Paul] Williams," a minister, who, promising to have the account published in England, added his own "Reflections" and included Hellier's "Admonition to all spectators at the Gallows."
Preliminary matter includes poetry.
JCB(2)2:1204; Sabin31252; WingV19; Swem5861; Torrence86.

0885, 1846 rev

BA680
X200s

Xaimes de Ribera, Juan, fl. 1679-1689.
Sermon Predicado En El Celebre Dia del gran Padre de la Iglesia S. Agustin. Por El P. Lec. Fr. Ioan Xaimes de Ribera... Año de 1679. Dedicale Al Sor D.^{or} D. Ignacio de Castelvi, Thesorero de la Ilustre Cathedral del Cuzco.
Con Licencia. Impresso En Lima, Por Luis de Lyra. Año de 1680.
8 p. ℓ., 9 numb. ℓ. 20.5cm. 4º
Includes (verso 8th p. ℓ.) Latin poetry by Melchor de Segura.
License dated (recto 4th p. ℓ.) 6 June 1680.
Medina(Lima)519.

5502, 1909

1681

D681
A164a

An Abstract, Or Abbreviation Of some Few of the Many (Later and Former) Testimonys From The Inhabitants Of New-Jersey, And Other Eminent Persons. Who have Wrote particularly concerning That Place.
London, Printed by Thomas Milbourn, in the Year, 1681.
32 p. 19cm. 4º
A collection of 16 letters by settlers in West New Jersey, with also an extract from Beauchamp Plantagenet's Description of... New Albion, 1st pub. London, 1648 (which includes an extract from Robert Evelyn's A direction for adventurers, 1st pub. London, 1641).
"Scottish Proprietors' Tracts" no. 2. Cf. Church 649n.

Dated (p. 17) "this present 5th. Moneth, 1681."
JCB(2)2:1222; Church669; Sabin53031; Vail (Front.)194; Baer(Md.)97; WingA147.

02900, 1861

C585
E96t
12

[Addison, Lancelot] 1632-1703.
The Moores Baffled: Being A Discourse Concerning Tanger, Especially when it was under the Earl of Teviot; ... In a Letter from a Learned person (long Resident in that place) at the desire of a person of Quality.
London: Printed for William Crooke, at the Green-Dragon without Temple-Bar. 1681.
2 p. ℓ., 27, [28-32] p. fold. plate. 20cm. 4º
"The Bookseller To The Reader" (2d p. ℓ.) signed William Crooke.
"Books Printed for, and are to be Sold by William Crooke...": p. [28-32]
Bound as no. 12 of 19 items in vol. with binder's title: Tracts 1681-1701.
Wing A525.

11352-12, 1918

B69
G643v
33

Agurto y Loaysa, Joseph de, fl. 1676-1688.
Villancicos Qve Se Cantaron En En [sic] La S. Iglesia Cathedral De Mexico: En los Maytines del Gloriosissimo Principe de la Iglesia el Señor San Pedro. ... Compuestos en metro musico por el B.^{r} Ioseph de Agurto, y Loaysa, Maestro Compositor de dicha Santa Iglesia.
Con licencia, en Mexico, por la Viuda de Bernardo Calderon. Año de 1681.
[8] p. 20cm. 4º
Woodcut title vignette (St. Peter within a decorative frame)
Bound, in contemporary vellum, as no. 33 with 42 other items.
Gonzalez(1952)219.

28933, 1941

E681
A499s

Amelot de La Houssaye, Abraham Nicolas, 1634-1706.
La Storia Del Governo Di Venezia Del Signor Amelotto della Houssaia. ...
In Colonia, Appresso Pietro del Martello. [i.e. Paris?] M. DC. LXXXI.

	3 pts. in 1 v.: pt.1, 8 p.ℓ., 247 [248-270] p.; pt.2, 14 p.ℓ., 72, 72(i.e. 73)-164(i.e. 165), 147(i.e. 166)-251(i.e. 250), 253(i.e. 251)-295 (i.e. 293) p.; [pt.3] 240, [6] p. 17cm. 12° Each part has special t.-p., separate paging and signatures. Title [pt.3]: Svpplimento Alla Storia Del Governo Di Venezia, ... Cut (armillary sphere) on title-pages. The same sphere appears on the t.-p. of [Dufour, P.S.] <u>Tractatus novi</u>, Parisiis, Apud Petrum Muguet, 1685. First pub. Paris, 1676-1677. Views the discovery of America as a cause of the economic decline of Venice. In this copy there is a blank leaf at end of each part. Parenti 54.
69-240	

F681 B741ℓu	[Bos, Lambert van den] 1610-1698. Ander Theil Der Durchleuchtigen See-Helden/ dieser Zeit. Worinnen gehandelt wird von den fürnehmsten Thaten und Zügen/der berühmtesten Holländischen Admiralen nebenst einziger Ausländischen Befehlchhabern und endiget sich mit dem Todt des Admirals Michael Adrians de Ruyter. Mit Churfürstlichem Sächsischem Gnaden-Privilegio. Nürnberg/In verlegung Johann Hofmanns/ Kunst-und Buchhändlers. M.DC.LXXXI. 402, [5] p. 17 plates (incl. 4 fold.), 6 ports., fold. map. 21cm. 4°. (Issued as a part of his <u>Leben und Thaten Der Durchläuchtigsten See-Helden</u>. Sultzbach / Nürnberg, 1681) Transl. from: <u>Leeven en Daden Der Doorluchtighste Zee Helden</u>, part 2. Amsterdam, 1676. Bound in contemporary vellum. JCB(1)2:890; JCB(2)2:1234; Leclerc(1878)73; Palmer 295.
03007A, 1865	

BA681 A958s	Avila, Juan de, fl. 1684. Sermon De El Glorioso Martyr S. Felipe De Iesvs, Patron, y Criollo de Mexico. Predicólo, En la Iglesia Cathedral El P. Fr. Ivan De Avila, Predicador del Convento de N.P.S. Francisco. Dedicalo ... Al ... Virrey ... Con licencia, en Mexico por Francisco Rodriguez Lupercio. Año de 1681. 8 p.ℓ., [20] p. 19.5cm. 4° Cut (dedicatee's coat of arms) on t.-p. License dated (6th p.ℓ.) 28 Febr. 1681. Palau(2)20459; Medina(Mexico)1220; Sabin 36790.
70-153	

DA681 B355f	Baxter, Richard, 1615-1691. Faithful Souls Shall Be With Christ, The Certainty Proved and their Christianity Described, and Exemplified in the truly-Christian Life and Death of that excellent amiable Saint, Henry Ashhurst Esq; Citizen of London. Briefly and truly Published for the Conviction of Hypocrites and the Malignant, the Strengthning of Believers, and the Imitation of all; especially the Masters of Families in London. By Richard Baxter. ... London, Printed for Nevil Simmons, at the Three Golden Cocks, at the West end of St. Pauls Church, 1681. 4 p.ℓ., 60 p. 20.5cm. 4° Dedication dated (4th p.ℓ.ᵛ) 7 Dec. 1680. Wing B1265; McAlpin 4:46.
68-486	

F681 B741ℓ	[Bos, Lambert van den] 1610-1698. Leben und Tapffere Thaten der aller-berühmtesten See-Helden/Admiralen und Land-Erfinder unserer Zeiten/angefangen mit Cristoforo Colombo Entdeckern der Neuen Welt/und geendigt mit dem Welt-berühmten Admiral M. A. de Ruyter, Rittern/&c. ...Unlängst in Nider-Teutscher Sprache aufgesetzt/durch V. D. B. Anjetzo aber in unsere Hoch-Teutsche reinlich überbracht/ Von Matthia Krämern/Sprachmeistern. Samt einem Anhange/Vieler Denckwürdigkeiten/welche der Niderländische Author den Helden-Thaten Almeyda/Albuquerque/und Acuniæ/entweder ausgelassen/oder nur kürtzlich gerühret/beygetragen und erstattet/Durch Erasmum Francisci. Nürnberg/ In Verlegung Christoph Endters Seel. Handlungs-Erben. Anno M DC LXXXI. 6 p.ℓ., 1090, [18] p. 22 plates (incl. 6 fold.), 9 ports., fold. map. 21cm. 4°. Errata: verso of final leaf. Added t.-p., engraved: Leben und Tapfere Thaten der Allerberühmtesten See-Helden. Title in red and black. Transl. from: <u>Leeven en Daden Der Doorluchtighste Zee-Helden</u>. Amsterdam, 1676, with the addition of Francisci's <u>Anhang Unterschiedlicher Denckwurdigkeiten</u> (p. 1009-90). Another German transl. was pub. Nürnberg, 1681 (without Francisci's <u>Anhang</u>) under title: <u>Leben und Tapffere Thaten der aller-berühmtesten See-Helden</u>.

F681 [Bos, Lambert van den] 1610-1698.
B741lu Leben und Thaten Der Durchläuchtigsten
See-Helden Und Erfinder der Länder dieser
Zeiten/Anfahend Mit Christoph Columbus Dem
Erfinder der neuen Welt/und sich endend mit
dem höchstberühmten Admiral M. A. de Ruyter,
Rittern u. s. f. Worinnen viel seltzame Fälle/
tapffere Verrichtungen/Grossmüthige Verwal-
tungen/und harte See-Treffen u. s. w. vorge-
stellet werden. Mit grossem Fleiss/aus vielen
glaubwürdigen Schrifften/und gewissen bewähr-
ten Urkünden /in Holländischer Sprache/
zusammen gebracht/und beschrieben/Durch
V. D. B. Nunmehr aber In die hochteutsche
Sprache übersetzt und heraus gegeben.
Gedruckt zu Sultzbach/In Verlegung Johann
Hofmanns/Kunst- und Buch-Händlers in
Nürnberg. [1681]
2 pt. in 1 v.: 4 p. ℓ., 451, [452-460] p.; 402, [5] p.
20 plates (incl. 6 fold.), 9 ports., fold. map.
21cm. 4°.
Added t.-p., engraved: Leben und Thaten
Der Durchleuchtigsten Seehelden
Transl. from: Leeven en Daden Der Doorluch-
tighste Zee-Helden. Amsterdam, 1676. Another
German transl. was pub. Nürnberg, 1681, under
title: Leben und Thaten Der Durchläuchtigsten See-
Helden... .
Title-page of part 2: Ander Theil Der Durch-
leuchtigen See-Helden. Nürnberg, 1681.
Bound in contemporary vellum.
JCB(2)2:1234; Leclerc(1878)73; Palmer295.
03007, 1865 rev

DA681 Burnet, Gilbert, Bp. of Salisbury, 1643-1715.
-B964h The History Of The Reformation Of The Church
of England. In Two Parts... The Second Edition,
Corrected. By Gilbert Burnet, D.D.
London, Printed by T. H. for Richard Chiswell,
at the Rose and Crown in St. Paul's Churchyard,
MDCLXXXI.
2 v.: v.1, 10 p. ℓ., 377, 324, 329-368, [4] p.
7 ports.; v.2, 14 p. ℓ., 227, 233-421, [7], 368,
(365)-(368), 369-416, [7] p. 9 ports. 32.5cm.
fol.
Titles in red and black.

Bound in contemporary vellum.
JCB(2)2:1233; Muller(1872)130; Sabin6441;
Palmer295.
03636, before 1866

Added title-pages, engr.; signed (v.1) R. White
Sculpsit.
First pub. London, 1679 (consisting of the 1st
part only).
Preliminary matter dated (v. 2, 1st p. ℓ.^{v})
5 Jan. 1680/1.
Errata, v. 2, 14th p. ℓ.^{v}, p. 416, and p. 4 at end.
Contents.—v.1. Of The Progress made in it
during the Reign Of K. Henry the VIII.—v. 2.
Of The Progress made in it till the Settlement
of it in the beginning Of Q. Elizabeth's Reign.
Each vol. includes "A Collection Of Records
And Original Papers; With Other Instruments
Referred to..." (v.1, p. 1-270, 2d count; v.2,
p. 1-379, 2d count). The "Collection", v. 2,
has a special t.-p. and separate paging but
continuous signatures. The special t.-p. has
imprint: London, Printed by J. D. for Richard
Chiswell. 1680.
"Books printed for, and sold by Richard
Chiswell": v. 2, p. [5-7] at end.
This copy of v. 2 has an additional, variant
copy of each port. (mounted).
Imperfect: v.1 wanting; description from
another copy at Brown University.
Wing B5798.
05728, before 1874 rev

D681 Carew, Thomas.
-C314h Hinc Illæ Lacrymæ; Or, An Epitome Of
The Life and Death Of Sir William Courten
And Sir Paul Pyndar Late of London K^{nts}.
Deceased, With their great Services and
Sufferings under the Crown of England. ...
Faithfully and Modestly Collected by Thomas
Carew Gent. with some Remarques thereupon.
London, Printed for the Persons Interested
[sic], Anno Dom. MDCLXXXI.
2 p. ℓ., 24 p. 33cm. fol.
Dated (2d p. ℓ.^{v}) 12 July 1681.
In this copy pages are red ruled in ms.
WingC563.
69-251

BA681 Carrasco de Saavedra, Diego José.
C313s Sermon De La Pvrissima Concepcion De
Maria Santissima Señora nuestra. Predicado Por El Dotor Don Diego Ioseph Carrasco de Saauedra, Cura, y Vicario del Pueblo
de Quilaquila, Visitador general deste Arçobispado de los Charcas, y de la Santa
cruzada. ...
Con licencia, impresso en Lima, Año
de 1681.

8 p. ℓ., 15 numb. ℓ. 19.5cm. 4°
Approbation dated (3d p. ℓ.) 4 May 1680.
Medina(Lima)521.

70-467

B681 Colón, Fernando, 1488-1539.
C719ℓ La Vie De Cristofle Colomb, Et La Decou-
cop.1 verte Qu'il A Faite Des Indes Occidentales vul-
gairement appellées le Nouveau Monde. Composée par Fernand Colomb son Fils, & traduite
en François. ... Premiere [-Seconde] Partie.
A Paris, Chez Claude Barbin, au Palais, sur
le second Perron de la Sainte Chapelle. Et
Chez Christophe Ballard, ruë S. Jean de Beauvais, au Mont Parnasse. M.DC.LXXXI. Avec
Privilege Du Roy.
2 v.: 12 p. ℓ., 262 p.; 12 p. ℓ., 260 p.
15.5cm. 12°
Translation by Charles Cotolendy of <u>Historie
del Sig. Don Fernando Colombo</u>, 1st pub.
Venice, 1571.
"Achevé d'imprimer pour la premier fois,
le neufiéme jour de Septembre mil six cent
quatre-vingt-un." (v.1, 7th p. ℓ., v.2, 7th p. ℓ.ᵛ).
"Recueil des Ceremonies de la Foy des Indiens,"
by Ramón Pane, v.2, p. 1-33.
There is a different cut on each t.-p.
The 2 v. of this copy are bound together in 1 v.

B681 —— ——Another copy. 16cm.
C719ℓ 2 v.
cop.2 JCB(2)2:1215; Sabin14677; Streit2:2152; cf.
Palau(2)57227; Leclerc(1878)143.

03631, before 1866
04712, before 1866

D681 Dryden, John, 1631-1700.
D799 The Indian Emperour, Or The, Conquest Of
Mexico By The Spaniards. Being the Sequel of
the Indian Queen. By John Dryden Esq; ...
London, Printed for H. Herringman, at the
Sign of the Blue Anchor in the Lower walk of the
New Exchange. 1681.
4 p. ℓ., 68, [2] p. 21.5cm. 4°.
First pub. London, 1667.
"Connexion of the Indian Emperour to the
Indian Queen" (4th p. ℓ.).
JCB(2)1216; Sabin20979; Macdonald(Dryden)69e;
WingD2292.

03633, before 1866

E681 Duval, Pierre, 1618-1683.
D983g Geographiæ Universalis Pars Prior [-posterior].
Das ist: Der Allgemeinen. Erd-Beschreibung
Erster [-anderer] Theil/ ... Anfangs in Franzö-
sischer Sprach beschrieben durch P. du Val. Ihrer
Königl. Maj. in Franckreich Geogr. Ordin.
Anjetzo aber ins Teutsche übersetzet/und in dieser
zweyten Edicion an unterschiedlichen Orten/wo es
die Noth erfordert/fast um die Helffte vermehret/
von Johann Christoff Beer.
Nürnberg In Verleg. Johann Hoffmañs Buch-und
Kunsthändlers/Gedruckt daselbst bey Christian
Siegmund Froberg. M.DC.LXXXI.
2 v.: 4 p. ℓ., 566, [2] p. 42 fold. maps; 4 p. ℓ.,
415, 418-449, [1] p. 12 plates (coats of arms),
30 fold. maps. 14cm. 12°
Each vol. has an added t.-p., engraved on two
leaves. Engraved t.-p., v.1, signed: Hipschman
scul.
Transl. from: <u>Le Monde ou La Géographie
Vniuerselle</u>, 1st pub. Paris, 1658. German transl.
1st pub. Nurenberg, 1678.
Vol. 1 covers America, Africa, and Asia;
vol. 2 covers Europe.
The 2 v. of this copy are bound together in 1 v.
Imperfect: p. 347-50 and 443-6, v.1, wanting.
JCB(2)2:1217; Palmer315.

02352, 1851

+Z The English Atlas ...
≡E58 Oxford, Printed at the Theater, for Moses Pitt
1681 ... MDCLXXX - MDCLXXXII.
5 v. 58.5cm. fol.
Imperfect: v.2 only: ... Description of Part of
the Empire of Germany... By William Nicolson,
M.A. Fellow of Queen's College, Oxon. Oxford,
1681.
The work was conceived by Moses Pitt, the
publisher. Bishop William Nicolson and Richard
Peers were generally responsible for the
geographical and historical descriptions.
"Books Printed at the Theatre in Oxford..."
v.2, last p.
Phillips(Atlases)2831, 3032.

05847, before 1923

B681 Escobar Salmeron y Castro, José de, d. 1684.
E74d Discvrso Cometologico, Y Relacion Del Nvevo
Cometa: Visto en aqueste Hemispherio Mexicano, y generalmente en todo el Mundo: el Año
de 1680; Y extinguido en este de 81: Observado,
y Regulado en este mismo Horizonte de Mexico.
Por Joseph De Escobar, Salmeron, Y Castro,

Medico, y Cathedratico de Cirugia, y Anothomia [sic], en esta Real Vniversidad: Dedicado, y Consagrado al gloriosissimo Patriarcha San Joseph, Esposo de Nuestra Señora, y amantissimo Patron de esta Nueva-España.

Con Licencia. En Mexico Por la Viuda de Bernardo Calderon, Año de 1681.

4 p. ℓ., 24 numb. ℓ. illus. 19.5cm. 4⁰

Cut of comet on t.-p.

License (verso 3d p. ℓ.) dated 18 Apr. 1681.

A reply to Carlos de Sigüenza y Góngora. Manifiesto filosófico contra los cometas. Mexico, 1681.

Imperfect: title leaf wanting; available in facsimile.

Palau(2)81248; Medina(Mexico)1224; Sabin75818.

5762, 1909

26 p. ℓ., xvi, 328, [4] p. illus. (engr.), 5 plates (incl. 3 fold.), 4 port., fold. map. 20.5cm. 4⁰

Title in red and black.

Transl. from: De Americaensche Zee-Roovers, Amsterdam, 1678.

The 2d issue; originally issued with text of Dedication shorter.

Preliminary matter includes poetry by the translator and by Miguel de Barrios and Duarte López Rosa.

"Descripcion De las Islas del Mar Athlantico Y De America." (p. i-xvi) - in verse - by Miguel de Barrios.

JCB(2)2:1218; Palau(2)85730; Sabin23471; Medina (BHA)1714; Church667; BLH 6:3194.

03632, before 1866

DA681 E96d
An Exalted Diotrephes Reprehended, Or the Spirit of Error and Envy In William Rogers against the Truth And many of the Antient and Faithful Friends thereof, Manifested in his late Monstrous Birth, or Work of Darkness, (viz.) his False and Scandalous Book, Intituled, The Christian-Quaker Distinguished ... Also a Comparison between his said Book, and many Exhortations and Reproofs, Contained in an Epistle, given forth under his Hand ... To be dispersed only among Friends, unless his Book is made more Publick. ...

London, Printed for John Bringhurst, Printer and Stationer, at the Sign of the Book in Grace-Church-Street. 1681.

48 p. 18.5cm. (19.5cm. in case) 4⁰

Signed: Richard Snead, Charles Harford, Richard Vickris, Charles Jones.

A reply to William Rogers, The Christian-Quaker Distinguished, 1st pub. London, 1680.

WingS4390; Smith(Friends)2:614; McAlpin 4:54.

68-72

BA681 E99h
Ezcaray, Antonio de, fl. 1681-1691.

Hvmilde Desempeño, Qve La Santa Provincia Del Santo Evangelio puso en el cuidado del menor de sus hijos el Padre Fray Antonio De Ezcaray, su Secretario: Natural de la Coronada Villa de Madrid. En las magnificas, y solemnes fiestas que en demonstracion de su afecto, y voto consagra en annuales cultos, al Misterio de la Purissima Concepcion de Maria Señora N. La grande entre las grandes, la Magnifica, y Real Vniversidad de Mexico: En cuya Capilla se predicò el primero Domingo de Quaresma. ...

Con Licencia. En Mexico, por la Viuda de Bernardo Calderon, año de 1681.

7 p. ℓ., 8 numb. ℓ. 19.5cm. 4⁰

License dated (4th p. ℓ.) 14 Apr. 1681.

Palau(2)85867; Medina(Mexico)1223.

69-765

F681 E96p
[Exquemelin, Alexandre Olivier]

Piratas De La America, Y luz à la defensa de las costas de Indias Occidentales. Dedicado A Don Bernardino Antonio De Pardiñas Villar de Francos, ... Por El Zelo Y Cuydado De Don Antonio Freyre, ... Traducido de la lengua Flamenca en Española, por el D^{or}. De Buena-Maison, Medico Practico en la Amplissima y Magnifica Ciudad de Amsterdam.

Impresso en Colonia Agrippina, en Casa de Lorenzo Struickman. Año de 1681.

BA681 E99s
Ezcaray, Antonio de, fl. 1681-1691

Sermon Panegyrico. Desagravios de Christo Vida Nuestra En su Cuerpo Sacramentado. Solemne demostracion, que hizo el Muy Religioso Convento de N. Madre Santa Clara de Mexico. el dia 27. de Abril de este presente año. En la Dominica III. despues de Pasqua. Sv Orador El P. Fr. Antonio de Ezcaray Religioso de N.P.S: Francisco, Secretario de la Provincia del S. Evangelio. Y Natural de la Coronada Villa de Madrid. Quien con rendimiento de hijo, discipulo, y criado. En demostracion de lo mucho que debe Al Ilust.^{mo} y Rev.^{mo} Señor D. Fr. Bartholome Garcia de Escañuela Obispo de

la Nueva-Vizcaya, del Consejo de su Magestad, y su Predicador, &c. Su Señor Padre, y Maestro, affectuoso, y reverente le dedica, y consagra.
 Con Licencia. En Mexico. Por la Viuda de Bernardo Calderon, Año de 1681.
 8 p. l., 9 numb. l. 19.5cm. 4°
 License (recto 7th p. l.) dated: 4 June 1681.
 Palau(2)85868; Medina(Mexico)1222.

1033, 1905

DA681
F791
 Fox, George, 1624-1691.
 Traitté De la Revelation, De la Prophetie, de la mesure, de la regle des Chrestiens Et de l'Inspiration & suffisance de l'Esprit. Par George Fox. Imprimé en Anglois 1676. Et maintenant mis en Francois par une autre personne, pour le bien & avantage du public.
 [Rotterdam?] Imprime [sic] 1681.
 38p. 20.5cm. 4°
 Transl. from: Concerning revelation, prophecy, measure and rule. [London], 1676.
 Signed: George Fox. Des Prisons de Worcestre, le 9. du 11. mois appellé Janvier 1674. ...
 Smith(Friends)1:675.

11439, 1918

EB
-W&A
226a
 France--Sovereigns, etc., 1643-1715 (Louis XIV). 26 July 1681
 Arrest Dv Conseil D'Estat, Portant que conformément à L'Adivdication Faite ce jourd'huy au Conseil: Me Iean Favconnet jouyra des Fermes Generales des Gabelles de France, Aydes, Entrées, Cinq grosses Fermes, & autres Droits y joints, à commencer du premier Octobre 1681. Et de la Ferme generale des Domaines du premier Ianvier 1682. Du vingt-sixiéme Iuillet 1681.
 [Paris] Au Palais, Chez la V. Saugrain, au dernier Pillier de la Grand'Salle, vis à vis la Grand'Chambre, à la Croix d'Or. [1681]
 12 p. 25cm. (32cm. in case). 4°
 Among the taxes granted to this tax farmer is that on "toutes sortes de Tabac en feüilles, cordes, rouleaux, & en poudre, parfumez & non parfumez dans tout le Royaume, Païs & Terres de l'obeïssance de Sa Majesté." (p. 7).

28298, 1938

EB
F8355
1681
1
 France--Laws, statutes, etc., 1643-1715 (Louis XIV). Aug. 1681.
 Ordonnance De Louis XIV. Roy De France Et De Navarre. Donnée à Fontainebleau au mois d'Aoust 1681. Touchant la Marine.
 A Paris, Chez <Denys Thierry, ruë saint Jacques, devant la ruë du Plâtre, à la Ville de Paris. Et Christophle Ballard, ruë S. Jean de Beauvais, au Mont Parnasse. M. DC. LXXXI. Avec Privilege de sa Majesté.
 4 p. l., 273, [53] p. 24.5cm. 4°
 Registration dated (p. 273) 8 Jan. 1682.
 In this copy the leaf bearing p. 15-16 is a cancel.
 "Explication des termes de Marine": p. [31-53] at end.
 Wroth&Annan227; Actes Royaux 15237.

69-17

BA681
F954e
 Fuenlabrada, Nicolás de, fl. 1681.
 Oracion Evangelica, Y Panegyrica Relacion, De Las Glorias, Y Maravillas grandes de la Soberana Reyna de los Angeles Maria Santissima Señora N. en su milagrosissima Imagen, del Español Gvadalvpe, en la Estremadura. Por el P. Fr. Nicolas De Fvenlabrada, indigno hijo de la muy Ilustre, y Religiosa Provincia del Santissimo Nombre de Jesvs, de esta Nueva-España; Lector de Theologia en el Convento de N. P. S. Augustin de Mexico. Predicose, en la Fiesta, que consagrò à la Magestad de tan Augusta Princesa, vn su Devoto; con ocasion de aver logrado su solicitud, devocion, y desvelo, vn Trasunto de tan Sagrada Reyna, tocado à su prodigiosissimo, y veneradissimo Original, que vino en esta presente Flota, del año de 1680. y quedò colocado en la Iglesia de dicho Convento de N. P. S. Augustin de Mexico; donde se solemniçò, y celebrò su venida, el dia 12. de Enero, de este año de 1681. La Dominica infra octavam, de la Epiphania del Señor. Dedicala humilde, y rendido, la ofrece, à las Soberanas plantas de tan Suprema Emperatriz (con el mismo Titulo de Gvadalvpe) en su terreno Parayso, ò en su escogido, y sin segundo florido cielo Mexicano.
 Con Licencia. En Mexico, por la Viuda de Bernardo Calderon. [1681]
 7 p. l., 19 numb. l. pl. 20.5cm. 4°
 License (verso 6th p. l.) dated 8 Mar. 1681.
 Imperfect: l. 19 wanting.
 Palau(2)95236; Medina(Mexico)1225; Santiago Vela 2:685-86.

1035, 1905

DA681 [Godwin, Morgan] fl. 1685.
G592s   A Supplement To The Negro's & Indian's Advocate: Or, Some further Considerations and Proposals for the effectual and speedy carrying on of the Negro's Christianity in our Plantations (Notwithstanding the late pretended Impossibilities) without any prejudice to their Owners. By M. G. A Presbyter of the Church of England. ...
    London Printed by J.[ohn] D.[arby] 1681.
    12 p. 18.5cm. 4°
    This copy is closely trimmed with some effect on side-notes and direction-lines.
    JCB(2)2:1231; Sabin27678; WingG973; Torrence87.
03635, before 1866   rev

F681   Grotius, Hugo, 1583-1645.
-G881h   Hugo De Groots Nederlandtsche Jaerboeken En Historien, Sedert het jaer M D L V tot het jaer M D C I X; Met De Belegering Der Stadt Grol en den aenkleven des jaers M DC XXVII; Als ook het Tractaet van De Batavische Nu Hollandtsche Republyk En De Vrye Zeevaert, Met Aenteeckeningen: Voorts met het Leven des Schrijvers, twee volkomen Registers, en veele koopere Platen verciert. Alles Vertaelt door Joan Goris.
    t' Amsterdam, By de Weduwe van Joannes van Someren, Abraham Wolfgangk en Hendrik en Dirk Boom, M DC LXXXI.
    22 p.ℓ., 591, [76], 19 p., 3 ℓ., 34 p., 4 ℓ., 43-74 p. 22 fold. plates, 20 ports., 5 fold. plans. 33cm. fol.
    Added t.-p., engr.
    Title in red and black. Printer's device (Bibliotheca belgica II 19 (Amsterdam) Someren 1) on t.-p.
    Imperfect: added t.-p. and all illus. except 1 plan wanting; available in facsim.
    Bound in contemporary vellum.
    Contents:
    "Nederlandtsche jaerboeken en historien" (22 p.ℓ., 591, [76] p.). Transl. (with some modification of prelims.) from Annales et historiae de rebus Belgicus, 1st pub. Amsterdam, 1657.
    "Beleegeringh der stadt Grol" (19 p., with special half-title and separate paging and signatures). Transl. from Grollae obsidio, 1st pub. Amsterdam, 1629.
    "Verhandelingh van de oudheit der Batavische ... republyke" (3 ℓ., 34 p., with special half-title and separate paging and signatures). Transl. from Liber de antiquitate reipublicae Bataviae, 1st pub. Leyden, 1610.

"Vrye see" (4 ℓ., 43-74 p., with special half-title but paging and signatures continued from the preceding). Transl. from Mare liberum, 1st pub. Leyden, 1609.
    Ter Meulen-Diermanse749(724, 704, 558).
12844, 1920   rev

DA681   [Hickeringill, Edmund] 1631-1708.
-H628n   The Naked Truth. The Second Part. In Several Inquiries Concerning the Canons And Ecclesiastical Jurisdiction, Canonical Abedience, Convocations, Procurations, Synodals and Visitations: Also Of The Church of England, And Church-wardens, And The Oath of Church-wardens. And Of Sacriledge. The Second Edition Corrected and Amended. ...
    London, Printed for Francis Smith, and are to be Sold at his Shop, at the Elephant and Castle near the Royal Exchange in Cornhill. 1681.
    2 p.ℓ., 36 p. 32cm. (33cm. in case). fol.
    First pub. London, 1681.
    Signed (p. 36): "I hereby allow ... Francis Smith ... to Print my Book, Entituled, The Naked Truth, the Second Part. Colchester, November 2d. 1680. Edmund Hiceringill."
    "... title suggested by 'The Naked Truth', 1675, by Herbert Croft ... with which it has nothing in common." -cf. DNB26:348.
    WingH1822; McAlpin4:59.
05116, before 1874

DA681   [Hickeringill, Edmund] 1631-1708.
-H628v   A Vindication Of The Naked Truth, The Second Part: Against The Trivial Objections and Exceptions (Of one Fullwood; (Stiling himself) D.D. Archdeacon of Totnes in Devonshire) In A Libelling Pamphlet With A Bulky and Imboss'd Title (Calling it) Leges Angliæ, Or, The Lawfulness of Ecclesiastical Jurisdiction In The Church of England: In Answer to Mr. Hickeringill's Naked Truth, the Second Part. By Phil. Hickeringill.
    London, Printed for Richard Janeway in Queens-head-Alley in Pater-noster Row, 1681.
    2 p.ℓ., 36 p. 31cm. fol.
    A reply to: Fullwood, Francis. Leges Angliæ. London, 1681, itself a reply to: Hickeringill, Edmund. The naked truth. The second part. London, 1681.
    WingH1832.
68-487

FC650 H737 31	Hollandse Mercurius, Verhalende de voornaemste Saecken van Staet, En andere Voorvallen, Die, in en omtrent de Vereenigde Nederlanden, En elders, In het Jaer 1680, Zijn geschiedt. Het Een-en-dertigste Deel. Tot Haerlem, Gedruckt, by Abraham Casteleyn, Stadts Drucker, op de Marckt, in de Blye Druck, Anno 1681. 3 p.ℓ., 219, [220-224] p. 2 plates. 20cm. 4° (Bound in [vol. 7] of Hollandse Mercurius) Added t.-p., engraved: Hollantse Mercurius By Abraham Casteleyn tot Haerlem A° 1681 JCB(3)2:410; Sabin32523.
8487EE, 1912	

B681 K56e	Kino, Eusebio Francisco, 1644-1711. Exposicion Astronomica De El Cometa, Que el Año de 1680. por los meses de Noviembre, y Diziembre, y este Año de 1681. por los meses de Enero y Febrero, se ha visto en todo el mundo, y le ha observado en la Ciudad de Cadiz, El P. Eusebio Francisco Kino De la Compañia de Jesvs. Con Licencia, en Mexico por Francisco Rodriguez Lupercio. 1681. 8 p.ℓ., 28 numb. ℓ. fold. chart. 20cm. (22 cm. in case). Cut (Virgin Mary) on t.-p. Licenses (5th-6th p.ℓ.) dated 24 Sept 1681. A reply to Sigüenza y Góngora, Carlos de. Manifiesto philosóphico contra los cometas, Mexico, 1681. Bound in contemporary vellum.
Me681 Y91d Print	———— ————Chart: Delineacion Y Dibvjo De Las Constelaciones Y Partes Del Cielo Por Donde Discvrrio El G^randioso Cometa ... Signed: Anto^o. Ysarti. Palau 128015; Medina(Mexico)1228; Backer 4:1044; Sabin37936; cf. Wagner p. 291; Streit 2:2155.
05742, 1909	

EA681 M334ℓ	Marie de l'Incarnation, mère, 1599-1672. Lettres De La Venerable Mere Marie De L'Incarnation Premiere Superieure Des Ursulines De La Nouvelle France, Divisées en deux Parties. A Paris, Chez Louis Billaine, au second Pillier de la grande Salle du Palais, au grand Cesar. M. DC. LXXXI. Avec Approbation des Docteurs, & Privilege de Sa Majesté. 5 p.ℓ., 675, [1] p. front. (port.) 25.5cm. 4° Cut on t.-p. "Achevé d'imprimer pour la premiere fois, le 5. jour de Mai 1681." (last page). Compiled and edited by Claude Martin. Pt. 1. Les lettres spirituelles. -Pt. 2. Les lettres historiques. Bound in contemporary calf. Sabin44562; Streit2:2711; Harrisse(NF)148.
05125, 1890	

B681 M385c	Martínez de la Puente, José, fl. 1681. Compendio De Las Historias De Los Descvbrimientos, Conqvistas, Y Gverras De La India Oriental, y sus Islas ... Con Privilegio En Madrid, En la Imprenta Imperial: Por la Viuda de Ioseph Fernandez de Buendia. Año de 1681. 8 p.ℓ., 288, 287-380, [34] p. 20cm. 4° Title in red and black Errata, p.ℓ. 6. "Suma de la Tassa" (p.ℓ. 6) dated 10 Jan 1681. Includes mention of the discovery of Brazil. Palau(2)155609; Sabin44953; Borba de Moraes 2:25.
63-103 rev	

BA681 -M519t	Meléndez, Juan, fl. 1681. Tesoros Verdaderos De Las Yndias En la Historia de la gran Prouincia De San Ivan Bavtista Del Perv De el Orden de Predicadores ... Por El Maestro F. Ivan Melendez Natural de Lima, Hijo de la misma Prouincia, y Sv Coronista ... En Roma, En la Imprenta de Nicolas Angel Tinassio. M. DC. LXXXI [-M. DC. LXXXII]. Con Licencia De Los Svperiores. 3 v.: v.1, 24 p.ℓ., 643, [644-667] p. fold. pl., port., fold. plan; v.2, 14 p.ℓ., 669, [670-688] p.; v.3, 18 p.ℓ., 857, [858-876] p. 30cm. fol. Imprint dated: v.2, 1681; v.3, 1682. Titles in red and black. Cut (coat of arms) on each t.-p. Each vol. has added t.-p., engr. Preliminary matter of each vol. includes poetry. In v.1 license dated (8th p.ℓ.^v) 7 Mar. 1681; in v.2 "Censura" dated (7th p.ℓ.^v) 6 Sept. 1681; in v.3 "Censura" dated (10th p.ℓ.^v) 6 May 1682. Imperfect: port., v.1, and engraved title-pages, v.1 and v.2, wanting; available in facsim. JCB(2)2:1220; Medina(BHA)1717; Palau(2)160165; Sabin47423; Zegarra212.
05669, before 1874 rev	

F681 Melton, Edward, pseud.?
M528e   Eduward Meltons, Engelsch Edelmans, Zeldzaame en Gedenkwaardige Zee- en Land-Reizen; Door Egypten, West-Indien, Perzien, Turkyen, Oost-Indien, en d'aangrenzende Gewesten ... Aangevangen in den jaare 1660. en geëindigd in den jaare 1677. Vertaald uit d'eigene Aanteekeningen en Brieven van den gedagten Heer Melton...
    t' Amsterdam, By Jan Ten Hoorn, Boek-verkooper over 't Oude Heeren-Logement, Anno 1681.
    4 p. ℓ., 495, [7] p. 18 plates (part. fold.), port. 20.5cm. 4⁰
    Added t.-p., engraved: Edward Meltons Zee-en Land, Reizen, Door verscheide Gewesten des Werelds.
    Cut (printer's monogram) on t.-p.
    A compilation of accounts from various sources, attributed by Tiele to Gotfried van Broekhuizen.
    The part relating to Egypt has been identified as a translation of Johann Michael Wansleben's Nouvelle relation en forme de iournal, d'un voyage fait en Egypte (1st pub. Paris, 1677). The part relating to New Netherland is an abridgment of Adriaen van der Donck's Beschrijvinge van Nieuw-Nederlant (1st pub. Amsterdam, 1655), with the introduction to that part being taken from Arnoldus Montanus' De nieuwe en onbekende weereld (1st pub. Amsterdam, 1671). The account of the West Indies is in part taken from Alexandre Olivier Exquemelin's De Americaensche Zee-Roovers (1st pub. Amsterdam, 1678).
    JCB(2)2:1221; Sabin47472; Asher16; Muller (1872)960; Tiele738; Scheepvaart Mus.118.
02838, 1861 rev

C681 Notice Et Justification Du Tiltre [sic], & bonne
N912e2 foy avec laquelle l'on a estably, la nouvelle Colonie du Sacrement de S. Vincent en la Situation appellée de S. Gabriel, sur les bords du Rio de la Pratta. Traitté Provisionel sur le nouvel incident, causé par le Gouverneur de Buenos Ayres, ajusté en cette cour de Lisbonne par le Duc de Jovenase, Prince de Chelemar, Ambassadeur Extraordinaire du Roy Catholique, avec les Plenipotentiaires de Son Altesse, approuvé, ratifié & confirmé, par les deux Princes.
    [Amsterdam] Suivant le Copie De Lisbonne, Avec les Privileges necessaires, A l'Imprimerie d'Antoine Craesbeck de Mello, Imprimeur de la Maison Royale, l'An 1681.
    129 p. 14cm. 12⁰
    Transl. from: Noticia e Iustificaçam do titulo, e boa fee com que se obrou a Nova Colonia Do Sacramento. Lisboa, 1681.

    Ratification dated (p. 125) 13 June 1681.
    JCB(2)2:1223; JCBAR35:49-50; Borba de Moraes 2:105; Sabin74790; Palau(2)193366.
03630, before 1866

C681 Noticia, E Ivstificaçam Do Titvlo, E Boa Fee
-N912e1 Com Qve Se Obrou A Nova Colonia Do Sacramento, Nas Terras Da Capitania De S. Vicente, No Sitio Chamado De S. Gabriel Nas Margens Do Rio Da Prata. E Tratado Provisional Sobre O Novo Incidente cauzado pelo Governador de Buenos Ayres, ajustado nesta Corte de Lisboa pelo Duque de Iovenaso Principe de Chelemar Embaxador Extraordinario de El Rey Catholico, com os Plenipotenciarios de Sua Alteza: approvado, ratificado, & confirmado por ambos os Principes.
    Em Lisboa. Com as licenças necessarias. Na Impressaõ de Antonio Craesbeeck de Mello Impressor da Casa Real Anno 1681.
    1 p. ℓ., 34, [12] p. 30cm. fol.
    Ratification dated (p. [11]) 13 June 1681.
    Borba de Moraes records a variant with the same imprint whose title reads: Noticia, E Iustificaçam Do Titulo ...
    With, as issued: Portugal--Treaties, etc.--1656-1683 (Alfonso VI), Dom Pedro Por Graça De Deos Principe De Portugal ... Tratado Provisional... [Lisboa, 1681], which is separately signed.
    JCBAR35:49-50; Sabin56001; cf. Borba de Moraes 2:104.
16732, 1935 rev

B681 Olmo, José Vicente del, 1611-1696.
-O51n   Nveva Descripcion Del Orbe De La Tierra. En Qve Se Trata De Todas Svs Partes Interiores, Y Exteriores, Y Circvlos De La Esphera, Y De La Inteligencia, Vso, Y Fabrica De Los Mapas, Y Tablas Geographicas, Assi Vniversales, Y Genralles [sic], Como Particvlares. Explicanse Svs Diferencias, Se Corrigen Los Errores, Y Imperfecciones De Las Antigvas, Y Se Añaden Otras Modernas. Con La Fabrica, Y Vso Del Globo Terrestre Artificial, Y De Las Cartas De Navegar. Tocanse Mvchas, Y Varias Cvriosidades De Philosophia Natvral, Y De Historia Sagrada, Y Profana, Con Las Noticias, Y Fvndamentos De La Chronologia, Y Origen, Y Principio De Las Mas Principales Eras, Y Epochas Del Mvndo. Dedicada Al Rey Nvestro Señor D. Carlos Segvndo Monarca De España. Por Ioseph Vicente Del Olmo Secretario Del Santo Oficio De La Inqvisicion De Valencia.

En Valencia: Por Ioan Lorenço Cabrera Año 1681.
14 p.ℓ., 590, [27] p. illus. (tables, diagrs.). 30cm. fol.
In this copy a printed label pasted in line 9 of the t.-p. corrects "Genralles" [sic] to read "Generales".
Added t.-p., engr.
"Censura" dated (7th p.ℓ.ᵛ) 26 Feb. 1675.
"De La America" p. 427-430.
Bound in contemporary calf.
Palau(2)201032; Sabin57230; Medina(BHA)1721.

11716, 1918

H681
P287g
Passerone, Lodovico, fl. 1674.
Gvida Geografica Ouero Compendiosa Descrittione Del Globo Terreno Premessa vna breue notitia di tutto l'Uniuerso. Di D. Lodovico Passerone Di Lantosca Dottor d'Ambe le Leggi. Ampliata d'Aggiunte. Dal Sig. Carlo Assonica Dottor. Dedicata Al Molt' Illustre Signor il Signor Gio: Battista Castelli.
In Venetia, M.D.C. LXXXI. Per Iseppo Prodocimo. Con Licenza de' Superiori, e Priuilegio.
6 p.ℓ., 321 [i.e.322], [10] p. illus. 14.5cm. 12°
Previously pub. Bologna, 1674.
Dedication dated (verso 5th p.ℓ.): 29. Marzo 1681.
In this copy there is a blank leaf following p. 321 [i.e.322] and at end.
"Dell' America": p. 303-321 [i.e.322].
Bound in contemporary vellum.

12765, 1920

DA681
P412e
Penn, William, 1644-1718.
A Brief Examination and State Of Liberty Spiritual, Both With Respect to Persons in their Private Capacity, and in their Church Society and Communion. Written for the Establishment of the Faithful, Information of the Simple-Hearted, and Reproof of the Arrogant and High Minded, by a Lover of True Liberty, as it is in Jesus, William Penn. ...
London, Printed by Andrew Sowle, and sold at his Shop in Devonshire Buildings, without Bishops-Gate, 1681.
2 p.ℓ., 15 p. 19cm. 4°.
Signed: William Penn. Warninghurst in Sussex, the 20th of the 9th Moneth, 1681.
Smith(Friends)2:298; McAlpin4:71; WingP1260.

11348, 1918

D681
P412k
[Penn, William] 1644-1718.
Een kort Bericht Van de Provintie ofte Landschap Penn-Sylvania genaemt, leggende in America; Nu onlangs onder het groote Zegel van Engeland gegeven aan William Penn, &c. Mitsgaders Van de Privilegien, ende Macht om het selve wel te Regeeren. Uyt het Engels overgeset na de Copye tot Londen gedrukt by Benjamin Clark, Boekverkooper in George Yard Lombardstreet, 1681. ... Als mede, De Copye van een Brief by den selven W. P. geschreven aan zekere Regeeringe Anno 1675. tegens de Vervolginge en voor de Vryheyt van Conscientie, aan alle &c.
Tot Rotterdam, Gedrukt by Pieter Van Wynbrugge, Boek-Drukker in de Leeuwestraat, in de Wereld Vol-Druk. Anno 1681.
24 p. 20.5cm. 4°
Translated by Benjamin Furly from Penn's Some account of ... Pennsylvania, London, 1681, and Christian liberty, 1st pub. London, 1675.
JCB(2)2:1227; Sabin59710; Vail(Front.)196; Kane(Promotion)7.

02306, 1853   rev

D681
P412n
[Penn, William] 1644-1718.
Eine Nachricht wegen der Landschaft Pennsilvania in America: Welche Jüngstens unter dem Grossen Siegel in Engelland an William Penn, &c. Sambt den Freyheiten und der Macht/so zu behöriger guten Regierung verselben nötig/übergeben worden/... Aus dem in London gedrucktem und aldar bey Benjamin Clarck, Buchhändlern in George-Yard Lombard-street befindlichem Englischen übergesetzet. Nebenst beygefügtem ehemaligem im 1675. Jahr gedrucktem Schreiben des oberwehnten Will. Penns.
In Amsterdam/gedruckt bey Christoff Cunraden, Im Jahr 1681.
31 p. 18.5cm. 4°
Translated from his Some account of ... Pennsilvania, London, 1681, and his Christian Liberty, 1st pub. London, 1675.
Translated probably by Jan Claus.
Includes "Eine kurtze Ausslegung etlicher Englischen Wörter/so hierinnen vorkommen/..." (p. 29-31).
JCB(2)2:1226; Sabin59719; Vail(Front.)197; Kane(Promotion)6; Palmer371.

03629, before 1866   rev

Blathwayt
15
[R]
[Penn, William] 1644-1718.
Reader, The Intention of this Map, is to give an account of some of the Province of Pennsylvania in America ...

[London, 1681]
1 strip. 20.5 x 56.5cm. (Issued as a part of <u>A Map of Some of the South and east bounds of Pennsylvania</u>, London, J. Thornton and J. Seller [1681]).
Title from beginning of text.
The text is printed (on the face only of the strip). The strip is pasted along the bottom edge of the map.
See <u>A Note on the William Penn map of Pennsylvania (London, 1681): to accompany the facsimile issued by the John Carter Brown Library</u>, Providence, R.I., 1943.
Baer(Md.)100; Phillips(Maps)670; Vail(Front.) 198n.
8181, 1911

D681
-P412s
[Penn, William] 1644-1718.
Some Account Of The Province Of Pennsilvania In America; Lately Granted under the Great Seal Of England To William Penn, &c. Together with Priviledges and Powers necessary to the well-governing thereof. Made publick for the Information of such as are or may be disposed to Transport themselves or Servants into those parts.
London: Printed, and Sold by Benjamin Clark Bookseller in George-Yard Lombard-street, 1681.
1 p.ℓ., 10 p. 29.5cm. fol.
Signed (p. 10): William Penn.
JCB(1)2:902; JCB(2)2:1225; Sabin59733; Church 671; Smith(Friends)2:297; Vail(Front)195; Kane (Promotion)1; WingP1365.
0530, 1846

C681
-N912e1
Portugal--Treaties, etc., 1668-1706 (Pedro II).
Dom Pedro Por Graça De Deos, Principe De Portugal, & dos Algarves daquem, & dalém, mar em Africa Senhor de Guiné, & da Cõquista, navegaçaõ, comercio da Ethiopia, Arabia Persia, & da India, &c. ... Faço saber aos q esta minha Carta patente, & de approvaçaõ, ratificaçaõ, & confirmaçaõ virè, que nesta Cidade de Lisboa, em os sete dias do mez de Mayo deste anno presente de mil, seiscentos, outenta, & hum, se ajustou concluio, & assinou hum Tratado provisional, feito entre Mim ... & o muito Alto, & Serenissimo Principe D. Carlos Segundo Rey Catholico das Espanhas ...
[Lisboa, 1681]
[12] p. 30cm. fol. (Issued as a part of <u>Noticia e iustificaçam do titulo e boa feé...</u>, Lisboa, 1681.)

Title from beginning of text.
Concerns Colonia del Sacramento.
Ratification dated (p. [11]) 13 June 1681.
JCBAR35:49-50; Sabin56001; cf. Borba de Moraes 2:104.
16732A, 1935

D681
P895p
The Practick Part Of the Office of A Justice of the Peace: Containing Precedents Upon Acts of Parliament. As Also Appeals, Informations, Indictments, And other Proceedings relating to the Office of a Justice of the Peace. Clerk of the Peace, And Clerk of Indictments, Either within, or out of the Sessions of the Peace.
London, Printed for George Downs at the Three Flower de Luces over against St. Dunstans-Church in Fleet-street, 1681.
2 p.ℓ., 372, 22 p. 15cm. 12°
In this copy there is a blank leaf at end.
Wing P3147.
16804, 1935

B681
R672
Rocha, Diego Andrés, 1607-1688.
Tratado Vnico, Y Singvlar Del Origen De Los Indios Occidentales del Piru, Mexico, Santa Fè, y Chile. Por El Doctor Don Diego Andres Rocha Oydor de la Real Audiencia de Lima. Dedicalo A La Proteccion Del señor Doctor D. Ioseph del Corral, Calvo de la Vanda, Oydor de la misma Audiencia.
Año de 1681. Con Licencia En Lima; En la Imprenta de Manuel de los Olivos, Por Ioseph de Contreras.
7 p.ℓ., 84 numb. ℓ., [24] p., 15 numb. ℓ. illus. 20cm. 4°
Cut on t.-p.
License (3d p.ℓ.ᵛ) dated 23 Apr. 1681.
"Copia De Carta Qve El Avtor Escrivio A Sv Hijo El General Don Iuan Enriquez de Sanguesa, Residente en la Villa de Cochabamba, donde fue Corregidor Iusticia Mayor, sobre el Cometa del año de 1680": p. [1-16].
Some copies are found with verse encomia of the author (7th p.ℓ.; present this copy) and with "Adiciones A Los Capitvlos Del Origen De Los Indios por su Autor" (15 numb. ℓ. at end); "Adiciones" wanting in this copy, available in facsim.
JCB(2)2:1229; Palau(2)271817; Medina (Lima)526; Sabin72290.
0520, 1846

E681 [Rochefort, Charles de] b. 1605.
R674h Histoire Naturelle Et Morale Des Iles Antilles De L'Amerique... Avec un Vocabulaire Caraïbe. Derniere Edition. Reveuë & augmentée par l'Autheur d'un Recit de l'Estat present des celebres Colonies de la Virginie, de Marie-Land, de la Caroline, du nouveau Duché d'York, de Penn-Sylvania, & de la nouvelle Angleterre, situées dans l'Amerique septentrionale, & qui relevent de la Couronne du Roy de la grand' Bretagne. Tiré fidelement des memoires des habitans des mêmes Colonies, en faveur de ceus, qui auroyent le dessein de s'y transporter pour s'y établir.
A Rotterdam, Chez Reinier Leers, M.DC.LXXXI.
18 p.ℓ., 583, [584-596], 43 p. illus. 3 fold. plates. 24cm. 4°
Added t.-p., engraved: Histoire Naturelle Et Morale Des Iles Antilles de l'Amerique. Derniere Edition reveuë et augmentée. A Rotterdam, Chez Reinier Leers, 1681.
Cut on t.-p., incl. motto: Labore Et Vigilantia.
First pub. Rotterdam, 1658. These are the same sheets as the Rotterdam, 1665, ed. except that the 1st gathering, a⁴, has been reprinted. The same plate was used for the added t.-p., revised for this edition.
With, as issued for this ed., his Recit de l'estat present des celebres colonies, Rotterdam, 1681, with special t.-p., and separate paging and signatures.
Dedication signed (recto 8th p.ℓ.): De Rochefort.
Preliminary matter by Louis de Poincy, de Valcroissant and Edward Graves, 13th-18th p.ℓ.
"Vocabulaire Caraïbe" by Raimond Breton: p. 571-583.
Bound in contemporary calf.
JCB(2)2:1230; Sabin72318; Pilling3349.

01910, 1854

E681 [Rochefort, Charles de] b. 1605.
R674h Recit De L'Estat Present Des Celebres Colonies De la Virginie, de Marie-Land, de la Caroline, du nouveau Duché d'York, de Penn-Sylvania, & de la nouvelle Angleterre, situées dans l'Amerique septentrionale, entre les trente deuxiéme & quarante sixiéme degrés de l'élevation du Pole du Nord, & établies sous les auspices, & l'autorité souveraine du Roy de la grand'Bretagne. Tiré fidelement des memoires des habitans des mêmes Colonies, en faveur de ceus, qui auroyent le dessein de s'y transporter & de s'y établir.
A Rotterdam, Chez Reinier Leers, M.DC.LXXXI.
43 p. 24cm. 4° (Issued as a part of his Histoire Naturelle Et Morale Des Iles Antilles De L'Amerique... Derniere Edition. Rotterdam, 1681.)
Cut on t.-p., incl. motto: Labore Et Vigilantia.
JCB(2)2:1230; Sabin72318.

01910A, 1854

bB681 Ronquillo, Pedro, b. 1635.
R774ℓ The Last Memorial Of The Spanish Ambassa-
[R] dor, Faithfully Translated into English.
London, Printed for Francis Smith at the Elephant and Castle near the Royal Exchange in Cornhil. 1681.
[2] p. 28.5cm. folio.
Caption title; imprint at end.
A protest of violations of the Treaty of Nijmegen by France, appealing for English support.
Wing R1916.

932, 1905

B681 Sandoval, Prudencio de, Bp. of Pamplona,
-S218h ca. 1560-1620.
[R] Historia de la Vida y Hechos Del Emperador Carlos V. Maximo, Fortissimo, Rey Catholico de España, y de las Indias, Islas, y Tierra Firme del Mar Oceano, &c. Por El Maestro Fray Prvdencio De Sandoval Su Coronista, Obispo De Pamplona. Nueva Impression...
En Amberes. Por Geronymo Verdussen, Impressor, y Mercader de Libros. Año M.DC.LXXXI.
2 v.: 12 p.ℓ., 672, [18] p. incl. coat of arms. fold. pl., 26 ports.; 2 p.ℓ., 674, [10] p. 4 fold. plates, 24 ports. 33cm. fol.
Cut (printer's device) on t.-p. (Peeters-Fontainas, 111).
Vol. 1 has an added engr. t.-p., signed: J. Lamorlet delin. Vol. 2 has an engr. t.-p. only.
Title (v.1) in red and black.
Dedication (v.1, 3d-4th p.ℓ.ᵛ) by Jérôme Verdussen.
Preliminary matter, v.2, includes poetry by Juan de Salcedo.
Approbation dated (v.1, p. [18] at end) 12 April 1676.
First pub. Valladolid, 1604-1606.
Bound in contemporary calf.
In this copy there is a blank leaf at end, v.1.
Sabin76427; Palau(2)297150; Peeters-Fontainas (1965)1160.

70-262

BA681　　Santoyo, Felipe de.
S237p　　　Panegyrica Dedicacion De El Templo, Para la
mejor Heroyna de las Montañas Sancta Isabel,
Mistica Cibeles de la Iglesia, Qve Al glorioso
Apostol Patron de las Españas Santiago Consagra
en musico concento que pulsò la lyra de su Musa,
D. Felipe De Santoyo Garcia, Galan, Y Con-
treras. Natural de la Ciudad de Toledo.
　　　Con licencia: en Mexico por Francisco Rodri-
guez Lupercio 1681.
　　　5 p. ℓ., [45] p. 20cm. 4º
　　　In verse.
　　　Approbation dated (3d p. ℓ.ᵛ) 2 Oct. 1681.
　　　Preliminary matter (poetry) by Francisco
Acevedo and Nicolas Portillo, 4th p. ℓ.
　　　Palau(2)301044; Medina(Mexico)1234; Sabin76894.

15653, 1930

BA681　　Sariñana y Cuenca, Isidro, 1630?-1696.
S245o　　　Oracion Fvnebre, Qve Dixo El Doctor D.
Ysidro Sariñana, Y Cvenca Chantre de la Santa
Iglesia Metropolitana de Mexico, Cathedratico
de Prima de Sagrada Escritura en la Real Vni-
versidad, Calificador del Tribunal del Santo
Officio de la Inquisicion, y Examinador Synodal
del Arçobispado. El dia 20. de Março de 1681.
Presente el Ex.ᵐᵒ Señor Marquès de la Laguna,
Conde de Paredes, Virrey desta Nueva-España.
En las Exequias de veinte y vn Religiosos de la
Regular Observancia del Seraphico P. S. Fran-
cisco, que murieron à manos de los Indios
Apostatas de la Nueva-Mexico, en diez de Agosto
del Año de 1680. Imprimela, y Dedicala à la
Catholica, y Real Magestad de el Rey N. Señor
D. Carlos Segvndo (que Dios guarde.) El R. P.
Predicador Fr. Francisco Ayeta, Custodio
habitual de aquella Custodia, actual Visitador de
ella, y Comissario General del Santo Officio de
la Inquisicion de la Nueva-España.
　　　Con Licencia. En Mexico, por la Viuda de
Bernardo Calderon, año de 1681.
　　　6 p. ℓ., 13 numb. ℓ. 19cm. (21cm. in case) 4º
　　　Dedication dated (3d p. ℓ.) 10 Apr. 1681.
　　　Palau(2)302137; Medina(Mexico)1235; Wagner54;
Streit2:2151.

28577, 1940

BA681　　Sedeño, Gregorio.
S447d　　　Descripciō De Las Funerales Exequias, Y
Sermon, que en ellas se predicó en la muerte
de la muy Noble, y piadosa Señora Doña Jacinta
de Vidarte, y Pardo, que se hizieron en el Con-
vento de Nuestro Padre Santo Domingo, Lunes
veinte y cinco de Agosto de este año de 1681. ...
Predicolo El Mvy Reuerendo P. Presentado Fray
Gregorio Sedeño, Lector de Sagrada Theologia
de dicha Religion.
　　　Con Licencia, En la Puebla de los Angeles,
en la Imprenta de la Viuda de Iuan de Borja, y
Gandia. Año de 1681.
　　　7 p. ℓ., 20 numb. ℓ., [1] p. illus. 20cm. 4º
　　　License dated (6th p. ℓ.ʳ) 15 Sept. 1681.
　　　Includes poetry (numb. ℓ. 5ᵛ-8ʳ).
　　　Page [1] at end consists entirely of woodcut
illus.
　　　In this copy some side-notes are shaved.

BA681　　————Another copy. 20cm.
S447d　　　Imperfect: 1st and last leaves wanting.
cop.2　　　Palau(2)305687; Medina(Puebla)76; Sabin78766.
69-1070
1034, 1905 rev

DA681　　Songhurst, John, d. 1688.
S698e　　　An Epistle Of Love And Tender Good Will To
the Called of God, that have in any measure
answered their Call. ... By ... John Songhurst. ...
　　　London, Printed by Andrew Sowle, and sold at
his Shop in Devonshire New-buildings, without
Bishops-Gate, 1681.
　　　23 p. 18.5cm. 4º
　　　Dated (p. 23): the 20th of the 2d Moneth, 1679.
　　　WingS4686; Smith(Friends)2:615.

12518, 1920

BB　　　Spain--Consejo de las Indias.
-S7329　　　Ordenanzas Del Consejo Real De Las Indias.
1681　　Nvevamente Recopiladas, Y Por El Rey Don
1　　　Felipe Qvarto N.S. Para Sv Govierno, Establecí-
das Año de M.DC.XXXVI.
　　　En Madrid: Por Ivlian De Paredes, Año de 1681.
　　　206, [14] p. 29.5cm. fol.
　　　Cut (coat of arms of the Council) on t.-p.,
signed: Pº perete. escul. Madrid. 1636.
　　　First pub. Madrid, 1636.
　　　JCB(2)2:1224; Medina(BHA)1722.

01519, 1847

BB　　　Spain--Laws, statutes, etc.
-S7333　　　Recopilacion De Leyes De Los Reynos De Las
1681　　Indias. Mandadas Imprimir, Y Pvblicar Por La

Magestad Catolica Del Rey Don Carlos II. Nvestro Señor. Va Dividida En Qvatro Tomos, con el Indice general, y al principio de cada Tomo el Indice especial de los titulos, que contiene. ...
En Madrid: Por Ivlian De Paredes, Año de 1681.
4 v.: v.1, 6 p.ℓ., 299 numb. ℓ.; v.2, 3 p.ℓ., 298 numb. ℓ.; v.3, 3 p.ℓ., 302 numb. ℓ.; v.4, 2 p.ℓ., 145, 144-364 numb. ℓ. 34cm. fol.
Cut (coat of arms of the Council of the Indies) on title-pages; engraved by Gregorius Fosman.
A compilation of the laws of the Indies, prepared chiefly by Antonio Rodríguez de León Pinelo, was completed in 1635. This remained in ms. until brought up to date and edited for this publication by Fernando Jiménez Paniagua.
Errata: v.1, 4 p.ℓ.^{v}; v.2, 3d p.ℓ.^{v}; v.3, 3d p.ℓ.^{v}; v.4, 2 p.ℓ.^{v}.
License (v.1, 2d p.ℓ.) dated 1 Nov. 1681.
Bound in contemporary limp vellum.
JCB(2)2:1228; Sabin 68386; Palau(2)137461; Harrisse(BAV)p. 395-396; Streit 1:684.
0521-0524, 1846 rev

bBB
S7336
1681
2
Spain--Sovereigns, etc., 1665-1700 (Charles II)
17 Dec 1679
El Rey Por quanto el Rey mi señor, y abuelo (que santa gloria aya) mandò dar, y dio en quinze de Julio del año de mil y seiscientos y veinte, vno cedula, cuyo tenor es como se sigue. ...
[Lima, 1681]
[4] p. 31.5 x 21.5cm. fol.
Title from caption and beginning of text.
Interprets the decree of 15 July 1620 to disqualify for judicial office in Spanish America anyone indebted to the Treasury; occasioned by an incident involving Miguel Hurtado of Cuzco.
Dated in Buen Retiro, 17 Dec 1679.
Manuscript certificate dated in Lima, 31 July 1681.
Papel sellado variously dated 1675-81.
28197, 1938

DA681
S857u
Stillingfleet, Edward, bp. of Worcester, 1635-1699.
The Unreasonableness of Separation: Or, An Impartial Account Of The History, Nature, and Pleas Of The Present Separation From The Communion of the Church of England. To which, Several late Letters are Annexed, of Eminent Protestant Divines Abroad, concerning the Nature of our Differences, and the Way to Compose Them. By Edward Stillingfleet, D.D. Dean of St. Pauls, and Chaplain in Ordinary to His Majesty.
London, Printed by T. N. for Henry Mortlock, at the Phœnix in St. Paul's Church-yard. MDCLXXXI.
1 p.ℓ., xciv p., 4 p.ℓ., 88, 91-449 p. 19.5cm. 4°.
McAlpin4:76; Dexter(Cong.)2162; Wing S5675.
5826, 1909

E681
T418r
Thévenot, Melchisédech, 1620?-1692.
Recueil De Voyages De Mr Thevenot. Dedié Au Roy.
A Paris, Chez Estienne Michallet ruë S. Jaques à l'Image S. Paul. M. DC. LXXXI. Avec Privilege du Roy.
1 p.ℓ., [8 parts] 17.5cm. 8°
Cut on t.-p.
This is a compilation of works not contained in Thevenot's folio Relation de divers voyages curieux, Paris, 1663-1696. Each part is separately paged and signed. The order of parts is differently arranged in various copies, but the order followed below in listing the contents is suggested by a list which is printed on the verso of the title ([part 8] in the listing below is not specifically mentioned in the printed list).
In this copy the arrangement of parts as bound is: 1 (incl. map of 2), 5, 2, 3, 4, 6, 7, 8.

E681
T418r
cop.2
———— Another copy. 16.5cm.
In this copy the imprint date on the title-page has been altered in ms. to read M. DC. LXXXII.
In this copy the arrangement of parts as bound is: 1 (incl. 5), 2, 4, 3, 6, 7, 8.
Contents:
[part 1] 16 p.
"Avis" p. 1-11.
"Relations de ce Recüeil, imprimées jusques à cette heure" p. 12-16. This gives the parts of the folio Relation de divers voyages curieux as well as those of the present octavo Recueil.
"Achevé d'imprimer pour la premiere fois le 8 Septembre 1681." (p. 16).
[part 2] 43 p. fold. map.
[Marquette, Jacques] "Decouverte De Quelques Pays Et Nations De L'Amerique Septentrionale."
[part 3] fold. map.
Includes text "Explication De La Carte De La Decouverte De La Terre D'Ielmer, au de-là de la Nouvelle Zemble, & des routes pour passer

par le Nort, au Japon, à la Chine, & aux Indes Orientales."

[part 4] 18 p.

[Baĭkov, Fedor Isakovich] "Voyage D'Un Ambassadevr Que Le Tzaar De Moscovie Envoya Par Terre A La Chine L'Année 1653."

[part 5] fold. map.

[Carte de la Route d'Abel Tasman autour de la Terre Australe] (title from list of contents, p. ℓ.^{v})

In some copies there are Arabic genealogies on the reverse side of the map, but in these copies the reverse side is blank.

[part 6] 32 p. plate.

"Discours Sur L'Art De La Navigation, Avec quelques Problémes qui peuvent suppléer en partie ce qui manque à un Art si necessaire."

In copy 1 the reverse side of the leaf on which the plate is printed has text: "Explication Des Lettres de la Figure suivante." In copy 2 the reverse side is blank.

[part 7] 2 p. ℓ., 20, 14, 8 p. incl. illus. (5 engr.), 6 plates. 2 fold. plates.

Swammerdam, Jan. "Les Histoires Naturelles De L'Ephemere Et Du Cancellus Ou Bernard L'Hermite Décrites & représentées par Figures par Mr Swammerdam, pour servir de Suplément à ce qu'Aristote & les autres en ont écrit..." First pub. as Ephemeri vita, Amsterdam, 1675.

"Errata" 2d p. ℓ. Applies to parts 1, 6, and 7.

[part 8] 16 p. illus.

Swammerdam, Jan. "Le Cabinet De Mr. Svvammérdam, Docteur En Medecine, Ou Catalogue De toutes sortes d'Insectes, & de diverses preparations Anatomiques..." First pub. as Catalogus musei instructissimi [Amsterdam] 1679.

JCB(2)2:1232; Sabin95332; 44666n; Church 672; Harrisse(NF)147; Streit 1:633; cf. Backer5:600.

0525, 1846 rev
05266, 1884 rev

D681
-T627t
To The Parliament Of England, The Case of the Poor English Protestants in Mary-Land Under the Arbitrary Power of their Popish Governour the Lord Baltimore, who, with his Father, hath made it their Business to have the whole Countrey subject to the Church of Rome ever since the first Planting of that Collony; as doth appear by all their Actions.
[London, 1681]
4 p. 30cm. (33.5cm. in case). fol.
Caption title.

63-161

D679
-H313s
The Triumphs Of Justice Over Unjust Judges: Exhibiting, I. The Names and Crimes of Four and Forty Judges Hang'd in one Year in England, as Murderers for their corrupt Judgments. ... Humbly Dedicated to the Lord Chief Justice Scroggs, ...
London, Printed for Benjamin Harris, at the Stationers Arms in the Piazza under the Royal Exchange. 1681.
2 p. ℓ., 36 p. 31cm. fol.
Dedication signed (2d p. ℓ.): Westminster-Hall this 23. of Dec. 1680. ... Philo-Dicaios.
Lord Chief Justice Scroggs is principal object of this attack.
Bound as no. 7 of 8 items.
WingT2297.

7086, 1910

HA681
V176c
[Valladolid, Juan Francisco de] fl. 1655.
Compendio Della Vita, Virtù, e Miracoli Del B. Toribio Alfonso Mogrobesio Arciuescouo di Lima Con Vna Breve Descrittione Della Solennità della Beatificatione del medesimo fatta nella Basilica di S. Pietro, e Chiefa di S. Maria di Monserrato, e nell'Antichissima Chiefa Collegiata di S. Anastasia nel primo Altare iui erettogli nel giorno della sua Festa. ...
In Roma, Per il Tinassi. MDCLXXXI. Con licenza de' Superiori.
62 p. 14.5cm. 12°
First pub. under title: Vita del Servo di Dio D. Toribio Alfonso Mogrobejo ... Rome, 1655.
Dedication signed: Gio. Francisco Valladolid.
Cut on t.-p.
In this copy there is a blank final leaf.
Sabin98369; Palau(1)7:107.

11541, 1918 rev

BA681
V433b
Velasco, Tomás de
Breviloqvio Moral Practico, En Qve Se Contienen Las sesenta y cinco proposiciones prohibidas por N. SS. P. Innocencio XI. declaradas por via de impugnacion, Con vn Appendice añadido al fin de las quarenta y cinco proposiciones prohibidas por el Santissimo Alexandro VII. que por estar declaradas por otros; se da de sus mismas razones vna breve elucidacion. Ofrece esta disposicion de impugnarlas, y reducirlas á sus proprias claces, ò materias Morales á que pertenecen El P. Fr. Thomas De Velasco, Lector de Visperas de Theologia, hijo de la Santa Provincia de San Diego de Mexico de Franciscanos Descalços en esta Nueva-España. A la Reyna

                de los Angeles Maria N. Señora.
                    Con Licencia en Mexico, por la Viuda de Bernardo Calderon. A su costa. Año de 1681.
                    10 p.ℓ., 35, xii numb. ℓ., [16] p. 14.5cm. 8°
                    Errata, p. [16] at end.
                    License (7th p.ℓ.^{r}) dated 17 May 1681.
                    Bound in contemporary vellum.
                    Palau(1)7:138; Medina(Mexico)1238.

4325, 1908

J681   Wagner, Johann Christoph.
W133c   Cometa Disparens, Das ist: Gründlicher Bericht von dem fernern Lauff Dess Komet-Sterns/Biss zu dessen völliger Verlöschung; ... Deme mit angefügt wird Was von der grossen Zusammen-Kunfft der beyden obern Planeten/Saturni und Jovis. Jtem der grossen 1684. erscheinenden Sonnen-Finsternuss zu halten. Aufgesetzt durch Johann Christoph Wagner/Noribergens.
    Augspurg/gedruckt bey Jacob Koppmayr/ Anno 1681.
    1 p.ℓ., [26] p. illus. (tables, diagrs.). 18.5cm. 4°
    Cut (diagr.) on t.-p.
    A continuation of his Gründlicher und warhaffter Bericht ... Augsburg, 1681.
    Erratum, at end.
    With this is bound his Gründlicher und warhaffter Bericht ... Augsburg, 1681.

69-718

J681   Wagner, Johann Christoph.
W133c   Gründlicher und warhaffter Bericht von dem Ursprung der Kometen/derselben Natur/Gestalt/Zeit/Farb/Grösse/und Lauff ... Aus Anlass dess gegenwärtigen schröcklichen Komet-Sterns/Welcher in dem November/ und ietzund den 26. December dess 1680. Jahrs sich widerumb sehen lässet. An den Tag gegeben durch Johann Christoph Wagner/ Noribergens.
    Augsburg/gedruckt bey Jacob Koppmayr / Anno 1681.
    1 p.ℓ., [14] p. illus. (tables), 2 plates (incl. 1 fold.) 18.5cm. 4°
    Title vignette.
    Bound with his Cometa Disparens, Das ist: Gründlicher Bericht ... Augsburg, 1681.

69-719

DA681   [Whitehead, George] 1636?-1723.
W592a   The Accuser of our Brethren Cast Down in Righteous Judgment Against That Spirit Of Hellish Jealousie Vented in a great Confused Book, falsly Entituled, The Christian-Quaker Distinguished from the Apostate and Innovator; ...
    London, Printed for John Bringhurst at the Sign of the Book in Grace-Church-street, near Cornhil, 1681.
    14 p.ℓ., 270, [2] p. 17cm. 8°
    A reply to William Rogers' The Christian Quaker distinguished, London, 1680.
    Endorsement of the Society of Friends dated (p. 262) in London "the 1st day of the 6th Moneth, 1681."
    Errata, p. [1] at end.
    Bookseller's advertisement, p. [2] at end.
    Bound in contemporary calf, rebacked.
    Smith(Friends)2:896; Wing W1887; McAlpin 4:82.

70-44

DA681   Willard, Samuel, 1640-1707.
W695n   Ne Sutor ultra Crepidam. Or Brief Animadversions Upon the New-England Anabaptists Late Fallacious Narrative; Wherein the Notorious Mistakes and Falshoods by them Published, are Detected. By Samuel Willard Teacher of a Church in Boston in New-England. ...
    Boston In New-England, Printed by S. Green, upon Assignment of S. Sewall. And are to be Sold by Sam. Philips, at the West end of the Exchange: 1681.
    4 p.ℓ., 27 p. 19cm. 4°
    "To the Reader." 2d-4th p.ℓ., signed: Boston New-Engl. Nov. 4. 1681. Increase Mather.
    A reply to John Russel, A Brief Narrative of some Considerable Passages ... London, 1680.
    Wing W2288; Evans 309; Sabin 104097; Holmes (I)167.

6458, 1910

bD681   Williams, Roger, mariner, fl. 1672-1681.
W726t   To the King's Most Excellent Majesty. The Humble Petition of Roger Williams of London Mariner, Your Majesty's most Loyal and Dutiful Subject.
    [London, ca. 1681]
    Broadside. 44.5 x 32.5cm. 1°
    Text in two columns.
    Petition for relief from a judgment of July 1681 in favor of Edward Melish, merchant and owner of ship Valentine. Williams had commanded the

ship on a voyage from London to Faro, Portugal, to Newfoundland in 1672-3 during which it had been captured by a Dutch privateer; in 1679 Williams had brought an action for wages.
WingW2771.

05848, before 1914

1682

B682
-A118*l*
Abarca, Pedro, 1619-1693.
Los Reyes De Aragon En Anales Historicos, Distribvidos En Dos Partes: ...Por El Padre Pedro Abarca De La Compañia De Iesvs, Maestro Del Gremio De La Vniversidad De Salamanca, Y Sv Cathedratico Jvbilado De Prima De Theologia: Y Prefecto De Los Estvdios De Sv Colegio Real. Primera [-segunda] Parte.
Con Privilegio. En Madrid: En la Imprenta Imperial, Año de M.DC.LXXXII [-1684].
2 v.: 10 p.*l*., 204, 203-323 numb. *l*., [2] p.; 6 p.*l*., 418 numb. *l*., [16] p. 29cm. fol.
Vol. 2 has title: Segvnda Parte De Los Anales Historicos De Los Reyes De Aragon Por El P. Maestro Pedro Abarca De La Compañia De Iesvs ... Con Privilegio: En Salamanca, Por Lvcas Perez, Impressor de la Vniversidad. Año de M.DC.LXXXIV.
Errata: v.1, 9th p.*l*.^{v}; v.2, p. [15-16]
"Tassa" dated: v.1, 13 Aug. 1682 (9th p.*l*.^{v}); v.2, 28 Sept. 1684 (6th p.*l*.^{v}).
Palau(2)429; Backer 1:5.

68-169

B682
A189r
Acuña, Cristóbal de, b. 1597.
Relation De La Riviere Des Amazones Tradvite Par feu Mr de Gomberville de l'Academie Françoise. Sur l'Original Espagnol du P. Christophle d'Acuña Jesuite. Avec une Dissertation sur la Riviere des Amazones pour servir de Preface. ...
A Paris, Chez Claude Barbin, au Palais, sur le Perron de la S^e Chapelle. M.DC.LXXXII. Avec Privilege du Roy.
2 v.: 1 p.*l*., 142, 153-199, [1], 238 p.; 2 p.*l*., 218, 3-206 p. fold. map. 16cm. 12°
Acuña's Relation, which is an account of the expeditions under Pedro Teixeira, was transl.
from: Nuevo descubrimiento del gran rio de las Amazonas, Madrid, 1641.
"Achevé d'imprimer pour la premiere fois le quinze Juillet 1682." (v.2, 2d p.*l*.^{v}).
Errata, v.1, p. 199-[1]. In some copies errata are corrected. In this copy errata are not corrected.
Includes in v.2: "Lettre Escrite De l'Isle de Cayenne au mois de Septembre mil six cens soixente quatorze" by Jean Grillet (p. 3-8, 2d count); "Iovrnal Dv Voyage qu'ont fait les Peres Jean Grillet & François Bechamel... dans la Goyane, l'an 1674" (p. 9-136, 2d count); "Nottes Du Voyage qu'ont fait les Peres Iean Grillet & Bechamel" (p. 137-178, 2d count); "Relation De La Guiane Et Du Commerce qu'on y peut faire" (p. 179-206, 2d count).
Also issued Paris, 1682, with imprint "Chez la Veuve Louis Billaine."
In this copy, v.2, p. 1-218 and 3-206 are reversed in the binding.
In this copy, v.1, there is a blank leaf at end.
Imperfect: fold. map wanting; supplied in facsimile.
Bound in contemporary calf.
JCB(2)2:1235; Palau(2)2484; Sabin151; Backer 1:39, 3:1828; Streit2:2166; Borba de Moraes 1:11note.

03639, before 1866

B69
G643v
17
Agurto y Loaysa, Joseph de, fl. 1676-1688.
Villancicos, Que Se Cantaron En La Santa Iglesia Metropolitana de Mexico: En honor de Maria Santissima Madre de Dios. En su Assvmpcion Triumphante. ... Pusolos en metro Musico, el B.^{r} Joseph de Loaysa, y Agurto, Compositor de los Villancicos en dicha S. Iglesia.
Con Licencia. En Mexico: Por la Viuda de Bernardo Calderon, año de 1682.
[8] p. 20cm. 4°
Imprint at end.
Woodcut title vignette (the Virgin surrounded by angels against a background of a heraldic two-headed eagle).
Bound, in contemporary vellum, as no. 17 with 42 other items.

28917, 1941

B682
-A635e
Antonio de Santa María, Carmelite.
España Trivnfante Y La Iglesia Lavreada, En Todo El Globo De El

70-574

Mvndo Por el Patrocinio de Maria Santissima en España. Finezas Qve Nvestra Señora Ha Obrado con España, obsequios, y servicios con que han correspondido nuestros Reyes Catolicos à tan Soberana Señora. Discvrsos Historiales Desde El Nacimiento de Maria Santissima, hasta la restauracion de la Ciudad de Mecina, y entrada de la Reina nuestra señora en su Real Corte, Reinando la Magestad Catolica de Don Carlos II Nvestro Señor, Qve Dios Gvarde. Por El Padre Fr. Antonio de Santa Maria, Religioso Descalço de Nuestra Señora del Carmen. ...
Año 1682. Con Privilegio. En Madrid: Por Iulian de Paredes, Impressor de Libros. Vendese en su casa, en la Plaçuela del Angel.
15 p.ℓ., 638, [13] p. 29cm. fol.
Chapters 39-41, p. 354-387, cover the discovery and conquest of Spanish America.
"Suma de la Tassa" dated (10th p.ℓ.) 13 Jan. 1682.
In this copy there is a blank leaf at beginning. Palau(2)298098; BLH5:3235.

BA682
A816e

Asenjo y Crespo, Ignacio de, 1648-1736.
Exercicio Practico De La Volvntad De Dios. Trabajos Qve Corresponden à cada grado de Oracion, y Compendio de la mortificacion. Sacado A Lvz. Por el Lic. Don Ignacio de Asenjo y Crespo, Canonigo de la Santa Iglesia Cathedral de la Puebla, y Limosnero que fue del Illmo, y Rmo. Sr. Doctr. D. Manuel Fernandez de Santa Cruz, Obispo de dicha Santa Iglesia. ...
Reimpresso en la Puebla, en la Imprenta de Miguel de Ortega. [1682?]
10 p.ℓ., 310, [5] p. 10.5cm. 16°
Also attributed to Manuel Fernández de Santa Cruz y Sahagún.
Approbation dated (10th p.ℓ.ᵛ) 26 Sept. 1681.
The only other edition recorded as seen is that of Mexico, 1682 (Medina (Mexico) 1239). However, Medina (Puebla) 77, following Beristain, records an edition of Puebla 1681.
Cf. Medina(Puebla)77; cf. Medina(Mexico) 1239; cf. Sabin 26777; Palau(2)18313n.

10860, 1915 rev

DA682
B355m

Baxter, Richard, 1615-1691.
Mr. Baxter's Vindication Of The Church of England In her Rites and Ceremonies, Discipline, And Church-Orders. As faithfully taken out of his own Writings, without either false Citation, or fraudulent Alteration. To which is prefixed: His Epistle to the Non-conformists: being a just and true Abstract of his Book, Entituled, A Defence of the Principles of Love. ...
London. Printed for Walter Kettilby at the Bishops-head in St. Pauls Church-yard. 1682.
3 p.ℓ., 37 p. 19.5cm. 4°
Includes extracts from various works by Baxter and commentaries on them. His A Defence of the Principles of Love was first pub. London, 1671.
WingB1449.

10594, 1915

D682
-B658c

Blome, Richard, d. 1705.
Cosmography And Geography In Two Parts: The First Containing the General and Absolute Part of Cosmography and Geography, Being A Translation From that Eminent and much Esteemed Geographer Varenius, Wherein are at large handled All such Arts as are necessary to be understood for the true knowledge thereof. To which is added the much wanted Schemes omitted by the Author. The Second Part, Being a Geographical Description of all the World, Taken from the Notes and Works of the Famous Monsieur Sanson, Late Geographer to the French King: To which are added About an Hundred Cosmographical, Geographical and Hydrographical Tables of several Kingdoms and Isles in the World, with their Chief Cities, Seaports, Bays, &c. drawn from the Maps of the said Sanson. Illustrated with Maps.
London, Printed by S. Roycroft for Richard Blome, MDCLXXXII.
4 p.ℓ., 364 p., 1 ℓ., 493 p. 24 fold. maps, 3 fold. charts. 34cm. fol.
First pt. transl. from Bernhard Varan, Geographia generalis, 1st pub. Amsterdam, 1650. With, as issued, his A geographical description of the world, taken from the works of ... Sanson, London, 1680, with special t.-p., separate paging and signatures.
Bound in contemporary calf.
WingV102; Sabin76720; Baer(Md.)101.

67-356

D682
B677s

[Bohun, Edmund] 1645-1699.
The Second Part Of The Address To The Freemen And Free-Holders Of The Nation. By the same Author.

London, Printed by A. Godbid and J. Playford for George Wells, at the Sun in St. Pauls Churchyard, 1682.
1 p.l., xxv, 90 p. 20.5cm. 4°
In this copy there is a blank leaf at end.
Wing B3460.

68-104

DA682
B711p
Bond, Samson.
A Publick Tryal Of The Quakers In Barmudas Upon the first Day of May, 1678. First, The Charge against them was openly read ... Secondly, The Whole Charge being Proved by the Testimony of the Holy Scriptures: was found by the Sheriffe, and Justices of Peace, a true and just Charge. Thirdly, Being found Guilty, they are here Sentenced, and brought forth unto the deserved Execution of the Presse. By Samson Bond late Preacher of the Gospel in Barmudas. ...
Boston In New-England: Printed by Samuel Green, upon Assignment of Samuel Sewall: 1682.
2 p.l., 100 (i.e. 104) p. 20cm. 4°
Errata, 2d p.l.^{v}
JCB(2)2:1236; Evans313; Sabin6285; Smith (Anti-Quak)76; WingB3585.

04633, 1876

D682
B853
A Brief Account Of The Province Of East-Jersey In America. Pulished [sic] by the present Propriators, For Information of all such Persons who are or may be inclined to Setle themselves, Families, and Servants in that Country.
London, Printed for Benjamin Clark in George-Yard in Lombard-street, Bookseller, MDCLXXXII.
1 p.l., 6 p. 19cm. 4°.
List of the twelve proprietors printed on a slip, pasted at bottom of page 6.
Another issue has proprietors' names printed on t.-p.
"Scottish Proprietors' Tracts" no. 3. Cf. Church649n.
JCB(2)2:1237; Sabin53078; WingB4517; cf.Church 674A.

01520, 1847

BA682
C146e
Calderón, Juan.
España Illvstrada. Con La Mysteriosa Lvz De N. Señora Del Pilar De Zaragoza. Sermon, Qve En El Convento De N. Padre S. Francisco de Mexico. Predicó El R.P. Fr. Ivan Calderon Lector Iubilado, y de Prima de dicho Convento. Cantando su primera Missa vn nuevo Sacerdote. ...
Con licencia, en Mexico, Por Francisco Rodriguez Lupercio. Año de 1682.
6 p.l., 8, 8-11 numb. l. 19.5cm. 4°
"Censvra" dated (6th p.l.^{v}) 16 Nov. 1682.
Palau(2)39719; Medina(Mexico)1240.

69-764

D682
-C167l
[F]
Calvert, Philip, 1626-1682.
A Letter From The Chancellour Of Mary-Land, To Col. Henry Meese, Merchant in London: Concerning the late Troubles in Mary-Land.
London: Printed for A.[llen] Banks, 1682.
[2] p. 31.5cm. fol.
Caption title; imprint at end.
Dated (p. [2]): From Patuxent River-side, this 29th. December, 1681.
JCBAR50:30-33; WingC320; Baer(Md.)102.

30560, 1949

D682
A819c
Carolina; Or A Description Of the Present State of that Country, And The Natural Excellencies thereof ... Published by T. A. Gent. Clerk on Board his Majesties Ship the Richmond, which was sent out in the Year 1680. with particular Instructions to enquire into the State of that Country, by His Majesties Special Command, and Return'd this Present Year, 1682.
London, Printed for W.C. and to be Sold by Mrs. Grover in Pelican Court in Little Britain, 1682.
2 p.l., 40 p. 24cm. 4°
The author, "T.A.", has long been identified with the name "Thomas Ash", although such a person is otherwise unknown. It seems more likely that "T.A." is Thomas Amy, who became a proprietor of Carolina.
With this are bound: A true description of Carolina, London [1682] and A generall mapp of Carolina ... printed for Ric. Bloome, London, 1672.
JCB(2)2:1633; Wing A3934; Sabin 2172; Church 673.

4817, 1908 rev

BA682
C363d
Catholic Church--Liturgy and ritual--Special offices--Liberata, Saint.
Die xx. Iunij. Officivm Sanctæ Liberatæ Virginis, Et Martyris. Patronæ Ecclesiæ, Et Dioecesis Segvntinæ, Dvplex Secundæ Clasis. A Sacra Rituum Congregatione recognitum, & approbatū, in Regnis Hispaniarum celebrandum die xx. Mensis Iulij, ab omnibus vtrivs-

que sexus qui ad Horas Canonicas tenentur, iuxta decretum eiusdem Sacræ Congregat. 26. Septembris 1682.
  [Mexico, 1682?]
  [8] p. 15cm. 8°
  Caption title.
  Also issued as part of a collection with general t.-p.: <u>Nova, et vltima officia Sanctorvm concessa, a SS. P. N. Innocentio XI. Supplementum Breviario</u>, Mexici, apud heredes Viudae Bernardi Calderon [1691?]
  Medina(Mexico)1948.
5761², 1909 rev

D682
C712s
Collins, John, 1625-1683.
  Salt And Fishery, A Discourse thereof ... By John Collins, Accomptant to the Royal Fishery Company. E Reg. Soc. Philomath.
  London, Printed by A. Godbid, and J. Playford, and are to be Sold by Mr. Robert Horne at the Royal Exchange, Mr. John Kersey, and Mr. Henry Faithorn, at the Rose in St. Pauls Churchyard, Mr. William Bury, Globe-maker, at the Globe near Charing-Cross, 1682.
  4 p.ℓ., 32, 49-164, [4] p. 18.5cm. 4°
  "Of The Newfound-Land Fishery": p. 93-101.
  "An Advertisement about Planting the Isle of Tobago": p. 161-164.
  Booksellers' advertisements, p. 163-164.
  Errata, last page.
  Imperfect: closely trimmed affecting some headlines and 2 lines of the imprint; t.-p. available in facsim.
  In this copy p. 57-64 are misbound between p. 72-73.
  Wing C5380; Sabin 14440; Kress 1553.
64-181

BA682
-C783d
Copia De Dos Cartas Escritas De Vn Missionero, y del Superior de las Missiones de los Maynas, en el Rio Marañon, jurisdiccion de la Real Audiencia de Quito, avisando al Padre Vice-Provincial de la Compañia de Iesvs, del Nuevo Reyno de Granada; el vno, el estado del Pueblo en que assiste; y el otro, el que tiene parte de aquella gloriosa Mission, que avia visitado el año passado de 1681.
  [Madrid, 1682]
  [4] p. 30cm. fol.
  Caption title.
  "Primera Carta." (p. [1-2]) signed: Desde San Xabier de Gayes 20. de Mayo de 1681. ... Francisco Fernandez de Mendoza.
  "Segvnda Carta." (p. [2-4]) signed: Laguna, y Iunio 3. de 1681 años. ... Iuan Lorenço Luzero.
  "Iuzgando estimables, y de edificacion estas dos Cartas, que vinieron en los Galeones de este año de 82. ha querido el Procurador de Indias en Madrid, participarlas à estas Provincias de Europa..." (p. 4).
  Palau(2)89244; Medina(BHA)6385, 6533; Sabin 47172; Streit 2:2164.
68-258

BA682
C824a
Correa, Antonio.
  Anillo De Salomon, Qve Al Inefable Misterio De La Santissima Trinidad, En su Fiesta, que celebrò la Iglesia Parrochial, de la Nobilissima Villa de Carrion, Valle de Atrisco, (manifiesto el Santissimo Sacramento en la mano del Padre Eterno) discurriò El P. Fr. Antonio Correa, Predicador Conventual, y Comissario Visitador de la Tercera Orden de dicha Villa de Carrion, de N.P. San Francisco, Dia primero de Junio, de 1681. ...
  Con licencia En Mexico: Por la Viuda de Bernardo Calderon. Año de 1682.
  5 p.ℓ., 7 numb. ℓ. 19.5cm. 4°
  Cut (Dominican coat of arms) on t.-p.
  "Censura" dated (4th p.ℓ.) 8 Jan. 1682.
  Includes poetry.
  Palau(2)62504; Medina(Mexico)1242.
69-762

B682
C962p
[R]
Cubero Sebastián, Pedro, 1640-ca. 1696.
  Peregrinacion Del Mvndo, Del Doctor D. Pedro Cvbero Sebastian, Predicador Apostolico. Dedicada Al Excelentissimo Señor D. Fernando Ioachin Faxardo, De Reqvesens, Y Zvñiga, Marqves De Los Velez, &c. Virrey, y Capitan General del Reyno de Napoles.
  En Napoles, Por Carlos Porsile 1682. Con licencia de los Superiores.
  7 p.ℓ., 451, [4] p. 2 ports. (incl. front.) 20.5cm. 4°
  Added half-title, engr., with inscription: Ad istanza del S.ʳ Gioseppe Criscolo A. 1682.
  Dedication dated (3d p.ℓ.ᵛ) 27 Oct. 1682.
  Preliminary matter includes poetry by Pedro Calderón de la Barca, Juan de Matos Fragoso, and Antonio de Cardenas.
  First pub. Madrid, 1680, under title: <u>Breve relación de la peregrinación</u>.
  Palau(2)65757;   Medina(BHA)1728; Retana 149; Streit 5:555.
10820, 1915

DA682 Davenport, John, 1597-1670.
D247s The Saints Anchor-Hold, In All Storms and Tempests. Preached in sundry Sermons. And published for the Support and Comfort of Gods People, in all times of Tryal. By John Davenport, B. D. sometime Minister of Stephens Coleman-street; London; and now Pastor of the Church of Christ in New-Haven in New-England. ...
London, Printed for Tho. Guy, at the Oxford Arms, on the West side of the Royal Exchange, 1682.
4 p. ℓ., 231 p. 14.5cm. 12º
Errata: verso 4th p. ℓ.
First pub. London, 1661.
"The Preface..." (2d-4th p. ℓ.) signed: William Hooke. Joseph Caryl.
Wing D367; cf. Dexter(Cong.)1878.
5088, 1909

B682 Evelino, Gaspar Juan.
E93e Especulacion Astrologica, Y Physica De La Natvraleza De Los Cometas, Y Jvizio Del Qve Este Año de 1682. Se ve en todo el Mundo. Por Gaspar Juan Evelino, Mathematico. M.M.S.D. C.C.
Con Licencia. En Mexico: Por la Viuda de Bernardo Calderon, en la calle de San Augustin, Año de 1682.
[8] p. 18.5cm. 4º
Medina(Mexico)1244; Sabin23207.
05867, 1896

F682 [Exquemelin, Alexandre Olivier]
E96p Piratas De La America. Y Luz à la defensa de las Costas de Indias Occidentales Dedicado Al muy Noble Señor Don Ricardo de Whyte, Cavallero del Orden Militar de Calatrava &cª. Traducido De la lengua Flamenca en Española, por el Dᵒʳ. de Bonne Maison. Impression Segunda.
En Colonia Agrippina, En casa de Lorenço Struikman, Año de 1682.
28 p. ℓ., 490, [8] p. plate (coat of arms). 13.5cm. 12º
Cut on t.-p.
Transl. from: De Americaensche Zee-Roovers, Amsterdam, 1678. Spanish transl. 1st pub. Cologne, 1681.
Preliminary matter includes short poetry by the translator and by Miguel de Barrios and Duarte López Rosa as well as "Descripcion De las Islas del Mar Athlantico Y De America..." (17th-28th p. ℓ.) - in verse - by Miguel de Barrios.

Another issue with 24 p. ℓ. has different t.-p. and dedication.
JCB(2)2:1240; Palau(2)85731; Sabin23473; Medina (BHA)1727; BLH 6:3194.
0886, 1846 rev

F682 [Exquemelin, Alexandre Olivier]
E96p* Piratas De La America. Y Luz à la defensa de las Costas de Indias Occidentales Dedicado Al muy Noble Señor Don Francisco Lopez Suazo. Traducido. De la lengua Flamenca en Española, por el Dᵒʳ. de Buena-Maison Medico Practico en la opulentissima Ciudad de Amsterdam. Segunda Impression.
En Colonia Agrippina, En casa de Lorenço Struikman, Año de 1682.
24 p. ℓ., 490, [8] p. 13.5cm. 12º
Cut on t.-p.
Transl. from De Americaensche Zee-Roovers, Amsterdam, 1678. Spanish transl. 1st pub. Cologne, 1681.
Preliminary matter includes short poetry by the translator and by Miguel de Barrios and Duarte López Rosa as well as "Descripcion De las Islas del Mar Athlantico Y De America..." (17th-28th p. ℓ.) - in verse - by Miguel de Barrios.
Another issue with 28 p. ℓ. has different t.-p. and dedication.
In this copy there is a blank ℓ. at end.
Bound in contemporary vellum.
Cf. JCB(2)2:1240; cf. Palau(2)85731; Sabin 23472; Medina(BHA)1726; BLH6:3194.
69-752

B69 Florido, Sylvestre, fl. 1682.
G643v Villancicos, Qve Se Cantaron En La S. Iglesia Cathedral de Mexico: En los Maytines del Gloriosissimo Principe de la Iglesia el Señor San Pedro. ... Que ofrece... El B.ʳ Sylvestre Florido. Compuestos en metro musico, por el B.ʳ Joseph de Agurto, y Loaysa, Maestro Compositor de dicha Santa Iglesia.
En Mexico: Por la Viuda de Bernardo Calderon, Año de 1682.
[8] p. 20cm. 4º
Imprint at end.
Woodcut title vignette (St. Peter within a decorative frame)
Bound, in contemporary vellum, as no. 29 with 42 other items.
28929, 1941

DA682 F791

Fox, George, 1624-1691.
    Concerning Persecution In All Ages To this Day. ... G. Fox.
    London, Printed by John Bringhvrst, at the Sign of the Book in Grace-Church-Street, 1682.
    19, [1], p. 19cm. (20cm. in case) 4°
    Signed (p.16): London, the 8th Month, 1682. G.F.
    Includes "To all the Elect of God..." (p. 17-19) signed: From Kingston upon Thames, the 2d of the 9th Moneth, 1682. G.F.
    "Books Printed and Sold by John Bringhurst at the Sign of the Book in Grace-Church-street, near Cornhil": p. [1] at end.
    Smith(Friends)1:681; WingF1769.

62-35

DA682 F791e

[Fox, George] 1624-1691.
    An Epistle To All Christians To keep to Yea, Yea, and Nay, Nay, And to fulfil their Words And Promises. By G.F.
    London, Printed for Benjamin Clark in George-Yard in Lonbard [sic]-street, Bookseller, 1682.
    1p.ℓ., 6p. 18.5cm. 4°
    Signed: G.F. Edmonton in the County of Middlesex 23-11 Month, 1681.
    Smith(Friends)1:681; WingF1804.

11441, 1918

DA682 F791s

Fox, George, 1624-1691.
    Something in Ansvver To all such as falsly say, The Quakers Are No Christians; ... By George Fox.
    London: Printed and Sold by Andrew Sowle, at the Crooked-Billet in Holloway-Lane, near Shoreditch, 1682.
    28p. 19.5cm. 4°
    Smith(Friends)1:681; WingF1913.

11463, 1918

EB F8355 1682 2

France--Laws, statutes, etc., 1643-1715 (Louis XIV).   Aug. 1681.
    Ordonnance De Louis XIV. Roy De France Et De Navarre. Donné à Fontainebleau au mois d'Aoust 1681. Touchant la Marine.
    Suivant la Copie imprimée A Paris, Chez Denys Thierry, & Christophle Ballard. M DC LXXXII.
    4 p.ℓ., 271, [272-345] p. 11.5cm. 16°
    First pub. Paris, 1681.

"Explication des Termes de Marine": p. [322-345].
    Includes (p. 265-271) "Reglement que le Roy veut estre observé par ses sujets qui acheteront, ou seront construire des Vaisseaux, Barques; & autres Bastimens de mer, tant en France que dans les Païs Estrangers... Fait à Strasbourg le vingt-quatriéme jour d'Octobre mil six cens quatre-vingts-un. ..."
    Title-page mutilated.
    In this copy there is a blank ℓ. at end.
    Bound in contemporary vellum.
    Wroth & Annan227.

15270, 1929 rev

EB F8355 1682 1

France--Sovereigns, etc., 1643-1715 (Louis XIV)   18 July 1682.
    Arrest Dv Conseil D'Estat Dv Roy, Du dix-huitiéme Juillet 1682. Portant Que faute par les Marchands Negocians, qui feront porter des Marchandises és Isles de l'Amerique & de Canada, pour y estre consommées, de raporter dans huit mois, Certificats de la Descente d'icelles, au bas des Acquits à Caution qui leur seront fournis, & de faire décharger leurs Soûmissions sur les Registres; Ils demeureront exclus de la décharge des Droits d'Entrée, & contraints au payement du Quatruple, &c. Extraict des Registres du Conseil d'Estat.
    [Paris, 1682]
    3 p. 25cm. 4°
    Caption title.
    Wroth & Annan234; Harrisse(NF)149.

14971, 1928

D682 -F853a

Free Society of Traders in Pennsylvania.
    The Articles, Settlement and Offices Of the Free Society Of Traders In Pensilvania: Agreed upon by divers Merchants And Others for the better Improvement and Government Of Trade In That Province.
    London, Printed for Benjamin Clark in George-Yard in Lombard-street, Printer to the Society of Pennsylvania, MDC LXXXII.
    3 p.ℓ., [10] p. 29cm. fol.
    "The Preface." signed (recto 3d p.ℓ.): London, 25. 1st. Mo. called March, 1682. Nicolas More, James Claypoole, Philip Ford.
    Only p. 1 numbered.
    Wing A3885; Sabin59897; Vail(Front.)205.

65-32

D682　　Gage, Thomas, 1603?-1656.
G133n　　　Nieuwe ende seer naeuwkeurige Reyse Door de Spaensche West-Indien Van Thomas Gage; Met seer curieuse soo Land-kaerten als Historische Figueren verciert ende met twee Registers voorsien. Overgeset door H. V. Q.
　　　Tot Utrecht, By Johannes Ribbius, Boeckverkooper in de korte St. Ians-straet. M. DC. LXXXII.
　　　10 p. ℓ., 168, 167-450, [66] p. 8 plates (incl. 2 fold.), 3 fold. maps. 21cm. 4º
　　　Cut on t.-p.
　　　Added t.-p., engraved: Nieuwe en seer Nauwkeurige Reijse...t. 'Utrecht bij Iohannes Ribbius. Aº 1682 J. Doesburgh, in. et fe.
　　　Dedication (3d-6th p. ℓ.) signed: H. V. Quellenburgh.
　　　Transl. by Henrik van Quellenburgh from: A New Survey of the West-Indies, first pub. London, 1648, under title: The English-American his Travail by Sea and Land.
　　　"Korte Onderwysinge, Om de Indiaensche Taele, welcke men Poconchi ofte Pocoman noemt, te leeren": p. [439]-450.
　　　JCB(2)2:1241; Streit 2:2167; Muller(1872)610; Sabin26310; Pilling1367.
01911, 1854

bDA682　　[Godwin, Morgan] fl. 1685.
G592r　　　The Revival: Or Directions for a Sculture, describing the extraordinary Care and Diligence of our Nation, in publishing the Faith among Infidels in America, and elsewhere; compared with other both Primitive and Modern Professors of Christianity.
　　　London, Printed by J. Darby, 1682.
　　　Broadside. 28 x 18cm. 1/2º
　　　At end: "Place this figure before, p. 111. of The Negro's Advocate."
　　　His The Negro's & Indians advocate was pub. London, 1680.
　　　Sabin70325; WingG972.
10566, 1914

D70　　Hickeringill, Edmund, 1631-1708.
-P769t　　　The Black Non-Conformist, Discover'd In More Naked Truth: Proving, That Excommunication & Confirmation, The Two Great Episcopal Appurtenances; And Diocesan Bishops, Are (as now in use) of Human Make and Shape; And, That not only some Lay-Men, but all the Keen-cringing Clergy Are Non-Conformists. ... By Edmund Hickeringill Rector of the Rectory of All-Saints in Colchester.
　　　London, Printed by George Larkin, and are to be Sold by Richard Janeway, and most Booksellers in London. M. DC. LXXXII.
　　　9 p. ℓ., 68, [10] p. 30.5cm. fol.
　　　Dedication dated (6th p. ℓ.ʳ) 4 Dec. 1681.
　　　Imperfect: 2d-3d p. ℓ. mutilated, 1st p. ℓ. and p. [7-10] wanting; available in facsim.
　　　Errata, last page.
　　　No. [3] in a volume with binder's title: Political tracts 1655-1702.
　　　WingH1796; McAlpin4:98.
9973-3, 1914

DA682　　Hickeringill, Edmund, 1631-1708.
-H628b　　　The Black Non-Conformist, Discover'd In More Naked Truth: Proving, That Excommunication, Confirmation, >the two Great Episcopal Appurtenances, & Diocesan Bishops, Are not (as now in use) of Divine, but Human Make and Shape; And, That not only some Lay-Men, but all the Keen-cringing Clergy Are Non-Conformists ... The Second Edition. ... By Edm. Hickeringill Rector of the Rectory of All-Saints in Colchester.
　　　London, Printed by G. Larkin, and are to be Sold by Richard Janeway, and most Booksellers in London. M. DC. LXXXII.
　　　9 p. ℓ., 68, [10] p. 31cm. fol.
　　　First pub. London, 1682; these are the same sheets with new t.-p.
　　　Errata, last page.
　　　In this copy there is a blank leaf at beginning.
　　　cf. WingH1797.
68-488

FC650　　Hollandse Mercurius, Verhalende de voor-
H737　　　naemste Saken van Staet, En andere Voor-
32　　　vallen, Die, in en omtrent de Vereenigde Nederlanden, En elders in Europa, In het Jaer 1681, Zijn geschiet. Het Twee-en-Dertigste Deel.
　　　Tot Haerlem, Gedruckt by Abraham Casteleyn, Stadts-Drucker, op de Marckt, in de Blye Druck. Anno 1682.
　　　4 p. ℓ., 256 p. 2 fold. plates. 20cm. 4º
　　(Bound in [vol. 8] of Hollandse Mercurius)
　　　Erratum: p. 256.
　　　Added t.-p., engraved: Hollandse Mercurius tot Haerlem by Abraham Casteleyn Anno 1681.
　　　JCB(3)2:410; Sabin32523.
8487FF, 1912

BA682　　Jesuits--Spain--Procurador General por las
-J58s　　　　Provincias de Indias.
　　　　　　Señor. Manuel Rodriguez de la Compañia de
　　　　　Iesvs, Procurador general por las Provincias de
　　　　　Indias, dize: ...
　　　　　　　[Madrid? 1682?]
　　　　　　　[4] p. 31.5cm. fol.
　　　　　　Jesuit trigram at head of title.
　　　　　　Memorial to the king recounting Jesuit mission-
　　　　　ary activities among the Mayna Indians, center-
　　　　　ing around San Francisco de Borja, Peru, and
　　　　　requesting that other missionary orders be
　　　　　excluded from the area.
　　　　　　　Palau(2) 273202; Sabin72525, 72526 (actual copy);
　　　　　Medina(BHA)6822; Streit2202.
11926, 1919

DA682　　[Keith, George] 1639?-1716.
K28t　　　　Truths Defence: Or, the Pretended Examina-
　　　　　tion By John Alexander of Leith, Of the Prin-
　　　　　ciples of those (called Quakers) Falsly termed
　　　　　by him Jesuitico-Quakerism, Re-Examined
　　　　　And Confuted, Together with Some Animad-
　　　　　versions on the Dedication of his Book to Sir
　　　　　Robert Clayton, then Major of London. By
　　　　　G. K.
　　　　　　　London, Printed for Benjamin Clark in
　　　　　George-Yard in Lombard-street, Bookseller,
　　　　　1682.
　　　　　　　1 p.ℓ., 254 p. 15.5cm. 8°.
　　　　　　Errata: slip mounted on verso of t.-p.
　　　　　　A reply to John Alexander, Jesuitico-Quaker-
　　　　　ism Examined. London, 1680.
　　　　　　　Smith(Friends)2:22-23; McAlpin4:103; Wing
　　　　　K225.
8389, 1912

bD682　　A Letter from Jamaica, to a Friend in London,
L651fj　　　　concerning Kid-Napping.
　　　　　　　[London? 1682]
　　　　　　　Broadside. 34 x 21cm. 1/2°
　　　　　　Signed: T.M. ... Jamaica, Decemb. 30.
　　　　　1681.
　　　　　　Includes mention of John Wilmer, who was
　　　　　tried in London, 1682, for kidnapping and
　　　　　transporting a boy to Jamaica.
　　　　　　　JCBAR65:25; Wing L1481.
64-182 rev

D682　　A Letter From New-England Concerning their
-L651f　　　　Customs, Manners, And Religion. Written upon
[R]　　　　occasion of a Report about a Quo Warranto
　　　　　Brought against that Government.
　　　　　　　London, Printed for Randolph Taylor near
　　　　　Stationers Hall, 1682.
　　　　　　　1 p.ℓ., 9 p. fol. 30cm. (33cm. in case).
　　　　　　Signed at end: J.W.
　　　　　　　Wing W59; Sabin52641; Church674; Dexter2214.
14290, 1925

D682　　[Loddington, William] 1626?-1711.
L821p　　　　Plantation Work The Work Of This Generation.
　　　　　Written in True-Love To all such as are weight-
　　　　　ily inclined to Transplant themselves and Fami-
　　　　　lies to any of the English Plantations in America.
　　　　　The Most material Doubts and Objections against
　　　　　it being removed ...
　　　　　　　London, Printed for Benjamin Clark in George-
　　　　　Yard in Lombard-street, 1682.
　　　　　　　1 p.ℓ., 18 p. 18cm. 4°
　　　　　　Signed (p. 10, 13): W. L. Authorship has
　　　　　also been variously ascribed to George Fox or
　　　　　William Penn.
　　　　　　Includes as "Postcript" (p. 14-17) "A little
　　　　　Model for Plantations" from Francis Bacon's
　　　　　The Essayes Or Covnsels, Civill And Morall ...
　　　　　Newly enlarged. First pub. London, 1625.
　　　　　　"An Abstract of some passages out of divers
　　　　　Letters from America relating to Pennsylvania",
　　　　　p. 17-18.
　　　　　　Closely trimmed at top affecting head-lines
　　　　　and 1st line of t.-p.
　　　　　　　JCB(2)2:1252; WingL2804; Sabin63318; Vail
　　　　　(Front.)209; Smith(Friends)2:128.
03640, before 1866

B682　　[López y Martínez, Juan Luis, marqués del
-L864p　　　　Risco] d. 1732, comp.
　　　　　　De Examine Symboli Politici, Ac Militaris
　　　　　Plvs Vltra. Apud Bartholomæum Leonardum
　　　　　Epistolica Exercitatio. ...
　　　　　　　Limæ, Anno 1682
　　　　　　　1 p.ℓ., 2 numb. ℓ., [2] p. 28cm. fol.
　　　　　　Dedication (1st p.ℓ.ᵛ) signed: Dabam bis Limæ
　　　　　III. Non. Decembris Ann. M.DC.LXXXII. ...
　　　　　D. Ioannes Ludovicus Lopez.
　　　　　　Relates to the passage about emperor Charles
　　　　　V's heraldic　　　　motto "Plus ultra" in:

	Leonardo y Argensola, Bartolomé Juan. <u>Primera parte de los anales de Aragon</u>, Saragossa, 1630. Contents: "Epistola I" by Juan Luis López y Martínez; "Epistola II" by Simón Plaza; and "Epistola III" by Francisco López. Bound as no. 3 in a vol. with binder's title: Luis Lopez Obras. Medina(Lima)535; Leclerc(1878)1826.3(this copy).
14009, 1925	

B682 -L864p	López y Martínez, Juan Luis, marqués del Risco, d. 1732. Parecer Del Doctor Don Ivan Lvis Lopez Del Consejo De S. M. Alcalde del Crimen de esta Real Audiencia, y Auditor General de la gente de Mar, y Guerra de este Reyno. Sobre Si Al Vasallo, Qve Ofrece Descubrir algun arbitrio en beneficio de la causa publica con exorbitantes condiciones, se le podra obligar â que lo manifieste, dandole la recompensa, que se tuviere por justa. Escrito De Orden Del Exmo Sor Don Melchor De Navarra, I Rocafvll, ... Virrey, Gouernador, y Capitan General de estos Reynos del Peru, Tierrafirme, y Chile. En illustracion de la ley 2. tit. I. ley 5. tit. 26. partit. 2 y ley 31 tit. 18. partit. 3. ... En Lima Año. 1682. 1 p.ℓ., 12 numb. ℓ. 28cm. fol. Dated (at end) in Lima, 10 Feb. 1682. Bound as no. 1 in a vol. with binder's title: Luis Lopez Obras. Palau(2)141405; Medina(Lima)534; Leclerc (1878)1826.1 (this copy).
14007, 1925	

EA682 M334r	Marie de l'Incarnation, mère, 1599-1672. Retraites De La Venerable Mere Marie De L'Incarnation Religieuse Ursuline. Avec Vne Exposition succinte du Cantique des Cantiques. A Paris, Chez la Veuve Louis Billaine, au second Pillier de la grand' Salle du Palais, à l'Image S. Augustin. M. DC. LXXXII. Avec Approbation, & Privilege du Roy. 19 p.ℓ., 248 p. 15.5cm. 12º Cut (incl. "IHS") on t.-p. "Achevé d'imprimer pour la premiere fois le 22. Janvier 1682." (recto 19th p.ℓ.). Edited by the author's son, Claude Martin. Bound in contemporary calf. Sabin70132; Leclerc(1878)759.
8562, 1912	

D. Math I.30^1	Mather, Increase, 1639-1723. Diatriba De Signo Filii Hominis, Et De Secundo Messiæ Adventu; Ubi de modo futuræ Judæorum Conversionis; Nec non de signis Novissimi diei, disseritur. Authore Crescentio Mathero ... Amstelodami, Apud Mercy Browning Juxta Bursam. 1682. 4 p.ℓ., 98, [6] p. 14.5cm. 8º Cut on t.-p. A sequel to his <u>The mystery of Israel's salvation</u>, Boston, 1669. Errata, last p. "Lectori veritatis studioso" dated (4th p.ℓ.): Bostoniæ in Nov. Angliâ, Decembris die 15. JCB(2)2:1243; Sabin46652; Holmes(I)30^1.
05857, before 1882	

D. Math I.62B1	Mather, Increase, 1639-1723. Heaven's Alarm To The World. Or A Sermon, wherein is shewed, That Fearful Sights And Signs in Heaven, are the Presages of great Calamities at hand. Preached at the Lecture of Boston in New-England; January, 20. 1680. By Mr. Increase Mather. The Second Impression. ... Boston In New-England, Printed for Samuel Sewall. And are to be sold by Joseph Browning at the Corner of the Prison-Lane Next the Town-House. 1682. 4 p.ℓ., 38 p., 1 ℓ., 32 p. 14.5cm. 8º Includes (1 ℓ., 32 p. at end) his <u>The Latter Sign Discoursed of, In A Sermon Preached at the Lecture of Boston in New-England; August 31. 1682</u> with half-title, separate paging but continuous signatures. Heaven's Alarm 1st pub. Boston, 1681. "To the Reader" dated (4th p.ℓ.^{v}): 16 Febr. 1680/1. The first sermon was occasioned by the comet of 1680, the second by Halley's comet in 1682. Some copies later issued as a part of his Kometographia, Boston, 1683. JCB(2)2:1244; Wing M1218; Evans320; Sabin 46691; Holmes(I)62B1.
05858, before 1882	

D. Math I.88A	Mather, Increase, 1639-1723. Practical Truths Tending to Promote the Power of Godliness: Wherein Several Important Duties, are Urged, and the Evil of divers common Sins, is Evinced; Delivered in Sundry Sermons. By Increase Mather, Teacher of a Church at Boston in New-England ...

[101]

Boston in New-England Printed by Samuel Green upon Assignment of Samuel Sewall. 1682.
    7 p.ℓ., 220 p., 1 ℓ. 15cm. 8°
    Dedication dated 19 July 1682.
    Errata, 7th p.ℓ.ʳ.
    Bookseller's advertisements, 7th p.ℓ.ʳ and last p.
    JCB(2)2:1246; WingM1237; Evans322; Sabin 46720; Holmes(I)88A.
05855, before 1882

D.Math I.117   Mather, Increase, 1639-1723.
A Sermon Wherein is shewed that the Church of God is sometimes a Subject of Great Persecution; Preached on a Publick Fast At Boston in New-England: Occasioned by the Tidings of a great Persecution Raised against the Protestants in France. By Increase Mather, Teacher to a Church of Christ. ...
    Boston In New-England: Printed for Samuel Sewall, in the Year, 1682.
    3 p.ℓ., 24 p. 18.5cm. 4°
    Occasioned by the revocation of the Edict of Nantes.
    "To The Reader" dated (3d p.ℓ.ᵛ): 1.M.28.D.1682.
    Errata, p. 24.
    Bookseller's advertisement, p. 24.
    In this copy there is a blank ℓ. at end.
    JCB(2)2:1247; WingM1251; Evans324; Sabin 46739; Holmes(I)117.
05856, 1878

BA682 -M491c   Medina, Baltasar de, d. 1696.
Chronica De La Santa Provincia De San Diego de Mexico, de Religiosos Descalços de N.S.P.S. Francisco en la Nueva-España. Vidas De Ilvstres, Y Venerables Varones, que la han edificado con excelentes virtudes. Escrivelas, y Consagralas al Glorioso San Diego De Alcalá Patron, y Tutelar de la misma Provincia, F. Balthassar De Medina, Natural de la Ciudad de Mexico, Lector de Theologia, Hijo, y Difinidor de la misma Provincia de San Diego, y Comissario Visitador, que fue, de la de San Gregorio de Philipinas.
    Con Licencia De Los Svperiores. En Mexico: Por Juan de Ribera, Impressor, y Mercader de Libros en el Empedradillo. Año de 1682.
    23 p.ℓ., 259 numb. ℓ., [20]p. map. 29cm. fol.
    Added t.-p., engraved.
    Dedication dated (7th p.ℓ.ᵛ) 4 Aug.1682.
    Errata, 20th p.ℓ.ᵛ.

Preliminary matter includes poetry by Pedro Antonio de Aguirre, 16th p.ℓ.
    Imperfect: added t.-p. wanting, outer margin of last 2 ℓ. mutilated; available in facsim.

    Bound in contemporary vellum.
    Palau(2)159373; Medina(Mexico)1250; Sabin 47336; Wagner55.
05868, 1899

BA681 -M519t 3   Melendez, Juan, fl. 1681.
Tesoros Verdaderos De Las Yndias.
Roma, M. DC. LXXXII.
See entry under v.1, 1681.
05669, before 1874

J682 -M549i   Mentzel, Christian, 1622-1701.
... Index Nominum Plantarum Universalis, Diversis Terrarum, Gentiúmque Linguis, quotquot ex Auctoribus ad singula Plantarum Nomina excerpi & juxta seriem A.B.C. collocari potuerunt, ad Unum redactus, videlicet: Europæorum Latinâ ... Asiaticorum ... Africanorum ... Americanorum ... Characteribus Latinorum, Græcorum & Germanorum maximè per Europam usitatis conscriptus ... Accessit in calce Indicis Pugillus Plantarum rariorum cum figuris aliquot æneis, & brevibus nonnullis descriptionibus, quarum mentio in Indice facta. His, ut Indicum multitudo evitaretur, intertextus est nonnullarum Brasiliæ Plantarum Indiculus, quarum nomina apud Clar:Pisonem & alios non extant, cum quibusdam Clar: Jac: Breynii rarioribus, quæ Prodromus ejus Fasciculi rariorum Plantarum habet, & aliis, partim Indice contentis, partim Indice absolutô, demum Appendicis locô adjectis. Adornavit & perfecit opus Christianus Mentzelius, Fürstenwald.March.Philosoph. & Medicin.D. Serenissimi Electoris Brandenburgici Consiliarius & Archiater.
    Berolini, Cum Gratiis & Privilegiis decennalibus S. Cæs. Maj. & Sereniss. Elect. Brandenb. Sumptibus Auctoris. Prostat apud Danielem Reichelium. Ex Officina Rungiana, M. DC. LXXXII.
    9 p.ℓ., 331 p. 2 ℓ., [13], [2] p. 11 plates. 33cm. fol.
    Title in red and black.
    Title in Greek at head of title.
    Added t.-p., engr. by Cornelius Nicolaus Schurtz from design of Rutger von Langerfeld.
    Errata, p. 331.
    Preliminary matter includes laudatory poetry by Johannes Michael Fehr and Johannes Gerlach Wilhelmi (9th p.ℓ.ᵛ).

69-321
    Includes "Pugillus Rariorum Plantarum" (ℓ. 1-2, p. [1-13] with both printed and engraved half-titles and the 11 plates. Partly taken from Jacobus Breynius' Podromus fasciculi rariorum plantarum anno 1679... 1st pub. Danzig, 1680.
    Register of engravings on pasted label at end.
    Bound in contemporary vellum.
    Pritzel 6093.

D682 M631n   Miege, Guy, 1644-1718?
    A New Cosmography, Or Survey Of the Whole World; In Six Ingenious and Comprehensive Discourses. With a Previous Discourse, being a New Project for bringing up Young Men to Learning. Humbly Dedicated to the Honourable Henry Lyttelton, Esq; By Guy Miege, Gent.
    London, Printed for Thomas Basset, at the George in Fleet-street, near St. Dunstans Church, 1682.
    2 p. ℓ., 128, 127-146 p. 2 plates. 16.5cm. 8°
    Bound in contemporary calf.
    Wing M2015.
9483, 1913

DA682 N173f2   [Nalson, John] 1638?-1686.
    Foxes And Firebrands: Or, A Specimen Of The Danger and Harmony of Popery and Separation. Wherein is proved from undeniable Matter of Fact and Reason, that Separation from the Church of England is, in the judgment of Papists, and by sad experience, found the most compendious way to introduce Popery, and to ruine the Protestant Religion. ... The Second Edition. In Two Parts.
    Dublin, Printed by Jos. Ray, for Jos. Howes, and are to be sold by Awnsham Churchill at the Black Swan in Pater-noster-Row, near Amen Corner, London. 1682.
    7 p. ℓ., 70 p., 1 ℓ., [5], 154 p. 17cm. 8°
    First pub. London, 1680, with a 2d ed. pub. London, 1681. Another edition, "The Second Edition. In Two Parts", with which was issued [Ware Robert] The second part of Foxes and Firebrands, was pub. with imprint "Dublin Printed by Joseph Ray for a Society of Stationers, and are to be sold by the booksellers of Dublin, 1682". The present book is the same Dublin, 1682, edition issued with a variant imprint; [Ware's] Second part has a special t.-p., separate paging, but continuous signatures. There is also another edition, a page-for-page reprint of the two parts of the present book, the t.-p. of which can be distinguished from the present book by "judgments" in line 11 of t.-p. and "Pater-nister" in the imprint.
    "To The Reader. Christian Reader..." (2d-4th p. ℓ.) signed at end: R.[obert] W.[are]
    Dedication (5th-7th p. ℓ.) signed: Philirenes [i.e. John Nalson]
    Errata, 7th p. ℓ.^{v}
    Bookseller's advertisement, p. 154.
    In this copy there is a blank ℓ. at beginning.
    Bound in contemporary calf.
    WingN105, W853; Smith(Anti-Quak.)23; cf. McAlpin4:108, 118-119.
06375, 1968

DA682 N173f3   [Nalson, John] 1638?-1686.
    Foxes And Firebrands: Or, A Specimen Of The Danger and Harmony of Popery and Separation. Wherein is proved from undeniable Matter of Fact and Reason, that Separation from the Church of England is, in the judgments of Papists, and by sad experience, found the most compendious way to introduce Popery, and to ruine the Protestant Religion. ... The Second Edition. In Two Parts.
    Dublin, Printed by Jos. Ray, for Jos. Howes, and are to be sold by Awnsham Churchill at the Black Swan in Pater-nister [sic]-Row, near Amen-Corner, London. 1682.
    7 p. ℓ., 70 p., 1 ℓ., [5], 154 p. 17cm. 8°
    First pub. London, 1680, with a 2d ed. pub. London, 1681. The present book is a page-for-page reprint of another edition, "The Second Edition. In Two Parts", with which was issued [Ware, Robert] The second part of Foxes and firebrands; that edition was issued with imprint "Dublin Printed by Joseph Ray for a Society of Stationers, and are to be sold by the booksellers of Dublin, 1682" and also in an issue with variant imprint similar to the present book, the t.-p. of which can be distinguished from the present book by "judgment" in line 11 of t.-p. and "Pater-noster" in the imprint.
    [Ware's] Second part has a special t.-p., separate paging, but continuous signatures.
    "To The Readbr [sic]. Courteous Reader..." (2d-4th p. ℓ.) signed at end: W. R. [i.e. Robert Ware]
    Dedication (5th-7th p. ℓ.) signed: Philirenes [i.e. John Nalson]
    Errata, 7th p. ℓ.^{v}
    Bookseller's advertisement, p. 154.
    In this copy there is a blank ℓ. at beginning.

68-115

        Contemporary ms. annotations.
        Bound in contemporary calf, rebacked.
        WingN105; W853; Smith(Anti-Quak.)23;
McAlpin4:108, 118-119.

D682
N285h

The Natural History Of Coffee, Thee, Chocolate, Tobacco. In four several Sections; With A Tract Of Elder and Juniper-Berries, Shewing how Useful they may be in Our Coffee-Houses: And also the way of making Mum, With some Remarks upon that Liquor. Collected from the Writings of the best Physicians, and Modern Travellers.
    London: Printed for Christopher Wilkinson, at the Black Boy over against St. Dunstan's Church in Fleetstreet. 1682.
    36, [4] p. 20.5cm. 4°
    Booksellers' advertisement at end.
    WingC1860; Sabin52041; Arents372.

05504, 1889

FB
N469
1682
1

Netherlands (United Provinces, 1581-1795)--
    Staten Generaal.
    Octroy Ofte fondamentele Conditien/onder de welcke haer Hoogh Mog. ten besten en voordeele van de Ingezetenen deser Landen/ de Colonie van Suriname hebben doen vallen in handen ende onder directie van de Bewindthebberen van de generale Nederlandtsche Geoctroyeerde West-Indische Compagnie.
    In 's Graven-Hage, By Jacobus Scheltus, Ordinaris Drucker van de Hoogh Mogende Heeren Staten Generael der Vereenighde Nederlanden. Anno 1682. Met Privilegie.
    15 p. 21.5cm. 4°
    Cut (coat of arms within border) on t.-p.
    Sabin 102903.

70-484

F682
=N678j

Nieuhof, Johan, 1618-1672.
    ... Gedenkwaerdige Zee en Lantreize Door de Voornaemste Landschappen van West en Oostindien.
    T Amsterdam By de Weduwe van Iacob van Meurs 1682
    6 p.ℓ., 47, 40-192, 195-240, [2] p. incl. illus., coat of arms. 3 plates (incl. double plate), port., double-page map; 2 p.ℓ., 218, 217-308, [4] p. illus., 41 plates (incl. 25 double plates), 4 double-page maps. 39cm. fol.
    At head of title: Joan Nieuhofs.
    Engraved t.-p.
    Edited by Hendrik Nieuhof.
    Two parts, each with special t.-p. and separate paging and signatures: [1]... Gedenkweerdige Brasiliaense Zee-en Lant-Reize. [2] ... Zee en Lant-Reize door... Oostindien.
    Preliminary matter includes poetry signed v.1: I.D.L., J. Nieuhof, and v.2: J. Nieuhof, P. Ketting, Jacob Steendam, Zacharias Kaheingh.
    Dedication dated (v.1, 4th p.ℓ.^{v}): Den 4 van Sprokkelmaent, 1682.
    JCB(2)2:1248; Sabin55278; Rodrigues1770; Muller(1872)1146; Borba de Moraes2:101.

03637-8, before 1866

F682
=N678j

Nieuhof, Johan, 1618-1672.
    ... Gedenkweerdige Brasiliaense Zee-en Lant-Reize. Behelzende Al het geen op dezelve is voorgevallen. Beneffens Een bondige beschrijving van gantsch Neerlants Brasil, Zoo van lantschappen, steden, dieren, gewassen, als draghten, zeden en godsdienst der inwoonders: En inzonderheit Een wijtloopig verhael der merkwaardigste voorvallen en geschiedenissen, die zich, geduurende zijn negenjarigh verblijf in Brasil, in d'oorlogen en opstant der Portugesen tegen d'onzen, zich sedert het jaer 1640. tot 1649. hebben toegedragen. ...
    t'Amsterdam, Voor de Weduwe van Jacob van Meurs, op de Keizers-gracht. 1682.
    5 p.ℓ., 47, 40-192, 195-240, [2] p. incl. illus., coat of arms. 3 plates (incl. double plate), port., double-page map. 39cm. fol. (Issued as the 1st part of his Gedenkwaerdige Zee en Lantreize Door de Voornaemste Landschappen van West en Oostindien. Amsterdam, 1682.)
    At head of title: Johan Nieuhofs.
    Title in red and black.
    Cut (Mercury) on t.-p.
    Edited by Hendrik Nieuhof.
    Preliminary matter includes poetry signed: I.D.L., J. Nieuhof.
    Dedication dated (4th p.ℓ.^{v}): Den 4 van Spokkelmaent, 1682.
    Errata, p. 240.

03637, before 1866

F682 =N678j	Nieuhof, Johan, 1618-1672. ... Zee en Lant-Reize door verscheide Gewesten van Oostindien, Behelzende veele zeltzaame en wonderlijke voorvallen en geschiedenissen. Beneffens Een beschrijving van lantschappen, steden, dieren, gewassen, draghten, zeden en godsdienst der inwoonders: En inzonderheit een wijtloopig verhael der Stad Batavia ... t'Amsterdam, Voor de Weduwe van Jacob van Meurs, op de Keizers-gracht. 1682. 2 p.ℓ., 218, 217-308, [1] p. illus., 41 plates (incl. 25 double plates), 4 double-page maps. 39cm. fol. (Issued as the 2d part of his <u>Gedenkwaerdige Zee en Lantreize, Door de voornaemste Landschappen van West en Oostindien</u>. Amsterdam, 1682.) At head of title: Joan Nieuhofs. Cut (Mercury) on t.-p. Edited by Hendrik Nieuhof. Preliminary matter includes poetry signed: J. Nieuhof, P. Ketting, Jacob Steendam, Zacharias Kaheingh. Errata, at end. 03638, before 1866		8 p. 17.5cm. 4º. "A Letter sent from New-Jersey in America to a Friend in London..." (p. 3) signed: Burlington the 12th of the 5th. Month, 1682. John Cripps. "An imitation of the Indian Marks" (p. 8) signed: Henry Jacobs Falckinburs, Interpreter. WingO127; Sabin56650; Smith(Friends)1:465; Church675. 8829, 1912
DA682 O11s	Oakes, Urian, 1631-1681. The Soveraign Efficacy of Divine Providence ... As Delivered in a Sermon Preached in Cambridge, on Sept. 10. 1677. Being the Day of Artillery Election there. By Mr. Urian Oakes, the late (and still to be Lamented) Reverend Pastor of the Church of Christ in Cambridge: And Learned President of Harvard Colledge. ... Boston In New-England: Printed for Samuel Sewall. 1682. 3 p.ℓ., 40 p., 1 ℓ. 18.5cm. 4º "To The Reader" (2d-3d p.ℓ.) signed: John Sherman. Bookseller's advertisement on last leaf. "Carmen funebre in obitum... Uriani Oakesii ..." by William Adams in ms. on verso of t.-p.; other ms. additions on a leaf at end. JCB(2)2:1249; Evans326; WingO23; Sabin56384. 04999, 1851	DA682 P451f [R]	Pain, Philip, d. 1668? [Daily Meditations: Or, Quotidian Preparations For And Considerations Of Death And Eternity. Second Edition. Boston: 1682.] 1 p.ℓ., 16, [5] p. 15cm. (16cm. in case) 8º First pub. Cambridge, Mass., 1668. "A Postcript [sic] To The Reader" p. [1-2] at end signed: M.[armaduke?] J.[ohnson?]. "Verses made by That worthy Knight, Sir. Walter Rawleigh, A little before his Death." (p. 3-5 at end). Imperfect: t.-p., p. 1-4, 9-12, and final ℓ. wanting; except t.-p., available in facsimile. Title and imprint from Evans. Bound with: Perkins, William. <u>The Foundation of Christian Religion</u>, Boston, <u>1682</u>. Evans327; WingP191A. 13021-6, 1921
D682 O16t	Ockanickon, Indian chief, d. 1682? A True Account Of The Dying UUords Of Ockanickon, An Indian King, Spoken to Jahkursoe, His Brother's Son, whom he appointed King After Him. London, Printed for Benjamin Clark, Bookseller, in George-Yard in Lombard-street, 1682.	BA682 P153v	Palafox y Mendoza, Juan de, bp., 1600-1659. Vida Interior Del Excelentissimo Señor D. Juan De Palafox Y Mendoza, Obispo antes de la Puebla de los Angeles, Virrey, y Capitan General de la Nueva España. Visitador de tres Virreyes de ella; Arçobispo electo de Mexico, de el Consejo Supremo de Aragon. La qual vida el mismo señor Obispo dexô escrita. En Brusselas, Por Francisco Foppens, Impressor, y Mercader de Libros, Año de 1682. 8 p.ℓ., 182, 185-380, 383-404 p. 20.5cm. 4º License dated (6th p.ℓ.ᵛ) 30 Jan. 1682. Preliminary matter includes poetry, 2d-4th p.ℓ.ʳ There is another edition of Brussels, 1682, with same title and imprint, which has 220 p. main paging. Bound in contemporary vellum. Sabin 58303; Peeters-Fontainas(1965)1033. 11823, 1919

D682
P412b
[Penn, William] 1644-1718.
A Brief Account Of The Province of Pennsylvania, Lately Granted by the King, under the Great Seal of England, to William Penn, and his Heirs and Assigns.
London: Printed for Benjamin Clark in George-Yard in Lombard-street, Bookseller. MDCLXXXII.
1 p.ℓ., 14 p. 19cm. 8°
Signed p. 14: William Penn.
First pub. London, 1681.
This edition is printed entirely in roman and italic type. The "Postscript" (p. 14) advises that further information is available "...at Philip Ford's... at Thomas Rudyard's or Benjamin Clark's... where the Mapps of Pensilvania are likewise to be sold: As also the Description belonging to the Maps; and likewise the Articles, Settlement and Offices of the Free-Society of Traders in Pennsilvania ..."
There is another edition with the same title and imprint and the same pagination which, however, is printed in 4° format and has p. 1-8 in black letter. The "Postscript" (p. 14) of that edition mentions, as above, where further information is available and the maps and description are sold. The "Articles, settlement and offices", however, are not mentioned.
JCBAR42:38.
29099, 1942

DA682
P412e
[Penn, William] 1644-1718.
An Epistle, Containing A Salutation To All Faithful Friends, A Reproof to the Unfaithful; And A Visitation to the Enquiring, In a Solemn Farewell to them all in the Land of my Nativity.
[London, Andrew Sowle, 1682]
8 p. 18.5cm. 4°.
Caption title.
Signed (p. 3, p. 6): William Penn. Signed (p. 7): From the Downs, the 30th of the 6th Mon. 1682. W. P.
"Books Printed and Sold by Andrew Sowle, at the Sign of the Crooked-Billet in Holloway-Lane in Shoreditch, and at his Shop without Bishops-Gate, 1682." (p. 8).
Smith(Friends)2:302; McAlpin4:111; Wing P1283.
11347, 1918

D682
-P412f
[Penn, William] 1644-1718.
The Frame of the Government Of The Province of Pennsylvania In America: Together with certain Laws Agreed upon in England By The Governour And Divers Free-Men of the aforesaid Province. To be further Explained and Confirmed there by the first Provincial Council and General Assembly that shall be held, if they see meet.
[London] Printed [by William Bradford] in the Year MDCLXXXII.
2 p.ℓ., 11 p. 30cm. fol.
Privately printed by William Bradford at the press of his master, Andrew Sowle.
There is a variant issue, otherwise the same as this issue but with the words "and General Assembly" omitted from the t.-p.
JCB(2)2:1251; Sabin59696; Church676; Smith (Friends)2:298; Vail(Front)208; Kane(Promotion) 10; WingP1292.
0529, 1846

DA682
P451f
Perkins, William, 1558-1602.
The Foundation of Christian Religion Gathered into Six Principles...By William Perkins.
Boston In New-England Printed by Samuel Green, and sold by Mary Avery near the Blue Anchor in Boston. 1682.
4 p.ℓ., 39, [1] p. 15cm. (16cm. in case) 8°
First pub. London, 1590.
"Proofs [of the six principles] out of the Word of God" (p. 1-11) signed: T.[homas?] S.[hepard?].
Title-ℓ. mutilated; available in facsimile.
With this are bound in contemporary calf: Mather, Increase, The surest way to the greatest honour, Boston, 1699; Willard, Samuel, The man of war, Boston, 1699; Mather, Cotten, ed., Thirty important cases, Boston, 1699; Belcher, Joseph, The worst enemy conquered, Boston, 1698; Pain, Philip [Daily meditations, Boston, 1682]; Bond, Samson, The sincere milk of the word, Boston, 1699; and Stone, Samuel, A short catechism, Boston, 1699.
In this copy all but the t.-p. of Perkins' Foundation is bound following Belcher's Worst enemy.
Evans328; WingP1569; Eames(N.E.Cat.)15.
13021-1, 1921

bBB P4716 1682 1
Peru(Viceroyalty)--Laws, statutes, etc., 1681-1689 (Navarra y Rocafull) 13 May 1682
Don Melchor de Nauarra y Rocafull, ... Duque de la Palata.... Por quanto su Magestad (Dios le guarde) por su Real Cedula de 13. de Febrero del año passado de 1680. reconociendo el excesso, con que se defraudan sus Reales quintos en la Plata labrada ...
[Lima, 1682]
[5] p. 31.5 x 21.5cm. fol.
Title from beginning of the text.
At end: "V. Exc. prohibe la extraccion, y saca de la Plata labrada de este Reyno."
Dated in Ciudad de los Reyes, 13 May 1682, with manuscript signature: El duque de la Palata.
Manuscript certifications of the city of Huamanga dated 10 June 1682.
Papel sellado variously dated 1667-83.
Medina(Lima) 538.
28199, 1938

bBB P4716 1682 2
Peru(Viceroyalty)--Laws, statutes, etc., 1681-1689 (Navarra y Rocafull) 13 May 1682
Don Melchor de Nauarra y Rocafull ... Duque de la Palata ... Por quanto vno de los efectos de mayor importancia de la Real Hazienda en estos Reynos es el de los Reales Quintos, que por Regalia, y de su Patrimonio Real pertenecen a su Magestad de la Plata, y Oro que se saca de las Minas y assientos de sus Prouincias ...
[Lima, 1682]
[12] p. 31.5 x 22cm. fol.
Title from beginning of the text.
At end: "V. Exc. renueua las penas contra los que extrauiaren la Plata, y Oro sin quintar, y da nueua forma a su execucion."
Dated in Ciudad de los Reyes, 13 May 1682, with manuscript signature: El duque de la Palata.
Manuscript certifications of the city of Huamanga dated 10 June 1682.
Papel sellado variously dated 1663-83.
Medina(Lima)537.
28198, 1938

B682 -L864p
Peru(Viceroyalty)--Real Audiencia.
Decission De La Real Avdiencia De Los Reyes. En Favor De la Regalia, i Real Jurisdicion, Sobre El Articulo, dos vezes remitido, en la Causa de Oliberos Belin, Llamado Comvnmente Don Carlos Clerqve. ...
En Lima Ano [sic] De 1682.
2 p.ℓ., 26,[1] p. 28cm. fol.
Written by Juan Luis López y Martínez.
"Belin" or "Clerque" was a member of Narbrough's expedition captured at Valdivia in 1670.
Dated (p. 26) in Lima, 20 May 1682.
Includes poetry.
Errata, p. 26
Marginal annotations in ms.
Bound as no. 2 in a vol. with binder's title: Luis Lopez Obras.
Medina(Lima)533; Leclerc(1878)1826.2(this copy).
14008, 1925

EA682 -P744d
Poeme De Six Religievses Ursulines Qui Sont Passées A La Martinique Pour L'Etablisement D'Un Monastere De Leur Ordre Dedié à Mademoiselle de Nantes, Par les Vrsulines du grand Convent de Paris.
A Paris. M. DC. LXXXII.
34 p. 26.5cm. 4º
Cut on t.-p.
Colophon: A Paris En la Boutique de George Iosse ruë S. Iacques à la Couronne d'Espines. 1682.
License (p. 34) dated 24 July 1682.
JCB(2)1253; Sabin 63600.
03793, 1868

CB -P8539 1682 1
Portugal--Treaties, etc.--1668-1706 (Pedro II).
Avtos De Las Conferencias De Los Comisarios De Las Coronas De Castilla, Y Portvgal, Que se juntaron en virtud del Tratado Prouisional, Echo Por El Dvqve De Iovenazo Embaxador Extraordinario, y Plenipotenciario de S.M. Catholica, Y El Dvqve De Caraval, Marqves De Frontera, Y Fray Don Manvel Pereira, Plenipotenciarios del Serenissimo Principe de Portugal en 7. de Mayo 1681. Sobre la diferencia ocasionada de la fundacion de vna Colonia, nombrada del Sacramento en la margen Septentrional del Rio de la Plata, frente de la Isla de San Gabriel. Atti Delle Conferenze Tra I Commissarii Delle Corone Di Castiglia, E Portogallo, Che si vnirono per esecutione del Trattato Prouisionale, Fatto Dal Dvca Di Giovenazzo Ambasciatore Straordinario, e Plenipotentiario di S. M. Cattolica, E Dalli Dvca Di Cadaval, Marchese Di Frontera, Et Fra D. Emmanvele Pereira, Plenipotentiarij del Serenissimo Principe di Portogallo ne, 7. di Maggio 1681. Intorno la differenza insorta per la fundatione della Colonia, detta uel Sacramento nel margine Settentrionale del Fiume della Plata, incontro la Isola di S. Gabriele.
[Rome, ca. 1682]

1 p.ℓ., 302 p. illus (diagrs.), 2 fold. tables. 32.5cm. fol.
José Eugenio Uriarte suggests in his Catálogo razonado that the compiler is Juan Carlos Andosilla.
Contains documents in Spanish and Portuguese with Italian translation in a parallel column.
In this copy there is a blank leaf in front and at the end.
JCBAR33:25; Palau(2)19924.

16436, 1933

D682 P933s
The Present State Of Carolina With Advice to the Setlers. By R. F.
London, Printed by John Bringhurst, at the Sign of the Book in Grace-Church-Street, 1682.
36 p. 18.5cm. 4°
The author, "R. F.", is probably Robert Ferguson.
Errata p. 36.
Includes (p. 36) "Advertisement. There is one Mr. Nathan Sumers Engineer for Carolina, that hath undertaken⟨by a new Engin of his own⟩ with the Lords Proprietors, and others, to un-burden and clear the Ground to fit if for Cultivation..."
Closely trimmed with some loss of text; available in facsim.
Wing F52A; Sabin 87919, Vail(Front.)204.

04823 rev

D682 P965
Proposals By The Proprietors Of East-Jersey In America, For the Building of a Tovvn On Ambo-Point, And for the Disposition of Lands in that Province And Also For Encouragement of Artificers and Labourers that shall Transport themselves thither out of England, Scotland, and Ireland.
London, Printed for Benjamin Clark in George-Yard in Lombard-street, Bookseller, M DC LXXXII.
1 p.ℓ., 6 p. 19cm. 4°
"Scottish Proprietors' Tracts" no. 4. Cf. Church 649n.
JCB(2)2:1238; Sabin1000; WingP3717.

01521, 1847

BA682 R422s
Rentería, Martín de, 1639-1689.
Sermon, Qve Predicò En El Convento de Señoras Religiosas de la Concepcion, A La Fiesta Titvlar De La muy Ilustre Congregacion de la Transfiguracion, El Padre Martin De Renteria, de la Compañia de Jesvs, y su Cathedratico de Visperas de Theologia, en el Colegio Maximo de San Pedro, y San Pablo de Mexico. ...
Con Licencia En Mexico: Por la Viuda de Bernardo Calderon, en la calle de San Augustin, Año de 1682.
5 p.ℓ., 9 numb. ℓ. 19.5cm. 4°
License dated (5th p.ℓ.^{v}) 12 Sept. 1682.
Palau(2)261199; Medina(Mexico)1255.

69-763

BA682 R666s
Robles, Juan de, 1628-1697.
Sermon, Qve Predicò El P. Ivan De Robles, Theologo de la Compañia de Jesvs, En La Civdad De Santiago De Queretaro, su Patria, el dia doze de Diziembre de 1681. En La Iglesia De N. Señora De Gvadalvpe, A la Annual memoria de la milagrosa Aparicion de su prodigiosa Imagen, que se Venera en el serro de Guadalupe Mexicano, Y celebra aqui en su Trassumpto La Ilustrissima Congregacion de Sacerdotes, que se honran con su titulo, y militan con su amparo. Dedicalo Al Br. D. Ivan Cavallero, y Ocio, su Fundador, Comissario de Corte del Santo Tribunal de la Inquisicion.
Con Licencia En Mexico. Por Juan de Ribera, Mercader de Libros en el Empedradillo. 1682.
4 p.ℓ., 8 numb. ℓ. 21cm. 4°
"Sentir" dated (2d p.ℓ.^{v}): 20 March 1682.
Medina(Mexico)1258; Sabin72250.

5247, 1909

DA682 R883t [R]
Rowlandson, Mary (White), ca.1635-ca.1678.
A True History Of The Captivity & Restoration Of Mrs. Mary Rowlandson, A Minister's Wife in New-England. Wherein is set forth, The Cruel and Inhumane Usage she underwent amongst the Heathens, for Eleven Weeks time: And her Deliverance from them. ... Whereunto is annexed, A Sermon of the Possibility of God's Forsaking a People that have been near and dear to him. Preached by Mr. Joseph Rowlandson, Husband to the said Mrs. Rowlandson: It being his Last Sermon.
Printed first at New-England: And Re-printed at London, and sold by Joseph Poole, at the Blue

Bowl in the Long-Walk, by Christs-Church Hospital. 1682.
3 p.ℓ., 46 p. 19cm. 4°
Preface (2d-3d p.ℓ.) signed: Per Amicum.
"A Sermon Preached at Weathersfield, Nov. 21. 1678. By Mr. Joseph Rowlandson, it being a day of Fasting and Humiliation." (p. 35-46).
Preface (p. 35-36) signed: B. W.
First pub. Cambridge, Mass., 1682, Mary Rowlandson's part under title <u>The sovereignty & goodness of God</u>, Joseph Rowlandson's part under title <u>The possibility of Gods forsaking a people</u>.

DA682
R883t
cop.2
——————Another copy. 19.5cm.
Margins closely trimmed, affecting text on 2d p.ℓ. and p. 37-38.
JCB(2)2:1255; WingR2094, R2091; Sabin 73579; Vail(Front.)214.
0528, 1846
05717, before 1874   rev

D682
A819c
[R]
A true Description Of Carolina.
London, Printed for Joel Gascoin at the Plat near Wapping old Stairs, and R[obert Greene] at the Rose and Crown in Budg-Row. [1682]
4 numb. ℓ. 19cm. (24cm. in binding) 4°
Caption title; imprint at end.
An abridgment of <u>The present state of Carolina with advice to the setlers by R. F.</u>, London, 1682. "R. F." is probably Robert Ferguson.
Printed on rectos only. Issued to accompany: Gascoyne, Joel. <u>A new map of the country of Carolina ... sold by Joel Gascoyne ... and Robert Greene</u>, London [1682] (cf. Cumming, W.P. The Southeast in early maps, no. 92).
Includes (numb. ℓ.4) "Advertisement. There is one Mr. Nathan Sumers Engineer for Carolina, that hath undertaken <by a new Engine of his own> with the Lords Proprietors, and others to unburden, and clear the Ground to fit it for Cultivation ..."
Closely trimmed affecting text on 2 leaves.
Bound with: <u>Carolina; or, A description of the present state of that country</u>, London, 1682, as the 2d of 3 items.
Sabin 97115; Wing G284; Vail(Front.)203.
4818, 1908   rev

E682
V131h
[Vairasse, Denis] fl. 1665-1681.
Historie Der Sevarambes, Volkeren die een Gedeelte van het darde Vast-land bewoonen, gemeenlijk Zuid-Land genaamd; ... Uit het Fransch in het Nederduitsch gebracht Door G. v. Broekhuizen. ...
t' Amsterdam, By Timotheus ten Hoorn, Boekverkooper in de Nes, by de Brakke Grond. 1682.
8 p.ℓ., 168, 171-253, 96 p. 16 plates. 19.5cm. 4°
Translated from the French original, 1st pub. under title: <u>Histoire des Sévarambes</u>, Paris, 1677-1679.
The 1st portion was pub. in English under title: <u>The history of the Sevarites</u>, London, 1675.
Added t.-p., engraved: Historie der Sevarambes. Behelzende een Beschrijving van het Onbekend Zuid-Land, Ian Luyken inven et Fecit. t'Amsterdam Bÿ Timotheus ten Hoorn, Boekverkoper inde Nes 1683.
Issued in 4 pts. with special title-pages for pts. 2-4 and separate paging and signatures for pt. 4.
Written under the pseudonym Captain Siden.
JCB(2)2:1256; Scheepvaart Mus. 287.
05668, before 1874

BA682
V645s
Victoria Salazar, Diego de, d. ca. 1700.
Sermon De La Gloriosa Virgen, Y Doctora Sagrada Santa Theresa De Jesvs, Que en el Convento de los Padres Carmelitas Descalços de la Ciudad de la Puebla predicò el dia de su fiesta El Doct. D. Diego De Victoria Salazar, Canonigo Magistral de la Santa Iglesia Cathedral de dicha Ciudad Examinador Synodal de su Obispado Calificador del Santo Officio Cathedratico de Prima de Theologia en los Reales Collegios de San Pedro, y San Juan, y Regente de sus estudios. ...
Con licencia: en Mexico. Por Francisco Rodriguez Lupercio. Año de 1682.
4 p.ℓ., [24] p. 19.5cm. 4°
License (3d p.ℓ.ᵛ) dated 12 Dec. 1682.
Dedication by Ignacio de Asenjo y Crespo.
Medina(Mexico)1265; Palau(1)7:169.
68-455

BA682
V649v
Vidal Figueroa, José, 1630-1702.
Vida Exemplar, Mverte Santa, Y Regocijada De el Angelical Hermano Migvel De Omaña, de la Compañia de Jesvs, en la Provincia de Nueva-España. Dispvesta Por el P. Ioseph Vidal su Confessor, de la misma Compañia. Para comun edificacion, y singular consuelo de los que en este Reyno le conocieron, y trataron. Dedicada A la vtilidad de la Iubentud Mexicana, que por cursar nuestros estudios le comunicó de cerca, y fue testigo ocular de sus heroycas virtudes.

Sacala A Lvz El B^r. D. Diego Pardo, y Aguiar, Presbytero, Notario de sequestros de el Santo Officio de Mexico.
 Con Licencia: en Mexico, por Juan de Ribera. Año de 1682.
 16 p.ℓ., 52 (i.e. 51), 54-66, 66-72 numb. ℓ., [13] p. 20.5cm. 4º
 License dated (6th p. ℓ.^r), 9 June 1682.
 Errata, p. [12-13] at end.
 JCB(2)2:1257; Palau(1)7:174; Medina(Mexico) 1266; Sabin99463; Backer8:646.

0797, 1846

CA679
V665s
1-2
 Vieira, Antonio, 1608-1697.
 Sermoens Do P. Antonio Vieira, Da Companhia De Jesu, Prégador de Sua Alteza. Segvnda Parte. ...
 Em Lisboa. Na Officina de Miguel Deslandes, E à sua custa, & de Antonio Leyte Pereyra Mercador de Livros. M. DC. LXXXII. Com todas as licenças, & Privilegio Real.
 4 p.ℓ., 470, [56] p. 21cm. 4º
 Cut (Jesuit trigram, floriated) on t.-p.
 License dated (4th p. ℓ.) 25 Nov. 1682.
 Contains 15 sermons preached in Rome [ca.1670], 1674, Lisbon 1644, 1645, 1651, 1652, 1655, 1659, 1662, 1670, São Luiz, Brazil, [1653-1661], 1654, and Bahia, Brazil, 1637.
 According to Leite "Deste volume de 1682, com a mesma data, conhecem se duas edições diferentes, com leves variantes.
 In this copy there is a blank ℓ. following p. 470.
 Bound with his Sermoens ... primeyra parte, Lisbon, 1679.
 Rodrigues2504; Backer8:659; Leite 9:194; Innocencio 1:290.

68-192.2

B682
V714m
 Villalobos, Juan de.
 Manifiesto Que A Sv Magestad (Que Dios Gvarde) Y Señores de su Real, y Supremo Consejo de las Indias, Haze El Capitan Don Jvan De Villalobos, Vezino de la Nueva Ciudad de la Veracruz en el Reyno de la Nueva España, Sobre La Introdvccion De Esclavos Negros en las Indias Occidentales.
 Impresso en Sevilla, año de 1682.
 24 numb. ℓ. 21.5cm. 4º
 Dated at end in Seville, 9 Feb. 1682.
 Cut (royal arms) on 1st ℓ.
 JCB(2)2:1258; Sabin99650.

0796, 1846

BA682
-V732i
 [Villegas, Manuel Juan]
 Informe Ivridico. Por Los Padres Españoles, Religiosos de la Serafica Orden de Nuestro Padre San Francisco de las Prouincias de los Doze Apostoles de Lima, y de San Antonio de los Charcas del Reyno del Perù. Qve Se Haze Al Capitulo General, para el Voto consultiuo que ha de hazer à la Sagrada Congregacion de Eminentissimos Cardenales de Obispos, y Regulares. Sobre La Alternatiua, que est à estatuida para la eleccion de Prouinciales, Custodios, Difinidores, Guardianes, y otros oficios honorificos, y de voz, y voto.
 [Madrid, 1682]
 28 numb. ℓ. 29cm. fol.
 Signed at end: En Madrid à 26. de Agosto de 1682. Fr. Manuel Ioseph de Villegas. Lic. D. Iuan de Contreras Herrera. Lic. D. Iuan Gutierrez Coronel.
 Palau(1)7, 203; Medina(BHA)1740; Sabin 99730.

70-576

F682
V982c
 Vries, Simon, b. 1630.
 Curieuse Aenmerckingen Der bysonderste Oost en West-Indische Verwonderens-waerdige Dingen; Nevens die van China, Africa, en andere Gewesten des Werelds. ... Door S. De Vries. In IV. Deelen. ...
 t' Utrecht, By Johannes Ribbius, Boeckverkooper in de korte Jans-straet. M. DC. LXXXII.
 4 v.: v.1, 88 p. ℓ., 496, [35] p. 13 plates (incl. 4 fold.), 2 fold. maps; v.2, 2 p.ℓ., 497-1328, [48] p. 16 plates (incl. 5 fold.), 12 fold. maps; v.3, 3 p.ℓ., 260, 602, [52] p. 21 plates (incl. 10 fold.); v.4, 4 p.ℓ., 603-1528, [58] p. 12 plates (incl. 1 fold.) 22.5cm. 4º
 Cut on title-pages.
 Each v. has an added t.-p., engraved.
 Title of v.1 in red and black.
 Foreword dated (v.1, 19th p. ℓ.^v): Utrecht, deesen 15 der Wijnmaend des Jaers 1681.
 In this copy the index for v.1 ([35] p.) is bound after the prelims. of v.2, and in v.4 p. 1513-1520 are misbound between p. 1496-1497.
 Bound in contemporary vellum.
 JCB(2)2:1259; Sabin100854; Scheepvaart Mus. 240; Muller(1872)1565; Tiele 1185.

03016, 1865

DA682 [Ware, Robert] d. 1696.
N173f2   The Second Part Of Foxes And Firebrands,
Or a Specimen Of the Danger and Harmony
of Popery and Separation ...
   Dublin, Printed by Joseph Ray, for Joseph
Howes, and are to be sold by Awnsham
Churchill Bookseller at the Black-Swan in
Pater-noster-row, London, 1682.
   1 p.ℓ., [5], 154 p. 17cm. 8° (Issued as
a part of [Nalson, John] Foxes and fire-
brands, Dublin, 1682.)
   This is an issue with variant imprint of the
edition pub. "Dvblin, Printed by Jos. Ray for
a Society of Stationers, and are to be sold by
the Booksellers of Dublin. MDCLXXXII."
   Bookseller's advertisement, p. 154.
   Bound in contemporary calf.
   WingW853; cf. Smith (Anti-Quak.)23; cf.
McAlpin4:118.
06375A, 1968

DA682 [Ware, Robert] d. 1696.
N173f3   The Second Part Of Foxes And Firebrands:
Or, A Specimen Of The Danger and Harmony
of Popery and Separation. ...
   Dublin, Printed by Jos. Ray, for Jos. Howes,
and are to be sold by Awnsham Churchill at the
Black Swan in Pater-hoster-Row, near Amen-
Corner, London. 1682.
   1 p.ℓ., [5], 154 p. 17cm. 8° (Issued as a
part of [Nalson, John] Foxes and firebrands,
Dublin, 1682.)
   This is a page-for-page reprint of another
Dublin, 1682, edition in whose imprint fore-
names are not abbreviated (and which was also
issued with variant imprint "Dublin, Printed
by Jos. Ray for a Society of Stationers, and
are to be sold by the Booksellers of Dublin.
MDCCXXII.").
   Bookseller's advertisement, p. 154.
   Contemporary ms. annotations.
   Bound in contemporary calf.
   WingW853; McAlpin4:118-119; cf. Smith
(Anti-Quak.)23.
68-115A

DC   VVeekly Memorials For The Ingenious: Or, An
W394m   Account of Books lately set forth in several
1-29   Languages. With Some other curious Novel-
ties relating to Arts and Sciences. [no. 1-7,
16 Jan. 1681/2 - 27 Feb. 1681/2].
   London: Printed for Henry Faithorne and John
Kersey, at the Rose in St. Pauls Church-yard.
1682.

   56 p. illus. 24cm. 4°
   Each no. has caption title and imprint at end.
   John Beaumont and James Petiver have been
suggested as the editors.
   Includes much material translated from Journal
des sçavans.
   Errata, p. 40.
   These 7 nos. are bound with and were edited by
the "author" of: Weekly memorials for the ingenious, London, R. Chiswell [et al.], 1683, a
different publication issued under the same title.
After the 7th no. the author left Faithorne and
conducted the rival series sold by Chiswell. The
original series was contemporaneously continued
by Faithorne.
   Bound in contemporary calf.
   Crane and Kaye 934.
2057A, 1906

D682   [Wilmer, John] fl. 1682-1693.
-W743c1   The Case Of John Wilmore Truly and Im-
partially Related: Or, A Looking-Glass For All
Merchants and Planters That are Concerned in
the American Plantations.
   London, Printed for Edw. Powell at the White
Swan in Little Brittain, MDC LXXXII.
   1 p.ℓ., 17 p. 29cm. fol.
   Signed (p. 17): John Wilmer.
   Wilmer was tried in London, 1682, for kid-
napping and transporting a boy to Jamaica.
   Next to last line of p. 7 begins "(said they)".
Line 19, page 17 ends "[See Heraclitus Num.
71]".

D682   ————Variant. 30cm.
-W743c2   Next to last line of p. 7 begins "hovvever
vve". Line 19, page 17 ends "[mark Heraclitus Num. 71]".
   WingW2883; Sabin104573; Cundall(Jam.
Supp.)264.
0617, 1846
02938, 1861 rev

D682   [Wilson, Samuel] fl. 1678-1682.
W753a1   An Account Of The Province Of Carolina In
America. Together With An Abstract of the
Patent, and several other Necessary and Useful
Particulars, to such as have thoughts of Trans-
porting themselves thither. Published for their
Information.
   London: Printed by G. Larkin for Francis

[III]

Smith, at the Elephant and Castle in Cornhil. 1682.

26 (i.e. 27) p. A-C⁴ D². fold. map. 19.5cm. 4°

Dedication signed (p. [4]) by Samuel Wilson, secretary to the Proprietors of Carolina.

Two variants of gathering B are known, corrected and uncorrected (the latter with typographical errors in the top paragraph of B2, e.g. in line 1 "strony" for "strong", and p. 10, 11, 14, 15 misnumbered respectively 9, 10, 13, 14). Two variants of gathering D are known, corrected and uncorrected (the latter with p. 25, 26, 27 misnumbered respectively 27, 25, 26).

This copy has gatherings B and D in the uncorrected variants.

D682
W753a2 ———— Another copy. 18cm.

This copy has gathering B in the corrected variant and gathering D in the uncorrected variant.

Without map.

JCB(2)2:1261; WingW2932; Sabin104685; Vail(Front)216; Church677 and 678.

1905, 1906
0526, 1846

1683

bD683
A244c Advertisment Concerning East-New-Jersey
Edinburgh, Printed by John Reid, Anno Dom. 1683.

Broadside. 30 x 18cm. 1/2°
"Scottish Proprietors' Tracts" [no. 8] (cf. Church 649n).
Vail(Front.)217A; WingA609A.

3312, 1907

B683
A681v1 Arenas, Pedro de, fl. 1611.
Vocabvlario Manual De Las Lengvas Castellana, y Mexicana. En Qve Se Contienen Las palabras, preguntas, y respuestas mas comunes, y ordinarias que se suelen ofrecer en el trato, y comunicacion entre Españoles, è Indios. Enmendado en esta vltima impression Compuesto por Pedro De Arenas.

Impresso con licencia, y Aprobacion. En Mexico. En La Imprenta De La Viuda De Bernardo Calderon. Año de M. DC. LXXXIII.

4 p.ℓ., 118, [2] p. 14.5cm. 8°
First pub. Mexico, 1611.

One of two distinct editions of 1683, as mentioned by García Icazbalceta. In this edition most gatherings are signed on the 1st leaf only.

Imperfect: lower margin closely trimmed, affecting text and signature marks in a few instances.

JCB(2)2:1262; Medina(Mexico)1271; Palau(2) 15924; Ugarte 18; Pilling153; Viñaza 211; Icazbalceta(Apuntes)6.

04344, before 1874

B683
A681v2 Arenas, Pedro de, fl. 1611.
[Vocabulario manual de las lenguas Castellana y mexicana]
[Mexico, Viuda de Bernardo Calderón, 1683]

4 p.ℓ., 118, [2] p. 13.5cm. 8°
First pub. Mexico, 1611.

One of two distinct editions of 1683 as mentioned by García Icazbalceta. In this edition most gatherings are signed on the first two leaves.

Imperfect: p.ℓ. 1-4 wanting; t.-p. of the other 1683 edition inserted. Three pages mutilated; copy closely trimmed with some loss of text.

Bound in contemporary vellum.

JCB(2)2:1262; Medina(Mexico)1271; Palau (2)15924; Ugarte 18; Pilling 153; Viñaza211; Icazbalceta(Apuntes)6.

04345, before 1923

D683
B677a [Bohun, Edmund] 1645-1699.
An Address To The Free-Men And Free-Holders Of The Nation. The Second Edition.
London: Printed for George Wells, in S. Pauls Church-Yard, 1683.

1 p.ℓ., xi, 66 p. 20.5cm. 4°
First pub. London, 1682.

In this copy there is a blank leaf at end.
WingB3445.

68-103

D683　[Bohun, Edmund] 1645-1699.
B677t　　The Third and Last Part Of The Address To
　　　The Free-Men And Free-Holders Of The Nation.
　　　By the same Author.
　　　　London, Printed for George Wells, at the Sun
　　　in St. Paul's Church-yard, 1683.
　　　　1 p. ℓ., xxii, 138 p.　20.5cm.　4°
　　　　An appendix "Advice To The Reader..."
　　　(p. 131-138) concerns "the case of Mr. Richard
　　　Thompson of Bristol Clerk."
　　　　In this copy there is a blank leaf at beginning.
　　　　A continuation of his Address..., and his
　　　Second part of the Address..., each 1st pub.
　　　London, 1682.

68-105

F683　[Bos, Lambert van den] 1610-1698.
B741ℓ　　Leeven en Daaden Der Doorluchtigste Zee-
　　　Helden, Beginnende met de Tocht na Damiaten,
　　　Voorgevallen in den Jare 1217. En eindigende
　　　met den beroemden Admirael M. A. de Ruyter,
　　　Hartog, Ridd. &c. Vertoonende alle de voor-
　　　naemste Zeedaden die de Hollanders en Zee-
　　　landers...Naeukeurigh, uyt veele geloofwaerdige
　　　Schriften, en Authentijcke Stucken, by een ge-
　　　bracht, en beschreven, Door V. D. B. Met veele
　　　curieuse koopere Plaeten verciert.
　　　　t'Amsteldam, By Jan ten Hoorn, en Jan Bouman,
　　　Boekverkoopers, in Compagnie. Anno 1683.
　　　　8 p. ℓ., 166, 177-289 p., 1 ℓ., 289-784, [7] p.
　　　18 plates (incl. 6 fold.), 9 ports., fold. map.
　　　24.5cm.　4°
　　　　Added t.-p., engraved: Leeven, en Daden,
　　　der Doorlughtige Zee-Helden. T'Amsterdam...
　　　1683.
　　　　This is an account of the principal Dutch
　　　naval achievements. It incorporates much
　　　material from another work which was pub.
　　　under the same title in Amsterdam, 1676.
　　　The 1676 work, however, was international
　　　in scope, including material on other nations,
　　　not only the Dutch.
　　　　"Aan Den Leezer" (4th p. ℓ.) dated 10 Dec-
　　　ember. 1682.
　　　　Bound in contemporary calf.
　　　　JCB(2)2:1264; Muller(1872)128; Sabin6440;
　　　Scheepvaart Mus. 843.
04713, before 1874

D683　A Brief Account of the Province Of East-New-
B853　　Jarsey In America: Published by the Scots
[R]　　Proprietors Having Interest there. For the
　　　Information of such, as may have a Desire
　　　to Transport themselves, or their Families
　　　thither. Wherein The Nature and Advantage
of, and Interest in a Forraign Plantation to
this Country is Demonstrated.
　　Edinburgh, Printed by John Reid, Anno Dom.
1683.
　　15 p.　20cm.　4°
　　Cut on t.-p.
　　"Scottish Proprietors' Tracts" no. 5. Cf.
Church 649n.
　　Church683; Sabin53079; Baer(Md.)107; Vail
(Front.)218; WingB4518.
04207, 1898-9

BA683　Calderon del Castillo, Antonio, fl. 1683.
C146p　　Platica De El Archangel San Migvel, En For-
　　　ma De Meditacion; Dicha en la Capilla de la
　　　Pvrissima. Dala á la Estampa, á su costa; para
　　　la comun vtilidad y devocion del Santo Archangel.
　　　Y Dedicala; Por su particular estimacion, A la
　　　muy Ilustre Congregacion de el mismo Arch-
　　　angel San Migvel: fundada en el Religiosissimo
　　　Convento de N. Señora de la Encarnacion, desta
　　　Corte. El B.r [sic] Antonio Calderon del Castillo,
　　　Prefecto de la misma Congregacion.
　　　　Con Licencia. En Mexico: Por la Viuda de
　　　Bernardo Calderon. Año de 1683.
　　　　3 p. ℓ., 29 numb. ℓ.　14.5cm.　8°
　　　　Cut (angel's head) on t.-p.
05821, before 1902

BA683　Catholic Church--Liturgy and ritual--Special
C363d　　offices--Edward, the Confessor, King of Eng-
　　　land, Saint.
　　　　Die xxij. Octobris. Officivm S. Edvardi Con-
　　　fessoris. Regis Angliæ. Semidvplex. Omnia de
　　　Communi Confessoris non Pontificis, exceptis
　　　Lectionibus secundi Nocturni & Oratione.
　　　　Mexici. Superiorum permissu. Apud Viduam
　　　Bernardi Calderon, in via Sancti Augustini, 1683.
　　　　[8] p.　15cm.　8°
　　　　Caption title; imprint at end.
　　　　First pub. under title: Die 13. Octobris. In
　　　festo S. Edvardi. Saragossa, 1681.
　　　　Dated (p. [7])　22 Aug. 1682.
5761¹², 1909

DA683　Church of England--Book of Common Prayer--
C562ℓ　　French.
　　　　La Liturgie, C'est à dire, Le Formulaire des
　　　Prieres Publiques, De l'Administration Des Sa-
　　　cremens, Et des autres Ceremonies & Coûtumes

de l'Eglise, Selon l'Usage de L'Eglise Anglicane: Avec Le Pseautier, Ou les Pseaumes De David, Ponctuez selon qu'ils doivent estre, ou Chantez, ou leûs dans les Eglises.

A Londres, Imprimée par R. E[veringham] pour R. Bentley, & S. Magnes, demeurant dans Russel-Street au Covent-Jardin. 1683.

18 p. ℓ., 347, [1] p. 15.5cm. 12º

Transl. by Jean Durell, from: The Book of Common Prayer. Cambridge, 1662. French transl. first pub. London 1667.

Bound in contemporary calf.

Wing D2690; McAlpin4:141.

8275, 1912

BA683
C824f

Correa, Antonio.

Fvnebre Panegyris, Qve A Las Honras Del Muy Piadoso, y nobilissimo Republicano Diego Del Castillo Comprador de Plata, consagrò como à Patrono de su Iglesia, El Muy Illustre Convento de las Señoras Religiosas Descalças de Sancta Ysabel de esta Ciudad de Mexico el dia 29. de Março de 1683. Predicò, El P. Fray Antonio Correa Predicador mayor del Convento de N.P.S. Francisco desta Ciudad. Dedicalo, A N. M. R.P. Fr. Francisco De Avila Lector jubilado, Qualificador del Santo Oficio, y Ministro Provincial de la Provincia del Santo Evangelio. Dalo A La Estampa A Expensas Svyas El Capitã Domingo de la Rea y Zarate, Natural de Eribe en la Provincia de Alava, y Comprador de Plata en la Imperial de Mexico.

Con liceucia [sic] en Mexico, Por Francisco Rodriguez Lupercio. Año de 1683.

9 p. ℓ., [19] p. 20cm. 4º

License dated (ℓ. 8^r) 17 May 1683.

Dedication includes poetry: ℓ. 4-5.

Palau(2)62505; Medina(Mexico)1276.

1036, 1905

BA683
C824s

Correa, Antonio.

Sylogismo Sacramental, Y Mariano. Sermon Panegyrico, Que al purissimo mysterio de la Concepcion sin mancha de Maria Santissi^{ma} Señora Nvestra, (Presente El SS. Sacramento de la Eucharistia⟩ en la solemne fiesta, que el dia Octavo de Diziembre, año de 1682. (con assistencia del Nobilissimo Consulado) consagrò generosamẽte devoto al instante primero de su originea gracia el muy illustre Convento de N.P.S. Francisco de Mexico. Predicò El P. Fr. Antonio Correa, Predicador mayor de dicho Convento. ...

Con Licencia En Mexico: Por la Uiuda de Francisco Rodriguez Lupercio. Año de 1683.

4 p. ℓ., 10 numb. ℓ. 19.5cm. 4º

License dated (3d p. ℓ.^{r}) 9 Oct. 1683.

Palau(2)62506; Medina(Mexico)1275.

69-760

E683
D861m

[Dufour, Philippe Sylvestre] 1622-1687.

Moral Instructions Of A Father To His Son, Upon His Departure for a long Voyage: Or, An Easie way to guide a Young Man towards all sorts of Virtues. With an hundred Maximes, Christian and Moral.

London, Printed for W. Crook, at the Green Dragon without Temple-Bar, near Devereux Court, 1683.

6 p. ℓ., 99 [100-108] p. 14.5cm. 12º

Translated by Peregrine Clifford Chamberlayne, from: Instruction d'un père à son fils qui part pour un long voyage, 1st pub. Lyon, 1677.

Dedication to Sir Thomas Grantham mentions (3d p. ℓ.) his part in pacifying Virginia during Bacon's Rebellion, 1676.

"Books Printed for William Crook...": p. [100]-[108] at end.

Bound in contemporary calf, rebacked.

Wing M2617.

1435, 1906

DA683
E81b

[Estlacke, Francis] fl. 1678-1683.

A Bermudas Preacher Proved A Persecutor Being a Just Tryal Of Sampson Bond's Book, Entituled, A Publick Tryal of the Quakers, etc. ... By those that have been more particularly concerned, and Eye and Ear-Witnesses in the Dispute at Bermudas; and those that have had the perusal of his Book, which manifests it self. ...

London, Printed by John Bringhurst at the Sign of the Book in Grace-Church-street, 1683.

1 p. ℓ., 92, 38 p., 1 ℓ. 19.5cm. 4º

A reply to: Samson Bond, A Publick Tryal Of The Quakers in Barmudas. Boston, 1682.

A collection of texts by Francis Estlacke, William Wilkinson, Richard Richardson, and John Tyso.

Page 18 (1st count) dated: Bermudas the 1st Month. 1683.

"The Truth Of Christ Jesus ... By ... Francis Estlacke" has half-title.

"Books Printed and Sold by John Bringhurst": 1 p. at end; in this copy supplied from another copy.

JCB(2)2:1265, 1276; WingE3354; Sabin23054; Smith(Friends)1:577, 2:937, 2:467, 2:837.

03641, 1866
2052, 1906

BA683 Ezcaray, Antonio de, fl. 1681-1691.
E99d Deseos De Asertar. Sermon Gratvlatorio Con Qve Vn Hvmilde, Y Rendido Hijo, y Subdito sirviò à su Madre la Santa Provincia del Santo Evangelio ... En La magnifica, y solemne fiesta, que celebrò en su Convento de N.P.S. Francisco de Mexico, el dia diez y seis de Agosto del Año passado de ochenta y dos; con la occurrencia de la Dominica de los Leprosos, y el Patron de ellos San Roqve. En hazimiento de gracias de la acertada eleccion, en que saliò electo por Ministro Provincial N.M.R.P. Fr. Francisco De Avila, Lector Jubilado, y Calificador del S. Oficio de la Inquisicion; ocupando aquel dia su P.M.R. las aras, con asistencia de toda la Provincia. Discvrrialos Fray Antonio De Escaray, entonces su Secretario, y oy Guardian actual del Convento de N. Seraphico P.S. Francisco de Mexico: Natural de la coronada Villa De Madrid. ...
Con Licencia. En Mexico. Por la Viuda de Bernardo Calderon, en la calle de S. Augustin, Año de 1683.
5 p.ℓ., 10 numb. ℓ. 19.5cm. 4⁰
License dated (5th p.ℓ.ᵛ) 13 March 1683.
Imperfect: numb. ℓ. 6-7 wanting.
Palau(2)80839; Medina(Mexico)1278.

69-759

BA683 Ezcaray, Antonio de, fl. 1681-1691.
E99e Oracion Panegirica, En La Magnifica, Y Solemne Fiesta, Que en demostracion de su affecto, devocion, y lealtad, celebrò la siempre Ilustre, y Noble Hermandad De Aranzazv, En Vizcaynos, Guipuzquanos, Alabeses, y Navarros. A La Reyna de los Angeles. Andrea Maria De Aranzazv. El dia octavo de su Assumpcion Gloriosa à los Cielos: en el Convento de N.P.S. Francisco de Mexico. Manifiesto Christo N. Bien Sacramentado. Deziala Fr. Antonio de Ezcaray Predicador, y Guardian actual de dicho Convento; Natural de la Coronada Villa de Madrid. Consagrala Con el rendimiento debido, à su R.ᵐᵒ Padre, y Prelado Fr. Jvan De Lvzvriaga, Lector Jubilado, Predicador Apostolico, Padre de las SS. Provincias de Cantabria, y Valencia, y Comisatio [sic] General de todas las de la Nueva-España, y Philipinas, &c. Imprimela A sus expensas, el Capitan Iuan Ortiz de Zarate, Saens de Maturana, y Torrealde.
Con Licencia. En Mexico. Por la Viuda de Bernardo Caldeton [sic], en la calle de S. Augustin, Año de 1683.
12 p.ℓ., 11 numb. ℓ. 20cm. 4⁰
License dated (12th p.ℓ.ᵛ) 11 Oct 1683.
Palau(2)85869; Medina(Mexico)1279.

1038, 1905

BA683 Florencia, Francisco de, 1619-1695.
F632s Sermon A La Festividad Del Bienaventvrado San Lvis Gonzaga De La Compañia De Jesvs, Marqves de Castellon, Principe del Imperio; Predicado En el Colegio Maximo de San Pedro, y San Pablo de Mexico. Por El P. Francisco De Florencia de la misma Compañia, Rector de èl, y Calificador de el Santo Officio de la Inquisicion, En su dia 21. de Junio, quarto de la Octava de el Santissimo Sacramento, en que estuvo patente. ...
Con Licencia En Mexico Por Juan de Ribera, en el Empedradillo. Año de 1683.
6 p.ℓ., 7, 7-14 numb. ℓ. 19.5cm. 4⁰
Dedication dated (4th p.ℓ.ᵛ) 26 Oct. 1683.
Palau(2)92335; Medina(Mexico)1280; Sabin 24819n; Backer3:795.

69-772

D683 [Ford, Philip] d. 1702.
-F711 A Vindication of William Penn, Proprietary
[R]   of Pennsylvania, from the late Aspersions spread abroad on purpose to Defame him.
London, Printed for Benjamin Clark in George-Yard in Lombard-street, 1683.
2 p. 30.5cm. fol.
Caption title; imprint at end.
Signed: London, 12th. 12th. Month, 1682/3. Philip Ford.
A reply to attacks on Penn attributed to Thomas Hicks, "William Penn having been of late Traduc'd as being a Papist, and Dead ..."
Includes (p. 2) "... Abstract of several Letters from William Penn Proprietary of Pennsylvania, to P.F. &c. Dated at Upland, Nov. 1. and from West-River, Decemb. 16. Mary-land, 1682."
Huth Catalogue 2:537 (this copy).
JCBAR 51:17-21; Church680; Sabin25067; Smith(Friends)1:621; Baer(Md.)106A; Vail (Front)221; Wing F1470.

30868, 1951

DA683 [Fox, George] 1624-1691.
F791   The Devil Was and Is the Old Informer Against The Righteous.
   London, Printed by John Bringhvrst, at the Sign of the Book in Grace-Church Street. 1682/3.
   12 p. 18cm. (20cm. in case) 4°
   Caption title; imprint at end.
   Signed: G. Fox.
   Smith(Friends)1:682; WingF1795.

62-37

DA683 Fox, George, 1624-1691.
F791t   Tythes, Offerings, And First-Fruits, Commanded by the Law in the Old Testament, Is Not Gospel, ... By George Fox. ...
   London, Printed for Benjamin Clark in George-Yard in Lombard-street, 1683.
   1 p.ℓ., 13, [1] p. 19.5cm. 4°
   Signed (p. 13): From South-gate 1682. G. Fox.
   Smith states that "the substance of this is in the tract entitled, The Beginning of Tythes" pub. [London] 1676.
   "Books Sold by Benjamin Clark in George-Yard in Lombard-street, Bookseller": p. [14]
   Smith(Friends)1:682-683; WingF1973.

11461, 1918

BA683 García, Francisco, 1641-1685.
G216v   Vida, Y Martyrio De El Venerable Padre Diego Lvis De Sanvitores, De La Compañia De Iesvs, Primer Apostol De Las Islas Marianas, Y Svcessos De Estas Islas, Desde El Año De Mil Seiscientos Y Sesenta Y Ocho, Asta El De Mil Seiscientos Y Ochenta Y Vno. Por El Padre Francisco Garcia, de la misma Compañia de Iesvs. ...
   Con Privilegio. En Madrid: Por Ivan Garcia Infanzon. Año de M.DC.LXXXIII.
   8 p.ℓ., 597, [10] p. port. 21.5cm. 4°
   "Svma De La Tassa" dated (7th p.ℓ.^{v}) 6 Sept. 1683.
   Errata, 7th p.ℓ.^{v}
   Preliminary matter includes poetry.
   Imperfect: port. wanting; available in facsim.
   Bound in contemporary vellum.
   Palau(2)97961; Medina(Filipinas)223; Sabin 26565; Backer3:1214; Streit 21:303.

70-526

BA683 García, Francisco, 1641-1685.
G216vm   Vida, Y Milagros De San Francisco Xavier, De La Compañia De Iesvs, Apostol De Las Indias, Por El Padre Francisco Garcia, Maestro de Theologia, de la misma Compañia de Iesvs. Tercera Impression, Coregida, Y Emendada
   Año 1683. Con Licencia. En Barcelona, En La Imprenta De Antonio Ferrer, Y Balthazar Ferrer Libreros, Vendense en sus Casas.
   4 p.ℓ., 401, [402-408] p. 21cm. 4°
   Cut (device of the Society of Jesus) on t.-p.
   First pub. Madrid, 1662.
   Palau(2)97881; Backer3:1209.

70-517

DB Gt.Brit.--Sovereigns, etc., 1660-1685 (Charles
-G7888 II)   26 July 1683
1683   At the Court at Whitehall, The 20th of July,
1   1683.
   London, Printed by the Assigns of John Bill deceas'd: And by Henry Hills, and Thomas Newcomb, Printers to the Kings most Excellent Majesty, 1683.
   4 p. 30cm. fol.
   Caption title; imprint at end.
   Cut (royal arms) on t.-p. (Steele 93).
   Announces issuance of a quo warranto against the charter of Massachusetts and orders Edward Randolph to New England to deliver notification.
   Includes a declaration of the king dated (p. 4) 26 July 1683.
   Sabin45929; WingE2893; Church681.

05935, 1888

H683 Gualdo Priorato, Galeazzo, conte, 1606-1678.
-G911t   Teatro Del Belgio, O'Sia Descritione Delle Diecisette Provincie Del Medesimo; Con le Plante delle Città, e Fortezze Principali; da chi al presente possesse; come, in qual modo, & in qual tempo acquistate. Aggiontovi vn succinto racconto di quanto è occorso dalla mossa d'armi del Re Christianissimo contro gli Stati Generali delle Provincie Unite sin' al fine del 1672. Descritta Dal Conte Galeazzo Gualdo Priorato.
   In Francofort M.DC.LXXXIII.
   6 p.ℓ., 148, [6] p. 13 ports., 2 fold. plates, fold. map, 120 double plans. 35cm. fol.
   Cut on t.-p. (storming of a fortress), engr. by Tobias Sadeler.

Added t.-p.: engr. compartment bearing coats of arms of the Netherlandish provinces; title in letterpress "Il Teatro Del Belgio".

Based in part on his Relatione delle Provincie Unite del Paese Basso, 1st pub. Cologne [i.e. Brussels?] 1668.

First pub. 1673 in both a Frankfurt and a Vienna issue. A version in German was also published in Vienna, 1673, under title Schauplatz dess Niederlandes. These are the same sheets as the Italian version of 1673 without 2 p.ℓ. of privileges found in the Frankfurt issue.

"Della Compagnia dell' Indie Occidentali" p. 79-81.

Imperfect: 13 ports. wanting; available in facsim.

In this copy on p. 17 the end of line 13 and all of line 14 are covered by pasted cancel slips.

Bound in contemporary half vellum.

69-410

E683 H515d
Hennepin, Louis, ca. 1640-ca. 1705.
Description De La Louisiane, Nouvellement Decouverte au Sud'Oüest de la Nouvelle France, Par Ordre Du Roy. Avec la Carte du Pays: Les Mœurs & la Maniere de vivre des Sauvages. Dediée A Sa Majesté Par le R.P.Louis Hennepin, Missionnaire Recollet & Notaire Apostolique.

A Paris, Chez la Veuve Sebastien Huré, rue Saint Jacques, à l'Image S. Jerôme, prés S. Severin. M.DC.LXXXIII. Avec Privilege Dv Roy.

6 p.ℓ., 312, 107 p. fold. map. 16cm. 12°

Cut (printer's device) on t.-p.

"Achevé d'imprimer pour la premiere fois, le 5. Janvier 1683." (6th p.ℓ.ᵛ).

Title leaf and map from another copy.

JCB(2)2:1226; Sabin31347; Harrisse(NF)150; Paltsits(Hennepin)xlix; Vail(Front.)222; Streit2:2721.

X01912, 1877

FC650 H737 33
Hollandse Mercurius, Verhalende de voornaemste Saken van Staet En Oorlog, Die, in en omtrent de Vereenigde Nederlanden, En elders in Europa, In het Jaer 1682, Zijn geschiedt. Het Drie-en-Dertigste Deel.

Tot Haerlem, Gedruckt by Abraham Casteleyn, Stadts-Drucker, op de Marckt, in de Blye Druck. Anno 1683.

3 p.ℓ., 253, [254-256] p. fold. map. fold. plate. 20cm. 4° (Bound in [vol. 8] of Hollandse Mercurius)

Added t.-p., engraved: Hollandse Mercurius Anno 1682 Tot Haerlem By Abraham Castelyn

JCB(3)2:410; Sabin32523.

8487GG, 1912

DB J2755 1683 1
Jamaica--Laws, statutes, etc.
The Laws Of Jamaica, Passed by the Assembly, And Confirmed by His Majesty In Council, Feb. 23. 1683. To which is added, A short Account of the Island and Government thereof. With an Exact Map of the Island.

London, Printed by H. Hills for Charles Harper at the Flower de Luce over against St Dunstan's-Church in Fleet-street. 1683.

32 p.ℓ., 218, [6] p. fold. map. 20cm. 8°

"To The Reader." p.ℓ. 2-13 is a description of the climate, geography, and government of the island. "The Preface." p.ℓ. 14-30, signed F.[rancis] H.[anson], is an account of the legal system and inhabitants, including Negro slaves.

"Law-Books Printed for, or Sold by Charles Harper ..." p. [220-224]

Bound in contemporary calf; from the library of William Blathwayt with marginal annotations on p. 46.

Sabin35622; Wing J124.

9290, 1913

F683 K85e
Kort En Opregt Verhaal Van het Droevig en avontuurlijk wedervaren/ Van Abraham Jansz Van Oelen, Schipper van nieu Vos-meer; Geschied in het Jaar 1682. op den 26. Januarij, in die bekende hooge Water vloed. En hoe hij op den 7 October van het selve Jaar/ op een wonderlijke en nooijt gehoorde wijs/ by St. Anna Land, een (so genaemde) Walvis, gevangen heeft. Beschreven uijt het verhaal van den Vanger selfs. Met schoone Kopere Plaaten versien, uijtbeeldende hoe de Vis eerst gesien, en daar na gevangen is. Midigaders, een naukeurige beschrijving van de hoedanigheijd van de Vis. Als mede een Rijm beschrijving hoedanig de Wal-Vissen in Groenland gevangen werden. Waar agter ook sijn bij gevoegt/ eenige bijsondere droevige/ wonderlijke/ en avontuurlijke voorvallen/ van sommige Commandeurs en Gasten in Groen-Land uijtgestaan. Nooijt voor desen gedrukt.

[Leyden? 1683]

51 [52-59] p. 5 fold. plates. 20cm. 4°

Added t.-p., engr.: Aenschou de Groenlands Visserij, In Prent, en ook in Rijmerij. Gedrukt

voor den Auteur, 1683. Wanting: available in facsimile.
"Die altijd is op't Land..." (p. 48-51) signed: P.P.V.S.
JCB(2)2:1250; Sabin56733.
05664, before 1882

BA683 Lascari de Torres, Antonio, fl. 1667-1683.
L341s Sermon A La Celebridad De Los Dolores de Maria Santissima Señora Nuestra, Viernes 6. de Quaresma, y del Consilio, este año de 82. Patente Como titular de los Viernes, la insigne Reliquia de la Santa, y prodigiosa Cruz de Guatulco Qve Predicò El Licenciado D. Antonio Lascari De Torres, Racionero antes de la S. Iglesia Cathedral de Michoacan, Actual Canonigo de esta de Antequera Obispado de Oaxaca, Comissario del Santo Officio de la Inquisicion, y Examinador Synodal, de dicho Obispado. Dedicalo Al Capitan, y Sargento mayor Don Fernando Nieto De Silva, Y Agviñiga, Alcalde mayor del Real de Minas de Chichicapa, Administrador de los Reales azogues, Encomendero perpetuo en Pueblos de esta Nueva-España.
Con Licencia De Los Svperiores En Mexico Por Juan de Ribera Impresor, y Mercader de Libros. Año de 1683.
4 p.ℓ., 6 numb. ℓ. 20.5cm. 4°
License dated (3d p.ℓ.ᵛ): 10 Jan 1683.
Palau(2)132356; Medina(Mexico)1286.
1039, 1905

BA683 [Ledesma, José]
L473s Silvos, Con Qve El Pastor Divino avissa á
[R] todos los Sacerdotes, Padres, y Ministros de su Iglesia, y Pastores de su Rebaño las graves obligaciones de tan alto ministerio, para que atendidas continuamente, aspiren siempre á mas perfecta vida, y costumbres en el camino de la virtud. El Ilustrissimo, y Reverendissimo Señor Doctor D. Francisco de Aguiar, y Seixas, del Consejo de su Magestad, Arçobispo de Mexico (cuyo zelo mandò se diessen á la estampa) concede quarenta dias de Indulgencia á todos los Padres Sacerdotes, que con la devida atencion los leyeren. Van al fin añadidos algunos puntos, que persuaden la obligacion de enseñar, y aprender la Doctrina Christiana.
Con Licencia. En Mexico: Por Juan de Ribera, Mercader de Libros en el Empedradillo. Año de 1683.
1 p.ℓ., [29] p. 14.5cm. 8°

First pub. Mexico, 1682.
"Pvntos, Qve Persvaden La grave obligacion que tienen de enseñar la Doctrina Christiana los Señores Sacerdotes, Curas, y Pastores de las almas..." (p.[18]-[29]) are taken from Ortigas, Manuel. Sumario de Misiones. Parte segvnda. Saragossa, 1671-1672.
Palau(2)134185; Medina(Mexico)1299.
05814, before 1923

BA683 Lemus, Diego de.
L562v Vida, Virtudes, Trabajos, Fabores, Y Milagros De La Ven. M. Sor Maria De Jesvs Angelopolitana Religiosa en el insigne Convento de la limpia Concepcion de la Ciudad de los Angeles, en la Nueva España; y natural de ella. Dedicada A La Soberana Emperatriz Del Cielo Maria Madre De Dios. Por El Licenciado Diego De Lemus Beneficiado de la Villa de Pedraza en el Obispado de Segovia.
En Leon, A Costa de Anisson, y Posuel. M. DC. LXXXIII. Con Privilegio.
10 p.ℓ., 553, [1] p. incl. port. 22cm. 4°
Cut on t.-p.
Ascribed also to Andrés Sáenz de la Peña (cf. Beristain no. 412). This is not the same work as the life of María de Jesús by Francisco García Pardo (Medina(Mexico) 1144).
Includes (6th-7th p.ℓ.) "Aprobacion del Señor... Diego De Victoria Salazar Canonigo Magistral de la Sancta Iglesia de la Puebla de los Angeles" and the "Licencia Del... Señor Obispo de la Puebla de los Angeles" which are thought to have been printed in Puebla de los Angeles, Mexico (cf. Palau).
Imperfect: 1st p.ℓ. (incl. port.) wanting; available in facsim.
JCB(2)2:1269; Palau(2)134872, 284388; Medina(BHA)1750; Sabin40020.
03987, 1869

D683 [Lockhart, George] fl. 1683.
L816f A Further Account of East-New-Jarsey By
[R] a Letter Write to One of the Proprietors Thereof, by a Countrey-man, who has a great Plantation there. Together With the Discription of the said Province, as it is in Ogilbies Atlas, Printed in the year, 1671.
Edinburgh, Printed by John Reid, Anno Dom. 1683.
7 p. 20cm. 4°

[118]

The letter (p. [3-4]) "For Robert Barkley, &c." is dated "London, June the 2d. 1683" and is signed "Geo: Lockhart."
"The Description of America, by John Ogilbie, Printed in the Year 1671 In his book, Fol. 168. 181. 182." (p. 5-7).
"Scottish Proprietors' Tract" (cf. Church 649n) [9].
JCBAR41:30-2; Vail(Front.)223; WingF2543.
28946, 1941

BA683 López, Francisco, 1648-1696.
L864s Sermon Panegirico De N. S.^{ra} Del Pilar, Qve Predico El R.^{mo} P. Francisco Lopez de la Compañia de Iesus ... en la Iglesia de N. Señora de los Desamparados de la Ciudad de Lima. ...
Con Licencia, Impresso En Lima, por Luis de Lyra, Año de 1683.
5 p.ℓ., 15 numb. ℓ. 19.5cm. 4°
Dedication by Juan Luis López y Martínez dated (2d p.ℓ.) 4 Nov. 1683.
Preliminary matter includes commendatory poetry by J.F.V., S.J.
Palau(2)139965; Medina(Lima)553; Backer 4:1946.
70-486

B682 López y Martínez, Juan Luis, marqués del
-L864p Risco, d. 1732.
Testimonio De La Sentencia Dada Y Pronvnciada En La Causa de Capitulos, que Gaspar Fernandez de Grado, Tesorero de la Santa Cruzada de la Ciudad de Ica, puso a Don Iuan de Villegas y Godoy, su Corregidor, y Justicia Mayor, y Teniente de Capitan General de la Costa de Barlovento. Por El Señor Doctor Don Ivan Lvis Lopez Del Consejo De S. M. Alcalde Del Crimen De la Real Audiencia de Lima, ... y Iuez de dicha Causa, por especial Comission del Real Acuerdo de Iusticia de este Reyno, en 31. de Agosto de 1683. ...
En Lima Ano [sic] De 1683.
1 p.ℓ., 6 numb. ℓ. 28cm. fol.
Dated at end 22 Sept. 1683.
Bound as no. 5 in a vol. with binder's title: Luis Lopez Obras.
Medina(Lima)556; Leclerc(1878)1826.5(this copy).
14011, 1925

J683 Major, Johann Daniel, 1634-1693.
M234d D. Johann-Daniel Majors See-Farth nach der Neuen Welt/ohne Schiff-und Segel; Anno 1670. zu erst/und nu wiederumb/der gelehrten Welt vorgestellet.
Hamburg/In Verlegung George Wolffen/Buchhändlers. clɔ lɔc LXXXIII.
12 p.ℓ., 258, [5] p. 12°
Added t.-p., engraved: D.I.D.Majors P.P. See-Farth nach der Neuen Welt. 1682.
First pub. Kiel, 1670.
Dedication dated (12th p.ℓ.): Kiel den 25. Sept. 1682.
This is not a voyage to the New World, as the title suggests, but a compendium of miscellaneous information on the sciences and arts.
Sabin44076; Palmer356.
01577, 1847

E683 Mallet, Alain Manesson, 1630?-1706?
M253d Description De L'Univers, Contenant Les Differents Systêmes Du Monde, les Cartes generales & particulieres de la Geographie Ancienne & Moderne: Les Plans & les Profils des principales Villes & des autres lieux plus considerables de la Terre; avec les Portraits des Souverains qui y commandent, leurs Blasons, Titres & Livrées: Et les Mœurs, Religions, Gouvernemens & divers habillemens de chaque Nation. Dediée Au Roy. Par Allain Manesson Mallet. Maistre de Mathematiques des Pages de la petite Escurie de sa Majesté, cy-devant Ingenieur & Sergent Major d'Artillerie en Portugal. ...
A Paris, Chez Denys Thierry, ruë S. Jacques, à l'Enseigne de la Ville de Paris, devant la ruë du Plâtre. M.DC.LXXXIII. Avec Privilege Du Roy.
5 v.: v.1, 9 p.ℓ., 228 p., 1 ℓ., 229-302, [9] p. incl. plates, maps, tables. 2 ports.; v.2, 4 p.ℓ., 299, [20] p. incl. plates, maps. 4 plates; v.3, 4 p.ℓ., 256, [15] p. incl. plates, maps. 10 plates; v.4, 5 p.ℓ., 328, [43] p. incl. plates, maps; v.5, 6 p.ℓ., 80 p., 81-96 numb. ℓ., 97-400 p., 21 ℓ. incl. plates, maps. 21.5cm. 8°
Errata: v.1, p. [7] at end; v.2, p. [19-20] at end; v.3, p. [13] at end; v.4, p. [41-43] at end; v.5, last leaf.
Cut on title-pages.
Each v. has an added, engr. t.-p. v.1: Description De L'Univers.—v.2: ... Asie Ancienne Et Moderne.—v.3: ... Afrique Ancienne Et Moderne.—v.4: ... L'Europe Ancienne Et Moderne.—v.5: ... Suite De L'Europe Ancienne Et Moderne Des Terres Australes Et De L'Amerique.
"Achevé d'imprimer pour la premiere fois

	...": v.1 (p. [9] at end) 1 Sept. 1682, v.3 (p. [15] at end) 1 Sept. 1682, v.4 (p. [40] at end) 31 Dec. 1682, v.5 (20th ℓ. at end) 31 Mar. 1683. Maps in v.3, p. 13, v.4, p. 181, and v.5, p. 47 have been pasted over what appears to be another impression of the same map. In this copy there is a blank leaf preceding the engraved added t.-p. in v.4. Bound in contemporary calf. Sabin 44130; Borba de Moraes 2:13. 12408-12412, 1919
D. Math I.67A	Mather, Increase, 1639-1723. ΚΟΜΗΤΟΓΡΑΦΙΑ. Or A Discourse Concerning Comets; wherein the Nature of Blazing Stars is Enquired into: With an Historical Account of all the Comets which have appeared from the Beginning of the World unto this present Year, M.DC.LXXXIII. Expressing The Place in the Heavens, where they were seen, Their Motion, Forms, Duration; and the Remarkable Events which have followed in the World, so far as they have been by Learned Men Observed. As also two Sermons Occasioned by the late Blazing Stars. By Increase Mather, Teacher of a Church at Boston in New-England. ... Boston In New-England. Printed by S: G.[reen] for S. S.[ewell] And sold by J. Browning At the corner of the Prison Lane next the Town-House 1683. 6 p.ℓ., 143 p., 1 ℓ., [6], 38 p., 1 ℓ., 32 p. 15cm. 8° Occasioned by the appearance of Halley's Comet, 1682. "To the Reader" (2d-3d p.ℓ.) signed: John Sherman; "To the Reader." (4th-5th^r p.ℓ.) signed: Boston N.E. Dec. 31. 1682. Increase Mather. Errata, p. 143; some copies have a slip with additional errata mounted on blank verso of p. 143. With this were issued 2 sermons previously separately issued: his <u>Heaven's Alarm To The World</u>. Boston, 1682, which itself includes his <u>The Latter Sign Discoursed of in a Sermon</u>. In this copy the 2 additional sermons are wanting; Library has, however, the separate issue. Imperfect: t.-p. wanting; supplied in pen and ink facsim. In this copy there is a blank leaf following p. 143. JCB(2)2:1290; Evans 352; Wing M1224; Sabin 46696; Holmes(I.)67A; Church 682. 06175, before 1874
D. Math M.90A	Mather, Samuel, 1626-1671. The Figures Or Types Of The Old Testament, By which Christ and the Heavenly things of the Gospel were preached and shadowed to the People of God of old; Explained and improved in sundry Sermons, By Mr. Samuel Mather, some-time Pastor of a Church in Dublin. [Dublin] Printed in the Year M.DC.LXXXIII. 4 p.ℓ., 678 p. 20.5cm. 4° Edited by Nathaniel Mather of Dublin. Errata, 4th p.ℓ.^{v}. In this copy p. 49-56 duplicated; there is a blank ℓ. at end. Bound in contemporary calf. Fly leaf inscribed: "Eliakim Mather the gift of Unkle Nath^{ll} Mather In Ireland only I pay for binding 18^d 1686 Nov 24 recd." Holmes(M)90A; Wing M1279. 4572, 1908
BA683 M491v	Medina, Baltasar de, d. 1696. Vida, Martyrio, Y Beatificacion del Invicto Proto-Martyr del Japon San Felipe De Jesvs, Patron de Mexico su Patria, Imperial Corte de Nueva España en el Nuevo Mundo, Que escrive, y Consagra al mismo Inclyto Proto-Martyr Fr. Balthassar De Medina, su Compatriota, Lector de Theologia, Diffinidor habitual, y Chronista de la S. Provincia de S. Diego de Religiosos Descalços de N.P.S. Francisco en Nueva-España, y Comissario Visitador, que fue, de la de S. Gregorio de Philipinas. Sale A Lvz A costa de Bienhechores devotos del Santo Martyr, y diligencias del Br. Diego Del Castillo Marqves Presbytero, Capellan de Coro de la Santa Iglesia Metropolitana. Con Licencia: En Mexico. Por Iuan de Ribera, Impressor, y Mercader de Libros en el Empedradillo. Año de 1683. 20 p.ℓ., 64 numb. ℓ., [16] p. pl. 20.5cm. 4° Title in red and black. License (9th p.ℓ.^{v}) dated 13 Jan 1683. Errata, ℓ. [1]^v at end. Bound in contemporary vellum. Medina(Mexico) 1287; Palau(2) 159375; Streit 5:1606. 12532, 1920
BA683 M763b [R]	Montalvo, Francisco Antonio de, 17th cent. Breve Teatro De las acciones mas notables De La Vida Del Bienaventvrado Toribio Arçobispo de Lima. Compvesto Por el Doctor D. Francisco Antonio De Montalvo Del Orden

69-643
de S. Antonio de Viena. Y Consagrado A La Real Magestad De La Reyna Nvestra Señora Por el Doctor Don Ivan Francisco De Valladolid Maestre Escuela de la Iglesia Metropolitana del Perù, y Procurador de su Canoniçazion.

En Roma, Por el Tinasi Ympr.[esor] Cam.[eral] 1683. Con licencia de los Superiores.

3 p.ℓ., 224 p. incl. [3], 40 plates. 20cm. 4°

Also issued with dedication variant.

In this issue the t.-p. is in letterpress surrounded by an engr. compartment. The other 2 p.ℓ. are copper plates surrounded by engr. compartments, and p.1 is an added engr. t.-p. by Benoît Thiboust after Giovanni Battista Gaetano.

Bound in contemporary vellum.

Sabin50069; Medina(BHA)1752; Palau(2)177318; Streit2:2184.

BA683
-M763s
Montalvo, Francisco Antonio de, 17th cent.

El Sol Del Nvevo Mvndo Ideado Y Compvesto En las esclarecidas Operaciones Del Bienaventvrado Toribio Arçobispo De Lima. Por El D.ᵒʳ D. Francisco Antᵒ. De Montalvo, Natural de Seuilla, del Orden de S. Antonio de Viena. Y Ofrecido Al Excellentissimo Señor D. Melchor De Navarra Y Rocafvll, Duque de la Palata, del Consexo de Estado, Virrey, Gouernador, y Capitan General del Reyno del Perù, Tierrafirme, y Chile. Por El Doctor D. Ivan Francisco De Valladolid. Maestreescuela de la Sancta Yglesia Metropolitana de los Reyes, y Procurador General en Roma de la causa de Canoniçacion del Glorioso Prelado.

En Roma, En la Imprenta de Angel Bernavò: M.DC.LXXXIII. Con Licencia De Los Svperiores

9 p.ℓ., 540, [27] p. front., port. 29.5cm. fol.

Cut (coat of arms) on t.-p.

Imperfect: front., port., half-title, and 6 ℓ. at end wanting; available in facsim.

Medina(BHA)1751; Palau(2)177319; Sabin50071; Zegarra205.

5503, 1909

BA683
M763v
Montalvo, Francisco Antonio de, 17th cent.

Vida Admirable Y Mverte Preciosa Del Venerable Hermano Pedro De S. Ioseph Betancvr Fundador de la Compañia Bethlemitica en las Yndias Occidentales Compvesta Por El Doctor D. Francisco Antonio De Montalvo Natvral De Sevilla Del Orden de S. Antonio de Viena, Y Dedicada A La Real Magestad De La Reyna Madre Doña Maria Ana De Avstria.

En Roma, MDCLXXXIII. Por Nicolas Angel Tinassi Ympresor Camer. Con licencia de los Superiores

9 p.ℓ., 416 p., 34 ℓ. port. 23.5cm. 4°

Added t.-p., engraved: Vida Exemplar ... Carlo Ascentii Inven. ... B. Thiboust Sculp.

Cut on t.-p.

Dedication dated (4th p.ℓ.ᵛ), Rome, 8 May 1683.

Errata, ℓ.18 at end.

Papal brief concerning the foundation of the order of the Bethlehemites: ℓ. 1-4 at end.

"Panegyrico Qve D. Geronimo Varona De Loaysa Predicò en las honras Del Venerable Hermano Pedro De S. Ioseph Betancvr", ℓ. 19-34 at end; 1st pub. Guatemala, 1668, under title: Elogio fúnebre.

Bound in contemporary sheep.

Palau(2)177321; Medina(BHA)1753; Sabin 50072.

11245, 1917

DB
-J2753
1683
A Narrative Of Affairs Lately received from his Majesties Island of Jamaica: Viz. I. His Excellency the Governour Sir Thomas Linch's Speech to the Assembly met Sept. 21. 1682. II. Samuel Bernard Esq; Speaker of the said Assembly, his Speech to the Governour. III. An humble Address from his Majesties Council, and the Gentlemen of the Assembly, to his most Sacred Majesty. IV. The Governour's Speech at the Proroguing the Assembly. London: Printed for Randal Taylor, near Stationers Hall. 1683.

1 p.ℓ., 6 p. 30cm. fol.

Cut (royal arms) on t.-p.

WingN169; Sabin35633; Cundall(Jam.)625.

1815, 1906

D683
O16t
Ockanickon, Indian chief, d. 1682?

A True Account Of The Dying Words Of Ockanickon, An Indian King. Spoken to Jahkursoe, His Brother's Son, whom he appointed King After Him.

[London] Printed in the Year 1683.

6 p. 19cm. 4°.

First pub. London, 1682.

"A Letter sent from New-Jersey in America to a Friend in London..." (p. 2) signed: Burlington

the 12th of the 5th. Month, 1682. John Cripps.
"An imitation of the Indian Marks." (p. 6). The marks are supplied in ms.
Signed (p. 6): Henry Jacobs Falckinburs, Interpreter.
WingO128; Sabin56650; Smith(Friends)1:465; Church675.

05723, before 1923

BA683
O48o
Olivares, José de, fl. 1683.
Oracion Panegyrica, Qve A La Festiva Solemnidad De La nueva Capilla, que se consagro à N. Señora de Gvadalvpe. Y translacion de la peregrina, y milagrosa efigie de Christo Crucificado, que por tiempo immemorial se adora, y venera en las Cuebas, y Santuario de S. Miguel de Chalma, del Orden de N. P. San Augustin. Predicò El P.M. Fr. Joseph de Olivares, de dicha Orden, Maestro en Sagrada Theologia por la Real Vniversidad de Mexico. Y por su Religion, en esta Provincia del Santissimo Nombre De Jesvs, de la Nueva-España. Dedicala A la mesma Santissima Imagen, de Christo Crvcificado.
Con Licencia. En Mexico, por la Viuda de Bernardo Calderon, en la calle de S. Augustin, Año de 1683.
9 p.ℓ., 11 numb. ℓ. 20.5cm. 4°
"Parecer" dated (6th p.ℓ.^{v}) 17 May 1683.
Some copies may incl. a plate, which is recorded by Medina as "una gran estampa en cobre del Christo de Chalma, grabada por Juan Añasco."
Palau(2)200408; Medina(Mexico)1289; Santiago Vela 6:72.

13058, 1921

BA683
P153p
[k]
Palafox y Mendoza, Juan de, Bp., 1600-1659.
Peregrinacion De Philotea Al Santa Templo, Y Monte De La Crvz. Del Illvstrissimo, Y Reverendissimo Señor Don Ivan de Palafox y Mendoza, del Consejo de su Magestad, Obispo de Osma, &c. ...
Con Licencia: En Barcelona, en casa Cormellas, por Iayme Cays, Año 1683. Vendese en Casa Francisco Llopis à la Libreria, y à su costa.
12 p.ℓ., 215, [1] p. 20.5cm. 4°
First pub. Madrid, 1659.
Approbation dated (4th p.ℓ.) 4 Jan. 1683.
Palau(2)209764.

70-527

bD683
P279
Paschall, Thomas, 1635-1718.
An Abstract of a Letter From Thomas Paskell Of Pennsilvania To his Friend J. J. of Chippenham.
London, Printed by John Bringhurst, at the Sign of the Book in Grace-Church-Street. 1683.
2 p. 30cm. fol.
Caption title, imprint at end.
Signed: Pensilvania, the last of January, 168$\frac{2}{3}$ Thomas Paskell.
Sabin58991; Church684; Vail(Front.)224; WingP647.

1433, 1906

D683
-P412ℓ
[R]
Penn, William, 1644-1718.
A Letter From William Penn Poprietary [sic] and Governour of Pennsylvania In America, To The Committee Of The Free Society of Traders' of that Province, residing in London. ... To which is added, An Account of the City of Philadelphia Newly laid out. ... With A Portraiture or Platform thereof, Wherein the Purchasers Lots are distinguished by certain Numbers inserted, directing to a Catalogue of the said Purchasors Names ...
Printed and Sold by Andrew Sowle, at the Crooked-Billet in Holloway-Lane in Shoreditch, and at several Stationers in London, 1683.
1 p.ℓ., 10 p. fold map. 32.5cm. fol.
Signed (p. 9) by William Penn in Philadelphia, 16 Aug. 1683.
With this is bound "Directions of Reference in the City-Draught of Philadelphia ..." (6 p. in ms.).
JCB(2)2:1271; WingP1319; Sabin54712; Church685(1); Vail(Front.)225.

01913a, before 1854 rev

B682
-L864p
Peru(Viceroyalty)--Auditor General de la Gente de Mar y Guerra.
Consvlta Del Avditor General De La Gente De Mar, I Guerra De Este Reino. Sobre La Fuga de veinte Soldados, de la Compañia de Leva del Capitan Don Sebastian de Carranza, que se huyeron del Navio San Pedro, con su Cabo, Ronda, y Centinelas: y demas excessos, que cometieron hasta que fueron aprehendidos. Al Excelentissimo Señor Don Melchor De Navarra I Rocafull, ... Virrey, Governador, y Capitan General de estos Reynos del Peru, Tierrafirme, y Chile, &c. En Illustracion de las Leyes 15. y 22. del Tit. 17. del Libro 3. del Sumario de las Leyes de las Indias. ...

[122]

En Lima Ano [sic] De 1683.
1 p.ℓ., 7 numb. ℓ., [1] ℓ. 28cm. fol.
Signed (7th numb. ℓ.ᵛ): Don Iuan Luis Lopez.
Viceroy's endorsement dated (last p.) 3 Mar 1683.
Bound as no. 4 in a vol. with binder's title: Luis Lopez Obras.
Leclerc(1878)1826.4 (this copy).

BB -S7336 1627 1 ——— ———Another copy. 28.5cm.
Bound in a vol. of Spanish folio pamphlets with foliation in ms. 221-229.
Medina(Lima)549.

14010, 1925
7491, 1910

bBB P4716 1683 1   Peru (Viceroyalty)--Laws, statutes, etc., 1681-1689 (Navarra y Rocafull)   3 Dec. 1683
Don Melchor De Navarra, y Rocaffull ... Duque de la Palata, ... Por quanto su Magestad (Dios le Guarde) considerando el desorden, y excesso conq̃ se ha extraviado a los Estrangeros la plata en pasta, ...
[Lima, 1683]
[6] p. 31.5cm. fol.
Title from beginning of text.
At end: "V. Exc. Manda, que no se pueda sacar plata en pasta, ni labrada deste Reyno, para el de Tierrafirme, ni otras partes, aunque estê quintada, y que se reduzga toda a moneda para poderla nauegar, y comerciar con ella fuera deste Reyno."
Dated in Lima, 3 Dec 1683 (day of month supplied in manuscript), with manuscript signature: El duque de la Palata.
Papel sellado variously dated 1670-83.
Medina(Lima)558.

28200, 1938

D683 P892p   Poyntz, John, fl. 1658-1695.
The Present Prospect Of The Famous and Fertile Island Of Tobago: With A Description of the Situation, Growth, Fertility and Manufacture of the said Island. To which is Added, Proposals for the Encouragement of all those that are minded to settle there. By Captain John Poyntz.
London: Printed by George Larkin for the Author, and are to be Sold by Thomas Malthus, at the Sun in the Poultrey. 1683.
2 p.ℓ., 47 p. 20cm. 4°.

"Advertisement. A nevv Map of the Island of Tobago...is to be sold by John Seller...", p. 47.
JCB(2)2:1272; WingP3130; Sabin64857; Cundall (WI)1885; Arents378.

0799, 1846

D683 P933s   The Present State Of Jamaica. With The Life Of the Great Columbus The first Discoverer: To which is Added An Exact Account of Sir Hen. Morgan's Voyage to, and famous Siege and taking of Panama from the Spaniards.
London, Printed by Fr. Clark for Tho. Malthus at the Sun in the Poultry, 1683.
5 p.ℓ., 117 p. 15cm. 12°
"Books lately printed for and sold by Tho. Malthus": 4th-5th p.ℓ.
"The Present State Of Jamaica" (p. 1-54).
"Sir Henry Morgan's Voyage To Panama,1670. London, Printed for Thomas Malthus at the Sun in the Poultry, 1683" (p. 55-97) has special t.-p. This is a collection of official papers also found in Cal.S.P.Col. 1669-1674.
"A short account of the Life of Christopher Collumb or Collumbus the first Doscoverer [sic] of Jamaica": p. 99-117.
JCB(2)2:1268; Wing P3268; Sabin35649; Cundall (Jam.)268.

0798, 1846

BA683 R763m   Romero, Diego, d. 1680.
Meditaciones De La Passion de Christo Vida Nuestra. Hechas Por El V. Padre Fray Diego Romero Religioso de N. Padre San Francisco, Hijo de la Provincia de el Santo Evangelio. Dalas A La Estampa, con vn Refumen breve para la Oracion, vn devoto, que las dedica, A Christo Nvestro Señor Crucificado.
Con Licencia, En la Puebla de los Angeles, en la Imprenta de Diego Fernandez de Leon. Año de 1683.
6 p.ℓ., 20 numb. ℓ. illus. 14.5cm. 8°
The earliest edition noted is that recorded by Medina(Mexico)1136 (from Andrade 1192) as "Reimpressa" Mexico, 1675.
License dated (5th p.ℓ.ʳ) 4 Jan. 1683.

05813, before 1923

BA683   Ruiz Blanco, Matías, 1643-1705?
R934m   Manval Para Catekizar, Y Administrar Los
Santos Sacramentos à los Indios que habitan la
Prouincia de la nueua Andaluzia, y nueua Bar-
celona, y San Christoval de los Cumanagotos.
Dirigido A La Santissima Trinidad. Por El
Padre Fr. Mathias Ruiz Blanco, de la Regular
Observancia de nuestro Padre San Francisco,
hijo de la Santa Prouincia de Andaluzia, Lector
de Theologia, y Predicador Apostolico en las
Santas Missiones de Piritu, y Examinador
Synodal en este Obispado de Puerto Rico.
    En Burgos: Por Iuan de Viar. Año 1683.
    8 p.ℓ., 101, [1] p. 14.5cm. 8°
    Half-title: Manval De Catecvmenos, En
Lengva Cvmanacota.
    License dated (6th p.ℓ.^{v}) 11 Jan. 1683.
    Errata, 8th p.ℓ.^{v}.
    JCB(2)2:1263; Palau(1)6:354; Medina(BHA)1743;
Sabin74018; Viñaza212; Streit 2:2263.
01664, 1853

B69   Salazar, Antonio de, fl. 1673-1698.
G643v   Villancicos, Qve Se Cantaron En La Sancta
34   Igleia [sic] Cathedral De La Puebla de los
Angeles, en los Maytines del Gloriosissimo
Principe de la Iglesia el Señor San Pedro, este
año de 1683. ... Compuestos En Metro Musico
Por Antonio de Salazar Maestro de Capilla de
esta Sancta Iglesia.
    Con Licencia, en la Puebla, por Diego Fer-
nandez de Leon. [1683].
    [8] p. 20cm. 4°.
    Woodcut title vignette (St. Peter)
    Bound, in contemporary vellum, as no. 34
with 42 other items.

28934, 1941

Z   Sanson, Nicolas, 1600-1667.
S229   L'Europe En Plusieurs Cartes, Et en divers
1683   Traittés De Geographie Et D'Histoire; Là où
sont décrits succinctement, & avec une belle
Methode, & facile Ses Empires, Ses Peuples, Ses
Colonies, Leurs Mœurs, Langues, Religions,
Richesses, &c. Et ce qu'il y a de plus beau, &
de plus rare dans toutes ses Parties, & dans ses
Iles. Par N. Sanson d'Abbeville, Geographe
Ordinaire du Roy.
    [Utrecht, Gisbert van Zyll] Sur la Copie
imprimée A Paris, Chez l'Autheur dans le Cloître
de Saint Germain de l'Auxerrois, joignant la
grande Porte du Cloître. M.DC.LXXXIII.

    [4] pts. in 1 v.: 4 p.ℓ., 40, 43-53 p., 1 ℓ.;
102 p., 2 ℓ.; 98; 83 p., 1 ℓ. 62 double-page
maps. 22.5cm. 4°
    Cut (armillary sphere: Rahir marque 64)
on t.-p.
    Added t.-p. (double), engr.: L'Evrope Dediée
a Monseigneur Monseigneur [sic] le Tellier
Secret.' d'Estat &c. Par N. Sanson le fils Geographe du Roy Súr la Copie A Paris chez
l'Autheur 1683. Jean. de. la. Aveleu. fecit.
    Parts [2-4] (L'Asie, L'Afrique, and L'Ameri-
que) each have half-title.
    Part [1] by Nicholas Sanson, the son, and
parts [3-4] by Nicolas Sanson, the father.
    First pub. Paris, 1656.
    Part 1: Text on reverse of maps with maps
included in paging (except last map).
    Contents.—[1]. L'Europe (first pub. Paris,
1648) p. 1-52.—[2]. L'Asie (first pub. Paris,
1652) p. 1-102, 2d count.—[3]. L'Afrique
(first pub. Paris, 1656) p.1-98, 3d count.—
[4]. L'Amerique (first pub. Paris, 1656)
p. 1-82, 4th count.
    "Cartes, Tables & Traités... que le Sr.
Sanson... a faire graver": last ℓ., pt. [2].
    Bound in contemporary vellum.
    Phillips(Atlases)494; Sabin76712

    Contents(maps):
L'Europe:
[1]   Evrope... A. d'Winter schu.
[2]   Isles Britanniqves... A. d'Winter scu:
[3]   Scandinavie ou les Estats de Dane-
      mark, de Svede &c. ... A: de Winter sculp.
[4]   Rvssie Blanche ou Moscovie... A. d'Winter
      sculp.
[5]   France... A. d'Winter fe:
[6]   Allemagne... A. d'Winter schul.
[7]   Estats de la Couronne de Pologne... A.
      d'Winter sculp.
[8]   Espagne... A. d'Winter scu:
[9]   Italie...
[10] Partie de Tvrqvie... A. d'Winter sculp.
[11] Hongrie... A. d'Winter sculp.
L'Asie:
[12] L'Asie...
[13] Tvrqvie en Asie... A. d'Winter fe:
[14] Anatolie... A. D'Winter schu.
[15] Mer Noire...
[16] Sorie, et Diarbeck divisés en leurs Parties
      ...
[17] Turcomanie Georgie Commanie...
[18] L'Arabie Petrée, Deserte Et Hevrevse...
      A: de Winter sculp.
[19] L'Empire du Sophy de Perses... A. d'
      Winter schu.
[20] L'Empire du Grand Mogol...
[21] Presqv'Isle De L'Inde deça la Gange, ou
      sont les Roÿaumes, de Decan, de Golconde
      de Bisnagar, et le Malabar...

[22] [Inset:] Le Malabar. Auec tous les Roÿaumes, qui sont sur sa Coste, dans la Terre, et dans les Montag^{nes}
[22] Partie De L'Inde au delà du Gange ... A. d'Winter schu:—Presqv-Isle De L'Inde au de là du Gange ...
[23] Royavme de la Chine ... A: de Winter fe: et.
[24] La Grande Tartarie ... A. d'Winter schu:
[25] Les Isles Dv Iapon ... A. d'Winter sculp.
[26] Les Isles Philippines ... Islas De Los Ladrones ou Isle Des Larrons. A: de Winter scu.
[27] Les Isles Molvcqves; Celebes, Gilolo, &c ... A. d'Winter sculp.
[Insets:] Isles De Banda.—Les Isles Molvcqves.
[28] Les Isles De La Sonde. entre lesquelles sont Svmatra, Iava, Borneo, &c. ... A. de Winter sculp.
[29] Ceylan, et les Maldives ...
[Inset:] Ceylan Isle Qui est la Taprobane des Anciens.
L'Afrique:
[30] Afriqve ... A. d'Winter schu.
[31] Royaume De Maroc divisé en sept Provinces &c. Tiré de Sanut, de Marmol, &c. ...
[32] Royaume De Fez divisé en sept Provinces Tire de Sanut Gc. ...
[33] Partie De Barbarie ou est La Royaume D' Alger divisé en ses Provinces. Part Du Biledulgerid, ou sont Tegorarin, Zeb, &c.
[34] Partie De Barbarie. ou sont les Royau^{mes} de Tunis, et Tripoli, Tires de Sanut, et d'Autres ... A d'Winter sc.
[35] Royau^{me} et Desert De Barca, et L'Ægypte divisée en ses Principales Parties ... A. d'Winter scul:
[36] Partie Du Biledulgerid ou Sont Tesset, Darha, et Segelmesse ...
[37] Egypte divisée en ses Douze Cassilifs, ou Gouvernemens. Tiree de Sanut, et de divers autres Autheurs ...
[38] Afrique ou Libie Ulterieure, ou sont Le Saara ou Desert, Le Pays Des Negres La Guinée, &c. ...
[39] La Guinée et Pays circomvoisins; Tires de Mercator, de Blommart &c. ...
[40] Partie De La Haute Æthiopie ou sont L' Empi^{re} des Abissins et la Nubie &c. Tirées de Sanut, de Mercator ... A. de Winter fec:
[41] Le Zanguebar Tire de Sanut &c. ... — Partie Du Zanguebar ou Sont les Costes d'Ajan et d'Abex &c. Tirée de Sanut de Marmol &c. ...
[42] Royaume De Congo, &c. ... A. d'Winter sculp.
[43] Pays, et Coste des Caffres: Empires de Monomotapa Monoemugi, &c. Tirés de Sanuto, et d'autres ... A. de Winter sculp:
[44] Isle De Madagascar ou de St Laurens. Tirée de Sanuto &c. ...

[45] Isles Du Cap Verd Coste, et Pays Des Negres aux environs du Cap Verd Tirés de Sanut, de Blomart. etc. ...
[46] Isles Canaries ...
[Inset:] Isle Madere.
[47] Les Isles De Malte, Goze, &c. ... A. de Winter sculp.
L'Amerique:
[48] Americqve Septentrionale ... A. d'Winter sculp.
[49] Le Canada, ou Nouvelle France, &c. Tirée de diverses Relations des. Francois, Anglois, Hollandais, &c. ...
[50] La Floride ...
[51] Audience De Mexico ... A. d'Winter scu.
[52] Audience De Guadalajara, Nouveau Mexique, Californie, &c. ...
[53] Audience De Guatimala ...
[54] Les Isles Antilles, &c. entre lesquelles sont Les Lucayes, et Les Caribes ...
[55] Ameriqve Meridionale ...
[56] Terre Ferme, Nou^{veau} Roy^{me} De Grenade, &c. ... A: d. Winter fe:
[57] Guiane divisée en Guiane et Caribane ...
[58] Le Perou et le cours de la Riv^{re} Amazone ...
[59] Le Chili. Tiré de Alf de Oualle de la C.d. I. et divise en treize Iurisdictions ...
[60] Le Bresil, dont la Coste est possedée par les Portugais et divisée en Quatorze Capitaineries ...
[61] Le Paraguay Subdivisé en ses principales Parties. suivantles dernieres Relaõns ...
[62] Destroit De Magellan, Terre Et Isles Magellanicques, &c. ... A: d. Winter fe.

05943, before 1923

BA683 S245s
Sariñana y Cuenca, Isidro, 1630?-1696.
    Sermon De El Gloriosissimo Principe De La Iglesia San Pedro, Qve En 29. de Junio de 1683. dia en que recibiò el Palio el Ilust.^{mo} y Rev^{mo} Señor D^r. D. Francisco De Agviar, Y Ceijas, Arçobispo de Mexico, Predicó En la Santa Iglesia Metropolitana el Ilust.^{mo} Senor D^r. D. Isidro Sariñana, Y Cvenca, Obispo electo de Oaxaca.
    Con Licencia. En Mexico: Por Juan de Ribera, Impressor de Libros en el Empedradillo. [1683]
    6 p. ℓ., 12 numb. ℓ. 19.5cm. 4°
    License dated (6th p. ℓ.^{v}) 21 July 1683. Preliminary matter includes poetry.
Palau(2)302138; Medina(Mexico)1294; Sabin 77056.

69-761

B683
S579t
[R]
 Sigüenza y Góngora, Carlos de, 1645-1700.
 Trivmpho Parthenico Qve En Glorias De Maria, Santissima immaculadamente concebida, celebrò la Pontificia, Imperial, y Regia Academia Mexicana En el biennio, que como su Rector la governò El Doctor Don Juan De Narvaez, Tesorero General de la Santa Cruzada en el Arçobispado de Mexico, y al presente Cathedratico de Prima de Sagrada Escritura. Describelo D. Carlos de Siguenza, y Gongora, Mexicano, y en ella Cathedratico proprietario de Mathematicas.
 En Mexico: Por Juan de Ribera, en el Empedradillo. IXI. DC. LXXX. III.
 8 p. ℓ., 118 numb. ℓ. 20.5cm. 4º
 Cut (winged horse) on t.-p.
 With passage on ℓ. 48 effaced as ordered by the Inquisition.
 License dated (7th p. ℓ.) 6 Apr 1683.
 Preliminary matter (poetry) by Francisco de Ayerra y Santa María, José de Mora y Cuéllar, Juan de Guevara, and Alonso Ramírez de Vargas.
 Includes poems by various authors entered in the competitions held 1682 and 1683 celebrating the Immaculate Conception.

B683
S579t
cop.2
 —— ——Another copy. 19cm.
 Bottom margin closely trimmed affecting some catchwords and signature marks.
 JCB(2)1273; Palau(1)515; Medina(Mexico)1297; Sabin 80986.
05768, before 1874
03642, before 1866

JA683
-T167g
 Tanner, Mathias, 1630-1692.
 Die Gesellschafft Jesu Biss zur vergiessung ihres Blutes wider den Götzendienst/ Unglauben/ und Laster/ Für Gott/ den wahren Glauben/ und Tugendten in allen vier Theilen der Welt streitend: Das ist: Lebens-Wandel/ und Todtes-Begebenheit/ der jenigen/ Die auss der Gesellschaft Jesu umb verthätigung Gottes/ des wahren Glaubens/ und der Tugenden/ gewaltthätiger Weiss hingerichtet worden: Vorhero Lateinisch beschrieben Von R. P. Mathia Tanner S.J. Theologo. anjetzo aber Von einem andern Priester gemeldter Societät in die Teutsche Sprach übersetzet. Mit Ihro Röm: Kayserl. und Königl. Majestät Freiheit und Begnadigung/ und Guttheissen der Obern.
 Gedruckt zu Prag/ in der Carolo-Ferdinandeischen Universität Buchdruckerey/ in dem Collegio der Societät Jesu/ im Jahr 1683.
 12 p. ℓ., 78, 89-136, 139-192, 191-328, 327-334, 337-562, [6], 563-737, [1] p. incl. illus., ports. (a)^4)o(^{4} A-B^2 C-Z^4 2A-5B^4 31.5cm. fol.
 Transl. by Bartholomaeus Christelius from: Societas Jesu Usque Ad Sanguinis Et Vitæ Profusionem Militans. Pragæ, 1675.
 Jesuits in America: last section, following p. 562.
 The illustrations in the text and the engraved added titles, which precede the general t.-p. and each of the four sections, are signed by Melchior Küsell, after Charles Screta.
 In this copy pages 525-6 are misbound between p. 522-3 because of missigning of 3X2.3.
 JCB(2)2:1274; Sabin 94331; Backer 2:1160, 7:1860; Streit 1:689; Palmer 396.
04700, before 1882

DA683
T243ℓ
 [Taylor, John] ca. 1638-1708.
 A Loving & Friendly Invitation To All Sinners To Repent, ... With a brief Account of the Latter Part of the Life of John Perrot, ... Also, a Testimony against Robt. Rich and John Perrot their filthy Books lately printed against God's People in Scorn called Quakers. With a Postscript by Another Hand.
 London, Printed by John Bringhurst, at the Sign of the Book in Grace-Church-street, 1683.
 20 p. 18.5cm. 4º
 Signed p. 10: John Taylor.
 Includes references to Taylor's encounters with Perrot and Rich in the West Indies, chiefly Barbados.
 A reply in part to Perrot's The vision of John Perrot, London, 1682, and to various works by Robert Rich.
 "A Postcript by Another Hand." (p. 19-20) signed: John Field. jun.
 Wing T535; Smith(Friends)2:704.
69-277

DA683
T294a
 [Tenison, Thomas] abp. of Canterbury, 1636-1715.
 An Argument For Union, Taken from the True Interest Of Those Dissenters in England, Who Profess, and call themselves Protestants.
 London, Printed for Tho. Basset, at the George in Fleet-street; Benj. Tooke, at the Ship in St. Pauls Church-yard; and F. Gardiner, at the White-Horse in Ludgate-street, 1683.

E696
=T418r
12688, 1920

Thévenot, Melchisédech, 1620?-1692.
Relations De Divers Voayges [sic] Curieux Qui N'Ont Point Esté Publiees; Ou Qvi Ont Esté Tradvites D'Haclvyt, de Purchas, & d'autres Voyageurs Anglois, Hollandois, Portugais, Allemands, Espagnols; Et De Quelques Persans, Arabes, Et Autres Auteurs Orientaux. ... Par Monsieur Thevenot. Premier [-Quatriesme] Partie.
A Paris, Chez André Pralard, ruë Saint Iacques, à l'Occasion. M.DC.LXXXIII. Avec Privilege du Roy.
4 pts. illus., plates, maps. fol.

This is the 1683 issue of Thévenot's Relations. There is really only one edition of Thévenot's collection, issued in five parts between 1663 and 1696. Part 1 was first issued in 1663, part 2 in 1664, part 3 in 1666, part 4 during 1672-1674, and part 5 in 1696. During the course of publication the parts of the collection already published were reissued with new title-pages in 1664, 1666, 1672, 1683, and 1696. Some sheets were reprinted for these reissues.

The contents and arrangement of individual copies vary. The Library has six copies and some miscellaneous fragments.

The issues of 1663, 1664, and 1666 are entered in JCB(3)3 at p. 102, 121, and 148, respectively. For the issue of 1696 see this catalogue under that year.

The 1683 issue consists of parts 1-4.
Contents:
(Locations in the Library's copies are indicated in the margin.)

1.ptie.: cop.5.1;
2.ptie.: cop.5.2;
3.ptie.: cop.5.3;
4.ptie.: cop.5.4

Each part has its own t.-p., as above, in red and black, with cut on title-pages. The verso of each t.-p. has a table of the contents of parts 1-4 of the Relations and of Thévenot's 8⁰ Recueil, 1st pub. Paris, 1681. The title-leaf of pt.1 is mutilated in the Library's copy.

For a listing of the other items in the 1683 issue (parts 1-4) see the complete listing of contents in the entry for the 1696 issue of Thévenot's Relations.
Cf. JCB(2)2:935, 936; (3)3:102, 121, 148; cf. Sabin95333, 95334; cf. Camus: Thévenot; cf. Lenox: Thévenot; cf. Bibl. Lindesiana 8830-8840.

04807, 1849   05132, 1884   04806, 1848
03923, 1868   05133, before 1884   01929, 1854

2 p.ℓ., 43 p. 20cm. 4⁰.
Errata: verso 2d p.ℓ.
McAlpin4:152; Dexter(Cong.)2244; WingT688.

DA683
T531ℓ

Three Letters Of Thanks To The Protestant Reconciler. 1. From the Anabaptists at Munster. 2. From the Congregations in New-England. 3. From the Quakers in Pensilvania.
London, Printed for Benj. Took, 1683.
1 p.ℓ., 26 p. 19.5cm. 4⁰.
A reply to Daniel Whitby, The Protestant Reconciler..., London, 1683. The three letters are probably a fabrication by a partisan of the Church of England intended to discredit the three dissenting sects and the idea of Protestant union.
JCB(2)2:1275; Sabin95739; Smith(Friends) 2:452; Dexter(Cong.)2230; WingT1098.
0531, 1846

DA683
T694p

Torrey, Samuel, 1632-1707.
A Plea For the Life of Dying Religion from the Word of the Lord: In A Sermon Preached to the General Assembly of the Colony of the Massachusets at Boston in New-England, May 16. 1683. Being the Day of Election there. By Mr. Samuel Torrey Pastor of the Church of Christ at Waymouth. ...
Boston In New-England Printed by Samuel Green for Samuel Sewall. 1683.
4 p.ℓ., 46 p., 1 ℓ. 18cm. 4⁰
"To The Reader" (2d-4th p.ℓ.) signed: Boston in N.England. August 31. 1683. Increase Mather.
Booksellers' advertisement, last leaf.
Evans353; Sabin96303; Holmes(I)161; WingT1918; Brinley 873(this copy).
16849, 1936

D683
T875d

[Tryon, Thomas] 1634-1703.
A Dialogue Between An East-Indian Brackmanny Or Heathen-Philosopher, And A French Gentleman Concerning the Present Affairs of Europe.
London: Printed and Sold by Andrew Sowle at the Crooked-Billet in Holloway-Lane, in Shoreditch, 1683.
1 p.ℓ., 22 p. 19cm. 8⁰
Chiefly concerns religious persecution.
Bookseller's advertisement, p.ℓ.ᵛ.
Includes, p. 21-22, lines from Ovid, Sandys translation, "To shew that the recommending Abstinence from Flesh, is no new upstart Conceit..."
Also issued bound with his The Way to health, London, 1683.
WingD1301.
68-193

CA683 V665q Vieira, Antonio, 1608-1697.
Qvinta Parte De Sermones Del Padre Antonio De Vieira, De La Compañia De Iesvs, Predicador De S.A. El Principe De Portvgal. Tradvcidos Del Original Del Mismo Autor, y con su aprobacion, por el Lic. D. Francisco de Cubillas Donyague, [pseud.] Presbytero, y Abogado de los Reales Consejos. ...
Año 1683. Con Privilegio. En Madrid: Por Antonio Gonçalez de Reyes. A costa de Gabriel de Leon, Mercader de Libros. Vendese en su casa enfrente de la Estafeta.
4 p.l., 479, [480-452] p. 21.5cm. 4°
Cut (incl. motto "De Forti Dulcedo") on t.-p. (cf. Vindel(Escudos) 501-508).
"Svma De La Tassa" dated (3d p.l.ᵛ) 8 July 1683.
Errata, 3d p.l.ᵛ
According to Uriarte this was translated (under the pseudonym Francisco de Cubillas Donyague) by Bartolomé Alcázar.
Contains 16 sermons preached in Rome [ca. 1670], 1674, Lisbon 1644, 1645, 1651, 1652, 1655, 1659, 1662, 1670, São Luiz, Brazil, [1653-1661] 1654, Bahia, Brazil, 1637, etc.
These were not published in the original Portuguese until 1682 in Lisbon as his Sermoens, 2. parte. That edition, however, contained only 15 sermons; the 16th in this Spanish edition appears not to have been published in Portuguese.
Bound in contemporary limp vellum.
Backer8:664; Leite9:326; BLH5:372.

68-336

CA679 V665s 3-4 Vieira, Antonio, 1608-1697.
Sermoens Do P. Antonio Vieira, Da Companhia De Iesv, Prégador de Sua Magestade. Terceira Parte.
Em Lisboa. Na Officina de Migvel Deslandes. A custa de Antonio Leyte Pereyra, Mercador de Livros. M.DC.LXXXIII. Com todas as licenças, & Privilegio Real.
5 p.l., 175, 179-574, [1] p. 21cm. 4°
Cut (Jesuit trigram, floriated) on t.-p.
"Taixaõ este Livro..." dated (4th p.l.ᵛ) 16 Dec. 1683.
Errata, 5th p.l.
Contains 15 sermons preached in Lisbon 1643, 1644, 1648, 1650, 1651, 1655, 1669, São Luiz, Brazil, 1656, 1657, 1659, Coimbra 1663, and Bahia, Brazil, 1639, 1640.
According to Leite "Deste volume, com a data de 1683, conhecem-se 3 impressões diferentes." In this issue there is a colophon on p. [1] at end.
In this copy there is a blank l. at end.
With this is bound his Sermoens...quarta parte, Lisbon, 1685.

Rodrigues 2505; Backer8:659; Leite9:195; Innocencio 1:290.

68-192.3

D683 V975o The Voyages Of The Ever Renowned Sr. Francis Drake Into the West Indies. Viz. His great Adventures for Gold, and Silver, with the Gaining thereof, and an Account of his Surprising of Nombre de Dios. A large Account of that Voyage wherein he Encompassed the World. His Voyage made with Francis Knollis, and others; their taking the Towns of St. Jago, Sancto Domingo, Carthagena, and Saint Augustin. His last Voyage (in which he Died) being Accompanied with several Valiant Commanders, and the Manner of his Burial. Collected out of the Notes of the most Aproved Authors. To which is added, An Account of his Valorous Exploits in the Spanish Invasion.
London, Printed for Thomas Malthus, at the Sign of the Sun, in the Poultry, 1683.
3 p.l., 168 p. 15cm. 8°
Abridged from Sir Francis Drake revived, London, 1653.
"Books lately printed for & sold by Tho. Malthus": 3d p.l.
WingV749; Sabin100842.

05725, before 1902

DC W394m 1-29 VVeekly Memorials For The Ingenious: Or, An Account Of Books lately set forth in Several Languages. With Other Accounts relating to Arts and Sciences.
London: Printed for the Author, and are to be sold by R. Chiswel, at the Rose and Crown in St. Pauls Church yard, Tho. Basset at the George in Fleetstreet, W. Crook at the Green Dragon without Temple-bar, and Sam. Crouch, at the Princes Arms the corner of Popes-head alley. 1683.
4 p.l., 72, 65-224 p. 24cm. 4°
Issued in parts numbered 1-29 and dated 20 Mar. 1681/2 - 25 Sept. 1682, each of which has caption title and imprint at end. Imprint of no. 8 variant: London: Printed for Henry Faithorne and John Kersey, at the Rose in St. Pauls Church-yard. 1682. (no. 8 dated 6 Mar. 1681/2). Imprint of no. 9 variant: London: Printed by J.C. and Freeman Collins, in Black-and-white-court in the Old Bayley. 1682. (no. 9 dated 13 Mar. 1681/2).
John Beaumont and James Petiver have been suggested as the editors.

Includes much material translated from Journal des sçavans.
Errata, p. 224.
Booksellers' advertisements, p. 128, 208, 224.
Bound in contemporary calf.
With this are bound nos. 1-7 only of a different publication issued under the same title: Weekly memorials for the ingenious ... , London, Printed for Henry Faithorne and John Kersey... , 1682. Nos. are dated 16 Jan. 1681/2 - 27 Feb. 1681/2. These 7 nos. were edited by the "author" of the Weekly memorials sold by Chiswell et al. After the 7th no. he left Faithorne and conducted the rival series sold by Chiswell. The original series was contemporaneously continued by Faithorne.
The no. 1 pub. by Chiswell, et al., contains the same matter as the no. 10 of the Faithorne series. Nos. 8 and 9 of the Chiswell series contain the same matter as nos. 8 and 9 of the Faithorne series; they were issued 8 May 1682, the date on which a no. 8 of the Chiswell series was expected.
Crane and Kaye 935, 934.

2057, 1906

DA683
W532s
Westminster Assembly of Divines.
The Shorter Catechism Composed by the Reverend Assembly Of Divines With the Proofs thereof Out of the Scriptures, In Words at length. ...
Boston In NevvEngland, Printed by Samuel Sewall. 1683.
1 p.l., 54 p. 15.5cm. 8°
First pub. London [1647] under title: The humble advice of the Assembly of Divines now...sitting at Westminster concerning a shorter catechism.
Evans354; Sabin80709; Brinley 739 (this copy); Eames(N.E.Cat.)71 (this copy).

70-100

DA683
W724c
[Williams, John] bp. of Chichester, 1636?-1709.
The Case Of Lay-Communion With The Church Of England Considered; And the Lawfulness of it shew'd from the Testimony of above an hundred eminent Non-Conformists of several Perswasions. Published for the satisfaction of the scrupulous, and to prevent the sufferings which such needlesly expose themselves to.
London, Printed for Richard Chiswell at the Rose and Crown in St. Paul's Church-Yard. 1683.
4 p.l., 75 p. 20cm. 4°
McAlpin4:156; Dexter(Cong.)2222; Wing W2692.

12690, 1920

B683
Y22p
Yangues, Manuel de, d. 1676.
Principios, Y Reglas De La Lengva Cvmmanagota, General En Varias Naciones, Qve Habitan En La Provincia De Cvmmana En Las Indias Occidentales. Compvestos Por El R. P. Predicador Fr. Manuel De Yangues, del Orden de N.P.S. Francisco...Dirigidos Al Reverendissimo Padre Fray Christoual del Viso, Comissario General de Indias, &c. Sacados A Lvz Aora Nvevamente, corregidos, y reducidos à mayor claridad, y breuedad, junto con vn Diccionario que ha compuesto el R. P. Fr. Mathias Blanco, Religioso de la misma Orden, Lector de Theologia, Examinador Synodal de el Obispado de San Iuan de Puerto-Rico ...
Con Licencia. En Bvrgos: Por. Iuan de Viar. Año de 1683.
4 p.l., 220 p. 20.5cm. 4°
License dated (3d p.l.^{v}) 11 Jan. 1683.
Errata, 4th p.l.^{v}
Palau(1)7:239; Medina(BHA)1742; Sabin105954; Viñaza213; Streit2:2263.

05884, before 1923

1684

Abarca, Pedro, 1619-1693.
Segunda parte de los anales históricos de los reyes de Aragon.
Salamanca, 1684.
See under his Los reyes de Aragon, Madrid, 1682.

B69
G643v
21
Agurto y Loaysa, Joseph de, fl. 1676-1688.
Villancicos, Qve Se Cantaron En La Santa Iglesia Metropolitana de Mexico; En honor de

Maria Santissima Madre de Dios, en su Assumpcion Triumphante. ... Pusolos en metro Musico el Br. Joseph de Loaysa, y Agurto Maestro de dicha Santa Iglesia.

Con Licencia En;[sic] Mexico: Por la Viuda de Bernardo Calderon. Año de 1684.

1 p.ℓ., [5] p. 20cm. 4°

Woodcut title vignette (the Virgin surrounded by angels).

Bound, in contemporary vellum, as no. 21 with 42 other items.

28921, 1941

BA684
A958a
Avila, Juan de, fl. 1684.

Amistad Geroglifica, Qve En La Conversion De S. Dimas Discurriô, Leyò, Y Entendiò El R.do P. Fr. Ivan De Avila, Predicador General jubilado, de la Orden de N. P. S. Francisco, y Guardian del Convento de S. Buenaventura de Quauhtitlan. En el sermon que predicó en el Convento de Religiosas de la Encarnacion, el dia Martes Santo 28. de Março de 1684. años. A La Memoria, Y Recverdo Qve De Tan grande milagro, haze, y celebra El Tribunal Sãcto de la Inquisiciõ, de esta Nueva-España, en cuya assistencia se dixo. ...

Con licencia en Mexico, por la Viuda de Francisco Rodriguez Lupercio 1684.

8 p.ℓ., [24] p. 20cm. 4°

License dated (7th p.ℓ.r) 12 May 1684.

Includes poetry.

Imperfect: 2d p.ℓ. wanting; available in facsim.

Palau(2)20461; Medina(Mexico)1303.

1040, 1905

BA684
A958m
[R]
Avila, Juan de, fl. 1684.

Mariano Pentilitero, Colvmna Evangelica, Qve Discvrriô, Leyô, Y Entendiô El Rdo P. Fr. Ivan De Avila, Predicador General Jvbilado, de la Orden de N. P. S. Francisco, Qualificador del Santo Officio, y Guardian actual del Convento de S. Buenaventura de Quauhtitlan. En el sermon que predicó en el Convento de Mexico á II. de Octubre del año de 1684. En la fiesta de N. Señora del Pilar De Zaragoza, Que le celebra anual vn devoto, à cuyas expensas se dio à la estampa. ...

Impresso en Mexico, por la Viuda de Francisco Rodriguez Lupercio. Año de 1684.

8 p.ℓ., 8 numb. ℓ., [8] p. 19.5cm. 4°

Dedication dated (4th p.ℓ.v) 30 Nov. 1684.

Preliminary matter includes poetry.
Palau(2)20462; Medina(Mexico)1302.

69-800

F684
A985v
[Ayres, Philip] 1638-1712, ed.

The Voyages and Adventures Of Capt. Barth. Sharp And others, in the South Sea: Being A Journal of the same. Also Capt. Van Horn with his Buccaniers surprizing of la Vera Cruz. To which is added The true Relation of Sir Henry Morgan his Expedition against the Spaniards in the West-Indies, and his taking Panama. Together with The President of Panama's Account of the same Expedition: Translated out of Spanish. And Col. Beeston's adjustment of the Peace between the Spaniards and English in the West Indies. Published by P. A. Esq;.

London Printed by B. W. for R. H. and S. T. and are to be sold by Walter Davis in Amen-Corner. MDC LXXXIV.

12 p.ℓ., 172 p. 17cm. 8°

The preface is chiefly a vindication of Henry Morgan in reply to Exquemelin's Bucaniers Of America, London, Crooke, 1684.

The account of Sharpe's voyage is based on a journal by John Cox.

Also includes an account of Capt. Charles Carlisle's actions against pirates in the West Indies.

JCB(2)2:1298; Sabin79781; WingA4315.

0620, 1846

BA684
B826o
Bravo Davila y Cartagena, Juan.

Oracion Panegyrica A Las Glorias Del Angelico Doctor S. Thomas De Aquino que celebrô el insigne Colegio de S. Antonio el Magno de la Ciudad del Cuzco a 7. de Março de 1684. en el ilustre Templo de los Predicadores. Dixola El Doct. D. Ivan Brabo Davila y Cartagena, Colegial del sobredicho Colegio, Canonigo de la Santa Iglesia Catedral del Cuzco, y Prouisor y Vicario general de su Obispado &c. Sacalo A Luz El M. R. P. M. F. Miguel De Lazarte, Prior del Conuento de Predicadores del Cuzco, y Vicario Prouincial de su Obispado, y del de Arequipa. Y Ofrecelo Al Ilustrissimo Y Reverendissimo Señor Doct. D. Manuel de Mollinedo y Angulo del Consejo de su Magestad, y Obispo de la Ciudad del Cuzco.

Con Licencia. En Lima. Por Ioseph de Contreras Año de 1684.

[130]

5506, 1909
  10 p. l., [32] p. 20cm. 4°
  License dated (8th p. l.ᵛ) 20 June 1684.
  Medina(Lima)562.

D684
C292d Carolina Described more fully then [sic] heretofore. Being an Impartial Collection Made from the several Relations of that Place in Print, since Its first planting (by the English,) and before, under the Denomination of Florida, From diverse Letters from those that have Transported themselves (From this Kingdom of Ireland.) And the Relations of Those that have been in that Country several years together. whereunto is added the Charter, with the Fundamental Constitutions of that Province. With Sundry Necessary Observations made thereon; usefull to all that have a Disposition to Transport themselves to that Place; with the Account of what Shipping bound Thither from this Kingdom, this present Summer. 1684. And the Charges of Transporting of Persons and Goods.
  Dublin, Printed 1684.
  1 p. l., 2-3, 16, [4], 17-56 p. []² A-B⁴ b² C-G⁴ 19.5cm. (20.5cm. in case) 4°
  Includes accounts of Carolina taken from Thomas Peake, Samuel Wilson, John Ogilby, Richard Blome, Samuel Clarke, and John Crawford.
  JCBAR55:20-25; WingC606; cf. Sabin10963; Church688; Vail(Front.)227.
31745, 1955

BA684
-C783d Copia De Vna Carta, Escrita Al Padre Fray Alonso Sandin, de la Orden de Predicadores, Difinidor, y Procurador General de la Prouincia del Santo Rosario de Philipinas en esta Corte; en que dà noticia de el estado de aquellas Islas.
  [Madrid? 1684?]
  14 numb. l. 29.5cm. fol.
  Caption title.
  Concerns the removal of Archbishop Felipe Fernández de Pardo.
  The letter itself (numb. l. 1-7) is dated at end 26 May 1683.
  Includes (numb. l. 8-14) "Pvntos Qve Hemos Sabido Se escriuen al Consejo contra nosotros este año, y respuesta à ellos ... Del mismo Autor de la Carta."
  Cf. JCBAR66:4; Palau(2)61285; Medina (Filipinas)363; Streit5:929; Retana197.
66-119

DA684
C789s
[R] Corbet, John, 1620-1680.
  Self-Imployment In Secret: Containing I. Evidences upon Self-Examination. II. Thoughts upon Painfull Afflictions. III. Memorials for Practice. Left under the Hand-Writing of that Learned and Reverend Divine, Mr. John Corbet, Late of Chichester. The Third Edition, carefully Corrected.
  Boston In New-England Printed by Richard Pierce for Joseph Brunning, And are to be sold at his Shop at the Corner of Prison-Lane next the Exchange 1684.
  6 p. l., 44 p. 16cm. (17cm. in case) 8°
  First pub. London, 1681.
  "To the Reader" signed (4th p. l.ʳ) Increase Mather. 27 Nov. 1684.
  Evans357; WingC6266; Sabin16746; Holmes(I) 136.
31383, 1954

H684
E74d Eschinardi, Francesco, 1623-1703.
  De Impetv Tractatvs Dvplex Primvs De Impetv In Commvni: De Motv Locali: Et De Machinis. Secvndvs De Flvidis In Commvni: De Comparatione Flvidorvm Cvm Solidis: Et De Mensvra Aqvarvm Cvrrentivm. ... Avctore Francisco Eschinardo E Societate Iesv Matheseos Professore in Collegio Romano.
  Romae, Ex Typographia Angeli Bernabò. M.DC.LXXXIV. Svperiorvm Permissv.
  4 p. l., 192, 185-336 p. 10 fold. plates (incl. diagrs.), tab. 22.5cm. 4°
  Cut on t.-p.
  License dated (4th p. l.ᵛ) 1 March 1684.
  "Qværes rationem ... , quam dicitur habuisse Columbus de nouo Mundo, ... ex Ventis spirantibus ab illa parte ... ?" p. 329-330.
  Bound in contemporary calf.
  Backer3:434.
69-546

F684
E96bl Exquemelin, Alexandre Olivier.
  Bucaniers Of America: Or, a true Account Of The Most remarkable Assaults Committed of late years upon the Coasts of The West-Indies, By the Bucaniers of Jamaica and Tortuga, Both English and French. Wherein are contained more especially, The unparallel'd Exploits of Sir Henry Morgan, our English Jamaican Hero, who sack'd Puerto Velo, burnt Panama, &c. Written originally in Dutch, by John Esquemeling, one of the Bucaniers, who was present at those Tragedies;

	and thence translated into Spanish, by Alonso de Bonne-maison, Doctor of Physick, and Practitioner at Amsterdam. Now faithfully rendred [sic] into English. London: Printed for William Crooke, at the Green Dragon with-out Temple-bar. 1684. 6 p.ℓ., 115, 151, [1], 124, [11] p. illus. (part engr.), 4 plates (incl. 1 fold., 1 double), 4 ports., map. 24cm. 4º Issued in 3 pts. Dutch original 1st pub. Amsterdam, 1678, under title: De Americaensche Zee-Roovers. This transl. is from the Spanish transl. 1st pub. Cologne, 1681, under title: Piratas De La America. "Books Printed for William Crooke this year 1684." following p. 151. With this is bound: Ringrose, Basil, Bucaniers Of America. The Second Volume. London, Crooke, 1685. JCB(2)2:1281; WingE3894; Sabin23479; Church 689. 01916, before 1854

at those Transactions" signed: W.D. [i.e. William Dick]
With this is bound: Ringrose, Basil. Bucaniers Of America. The Second Volume. London, Crooke, 1685.
JCB(2)2:1282; WingE3896; Sabin23481.
04489-1, before 1882

F684 E96b2	Exquemelin, Alexandre Olivier. Bucaniers Of America: Or, a True Account Of The Most Remarkable Assaults Committed of late Years upon the Coasts of The West-Indies, By the Bucaniers of Jamaica and Tortuga, Both English and French. Wherein are contained more especially, The unparallel'd Exploits of Sir Henry Morgan, our English Jamaican Hero, who sack'd Puerto Velo, burnt Panama, &c. Written originally in Dutch, by John Esquemeling, one of the Bucaniers, who was present at those Tragedies, and Translated into Spanish by Alonso de Bonne-maison, M.D. &c. The Second Edition, Corrected, and Inlarged with two Additional Relations, viz. the one of Captain Cook, and the other of Captain Sharp. Now faithfully rendred [sic] into English. London: Printed for William Crooke, at the Green Dragon without Temple-bar. 1684. 6 p.ℓ., 49, 42-43, 52-53, 46-47, 80, 84, [12] p. illus. (part engr.), 4 plates (incl. 2 fold.), 4 ports., fold. map. 22cm. 4º Issued in 3 pts. Dutch original 1st pub. Amsterdam, 1678, under title: De Americaensche Zee-Roovers. This transl. is from the Spanish transl. 1st pub. Cologne, 1681, under title: Piratas De La America. This transl. 1st pub. London, the same year. Two chapters added in this edition, p. 61-84 at end. Added material about Bartholomew Sharpe, "given by one of the Bucaniers, who was present

F684 E96h	Exquemelin, Alexandre Olivier. The History Of The Bucaniers: Being An Impartial Relation Of all the Battels, Sieges, and other most Eminent Assaults committed for several years upon the Coasts of the VVest-Indies By the Pirates of Jamaica and Tortuga. Both English, & other Nations. More especially the Unparallel'd Atchievements of Sir H.[enry] M.[organ] Made English from the Dutch Copy: Written by J. Esquemeling, one of the Bucaniers, very much Corrected, from the Errours of the Original, by the Relations of some English Gentlemen, that then resided in those Parts. ... London, Printed for Tho. Malthus at the Sun in the Poultrey. 1684. 12 p.ℓ., 192 p. 2 plates (ports.) 15.5cm. 12º Dutch original 1st pub. Amsterdam, 1678, under title: De Americaensche Zee-Roovers. "The Publisher To The Reader" (2d-6th p.ℓ.) criticizes the veracity of the Exquemelin account published in translation under title: Bucaniers Of America by Crooke, London, the same year. Dedicatory verses (p.ℓ. 7) signed: A.B. JCB(2)2:1283; WingE3898; Sabin23480. 01918, 1854

BA684 L525v1	Florencia, Francisco de, 1619-1695. Relacion De La Exemplar, Y Religiosa vida del Padre Nicolas De Gvadalaxara, Professo de nuestra Compañia de Jesvs, A Los Reverendos Padres, y charissimos Hermanos de la V. y Religiosa Provincia de Nueva-Espana. A Qvienes La Dirige, y dedica el P. Francisco de Florencia de la misma Compañia de Iesvs. Con quatro breves tratados espirituales, para las almas, que tratan de virtud, compuestos por el mesmo Padre Nicolas de Guadalaxara. Con Licencia De Los Svperiores. [Mexico] Por Juan de Ribera, Impressor, y Mercader de Libros en el Empedradillo. Año de 1684. 4 p.ℓ., 32 numb. ℓ., 23 numb. ℓ., [2] p. 19.5cm. 4º License dated (last p.) 29 May 1684. Bound with: Leiba, Diego de. Vida De El Venerable Padre Fr. Diego Romero. [Mexico], 1684.

	JCB(2)2:1285; Palau(2)92336; Medina(Mexico) 1305; Sabin24818; Backer3:795.
03982, 1869	

DA684 F785d	[Fowler, Edward, bp. of Gloucester] 1632-1714. A Defence Of The Resolution Of This Case, Viz. Whether the Church of England's Symbolizing so far as it doth with the Church of Rome, makes it Unlawfull to hold Communion with the Church of England. In Answer to a Book Intituled A Modest Examination Of That Resolution. London, Printed by J. H. for B.[rabazon] Aylmer, at the Three Pigeons, against the Royal Exchange in Cornhill. 1684. 1 p.ℓ., 52 p., 1 ℓ. 20cm. 4° A reply to A modest examination of the resolution of this case of conscience, London, 1683. Errata, p. 52. Booksellers' advertisement, last page. WingF1697.
12945, 1920	

DA684 F791	[Fox, George] 1624-1691. A Declaration From The Harmless & Innocent People of God, called, Quakers Against All Sedition Plotters & Fighters In the World. ... Presented unto the King upon the 21th day of the 11th moneth, 1660. [London, 1684?] 7, [1] p. 20.5cm. (25.5cm. in case) 4° Caption title. First pub. London, 1660. Includes, last p., "Added in the Reprinting. ... This was our Testimony above Twenty Years ago ..." A variant of this edition has imprint at end "London, Reprinted by John Bringhurst..., 1684." The variant is signed (p. 6) by George Fox and 11 others; its title reads "... Against all Plotters..." and "... given unto the King...". Smith(Friends)1:662; 2:445; WingF1788; McAlpin4:167-68.
15584, 1930	

DA684 F791d	[Fox, George] 1624-1691. A Declaration From The Harmless & Innocent People of God, called, Quakers Against All Plotters and Fighters In the World. ... This Declaration was given unto the King, upon the 21th day of the 11th moneth, 1660. London, Reprinted by John Bringhurst, at the Sign of the Book and Three Black-Birds, in Leaden-Hall Mutton-Market, 1684. 7, [1] p. 20.5cm. (21.5cm. in case) 4° Caption title; imprint at end. Signed (p. 6) by George Fox and 11 others. First pub. London, 1660. Includes, last p., "Added in the Reprinting. ... This was our Testimony above Twenty Years ago ..." A variant of this edition, [London, 1684?], lacks imprint and names on p. 6; its title reads "... Against all Sedition Plotters..." and "... Presented unto the King...". WingF1789; Smith(Friends)1:662, 2:445; McAlpin4:167.
68-81	

EB F8355 1684 1	France--Sovereigns, etc., 1643-1715. (Louis XIV). 21 Jan 1684 Arrest Du Conseil D'Estat: Qui Commet Les Sieurs Morel de Boistiroux & Mesnager pour avoir la direction & conduite des affaires de la Compagnie & Domaine d'Occident. Du 21. Janvier 1684. A Paris, Par Sebastien Mabre-Cramoisy, Imprimeur du Roy. M. DC. LXXXIV. De l'exprés commandement de Sa Majesté. 7 p. 25cm. 4° Cut (royal arms) on t.-p. Wroth & Annan 254.
1455, 1906	

F690 B645g	Gronovius, Jacobus, 1645-1716. Jacobi Gronovii Dissertatio De Origine Romuli, Recitata die xxiij Octobris, Quum alterum stationis suæ quinquennium commendaret. Lugd. Batavorum. Apud Jordanum Luchtmans. cIↃ Ic C LXXXIV [sic]. 3 p.ℓ., 48 p. 20cm. 8° Cut (engr. of Roman coins) on t.-p. Bound with: Blaeu, W. J. ... Institutio astronomica, Leyden, 1690, as the 5th of 5 items.
12022.5, 1919	

F690 B645g   Gronovius, Jacobus, 1645-1716.
        Jacobi Gronovii Responsio Ad Cavillationes Raphaelis Fabretti.
        Lugd. Batavorum. Apud Jordanum Luchtmans. cIɔIɔCLXXXIV.
        56 p. 20cm. 8°
        Cut (printer's device incl. motto: Spes Alit Agricolas) on t.-p.
        A reply to: Fabretti, Raffaele. De aquis et aquæductibus veteris Romae, Rome, 1680.
        Bound with: Blaeu, W.J. ...Institutio astronomica, Leyden, 1690, as the 4th of 5 items.

12022.4, 1919

D684 -H251c   Hanson, Samuel, defendant.
        The Case Of Samuel Hanson, Merchant and Planter in Barbadoes, Humbly offer'd and submitted to the Kings Most Excellent Majesty's Consideration, and Royal Determination in Council.
        [London? 1684?]
        19 p. 30cm. fol.
        Caption title.
        Latest date mentioned in text is 10 Apr. 1684.
        WingH664; cf. Sabin30273.

12041, 1919

FA678 -H428k   Hazart, Cornelius, 1617-1690.
        Kirchen-Geschichte/Das ist: Catholisches Christenthum/durch die gantze Welt aussgebreitet/ Insonderheit Bey nächst-verflossenen/ und anjetzo fliessenden Jahr-Hundert... In vilfältigen Kupffern zu füglicher Erkandnuss abgebildet Erstlich beschriben/und an Tag gegeben/durch R.P. Cornelium Hazart, Nunmehr aber Auss der Nider-in die Hoch-Teutsche Sprach übersetzet/und vermehret/ durch R.P. Mathiam Soutermans, Beyde der Gesellschafft Jesu Priestern. Der ander Theil/In sich begreiffend Die Africanische Länder/Abassia, Guinea, Angola, Congo, Monomotapa, Marocco, und Fessa: Demnach die Americanische/Perù, Paraquaria, Brasilia, Florida, Canada, Mexico, und Maragnan.
        Cum Gratia, & Privilegio Sacræ Cæsareæ Majestatis Permissu Superiorum. Gedruckt/ und verlegt/zu Wienn in Oesterreich/Durch Leopoldum Voigt / einer Löblichen Universitæt Buchdrucker/Anno M.DC.LXXXIV.
        9 p.ℓ., 606, [31] p. illus. (engr., incl. port.) 30cm. fol. (Issued as a part of his Kirchen-Geschichte, Vienna, 1678-1684)
        Transl. from: Kerckelycke Historie Van de Gheheele Wereldt. Vol.2. Antwerp, 1671.
        Title in red and black.
        Added t.-p., engraved: Catholisches Christenthum...
        Privilege dated (9th p.ℓ.ᵛ) 23 March 1683.
        Errata, last page.
        JCB(2)2:1287; Sabin31114; Backer7:1407; Streit1:668.

03011A, 1865 rev

E684 H515d   Hennepin, Louis, ca. 1640-ca. 1705.
        Description De La Louisiane, Nouvellement Decouverte au Sud' Oüest de la Nouvelle France, Par Ordre Du Roy. Avec la Carte du Pays: Les Mœurs & la Maniere de vivre des Sauvages, Dediée A Sa Majesté. Par le R.P. Loüis Hennepin, Missionaire Recollet & Notaire Apostolique.
        A Paris, Chez Amable Auroy, ruë Saint Jacques, à l'Image S. Jerôme, Proche la fontaine S. Severin. M.DC.LXXXIV. Avec Privilege, du Roy.
        6 p.ℓ., 312, 107 p. fold. map. 16.5cm. 12°
        Cut (printer's device) on t.-p.
        First pub. Paris, 1683. These are the same sheets with cancel t.-p.
        "Achevé d'imprimer pour la premiere fois, le 5. Janvier 1683." (6th p.ℓ.ᵛ).
        Bound in contemporary calf.
        Cf. Sabin31347; Paltsits(Hennepin)ℓ; Streit 2: 2723.

05846, 1885

FC650 H737 34   Hollandse Mercurius, Verhalende de voornaemste Saken van Staet En Oorlog, Die, in en omtrent de Vereenigde Nederlanden, En elders in Europa, In het Jaer 1683, Zijn geschiedt. Het Vier-en-Dertigste Deel.
        Tot Haerlem, Gedruckt by Abraham Casteleyn, Stadts-Drucker, op de Marckt, in de Blye Druck. Anno 1684.
        4 p.ℓ., 250, [6]p. 3 plates (1 fold.) 20cm. 4° (Bound in [vol. 8] of Hollandse Mercurius)
        Added t.-p., engraved: Den Hollandschen Mercurius Anno 1683. Tot Haerlem: By Abraham Casteleyn.
        JCB(3)2:410; Sabin32523.

8487HH, 1912

D684
-H745f
    Holloway, James, d. 1684.
       The Free and Voluntary Confession and Narrative Of James Holloway (Addressed to His Majesty) ... As also The Proceedings against the said James Holloway ... And his Petition to His Majesty. Together With a particular Account of the Discourse as passed between the Sheriffs of London and the said James Holloway at the time of his Execution for High-Treason at Tyburn, April 30. 1684. With his Prayer immediately before, and the true Copy of the Paper Delivered them at the same Time and Place.
      London, Printed for Robert Horn, John Baker, and John Redmayne. 1684.
      16 p. 30cm. fol.
      Caption title; imprint at end.
      Holloway was involved in the Whig conspiracy and Rye House Plot, 1683. He describes his flight to the West Indies and arrest in St. Eustachius.
      Wing H2509.

71-251

BA684
J58m
    Isidoro de Jesús María.
      Maria Sanctissima Victoriosa, Y Victoreada En Sv Immacvlada Concepcion. Por Fr. Isidoro De Iesvs Maria Religioso Augustino Descalço, Provincial actual de la Provincia de S. Nicolas de Philipinas. En la fiesta que celebrò la Milicia en la Capilla Real de la Ciudad de Manila. En El Domingo Quarto De Adviento, dia del Apostol Santo Thomas. Año de 1681. Patente El Santissimo Sacramento.
      Con Licencia De Nvestros Svperiores En Mexico, por la Viuda de Francisco Rodriguez Lupercio. 1684.
      10 p. ℓ., [28] p. 20.5cm. 4°
      "Parecer" dated (8th p. ℓ.^{r}) 17 Feb. 1684.
      Imperfect: 2d-3d p. ℓ. wanting.
      Palau(2)123732; Medina(Mexico)1307.

1042, 1905 rev

DB
-J2755
1684
1
    Jamaica--Laws, statutes, etc.
      The Laws Of Jamaica, Passed by the Assembly, And Confirmed by His Majesty In Council, April 17. 1684. To which is added, The State of Jamaica, As it is now under the Government of Sir Thomas Lynch. With a large Mapp of the Island.
      London, Printed by H.H. Jun. for Charles Harper, at the Flower-de-Luce over against St. Dunstan's Church in Fleet-street. M.DC.LXXXIV.
      1 p. ℓ., xix, [xx-xxii], 86 p., 1 ℓ., 87-151, [1] p. fold. map. 31.5cm. fol.
      "The State Of Jamaica" (p. i-xix, dated at end: Octob. 1. 1683.) was written by Sir Thomas Lynch.
      Includes certificate of royal approval (signed: John Nicholas) on leaf inserted between p. 86-87.
      The first part, p. 1-86, was 1st pub. under title: The laws ... confirmed ... in council Feb. 23. 1683, 4°, London, 1683. The second part, p. 87-151, and "The State of Jamaica", p. i-xix, were also pub. under title: The laws ... confirmed ... April 17, 1681, vol. II, 4°, London, 1684.
      A continuation was pub. under title: The continuation of the laws of Jamaica, folio, London, 1698.
      "Law-Books Printed for, or sold by Charles Harper ...", last p.
      Bound in contemporary calf rebacked; from the library of William Blathwayt.
      Sabin 35623; Cundall(Jam.)626; Wing J125; Tower 119.

X4486, 1913

DA684
K28d
    [Keith, George] 1639?-1716.
      Divine Immediate Revelation And Inspiration, Continued in the True Church, Second Part. In Two Treatises: The First being an Answer to Jo. W. Bajer ... The Second being an Answer to George Hicks ... Together, with some Testimonies of Truth, Collected out of diverse Ancient Writers and Fathers, so called. By G. K.
      London, Printed in the Year, 1684.
      7 p. ℓ., 206 p. 17.5cm. 8°
      Cancel t.-p. The title of another issue, also London, 1684, omits the designation "Second Part".
      A reply to Johann Wilhelm Bajer, Synopsis theologiae enthusiastarum recentiorum, seu Quakerorum, Jena, 1682, and to George Hickes, Spirit of enthusiasm exorcised, London, 1680.
      First treatise 1st pub. under title Ab J. G. Bajeri ... dissertationem primam contra Quakeros, Amsterdam, 1683.
      Errata, 7th p. ℓ.^{v}
      In this copy there is a blank ℓ. at beginning and at end.
      Wing K159; Smith(Friends)2:23; Smith(Anti-Quak)55, 225.

15950, 1930

BA684
L525v1
Leiba, Diego de.
Vida De El Venerable Padre Fr. Diego Romero, De La Regvlar Observancia De N.S.P.S. Francisco, Sacerdote, é Hijo de esta Provincia de el Santo Evangelio.
... Escrita Por el P. Predicador Fr. Diego De Leiba, Natural de la Puebla de los Angeles.
Con Licencia De Los Svperiores. [Mexico] Por Juan de Ribera, Impressor, y Mercader de Libros en el Empedradillo. Año de 1684.
12 p. ℓ., 62 numb. ℓ., [4] p. illus. 19.5cm. 4°
License dated (11th p. ℓ.v) 23 Aug. 1684.
Errata, last page.
Imperfect: 2d-3d p. ℓ. wanting; available in facsim.
With this is bound: Florencia, Francisco de. Relacion De La Exemplar, Y Religiosa vida del Padre Nicolas De Gvadalaxara. [Mexico], 1684.
JCB(2)2:1288; Palau(2)134640; Medina(Mexico)1308; Sabin39892; Wagner57; Streit 2:2198.

03981, 1869 rev

BA684
L525v2
Leiba, Diego de.
Vida De El Venerable Padre Fr. Diego Romero, De La Regvlar Observancia de N.S.P.S. Francisco, Sacerdote, è Hijo de esta Provincia de el Santo Evangelio.
... Por su mas indigno Esclavo El R. P. Fr. Diego De Leyba, Predicador, Pro-Ministro de la misma Provincia del Santo Euangelio de Mexico, y Procurador en la Curia Romana de la Canonizacion del V. Padre Fr. Sebastian de Aparicio.
[Sevilla? 1687?] Con Licencia De Los Svperiores. Por Juan de Ribera, Impressor y Mercader de Libros en el Empedradillo, [Mexico] Año de 1684.
12 p. ℓ., 62 numb. ℓ., [4] p. illus. 20.5cm. 4°
Reprinted from 1st ed. [Mexico] 1684, almost page-for-page the same; errata listed in the [Mexico] 1684 edition are here corrected. The fact that here on the t.-p. Leiba is styled "Procurador en la Curia Romana de la Canonizacion del V. Padre Fr. Sebastian de Aparicio" and the fact that Leiba published a biography of Aparicio in Seville, 1687 (on the t.-p. of which he is similarly styled) suggest that this was pub. in Seville at the same time.
License dated (11th p. ℓ.v) 23 Aug. 1684.
Bound in contemporary vellum.

BA684
L525v2
cop.2
———— Another copy. 19.5cm.
In this copy 4th, 8th, 12th p. ℓ. and ℓ. 4, 49 mutilated with some loss of text.
JCB(2)2:1289; Palau(2)134640; Medina(BHA)7852; Sabin39892; Wagner57a; Streit 2:2199.

68-462
03983, 1869

BA684
-L732c
Lima(Ecclesiastical province).
Concilia Limana, Constitvtiones Synodales, Et alia vtilia Monumenta: Qvibvs Beatvs Toribivs Archiepisc. Limanvs Ecclesias Peruani Imperij mirificè illustrauit. Nunc denuò exarata studio & diligentia D.ris D. Francisci Antonii De Montalvo, Hispalensis, Ordinis Sancti Antonij.
Romæ, Ex Typographia Iosephi Vannaccij. M.DC.LXXXIV. Svperiorvm Permissv.
18 p. ℓ., 355, [1] p. 2 ports. 30.5cm. fol.
Cut (ecclesiastical coat of arms) on t.-p.
First pub. under title: Lima Limata, Constitvtionibvs Synodalibvs Et Aliis Monvmentis, Rome, 1673.
Dedication dated (4th p. ℓ.v) 1 March 1684.
JCB(2)2:1280; Palau(2)177322; Medina(BHA)1767; Sabin50070; Streit 2:2200.

0800, 1846

BA684
L864s
Lopez, Francisco, 1648-1696.
Sermon En La Honoracion Annua, Y Vniversal Sufragio, Que De Orden de la Magestad Catolica del Rey N.S. D. Carlos II. El Deseado se fundó en la S. Iglesia Metropolitana de Lima, por todos los Soldados, que an muerto en su Real servicio, el dia 3 de Noviembre de 1684. Dedicalo ... El P. Francisco Lopez de la Compañia de Iesus.
Con licencia de todos los Superiores. En Lima, Año de 1684. Por Joseph De Contreras.
5 p. ℓ., [26] p. 20cm. 4°
Dedication dated (3d p. ℓ.v) 12 Dec. 1684.
Medina(Lima)571; Backer4:1946-47.

5505, 1909

EA684
L934v
[Lucchesini, Giovanni Lorenzo] 1638-1716.
La Vie De Sainte Rose De Ste Marie, Religieuse du Tiers Ordre de saint Dominique, Originaire du Perou dans les Indes Occidentales, Canonizée par N.S.P. le Pape Clement X. le 12.

Avril 1671. Par le R. P. Jean Bapt. Feüillet, de l'Ordre des FF. Prêcheurs de la Province de S. Louis, & Missionaire Apostolique dans les Antisles de l'Amerique. Quatrieme Edition.

A Paris, Chez André Cramoisy, ruë de la Harpe, au Sacrifice d'Abraham. M. DC. LXXXIV. Avec Approbation & Privilege.
    12 p. ℓ., 276 p. 14cm. 12°
    Also attributed to Antonio González de Acuña.
    Translated, by Jean Baptiste Feuillet, from Compendium admirabilis vitæ Rosae de S. Maria... Rome, 1665. French transl. 1st pub. Paris, 1668.
    "Extrait du Privilege du Roy" dated (10th p. ℓ.) 18 Sept. 1668.
    JCB(2)2:1284.
03643, before 1866

BA684 María de la Antigua, madre, 1566-1617.
M332e   Estaciones De La Passion Del Señor, Qve Exercitava la V. M. Maria De La Antigva, Religiosa Professa de nuestra Madre Santa Clara. Y Le Mandó N. Señor las publicase para gloria suya, memoria de su SS. Passion, y mayor aprovechamiento de las almas. Dedicadas A el Licenciado Diego Calderon Benabides Comissario del S. Oficio de la Inquisicion, y Capellan del Hospital de N. Señora de la Concepcion.
[R]

Año de 1684. Con licencia, en Mexico, por Juan de Ribera en el Empedradillo.
    1 p. ℓ., [22] p. 15cm. 8°
    Cut (Franciscan device) on t. -p.
    Includes poetry.
    "Oracion, Que compuso San Augustin, en memoria de la Passion de el Señor." (p. [22]).
    Last ℓ. mutilated.
12730-1, 1920

EA684 Marie de l'Incarnation, mère, 1599-1672.
M334e   L'Ecole Sainte Ou Explication Familiere Des Mysteres De La Foy. Pour toutes fortes de Personnes qui sont obligées d'apprendre, ou d'enseigner la Doctrine Chrétienne. Par la Venerable Mere Marie De L'Incarnation, Religieuse Ursuline.

A Paris, Chez Jean Baptiste Coignard, Imprimeur & Libraire ordinaire du Roy, ruë Saint Jacques, à la Bible d'or. M. DC. LXXXIV. Avec Privilege du Roy, & Approbations.

    16 p. ℓ., 275, [10]**, 276-562, [2] p. illus. (engr.) 17cm. 12°
    Cut on t. -p.
    Edited by Claude Martin.
    Privilege dated (last p.) 4 July 1683.
    Includes "Sixiéme precepte. Vous ne commettrez point d'adultere", 10 pages, each paged**.
    In this copy there is a blank leaf following p. 562. The [2] p. at end contain an "Approbation" and the privilege.
    Bound in contemporary calf.
8563, 1912

D. Math Mather, Increase, 1639-1723.
I.45   The Doctrine Of Divine Providence Opened And Applyed: Also Sundry Sermons on Several other Subjects, By Increase Mather. Teacher of a Church at Boston in New-England ...

Boston In New-England [sic] Printed by Richard Pierce for Joseph Brunning, And are to be sold at his Shop at the Corner of Prison-Lane next the Exchange 1684.
    4 p. ℓ., 148 p., 1 ℓ., 28 p., 2 ℓ. 14.5cm. 8°
    In this issue the 4th p. ℓ.ᵛ is blank and "The Contents" is on the next to last leaf at end.
    "To the Reader." dated (4th p. ℓ.) 25 Oct 1684.
    Erratum, p. 148 (1 line).
    Bookseller's advertisement, final ℓ.
    With, as issued, Nathaniel Mather, A sermon wherein is shewed..., Boston, 1684, with special t. -p. and separate paging and signatures.
    Bound in contemporary calf.
    Imperfect: p. 81-82, 93-94, 21-22 (2d count), and part of final ℓ. wanting; some tears affect text.
    In this copy there is a blank ℓ. after p. 148.
    Annotations in ms. by Rev. Solomon Townsend, 1716-1791, of Barrington, R.I.

D. Math ——— Another copy. 14.5cm.
I.45   Errata, p. 148 (2 lines).
cop. 2   In this copy a leaf from his The mystery of Christ opened, Boston, 1686, listing contents and with bookseller's advert. on verso, has been inserted following 4th p. ℓ.
    Evans371; Sabin46671; WingM1204; Holmes (I)45.
9635, 1914
05860, 1878

D. Math Mather, Increase, 1639-1723.
I. 52C   An Essay For The Recording Of Illustrious
[R]   Providences: Wherein, An Account is given of
many Remarkable and very Memorable Events,
which have happened in this last Age; Especially
In New-England. By Increase Mather, Teacher
of a Church at Boston in New-England. ...
   Printed at Boston in New-England, and are to
be sold by George Calvert at the Sign of the
Half-moon in Pauls Church-yard, London, 1684.
   11 p.ℓ., 372, [8] p., 1ℓ. 14cm. 8º
   Errata, p. 372.
   Cancel t.-p. 1st issued with imprint: Boston
in New-England Printed by Samuel Green for
Joseph Browning ... 1684.
   Preface dated (11 p.ℓ.ʳ) Jan. 1, 1683/4.
   JCB(2)2:1291; WingM1208; Evans373; Sabin
46680; Holmes(I)52C; Church691.

03644, 1866

D. Math Mather, Nathaniel, 1631-1697.
I. 45   A Sermon Wherein Is Shewed That it is the
Duty and should be the Care of Believers on
Christ, to Live in the Constant Exercise of
Grace. By Mr. Nathanael Mather Pastor of a
Church at Dublin in Ireland. ...
   Printed at Boston in New-England By R.[ichard]
P.[ierce] for Joseph Browning Stationer. Anno
1684.
   1 p.ℓ., 28 p. 14.5cm. 8º (Issued as a part
of Increase Mather, Doctrine of divine provi-
dence, Boston, 1684.)
   Bound in contemporary calf.
   Imperfect: p. 21-22 wanting; some tears
affect text.

D. Math ———Another copy. 14.5cm.
I. 45
cop. 2

9635A, 1914
05860A, 1878

BA684 Pedroche, Cristóbal, 1640-1715.
-P372b   Breve, Y Compendiosa Relacion De la
Prision, y Destierro del señor Arçobispo,
Don Fray Phelipe Pardo, por la gracia de
Dios, y de la Santa Sede Apostolica, Arço-
bispo de Manila, Metropolitano de estas
Islas, del Consejo de su Magestad Catholica,
&c. que se executò Miercoles quinto de
Quaresma, treinta y vno de Março del año
de 1683. à las tres de la mañana, por el
Oydor Don Christoual Grimaldo, el Alcalde
Ordinario Iuan de Veristain, Sargento Mayor
del campo Don Alonso de Aponte, y Secre-
tario de Camara Iuan Sanchez, &c. Escriuela,
por mandado de su Prouincial, Fray Christoual
de Pedroche, del Orden de Predicadores.
   [Madrid? 1684?]
   12 numb. ℓ. 29.5cm. fol.
   Caption title.
   Dated at end: 24 May 1683.
   First pub. under title: Breve, y compendiosa
relacion de la estrañez ... [Madrid? 1683]
   Cf. JCBAR66:4; Palau(2)216260; Medina
(Filipinas)225; Streit5:936; Retana 199.

66-113, 1965

BA684 [Peguero, Juan] d. 1691.
-P376i   Informacion Ivridica, Qve remite la Prouincia
de el SS.ᵐᵒ Rosario de Philipinas, de la Orden de
Predicadores, à su Magestad, à fauor de sus
Religiosos, por ocasion de auer intentado sus
emulos el desacreditarla en estos Reynos, y
ante su Magestad. ...
   [Madrid? ca. 1684]
   10 numb. ℓ. 28.5cm. fol.
   Caption title.
   Prepared by "Fray Iuan Peguero, Procurador
General de esta Prouincia de el Santissimo Rosario de Philipinas, Orden de Predicadores"
(numb. ℓ. 1).
   Dated (numb. ℓ. 9ᵛ) in Manila, 10 Jan. 1682.
   Answers accusations circulated by the Jesuits
against the Dominicans in connection with the
controversy between the Jesuits and the Dominican Archbishop Felipe Fernández de Pardo.
Includes testimonials in favor of the Dominicans
by several prominent persons in Manila.
   Cf. JCBAR66:4; Palau(2)119324; Medina(Filipinas)
222; Streit5:924; Retana198.

66-123

D684 [Penn, William] 1644-1718.
P412b   Beschreibung Der in America neu-erfundenen
Provinz Pensylvanien. Derer Inwohner/Gesetz/
Arth/Sitten und Gebrauch: Auch sämtlicher Re-
viren des Landes/Sonderlich der Haupt-Stadt
Phila-Delphia Alles glaubwurdigst Auss des
Gouverneurs darinnen erstatteten Nachricht.
   [Hamburg] In Verlegung bey Henrich Heuss
an der Banco/im Jahr 1684.
   1 p.ℓ., 32 p. fold. plan. 19.5cm. 4º.

"Send-Schreiben vom William Penn/Eigenthümer und Stadthalter zu Pensilvania in America; geschrieben an die Commissarien der freyen Societät der Kauffleute... welche sich in Londen auffhalten... Erstlich in Englischer Sprache beschrieben/nachmahls auss der Holländischen in der Hochdeutschen Sprache übergesetzet. durch J.W. Hamburg. Bey Henrich Heusch in Jahr 1684": p. 1.

Translation of Missive van William Penn, Amsterdam, 1684. That itself is a transl. by Benjamin Furly, of A Letter From William Penn... To the Committee Of The Free Society of Traders, London, 1683, and of Thomas Paschell, An Abstract of a Letter from Thomas Paskell, London, 1683.

JCB(1)2:932; JCB(2)2:1295; Baer(Md)108; Vail (Front)231; Kane(Promotion)15, Palmer371.

0532, 1846

D684   Penn, William, 1644-1718.
P412m   Missive Van William Penn, Eygenaar en Gouverneur van Pennsylvania, In America. Geschreven aan de Commissarissen van de Vrye Societeyt der Handelaars op deselve Provintie, binnen London residerende. ... Waar by noch gevoeght is een Beschrijving van de Hoost-Stadt Philadelphia. ...
   t'Amsterdam, By Jacob Claus, Boekverkooper in de Prince-straat, 1684.
   28 p. fold. plan. 19.5cm. 4°.
   Contents.-[I] "Aan den Lezer" (p. 3-6) signed: Rotterdam den 6. der 3. Maand. 1684. Benjamin Furly.-[II] "Missive" (p. 7-22) signed: Philadelphia 26. der 8. maand genaamt Augustus. 1683. William Penn.-[III] "Een kort Verhaal Wegens de Situatie ... Philadelphia" (p. 22-23) by Thomas Holmes.-[IV] "De Declaratie des Conings, aan de Inwoonders en Coloniers der Provintie van Pennsylvania" (p. 24).— [V] "Extract Uyt een Brief uyt Pennsylvania, geschreven by Thomas Paskell, aan J. J. van Chippenham ..." (p. 25-28) signed: Pennsylvania den 10. February, 1683. Hollandse Stijl. Thomas Paskell.
   Transl. by Benjamin Furly from: A Letter From William Penn... To the Committee Of The Free Society of Traders. London, 1683; and Paschall, An Abstract of a Letter from Thomas Paskell. London, 1683.
   JCB(1)2:939; JCB(2)2:1293; Sabin59717; Vail (Front.)232; Kane(Promotion)16; Baer(Md.) 109.

02307, 1853

D684   [Penn, William] 1644-1718.
P412r   Recueil De Diverses Pieces, Concernant La Pensylvanie.
   A La Haye, Chez Abraham Troyel, Marchand Libraire, dans la Grand Sale de la Cour, M.DC.LXXXIV.
   118 p. 13cm. 12°.
   A collection of 5 articles on Pennsylvania transl. by Benjamin Furly from Penn's Some Account of... Pennsilvania, London, 1681, Penn's Letter... To The Committee of Free Traders, London, 1683, and Paschall's Abstract of a Letter from Thomas Paskell, London, 1683.
   "Eclaircissemens De Monsieur Furly" includes prefatory materials used in his Dutch translations of these works.
   JCB(1)2:942; JCB(2)2:1294; Church692; Sabin 60445; Leclerc(1867)1249; Vail(Front.)233; Baer(Md.)110; Kane(Promotion)14.

03645, before 1866

E684   Recueil De Divers Voyages Faits En Afrique
R311d   Et En L'Amerique, Qui N'Ont Point Esté Encore Publiez ... Le tout enrichi de Figures, & de Cartes Geographiques, qui servent à l'intelligence des choses contenuës en ce Volume.
   A Paris, Chez la Veuve Ant. Cellier, ruë de la Harpe, à l'Imprimerie des Roziers. M.DC. LXXXIV. Avec Privilege Du Roy.
   4 p. ℓ., [10 parts] 25cm. 4°
   Compiled by Henri Justel.
   First pub. Paris, 1674; these are the same sheets with cancel t.-p. "Achevé d'imprimer": 4 Oct. 1673 (4th p. ℓ.^{v}).
   Each part has special half-title.
   Order of parts differs in various copies, but sequences of paging and signatures determine sectional groupings as indicated in Contents.
   This copy bound in contemporary calf as follows.
   Contents:
   [section] a^4 A-2H^4 2I^2 2K^4 2L^2
   Ligon, Richard. Histoire de l'isle des Barbades. 1 ℓ., [6], 204 p. 6 plates, fold. map, 3 fold. diagrs. Transl. from: A true & exact history of the Island of Barbados; 1st pub. London, 1657. (In this copy fold. map is bound at end of section; p. [1-4] wanting, available in copies of 1674 issue.)
   [Lobo, Jeronymo] Relation de la riviere du Nil. 1 ℓ., 207-252 p. Transl. from: A short relation of the river Nile, 1st pub. London, 1669, itself transl. by Sir Peter Wyche from the Portuguese original in ms. "Itinerario das suas viagems".

Extrait de l'histoire d'Ethiopie. [2], 253-262 p. incl. map. Transl. from Historia geral da Ethiopia... composta... pelo Padre Manoel d'Almeyda... abreviada... pelo Padre Balthezar Tellez, Coimbra, 1660. French transl. 1st pub. Rouen, 1671. (This part wanting in this copy; available in copies of 1674 issue.)
[section] §-4§⁴ 5§²
Description de l'empire du Prete-Jean. 1 ℓ., 3-35 p. fold. map. Includes errata, p. 35. Transl. from Historia geral da Ethiopia... composta... pelo Padre Manoel d'Almeyda... abreviada... pelo Padre Balthezar Tellez, Coimbra, 1660. (In this copy fold. map wanting; available complete in copy 1 of 1674 issue.)
[section] **A-**C⁴
Relation du voyage fait sur les costes d'Afrique. 1 ℓ., 3-23 p.
[section] a² b-g⁴ *A-*K⁴ *L²
La Borde, sieur de. Relation de l'origine, moeurs, coustumes, religion, guerres et voyages des caraibes. 1 ℓ., 3-40 p. 3 plates. (In this copy plates are misbound with Ligon's Barbades.)
Relation de la Guiane. 1 ℓ., 43-49 p.
[Blome, Richard] Description de l'isle de la Jamaique et de toutes celles que possedent les anglois dans l'Amerique. 1 ℓ., 81 p. 2 fold. maps. Transl. from: A description of the island of Jamaica, 1st pub. London, 1672. Includes additional half-titles: "Relation de l'isle des Barbades" (p. 29), "Colonies angloises" (p. 47). (In this copy half-title (p. 47) and fold. map of North American colonies wanting; half-title available in facsim. and map in copy 1 of 1674 issue.)
JCB(2)2:1296; Sabin68430; Streit1:695.

01914, 1854 rev

BA684 Reyes, Gaspar de los, 1655-1706.
R457s Sermon, Que predicó El P. Gaspar De Los Reyes de la Compañia de Jesus, En las honrras, que la Santa Iglesia Cathedral de Antequera hizo Al Ex.ᵐᵒ Ill.ᵐᵒ, y R.ᵐᵒ Señor Maestro D. Fr. Payo Enrriqvez De Ribera. Sacalo A Lvz, El Doctor D. Gonzalo Dominguez Guerra de el Corral, Dean de dicha Santa Iglesia. Dedicalo, A su dignissimo Prelado, el Ill.ᵐᵒ y R.ᵐᵒ Señor Doctor Don Isidro Sariñana y Cuenca, del Consejo de su Magestad, &c.
En Mexico: por la Viuda de Francisco Rodriguez Lupercio. 1684.
6 p.ℓ., [24] p. 20cm. 4°
"Sentir" dated (4th p.ℓ.ʳ) 19 Dec. 1684.
Imperfect: p. [2-3] wanting.

Palau(2)265547; Medina(Mexico)1323; Backer 6:1690.

1041, 1905

B684 [Rodríguez, Manuel] 1633-1701.
-R696m Compendio Historial, E Indice Chronologico Pervano, Y Del Nvevo Reyno De Granada, desde el principio de los descubrimientos de las Indias Occidentales, tocando varias cosas memorables de ellas, assi Eclesiasticas, como Seculares. [Madrid, 1684]
[24] p. 29.5cm. fol. (With (as issued?) his El Marañon, Y Amazonas... Madrid, 1684.)
Caption title.
JCB(2)1297; Palau(2)273204; Sabin72524; Medina(BHA)1771; Streit2:2201; Backer6:1965.

0209A, 1840

B684 Rodríguez, Manuel, 1633-1701.
-R696m El Marañon, Y Amazonas. Historia De Los Descvbrimientos, Entradas, Y Redvccion De Naciones. Trabajos Malogrados De Algvnos Conqvistadores, Y Dichosos De Otros, Assi Temporales, Como Espiritvales, En Las Dilatadas Montañas, Y Mayores Rios De La America. Escrita Por El Padre Manvel Rodrigvez, De La Compañia De Iesvs, Procvrador General De Las Provincias De Indias, En La Corte De Madrid.
Con Licencia. En Madrid, En La Imprenta de Antonio Gonçalez de Reyes. Año de 1684.
12 p.ℓ., 444, [7] p. 29.5cm. fol.
Contains extensive extracts from Cristóbal de Acuña's Nuevo descubrimiento del gran río de las Amazonas, Madrid, 1641 (p. 101-141, 425-428).
Errata: verso 8th p.ℓ. (dated 13 Mar 1684).
Imperfect: half-title wanting, available in facsim.
With (as issued?) his Compendio Historial, E Indice Chronologico Pervano, Y Del Nvevo Reyno De Granada... [Madrid, 1684], with separate paging and signatures.
JCB(2)2:1297; Palau(2)273202; Sabin72524; Medina(BHA)1771; Streit2:2201; Backer6:1965; Borba 2:212-213.

0209, 1840

B684 San Buenaventura, Gabriel de, fl. 1684.
S194a Arte De La Lengva Maya, Compuesto por el R.P. Fr. Gabriel de San Buenaventura Predica-

dor, y difinidor habitual de la Provincia de San Joseph de Yucathan del Orden de N.P.S. Francisco.

 Año de 1684. Con Licencia: En Mexico, por la Viuda de Bernardo Calderon.

 9 p.l., 6 p., 6-9 numb. l., [4] p., 10-41 numb. l. 20cm. 4º

 Cut (Franciscan coat of arms) on t.-p.

 Approbation dated (6th p.l.^{v}) 11 May 1684.

 Imperfect: [4] p. between numb. l. 9 and 10 wanting; text available in Mexico, 1888, reprint.

 JCB(2)2:1279; Palau(2)290362; Medina(Mexico) 1325; Sabin76007; Pilling516; Viñaza216; Ugarte 386.

04086, 1870

BA684 -S217r Sandín, Alonso, 1630-1701.

 Respvesta A Vna Relacion Sumaria, que salió à luz, y se publicó en el Reyno de la Nueua España, por parte de los Ministros de su Magestad de la Real Audiencia de la Ciudad de Manila en las Islas Philipinas, en que intentan dar satisfacion de lo obrado por dichos Ministros, en las repetidas competencias, que estos años han tenido con Don Fray Phelipe Pardo, Arçobispo de dicha Ciudad de Manila. Responde A Ella Fray Alonso Sandin, de la Orden de Predicadores, Definidor, y Procurador General de la Prouincia del Santissimo Rosario en dichas Islas Philipinas, poder aviente de dicho señor Arçobispo en la Corte de su Magestad.

 [Madrid, ca. 1684]

 70 numb. l. 28.5cm. fol.

 Caption title.

 A reply to: [Ortega, Jerónimo de] Relacion sumaria de los sucessos de la ciudad de Manila, Manila, 1683.

 Palau(2)297028; Medina(Filipinas)373; Retana 201; Streit 5:937.

66-117

BA684 S237m Santoyo, Felipe de.

 Mistica Diana, Descripcion Panegyrica De Sv Nvevo Templo, Qve, Con La advocacion de Nuestra Señora de la Antigva, de Santa Teresa de Jesvs de Carmelitas Descalças, erigió el fervoroso zelo del Capitan Estevan de Molina Mosquera. Que escrivia Don Phelipe de Santoyo, y la consagra humilde, A la Soberana Reyna de los Angeles Maria Santissima de la Antigva.

 Con Licencia en Mexico, por Juan de Ribera.

 Año de 1684.

 4 p.l., 19 numb. l. 19.5cm. 4º

 Cut (Virgin Mary) on t.-p.

 In verse.

 License dated (3d p.l.) 20 Oct. 1684.

 Preliminary matter includes poetry by Francisco de Ayerra y Santa Maria, Alonso Ramírez de Vargas, Juan Marin Falconi, and Nicolas, marqués de los Rios.

 This copy closely trimmed at outer margin affecting some marginal notes.

 Palau(2)301045; Medina(Mexico)1327; Gonzalez(1952)226; Sabin76892.

15652, 1930

F684 S464e De Seldsaame en Noit Gehoorde Wal-Vis-Vangst, Voorgevallen by St. Anna-Land in't jaar 1682. den 7. October. Midsgaders, Een Pertinente Beschrijvinge, Van de geheele Groen-Landse-Vaart. Verhandeld in Prose, en Versen. Nevens Verscheide Saaken tot die Materie dienende; Gelijk op d'and're sijde van dit Blad kan gesien worden. Door P: P: v: S. Med schoone Kop're Prentverbeeldingen verciert. Dese 2de. Druk, merkelijk verbetert, En, bij na de helft, vermeerdert.

 Tot Leiden [Abraham Elzevier] in't Jaar 1684.

 1 p.l., 72, [6] p. 7 plates (incl. 5 fold.). 20cm. 4º []1 A-I^4 K^4(-K1=[]1)

 Cut (Rahir fleuron 60) on t.-p.

 This is an enlarged version of Kort En Opregt Verhaal Van het Droevig en avontuurlijk wedervaren... [Leiden? 1683].

 This version 1st pub. Leyden, 1684.

 A3 missigned: B3.

F684 S464e cop.2 ———— Another copy. 19.5cm.

 A3 signed correctly.

 JCB(2)2:1286; Sabin74630; Muller(1872)1788; Knuttel 12249.

05665, probably before 1874 rev
05666, before 1882

BA684 S579p Sigüenza y Góngora, Carlos de, 1645-1700.

 Parayso Occidental, plantado y cultivado por la liberal benefica mano de los muy Catholicos, y poderosos Reyes de España Nuestros Señores en su Magnifico Real Convento de Jesus Maria de Mexico: De Cuya Fundacion, Y Progressos, y de las prodigiosas maravillas, y virtudes, con que exalando olor suave de perfeccion, florecieron en su clausura la V. M. Marina De La

Crvz, y otras exemplarissimas Religiosas Da Noticia En Este Volumen D. Carlos de Siguenza, y Gongora Presbytero Mexicano.
 Con Licencia De Los Svperiores En Mexico: por Juan de Ribera, Impressor, y Mercader de libros. Año de M.DC.LXXX.IIIJ.
 12 p.ℓ., 206 numb. ℓ., 1 ℓ. 22cm. 4°
 Royal arms on 1st ℓ., preceding t.-p.
 Cut (winged horse) on t.-p.; incl. motto: Sic Itvr Ad Astra.
 License dated (8th p.ℓ.ᵛ) 20 July 1682.
 Errata, final leaf.
 JCB(2)2:1299; Palau(2)312973; Medina(Mexico) 1328; Sabin 80980.
05769, 1870

B684 -S687h [R]   Solís y Rivadeneyra, Antonio de, 1610-1686.
 Historia De La Conqvista De Mexico, Poblacion, Y Progressos De La America Septentrional, Conocida Por El Nombre De Nveva España. Escriviala Don Antonio De Solis, Secretario de su Magestad, y su Chronista mayor de las Indias. Y La Pone A Los Pies Del Rey Nvestro Señor, Por Mano Del Excelentissimo Señor Conde de Oropesa.
 En Madrid. En la Imprenta de Bernardo de Villa-Diego, Impressor de su Magestad. Año M.DC.LXXXIV.
 17 p.ℓ., 548, [15] p. 29.5cm. fol.
 Added t.-p., engr.: Historia de la Nueva España... Theod. Ardeman inv. I F Leonardo sculp.
 "Tassa" dated (12th p.ℓ.) 6 Dec. 1684.
 Errata, 12th p.ℓ.
 JCB(2)2:1300; Sabin 86446; Palau(1)6:529; Medina(BHA)1773; Arocena IV 2.1.
01915, 1854

E684 T418v   Thévenot, Jean de, 1633-1667.
 Voyages De Mʳ De Thevenot, Contenant La Relation de l'Indostan, des nouveaux Mogols, & des autres Peuples & Pays des Indes.
 A Paris, Chez La Veuve Biestkins, ruë de la Harpe, à l'Imprimerie des Roziers. M.DC.LXXXIV. Avec Privilege du Roy.
 10 p.ℓ., 338, [19] p. tables. 23.3cm. 4°
 Also pub. as his Troisième partie des voyages de M. Thevenot, contenant la relation de l'Indostan...Paris, C. Barbin, 1684, forming the 3d part of his Relation d'un voyage fait au Levant... Paris, 1665-1684.
 Printer's device on t.-p.
 Includes tables (4 p.) "Alphabeth Malabar."
 According to binder's directions (p.[19] at end) these are to be placed between p. 264 and 265, but in this copy they are bound at end.
 "Achevé d'imprimer le 30. Septembre 1684." (2d p.ℓ.ᵛ)
04711, before 1874

D684 T875c   [Tryon, Thomas] 1634-1703.
 The Country-Man's Companion: Or, A New Method Of Ordering Horses & Sheep So as to preserve them both from Diseases and Causalties [sic], Or, To Recover them if fallen Ill ... And particularly to preserve Sheep from that Monsterous, Mortifying Distemper, The Rot. By Philotheos Physiologus, The Author of The Way to Health, long Life and Happiness, &c.
 London, Printed and Sold by Andrew Sowle, at the Crooked-Billet in Holloway-Court in Holloway-Lane, near Shoreditch. [1684?]
 4 p.ℓ., 173, [174-176] p. 14.5cm. 8°
 "The Planters Speech To his Neighbours & Country-men in Pennsylvania, East and West-Jersey..." (p. 100-141)
 Booksellers' advertisement, p.[174-176] at end.
 Wing T3176; Sabin 97285; Vail(Front.)234.
4480, 1908

D684 T875f   [Tryon, Thomas] 1634-1703.
 Friendly Advice To The Gentlemen-Planters Of The East and West Indies. In Three Parts. I. A brief Treatise of the most principal Fruit and Herbs that grow in the East & West Indies; giving an Account of their respective Vertues both for Food and Physick, and what Planet and Sign they are under. Together with some Directions for the Preservation of Health and Life in those hot Climates. II. The Complaints of the Negro-Slaves against the hard Usages and barbarous Cruelties inflicted upon them. III. A Discourse in way of Dialogue, between an Ethiopean or Negro-Slave, and a Christian that was his Master in America. By Philotheos Physiologus.
 [London] Printed by Andrew Sowle, in the Year 1684.
 1 p.ℓ., 222 p. 14cm. 8°

          The t.-p. of another issue reads "Friendly Advcie... [sic]" and has imprint "London, Printed by Andrew Sowle at the Crooked Billet in Holloway-Lane near Shoreditch."
          In this copy t.-p. closely trimmed at outer margin. Closely trimmed at top with some loss of text, p. 85-87; available in facsim.
          JCB(2)2:1302; WingT3179; Sabin25947; Cundall (WI)1987.

0533, 1846

DB   Virginia(Colony)--Laws, statutes, etc.
-V8175   A Complete Collection Of All The Lavvs Of
1684   Virginia Now In Force. Carefully Copied
1   from the Assembly Records. To which is Annexed an Alphabetical Table.
          London, Printed by T.J. for J.P. and are to be sold by Tho. Mercer at the Sign of the Half Moon the Corner Shop of the Royal-Exchange in Cornhil. [1684?]
          3 p.ℓ., 148, (145)-(148), 149-300, [22] p. 29.5cm. (30.5cm. in case) fol.
          Dedication signed by the compiler, [J.]ohn [P.]urvis.
          Bound in contemporary calf.
          Sabin100381; Wing V636; Torrence89; Swem4437, 22379; Tower904.

457, 1904

DA684   Willard, Samuel, 1640-1707.
W695m   Mercy Magnified On A Penitent Prodigal, Or A Brief Discourse, wherein Christs Parable of the Lost Son found, is Opened and Applied, As it was Delivered in Sundry Sermons, By Samuel Willard Teacher of a Church in Boston in New-England. ...
          Boston in New-England Printed by Samuel Green, for Samuel Philips, and are to be Sold at his Shop at the West end of the Town-House. 1684.
          3 p.ℓ., 391, [1] p. 15cm. 8º
          Errata, last page.
          In this copy there is a blank leaf at front.
          WingW2285; Evans379; Sabin104094.

5796, 1909

1685

DA685   Adams, William, 1650-1685.
A197g   God's Eye On The Contrite Or A Discourse Shewing That True Poverty and Contrition of spirit and Trembling at God's Word is the Infallible and only way for the Obtaining and Retaining of Divine Acceptation. As it was made in the Audience of the General Assembly of the Massachusetts Colony at Boston in New-England; May 27. 1685. being the Day of Election there. By Mr. William Adams. ...
          Boston in New-England, Printed by Richard Pierce for Samuel Sewall 1685.
          1 p.ℓ., 41 p. 18cm. 4º
          In this copy the blank portion of p. 41 below the text has been excised.
          Evans381; Sabin347; WingA498.

16850, 1936

D685   An Advertisement Concerning the Province of
A244c   East-New-Jersey In America. Published for the Information of such as are desirous to be concerned therein, or to transport themselves thereto.
          Edinburgh, Printed by John Reid, Anno Dom. 1685.
          1 p.ℓ., 22 p. 19.5cm. 4º
          Includes letters and testimonies about the province, the latest dated (p. 13): at Aberdeen the 5th day of March, 1685.
          Errata, p. 22.
          "Scottish Proprietors' Tracts" no. 7. Cf. Church 649n.
          Church695; Baer117; Vail(Front)237; WingP1672.

9340, 1913

B69   Agurto y Loaysa, Joseph de, fl. 1676-1688.
G643v   Villancicos, Qve Se Cantaron En La Santa
18   Iglesia Metropolitana de Mexico: en honor de Maria Santissima Madre De Dios, En Sv Assumpcion Triumphante. ... Año de 1685. Pusolos en metro Musico el Br. Joseph de Loaysa, y Agurto Maestro de Capilla de dicha Santa Iglesia.
          Con licēcia, en Mexico: Por los Herederos de la Viuda de Bernardo Calderon, [1685].
          [8] p. 20cm. 4º
          Woodcut title vignette (the Virgin, crowned, standing on the shoulders of angels; inscribed in lower corners: ADC; AT)
          Bound, in contemporary vellum, as no. 18 with 42 other items.
          cf. Medina(Mexico)1339.

28918, 1941

F685 [Aysma, Joannes] b. ca. 1636.
A987s Spiegel Der Sibyllen, Van Vierderley Vertooningen. ... Vertoonende sich daar in ook seer Eerbiediglijk, de Persoonen der XII. Voornaamste Sibyllen, met hare seer Aanmerkelijke Leeringen en Wonderbaarlijke Voorseggingen, over Kerkelijke, Staatsche, en Particuliere Saken; ook die de Tegenwoordige Rijken en Staten in Asia en Europa betreffen, en noch staan te geschieden, ja tot 's Weerelds Eynde. t'Samengestelt ... Door J. A. Seer rykelijk verçiert met allerhande raare Kopere Plaaten, ... De Tweede Druk naaukeurig oversien, en van veel Drukfauten verbetert.
t'Amsterdam. Gedrukt voor d'Autheur, waar by dit Werk ook te bekomen is, op de Bloemgraft, omtrent de Drukkery van d'Heer Blaauw: en by Timotheus ten Hoorn, Boekverkooper in de Nes, naast de Brakke Gront. 1685.
8 p.ℓ., 938, [30] p. 36 plates (incl. 20 fold.) 20.5cm. 4°
Added t.-p., engraved.
Colophon: t'Amsterdam, Gedrukt by Hendrik Harmensz. Boekdrukker in de Lange-straat, by de Brouwers-Graft, 1685.
First pub. Amsterdam, 1685.
A chapter on "Heydensche Religion" (p. 293-338) includes sections on Nieuw-Nederland, Virginia, Florida, Kuba, and Hispaniola.
Muller(1872)2382.

69-646

DA685 [Bayly, Lewis, Bp. of Bangor] d. 1631.
B359m Manitowompae Pomantamoonk Sampwshanau Christianoh Uttoh woh an Pomantog Wnssikkitteahonat [sic] God. ...
Cambridge [Mass.]. Printed for the right Honerable [sic] Corperation [sic] in London for the Gospelizing the Indins [sic], in New-England. 1685.
288, 273-333, [334-335] p. 15cm. 8°
An abridged transl., by John Eliot, of The practice of piety, 1st pub. London, 1612; transl. into Massachuset language 1st pub. Cambridge, 1665.
JCB(2)2:1313; Evans383; WingB1476; Sabin 4076; Pilling1189; CP181.

03647, before 1860

BA685 Becerra Tanco, Luis, 1602-1672.
B389f Felicidad De Mexico En El Principio, Y Milagroso Origen, Qve tvvo El Santvario De La Virgen Maria Nvestra Señora De Gvadalvpe, Extramuros: En la Aparicion admirable desta Soberana Señora, y de su prodigiosa Imagen. Sacada à luz, y añadida por el Bachiller Luis Bezerra Tanco, Presbytero, difunto, para esta segunda impression que ha procurado el Doctor D. Antonio de Gama ...
Con licencia, en Sevilla por Thomás Lopez de Haro, Año de 1685.
8 p.ℓ., 64 p., 4 plates, 20.5cm. 4°
First pub. under title: Origen milagroso del Santuario de Nuestra Señora de Guadalupe. Mexico, 1666.
Imperfect: plates wanting; available in facsim.
JCB(2)2:1305; Palau(2)26231; Sabin4216; Medina (BHA)1776; BLH6:3574.

03980, 1869

BA685 [Berart, Raimundo] 1651-1713.
-B483r Relacion Con Insercion De Avtos Sobre Todo Loqve a Passado Para Restitvir A Sv Silla al Illustrissimo Señor Maestro D. Fr. Pheliппe Pardo Arzobispo Metropolitano de Manila del Consejo de su Magestad &c. Y de las demas consequencias, segun consta en este Iuzgado Ecclesiastico: mandada referir por dicho Illustrissimo Señor a fin de poderse imprimir, y remitir; por quanto segun el corto tiempo es impossible hacer los tantos necessarios para remitir a la Europa a los Tribunales, que quiere su Señoria Illustrissima.
En Manila por el Capitan D. Gaspar de los Reyes impressor de libros. En 19. de Mayo de 1685.
77 numb. ℓ. 29cm. fol.
Caption title; imprint at end.
Ms. certification at end dated: Manila, 30 May 1685.
Each leaf of this copy bears the manuscript authentication of the archbishop's secretary, Domingo Diaz, as well as his signature at end, along with the signatures of three notaries.
Cf. JCBAR66:4; Palau(2)27669; Medina (Manila)106; Streit5:941; Retana156.

66-124

F685 Beughem, Cornelius à, fl. 1678-1710.
B566b Bibliographia Historica, Chronologica & Geographica Novissima, Perpetuo Continuanda ... Opera ac Studio Corneli à Beughem, Embricensis. Accedit Ejusdem Musæum seu Syllabus Iconum sive Imaginum illustrium à sæculo hominum, quæ in ejus Musæo spectantur.

70-338	Amstelædami, Apud Janssonio-Waesbergios, cIɔ Iɔc LXXXV. 8 p.ℓ., 788 p., 13.5cm. 12° The bibliography covers books pub. through 1683. In this copy there is a blank ℓ. at end. Bound in contemporary calf. Sabin 5102; Besterman(4) 2440, 2865.

DA685 B582m	Bible--Massachuset--Eliot--1685. Mamusse Wunneetupanatamwe Up-Biblum God Naneeswe Nukkone Testament Kah Wonk Wusku Testament. Ne quoshkinnumuk nashpe Wuttinneumoh Christ noh asoowesit John Eliot. Nahohtôeu ontchetôe Printeuoomuk. Cambridge. [Mass.] Printeuoop nashpe Samuel Green. MDCLXXXV. 2 v. in 1: 1 p.ℓ., [850] p., 1 ℓ.; 1 p.ℓ., [257, 102] p. 20cm. 4° Eliot Indian Bible, 2d ed.; 1st pub. Cambridge, Mass., 1663. Revised by John Eliot with the assistance of John Cotton. In the Massachuset language. In this copy a dedication ℓ. dated in Boston, 23 Oct. 1685, is inserted following t.-p. Also there is a blank ℓ. at beginning and at end. Erratum, last ℓ. O.T. The N.T. has a special t.-p. dated 1680 and separate signatures. Printing of the Bible commenced in 1680 with the N.T., which was finished late in 1681. A metrical version of the Psalms and rules for Christian living, which are found at the end of the N.T., were completed next in 1682. At that time a few copies may have been issued. Printing of the O.T. began in 1682, and the whole Bible was completed in 1685 (cf. Pilling). Bound in contemporary calf. Brinley 789 (this copy).

DA685 B582m cop.2 06269, 1884 03622-3, before 1858	——————Another copy. 19cm. Without dedication ℓ. Closely trimmed at bottom with slight effect on text. Bound in contemporary calf, rebacked. JCB(2)2:1312, 1201; Evans 385, 279; WingB2756-7; CP180, 179; Pilling(Algonquian)153-169; Darlow and Moule 6738.

DA685 B582p	Bible--O.T.--Ecclesiastes--English--Paraphrases--1685. A Paraphrase Upon The Books Of Ecclesiastes And The Song of Solomon. With Arguments to each Chapter, and Annotations thereupon. By Symon Patrick D.D. Dean of Peterburgh, and one of His Majesties Chaplains in Ordinary. London, Printed for Rich. Royston, Bookseller to the King's most Sacred Majesty. MDCLXXXV. 3 p.ℓ., xxiii, 380 p., 1 ℓ., xiv, 215, [216-220] p. port. 17.5cm. 8° Bookseller's advertisement, [216-220] p. at end. With as issued: The Song of Solomon Paraphrased. London, 1685, with special t.-p., separate paging but continuous signatures. In this copy there is a blank leaf at beginning. Imperfect: port. wanting; available in facsim. Wing B2642; McAlpin 4:205.
16522, 1934	

DA685 B582p	Bible--O.T.--Song of Solomon--English--Paraphrases--1685. The Song of Solomon Paraphrased. With Annotations. By the same Author. London, Printed for Rich. Royston, Bookseller to the Kings most Sacred Majesty. MDCLXXXV. 1 p.ℓ., xiv, 215, [216-220] p. 17.5cm. 8°. (Issued as a part of A paraphrase upon the books of Ecclesiastes and the Song of Solomon, London, 1685.) By Simon Patrick. Cut on t.-p. Bookseller's advertisement, p.[216-220] at end. Bound in contemporary calf. Wing B2642; McAlpin 4:205.
16522A, 1934	

DA685 B582m	Bible--N.T.--Massachuset--Eliot--1685. VVusku Wuttestamentum Nul-Lordumun Iesus Christ Nuppoquohwussuaeneumun. Cambridge, [Mass.] Printed for the Right Honourable Corporation in London, for the propogation [sic] of the Gospel among the Indians in New-England 1680 [i.e. 1685]. 1 p.ℓ., [257, 102] p. 20cm. 4° (Issued as a part of Bible--Massachuset--Eliot--1685, Mamusse ... , Cambridge, Mass., 1685.) Eliot Indian Bible, New Testament, 2d ed.; 1st pub. Cambridge, Mass., 1663. Revised by John Eliot with the assistance of John Cotton. In the Massachuset language. Includes (p. 1-102, 2d count) metrical version of the Psalms and rules for Christian living. Printing of N.T. began in 1680 and was finished in 1681. The metrical version of the Psalms and rules for Christian living at the end of the N.T.

	were completed next in 1682, at which time a few copies may have been issued. Printing of the O.T. began in 1682, and the whole Bible was completed in 1685 (cf. Pilling). Bound in contemporary calf. Brinley 789 (this copy).
DA685 B582m cop.2	———— Another copy. 19cm. Bound in contemporary calf, rebacked. JCB(2)2:1312, 1201; Sabin22156-7; Evans385, 279; WingB2756-7; CP180, 179; Pilling(Algonquian)153-169; Darlow and Moule6738.
06269A, 1884 03622-3A, before 1858	
DA685 B923s2	Buckingham, George Villiers, 2d duke of, 1628-1687. A Short Discourse Upon The Reasonableness Of Men's having a Religion, Or Worship of God. By his Grace, George Duke of Buckingham. The Second Edition. London, Printed by John Leake, for Luke Meredith, at the King's Head, at the West End of St. Paul's Church-Yard, MDCLXXXV. 3 p.ℓ., 21 p. 20.5cm. 4° First pub. London, same year. Cf. WingB5329.
67-427	
D685 B927g [R]	Budd, Thomas, d. 1698. Good Order Established In Pennsilvania & New-Jersey In America, Being a true Account of the Country; With its Produce and Commodities there made. ... Likewise, several other things needful to be understood by those that are or do intend to be concerned in planting in the said Countries. ... By Thomas Budd. [Philadelphia, William Bradford] Printed in the Year 1685. 39, [1] p. 20cm. 4° Errata, at end. Signed: London, the 29th of the 8th Month, 1684. "A Letter from New-Jersey ..." (signed: John Cripps) and "The Dying-Words of Ockanichon ...": p. 30-31. First pub. under title: A true account of the dying words of Ockanickon. London, 1682. JCB(1)2:943; JCB(2)2:1308; Church694; Sabin 8952; Evans386; Vail(Front.)239; WingB5358.
02852, 1861	
DA685 C271r	[Care, George] A Reply To The Answer Of The Man of No Name, To His Grace the Duke of Buckingham's Paper of Religion, and Liberty of Conscience. By G.C. an Affectionate Friend, and true Servant of his Grace the Duke of Buckingham's. London, Printed by John Leake, for Luke Meredith, at the King's Head, at the West End of St. Paul's Church-Yard, MDCLXXXV. 1 p.ℓ., 32, 35-36 p., 1 ℓ. 20.5cm. 4° A defence of: George Villiers, 2d duke of Buckingham, A short discourse upon the reasonableness of men's having a religion, London, 1685, in reply to: A short answer to his grace the D. of Buckingham's paper concerning toleration and liberty of conscience, London, 1685. Booksellers' advertisement, 1 ℓ. at end. WingC504.
69-456	
BA685 C363of	Catholic Church--Liturgy and ritual--Officium de Septem Doloribus Beatae Mariae Virginis. Officivm Septem Dolorvm B. Mariæ Virginis. In omnibus Hispaniarum Regnis, & ditionibus recitandum. [Mexico? ca. 1685] [8] p. 15cm. 8° Caption title. In Mexico 1st pub. 1673. In this copy p. [3-8] mutilated with some loss of text.
5761-17, 1909	
BA685 C363dd	Catholic Church--Liturgy and ritual--Special offices--Antoninus, Saint, Abp. of Florence. Die X. Maii. Officium In Festo S. Antonini Archiepiscopi Florentini, & Confessoris Ordinis Prædicatorum. Semiduplex ad libitum. Superiorum Permissu. Mexici: Apud Heredes Viduæ Bernardi Calderon. Donde se hallarâ. [ca. 1685]. 1 p.ℓ., [6] p. incl. illus. 15cm. 8° Cut (St. Anthony) on t.-p.
5761-13, 1909	
BA685 C363di	Catholic Church--Liturgy and ritual--Special offices--Cajetanus, Saint. Die vij. Augusti. In Festo S. Caietani Confessoris, Clericorum Regularium Fundatoris. Semiduplex ... [Mexico? ca. 1685]

[8] p. 15cm. 8º
Caption title.
"Die xxx. Augusti. Officivm Sanctæ Rosæ A
S. Maria Virginis Limanæ. Tertij Ordinis. S.
Dominici. Dvplex Prim. Clas.": p. [6-8].

5761-16

BA685   Catholic Church--Liturgy and ritual--Special
C363o   offices--Francisco de Borja, Saint.
            Officivm S. Francisci Borgiæ Societatis Iesu
        A Sacra Rituum Congregatione recognitum, &
        aprobatum ...
            Superiorum Permissu Mexici, apud Heredes
        Viduae Bernardi Calderon 1685.
            [8] p. 15cm. 8º
            Cut (Jesuit device) on t.-p.
            Promulgation dated (last p.) 17 June 1684.
            Medina(Mexico)1348.

5761^{11} 1909

BA685   Catholic Church--Liturgy and ritual--Special
C363os   offices--Gabriel, Archangel.
            Officium Sancti Gabrielis Archangeli Duplex
        maius Die 18. Martij.
            Superiorum permisu, Mexici apud Heredes
        Viduæ Bernardi Calderon; Anno 1685.
            [18] p. 15cm. 8º
            Cut (Annunciation) on t.-p.; incl. motto:
        Ave Maria Gratia Plena.
            First pub. Madrid, 1685.
            Includes poetry.
            Imperfect: last ℓ. wanting.
            Medina(Mexico)1350.

5761^6, 1909

BA685   Catholic Church--Liturgy and ritual--Special
C363dj   offices--Giovanni Gualberto, Saint.
            Die xij. Iulij. In Festo S. Ioannis Gvalberti.
        Semiduplex. Ad libitum. Omnia de Comm.
        Abbatum præter Lectiones secundi, & tertij
        Nocturni.
            Superiorum permissu. Mexici, apud Viduam
        Bernardi Calderon. [ca. 1685]
            [8] p. 15cm. 8º
            Caption title; imprint at end.
            In Mexico 1st pub. 1672.
            "Die xv. Iulij. In Festo S. Henrici Impera-
        toris." p. [5-8]
            "Die xxx. Maij. In Festo S. Ferdinandi Regis
        Hisp." p. [8]

5761-15, 1909

BA685   Catholic Church--Liturgy and ritual--Special
C363de   offices--Isidorus, Saint, patron of Madrid.
            Die 15. Maij. In Festo S. Isidori Agricolæ
        Confessoris, Matriti Patroni. Dvplex.
            [Mexico? ca. 1685]
            [4] p. 15cm. 8º
            Caption title.
            In Mexico 1st pub. 1663.

5761-14

BA685   Catholic Church--Liturgy and ritual--
C363d   Special offices--Rosa, of Lima, Saint.
            Die xxx. Augusti. In Festo S. Rosæ. A
        Sancta Maria, Uirginis Limanæ, Tertij
        Ordinis Sancti Dominici. Omnia de Communi
        Virginam, præter orationem, & lectiones
        secundi Nocturni.
            Mexici, apud Heredes Viduae Bernardi
        Calderon. [1685?]
            [8] p. 15cm. 8º
            Caption title; imprint at end.
            In Mexico 1st pub. 1672.

5761-5, 1909

BA685   Catholic Church--Liturgy and ritual--Special
C363dt   offices--Rosa, of Lima, Saint.
            Die XXX. Augusti. In Festo Sanctæ Rosæ
        A Sancta Maria, Virginis Limanæ, Tertii Or-
        dinis S. Dominici. Duplex Primæ Classis
        Cum Octava. ...
            [Mexico? ca. 1685]
            11 p. 16cm. 12º
            Caption title.
            In Mexico 1st pub. 1672.

11281, 1918

DA685   Church of England--Liturgy and ritual.
C562f   A Form Of Prayer, With Thanksgiving To
        Almighty God for having put an end to The Great
        Rebellion by the Restitution of the King and Royal
        Family. And the Restauration of the Govern-
        ment after many years Interruption: Which un-
        speakable Mercies were wonderfully Compleated
        upon the 29th of May, in the year, 1660. And
        in Memory thereof, that Day in every Year is
        by Act of Parliament Appointed to be forever
        kept Holy. By his Majesties special Command.
            London, Printed by the Assigns of John Bill
        deceas'd: And by Henry Hills, and Thomas New-
        comb, Printers to the Kings most Excellent
        Majesty. 1685.

2 p.ℓ., [11] p. 18.5cm. 4º
Order to print (2d p.ℓ.ᵛ) dated 29 Apr 1685.
WingC4173; cf. McAlpin4:195-6.

9759, 1914

B685 Colón, Fernando, 1488-1539
C719h Historie Del Signor D. Fernando Colombo. Nelle quali s'hà particolare, & vera relatione della vita, e de' fatti dell' Ammiraglio. D. Christoforo Colombo suo Padre, E dello scoprimento, ch'egli fece dell'Indie Occidentali, dette Mondo Nuouo, hora possedute dal Serenissimo Rè Cattolico. Nuouamente di lingua Spagnuola tradotte nell' Italiana dal Sign. Alfonso Vlloa. ...
In Venetia, M.DC.LXXXV. Appresso Giuseppe Tramontin. Con licenza de' Superiori, e Priuileg.
24 p.ℓ., 336, 339-494, [11] p. 13cm. 12º.
Half-title: Historie Del Colombo.
First pub. Venice, 1571.
"Scrittura di Frà Roman [i.e. Ramón Pane] delle antichità de gl'Indiani...": p. 253-290.
JCB(2)2:1310; Sabin14676; Palau(2)57213.

04715, before 1874

D685 [Crouch, Nathaniel] 1632?-1725?
C952e The English Empire In America: Or a Prospect of His Majesties Dominions in the West-Indies. ... With an account of the Discovery, Scituation, Product, and other Excellencies of these Countries. To which is prefixed a Relation of the first Discovery of the New World called America, by the Spaniards. And of the Remarkable Voyages of several Englishmen to divers places therein. Illustrated with Maps and Pictures. By R.[ichard] B.[urton, pseud.] Author of Englands Monarchs, &c. Admirable Curiosities in England, &c. ...
London, Printed for Nath. Crouch at the Bell in the Poultrey near Cheapside. 1685.
2 p.ℓ., 209, [210-212] p. 2 plates, 2 maps. 14.5cm. 12º
Bookseller's advertisement, p. 209-[212].
Includes poetry.
Imperfect: last ℓ. wanting.

D685 ——— ———Another copy. 14.5cm.
C952e Imperfect: 2 plates wanting; map mutilated, completed in pen and ink facsim.
cop.2 JCB(2)2:1309; WingC7319; Sabin9499.
0801, 1846
05938, before 1874?

DA685 A Defence Of The Duke of Buckingham,
D313o Against the Answer to his Book, And the Reply to his Letter. By the Author of the late Considerations.
Entered according to Order. London, Printed for W.C. 1685.
8 p. 20.5cm. 4º
"the Author of the late Considerations" (i.e. of Considerations moving to a toleration and liberty of conscience, London, 1685) is supposed by Smith to be William Penn (cf. Smith(Friends)1:42 and 2:303).
Caption title; imprint at end.
This is a defence of: George Villiers, 2d duke of Buckingham, A short discourse upon the reasonableness of men's having a religion, London, 1685, and is one of a series of pamphlets pub. London, 1685, which were engendered by it. The following is the sequence of replies and counter-replies which preceded the present work and are mentioned in its title: A short answer to his grace the D. of Buckingham's paper concerning toleration and liberty of conscience; The duke of Buckingham his grace's letter to the unknown author of a paper entituled A short answer to his grace the Duke of Buckingham's paper; A reply to his grace the duke of Buckingham's letter to the author of a paper entituled An answer to his graces discourse. Considerations moving to toleration [attributed to William Penn] is another pamphlet engendered by Buckingham's Short discourse and was issued in support of it.
WingD816A.

69-453

E685 [Dufour, Philippe Sylvestre] 1622-1687.
D861t Tractatvs Novi De Potv Caphé; De Chinensivm Thé; Et De Chocolata.
Parisiis, Apud Petrum Muguet. M.DC.LXXXV.
3 p.ℓ., 202, [4] p. front., 3 plates. 15cm. 12º
Cut (armillary sphere) on t.-p.
Transl. by Jacob Spon, from: Traités nouveaux et curieux du caffé, du thé et du chocolate, Lyon, 1685, 1st pub. under title: De l'vsage dv caphé, dv thé, et dv chocolate, Lyon, 1671.
"Tractavs De Potv Caphé" (p. 1-100) is taken from Antonio Fausto Naironi's Discursus de saluberrima potione cahue seu cafe, Rome, 1671; "Tractatvs De Chinesivm Thé" (p. 101-140) from Alexandre de Rhodes's Divers voyages et missions dv P. Alex. de Rhodes's en la Chine..., 1st pub. Paris, 1653, and Johan Nieuhof's Gesandshap der Nederlandische Oost-Indische Compagnie..., 1st pub. Am-

sterdam, 1665; "Tractatvs De Chocolata" (p. 141-191) from Antonio Colmenero de Ledesma's Du Chocolate, discours curieux (transl. from the Spanish by René Moreau), Paris, 1643; "Dialogvs De Chocolata" (p. 192-202) from Bartolomé Marradon's Dialogus del uso del Tabaco y los daños que causa, etc., y del chocolate... , 1st pub. Seville, 1618.
    In this copy the paste-down at end is an integral blank leaf.
    Bound in contemporary calf.

30759, 1950

E685   Dufour, Philippe Sylvestre, 1622-1687.
D861tr   Traitez Nouveaux & curieux Dv Café, Dv Thé Et Dv Chocolate. Ouvrage également necessaire aux Medecins, & à tous ceux qui aiment leur santé. Par Philippe Sylvestre Dvfovr.
    A Lyon, Chez Iean Girin, & B. Riviere, ruë Merciere, à la Prudence. M. DC. LXXXV. Avec Privilege Dv Roy.
    11 p. ℓ., 445, [446-450] p. incl. plate. 2 plates. 12°
    Title in red and black.
    Cut on t.-p.
    Added t.-p., engr.
    "Achevé d'imprimer pour la premiere fois le 30. Septembre 1684." (11th p. ℓ.)
    First pub. Lyon, 1671, under title: Du l'usage du caphé, du thé, et du chocolate.
    Jacob Spon, to whom this work has been attributed, was the translator of a Latin version pub. Paris, 1685, under title: Tractatus novi de potu caphé...
    "Traité Dv Café" (p. 1-216) is taken from Antonio Fausto Naironi's Discursus de saluberrima potione cahue seu cafe, Rome, 1671; "Traité Dv Thé" (p. 223-304) from Alexandre de Rhode's Divers voyages et missions du P. Alex. de Rhodes en la Chine... , 1st pub. Paris, 1653, and Johan Nieuhof's Gesandshap der Nederlandische Oost-Indische Compagnie... , 1st pub. Amsterdam, 1665; "Traité Du Chocolate" (p. 305-421) from Antonio Colmenero de Ledesma's Du Chocolate, discours curieux (transl. from the Spanish by René Moreau), Paris, 1643; "Dialogue Du Chocolate" (p. 423-445) from Bartolomé Marradón's Dialogus del uso del Tabaco y los daños que causa, etc., y del chocolate... , 1st pub. Seville, 1618.
    In this copy there is a blank ℓ. at end.
    Bound in contemporary calf.
    Arents(Adds.) 492.

70-33

BA685   Florencia, Francisco de, 1619-1695.
F632m   La Milagrosa Invencion De Vn Tesoro Escondido En Vn campo, que halló vn venturoso
[R]   Cazique, y escondió en su casa, para gozarlo á sus solas. Patente Ya En El Santvario De los Remedios en su admirable Imagen de N. Señora; señalada en milagros; invocada por Patrona de las lluvias, y temporales; Defensora De Los Españoles, Abogada de los Indios, Conquistadora de Mexico... Noticias De Sv Origen, Y venidas á Mexico; maravillas, que ha obrado con los que la invocan; descripcion de su Casa, y meditaciones para sus Novenas. Por el P. Francisco De Florencia, de la Compañia de Jesus. Dalas A La Estampa El Br. D. Lorenzo de Mendoza, Capellan, y Vicario de la Santa Imagen, y Comissario del Santo Officio...
    Con Licencia De Los Superiores: [Mexico] Por Doña Maria de Benavides, Viuda de Juan de Ribera. Año de 1685.
    8 p. ℓ., 80 numb. ℓ., [4] p. front. 20cm. 4°
    License dated (7th p. ℓ.^{v}) 16 Oct. 1685.
    Errata, last p.
    With this is bound: Loaisaga, Manuel de, Historia De La Milagrosissima Imagen De N^{ra}. S^{ra}. De Occotlan. Mexico, 1750.
    Palau(2)92338; Medina(Mexico)1337; Sabin 24813; Backer3:796.

29054, 1941

DA685   [Fox, George] 1624-1691.
F791   To All Kings, Princes, Rulers, Governours, Bishops and Clergy. That Profess Christianity in Christendom Being A Distinction between the Laws, Commandments and Ordinances of the Higher Powers, for the Punishment of Evil Doers, and for the Praise of them that do Well ... By G. F.
    London, Printed by John Bringhurst in Leaden-Hall, 1685.
    27p. 19cm. (20cm. in case) 4°
    Signed(p. 21): London the 30th of the 3d Moneth, 1685. G. F.
    "Postscript": p. 22-27.
    Smith(Friends)1:685; WingF1938.

62-40, 1961

EB   France--Sovereigns, etc., 1643-1715.
F8355   (Louis XIV).   8 Feb.1685
1685   Arrest Du Conseil D'Estat, Sa Majesté Y
1   Estant, Pour Le Rétablissement De La Fabrique des purs Castors de Canada. Du 8 Février 1685.
    A Paris, Par Sebastien Mabre-Cramoisy, Imprimeur du Roy. M. DC. LXXXV. De

EB France--Sovereigns, etc., 1643-1715.
F8355   (Louis XIV).   12 Apr. 1685
1685   Arrest Du Conseil D'Estat, Sa Majesté Y
2   Estant, Pour Le Rétablissement De La Fabrique des purs Castors de Canada. Du 12. Avril 1685.
    A Paris, Par Sebastien Mabre-Cramoisy, Imprimeur du Roy. M. DC. LXXXV. De l'exprés commandement de Sa Majesté.
    2 (i.e. 4) p. 25.5cm. 4°
    Cut (royal arms) on t.-p.
    Wroth&Annan274; Harrisse(NF)154; Sabin56073.
14973, 1928

EB France--Sovereigns, etc., 1643-1715.
F8355   (Louis XIV).   12 Apr. 1685
1685   Arrest Du Conseil D'Estat, Sa Majesté Y
2   Estant, Pour Le Rétablissement De La Fabrique des purs Castors de Canada. Du 12. Avril 1685.
    A Paris, Par Sebastien Mabre-Cramoisy, Imprimeur du Roy. M. DC. LXXXV. De l'exprés commandement de Sa Majesté.
    8 p. 25.5cm. 4°
    Cut (royal arms) on t.-p.
    Wroth&Annan279; Harrisse(NF)155; Sabin56074.
14974, 1928

BA685 Franciscans.
F819i   Instrvccion, Y Doctrina De Novicios, Sacada De La De San Bvenaventvra, Y De La De Las Provincias De Descalsos De N.P. San Francisco, de San Ioseph, y de San Pablo, nuevamente emmendada, añadida, y ajustada al vso, y estilo de esta de San Diego de Mexico. Por Nvestro Hermano Fr. Ioseph Veedor Predicador, y Deffinidor actual de ella, de orden de N. Hermano Fr. Sebastian De Castrillon, Y Gallo, Predicador, y Ministro Provincial de la misma Provincia. Año de mil seiscientos y ochenta y cinco. ...
    Con Licencia. En la Puebla, por Diego Fernandez de Leon. Año de 1685.
    6 p.ℓ., 114 numb. ℓ. 20cm. 4°
    Cut (San Diego) on t.-p.
    A rev. and enl. of its: Primera parte de la Instrvccion Y doctrina, con que se han de criar los nuevos Religiosos ... first pub. Madrid, 1595.
    License dated (4th p.ℓ.ʳ) 20 Apr. 1685.
    With this is bound: Muñoz de Castro, Pedro. Exaltacion Magnifica De La Betlemitica Rosa ... Mexico, 1697.
    Palau(1)7:124; Medina(Puebla)97; Sabin98737.
05981, before 1923

BA685 García, Francisco, 1641-1685.
G216v   Vida, Y Milagros De S. Francisco Xavier, De La Compañia De Iesvs, Apostol De Las Indias. Por El Padre Francisco Garcia, Maestro de Theologia, de la misma Compañia de Iesvs.
    Con Privilegio. En Madrid: Por Ivan Garcia Infanzon. Vendese en casa de Marcos Alvarez de Arellano, Librero, debaxo de los Estudios de la Compañia. Y el librito de la Nouena. [1685?].
    5 p.ℓ., 213, 216-490 p. front. (port.). 20cm. 4°
    Cut (device of the Society of Jesus) on t.-p.
    First pub. Madrid, 1662. There is another edition, apparently also of 1685 (errata are dated 13 Dec. 1685), with imprint "En Madrid: Por Juan García Infanzon. Se hallará en la Portería de la Casa de Noviciado de la Compañia de Jesus de esta Corte."
    Errata, 3d p.ℓ.ᵛ; dated 15 Dec. 1685.
    Preliminary matter includes poetry, 4th-5th p.ℓ.
    "Novena De S. Francisco Xavier": p. 465-487.
    "Litaniae": p. 488-490.
    Imperfect: port. wanting; available in facsim. Bound in contemporary vellum.
    Backer3:1209; cf. Palau(2)97882; Streit5:583.
5504, 1909

BA685 García, Francisco, 1641-1685.
G216vy   Vida, Y Milagros De San Francisco Xavier, De La Compañia De Jesus, Apostol De Las Indias. Por El Padre Francisco Garcia, Maestro de Theologia, de la misma Compañia de Jesus.
    Con Privilegio En Madrid: Por Juan Garcia Infanzon. Se hallará en la Portería de la Casa de Noviciado de la Compañia de Jesus de esta Corte. [1685?]
    5 p.ℓ., 212, 215-490 p. 21.5cm. 4°
    Cut (device of the Society of Jesus) on t.-p.
    First pub. Madrid, 1662. There is another edition, apparently also of 1685 (errata are dated 15 Dec. 1685) with imprint: En Madrid: Por Ivan Garcia Infanzon. Vendese en casa de Marcos Arellano, Librero, debaxo de los Estudios de la Compañia. Y el librito de la Nouena.
    Errata, 3d p.ℓ.ᵛ dated 13 Dec. 1685.
    Preliminary matter includes poetry, 4th-5th p.ℓ.
    Woodcut port. "S. Francisco Xavier" is used as a tailpiece, p. 262, 334, 457, and 464.
    "Novena De S. Francisco Xavier" p. 465-487. "Litaniae": p. 488-490.
    Imperfect: p. 465-490 wanting; available in facsim.
    Palau(2)97882; Backer3:1209; Streit 5:583n.
70-528

H685 Giannettasio, Niccolò Partenio, 1648-1715.
G433n   Nic. Parthenii Giannettasij Soc. Jesu. Piscatoria et Nautica.
    Neap. apud Ia. Raillard, an. MDCLXXXV
    5 p. l., 246, [2] p. 10 plates. 16cm. 8º
    Engraved t.-p. ("F. De Louuemont Fec.").
    In some copies the imprint on the engr. t.-p. reads "Neapoli typis regiis an. MDCLXXXV".
    "Piscatoria", p. 7-48, consists of 13 eclogues of fishermen; "Nautica", p. 49-246, is a didactic and descriptive poem on navigation.
    "Novi Orbis detecti author" p. 236-244.
    "Ejusdem descriptio" p. 244-246.
    Errata, 2d p. l.^{v}
    Dedication dated (5th p. l.^{v}) Aug. 1685.
    Sabin 58926; Backer 3:1387; Palau(2) 101781.
70-498

DA685 Godwin, Morgan, fl. 1685.
G592t   Trade preferr'd before Religion, And Christ made to give place to Mammon: Represented in a Sermon Relating to the Plantations. First Preached at Westminster-Abby, And afterwards divers Churches in London. By Morgan Godwyn, sometime Student of Christ-Church in Oxford. ...
    London, Printed for B. Took at the Ship in St. Paul's Church-yard, and for Isaac Cleave at the Star in Chancery-Lane, 1685.
    3 p. l., 12, 34 p. 20.5cm. 4º
    Errata: p. 12 (1st count.)
    Imperfect: p. 33-34 wanting; available in facsim.
    JCB(2)2:1314; Sabin 27679; Wing G974.
03873, 1868

DB   Great Britain--Treaties, etc., 1660-1685
G7895   (Charles II).
1685   Several Treaties Of Peace and Commerce Concluded between the late King Of Blessed Memory Deceased, And Other Princes and States. Reprinted and Published by His Majesties Special Command.
    London, Printed by the Assigns of John Bill deceas'd: and by Henry Hills, and Thomas Newcomb, Printers to the Kings most Excellent Majesty. 1685.
    2 p. l., 269 p., 1 l. 24cm. 4º
    Collected and reprinted upon the accession of James II.
    Order to print (1st p. l.) dated 1 March 1684/5; cut (royal arms: Steele 98) at head.
    Contents.—Treaty of peace and commerce with Spain, Madrid, 13/23 May 1667, p. 1-38.—Treaty of peace with France, Breda, 21/31 July 1667, p. 39-47.—Treaty of peace with Denmark, Breda, 21/31 July 1667, p. 49-54.—Treaty of peace with Holland, Breda, 21/31 July 1667, p. 55-78.—Treaty of navigation and commerce with Holland, Breda, 21/31 July 1667, p. 79-92.—Treaty of navigation and commerce with Holland, Hague, 7/17 Feb. 1667/8, p. 93-106.—Treaty of friendship and commerce with Savoy, Florence, 19 Sept. 1669, p. 107-122.—Treaty with Spain for settling differences in America, Madrid, 8/18 July 1670, p. 123-130.—Treaty of alliance and commerce with Denmark, Copenhagen, 11 July 1670, p. 131-155.—Treaty of peace with Tunis, 5 Oct. 1662, confirmed 4 Feb. 1674/5, p. 157-162.—Treaty of peace and commerce with Tripoli, 1 May 1676, p. 163-175.—Treaty of peace with Holland, Westminster, 9/19 Feb. 1673/4, p. 177-183.—Treaty marine with Holland, London, 1 Dec. 1674, p. 185-200.—Explanatory declaration of the marine treaties with Holland, Hague, 30 Dec. 1675, p. 201-202.—Capitulations and articles of peace with the Ottoman Empire, Adrianople, Sept. 1675, p. 203-242.—Treaty marine with France, St. Germain-en-Laye, 24 Feb. 1676/7, p. 243-256.—Treaty of peace and commerce with Algiers, 10 April 1682, p. 257-269.—Table of Treaties, last l.
    In this copy there is a blank l. before the last printed l.
    Bound in contemporary calf, rebacked.
    Wing C3604B; Kress 1625.
67-46

C685   Gusmão, Alexandre de, 1629-1724.
G982h   Historia Do Predestinado Peregrino, E Seu Irmam Precito. Em a qual de baxo [sic] de huma misterioza parabola se descreve o sucesso feliz, do que se ha de salvar, & infeliz sorte do que se ha de condenar. Dedicada Ao Peregrino Celestial, S. Framcisco Xavier Apostolo do Oriente. Composta Pello P. Alexandre De Gvsmam da Companhia de Iesv, da Provincia do Brazil.
    Evora, Com todas as licenças necessarias na Officina da Universidade. Anno de 1685.
    4 p. l., 364, [9] p. 14.5cm. 8º
    First pub. Lisbon, 1682.
    "Taixam ..." dated (4th p. l.^{v}) 8 May 1685.
    Bound in contemporary vellum.
    Borba de Moraes 1:323; Backer 3:1961; Innocencio 1:32-33.
32571, 1960

C685 H673d Histoire De La Conqueste De La Floride, Par Les Espagnols, Sous Ferdinand De Soto. Ecrite en Portugais par un Gentil-homme de la ville d'Elvas. Par M.[onsieur] D.[e] C.[itry]
A Paris, Chez Denys Thierry, ruë saint Jacques, devant la ruë du Plâtre, à l'Enseigne de la Ville De Paris. M. DC. LXXXV. Avec Privilege Du Roy.
12 p. ℓ., 300 p. 16.5 cm. 12°
Cut on t.-p.
Transl. by S. de Broë, seigneur de Citry from: Relaçam verdadeira dos trabalhos que o governador dom Fernando de Souto . . . , 1st pub. Evora, 1556.
"Achevé d'imprimer": 27 Feb. 1685. (12th p. ℓ.)
JCB(2)2:1324; Palau(2)256843n; Sabin24864.

0803, 1846

FC650 H737 35 Hollandse Mercurius, Verhalende de voornaemste Saken van Staet, En andere Voorvallen, Die, in en omtrent de Vereenigde Nederlanden, En elders in Europa, In het Jaer 1684, Zijn geschiet. Het Vijf-en-Dertigste Deel.
Tot Haerlem, Gedruckt by Abraham Casteleyn, Stadts-Drucker, op de Marckt, in de Blye Druck. Anno 1685.
3 p. ℓ., 311, [312-318] p. 3 plates, fold. map. 20 cm. 4° (Bound in [vol. 9] of Hollandse Mercurius)
Errata: p. [312]
Added t.-p., engraved: Hollandsche Mercurius A° 1685 Tot Haerlem By Abraham Casteleyn
JCB(3)2:410; Sabin32523

8487 II, 1912

J685 K58q Kirchmayer, Georg Kaspar, 1635-1700.
. . . De Atlantide ad Timaeum atqve Critiam Platonis, Disseret In Almâ Leucorea, Praeside Georgio Caspare Kirchmajero, Orator. Prof. Publ. Ord. Philosoph. h.t. Spect. Decano, M. Johann. Christianus Bock/Grimmâ-Misnicus, Ad D. VII. Martii, in Auditorio Majori, horis matutinis, Anno cIↄ Iↄc LXXXV.
Witenbergae, Typis Christiani Schrödteri, Acad. Typ. [1685].
1 p. ℓ., 22 p. 20 cm. 4°
Diss.—Wittenberg (Johannes Christian Bock, respondent)
At head of title: Q. B. V. D.
Text in Latin and Greek.

32766, 1960

E685 L217d La Martinière, Pierre Martin de, 1634-1690.
De Noordsche Weereld; Vertoond In twee nieuwe, aenmercklijcke, derwaerts gedaene Reysen: D'eene, van de Heer Martiniere, Door Noorweegen, Lapland, Boranday, Siberien, Samojessie, Ys-land, Groenland en Nova-Zembla: Met de Beschrijvingh van der Inwoonderen Seeden, Gewoonten, Overgeloven, Gestalte, Dragten, en Huysen: De Koophandel, met haer gedreven: En dwalingh der Weereld-beschrijvers, soo in de plaetsingh als uytstreckingh van Groenland en Zembla. D'andere, van de Hamburger Frederick Martens, Verright nae Spitsbergen, of Groenland, in't Jaer 1671. Met nauwkeurige Aenteeckeningh van de gelegenheyd deses Lands, en desselven uyterste Deelen: Van de Zee; 't Ys; de Lught; de daer wassende verscheydene Kruyden; de sigh daer onthoudende Vogelen, Dieren, Visschen, Walvisschen en Zee-qualmen. Vertaeld, en doorgaens met Toe-Doeningen verrijckt, Door S. De Vries. Met een goed getal nae 't leven afgeteeckende Figueren.
t'Amsteldam, By Aert Dircksz. Ooszaen, Boeckverkoper op den Dam. M. DC. LXXXV.
6 p. ℓ., 334, [17] p. incl. illus. (map). 20 plates (incl. 6 fold.), map. 20.5 cm. 4°
Added t.-p., engraved.
Foreword (3d-6th p. ℓ.ʳ) signed: Utrecht, deesen 4. der Lente-maend des Jaers 1685. Simon De Vries.
The first account is a transl. of: Pierre Martin de La Martinière, Voyage Des Pais Septentrionaux, 1st pub. Paris, 1671; the second is a transl. of: Friedrich Martens, Spitzbergische oder Groenlandische Reise, 1st pub. Hamburgh, 1675. Both have extensive notes added by the editor, Simon de Vries.
JCB(2)2:1316; Sabin38712; Muller(1872)672.

02837, 1861

bBA685 L587c Leopold I, Emperor of Germany, 1640-1705.
Copia De La Promesa, Qve El Invictissimo Señor Emperador Leopoldo II. [sic] De Este Nombre (Qve Dios Gvarde) Hizo En Veneracion De Los Santos Lvgares De Gervsalen. Cvyo Original Traslado Desde Sv Avgvstissima Mano, En La De Nuestro Reverendissimo . . . Ministro General de toda la Orden de Nuestro Serafico Padre San Francisco, el dia dos de Agosto de este año de mil secientos y ochenta y cinco . . . Remitió dicha Copia su Reverendissima al Reverendo Padre Fray Alonso de Robles, Comissario General de los Santos Lugares, en esta Corte de España.
Con Licencia en la Puebla de los Angeles por Diego Fernandez de Leon vendese en su tienda en la esquina de la Plaça à la entrada

de la calle de cholula. [1685]
[4] p. 31.5cm. fol.
Issued to promote donations for support of the Franciscan establishments in the Holy Land.
Removed from the binding of: Ponce de León, Nicolás, Historia de la singular vida de el ... Fray Christoval de Molina, Puebla, Diego Fernández de León, 1686.

1513, about 1906

BA685 Liñán y Cisneros, Melchor, Abp., d.1708.
-L735e   Ofensa, Y Defensa De La Libertad Eclesiastica. La Primera En Veinte Y Qvatro Capitulos, que mandò publicar el Excelentissimo señor Duque de la Palata, Virrey del Perú, en despacho de 20. de Febrero de 1684. Y La Segvnda Armada Con Los escudos Catolicos de la ley, y la razon, que establecen los dominios de su Magestad, y dictò su propria obligacion Al Excelentissimo Señor D^r. D. Melchor De Liñán Y Cisneros, Arçobispo de Lima.
[Lima? 1685?]
104 numb. l. 29.5cm. fol.
Cut (incl. "IHS" and motto "Ad Maiorem Dei Gloriam") on t.-p.
In reply to: Peru(Viceroyalty)--Laws, statutes, etc., 1681-1689 (Navarra y Rocafull). Ordenanza, Lima, 20 Feb. 1684; Frasso, Pedro. Consulta y parecer sobre las dudas, Lima, 1684; López y Martínez, Juan Luis, marqués del Risco. Alegacion juridica, historico-politica.
In a contemporary hand on t.-p. of this copy, "Escriuiola el D.^{or} D. Diego Montero del Aguila."
Palau(2)138613; Medina(BHA)8479.

5518, 1909

BB   López, Francisco, 1648-1696.
-P4716   Gemino Lvminari Toleto, Ac Navarræ, Vtrivs-
1685   qve Orbis Miracvlo, Primævo Alteri, Alteri Non
1   Secvndo Pervviani Imperii Proregi, Gratulatio, Qua Tantos Uiros Franciscvs Lopez Societatis Iesv à Confessionibus Excell. D. Ducis Palatæ Ter Magnos Confitetvr.
[Lima, Joseph de Contreras, 1685]
[12] p. 30cm. fol. (Issued as a part of Tomo primero de las ordenanzas del Peru, Tomás de Ballesteros, comp., Lima, 1685.)
Laudatory verses.
Bound in contemporary vellum.

B682   ———————Another copy. 28cm.
-L864p   Bound as no. 9 in a vol. with binder's title: Luis Lopez Obras.

Cf. Medina(Lima)577, 633; Backer4:1947; Leclerc(1878)1826.13(this copy); cf. Sabin2962.

5508A, 1909
14015, 1925

B682   [López, Francisco] 1648-1696.
-L864p   Noticias Del Sur. Despacho, Y Felizes Svcesos De La Armada del Año de 1685. En El Govierno Del Excelentissimo Señor D. Melchor de Nauarra y Rocaffull Duque de la Palata, ... Virrey, y Capitan General de los Reynos del Peru, Tierrafirme, y Chile.
[Lima, 1685]
[26] p. 28cm. fol.
Caption title.
An account of the principal events in the viceroyalty of Peru 1681-1685.
Bound as no. 6 in a vol. with binder's title: Luis Lopez Obras.
Palau(2)139975; Medina(Lima)586; Backer 4: 1947; Leclerc(1878)1826.10 (this copy).

14012, 1925 rev

B682   López y Martínez, Juan Luis, marqués del
-L864p   Risco, d. 1732.
Discurso Ivridico, Historico-Politico, En Defensa De La Jurisdiction Real Ilvstracion De La Prouision De Veinte De Febrero del año passado de 1684. ... Sobre Qve En Recibir Los Corregidores Deste Reyno informaciones secretas de oficio, ... en orden à averiguar como observan los Curas, y Doctrineros las disposiciones Canonicas, Synodales, Cedulas, y Ordenanças de su Magestad, ... à fin solo de dar cuenta con ellas à sus Prelados, y al Govierno Superior destos Reynos, paraque lo remedien, no se contraviene en cosa alguna à la Immunidad de la Iglesia. Escrito De Orden Del Exc^{mo} Señor Dvque De La Palata, Virrey Destos Reynos. Por El Doctor Don Juan Luis Lopez, del Consejo de su Magestad, Alcalde del Crimen mas antiguo de la Real Audiencia de los Reyes, y Governador de Guancabelica.
Impresso Año De M.DC.LXXXV. Con Licencia Del Govierno, En Lima.
5 p.l., 5-146 p. 28cm. fol.
Dated (p. 133) in Guancavelica, 13 Nov. 1684.
Includes an "Ordenanza..." dated in Lima, 20 Feb. 1684 (p. 135-146).
Another version of the text pub. Lima, the same year, under title: Discurso legal, theológico-práctico.
Bound as no. 11 in a vol. with binder's title: Luis Lopez Obras.

BA685
-L864p
López y Martínez, Juan Luis, marqués del Risco, d. 1732.
Discvrso Legal. Theologico-Practico. En Defensa De La Provision Y Ordenanza De Govierno De XX. De Febrero De El Año M. DC. LXXXIV. Impressa En El Tomo Primero De Las Ordenanzas Del Perv, Fol. CCC.XI. Escrito De Orden De El Excelentissimo Señor Don Melchor de Navarra y Rocafull, Duque de la Palata, ... Virrey, y Capitan General de los Reynos, y Provincias de el Perù, Tierrafirme, y Chile. Por Don Ioan Lvys Lopez, de el Consejo de su Magestad, Alcalde de el Crimen mas antiguo de la Real Audiencia de los Reyes, y Governador de Guancabelica. ...
Impresso en Lima. Con licencia de el Govierno. Año M.DC.LXXXV.
4 p.ℓ., 192, 63 p. 30cm. fol.
Dated (3d p.ℓ.^{v}) in Guancabelica, 23 Nov. 1684.
Another version of the text pub. Lima, the same year, under title: Discurso iuridico, historico-politico, en defensa de la jurisdicion real.
With, as issued, "Despachos Y Cartas De Govierno. Acerca De La Execvcion De La Provision, Y Ordenanza De XX. De Febrero De El Año M.DC.LXXXIV." with half-title, separate paging and signatures.

B682
-L864p
————Another copy. 28cm.
Bound as no. 12 in a vol. with binder's title: Luis Lopez Obras.
Leclerc(1878)1826.7(this copy).

B661
-L585m
————Another copy. 29cm.
Bound as no. 2 of 3 items in vol. with binder's title: Tratamiento de los indios.
JCB(2)2:1315, 1311; cf. Palau(2)141409; Medina (Lima)582; Sabin 61115.

Palau(2)141399; Medina(Lima)581; Leclerc (1878)1826.6(this copy); Sabin 61114.

14017, 1925

03651, before 1866
14018, 1925
5671, 1909

D685
M393c
Maryland (Colony)--Charters.
The Charter Of Mary-Land.
[London, ca. 1685?]
23 p. 18cm. (19cm. in case) 8°
Caption title.
Cut (royal arms) at head of title.
This has been dated [1632]; see Wroth, L.C., "The Maryland colonization tracts" in Essays offered to Herbert Putnam, New Haven, 1929, p. 539 ff. For dating [ca. 1685?] see Wyllie, J.C., "The first Maryland tract" in Essays honoring Lawrence C. Wroth, Portland, Me., 1951, p. 475 ff.
With contemporary ms. annotations.
JCB(3)2:243; Baer(Md.)18.

8084, 1911

D.Math
I.19B
Mather, Increase, 1639-1723.
A Call From Heaven, To the Present And Succeeding Generations Or A Discourse Wherein is Shewed I. That the Children of Godly Parents are under special Advantages and Encouragements to seek the Lord. II. The Exceeding danger of Apostasie, especially as to those that are the Children and Posterity of such as have been Eminent for God in their Generation. III. That Young men ought to remember God their Creator. The Second Impression. By Increase Mather, Teacher of a Church in Boston in N. England. ...
Boston, Printed by R.[ichard] P.[ierce] for I.[ohn] Brunning, 1685.
4 p.ℓ., 198 p., 1 ℓ., 38 p. 15.5cm. 8°
First pub. Boston, 1679.
Includes his A discourse concerning the danger of apostasy, [Boston] 1685, p. [45]-159, and his Pray for the rising generation, [Boston] 1685, p. [161]-198, each of which has a special t.-p. but continuous paging and signatures.
With, as issued, his A sermon (preached at the lecture in Boston in New England the 18th of the I. month 1674 ...), Boston, 1685, with special t.-p. and separate paging and signatures.
In this copy there is a blank ℓ. at the end of Pray for the rising generation.
Bookseller's advertisement, 4th p.ℓ.^{v}
"To the Reader" dated (4th p.ℓ. recto): Boston, 3. m. 16. d. 1679.
Imperfect: p.ℓ. 1-3 wanting; available in facsim.
Bound in contemporary sheep.
JCB(2)2:1318; Evans 393; Sabin 46645; Holmes (I) 19B; Wing M 1191.

05127, before 1882

D.Math
I.19B
Mather, Increase, 1639-1723.
A Discourse Concerning the Danger of Apostacy Especiall as to those that are the Children and Posterity of such as have been eminent for God in their Generation. Delivered in a Sermon preached in the Audience of the General Assembly of the Massachusetts Colony, at Boston in New-England, May 23. 1677. being the Day of Election there. By Increase Mather. Teacher

[154]

	of a Church in Boston in New-England. ... [Boston] Printed by R.[ichard] P.[ierce] Anno Domini. 1685. [45]-159 p. 15.5cm. 8° (Issued as a part of his A Call from Heaven, Boston, 1685.) First pub. Boston, 1679. 05127A, before 1882
D.Math I.19B	Mather, Increase, 1639-1723. Pray For The Rising Generation. Or A Sermon Wherein Godly Parents are encouraged to Pray and Believe for their Children. Preached the third day of the 5th Moneth 1678. Which day was set apart by the Second Church in Boston in New-England, humbly to seek unto God by Fasting and Prayer, for a Spirit of Converting Grace to be poured upon the Children and Rising Generation in N. England. The Third Impression. By Increase Mather. Teacher of that Church.... [Boston] Printed by R.[ichard] P.[ierce] Anno Domini. 1685. [161]-198 p. 15.5cm. 8° (Issued as a part of his A Call from Heaven, Boston, 1685.) First pub. Cambridge, Mass., 1678. "To the Reader" signed (p. [164]): Boston, August 22. 1678. Holmes(I)89c. 05127B, before 1882
D.Math I.19B	Mather, Increase, 1639-1723. A Sermon (Preached at the Lecture in Boston in New-England the 18th of the I. Moneth 1674. When two men were Executed, who had Murthered their Master) Wherein Is Shewed That Excess in wickedness doth bring Untimely Death. The Second Impression. By Increase Mather, Teacher of a Church of Christ. ... [Boston] Printed by R.[ichard] P.[ierce] for J.[oseph] Brunning in Boston 1685. 1 p.ℓ., 38 p. 15.5cm. 8° (Issued as a part of his A Call from Heaven, Boston, 1685.) First pub. as The Wicked mans Portion Or A Sermon (Preached at the Lecture ...), Boston, 1675. JCB(2)2:1319; Evans394; Sabin46736; Holmes (I)174B; WingM1250. 05128, before 1882
DA685 M454a	[Maurice, Henry] 1648-1691. The Antithelemite, Or An Answer To Certain Quæres By the D. of B. And to the Considerations of an unknown Author Concerning Toleration.

	This may be Printed, June 12. 1685. R. L S. London, Printed for Sam. Smith, at the Prince's Arms in St. Paul's Church-Yard. 1685. 1 p.ℓ., 76 p. 20cm. 4° A reply to: George Villiers, 2d duke of Buckingham, A short discourse upon the reasonableness of men's having a religion, London, 1685, and to: Considerations moving to a toleration and liberty of conscience ... occasioned by an excellent discourse upon that subject ... by ... the Duke of Buckingham [attributed to William Penn] London, 1685. With references to New England, p. 31 ff. JCB(2)2:1304; WingM1359; Sabin46954. 05936, before 1870 rev
BA685 M539s	Mendoza, Juan de, fl. 1656-1686. Sermon De La Milagrosa Aparicion De La Imagen Santa De Aranzanzv [sic], Qve En La Dominica Infra Octava De la Assumpcion de Nuestra Señora. Predicò El R.P. Fr. Ioan De Mendoza Ayala Predicador General Jvbilado, Chronista de esta Provincia del Santo Evangelio, y Difinidor en acto de dicha Provincia. ... Con licencia, En Mexico, por la Viuda de Francisco Rodriguez. Lupercio. Año de 1685. 10 p.ℓ., [28] p. 20.5cm. 4° License dated (8th p.ℓ.ʳ) 18 Sept. 1685. Palau(2)163875; Medina(Mexico)1342. 1043, 1905
BA685 M798s	Montoro, José. Sermon, Qve En La Dedicacion De La Capilla De La Venerable, E Ilvstre Tercera Orden Sita En El Convento De N.P.S. Francisco de la Ciudad de Oaxaca Predicò El P. Predicador Fr. Joseph Montoro Religioso Descalço de N.P.S. Francisco, Hijo de la Santa Provincia de San Diego de Mexico, y Comissario Visitador de la Dicha Tercera Orden, en 18. de Febrero de 1685. años. ... Con Licencia De Los Svperiores: En Mexico, por Doña Maria de Benavides, Viuda de Juan de Ribera, en el Empedradillo. Año de 1685. 6 p.ℓ., 13 numb. ℓ. 20.5cm. 4° License dated (6th p.ℓ.ᵛ) 26 Aug. 1685. Dedication (2d-3d p.ℓ) by Juan Ruiz de Torres. Palau(2)179465; Medina(Mexico)1343. 1044, 1905

1685

DA685 M817p
Moody, Joshua, 1633-1697.
A Practical Discourse Concerning The Choice Benefit of Communion with God in His House, Witnessed unto by the Experience of Saints as The best Improvement of Time. Being the Summe of several Sermons on Psal. 84. 10. Preach'd in Boston on Lecture-Dayes By Joshua Moody Minister of the Gospel. ...
Boston In New-England Printed by Richard Pierce for Joseph Brunning, And are to be sold at his Shop at the Corner of Prison-Lane next the Exchange. 1685.
4 p. ℓ., 109 p., 1 ℓ. 15cm. (16cm. in case). 8°
Errata, 1st p. ℓ.^{v}.
Bookseller's advertisement, last page.
Imperfect: 1st p. ℓ. wanting; available in facsim.
Bound in contemporary calf.
WingM2523; Evans396; Sabin50298.

3035, 1907

B69 G643v 8
Muñoz de Castro, Pedro.
Descripcion De La Solemne Venida de la Imagen milagrosa de Nuestra Señora De Los Remedios à esta nobilissima Ciudad de Mexico este presente año de 1685. ...
Con Licencia. En Mexico: Por Juan de Ribera. Año de 1685.
[8] p. 20cm. 4°
Woodcut title vignette (statue of the Virgin with votary offerings between two lamps,
labelled, at bottom: NR. S^A ÐLOS REMEDIOSM)
Bound, in contemporary vellum, as no. 8 with 42 other items.

28908, 1941

DA685 N173t
[Nalson, John] 1638?-1686, supposed author.
Toleration And Liberty Of Conscience Considered, And Proved Impracticable, Impossible, And, even in the Opinion Of Dissenters, Sinful and Unlawful.
London, Printed for Thomas Dring, at the Corner of Chancery Lane next Fleet-Street, 1685.
40 p. 19.5cm. 4°
Title is on p. [3], verso blank.
Includes bookseller's advertisements on p. [2] (recto blank) and p. 40.
A reply to Considerations moving to a toleration and liberty of conscience [attributed to William Penn], London, 1685.
Imperfect: 1st ℓ. wanting; available in facsim.
WingN115; McAlpin4:211.

69-455

BA685 N322e
Navarro de San Antonio, Bartolome, 1658?-1752.
Evangelico Panegiris En La Fiesta, Qve haze annualmente (pidiendo la salud, y prosperidades de esta Republica de los Angeles) la Coffradia de Iesvs Nazareno de las Caydas. Predicado El Domingo Treinta de Septiembre, dia de S. Geronimo, y vltimo de la Octava, que solemnizò con Missas cantadas, y Sermones la Dedicacion de vna Capilla al mismo Señor divinissimo, y dos Collaterales el vno à la Purissima Virgen Maria Sanctissima de Guadalupe, y al Gloriosissimo Patriarcha Esposo suyo S. Ioseph el otro. ... Dixolo el R. P. Fr. Bartholome Navarro de San Antonio ...
Con Licencia en la Puebla de los Angeles. Por Diego Fernandez de Leon. Año de 1685.
6 p. ℓ., 10 numb. ℓ. 19.5cm. 4°
License dated (4th p. ℓ.^{r}) 24 Nov. 1685.
Dedication (2d p. ℓ.^{r}) by Juan de Gorospe.
Palau(2)188587; Medina(Puebla)93.

1045, 1905

BA685 N841s
Noriega, José de, 17th cent.
Sermon Panegirico En rogativa por Agua, hecha à la milagrosissima Imagen de Nuestra Señora de los Remedios, En la Santa Iglesia Metropolitana de Mexico; el dia Sexto del solemne Octavario... Predicolo El P. Presentado Fray Joseph de Noriega, Menor hijo de tan Sagrada Familia, Secretario actual de esta Provincia de la Visitacion de Nueva-España, y Lector de Prima de Sagrada Theologia en el Convento grande de Mexico. ...
Con Licencia, En Mexico Por Los Herederos de la Viuda de Bernardo Calderon, Año 1685.
7 p. ℓ., 10 numb. ℓ. illus. 20.5cm. 4°
Dedication dated (3d p. ℓ.^{r}) 23 June 1685.
Palau(2)192969; Medina(Mexico)1345.

1046, 1905

E685 N934r [R]
Nouvelle Relation de la Caroline Par Un Gentilhomme François arrivé, depuis deux mois, de ce nouveau pais. Où il parle de la route qu'il faut tenir pour y aller le plus sûrement, & de l'état où il a trouve cette Nouvelle contrée.

[156]

A La Haye. Chez Meyndert Uytweft [i.e. Uytwerf] Marchand Libraire de Meurant dans le Gortstraet. [1685?]
36 p. 13 cm. (14.5cm. in case) 12°
Cut (armillary sphere; Rahir marque 72) on t.-p.
"L'auteur y a passé un Printems, & une partie de l'esté de l'an 85." (p. 12).
JCBAR28:14; Vail246.

15099, 1928

B685 Osorio y Peralta, Diego.
O83p Principia Medicinae, Epitome, Et Totius Humani Corporis Fabrica seu ex Microcosmi Armonia Divinum, Germen, A D.D. D. Didaco Ossorio, Et Peralta, diu, iam Chirurgicæ & Anathomicę Cathedrę Methodicę, & nunc Vespertinae in Mexicana Academia Moderatore, S. Inquisitionis Tribunalis à Secretis Regalisque ergastatuli fidelissimo Medico & huius Novi-Regni Prothomedico.
1685. Cvn [sic] Licentia. Mexici, apud Heredes Viduæ Bernardi Calderon.
6 p. ℓ., 104 (i.e. 105) numb. ℓ. illus.. 20cm. 4°
Approbation dated (6th p. ℓ.ᵛ) 28 Apr. 1684.
Text in Latin and Spanish.
Title-page mutilated; completed in pen-and-ink facsimile.
Bound in contemporary vellum.
Palau(2)206757; Medina(Mexico)1354; Sabin 57817.

32235, 1958

BA685 Peña, Pedro de la.
P397s Signo Evcharistico, Predicado, En La Festiva Pompa, Y Celebridad annual, que acostumbra hazer el Convento Imperial de Predicadores Al SSᵐᵒ Sacramento, En concurrencia de el Sagrado Precursor San Jvan Baptista. Con Assistencia De el Exᵐᵒ Señor Conde de Paredes, Marquès de la Laguna, Virrey de esta Nueva-España, &c. Y desta Nobilissima Ciudad de Mexico. Por El M. R. P. M. Fr. Pedro De LaPeña del mesmo Orden Vicario del Convento de Predicadores de los Santos Apostoles S. Phelipe, y San Tiago del Pueblo de Azcapotzalco. ...
Con Licencia De Los Svperiores. En Mexico, por la Uiuda de Francisco Rodriguez Lupercio de 1685.
1 p. ℓ., [22] p. 20.5cm. 4°
License (p. [10]) dated 30 July 1685.
Medina(Mexico)1356; cf. Palau(2)217420.

68-427

DA685 [Penn, William] 1644-1718.
P412d1 A Defence Of The Duke of Buckingham's Book Of Religion & Worship, From The Exceptions of a Nameless Author. By the Pensilvanian. ...
London, Printed for A. Banks, in the Year 1685.
2 p. ℓ., 13 (i.e. 31) p. 19.5cm. 4°
"To the Reader" (2d p. ℓ.) signed: W.P.
A defence of: George Villiers, 2d duke of Buckingham, A short discourse upon the reasonableness of men's having a religion, London, 1685, in reply to: A short answer to his grace the D. Buckingham's paper concerning toleration and liberty of conscience, London, 1685.
Pages 26, 27, 41 are misnumbered respectively 12, 9, 13.

DA685 ———Corrected issue.
P412d2 2 p. ℓ., 31 p. 19cm. 4°
Pages are correctly numbered.
Errata, p. 31.
Smith(Friends)2:303; WingP1275.

30131, 1947 rev
11515, 1918 rev

D685 [Penn, William] 1644-1718.
P412f A Further Account of the Province of Pensylvania, and its Improvements. For the Satisfaction of those that are Adventurers, and Inclined to be so.
[London? 1685?]
16 p. 19.5cm. 4°.
Caption title.
Signed (p. 16): Worminghurst-Place, 12th of the 10th Month 85. William Penn.
Includes (p. 9-11) a letter to Penn dated in Philadelphia 3 Aug. 1685 and signed by Robert Turner, giving "a short account of proceedings, as to settlements here ..."
There is another 4° edition also pub. [London? 1685?], but with 20 p.
JCB(2)2:1321; Church696n; Sabin59702; Baer (Md.)118B; Vail(Front.)241; WingP1294.

03650, before 1866

D685 [Penn, William] 1644-1718.
P412f A Further Account Of the Province of
1 Pennsylvania And Its Improvements. For the Satisfaction of those that are Adventurers, and enclined to be so.

[157]

[London? 1685?]
20 p. 19cm. 4⁰
Caption title.
Signed (p. 20): Worminghurst-Place, 12th of the 10th Month 85. William Penn.
Includes (p. 11-14) a letter to Penn dated in Philadelphia 3 Aug. 1685 and signed by Robert Turner, giving "a short account of proceedings, as to settlements here ..."
Also issued (cf. Baer; Church) with an errata slip pasted at end (p. 20). An errata slip is not present in this copy.
There is another 4⁰ edition also pub. [London? 1685?], but with 16 p.
JCB(2)2:1320; Church696; Baer(Md.)118A; Smith(Friends)2:303; Vail(Front.)240; Sabin 59701; WingP1294.
03649, before 1866

BB   Peru(Viceroyalty)--Laws, statutes, etc.
-P4716   Tomo Primero De Las Ordenanzas Del
1685   Peru. Dirigidas. Al Rey Nvestro Senor [sic]
1   En su Real y Supremo Consejo de las Indias.
Por Mano Del Exc.ᵐᵒ Senor [sic] D. Melchor De Navarra Y Rocafull ... Virrey Gouernador, y Capitan General de estos Reynos. Recogidas, Y Coordenadas. Por El Lic. D. Thomas De Ballesteros Relator del Gouierno Superior, Real Acuerdo, Sala del Crimen, y Tribunal de Cuentas de este Reyno, y de la Santa Inquisicion, y Abogado de presos de sus Carceles secretas, y Alcalde mayor de la casa de moneda de esta Ciudad.
Con Licencia En Lima Por Joseph de Contreras. Año de M. DC. LXXXV.
21 p.ℓ., 320 numb. ℓ., [47] p. 30cm. fol.
Cut (royal arms) on t.-p.
License and approbation dated (8th p.ℓ.ᵛ, 10th p.ℓ.ᵛ) 7 Dec. 1683.
Errata, 19th p.ℓ.
With, as issued, López, Francisco. Gemino luminari [Lima, 1685] with half title and separate signatures.
No more published.
Bound in contemporary vellum.
Palau(2)23045; Medina(Lima)577; Sabin 2962.
5508, 1909

BA685   Peru(Viceroyalty)--Viceroy, 1681-1689
-L864p   (Navarra y Rocafull).
Despachos, Y Cartas De Govierno. Acerca De La Execvcion De La Provision, Y Ordenanza De XX. De Febrero De El Año M. DC. LXXXIV.

[Lima, 1685] (Issued as a part of López y Martínez, J.L. Discurso legal theologico-practico, Lima, 1685.)
63 p. 30cm. fol.
Dated (p. 63) 13 Dec. 1684.
"Ordenanza..." dated in Ciudad de los Reyes 20 Feb. 1684 (p. 28-40).

B682   ———— Another copy. 28cm.
-L864p   A part of item bound as no. 12 in a vol. with binder's title: Luis Lopez Obras.
Leclerc(1878)1826.7 (this copy).

B661   ———— Another copy. 29cm.
-L585m   A part of item bound as no. 2 of 3 items in vol. with binder's title: Tratamiento de los indios.
JCB(2)2:1311; cf. Palau(2)141409; Medina(Lima) 582.
03651A, before 1866
14018A, 1925
5671A, 1909

JA685   Pfeiffer, August, 1640-1698.
P526p   ... Pansophia Mosaica E Genesi Delineata, Das ist/Der Grund-Riss aller Weissheit/Darinnen aus dem Ersten Buch Mosis Alle Glaubens-Articul ... von D. Augusto Pfeiffern.
Leipzig/In Verlag Joh. Friedrich Gleditschens Druckts Christian Götze/ M DC LXXXV.
10 p.ℓ., 636, [24] p. front. 13.5cm. 12⁰
Title in red and black.
Motto in Hebrew at head of title.
Dedication dated (9th p.ℓ.ʳ) 20 Dec. 1684.
Errata, p. [23-24] at end.
"Die Americanischen Sprachen": p. 399-401.
Bound in contemporary vellum.
62-159, 1961

J685   Pufendorf, Samuel, Freiherr von, 1632-1694.
P977i   Introduction à L'Histoire. Des principaux Etats, Tels qu'ils sont aujourd'hui dans L'Europe. Premiere [-Seconde] Partie. Traduit de l'original Allemand de Samuel Pufendorf, par Claude Rouxel.
à Utrecht, Chez Jean Ribbius, M. DC. LXXXV.
2 v.: 8 p.ℓ., 545, [546-629] p.; 442, [38] p. 14cm. 12⁰
Cut on title-pages.
Transl. from: Einleitung zu der Historie der vornehmsten Reiche und Staaten ... Frankfurt, 1682.
Includes references to American colonies.

70-331
Errata, v. 1, p. [629].
In this copy there is a blank leaf at end of v.1..

D685
-Q1e
The Quakers Elegy On The Death Of Charles Late King of England. Written by W.P. a sincere Lover of Charles and James.
London, Printed by J.P. for Henry Playford, near the Temple-Church: 1685.
4 p. 33cm. (33.5cm. in case). fol.
Caption title; imprint p. 4.
William Penn wrote Fiction found out [London? 1685] to deny authorship.
WingP1349; Smith(Anti-Quak)348.
31774, 1955

B69
G643v
35
[Ramirez de Vargas, Alonso]
Villancicos, Que se cantaron en la Santa Iglesia Metropolitana, la noche de los Maytines del Principe de los Apostoles San Pedro. ...
Con licencia en Mexico, por los Herederos de la Viuda de Bernardo Calderon. Año de 1685.
[8] p. 20cm. 4°
"Compuestos en Metro musico por el Br. Joseph de Agurto, y Loaysa, Maestro de Capilla de dicha Santa Iglesia." (p.[8]).
Woodcut title vignette (St. Peter enthroned; inscribed at base: San Pedro.)
Authorship: cf. González(1952)232.
Bound, in contemporary vellum, as no. 35 with 42 other items.
28935, 1941

F684
E96b1
Ringrose, Basil, d. 1686.
Bucaniers Of America. The Second Volume. Containing The Dangerous Voyage and Bold Attempts of Captain Bartholomew Sharp, and others; performed upon the Coasts of the South Sea, for the space of two years, &c. From the Original Journal of the said Voyage. Written By Mr. Basil Ringrose, Gent. Who was all along present at those Transactions.
London: Printed for William Crooke, at the Sign of the Green Dragon without Temple-bar. 1685.
8 p.l., 143, 140-212, [24] p. illus. (incl. maps), 2 maps (incl. 1 fold.). 24cm. 4°
Errata, 8th p.l. verso.

With headlines numbering it as pt. 4 of Exquemelin, A.O., Bucaniers Of America, London, Crooke, 1684.
The preface replies to criticisms made in [Ayres, Philip] The voyages and adventures of Capt. Barth. Sharp, London, 1684, against Exquemelin, Bucaniers of America, London, Crooke, 1684.
Includes 42 coastal profiles.
"A Catalogue of Books printed and sold by William Crooke, Bookseller..." p. [18-24].
Bound with: Exquemelin, A.O. Bucaniers Of America, London, Crooke, 1684.

F684
E96b2
—— ——Another copy. 22cm. Bound with: Exquemelin, A.O. Bucaniers Of America, The Second Edition. London, Crooke, 1684.
JCB(2)2:1281; WingE3897; Sabin23479; Church 689.
01917, before 1854
04489-2, before 1882

D685
S424b
[Scot, George] d. 1685.
A Brief Advertisement, Concerning East-New-Jersey, in America.
[Edinburgh? John Reid? 1685]
3 p. 16cm. 4°
Caption title.
Refers at end to An Advertisement concerning the Province of East-New-Jersey, Edinburgh, 1685.
"Scottish Proprietors' Tracts" [no. 10]. Cf. Church 649n.
JCBAR53:62-63.
31138, 1952

D685
S424m
[Scot, George] d. 1685.
The Model Of The Government Of the Province Of East-New-Jersey In America; And Encouragements for such as Designs to be concerned there. Published for Information of such as are desirous to be Interested in that place.
Edinburgh, Printed by John Reid, And Sold be[sic] Alexander Ogston Stationer in the Parliament Closs. Anno Dom. 1685.
4 p.l., 272 p. 14cm. 8°.
Dedication signed (4th p.l.): George Scot.
First issue: last paragraph of p. 37 begins "I find removal likewise allowable in case of persecution..." Cf. Church 697.
Contains also letters and reports of settlers, including those 1st pub. in An advertisement concerning the Province of East-New-Jersey, Edinburgh, 1685, and (at end) [his] A brief

advertisement concerning East-New-Jersey, 1st pub. [Edinburgh? 1685]
"Scottish Proprietors' Tracts" [no. 11].
Cf. Church 649n.
In this copy 1st p.ℓ. with signature mark, otherwise blank, is wanting.
JCB(2)2:1323; Church 697; Sabin 78186; Vail (Front.)243; Baer(Md.)120; WingS2036.

0802, 1846

D685 Shakespeare, William, 1564-1616.
=S527m M^r· William Shakespear's Comedies, Histories, And Tragedies. Published according to the true Original Copies. Unto which is added, Seven Plays, Never before Printed in Folio: Viz. Pericles Prince of Tyre. The London Prodigal. The History of Thomas Lord Cromwel. Sir John Oldcastle Lord Cobham. The Puritan Widow. A Yorkshire Tragedy. The Tragedy of Locrine. The Fourth Edition.
London, Printed for H.[enry] Herringman, E.[dward] Brewster, and R.[ichard] Bentley, at the Anchor in the New Exchange, the Crane in St. Pauls Church-Yard, and in Russel-Street Covent-Garden. 1685.
6 p.ℓ., 96, 99-160, 163-243 (i.e. 255), 254-272 p., 1 ℓ., 328, 303 p. incl. front. (port.) 37cm. fol.
Cut (fleur-de-lis; McKerrow(Devices) 263) on t.-p.
First pub. London, 1623.
This t.-p. also was issued with a variant imprint adding the name of another bookseller, R.[ichard] Chiswell. Also issued with the t.-p., in another setting in which the only booksellers' names included in the imprint are H. Herringman, Joseph Knight, and Francis Saunders.
The three groups of paging have separate signature sequences. The printing of the first paging group and the preliminaries has been attributed to Robert Roberts (cf. F. Bowers, "Robert Roberts," Shakespeare Quarterly, II(1951)241-246). Another printing is known of some of the sheets of the second paging group in which the side and foot rules were omitted (cf. G. E. Dawson, "Some bibliographical irregularities in the Shakespeare Fourth Folio," Bibliographical Society of the University of Virginia. Papers IV(1951-52), 93-103.)
Preliminary matter includes commendatory poetry by Leonard Digges, J. M. (James Mabbe?), Ben Jonson, J.M.S., John Milton, and Hugh Holland.
WingS2915; Church(Eng.Lit.)620; cf. Pforzheimer 910.

06722, 1884

E685 [Verbiest, Ferdinand] 1623-1688.
V478v Voyages De L'Empereur De La Chine Dans La Tartarie, Ausquels On A Joint une nouvelle découverte au Mexique.
A Paris, Chez Estienne Michallet, ruë S. Jacques, à l'Image S. Paul. M. DC. LXXXV. Avec Approbation.
4 p.ℓ., 110 p. 14.5cm. 12°
Dedication signed (4th p.ℓ.^{v}) D.D.
Approbation dated (p. 110) 20 July 1685.
"Voyages de l'empereur de la Chine" (p. 1-78) transl. from letters of Ferdinand Verbiest, one of which was pub. under title: Lettre du P. Ferdinand Verbiest de la Compagnie de Jesus. Paris, 1684. "Nouvelle descente des espagnols dans l'isle de Californie, l'an 1683" (p. 79-110) transl. from letters of Isidro Otondo y Antillón (cf. p. 82).
JCB(2)2:1325; Sabin 98928; Backer 8:583; Streit 2:2223; Wagner 58a.

03646, before 1866

CA679 Vieira, Antonio, 1608-1697.
V665s Sermoens Do P. Antonio Vieira, Da Companhia De Jesu, Prègador de Sua Magestade. Quarta Parte.
3-4 Em Lisboa. Na Officina de Miguel Deslandes. A custa de Antonio Leyte Pereyra, Mercador de Livros. M. DC. LXXXV. Com todas as licenças, & Privilegio Real.
6 p.ℓ., 600 p. 21cm. 4°
Cut (Jesuit trigram, floriated) on t.-p.
License dated (5th p.ℓ.) 25 Jan. 1685.
Errata, 6th p.ℓ.
Contains 15 sermons preached in Bahia, Brazil, 1640, Lisbon 1643, 1644, 1651, 1652, 1655, 1662, [Lisbon?] 1649, Rome 1674, São Luiz, Brazil, 1654, São Miguel Island, Azores, [1641?], Pará, Brazil, 1656.
According to Leite "Deste volume de 1685 há duas impressões diferentes."
Bound with his Sermons... terceira parte, Lisbon, 1683.
Rodrigues 2506; Backer 8:659; Leite 9:195; Innocencio 1:290.

68-192.4

1686

B69
G643v
19
Agurto y Loaysa, Joseph de, fl. 1676-1688.
Villancicos Qve Se Cantaron En La Santa Iglesia Metropolitana de Mexico: en honor de Maria Santissima Madre de Dios, en su Assumpcion Trivmphante. ... Pusolos en metro Musico, el Br. Joseph de Loaysa, y Agurto, Maestro de Capilla de dicha Santa Iglesia. Año 1686.
Con licencia en Mexico: Por los Herederos de la Viuda de Bernardo Calderon. [1686]
[8] p. 20cm. 4°
Woodcut title vignette (the Virgin surrounded by angels)
Bound, in contemporary vellum, as no. 19 with 42 other items.
Medina(Mexico)1375.

28919, 1941

B619
M737r
Alvarez Ossorio y Redín, Miguel.
Discvrso Vniversal, de las Causas que ofenden esta Monarquia, y Remedios eficaces para todas. Señor. Don Miguel Alvarez Ossorio y Redin, vassallo de V. Mag. vezino de Madrid, dize: ...
[Madrid? 1686]
32 p. 20cm. 4° (Issued as a part of his Señor. Con estos dos memoriales ... [Madrid? 1686])
Title from caption and beginning of text.
Includes poetry (p. 30-32).
Bound in contemporary vellum with: Moncada, Sancho de. Restauración política de España, Madrid, 1619, as part of the 4th of 10 items.
Palau(2)9784; Colmeiro18.

12570-4B, 1920

B619
M737r
[Alvarez Ossorio y Redín, Miguel]
Extension Politica, Y Economica, y la mejor Piedra de Toque, y Crisol de Verdades, para descubrir los Tesoros que necessita esta Catolica Monarquia.
[Madrid? 1686]
49 p. incl. tables. 20cm. 4° (Issued as a part of his Señor. Con estos dos memoriales ... [Madrid? 1686])
Caption title.
Signed at end: Octubre, y 11. de 1686.
D. Miguel Albarez Ossorio, y Redin.
Bound in contemporary vellum with: Moncada, Sancho de. Restauración política de España, Madrid, 1619, as part of the 4th of 10 items.
Palau(2)9783; Colmeiro18.

12570-4A, 1920

B619
M737r
Alvarez Ossorio y Redín, Miguel.
Señor. Con Estos Dos Memoriales, se descubren medios para quitar los tributos, y sustentar continuamente quatro millones de personas pobres: Con Svs Labores, Se enriquezerà esta Monarquia, y valdràn las Rentas de V. Mag. mas de cien millones de pesos todos los años: Se podràn defender los Reynos, y pagar todas las deudas en que està empeñada la Hazienda Real. Segundo Memorial, De Don Miguel Albarez Ossorio, y Redin.
[Madrid? 1686]
1 p. ℓ., 49, 32 p. incl. tables. 20cm. 4°
The memorials contained are entitled Extension política y económica ... and Discurso universal ... . These are the 2d and 3d of several memorials prepared by Alvarez Ossorio for the Spanish king on economic conditions and policies. Each memorial has a caption title and separate paging and signatures.
Dated (p. 49) 11 Oct. 1686.
Errata, 1st p. ℓ.ᵛ
Includes poetry (p. 30-32, 2d count).
Bound in contemporary vellum with: Moncada, Sancho de. Restauración política de España, Madrid, 1619, as the 4th of 10 items.
Palau(2)9783, 9784; Colmeiro18.

12570-4, 1920

CA686
A663c
Araujo, Antonio de, 1566-1632.
Catecismo Brasilico Da Doutrina Christãa, Com o Ceremonial dos Sacramentos, & mais actos Parochiaes. Composto Por Padres Doutos

da Companhia de Jesus, Aperfeiçoado, & dado a luz Pelo Padre Antonio De Araujo da mesma Companhia Emendado nesta segunda impressaõ Pelo P. Bertholameu De Leam da mesma Companhia.
    Lisboa. Na Officina de Miguel Deslandes M.DC.LXXXVI. Com todas as licenças necessarias.
    16 p.ℓ., 371, [372-380] p. illus. 14cm. 8°
    Cut on t.-p.
    First pub. Lisbon, 1618.
    License dated (15th p.ℓ.ʳ) 26 Oct. 1685.
    Errata, 15th p.ℓ.ᵛ-16th p.ℓ.ʳ.
    "Poemas Brasilicos Do Padre Christovaõ Valente": 3d p.ℓ.-6th p.ℓ.ᵛ.
    JCBAR40:27; Borba de Moraes1:39; Backer 1:507; Viñaza217.

28598, 1940

BA685 Argote y Valdés, Juan de.
A693o   Oracion Panegyrica A Sancto Thomas De Aqvino, Dotor de la Iglesia, Qve Dedica Al Il.ᵐᵒ S.ᵒʳ D.ᵒʳ D. Ivan Queipo de Llano Valdes, Obispo de la Paz... Y Predico En El Convento de Predicadores de dicha Ciudad el dia 7. de Marzo deste año de 1686. El Doct. D. Juan de Argote y Valdes, Cura del Pueblo de Calacoto, Vicario Eclesiastico, y Comissario del S. Oficio de la Inquisicion en la Prouincia de Pacaxes.
    Con licencia: Impresso en Lima, por Ioseph de Contreras. Año de 1686.
    6 p.ℓ., [18] p. 18.5cm. 4°
    License dated (2d p.ℓ.ᵛ) 21 Oct. 1686.
    Medina(Lima)588.

70-464

BA686 Avila, Juan de, fl. 1684.
A958p   Pvreza Emblematica Discvrrida En la Profession de la M. Maria Ana De San Francisco, Religiosa de Santa Clara, Sermon, Que el Sabado ocho de Diziembre, dia de la Concepcion Purissima de Maria Señora Nuestra, presente el Santissimo Sacramento del Altar, predicaba, y dezia El R.P. Fr. Jvan De Avila, Predicador General del Orden de N.P.S. Francisco, y Qualificador del Santo Officio de la Inquisicion. ...
    Con Licencia De Los Superiores. En Mexico, por Doña Maria de Benavides, Viuda de Juan de Ribera, en el Empedradillo. Año de 1686.
    4 p.ℓ., 10 numb. ℓ. 19cm. 4°
    Dedication signed: Francisco de Murga.
    License (3d p.ℓ.ᵛ) dated 6 Mar. 1686.
    Medina(Mexico)1366.

68-425

BA686 Catholic Church--Liturgy and ritual--Officium
C363o   Beatissimae Virginis Mariae de Mercede Redemptionis captivorum.
    Officivm B. Virginis Mariæ De Mercede Redemptionis Captivorvm. ...
    Cvm Licentia. Mexico, apud Dñam Mariam de Benavides, Viduam Ioannis de Ribera. Anno 1686.
    [8] p. 15cm. 8°
    In Mexico 1st pub. Puebla de los Angeles, 1680.
    Promulgation dated (p.[8]) 18 Jan. 1680.

5761¹⁰, 1909

BA686 Catholic Church--Liturgy and ritual--Officium
C363dd   de Nomine Beatissimae Virginis Mariae.
    Die Dña infra Oct. Nativ. B. Maria Virginis. Officium De Sanctissimo Nomine B. Mariæ Virginis. ...
    Svperiorum Permissv. Mexici, apud Heredes Viduæ Bernardi Calderon anno 1686.
    [8] p. 15cm. 8°
    Caption title; imprint at end.
    In Mexico first pub. ca. 1673 under title: Die xvij. Septembris. Officivm De Nomine Beatissimæ Virginis Mariæ.
    Medina(Mexico)1385.

5761⁹, 1909

BA686 Catholic Church--Liturgy and ritual--Special
C363d   offices--Jean de Matha, Saint.
    Die viii. Februarii In Festo S. Ioannis De Matha Confessoris. Dvplex. Omnia de Communi Confessoris non Pontific. exceptis his quæ sunt propria.
    Mexici, apud Hæredes Viduæ Bernaridi [sic] Calderon. Anno 1686.
    [2] p. 15cm. 12°
    Caption title; imprint at end.
    First pub. under title: Officium S. Ioannis de Matha. Barcelona, 1676.

5761⁸, 1909

BA686 Catholic Church--Liturgy and ritual--Special
C363os   offices--Patrick, Saint.
    Officivm. Sancti Patritij Hiberniæ Episcopi. Semidvplex. ...
    Superiorum permissu. Mexici, apud Hæredes

5761⁷, 1909

Uiduæ Bernardi Calderon. Anno Domini 1686. [4] p. 15cm. 8º
Caption title; imprint at end.
Promulgation dated (p. [4]) 24 Nov. 1685.

BA686
C363n
[R]

Catholic Church in Spain--Councils.
Notitia Conciliorvm Hispaniae, Atqve Novi Orbis, Epistolarvm Decretalivm, Et Aliorvm Monvmentorvm Sacræ Antiquitatis, ad ipsam spectantium, magna ex parte hactenus ineditorum: Qvorvm Editio Paratvr Salmanticæ, cum Notis & Dissertationibus. Svb Avspiciis Catholici Monarchæ Caroli Secvndi: Stvdio Et Vigiliis M. Fr. Iosephi Saenz De Agvirre, ...
Salmanticæ: Apud Lvcam Perez, Vniversitatis Typographum. Anno M.DC.LXXXVI. Svperiorvm Permissv.
495,[1] p. 15.5cm. 8º
Half-title: Agvirre, Notitia Compendiaria, Sive Epitome Brevis Ac Dilvcida Conciliorvm Omnivm Hispaniæ...
Dedication dated (p. 14) 29 Nov. 1685.
Errata, last p.
Sabin74856; Palau(2)284300; Medina(BHA) 1796.

68-239

BA686
C414o

Cereceda, Juan Alonso de, 1632-ca.1691.
Oracion Panegirica, Y Fvnebre, Qve En Las Honrras De La Venerable Sierua de Dios Soror Ana de los Angeles, ô Monteagudo, Religiosa, y Madre del obseruantissimo Monasterio de Santa Catalina de Sena de la Ciudad de Arequipa. Dixo El M. R. P. Ivan Alonso De Cereceda Rector del Colegio de la Compañia de Iesus de la misma Ciudad, Cathedratico de Prima que ha sido en su Provincia. ...
Con Licencia Impresso En Lima por Luis de Lyra, Año de 1686, [sic]
8 p.ℓ., 12 numb. ℓ. 20.5cm. 4º
Approbation dated (4th p.ℓ.ʳ) 27 Apr. 1686.
Palau(2)51664; Medina(Lima)589.

5507, 1909

F686
=D212d

Dapper, Olfert, 1636-1689.
Description De L'Afrique, Contenant Les Noms, la Situation & les Confins de toutes ses Parties, leurs Rivieres, leurs Villes & leurs Habitations, leurs Plantes & leurs Animaux; les Mœurs, les Coûtumes, la Langue, les Richesses, la Religion & le Gouvernement de ses Peuples. Avec Des Cartes ... & des Figures en taille-douce, ... Traduite du Flamand D'O. Dapper, D.M.
A Amsterdam, Chez Wolfgang, Waesberge, Boom & van Someren, M.DC.LXXXVI.
4 p.ℓ., 534, [22] p. illus. (engr.), 30 fold. plates, 13 fold. maps. 37cm. fol.
Cut (publisher's device) on t.-p.; incl. motto "Tandem Fit Arbor Surculus" and initials "HDB".
Added t.-p., engr.
Transl. from: Naukeurige Beschrijvinge der Afrikaensche gewesten and Naukeurige Beschrijvinge der Afrikaensche eylanden, 1st pub. Amsterdam, 1668.
Bound in contemporary calf.
Tiele298n.; Streit4738; Scheepvaart Mus. 199.

69-348

C619
A949n

Decima Relaçam Historica, Pertencente Ao Estado, Successos, & Progressos da Liga Sagrada contra Turcos: Publicada nesta Corte de Lisboa a 27. de Setembro, Do Anno de 1686. ...
Lisboa. Na Officina de Miguel Deslandes, Na Rua da Figueira. Anno 1686. Com todas as licenças necessarias.
16 p. 19.5cm. 4º
Cut on t.-p.
The 10th of 17 such "Relações" of the war of the Holy League against the Turks, issued irregularly in Lisbon, by Miguel Deslandes, July-December, 1686.
Bound as the 4th in a volume of 58 pamphlets, 1619-1702.
Innocencio 18:241-242.

9345, 1913

C619
A949n

Decima-Setima Relaçam Historica, Pertencente Ao Estado, Successos, & Progressos da Liga Sagrada contra Turcos: Publicada nesta Corte de Lisboa a 6. de Dezembro. Do Anno de 1686. ...
Lisboa. Na Officina de Miguel Deslandes. Na Rua da Figueira. Anno 1686. Com todas as licenças necessarias.
12 p. 19.5cm. 4º
Cut on t.-p.
The 17th of 17 such "Relações" of the war of the Holy League against the Turks issued irregularly in Lisbon, by Miguel Deslandes,

F686 E96h Exquemelin, Alexandre Olivier.
Histoire Des Avanturiers Qui Se Sont Signalez Dans Les Indes, Contenant Ce Qu'ils Ont Fait De Plus Remarquable Depuis Vingt Années. Avec La Vie, les Mœurs, les Coûtumes des Habitans de Saint Domingue & de la Tortuë, & une Description exacte de ces lieux; Où l'on voit L'établissement d'une Chambre des Comptes dans les Indes, & un Etat, tiré de cette Chambre, des Offices tant Ecclesiastiques que Seculieres, où le Roy d'Espagne pourvoit, les Revenus qu'il tire de l'Amerique, & ce que les plus grands Princes de l'Europe y possedent. ... Par Alexandre Olivier Oexmelin. ...
A Paris, Chez Jacques Le Febvre, au dernier pillier de la Grand' Salle, vis-à-vis les Requestes du Palais. M. DC. LXXXVI. Avec Privilege Du Roy.
2 v.: 16 p.ℓ., 342, [24] 3 plates (incl. 1 fold.) 2 fold. map; 3 p.ℓ., 286, 281-384, [24] p. pl., fold. map.   17cm. 12°
Added t.-p., engr.: Histoire Des Avanturiers Des Boucaniers Et De La Chambre Des Comptes, établie dans les Indes 1686. A Paris, Chez Jacques Le Febvre, au dernier, pillier de la Grand' Salle, vis-à-vis les Requestes du Palais. Avec Privilege du Roy. N. Guerard In. et Sculp.
Based on Exquemelin's account 1st pub. under the title De Americaensche Zee-Roovers, Amsterdam, 1678, but greatly altered and enlarged.
Dedication signed (verso 5th p.ℓ., v.1): De Frontignieres.
"Achevé d'imprimer le premier Juin 1686." (verso 16th p.ℓ., v.1).
"Livres imprimez à Paris chez Jacques Le Fevre..." (p. [23-24], v.2).
Imperfect: v.2, p. [23-24] wanting; available in facsim.
JCB(2)2:1328; Sabin 23475.

02311, 1850

BA686 E99s Ezcaray, Antonio de, fl. 1681-1691.
Sermon En El Entierro De Nvestro Redemptor Jesu-Christo, En el culto, y demostracion, que el Vienes [sic] Santo por la noche haze el muy Religioso Convento de S. Clara de la Ciudad de Santiago de Queretaro. Predicole El R.P. Fr. Antonio De Escaray, Predicador de su Magestad, y Apostolico del Colegio de la Santa Cruz de dicha Ciudad. ...
Con Licencia, En Mexico: Por los Herederos de la Viuda de Bernardo Calderon, en la calle de San Augustin. Año de 1686.
5 p.ℓ., 18 numb. ℓ. 19.5cm. 4°
License dated (4th p.ℓ.) 12 July 1686.
Medina(Mexico)1368; Palau(2)80841.

70-155

EB -W&A 290 France--Sovereigns, etc., 1643-1715 (Louis XIV).   30 Oct. 1686
Arrest Du Conseil D'Estat Du Roy, Qui exempte de tous droits les Sucres provenans de la Rafinerie établie à la Guadeloupe, par M. Château-du-Bois. Du trentiéme Octobre 1686.
A Paris, Chez la V. Saugrain, à l'entrée du Quay de Gêvres, au Paradis. [1686]
Broadside. 26.5 x 20.5cm. (32cm. in case) 1/4°
Wroth & Annan 290.

29351, 1943

bDB G7888 1686 1 Gt.Brit.--Sovereigns, etc., 1685-1688 (James II)   26 Mar.1686
At the Court at Whitehall, This 26th day of March 1686. ...
London, Printed by Charles Bill, Henry Hills, and Thomas Newcomb, Printers to the Kings most Excellent Majesty, 1686.
Broadside. 2 sheets. 56.5 x 35.5cm. 1°
Cut (royal arms, Steele 102) at head of title.
Caption title; imprint at end.
Concerns "the Hiring of Servants for His Majesties Plantations."
First pub. London, 1682.
Wing E2896; Steele E3830.

4446, 1908

DB G7895 1686 3 Gt.Brit.--Treaties, etc., 1660-1685 (Charles II)
Several Treaties Of Peace and Commerce Concluded between the late King Of Blessed Memory Deceased, And Other Princes and States; With Additional Notes in the Margin, Referring to the several Articles in each Treaty, and a Table. Reprinted and Published by His Majesties Especial Command.

July-December, 1686.
Bound as the 5th in a volume of 58 pamphlets, 1619-1702.
Innocencio 18:241-242.

9346, 1913

London, Printed by His Majesties Printers, and sold by Edward Poole at the Sign of the Ship over against the Royal Exchange. 1686.
2 p. ℓ., 269 p. 19.5cm. 4°
This collection was 1st pub. London, 1685. These are the same sheets reissued with a cancel t.-p. In this issue an order to print, 1st p. ℓ. of the 1685 issue, also has been canceled, and the "Table of the Treaties", last ℓ. of the 1685 ed., is bound as the 2d p. ℓ.
Sabin 79375; Wing C3605.

70-175

DB G7895 1686 1
Gt. Brit.--Treaties, etc., 1685-1688 (James II) 6/16 Nov. 1686
Tractatus Pacis, Bonæ Correspondentiæ, Et Neutralitatis in America, Inter Serenissimum & Potentissimum Principem Jacobum II. Dei Gratiâ Magnæ Britanniæ, Franciæ & Hiberniæ Regem, Fidei Defensorem, &c. Et Serenissimum & Potentissimum Principem Ludovicum XIV. Eadem Dei Gratia Regem Christianissimum, Conclusus $\frac{6}{16}$ Die Mensis Novembris, Anno Dom. 1686.
Cum Privilegio. [Londini] Typis Thomæ Newcomb, unius ex Typographis Regiis in vico vulgò dicto The Savoy, 1686.
15 p. 20cm. 4°
"Whitehall Treaty of Neutrality." Also pub. in English, London, 1686, under title: Treaty of Peace ...
Wing J392; Sabin 96532; Davenport 79.

10817, 1915

DB G7895 1686 2
Gt. Brit.--Treaties, etc., 1685-1688 (James II) 6/16 Nov. 1686
Treaty Of Peace, Good Correspondence & Neutrality In America, Between the most Serene and Mighty Prince James II. By the Grace of God, King of Great Britain, France and Ireland, Defender of the Faith, &c. And the most Serene and Mighty Prince Lewis XIV. The Most Christian King: Concluded the $\frac{6\text{th}}{16}$ Day of Novemb. 1686.
Published by His Majesties Command. [London] In the Savoy: Printed by Thomas Newcomb, One of His Majesties Printers. MDCLXXXVI.
19, [1] p. 19.5cm. 4°
"Whitehall Treaty of Neutrality." Also pub. in Latin, London, 1686, under title: Tractatus Pacis ...
Bookseller's advertisement, last p.
JCB(2)2:1331; Wing J393; Sabin 96532; Davenport 79.

03684, before 1866

CA686 G982s
Gusmão, Alexandre de, 1629-1724.
Sermão Que Pregou Na Cathedral Da Bahia De Todos os Santos. O P. Alexandre De Gvsmam Da Cõpanhia de Iesu, Provincial da Provincia do Brasil. Nas Exequias Do Illustrissimo Senhor D. Fr. Ioam Da Madre De Deos, Primeiro Arcebispo Da Bahia, Que faleceo do mal commum que nella ouve neste Anno de 1686. ...
Lisboa. Com todas as licenças necessarias. Na Officina de Miguel Manescal Impressor do Santo Officio, Anno de 1686. A custa de Manoel Lopes Fereira, mercador de Livros.
2 p. ℓ., 19 p. 19cm. 4°
Dedication (2d p. ℓ.) signed: Bahia de Iulho 16. de 1686. Francisco Pereira.
Sabin 29322; Borba de Moraes 1:324; Backer 3:1961.

70-151

E686 H515d
Hennepin, Louis, ca. 1640-ca. 1705.
Descrizione Della Lvigiana; Paese nuouamente scoperto nell' America Settentrionale, sotto gl' auspicij Del Christianissimo Lvigi XIV. Con la Carta Geografica del medesimo, costumi, e maniere di viuere di que' Seluaggi. Del P. Lvigi Hennepin Francescano Recolletto, e Missionario Apostolico in questa Scoperta. Tradotta dal Francese, e Dedicata Al Reverendiss. P.D. Lodovico de' Conti Gverra Abbate Casinense di S. Procolo, di Bologna.
In Bologna, per Giacomo Monti. 1686. Con licenza de' Superiori.
6 p. ℓ., 396 p. fold. map. 13.5cm. 12°
Dedication (2d-6th p. ℓ.) signed: Bologna li 21. Gennaro 1686. Casmiro Freschot.
Transl. from Description de la Louisiane, 1st pub. Paris, 1683.

E686 H515d cop.2
——— ——Another copy. 15.5cm.
Uncut.
Imperfect: map wanting.
JCB(2)2:1326; Sabin 31356; Harrisse(NF)157; Paltsits(Hennepin) ℓi; Streit 2:2732.

01588, 1847
06005, before 1902

DA686 H637o
Higginson, John, 1616-1708.
Our Dying Saviour's Legacy of Peace To His Disciples in a troublesome World, from John 14. 27. My Peace I give unto you, &c. Also a Discourse On the Two Witnesses: Shewing that it is the Duty of all Christians to be Witnesses unto Christ, from Rev. 11.3. I will give to my

two Witnesses, &c: Unto which is added, Some Help to Self-Examination. By John Higginson Pastor of the Church in Salem. ...
 Boston, Printed by Samuel Green for John Usher near the Town-House, 1686.
 7 p. ℓ., 205 p., 1 ℓ. 14.5cm. (15.5cm. in case). 8º
 "To the Church and People of God..." dated (5th p. ℓ.^{r}) 6 Aug. 1686.
 "Christian Reader..." signed (7th p. ℓ.^{r}) Samuel Willard.
 Bookseller's advertisement, last leaf.
 In this copy there is a blank ℓ. at beginning.
 Bound in contemporary calf.
 WingH1956; Evans407; Sabin31745.

3036, 1907

FC650
H737
36
 Hollandse Mercurius, Verhalende de voornaemste Saken van Staet, En andere Voorvallen, Die, in en omtrent de Vereenigde Nederlanden, En elders in Europa, In het Jaer 1685, Zijn geschiet. Het Ses-en-Dertigste Deel.
 Tot Haerlem, Gedruckt by Abraham Casteleyn, Stadts-Drucker, op de Marckt, in de Blye Druck. Anno 1686.
 3 p. ℓ., 265, [5] p. 4 fold. plates. 20cm. 4º (Bound in [vol. 9] of Hollandse Mercurius)
 Added t.-p., engraved: Hollandsche Mercurius Anno 1685 Tot Haerlem by Abraham Casteleyn
 JCB(3)2:410, Sabin32523.

8487JJ, 1912

B686
-L182m
 Lagúnez, Matías, d. 1703.
 Memorial, Qve El Licenciado Don Matias Lagunez, del Consejo de su Magestad, y Oydor de la Real Audiencia de San Francisco de Quito, haziendo oficio de Fiscal en ella, diò, y presentò en dicha Real Audiencia, à cerca del beneficio, y cobrança de los tributos de los Indios. Y De los medios que se pueden poner, para que se eviten los fraudes, que en dicha cobrança se cometen, en daño, y perjuicio de la Real Hazienda.
 Impresso en Madrid. Año de 1686.
 12 numb. ℓ. 28.5cm. fol.
 Palau(2)130101; Medina(BHA)1789.

68-286

BA686
-L979p
[R]
 Luzuriaga, Juan de.
 Paranympho Celeste Historia De La Mystica Zarza, Milagrosa Imagen, y prodigioso Santuario de Aranzazu De Religiosos Observantes De N. Seraphico Padre San Francisco En La Provincia De Gvypvzcoa De La Region De Cantabria, Escribela ... El M.R.P. Fr. Jvan De Lvzvriaga, Predicador Apostolico, Lector Jubilado, Padre de las Santas Provincias de Cantabria, y Valencia, y Comissario General de todas las de Nueva-España de Nuestro Padre San Francisco.
 Con Licencia De Los Svperiores: En Mexico, por los Herederos de la Viuda de Bernardo Calderon. Año de 1686.
 18 p. ℓ., 114, 96, 112, [16] p. pl. 27cm. 4º
 License dated (13th p. ℓ.^{r}) 26 Aug. 1685.
 Errata, p.[2] at end.
 Imperfect: plate and 5th p. ℓ. wanting, p.[11-16] at end mutilated; available in facsim.
 Palau(2)144367; Medina(Mexico)1376.

5509, 1909

E686
M253d
 Mallet, Alain Manesson, 1630?-1706?
 Description De L'Univers, Contenant Les Differents Systemes Du Monde, Les Cartes generales & particulieres de la Geographie Ancienne & Moderne: Les Plans & les Profils des principales Villes & des autres lieux plus considerables de la Terre; avec les Portraits des Souverains qui y commandent, leurs Blasons, Titres & Livrées: Et les Mœurs, Religions, Gouvernemens & divers habillemens de chaque Nation. Dediée Av Roy. Par Allain Manesson Mallet, Maistre de Mathematiques des Pages de la petite Escurie de Sa Majesté, cy-devant Ingenieur & Sergent Major d'Artillerie en Portugal. Tome Cinqvième.
 Suivant la Copie Imprimée a Paris. Francfourt sur le Main, Chez Jean David Zunner. M DC LXXXVI.
 6 p. ℓ., 234, [36] p. 59 plates, 7 ports., 74 maps (incl. 2 fold.), 3 plans. 21.5cm. 4º
 Added t.-p., engraved: Suite De L Europe Ancienne Et Moderne Des Terres Australes Et De L Amerique Tome V die Fortsetzung des alten und Neuen Europæ, wie auch der Australischen, oder Mittägigen Länder, und America Fünffter theil.
 Vol. 5 of 5 v. pub. 1685-1686. First pub. Paris, 1683. Also issued Frankfurt, Zunner, 1684-1685, in German transl. under title: Beschreibung des gantzen Welt-Kreisses.
 Captions of illustrations are in German.
 Bound in contemporary calf.
 Sabin44130; Borba de Moraes2:13.

05724, before 1874

D. Math I.115A[1]	Mather, Cotton, 1663-1728. The Call Of The Gospel Applyed unto All men in general, and unto a Condemned Malefactor in particular. In A Sermon Preached on the 7th d. of the 1st. m. 1686. At the Request, and in the Hearing of a man under a just Sentence of Death for the horrid Sin of Murder. By Cotton Mather, Pastor to a Church at Boston in N.E. ... Printed at Boston, by R.[ichard] P.[ierce] Anno Supradict: [i.e. 1686] 1 p.l., 54 p. 14.5cm. 8º (Issued as a part of Increase Mather's A sermon occasioned by the execution of a man, Boston, 1686.) With, as issued, Joshua Moody's An exhortation to a condemned malefactor, Boston, 1686, with special t.-p. but continuous paging and signatures. Occasioned by the execution of James Morgan. Bound in contemporary calf. In this copy there is a blank l. counted as p. 55-56. Tears and worn edges affecting text of numerous pages including t.-p.	D. Math I.77[1]	Mather, Increase, 1639-1723. The Mystery Of Christ Opened And Applyed. In Several Sermons, Concerning the Person, Office, and Glory of Jesus Christ. By Increase Mather, Teacher of a Church at Boston in N. England. ... Printed at Boston in New-England Anno 1686. 1 p.l., 6, 212, [2] p. 14.5cm. 8º Printed by Richard Pierce for Joseph Brunning (cf. Holmes). Errata, 9 lines, verso t.-p. "Books printed for, and sold by Joseph Brunning..." last p. Also issued with imprint "Printed in the year MDCLXXXVI." In this copy there is a blank l. between p. 74-75 and a blank l. counted as p. 179-180. JCB(2)2:1327; Evans416; WingM1228; Holmes (I)77[1]. 03653, 1866
D. Math I.115A[1] cop. 2	———— Another copy. 14.5cm. Bound in contemporary calf. In this copy there is a blank l. counted as p. 55-56. Imperfect: p. 1-2 wanting. Evans413; Sabin46244; WingM1087; Holmes (C)43A; cf. Holmes(I)115A. 16771A, 1935 6109A, 1909	D. Math I.115A[1] [F]	Mather, Increase, 1639-1723. A Sermon Occasioned by the Execution of a Man found Guilty of Murder: Preached at Boston in New-England, March 11th 168⅖. (Together with the confession, Last Expressions, and Solemn Warning of that Murderer, to all Persons; especially to Young Men; to beware of those Sins which brought him to his Miserable End.) By Increase Mather. Teacher of a Church of Christ. ... Boston, Printed for John Dunton Book-Seller, lately Arrived from London; and are to be Sold by him, both at his Shop over against the Town-House, and his Shop in Salem. 1686. 2 p.l., 44, [2], 94 p. 14.5cm. 8º Preached at the Boston Thursday Lecture. Occasioned by the execution of James Morgan. "To the Reader" dated (2d p.l.[v]) 26 Mar.1686. Errata, p. 44 (1st count). With, as issued, Cotton Mather's The call of the gospel applyed, Boston, 1686, and Joshua Moody's An exhortation to a condemned malefactor, Boston, 1686, with special title-pages, separate paging, but continuous signatures. Also issued with Joseph Brunning's imprint. Bound in contemporary calf. In this copy there is a blank l. counted as p. 55-56 (2d count). Tears and worn edges affecting text of numerous pages, including title-pages.
D. Math I.77[2]	Mather, Increase, 1639-1723. The Mystery Of Christ Opened And Applyed. In Several Sermons, Concerning the Person, Office, and Glory of Jesus Christ. By Increase Mather, Teacher of a Church at Boston in N. England. ... [Boston] Printed in the year MDCLXXXVI. 1 p.l., 6, 212,[2] p. 14.5cm. 8º Printed by Richard Pierce for Joseph Brunning (cf. Holmes). Errata, 10 lines, verso t.-p. "Books printed for, and sold by Joseph Brunning..." last p. Also issued with imprint "Printed at Boston in New England Anno 1686." "Ex dono Rev. authoris Octbr. 1687" inscribed on fly leaf. In this copy there is a blank l. between p. 74-75 and a blank l. counted as p. 179-180. Bound in contemporary calf. Sabin46706; WingM1229; Holmes(I)77[2]. 2515, 1906		

D.Math I.115A[1] cop.2 [F]	——— ———Another copy. 14.5cm. 　　In this copy there is a blank *l*. counted as p. 55-56 (2d count). 　　Imperfect: t.-p., 2d p. *l*., p. 1-2 (2d count), 89-94 (2d count) wanting. 　　Bound in contemporary calf. 　　Sabin46735; WingM1247; Holmes(I)115A[1].		Trbajo [sic] Vna denunciacion, que se hizo ante el Tribunal de la Santa Cruzada, de vn Sumario de Indulgencias de la Cofradia de la Sangre de Christo, fundada en su Capilla de la Parrochia de Santa Catharina Martir de esta Ciudad de Mexico. Escriviala De nuevo, con algunos reparos, para los aficionados à la verdad, y deseosos de saberla, El Padre Fray Nicolas De Merlo, del Orden de Predicadores. Ponese Lo Primero la dicha denunciacion; siguense despues dos Sumarios de dicha Cofradia, vno impresso por el mes de Enero del año de 1686. y otro impresso por Março de el proprio año: vno, y otro falso. Y por vltimo se ponen para los curiosos algunos reparos que han parecido à proposito. ... 　　[Mexico, 1686] 　　21 numb. *l*. 30cm. (31cm. in case) fol. 　　At head of title: Lex veritatis fuit in ore eius. ... 　　With verso of *l*.1 and of *l*. 21 blank. 　　Dated at end 22 May 1686. 　　"Denunciacion": 2d-4th numb. *l*. 　　"Sumario de las indulgencias": 4th-7th[V] numb. *l*. 　　"Reparos notables": 7th[V]-21st numb. *l*. 　　Palau(2)165837; Medina(Mexico)1381.
16771, 1935 6109, 1909			
BA686 M539i	Mendoza, Juan de, fl. 1656-1686. 　　Impression Mysteriosa. De Las Llagas De N. Redemptor En El Cverpo Del Seraphin Humano. La predicó el R. P. Fr. Ioan De Mendoza Ayala Predicador General, jubilado, Chronista de esta Provincia del Santo Evangelio, y Diffinidor en acto de dicha Provincia. El Dia 17. De Septiembre De Este Año de 1685. ... 　　Con Licencia, En Mexico, Por la Viuda de Francisco Rodriguez Lupercio. Año de 1686. 　　8 p. *l*., [28] p. 18.5cm. 4[o] 　　Approbation dated (5th p. *l*.[v]) 3 Dec. 1685. 　　Medina(Mexico)1380; Palau(2)163876.		
		5165, 1909	
68-414		D.Math I.115A[1]	Moody, Joshua, 1633-1697. 　　An Exhortation To a Condemned Malefactor Delivered March 6th 168[5]/[6] By Joshua Moodey, Preacher of the Gospel at Boston in N. England. ... 　　Printed at Boston in N. England. Anno prædict. [i.e. 1686] 　　2 p. *l*., 61-94 p. 14.5cm. 8[o] (Issued as a part of Increase Mather's <u>A sermon occasioned by the execution of a man</u>, Boston, 1686, and of Cotton Mather's <u>The call of the gospel applyed</u>, Boston, 1656.) 　　Occasioned by the execution of James Morgan. 　　Bound in contemporary calf. 　　Tears and worn edges affecting text of numerous pages.
BA686 M539v	Mendoza, Juan de, fl. 1656-1686. 　　Virtvd Jviziosa, Santidad Prvdente De San Gregorio Thavmatvrgo Obispo de Neocesarea, Patron de esta Ciudad de Mexico, Qve En el dia 17. de Noviembre de el Año passado de 1685. en la Iglesia Cathedral, con assistencia de el Excelentissimo Señor Marques de la Laguna Virrey de esta Nueva-España: Real Audiencia· Cabildo Ecclesiastico: Ciudad, y Regimiento Predicò El R. P. Fr. Ivan De Mendoza Ayala Predicador General Jubilado, Chronista, y Difinidor en acto de esta Provincia de el Santo Evangelio ... 　　Con Licencia De Los Superiores. En Mexico, por Doña Maria de Benavides, Viuda de Juan de Ribera, en el Empedradillo. Año de 1686. 　　7 p. *l*., 13 numb. *l*. 20.5cm. 4[o] 　　License dated (6th p. *l*.[r]) 15 Feb. 1686. 　　Medina(Mexico)1379; Palau(2)163877.		
		D.Math I.115A[1] cop.2	——— ———Another copy. 14.5cm. 　　Imperfect: p. 89-94 wanting. 　　Bound in contemporary calf. 　　cf. Holmes(I)115A; Holmes(C)43A.
		16771B, 1935 6109B, 1909	
68-421			
BA686 -M565e	Merlo, Nicolás. 　　... Espejo De Indvlgencias, Donde Con Gran Claridad Se Ven las falsas, y verdaderas. Tomase Por Assvmpto De Este		

[168]

D686 Moxon, Joseph, 1627-1691.
M937t   A Tutor To Astronomy and Geography. Or an easie and speedy way to know the Use of both the Globes, Cœlestial and Terrestrial. In Six Books. The <1. Teaching the Rudiments of Astronomy and Geography. 2. 3. 4. 5. 6.> Shewing by the Globes the solution of < Astronomical and Geographical Problemes. Problemes in Navigation. Astrological Problemes. Gnomonical Problemes. Trigonometrical Problemes. ... With an Appendix shewing the Use of the Ptolomaick Sphere. The Fourth Edition Corrected and Enlarged. By Joseph Moxon. Whereunto is added the Antient Poetical Stories of the Stars: shewing Reasons why the several Shapes and Forms are pictured on the Cœlestial Globe. As also a Discourse of the Antiquity, Progress and Augmentations of Astronomy. ...
   London. Printed by S. Roycroft, for Joseph Moxon: and Sold at his Shop in Ludgate Street, at the sign of Atlas. 1686.
   3 p.ℓ., 271, [1], [8] p. incl. illus., tables. front. (port.) 20.5cm. 4°
   A rev. and enl. of the 1st ed., London, 1659.
   "The Ancient Stories Of the several Stars and Constellations ... Collected from Dr. Hood": p. 208-232.
   "A Discourse Of the Antiquity, Progress and Augmentation Of Astronomy" by Pierre Gassendi: p. 233-271.
   "A Catalogue of Books, Maps, and Instruments, Made and Sold by Joseph Moxon": p. [272].
   Imperfect: portrait wanting; available in facsim.
   Bound in contemporary calf.
   WingM3025.
9932, 1914

D686   Nader Informatie en Bericht Voor die gene die
N135i   genegen zijn, om zich na America te begeeven, en in de Provincie van Pensylvania Geinteresseerd zijn, of zich daar zoeken neder te zetten. Met een Voorreden Behelzende verscheydene aanmerkelijke zaken vanden tegenwoordige toestand, en Regeering dier Provincie; Nooit voor dezen in druk geweest: maar nu eerst uytgegeven door Robert Webb.
   t'Amsterdam, By Jacob Claus, Boekverkoper in de Prinse-straat, 1686.
   8, 11 p. 19cm. 4°
   Consists of "Voorreden" (1st count, p. 2-8; signed at end "Robert Webb") and of text (2d count, p. 1-11) with caption title "Nader Informatie of Onderrechtinge voor die gene die genegen zijn ..."
   Only the preface is by Robert Webb. It is first published here.
   The text is by William Penn, a transl. of Information and direction to such persons as are inclined to America, more especially those related to the Province of Pennsylvania, 1st pub. [London, ca. 1684]
   Errata, 1st count, p. 8.
   There is a colophon identical to the imprint.
   JCB(2)2:1332; Sabin102227; Vail(Front.)249, 250.
02309, 1850   rev

D686   [Penn, William] 1644-1718.
N135i   Nader Informatie of Onderrechtinge voor de gene die genegen zijn om na America te gaan, en wel voornamentlijk voor die geene die in de Provintie van Pensylvania geintresseert zijn.
   t'Amsterdam, By Jacob Claus, Boekverkooper, in de Prince-straat, 1686.
   11 p. 19cm. 4° (Issued as a part of Nader Informatie en Bericht..., Amsterdam, 1686.)
   Caption title; imprint at end.
   Transl. of: Information and direction to such persons as are inclined to America, more especially those related to the Province of Pennsylvania, 1st pub. [London, ca. 1684]
   JCB(2)2:1332; Sabin102227; Vail(Front.)250.
02309A   rev

DA686   [Penn, William] 1644-1718.
P412pA   A Perswasive To Moderation To Church Dissenters, In Prudence and Conscience:
[R]   Humbly Submitted to the King And His Great Councel. By one of the Humblest and most Dutiful of his Dissenting Subjects. ...
   [London, 1686]
   4 p.ℓ., 52 p., 1 ℓ. 19.5cm. (20.5cm. in case). 4° []1 []1 []2 A-F4 G2 []1
   First pub. London, 1685, under title: A perswasive to moderation to dissenting Christians ...
   Errata, leaf at end.
   Readings: last line of t.-p., "... Charls [sic] ..."; p. 38, line 1, "Age, the present Government...". Catchword, p. 47: "as".
   Smith(Friends)2:303; WingP1338A; McAlpin 4:226-227.

DA686   ——Another edition. [London, 1686]
P412pB   4 p.ℓ., 52 p. 19cm. (20cm. in case).
[R]   4° []4 A-F4 G2.
   The title reads the same as the preceding, but this book is mostly a different setting of type. It consists partly of the same sheets and/or the same type-setting as the preceding.

The type-settings of both editions are very similar.
In this edition there is no errata list. Most of the corrected readings of the list in the preceding edition are followed.
Readings: last line of t.-p., "... Charles ..."; p. 38, line 1, "Age, the present Frame of Government...". Catchword, p. 47: "Thirdly,".
Smith(Friends)2:303; WingP1338A.
30129, 1947 rev
62-242

D686 P412t
Penn, William, 1644-1718.
Tweede Bericht ofte Relaas Van William Penn, Eygenaar en Gouverneur van de Provintie van Pennsylvania, In America. Behelsende een korte Beschrijvinge van den tegenwoordige toestand en gelegentheid van die Colonie. ... Uyt het Engels overgeset.
t'Amsterdam, By Jacob Claus, Boekverkoper in de Prince-straat. [1686]
20 p. 19.5cm. 4º.
Signed (p. 20): Wm. Penn. Worminghurst den 12 October, 1685.
Transl. by William Sewel from: A further account of the Province of Pennsylvania [London? 1685?]
JCB(2)2:1322; Church696n; Sabin59738; Baer(Md.)119; Vail(Front.)242.
02308, 1850-51

E686 P699p [R]
Plan pour former un Establissement en Caroline.
A La Haye. Chez Meindert Uytwerf, Marchand Libraire dans l'Acterum. l'An 1686.
15 p. 20cm. 4º
Caption title; imprint at end.
JCBAR28:13; Vail251.
06219, 1895

BA686 P792h
Ponce de León, Nicolás.
Historia De La Singvlar Vida, De El Venerable Hermano Fray Christoval de Molina Religioso Lego de la Orden de N. P. San Augustin. Hijo de el illustrissimo Convento de Nuestra Señora de Gracia de la misma Orden; de la Ciudad de la Puebla de los Angeles donde reciviò el habito, y muriò. Escrita Por El Padre Lector Fr. Nicolas Ponze de Leon, Religioso de la misma Orden. Año de 1686. ...

Con Licencia En la Puebla de los Angeles por Diego Fernandez de Leon. Año de 1686. Vendense en su Tienda en la esquina de la Plaça en la Calle de Cholula.
19 p. ℓ., 117 numb. ℓ., [34] p. 20cm. 4º
Cut (Augustinian device) on t.-p.
License dated (7th p. ℓ.^{r}) 22 Dec. 1685.
Errata, 19th p. ℓ.
Bound in contemporary vellum.
Palau(2)231035; Medina(Puebla)101; Sabin63976; Santiago Vela6:382:1; Streit 2:2229.
06004, before 1923

H686 P833i
Porcacchi, Tommaso, 1530(ca.)-1585.
L'Isole Piv Famose Del Mondo, Descritte Da Tomaso Porcacchi Da Castiglione Arretino, Di nuovo corrette, & illustrate con l'aggiunta dell' Istria, & altre Isole, Scogli, e nuove curiosità. Essendovi una distinta descrittione della Città di Costantinopoli, e della Penisola di Morea. ...
In Venetia, M.DC.LXXXVI. Presso Pietr' Antonio Brigonci. Con Licenza de' Superiori, e Privilegio.
2 p. ℓ., 144, 155-194, 197-200 p. 46 maps. 21.5cm. 4º
Cut on t.-p.
First pub. Venice, 1572.
Includes maps and descriptions of "Città et isole del Temistitan" (i.e. Mexico City), "Isola, E Terra Di Santa Croce, Overo Mondo Nvovo", "Spagnuola", Cuba, Jamaica, and "San Giovanni Detta Borichen" (i.e. Puerto Rico).
Dedication, 2d p. ℓ., signed: Venetia li 22. Luglio 1686... Pietr' Antonio Brigonci.
Phillips(Atlases)5680 describes what appears to be a similar but not identical issue: The Phillips title mentions Girolamo Porro, the engraver of the maps and joint publisher of the 1st ed., while the title of the present issue does not mention Porro. Phillips notes the omission of nos. 145-154 in the paging but not also nos. 195-196 as in the present issue. Although "Istria" is mentioned in the Phillips title it is noted as wanting from the contents and as not mentioned in the table of contents; in the present issue a description of Istria appears without map, p. 184-188, and is listed in the table of contents, p. 200, as the 11th of 13 parts of the "terzo libro". Plate [20] as listed by Phillips, "Conflitto navale ...", is not included in the present copy, although a corresponding text appears at p. 86-93. The maps in the present copy are bound up slightly differently from what is described in Phillips.
Sabin64153; cf. Phillips(Atlases)5680.
70-342

J686
=P966d
Prospect Des ganzen Erdkreisses/In Fünff absonderlichen Carten/Namentlich Europa/ Asia/Africa Und Dem Mitternächtig-und Mittägigen America/Samt einer ausführlichen Beschreibung derselben Länder/ Provinzien/Königreiche/Herrschafften/ Fürstenthümer/und Inseln/Wie auch Städte/ Vestungen und Schlösser bestehend/Vor Augen gestellet und zum Druck übergeben. Nürnberg/Zu finden bey Johann Hoffmann/ Buch-und Kunsthändlern. Gedruckt bey Andreas Knorzen Seel. Wittib. Anno M.DC.LXXXVI.
60 p. 35.5cm. fol.
Cut on t.-p.
Without maps.
Palmer373.

10834, 1915

C686
R382o
A Relation Of The Invasion and Conquest Of Florida By The Spaniards, Under the Command of Fernando de Soto. Written in Portuguese by a Gentleman of the Town of Elvas. Now Englished. To which is Subjoyned Two Journeys of the present Emperour of China into Tartary in the Years 1682, and 1683. With some Discoveries made by the Spaniards in the Island of California, in the Year 1683.
London: Printed for John Lawrence, at the Angel in the Poultry over against the Compter. 1686.
8 p.ℓ., 272 p. 16.5cm. 8º
"A Relation Of The Invasion and Conquest Of Florida..." (p. 1-220) transl. from: Histoire De La Conqueste De La Floride... Paris, 1685, itself transl. from: Relaçam verdadeira dos trabalhos... 1st pub. Evora, 1556.
The "Two Journeys... into Tartary..." by Ferdinand Verbiest and "... Spaniards in... California..." by Isidro Otondo y Antillón (p. 221-272) transl. from: Voyages De L'Empereur De La Chine... ausquels on a joint une nouvelle découverte du Mexique, Paris, 1685. Includes special t.-p. (p. 221): A Journey Of The Emperor of China Into East-Tartary. In the Year 1682. London: Printed by Freeman Collins, for John Lawrence, over-against the Poultry-Compter. 1686."
License dated (1st p.ℓ.ᵛ) 7 June 1686.
Errata, 8th p.ℓ.ᵛ
JCB(2)2:1329; WingR840; Sabin24865; Wagner 58b.

01919, 1854

DA686
R823r
Ross, Alexander, 1590-1654
Les Religions Du Monde, Ou Demonstration de toutes les Religions & heresies de L'Asie, Afrique, Amerique, & de L'Europe, Depuis le commencement du monde jusqu'à present. Escrites par le Sʳ. Alexandre Ross. Et traduites par le Sʳ. Thomas La Grue, Maistre és Arts, & Docteur en Medecine. Enrichy par tout de figures en taille douce.
A Amsterdam, Chez Abraham Wolfgang. MDCLXXXVI.
6 p.ℓ., 570 p., 1 ℓ., 579-867, [868-879] p. front., 15 fold. plates. 16cm. 12º
Cut on t.-p.
Transl. from: Πανσέβεια, or a view of all religions in the world. First pub. London, 1653.
Includes half-titles: "Seconde Partie" (p.289) and "Troisieme Partie" (ℓ. preceding p. 579).
In this copy there is a blank leaf following p. 570.
Bound in contemporary calf.
Sabin73318n.

69-596

BA686
-S217b
Sandín, Alonso, 1630-1701.
Breve, Y Compendiosa Relacion De Lo Obrado por Don Fr. Phelipe Pardo, Arçobispo de la Iglesia Metropolitana de Manila en las Islas Philipinas, despues de restituido à su Iglesia, sacada legalmente de los Autos, que nuevamente han venido al Consejo. Recopilados Por Fr. Alonso Sandin, del Orden de Predicaderes [sic], Difinidor, y Procurador General de la Prouincia del Santo Rosario de Philipinas, poder habiente de dicho Arçobispo.
[Madrid? 1686?]
24 numb. ℓ. 29.5cm. fol.
Caption title.
Based on documentation also published in Raimundo Berart's Relación con inserción de autos... Manila, 1685.
Cf. JCBAR66:4; Palau(2)297029; Medina (Filipinas)377; Streit5:948; Retana 204.

66-118

B69
G643v
36
Téllez Giron, Juan Alejo.
Villancicos, Que se Cantaron en la Santa Iglesia Metropolitana, la noche de los Maytines del Principe de los Apostoles San Pedro. ... Escrivelos el Br. Don Juan Alejo Tellesgiron.
Con licencia; en Mexico, por los Herederos de la Uiuda de Bernardo Calderon, año de 1686.

1686

[8] p. 20cm. 4º
"Compuestos en Metro musico, por el Br. Joseph de Agurto, y Loaysa, Maestro de Capilla de dicha Santa Iglesia." (p. [8]).
Woodcut title vignette (St. Peter; inscribed in lower left corner: AD).
Bound, in contemporary vellum, as no. 36 with 42 other items.
Gonzalez(1952)233.

28936, 1941

H686 T323r
Terra Rossa, Vitale.
Riflessioni Geografiche Circa Le Terre Incognite Distese in ossequio perpetuo della Nobiltà Veneziana, Nelle quali I. Si pruoua, che i Patrizi di Venezia prima d'ogni altro hanno all' Italia, & all' Europa, discoperte tutte le Terre anticamente Incognite, anco l'America, e la Terra Australe. II. Si desidera vna esatta, e perfetta Concordia della vecchia, e nuoua Geografia, in onore de' Signori Veneziani. III. Si difende contra il moderno Braudrand [sic], che niuno infra i racconti Geografici, dagli stessi Gentiluomini dell' Adria publicati, è stato finto, ò fauoloso. ... Dal P. D. Vitale Terra Rossa da Parma, Priore Casinense di Lerino, Dottore di Filos. e Teol. già Publico Lettore nell' Vniuersità di Bologna, ed ora Filosofo Ordinario in quella di Padoua.
In Padova, MDCLXXXVI. Per il Cadorino, Con licenza de' Sup. Et Privilegio Del Serenissimo Principe.
16 p.ℓ., 298, [10] p. incl. port. 23cm. 4º
Cut on t.-p.; incl. caption: Pace.
The same sheets were also issued with variant imprint "... MDCLXXXVII ... Privilegio Del ... Senato."
Dedication dated (13th p.ℓ.ʳ) 2 June 1686.
Defends the claim of the discovery of America by the brothers Zeni in reply to: Michel Antoine Baudrand, Geographia ordine litterarum disposita, Paris, 1681-1682 [v.1, 1682].
Errata, p. 298.
Bound in contemporary vellum.
JCB(2)2:1330; Sabin94858.

03655, before 1866

CA679 V665s 9
Vieira, Antonio, 1608-1697.
Maria Rosa Mystica. Excellencias, Poderes, E Maravilhas do seu Rosario, Compendiadas Em Trinta Sermoens Asceticos, & Panegyricos sobre os dous Evangelhos desta solennidade Novo, & Antigo ... Pelo P. Antonio Vieira da Companhia de Jesv Da Provincia do Brasil ... I. Parte.
Lisboa. Na Officina de Migvel Deslandes, Na Rua da Figueyra. A custa de Antonio Leyte Pereyra, Mercador de Livros. M.DC.LXXXVI. Com todas as licenças, & Privilegio Real.
4 p.ℓ., 116, 127-521, 146-178, 46 p. 21cm. 4º [His Sermoens, 9. parte]
Cut (Jesuit trigram, floriated) on t.-p.
"Tayxaõ este Livro ..." dated (4th p.ℓ.) 12 Nov. 1686.
Errata, 4th p.ℓ.ᵛ
According to Leite "Deste vol. de 1686 conhecem-se três impressões diferentes."
In this copy a few lines of text on p.ℓ. 1-2 are affected by disintegration.
Bound in contemporary calf.
Rodrigues2511; Backer8:659-650; Leite 9:197-198; Innocencio 1:290.

68-343

A582 M517p
Vossius, Isaac, 1618-1689.
Isaaci Vossii Observationum Ad Pomp. Melam Appendix. Accedit ejusdem ad Tertias P. Simonii Objectiones Responsio. Subjungitur Pauli Colomesii ad Henricum Justellum Epistola.
Londini, Prostant apud Robertum Scott, Bibliopolam, MDCLXXXVI.
2 p.ℓ., 136 p. 20.5cm. 4º
A reply to Jacobus Gronovius' notes in Pomponius Mela's ... Libri tres de situ orbis, Leiden, 1685, and to Richard Simon's ... Opuscula critica adversus I. Vossium, Edinburgh, 1685.
Colomiès' letter deals with Richard Simon's Histoire critique du Vieux Testament, 1st pub. Paris, 1678.
Errata, 2d p.ℓ.ᵛ
Bound with: Mela, Pomponius. ... De situ orbis libri tres, Bordeaux, 1582.

06683, 1887

1687

B619 M737r
Alvarez Ossorio y Redín, Miguel.
Señor. Don Miguel Albarez Ossorio y Redin, dize: Que para mayor aumento de las Rentas Reales, y vniversal alivio de la causa publica, ha puesto tres Memoriales en la Real mano de V. Mag.
[Madrid? 1687?]
1 ℓ. 20cm. 4º
Title from caption and beginning of text.
Draws attention to the memoriales, Defensa,

unión y restauración [Madrid? 1686?], Extensión política y económica [Madrid? 1686?], and Discurso universal de las causas [Madrid? 1686], concerning economic conditions and policies which were prepared for the Spanish king by Alvarez Ossorio.
    Bound in contemporary vellum with: Moncada, Sancho de. Restauración política de España, Madrid, 1619, as the 6th of 10 items.

12570-6, 1920

B619 Alvarez Ossorio y Redín, Miguel.
M737r   Zelador General Para el bien comun de todos. Indice, y Resumen de los Memoriales de Don Miguel Albrrez [sic] Oslorio [sic], y Redin. [Madrid? 1687]
    14 p. 20cm. 4°
    Caption title.
    Summarizes his: Defensa, unión y restauración de esta monarquía [Madrid? 1686?], Extensión política y económica [Madrid? 1686], and Discurso universal de las causas [Madrid? 1686]
    In this copy there is a blank l. at end. This copy is closely trimmed at outer margin with some effect on text.
    Bound in contemporary vellum with: Moncada, Sancho de. Restauración política de España, Madrid, 1619, as the 5th of 10 items.
    Colmeiro18.

12570-5, 1920

D687 [Blome, Richard] d. 1705.
B653p   The Present State Of His Majesties Isles and Territories In America, Viz. Jamaica, Barbadoes, S. Christophers, Mevis [sic], Antego, S. Vincent, Dominica, New-Jersey, Pensilvania, Monserat, > <Anguilla, Bermudas, Carolina, Virginia, New-England, Tobago. New-Found-Land. Mary-Land, New-York. With New Maps of every Place. Together with Astronomical Tables, ...
    Licens'd, July 20. 1686. Roger L'Estrange. London: Printed by H. Clark, for Dorman Newman, at the Kings-Arms in the Poultrey, 1687.
    4 p. l., 262 p., 1 l., [40] p. front. (port.), 7 maps (incl. 1 fold.), diagr. 18.5cm. 8°
    Dedication signed (2d p. l.^{r}): Richard Blome.
    A revision and enlargement of his A description of the island of Jamaica, 1st pub. London, 1672.
    "The Proposals lately made by Captain John Poyntz..." (1st pub. under title: The Present Prospect Of The Famous and Fertile Island Of Tobago. London, 1683): p. 259-262.
    Bookseller's advertisement, p. [35-40] at end.
    JCB(2)2:1333; WingB3215; Sabin5972; Church 699; Baer(Md.)124; Dexter(Cong.)2300.

01920, 1854

F687 Brandt, Geeraert, 1626-1685.
-B821l   Leben und Thaten des Fürtreflichen und Sonderbahren See-Helden Herrn Michaels de Ruiter, Hertzogs/Ritters/u.s.f. L. Admirals Generals von Holland und West-Friesland. In Niederländischer Sprache beschrieben/durch Herrn Gerhard Brand. Worinnen nicht allein diesses Ungemeinen und zum höchsten Lob-und Ruhm-würdigen Selden Unvergleichliches Leben/... wie auch der Ost-und West-Indien/und verschiedener Heidnischer Länder Beschaffenheit und Begebenheiten... zu finden seind. ...Aus der Niederländischen in die Hochdeutsche Sprache treulich übergesetzet.
    Zu Amsterdam/Bei Wolfgang/Waasbergen/Boom/von Someren/und Goethals. MDCLXXXVII.
    4 p. l., 150, 153-346, 349-472, 170, 187-250, 261-288, [32] p. 8 plates (incl. 7 double plates), port. 30.5cm. fol.
    Added t.-p., engraved.
    Cut on t.-p.
    Edited by Kaspar and Johannes Brandt.
    Transl. from: Het Leven en Bedryf van den Heere Michiel de Ruiter. Amsterdam, 1687.
    JCB(2)2:1334; Sabin7408; Palmer296.

03933, 1868

F687 Brandt, Geeraert, 1626-1685.
-B821le   Het Leven En Bedryf Van Den Heere Michiel De Ruiter, Hertog, Ridder, &c. L. Admiraal Generaal van Hollandt en Westvrieslandt. Beschreeven Door Gerard Brandt. Met schoone koopere plaaten verciert.
    Te Amsterdam, Voor Wolfgang, Waasberge, Boom, Van Someren en Goethals. MDCLXXXVII.
    5 p. l., 1065, [1066-1088] p. 8 plates (incl. 7 double), port. 32.5cm. fol.
    Edited by Kaspar and Johannes Brandt.
    Cut on t.-p., incl. motto: Indefessus Agendo.
    Added t.-p., engr., with imprint: Tot Amsterdam, Uyt de Drukkerye van P. en J. Blaeu, Voor de Compagnie, MDCXCIX.
    Various issues of this work were made by the same group of publishers. Although this copy has a printed t.-p. dated 1687 and an engr. t.-p. dated 1699, the copy, which is bound in contemporary calf, appears to represent a genuine issue. Some other recorded

1687

copies have a printed t.-p. dated 1687 with an engr. t.-p. dated 1686; others have a printed t.-p. dated 1701 with an engr. t.-p. dated 1699.

"Eenige der voornaamste Gedichten, Op 't afsterven van den Heere Michiel De Ruiter..." (p. [1015]-1065) includes poetry by Joachim Oudaan, Nicolaas Heinsius, Joannes Vollenhove, Arnold Moonen, Joannis Antonides van der Goes, D. Schelte, and Geeraert Brandt. Preliminary matter includes poetry by Joannes Vollenhove.

Sabin 7405; Scheepvaart Mus. 843.

70-37 rev

F687
B853v

Brief, Van seeker Frans Heer, Geschreeven uyt Cadix Den 17 April 1687. Behelsende, hoe dat die van de Gereformeerde Religie uyt Vrankrijk na de Eylanden van America werden toegevoert, en aldaar tot slaven verkogt.

Tot Rotterdam, By Heyndrik de Graef, Boeck-verkooper op de Marct. 1687.

6 p. 21cm. 4°

Cut on t.-p.

Also issued [1687?] in at least two other Dutch versions, a 4° and a folio, without imprint but "Na de Copye tot Rotterdam". Also issued 1687 in a German transl. under title: Unerhörter Christen-Verkauff.

In this copy there is a blank leaf at the end.

Cf. JCBAR 55:25-30; Knuttel 12568; Meulman 6153.

32293, 1958

H687
C282m

Carli, Dionigi, ca. 1637-ca. 1695.
Il Moro Trasportato Nell' Inclita Città Di Venetia, O Vero Curioso racconto de Costumi, Riti, e Religione de Popoli dell' Africa, America, Asia, & Europa. Rauisati dal Molto Reuerendo Padre Dionigio Carli Da Piacenza Predicatore Capuccino, e Missionario Apostolico in quelle parti. Diviso In Doi [sic] Libri. ...

In Bassano, M.DC.LXXXVII. Appresso Gio: Antonio Remondinj. Con Licenza De' Svperiori, E Privilegio.

8 p.ℓ., 402, [18] p. plate. 24.5cm. 4°

Cut on t.-p.

Half-title: Le Qvattro Parti Del Mondo.

The first part concerns the voyage of Carli and Michele Angelo Guattini, Capuchin missionaries, from Bologna through Lisbon to Brazil and West Africa and back. The account of this voyage was 1st pub. under title: Viaggio del P. Dionigi de'

69-323

Carli da Piacenza, e del P. Michel Angelo de' Guatini. Reggio Emilia, 1671. The second part concerns travels through the Near East.

Dedication dated (3d p.ℓ.ᵛ) 30 June 1687.

Preliminary matter includes commendatory poetry by Adriano Chisini, Giuseppe Chisini, Giovanni Battista Mutio, Stefano Conti, and Antonio Crestani.

Imperfect: 1st p.ℓ. wanting; available in facsim.

Borba de Moraes 1:131; Streit 16:4772.

C619
A949n

Catholic Church--Pope, 1676-1689. (Innocentius XI)   28 Aug. 1687
Bula De La Santidad De Inocencio XI. En Qve Condena Sesenta y ocho Proposiciones De Migvel De Molinos

Lisboa. Na Officina de Miguel Deslandes Na Rua da Figueyra. Com todas as licenças necessarias.   Anno 1687.

15 p. 19.5cm. 4°

Cut (papal device) on t.-p.

Text in Spanish.

Prohibits and condemns all works of Molinos, printed or in manuscript.

First pub. in Rome, 28 Aug. 1687.

Certificate of publication dated (p. 15) 3 Sept. 1687.

Bound as the 6th in a volume of 58 pamphlets, 1619-1702.

Palau (2) 119848.

9347, 1913

BA687
C828c

[Cortés Osorio, Juan] 1623-1688.
Conferencia Cvriosa De La Assamblea Popvlar, Qve Convocó En La Pverta Del Sol Catalina De La Parra; Explicada En Vna Carta Qve Escrive A Emerico Tekeli, Sv Correspondiente, Y Contenida En La Conversacion De Vn Forastero, Con Vn Cortesano.

Impresso en Peralta [i.e. Madrid?]. Por Pedro Ximenez.   Año de 1687.

1 p.ℓ., 55 p. 20cm. 4°

A defence of the Jesuits in fictional form.

"En el mismo año se hicieron dos tiradas. El pie de imprenta es supuesto. Probablemente se imprimió en Madrid, donde residia el P. Cortés, fallecido allí en 1688." (Palau)

Palau (2) 63425.

70-524

D687　　[Crouch, Nathaniel] 1632?-1725?
C952e　　　The English Heroe: Or, Sir Francis Drake
　　　　Revived. Being a full Account of the Dangerous
　　　　Voyages, Admirable Adventures, Notable Dis-
　　　　coveries, and Magnanimous Atchievements of
　　　　that Valiant and Renowned Commander. ... Re-
　　　　vised, Corrected, very much Inlarged, reduced
　　　　into Chapters with Contents, and beautified with
　　　　Pictures. By R.[ichard] B.[urton, pseud.]
　　　　　Licensed and Entred according to Order,
　　　　March 30. 1687. London, Printed for Nath.
　　　　Crouch at the Bell in the Poultrey near Cheapside.
　　　　1687.
　　　　　2 p.ℓ., 206, [6] p. illus. 15cm. 12º
　　　　　Booksellers' advertisement, p. [1-6] at end.
　　　　　JCB(2)2:1335; WingC7321A; Sabin9500.
06010, before 1882

E687　　[Dellon, Gabriel] b. ca. 1649.
D358r　　　Relation De L'Inquisition De Goa.
　　　　A Leyde, Chez Daniel Gaasbeek, Marchand
　　　　Libraire. 1687 [i.e. 1688?]
　　　　　4 p.ℓ., 220 p. 14.5cm. 12º
　　　　　Cut (armillary sphere) on t.-p.
　　　　　"Mon départ de Goa, mon arrivée au Brésil,
　　　　puis à Lisbonne." (p. 189-192).
　　　　　First pub. Paris with t.-p. dated 1688 but
　　　　with printer's imprint at end dated 1687 and
　　　　with 437 p. main paging. There is another ed.,
　　　　which is really a Dutch counterfeit, with Paris,
　　　　1688, on t.-p. and with printer's imprint at end
　　　　dated 1688 and 251 p. main paging.
　　　　　This edition is an abridged reprint.
　　　　　Perhaps also issued with 6 plates (cf.Rahir).
　　　　　Cf. Borba de Moraes 1:216-217; Rahir 2847;
　　　　Vekené 271.
69-640

E687　　[Durand,　　of Dauphiné] fl. 1685-1687.
D948v　　　Voyages D'Un Francois, Exilé pour la Re-
[R]　　ligion, Avec Une Description de la Virgine
　　　　& Marilan Dans L'Amerique.
　　　　A La Haye, Imprimé pour l'Autheur, 1687.
　　　　　140 p. 14cm. 12º
　　　　　Cut (angel's head) on t.-p.
　　　　　"Achevé d'imprimer ce 7. Juillet 1687.":
　　　　p. 136.
　　　　　"Propositions Pour la Virgine." (p. 137-
　　　　140) dated in London, 30 May 1687, "de la
　　　　part des Proprietaires Nic: Hayward."
　　　　　In this copy there are 2 blank leaves at
　　　　end.
　　　　　With this is bound, in contemporary calf:

　　　　Chavigny de La Bretonnière, François de.
　　　　La religieuse cavalier. Brussels, 1696.
　　　　　Sabin100837; Vail(Front.)256; Arents394;
　　　　Baer125; Torrence90.
1180-1, 1906

C687　　Figueira, Luiz, 1573-1643.
F475a　　　Arte De Grammatica Da Lingua Brasilica,
　　　　Do P. Luis Figueira, Theologo da Companhia
　　　　de Jesus.
　　　　　Lisboa. Na Officina de Miguel Deslandes,
　　　　Na Rua da Figueira. Anno 1687. Com todas
　　　　as licenças necessarias.
　　　　　4 p.ℓ., 167, [1] p. 14.5cm. 8º
　　　　　Cut (Jesuit device) on t.-p.
　　　　　First pub. Lisbon, [1621]. This edition
　　　　edited by João Filippe Bettendorf.
　　　　　License dated (4th p.ℓ.ᵛ) 16 Dec. 1686.
　　　　　Errata, last p.
　　　　　JCB(2)2:1337; Sabin24313; Backer3:721;
　　　　Viñaza 221; Borba de Moraes 1:263.
06251, 1867?

EB　　France--Treaties, etc., 1643-1715 (Louis XIV)
F8455　　　　　　　　　　　　　　　16 Nov.1686
1687　　　Traité De Neutralité, Conclv A Londres le
1　　16. Novembre 1686. Entre Les Rois De France
　　　　Et D'Angleterre toûchant les Païs des deux Rois
　　　　en Amerique.
　　　　　Iouxte la Copie Imprimée à Paris. A Bordeaux,
　　　　Chez la Veuve de G. De La Court, Et N. De La
　　　　Court, Imprimeur du Roy, de Monseigneur l'Ar-
　　　　chevêque, & de l'Université. M.DC.LXXXVII.
　　　　De l'exprés commandement de sa Majesté.
　　　　　8 p. 22cm. (23.5cm. in case)
　　　　　Cut (royal arms) on t.-p.
　　　　　First pub. Paris, 1686.
　　　　　"Whitehall Treaty of Neutrality."
　　　　　Davenport 79.
31684, 1955

D687　　Franck, Richard, 1624?-1708.
F822p　　　A Philosophical Treatise Of The Original And
　　　　Production Of Things. Writ in America in a
　　　　Time of Solitudes. By R. Franck.
　　　　　London, Printed by John Gain, and are to be
　　　　sold by S. Tidmarsh at the King's Head in Corn-
　　　　hill: and S. Smith at the Prince's Arms in Sᵗ.
　　　　Paul's Church-Yard. 1687.
　　　　　13 p.ℓ., 170 p. 14.5cm. (15.5cm. in case) 8º
　　　　　Caption (p. 1) and running title: Rabbi Moses.
　　　　　Preliminary matter signed: Philanthropus.
　　　　　WingF2065; Sabin25467.
29952, 1947

BA687 Gorosito, Francisco de.
G672s   Sermon De N. Glorioss.^{mo} Padre San Pedro Nolasco Qve Dedica A N. R^{mo} P.M. Fr. Francisco Martines Falcon ... Diffinidor, y Secretario de la Provincia de Castilla, y Vicario General de estas de Nueua-España de el Real Orden de Nuestra Señora de la Merced Redempcion de Cautivos El P. P^{dor} Fr. Francisco De Gorosito, Commendador de el Convento de dicho Orden de la Villa de Carrion Valle de Atlixco.
    Con licencia en la Puebla de los Angeles en la Imprenta de Diego Fernandez de Leon en la calle de Cholula. [1687]
    6 p.ℓ., 16 p. 19.5cm. 4°
    License dated (4th p.ℓ.^{v}) 20 Dec. 1687.
    Palau(2)106253; Medina(Puebla)103; Sabin28027.
1047, 1905

C619   Gt.Brit.--Sovereigns, etc., 1685-1688 (James II).
A949n   4 Apr. 1687
    Favoravel declaraçaõ de El Rey de Inglaterra a todos os seus amados subditos para liberdade de conciencia.
    Lisboa, Na Officina de Miguel Deslandes, Na Rua da Figueira. Anno 1687. Com todas as licenças necessarias.
    7 p. 19.5cm. 4°
    Caption title; imprint at end.
    First pub. London, 1687; dated (p. 7): Dada em nossa Corte de Withall a 4. de Abril de 1687. annos ...
    Bound as the 7th in a volume of 58 pamphlets, 1619-1702.
9348, 1913

J687   Happel, Eberhard Werner, 1647-1690.
H252e   ... Mundus Mirabilis Tripartitus, Oder Wunderbare Welt/in einer kurtzen Cosmographia fürgestellet: Also/dass Der Erste Theil handelt Von dem Himmel/beweg-und unbeweglichen Sternen/... Der Andere Theil/ Von den Menschen und Thieren der Erden/... Der Dritte Theil/ Von den Universitäten/Seehafen/Vestungen/Residentzien/ ... mit vielen Kupffern und schönen Figuren ausgezieret/...
    Ulm/druckts und verlegts Matthæus Wagner/ 1687 [-1689]
    3 v.: v. 1, 9 p.ℓ., 800, [28] p. illus. incl. 2 diagrs. front. (port.), 15 plates (incl. 8 fold.), fold. map, fold. tab.; v.2, 6 p.ℓ., 1154, [1155-1178] p. front., 2 fold. maps; v.3, 8 p.ℓ., 1299, [1] p., 10 ℓ. front. 20.5cm. 4°
    Titles in red and black. Author's name at head of titles. Titles vary slightly.
    Imprint, v.2, dated: 1688; v.3: 1689.
    Dedications signed by printer, v. 1 dated (3d p.ℓ.^{v}) 14 March 1687; v. 2 dated (2d p.ℓ.^{v}) 15 Apr. 1688.
    "Von den Americanischen Sprachen": v.2, p. 1144-1147.
    Imperfect: v.3 wanting; data from copy in The New York Public Library.
    JCB(2)2:1338; Sabin30278; Palmer333; Muller (1878)734; Scheepvaart Mus.640.
06405, before 1874

FC650 Hollandse Mercurius, Verhalende de voor-
H737   naemste Saken van Staet, En andere Voor-
37   vallen, Die in en omtrent de Vereenigde Nederlanden, En elders in Europa, In het Jaer 1686 Zijn geschiet. Het Seven-en-Dertigste Deel.
    Tot Haerlem, Gedruckt by Abraham Casteleyn, Stads-Drucker, op de Marckt, in de Blye Druck. Anno 1687.
    3 p.ℓ., 250, [5] p. 3 plates. 20cm. 4°
    (Bound in [vol. 9] of Hollandse Mercurius)
    Added t.-p., engraved: Hollandse Mercurius A°.1686, Tot Haerlem by Abraham Casteleyn.
    JCB(3)2:410; Sabin32523.
8487KK, 1912

DA687 Keith, George, 1639?-1716.
K28b   The Benefit, Advantage, and Glory of Silent Meetings ... By George Keith.
    London, Printed, by Andrew Sowle, in the Year 1687.
    27 p. 18.5cm. 4°
    "Post-Script. The Copy of a Letter written from Germany, by Stephen Crisp..." (p. 24-27).
    First pub. London, 1670.
    Wing K145; Smith(Friends)2:19; McAlpin4:250.
8390, 1912

DA688 Keith, George, 1639?-1716.
K28f   Concerning Prayer. I. Some Questions answered. II. Some Reasons given, why all Prayer in Words, whether only conceived in the Heart, or uttered and expressed by the Mouth, should be by the help of the Holy Spirit, helping us to conceive those Words. III. Some Objections or seeming Reasons brought, for using set Forms of Prayer, read out of a Book; as if that reading were Prayer, Answered: Also a few Words con-

cerning Singing or Praising God with a Psalm. By G. K.

[London] Printed in the Year 1687.

5 p.ℓ., 6, 17-128 p. 15cm. 8° (Issued as a part of his The fundamental truths of Christianity, London, 1688.)

McAlpin4:250; cf. WingK168; cf. Smith(Friends) 2:23; cf. McAlpin4:292.

11475A, 1918

E702 Korte, Beknopte, en Nette Beschryving, Van de
H515n Koningrijken Hungarien, Dalmatien, en Morea. Mitsgaders de Vorstendommen Zeevenbergen, Walachien, Moldavien, Bulgarien &c. En der zelver Vestingen en Steeden. Nevens een omstandig Verhaal; van het geene, dat omtrent, en zedert de Verovering van Offen, door der Christenden Wapenen is ingenomen.

t'Amsterdam, By Aart Dirksz. Ooszaan, Boekverkooper op den Dam. M.DC.LXXXVII.

32, 84, 115 p. 25.5cm. 4°

Imprint covered by label: t'Amsterdam... [mutilated].

Bound with Hennepin, Louis. Nieuwe ontdekkinge, Amsterdam, 1702.

06007-2, before 1870

A68 [Lea, Philip] d. 1700.
Le   An Alphabet Of Africa And The Parts
4   Adjacent: By Which, With much Ease and
Map Readiness may be found any Kingdom, Country, City, Town, &c. in the Map. ...

London, Printed by H.[enry] C.[lark] for John Overton at the White-Horse without Newgate. Collected by Philip Lea, Globe-maker, at the Atlas and Hercules, near the Corner of Friday-street, in Cheap-side. [1687?]

2 sheets. 50.5 x 34.5cm. 1°

Caption title; imprint at end.
Sheets are printed on one side only.
Tables, sheet [1] formed into 2 vertical sections, each with 4 columns; sheet [2] formed into 3 horizontal sections, top and middle sections each with 8 columns, bottom section with 4 columns.

Issued to accompany his A new mapp of Africa, London, J. Overton and P. Lea [1687?]

A68 ——————Another copy. 50.5 x 34.5cm.
Le   TC II336.
4(b)
Map

C-0034 index
C-6504 index

A68 [Lea, Philip] d. 1700.
Le   An Alphabet of America, and the Parts
1   Adjacent: By which, with much ease and
Map readiness may be found any Country, City, Town, &c. in the Map. ...

[London, 1687?]
1 sheet. 50 x 34.5cm. 1°
Caption title.
Printed on one side only.
Tables formed into 2 vertical sections, each with 4 columns.

Issued to accompany his A new mapp of America, London, P. Lea and I. Overton [1687?]

Bookseller's advertisement at end.

A68   ——————Another copy. 50 x 34.5cm.
Le(b) TC II336
1
Map

C-0031 index
C-6501 index

A68 [Lea, Philip] d. 1700.
Le   An Alphabet of Asia, and the Parts
3   Adjacent: By which, with much ease and
Map readiness may be found any Kingdom, Country, City, Town, &c. in the Map. ...

London, Printed by H.[enry] C.[lark] for John Overton, at the White-Horse without Newgate, and collected by Phillip Lea Globemaker, at che [sic] Atlas and Hercules in Cheap-side, next to the Corner of Friday-street. [1687?]

2 sheets. 50 x 35cm. 1°
Caption title; imprint at end.
Sheets are printed on one side only.
Tables, sheet [1] formed into 2 vertical sections, each with 4 columns; sheet [2] formed into 3 horizontal sections, each with 9 columns.

Issued to accompany his A new mapp of Asia, London, I. Overton and P. Lea [1687?]

A68   ——————Variant. 50 x 35cm.
Le   Imprint reads "... at che [sic] Atlas ...
3(b) Friday-streee [sic]."
Map   TC II336.

C-0033 index
C-6503 index

A68 [Lea, Philip] d. 1700.
Le   An Alphabet of Europe, and the Parts
2   Adjacent. By which, with much ease and
Map readiness may be found any Kingdom,

Province, City, Town, &c. in the Map. ...
London, Printed by H.[enry] Clark, for Philip Lea, Globemaker, at the Atlas and Hercules in the Poultrey against the Old-Jury, where you may have the other three Quarters 1687.
2 sheets. 50 x 35cm. 1°
Caption title; imprint at end.
Sheets are printed on one side only.
Tables, sheet[1] formed into 2 vertical sections, left section with 5 columns, right section with 6 columns; sheet[2] formed into 3 horizontal sections, each with 12 columns.
Issued to accompany his <u>A new mapp of Europe</u>, London, P. Lea and I. Overton [1687?]

A68
Le
2(b)
Map
——— ———Variant. 1 sheet. 50 x 35cm.
Same text printed on the two sides of the sheet.
TC II 200, 336.

C-0032 index
C-6502 index

DA687
L481c
Lee, Samuel, 1625-1691.
Χαρα' της Πιςεως   The Joy of Faith, Or A Treatise Opening the true Nature of Faith, its lowest Stature and Distinction from Assurance, with a Scripture Method to attain both; by the Influence and Aid of Divine Grace: with a preliminary Tract evidencing the Being and actings of Faith, the Deity of Christ, and the Divinity of the Sacred Scriptures. ... By Samuel Lee. M.A. Sometime Fellow of Wadham Colledge. Oxon.
Boston, Printed by Samuel Green. 1687.
9 p.ℓ., 247 p., 1 ℓ. 15.5cm. 8°
"Epistle dedicatory" signed (4th p.ℓ.^{v}): Abbots Langly Jan. 16. 1685. Samuel Lee.
Errata, last leaf.
In this copy there is a blank ℓ. at beginning and at end.
Evans429; Sabin39796; WingL819.

4395, 1908

BA687
-L525v
Leiba, Diego de.
Virtvdes, Y Milagros En Vida, Y Muerte Del Venerable Padre Fr. Sebastian De Aparicio, Religioso Lego De La Regvlar Observancia de nuestro Serafico Padre San Francisco, è hijo de la Provincia del Santo Evangelio de Mexico, en la Nueva España, que floreciò en el Convento de la Puebla de los Angeles. ... Por El R. P. Fr. Diego De Leyba, Predicador, Pro-Ministro de la misma Provincia del Santo Evangelio, y Procura-
dor en la Curia Romana de la Canonizacion del dicho Siervo de Dios.
Con Privilegio. Y por su Original Impresso en Sevilla. [Madrid? 1687?].
7 p.ℓ., 387 p. port. 28.5cm. fol.
First pub. Seville, 1687.
"Tassa" dated (4th p.ℓ.^{r}) Madrid, 10 Apr. 1687.
Errata, 4th p.ℓ.^{r}
Bound in contemporary vellum.

11834, 1919

EA687
L646d
[Le Tellier, Michel] 1643-1719.
Defense Des Nouveaux Chrestiens Et Des Missionnaires de la Chine, du Japon, & des Indes. Contre deux Livres intitulez La Morale Pratique Des Jesuites, Et L'Esprit De M. Arnauld.
A Paris, Chez Estienne Michallet, premier Imprimeur du Roy, ruë S. Jacques, à l'Image S. Paul. M.DC.LXXXVII. Avec Approbation & Privilege de Sa Majesté.
28 p.ℓ., 568,[8] p. illus. 18.5cm. 12°
Bears designation (p. 568) "Fin de la premiere Partie."
A reply to La morale pratique des Jésuites, v.1-2, Cologne, 1669-1683, by Sébastien Joseph de Coislin du Cambout, abbé de Pontchâteau, and Antoine Arnauld and to Pierre Jurrieu's L'Esprit de M. Arnauld, Deventer, 1684.
"Achevé d'imprimer pour la premiere fois le 15. Novembre 1687." (28th p.ℓ.)
Errata, 28th p.ℓ.^{v}, p. 568.
Bound in contemporary calf.
Streit5:2570; Backer7:1913; cf. Palau(2) 69677n.

69-25

D. Math
I.130A
Mather, Increase, 1639-1723.
A Testimony Against several Prophane and Superstitious Customs, Now Practised by some in New-England, The Evil whereof is evinced from the Holy Scriptures, and from the Writings both of Ancient and Modern Divines. By Increase Mather, Teacher of a Church in Boston, and Rector of Harvard Colledge at Cambridge in New-England. ...
London: Printed in the Year, 1687.
4 p.ℓ., 23, 34-41 p. 18.5cm. 8°
Written against stage plays, health-drinking, gambling, Christmas celebrations, and the celebration of other holidays.
"The Preface" dated (4th p.ℓ.^{v}) 30 Oct 1686.
Evans451; Sabin46752; Wing M1256; Holmes (I)130A.

30954, 1951

D687 More, Nicholas, d. 1689.
M836l   A Letter From Doctor More, With Passages out of several Letters from Persons of good Credit. Relating to the State and Improvement of the Province of Pennsilvania. Published to prevent false Reports.
    [London?] Printed in the Year 1687.
    11 p. 19.5cm. 4°.
    Preface (p. 3) signed: William Penn.
    "A Letter from Dr. More. Honored Governour...Green-Spring the 13th of September, 1686. ... Nicholas More." (p. 4-7).
    Other letters (p. 8-11) from "the Governors Steward," "the Governers Gardiner," Robert Turner, David Lloyd, Thomas Holmes, James Claypole.
    JCB(2)2:1339; Church701; Vail(Front.)257; WingM2684.
03656, before 1866

F687 [Muys van Holy, Nicolaas] 1653 or 4-1717.
M993m   Middelen en motiven om het kopen en verkopen van Oost- en West-Indische actien, die niet getransporteert werden, mitsgaders ook die de verkoper ten dage van den verkoop niet in eigendom heeft, als mede optie partyen der actien, te beswaren met een Impost, ten behoeve van het gemeene Land en de stad Amsterdam.
    Gedrukt tot Amsterdam: 1687.
    8 p. 22cm. 4°
    Signed (at end): Nicolaes Muys van Holy.
    Caption title; imprint at end.
    Sabin51613; Muller(1872)438; Knuttel 12622.
69-267

H687 [Nigrisoli, Francesco Maria] 1648-1727, ed.
N689f   Febris China Chinæ Expvgnata, Sev Illvstrivm Aliqvot Virorvm Opvscvla, Quæ veram tradunt Methodum, Febres China Chinæ Cvrandi. ... Collegit, argumenta, notas, obseruationes addidit Med. Ferrariensis.
    Ferrariæ, M.DC.LXXXVII. Typis Bernardini Pomatelli. Superiorum permissu.
    xvi, 204 p. 2 plates. 24cm. 4°
    Cut on t.-p.
    A collection of works on Cinchona or quinine, consisting of works by Nicolas de Blégny (1st pub. Paris, 1680, under title: La découverte de l'admirable remède anglois pour la guérison des fièvres), François de Monginot (1st pub. Lyon, 1679, under title: Traité de la guérison des fièvres par le quinquina), Raymond Restaurand (1st pub. Lyon, 1681, under title: Hippocrate; de l'usage du China-China pour la guérison des fièvres) and Jacob Spon (1st pub. Lyon,

1681, under title: Observations sur les fièvres et les fébrifuges).
    Melzi 1:399; Waring 339.
70-582

C619 Paiva, Sebastião da Fonseca e, 1625-1705.
A949n   Relaçam Da Feliz Chegada Da Serenissima Senhora D. Maria Sofia Isabel, Raynha de Portugal, à Cidade, & Corte de Lisboa, em 11. de Agosto de 1687. & descripçaõ da ponte da Casa da India. ... Por Sebastião de Affonseca, & Payva, Freire Conventual do Convento Real de Palmela, da Ordem de Sanct-Iago da Espada, & Mestre da Capella no Hospital Real de todos os Santos.
    Lisboa. Com todas as licenças necessarias. Na Officina de Domingos Carneyro. M.DC.-LXXX.VII.
    16 p. 19.5cm. 4°
    In verse.
    Dedication (p. 3) dated 4 Sept. 1687.
    Bound as the 9th in a volume of 58 pamphlets, 1619-1702.
    Innocencio7:207.
9350, 1913

BA687 Palafox y Mendoza, Juan de, Bp., 1600-1659.
P153v   Vida Interior Del Excelentissimo Señor Don
[R] Jvan De Palafox Y Mendoza, Obispo Antes De La Puebla De Los Angeles, Virrey, y Capitan General de la Nueva España. Visitador De Tres Virreyes De Ella, Arzobispo Electo De Mexico, de el Consejo Supremo de Aragon. La Qval Vida El Mismo Señor Obispo dexò escrita.
    En Barcelona: Por Antonio Ferrer, y Compañia, con las licencias ordinarias, Año de 1687.
    4 p.l., 327 p. 20cm. 4°
    First pub. Brussels, 1682.
    Preliminary matter includes poetry.
    Bound in contemporary vellum.
    Palau(2)209800; Medina(BHA)1804; Sabin 99456n.
69-797

DA687 Penn, William, 1644-1718.
-P412s   The Speech Of William Penn To His Majesty, Upon His Delivering the Quakers Address.
    [London, 1687]
    2 p. 30cm. fol.
    Caption title.

70-49
    Includes (p. 2) "His Majesties most Gracious Answer."
    Occasioned by the Declaration of Indulgence, 4 April 1687.
    Also issued under title "Mr. Penn's speech to the king" with imprint "London, Printed for J. H. and T. S. ... 1687".
    Wing P1372A; Smith(Friends)2:304.

DA687
P412t

[Penn, William] 1644-1718.
    A Third Letter From a Gentleman in the Country, To his Friends in London, Upon the Subject of the Penal Laws and Tests.
    Licensed, May the 16th 1687. London, Printed, for J. H. and T. S. and to be had of most Booksellers in London and Westminster. 1687.
    19 p. 20cm. 4°
    Wing P1381; Smith(Friends)2:304; McAlpin 4:257.

67-340

bBB
P4716
1687
1

Peru(Viceroyalty)--Laws, statutes, etc., 1681-1689 (Navarra y Rocafull)   1687
    Aranzel De Los Jornales, Que Se Han De Pagar A Los Indios assi voluntarios, Mingados, Alquilas, y agregados à las Haziendas de Españoles, como Mitayos, y de obligacion, en todo genero de trabajo. ...
    [Lima, 1687]
    1 p.l., 13 numb. l. 32cm. fol.
    Dated in "Ciudad de los Reyes", 1687, with blanks for insertion of day and month.
    With ms. signature: El duque de la Palata.
    Royal coat of arms at head of title.
    Medina(Lima)593; Palau(2)14736.

28201, 1938

E687
P489p

Petit, Pierre, 1617-1687.
    Petri Petiti, Philosophi, & Doct. Medici De Amazonibus Dissertatio, Quâ an verè extiterint, necne, variis ultro citroque conjecturis & argumentis disputatur. ... Editio Secunda, Auctior & Correctior.
    Amstelodami, Apud < Johannem Wolters & Ysbrandum Haring, > 1687.
    6 p.l., 398, [399-401], [8] p. illus., fold. map. 16.5cm. 12°
    Cut (Rahir fleuron 87) on t.-p.
    Added t.-p., engr., signed by Joannes van den Avele, 1687.
    First pub. Paris, 1685.
    The subject is treated in terms of evidence from classical and medieval authorities.
    In this copy the "Index Rerum Memorabilium ..." ([8] p.) is misbound among the preliminary leaves (as printed) instead of at end.
    Sabin 61256.

71-06

C585
E96t
13

[Puccini, Vincenzio]
    The Life Of S.t Mary Magdalene Of Pazzi, A Carmelite Nunn. Newly translated out of Italian by the Reverend Father Lezin de Sainte Scholastique, Provincial of the Reformed Carmelites of Touraine. At Paris, For Sebast. Cramoisy in St. James's Street, at the Sign of Fame. 1670. And now done out of French: With a preface concerning the nature, causes, concomitants, and consequences of Ecstasy and Rapture, and a brief discourse added about discerning and trying the Spirits, whether they be of God.
    London, Printed; And are to be sold by Randal Taylor near Stationers Hall. 1687.
    2 p.l., 134 p., 1 l. 20cm. 4°.
    Errata: recto of final leaf.
    English transl. first pub. London, 1670.
    Transl. by Thomas Smith, D.D., who also wrote the anti-papist Preface (p. 1-33), and "A brief discourse..." which follows the 'Life'.
    The 'Life' (p. [35]-84) has a separate t.-p., transl. from the t.-p. of the French edition, Paris, 1670.
    "Imprimatur" dated (2d p.l.v) 9 July 1687.
    Bound as the 13th of 19 items in a volume with binder's title: Tracts 1681-1701.
    Wing P4158.

11352-13, 1918

B687
-R173m

Ramírez de Arellano, José.
    Memorial, Y Discvrso Informativo, Qve Presenta Al Rey N.o Señor En Sv Real Y Svpremo Consejo De Las Indias, Por La Provincia De Venezvela, y Encomenderos de Indios de todas las Ciudades de ella, El Sargento Mayor Don Joseph Ramirez de Arellano, su Procurador General en esta Corte. Sobre La prompta execucion dada à la Real Cedula de su Magestad de 20. de Iunio de 1686. en que se prohibe el seruicio personal de los Indios: ...
    [Madrid? 1687?]
    1 p.l., 28 numb. l., [2] p. 29cm. fol.
    "Avtos, E Instrvmentos Qve Se presentan con este Memorial", p. [1-2] at end.
    Palau(2)246936; Vindel 2354.

13766, 1924

E687   Relation D'Un Grand Combat Donné Dans La
R382d   Nouvelle France Entre Les Troupes Du
        Roy Et Les Iroquois.
          [Bordeaux, Lacourt, 1687?]
          7 p. 23.5cm. (24.5cm. in case). 4°
          Caption title.
          An account of the expedition of the marquis
        de Denonville from June to July 1687.
          Booksellers' advertisement, p. 7: Le Sieur
        Lacourt le jeune, Libraire, au Grand Marché,
        donne toûjours à lire chez lui la Gazette d'
        Hollande... & autres Livres..."
          JCBAR 16:9.
10925, 1916

C619   Ribeiro Coutinho, Paschoal, d. 1729.
A949n   Arco Triunfal Idea, E Allegoria, Sobre a
        Fabula de Paris em o Monte Ida. Cuja Ficçam
        Ha De Servir Para o Arco Triunfal, que a Rua
        dos Ourives do Ouro celebra, em applauso dos
        felicissimos Desposorios das Augustas, &
        Lusitanas Magestades. Descreve-A Pascoal
        Ribeiro Coutinho.
          Lisboa. Com todas as licenças necessarias.
        Na Officina de Miguel Manescal, Impressor
        do Sancto Officio. Anno de 1687.
          14 p. 19.5cm. 4°
          Cut (royal arms) on t.-p.
          Includes poetry.
          In this copy there is a blank ℓ. at end.
          Bound as the 10th in a volume of 58
        pamphlets, 1619-1702.
          Innocencio 6:353.
9351, 1913

BA687   [Ripalda, Gerónimo de] 1536?-1618.
R588d   [Doctrina Christiana, traducida de la Lengua
        Castellana, en Lengua Zapoteca Nexitza. Con
        otras addiciones vtiles, y necessarias para la
        educacon Catholica y exitacion a la devocion
        Christiana. Por D. Francisco Pacheco de Sylva,
        Cura Beneficiado presentado por su Magestad de
        el Partido de S. Juan Yahee, y Taneche. Dedica
        este Corto trabajo á la Emperatriz de los Cielos
        Nuestra Señora la siempre Virgen Maria.
          Mexico, 1687]
          28 p.ℓ., 135 [+] numb. ℓ. 14cm. 8°
          Text in Spanish and Zapotec in parallel
        columns.
          Transl. from: Doctrina Christiana, con una
        exposicion breve, 1st pub. Burgos, 1591.
          License dated (15th p.ℓ.ᵛ) 27 May 1687.
          Imperfect: t.-p. and ℓ. 136-[140?] wanting;
        data from Ugarte. No perfect copy known.
          Bound in contemporary vellum.
          Palau(2)269101; Medina(Mexico)1400; Pilling
        2871; Ugarte279; Backer6:1869.
06260, before 1902 (1884?)

BA687   Robles, Juan de, 1628-1697.
R666s   Sermon Del Gloriossissimo Patriarcha, Padre
        existimado del Hijo Vnigenito de Dios. Esposo
        dignissimo de la Madre del Eterno Verbo huma-
        nado. Nvestro Señor San Joseph. Predicado En
        Sv Dia En El Colegio del Espiritu Santo de la
        Compañia de Jesvs de la Ciudad de la Puebla de
        los Angeles, este año de 1687. Dixòlo El Padre
        Jvan De Robles, Professo de la misma Compañia.
        ...
          Con Licencia De Los Svperiores. En Mexico:
        por Doña Maria de Benavides, Viuda de Juan de
        Ribera, En el Empedradillo. Año de 1687.
          6 p.ℓ., 8 numb. ℓ. 19.5cm. 4°
          License dated (6th p.ℓ.ᵛ) 20 Aug. 1687.
          Palau(2)271182; Medina(Mexico)1401; Backer
        6:1926.
4921, 1908

H687   Terra Rossa, Vitale.
T323r   Riflessioni Geografiche Circa Le Terre
        Incognite Distese in ossequio perpetuo della
        Nobiltà Veneziana, Nelle quali I. Si pruoua,
        che i Patrizi di Venezia prima d'ogni altro
        hanno all'Italia, & all'Europa, discoperte
        tutte le Terre anticamente Incognite, anco
        l'America, e la Terra Australe. II. Si
        desidera vna esatta, e perfetta Concordia
        della vecchia, e nuoua Geografia, in onore
        de' Signori Veneziani. III. Si difende contra
        il moderno Braudrand [sic], che niuno infra
        i racconti Geografici, dagli stessi Gentiluo-
        mini dell'Adria publicati, è stato finto, ò
        fauoloso. ... Dal P. D. Vitale Terra Rossa
        da Parma, Priore Casinense di Lerino, Dot-
        tore di Filos. e Teol. già Publico Lettore nell'
        Vniuersità di Bologna, ed ora Filosofo Ordinario
        in quella di Padoua.
          In Padova, MDCLXXXVII Per il Cadorino, Con
        licenza de' Sup. Et Privilegio Del Serenissimo
        Senato.
          16 p.ℓ., 298, [10] p. incl. port. 24cm. 4°
          Cut on t.-p., incl. caption: Pace.
          The same sheets were also issued with variant
        imprint "...MDCLXXXVI...Privilegio Del...
        Principe."
          Dedication dated (13th p.ℓ.ʳ) 2 June 1686.
          Defends the claim of the discovery of America
        by the brothers Zeni in reply to: Michel Antoine
        Baudrand, Geographia ordine litterarum disposita,
        Paris, 1681-1682 [v.1, 1682].
          Errata, p. 298.
          JCB(2)2:1341; Sabin94858.
06245, before 1874

BA687　Traslado De Vna Consvlta Fecha A Los Illvs-
-T775d　trissimos Señores Avxiliares Por El Illvstrissimo Señor Maestro D. Fray Phelippe
Pardo Arzobispo de Manila Metropolitano
destas Islas mi Señor, de las respuestas
de sus Illustrissimas, y de la Prouision
Real, que dió motiuo a dicha consulta, que
manda imprimir su Illustrissima mi Señor
por no dar lugar el tiempo a escriuir los
traslados necessarios.
[Manila, Gaspar de los Reyes, 1687]
145 numb. ℓ. 29cm. fol.
Caption title.
Certification dated at end: Manila, 15 June
1687.
First pub. Manila, 1685, under the same
title but in a shorter version.
Each leaf of this copy bears the manuscript
authentication of the archbishop's secretary
Domingo Diaz as well as his signature at end
along with the signatures of three notaries.
JCBAR66:4; Retana160; Palau(1)7:64n; Medina
(Manila)107n.

66-122

F687　Unerhörter Christen-Verkauff/Das ist/Traurige
U56c　Hinführung der in Banden und Ketten beständig
gewesnen Bekenneren und Bekennerinnen Jesu
Christi/Auss den Französischen Kerkeren in
die Insul Canada in America/allwo sie als
Leibeigne verkauft und den bekandten Gewüs-
senspeinigeren übergeben werden sollen. ...
[Brandenburg (Electorate)?] MDCLXXXVII.
1 p.ℓ., [5] p. 21.5cm. 4º
A translation, with an additional one-page introduction and final paragraph, of: Brief van
seeker Frans Heer, geschreeven uyt Cadix den
17 April 1687, Rotterdam, 1687.
This pub. is perhaps related to the fact that
Frederick William, Elector of Brandenburg,
admitted refugee French Protestants into his
territories after the Revocation of the Edict of
Nantes.
JCBAR55:25-30.

31800, 1955

BA687　Valdés, Rodrigo de, 1609-1682.
V145p　Poema Heroyco Hispano-Latino Panegyrico
De La Fvndacion, Y Grandezas de la muy
Noble, y Leal Ciudad de Lima. Obra Postvma
Del M.R.P.M. Rodrigo De Valdes, de la Com-
pañia De Jesvs, Cathedratico de Prima jubilado,
y Prefecto Regente de Estudios en el Colegio
Maximo de San Pablo. Sacale A La Lvz El Doct.
D. Francisco Garabito de Leon y Messia, Cura-
Rector de la Iglesia Metropolitana de Lima, ...

En Madrid, en la Imprenta de Antonio Roman,
año 1687.
28 p.ℓ., [56], 184, [8] p. 20.5cm. 4º
Preliminary matter includes poetry by
Francisco Cruzado y Aragón, Esteban
Cruzado y Ferrer, Francisco Cruzado y Ferrer,
and Bartolomé Cruzado.
Errata, (12th p.ℓ.ʳ) dated 7 July 1687.
"Carta ... que escriuió ... Francisco del
Quadro, ... en la muerte de el Padre Rodrigo
de Valdès." p. [1-56]
JCB(2)2:1343; Palau(1)7:98; Medina(BHA)1806;
Sabin98322; Backer8:376-377; Zegarra162.

03657, before 1866

B69　Villancicos A Los Maytines, Que Se Han
G643v　De Celebrar El Dia De El Glorioso Apostol,
37　Principe De La Iglesia San Pedro. ...
Con licencia, en Mexico. Por los Herederos de la Viuda de Bernardo Calderon. Año
de 1687.
[8] p.? 23cm. 4º
Imprint at end.
Woodcut title vignette (St. Peter within a
decorative frame).
Fragment: 1st and last leaves only; t.-p.
mutilated.
Bound, in contemporary vellum, as no. 37
with 42 other items.

28937, 1941

F687　Vries, Simon de, b. 1630.
V982w　Wonderen Soo aen als in, En Wonder-Gevallen
Soo op als ontrent De Zeeën, Rivieren, Meiren,
Poelen en Fonteynen: ... verhandeld Door S. De
Vries.
Amsterdam, By Jan ten Hoorn, Boeckverkooper
over 't Oude Heeren-Logiment. MDCLXXXVII.
8 p.ℓ., 688, [53] p. 22.5cm. 4º
Added t.-p., engraved, signed: I. Luyken.
Cut on t.-p.
First pub. Amsterdam, 1667.
"Voor-Beright" dated (8th p.ℓ.ᵛ): "30. der
Wijnmaend O. S. des Jaers 1686."
Errata, 6th p.ℓ.ᵛ - 7th p.ℓ.ʳ.
Imperfect: p. 431-432 wanting; available in
facsim.
Bound in contemporary vellum.
JCB(2)2:1344; Scheepvaart Mus. 716.

03017, 1865

BA687 Xarque, Francisco, 1609-1691.
X2i   Insignes Missioneros De La Compañia De Jesvs
En La Provincia Del Paraguay. Estado Presente
De Sus Missiones En Tucumàn, Paraguay, y Rio
de la Plata, que comprehende su Distrito. Por
El Doct. D. Francisco Xarqve... Que remite, y
consagra à los Religiosos Operarios, y Apostoli-
cos Missioneros, que al presente prosiguen sus
heroycas empressas, Por mano del Rmo. P. y
Sapientissimo Doctor el Padre Thirso Gonçalez
de Santalla, Preposito General, y Atlante de las
Missiones que por todo el Orbe exercita la Reli-
gion amplissima de la Compañia de Jesvs.
En Pamplona, por Juan Micòn, Impressor.
Año 1687.
12 p. ℓ., 217, 220-432 p. 21.5cm. 4°
Errata, 11th p. ℓ.ᵛ-12th p. ℓ.ʳ.
"Tassa" statement dated (12th p. ℓ.ᵛ) 29 Dec. 1687.
Contents.—bk. 1, life of Simon Maceta.—bk.
2, life of Francisco Diaz Taño.—bk. 3, "El
Estado Qve Al Presente gozan las Missiones..."
JCB(2)2:1345; Sabin105716; Medina(BHA)1808;
Streit2:2236; Backer11:1349; Borba de Moraes2:382.
0804, 1846

1688

BA688   Alvarez de Toledo, Domingo.
-A473c Copia De La Espantosa Carta, Escrita Por
el P. Fr. Domingo Albarez de Toledo, Procurador General de Corte, del Orden de N. P. S.
Francisco, embiada desde la Ciudad de Lima,
al Rᵐᵒ P. Comissaeio [sic] General en Este
charque, que su fecha es de 29. de Octubre de
1687. años, dandole quenta de los lastimosos
estragos, y desgracias que han sucedido en
dicha Ciudad.
[Barcelona?] Publicado oy Viernes, à dos
de Iulio de este año de 1688.
[4] p. 31cm. fol.
Caption title; imprint at end.
An account of the earthquake in Lima,
20 Oct. 1687.
Another issue of this text pub. Barcelona,
Vicente Suriá, 1688, is recorded at Medina
(BHA)1809 and Sabin 644.
For a ms. version of the text cf. Maffei
64 (repeated Medina(Lima)602n).
In this copy the lower margins are repaired,
affecting one line of text on p. [2].
32612, 1960

BA688   Alvarez de Toledo, Domingo.
A473cv Copy van een Brief, Die den Pater Fr.
Domingo Alvares de Toledo, Procureur Gen.
van 't Hof, van Sᵗᵉ. Franciscus Order, Aen den
Commissaris Generael binnen dese Provineie [sic],
geschreven heeft, in dato den 29 October 1687.
Aengaende het verdestrueren der Stadt Lima, in
America.
[Antwerp?] Anno 1688.
8 p. 19.5cm. 4°
Cut on t.-p.
Transl. from: Copia de la espantosa carta,
[Barcelona?] 1688.
JCB(2)2:1365; Sabin972; Knuttel 12677.
02312, 1850

D688   An Answer By An Anabaptist To The Three
A626a   Considerations Proposed to Mr William Penn,
By a pretended Baptist, Concerning A Magna
Charta For Liberty of Conscience. Allowed
to be Published this 10th Day of September,
1688.
London. Printed in the Year MDCLXXXVIII.
14 p. 21cm. 4°.
A reply to [Thomas Comber] Three Consider-
ations proposed to Mr. William Pen. [London,
1688].
In this copy there is a blank ℓ. at end.
JCB(2)2:1346; Smith(Anti-Quak)25; McAlpin4:272;
Wing A3275.
03659, before 1866

BA688   Arequipa, Peru (Diocese)--Synod, 1684.
-A681c Constitvciones Synodales, del Obispado
de Arequipa. Hechas, Y Ordenadas Por
El Ilvstrissimo y Reuerendissimo Señor
Doctor Don Antonio de Leon su Obispo,
del Consejo de su Magestad. En La Synodo
Diocessana Qve Celebro Año de 1684.
En Lima por Ioseph de Contreras Año de
1688.
2 p. ℓ., 103 numb. ℓ., 15 ℓ. 30cm. fol.
Cuts (the Virgin; bishop's coat of arms)
on t.-p.
License dated (2d p. ℓ.ᵛ) 15 June 1686.
Palau(2)60182; Medina(Lima)607; Sabin
16069; Streit2:2249.
68-168

G688
L257s
[Ari Thorgilsson, Fródi] 1068?-1148.
Schedæ Ara Prestz Froda Vm Island. Prentadar i Skalhollte af Hendrick Kruse. Anno 1688.
1 p.ℓ., 14, [8] p. incl. illus. 20cm. 4°
Also known under title: Islendingabók.
Preliminary matter (p.ℓ.^{v}) by Thórdur Thorláksson, dated in Skálholt 1 May 1688.
With ms. annotations.
See Hermannsson, Halldór, Icelandic books of the seventeenth century, Ithaca, New York, p. 4.
Bound (as the 2d of 4 items) with 3 other works printed in Skálholt by Hendrik Kruse, 1688: Landnámabók. Sagan Landnama ... —Kristnisaga. Christendoms saga ... —Jónsson, Arngrímur. Gronlandia, edur Grænlandz saga ...
JCBAR41:14-20; Sabin34158.

28998, 1941

BA688
A951s
Avendaño Suares de Sousa, Pedro de, b. ca. 1654.
Sermon Qve En La Fiesta Titvlar Qve Celebra La Compañia de Bethlem en su Hospital de Convalecientes de aquesta Ciudad de Mexico. Predicó El P. Pedro De Avendaño de la Compañia de Iesvs. A veinte y siete de Diziembre, tercero de Pasqua de Navidad, dia del Evangelista S. Jvan. Patente el Santissimo Sacramento. Año de 1687. Sacanlo à luz dos devotos benefactores de el Hospital de Convalecientes de Mexico.
Con Licencia De Los Svperiores, En Mexico: por Doña Maria de Benavides, Viuda de Juan de Ribera. En el Empedradillo. Año de 1688.
6 p.ℓ., 12 numb. ℓ. 20.5cm. 4°
Dedication (2d-3d p.ℓ.) signed: El Prefecto, y Sujetos de la Compañia de Bethlem de Mexico.
License dated (6th p.ℓ.^{r}) 20 Feb. 1688.
Palau(2)20148; Medina(Mexico)1406; Backer 1:683.

12894, 1921

BA688
A958c
Avila, Juan de, fl. 1684.
Coronado Non Plvs Vltra Franciscano. El Santo Cardenal de Albania S. Bvenaventvra. Sermon, Que en la fiesta, que le celebró, en el Convento de Tepetitlan El P. Predicador, y Guardian Fr. Alonso De Avila, Predicó El R.P. Fr. Ivan De Avila, Y Rosas, Predicador General Iubilado, Calificador del S. Officio, y Hermano de el dicho P. Guardian. ...
Con Licencia De Los Svperiores: En Mexico: por Doña Maria de Benavides, Viuda de Juan de Ribera En el Empedradillo. Año de 1688.

6 p.ℓ., 15 numb. ℓ. 19.5cm. 4°
Approbation dated (5th p.ℓ.^{r}) 20 May 1688.
Medina(Mexico)1408; Palau(2)20465.

68-422

BA688
A958s
Avila, Juan de, fl. 1684.
Sagrado Notariaco. Mexoras De La Pvebla, Civdad de la Purissima. Panegirico En el tercero dia del Novenario, que se hizo à la Dedicacion Solemne del Templo de la Concepcion de Maria SS. con el superlativo renombre Purissima, que antes fue de San Christobal, y era, y es, Casa de los niños expuestos, desamparados. Predicólo Fl [sic] R. P. Fr. Jvan De Avila, Y Rosas, Predicador General Jubilado, Calificador del S. Officio, y humilde Religioso de S. Francisco. ...
Con Licencia De Los Svperiores: En Mexico: por Doña Maria de Benavides, Viuda de Juan de Ribera En el Empedradillo. Año de 1688.
8 p.ℓ., 19 numb. ℓ., 1 ℓ. 19.5cm. 4°
Approbation dated (5th p.ℓ.^{r}) 29 March 1688.
Palau(2)20466; Medina(Mexico)1407.

69-757

BA688
-A977s
Ayeta, Francisco de.
Señor. Fray Francisco de Ayeta, Ex-Custodio, y Padre de la S. Provincia de Mexico, y Procurador General de todas las de las Indias, dize: Que estando à cargo de la Religiõ las Conversiones del Rio Verde, Panuco, y Tampico, en que se exercitan sus Religiosos, procurando la reduccion de los Indios Chichimecos. ...
[Madrid? ca. 1688]
[11] p. 30.5cm. fol.
Title from caption and beginning of text.
Cites document (p. [10]) dated 7 Nov. 1688.
"Memorial, Tocante A Qve El Azeyte Qve su Magestad manda dar de limosna para alumbrar el Santissimo Sacramento, en los Conventos de la Prouincia de Xalisco, se entregue à la Religion, sin interuencion alguna del Diocesano": p. [5-8].
"Representacion Hecha A Nvestro Reverendissimo Padre Comissario General de las Indias; quenta que se diò al Consejo, y su resolucion, en orden à lleuar vna Mission à la Prouincia de Nicaragua, con ciertas condiciones, &c.": p. [8-11].

5050, 1909

BA688
-A977sf

Ayeta, Francisco de.
  Señor. Fray Francisco De Ayeta, Ex-Custodio, y Padre de la Santa Provincia del Santo Evangelio de Mexico, y Procurador General de todas las de las Indias, dize: Que por dos Reales Cedulas, sus datas de 24. de Septiembre de 1688 ...
  [Madrid? 1688?]
  58 numb. ℓ. 30cm. fol.
  Title from caption and beginning of text.
  Concerns Franciscan doctrinas in the Province of Zacatecas.
  Palau(2)20800(this copy?)

70-579

F688
B566i

Beughem, Cornelius à, fl. 1678-1710.
  Incunabula Typographiæ Notitiam exhibentia. Catalogus Librorum Scriptorumque proximis ab inventione Typographiæ annis, usque ad Annum Christi M.D. inclusive, in quavis linguâ editiorum: ubi simul etiam exhibentur, de quibus non constat, quo præcise anno sint impressi; cum appendice Anonymorum. ... Corneli à Beughem Embric.
  Amstelodami, Apud Joannem Wolters 1688.
  6 p. ℓ., 168, 171-191 p. 13.5cm. 12°
  Cut on t.-p. (armillary sphere; Rahir marque 61 but with terminal of stem present, not shown by Rahir).
  Dedication dated (2d p. ℓ.ᵛ) Nov. 1687.
  In this copy there is a blank leaf at end.
  Rahir 2850.

64-127

DA688
B582p
[R]

Bible--O.T.--Psalms--English--Paraphrases--1688--Bay Psalm Book.
  The Psalms, Hymns, And Spiritual Songs of the Old and New Testament, faithfully translated into English Meeter. For the Use, Edification and Comfort of the Saints in publick and private, especially in New-England. ... The Sixth Edition.
  London, Printed for Richard Chiswell at the Rose and Crown in St. Paul's Church-yard. 1688.
  6 p. ℓ., 84 p. 15.5cm. 12°
  Bay Psalm book; 1st pub. Cambridge, Mass., 1640.
  Bound in contemporary calf.

68-381

DA688
B582b

Bible--O.T.--Psalms--Hebrew--1688.
  ... The Book of Psalmes With the New English Translation, Published By John Leusden, Professor of the Hebrew tongue in the University of Utrecht.
  London, Printed by Samuel Smith [i.e. Utrecht?], and are to be fold [sic] by him at his Shop in the sign of the Princes Armes in S. Pauls Church-Yard, 1688.
  4 p. ℓ., 240 numb. ℓ., [4] p. 13cm. 12°
  Title in Hebrew at head of title.
  Cut (cupidon on bough) on t.-p.
  Text in Hebrew and English on opposite pages.
  Paged from right to left.
  Also issued with imprint: Printed at Utrecht by John van de Water, 1688.
  The same setting of the Hebrew type (and of a table at the end of the book) was used for other editions of the Psalms edited by Leusden: Liber Psalmorum in Hebrew and Latin, which was issued with London and Utrecht imprints dated 1688, and Het Hebreus Psalmboeck in Hebrew and Dutch, which was issued with a Utrecht imprint dated 1688. Leusden had previously edited the Psalms in Hebrew in an edition of the Old Testament in Hebrew (1st pub. 1661) and in an edition of the Psalms alone in Hebrew (1st pub. 1666) which were issued in Amsterdam by Joseph Athias.
  Dedicated to John Eliot and to "the Twenty Four American [i.e. Indian] Ministers. Lately Gentiles but now converted to the Christian Religion (by the Grace of God, and Labour of the Reverend John Eliot ...)".
  The preface refers to Increase Mather and his letter to Leusden pub. under title De successu evangelii.
  Preface dated (4th p. ℓ.ᵛ) 15 Mar. 1688.
  JCB(2)2:1358; Wing B2744; Sabin 66452.

04635, before 1882

FA688
B582h

Bible--O.T.--Psalms--Hebrew--1688.
  ... Het Hebreus Psalmboeck Met de Nieuwe Nederlantsche oversettinge, Uytgegeven Door Johannes Leusden Professor der Heylige Tale in de Universiteyt tot Urecht [sic].
  t'Utrecht, By Johannes van de Water, A. cIɔ Iɔ c LXXXVIII.
  4 p. ℓ., 240 numb. ℓ., [4] p. 13cm. 12°
  Title in Hebrew at head of title.
  Cut (cupidon on bough) on t.-p.
  Text in Hebrew and Dutch on opposite pages.
  Paged from right to left.
  The same setting of the Hebrew type (and of a table at the end of the book) was used for other editions of the Psalms edited by Leusden: Liber Psalmorum in Hebrew and Latin, which was issued with London and Utrecht imprints dated 1688, and The Book of Psalmes in Hebrew and English, which also was issued with London and Utrecht imprints dated 1688. Leusden had previously edited the Psalms in Hebrew in an

edition of the Old Testament in Hebrew (1st pub. 1661) and in an edition of the Psalms alone in Hebrew (1st pub. 1666) which were issued in Amsterdam by Joseph Athias.
Preface contains references to Increase Mather and John Eliot.
Preface dated (4th p. $\ell.^v$) 15 Mar. 1688.
JCBAR21:12; Muller(1877)2057; Sabin66454n.

13116, 1921

FA688 Bible--O.T.--Psalms--Hebrew--1688.
B582ℓ ... Liber Psalmorum, Editus A Johanne Leusden, Linguæ Sanctæ in Academia Ultrajectina Professore Ordinario.
Londini, [i.e. Utrecht?] Sumptibus Samuelis Smith, ad insigne Principis in Cæmiterio D. Pauli. A. 1688.
8 p., 240 numb. ℓ., [4] p. 13.5cm. 12°
Title in Hebrew at head of title.
Cut (cupidon on bough) on t.-p.
Text in Hebrew and Latin on opposite pages.
Paged from right to left.
Also issued with imprints: Utrecht, B. Lobee, 1688; Utrecht W. vande Water, 1688.
The same setting of the Hebrew type (and of a table at the end of the book) was used for other editions of the Psalms edited by Leusden: Het Hebreus Psalmboeck in Hebrew and Dutch, which was issued with a Utrecht imprint dated 1688, and The Book of Psalmes in Hebrew and English, which was issued with London and Utrecht imprints dated 1688. Leusden had previously edited the Psalms in Hebrew in an edition of the Old Testament in Hebrew (1st pub. 1661) and in an edition of the Psalms alone in Hebrew (1st pub. 1666) which were issued in Amsterdam by Joseph Athias.
Dedicated to Increase Mather.
Preface dated (p. 8) 1 Apr. 1688.
Bound in contemporary vellum.

FA688 ———Another copy. 13.5cm.
B582ℓ Leaf 145 misnumb.: 155.
cop. 2 JCB(2)2:1357; WingB2745; Muller(1872)3491; Sabin66454.

04637
04636, before 1882

D688 [Blome, Richard] d. 1705.
B653a L'Amerique Angloise, Ou Description Des Isles Et Terres Du Roi D'Angleterre, Dans L'Amerique. Avec de nouvelles Cartes de cha-

que Isle & Terres. Traduit de l' Anglois.
A Amsterdam, Chez Abraham Wolfgang, prés la Bourse. M. DC. LXXXVIII.
2 p. ℓ., 331, [1] p. 7 fold. maps. 15cm. 12°
Transl. from: The Present State Of His Majesties Isles and Territories In America, London, 1687.
JCB(2)2:1347; Sabin5969; Baer(Md.)126; Cundall (Jam. Supp.)207a; Muller(1872)119.

0805, 1846

D689 A Collection of Papers Relating to the
C697o Present Juncture of Affairs in England. Viz.
cop. 3 1. The Humble Petition of Seven Bishops to his Majesty. ...
[London] Printed in the Year 1688.
1 p. ℓ., 34 p. 20cm. 4°
Contains the texts of 11 "papers".
Also known with t.-p. in a variant state as recorded by McAlpin 4:279-280n.
Also issued as part 1 of A compleat collection of papers in twelve parts. London, 1689.
Bound in contemporary calf, rebacked, as the 1st of 11 items.
JCB(2)2:1351; WingC5169A; McAlpin4:279-80.

06843A

D688 [Comber, Thomas] 1645-1699.
C729t Three Considerations proposed to Mr. William Pen, concerning the Validity and Security of his New Magna Charta for Liberty of Conscience, by a Baptist; which may be worthy the Consideration of all the Quakers, and of all my Dissenting Brethren also, that have Votes in the Choice of Parliament-Men.
[London, 1688]
4 p. 20.5cm. 4°.
Caption title.
A reply to Penn, Great and Popular Objection, London, 1688.
Smith(Anti-Quak)25, 135; McAlpin4:280; WingC5496.

30130, 1947

E688 [Dellon, Gabriel] b. ca. 1649.
D358a Aanmerkelijk Historisch-Verhaal Van De Inquisitie Der Portugeesen in Goa, en andere gewesten van Oost-Indiën. Uut [sic] het Frans vertaalt.
Tot Middelburg, By Gillis Horthemels De Jonge. 1688.
6 p. ℓ., 282, [17] p. 6 plates (incl. 3 fold.). 14.5cm. 12°

70-36	Cut (engr.) on t.-p., incl. motto: Misericordia Et Ivstitia. "Mijn vertrek van Goa; aankomst aan Brasil: korte beschrijving van dit Land." (p. 224-235). First pub. Paris, 1688, under title <u>Relation de l'Inquisition de Goa</u> in a 12⁰ edition with 437 p. main paging. Another 12⁰ edition, with Paris, 1688, imprint statement on the t.-p., but with 251 p. main paging, is really a Dutch reprint. A Leyden edition dated on the t.-p. 1687 [i.e. 1688?] is an abridged reprint. Muller(1872)147; cf. Borba de Moraes 1:216-217.

69-820 rev	Lambin, 1687." (p. 437). These same sheets were also issued with inserted plates, engr. title vignette, and engr. headpieces. The page areas bearing engravings in that issue are left blank in this. Another 12⁰ edition with the same imprint statement on the t.-p., but with 251 p. main paging, is really a Dutch reprint. A Leyden edition dated on the t.-p. 1687 [i.e. 1688?] is an abridged reprint. In this copy there is a blank ℓ. at end. Bound in contemporary calf. Cf. Borba de Moraes 1:216-217; Vekené 275.

E688 D358h 69-457	[Dellon, Gabriel] b. ca. 1649. The History Of The Inquisition, As it is Exercised at Goa. Written in French, by the Ingenious Monsieur Dellon, who laboured five years under those severities. With an Account of his Deliverance. Translated into English. London, Printed for James Knapton, at the Queens-Head, in St. Paul's Church-yard. MDCLXXXVIII. 4 p.ℓ., 70 p. 23cm. 4⁰ []² A-S² [T]² (-[T]2) 4⁰ Translated and abridged by Henry Wharton from <u>Relation de l'Inquisition de Goa</u>, Paris, 1688. English transl. 1st pub. the same year without the bookseller's name on the t.-p. and with only 3 p.ℓ. This is the 2d issue with new t.-p. and a preface (2d p.ℓ.) added "to satisfie the World that these Papers came not abroad with any design of insinuating to the People a probability of the Inquisition, being about to be introduced into England." There was another edition the same year whose sheets are gathered in fours. Wing D942; cf. Borba de Moraes 1:216-217; Vekené 276a.

E688 D358r2 68-273 rev 2	[Dellon, Gabriel] b. ca. 1649. Relation De L'Inquisition De Goa. A Paris, Chez Daniel Horthemels, ruë Saint Jacques, au Mecœnas. [i.e. Netherlands] M.DC.LXXXVIII. Avec Privilege Du Roi. 8 p.ℓ., 251, [252-264] p. 6 plates (incl. 3 fold.) 16.5cm. 12⁰ Cut (engr.) on t.-p., incl. motto: Misericordia Et Ivstitia. "Mon départ de Goa; arrivée au Bresil; briéve description de ce Pays." (p. 199-209). "Achevé d'imprimer pour la premiere fois lederniér [sic] Octobre 1687." (1st p.ℓ.ᵛ). "A Paris. De l'Imprimerie d'Antoine Lambin. 1688." (p. 251). First pub. Paris, 1688, in another 12⁰ edition with the same imprint statement on the t.-p., but with 437 p. main paging. The present edition is really a Dutch reprint. A Leyden edition dated on the t.-p. 1687 [i.e. 1688?] is an abridged reprint. Cf. Borba de Moraes 1:216-217.

E688 D358r1	[Dellon, Gabriel] b. ca. 1649. Relation De L'Inquisition De Goa. A Paris, Chez Daniel Horthemels, ruë Saint Jacques, au Mecœnas. M.DC.LXXXVIII. Avec Privilege Du Roi. 13 p.ℓ., 437, [438-462] p. 16cm. 12⁰ "Mon départ de Goa; arrivée au Bresil; briéve description de ce Pays." (p. 343-361). Errata, p. [460] "Achevé d'imprimer pour la premiere fois lederniér [sic] Octobre 1687." (p. [462]). "A Paris, De l'Imprimerie d'Antoine

E688 H515 cop.1	Denys, Nicolas, 1598-1688. Geographische en Historische Beschrijving der Kusten Van Noord-America, Met de Natuurlijke Historie des Landts: Door den Heer Denys, Gouverneur Lieutenant Generaal poor den Koning van Vrankrijk, en Eigenaar van alle de Landen en Eilanden welke gelegen zijn van Cap de Campseaux af tot aan Cap des Roziers. t' Amsterdam, By Jan Ten Hoorn, Boekverkooper over 't Oude Heeren Logement, in de Histori-Schryver. A. 1688. 2 p.ℓ., 200, [4] p. 2 plates. 20.5cm. 4⁰ (Issued as a part of Hennepin, Louis. <u>Beschryving van Louisania</u>, Amsterdam, 1688.)

	Cut on t.-p. Half title (p. 85): Natuurlyke Historie... Transl. from <u>Description géographique et historique des costes de l'Amérique septentrionale</u>, Paris, 1672. JCB(2)2:1352; Sabin19616; Harrisse(NF)161; Muller(1872)516.
03665, before 1866	

H688 D421d	La Deplorable Desolation Generale Arrivé au Royaume de Naples, le 5. & 6. de Iuin 1688. veille & jour de Pentecoste, a onze heures du matin; qui a abîmé plusieurs Villes, Bourgs, & Villages & Châteaux. Avec le Tremblement de terre arrivée au Perou. Traduit d'Italien en François. [France?] Sur l'Imprimé, A Tvrin, Chez Antoine Gianelly, Imprimeur de son Altesse Royale de Savoye. Avec Permission des Superieurs. [1688?] 12 p. 14cm. 12° Cut on t.-p.
5756, 1909	

BA688 -E18e	Echave y Assu, Francisco de, fl. 17th cent. La Estrella De Lima Convertida En Sol Sobre Svs Tres Coronas El B. Toribio Alfonso Mogrobexo, Sv Segvndo Arzobispo: Celebrado Con Epitalamios Sacros, y solemnes Cultos, por su Esposa la Santa Iglesia Metropolitana de Lima, Al Activo, Y Soberano Inflvxo del Ex$^{mo.}$ è Ill$^{mo.}$ señor Doct D. Melchor de Liñan y Cisneros, ... Arçobispo (octavo en orden) de la Santa Iglesia de Lima; Virrey, Governador, y Capitan General, que ha sido de los Reynos del Perù, Tierra-firme, y Chile. Descripcion Sacro Politica De Las Grandezas de la Ciudad de Lima, y compendio historico <u>Eclesiastico de su Santa Iglesia</u> Metropolitana: Qve Descrive D. Francisco de Echave y Assu, Cavallero del Orden de Santiago, Corregidor del Cercado de Lima por su Magestad, ... Amberes. Por Juan Baptista Verdussen, año 1688. 11 p.ℓ., 239, 230-381, [382-383] p. pl. 32cm. fol. Cut on t.-p. Added half-title, engr. Authorship has been erroneously ascribed to José de Buendía. Occasioned by the ceremonies in Lima, 1680, celebrating the beatification of Toribio Alfonso Mogrovejo; includes poetry. "Cet ouvrage, semble, avoir été imprimé en ... Séville, chez Tomás López de Haro

	..." (Peeters-Fontainas). "Tassa" dated (8th p.ℓ.) 11 Nov. 1688. Errata, 7th p.ℓ.^{v} Issued with alternative dedications, either to Pope Innocent XI or to Carlos II, King of Spain. In this copy the t.-p. includes a statement of dedication to Innocent XI; the full text of the dedication (3d p.ℓ.) however, is wanting. A map of Lima is found in some copies.
Col.G.E. Church Collection	—————Variant. 29.5cm. The t.-p. of this copy includes a statement of dedication to Carlos II, King of Spain. This copy includes the full text of the dedication to Carlos II (3d p.ℓ.). Another leaf containing the dedication to Innocent XI is also bound in. JCB(2)2:1353; Medina(BHA)1813; Palau(2) 78066; Sabin21765; Backer2:338; Peeters-Fontainas(1965)366; Streit2:2242.
03661, before 1866	

F688 E96h	Exquemelin, Alexandre Olivier. Histoire Des Avanturiers Qui Se Sont Signalez Dans Les Indes, Contenant Ce Qu'ils Ont Fait De Plus Remarquable Depuis Vingt Années. Avec La Vie, les Mœurs, les Coûtumes des Habitans de Saint Domingue & de la Tortuë, & une Description exacte de ces lieux; Où l'on voit L'établissement d'une Chambre des Comptes dans les Indes, & un Etat, tiré de cette Chambre, des Offices tant Ecclesiastiques que Seculiers, où le Roy d'Espagne pourvoit, les Revenus qu'il tire de l'Amerique, & ce que les plus grands Princes de l'Europe y possedent. ... Par Alexandre Olivier Oexmelin. ... A Paris. Chez Jacques Le Febure, au dernier pillier de la Grand'Salle, vis-à-vis les Requestes du Palais. M. DC. LXXXVIII. Avec Privilege Du Roy. 2v.: 12 p.ℓ., 448 (i.e. 248), [16] p. incl. illus., plates. 2 fold. maps; 3 p.ℓ., 285, [17] p. incl. pl. fold. map. 13cm. 12° Added t.-p., engr.: Histoire Des Avanturiers Des Boucaniers Et De La Chambre Des Comptes, établie dans les Indes 1688. A Paris, Chez Jacques Le Febvre, au dernier pillier de la Grand Salle, Vis-a-Vis les Requestes du Palais. Gasp: Bouttats fecit Based on Exquemelin's account 1st pub. under the title <u>De Americaensche Zee-Roovers</u>, Amsterdam, 1678, but greatly altered and enlarged. This version 1st pub. Paris, 1686. Dedication signed (verso 5th p.ℓ., v.1): De Frontignières. "Achevé d'imprimer le premier Juin 1687." (v.2, p. [17] at end).

B688　　Fernández de Medrano, Sebastián, 1646-1705.
F363b1　　　Breve Descripcion Del Mundo O Guia Geo-
[R]　　graphica De Medrano. Lo mas principal de
ella en Verso. ...
　　En Brusselas, En casa de Lamberto Marchant,
Mercader de Libros. M. DC. LXXXVIII.
　　108 p. 15cm. 12°
　　Cut on t.-p.
　　Abridged from his Breve descripción del
mundo, Brussels, 1686. "De La Descripcion
Del Mundo En General" (p. 17-33) versified by
Manuel de Pellicer y Velasco.
　　Preliminary matter includes author's dedica-
tion in verse and commendatory poetry by
Nicolás de Oliver y Fullana and Manuel de
Pellicer y Velasco.
　　Bound in contemporary calf.
　　Medina(BHA)1815; Sabin47359; Peeters-
Fontainas(1965)436; Borba de Moraes 1:260.

13141, 1921

B688　　Fernández de Medrano, Sebastián, 1646-1705.
F363b2　　　Breve Descripcion Del Mvndo, O Gvia Geo-
[R]　　graphica De Medrano. Lo mas principal de
ella en Verso. ...
　　En Brvsselas: En casa de Lamberto Marchant,
Mercader de Libros. M. DC. LXXXVIII. Ven-
dese en Barcelona, en casa de Ioseph Texidò,
Impressor del Rey nuestro Señor.
　　8 p.ℓ., 103 p. 15cm. 8°
　　First pub. Brussels, 1688.
　　Abridged from his Breve descripción del
mundo, Brussels, 1686. "De La Descripcion
Del Mundo En General" (p. 1-15) versified by
Manuel de Pellicer y Velasco.
　　Preliminary matter includes author's dedication
in verse and commendatory poetry by Nicolás de
Oliver y Fullana and Manuel de Pellicer y Velasco.
　　In this copy caption title (p. 76) "De Las Civdades
De Africa, ..." is corrected by pasted label to
read "... America, ..."
　　Bound in contemporary vellum.
　　JCB(2)2:1360; Palau(2)89226.

06402, before 1874

　　In this copy there are 2 blank leaves at the
end of v. 2.
　　Bound in contemporary vellum, 2 v. in 1.
　　JCB(2)2:1362; Sabin23476; Palau(2)85743.

0887, 1846
0888, 1846

B688　　[Fernández de Piedrahita, Lucas] 1624-1688.
-F363h　　　Historia General De Las Conqvistas Del
Nuevo Reyno De Granada.
　　Amberes. Por Juan Baptista Verdussen.
[i.e.? Seville, Tomás López de Haro] [1688]
　　11 p.ℓ., 62 p., 1 ℓ., 63-599, [600-606] p.
29cm. fol.
　　"Cette impression semble être exécutée en
Espagne, à Séville, par Tomás López de
Haro ..." (cf. Peeters-Fontainas).
　　Covers through 1563; this is part 1 only
of 2 parts projected to cover through 1630; no
more published.
　　Divided into 12 books; there is an added
general t.-p., engr.; an added t.-p., engr., is
prefixed to "Libro primero" and to "Libro
tercero."
　　"Tassa" dated (7th p.ℓ.ʳ) 9 Aug. 1688.
　　Errata, 7th p.ℓ.ʳ
　　Preliminary matter includes commendatory
poetry by Juan Meléndez, Diego de Figueroa,
and Ignacio Martínez de Aibar.
　　Bound in contemporary calf.
　　JCB(2)2:1364; Palau(2)89568; Medina(BHA)
1816; Peeters-Fontainas(1965)455; Sabin
62704; Vindel 1006.

0537, 1846

BA688　　Ferro Machado, Juan, d. 1724.
-F395s　　　Señor. El Bachiller Don Juan Ferro
Machado, Presbitero, natural, y Domi-
ciliario de la Ciudad de la Havana, Obis-
pado de Cuba, Visitador General de las
Provincias de la Florida. Sobre. La
Visita de ellas, puntos, y reparos cometidos
por Cedulas ...
　　[Madrid? 1688?]
　　22 numb. ℓ. 28.5cm. fol.
　　Title from caption and beginning of text.
　　Memorial concerning his ecclesiastical
visitation of the mission centers in Florida
conducted in 1688.
　　With this is bound, in contemporary vellum:
Ayeta, Francisco de. Señor Al mas modesto...
[Madrid? ca. 1690]

1449, 1906

D689　　A Fifth Collection of Papers Relating to the
C697o　　　Present Juncture of Affairs in England.
Viz. I. The hard Case of Protestant Subjects
under the Dominion of a Popish Prince. ...
Licensed and Entred according to Order.
　　London printed, and are to be sold by Rich.
Janeway in Queen's-head-Court in Pater-
Noster Row, 1688.
　　1 p.ℓ., 24, 33-40, 33-34 p. []¹ B-E⁴
F²(-F1=[]1). 19cm. 4°

Contains the texts of 8 "papers".
Also issued as part 5 of <u>A compleat collection of papers in twelve parts.</u> London, 1689.
"A Letter To The King, When Duke of York..." [by Leoline Jenkins], paged 33-40, signed E^4, was also issued separately, paged 1-8, signed A^4, and with a colophon of London, Janeway, 1688. The "separate issue" is found in some copies of the <u>Fifth collection</u> (cf. McAlpin 4:284n, 4:291). The <u>t.-p.</u> of the <u>Fifth collection</u> is also known in variant state (cf. McAlpin 4:284n).
In this copy C4 is figured * and E2 is missigned "A2".
Bound in contemporary calf as the 5th of 12 items after collective t.-p.

D689
C697o
cop.2
——— ———Variant. 19cm.
In this copy C4 is figured * and E2 is correctly signed.
Bound as the 5th of 12 items.

D689
C697o
cop.3
——— ———Variant. 20cm.
In this copy C4 is figured * and E2 is correctly signed.
Bound in contemporary calf, rebacked, as the 5th of 11 items.
Wing F889; McAlpin 4:284; cf. JCB(2) 2:1351n; cf. Sabin 81492n.
12463E, 1920
06842E, before 1882
06843

BA688
F632e
Florencia, Francisco de, 1619-1695.
La Estrella De El Norte De Mexico, Aparecida Al Rayar El Dia De la luz Evangelica en este Nuevo-Mundo, en la cumbre de el cerro de Tepeyacac orilla del mar Tezcucano, à vn Natural recien convertido; ... En la Historia de la Milagrosa Imagen de N. Señora de Guadalupe de Mexico, que se apareciò en la manta de Juan Diego. Compvsola El P. Francisco De Florencia de la Compañia de Iesvs. ... Con las Novenas proprias de la Aparicion de la Santa Imagen.
Con Licencia De Los Svperiores: En Mexico: por Doña Maria de Benavides, Viuda de Juan de Ribera En el Empedradillo. Año de 1688.
22 p.ℓ., 241 numb. ℓ., [6] p. incl. front. 21cm. 4°
"Protesta" dated (numb. ℓ. 241^v) 2 Oct. 1688.
Errata, at end.
Bound in contemporary vellum.
Palau(2)92340; Medina(Mexico)1412; Sabin 24806; Backer3:796-97.
06404, before 1902

DA688
F791
Fox, George, 1624-1691.
An Answer To The Speech or Decalration [sic] Of the Great Turk, Sulton Mahomet. Which He sent to Leopold Emperor of Germany. ... Written, by George Fox, five Years since, being 1683. ...
[London] Printed, and Sold, by A. Sowle, at the Three Keys in Nags-Head Court, in Grace-Church-Street, over-against the Conduit 1688.
16p. 19cm. (20cm. in case) 4°
"The Speech or Declaration of Sultan Mahomet the great Turk ... translated out of High Dutch" p. 3-4.
Smith(Friends)1:687; Wing F1746.
11465, 1918

B688
-G216r
[R]
Garcilaso de la Vega, el Inca, 1539-1616.
The Royal Commentaries Of Peru, In Two Parts. The First Part. Treating of the Original of their Incas or Kings: Of their Idolatry: Of their Laws and Government both in Peace and War: Of the Reigns and Conquests of the Incas: With many other Particulars relating to their Empire and Policies before such time as the Spaniards invaded their Countries. The Scond [sic] Part. Describing the manner by which that new World was conquered by the Spaniards. Also the Civil Wars between the Piçarrists and the Almagrians, occasioned by Quarrels arising about the Division of that Land. Of the Rise and Fall of Rebels; and other Particulars contained in that History. Illustrated with Sculptures. Written originally in Spanish, By the Inca Garcilasso De La Vega, And rendred into English, by Sir Paul Rycaut, K^t.
London, Printed by Miles Flesher, for Jacob Tonson at the Judge's-Head in Chancery-Lane near Fleetstreet, MDCLXXXVIII.
2 pts. in 1 v.: 4 p.ℓ., 22, 27-412 p., 1 ℓ., 417-1019, [8] p. front. (port.), 10 plates. 33cm. fol.
Title in red and black.
Transl. from: <u>Primera parte de los commentarios reales</u>, 1st pub. Lisbon, 1609, and <u>Historia general del Perv</u>, 1st pub. Córdova, 1617.
Also issued London, 1688, with other variant imprints.
License dated (verso of t.-p.) 3 Aug. 1685.
In this copy there is a blank leaf following p. 412.
JCB(2)2:1368; Wing G217; Palau(1)7:127; Medina(BHA)658n; Sabin 98760.
01747, 1855

bDB
G7888
1688
2
Gt.Brit.--Sovereigns, etc., 1685-1688 (James II).   20 Jan. 1687/8
By the King, A Proclamation For the more effectual Reducing and Suppressing of Pirates

and Privateers in America.
London, Printed by Charles Bill, Henry Hills, and Thomas Newcomb, Printers to the Kings most Excellent Majesty. 1687/8.
Broadside. 2 sheets. 56.5 x 35.5cm. 1°
Cut (royal arms, Steele 103) at head of title.
Caption title; imprint at end.
Dated at end, 20 Jan. 1687/8.
Sabin 65939n; Wing J355; Steele E3857.

4447, 1908

bDB
G7888
1688
3

Gt. Brit.--Sovereigns, etc., 1685-1688
(James II).   31 Mar. 1688
By the King, A Proclamation Prohibiting His Majesties Subjects to Trade within the Limits Assigned to the Governour and Company of Adventurers of England, Trading into Hudson's Bay, except those of the Company.
London, Printed by Charles Bill, Henry Hills, and Thomas Newcomb, Printers to the Kings most Excellent Majesty, 1688.
Broadside. 46 x 35.5cm. 1°
Cut (royal arms, Steele 102a) at head of title.
Dated at end 31 Mar. 1688.
Wing J366; Steele E3862.

4448, 1908

DB
-G7888
1688
1

Gt. Brit.--Sovereigns, etc., 1685-1688
(James II)   27 Sept. 1688
Grant of The Northern Neck In Virginia To Lord Culpepper.
[London, 1688]
6 p., 1 ℓ. 28.5cm. fol.
Docket title.
Caption title: Septima Pars Patentium de Anno Regni Regis Jacobi Secundi Quarto.
Dated (p. 6) 27 Sept.
JCB(2)2:1369; Sabin 99889; Wing J386B; NYPL(Va. 1907)30.

0534, 1846

J688
-H252t

Happel, Eberhard Werner, 1647-1690.
Thesaurus Exoticorum. Oder eine mit Aussländischen Raritäten und Geschichten Wohlversehene Schatz-Kammer Fürstellend die Asiatische, Africanische und Americanische Nationes Der Perser/Indianer/Sinesen/Tartarn/Egypter/ Barbarn/Libyer/Nigriten/Guineer/Hottentotten/ Abyssiner/Canadenser/Virgenier/Floridaner/ Mexicaner/Peruaner/Chilenser/Magellanier und Brasilianer etc. ... Darauff folget eine Umständliche Beschreibung von Türckey: ... Wie auch ihres Propheten Mahomets Lebens-Beschreibung/ und sein Verfluchtes Gesetz-Buch oder Alkoran. Alssdann eine Kürtzbündige Beschreibung von Ungarn: ... Hiernechst eine umbständliche Beschreibung des Lebens-Lauffs Ihrer Käyserl. Mayest. Leopoldi I. ... herausgegeben Von Everhardo Gvernero Happelio.
Hamburg, Gedruckt und Verlegt durch Thomas von Wiering, Buchdrucker und Formschneider bey der Börse/im Gülden A.B.C. Jm Jahr 1688. Sind auch zu bekommen in Franckfurth bey Zacharias Herteln.
8 p.ℓ., 5 pts. in 1 v.: pt.1, 1 ℓ., 120 p. illus.; pt.2, 1 ℓ., 192 p. 3 fold. plates, 11 ports. (incl. 5 fold.) fold. map; pt.3, 1 ℓ., 77, 88-114, 105-144, 149-160 p. illus., 10 fold. plates, 2 fold. ports., 2 fold. maps; pt.4, 1 ℓ., 288 p. illus., 3 fold. plates; pt.5, 2 ℓ., 115 p. 34cm. fol.
Title in red and black. Illustrated initials on t.-p.
Added t.-p., engraved.
Each part has separate paging and signatures; a half-title was issued for each part. Copies are found with varying number of half-titles; this copy has only the half-title for pt.5; others available in facsim.
Also issued with variant title-pages (cf. line 20, which in this copy reads "... Alkoren..." vs. "... Alkoran..." in other copies, etc.).
Also issued with variant "Vor-Rede" (e.g. in this copy there are 22 lines on last page vs. 27 in other copies).
Imperfect: p.ℓ. 7-8, p. 115-118 (1st count) wanting; available in facsim. Title-page closely trimmed at bottom affecting last line of imprint; available in facsim.
Bound in contemporary calf.
Sabin 30279; Palmer 333; Palau(2)112243.

29976, 1947

E688
H515b

Hennepin, Louis, ca. 1640-ca. 1705.
Beschryving Van Louisania, Nieuwelijks ontdekt ten Zuid-Westen Van Nieuw-Vrankryk, Door order van den Koning. Met de Kaart des Landts, en een nauwkeurige verhandeling van de Zeden en manieren van leeven der Wilden. Door Den Vader Lodewyk Hennepin, Recolletsche Missionaris in die Gewesten, en Apostolische Notaris. Mitsgaders de Geographische en Historische Beschrijving der Kusten Van Noord-America, Met de Natuurlijke Historie des Landts. Door den Heer Denys ...
t' Amsterdam, By Jan Ten Hoorn, Boekverkooper over 't Oude Heeren Logement, in de Histori-Schryver. A. 1688.
4 p.ℓ., 158, [5] p., 1 ℓ., [2], 200, [4] p. 6

plates, fold. map. 20.5cm. 4º
Cut (arms of Amsterdam) on t.-p.
Added t.-p., engr.: Ontdekking van Louisania Door den Vader L. Hennepin. Benevens de Beschryving van Noord-America Door den Heer Denys ...
With, as issued, Denys' Geographische en historische beschrijving, Amsterdam, 1688, with special t.-p. and separate paging and signatures.
Hennepin text transl. from Description de la Louisiane, 1st pub. Paris, 1683. Denys text transl. from Description géographique et historique des costes de l'Amérique septentrionale, Paris, 1672.
Imperfect: fold. map, added t.-p. (1st p.ℓ.), and 4th p.ℓ. wanting.

E688
H515b
cop. 2
————————Another copy. 20.5cm.
Imperfect: Denys' Geographische en historische beschryving wanting.
JCB(2)2:1355; Sabin31357; Harrisse(NF)161; Paltsits(Hennepin)li; Muller(1872)908; Streit 2:2738.
03664, before 1866
03665, before 1866
0366³, before 1866

E688
H515d
Hennepin, Louis, ca. 1640-ca. 1705.
Description De La Louisiane, Nouvellement Decouverte au Sud'Oüest de la Nouvelle France, Par Ordre Du Roy. Avec la Carte du Pays: Les Mœurs & la Maniere de vivre des Sauvages. Dediée A Sa Majesté Par le R. P. Loüis Hennepin Missionnaire Recollet & Notaire Apostolique.
A Paris, Chez Amable Auroy, ruë Saint Saint [sic] Jacques à l'Image S. Jerôme, attenant la Fontaine S. Severin. M.DC.L.XXXVIII. Avec Privilege Du Roy.
6 p.ℓ., 312, 107 p. fold. map. 16cm. 12º
Cut (monogram) on t.-p.
"Achevé d'imprimer pour la secon. de [sic] fois, le 10. Mars 1688. De l'Imprimerie de Laurent Rondet." (6th p.ℓ.ᵛ)
First pub. Paris, 1683.
Imperfect: map (same as in Paris, 1683 ed.) wanting.
JCB(2)2:1354; Sabin31348; Harrisse(NF)160; Paltsits(Hennepin)ℓi; Streit 2:2737.
03666, before 1866

FC650
H737
38
Hollandse Mercurius, Verhalende de voornaemste Saken van Staet, En andere Voorvallen, Die in en omtrent de Vereenigde Nederlanden, En elders in Europa, In het Jaer 1687 Zijn geschiet. Het Acht-en-Dertigste Deel.
Tot Haerlem, Gedruckt by Abraham Casteleyn, Stads-Drucker, op de Marckt, in de Blye Druck. Anno 1688.
3 p.ℓ., 230, [6] p. 5 plates. 20cm. 4º
(Bound in [vol. 10] of Hollandse Mercurius)
Added t.-p., engraved: Hollandse Mercurius Anno 1687. Tot Haerlem by Abraham Casteleyn
JCB(3)2:410; Sabin32523.
8487LL, 1912

F688
H813g
Horn, Georg, 1620-1670.
Georgi Horni Orbis Politicus Imperiorum, Regnorum, Principatuum, Rerumpublicarum, Cum Memorabilibus Totius Mundi, & Geographia veteri ac recenti: Adjectis Animadversionibus extantiora quædam controversa loca illustrantibus, Editio Tertia, Auctior & Emendatior.
Veronæ [i.e. Leipzig?], Anno MDCLXXXVIII.
12 p.ℓ., 576, [44] p. 14cm. 12º
Added t.-p., engr.
First pub. Leiden, 1667.
These may be mainly the same sheets as the Leipzig, 1685, edition with cancel title-pages.
In this copy there are two blank leaves at end.
Bound in contemporary calf.
12565, 1920

G688
L257s
Jónsson, Arngrímur, 1568-1648.
Gronlandia Edur Grænlandz Saga Vr Islendskum Sagna Bookum og Añalum samañtekiñ og a Latinskt maal Skrifud Af theim Heidurliga & Halœrda Manni/ Syra Arngrime Ionssine Fordum Officiali Hola Stiftis og Soknarpreste ad Melstad Eñ a Norrænu utlǿgd af Einare Eiolfssine.
Dryckt i Skalhollte/Af Hendrick Kruse Anno 1688.
1 p.ℓ., 41, [42-46] p. incl. illus. 20cm. 4º
Dedication by Einar Eyjólfsson (p.[2]), dated in Skálholt 9 March 1688.
"Appendix Vm Sigling oc Stefnu fra Noreg oc Islande til Grœnlands. Epter Blǿdum nockrum sem fundust i Skalhollte" (p.[42]-[43]) signed: Th.[órdur] Th.[orláksson] S.
With ms. annotations.
See Hermannsson, Halldór, Icelandic books of the seventeenth century, Ithaca, New York, p. 52.
Bound (as the 4th of 4 items) with 3 other works printed in Skálholt by Hendrik Kruse, 1688: Landnámabók. Sagan Landnama ...

	—Ari Thorgilsson, Fródi. <u>Schedæ ara prestz froda vm Island.</u>—Kristnisaga. <u>Christendoms saga</u> ... JCB(2)2:1356; JCBAR41:14-20; Sabin2058, 28646, 74880. 29000, 1941
DA688 K28f	Keith, George, 1639?-1716. The Fundamental Truths Of Christianity, Briefly hinted at by way of Question and Answer. To which is added a Treatise Of Prayer In the same Method. By George Keith. London, Printed in the Year MDC LXXXVIII. 3 p. ℓ., 16 p., 5 ℓ., 6, 17-128 p. 15cm. 8º "The Preface" signed (3d p. ℓ.ʳ): Thy Sincere Friend R.[obert] B.[arclay] London the 27th. of the 5th. Month, 1687. Errata, 3d p. ℓ. ᵛ. With, as issued, his <u>Concerning prayer</u>, [London] 1687, with special t.-p., separate paging and signatures. Bound in contemporary calf, rebacked. WingK168; Smith(Friends)2:23; McAlpin4:292. 11475, 1918
G688 L257s	Kristnisaga. Christendoms Saga Hliodande um thad hvornenn Christen Tru kom fyrst a Island/ at forlage thess haloflega Herra/Olafs Tryggvason ar Noregs Kongs. Cum gratia & Privilegio Sacræ Regiæ Maiestatis Daniæ & Norvegiæ. Prentud i Skalhollti af Hendrick Kruse/Anno M.DC. LXXXVIII. 2 p. ℓ., 26, [2] p. incl. port. 20cm. 4º An account of early Christianity in Iceland. Preliminary matter (2d p. ℓ.) by Thórdur Thorláksson, dated in Skálholt, 2 June 1688. With ms. annotations. See Hermannsson, Halldór, <u>Icelandic books of the seventeenth century</u>, Ithaca, New York, p. 61. Bound (as the 3d of 4 items) with 3 other works printed in Skálholt by Hendrik Kruse, 1688: Landnámabók. <u>Sagan Landnama</u> ...—Ari Thorgilsson, Fródi. <u>Schedæ ara prestz froda vm Island.</u>—Jónsson, Arngrímur. <u>Gronlandia, edur Grænlandz saga</u> ... JCBAR41:14-20; Sabin74880n. 28999, 1941
G688 L257s	Landnámabók. Sagan Landnama Vm fyrstu bygging Islands af Nordmønnum. ... Skalhollte/Dryckt af Hendr: Kruse/A. MDCLXXXVIII. 5 p. ℓ., 182, [20] p. incl. illus. 20cm. 4º Title in red and black, within frame of woodcuts. Cut (with royal monogram) on t.-p. A compilation of place histories and of the personal and family histories of the first settlers in Iceland. Edited by Einar Eyjólfsson. Preliminary matter (2d-4th p. ℓ.) by Thórdur Thorláksson, dated in Skálholt, 18 April 1688. Includes poetry (p. [18]-[20] at end) by Einar Eyjólfsson, Thórdur Thorláksson and Thorlákur Grímsson. Errata, p. [17] at end. With ms. annotations. See Hermannsson, Halldór, <u>Icelandic books of the seventeenth century</u>, Ithaca, New York, p. 61-62. With this are bound 3 other works printed in Skálholt by Hendrik Kruse, 1688: Ari Thorgillson, Fródi. <u>Schedæ ara prestz froda vm Island.</u>—Kristnisaga. <u>Christendoms saga hliodande um thad hvornenn Christen tru kom fyrst a Island</u> ...—Jónsson, Arngrímur. <u>Gronlandia, edur Grænlandz saga</u> ... JCBAR41:14-20; Sabin74880. 28997, 1941
D688 L651f	A Letter From a Minister of the Church of England, To the pretended Baptist, Author of the Three Considerations Directed to Mr. Penn. Allowed to be Published this 10th Day of September, 1688. [London] Sold [by Andrew Sowle] at the Three Keys, in Nags-Head-Court, in Grace-Church-Street, over-against the Conduit, 1688. 8 p. 19cm. 4º A reply to [Thomas Comber] <u>Three Considerations proposed to Mr. William Pen.</u> [London, 1688] WingL1417. 30132, 1947
DA688 L722d	The Life & Death, Travels And Sufferings Of Robert VVidders Of Kellet in Lancashire; Who Was one of the Lords Worthies, together with several Testimonies of his Neighbours and Friends concerning him. London: Printed in the Year, 1688. 16(i.e. 28) p. 19cm. 4º

"G.[eorge] F.[ox]'s Testimony concerning Robert Widders" (p. 27-end).
Wing L2019; Sabin103883; Smith(Friends)2:926.
15289, 1928

B682 -L864p [López, Francisco] 1648-1696.
Noticias Del Svr Continvadas Desde 6. De Nouiembre de 1685. hasta Iunio de 1688.
[Lima, 1688]
[35] p. 28cm. fol.
Caption title.
Continuation of [his] Noticias del sur [Lima, 1685].
Bound as no. 7 in a vol. with binder's title: Luis Lopez Obras.
Palau(2)139976; Medina(Lima)610; Backer4: 1947; Leclerc(1878)1826.11 (this copy); Sabin 61149n.
14013, 1925

B682 -L864p [López, Francisco] 1648-1696.
Vltimas Noticias Del Svr, Y Felizes operaciones del Navio San Ioseph, de la Esquadra de N. Señora de Guia contra Piratas.
[Lima, 1688]
[3] p. 28cm. fol.
Caption title.
Continuation of [his] Noticias del sur continuadas, [Lima, 1688]
Bound as no. 8 in a vol. with binder's title: Luis Lopez Obras.
Medina(Lima)611; Backer4:1947; Leclerc(1878) 1826.12(this copy); Sabin61149n.
14014, 1926

BA688 -L864h López de Cogolludo, Diego, ca. 1612-1665.
Historia De Yucathan. Compuesta Por El M.R.P. Fr. Diego Lopez Cogollvdo, Lector Jvbilado, Y Padre Perpetvo De Dicha Provincia. ... Sacala A Lvz El M.R.P. Fr. Francisco De Ayeta...
Con Privilegio. En Madrid: Por Jvan Garcia Infanzon, Año 1688.
15 p.ℓ., 760, [31] p. incl. illus. 30cm. fol.
Added t.-p., engr.: Historia De La Provincia De Yvcathan ... Avthor El R.P.F. Juan [sic] Lopez de Cogolludo.
Dedication dated (9th p.ℓ.^{v}) 16 Febr. 1688.
Errata, 15th p.ℓ.^{r}
Palau(2)141001; Medina(BHA)1821; Sabin 14210; Streit2:2245.
29094, 1942

D688 L897g Love, John, fl. 1688.
Geodæsia: Or, The Art Of Surveying And Measuring of Land, Made Easie. ... As Also, How to Lay-out New Lands in America, or elsewhere: And how to make a Perfect Map of a River's Mouth or Harbour; with several other Things never yet Publish'd in our Language. By John Love, Philomath. ...
London: Printed for John Taylor at the Ship in S. Paul's Church-Yard, MDCLXXXVIII.
12 p.ℓ., 196, [52] p. incl. illus. (diagrs.), tables. 20.5cm. 4°
Title in red and black.
License dated (2d p.ℓ.^{v}) 16 Febr. 1688.
Booksellers' advertisement, 12th p.ℓ.
Instrument makers' advertisement, 6th p.ℓ.^{v}
In this copy the last 4 p. are bound between p. 194 and 195.
Bound in contemporary calf.
WingL3191; Taylor (Mathematical practitioners: Tudor & Stuart) 468.
31935, 1956

D. Math I.128A Mather, Increase, 1639-1723.
De Successu Evangelij Apud Indos In Novâ-Angliâ Epistola. Ad Cl. Virum D. Johannem Leusdenum, Linguæ Sanctæ in Ultrajectinâ Academiâ Professorem, Scripta. A Crescentio Mathero Apud Bostonienses V.D.M. nec non Collegij Harvardini quod est Cantabrigia Nov-Anglorum, Rectore.
Londini, Typis J.G. 1688.
1 p.ℓ., 13 p. 14.5cm. 8°
Dated at end in Boston, 12 July 1687.
Sabin46749; Holmes(I)128A; Church704; WingM1197.
02323, 1850

D. Math I.79A [R] [Mather, Increase] 1639-1723.
A Narrative Of the Miseries of New-England, By Reason of an Arbitrary Government Erected there.
[London, Richard Baldwin? 1688]
8 p. 19cm. 4°
Caption title.
Another edition reprinted by W.H. Whitmore in The Andros Tracts, v.2, p. 1-14.
Wing M1231; Holmes(I)79A.
03831, before 1874

E688 M688w Mocquet, Jean, b. 1575.
Wunderbare Jedoch Gründlich-und warhaffte Geschichte und Reise Begebnisse In

[194]

Africa/Asia/Ost-und West-Indien von Jan Mocquet aus Frankreich/Ihrer Königlichen Majestät Heinrichs des Grossen oder IV. und Ludwigs des XIII. daselbst gewesnen geheimen Hof-und Cammer-Apothekers/wie auch wolbestellten Verwesers/derer daselbst befindlichen fremden/ausländischen/ und in unsern Landen unbekannten Früchten/ Gewächsen/Kräutern und Blumen/in dero Königlichen Residenz-Stadt zu Paris/in der Tuillerie... aus dem Französischen in Hochteutsche Sprache übersetzet und entdecket durch Johann Georg Schochen.

Lüneburg/In Verlegung Johann Georg Lippers. [1688]

30 p. ℓ., 632 p. front., 10 plates, double plan. 21cm. 4°

Transl. from: <u>Voyages En Afriqve, Asie, Indes Orientales & Occidentales</u>, 1st pub. Paris, 1616.

"Vor-Bericht" dated (30th p. ℓ.^v) 30 March 1688.

JCB(2)2:1361; Sabin49793; Palmer359; Borba de Moraes 2:66-67.

03662, before 1866

D688
M689f
[R]

A Model For Erecting a Bank of Credit: With A Discourse In Explanation thereof. Adapted to the Use of any Trading Countrey, where there is a Scarcity of Moneys: More Especially for his Majesties Plantations in America. ...

London, Printed by J. A. for Thomas Cockeril at the Three Leggs in the Poultrey, over against the Stocks-Market, 1688.

1 p. ℓ., 38 p. 16cm. 8°

Scheme for a bank in Boston proposed by John Blackwell. In this and other known copies canceling leaves bearing p. 7-8 and p. 13-14 with additions to the text have been supplied. These are of the same kind of paper as p. 31-38, added as "A Supplement or Appendix ... " The additions were presumably made in Boston at the behest of Gov. Andros. The cancelland leaf bearing p. 13-14 and others of the same gathering (but not the leaf bearing p. 7-8) have survived as fly leaves in a book in the Prince Library. A reprint of the <u>Model</u>, Boston, 1714, did not include the supplement and followed an unrevised text for p. 7-8 and p. 13-14.

Sabin49795; WingM2312.

68-257

D688
M728d

Molloy, Charles, 1646-1690.
De Jure Maritimo Et Navali: Or, A Treatise Of Affairs Maritime And Of Commerce. ... The Fourth Edition. By Charles Molloy.

London, Printed for John Bellinger in Clifford's Inn Lane, against the West Door of St. Dunstan's Church; and John Walthoe against the St. John's-Head Tavern in Chancery-Lane, near Lincolns-Inn, 1688.

13 p. ℓ., 433, [13] p. front. 21cm. 8°

Added t.-p., engr. (signed by John Drapentier).

First pub. London, 1676.

Bound in contemporary calf.

Sabin49924; Wing M2398; Kress1677.

71-14

Z
M834
1688

Morden, Robert, d. 1703.
Geography Rectified: Or, A Description Of The World... Illustrated with Seventy six Maps. The Second Edition, Enlarged with above Thirty Sheets more in the Description, and about Twenty New Maps. ... By Robert Morden.

London: Printed for Robert Morden and Thomas Cockerill, at the Atlas in Cornhill, and at the Three Legs in the Poultrey, over against the Stocks-Market. MDCLXXXVIII.

8 p. ℓ., 304, 321-495, 486-544, [2], 545-596 p. A⁴a⁴ B-2Q⁴ 3A-4G⁴ (4G1+1) 4H-4N⁴ (-4N4). illus. (77 maps). 20.5cm. 4°

Title in red and black.

Maps engr. in text.

In this copy the maps are hand colored.

First pub. London, 1680.

The section on America occupies p. 513-595.

Bound in contemporary calf, rebacked.

Sabin50535; Wing M2620; Phillips(Atlases)498.

11646, 1918

F688
M958v

[Muller, Andreas] secretarius.
Vervolg Van 't Verwerd Europa, Of Politijke en Historische Beschryving van alle gedenkwaardigste Staats- en Krygs-Voorvallen zoo binnen, als buyten 't Christen-Ryk Voornamentlijk in en omtrent Hoog- en Neder-Duytsland, en derzelver aangrenzende Rijken en Staaten, zedert den Jaare 1672. tot 1675. door de Fransche Wapenen veroorsaakt. ... Met bygevoegde Authentijke Stukken.

t'Amsterdam, By Abraham van Someren, in de Kalverstraat. MDCLXXXVIII.

12 p. ℓ., 176, 179-1058, [31], 96 p. 20cm. 4°

Cut (swag) on t.-p.

Includes a documentary appendix (at end).

A continuation of: Pieter Valckenier. <u>'t Verwerd Europa, Ofte Politijke en Historische Beschryvinge</u>, 1st pub. Amsterdam, 1668.

Transl. from: <u>Des Verwirrten Europæ Continuation</u>, Amsterdam, 1680.

Another issue appeared with imprint: Amsterdam, Hendrik en de weduwe van D. Boom, 1688.

68-256

D688　　[Penn, William] 1644-1718.
P412g　　The Great and Popular Objection Against the Repeal of the Penal Laws & Tests Briefly Stated and Consider'd, And Which May serve for Answer to several late Pamphlets upon that Subject. By a Friend to Liberty for Liberties sake Licensed February the 4th 1687.
　　　　London, Printed, and Sold, by Andrew Sowle, at the Three-Keys, in Nags-Head-Court, in Grace-Church-Street, over-against the Conduit, 1688.
　　　　23 p.　19.5cm.　4°.
　　　　Smith(Friends)2:305; McAlpin4:300; Wing P1298.
11350, 1918

D688　　[Penn, William] 1644-1718.
P412t　　Three Letters Tending to demostrate [sic] how the Security of this Nation Against al [sic] Future Persecution For Religion, Lys [sic] in the Abolishment of the Present Penal Laws and Tests, and in the Establishment of A New Law For Universal Liberty of Conscience: With Allowance.
　　　　London, Printed, and Sold, by Andrew Sowle, at the Three Keys, in Nags-Head-Court, in Grace-Church-Street, over-against the Conduit, 1688.
　　　　27 p.　19cm.　4°.
　　　　Smith(Friends)2:304; McAlpin4:313; Wing P1385; Sabin95740.
31119, 1952

E688　　Petit, Pierre, 1617-1687.
P489p　　Petri Petiti Philosophi & Doctoris Medici De Natura & Moribus Anthropophagorum Dissertatio.
　　　　Trajecti Ad Rhenum, Ex Officina Rudolphi a Zyll, Bibliop. cIɔ. Iɔ. c. LXXXVIII.
　　　　152 p.　19cm.　8°
　　　　Cut (printer's device) on t. p., incl. motto "Pax Artivm Altrix" and label "Minerva Traiectina".
　　　　"Caput. VI. Anthropophagi frequentes in novo orbe" (p. 24-27).
　　　　Sabin61257.
69-651

D585　　[Picard, Jean] 1620-1682.
-B633m　　The Measure Of The Earth: Being An Account of several Observations made for that Purpose by divers Members of the Royal Academy of Science at Paris. Translated out of the French by Richard Waller, Fellow of the Royal Society.
　　　　London: Printed by R. Roberts: And are to be Sold by T. Basset, at the George near Temple-Bar; J. Robinson, at the Golden Lyon in St. Paul's Church-Yard; B. Aylmer, at the Three Pigeons over against the Royal Exchange; J. Southby, at the Harrow in Cornhil; and W. Canning in the Temple, MDCLXXXVIII.
　　　　2 p.ℓ., 40 p. illus., 5 plates. 27cm. fol.
　　　　(Issued as a part of Académie des Sciences, Paris. Memoir's [sic] for a natural history of animals, London, 1688.)
　　　　Cut (fleur-de-lis) on t.-p.
　　　　Imprimatur (1st p. ℓ.ᵛ) dated 28 Oct. 1687.
　　　　Errata, p. 40.
　　　　Translated from Mesure de la terre, 1st pub. Paris, 1671.
　　　　Bound with Blagrave, John. The mathematical iewel, London [1585], as the 3d of 3 items.
　　　　Wing M1582; Taylor Mathematical practitioners (Tudor & Stuart) 472.
13967-3, 1925

DA688　　[Popple, Sir William] d. 1708.
P831ℓ　　A Letter To Mʳ Penn: With His Answer.
1　　　　London: Printed for Andrew Wilson, and are to be sold by the several Booksellers in London & Westminster, 1688.
　　　　20 p.　20.5cm.　4°.
　　　　Letter to Penn (p. 3-9) dated: London, October the 20th. 1688. "Mr. Penn's Answer" (p. 10-20) signed: Teddington, October the 24th. 1688. ... W. P.
　　　　Church705; Smith(Friends)2:305; Wing P2961.
11516, 1918

DA688　　[Popple, Sir William] d. 1708.
P831ℓ　　A Letter To Mʳ Penn With His Answer.
2　　　　London: Printed for Andrew Wilson, And are to be Sold by the several Booksellers in London and Westminster. 1688.
　　　　10 p.　21.5cm.　4°.
　　　　Text in two columns.
　　　　Letter to Penn (p. 3-5) dated: London, October the 20th. 1688. "Mr. Penn's Answer" (p. 6-10) signed: Teddington, October the 24th. 1688. ... W. P.
　　　　Includes a postscript, p. 10.
　　　　This edition was also issued the same year without the postscript. First pub. the same year in an edition of 20 p. (without the postscript).
　　　　JCB(2)2:1363; Church706; Sabin59714; Smith(Friends)2:305; Wing P2962.
03660, before 1866

C619 Relaçam Do Exemplar Castigo mandado por Deos
A949n à Cidade De Lima, Cabeça do Perù, & â sua
Costa de Barlovento, com os horriveis tremo-
res da terra, que succédérão a 20. de Outubro
de 1687.
Lisboa, Na Officina de Miguel Deslandes Im-
pressor de Sua Magestade. Anno 1688. Com
todas as licenças necessarias.
11 p. 19.5cm. 4º
Caption title; imprint at end.
First pub. Lima, 1687.
Attributed to Francisco López or José Buendía.
Bound as the 8th in a volume of 58 pamphlets, 1619-1702.

9349, 1913

B688 Relacion Del Exemplar Castigo Que embió Dios
-R382d á la Ciudad de Lima Cabeça del Perú, y à su
Costa de Barlovento con los espantosos Tem-
blores del dia 20. de Octubre del Año de 1687.
Con licencia en Lima, y por su original en
Mexico, por la Viuda de Francisco Rodriguez
Lupercio. Año de 1688. Qvinta Impression.
[8] p. 30cm. fol.
Caption title; imprint at end.
First pub. Lima, 1687.
Attributed to Francisco López or José
Buendía.
Palau(2)258928; Medina(Mexico)1421; cf.
Medina(Lima)602n; cf. Backer2:337-8, 4:1947.

29628, 1944

E688 Rennefort, Urbain Souchu de, ca.1630-ca.1689.
R415h2 Histoire Des Indes Orientales. Par Monsieur
Souchu De Rennefort.
Suivant la Copie de Paris. A Leide, Chez
Frederik Harring, Marchand Libraire. 1688.
12 p.ℓ., 571 p. 15.5cm. 12º
Cut (swag) on t.-p.
First pub. Paris, 1688.
Bound in contemporary calf.
Borba de Moraes2:270.

68-49

BA688 Reyes, Gaspar de los, 1655-1706.
R457s Sermon Al Glorioso San Francisco De Borja,
Dvque Qvarto De Gandia. Tercero General De
La Compañia De Jesus. Predicoló El P. Gaspar
De Los Reyes Angel. De la mesma Compañia.
En Presencia del Excelentissimo Señor Conde
de la Monclova, Virrey desta Nueva-España,
Electo de los Reynos del Perû.
Con Licencia en Mexico, por los Herederos
de la Viuda de Bernardo Calderon. Año de 1688.
En la Imprenta de Antuerpia.
4 p.ℓ., 18 numb. ℓ. 19.5cm. 4º
License dated (4th p.ℓ.ʳ) 27 Oct. 1688.
Palau(2)265548; Medina(Mexico)1422; Sabin 70397; Backer6:1690.

4922, 1908

BA688 [Riofrío, Bernardo de] d. 1700.
-R585p Por El Venerable Dean, Y Cavildo
De La Santa Iglesia de Mechoacan, como
Patron de los dos Hospitales, intitulados de
Santa Fee, el vno en distancia de dos leguas
de Mexico, y el otro en el Obispado de
Mechoacan Cerca De Que Se Declare, No
dever pagar el Real Tributo los Naturales
de ellos. en virtud de privilegio, que por
su parte se alega, y por el qual, nunca le
han pagado, y cerca de que haviendoseles
perdido, no lo deven presentar especifico,
sino probarlo juntamente con las causas,
que precedieron à su concession.
[Mexico, 1688]
1 p.ℓ., 11 numb. ℓ. 29cm. fol.
Signed at end: Mexico, y Febrero 4. de
1688. años. Lic.ᵈᵒ Don Bernardo de Rio-
Frio.
Palau(2)268389; Medina(Mexico)1423.

15642, 1930

EA688 Saint Vallier, Jean Baptiste de la Croix
S155e Chevrières de, Bp. of Quebec, 1653-1727.
Estat Present De L'Eglise Et De La Colonie
Françoise Dans La Nouvelle France, Par M.
l'Evêque de Quebec.
A Paris, Chez Robert Pepie, ruë S. Jacques,
à l'image S. Basile, au dessus de la Fontaine
S. Severin. M. DC. LXXXVIII. Avec Privi-
lege Dv Roy.
1 p.ℓ., 267, [1] p. 18.5cm. 8º
Cut on t.-p.
Colophon (p. 267): A Paris, De l'Im-
primerie de la veuve Denis Langlois, ruë S.
Estienne des Grecs. 1688.
"Achevé" dated (last p.) 11 Mar. 1688.
The same sheets also issued Paris, the
same year, under title Relation Des Missions
De La Nouvelle France.
JCB(2)2:1366; Sabin66978; Church707n;
Harrisse(NF)159.

0535, 1846

EA688　Saint Vallier, Jean Baptiste de la Croix
S155r　　Chevrières de, Bp. of Quebec, 1653-1727.
　　　Relation Des Missions De La Nouvelle
　　France, Par M. l'Evêque de Quebec.
　　　A Paris, Chez Robert Pepie, ruë S. Jacques,
　　à l'image S. Basile, au dessus de la Fontaine
　　S. Severin. M. DC. LXXXVIII. Avec Pri-
　　vilege Dv Roy.
　　　1 p.l., 267, [1] p. 18.5cm. 8°
　　　Cut on t.-p.
　　　Colophon (p. 267): A Paris, De l'Im-
　　primerie de la veuve Denis Langlois, ruë S.
　　Estienne des Grecs. 1688.
　　　"Achevé" dated (last p.) 11 Mar. 1688.
　　　The same sheets also issued Paris, the
　　same year, under title: Estat present de
　　l'église et de la colonie françoise dans la
　　Nouvelle France.
　　　JCB(2)2:1367; Sabin66979; Church707.
03667, before 1866

B69　　Santillana, Gabriel de.
G643v　　Villancicos, Que Se Cantaron En Los May-
38　　tines Del gloriosissimo Principe de la Iglesia
　　el Señor San Pedro... Escrivelos: El Br. Don
　　Gabriel de Santilla [sic]... Pusolos en Metro
　　Musico el Br. Joseph de Loaysa, y Agurto,
　　Maestro de Capilla de dicha Santa Iglesia.
　　　En Mexico, Por los Herederos de la Uiuda
　　de Bernardo Calderon, año 1688.
　　　[8] p. 20cm. 4°
　　　Woodcut title vignette (St. Peter within a de-
　　corative frame)
　　　Bound, in contemporary vellum, as no. 38
　　with 42 other items.
　　　Medina(Mexico)1425.
28938, 1941

BA688　Sariñana y Cuenca, Isidro, 1630?-1696.
S245s　　Sermon De N.S.P.S. Francisco, Que En su
　　dia, y Convento de la Descalçes Seraphica de
　　la Ciudad de Antequera Valle de Oaxaca Predicó
　　El Ill.mo y Rev.mo Señor Dr. D. Isidro Sariñana,
　　Y Cvenca, del Consejo de su Magestad, y Obispo
　　de la misma Ciudad, este Año de 1687. ...
　　　Con Licencia De Los Svperiores. En Mexico:
　　por Doña Maria de Benavides, Viuda de Juan de
　　Ribera en el Empedradillo. Año de 1688.
　　　12 p.l., 12 numb. l. 19.5cm. 4°
　　　Approbation dated (12th p. l.v) 16 Dec. 1687.
　　　Palau(2)302140; Medina(Mexico)1427.
69-758

D689　　A Second Collection of Papers Relating to the
C697o　Present Juncture of Affairs in England.
cop. 3　　Viz. I. An Enquiry into the Measures of
　　Submission to the Supreme Authority ...
　　[London] Printed in the Year, 1688.
　　　1 p.l., 34 p. 20cm. 4°
　　　Contains the texts of 7 "papers".
　　　Also issued as a part of A compleat collection
　　of papers in twelve parts. London, 1689.
　　　Bound in contemporary calf, rebacked, as the
　　2d of 11 items.
　　　Wing S2264; McAlpin4:306-07; cf. JCB(2)2:
　　1351n; cf. Sabin81492n.
06843B

B688　　Seixas y Lovera, Francisco de.
S462t　　Theatro Naval Hydrographico, De Los Flvxos,
　　Y Reflvxos, Y De Las Corrientes De Los Mares,
　　Estrechos. Archipielagos, Y Passages Aquales
　　Del Mundo, Y De Las Diferencias De Las Uaria-
　　ciones De La Aguja De Marear, Y Efectos De La
　　Luna, Con Los Uientos Generales, Y Particv-
　　lares Qve Reynan En Las Quatro Regiones
　　Maritimas Del Orbe. Dirigido Al Rey Nuestro
　　Señor, En Sv Real Consejo de Indias, siendo
　　Presidente en èl, el Excelentissimo Señor
　　Marquès de los Velez, &c. Compvesto Por Don
　　Francisco de Seyxas y Lovera.
　　　Con Privilegio. En Madrid: Por Antonio de
　　Zafra, Criado de su Magestad. Año de 1688.
　　　8 p.l., 104 numb. l., [8] p.　fold. table.
　　20.5cm. 4°
　　　Cut (royal arms) on t.-p.
　　　Errata: recto 7th p. l.
　　　Dedication dated (recto 3d p. l.) 25 Dec. 1688.
　　　Palau(2)306607; Sabin78961; Medina(Chile)181;
　　Borba de Moraes2:246.
63-206

CA679　Vieira, Antonio, 1608-1697.
V665s　　Maria Rosa Mystica. Excellencias, Poderes,
10　　E Maravilhas Do Seu Rosario: Compendiadas
　　Em Trinta Sermoens Asceticos, E Panegyricos,
　　sobre os dous Evangelhos desta Solennidade,
　　Novo, & Antigo ... Pelo P. Antonio Vieira, Da
　　Companhia De Jesu ... II. Parte.
　　　Lisboa, Na Impressaõ Craesbeeckiana.
　　Anno M.DC.LXXXVIII. A custa de Antonio
　　Leyte Pereyra, Mercador de Livros. Com
　　todas as Licenças, & Privilegio Real.
　　　4 p.l., 64 p., 65-66 numb. l., 67-518,
　　32, 24 p. 21cm. 4° [His Sermoens, 10.
　　parte]
　　　Cut (putto) on t.-p.
　　　Permission dated (4th p. l.) 4 Feb. 1688.

68-342	Errata, 4th p. ℓ.ᵛ ("Outras Erratas do Primeiro Tomo do Rosario... Erratas deste Segundo Tomo do Rosario.") According to Leite "Com a data de 1688 há duas impressões..." Bound in contemporary limp vellum. Rodrigues 2512; Backer 8:650; Leite 9:198; Innocencio 1:290.

B688 =Y36d [R] Ybáñez de Faria, Diego, fl. 1660.
D. D. Didacus Covarruvias A Leiva Toletanus, Segobiensis Episcopus, Supremique Castellæ Senatus Præses; Enucleatus Et Auctus Practicis In Quæstionibus Per D. Didacum Ybañez De Faria Gaditanum, Præpotentis Monarchæ Caroli II. Hispaniarum Indiarumque Regis Catholici A Consiliis, In Cancellaria De Buenos Aires Regii Fisci Patronum, & in Goatemalensi Prætorio apud Americam primarios inter Judices adscriptum. ...
Lugduni, Sumpt. Petri Borde, Joan. & Petri Arnaud. M. DC. LXXXVIII. Cum Privilegio Regis.
2 p.ℓ., 330, [44] p. 36cm. fol.
Title in red and black.
Cut (coat of arms) on t.-p.
Privilege dated (2d p. ℓ.ᵛ) 14 Apr. 1688.
Forms the 2d volume of his ... Novæ additiones, observationes et notæ ad libros variarum resolutionum ... D. Didaci Covarruvias a Leiva... , Leyden, 1688.
First pub. Madrid, 1660.
In this copy there is a blank ℓ. at end.
Bound in contemporary calf.
Medina(BHA)1820n; Palau(2)117454.

5755, 1909

1689

F689 A111b A. B. C. Boek, Voor Jacobus de Tweede, Waar uyt hy kan leeren (dewyl hy nu tyt fal hebben) hoe ontrou welijk door hem alle onheylen en Oorlogen tegen Hollant sijn gebrouwen, door het aenraden en gehoor geven vande Paters Jesuyten.
Gedrukt tot Molevelt, By Pater Peters. inde gekroonde Molenaers Soon, aldernaest den Paepsche Luypert, 1689.
32 p. 20cm. 4⁰
Cut on t.-p.
Knuttel 13220; Backer 11:1089.

28615, 1945

D689 A172o [R] An Account of the Late Revolutions in New-England; In a Letter.
[Boston, Benjamin Harris, 1689?]
7 p. 20.5cm. 4⁰
Caption title.
Signed at end: Boston, June 6. 1689: Sir, Your Servant A. B.
At foot of p. 7: The foregoing Account, being very carefully and critically Examined, by divers very Worthy and Faithful Gentlemen, was advised to be Published for the preventing of False Reports: And is to be Sold at the London-Coffee-House.
Reprinted by W. H. Whitmore in The Andros Tracts, v.2, p. 189-202.
Not the same as a pamphlet by Nathaniel Byfield pub. the same year under title: An Account of the late revolution [sic] in New-England.
JCB(2)2:1370; Sabin 1547; cf. Evans 462; cf. Wing B6381.

05887, before 1865

B69 G643v 39 Acevedo, Francisco.
Villancicos Que Se Cantaron En Los Maytines del gloriosissimo Principe de la Iglesia el Señor San Pedro En la Santa Iglesia Cathedral Metropolitana de Mexico. ... Escrivelos: El Br. Don Francisco de Azevedo Pusolos en Metro Musico Antonio de Salazar Maestro de Capilla de dicha Santa Iglesia.
En Mexico. Por los Herederos de la Viuda de Bernardo Calderon. Año de 1689.
[8] p. 20cm. 4⁰
Imprint at end.
Woodcut title vignette (St. Peter within a decorative frame)
Bound, in contemporary vellum, as no. 39 with 42 other items.

28939, 1941

E689 A238q Les Admirables Qualitez Du Kinkina, Confirmées Par Plusieurs Experiences, Et La Maniere De S'En servir dans toutes les fiévres pour toute sorte d'âge, de sexe, & de complexions.
A Paris, Chez Martin Jouvenel, Marchand Libraire, au bas de la ruë de la Harpe, à l'Image S. Augustin, proche le Pont S. Michel. M. DC. LXXXIX. Avec Privilege & Approbations.
12 p.ℓ., 164, [2], 4 p. 16.5cm. 12⁰
"Cut (monogram) on t.-p.
"... Il y trouvera encore non seulement ce qu'en a dit & enseigné le Chevalier Talbot Anglois, mais aussi tout ce qu'il y a de meilleur

dans Sebastien Bade...", 7th p.l.
"Achevé d'imprimer pour la premiere fois le 9. Avril 1689... A Paris. De l'Imprimerie de la Veuve de Denis Langlois. 1689." (p. [2] at end).
Booksellers' advertisement, 4 p. at end.
In this copy there is a blank leaf preceding the final 4 pages.
Bound in contemporary calf.
Waring339.

69-951

BA689 A283s Aguilera, Francisco de, d. 1704.
Sermon, Qve Predico El P. Francisco De Agvilera, Professo De La Compañia De Jesvs. En La Solemne Fiesta A La Colocasion de vn nuevo Sumptuoso Retablo, que dedicò al Gloriosso Apostol de las Indias S. Francisco Xavier, El Colegio Del Espiritv Sancto en su Iglesia de la misma Compañia, en Concurrencia de vna Missa Nueva. ...
Con liçencia en la Puebla, en la Imprenta de Diego Fernandez de Leon, este año de 1689.
5 p.l., 13 numb. l. 19.5cm. 4°
Approbation dated (4th p.l.ᵛ) 21 Nov. 1689.
Palau(2)3748; Medina(Puebla)112; Backer1:90.

13059, 1921

BA689 -A977d [Ayeta, Francisco de]
Defensa De La Verdad, Consagrada A La Luz De La Justicia; Svjeta A La Comun Censvra, Para Qve Sea Patente Al Teatro Del Mvndo.
[Madrid? ca. 1689]
2 p.l., 14, 302, 17 numb. l. 28.5cm. fol.
Signed (numb. l. 302): Fr. Francisco de Ayeta.
The Franciscan case in a controversy over missions with the Bishop of Guadalajara, Mexico, Juan de Santiago León Garabito.
"Bvllas Apostolicas": numb. l. 1-14.
In this copy there is a blank leaf at end.
Bound in contemporary vellum.
With this is bound a collection of the relevant royal cedulas and a papal bull. Text begins: Yo Pedro de Arce y Andrade, Escrivano del Rey... Certifico, y doy fee... [Madrid, 1689].
Palau(2)20798; Medina(BHA)6238; Streit2:2290; Andrade2261.

28526, 1940

BA673 -P434m Ayeta, Francisco de.
Señor. Fray Francisco de Ayeta, Ex-Custodio, y Padre de la Provincia del Santo Evangelio de Mexico, y Procurador General de todas las de las Indias, dize: Que por decreto de 26. de Enero deste año, se sirviò V. Magestad de mandar se hiziesse, notorio al Suplicante el pedimento del Licenciado Don Antonio Arguellez, Fiscal del Consejo por la negociacion de Nueua España, sobre si ay, ò no obligacion en los Prelados Regulares de dar las causas de la remocion de sus subditos Doctrineros al Obispo, como al Vice-Patron con las respuestas fiscales ...
[Madrid? ca. 1689]
15 numb. l. 31.5cm. fol.
Title from caption and beginning of text.
Includes commentary on "las respuestas fiscales del Licenciado Don Ioseph de Ortega, y Don Antonio Arguellez".
Cites (10th, 14th numb. l.) his Defensa de la verdad. [Madrid? ca. 1689]
Bound as the 3d of 5 items with: Perea Quintanilla, Miguel de. Manifiesto a la reyna ... [Mexico? 1673?]

BA689 -A977s ——— ———Another copy. 30.5cm.
In this copy there is a blank l. at end.
Palau(2)20800 (this copy?).

04154, 1870
70-578

DA689 B154m Bailey, John, 1644-1697.
Man's chief End To Glorifie God; Or Some Brief Sermon-Notes On I Cor.10.31. By the Reverend Mr. John Bailey, Sometime Preacher and Prisoner of Christ at Limerick in Ireland, And now Pastor to the Church of Christ in Watertown in New-England. ...
Boston Printed by Samuel Green, and are to be Sold by Richard Wilkins Book-Seller near the Town-House. Anno. 1689.
4 p.l., 160, 40, [3] p. 15cm. 8°
"To the Reader" signed (4th p.l.ᵛ): J.M.
With, as issued, "To my Loving and Dearly Beloved Christian Friends, in and about Lymerick" with caption title, separate paging and signatures.
In this copy there is a blank l. at end.
Bound in contemporary calf.
Evans456; WingB448; Sabin2734.

3037, 1907

DA689 B154m [Bailey, John] 1644-1697.
To my Loving and Dearly Beloved Christian Friends, in and about Lymerick.
[Boston, Printed by Samuel Green for Richard Wilkins, 1689.]

40, [3] p. 15cm. 8⁰ (Issued as a part of his Man's chief End To Glorifie God. Boston, 1689.)
Dated (p. 40) 8 May 1684.
In this copy there is a blank leaf at end.
Evans 457; Wing B449; Sabin 2734.

3037A, 1907

D689
B264a
[Barbon, Nicholas] d. 1698.
An Apology For The Builder; Or A Discourse Shewing The Cause and Effects Of The Increase of Building.
London, Printed in the Year, MDCLXXXIX.
1 p.ℓ., 37 p. 19cm. 4⁰
Occasioned by a building tax passed June 17, 1685; argument illustrated with American examples.
First pub. London, 1685.
Bound in contemporary calf, rebacked.
Wing B705; Sabin 1765; Kress 1683.

11369, 1918

H689
B817h
Brandano, Alessandro.
Historia Delle Guerre Di Portogallo Succedute per l'occasione della separazione di quel Regno dalla Corona Cattolica Descritte ... Da Alessandro Brandano.
In Venezia, M.DC.LXXXIX. Presso Paolo Baglioni. Con Licenza De' Svperiori, E Privilegio.
4 p.ℓ., 512, [27] p. front. 23.5cm. 4⁰
Cut (printer's device) on t.-p.
Half-title: Historia Di Portogallo.
License dated (last page) 28 Sept. 1688.
Errata, p. [26] at end.
Includes material on the Dutch conquests in Brazil.
Bound in contemporary paper boards.
Palau(2) 34446.

12857, 1920

D689
B993aL1
[R]
Byfield, Nathaniel, 1653-1733.
An Account Of The Late Revolution In New-England. Together with the Declaration Of The Gentlemen, Merchants, and Inhabitants of Boston, and the Country adjacent. April 18. 1689.
Written by Mʳ. Nathanael Byfield, a Merchant of Bristol in New-England, to his Friends in London.
Licensed, June 27. 1689. J. Fraser. London: Printed for Ric. Chiswell, at the Rose and Crown in St. Paul's Church-Yard. MDCLXXXIX.
20 p. 18cm. 4⁰
"The Declaration Of The Gentlemen, Merchants, and Inhabitants of Boston, and the Country Adja-

cent. April 18. 1689" (p. 7-19), drawn up by Cotton Mather, 1st pub. Boston, 1689, as broadside.
Includes (p. 20) copy of broadside addressed to Sir Edmund Andros "At the Town-House in Boston, April 18. 1689." signed by Waite Winthrop and others.
Reprinted by W. H. Whitmore in The Andros Tracts, v.1, p. 1-10.

D689
B993aL2
[R]
————Another issue. 19.5cm.
With "Printed according to the Copy Printed in New-England by Samuel Green. 1689." added to bottom of p. 19.
JCB(2)2:1372; JCBAR 24:16-17; Sabin 9708; Church 708; Wing B6379; Holmes(C) 85B.

13582, 1923
05886, before 1865

D689
B993aE
[R]
Byfield, Nathaniel, 1653-1733.
An Account Of The Late Revolution In New-England. Together with the Declaration of the Gentlemen, Merchants, and Inhabitants of Boston, and the Countrey adjacent, April 18. 1689.
Written by Mr. Nathanael Byfield, a Merchant of Bristol in New England, to his Friends in London.
Licensed, June 27. 1689. J. Fraser.
Edinburgh, Re-Printed in the Year. 1689.
7 p. 18cm. 4⁰
Caption title; imprint at end.
First pub. London, 1689.
"The Declaration of the Gentlemen, Merchants, and Inhabitants of Boston, and the Countrey adjacent, April 18. 1689" (p. 3-7), drawn up by Cotton Mather, 1st pub. Boston, 1689, as broadside.
Includes (p. 7) copy of broadside addressed to Sir Edmund Andros "At the Town-House in Boston, April 18. 1689." signed by Waite Winthrop and others.
Reprinted by W. H. Whitmore in The Andros Tracts, v.1, p. 1-10.
JCB(2)2:1373; JCBAR 24:16-17; Sabin 9708; Church 709; Wing B6380; Holmes(C) 85c.

02316, 1850

B689
C335p
Casas, Bartolomé de las, Bp. of Chiapa, 1474-1566.
Popery Truly Display'd in its Bloody Colours: Or, a Faithful Narrative Of The Horrid and Unexampled Massacres, Butcheries, and all manner of Cruelties, that Hell and Malice could invent, committed by the Popish Spanish Party on the Inhabitants of West-India: Together With the Devastations of several Kingdoms in America by Fire

and Sword, for the space of Forty and Two Years, from the time of its first Discovery by them. Composed first in Spanish by Bartholomew de las Casas, a Bishop there, and an Eye-Witness of most of these Barbarous Cruelties; afterward Translated by him into Latin, then by other hands, into High-Dutch, Low-Dutch, French, and now Taught to speak Modern English.
London, Printed for R. Hewson at the Crown in Cornhil, near the Stocks-Market. 1689.
4 p.ℓ., 80 p. 20cm. 4°
Transl. from: Breuissima relacion de la destruycion de las Indias... 1st pub. Seville, 1552.
JCB(2)2:1374; WingC798; Palau(2)46969; Sabin 11288; Cundall(WI)1989; Streit 1:711; Medina (BHA)v. 2, p. 475.

06014, before 1882

D689
C591d
[Claridge, Richard] 1649-1723.
A Defence Of The Present Government Under King William & Queen Mary. Shewing The Miseries of England under the Arbitrary Reign Of The Late King James II. The Reasonableness of the Proceedings against him, and the Happiness that will certainly follow a peaceable Submission to, and Standing by King William and Q. Mary. By a Divine of the Church of England.
London, Printed for R. Baldwin in the Old-Bayly. 1689.
1 p.ℓ., 10 p. 21.5cm. 4°
License (p.ℓ.^{v}) dated: May 16. 1689.
Wing C4432; Smith(Friends)1:408.

65-242

D689
C611n
Clarke, Samuel, 1599-1683.
A New Description Of The World. Or A Compendious Treatise of the Empires, Kingdoms, States, Provinces, Countries, Islands, Cities and Towns of Europe, Asia, Africa and America ... Faithfully Collected from the best Authors, By S. Clark.
London, Printed for Hen. Rhodes next Door to the Swan Tavern, near Brides-Lane, in Fleet-Street, 1689.
3 p.ℓ., 232 p. front. 14.5cm. 12°
License dated (verso of t.-p.) 11 Aug. 1688.
Bound in contemporary calf.
JCB(2)2:1375; WingC4554.

04236, 1871

BA689
C626t
Clemente, Claudio, 1594?-1642 or 3.
Tablas Chronologicas, En Qve Se Contienen Los Svcessos Eclesiasticos, y Seculares de España, Africa, Indias Orientales, y Occidentales, desde su principio, hasta el año 1642. de la Reparacion Humana. ... Compuestas Por El Padre Claudio Clemente, De La Compania de Iesvs, ... Ilvstradas, Y Añadidas Desde El Año 1642. Hasta el presente de 1689. con las noticias que se hallan entre estas** Por El Licenciado Vicente Ioseph Migvel, Natvral De la muy Antigua, Leal, y Coronada Ciudad de Valencia.
En Valencia, en la Imprenta de Jayme De Bordazar, año 1689. A costa de la Compañia de Libreros.
8 p.ℓ., 275 p. 20.5cm. 4°
Cut on t.-p.
Dedication dated (2d p.ℓ.^{v}) 21 Mar. 1689.
Palau, alone among the authorities cited, considers Claudio Clemente a pseudonym and enters his works under Juan Eusebio Nieremberg.
Revised and augmented by Vicente José Miguel, including the addition of material taken from Théophile Raynaud and Philippe Labbé.
Tables by Clemente are recorded as pub. Madrid, 1641-1644 (cf. Palau(2)190949-190950). His tables were also issued Saragossa, 1676-1677 with additions by Diego José Dormer (cf. Palau(2)190949, 190951). Errata, 8th p.ℓ.^{r}
Bound in contemporary calf with 3 p. of contemporary ms. notes at end.
JCB(2)2:1376; Palau(2)190952; Medina(BHA) 1834; Sabin13632; Backer2:1227; Streit 1:707.

0807, 1846

D689
C697o
A Collection of Papers Relating to the Present Juncture of Affairs in England. Viz. 1. The Humble Petition of Seven Bishops to his Majesty. ... The Third Edition.
Licensed and Entred according to Order.
London printed, and are to be sold by Richard Janeway in Queen's-head-Court in Paternoster-Row, 1689.
1 p.ℓ., 34 p. 19cm. 4°
Contains the texts of 15 "papers".
First pub. [London] 1688.
Also issued as part 1 of A compleat collection of papers in twelve parts. London, 1689.
Bound in contemporary calf as the 1st of 12 items after collective prelims.

D689
C697o
cop. 2
———— Another copy. 19cm.
Title-page disintegrated with slight loss of text.
Bound as the 1st of 12 items.

Wing C5169B; cf. JCB(2)2:1351n; cf. Sabin 81492n.
12463A, 1920
06842A, before 1882

D689
C697o
A Compleat Collection Of Papers, In Twelve Parts: Relating to the Great Revolutions In England and Scotland, From the Time of the Seven Bishops Petitioning K. James II. against the Dispensing Power, June 8. 1688. to the Coronation of King William and Queen Mary, April 11. 1689.
London; Printed by J.D. for R.Clavel at the Peacock, Henry Mortlock at the Phenix, and Jonathan Robinson at the Golden Lion in St. Paul's Church-Yard, 1689.
4 p.ℓ., 12 pts. in 1 v. 19cm. 4°
The editing of these twelve collections has been ascribed to Gilbert Burnet, either by confusing them with his Collection of eighteen papers relating to the affairs of church and state and his Six papers, both London, 1689, or on account of a similarity between the contents of the present collections and Burnet's.
Each part has separate paging and signatures and a special t.-p. reading "... Collection of papers relating to the present juncture of affairs in England... London printed, and are to be sold by Richard Janeway..."
More than one edition of some of the collections is recorded -- 1st collection: 1688, "3d" ed. 1689; 2d collection: 1688, "3d" ed. 1689; 3d collection: 1688, "2d" ed. 1689; 4th collection: 1688, 1689. The 5th collection is dated 1688, and the 6th-12th are dated 1689.
On some copies of the collective t.-p. the imprint reads "... Phoenix...".
Although a booksellers' advertisement, 2d p.ℓ.ᵛ, and the t.-p. of the 12th collection ("The Twelvth and Last Collection of Papers (Vol.I.)") provide for the issuance of further collections, no more were published.
Rival 6th, 7th, and 8th "Collections of papers" were pub. London, 1689, but these have completely different contents. The 7th of these bears Richard Baldwin's name in the imprint, and he is probably also responsible for the 6th and the 8th.
In this copy Collection 1 is 3d ed., 1689, Collection 2 is 3d ed., 1689, Collection 3 is 2d ed., 1689, and Collection 4 is the 1689 ed.
Bound in contemporary calf.

D689
C697o
cop.2
——— Another copy. 19cm.
Collective prelims. wanting.
In this copy the Collections are dated the same as in the preceding copy.

D689
C697o
cop.3
——— Another copy. 20cm.
Collective prelims. and Collection 11 wanting.
In this copy Collection 1 is the 1688 ed., Collection 2 is the 1688 ed., Collection 3 is 2d ed., 1689, and Collection 4 is the 1689 ed.
Bound in contemporary calf, rebacked.
JCB(2)2:1351; Wing C5638A; McAlpin 4:332; Sabin81492n; Holmes(I.)79n; Dexter(Cong.)2347.
12463, 1920
06842, before 1882
06843

F689
C783v
Copia van't Octroy Door de Hoogh Mog. Heeren Staten Generael der Vereenighde Nederlanden gegeven aen Jan Reeps, en syne mede Participanten, om een Colonie op te rechten aen de Westzyde van Rio de Las Amasones, tot aen Cabo d'Orange. Midtsgaders Een korte beschryvinge van de Landen, Vruchten Gedierten, ende Visschen, &c. nevens eenige opgestelde Conditien, on een Compagnie te maecken, tot voortsettinge van dese Colonie, ten meesten voordeele van de gemene Participanten.
In 's Graven-hage, By Jacobus Scheltus, Ordinaris Drucker van de Hoogh Mogende Heeren Staten Generael der Vereenighde Nederlanden. Anno 1689. Met Privilegie.
16 p. 20.5cm. 4°
Cut on t.-p.
"Octroy" (p. 3-6) dated 7 Jan. 1689.
JCB(2)2:1377; Sabin16674; Borba de Moraes 1:177-78; Muller(1872)713; Knuttel13299.
03672, before 1866

F689
C864h
[Courtilz, Gatien de, sieur de Sandras] 1644-1712.
Histoire De La Guerre De Hollande. Où l'on voit ce qui est arrivé de plus remarquable depuis l'année 1672. jusques en 1677. Premiere [-Seconde] Partie.
Suivant la Copie de Paris, A La Haye, Chez Henri van Bulderen, Marchand Libraire dans le Pooten, à l'Enseigne de Mezeray. M.DC.LXXXIX.
2 v.: 4 p.ℓ., 359 p.; 1 p.ℓ., 119 (i.e. 219) p. 15.5cm. 12°
Cut on title-pages.
Added t.-p., engr., v.1.
An earlier Paris printing, as implied by the imprint, is fictitious.
Also issued with variant imprint, the same as the present copy's but with an additional line "Avec Privilege des Etats de Hollande & West-

frise."
  Also issued with a different imprint, Cologne, P. Marteau, 1689.
  Some copies have an additional p.ℓ. bearing the privileges of the Estates of Hollande and West Friesland.
  There are variant versions of the preface. In this copy the 1st line reads "I'Ai balancé quel-". There are other copies with 1st line reading "Il seroit à souhai-".
  Cf. Cioranescu(17)22314.

71-82

D689 The Declaration Of The Reasons and Motives
-D295o   For the Present Appearing in Arms Of Their Majesties Protestant Subjects In the Province of Maryland. Licens'd, November 28th 1689. J.[ames] F.[raser].
  Published by Authority. Maryland, Printed by William Nuthead at the City of St. Maries. Re-printed in London, and Sold by Randal Taylor near Stationers Hall, 1689.
  8 p. 30.5cm. fol.
  Caption title; imprint at end.
  First pub. Saint Marys City, 1689.
  JCB(2)2:1380; WingP3823; Sabin19180; Evans466; Baer(Md.)134; Wroth(Md.)2.

03671, before 1866

D689 The Eighth Collection of Papers Relating to the
C697o   Present Juncture of Affairs in England. Viz. I. Proposals to the present Convention for Setling the Government. ...
  London printed, and are to be sold by Rich. Janeway in Queen's-head Court in Pater-Noster Row, 1689.
  1 p.ℓ., 34 p. 19cm. 4°
  Contains texts of 7 "papers".
  Also issued as a part of A compleat collection of papers in twelve parts. London, 1689.
  Not the same as An Eighth Collection of papers relating to the present Juncture of Affairs, London [R. Baldwin?] 1689.
  Bound in contemporary calf as the 8th of 12 items after collective prelims.

D689   ——— Another copy. 19cm.
C697o   Bound as the 8th of 12 items.
cop.2

D689   ——— Another copy. 20cm.
C697o   Bound in contemporary calf, rebacked, as the 8th of 11 items.
cop.3

  Wing E265A; McAlpin 4:336; cf. JCB(2)2: 1351n; cf. Sabin81492n.

12463H, 1920
06842H, before 1882
06843H

D689 Eleventh Collection of Papers Relating to the
C697o   Present Juncture of Affairs in England and Scotland. Viz. I. An Answer to the Desertion Discuss'd, being a Defence of the late and present Proceedings. ...
  London printed, and are to be sold by Richard Janeway in Queen's-head-Court in Pater-noster-Row, 1689.
  1 p.ℓ., 34 p. 19cm. 4°
  Contains the texts of 7 "papers".
  Also issued as a part of A compleat collection of papers in twelve parts. London, 1689.
  Bound in contemporary calf as the 11th of 12 items after collective prelims.

D689   ——— Another copy. 19cm.
C697o   Bound as the 11th of 12 items.
cop.2   Wing E498; McAlpin4:336-37; cf. JCB(2) 2:1351n; cf. Sabin81492n.

12463K, 1920
06842K, before 1882

F689 Engeland Beroerd Onder de Regeering Van
E57b   Koning Jacobus de II. En hersteld door Willem En Maria, Prins en Princesse van Orangie, Verkoozen en Gekroond tot Koning en Koningin Van Engeland, Schotland, Vrankrijk en Yerland. ... Seer naeukeurig na de Engelsche Orgineelen, en Autentijke Stukken en Bewijsen, in het Nederduytsch by een gebragt. Verciert met konstige koopere Plaaten en Medalien.
  t'Amsterdam, By Jan ten Hoorn, Boekverkooper, tegen over het Oude Heeren Logement. 1689.
  4 p.ℓ., 256, 259-327, 128, [4] p. illus., 11 plates (incl. 3 fold.) 22cm. 4°
  Added t.-p., engr.
  Preliminary matter includes poetry by Ludolf Smids (4th p.ℓ.ᵛ).
  Errata, at end.

13746, 1923

BA673　[Fernández de Santa Cruz y Sahagún
-P434m　　Manuel, Bp.] 1637-1699.
　　Consvlta Qve Haze A Su Magestad El
Obispo De La Pvebla De Los Angeles,
Aviendo Visto Vn Libro, Intitvlado: Defensa De La Verdad.
　　[Puebla de los Angeles? ca. 1689]
　　1 p. ℓ., 18 numb. ℓ. 31.5cm. fol.
　　Signed at end: Manuel, Obispo de la Puebla.
　　A reply to Ayeta, Francisco de. Defensa de la verdad. [Madrid? ca. 1689]
　　Bound as the 5th of 5 items with: Perea Quintanilla, Miguel de. Manifiesto a la reyna ... [Mexico? 1673?]
　　Palau(2)89730; Medina(Puebla)213; Sabin 76776.
04156, 1870

BA689　Florencia, Francisco de, 1619-1695.
F632c　　La Casa Peregrina, Solar Ilvstre, En Qve Nacio La Reyna De Los Angeles; Albergue Soberano, en Que Se Hospedo El Rey Eterno Hecho Hombre En Tiempo: Cielo Abreviado, En Que El Sol De Justicia Puso Su Thalamo, Para Desposarse Con La Humana Naturaleza La Casa De Nazareth, Oy De Loreto, Trasladada Por Ministerio De Angeles, Primero A Dalmacia, Despves A Italia. Copiada, Y Sacada A Luz De Los Escritores Antigvos De Ella Por El Padre Francisco De Florencia De La Compañia De Jesvs De La Provincia De Nueva-España. ...
　　En Mexico, en la Imprenta de Antuerpia de los Herederos de la Viuda de Bernardo Calderon. Año de 1689.
　　9 p. ℓ., 123 numb. ℓ., [10] p. 20cm. 4°
　　"Protesta" dated (p. [10] at end) 12 May 1689.
　　Errata, p. [9] at end.
　　Bound in contemporary vellum.
　　Palau(2)92346; Medina(Mexico)1440; Backer3: 797-8; Sabin24819n.
06408, before 1923

BA689　Florencia, Francisco de, 1619-1695.
F632d　　Descripcion Historica, Y Moral Del Yermo De San Migvel, De Las Cvevas En El Reyno de la Nueva-España, y invencion de la milagrosa Imagen de Christo nuestro Señor Crucificado, que se venera en ellas. Con Vn Breve Compendio De la admirable vida del Venerable Anacoreta Fray Bartolomè de Iesus Maria, y algunas noticias del Santo Fray Iuan de S. Ioseph su compañero. Por El Padre Francisco De Florencia, de la Compañia de Jesus.
　　Impresso en Cadiz en la Imprenta de la Compañia de Iesus, por Christoval de Requena. [1689?]
　　16, [6], 57, 60-300 p. 15cm. 8°
　　License dated (p. 15, 1st count) 1 Nov. 1689.
　　Bound in contemporary vellum.
　　Palau(2)92345; Medina(BHA)6466; Sabin 24805; Backer3:798.
06409, before 1923

BA689　[Florencia, Francisco de] 1619-1695.
F632v　　Vida Admirable, Y Mverte dichosa del Religioso P. Geronimo De Figveroa. Professo de la Compañia de Jesvs en la Provincia de Nueva-España. Missionero De quarenta años entre los Indios Taraumares, y Tepehuanes de la Sierra Madre: y despues Rector del Colegio Maximo, y Preposito de la Casa Professa de Mexico. ...
　　Con Licencia De Los Svperiores. En Mexico: por Doña Maria de Benavides, Viuda de Juan de Ribera en el Empedradillo. Año de 1689.
　　4 p. ℓ., 40 numb. ℓ. 21cm. 4°
　　Dedication signed (2d p. ℓ.^{v}) Francisco de Florencia.
　　License dated (4th p. ℓ.^{r}) 12 Dec. 1689.
　　Palau(2)92353; Medina(Mexico)1462; Sabin 24819n, 99450; Backer3:797; Wagner59; Streit2:2259.
28578, 1940

D689　A Fourth Collection of Papers Relating to the
C697o　　Present Juncture of Affairs in England.
　　Viz. I. The Prince of Orange's first Declaration from the Hague, Octob. 10. 1688. ...
　　Licensed and Entred according to Order. London printed, and are to be sold by Richard Janeway in Queen's-head-Court in Paternoster-Row, 1689.
　　1 p. ℓ., 34 p. 19cm. 4°
　　Contains the texts of 12 "papers".
　　First pub. London, 1688.
　　Also issued as part 4 of A compleat collection of papers in twelve parts. London, 1689.
　　Bound in contemporary calf as the 4th of 12 items after collective prelims.

D689   ——— ———Another copy. 19cm.
C697o   Bound as the 4th of 12 items.
cop. 2

D689   ——— ———Another copy. 20cm.
C697o   Bound in contemporary calf, rebacked,
cop. 3   as the 4th of 11 items.
                   Wing F1687; cf. JCB(2)2:1351n; cf. Sabin
               81492n.
12463D, 1920
06842D, before 1882
06843D

DA689   [Fox, George] 1624-1691.
F791   The True Christians Distinguished From such as
           go under the Name of Christians. With a Short
           Epistle Concerning The Holy Scriptures of Truth.
           ... By G.F.
           London, Printed for Thomas Northcott in George-
           Yard in Lombard-Street, MDCLXXXIX.
               1 p.ℓ., 16, [2] p. 19cm. 4°
           Dated (p. 13) "the seventh of first Month, [16]88/9."
           Bookseller's advertisement, [2] p. at end.
           Smith(Friends)1:688; Wing F1966.
11464, 1918

EB   France--Sovereigns, etc., 1643-1715 (Louis
-W&A   XIV).   13 Dec 1689
317   Arrest Du Conseil D'Estat Du Roy, Qui Or-
           donne que les Droits seront levez & perceus sur
           les Castors en Peau & en Poil qui viendront des
           Pays Estrangers dans les Ports du Royaume,
           permis par les Arrests des 24. Mars 1685. &
           25. Janvier 1687. même dans les Vaisseaux qui
           seront pris par les Armateurs François. Du
           treiziéme Decembre 1689.
           [Paris] De l'Imprimerie de Frederic Leonard,
           Premier Imprimeur du Roy, & seul pour les
           Finances. 1689.
               4 p. 25cm. (32cm. in case) 4°
           Caption title; imprint at end.
           Wroth & Annan317; Harrisse(NF)162; Sabin56075.
15716, 1930

EB   France--Treaties, etc., 1643-1715 (Louis XIV)
F8455   16 Nov.1686
1689   Traité De Neutralité Conclu A Londres le
1   seiziéme Novembre 1686. Entre Les Roys De
           France Et D'Angleterre, Touchant Les Pays

Des Deux Roys En Amerique.
     A Paris, De l'Imprimerie de Frederic
Leonard, premier Imprimeur du Roy, de
Monseigneur, & seul pour les Finances.
M. DC. LXXXVI. [i.e. 1689] Avec Privilege
De Sa Majesté.
        1 p.ℓ., 12 p. 25.5cm. 4°
     Colophon: De l'Imprimerie de Frederic
Leonard, Premier Imprimeur ordinaire du
Roy, de Monseigneur, du Clergé de France,
& seul pour les Finances. 1689. Avec Privi-
lege De Sa Majesté.
        First pub. Paris, 1686.
        "Whitehall Treaty of Neutrality."
        Sabin96531; Leclerc(1878)2623; Davenport79.
15495, 1929

DB   Gt.Brit.--Parliament--House of Commons.
-G7875   [Votes of the House of Commons, 1689-1758].
1689   [London, 1689-1758].
1-34   34 v. 29cm. fol.
     This collection, from the library of the earls
of Marchmont, consists of printed Votes (with
many manuscript annotations) among which are
interspersed other separately issued parliamen-
tary and non-parliamentary papers and other
papers in ms. (24 v.); a ms. "Index to the Votes
...Anno 1680: and from the year 1688 to the
year 1728 inclusive" (1 v.); and additional notes
in ms. for the years 1689-91, 1694-1705, 1709-
1719 (9 v.).
10376-10473, 1914

DB   Gt.Brit.--Parliament, 1689-1690--House of
-G7875   Commons.
1689   Votes Of The House of Commons, Mercurij
1   23. Octobris, 1689 [-Lunae 27° die Januarij,
           1689 [/90]].
           London, Printed by Charles Bill and Thomas
Newcomb, Printers to the King and Queens most
Excellent Majesties. 1689 [-1689/90].
             148 p. 29cm. fol.
           Caption titles; imprint at end of each number.
           Issued in pts. numbered 1-74.
           Bound in Votes of the House of Commons, v.1.
10376-1, 1914

DB   Gt. Brit.--Parliament, 1689-1690--House of
-G7875   Commons--Speaker.
1689   The Speech Of the Right Honourable Henry
1   Powle, Esq; Speaker Of The House of Commons:
                   On Munday the Sixteenth of December, 1689. At
                   The Passing of Four Bills, Entituled, I. An Act
                   for a Grant to Their Majesties of an Aid of Two
                   shillings in the Pound for One Year. II. An Act
                   for Declaring the Rights of the Subject, and
                   Settling the Succession of the Crown. III. An
                   Act for Naturalizing William Watts, an Infant.
                   IV. An Act for Declaring and Enacting John Roger-
                   son to be a Natural born Subject of this Realm.
                      London, Printed by Charles Bill, and Thomas
                   Newcomb, Printers to the King and Queens most
                   Excellent Majesties. MDCLXXXIX.
                      1 p.ℓ., 2 p. 29cm. fol.
                      Bound in Votes of the House of Commons, v.1,
                   after Votes for 16 Dec. 1689.
                      Wing P3115
10378, 1914

D689   Gt. Brit.--Sovereigns, etc., 1689-1694.
G786d   (William and Mary)   7 May 1689
                     Declaracion De La Guerra Por Su Magestad
                  Britanica, Contra El Rey De Los Franceses.
                     [Saragossa, 1689]
                     3 p. 19.5cm. 4°
                     Caption title.
                     Dated (p. 3) "17. [i.e. 7] de Mayo de 1689."
                     Transl. from: Their majesties declaration against
                  the French king, London, 7 May 1689.
                     Palau(2)69421.
66-67

bDB   Gt. Brit.--Sovereigns, etc., 1689-1694
G7888   (William and Mary)   7 May 1689
1689   Their Majesties Declaration Against the
1   French King.
                     London, Printed by Charles Bill, and Thomas
                  Newcomb, Printers to the King and Queen's
                  most Excellent Majesties. 1689.
                     Broadside. 43 x 35.5cm. 1°
                     Declaration of war.
                     Dated at end: 7 May 1689.
                     Steele records three London editions of
                  this same year.
                     Wing W2502; Steele E4001.
4449, 1908

DB   Gt. Brit.--Sovereigns, etc., 1689-1694 (William
-G7875   and Mary)   19 Oct. 1689
1689   His Majesties Most Gracious Speech To both
1   Houses of Parliament, On Saturday the 19th. Day
                   of October, 1689.
                      London, Printed by Charles Bill, and Thomas
                   Newcomb, Printers to the King and Queens most
                   Excellent Majesties. MDCLXXXIX.
                      4 p. 29cm. fol.
                      Cut (royal arms) on t.-p. (Steele 113).
                      Calls for supplies necessary for the war against
                   France.
                      Bound in Votes of the House of Commons, v.1,
                   before Votes for 23 Oct 1689.
                      Wing W2381.
10377-1, 1914

E689   Hennepin, Louis, ca. 1640-ca. 1705.
H515b   Beschreibung Der Landschafft Lovisiana
                  Welche/Auf Befehl des Königs in Frankreich/neu-
                  lich gegen Sudwesten Neu-Frankreichs In Ameri-
                  ca entdecket worden. Nebenst einer Land-Carten
                  und Bericht von den Sitten und Lebens-Art der
                  Wilden in selbiger Landschafft. In Französi-
                  scher Sprache herausgegeben durch P. Ludwig
                  Hennepin/Mission. Recoll. und Notarium Apos-
                  tolicum. Nun aber ins Teutsche übersetzt.
                     Nürnberg/In Verlag Andreä Otto 1689.
                     425 p. 2 fold. maps. 13.5cm. 12°
                     Cut on t.-p.; t.-p. in red and black.
                     Transl. from Description de la Louisiane, 1st
                  pub. Paris, 1683.
                     Includes Marquette's "Beschreibung Einer son-
                  derbaren Reise Etlicher bisher noch unbekannter
                  Länder und Völcker im Mitternächtigen America.
                  Welche im Jahr 1673. Durch P. Marquette S.J.
                  und Herrn Jolliet verrichtet worden. Aus dem
                  Französischen ins Teutsche übersetzet." (p. 353-
                  425) transl. from "Découverte de quelques pays
                  et nations de l'Amerique septentrionale" which
                  appeared in Melchisédech Thevenot's Recueil de
                  voyages, Paris, 1681.
                     In this copy there are three blank leaves at
                  end.
                     JCB(2)2:1379; Harrisse(NF)163; Palmer335;
                  Paltsits(Hennepin)lii; Streit 2:2742.
03012, 1865

FC650   Hollandse Mercurius, Verhalende de voor-
H737   naemste Saken van Staet, En andere Voor-
39   vallen, Die in en omtrent de Vereenigde

	Nederlanden, En elders in Europa, In het Jaer 1688 Zijn geschiet. Het Negen-en-Dertigste Deel. Tot Haerlem, Gedruckt by Abraham Casteleyn, Stads-Drucker', op de Marckt, in de Blye Druck. Anno 1689. 3 p.ℓ., 318, [6] p. 5 plates (incl. 1 fold.), map. 20cm 4° (Bound in [vol. 10] of <u>Hollandse Mercurius</u>) Added t.-p., engraved: Holland Mercurius Anno 1688. Haerlem By Abraham Casteleyn. 1689. JCB(3)2:410; Sabin32523.
8487MM, 1912	

BA689 L473v	Ledesma, Clemente de. Vida Espiritval Comvn De La Serafica Tercera Orden, que instituyó Serafico, que fundó Evangelico y que propagó Apostolico N.P. Angelico, y Ilagado Patriarca S. Francisco. Da Noticia General El P. Fr. Clemente De Ledesma hijo indigno de la Santa Provincia del Santo Evangelio Ex-Lector de Philosophia, y Theologia Moral, Predicador Iubilado, y Comissario Visitador de la Tercera Orden fundada en este Convento de N.P.S. Francisco de esta Ciudad de Mexico. Primero Tomo.... Con Licencia De Los Svperiores. En Mexico: por Doña Maria de Benavides, Viuda de Juan de Ribera en el Empedradillo. Año de 1689. 24 p.ℓ., 208 numb. ℓ., [8] p. 20cm. 4° No more published. License dated (14th p.ℓ.ʳ) 10 Dec. 1689. Preliminary matter includes poetry by Bernabé Pérez y Turcios. Bound in contemporary vellum. Palau(2)134128; Medina(Mexico)1446.
4924, 1908	

C585 E96t 14	[Leopold I, Emperor of Germany] 1640-1705. A Letter Written by the Emperor To The Late King James, Setting forth The True Occasion of his Fall, And The Treachery and Cruelty of the French. Licensed May 2. 1689. J. Fraser. London, Printed for Ric. Chiswell at the Rose and Crown in St. Paul's Church-Yard. 1689. 1 p.ℓ., 9 p. 20cm. 4°

	Text in Latin and English in parallel columns. Dated (p. 9): At Vienna the 9th of April 1689. Title-page this copy mutilated, with slight loss of text. Bound as no. 14 of 19 items in vol. with binder's title: Tracts 1681-1701. Wing L1113.
11352-14, 1918	

D689 L781g	[Littleton, Edward] b. 1626 The Groans of the Plantations: Or A True Account of Their Grievous and Extreme Sufferings By the Heavy Impositions Upon Sugar, And other Hardships. Relating more particularly to the Island of Barbados. London, Printed by M. Clark in the Year M DC LXXXIX. 1 p.ℓ., 35 p. 20.5cm. 4° JCB(2)2:1371; WingL2577; Sabin3271; Cundall(W.I.)10; Kress1700.
05945, before 1866	

DB M4143 1689 1	Massachusetts (Colony)--Convention, 24 May 1689. At a Convention of the Representatives Of The Several Towns and Villages of the Massachusets Colony in New-England. Printed at Boston by R.[ichard] P.[ierce] and Reprinted at London, 1689. 4 p. 19cm. (20 cm. in case) 4° Caption title; imprint at end. First pub. Boston, 1689.
70-117	

D.Math C.100B	[Mather, Cotton] 1663-1728. Early Piety, Exemplified In The Life and Death Of Mr. Nathanael Mather, Who Having become at the Age of Nineteen, an Instance of more than Common Learning and Virtue, Changed Earth for Heaven, Oct. 17. 1688. Whereto are added, Some Discourses on the true Nature, the great Reward, and the best Season of such A Walk With God as he left a Pattern of. The Second Edition. With a Prefatory Epistle by Mr. Matthew Mead. London, Printed by J. Astwood for John Dunton at the Black Raven in the Poultrey, 1689. 7 p.ℓ., 53, 52-60 p., 1 ℓ., 86 p. 15cm. 8° First pub. London, the same year. "To the Reader." (2d-3d p.ℓ.) signed: London,

June 17. 1689. Matthew Mead.
"To the Reader." (4th-5th p. ℓ.ʳ) signed:
London, February, 5ᵗʰ· 1689. Samuel Mather.
Bookseller's advertisement, 7th p. ℓ.ᵛ.
With, as issued, his Several sermons concerning walking with God, London, 1689, with special t.-p., separate paging, but continuous signatures.
JCB(2)2:1389; Sabin46293; Holmes(C)100B; Wing M1097.
03670, before 1866

D. Math
C. 228A
Mather, Cotton, 1663-1728.
Memorable Providences, Relating to Witchcrafts And Possessions. A Faithful Account of many Wonderful and Surprising Things, that have befallen several Bewitched and Possessed Persons in New-England. Particularly, A Narrative of the marvellous Trouble and Releef Experienced by a pious Family in Boston, very lately and sadly molested with Evil Spirits. Whereunto is added, A Discourse delivered unto a Congregation in Boston, on the Occasion of that Illustrious Providence. As also A Discourse delivered unto the same Congregation; on the occasion of an horrible Self-Murder Committed in the Town. With an Appendix, in vindication of a Chapter in a late Book of Remarkable Providence, from the Calumnies of a Quaker at Pen-silvania. Written By Cotton Mather, Minister of the Gospel. And Recommended by the Ministers of Boston and Charleston.
Printed at Boston in N. England by R.[ichard] P.[ierce] 1689. Sold by Joseph Brunning, at his Shop at the Corner of the Prison-Lane next the Exchange.
5 p. ℓ., 75, 21, 40 p., 1 ℓ., 14 p. 14.5cm. 8⁰
Imperfect: 3d and 4th p. ℓ. wanting; supplied in pen and ink facsim.; p. 11-14 at end remargined, text supplied in pen and ink facsim.
"To the Reader." signed (4th p. ℓ.ᵛ): Charles Morton, James Allen, Joshua Moodey, Samuel Willard.
The "Appendix" is a reply to George Keith's The Presbyterian and independent visible churches in New England, Philadelphia, 1689.

D. Math
C. 373
———— Another copy. 14.5cm.
Bound with his Speedy repentance, Boston, 1690.
Imperfect: t.-p. wanting; 2d-4th p. ℓ. misbound after p. 87 of his Speedy repentance.
JCB(2)2:1383; Sabin46407; Holmes(C)228A; WingM1123; Church711.
05877, before 1882 rev
03673, before 1866

D. Math
C. 100B
Mather, Cotton, 1663-1728.
Several Sermons Concerning Walking With God, And That In the Dayes of Youth: Preached At Boston in New-England. By Cotton Mather, Pastor of a Church there. ...
London, Printed by J. Astwood for J. Dunton, at the Black Raven in the Poultrey, over against the Compter. 1689.
1 p. ℓ., 86 p. 15cm. 8⁰ (Issued as a part of his Early piety exemplified, 2d ed., London, 1689.)
JCB(2)2:1381; Sabin46506; Holmes(C)100Bn.
03670A, before 1866

D. Math
C. 371
Mather, Cotton, 1663-1728.
Souldiers Counselled and Comforted. A Discourse Delivered unto some part of the Forces Engaged in the Just War of New-England Against the Northern & Eastern Indians. Sept. 1. 1689. By Cotton Mather Minister of the Gospel in Boston ...
Boston Printed by Samuel Green. 1689.
5 p. ℓ., 38 p. 14.5cm. 8⁰
Dated at end: At the North Meeting House in Boston 1 d. 7 m. Afternoon. 1689.
Delivered to troops going to defend Maine after the capture of Pemaquid.
Imperfect: p. 31-32 wanting. Closely trimmed, affecting imprint and some headlines.
JCB(2)2:1382; Sabin46526; Holmes(C)371; Wing M1154; Evans488.
03668, before 1866

D. Math
C. 456
Mather, Cotton, 1633-1728.
Work upon the Ark. Meditations upon the Ark As a Type of the Church; Delivered in a Sermon at Boston, And now Dedicated unto the Service of All, but especially of those whose Concerns Lye in Ships. By Cotton Mather. ...
Boston Printed by Samuel Green, and Sold by Joseph Browning at the corner of the Prison Lane. 1689.
5 p. ℓ., 54 p. 14.5cm. 8⁰
Dated at end: At the North Meeting-House in Boston, Nov. 17. 1689. Afternoon.
Pages 15-16 remargined with some text supplied in pen and ink.
JCB(2)2:1384; Sabin46609; Holmes(C)456; Wing M1177; Evans489.
05879, 1878

D.Math
I.17A
[R]

[Mather, Increase] 1639-1723.
A Brief Relation Of The State Of New England, From the Beginning of that Plantation To this Present Year, 1689. In a Letter to a Person of Quality.
Licenced, July 30th. 1689. London, Printed for Richard Baldwine, near the Black Bull in the Old-Baily, 1689.
18, [2] p. 20cm. 4º
"To Her Royal Highness the Princess of Orange, &c." (p. 13-15) signed: Hague the First of February, 1689. S. N. Abraham Kick.
Includes (p. 15-18) an English transl. of his De successu evangelij apud Indos in Nova-Anglia, 1st pub. London, 1688.
"Books lately Printed for R. Baldwin." (p.[1-2] at end).
Reprinted by W. H. Whitmore in The Andros Tracts, v.2, p. 149-170.
JCB(2)2:1386; Sabin46642; Holmes(I)17A; WingM1189; Church713.

0538, 1846

D.Math
I.81A
[R]

[Mather, Increase] 1639-1723.
New-England Vindicated, From the Unjust Aspersions cast on the former Government there, by some late Considerations, Pretending to Shew, That the Charters in those Colonies were Taken from them on Account of their Destroying the Manufactures and Navigation of England.
[London, Richard Baldwin? 1689]
8 p. 19cm. 4º
Caption title.
A reply to: Considerations humbly offered to the Parliament, London [1689] and An Abstract of the printed laws of New England, London, [1689]
Reprinted by W. H. Whitmore in The Andros Tracts, v.2, p. 111-124.
JCBAR 54:9-12; Sabin46712; Holmes(I.)81A; WingM1233.

31329, 1954

bBB
M6113
1689
1

Mexico(Viceroyalty)--Laws, statutes, etc., 1688-1696 (Galve).   1 Nov.1689
Don Gaspar de Sandoval, Cerda, Silva, y Mendoça Conde de Galve, Gentil hombre de la Camara de su Magestad, ... Virrey, Governador, y Capitan General desta Nueva-España, y Presidente de la Real Audiencia della, &c. Por quanto Por la Ley primera Titulo veinte, y seis Libro nono de la Recopilacion de las de Indias ...
[Mexico, 1689]
[2] p. 30.5cm. fol.
Title from caption and beginning of text.
Dated in Mexico, 1 Nov. 1689 (day and month supplied in manuscript), with manuscript signature "El Conde de Galve" and other authentications in ms.
Concerns the registration of immigrants.
Blanks left for insertion of the name of the particular jurisdiction addressed are completed in ms.
Papel sellado dated 1688.

12731-30, 1920

bBB
M6113
1689
2

Mexico(Viceroyalty)--Laws, statutes, etc., 1688-1696 (Galve).   12 Nov.1689
Don Gaspar de Sandoval, Cerda, Silva, y Mendoça Conde de Galve, Gentil hombre con exersicio de la Camara de su Magestad, ... Virrey, Governador, y Capitan General desta Nueva-España, y Presidente de la Real Audiencia della. Por quanto en cumplimiento de lo mandado por su Magestad por mandamiento de veinte y tres del passado ...
[Mexico, 1689]
[2] p. 30.5cm. fol.
Title from caption and beginning of text.
Dated in Mexico, 12 Nov. 1689, with manuscript signature "El Conde de Galve" and other authentications in ms.
Concerns the registration of immigrants.
Blanks left for insertion of the name of the particular jurisdiction addressed are completed in ms.
Papel sellado dated 1688.
With this copy there is present a conjugate blank leaf which bears ms. certifications.

12731-33, 1920

bBB
M6113
1689
3

Mexico(Viceroyalty)--Laws, statutes, etc., 1688-1696 (Galve).   12 Nov. 1689
Sirva esta de instruccion secreta, sobre lo que Vmd. ha de observar, en la execucion de los mandamiento, adjuntos. ...
[Mexico, 1689]
[2] p. 30cm. fol.
Title from beginning of text.

Dated in Mexico, 12 Nov. 1689, with manuscript signature "El Conde de Galve."
Concerns the registration of immigrants.
Papel sellado dated 1688.
With this copy there is present a blank conjugate leaf.
12731-29, 1920

D689 C697o
A Ninth Collection of Papers Relating to the Present Juncture of Affairs in England. Viz. I. A Dialogue between two Friends, wherein the Church of England is vindicated in joyning with the Prince of Orange in his Descent into England. ...
London printed, and are to be sold by Richard Janeway in Queen's-head-Court in Pater-noster-Row, 1689.
1 p.ℓ., 34 p. 19cm. 4º
Contains text of 7 "papers".
Also issued as a part of A compleat collection of papers in twelve parts. London, 1689.
Booksellers' advertisement at end.
Bound in contemporary calf as the 9th of 12 items after collective prelims.

D689 C697o cop.2
——— Another copy. 19cm.
Bound as the 9th of 12 items.

D689 C697o cop.3
——— Another copy. 20cm.
Bound in contemporary calf, rebacked, as the 9th of 11 items.
Wing N1164; McAlpin4:355; cf. JCB(2)2:1351n; cf. Sabin81492n.
12463 I, 1920
06842 I, before 1882
06843 I

BA689 O77s
Ortiz, Francisco Antonio, 1637-1720.
Sermon Qve Predicó El P. M. y Doctor Francisco Antonio Ortiz, Professo de quarto voto, Prefecto de la illustre Congregacion de el Salvador. En la fiesta del Gloriosissimo Patriarcha, y Fundador de la Compañia de Jesvs S. Ignacio De Loyola en la Casa Professa de Mexico el dia 31. de Julio de 1689. Dedicalo A las Aras de el mismo Santo Patriarcha.
Con Licencia De Los Svperiores. En Mexico: por Doña Maria de Benavides, Viuda de Juan de Ribera en el Empedradillo. Año de 1689.
4 p.ℓ., 12 numb. ℓ. 19.5cm. 4º

License dated (recto 4th p.ℓ.) 3 Sept 1689.
Palau(2)205634; Medina(Mexico)1449; Backer 5:1962.
4923, 1908

F689 -P469e
Pertinent en Waarachtig Verhaal van alle de Handelingen den Directie van Pedro Van Belle, ontrent Den Slavenhandel, ofte, het Assiento de Negros, eerst door D. Juan Barosso y Posso, bij zijn overlijden door D. Nicolas Porsio, en daar na door Balthasar Coijmans met den Koning van Spangien aangegaan, zoo in Spangien, de West-Indijes, als op Curaçao: Dienende Tot onderrichtinge van alle die gene, die bij het voorsz. Assiento, ofte de Compagnie van Coijmans en Van Belle tot Cadix, eenigsints zouden mogen wezen geinteresseert.
Te Rotterdam, Bij Reinier Leers, MDCLXXXIX.
1 p.ℓ., 126, 181, [182-184] p. 33.5cm. fol.
Cut (printer's device incl. motto "Tenet Meliora") on t.-p.
Errata, p. [184].
2302, 1906

D689 P685r
Pitman, Henry
A Relation Of The Great Sufferings And Strange Adventures Of Henry Pitman, Chyrurgion to the late Duke of Monmouth ...
Licensed, June 13th, 1689. London, Printed by Andrew Sowle; And are to be Sold by John Taylor, at the Sign of the Ship in Paul's Church-Yard, 1689.
38 p., 1 ℓ. 20cm. 4º
Pitman was transported to Barbados as a convict, escaped, and became involved with pirates.
Includes "An Account of the Adventures of my Companions since I left them ..., communicated to me by John Whicker...": p. 32-38.
"Advertisements. ... Medicines ... Prepared and Sold ... by Henry Pitman": last leaf.
WingP2298; Sabin63047; Church715; Cundall (WI)9b.
4007, 1908

DA689 P831ℓ
[Popple, Sir William] d. 1708.
Een Brief Van een zeker Heer aan William Penn, Eygenaar en Gouverneur van Pennsylvania; Beneffens zyn Antwoord daar op. Uyt

[211]

het Engelsch vertaald.
 t'Amsterdam, by de Wed: van Steven Swart, bezyde de Beurs, 1689.
 16 p. 20cm. 4º.
 Cut (Rahir fleuron 127?) on t.-p.
 "Goedwillige Leezer" (p. [2]) signed: W.[illem] S.[ewel]
 Letter to Penn (p. 3-8) dated: London, den 20 October, 1688. Answer (p. 9-16) signed: Teddington den 24sten Octob. 1688. ... W.P.
 Transl. by Willem Sewel of, A Letter To Mr. Penn: With His Answer, London, 1688.
 JCB(2)2:1390; Sabin 59684; Knuttel 13333.

02310, 1853

J689 P977s   Pufendorf, Samuel, Freiherr von, 1632-1694.
 Suite de L'Introduction à L'Histoire Des Principaux Etats De L'Europe, Qui comprend l'Histoire de Suede ... Premiere [-Seconde] Partie. Traduite de l'original Allemand, De Samuel Pufendorf, Par Claude Rouxel.
 à Utrecht, Chez Jean Ribbius, M. DC. LXXXIX.
 2 v.: 42 p. ℓ., 624 p.; 1 p. ℓ., 525, [526-617] p. 13.5cm. 12º
 Cut on each title-page.
 Introduction à l'histoire des principaux Etats, which this continues, was pub. Utrecht, 1687. The German originals, Einleitung zu der Historie der vornehmsten Reiche und Staaten so jetziger Zeit in Europa sich finden and Continuierte Einleitung were pub. Frankfurt, 1682 and [1685?] respectively.
 Includes references to American colonies.
 Errata, v. 1, 42d p. ℓ.ᵛ
 In this copy the t.-p. of v.1 is a cancel.

70-332

D696 -C737c   Reasons, why in this Juncture, no alteration should be made in the Government of the Church of Scotland.
 [Edinburgh? 1689]
 Broadside. 31 x 18.5cm. 1/2º
 Against the establishment of Presbyterianism.
 Bound in a volume of Scottish imprints and mss. as the 45th of 58 items.

7135, 1910

C619 A949n   Relaçam Verdadeira da ultima enfermidade, & morte de N. Santissimo Padre Innocencio XI. Pontifice Maximo, & do enterro que se fez do seu cadaver, do Monte Quirinal atè á Igreja de Saõ Pedro. Da-Se Noticia Do Numeroso Acompanhamento das guardas, & juntamente hũa demonstraçaõ das pedras, que se acháraõ dentro em o mesmo corpo, quando ò abriraõ para ser embalsamado, & outras circunstancias dignas de ponderaçaõ, & de se saberem.
 Foy impresso em Roma Por Francisco Leon. Anno 1689. E em Lisboa Por Domingos Carneyro, Impressor das Tres Ordens Militares.
 8 p. illus. 19.5cm. 4º
 Cuts (Saint Peter, archangel Michael) on t.-p.
 Imprint from colophon.
 "Debuxo ao natural, tanto da justa grandesa, cuanto da verdadeira forma das duas pedras, achadas pelos Cirurgiaens em os rins do defunto Summo Pontifice Innocencio XI. quando lhe abriraõ o corpo para o embalsama." (p. 4-5)
 Bound as the 11th in a volume of 58 pamphlets, 1619-1702.

9352, 1913

E689 R395d   [Renau d' Eliçagaray, Bernard] 1652-1719.
 De La Theorie De La Manœuvre Des Vaisseaux.
 A Paris, Chez Estienne Michallet, premier Imprimeur du Roy, ruë S. Jacques, à l'Image S. Paul M. DC. LXXXIX. De l'exprés commandement de Sa Majesté.
 6 p. ℓ., 64, 67-117 p. 25 fold. diagrs. 19cm. 8º
 Cut (monogram) on t.-p.
 Added t.-p., engr.: La Theorie de la Manoeuure des Vaisseavx par Mʳ le Chevalier Renau. ... Signed "F:Ertinger:del:et sculp:"
 Rev. and ed. by Joseph Sauveur.
 Bound in contemporary calf.

69-16

BA689 R457s   Reyes, Gaspar de los, 1655-1706.
 Sermon Del Gran Privado De Christo El Evangelista San Juan En La Titvlar Fiesta, Qve Patente El SS. Sacramento Celebra La Compañia De Bethlem En Su Hospital De Convalecientes De Mexico. Dixolo El P. Gaspar De Los Reyes Angel, De La Compañia De Jesus, En presencia del Excelentissimo Señor Conde de Galve, Virrey desta Nueva-España. ...
 Con licencia, en Mexico: Por los Herederos de la Viuda de Bernardo Calderon. En la Imprenta de Antuerpia. 1689
 5 p. ℓ., 15 numb. ℓ. 20cm. 4º

	License dated (5th p.ℓ.ʳ) 20 Febr. 1689.
	Palau(2)265549; Medina(Mexico)1454;
	Backer6:1690.
		CA689
		S111s
			Sá, Antonio de, 1620-1678.
			    Sermão Dos Passos Qve Pregov Ao Recolher Da Prociçam O P. Antonio De Saa da Companhia de Iesus,
			    Em Coimbra, Com as licenças necessarias Na Officina de Ioseph Ferreyra Impressor da Vniversidade, Anno 1689. A custa de Ioão Antunes mercador de livros.
			    16 p. 20cm. 4º
			    Cut (Jesuit trigram floriated) on t.-p.
			    First pub. Lisbon, 1675.
			    Palau(2)283208; Borba de Moraes 2:222; Backer7:355.

12530, 1920			
		69-186	

BA689
R588d
	[Ripalda, Gerónimo de] 1536?-1618.
	    Doctrina christiana, traducida de la Lengua Castellana, en Lengua Zapoteca Nexitza. Con otras addiciones vtiles, y necessarias, para la educacion Catholica, y excitacion à la devocion Christiana. Por D. Francisco Pacheco de Silva, Cura Beneficiado Presentado por su Magestad, de el Partido de San Joan Yahee y Taneche. Dedica este corto trabajo à la Emperatriz de los Cielos Nuestra Señora la siempre Virgen Maria.
	    Con licencia de los Svperiores, En la Puebla, en la Imprenta Plantiniana de Diego Fernandez de Leon. Año de 1689.
	    28 p.ℓ., 133 numb. ℓ. incl. woodcut. 14.5cm. 8º
	    Text in Spanish and Zapotec in parallel columns.
	    Transl. from: <u>Doctrina Christiana, con una exposicion breve,</u> 1st pub. Burgos, 1591. Transl. into Zapotec language 1st pub. Mexico, 1687.
	    License dated (15th p.ℓ.ᵛ) 1 June 1689.
	    Imperfect: t.-p. and 8th p.ℓ. wanting; title from Medina.
	    Bound in contemporary calf.
	    Palau(2)269101; Medina(Puebla)119; Ugarte280.
		BA689
		S245s
			Sariñana Y Cuenca, Isidro, 1630?-1696.
			    Sermon Qve En las honras del V. P. Fr. Christoval Mvñoz De La Concepcion, hijo, y Difinidor habitual de la Santa Provincia de S. Diego de Religiosos Descalzos de N.P.S. Francisco de esta Nueva-España. Predicò El Ilustmo.y Revmo. Señor Dr. D. Ysidro Sariñana, Y Cvenca, del Consejo de su Magestad, y Obispo de la Ciudad de Oaxaca. En el Convento de N.P.S. Francisco de la misma Ciudad, en el dia veinte y fiete de Junio de mil seiscientos y ochenta y nueve años. ...
			    Con Licencia De Los Svperiores. En Mexico: por Doña Maria de Benavides, Viuda de Juan de Ribera en el Empedradillo. Año de 1689.
			    12 p.ℓ., 16 numb. ℓ. 20cm. 4º
			    Dedication (2d-7th p.ℓ.ʳ) by José Montoro.
			    Approbation dated (8th p.ℓ.ᵛ) 20 Sept. 1689.
			    Medina(Mexico)1458; Palau(2)302141.

06262, before 1902?		68-424	

BA689
R666s
	Robles, Juan de, 1628-1697.
	    Sermon De La Pvrissima Concepcion de Maria Señora libre en su primer instante de la comun deuda de la culpa. Predicado Por el P. Ivan De Robles Professo de la Compañia de Iesus, el Domingo quarto de Adviento, en fiesta que celebrò el Capitan Bernardo de Ita, como Prefecto de la Congregacion de la Santissima Virgen, fundada en el Colegio de la Compañia de Iesvs de la Ciudad de Santiago de Queretaro. Con titulo de la Concepcion Immaculada. ...
	    Con Licencia De Los Svperiores. En Mexico: por Doña Maria de Benavides, Viuda de Juan de Ribera en el Empedradillo. Año de 1689.
	    5 p.ℓ., 13 numb. ℓ. 19.5cm. 4º
	    License dated (5th p.ℓ.ʳ) 9 [May] 1689.
	    Palau(2)271183; Medina(Mexico)1455; Sabin72250n; Backer6:1926.
		D689
		C697o
			A Second Collection of Papers Relating to the Present Juncture of Affairs in England. Viz. I. An Enquiry into the Measures of Submission to the Supreme Authority; and of the Grounds on which it may be lawful or necessary for Subjects to defend their Religion, Lives, and Liberties. ... The Third Edition.
			    Licensed and Entred according to Order. London printed, and are to be sold by Richard Janeway in Queen's-head-Court in Paternoster-Row, 1689.
			    1 p.ℓ., 34 p. 19cm. 4º
			    Contains texts of 7 "papers".
			    First pub. [London] 1688.
			    Also issued as part 2 of <u>A compleat collection of papers in twelve parts.</u> London, 1689.
			    Bound in contemporary calf as the 2d of 12 items after collective prelims.

69-773			

D689 C697o cop.2 12463B, 1920 06842B, before 1882	——— ———Another copy. 19cm. Bound as the 2d of 12 items. Wing S2265; cf. JCB(2)2:1351n; cf. Sabin 81492n.	D689 C697o cop.2	——— ———Another copy. 19cm. Bound as the 7th of 12 items.
		D689 C697o cop.3 12463G, 1920 06842G, before 1882 06843G	——— ———Another copy. 20cm. Bound in contemporary calf, rebacked, as the 7th of 11 items. Wing S2744; McAlpin4:364; cf. JCB(2)2:1351n, cf. Sabin81492n.
D689 S497cB 70-348	A Seventh Collection of Papers Relating to Parliaments, And The Penal Laws and Tests. ... [London, Richard Baldwin?] Printed in the Year 1689. 1 p.ℓ., 36 p., 1 ℓ. 19.5cm. 4° Contains texts of 7 "papers". Not the same as A seventh collection of papers relating to the present juncture of affairs in England, London, R. Janeway, 1689. The present Seventh Collection was probably issued by Richard Baldwin; Baldwin issued a Sixth Collection of Papers, London, 1689, in imitation of a Sixth Collection issued by Janeway, London, 1689. "Some Queries Concerning Liberty of Conscience Directed to William Pen And Henry Care" p. 27-33; 1st pub. [London, 1688]. "Three Considerations proposed to Mr. William Pen, concerning the Validity and Security of his New Magna Charta for Liberty of Conscience, by a Baptist [Thomas Comber] ..." p. 33-36; 1st pub. [London, 1688] Wing S2743; McAlpin4:364.	DA689 S547s 06414, before 1882	Shepard, Thomas, 1605-1649. Sampwutteahae Quinnuppekompauaenin. Wahuwômook oggussemesuog Sampwutteabáe Wunnamptamwaenuog, Mache wussukhúmun ut English-Mâne Unnontoowaonk nashpe Né muttáe-wunnegenúe Wuttinneumoh Christ Noh asoowesit Thomas Shephard Quinnuppenúmun en Indiane Unnontoowaonganit nashpe Ne Quttianatamwe wuttinneumoh Christ Noh assoowesit John Eliot. Kah nawhutche ut aiyeuongash oggussemese ontcheteauun Nashpe Grindal Rawson ... Cambridge [Mass.] Printed by Samuel Green, in the Year, 1689. 2 p.ℓ., 161 p. 14.5cm. 8° Transl. by John Eliot from: The sincere convert, 1st pub. London, 1640; with revisions by Grindall Rawson. JCB(2)2:1391; WingS3116; Evans497; Sabin 80217; Pilling1199; Brinley803 (this copy); CP183.
D689 C697o 	A Seventh Collection of Papers Relating to the Present Juncture of Affairs in England. Viz. I. Proposals humbly offered in behalf of the Princess of Orange. ... Licensed and Entred according to Order. London printed, and are to be sold by Richard Janeway in Queen's-head-Court in Pater-noster-Row, 1689. 1 p.ℓ., 34 p. 19cm. 4° Contains texts of 6 "papers". Also issued as a part of A compleat collection of papers in twelve parts. London, 1689. Not the same as A Seventh Collection of Papers [London, R. Baldwin?] 1689. Bound in contemporary calf as the 7th of 12 items after collective prelims.	D689 S625cB 71-174	A Sixth Collection Of Papers Relating To the Present Juncture of Affairs. Containing I. A Character of the Prince of Orange. ... Licensed according to Order. London, Printed, and sold by R.[ichard] Baldwin. 1689. 8, 16, 15 p. 20cm. 4° Contains texts of 6 "papers". Not the same as A Sixth Collection of Papers relating to the present juncture of affairs in England, London, R. Janeway, 1689. WingS3929; McAlpin4:366.

D689 A Sixth Collection of Papers Relating to the
C697o Present Juncture of Affairs in England.
Viz. I. Five Letters from Scotland, giving
Account of expelling Popery from thence. ...
Licensed and Entred according to Order.
London printed, and are to be sold by Richard
Janeway in Queen's-head-Court in Pater-noster-
Row, 1689.
1 p.ℓ., 34 p. 19cm. 4° []1 B-E⁴ F² (-F1
=[]1)
Contains texts of 10 "papers".
Also issued as part 6 of A compleat collection of papers in twelve parts. London, 1689.
"A Narrative of the Miseries of New-England, by reason of an Arbitrary Government Erected there" [by Increase Mather] p. 29-34; 1st pub. [London, 1688].
Not the same as A Sixth Collection of papers relating to the present juncture of affairs, London, R. Baldwin, 1689, which is noted in an "Advertisement", 1st p.ℓ.ᵛ
In this copy D3ᵛ and E1 are figured *; catchword, p. 30: uwn [sic], p. 31: made; catchword p. 20 is wanting, and on p. 24 the last line of the text and the direction line are partially masked.
Bound in contemporary calf as the 6th of 12 items after collective prelims.

D689 ———Another copy. 19cm.
C697o This copy is figured the same as the preceding; catchword, p. 30: uwn [sic], p. 31: mads [sic].
cop. 2 Bound in contemporary calf, rebacked, as the 6th of 11 items.

D689 ———Another copy. 20cm.
C697o This copy is figured the same as the preceding; catchword, p. 30: uwn [sic], p. 31: made.
cop. 3

D689 ———Another copy. 20cm.
S625c This copy is figured the same as the preceding; catchword, p. 30: uwn [sic], p. 31: made.

D705 ———Another copy. 19cm.
A172o2 This copy is figured the same as the preceding; catchword p. 30: uwn [sic], p. 31: mads [sic].
In this copy the first 3 leaves are mutilated, affecting text.
Bound with: An account of the progress of the reformation of manners... London, 1705.

JCB(2)2:1388, 1351n; Wing S3930; Sabin 81492; Church 714; Holmes(I.)79B, C; McAlpin 4:366.
12463F, 1920
06842F, before 1882
06843F
11910, 1919
06754

D689 Some Considerations humbly Offered to the
-S693c Parliament: Being a Short Discourse Shewing The great Inconvenience of joyning the
[R] Plantation Charters with those of England in the General Act of Restoration, and the Necessity of having for them a Particular Act. Wherein is Contained, A full Answer to a late Pamphlet Intituled, New-England Vindicated, &c. By a true Lover of his Country, and a hearty Wisher of the Prosperity of the said Plantations.
London, Printed for J. Prideaux, 1689.
4 p. 29cm. (30.5cm. in case). fol.
Caption title; imprint at end.
Also issued under title: A short discourse shewing the great inconvenience..., in the same setting of type but without imprint.
Reprinted by W. H. Whitmore in The Andros Tracts, v. 2, p. 135-148.
A reply to Increase Mather, New-England vindicated [London, 1689].
Cf. Sabin80621; cf. WingS3585.
63-259

D70 [Somers, John Somers, baron] 1651-1716.
-P769t A Brief History Of The Succession Of The Crown Of England, &c. Collected out of the Records, And the most Authentick Historians. Written for the Satisfaction of the Nation.
London, Printed, and are to be sold by Richard Janeway in Queens-Head-Court in Pater-Noster Row. 168⁸⁄₉.
1 p.ℓ., 18 p. 30.5cm. fol.
First pub. London, 1680.
Manuscript annotations.
No.[4] in a volume with binder's title: Political tracts 1655-1702.
WingS4639.
9973-4, 1914

D692　　State Tracts: Being A Collection Of Several
-S797t　　　Treatises Relating to the Government.
　　　　　Privately Printed in the Reign of K. Charles
　　　　　II.
　　　　　　London: Printed in the Year, 1689.
　　　　　　2 p.l., 240, 367-379, 383-391, 396-468 p.
　　　　　32cm. fol.
　　　　　　Bound in contemporary calf, rebacked, with
　　　　　binder's title: State Tracts Vol. IV.
　　　　　　Bound with: State tracts: being a farther
　　　　　collection of several choice treatises ...
　　　　　London, 1692.
　　　　　　Wing S5329.
831², 1905

D689　　A Tenth Collection of Papers Relating to the
C697o　　　Present Juncture of Affairs in England.
　　　　　Viz. I. Reflections upon our late and
　　　　　present Proceedings. ...
　　　　　　London printed, and are to be sold by
　　　　　Richard Janeway in Queen's-head-Court in
　　　　　Pater-noster-Row, 1689.
　　　　　　1 p.l., 34 p. 19cm. 4°
　　　　　　Contains texts of 5 "papers".
　　　　　　Also issued as a part of A compleat col-
　　　　　lection of papers in twelve parts. London,
　　　　　1689.
　　　　　　Booksellers' advertisement at end.
　　　　　　Also issued without the advertisement.
　　　　　　Bound in contemporary calf as the 10th
　　　　　of 12 items after collective prelims.

D689　　—— ——Another copy. 19cm.
C697o　　　Bound as the 10th of 12 items.
cop.2

D689　　—— ——Another copy. 20cm.
C697o　　　Bound in contemporary calf, rebacked,
cop.3　　as the 10th of 11 items.
　　　　　　Wing T727; McAlpin4:369; cf. JCB(2)2:
　　　　　1351n; cf. Sabin81492n.
12463J, 1920
06842J, before 1882
06843J

D689　　A Third Collection of Papers Relating to the
C697o　　　Present Juncture of Affairs in England.
　　　　　Viz. I. The Expedition of the Prince of
　　　　　Orange for England ... The Second Edition.
　　　　　Licensed and Entred according to Order.
　　　　　London printed, and are to be sold by Richard
　　　　　Janeway in Queen's-head-Court in Pater-noster-
　　　　　Row, 1689.
　　　　　　1 p.l., 38 p. 19cm. 4° []1 B-E⁴ F⁴ (-F1
　　　　　=[]1).

　　　　　　Contains texts of 4 "papers".
　　　　　　First pub. London, 1688.
　　　　　　Also issued as part 3 of A compleat col-
　　　　　lection of papers in twelve parts. London,
　　　　　1689.
　　　　　　This copy is figured * on B2, B4ᵛ, and C2ᵛ.
　　　　　　Bound in contemporary calf as the 3d of
　　　　　12 items after collective prelims.

D689　　—— ——Another copy. 19cm.
C697o　　　This copy is figured * on B2 and B4ᵛ only.
cop.2　　Bound as the 3d of 12 items.

D689　　—— ——Another copy. 20cm.
C697o　　　This copy is figured * on B2 and B4ᵛ, and
cop.3　　C2ᵛ.
　　　　　　Bound in contemporary calf, rebacked, as
　　　　　the 3d of 11 items.
　　　　　　Wing T901; McAlpin4:369; cf. JCB(2)
　　　　　2:1351n; cf. Sabin81492n.
12463C, 1920
06842C, before 1882
06843C

D689　　The Twelfth and Last Collection of Papers
C697o　　　(Vol. I.) Relating to the Present Juncture
　　　　　of Affairs in England and Scotland. Viz.
　　　　　I. The Secret League with France proved.
　　　　　...
　　　　　　London printed, and are to be sold by Richard
　　　　　Janeway in Queen's-head-Court in Pater-noster-
　　　　　Row, 1689.
　　　　　　1 p.l., ii, 40 p. 19cm. 4°
　　　　　　Contains texts of 13 "papers".
　　　　　　Also issued as a part of A compleat collection
　　　　　of papers in twelve parts. London, 1689.
　　　　　　Bound in contemporary calf as the 12th of 12
　　　　　items after collective prelims.

D689　　—— ——Another copy. 19cm.
C697o　　　Bound as the 12th of 12 items.
cop.2

D689　　—— ——Another copy. 20cm.
C697o　　　Inserted in a contemporary calf binding, re-
cop.3　　backed, as the 11th of 11 items.
　　　　　　Wing T3392; McAlpin4:371; cf. JCB(2)2:
　　　　　1351n; cf. Sabin81492n.
12463L, 1920
06842L, before 1882
06843L

B689 V393a [R] Vázquez Gaztelu, Antonio.
Arte De Lengva Mexicana Compvesto Por el Bachiller Don Antonio Vazquez Gastelu el Rey de Figueroa: Cathedratico de dicha Lengua en los Reales Collegios de S. Pedro, y S. Juan Sacalo A Lvz Por orden del Illustrissimo Señor Doctor Don Manuel Fernandez de Sancta Cruz, Obispo de la Puebla de los Angeles: Diego Fernandez de Leon. ...
Con Liçencia en la Puebla de los Angeles, en la Imprenta nueva de Diego Fernandez de Leon, año de 1689. Impresso à su costa: Hallarase en su Libreria
6 p. ℓ., 42 numb. ℓ. incl. illus. 20.5cm. 4º
Cut (printer's device) on t.-p.
License (6th p. ℓ.^{r}) dated 29 Aug. 1689.
Imperfect: ℓ. 10, 11, 22, and 23 wanting; available in facsim.
JCB(2)2:1378; Sabin 26746; Medina(Puebla)125; Streit 2:p. 731; cf. Ugarte 410.
06069, before 1882

CA679 V665s 5 Vieira, Antonio, 1608-1697.
Sermoens Do P. Antonio Vieira, Da Companhia De Jesu, Visitador Da Provincia Do Brasil, Prégador de Sua Magestade. Qvinta Parte.
Lisboa, Na Officina de Miguel Deslandes, Impressor de Sua Magestade. A custa de Antonio Leyte Pereyra, Mercador de Livros. M.DC.LXXXIX. Com todas as licenças necessarias, & Privilegio Real.
6 p. ℓ., 624 p. 21cm. 4º
Cut (Jesuit trigram floriated) on t.-p.
"Taixaõ" dated (5th p. ℓ.) 21 Feb. 1689.
Errata, 6th p. ℓ.
Contains 15 sermons preached in Saõ Luis, Brazil, Pará, Brazil, in Bahia, Brazil, 1634, Alcántara, Spain, 1644, etc.
According to Leite "Deste vol. conhecem-se duas impressões com a mesma data de 1689."
Bound in contemporary vellum.
Rodrigues 2507; Backer 8:659; Leite 9:195-196; Innocencio 1:290.
68-346

BA689 X200h Xaimes de Ribera, Juan, fl. 1679-1689.
Hazer De Si Mismo Espejo Sermon. Que En Penitente Novenario, Dedico Al Mejor Mezenas de las almas, Christo Crucificado, el Convento grande de N.P. San Augustin en memorias de las lamentables ruinas, que á veinte de Otubre. Año de 87 padeciò esta, si antes ergida pompa, oy abatida Ciudad de Lima. Predicole. Descvbierto El SS. Sacramento. El R.P. Fr. Ioan Xaymes De Ribera... Ofrecele. Al Deuoto, Y Exemplar Ministro, el bachiller Melchor de Sigura, ...
Con Licencia. En Lima; En la Imprenta de Manuel de los Olivos. En la calle de las Mantas. Año de 1689.
9 p. ℓ., 8 numb. ℓ. 20.5cm. 4º
Approbation dated (verso 5th p. ℓ.) 5 June 1689.
Medina(Lima)623.
5510, 1909

BA689 -A977d Yo Pedro de Arce y Andrade, Escrivano del Rey nuestro Señor, residente en su Corte, y Prouincia. Certifico, y doy fee, que oy dia de la fecha deste, el M.R.P. Fr. Francisco de Ayeta, Religioso de la Orden de N.P.S. Francisco, Predicador, Comissario general del Santo Oficio, Custodio de la Prouincia de Mexico, y Procurador General de todas las que su Sagrada Religion tiene en los Reynos de la Nueua España, y Perù, de las Indias Occidentales, exhibiò ante mi treinta y nueve Cedulas de su Magestad, y vna Bula del Señor Clemente X. y vna certificacion que cõtiene tres Cedulas ...
[Madrid, 1689]
29 numb. ℓ. 28.5cm. fol.
Title from beginning of text.
A collection of documents concerning the controversy over missions between the Franciscan order and the Bishop of Guadalajara, Mexico, Juan de Santiago León Garabito. Contains royal cédulas variously dated 24 Sept. 1688, 26 March 1689, or 16 Apr. 1689, a papal bull dated 12 May 1673, and a certificate (dated 21 Nov. 1686) containing royal cédulas dated 8 Apr. 1672, 26 Sept. 1673, and 9 Oct. 1686.
Certifications (numb. ℓ. 29^v) dated in Madrid, 9 and 10 March 1689.
Papel sellado dated 1689.
Bound with: Ayeta, Francisco de. Defensa de la verdad. [Madrid? ca. 1689]
28527, 1940

1690

bD690 A172o An Account Of the Late Dreadful Earth-Quake In the Island of Mevis [sic], St. Christophers, &c. Which happen'd in the Beginning of April, of this present Year 1690. In a Letter to a Friend in London.
London Printed for A. Smith, 1690.

[217]

2 p. 28cm. fol.
Caption title; imprint at end.
Dated in contemporary hand on p. 1: 24 June 1690.

68-173

B619 Alvarez Ossorio y Redín, Miguel.
M737r   Compañia Vniversal de Fabricas, y Comercios, y breve resumen de los medios mas ciertos, y practicables, para vnico remedio de esta Corona. Señor. Don Miguel Albarez Ossorios y Redin, digo: ...
[Madrid? ca. 1690]
16 p. 20cm. 4°
Title from caption and beginning of text.
Bound in contemporary vellum with: Moncada, Sancho de. Restauración política de España, Madrid, 1619, as the 8th of 10 items.
Colmeiro18.

12570-8, 1920

B619 Alvarez Ossorio y Redín, Miguel.
M737r   Medios Ciertos, Y Conclusiones Generales, que satisfacen à todas las dudas que se pueden ofrecer contra los Memoriales de Don Miguel Albarez Oslorio [sic] y Redin.
[Madrid? ca. 1690]
9 p. 20cm. 4°
Caption title.
In support of his memorials, Defensa unión y restauración [Madrid? 1686?], Extensión política y económica [Madrid? 1686], and Discurso universal de las causas [Madrid? 1686], concerning economic conditions and policies which were prepared for the Spanish king.
This copy is closely trimmed at bottom with some effect on text.
Bound in contemporary vellum with: Moncada, Sancho de, Restauración política de España, Madrid, 1619, as the 7th of 10 items.
Colmeiro18.

12570-7, 1920

B690   [Aranda Sidrón, Bartolomé de] fl. 1683-1699.
-A662p   Por Doña Ysabel Picaso De Ynojosa, Viuda del Capitan Juan Vasqvez De Medina, y el Licenciado D. Uentura de Medina Picasso su hijo. En El Pleyto, Que contra la susodicha movió el Capitan D. Theovaldo de Gorraez Vaumont, y Navarra, por si, y en nombre de el Mariscal de Castilla Don Carlos Antonio de Luna, y Arellano, en cuya vida corre el Officio de Guarda-mayor de la Real Casa de la Moneda de este Reyno. Sobre, Que se debe estar al contrato, y declaracion hecha por dicho Mariscal de pertenecer todo el valor, y emolumentos de dicho Officio, â dicho Licenciado, y que se debe poner perpetuo silencio à las pretenciones de dicho Mariscal.
[Mexico, 1690]
21 numb. ℓ. 28.5cm. (30cm. in case). fol.
Signed at end "Mexico, y Agosto 23. de 1690. ... L.^{do} Don Bartholome de Aranda Sidron."
Medina(Mexico)1466; Palau(2)14968.

70-482

B690   Arenas, Pedro de, fl. 1611.
A681v   Vocabvlario Manval De Las Lengvas Castellana y Mexicana. En Que Se Contienen Las palabras, preguntas y respuestas mas comunes y ordinarias que se suelen ofrecer en el trato y communicacion entre Españoles, è Indios. Compuesto por Pedro De Arenas.
Con Licencia, En Mexico. Por la Viuda de Francisco Rodriguez Lupercio, en la puente de Palacio. Año de 1690.
4 p.ℓ., 118, [2] p. 15cm. 4°.
First pub. Mexico, 1611.
JCB(2)2:1392; Sabin1936; Medina(Mexico)1467; Palau(2)15925; Pilling154; Viñaza225; Ugarte19.

02418, 1851

E690   [Arnauld, Antoine] 1612-1694.
A745h1   Histoire De Dom Jean De Palafox, Evêque d'Angelopolis, & depuis d'Osme. Et Des differens qu'il a eus avec les PP. Jesuites.
[Amsterdam?] M. DC. XC.
10 p.ℓ., 478, [2] p. 15.5cm. 12°
Cut (swag of fruit and flowers) on t.-p.
Chiefly a compilation from biographies of Palafox by Pierre Champion and Antonio González de Rosende, from Palafox's own writings, and from documents and controversial literature relating to Palafox.
With 38 lines per page. The type set for this edition was reimpressed in a different 12° imposition with new headlines and with 33 lines per page resulting in 548 p. main paging; the reimpression was issued with a t.-p. also dated 1690, which is typographically similar to and bears the same cut as the t.-p. of the present book, but which was printed from a different setting of type.
This edition is also found with a half-title bearing the designation of the series La morale pratique des Jesuites, t.4; wanting in this copy.
Errata: p. [1-2] at end.

	In this copy the leaf bearing p. 201-202 is a cancel. JCB(2)2:1402; Sabin 58293; Backer 11:109, 1333, 2:1055; Streit 2:2270.
02818, 1859	

EA690 A745h2	[Arnauld, Antoine] 1612-1694. Histoire De Dom Jean De Palafox, Evêque d'Angelopolis, & depuis d'Osme. Et Des differens qu'il a eus avec les P. P. Jesuites. [Amsterdam?] M. DC. XC. 11 p.ℓ., 548, [2] p. 14cm. 12° Cut (swag of fruit and flowers) on t.-p. Chiefly a compilation from biographies of Palafox by Piere Champion and Antonio González de Rosende, from Palafox's own writings, and from documents and controversial literature relating to Palafox. With 33 lines per page. This is a reimpression of type 1st pub. the same year in a different 12° imposition with 38 lines per page and 478 p. main paging (copies of which are found with a half-title bearing the designation of the series <u>La morale pratique des Jesuites</u>, t.4). This reimpression has new headlines and a reset t.-p. which is typographically similar to the original and bears the same cut. Errata: p. [1-2] at end. In this copy the leaf bearing p. 229-230 has been cancelled (leaving a broad stub showing text of the cancelled leaf) and another leaf has been substituted. In this copy there is a blank ℓ. at end. Bound in contemporary paper boards. Palau(2)209828; Streit 2:2270.
960, 1905	

BA690 A958m	Avila, Juan de, fl. 1684. Mercurio Panegyrico, Que Explicò, Y Leyó El R. P. Fray Juan De Avila, Predicador General Jubilado, Calificador del Santo Oficio, y Guardian del Convento de San Gabriel de Cholula, de el Orden de N.P.S. Francisco. Sermon, Que dixo en la Segunda Dominica de Adviento, en la Publicacion de la Santa Bulla de Cruzada en la Iglesia Cathedral de la Puebla de los Angeles. Año de 1689. ... Con Licencia, En la Puebla, Por Diego Fernandez de Leon. Año 1690. 8 p.ℓ., 10 numb. ℓ. 20cm. 4° "Sentir" dated (6th p.ℓ.ᵛ) 24 Dec. 1689. In this copy p.ℓ. 2-5 are mutilated with slight loss of text; available in facsimile. Palau(2)20468; Medina(Puebla)128.
69-778	

BA688 -F395s	[Ayeta, Francisco de] Señor. Al mas modesto, y prudente, nunca pudiera causar admiracion... [Madrid? ca. 1690] 227 numb. ℓ. 28.5cm. fol. Title from caption and beginning of text. Signed at end: Fr. Francisco de Ayeta. Bound with: Ferro Machado, Juan. <u>Señor... sobre la visita</u>, [Madrid? 1688?], to which this is a reply. Bound in contemporary vellum, lettered on spine: Ayeta. Verdad defendida.
1449-1, 1906	

D690 B412w	Behn, Aphra (Amis), 1640-1689. The Widdow Ranter Or, The History of Bacon in Virginia. A Tragi-Comedy, Acted by their Majesties Servants. Written by Mrs. A. Behn. London, Printed for James Knapton at the Crown in St. Paul's Church-Yard. 1690. 4 p.ℓ., 56 p. 22cm. 4° Dedication (2d p.ℓ.) signed: G.[eorge] J.[enkins] "Prologue By Mr. Dryden. ... Epilogue..." (3d p.ℓ.). "Books Newly Printed for James Knapton..." (4th p.ℓ.ᵛ) JCB(2)2:1393; Sabin 4372; NYPL(Va.1907)29; Wing B1774.
0544, 1846	

F690 B645g	Blaeu, Willem Janszoon, 1571-1638. Guilielmi Blaeu Institutio Astronomica De usu Globorum & Sphærarum Cælestium ac Terrestrium: Duabus Partibus Adornata, Una, secundum hypothesin Ptolemæi, Per Terram Quiescentem. Altera, juxta mentem N. Copernici, Per Terram Mobilem. Latinè reddita à M. Hortensio, in Ill. Amstelamensium Schola, Matheseos Professore. Amstelædami, Ex Officina Joannis Wolters. M DC LXXXX. 8 p.ℓ., 243 p. illus. (incl. tables, diagrs.). 20cm. 8° Title in red and black. Cut (Rahir fleuron 203) on t.-p. Transl. from: <u>Tweevoudigh onderwiis van de hemelsche en aerdsche globen</u>, 1st pub. Amsterdam, 1620. Latin transl. 1st pub. Amsterdam, 1634. Preliminary matter includes poetry by Kaspar van Baerle. With this are bound: Perizonius, J. ... <u>Dissertatio de morte Judae</u>, Leyden, 1702; Perizonius, J. ... <u>Responsio ad nuperam notitiam</u>, Leyden, 1703, Gronovius, J. ... <u>Responsio ad cavillationes Raphaelis Fabretti</u>, Leyden, 1684,

12022.1, 1919	and Gronovius, J. ... Dissertatio de origine Romuli, Leyden, 1684. Poggendorf 1:206.

H691
F228i
	Bobowski, Albert, afterwards Ali Bey, d. 1676.
	    Tractatus Alberti Bobovii Turcarum Imp. Mohammedis IV^{ti} olim Interpretis primarii, De Turcarum Liturgia, Peregrinatione Meccana, Circumcisione, Aegrotorum Visitatione, &c. Nonnullas Annotatiunculas, pro ut occasio se obtulit, passim adjecit Thomas Hyde S.T.D. è Coll. Reginæ Oxon. Protobibliothecarius Bodlejanus. Subjungitur Castigatio in Angelum à Sancto Joseph, Carmelitarum discalceatorum in Perside Præfectum olim generalem.
	    Oxonii, E Theatro Sheldoniano 1690.
	    2 p.ℓ., 31 p. 20.5cm. 4° (Issued as a part of Abraham Farissol, ... Itinera Mundi Sic Dicta Nempe Cosmographia. Oxford, 1691.)
	    Texts and notes in Latin with many passages in Arabic.
	    "Castigatio In Angelum à S^{to} Joseph ..." (p. 25-31) is a reply, by Thomas Hyde, to: Ange de Saint-Joseph, Pharmacopæa persica, Paris, 1681.
	    Wing F439; Sabin 60934; Muller(1872)1213.

06420A, 1874?	

D70
-P769t
	Brady, Robert, 1627?-1700.
	    An Historical Treatise Of Cities, And Burghs or Boroughs. Shewing, Their Original, and Whence, and from Whom they Received their Liberties, Privileges and Immunities; What they were, and what Made and Constituted a Free Burgh, & Free Burgesses. As Also, Shewing When they first sent their Representatives to Parliament. With A Concurrent Discourse Of most Matters, and Things incident, or Relating thereto. By Rob. Brady, Dr. in Physick.
	    London: Printed for Samuel Lowndes over against Exeter-Exchange in the Strand. MDCXC.
	    1 p.ℓ., iv, 79, 81-88 (i.e. 90), 41 (i.e. 43) p. [A]² (-[A]2 +'A2'·3) B-L⁴ M² [ ]¹ [ ]² 2A-D⁴ E⁴(E1 +'E2'·3) $2 signed (-M2). 30.5cm. fol.
	    Numerous errors in paging.
	    This copy contains two versions of the preface, iv p. (A2·3, a cancel) and [2] p. ([A]2, the cancelland).
	    Pages are misnumbered, 1st count, "25-26" for 85-86, "89-91" for 87-89, "88" for 90, and, 2d count, "35-38" for 39-42, "41" for 43.
	    In this copy 2d count p. "35-38" (i.e. 39-42) are misbound following 1st count p. 79.
	    Imperfect: 1st count p. 81-84, 25-26 (i.e. 85-86) and 2d count p. 35-38 wanting; available in facsim.
	    No. [5] in a volume with binder's title: Political tracts 1655-1702.
	    Wing B4192.

9973-5, 1914	

DB
-G7875
1689
1
	The Case of the Lord Mayor and Aldermen Of London, Upon The Petition of some of the Common-Council Men, presented to the Honourable House of Commons, with his Lordships and the Aldermens Answer to the Charge exhibited against them in the said Petition.
	    London, Printed for John Harris at the Harrow in the Poultrey, 1690.
	    [2] p. 34.5cm. 1/2°
	    Caption title; imprint at end.
	    "Licens'd Decemb. 13. 1690."
	    A reply to the petition To the honourable the knights, citizens and burgesses in Parliament assembled, the humble petition of the members of the Common Council of the city of London..., London, 1690, concerning the liberties and franchises of the city of London.
	    Bound in Votes of the House of Commons, v.1, after Votes for 15 Dec. 1690.
	    Wing C1106.

10382, 1914	

BA690
C363m
	Catholic Church--Liturgy and ritual--Ritual.
	    Manval De los Santos Sacramentos en el Idioma de Michuacan. Dedicalo ... El Bachiller. Ivan Martinez De Aravjo, primer Colegial de el Colegio de S. Ramon Nonnato, Abogado de la Real Audiencia de Mexico, Comissario del Santo Officio de la Inquisicion de esta Nueva-España, ...
	    Con Licencia De Los Svperiores. En Mexico: por Doña Maria de Benavides, Viuda de Juan de Ribera en el Empedradillo. Año de 1690.
	    7 p.ℓ., 93 numb. ℓ., [2] p. 21cm. 4°
	    Text in Spanish and Tarascan language.
	    License dated (4th p.ℓ.^{v}) 1 March 1690.
	    In this copy there is a blank leaf at end.
	    Palau(2)154733; Medina(Mexico)1476; Sabin 44956; Pilling 146; Ugarte 225.

06403, 1896	

BA690 C363b	Catholic Church--Pope, 1623-1644 (Urbanus VIII). Breve De N. Santissimo Padre el Señor Vrbano VIII. à cerca de la Ternativa de los Religiosos

70-239
    de N.P.S. Francisco de esta Provincia del Santo Evangelio de Mexico.
    Con Licencia De Los Superiores En Mexico: Por Doña Maria de Benavides, Viuda de Juan de Ribera, en el Empedradillo. Año de 1690.
    1 p.ℓ., [10] p. 20cm. 4º
    Cut (Franciscan coat of arms) on t.-p.
    Dated (at end) in Rome, 12 Nov. 1625.
    Also issued Mexico, 1690, in Latin under title: <u>Breve Sanctissimi Domini Nostri Vrbani Papæ VIII. ...</u> The Latin version is bound with this copy.
    Medina(Mexico)1486; Sabin98108; Streit 2:2264.

BA690
C363b
    Catholic Church--Pope, 1623-1644 (Urbanus VIII).
    Breve Sanctissimi Domini Nostri Vrbani Papæ VIII. Super Ternativa Religiosorum Fratrum Nostri Patris Sancti Francisci huius Novæ-Hispaniæ Provinciæ Mexicanæ Sancti Evangelij nuncupatæ
    Superiorvm Præmissu Mexici: Apud Dñam Mariam de Benavides Viduam Ioannis de Ribera. Anno 1690.
    1 p.ℓ., [9] p. 20cm. 4º
    Cut (Franciscan coat of arms) on t.-p.
    Dated (at end) in Rome, 12 Nov. 1625.
    Also issued Mexico, 1690, in Spanish under title: <u>Breve De N. Santissimo Padre el Señor Vrbano VIII. ...</u> This copy is bound with the Spanish version.
70-240
    Medina(Mexico)1487; Sabin98109; Streit 2:2265.

HA690
C377c
    Cavazzi, Giovanni Antonio, 1621-1678.
    Istorica Descrittione De' Tre Regni Congo, Matamba, Et Angola Sitvati Nell' Etiopia Inferiore Occidentale E Delle Missioni Apostoliche Esercitateui da Religiosi Capuccini, Accvratamente Compilata Dal P. Gio. Antonio Cavazzi Da Montecvccolo Sacerdote Capvccino; Il Qvale Vi Fv' Prefetto. E nel presente stile ridotta Dal P. Fortvnato Alamandini ...
    In Milano, MDCXC. Nelle Stampe Dell' Agnelli. Con Licenza De' Svperiori, [sic]
    8 p.ℓ., 785, [1] p. front., 40 plates (incl. 1 fold.), fold. map. 25cm. 4º
    Cut (lamb on book) on t.-p.; incl. motto "Ecce Agnu Dei".
    First pub. Bologna, 1687.
    Includes material on Brazil.
63-208
    Sabin11592; Borba1:147-8; Streit 16:4809.

H690
D671r
    Dominicans.
    Regula S. Augustini Et Constitutiones FF. Ordinis Prædicatorum Nunc recentèr reimpressæ Jussu Reverendiss. Patris Antonini Cloche, ejusdem Ordinis Magistri Generalis.
    Romæ, M.DC.XC. Typis Nicolai Angeli Tinassij. Superiorum permissu.
    3 pts. in 1 v.: pt.1, 10 p.ℓ., 344, [22] p.; pt.2, 116 (i.e. 316) p.; pt.3, 120, [16] p. 21cm. 8º
    Cut (engr. of St. Dominic) on t.-p.
    The text derives from Vincenzo Bandello's edition of the Rule of St. Augustine, 1st pub. Milan, 1505.
    Preface (2d-3d p.ℓ.) signed: 13. Aprilis. 1690. Fr. Antoninus Cloche.
    Contents: pt.1, Regula S. Augustini et Constitutiones Ff. Ordinis Prædicatorum.—pt.2, Constitutiones Sororum Ordinis Prædicatorum, Regula Tertii Ordinis Prædicatorum, De Instructione Officialium Ordinis Fratrum Prædicatorum, De Judiciis, Formularium.—pt.3, Compendiosa Chronica Reverendissorum Generalium Ordinis Fratrum Prædicatorum.
    The chronicle covers through the year 1686.
    Bound in contemporary calf.
70-506

E690
D983g
    Duval, Pierre, 1618-1683.
    Geographiæ Universalis Pars Prior. Das ist: Der allgemeinen Erd-Beschreibung Erster Theil. Darinnen die Drey Theil der Welt/ Nemlich America/ Africa und Asia/ ... enthalten. Anfangs in Frantzösischer Sprach beschrieben durch P. du Val, Ihrer Kön. Majt. in Franckreich Geogr. Ordin. Anjetzo aber ins Teutsche übersetzet/ und in dieser dritten Edition/ an unterschiedlichen Orten/ fast um die Helffte vermehret/ auch in dieser vierdten/ mit zweyen vollständigen Registern/ versehen von Johann Christoph Beer.
    Nürnberg/ Verlegts Johann Hoffmann/ Buch- und Kunst-Händler/ 1690.
    2v.: 8 p.ℓ., 566, [40]p.; [?] 5 plates, 51 maps (incl. 40 double, 10 fold.) 13.5cm. 12º
    Added t.-p., engraved, on two leaves: Petri Du Val Erster Theil Der allgemeinen Weltbeschreibung Von America, Africa, und Asia. Hipschman scul.
    Transl. from: <u>Le Monde ou La Géographie Universelle</u>, first pub. Paris, 1658. German transl. first pub. Nuremberg, 1678.
    "America": p. 35-215.
    "Zu gedencken/dass diese Register An. 1689 eingerichtet sind" (p. [40] at end).
    In this copy there is a blank ℓ. at end of v.1.
    Imperfect: vol. 2 wanting.
    Palmer315.
12762, 1920

D696
-C737c
    Episcopal Church in Scotland.
        Unto His Grace William Duke of Hamilton Their Majesties High Commissioner And The Honourable Estates of Parliament The Humble Petition of the Ministers who Conformed to Episcopacy.
        [Edinburgh? 1690]
        Broadside. 29.5 x 15cm. 1/2°
        Occasioned by the re-establishment of Presbyterianism.
        This copy is mutilated along left edge affecting text.
        Bound in a volume of Scottish imprints and mss. as the 37th of 58 items.
7132, 1910

DA690
F791
    Fox, George, 1624-1691.
        Spiritualis Necnon Divina Salutatio, In Qua Omnes qui profitentur Christianitatem, ... invitantur ... Georgius Fox.
        Londini, Impensis Thomæ Northcott, in Area Georgina, in Vico vulgo vocato Lumbard street, 1690.
        16p. 20.5cm. (25.5cm. in case) 4°
        "Errata inter legendum corrigenda": slip mounted on p.16.
        Transl. from: A Spiritual or Heavenly Salutation. London, 1690.
        "Postscriptum": p.7-12; "Testimonium Scripturis consonum, Persecutioni vero Religionis causa maxime contrarium": p.12-16.
        Smith(Friends)1:689; WingF1920.
62-39

BA690
G585p
    Godínez, Miguel, 1591-1644.
        Practica De La Theologia Mystica. Por El M.R.P.M. Migvel Godinez de la Compañia de Iesus Cathedratico de Theologia en el Colegio de S. Pedro, y S. Pablo de la Ciudad de Mexico. Sacala A Lvz El Licenc. D. Iuan de Salazar y Bolea, Presbytero, Secretario de Camara, y Govierno ... en la Puebla de los Angeles de la Nueva España.
        En Sevilla: por Iuan Vejarano, Año 1690. Vendese en Logroño, en casa de Luis Rodriguez, Mercader de libros, en los quatro cantones.
        11 p.ℓ., 385, [386-394] p. 15.5cm. 8°
        First pub. Puebla de los Angeles, 1681.
        Bound in contemporary vellum.
        Backer2:1571.
71-372

B69
G643v
1
    González de la Sancha, Lorenzo Antonio.
        Villancicos, Que Se Cantaron En La Santa Iglesia Metropolitana de Mexico: en los Maytines de la Natividad De Maria SS. N. Señora, ... Escriuelos el Br. D. Lorenzo Antonio Gonzalez de la Sancha, Presbytero. Y los dedica â dicho Señor Obispo. Compuestos en metro-Musico: por Antonio de Salazar, Maestro de Capilla de dicha Sancta Yglesia.
        Mexici apud Hæredes Viduæ Bernardi Calderon [169-]
        [8] p. 20cm. 4°
        Imprint at end.
        Woodcut title vignette (statue of the Virgin within an armorial border).
        Bound in contemporary vellum, as no.1 with 42 other items.
28901, 1941

DB
-G7875
1689
1
    Gt. Brit.--Parliament, 1690--House of Commons.
        Votes Of The House of Commons In The Parliament Began at Westminster The 20th day of March, in the Second Year of the Reign of King William and Queen Mary, Anno Domini, 1689 [/90].
        London, Printed by Richard Bently, Thomas Braddyll and Robert Everingham, and are to be Sold at the Post-Office in Russel-street Covent-Garden, and at the Seven Stars in Ave-Mary-Lane. M DC XC.
        2 p.ℓ., [12], 5-94 p. 29cm. fol.
        Issued in pts. numbered 1-47 and dated 21 Mar 1689 - 23 May 1690, each of which has caption title and imprint at end.
        Errata, p. 22, 30.
        Bound in Votes of the House of Commons, v.1.
10376-2, 1914

DB
-G7875
1689
1
    Gt. Brit.--Parliament, 1690-1691--House of Commons.
        Votes Of The House of Commons, Jovis 2. die Octobris Anno Gulielmi & Mariæ secundo Annoq; Domini, 1690 [-Martis 28 die Aprilis. 1691].
        London, Printed by Thomas Braddyll and Robert Everingham, and are to be Sold at the Seven Stars in Ave-Mary-Lane. M DC XC [-M DC XCI].
        158, 161-164 p. 29cm. fol.
        Caption titles; imprint at end of each number.
        Issued in pts. numbered 1-79.
        Imprint of nos. 78-79 dated "M DC XCI".
        Bound in Votes of the House of Commons, v.1.
10376-2.1, 1914

DB -G7875 1689 1	Gt. Brit. --Parliament, 1690-1691--House of Commons.
	    Votes Of The House of Commons, Mercurii 8. die Octobris 1690.
	    London, Printed by Thomas Braddyll and Robert Everingham, and are to be Sold at the Seven Stars in Ave-Mary-Lane. M DC XC.
	    [2] p. 29cm. 1/2°
	    Caption title; imprint at end.
	    Addresses of thanks to the sovereigns; to the king for his victories in Ireland.
	    Presented 10 Oct 1690.
	    Bound in Votes of the House of Commons, v.1, after Votes for 8 Oct. 1690.
	10376-2.11, 1914
		bDB G7888 1690 1	Gt. Brit. --Sovereigns, etc., 1689-1694 (William and Mary) 18 Feb. 1690.
			    A Second Brief for Irish Protestants.
			    [London, 1690]
			    Broadside. 51 x 41cm. 1°
			    Cut (royal arms) at head of sheet.
			    Dated at end 18 Feb. 1690.
			    Wing W2632; Steele E4029.
			11957, 1919

DB -G7875 1689 1	Gt. Brit. --Parliament, 1690-1691--House of Lords.
	    Two Several Addresses From The House of Peers, Presented to Their Majesties, On Thursday the 9th of October, 1690. With Their Majesties Most Gracious Answers.
	    London: Printed for Tim. Goodwin at the Maiden-Head against St. Dunstan's Church in Fleetstreet. 1690.
	    2 p.l., 4 p. 29cm. fol.
	    Addresses of thanks to the sovereigns; to the king for his victory in Ireland.
	    Bound in Votes of the House of Commons, v.1, before Votes for 9 Oct. 1690.
	    Wing E2854
	10379, 1914
		DB -G7875 1689 1	Gt. Brit. --Sovereigns, etc., 1689-1694 (William and Mary) 21 Mar. 1689/90
			    His Majesties Most Gracious Speech To both Houses of Parliament, On Friday the 21th [sic] of March 1689[/90].
			    London, Printed by Charles Bill and Thomas Newcomb, Printers to the King and Queens most Excellent Majesties. MDCLXXXIX [i.e. 1690].
			    4 p. 29cm. fol.
			    Cut (royal arms) on t.-p. (Steele 115).
			    Calls for supplies necessary for the war against France.
			    Bound in Votes of the House of Commons, v.1, before Votes for 21 Mar 1689[/90].
			    Wing W2379.
			10377-3, 1914 rev 3

DB -G7875 1689 1	Gt. Brit. --Sovereigns, etc., 1689-1694 (William and Mary) 27 Jan. 1689/90
	    His Majesties Most Gracious Speech To both Houses of Parliament, On Munday the 27th of January 1689[/90].
	    London, Printed by Charles Bill, and Thomas Newcomb, Printers to the King and Queens most Excellent Majesties. MDCLXXXIX [i.e. 1690].
	    4 p. 29cm. fol.
	    Cut (royal arms) on t.-p.
	    Announces preparations for war in Ireland and prorogues Parliament.
	    Bound in Votes of the House of Commons, v.1, after Votes for 27 Jan 1689[/90].
	10377-2, 1914 rev 3
		DB -G7875 1689 1	Gt. Brit. --Sovereigns, etc., 1689-1694 (William and Mary) 2 Oct. 1690
			    His Majesties Most Gracious Speech To both Houses of Parliament, On Thursday the Second of October, 1690.
			    London, Printed by Charles Bill and Thomas Newcomb, Printers to the King and Queens most Excellent Majesties. 1690.
			    4 p. 29cm. fol.
			    Cut (royal arms) on t.-p. (Steele 118).
			    Calls for funds to meet military expenses.
			    Bound in Votes of the House of Commons, v.1, before Votes for 2 Oct 1690.
			    Wing W2383.
			10377-4, 1914

		FC650 H737 40	Hollandse Mercurius, Verhalende de voornaemste Saken van Staet En Oorlog, Die in en omtrent de Vereenigde Nederlanden, En elders in Europa, In het Jaer 1689 Zijn geschiet. Het Veertigste Deel. Tot Haerlem, Gedruckt by Abraham Casteleyn, Stads-Drucker, op de Marckt, in de Blye

<blockquote>
Druck. Anno 1690.
4 p. l., 286, [6] p. 3 plates, 20cm. 4°
(Bound in [vol. 11] of <u>Hollandse Mercurius</u>)
Errata: p. 286.
Added t.-p., engraved: Hollandsche Mercurius. Tot Haerlem by Abraham Casteleyn. Anno 1690.
JCB(3)2:410; Sabin32523.
</blockquote>

8487NN, 1912

BA690 J91c — Juana Inés de la Cruz, sister, 1651-1695.
Carta Athenagorica De La Madre Jvana Ynes De La Crvz Religiosa Profesa De Velo, y Choro en el muy Religioso Convento de San Geronimo de la Ciudad de Mexico cabeça de la Nueba España. Qve Imprime, Y Dedica A La Misma Sor, Phylotea De La Crvz [pseud.] Su estudiosa aficionada en el Convento de la Santissima Trinidad de la Puebla de los Angeles.

Con licencia en la Puebla de los Angeles en la Imprenta de Diego Fernandez de Leon: Año de 1690. Hallarase este papel en la librería de Diego Fernandez de Leon debajo de el Portal de las Flores.
4 p. l., [28] p. 20cm. 4°
"...haze juiçio de vn Sermon del Mandato, que predicò el Reverendissimo P. Antonio de Vieyra..." (p. [1]: i.e. Vieira's "Sermam Do Mandato Na Capella Real. Anno 1650" pub. in his <u>Sermoens...7. parte</u>, Lisboa, 1692, p. 333-374).
License dated (1st p. l.ᵛ) 25 Nov. 1690.
"Phylotea de la Cruz" is a pseudonym of Manuel Fernández de Santa Cruz y Sahagún.
Palau(2)65265; Medina(Puebla)131; Backer 8:661; Sabin11091, 76775.

1048, 1905

DA690 K28p — Keith, George, 1639-1716.
The Pretended Antidoe [sic] Proved Poyson: Or, The true Principles of the Christian & Protestant Religion Defended, And the Four Counterfit Defenders thereof Detected and Discovered; the Names of which are James Allen, Joshua Moodey, Samuell Willard and Cotten Mather, who call themselves Ministers of the Gospel in Boston, in their pretended Answer to my Book, called, The Presbyterian & Independent Visible Churches in New-England...By George Keith. With an Appendix by John Delavall...

Philadelphia, Printed by Will. Bradford, 1690.
1 p. l., 224 p. 15.5cm. 8°
A reply to [Cotton Mather and others] <u>The Principles of the protestant religion maintained</u>, Boston, 1690.
Delavall's "Appendix" (p. 213-224) is a reply to Cotton Mather's <u>The serviceable man</u>, Boston, 1690.
Errata, p. 224.
In this copy there is a blank l. at the beginning.
Imperfect: p. 223-224 wanting; available in facsim.
Bound in contemporary calf.
Evans515; WingK192; Sabin37209; Smith(Friends)2:24; Hildeburn22.

32242, 1958

EA690 L646d — [Le Tellier, Michel] 1643-1719.
Defensa De Los Nvevos Christianos, Y Missioneros De La China, Japon, Y Indias. Contra Dos Libros Intitulados, La Practica Moral de los Jesuitas, y el Espiritu de M. Arnaldo. Traducida De Frances En Español De La segunda impression, hecha en Paris, en Casa de Estevan Michallet, Impressor Mayor del Rey, en la Calle de Santiago, à la Insignia de San Pablo, año 1688. Por Don Gabriel De Parraga, Gentil-Hombre De La Casa de su Magestad ...

Con Licencia. En Madrid: Por Antonio Roman. Año de 1690.
14 p. l., 266, [4] p. 20.5cm. 4°
Cut (crucifixion) on t.-p.
Transl. from <u>Défense des nouveaux chrétiens</u>, Paris, 1688. First pub. Paris, 1687.
Translation attributed by Backer to José López Echaburu y Alcaraz.
A reply to <u>La morale pratique des jésuites</u>, v.1-2, Cologne, 1669-1683, by Sébastien Joseph de Coislin du Chambout, abbé de Pontchâteau, and Antoine Arnauld and to Pierre Jurrieu's <u>L'esprit de M. Arnauld</u>, Deventer, 1684.
Bears designation (p. 266) "Fin de la primera Parte."
"Tassa" dated (4th p. l.ʳ) 13 June 1690.
Errata, 3d-4th p. l.
In this copy there is a blank l. at end.
Bound in contemporary vellum.
Medina(BHA)1851; Backer3:323, cf. 7:1913; Palau(2)4:69677; cf. Streit5:2570.

63-274 rev

BA690 -L979p [R] — Luzuriaga, Juan de.
Paranynfo Celeste Historia De La Mystica Zarza, Milagrosa Imagen, Y Prodigioso Santvario De Aranzazv, De Religiosos Observantes De Nvetro [sic] Serafico Padre San

68-275

Francisco En La Provincia De Gvipvzcoa, De La Region De Cantabria, Escrivela ... El M.R.P. Fr. Ivan De Lvzvriaga, Predicador Apostolico, Lector Iubilado, Padre de las Santas Provincias de Cantabria, y Valencia, y Comissario General de todas las de Nueva España de Nuestro Padre San Francisco.
  Con Licencia. En Madrid: Por Jvan Garcia Infanzon. Año de 1690.
  18 p.ℓ., 114, 96, 112 p., 1 ℓ., [14] p. 29.5cm. fol.
  First pub. Mexico, 1686.
  "Tassa" (7th p.ℓ.ᵛ) dated 27 May 1690.
  Errata, 7th p.ℓ.ᵛ.
  In this copy there is a blank ℓ. at end.
  Bound in contemporary vellum.
  Palau(2)144368; Medina(BHA)7864.

BA690
M385s

Martínez de la Parra, Juan, 1655-1701.
  Sermon Panegyrico A Las Virtudes, Y Milagros De El Prodigioso Apostol De La India Nuevo Thavmaturgo Del Oriente. San Francisco Xavier. Predicado En Su Dia Tres De Diziembre en la Casa Professa de la Compañia de Jesus de Mexico año de 1689. Por el R.P. Juan Martinez De La Parra, Professo de la mesma Compañia ...
  Con Licencia. En Mexico: Por los Herederos de la Viuda de Bernardo Calderon. Año de 1690.
  4 p.ℓ., 12 numb. ℓ. 19.5cm. 4º
  License dated (4th p.ℓ.ʳ) 24 Dec. 1689.
  Medina(Mexico)1477; Backer5:635.

68-413

D. Math
C. 67

Mather, Cotton, 1663-1728.
  A Companion for Communicants. Discourses Upon The Nature, the Design, and the Subject of the Lords Supper; With Devout Methods of Preparing for, and Approaching to that Blessed Ordinance. By Cotton Mather, Pastor of a Church at Boston. ...
  Printed at Boston by Samuel Green for Benjamin Harris at the London Coffee House, 1690.
  4 p.ℓ., 167, [1] p. 14.5cm. (16.5cm. in case) 8º
  Prepared for the use of members of the Second, or "North", Church in Boston.
  Errata, p. 167.
  "Books Printed for, and Sold by Benjamin Harris ..." (last p.).
  Imperfect: t.-p. mutilated, 2d-3d p.ℓ. wanting; available in facsim.
  Bound in contemporary calf.
  JCB(2)2:1395; Sabin46267; Evans535; Holmes(C) 67; Wing M1091.

05934, before 1882

D. Math
C. 304

Mather, Cotton, 1663-1728.
  The Present State Of New-England. Considered in a Discourse On the Necessities and Advantages of a Public Spirit In every Man; Especially, at such a time as this. Made at the Lecture in Boston 20. d. I. m. 1690. Upon the News of an Invasion by bloody Indians and French-Men, begun upon Us. By Cotton Mather. ...
  Boston Printed by Samuel Green. 1690.
  1 p.ℓ., 52 p. 14cm. (15cm. in case) 8º
  "By The Governour and General Court Of the Colony ..." signed at end: Isaac Addington Secr. March 13. 1689/90 (p. 47-52). First pub. Cambridge, Mass., 1689/90, as a broadside.
  JCBAR30:27; Sabin46465; Evans537; Holmes (C)304; WingM1143.

15480, 1929

D. Math
C. 305

[Mather, Cotton] 1663-1728.
  The Principles of the Protestant Religion Maintained, And Churches of New-England, in the Profession and Exercise thereof Defended, Against all the Calumnies of one George Keith, a Quaker, in a Book lately Published at Pensilvania, to undermine them both. By the Ministers of the Gospel in Boston, ...
  Boston, in New-England, Printed by Richard Pierce, and sold by the Booksellers. MDC XC.
  5 p.ℓ., 156 p. 15cm. 8º
  "The Preface" (2d-5th p.ℓ.) is signed by James Allen, Joshua Moody, Samuel Willard, and Cotton Mather; Mather is thought to be chiefly responsible for the work.
  A reply to George Keith's Presbyterian and independent visible churches, Philadelphia, 1689.
  Sabin46466; Evans502; WingA1029; Holmes(C) 305.

05941, before 1916

D. Math
C. 351

Mather, Cotton, 1663-1728.
  The Serviceable Man. A Discourse Made unto the General Court Of The Massachusets Colony, New-England, At the Anniversary Election 28 d. 3 m. 1690. By Cotton Mather Minister of the Gospel. ...
  Boston, Printed by Samuel Green, for Joseph Browning at the corner of the Prison Lane next the Exchange. 1690.
  2 p.ℓ., 64p. 14cm. 8º
  Order to print (1st p.ℓ.ᵛ) dated May 29, 1690.
  Imperfect: p. 59-64 wanting; available in facsim. Title-page mutilated, affecting text, completed in pen and ink facsim.
  Sabin46504; Evans538; WingM1150; Holmes(C) 351; Brinley1224(this copy).

16851, 1936

1690

<table>
<tr><td>D. Math
C. 373</td><td>Mather, Cotton, 1663-1728.
    Speedy Repentance urged. A Sermon Preached at Boston, Decemb. 29. 1689. In the Hearing, and at the Request of One Hugh Stone, A Miserable Man Under a just Sentence of Death, for a Tragical and Horrible Murder. Together with some Account concerning the Character, Carriage, and Execution of that Unhappy Malefactor. To which are Added, certain Memorable Providences Relating to some other Murders; & some great Instances of Repentance which have been seen among us. By Cotton Mather Pastor of a Church in Boston.
    Boston, Printed by Samuel Green, and Sold by Joseph Browning at the corner of the Prison Lane, and Benj. Harris at the London Coffee House. 1690.
    3 p.ℓ., 87, 15,[1] p. 14.5cm. 8°
    Erratum, last p.
    With this is bound: his Memorable providences, Boston, 1689 (with 2d-5th p.ℓ. misbound after p. 87 of his Speedy repentance).
    JCB(2)2:1396; Sabin46528; Evans539; WingM1154; Holmes(C)373.</td></tr>
<tr><td>03673, before 1866</td><td></td></tr>
<tr><td>D. Math
C. 453</td><td>Mather, Cotton, 1663-1728.
    The Way to Prosperity. A Sermon Preached to the Honovrable Convention Of the Governovr Council, and Representatives of the Massachuset-Colony in New-England; on May 23. 1689. By Cotton Mather. ...
    Boston. Printed by R. Pierce, for Joseph Brunning, Obadiah Gill, and James Woode, MDCXC.
    1 p.ℓ., [5], 26 (i.e. 36), 5, [7] p. 14.5cm. (15.5cm. in case). 8° (Issued as a part of his The wonderful works of God, Boston, 1690).
    Also issued with imprint: ...Printed by Richard Pierce for Benjamin Harris... Both issues are found with The wonderful works, and both may also have been issued separately.
    Pagings 1-26 (i.e. 36) and the following 1-5 begin on versos.
    Occasioned by: "To the King and Queens Most Excellent Majesties. The Humble Address of The President and Council for the Safety of the People..." dated in Boston, 20 May 1689. First pub. in Two addresses, London, 1689, and excerpted in the preface to the present work (p. [1-5]).
    "An Appendix Touching Prodigies In New-England." ([7] p. at end).
    Errata, at end.
    Bound in contemporary calf.</td></tr>
<tr><td>D. Math
C. 443</td><td>——Another copy. 14cm.
    Sabin46591; Evans540(2d title); WingM1169; Holmes(C)443.</td></tr>
<tr><td>32893, 1963
29463, 1944</td><td></td></tr>
</table>

<table>
<tr><td>D. Math
C. 453</td><td>Mather, Cotton, 1663-1728.
    The Wonderful Works of God Commemorated. Praises Bespoke for the God of Heaven, In a Thanksgiving Sermon; Delivered on Decemb. 19. 1689. Containing Just Reflections upon the Excellent Things done by the Great God, more Generally in Creation and Redemption, and in the Government of the World; But more Particularly in the Remarkable Revolutions of Providence which are everywhere the matter of present Observation. With a Postscript giving an Account of some very stupendous Accidents, which have lately happened in France. By Cotton Mather. To which is Added a Sermon Preached unto the Convention of the Massachuset-Colony in New-England. With a short Narrative of several Prodigies, which New-England hath of late had the Alarms of Heaven in.
    Printed at Boston by S. Green. & Sold by Joseph Browning at the corner of the Prison Lane, and Benj. Harris at the London Coffee-House, 1690.
    4 p.ℓ., 62(i.e. 64); [7], 26(i.e. 36), 5, [7] p. A⁴ B-E⁸ 2A-C⁸ D⁴. 14.5cm. (15.5cm. in case). 8°
    Pagings 1-26 (i.e. 64); and the following 1-5 begin on versos.
    Proclamation of a thanksgiving "At The Convention of the Governour and Council, and Representatives of the Colony of the Massachusets Bay..." dated in Boston, 3 Dec. 1689 (verso t.-p.).
    Dighton Rock is described, with an illus. of a portion of the inscription (4th p.ℓ.ᵛ).
    With, as issued, his The way to prosperity, Boston, 1690, with special t.-p. and separate paging and signatures.
    Errata, at end.
    In this copy outer margin 1st p.ℓ. worn, affecting text, and p. 1-2 mutilated; title and imprint completed from facsim. in Holmes; 1st p.ℓ.ᵛ and p. 1-2 available in facsim.
    Bound in contemporary calf.
    Sabin46602; Evans540; WingM1171; Holmes(C)453.</td></tr>
<tr><td>32892, 1963</td><td></td></tr>
<tr><td>EC
M557g
1691
[1]</td><td>Mercure Galant Dedié A Monseigneur Le Dauphin. Janvier 1691.
    A Paris, Galerie-Neuve Du Palais. [1690]
    339, [340-345] p. 3 plates (incl. 2 fold.: music). 15cm. 12°
    Cut (coat of arms) on t.-p.
    Edited by Jean Donneau de Vizé.
    "A Paris, Chez G. De Luyne, ... T. Girard, ... Et Michel Guerout, ... M. DC. LXXXX. Avec Privilege Du Roy." (p. 2).
    Includes poetry.
    In this copy there is a blank ℓ. at end.</td></tr>
</table>

bBB Mexico (Viceroyalty)--Laws, statutes, etc.,
M6113 1688-1696 (Galve).   12 Dec. 1690
1690 Don Gaspar de Sandoval, Cerda, Silva, y
1 Mendoza Conde de Galve, Gentil-hombre de
la Camara de su Magestad, ... Virrey Governador, y Capitan General desta Nueva-España, y Presidente de la Real Audiencia de ella, &c. Considerando su Magestad (que Dios guarde) la imposibilidad de medios con que al presente se halla su Real Hazienda, y los inescusables gastos, que pide la efectuacion de su casamiento ...
[Mexico, 1690]
[2] p. 30.5cm. fol.
Title from caption and beginning of text.
Dated in Mexico, 12 December 1690, with manuscript signature "El Conde de Galve" and other authentications in ms.
Directs each alcalde mayor to solicit from residents within his jurisdiction a donation intended chiefly to defray the extraordinary expenses of the king's marriage.
Blanks left for insertion of the name of the particular jurisdiction addressed are completed in ms.
Papel sellado dated 1690, 1691.
With this copy there is present a conjugate blank leaf which bears ms. certifications.
12731-31

Imperfect: p. 65-70, 227-228, 333-334, and plates wanting.
Hatin24.
4641, 1908

Z Morden, Robert, d. 1703.
M834 Atlas Terrestris. by Robt. Morden.
1690 [London] sold by Robt. Morden at ẏ Atlas in Cornhill. [ca. 1690].
1 p.ℓ., double plate, 78 double maps.
16.5cm. 8°
Engraved throughout.
This atlas was first issued sometime between 1688 and November of 1692. Each map bears an engraved page number. These numbers were not on the maps as they appeared in Morden's Geography Rectified, London, 1688. The numbers do appear, however, in the edition of 1693 (T.C. II 434: Nov. 1692).
The issue of the atlas here with undated title-page appeared sometime after May of 1693 but before 1699 because sixteen of the maps bear the numbers corresponding to their position in Patrick Gordon's Geography Anatomized, London,

1693 (T.C. II 457: May 1693). None, however, bear the altered numbers that appear in the 1699 edition of Gordon's book.
Bound in contemporary calf, rebacked.
Contents (maps):
(When the engraved page number on the map does not correspond to its position in the atlas, the page number that appears on the map, corresponding to its position in Gordon's Geography Anatomized, 1693, is included. Numbers already erroneous in Morden's 1693 Geography Rectified are not distinguished.)

1. A New Map of y̆ᵉ World by Robᵗ Morden.
[2] Evrope by Robᵗ. Morden. Pa. 19.
3. England Scotland & Ireland by Robᵗ Morden.
[4] England by Robᵗ Morden. Pa. 77.
[5] Wales by Robᵗ Morden. Pa. 79.
[6] Scotiæ Nova Descriptio per. Robert Morden. Pa. 73.
[7] Ireland. By Rob. Morden. Pa. 81.
8. Denmark by Robᵗ Morden at y̆ᵉ Atlas in Cornhil London.
[9] Sweden & Norway by Robᵗ. Morden. Pa. 21.
[10] Moscovie or Rvssie. Pa. 25.
[11] Poland by Robᵗ. Morden. Pa. 49.
12. Tartaria in Europe by Robᵗ Morden.
13. Transilvania Moldavia Valachia Bvlgaria &c by Robᵗ Morden.
14. A New Map of Hungary by Robᵗ Morden.
[15] A New Map of Germany By Robᵗ. Morden. Pa. 37.
[16] The Vnited Provinces Vulgo Holland by Robert Morden. Pa. 38.
[17] The Spanish Provinces Vulgo Flanders by Robert Mordon at y̆ᵉ Atlas in Cornhil. Pa. 38.
[18] France. Pa. 27.
[19] A New Map of Hispania and Portugallia By Robᵗ. Morden. Pa. 53.
20. A New Map of Portvgal by Robᵗ. Morden.
[21] Italia by Robert Morden at the Atlas in Cornhil London. Pa. 59.
22. Svisse by Rᵗ Morden.
23. Savoy and Piedmont by Rob. Morden.
24. Sicilia.
25. A New Map of Sclavonia Croatia. Dalmatia. Bosnia et Repub. Ragusa By Robᵗ. Morden.
26. A New Map of Servia Bulgaria en Romania By Robᵗ. Morden.
27. Grecia Novæ Descriptio Per Robᵗ. Morden London.
[28] Asia a New Description by Robᵗ. Morden. Pa. 85.
29. The Turkish Empire in Asia. By Rob: Morden.
30. Canaan by Rob. Morden.
31. Cypri Insula.
32. A New Map of the Turkish Empire By Robᵗ. Morden.
33. Armenia & Georgia-Comania &c By Robᵗ.

Morden.
34. A New Map of Arabia By Robt Morden.
35. A New Map of Persia by Robt Morden.
36. A New Description of Tartarie by Robt Morden.
37. Empire de Mogol by Robt Morden.
38. India on this side Ganges by R. Morden.
39. A New Map of India Beyond Ganges by R: Morden.
40. China a New Description by Robert Morden.
41. Japonæ ac Terræ Iessonis Novissima Descriptio Robt Morden.
42. The Maldives and Ceylon Ilands by Robt Morden.
43. A New Map of Ceylon by Rob Morden.
44. The Isles of Sonda By Robt Morden.
45. The Philipine Isles By Robt Morden.
46. The Molucca Ilands &c. By R. Morden.
[47] Africa by R. Morden. [unnumbered]
48. West Barbarie by Robt Mordon [sic]. East Barbarie by Robt Morden.
49. A New Map of the Kingdoms of Fez & Marocco by R. Morden.
50. A New Map of the Kingdome of Algier by Rob. Morden.
51. Ægypt by R. Morden.
52. Biledulgerid Sarra Terra Nigritarum Guine Nova Descriptio Robt Morden.
53. Habessinia Seu Abassia at Ethiopia By R. Morden.
54. Congo by Robt Morden at ye Atlas in Cornhil London.
55. The Empire of Monomotapa and ye Coast of Cafres.
56. The Coast Of Zanguebar and Aien by Robt Morden.
57. The Isles of Azores by Robt Morden.
58. The Canarie or Fortvnate Ilands by R.^t Morden.
59. Cape Verde Ilands by R.^t Morden.
60. Madagascar or St Laurance by Rob. Morden.
61. Maltha by Rob. Morden.
[62] America. Pa. 103.
63. Terra. Magellanica By Rob: Morden.
64. Chili and Paragay by Robt Morden.
65. Brazile A New Decription by Robt Morden.
66. Castilla del Or Gviana Perv The Country of ye Amasones by Robt Morden.
67. A Map of The Western Islands By R. Morden.
68. Insula Iamaicæ By Robt Morden.
69. The Island of Barbados. By Robert Morden.
70. Æstivarum Insulæ at Barmudas... by R Morden.
71. Mexico or New Spaine by Robt Morden.
72. New Mexico vel New Granata et Marata et California by R. Morden.
73. A Map of Florida and y̆ Great Lakes of Canada By Robt Morden.
74. A New Map of Carolina By Robert Morden.
75. A New Map of Virginia. By Robt Morden.
76. A New Map of New Jarsey and Pensilvania By Robt Morden.
77. A New Map of New England and New York By Robt Morden.
78. The North West Part of America by R. Morden At ye Atlas in Cornhill.

11708, 1918

D690　New-England's Faction Discovered; Or, A Brief
N532e　and True Account of their Persecution of the
[R]　Church of England; the Beginning and Progress of the War with the Indians; and other Late Proceedings there, in a Letter from a Gentleman of that Country, to a Person of Quality. Being, an Answer to a most false and scandalous Pamphlet lately Published; Intituled, News from New-England, &c.
London, Printed for J. Hindmarsh, at the Sign of the Golden Ball, over against the Royal Exchange in Cornhill. 1690.
8 p.　23cm.　4º
Caption title; imprint at end.
Signed at end: C.D.
Attributed to Joseph Dudley or Edward Randolph. Dudley is more likely the author, and it is likely that Randolph at least contributed to the work (cf. C.M. Andrews, Narratives of the insurrections, p. 227-228). Sabin attributes the work to a "C. Dove".
A reply to News from New England: in a letter written to a person of quality [London, 1689] (cf. Holmes(I) p. 637-41).
Reprinted by W.H. Whitmore in The Andros Tracts, v.2, p. 203-221.
JCB(2)2:1400; Sabin18229, 52757; WingD6.

0540, 1846

BA690　Octava Maravilla Del Nvevo Mundo En La
O21m　Gran Capilla Del Rosario. Dedicada Y aplaudida en el Convento de N.P.S. Domingo de la Ciudad [sic] de los Angeles. El dia 16. del Mes de Abril de 1690. Al Illvs.^{mo} Y Rev.^{mo} Señor D.D. Manvel Fernandez de Santa Crvz Obispo de la Puebla del Consejo de su Magestad.
Con licencia en la Puebla, en la Imprenta Plantiniana de Diego Fernandez de Leon, Impressor, y Mercader de libros. Año de 1690.
8 p. ℓ., 208 p.　illus.　4º
Cut (Dominican device) on t.-p.
License dated (8th p. ℓ.^v) 14 Aug. 1690.
Contains 8 sermons (the first 3 with special part-titles) by Diego Victoria Salazar, Juan Gorospe e Irala, José Salgado, José Valle, Pedro Zepeda, José Espinosa, Diego Gorospe,

and Jacinto Pérez.
   In this copy p. 179-208 mutilated, with some loss of text.
   Bound in contemporary vellum.
   Medina(Puebla)133; Palau(2)198576; Sabin66568.
6548, 1910

BA690   Osera y Estella, José Miguel, fl. 1672-1690.
O81f   El Fisico Christiano. Parte Primera. Libro De La Entrada A Sv Noble Exercicio. Obra Politica. Escrita Por El Doc. D. Ioseph Migvel de Ossera y Estella Medico de Camara del Rey N. Señor, Limosnero de la Santa Iglesia Cathedral de Tarazona, y Prothomedico General de los Reynos del Peru, y de la Armada Real del Mar del Sur. ...
   Con Licencia. Impresso en Lima, por Luis de Lyra. Año de 1690.
   7 p. ℓ., 50 numb. ℓ., 1 ℓ. 20.5cm. 4º
   Title in red and black.
   "Censvra" dated (4th p. ℓ.^{v}) 24 Aug. 1690.
   Errata, last leaf.
   No more published.
   Medina(Lima)629; Sabin57811.
06028, 1883

D690   Palmer, John, ca. 1650-1700.
P331i   An Impartial Account Of The State Of New England: Or, The Late Government there, Vindicated. In Answer to the Declaration Which the Faction set forth, when they Overturned That Government. With a Relation Of the Horrible Usage they treated the Governour with, and his Council; and all that had His Majesty's Commission. In a Letter to the Clergy there. By John Palmer.
   London: Printed for Edward Poole, at the Ship over against the Royal Exchange, in Cornhill, 1690.
   40 p. 22.5cm. 4º
   Dated at end: From the Castle the Twentieth Day of June, 1689.
   A revision of his The present state of New-England impartially considered [Boston, 1689]
   A reply to Cotton Mather's The declaration of the gentlemen, merchants, and inhabitants of Boston, Boston, 1689.
   Reprinted by W. H. Whitmore in The Andros Tracts, v.1, p. 21-62.
   JCB(2)2:1403; Sabin58359; Church716; Wing P246.
9539, 1846

D690   [Pepys, Samuel] 1633-1703.
P425m1   Memoires Relating to the State Of The Royal Navy Of England, For Ten Years, Determin'd December 1688. ...
[R]   [London] Printed Anno MDCXC.
   1 p. ℓ., 214, [17] p. front. (port.), fold. tab. [A]² B-M⁸ N-Q⁴ R⁸ S⁴ 17cm. 8º
   Title in red and black.
   This issue probably intended for private distribution. The same sheets were also issued with t.-p. bearing imprint: London ... for Ben. Griffin, and ... sold by Sam. Keble ... 1690.
   Copies are commonly found with additions in contemporary hand. In this copy p. 11, 33, 38-40, 42, 57, 70, 89, 90, 92, 103, 120, 138, 142 bear contemporary ms. corrections, and t.-p. is similarly marked.
   In this copy leaves B7, C2, 4, 6, D6, E8, K2, 3, L6, 7 are cancels.
   Imperfect: front. and tab. wanting.
   Wing P1449.
29743, 1945

D690   [Pepys, Samuel] 1633-1703.
P425m2   Memoires Relating to the State Of The Royal Navy Of England, For Ten Years, Determin'd December 1688. ...
[R]   London: Printed for Ben. Griffin, and are to be sold by Sam. Keble at the Great Turks-Head in Fleet-street over against Fetter-Lane, 1690.
   1 p. ℓ., 214, [17] p. front. (port.), fold. tab. [A]² B-M⁸ N-Q⁴ R⁸ S⁴ 17cm. 8º
   Title in red and black.
   The same sheets were also issued, probably for private distribution, with t.-p. bearing as imprint only: Printed Anno MDCXC.
   Copies are commonly found with additions in contemporary hand. In this copy p. 11, 33, 38-40, 42, 57, 70, 89, 90, 92, 103, 120, 138, 142 bear contemporary ms. corrections.
   In this copy leaves B7, C2, 4, 6, D6, E8, K2, 3, L6, 7 are cancels.
   Wing P1450.
68-08

B690   Pozuelo y Espinosa, Francisco, fl. 1651-1691.
P893c   Compendio De Los Esquadrones Modernos, Regvlares, E Irregvlares, Y De Algvnos Qve Los Romanos vsaron en lo antiguo; origen de la Milicia, y Armas: Con Vn Tratado De Los Cabos Principales de vn Exercito ... Compvesto Por El Capitan De Cavallos Coraças Españolas, D Francisco Pozuelo y Espinosa, Gouernador que fue de la Caualleria, que se juntò el año de 1683. para el socorro de la Ciudad de la Nueua Vera-Cruz y Regidor perpetuo de la Villa de Ocaña por

el estado de Hijosdalgo...
Con Privilegio En Madrid, por Francisco Sanz, Impressor del Reyno, y Portero de Camara de Su Magestad, Año de 1690. A costa de Angelo Garcia, Librero en la Villa de Ocaña.
8 p.ℓ., 156, [3] p. illus. 21cm. 4°
"Tassa" dated (7th p.ℓ.^{v}) 1 Dec. 1690.
Errata, 7th p.ℓ.^{r}
Bound in contemporary vellum.
Palau(2)234589; Medina(BHA)1858; Navarrete 1:485.

13139, 1921

E690
R253j
Raveneau de Lussan, -----, b. 1663.
Journal Du Voyage Fait A La Mer De Sud, Avec Les Flibustiers De L'Amerique En 1684. & années suivantes. Par le Sieur Raveneau De Lussan.
A Paris, Chez Jean Baptiste Coignard, Imprimeur ordinaire du Roy, Ruë S. Jacques, à la Bible d'or. 1690. Avec Privilege de Sa Majesté.
8 p.ℓ., 272 p. 13.5cm. 12°
First pub. Paris, 1689.
Cut on t.-p.
Privilege (verso 8th p.ℓ.) dated 8 July 1689.
Manuscript annotations.
Includes a recommendation of the author by le sieur de Cussy, governor of Saint Domingue (6th-8th p.ℓ.).
JCB(2)2:1394; Sabin67984.

01613, 1847

DB
-G7875
1689
1
Remarks Upon The Petition and Petitioners, Against the Lord Mayor, and Court of Aldermen, of London. December, 1690.
[London, 1690].
[2] p. 35.5cm. 1/2°
Caption title.
A reply to the petition To the honourable the knights, citizens and burgesses in Parliament assembled, the humble petition of the members of the Common Council of the city of London..., London, 1690, concerning the liberties and franchises of the city of London.
Bound in Votes of the House of Commons, v. 1, after Votes for 15 Dec. 1690.
Wing R951.

10381, 1914

bB690
R397u
Rendón de Soria, Diego.
Vsque Quaque Extensa Lucis, Et Ductus Lucens, Et Ducens Arctos: Portus Et Ortus, Portans Et Hortans Pharos...
Anno Domini 1690. Angelopoli: Ex Officina Plantiniana Didaci Fernandez de Leon.
Broadside. 42.5cm. x 30.5cm. 1°
Border of woodcuts, including coat-of-arms of Mercedarian order, and of type ornaments surrounds area of letter-press.
Thesis -- College of Saints Peter and John, Puebla de los Angeles, Mexico.
Fragmented, especially in lower half; removed from a binding of Franciscan Informaciones.

06514, before 1902

BA690
R934c
[R]
Ruiz Blanco, Matías, 1643-1705?
Conversion De Piritv. De Indios Cvmanagotos, Palenqves, Y Otros. Svs Principios, Y Incrementos que oy tiene, con todas las cosas mas singulares del Pais, politica, y ritos de sus naturales, practica que se observa en su Reduccion, y otras cosas dignas de memoria. Sacalas Nvevamente A Lvz El P. Fr. Matias Rviz Blanco, De La Observancia de N.P.S. Francisco, Lector de Theologia, Examinador del Obispado de Puerto-Rico, y Comissario Prouincial que ha sido dos vezes en dicha Conversion. ...
Con Privilegio. En Madrid: Por Iuan Garcia Infançon Año 1690.
8 p.ℓ., 160, [8], 250, [6] p. 15cm. 4°
"Tassa" dated (7th p.ℓ.^{v}) 10 July 1690.
Errata, 7th p.ℓ.^{r} and p. [4] at end.
"Practica Qve Ay En La Enseñança de los Indios..." (p. 112-160), 1st pub. under title: Manval Para Catekizar, Y Administrar Los Santos Sacramentos à los Indios... Burgos, 1683.
"Reglas Para La Inteligencia de la lengua de los Indios de Piritu [by Manuel de Yangues]. Dispuestas por el mismo Autor." (p. 1-46, 2d count). "Tesoro De Nombres, Y verbos de esta lengua, con algunas frases, y modos de hablar particulares. Compuesto por el mismo Autor." (p. 47-250, 2d count). These were 1st pub. together under title: Principios, y reglas de la lengua cummanagota, Burgos, 1683.
JCB(2)2:1404; Palau(2)281728; Medina(BHA) 1862; Sabin74017; Viñaza 226; Streit2:2263.

05950, before 1882

B690
S462d
Seixas y Lovera, Francisco de.
Descripcion Geographica, Y Derrotero De La Region Avstral Magallanica. ... Año de 1690.
Compvesto Por El Capitan Don Francisco de

Seixas y Lovera ...
Con Privilegio. En Madrid: Por Antonio de Zafra, Criado de su Magestad. [1690]
20 p. ℓ., 90 numb. ℓ. 21cm. 4°
Cut (royal arms) on t.-p.
"Al ... Real, y Supremo Consejo de Indias" dated (10th p. ℓ.ʳ) 18 June 1690.
Errata, 15th p. ℓ.ᵛ
"Los demàs Libros que el Autor tiene promptos para dàr à la Imprenta, son. ..." 20th p. ℓ.
JCB(2)2:1405; Palau(2)306613; Sabin78960; Medina(Chile)185; Borba de Moraes 2:247n.
0890, 1846

D690
S559a
A Short Account Of The Present State Of New-England. Anno Domini 1690.
[London? 1690]
12 p. 23cm. 4°
Caption title.
Signed (p. 12): N.N.
Wing N57.
05890, 1888

B690
S579ℓ
Sigüenza y Góngora, Carlos de, 1645-1700.
Libra Astronomica, Y Philosophica En Que D. Carlos de Siguenza y Gongora Cosmographo, y Mathematico Regio en la Academia Mexicana, Examina no solo lo que à su Manifiesto Philosophico contra los Cometas opuso el R. P. Eusebio Francisco Kino de la Compañia de Jesus; sino lo que el mismo R.P. opinò, y pretendio haver demostrado en su Exposicion Astronomica del Cometa del año de 1681. Sacala à luz D. Sebastian De Gvzman Y Cordova ...
En Mexico: por los Herederos de la Viuda de Bernardo Calderon IXI. DC. XC.
12 p. ℓ., 188 p. tables, diagrs. 20.5cm. (22.5cm. in case). 4°
Cut (winged horse) on t.-p.; incl. motto: Sic Itvr Ad Astra.
"Prologo" dated (p. ℓ. 11) 1 Jan 1690.
Dedication (p. ℓ. 3-7) by Sebastián Guzman y Córdova.
A reply to Kino, E. F. Exposición astronómica, Mexico, 1681, and Torre, Martin de la, Manifiesto cristiano en favor de los cometas, Mexico, 1681.
Includes (p. 8-19) his Manifiesto philosóphico contra los cometas, 1st pub. Mexico, 1681.
Palau(2)312974; Medina(Mexico)1484; Sabin 80976; Wagner62a.
28581, 1940

DA690
S693t
Some Testimonies Concerning the Life and Death Of Hugh Tickell; As Also His Convincement, Travels, Sufferings and Service for the Lord, and his Eternal Truth. ...
London, Printed for Thomas Northcott, in George-Yard, in Lombard-street, MDCXC.
1 p. ℓ., 10 p. 18.5cm. 4°.
Contents.-Testimonies of 1. His wife, Dorothy Tickell (p. 1-4). 2. "Mens Meeting, to which the said Hugh Tickell did belong" (p. 4-5). 3. Thomas Laythes (p. 5-6). 4. Thomas Dockrey (p. 6-8). 5. George Fox (p. 8-10).
Dated (p. 9, 10) "the 6th. the 4th. Month, 90.
Smith(Friends)2:744; WingS4622.
11449, 1918

D690
T455h
[Thomas, Sir Dalby] fl. 1690-1711.
An Historical Account Of The Rise and Growth of the West-India Collonies, And of the Great Advantages they are to England, in respect to Trade.
Licenced According to Order. London, Printed for Jo Hindmarsh at the Golden-Ball, over against the Royal-Exchange. 1690.
3 p. ℓ., 53 p. incl. tab. 19cm. 4°
Dedication (2d-3d p. ℓ.) signed: Dalby Thomas.
JCB(2)2:1406; WingT961; Sabin32056; Cundall (WI)1990; Kress1749; Baer(Md.)137; Arents410.
01522, 1847

bDA690
T627o
To our Rev[erend] ... Ministers of the several Parishes ... the Second Brief for Relief of the Poor [P]rotestants of Ireland shall come. [London? 1690].
Broadside. 30 x 20cm. fol.
Signed by five English bishops as "Commissioners among others appointed by their Majesties for the making of a general Collection for Relief of the poor Protestants of Ireland": H[enry Compton, bp. of] London, W.[illiam Lloyd, bp. of St.] Asaph, H.[umphrey Humphreys, bp. of] Bangor, N.[icholas Stratford, bp.] Cestriens [i.e. of Chester], and E.[dward Stillingfleet, bp.] Wigorniens [i.e. of Worcester].
In support of the royal proclamation: A second brief for Irish Protestants, dated at Westminster, 18 Feb. 1690 (Steele E4029).
Imperfect: part of top torn away.
05117, before 1874

DB -G7875 1689 1	To The Honourable The Knights, Citizens and Burgesses, In Parliament Assembled, The Humble Petition of the Members of the Common-Council of the City of London, hereunto Subscribing. London, Printed by Thomas Braddyll and Robert Everingham, and are to be Sold at the Seven Stars in Ave-Mary-Lane. M DC XC. [2] p. 27.5cm. 1/2° Caption title; imprint at end. Petitions for restoration of the liberties and franchises of the city of London which were revoked by Charles II. Bound in <u>Votes of the House of Commons</u>, v. 1, after <u>Votes</u> for 15 Dec. 1690. 10380, 1914		Includes "Palavra Do Prégador Empenhada, & Defendida: Empenhada publicamente No Sermam De Acçam De Graças Pelo Nascimento Do Principe D. João, Primogenito de SS. Magestades que Deos guarde; Defendida depois de sua morte, Em Hum Discurso Apologetico, Offerecido secretamente A Rainha N. S. Para alivio das saudades do mesmo Principe." (p. 121-239). According to Leite "Com a data de 1690 há duas edições diferentes." Bound in contemporary calf. With this is bound his <u>Sermoens ... tomo XIV</u>, Lisbon, 1710. Rodrigues 2515; Backer 8:660; Leite 9:199; Innocencio 1:290. 68-337
DA690 T627t	To the Right Reverend, and Reverend the Bishops, and Clergy of the Province of Canterbury, to be Assembled in Convocation at Westminster, A.D. 1690. The humble Petition of many Divines, and others of the Classical, Congregational, and other Perswasions, in the Name of themselves, and Brethren both of Old England and New, who have born Witness to the Truth in the day of Tryal. [London? 1690?] 8 p. 21cm. 4° Caption title. Wing T1717; Sabin 96029; McAlpin 4:370; Dexter(Cong.)2363. 03674, before 1866	CA679 V665s 6	Vieira, Antonio, 1608-1697. Sermoens Do P. Antonio Vieyra da Companhia de Jesu, Visitador Da Provincia Do Brasil, Prégador de Sua Magestade, Sexta Parte. Lisboa, Na Officina de Miguel Deslandes, Impressor de Sua Magestade. A custa de Antonio Leyte Pereira, Mercador de Livros. M. DC. LXXXX. Com todas as licenças necessarias, & Privilegio Real. 4 p.ℓ., 595 p. 21.5cm. 4° Cut (Jesuit trigram, floriated) on t.-p. Permission dated (3d p. ℓ.ᵛ) 8 July 1690. Errata, 4th p. ℓ. Contains 16 sermons preached in Lisbon, 1647, Rome, Bahia, 1638, 1639, and Tôrres Vedras, Portugal, 1652, etc. According to Leite "Deste vol., com a data de 1690, conhecem-se duas impressões diferentes." Rodrigues 2508; Backer 8:659; Leite 9:196; Innocencio 1:290. 68-394
CA679 V665s 13-14	Vieira, Antonio, 1608-1697. Palavra De Deos Empenhada, E Desempenhada: Empenhada No Serman Das Exequias Da Rainha N. S. Dona Maria Francisca Isabel de Saboya; Desempenhada No Sermam De Acçam De Graças pelo nascimento Do Principe D. João Primogenito de SS. Magestades, que Deos guarde. Prègou hum, & outro O P. Antonio Vieyra da Companhia de Jesu, Prégador de S. Magestade: O primeyro Na Igreja da Misericordia da Bahia, em 11. de Setembro, anno de 1684. O segundo Na Cathedral da mesma Cidade, em 16. de Dezembro, anno de 1688. Lisboa, Na Officina de Miguel Deslandes, Impressor de S. Magestade. Com todas as licenças necessarias. Anno 1690. 8 p. ℓ., 260 p. 19.5cm. 4° [His <u>Sermoens</u>, 13. parte] Cut on t.-p. Permissions dated (8th p. ℓ.) 6 Mar. 1690.	DA604 B258s [R]	A Vindication of Nevv-England. From The Vile Aspersions Cast upon that Country By a Late Address of a Faction there, Who Denominate themselves of the Church of England In Boston. Printed with Allowance. [Cambridge, Mass., 1690?] 1 p. ℓ., 27 p. 18.5cm. 4° Has been attributed to Increase Mather, but probably by Charles Morton of Charlestown, possibly from material supplied by Cotton Mather. Reprinted by W. H. Whitmore in <u>The Andros tracts</u>, v. 2, p. 19-78. Bound in early 18th century calf, as the 5th

in a vol. of six 17th century works.
Sabin 46756; Evans 452; Holmes(I) p. 615, 635-637; Wing V486.

689, 1905

+Z
≡V834
1690

Visscher, Nicolaes, 1649-1702.
Atlas Minor Sive Geographia Compendiosa, Qua Orbis Terrarum, Per Paucas Attamen Novissimas Tabulas Ostenditur.
Amstelædami, Ex Officina Nicolai Visscher. [ca. 1690]
2 p. l., engr. maps. 53cm. fol.
Added t.-p., engr.: Atlas Minor Sive totius Orbis Terrarum Contracta Delinea[ta] ex conatibus Nico[lai] Visscher Amst: Bat: Amstelædami apud Nicholaum Visscher cum Privil: Ordin: General: Belgii Fœderati. Ger: de Lairesse delin: & Sculp:
Dates are indicated on some maps; the years range from 1652 to 1685.
Maps are double-page size, except nos. [16], [24], and [51 bis], which are folded to double-page size.
In this copy the title-pages (p. l. 1-2) and maps are colored.
Includes contemporary manuscript index listing maps numbered 6-91. These are the same as the following contents listing except as indicated.
With this is bound: <u>A Geographical and Historical Account of the several Empires, Kingdoms, Republicks, Principalities and Dukedoms of Europe ... The Second Edition...</u>, London, 1721.
Bound in contemporary calf, rebacked.
JCBAR 65:53; Koeman Vis 10-19.

Made up of the following maps:
[1] Orbis Terrarum Nova Et Accuratissima Tabula. Auctore Nicolao Visscher.
[2] Europa delineata et recens edita per Nicolaum Visscher.
[3] Regni Daniæ, Novissima et Accuratissima Tabula Per Nicolaum Visscher.
[4] Scania Vulgo Schonen. apud Nic: Visscher.
[5] Tabula exactissima Regnorum Sueciæ et Norvegiæ nec non Maris Universi Orientalis, Terrarumq. adjacentium, summo studio ab Andræa Bureo Sueco in lucem edita ... A Nicolao Iohannide Piscatore.
[6] Nova Totius Livoniæ accurata Descriptio. Apud Janssonio-Waesbergios, et Mosem Pitt.
[7 Wanting. According to ms. index "Russia"].
[8] Tabula nova totus Regni Poloniæ ... Authore N. Sansonio Abbevillensj Geographus Regis Galliæ Amstelodami apud Nicolaum Visscher.
[9] Tabula Prussiæ Eximiâ Curâ Conscripta Per Casparum Henneberch Erlichensem et denuo edita, per Nicolaum Visscher... [Inset:] Konigsberg.
[10] S. Imperium Romano-Germanicum ... Neulich entworffen und theils gezeichnet durch Iulium Reichelt ... aber aussgeführt und aussgegeben durch Nicolaum Visscher...
[11] Carta Noua accurata del Passagio et strada dalli Paesi Bassi per via de Allemagna per Italia et per via di Paesi suizeri à Geneua, Lione et Roma ... dato in luce da Frederico de Wit di Amsterdam l'anno 1671.
[12] Electoratvs Brandenburgi Mekelenburgi, Et maximæ Partis Pomeraniæ novissima Tabula. Apud Nicolaum Visscher...
[13] Serenissimo, Celsissimo ac Invictissimo Principi, Frederico Guilielmo ... Hanc Pomeraniæ Ducatus Tabulam, D.D.D. Nicolaus Visscher...
[14] Ducatus Bremæ et Ferdæ, Maximæque partis Ducatus Stormariæ, Comitatus Oldenburgi, Albis, Visurgisque Fluminum Novissima Descriptio, per Nicolaum Visscher...
[15] Ducatus Brunsvicensis Fereque Lunæburgensis ... nova et locupletissima Descriptio Geographica. Correcta, innovata, edita, Per Nicolaum Visscher...
[16] Dvcatvs Lvnebvrgensis ... Apud Janssonio-Waesbergios, Mosem Pitt et Stephanum Swart.
[17] Totius Circuli Westphalici accurata descriptio P.r Nic Visscher...
[18] Ducatus Iuliacensis Montensis: et Comitatus Marciæ et Rapens-Bergæ ... de nova accuratè in lucem editæ: per Nicolaum Visscher. [Inset:] ... Orientalis Marciæ partes...
[19] Leodiensis ... Per Nicolaum Visscher...
[20] Totius Fluminis Rheni Novissima Descriptio ex Officina N: Visscher.
[21] Palatinatus Rheni Nova, Et Accurata Descriptio. ... editum per Nicolaum Joannis Piscatore. A.o 1652.
[22] Superioris Alsatiæ nec non Brisigaviæ et Suntgaviæ Geographica Tabula ... ex conatibus Nicolai Visscher...
[23] Landgraviatus Alsatiæ Inferioris Novissima Tabula, in qua simul Marchionatus Badensis, Ortenavia. Cæteraqtam Lotharingica quam alia Confinia, Accuratissimè describuntur per Nicolaum Visscher.
[24] Exactissima Helvetiæ Rhætiæ, Valesiæ ... Tabula. Ex conatibus Nicolai Visscher...
[25] Totius Regni Hungariæ et adjacentium Regionum Tabula A.o 1685 ... de novo correcta ac innumeris locis aucta per Nicolaum Visscher.

[26] Novissima et accuratissima XVII Provinciarum Germaniæ Inferioris Delineatio. Ex Officina Nicolai Visscher...

[27] Belgii Regii Tabula, in qua omnes Provinciæ ab Hispanis ad Annum 1684 possessæ, nec non tam a Rege Galliæ quam Batavis acquisitæ, accurratissime et distincte ostenduntur per Nicolaum Visscher.

[28] Tabula Ducatus Brabantiæ ... Per Nicolaum Visscher.

[29] Prima Pars Brabantiæ cuius caput Lovanivm Auctore Michaele Florentio a Langren... Apud Janssonio-Waesbergios, Mosem Pitt et Stephanum Swart.

[30] Secvnda Pars Brabantiæ cuius urbs primaria Brvxellæ Descr Michaele Florentio a Langren ... Apud Janssonio-Waesbergios, Mosem Pitt et Stephanum Swart.

[31] Tertia Pars Brabantiæ qua continetur Marchionat. S.R.I. horum urbs primaria Antverpia Ex Archetypo Michaelis Florenty a Langren ... Apud Janssonio-Waesbergios, Mosem Pit et Stephanum Swart.

[32] Qvarta Pars Brabantiæ cujus caput Sylvadvcis. Willebordus vander Burght describ. Excudebant Janssonio-Waesbergii, Moses Pitt et Stephanum Swart.

[33] Limburgi Ducatus et Comitatus Valckenburgi Nova Descriptio Per N: Visscher.

[34] Ducatus Lutzenburgi Novissima et accuratissima Delineatio, Per Nic: Visscher ...

[35] Flandriæ Comitatus Accuratissima Descriptio, edita per Nicolaum Visscher.

[36] Flandriæ Tevtonicæ Pars Orientalior Apud Janssonio-Waesbergios, Mosem Pitt et Stephanum Swart.

[37] Flandriæ Pars Occidentalis ... Apud Janssonio-Waesbergios, Mosem Pitt et Stephanum Swart.

[38] Flandriæ Pars duæ... Apud Janssonio-Waesbergios, Mosem Pitt et Stephanum Swart.

[39] Flandria Gallica ... Amstelodami Ioannes Ianssonius exe.

[40] Geographica Artesiæ Comitatus Tabula, per Nicolaum Visscher edita. ...

[41] Comitatus Hannoniæ et Archiepiscopatus Cameracensis Tabula, Per Nicolaum Visscher.

[42] Comitatus Namurci Emendata Delineatio, Nuperrimè in lucem edita, per Nicolaum Visscher ...

[43] Marchionatus Sacri Romani Imperii. ... C J Visscher Excudebat.
[Inset:] Tabella hæc in gratiam Spectatorum addita ut Ostium Scaldis videant simul etiam propugnacula, Aggares, Terras que à Mare absorptas.

[44] Mechlinia Dominium et Aerschot Ducatus Auctore Nicolao Visscher. ...

[45] Belgium Foederatum emendatè auctum et novissimè editum, per Nicolaum Visscher.

[46] Ducatus Geldria et Zutphania Comitatus per Nicolaum Visscher ...

[47] Tetrachia Ducatus Geldriæ Neomagensis Amstelodami apud F. de Wit.

[48] Tetrachia Ducatus Geldriæ Ruremondana Sive Hispanica Amstelodami apud F. de Wit.

[49] Novissima Comitatus Zutphaniæ, Totiusq Fluminis Isulæ Descriptio, per Nic: Visscher ...

[50] Ducatus Geldriæ Tetrachia Arnhemiensis Sive Velavia Gedruckt t'Amsterdam by F. de Wit ...

[51] Comitatus Hollandiæ Tabula Pluribus Locis Recens Emendata A Nicolao Visscher.
[Inset:] De resterende Eylanden van Hollant ...

[51 bis. Not listed on ms. index] Le Comté De Hollande Dressé sur les Memoires les plus Nouueaux Par le S.r Sanson, Geographe ordinaire du Roy. Presenté A Monseignevr Le Davphin ... Alexis Hubert Iaillot. ... A Amsterdam Chez P. Mortier ...

[52] Hollandiæ Pars Meridionalior, Vulgo Zuyd-Holland. Auctore Nic: Visscher. ...

[53] Delflandia, Schielandia et circumjacentes Insulæ ut Voorna, Overflackea, Goerea, Yselmonda et aliæ, ex conatibus Geographicis Nicolai Visscher ...

[54] Rhenolandia, Amstelandia ... Accurate et distincte edita per Nicolaum Visscher. ...

[55] Noordt Hollandt. Frederick de Wit Excudit.

[56] Comitatvs Zelandiæ Novissima Delineatio per Nicolaum Visscher.

[57] Ultraiectini Dominii Tabula Multo aliis auctior et correctior, per Nic: Visscher.

[58] Dominii Frisiæ Tabula, inter Flevum et Lavicam, Auctore B. Schotano à Sterringa ex Officina Nicolai Visscher.
[Inset:] Caerte vande Vriese Eylanden.

[59] Transisalania Provincia; Vulgo Overyssel. Auctor. N. ten-Have. Sch. Zwol. Conrect. edita vero per Nicolaum Visscher.

[60] Groningæ Et Omlandiæ Dominium vulgo De Provincie Van Stadt En Lande, ... per Lud: Tjardæ â Starckenburg et Nicol: Visscher ...

[61] Drentia Comitatvs. Transisulaniæ Tabula II. Auctore Cornelio Pynacker I.C. Apud Janssonio-Waesbergios, Mosem Pit et Stephanum Swart.

[62] Typvs Frisiæ Orientalis. Auctore Vbbone Emmio.
[Inset:] Rideriæ Portionis facies, ante inundationem ...
[63] Nova Totius Angliæ, Scotiæ, Et Hiberniæ Tab: Auctore Frederick de Wit.
[64] Gallia Vulgo La France, Ex Officina Nicolai Visscher.
[65] Vtrivsqve Bvrgvndiæ, tum Ducatus tum Comitatus, Descriptio. Amsterdami Apud Joannem Janssonium.
[66] Exactissima Lotharingia ... T Amsterdam Gedruckt by Carel Allardt ...
[67] Sabavdia Dvcatvs. Savoye Amsterdami. Apud Joan: Janssonium.
[68] Hispaniæ Et Portugalliæ Regna Per Nicolaum Visscher ...
[69] Accuratissima Principatus Cataloniæ, et Comitatuum Ruscinonis, et Cerretaniæ Descriptio per F. De Wit.
[70] Portugalliæ et Algarbiæ Regna, Per Nicolaum Visscher. ...
[71] Totius Italiæ Tabula, Per Nicolaum Visscher ...
[72] Accuratissima Dominii Veneti In Italia ... Tabula quæ est Lombardia Inferior Per F. de Wit ...
[73] Stato Di Milano. [For 73 ms. index lists "Dominium Eccleiasticum [sic]"
[74] Toscana Inferiore: Detta Anticamente Tvscia Svbvrbicaria.
[75] Regnum Neapolis in quo sunt Aprutium Ulterius et Citerius, Comitatus Molisius, Terra Laboris, Capitaniata Principatus Ulterior et Citerior Terra Bariensis et Hidruntina Basilicata Calabria Citerior et Ulterior Per Fredericum De Wit Amstelodami.
[76] Regnum Siciliæ ... editum per Nicolaum Visscher.
[77] Insularum Melitæ Vulgo Maltæ et Gozæ Novissima Delineatio, per Nicolaum Visscher.
[Inset:] Maximæ Partis Maris Mediterranei Tabella ...
[78] Exactissima totius Archipelagi nec non Græciæ Tabula ... per Nicolaum Visscher ...
[79 Wanting. According to ms. index "Candia insula"]
[80] Asiæ Nova Delineatio Auctore N. Visscher.
[81] Terra Sancta, Sive Promissionis, olim Palestina recens delineata, et in lucem edita per Nicolaum Visscher Anno 1659.
[82] Tvrcicvm Imperivm Apud F. de Wit Amstelodami.
[83] Nova Persiæ Armeniæ Natoliæ et Arabiæ Descriptio per F. de Wit.
[84] Tabula Tartariæ et majoris partis Regni Chinæ. edita a F. de Wit.
[85] Imperii Sinarvm Nova Descriptio. Auctore Joh van Loon.

[86] Indiæ Orientalis, nec non Insularum Adiacentium Nova Descriptio, Per Nicolaum Visscher.
[87] Africæ Accurata Tabula ex officina Nic. Visscher.
[88] Novissima et Accuratissima Totius Americæ Descriptio. per N. Visscher.
[89] Insulæ Americanæ in Oceano Septentrionali ac Regiones Adiacentes, a C. de May usque ad Lineam Æquinoctialem. Per Nicolaum Visscher. ...
[90] Novi Belgii Novæque Angliæ Nec Non Partis Virginiæ Tabula ... per Nicolaum Visscher.
[Inset:] Nieuw Amsterdam op t Eylant Manhattans.
[91] Insula Matanino Vulgo Martanico in lucem edita per Nicolaum Visscher ...

62-690

D690 W687s Wilkinson, William, commander of ship "Henry and William."
Systema Africanum: Or A Treatise, Discovering the Intrigues and Arbitrary Proceedings Of The Guiney Company. And Also How prejudicial they are to the American Planters, the Woollen, and other English Manufactures: To the visible Decay of Trade, and consequently greatly Impairing the Royal Revenue, which would be Infinitely Encreased, provided Merchants and Mariners were Encouraged, who can discover several Places not yet Known, or Traded unto, by the African Company. Together With a True Account of their Fortifications. Humbly Submitted to Their Majesties, and to the Consideration of Both Houses of Parliament. By William Wilkinson Mariner.
London, Printed in the Year M. DC. XC.
2 p. ℓ., 26 p. 19cm. 4°
Errata, p. 26.
In this copy there is a blank leaf at the end.
JCB(2)2:1407; WingW2256; Sabin104036.

0545, 1846

1691

BA691 -A441c Alloza, Juan de, 1598-1666.
Cielo Estrellado De Mil Y Veinte Y Dos Exemplos De Maria. Paraiso Espiritval, Y Tesoro De Favores, Y Regalos con que esta

Gran Señora ha favorecido, â los que se acogen à su proteccion, y amparo. Por El Padre Ivan De Alloza. Sacerdote Professo de la Compañia de Iesvs. Natvral De Lima, Civdad de los Reyes en el Perv. ...
  En Valencia: Con licencia: En la Imprenta de Vicente Mace, Maestro de Filosofia, junto el Real Colegio de Corpus Christi. Año 1691. A costa de Claudio Macè, y Iuan Baptista Macé, Mercaderes de Libros.
  18 p.ℓ., 489, [490-500] p. 29.5cm. fol.
  Author statement within two concentric circles with Latin legends.
  First pub. Madrid, 1655.
  "Epistola Lavdatoria" (p.ℓ. 9-13) signed: Gregorio Lopez.
  Imperfect: half-title wanting. This copy closely trimmed at bottom of p. 165-167 with slight loss of text; available in facsim.
  Medina(BHA)1866; Palau(2)10320n; Backer 1:184, 4:1957.
12628, 1920 rev

C619
A949n
Alvin, Juan.
  Elucidatio Veritatis In Casv Fatalivm Accvsationvm per quadringentos Fratres coadunatos contra Patres Provinciæ Algarbiorum, In Sacra Episcoporvm, & Regularium Congregatione factarum; Per Reverendissimvm Patrem Fr. Ioannem Alvin, Lectorem Ivbilatvm, totiusque Fratrum Minorum Ordinis Ministrum Generalem confecta; Ac Ad Eandem Sacram Congregationem remissa.
    [Lisboa? 1691]
  72, [2] p. 19.5cm. 4°
  Dated (p. 72) 9 Jan. 1691.
  Bound as the 12th in a volume of 58 pamphlets, 1619-1702.
9353, 1913

EA691
A745h
[Arnauld, Antoine] 1612-1694.
  Histoire De La Persecution De deux Saints Evêques par les Jesuites: L'Un Dom Bernardin De Cardenas, Evêque du Paraguay dans l'Amerique Meridionale. L'Autre Dom Philippe Pardo, Archevêque de l'Eglise de Manile Metropolitaine des Isles Philippines dans les Indes Orientales.
    [Amsterdam?] M. D. C. XCI.
  252, 149-503 (i.e. 504) p. 14cm. 12°
  Cut on t.-p.
  Chiefly a compilation of texts by Juan de San Diego y Villalón, Alonso Carrillo, Christoval Pedroche, and Alonso Sandin.
  "Reponse Au Jugement sur le Troisiéme Volume De La Morale Pratique Des Jesuites."

(p. [405]-end) is a reply to Michel Le Tellier's Defense des nouveaux Chrestiens, Paris, 1687.
  There is also a variant pub. the same year with half-title bearing designation of the series La morale pratique des Jesuites, t.5.
  Copies are found with errata, [2] p. at end; available in facsim.
  Bound in contemporary calf.
  JCB(2)2:1410; Sabin10804; Backer11:109,1349; Streit2:2278; Retana164.
03678, before 1866 rev

C585
E96t
15
Ashby, Sir John, d. 1693.
  The Account Given By Sir John Ashby Vice-Admiral, And Reere-Admiral Rooke To The Lords Commissioners, Of The Engagement At Sea, Between the English, Dutch, and French Fleets. June the 30th. 1690. With A Journal of the Fleet since their departure from St. Hellens, to their return to the Buoy-in-the-Nore, and other Material Psssages relating to the said Engagement.
    London, Printed for Randal Taylor near stationers-Hall, 1691.
  1 p.ℓ., 32 p. 20cm. 4°
  Concerns the Battle of Beachy Head, June 30, 1690.
  Includes Ashby's account (p. 1-3) and Rooke's (p. 3-5), signed and dated 11th of July, 1690; "The Lords Commissioners Letter, to the Queen's Majesty" (p. 5-8), signed: Sheerness the 18th. of July, 1690. Pembrooke, Maclesfield, R. Howard, H. Goodricke, Tho. Lee; "The Examinations of the Captains" (p. 9-26); the "Journal" (p. 27-32), dated: From the Buoy of the Nore, the 18th of July, 1690.
  Bound as no. 15 of 19 items in a vol. with binder's title: Tracts 1681-1701.
  WingA3937; Knuttel13590.
11352-15, 1918

FA691
B424b
Bekker, Balthasar, 1634-1698.
  De Betoverde Weereld, Zynde een Grondig Ondersoek Van't gemeen gevoelen aangaande de Geesten, derselver Aart en Vermogen, Bewind en Bedryf: als ook't gene de Menschen door derselver kragt en gemeenschap doen. In vier Boeken ondernomen Van Balthasar Bekker S.T.D. Predikant tot Amsterdam.
    t'Amsterdam, By Daniel Van Den Dalen, Boek-verkoper op't Rockin/bezijden de Beurs. 1691 [-1693].
  4 v. in 1: v.1, 11 p.ℓ., 138, [2] p. front. (port.); v.2, 4 p.ℓ., 262, [2] p.; v.3, 4 p.ℓ., 32, 188, [3] p.; v.4, 3 p.ℓ., 224, (217)-(224), (217)-(224), 225-277, [278-280] p. illus. 21cm. 4°

Cut on title-pages; incl. motto: Al Daalende.
Sub-titles vary: v.2, 3 "... Waar in de leere van de Geesten, derselver vermogens en werkingen, en besonderlik des Duivels, uit de natuurlike Reden en de H. Schriften ondersocht word ..."; v.4 "... Waar in't bewijs, dat uit d'Ervarentheid genomen word, ten gronde toe word ondersocht ..."
Imprint dated, v.1, 2: 1691; v.3, 4: 1693.
Volumes 1, 2 first pub. Leeuwarden, 1691. "De Leser zy versekerd/dat van dit boek niets uitgelaten is/'t gene in den Leewarder druk gestaan heeft. Dan wel op weinig plaatsen tot uitbreidinge der beknopte stoffe iets ingevoegd." (v.1, 11th p. ℓ.^{v}).
"Also voor den eersten druk der twee eerste boeken deses werks in 8°. by Hero Nauta tot Leewarden een acte van Privilegie staat/op den naam van Barend Beek, Boekverkeper in den Hage/ende daar in gemeld word/dat hy besig was met dat Boek te drukken: so verklaart den Auteur hier met sijne eigene hand/dat hy Barend Beek niet en kent/ende hem directelik noch indirectelik nooit iets te drukken gegeven heeft; maar desen druk van alle de vier boeken in 4°. aan niemant anders dan aan Daniel vanden Dalen toegestaan." (v.1, 4th p. ℓ.^{v}).
Each volume is signed in ms. by the author (v.1, 4th p. ℓ.^{v}; v.2, 1st p. ℓ.^{v}; v.3, 4th p. ℓ.^{v}; v.4, 3d p. ℓ.^{v}).
Also issued with the title-pages dated the same as the present issue but at least partially in a different setting of type.
Commendatory verses dated (v.1, 3d p. ℓ.^{v}) 16 Aug. 1691; prefaces dated (v.2, 4th p. ℓ.^{v}) 31 July 1691, (v.3, 4th p. ℓ.^{v}) 20 June 1693, (v.4, 3d p. ℓ.^{v}) 15 Sept. 1693.
"In Amerika salmen 't mede niet veel anders vinden." (v.1, p. 41-49).
"Register Der Boeken, gemaakt door Balthasar Bekker ... en die by Daniel vanden Dalen te bekomen zijn." (v.4, p. [280]).
Bound in contemporary vellum.

71-16

D691
B677g
Bohun, Edmund, 1645-1699.
A Geographical Dictionary: Representing the Present and Ancient Names Of All The Countries, Provinces, Remarkable Cities, Universities, Ports, Towns, Mountains, Seas, Streights, Fountains, and Rivers Of the whole World: Their Distances, Longitudes, and Latitudes. With a short Historical Account of the same; And Their Present State: To which is added an Index of the Ancient and Latin Names. ... By Edmund Bohun, Esquire. The Second Edition, Corrected and Enlarged, together with several Useful Maps not in the former Edition.
London: Printed for Charles Brome, at the Gun, at the West-End of S. Pauls. 1691.
8 p. ℓ., [808] p. incl. map. 4 fold. maps. 18cm. 8°
Title in red and black.
Added t.-p., engr. (dated 1688).
First pub. London, 1688.
Errata, last page.
In this issue "By Edmund Bohun, Esquire." is line 22 of the t.-p. Also issued with the same author statement immediately preceding the imprint, as line 24 of the t.-p.
Imperfect: added t.-p. wanting; available in facsimile.
Bound in contemporary calf.
WingB3453.

14975, 1928

DA691
B967t1
Burnyeat, John, 1631-1690.
The Truth Exalted In The Writings Of That Eminent and Faithful Servant of Christ John Burnyeat, Collected Into this Ensuing Volume as a Memorial to his Faithful Labours in and for the Truth. ...
London: Printed for Thomas Northcott in George-Yard in Lumbard-Street. 1691.
4 p. ℓ., 20, 264 (i.e. 260) p. 18.5cm. 4°
"The Preface To The Reader" [by William Penn] (2d-4th p. ℓ.).
"Go, Little Book..." (eulogistic verses) 6 lines (4th p. ℓ.^{v}).
Includes "A Testimony Concerning the Life and Death Of ... John Burnyeat" by George Fox and other testimonies, p. 1-20, the latest of which are dated 22d of the second month, 1691.
"A Testimony Concerning... John Burnyeat" (p. 1-20) dated in Dublin the 22th of the Second Month, 1691. Signed by Anthony Sharp and 5 others.
Includes his "The Innocency Of The Christian Quakers Manifested" (p. 187-220), 1st pub. [Dublin] 1688, and "The Holy Truth And Its Professors Defended... By John Burnyeat, and John Watson" (p. 221-254), 1st pub. London, 1688.
Bound in contemporary calf.

DA691
B967t2
———Another issue.
5 p. ℓ., 20, 72, [2], 73-264 (i.e. 260) p. 20cm. 4°
Same as 1st issue but with additional eulogistic verses, "On John Burnyeat's Book. Go, Little Book..." 9 lines (5th p. ℓ.) and "A Paper of John Burnyeat's, that came to hand, since his Works were Printed" ([2] p. between p. 72-73).
Bound in contemporary calf, rebacked.

JCB(2)2:1409; Wing B5968; Sabin 9417; Smith (Friends)1:349-50; McAlpin 4:411; Baer(Md.)138.
03676, before 1866
6617, 1910

B691 C327m Cartilla Mayor, En Lengua Castellana, Latina, y Mexicana. Nuevamente Corregida, y Enmendada, y Reformada en esta vltima Impression. ...
Con Licencia, Y Privilegio. En Mexico en la Imprenta de la Uiuda de Bernardo Calderon en la calle de San Agustin, Y con prohibicion, que ninguna otra persona sino la dicha Viuda, en toda la Nueva-españa pueda imprimir Cartillas ni Doctrinas pena de ducientos [sic] pesos, y los moldes perdidos. Año de 1691.
[16] p. 20cm. 4°
Cut (Franciscan arms) on t.-p.
Imprint on last p.
JCBAR 10:79.
05880, 1910

BA691 C363m Catholic Church--Liturgy and ritual--Ritual.
Manual De Los Santos. Sacramentos Conforme Al Ritual De Pavlo V. Formado Por mandado del Illustrissimo, y Excelentissimo Señor D. Juan De Palafox, Y Mendoza, Siendo Obispo de la Puebla de los Angeles, Electo Arçobispo de Mexico ... Impresso con Privilegio en Mexico el Año de 1642. Repetida segunda vez su ediccion el Año de 1671. en Mexico con las dos licencias del Superior govierno, y Ecclesiastica. Y esta tercera, y vltima vez corregido, emmendado, y dado â luz por orden del Illustrissimo, y Reverendissimo Señor Doctor D. Manuel Fernandez De Santa Crvz Actual Obispo de la Puebla de los Angeles del Consejo de su Magestad. &c.
Con licencia en la Puebla por Diego Fernandez de Leon. Año de 1691. Hallarase este Manual en el Palacio Episcopal en poder de Don Geronimo Perez de Soto Notario Publico de juzgado Eclesiastico.
12 p.ℓ., 56 [i.e. 59], 90-270, [4] p. 19.5cm. 4°
Title in red and black.
Edited by Andrés Sáenz de la Peña.
Reprinted from the edition of Mexico, 1671; 1st pub. Mexico, 1642.
"A Los Cvras ..." dated (12th p.ℓ.r) 23 May 1691.
Includes numerous passages in Aztec (p. 31-117).
Bound in contemporary vellum.
Palau(2)284386; Medina(Puebla)144; Sabin 74864; Pilling 3430; Viñaza 231.
3767, 1907

B691 C783d [R] Copia De Vna Carta, que escriviò vn Piloto del Patache de la Real Armada de Barlovento a vn amigo suyo, vezino de la Ciudad de la Havana, dandole cuenta diaria de los sucessos, y victorias de dicha Armada sobre los Puertos de Mançanilla, y el Guarico, habitados de Franceses Cosarios, a los quales han apresado doze embarcaciones, y assolado dichos Puertos.
Con licencia en Cadiz por Christoval de Requena: y por su original en Sevilla por Thomas Lopez de Haro, año de 1691.
[4] p. 19.5cm. 4°
Caption title; imprint at end.
By Tomás de Torres, captain of "el patache Santo Christo de San Román" [?] (mentioned by Sigüenza y Góngora, Trofeo de la justicia española, Mexico, 1691, p. 43).
Palau(2)61302; Medina(BHA)1869.
13487, 1923

+Z ≡C822 1691 Coronelli, Vincenzo, 1650-1718.
Atlante Veneto, Nel quale si contiene La Descrittione Geografica, Storica, Sacra, Profana, e Politica, Degl'Imperij, Regni, Provincie, e Stati, Dell'Universo, Loro Divisione, e Confini, Coll'aggiunta di tutti li Paesi nuovamente scoperti, Accresciuto di molte Tavole Geografiche, non più publicate. Opera, E Studio Del Padre Maestro Coronelli Min: Convent: Cosmografo della Serenissima Republica, e Professore di Geografia Nell' Università di Venetia, Ad Uso Dell' Accademia Cosmografica Degli Argonauti. Tomo I.
In Venetia MDCXCI.
6 p.ℓ., 154, 26, [14] p. double front., illus., 30 plates (incl. 8 double plates), port., 41 maps (incl. 39 double-page maps). fol.
The title, half-title, and 1st p. of the dedication (3d p.ℓ.r) are engraved.
Colophon (p. [13] at end): In Venetia, Appresso Girolamo Albrizzi. M.DC.XCI. A spese dell'Autore con Privilegio dell' Eccellentissimo Senato per anni venticinque.
Dedication dated (3d p.ℓ.v) 1691.
First pub. Venice, 1690; for this issue only the imprint and the colophon have been changed.
This is the 1st of 13 volumes which form his series also known as Atlante Veneto, issued Venice, 1690-1698.
Errata, p. [1] at end.
"Altre Opere, e Tavole Geografiche Publicate dall'Autore alle stampe, non comprese in questo Volume": p. [13] at end.
In this copy the imprint date on the t.-p. has been changed in ms. to MDCXCIII.
Bound in contemporary calf.
Armao 49.

Contents (maps):
[1] Primi Elementi, ò Introdutione Al Corso Geografico ...
[2] Planisferii Celesti, Calcolati Per L'Anno MDCC, Corretti, Et Aumentati Di Molte Stelle.
[3] Planisfero Settentrionale, Corretto, Et Accresciuto Di Molte Stelle. Calcolato all'Epoca dell'Anno 1700 ...
[4] Planisfero Meridionale, Corretto, Et Accresciuto Di Molte Stelle. Calcolato all'Epoca dell'Anno 1700 ...
[5] Ævi Veteris Usque Ad Annum Salutis Nonagesimum Supra Milles Quadringentos Cogniti Tantum, Typus Geographic: ... Descriptus, Anno Domini MDC LXXXVIII II [sic].
[6] Planisfero Del Mondo Vecchio ...
[7] Planisfero Del Mondo Nuovo ...
[8] Parte Orientale Dell'Europa ...
[9] Parte Occidentale Dell'Europa ...
[10] Asia [Parte Occidentale]
[11] [Asia Parte Orientale]
[12] L'Africa [Parte Occidentale]
[13] [Africa Parte Orientale]
[14] America Settentrionale Colle Nuoue Scoperte fin all'Anno 1688 ... [Parte Occidentale]
[15] [America Settentrionale Parte Orientale]
[16] [America Meridionale Parte Occidentale]
[17] America Meridionale [Parte Orientale]
[18] Terre Artiche ...
[19] [Polo Artico]
[20] Mare Del Svd, detto altrimenti Mare Pacifico. ...
[21] Mare Del Nord ...
[22] Ristretto Del Mediterraneo ...
[23] Parte Orientale Del Mediterraneo ...
[24] Canale Di Costantinopoli, Già detto Bosforo Tracio ...
[Inset:] Canale Di Costantinopoli ...
[25] Golfo Di Venezia ... 1688.
[26] Disegno Topografico Del Canale Di Cattaro ... MDCLXXXVIII.
[27] Golfo Della Prevesa ...
[Inset:] La Prevesa.
[28] Corso delli Fiumi Drino, e Boiana nella Dalmatia ...
[29] Disegno Idrografico Del Canale Reale Dell' Unione di due Mari In Lingua docca ...
[30] Abissinia, doue sono le Fonti del Nilo ...
[Inset:] Origine, e Corso del Nilo ...
[31-36] Corso Del Danubio da Vienna Sin'à Nicopoli e Paesi Adiacenti ...
[37] Citta, Porto, e Rada Di Brest, e Luoghi conuicini nella Bretagna ... 1689.
[Inset:] Porto Di Brest
[38] Corso Del Reno, Parte Settentrio: ...1690.
[39] Corso Del Reno, Parte Meridionale ... 1690.

[40] Bocche Del Fivme Negro et Isole Di Capo Verde ...
[Inset:] Isola Goree ...
[41] Corso del Fiume Dell Amazoni ...

12760, 1920

DA691 Cotton, John, 1584-1652.
C851n   Nashauanittue Meninnunk wutch Mukkiesog, Wussesèmumun wutch Sogkodtunganash Naneeswe Testamentsash; Wutch Ukkesitchippooonganoo Ukketeahogkounoh. Negonáe wussukhùmun ut Englishmánne Unnontoowaonganit, nashpe ne ánue, wunnegenùe Nohtompeantog. Noh asoowèsit John Cotton. Kah yeuyeu qushkinnúmun en Indiane Unnontoowaonganit wutch oonenehikqunàout Indiane Mukkiesog, Nashpe Grindal Rawson. Wunnaunchemookáe Nohtompeantog ut kenugke Indianog. ...
Cambridge [Mass.]: Printeuoop nashpe Samuel Green, kah Bartholomew Green. 1691.
13 p. 15cm. 8°
Transl. by Grindall Rawson, from: <u>Spiritual milk for babes</u>. London, 1668; 1st pub. under title: <u>Milk for babes</u>. London, 1646.
In this copy there is a blank leaf at end.
JCB(2)2:1411; WingC6446; Evans550; Sabin 17071; Pilling3202; CP185; Eames(N.E.Cat.) 62; Brinley783(this copy).

06419, 1878

H691   [Farissol, Abraham] 1451-1525?
F228i   ... Itinera Mundi, Sic Dicta Nempe Cosmographia, Autore Abrahamo Peritsol. Latinâ Versione donavit & Notas passim adjecit Thomas Hyde S.T.D. è Coll. Reginæ Oxon. Protobibliothecarius Bodlejanus. Calce exponitur Turcarum Liturgia, Peregrinatio Meccana, Ægrotorum Visitatio, Circumcisio, &c. Accedit Castigatio In Angelum à S^{to} Joseph, al.dictum de la Brosse, Carmelitam discalceatum, sui Ordinis in Ispahân Persidis olim Præfectum. Contentorum in Notis Elenchus Præfationem sequitur.
Oxonii, E Theatro Sheldoniano, MDCXCI. Impensis Henrici Bonwick Bibliopolæ Londinensis, apud quem prostant sub Signo Rubri Leonis in Cœmiterio Paulino.
8 p.ℓ., 196 p., 1 ℓ., [2], 31 p. 20.5cm. 4°
At head of title: [title in Hebrew] Id Est, With, as issued, Bobowskii, A. <u>Tractatus ... de Turcarum Liturgia</u>, Oxford, 1690, with special t.-p. and separate paging but continuous signatures.
Text of <u>Itinera mundi</u> in Hebrew and Latin in

parallel columns. Notes in Latin, with many passages in Greek, Arabic, and other exotic types.
    Itinera mundi 1st pub. in Hebrew under title: Iggeret Orechot Olam. Venice, 1586.
    Imprimatur dated (1st p. ℓ.ᵛ) 6 Aug. 1690. Addenda, 4th p. ℓ.ᵛ; errata, 8th p. ℓ.ᵛ
    JCB(2)2:1424; JCBAR55:45-47; Wing F438, 439; Sabin60934; Muller(1872)1213.

06420, 1874?

J691 F979i

Funck, David, ed.
    Der in Europa und America verehrliche Thron und Kron Gross-Britanniens Oder Des Königreichs Engel-Schott-und Irrlands gründliche Abschilderung ... angehängt eine genaue Erzehlung und Bericht von der letzten Enttrohnung König Jacobs II. und neue Betrohnung König Wilhelms des III. Samt allen dabey fürgelauffenen Begebenheiten und darzu gehörigen Kupffern/benebst einer jetzigen Zeit best berühmtesten Land-Mappe dieser Königreich.
    Hervorgegeben und verlegt Von David Funcken/ Kunst-und Buchhändl. in Nürnberg. [ca. 1691]
    1 p. ℓ., 308 p. 6 plates (incl. 2 fold.), 5 ports. 13.5cm. (14.5cm. in case). 12°
    Added t.-p., engr.: Der Gross-Brittanische Thron und Cron.
    In this copy there is a blank ℓ. at end.
    Baginsky219.

10828, 1915

DB -G7875 1689 1

Gt.Brit.--Parliament, 1691-1692--House of Commons.
    Votes Of The House of Commons, In The Parliament; Began at Westminster The 22th [sic] Day of October, in the Third Year of the Reign of King William and Queen Mary, Anno Domini, 1691.
    London: Printed by Thomas Braddyll and Robert Everingham, and are to be Sold at the Seven Stars, in Ave-Mary-Lane, M DC XCI [-1691/2].
    1 p. ℓ., 42, 41-283, [1] p. 29cm. fol.
    Issued in pts. numbered 1-98 [i.e. 99] and dated 22 Oct 1691 - 24 Feb 1691[/2], each of which has caption title and imprint at end.
    Numerous errors in paging.
    Errata, p. 112.
    Booksellers' advertisements, p. 20, 22, last p.
    Bound in Votes of the House of Commons, v.1.

10376-3, 1914

DB -G7875 1689 1

Gt.Brit.--Parliament, 1691-1692--House of Commons.
    Votes Of The House of Commons, Jovis 29. die Octobris, 1691.
    London, Printed by Thomas Braddyll and Robert Everingham, and are to be Sold at the Seven Stars in Ave-Mary-Lane, M DC XCI.
    [2] p. 29cm. 1/2°
    Caption title; imprint at end.
    Addresses of thanks to the sovereigns; to the king for his prosecution of the war against France. Presented 29 Oct. 1691.
    Bound in Votes of the House of Commons, v.1, after Votes for 28 Oct. 1691.

10376-3.1, 1914

FC650 H737 41

Hollandse Mercurius, Verhalende de voornaemste Saken van Staet, En andere Voorvallen, Die in en omtrent de Vereenigde Nederlanden, En elders in Europa, In het Jaer 1690 Zijn geschiet. Het Een-en-veertigste Deel.
    Tot Haerlem, Gedruckt by Abraham Casteleyn, Stads-Drucker, op de Marckt, in de Blye Druck. Anno 1691.
    5 p. ℓ., 349, [350-356] p. plate. 20cm. 4° (Bound in [vol. 11] of Hollandse Mercurius)
    Errata: p. 349.
    Added t.-p., engraved: Hollandsche Mercurius Tot Haerlem, by Abraham Casteleijn Aº 1691.
    JCB(3)2:410; Sabin32523.

8487-OO, 1912

E691 H888t

Huet, Pierre Daniel, Bp., 1630-1721.
    Traitté De La Situation Du Paradis Terrestre. ... Par Messire Pierre Daniel Huet, nommé à l'Evesché d'Avranches, de l'Academie Françoise.
    A Paris, Chez Jean Anisson, Directeur de l'Imprimerie Royale, ruë Saint Jacques, à la Fleur de Lis de Florence. M. DC. XCI. Avec Privilege Du Roy.
    11 p. ℓ., 240, [19] p. fold. map. 16cm. 12°
    Cut (printer's device: fleur de lis) on t.-p.
    Added t.-p., engr.
    "Achevé d'imprimer pour la premiere fois le 20. Novembre 1691." (11th p. ℓ.ᵛ).
    The author maintains that the Garden of Eden was located in Mesopotamia rather than in America or elsewhere.
    In this copy p. 171-172 and 189-190 are ripped as leaves to be cancelled. The cancellans of these leaves are bound (as printed) between p. [10] and [11] at end.
    Bound in contemporary calf.

70-107

D691 H919a [R]   The Humble Address Of The Publicans Of New-
England, To which King you please. With some
Remarks Upon it. ...
London: Printed in the Year, 1691.
35 p. 19.5cm. 4⁰
A reply to "To the King's most Excellent Majesty.
The Humble Address of divers Gentry, Merchants
and others ... Inhabiting in Boston, Charlestown..."
[London, 1691] which is reprinted here, p. 6-8.
Errata, p. 35.
Reprinted by W.H. Whitmore in The Andros
Tracts, v. 2, p. 231-269.
This has been attributed to Charles Morton of
Charlestown (cf. Holmes(I)p. 615, 635-7).
Sabin33688; WingH3386; Church720.

0548, 1846 rev

D691 I61n   The Interest Of The Nation, As it respects all
the Sugar-Plantations Abroad, And Refining
of Sugars At Home, Truly Stated; And Humbly
offered to the Honorable House of Commons.
London: Printed by B. Motte, 1691.
11 p. 18.5cm. 4⁰
This petition submitted by the "refiners of
sugar in England" is recorded in the Journals
of the House of Commons as read 21 Dec. 1641,
in reply to a petition by "several merchants
and planters" read 18 Dec. 1691.
JCB(2)2:1430; WingI269; Sabin34886; Kress
S1731.

02411, 1851

BA691 J91p [R]   Juana Inés de la Cruz, sister, 1651-1695.
Poëmas De La Vnica Poetisa Americana,
Musa Dezima, Soror Juana Ines De La Cruz,
Religiosa Professa En El Monasterio de San
Geronimo de la Imperial Ciudad de Mexico.
Que En Varios Metros, Idiomas, Y Estilos,
Fertiliza varios Assumptos: Con Elegantes,
Sutiles, Claros, Ingeniosos, Vtiles Versos:
Para Enseñanza, Recreo, Y Admiracion.
Sacolos A Luz Don Juan Camacho Gayna,
Cavallero Del Orden de Santiago, Governador
actual de la Ciudad del Puerto de Santa Maria.
Tercera Edicion, corregida, y añadida por su
Authora.
Impresso en Barcelona, por Joseph Llopis,
y á su costa. Año 1691.
8 p.l., 406, [10] p. 20cm. 4⁰
Cut (printer's device) on t.-p.; incl. motto:
En Lupus In Fabula.
Forms v.1 of the author's works.
First pub. under title: Inundación Castálida
..., Madrid, 1689.
There are two other so-called 3d editions:
Saragossa, 1692, and Valencia, 1709.

Preliminary matter includes commendatory
poetry by José Pérez de Montoro (2d-3d p.ℓ.ʳ),
and Catalina Alfaro Fernández de Cordova
(3d p.ℓ.ʳ).
Section title (Villancicos, Al Glorioso S.
Pedro) on printed label mounted over running
title on p. 217.
Imperfect: t.-p. slightly mutilated; p. 305-
306 wanting; available in facsimile.
Bound in contemporary vellum.
Palau(2)65222; Medina(BHA)1870; Sabin17735.

29671, 1945

B69 G643v 7   Juana Inés de la Cruz, sister, 1651-1695.
Villancicos, Con Que Se Solemnizaron en la
Santa Iglesia, y primera Cathedral de la Ciudad
de Antequera, Valle de Oaxaca, los Maytines de
la Gloriosa Martyr Santa Catharina, ... Dis-
curriolos La Erudicion sin segunda, y admirable
entendimiento de la Madre Juana Ynes de la
Cruz ... Pusolos En Metro Musico el Licenciado
Don Matheo Vallados Maestro de Capilla ...
Con Licencia, en la Puebla de los Angeles,
en la Imprenta de Diego Fernandez de Leon.
Año de 1691.
[28] p. 20cm. 4⁰
License dated (p.[2]) 3 Sept 1691.
Bound, in contemporary vellum, as no. 7
with 42 other items.
Medina(Puebla)137; Palau(2)65261.

28907, 1941

DA691 K28p   Keith, George, 1639?-1716.
The Presbyterian and Independent Visible
Churches In New-England And else-where,
Brought to the Test, and examined according to
the Doctrin of the holy Scriptures...With A Call
and Warning from the Lord to the People of
Boston and New-England, to Repent, &c. And
two Letters to the Preachers in Boston; and an
Answer to the gross Abuses, Lies and Slanders
of Increase Mather, and Nath. Morton, &c. By
George Keith.
London: Printed for Thomas Northcott, in
George-Yard in Lombard-street, 1691.
5 p.l., 230 p. 16.5cm. 8⁰
First pub. Philadelphia, 1689.
In part a reply to Increase Mather's An essay
for the recording of illustrious providences,
Boston, 1684, and to Nathaniel Morton's New-
England's memoriall, Cambridge, Mass., 1669.
Letter to Boston ministers dated (p. 212): The
21st of the 7th Month, 1688.
WingK191; Sabin37208; Smith(Friends)2:23;
McAlpin4:419.

01684, 1854

EA691 [Le Clercq, Chrétien] fl. 1641-1695.
L462e Etablissement De La Foy Dans La Nouvelle
[R] France, Contenant L'Histoire Des Colonies
Françoises, & des Découvertes qui s'y sont
faites jusques à present. Avec Une Relation
Exacte Des Expeditions & Voyages entrepris
pour la Découverte du Fleuve Mississipi jus-
ques au Golphe de Mexique. Par Ordre Du
Roy. Sous la conduite du Sieur de la Salle, &
de ses diverses avantures jusques à sa mort.
Ensemble Les Victoires remportées en Canada
sur les Anglois & Iroquois en 1690, par les
Armes de Sa Majesté sous le Commandement
de Monsieur le Comte de Frontenac, Gouver-
neur & Lieutenant General de la Nouvelle France.
Par le P[ère] C.[hrétien] L.[e] C.[lercq] ...
  A Paris, Chez Amable Au Roy, ruë Saint
Jacques attenant la Fontaine Saint Severin, à
l'Image Saint Jerôme. M. DC. LXXXXI. Avec
Privilege du Roy.
  2 v.: 10 p.ℓ., 559 p. fold. map; 5 p.ℓ.,
458 [i.e. 454], [19] p. 16cm. 12º
  Also issued with variant prelims. under
titles: Premier Etablissement De La Foy Dans
La Nouvelle France, Paris, 1691; and: Histoire
Des Colonies Françoises, Paris and Lyon, 1692.
  This copy was issued with "Achevé d'im-
primer" (v.1, 10th p.ℓ.ᵛ) dated 26 July 1691.
The "Table Des Chapitres" is bound as v.2,
p.ℓ. 2-5.
  Has also been ascribed to Louis de Buade
Frontenac and Valentin le Roux.
  Vol. 2, (p. 167-377) includes the narratives
of La Salle's discoveries written by the Re-
collect missionaries Zénobe Membré and
Anastase Douay.
  Booksellers' advertisement, v.2, [19] p.
at end.
  JCB(2)2:1413; Wagner61; Church718n; cf.
Sabin39650, 39651; cf. Streit 2:2749; cf.
Harrisse(NF)169.
01923, 1854 rev

E691 Le Clercq, Chrétien, fl. 1641-1695.
L462n Nouvelle Relation De La Gaspesie, Qui
[R] Contient Les Mœurs & la Religion des Sau-
vages Gaspesiens Porte-Croix, adorateurs
du Soleil, & d'autres Peuples de l'Amerique
Septentrionale, dite le Canada. ... Par le
Pere Chrestien Le Clercq, Missionaire
Recollet de la Province de Saint Antoine de
Pade en Artois, & Gardien du Convent de Lens.
  A Paris, Chez Amable Auroy, ruë Saint
Jacques, à l'Image S. Jerôme, attenant la
Fontaine S. Severin. M. DC. XCI. Avec
Privilege Du Roy.
  14 p.ℓ., 572 p. 17cm. 12º
  Colophon: De L'Imprimerie de Laurent
Rondet.
  "Achevé d'imprimer pour la premiere fois,
le vingtiéme Avril 1691." (14th p.ℓ.ᵛ)
  Examples of Micmac language: p. 158-164.
  In some copies a "Table Des Chapitres"
([4] p.) is inserted; available in Library's
copy of 1692 ed.
  Cf. Paltsits, V.H., "Bibliographical de-
scription..." in Champlain Society edition,
Toronto, 1910.
  Bound in contemporary calf.
  JCB(2)2:1415; Sabin39649; Church717; Streit
2:2750; Pilling(Algonquian)305; Harrisse(NF)
170.
0550, 1846

B682 [López, Francisco] 1648-1696.
-L864p Copia De Carta Escrita A Vn Cavallero De La
Civdad de los Reyes, dandole cuenta de la muerte
del Excelentissimo Señor Dvqve De La Palata, En
La Civdad De Portovelo, Viernes Santo 13. de
Abril de 1691.
  [Lima, 1691]
  [4] p. 28cm. fol.
  Caption title.
  Dated at end: San Felipe de Portovelo, y
Abril 15. de 1691.
  Bound as no. 10 in a vol. with binder's title:
Luis Lopez Obras.
  Palau(2)61299; Medina(Lima)634; Leclerc(1878)
1826.14(this copy); Sabin61105.
14016, 1925

BA691 [Martínez de la Parra, Juan] 1655-1701.
M385ℓ Lvz De Verdades Catholicas Y Explica-
[R] cion De La Doctrina Christiana. Que segun
la costumbre de la Casa professa de la Com-
pañia de Jesvs de Mexico, todos los Jueves
del año le platica en su Iglesia. Dala â la
Estampa el Padre Alonso Ramos de la mesma
Compañia, y Preposito actual de dicha Casa
Professa. ...
  Con Licencia de los Superiores; en Mexico,
en la Casa Professa, en la Imprenta de Diego
Fernandez de Leon, año 1691-[1696].
  3 v.: v.1, 17 p.ℓ., 400 p.; v.2, 8 p.ℓ.,
657 (i.e. 660) p.; v.3, 8 p.ℓ., 740 (i.e. 734),
[24] p. 19.5cm. 4º
  Title of v.1, 3 in red and black.
  Title, v.2: ... se contienen los mandamien-
tos del decalogo...; title, v.3: ... se con-
tienen los santos siete sacramentos ...
  Vol. 2 dated 1692; vol. 3 dated 1696.
  Imprint varies, v.3: Juan Joseph Guillena
Carrascoso Impressor y Mercader de libros,
â cuya costa se imprime en Mexico ...
  License dated, v.1 (13th p.ℓ.ᵛ) 10 July 1691.
Dedication dated, v.2 (5th p.ℓ.ᵛ) 1 July 1692.
Dedication, v.3, dated 23 Nov. 1696.

Imperfect: v.1, p. 293-294 wanting, available in facsim.; v.3 wanting, available in microfilm (except p. 522-529).

Palau(2)155509, 155510, 155511; Medina (Mexico)1494, 1524, 1640; Backer5:636.

62-339
68-277

D.Math C.228B Mather, Cotton, 1663-1728.

Late Memorable Providences Relating to Witchcrafts and Possessions, Clearly Manifesting, Not only that there are Witches, but that Good Men (as well as others) may possibly have their Lives shortned by such evil Instruments of Satan. Written by Cotton Mather Minister of the Gospel at Boston in New-England. The Second Impression. Recommended by the Reverend Mr. Richard Baxter in London, and by the Ministers of Boston and Charlestown in New-England.

London, Printed for Tho. Parkhurst at the Bible and Three Crowns in Cheapside near Mercers-Chapel. 1691.

11 p.ℓ., 62, 65-144 p. 15cm. 8°

First pub. under title Memorable providences, Boston, 1689.

"To The Reader" (3d-4th p.ℓ.) signed by Charles Morton, James Allen, Joshua Moody, and Samuel Willard.

"The Preface" (5th-9th p.ℓ.r) signed: London, Septemb. the 30th. 1690. Rich. Baxter.

"A Catalogue of Books Printed for, and Sold by Thomas Parkhurst..." (9thv-10th p.ℓ.).

"Appendix" (p. 132-144) is a reply to George Keith's The Presbyterian and independent visible churches in New England, Philadelphia, 1689.

JCB(2)2:1417; Sabin46375; WingM1118; Holmes (C)228B.

03675, before 1866

D.Math C.409C Mather, Cotton, 1663-1728.

The Life and Death Of The Renown'd Mr. John Eliot, Who was the First Preacher Of The Gospel To The Indians in America. With an Account of the Wonderful Success which the Gospel has had amongst the Heathen in that part of the World: And of the many strange Customes of the Pagan Indians, In New-England. Written by Cotton Mather. ... The Second Edition carefully corrected.

London: Printed for John Dunton, at the Raven in the Poultrey. MDCXCI.

3 p.ℓ., 138 p. 15cm. 8°

First pub. under title: The triumphs of reformed religion in America. The life of the renowned John Eliot, Boston, 1691.

"A Letter concerning the Success of the Gospel amongst the Indians in New-England. Written by Mr. Increase Mather..." (p. 79-83) is Cotton Mather's transl. of De Successu Evangelii, London, 1688.

Inserted in this copy at end is a copy of "Mr. Baxters Letter, to Mr Increase Mather, upon ye sight of this life of Mr Elliot" dated Aug. 3, 1691, in the hand of the Rev. Francis Tallents.

JCB(2)2:1419; Sabin46382; WingM1120; Holmes (C)409C; Holmes(I)128Gn.

0547, 1846

D.Math C.392 Mather, Cotton, 1663-1728.

Things to be Look'd for. Discourses On the Glorious Characters, With Conjectures on the Speedy Approaches of that State, Which is Reserved for the Church of God in the Latter Dayes. Together with an Inculcation of Several Duties, which the Undoubted Characters and Approaches of that State, Invite us unto: Delivered unto the Artillery Company of the Massachusets Colony: New England; at their Election Of Officers, for the Year 1691. By Cotton Mather. ...

Cambridge: [Mass.] Printed by Samuel Green, & Barth. Green, for Nicholas Buttolph, at Gutteridg's Coffee-House, in Boston. 1691.

83, [1] p. 13cm. 12°

Running title: Expectanda; Or, Things to be Look'd for.

In this copy there is a leaf containing "Advertisement" and "Errata" pasted on inside of front cover.

Imperfect: p. 1-10, 29-32 wanting, p. 11-12, 55-56 disintegrated with slight loss of text; available in facsimile.

Bound in contemporary sheep.

WingM1159; Evans567; Sabin46548; Holmes(C.) 392.

6112, 1909

D.Math C.409A Mather, Cotton, 1663-1728.

The Triumphs of the Reformed Religion, in America. The Life of the Renowned John Eliot; A Person justly Famous in the Church of God, Not only as an Eminent Christian, and an Excellent Minister, among the English, But also, As a Memorable Evangelist among the Indians, of New-England; With some Account concerning the late and strange Success of the Gospel, in those parts of the World, which for many Ages have lain Buried in Pagan Ignorance. Written by Cotton Mather. ...

Boston, Printed by Benjamin Harris, and John Allen, for Joseph Brunning at the corner of the Prison-Lane, 1691.

4 p.ℓ., 152 p. 15cm. (16cm. in case) 8°
"A Letter Concerning the Success of the Gospel, amongst the Indians in New-England. Written by Mr. Increase Mather..." (p. 88-93) is Cotton Mather's transl. of De Successu Evangelii, London,1688.
Errata, p. 152.
Bound in contemporary calf.
JCB(2)2:1418; Sabin46561; Evans568; WingM 1163; Holmes(C)409A; Holmes(I)128G.
8478, 1912

D. Math I. 14A [R]
[Mather, Increase] 1637-1723.
A Brief Account Concerning Several of the Agents Of New-England, Their Negotiation at the Court Of England: With Some Remarks on the New Charter Granted to the Colony of Massachusets. Shewing That all things duely Considered, Greater Priviledges than what are therein contained, could not at this Time rationally be expected by the People there.
London, Printed in the Year 1691.
24 p. 19cm. 4°
Signed (p. 22): London, Novemb. 16. 1691. Increase Mather.
"An Extract of a Letter ... Concerning the New Charter ..." (p. 23-24) signed by William Bates and 12 others: London, Octob. 17. 1691.
Reprinted by W. H. Whitmore in The Andros Tracts, v. 2, p. 271-299.
JCB(2)2:1420; Sabin46637; Holmes(I)14A; Wing M1184; Church719.
05888, 1878

E691 M666d
Minot, Jacques.
De La Nature, Et Des Causes De La Fièvre: Du Legitime Usage de la Saignée & des Purgatifs. Avec des Experiences sur le Quinquina, & des Réfléxions sur les effets de ce Remede. Par M. Minot, Docteur en Medecine. Seconde Edition, reveuë & augmentée.
A Paris, Chez Laurent D'Houry ruë Saint Jacques, devant la Fontaine Saint Severin, au Saint Esprit. M. DC. XCI. Avec Privilege & Approbation.
4 p.ℓ., 360, [24] p. 16.5cm. 12°
"Achevé d'imprimer pour la premiere fois en vertu du present Privilege le 4. Novembre 1691." (at end).
First pub. Paris, 1684.
It appears that the imprint date of this copy was misprinted "M. DC. LXCI" and that the date has been corrected by erasing the extraneous "L".
Bound in contemporary calf.
70-82

BA691 N238s
Narváez, Juan de, ca. 1650-1706.
Sermon Panegyrico, De El Dia Octavo De La Solemne Dedicacion del Templo con el titulo del nombre De Maria SS^ma^ De Gvadalvpe, y S. Bernardo: dia de la Visitacion de Santa Ysabel. Cuya solemnidad autorizó, assistiendo la Illma y Uenerabilissima Congregacion del Principe, y Cabeza suprema de la Iglesia nuestro gran Padre el Señor San Pedro, con su doctissimo, y nobilissimo Abad, y Cabeza el Sr. Doct. D. Manuel de Escalante, Colombres y Mendoza, Thesorero de esta Santa Iglesia Metropolitana. Examinador Synodal deste Arçobispado. Cathedratico jubilado de Prima de Sagrados Canones en esta Real Vniversidad, y Rector q̃ fue de ella. Predicado Por el Doctor D. Ivan De Narbaez, Racionero de la misma Iglesia, Examinador Synodal de dicho Arçobispado, Cathedratico proprietario de Prima de Sagrada Escriptura en la Real Vniversidad, y Rector que fue de ella dos vezes.
Cō licēcia en Mexico por la Viuda de Frãcisco Rodriguez Lupercio. 1691.
1 p.ℓ., 98-104, 106-112 numb. ℓ. 20.5cm. 4°
Also issued as a part of: Ramirez de Vargas, Alonso. Sagrado padron y panegyricos sermones. Mexico, 1691; these are the same sheets with the imprint added to the title-page.
Cf. Medina(Mexico)1500.
13426, 1923

BA691 N638s
Nicolás de la Trinidad.
Sermon A S. Antonio De Padua. En La Rogativa, Qve Por El buen viage de la Flota hizo la Mission, en el Convento de N. P. S. Francisco de la Ciudad de Cadiz, Año de 1687. Predicolo, El Padre Fr. Nicolas De La Trinidad, Lector de Theologia, Ex-Custodio de Tampico, Comissario del Santo Officio, y Guardian del Convento de la Milpa. ...
Con licencia, en Mexico por la Viuda de Francisco Rodriguez Lupercio, en la puente de Palacio. Año de 1691.
12 p.ℓ., 10 numb. ℓ. 20.5cm. 4°
Title in red and black.
Licenses dated (6th p.ℓ.^v^, 10th p.ℓ.^r^) 14 Aug. 1691.
Medina(Mexico)1510; Palau(1)7:70.
68-409

B691 O65h [R]
Ordóñez de Ceballos, Pedro, b. 1550?
Historia, Y Viage Del Mundo Del Clerigo Agradecido Don Pedro Ordoñez De Zevallos,

Natural De La Insigne Civdad De Jaen, à las cinco partes de la Europa, Africa, Asia, America, y Magalanica, con el Itinerario de todo èl. Contiene Tres Libros.

Con Licencia. En Madrid: Por Jvan Garcia Infanzon, Año de 1691. A costa de Joseph Vascones, Mercader de libros, vendese en las Gradas de San Felipe.

6 p. ℓ., 432, [7] p. 20cm. 4º

Title in red and black.

First pub. under title: Viage del mundo..., Madrid, 1614.

Errata (3d p. ℓ.ᵛ) dated 6 March 1691.

Imperfect: 6th p. ℓ. mutilated with some loss of text; available in facsim.

Bound in contemporary vellum.

Palau(2)203654; Medina(BHA)1874; Sabin 57525; Streit 1:717; Vindel 2001.

69-322

BA691 O77c
Ortiz de Salzedo, Francisco, 17th cent.
Curia Eclesiastica, Para Secretarios De Prelados, Juezes Eclesiasticos, Ordinarios, y Apostolicos, y Visitadores, y Notarios Ordinarios Apostolicos, y de Visita. Añadida en lo principal glossas, y autoridades por su mismo Autor. Con Una Relacion De Los Arzobispados, y Obispados de España, y Indias. ... Por Francisco Ortiz De Salcedo, Notario publico, Apostolico, y Real, descripto en el Archivo de la Curia Romana, Natural de Madrid, y Relator del Cõsejo de S. A. el Serenissimo Cardenal Infante D. Fernando mi señor, dignissimo Prelado de dicha Santa Iglesia, y Arçobispo de Toledo.

En Pamplona: Por Juan Micón. Año 1691.

8 p. ℓ., 152, 155-233 numb. ℓ., [17] p. 20cm. 4º

First pub. Madrid, 1610.

Palau(2)205993.

12650, 1920

BA691 P153v [R]
Palafox y Mendoza, Juan de, Bp., 1600-1659.
Vida Interior Del Ilvstrissimo, Excelentissimo, y Venerable Señor D. Juan De Palafox Y Mendoza, Del Consejo De Su Magestad, y su Consejero en los Supremos de Guerra, Indias, y Aragon, Obispo de la Puebla de los Angeles, Arçobispo electo de Mexico, Virrey, Presidente, Governador, y Capitan General de la Nueva-España, Visitador de todos sus Tribunales, Juez de residencia de tres Virreyes, y Obispo de la Santa Iglesia de Osma. Copiada Fielmente Por La Qve El Mismo Escrivio con titulo de Confessiones, y Confusiones, que Original se conserva oy en el Archivo del Convento de S. Hermenegildo de Madrid de la Esclarecida Religion de Carmelitas Descalços. ... Sacala A Lvz Don Migvel De Vergara, Cavallero Del Avito de Santiago, para el mayor aprovechamiento de las Almas.

Con Privilegio. En Sevilla, Por Lvcas Martin, Año 1691.

32 p. ℓ., 465, [33] p. port. 21cm. 4º

A rev. and enl. of the 1st ed., Brussels, 1682. Palau records an edition with the same imprint dated [1691] with 583 p. main paging.

Errata (18th p. ℓ.ʳ) dated 20 Dec. 1691.

Preliminary matter includes poetry.

Imperfect: p. 151-154 wanting (substituted by duplicate p. 455-458); available in facsim.

Bound in contemporary vellum.

Palau(2)209802; Medina(BHA)1875; Sabin 99456n.

11241, 1917

BA691 P155s
Palavicino y Villarrasa, Francisco Javier, fl. 1691-1694.
Sermon Panegyrico. Predicado, à la solemnidad de el Patrocinio de N. Señora, en la Iglesia del Real, y Religiosissimo Convento de Jesus Maria; de esta Imperial Ciudad de Mexico; en concurso de la primera Missa que en dicho dia, è Iglesia, cantó el Br. D. Antonio Bernardino Dominguez, Zamudio. Dixolo El Ldo. D. Francisco Xavier Palavicino, Y Villa. Rasa, Clerigo Presbytero, Valenciano. ...

Con Licencia De Los Svperiores. En Mexico: por Doña Maria de Benavides, Viuda de Juan de Ribera en el Empedradillo. Año de 1691.

5 p. ℓ., 7 numb. ℓ. 20cm. 4º

License dated (5th p. ℓ.ᵛ) 19 Dec. 1690.

Text of t.-p. slightly affected by mutilation.

Medina(Mexico)1498; Palau(2)210098.

70-152

BA691 R173s
Ramírez de Vargas, Alonso, ed.
Sagrado Padron Y Panegyricos Sermones A La Memoria Debida Al Svmptvoso Magnifico Templo, y curiosa Basilica del Convento de Religiosas del glorioso Abad San Bernardo, Que Edificò En Su Mayor Parte El Capitan D. Ioseph de Retes Largache, difũto Cavallero del Orden de Santiago, y consumaron en su cabal perfeccion su Sobrino Don Domingo De Retes, Y Doña Teresa De Retes Y Paz, su hija, en esta dos vezes Imperial, y siempre leal Ciudad de Mexico, con la Pompa funebre de la translacion de sus huessos, Qve Erige En Descripcion Historica Panegyrica, Don Alonso Ramirez de Vargas, Natural de esta Ciudad. ...

Con Licencia, En Mexico por la Viuda de

Francisco Rodriguez Lupercio en la puente de Palacio. Año de 1691.
9 p.ℓ., 1 ℓ., 18 numb. ℓ., 1 ℓ., [2] p., 22-52, 54-73 numb. ℓ., 1 ℓ., 74-97 numb. ℓ., 1 ℓ., 98-104, 106-135 numb. ℓ., [2] p. illus. 20.5cm. 4°
License dated (9th p.ℓ.ᵛ) 19 Oct. 1690.
Errata, [2] pages at end.
Contents:
All but the last item have special half-title.
[1]. Vidal de Figueroa, José. Sermon a la dedicacion del templo. (1 ℓ., numb. ℓ. 1-6)—[2]. Manso, Pedro. Sermon panegyrico. (numb. ℓ. 7-18)—[3]. Argüello, Manuel de. Sermon panegyrico. (1 ℓ., [2] p., 22-35 numb. ℓ.)—[4]. Rueda, Juan de. Sermon panegyrico. (numb. ℓ. 36-44)—[5]. Matías de San Juan Bautista. Sermon en la dedicacion. (numb. ℓ. 45-52, 54-62)—[6]. Méndez, Luis. Sermon Panegyrico. (numb. ℓ. 63-73)—[7]. Núñez de Miranda, Antonio. Sermon panegyrico. (1 ℓ., numb. ℓ. 74-97)—[8]. Narváez, Juan de. Sermon panegyrico. (1 ℓ., numb. ℓ. 98-104, 106-112)—[9]. Pompa funebre. (numb. ℓ. 113-118)—[10]. Casas Zeinos, Diego de las. Sermon funebre. (numb. ℓ. 119-129)—[11]. Fama postuma [poem] (numb. ℓ. 130-135).
Items [2] and [8] also circulated as separates, the same sheets with imprint added at bottom of title-page.
Bound in contemporary vellum.
JCBAR21:9; Palau(2)247201; Medina(Mexico) 1500; Sabin67659.

13069, 1921

D691
R262r
1
[R]
[Rawson, Edward] 1615-1693, supposed author.
The Revolution In New England Justified, And the People there Vindicated From the Aspersions cast upon them By Mr. John Palmer, In his Pretended Answer to the Declaration, Published by the Inhabitants of Boston, and the Country adjacent, on the day when they secured their late Oppressors, who acted by an Illegal and Arbitrary Commission from the Late King James.
Printed for Joseph Brunning at Boston in New England. 1691.
3 p.ℓ., 48, 12 p. 19cm. (22cm. in case) 4°
"To The Reader." signed (3d p.ℓ.ᵛ): E.[dward] R.[awson] S.[amuel] S.[ewall].
A reply to John Palmer's The present state of New England [Boston, 1689].
With, as issued, William Stoughton's A narrative of the proceeding of Sir Edmund Androsse [Boston] 1691, with special t.-p., separate paging and signatures.
Authorship has been attributed to Increase Mather.
This copy bound separately, cased with Stoughton item.
Reprinted by W. H. Whitmore in The Andros Tracts, v.1, p. 63-148.
JCB(2)2:1421; Evans575; Sabin46731; Church721; WingR376.

0546, 1846

E691
R382d
Relation De Ce Qui S'Est Passé En Canada, à la descente des Anglois à Quebec au mois d'Octobre 1690. faite par un Officier qui s'est trouvé dans l'occasion, & passé de Quebec à Port-Louïs, où a descendu Mr. de Vilbon Capitaine chargé des Paquets du Roy, & depuis arrivé à la Rochelle le 21. Janvier 1691. dans le Vaisseau la Fleur de May commandé par lé [sic] Capitaine Javelau de la Tremblade.
[La Rochelle? 1691?]
4 p. 21.5cm. 4°
Caption title.
At end: Avec Permission.
JCB(2)2:1426; JCBAR49:22; Sabin69258; Harrisse(NF)168; Leclerc(1867)1286.

03800, 1868

E691
R382dℓ
Relation De La Levée Dv Siège De Quebec, Capitale de la Nouvelle France.
A Paris du Bureau d'Adresse, aux Galleries du Louvre devant la ruë saint Thomas le 7. Février. 1691. Avec Privilege.
7, [1] p. 23cm. (24cm. in case) 4°
Caption title; imprint at end.
This is another edition of the account 1st pub. as an Extraordinaire of the Mercure de France, Paris, February 7th, 1691.
cf. Sabin69266; cf. Harrisse(NF)166.

31685, 1955

BA691
R457s
[R]
Reyes, Francisco de los.
Sagrado Dvo De Las Dos Mas Levantadas Vozes De Marcella, Y El Baptista Cantado al primero, instante, sin segundo, de la Concepcion purissima de Maria, Por El P. Fr. Francisco De Los Reyes, Ex-Lector, y Predicador mayor del Convento de San Francisco de Mexico En La Annval Fiesta, Qve a Mysterio tanto, celebra la Imperial Vniversidad Mexicana ...
En Mexico por la Viuda de Francisco

69-756
 Rodriguez Lupercio. 1691.
 7 p. l., 9 numb. l. 19.5cm. 4°
 License dated (5th p. l.v) 11 Jan. 1691.
 Palau(2)265539; Medina(Mexico)1503.

BA691
-S161c
 [Salazar, Martín de]
 Competentia Ivrisdictionis Inter Reverendissimvm Ministrum Generalem, Et Commissarivm Indiarvm Matriti Residentem, Ordinis Minorvm Sancti Francisci De Observantia.
 [Madrid, 1691]
 23 numb. l. 30.5cm. fol.
 Cut (engr.) at head of title.
 Signed at end: Fr. Martinus de Salazar, Concionater Regius, Pater, & Custos Provinciæ Castellæ, ac R^{mi}· Ministri Generalis Procurator.
 Medina(BHA)1879; Streit 2:2276; Palau(2) 286703.
71-244

BA691
S211i
 Sanchez, Francisco.
 Informe, Y Parecer Acerca De Las Razones Qve Ay En derecho para que los terceros de algunas de las Sagradas Religiones lo puedan ser juntamente de otras qualesquier. Por El R.P.M. Fr. Francisco Sanchez Del Orden de Predicadores, y su Provincia del Ss. Rosario de Filipinas.
 Con licencia de los Superiores en la Puebla, en la Imprenta de Diego Fernandez de Leon año 1691.
 1 p. l., 29 p. 21cm. 4°
 Cut (Dominican symbol) on t.-p.
 License dated (verso of t.-p.) 22 Jan. 1691.
 Palau(2)294119; Medina(Puebla)147; Sabin 76273.
14717, 1927

B691
S211a
 Sancho de Melgar, Estevan.
 Arte De La Lengva General Del Ynga llamada Qquechhua. Compvesto Por El Bac. D. Estevan Sancho de Melgar natural de esta Ciudad de los Reyes Cathedratico de dicha Lengua en esta Santa Iglesia Metropolitana, y Examinador Synodal de ella en este Arçobispado. ...
 Con Licencia. Impresso en Lima, en la Calle de las Mantas por Diego de Lyra Año de 1691.
 12 p. l., 50 (i.e. 54) numb. l., [3] p. 14.5cm. 8°
 License dated (8th p. l.r) 6 Feb. 1691.

 Leaves 20, 49-54 misnumbered respectively 10, 48-51, 48, 50.
 Preliminary matter includes poetry by Juan Ramón.
 Palau(2)296815; Medina(Lima)635; Sabin 47424; Viñaza230.
06425, 1884

BA691
S235s
 Santiago de Chile (Diocese)--Synod, 1691.
 Synodo Diocesana Con La Carta Pastoral Convocatoria para el; Y otra en orden, a la paga de los Diezmos. Celebrola El Illmo· Y Rev^{mo}· S^{or}· D^{or}· M^{tro}· Don Fray Bernardo Carrasco de Saavedra Obispo de Santiago de Chile del Consejo de su Magestad, en la Iglesia Cathedral de dicha Ciudad. A Qve Se Dio Principio Domingo diez y ocho de Enero de mil y seiscientos y ochenta, y ocho años, y se publicò en en [sic] dos de Mayo de dicho año.
 Con licencia en Lima en [sic]; en la Imprenta de Ioseph de Contreras, y Alvarado. Año de 1691.
 8 p. l., 79 numb. l., 12 l. 21cm. 4°
 Added t.-p. with cut (coat of arms).
 "Compvtatio Chronologica Kabballistica" (8th p. l.).
 Includes pastoral letters occasioned by the Lima earthquakes of 1687 and 1690 (numb. l. 75v-79v).
 License dated (7th p. l.v) 27 Nov. 1690.
 In this copy there is a blank l. at end.
 In this copy the added t.-p. is disintegrated affecting imprint.
 Bound in contemporary vellum.
 Palau(2)45111; Medina(Lima)631; Medina (Chile)186; Streit 2:2279.
5511, 1909

D691
S264a
[R]
 Savage, Thomas, 1640-1705.
 An Account Of The Late Action Of The New-Englanders, Under the Command of Sir William Phips, Against the French At Canada. Sent in a Letter from Major Thomas Savage of Boston in New-England, (who was present at the Action) to his Brother Mr. Perez Savage in London. Together with the Articles of War composed and agreed upon for that purpose.
 Licensed April 13. 1691. London, Printed for Thomas Jones at the White Horse without Temple-Bar. 1691.
 12, [3] p. 19.5cm. 4°
 The "Account" concludes with further information from other letters from New-England (p. 11-12) and a facsimile of one of the ten shilling bills issued by the Massachusetts Colony to pay the costs of the expedition (p. [1] at end).

Booksellers' advertisement, p. [2-3] at end.
JCBAR49:22; WingS771; Sabin77246; Church722; Dionne2:230.
06524, 1888

B691
S579t
[R]
Sigüenza y Góngora, Carlos de, 1645-1700.
Trofeo De La Jvsticia Española En El Castigo De La Alevosia Francesa Que Al Abrigo De La Armada de Barlovento, executaron los Lanzeros de la isla de Santo Domingo, en los que de aquella nacion ocupan sus costas. Debido todo à providentes ordenes del Ex.mo Señor D. Gaspar De Sandoval Cerda Silva Y Mendoza, Conde de Galve, Virrey de la Nueva-España. Escribelo D. Carlos de Siguenza y Gongora Cosmographo, y Cathedratico de Mathematicas del Rey N.S. en la Academia Mexicana.
En Mexico por los Herederos de la Viuda de Bernardo Calderon: Año de M. DC. XCI.
4 p. ℓ., 100 p. 19.5cm. (21cm. in case) 4°
Cut (winged horse) on t.-p.; incl. motto: Sic Itvr Ad Astra.
"Sucesos fatales de Monsiur [sic] de Lasalle en el lago de San Bernardo ..." p. 66-76.
"Hostilidades que se les hazen à los piratas que ocupaban la laguna de Terminos en el seno mexicano hasta desalojarlos de alli." p. 76-80.
"Epinicios Gratulatorios Con que algunos de los cultissimos Ingenios Mexicanos ... Celebraron al Exmo. Senor Don Gaspar de Sandoval, Cerda, Silva, Y Mendoza, Conde de Galve, &c. Virrey de la Nueva-España. Con ocasion de ... La Victoria, que por mar y tierra, consiguieron las catolicas armas americanas, de los Franceses poblados en El Guarico, lugar en la costa septentrional de la Isla Española, el dia 21. de Henero de este año de 1691." (p. 81-100), by Juana Inés de la Cruz, Francisco de Ayerra y Santa María, Francisco Xavier Zapata, Alonso Ramírez de Vargas, Antonio de Peralta, Francisco Acevedo, Diego Joseph de Bustos, Gaspar de Guevara, Antonio Morales Pastrana, and Juan de Guevara.
With this is bound, in ms., his: Relacion de lo sucedido á la Armada de Barlovento á fines del año pasado y principios de este de 1691.
Dorothy Schons, Bibliografía de Sor Juana Inés de la Cruz, Mexico, 1927, p. 31.
JCBAR40:20-21; Palau(2)312978; Medina (Mexico)1508; Sabin80987; Bissainthe7978; Wagner62; Jones(1938)352(this copy).
28579, 1940

B691
-S687hb
[R]
Solís y Rivadeneyra, Antonio de, 1610-1686.
Histoire De La Conquête Du Mexique, Ou De La Nouvelle Espagne. Traduite de l'Espagnol de Don Antoine De Solis.
A Paris, Chez Jeremie Bouillerot, ruë Saint Jacques, au Prophete Jeremie. M. DC. XCI. Avec Privilege Dv Roy.
15 p. ℓ., 630, [26] p. 12 plates (incl. 10 fold.), 2 maps. 26cm. 4°
Cut on t.-p.
Transl. by S. de Broë, seigneur de Citry et de La Guette, from Historia de la conquista de Mexico, Madrid, 1684.
One of a group of simultaneous issues by different booksellers, Paris, 1691, which differ only as to t.-p.
"Achevé d'imprimer pour la premiere fois, le vingt-deuxiéme jour de Fevrier mil six cens quatre-vingt onze." (15th p. ℓ.v)
"De l'Imprimerie de Laurent Rondet. 1691." (p. [25] at end)
Errata, p. [26] at end.
Bound in contemporary calf.
JCB(2)2:1427; Sabin86475; Palau(2)318665; cf. Arocena IV 2, 3n; cf. Medina(BHA)1772n.
03677, before 1866

B691
-S687hp
[R]
Solís y Rivadeneyra, Antonio de, 1610-1686.
Histoire De La Conquête Du Mexique, Ou De La Nouvelle Espagne. Traduite de l'Espagnol de Don Antoine De Solis.
A Paris, Chez Robert Pepie, ruë Saint Jacques, à l'Image S. Basile, au dessus de la Fontaine S. Severin. M. DC. XCI. Avec Privilege Dv Roy.
15 p. ℓ., 630, [26] p. 12 plates (incl. 10 fold.), 2 maps. 26cm. 4°
Cut on t.-p.
Transl. by S. de Broë, seigneur de Citry et de La Guette, from Historia de la conquista de Mexico, Madrid, 1684.
One of a group of simultaneous issues by different booksellers, Paris, 1691, which differ only as to t.-p.
"Achevé d'imprimer pour la premiere fois, le vingt-deuxiéme jour de Fevrier mil six cens quatre-vingt onze." (15th p. ℓ.v)
"De l'Imprimerie de Laurent Rondet. 1691." (p. [25] at end)
Errata, p. [26] at end.
Bound in contemporary calf.
JCB(2)2:1428; Sabin86475; Medina(BHA)1773n; Palau(2)318666; Arocena IV 2.6.
03816, 1868

B691
-S687h
[R]
Solís y Rivadeneyra, Antonio de, 1610-1686.
Historia De La Conqvista De Mexico, Poblacion, Y Progressos De La America Septentrional, Conocida Por El Nombre De Nveva España. Escriviala Don Antonio De Solis,

Secretario De Sv Magestad, Y Sv Chronista mayor de las Indias. Dedicase Al Illvstrissimo Señor Don Gvillen De Rocafvll Y Rocaberti, Por La Gracia De Dios Vizconde de Rocabertí, Conde de Peralada, y de Albatera, &c.

Año 1691. Barcelona. En la Imprenta de Ioseph Llopis. Impressor de Libros; y à su costa. Vendese en su Casa, en la calle de Santo Domingo.

10 p. ℓ., 384, 383-398, 401-548, [15] p. 31.5cm. fol.

Title in red and black.

Cut (printer's device) on t.-p.; incl. motto: En Lupis In Fabula.

Dedication (3d-4th p. ℓ.) signed: Barcelona, y Março à 18. de 1691. ... Ioseph Llopis.

First pub. Madrid, 1684.

Imperfect: half-title (1st p. ℓ.) wanting; available in facsim.

Bound in contemporary vellum.

Sabin86447; Palau(2)318603; Medina(BHA) 1880; Arocena IV 2.2.

06168, 1895

D691
S693ℓ
Some Letters And An Abstract of Letters From Pennsylvania, Containing The State and Improvement of that Province. Published to prevent Mis-Reports.

[London] Printed, and Sold by Andrew Sowe [sic], at the Crooked-Billet in Holloway-Lane, in Shoreditch, 1691.

12 p. 20cm. 4°

JCB(2)2:1423; WingS4515; Sabin60621; Smith (Friends)1:848-9; Vail(Front.)262.

02906, 1861

D691
S746t
[R]
Spencer, Thomas, secretary to Sir Timothy Thornhill.

A True and Faithful Relation Of The Proceedings Of The Forces of Their Majesties K. William and Q. Mary, In their Expedition against the French, In The Caribby Islands In The West-Indies: Under the Conduct of His Excellency Christopher Codrington, Captain General and Commander in Chief of the said Forces, In the Years 1689, and 1690. Written by Thomas Spencer, Jun. Secretary to the Honourable Sir Timothy Thornhil Baronet, to whose Regiment he was Muster-Master, and supplied the Place of Commissary.

London, Printed for Robert Clavel at the Peacock, at the West-End of St. Paul's Church-yard, 1691.

2 p. ℓ., 12 p. 19.5cm. 4°

Bound in contemporary calf.

JCB(2)2:1429; Wing S4963; Sabin89383; Cundall (WI)1991.

03679, before 1866

G691
S762d
Spole, Anders, 1630-1699, praeses.

... Dissertatione Graduali Americam Noviter Detectam Cum consensu Amplissimæ Facultatis Phisosophicæ [sic] in Regia ad Upsaliam Academia Præside Viro Celeberrimo Amplissimoqve Dn. Andrea. Spole Math. Sup. Profess. Reg. & Ord. Publico bonorum examini subjicit Olaus Beronius Upsal. Solitis ante meridiem horis in Audit. Gust. Majori ad d. 16. Novemb. Anni M DC XCI.

Holmiæ [Stockholm] Excudit Henricus Keyser/ S:æ R:æ M:tis & Ups. Acad. Typog. [1691]

2 p. ℓ., 15, [1] p. 16.5cm. 8°

At head of title: Q. F. F. S.

Diss. - Uppsala (Olaus Beronius, respondent)

14988, 1928

F691
S839z
Sterre, Dionysius van der, d. 1691.

Zeer Aanmerkelijke Reysen Gedaan door Jan Erasmus Reining, Meest in de West-Indien en ook in veel andere deelen des Werelds. &c. ... Samengesteld door D. vander Sterre, Med. Doct. op Curaçao. Met Figuren.

t' Amsterdam, By Jan ten Hoorn, Boekverkooper over 't Oude Heere Logement in den History-Schryver. 1691.

3 p. ℓ., 26, 25-134, [6] p. 6 plates (incl. 2 fold.) 19cm. 4°

Added t.-p., engr.

Cut (ship) on t.-p.

"Tot den Leezer" dated (3d p. ℓ.^{v}) 12 Oct. 1688.

JCB(2)2:1425; Sabin69119; Cundall(WI)1992; Muller(1872)1280; Scheepvaart Mus. 118.

02951, 1861

D691
R262r
2
[R]
[Stoughton, William] 1632-1701.

A Narrative Of The Proceedings Of Sir Edmond Androsse and his Complices, Who Acted by an Illegal and Arbitrary Commission from the Late K. James, during his Government in New England. By several Gentlemen who were of his Council.

[Boston] Printed [by Joseph Brunning] in the Year 1691.

12 p. 20cm. (22cm. in case) 4° (Issued as a part of [Rawson, Edward] The revolution in New England, Boston 1691).

Signed at end by William Stoughton, Thomas Hinckley and three others, although probably chiefly the work of Stoughton.

In part a reply to John Palmer's The present state of New England [Boston 1689] and to New England's Faction discovered, London, 1690.

"To The Reader" dated (p.3): B.N.E. Feb. 4. 1690/1.

Reprinted by W. H. Whitmore in The Andros Tracts, v.1, p. 133-148.

This copy bound separately, cased with Rawson item.

JCB(2)2:1408; Evans572; Sabin92350; Church 723; WingS5762.

0549, 1846

CA691 S985o Sylva, Antonio da, b. 1639.
Oraçam Funebre, Que Disse O Licenciado Antonio da Sylva, Vigario do Arrecife: Nas Exeqvias Da Serenissima Princesa D. Isabel Luisa Josepha, celebradas na Misericordia da Cidade de Olinda, aos 5. de Fevereiro de 1691. ...
Lisboa. Com todas as licenças necessarias. Na Officina de Miguel Manescal, Impressor do S. Officio. Anno M.DC.XCI.
5 p.ℓ., [20] p. 20cm. 4°
Preliminary matter includes poetry.
Sabin81075; Borba de Moraes2:255; Innocencio1:268.

69-641

D691 T627t [R] To The King's Most Excellent Majesty. The Humble Address of divers of the Gentry, Merchants and others, Your Majesties most Loyal and Dutiful Subjects, Inhabiting in Boston, Charlestown and Places adjacent, within Your Majesties Territory and Dominion of New-England, in America.
Licensed April the 28th. 1691. London, Printed by Henry Hills in Black-Fryars 1691.
8 p. 19cm. 4°
Caption title; imprint at end.
The "second petition of the Episcopalians" remonstrating the overthrowing of the Andros government (cf. W.N.Whitmore, The Andros Tracts, v.2, p. xxv).
Includes the petition (p. 1-2) and a letter (p. 3-8) dated "Charlestown New-England, November the 22d. 1690", signed L.[awrence] H.[ammond], which has special reference to the Quebec Expedition of 1690.
In this copy the sheet was turned the wrong way round when being perfected with the result that the pages of the gathering as printed run: p. 1, 6-7, 4-5, 2-3, 8.
JCBAR49:22; WingT1501; Sabin95946.

06525, before 1923

BA691 V422o Vega, José de la, fl. 1672-1691.
Oracion Espiritual A Sor Maria Francisca Novicia desde edad de cinco años, en el Religiosissimo Convento de San Phelipe de Jesus, de Religiosas Capuchinas de esta Ciudad de Mexico; Dicha En El Dia De Sv Profession Por el M.R.P. M. Fr. Joseph De La Vega del Real Orden de N. Señora de la Merced, Redempcion de Cautivos. ...
Con Licencia En Mexico Por los Herederos de la Viuda de Bernardo Calderõ año 1691
4 p.ℓ., 8 numb. ℓ., [2] p. 20cm. 4°
Approbation dated (4th p.ℓ.ᵛ) 24 Oct. 1691.
Medina(Mexico)1511; Sabin98762.

1049, 1905

DA691 W695m Willard, Samuel, 1640-1707.
The Mourners Cordial Against Excessive Sorrow Discovering what Grounds of Hope Gods People have concerning their Dead Friends By Samuel Willard, Teacher of a Church in Boston. ...
Boston, Printed by Benjamin Harris, and John Allen. 1691. Very Suitable to be given at Funerals.
4, 137, [1] p. 15cm. 8°
Booksellers' advertisement, last p.
Imperfect: p. 135-137 and last p. wanting; available in facsimile.
Bound in contemporary calf.
Mounted inside front cover: [Sewall, Samuel] Mrs. Judith Hull Of Boston... [Boston, 1695]
Evans583; WingW2287; Sabin104096.

-6682, 1910

H691 Z31g [Zani, Valerio] conte, d. 1696.
Il Genio Vagante Biblioteca curiosa Di cento, e più Relazioni Di Viaggi Stranieri de' nostri tempi Raccolta dal Signor Conte Avrelio degli Anzi [pseud.] Ed estratta da diverse Lettere private, Informazioni particolari, e Libri di varij Scrittori Italiani, Francesi Spagnuoli, Alemani, Latini, ed altri Autori del corrente Secolo. Parte Prima [-Parte Qvarta]. ...
In Parma, per Giuseppe dall'Oglio, & Ippolito Rosati MDCXCI [-MDCXCIII]. Cõ lic de' Sup. A spese di Lodovico Maria Rvinetti.

4 v.: v.1, 1 p.ℓ., iii-xxxxvi p., 1 ℓ., 508 p. front., 4 double plates, 3 fold. maps; v.2, 1 p.ℓ., iii-xxiii, [1], 186 (i.e. 486) p. fold. pl., 2 fold. maps, plan; v.3, 1 p.ℓ., iii-xii p., 1 ℓ., 504, 525-527 p. fold. pl., 2 fold. maps; v.4, 1 p.ℓ., iii-xxiii, [1], 581 p. 13.5cm. 12°

Imprint varies: v.2-4, by Ippolito e Francesco Maria Rosati, v.2, "A spese di Lodovico Maria Rvineti", v.3-4, "A spese di Giuseppe dall'Oglio"; dated, v.2, 1691, v.3, 1692, v.4, 1693.

Dedications dated: v.1 (p.x) 1690; v.3 (p. vii) 29 Sept. 1692; v.4 (p. iv) 10 May 1693.

In this copy there is a blank leaf at end of vols. 1, 2, 4, and following p. 486 in v.1.

Bound in contemporary vellum.

Palau(2)13565; Streit 1:715.

Contents of American interest: La Martinière, Pierre Martin de. Viaggi del Sig. della Martiniera ne' paesi settentrionale (v.1, p.1-29), an abridged transl. of Voyage des pais septentrionaux. Paris, 1671.—Negri, Francesco. Relazione della Lapponia (v.1, p.30-41).—Scheffer, Johannes. Storia della Lapponia, e dè suoi abitanti (v.1, p.42-48), an abridged transl. of Histoire de la Laponie. Paris, 1678, 1st pub. under title: Lapponia; id est regionis Lapponum. Frankfurt, 1673.—Martens, Friedrich. Viaggio di Spitzberga, o Gronlanda (v.1, p.49-57), an abridged version of Viaggio di Spizberga... Bologna, 1680, 1st pub. under title: Spitzbergische oder groenlandische Reise. Hamburg, 1675.—Notizie delle Terre Artiche (v.1, p.86-92).—Dell'Islanda (v.1, p.92-94), transl. from the French.—Della Gronelanda, o Groenlanda (p.94-102), transl. from the French.—Di alcune particolarità singolari, e poco cognite dell'Islanda estratte dal Giornale dè Letterati d'Inghilterra [i.e. Royal Society of London. Philosophical transactions] (v.1, p.102-106).—La Peyrère, Isaac de. Relazione della Groenlanda (v.1, p.106-115), an abridged transl. of Relation du Groenland. Paris, 1647. —Dell'Islanda (v.1, p.115-119).—Nuova division della terra, ... inviata da un signore celebre, e famoso per gli diversi viaggi al Sig. Abbate Della Sciambre... (v.1, p.387-400), first appeared in: Journal des Sçavans, 1684, under title: Nouvelle division de la terre, par les differentes especes ou races. —Exquemelin, Alexandre Olivier. Istoria de venturieri, che segnalati si sono nell'America... (v.2, p.395-416), an abridged transl. of Histoire des avanturiers... Paris, 1686.— Acuña, Cristóbal de. Relazione del Rio, ò fiume delle Amazoni nell'America Meridionale... (v.2, p.417-422), an abridged transl. of Relation de la Riviere des Amazones traduite par feu Mʳ de Gomberville. Paris, 1682, 1st pub. under title: Nuevo descubrimiento del gran Rio de las Amazonas. Madrid, 1641.—Hennepin, Louis. Descrizione della Luigiana (v.2, p.423-455), an abridged version of Descrizione della Luigiana. Bologna, 1686, 1st pub. under title: Description de la Louisiane. Paris, 1683.—Bergamori, Giuseppe Gaetano. Estratto da due lettere del Brasile degli 8. e 10. Nouembre 1674 (v.4, p. 61-70). —Dutertre, Jean Baptiste. Istoria general dell'Isole Antiglie (v.4, p.71-80), an abridged transl. of Histoire generale des Antilles. Paris, 1667-1671, 1st pub. under title: Histoire general des isles de S. Christophe, de la Guadeloupe... Paris, 1654.—Acarete du Biscay. Relazione di alcuni viaggi nella Riviera de la Plata, e di là per terra al Perù (v.4, p.81-86), an abridged transl. of Relation des voyages du Sieur..., which first appeared in pt.4 of Melchisédech Thévenot's Relations de divers voyages. Paris, 1672.—Allè, Francesco. Copia di lettera del venerabil Padre Fra' Francesco degli Alè da Bologna Zoccolante riformato dell' osservanza al secolo Antonio di Girolamo Alè, scritta l'anno 1634 [i.e. 1534] dal Messico cavata dall'originale (v.4, p.87-93).—Palafox y Mendoza, Juan de. L'Indiano o vero il ritratto al naturale (v.4, p.95-98), an abridged transl. of Virtudes del Indio, 1st pub. ca. 1650.— Crestien, ----. Estratto d'una lettera di M. Crestien scritta dall'Isola Martinica... 23. Maggio 1671. Colla relazione di alcune sirene ritrovatesi ni mari orientali (v.4, p.99-112). —Núñez de la Peña, Juan. Notizia delle antichità, e conquista dell'Isole della Gran Canaria (v.4, p.265-274), an abridged transl. of Conquista, y antigüedades de las islas de la Gran Canaria. Madrid, 1676.—Osservazioni curiose sopra il Lago del Messico (v.4, p.275-276), 1st appeared in: Journal des sçavans, 1676, under title: Remarques & observations curieuses touchant le Lac de Mexique.—Savary, Jacques. Il perfetto negoziante (v.4, p.351-354), an abridged transl. of Le Parfait negociant. Paris, 1675.—Pyrard, François. Viaggio di Francesco Pirard della Valle all'Indie Orientali, Maldive, Molucche, e al Brasile (v.4, p. 513-519), an abridged transl. of Voyage de François Pyrard de Laval. Paris, 1679, 1st pub. under title: Discours du voyage... Paris, 1611.

69-462

1692

B682 A Don Juan Luis Lopez hizo merced su Mag.
-L864p de Alcalde del Crimen de la Real Audien-
cia de los Reyes, ...
[Madrid, 1692]
27 p. 28cm. fol. (Issued as a part of Al
Doctor Don Jvan Lvis Lopez, despues de
treze años de estudios mayores en la Vniver-
sidad de Zaragoza [Madrid, 1692]).
Title from beginning of text.
A Relacion de servicios; performed in
Lima and Huancavelica, Peru.
List of Lopez' works, p. 19-21.
Ms. annotations, perhaps in Lopez' hand.
Bound as no. 17 in a vol. with binder's title:
Luis Lopez Obras.
14023, 1925

B682 Al Doctor Don Jvan Lvis Lopez, despues de treze
-L864p años de estudios mayores en la Vniversidad de
Zaragoza ...
[Madrid, 1692]
12, 27 p. 28cm. fol.
Title from beginning of text.
A Relacion de servicios; performed in
Saragossa, Spain.
With, as issued, A Don Juan Luis Lopez hizo
merced su Mag. [Madrid, 1692] with separate
paging and signatures.
Bound as no. 16 in a vol. with binder's title:
Luis Lopez Obras.
14022, 1925 rev

D692 Ampel en Breed Verhaal Van de jongst-gewesene
A616b Aardbevinge Tot Port-Royal in Jamaica, Op den
7/17 Juny 1692. In twee brieven van den Predikant der zelver Stad geschreven, van 't boort
het Schip de Granada, in de haven van Port-
Royal leggende. Waar van d'eene gedateert
is den 22. en d'ander den 28 Juny, oude Stijl.
...
Te Rotterdam, By Barent Bos, Boekverkooper.
1692.
8 p. 20.5cm. 4º
Cut on t.-p.
Transl. from A full account of the late dreadful earthquake at Port Royal in Jamaica, 1st pub.
London, 1692.
The "predikant der zelver Stad" was probably
a Dr. Heath (cf. Cundall(Jam.)251).

JCB(2)2:1433; Sabin64183; Knuttel13752;
Muller(1872)812.
05939, 1872

BA692 Andrés de San Agustín.
S194d Dios Prodigioso En El Jvdio Mas Obstinado,
En El Penitenciado Mas Penitente, Y En El
Mas Ciego En Errores, Despues Clarissimo
En Virtudes El Venerable Hermano Fray
Antonio De San Pedro Religioso Lego Del
Orden Esclarecido de Mercedarios descalços
Redencion de Cautivos. Cvya Admirable Vida,
Y Maravillosa Reduccion del Judaismo a nuestra
Santa Fè Escrive El P. Fr. Andres De S. Avgvs-
tin Cronista General de dicho Orden. Segunda
Vez La Saca A Lvz Fr. Luis de la Presentacion
Agente, y Procurador del Siervo de Dios ...
Con licencia de los Superiores, En Lima en
la Imprenta de Joseph de Contreras, y Alvarado.
Año de 1692.
14 p.ℓ., 198 (i.e. 200), 199-668, 667-698 p.
20.5cm. 4º
First pub. Seville, 1688.
License dated (9th p.ℓ.^{v}) 18 March 1692.
Preliminary matter includes poetry.
Imperfect: p. 565-572 wanting.
JCB(2)2:1431; Palau(2)289421; Medina(Lima)
646; Sabin75995.
03681, before 1866

BA692 Barrera Varaona, Joseph de la, fl. 1692-1695.
B272s Sagrado Escvdo De Armas De La Nobleza
De Christo, Padron de Nobles, Divisa De
Caballeros Sermon Panegyrico En glorias de
la Invencion De La Crvz, Titular Fiesta de la
Nobilissima Archi-Cofradia de Caballeros de
la Santa Vera-Crvz de esta Ciudad Mexicana,
... lo ofrece en humilde obsequio Sv Avthor
El Bachiller D. Joseph De La Barrera Varaona,
Presbytero de este Arçobispado, Mayordomo
Diputado ad honorem de dicha Archi-Cofradia
de la Santa Vera-Cruz.
Con licencia, en Mexico, por la Uiuda de
Francisco Rodrigvez Lupercio, en la Puente
de Palacio. Año de 1692.
4 p.ℓ., 8 numb. ℓ. 19.5cm. 4º
License dated (4th p.ℓ.^{v}) 27 May 1692.
Imperfect: 2d p.ℓ. mutilated; available in
facsimile.
Palau(2)24700; Medina(Mexico)1514.
1051, 1905

J692
B398h
[Becmann, Johann Christoph] 1641-1717.
Historia Orbis Terrarum, Geographica Et Civilis, De Variis Negotiis Nostri potiss. & Superioris Seculi, Aliisve rebus selectioribus. Editio IV. Correctior.
Francofurti Ad Oderam, Impensis Jeremiæ Schrey, & Henr. Joh. Meyeri Hæred. Anno M DC XCII.
2 pts. in 1 v.: 8 p.ℓ., 386, 389-434 p., 1 ℓ., 435-775, [62] p. 20cm. 4º
Title in red and black.
Added t.-p., engraved.
Cut (printer's device) on t.-p., incl. motto: Utilitas Junxit. Labor Ac Industria Servat.
Signed (4th p.ℓ.ᵛ): J. C. Becmanus, D.
First pub. Frankfurt au der Oder, 1673.
Bound in contemporary calf.
Cf. Sabin4255.

69-124

D692
B792g
Boyle, Hon. Robert, 1627-1691.
General Heads For the Natural History Of A Country, Great or Small; Drawn out for the Use of Travellers And Navigators. Imparted by the late Honourable Robert Boyle, Esq; Fellow of the Royal Society. Ordered to be published in his Life-time, at the Request of some Curious Persons. To which is added, other Directions for Navigators, &c. with particular Observations of the most noted Countries in the World: By another Hand.
London, Printed for John Taylor at the Ship in S. Paul's Church-yard, and S. Holford, at the Crown in the Pall Mall. 1692.
2 p.ℓ., 138, [2] p. 14cm. 12º
Based on his three papers pub. under the same title in Philosophical Transactions of the Royal Society, London, 1666, enl. probably by Denis Papin.
Advertisement for Papin's devices, p. [1] at end.
Bookseller's advertisement, p. [2] at end.
Bound in contemporary calf, rebacked.
WingB3980; Sabin7139; Fulton(Boyle)195.

32656, 1960

DA692
C146p
[Calderwood, David] 1575-1650.
The Pastor And The Prelate, Or Reformation And Conformity Shortly Compared ... Shewing Whether of the Two is to be followed by the true Christian and Countryman. ...
Edinburgh. Printed for Alexander Henderson, and are to be Sold at his Shop in the upper end of the Locken-Booths. 1692.
47 p. 19cm. 4º
First pub. Leyden, 1628.
WingC278; McAlpin4:439.

6445, 1910

BA692
C355f
Castro, Juan de.
Fabrica De Lvz Sacada Con fundamentos de Sabiduria, hecha à el dia del instante, en que se concibio sin mancha Maria Santissima Señora Nuestra. Manifestada en la Sacra, Noble, Docta, y Real Vniversidad de Mexico el quinto dia del Solemne Octavario, que los Señores Rector, D.D. y Sagradas Religiones hazen a la limpieza del instante Purissimo de Maria, dia que le cupo à la Sagrada, Real, y Militar Religion de Nuestra Señora de la Merced Redempcion de Cautivos à 13 de Diziembre de 1691. Dixola El P. Predicador Fr. Ioan De Castro, hijo de tan Sagrada Familia, y Predicador Conventual en el Convento grande de Mexico. ...
Con Licencia en Mexico, por los Herederos de la Viuda de Bernardo Calderon. Año de 1692.
8 p.ℓ., 11 numb. ℓ. 20.5cm. 4º
License dated (7th p.ℓ.ᵛ) 19 Jan. 1692.
Palau(2)48763; Medina(Mexico)1515.

1050, 1905

J692
C393c
Cellarius, Christoph, 1638-1707.
Christophori Cellarii Smalcaldiensis Geographia Antiqva iuxta & Nova, Recognita & ad veterum nouorumque scriptorum fidem historicorum maxime, idemtidem castigata, & plurimis locis aucta ac immutata.
Ienae Sumtu Io. Bielckii, Bibliop. Literis Wertherianis, M DC XCII.
2 pts. in 1 v.: 12 p.ℓ., 414,[62] p., 1 ℓ.; 3 p.ℓ., 264, [64] p. 14cm. 12º
Title in red and black.
Added t.-p., engr.: Christophori Cellari Nvclevs Geographiæ Antiqvæ Et Novæ. ...
Special t.-p., pt. [1]: ... Geographia Nova, Siue Hodiernam Terrarum Orbis faciem clarissime illustrans, Ad nostrorum temporum Historias accomodata. Ienae ... MDCXCII.
Special t.-p., pt. [2]: ... Geographia Antiqva Ad veterum Historiarum, siue a principio rerum ad Constantini Magni tempora deductarum, faciliorem explicationem adparata, & denuo auctius edita. Præmissa est in omnium temporum Geographiam brevis Introductio. Ienae ... M DC XCI.
Parts [1] and [2] have separate paging and signatures.
First pub. under title: ... Nucleus geographiae antiquae et novae. Jena, 1676.
Errata: 1 ℓ. at end of pt[1]; pt[2], 3d p.ℓ.
In this copy there is a blank leaf at the end of pt[1].

69-256

[253]

DA692 C498n
Chauncy, Isaac, 1632-1712.
　Neonomianism Unmask'd: Or, The Ancient Gospel Pleaded, Against the Other, Called A New ∠ Law Or Gospel. In A Theological Debate, occasioned by a Book lately Wrote by Mr. Dan. Williams, Entituled, Gospel-Truth Stated and Vindicated: Unwarily Commended and Subscribed by some Divines. Applauded and Defended by the late Athenian Clubb. ... By Isaac Chauncy, M.A.
　London, Printed for J. Harris at the Harrow in the Poultry, 1692.
　4 p.l., 40 p. 20cm. 4°
　A reply to: Williams, Daniel. Gospel-truth stated and vindicated. London, 1692, and to a notice in John Dunton's Athenian Gazette.
　Wing C3754; Sabin 12333; McAlpin 4:440.
4835, 1908

B660 -P171p
Colón de Portugal, Pedro Manuel, duque de Veragua, 1651-1710.
　Señor. Don Pedro Manuel Colòn de Portugal, Almirante, y Adelantado Mayor de las Indias, Duque de Veragua, Marques de Jamayca, Conde de Gelves, Capitan General de las Galeras de España, dize:Que bien notorio es à V. Mag. y à su Real Consejo de las Indias ...
　[Madrid, 1692?]
　4 numb. l. 32.5cm. fol.
　Title from caption and beginning of text.
　Petition calling for payment of the annuity granted by the Spanish crown to the descendents of Columbus.
　Bound as the 3d of 7 items in a vol. with binder's title: Pleytos de Mariano Colón.
　Cf. Bibliografía Colombina p. 190.
06522-3, before 1874

DC C737l 1692 Aug.
The Compleat Library: Or, News for the Ingenious. Containing an Historical Account of the Choicest Books newly Printed in England, and in the Forreign Journals. As Also, The State of Learning in the World. To be Published Monthly. August, 1692. By a London Divine, &c.
　London, Printed for John Dunton at the Raven in the Poultrey. Of whom is to be had the Compleat Library for May, June, and July being the three first that were Published. [1692]
　1 p.l., 213-282 p. 21.5cm. 4°
　Cut on t.-p., incl. mottos "Sic nos non nobis mellificamus apes" etc.
　Edited by Richard Wooley.
　Booksellers' advertisement, at end.
　Crane & Kaye 116.
7554, 1910

DC C373l 1692 Dec.
The Compleat Library: Vol. II. Containing several Original Pieces, with an Historical Account of the Choicest Books newly Printed in England and in the Forreign Journals. As Also, The State of Learning in the World. To be Published Monthly. December, 1692. By a London Divine, &c.
　London, Printed for John Dunton at the Raven in the Poultrey. Of whom is to be had the First Volume of the Compleat Library. [1692]
　72 p. 21.5cm. 4°
　Cut on t.-p., incl. mottos "Sic nos non nobis mellificamus apes" etc.
　Edited by Richard Wolley.
　Booksellers' advertisement, at end.
　Crane & Kaye 116.
7555, 1910

FB D397 1692 1
Denmark--Treaties, etc., 1670-1699
　(Christian V)　　30 June 1691
　Conventie Tusschen den Koningh van Denemarcken ter eenre; ende den Koningh van Groot Brittannien, ende vande Hoogh Mogende Heeren Staten Generael der Vereenighde Nederlanden, ter andere zyde: Over de Vaert en Commercie van de Deensche Schepen en Onderdanen op Vranckrijck.
　In 's Graven-Hage, By Jacobus Scheltus, Ordinaris Drucker van de Hoog Mogende Heeren Staten Generael der Vereenighde Nederlanden. Anno 1692. Met Privilegie.
　1 p.l., [14] p. 19cm. (21cm. in folder) 4°
　Cut (coat of arms within border) on t.-p.
　Dated (p. [3]) 30 June 1691.
　Knuttel 13752b.
12477, 1920

DA692 F79lv
[Fox, George] 1624-1691.
　A Vision Concerning The Mischievous Seperation[sic] Among Friends In Old England.
　Printed and Sold by Will. Bradford at Philadelphia, 1692.
　7p. 17.5cm. 4°
　Signed (p. 5): G. F. This has also been attributed to George Keith.
　"A General Epistle Against Seperation [sic]" (p. 5-7) concludes: Bednell-Green, near London, the 25. 10. Mo. 1686.
　Authorship: cf. Bulletin of Friends' Historical Association 24: 87-8.
　Sabin 25357; Evans 610; Smith (Friends) 2:26; Hildeburn 53; Wing K230.
04589, Before 1915

EB
-W&A
328a
	France--Laws, statutes, etc., 1643-1715
	(Louis XIV). Jan 1692
	    Edit Du Roy, Faisant défenses à toutes personnes, autres que ceux qui auront de Nous la permission, de vendre tout Caffé en Féve & en Poudre, Thé, Chocolat, Sorbec, Cacao, & Vanille. Du mois de Janvier 1692. Registré en Parlement le 21. Avril audit an.
	    A Rennes, Chez François Vatar, Imprimeur & Libraire ordinaire du Roy & du Parlement, au Palais, à la Palme d'or. M. DC. XCII. Avec Privilege de S^a Majesté.
	    8 p. 22.5cm. (32cm. in case) 4°
	    Cut (royal arms) on t.-p.
	    First pub. Paris, 1692.
	16529, 1934
			Bound in contemporary calf.
			JCBAR50:61; Palau(2)100974; Medina (BHA)1886; Navarrete1:134-135.
			30534, 1949

bD692
F965f
	A full Account of the Late Dreadful Earthquake At Port Royal in Jamaica; Written in two Letters from the Minister of that Place. From a Board the Granada in Port Royal Harbour...
	    London, Printed for Jacob Tonson, and Sold by R. Baldwyn. 1692.
	    2 p. 30.5cm. fol.
	    Caption title; imprint at end.
	    Letters dated June 22 and 28, 1692.
	    "Licensed Sept. 9, 1692" (p. 1).
	    The "minister of that place" was probably a Dr. Heath (cf. Cundall).
	    WingF2267; Sabin64185n; cf. Cundall(Jam.)251.
	05940, after 1882
		DB
		-G7875
		1689
		1
			Gt. Brit.--Parliament, 1692-1693--House of Commons.
			    The Address Of The House of Commons...
			    London, Printed by Thomas Braddyll and Robert Everingham, and are to be Sold at the Seven Stars in Ave-Mary-Lane, MDCXCII.
			    15-18 p. 29cm. fol. (Issued as a part of Gt. Brit.--Parliament, 1692-1693--House of Commons. Votes..., London, 1692-1693.)
			    Addresses of thanks to the sovereigns; presented 14 Nov 1692; to the king for his prosecution of the war against France.
			    "...To The King." (p. 15-16); "...To The Queen." (p. 17-18).
			    Caption title for each address; imprint at end.
			    Bound in Votes of the House of Commons, v.1.
			10376-4A, 1914

B692
-G291n
[R]
	Gaztañeta y de Iturribálzaga, Antonio, 1656-1728.
	    Norte De La Navegacion Hallado Por El Qvadrante De Redvccion, Qve Ofrece... El Capitan D. Antonio De Gaztañeta, Ytvrrivalzaga, Piloto mayor de la Real Armada del Mar Occeano.
	    Con Privilegio. En Sevilla, por Jvan Francisco De Blas, Impressor mayor de dicha Ciudad. Año de 1692.
	    15 p. ℓ., 185 numb. ℓ. [2] p. incl. illus. (diagrs.), chart, tables. fold. chart, diagr. 27cm. fol.
	    Title in red and black.
	    Added t.-p., engr.; signed: Mathias Arteaga. f. Hisp.
	    Based on: Blondel Saint-Aubin, Guillaume. Le veritable art de naviger par le quartier de reduction, 1st pub. 1671.
	    "Tassa" dated (9th p. ℓ.^{v}) 13 Nov. 1692.
	    Errata, 9th p. ℓ.^{v}
	    Imperfect: half-title wanting; available in facsimile.
		DB
		-G7875
		1689
		1
			Gt. Brit.--Parliament, 1692-1693--House of Commons.
			    Votes Of The House of Commons In The Parliament Began at Westminster The 4th day of November, in the Fourth Year of the Reign of King William and Queen Mary, Anno Domini, 1692.
			    London, Printed by Thomas Braddyll and Robert Everingham, and are to be Sold at the Seven Stars in Ave-Mary-Lane. MDC XCII [-1692/3].
			    254, 251-278, 281-306 p. 29cm. fol.
			    Issued in pts. numbered 1-102 and dated 4 Nov 1692 - 13 Mar 1692[/3], each of which has caption title and imprint at end.
			    Erratum, p. 112.
			    Imperfect? Parliament sat until 14 Mar 1692/3. The last no. present in this collection is for 13 Mar. 1692/3.
			    Bound in Votes of the House of Commons, v.1.
			10376-4, 1914

		DB
		-G7875
		1689
		1
			Gt. Brit.--Sovereigns, etc., 1689-1694 (William and Mary)
			    His Majesties Most Gracious Speech To both Houses of Parliament, On Friday the Fourth of November, 1692.
			    London, Printed by Charles Bill and the Executrix of Thomas Newcomb, deceas'd; Printers to

the King and Queens most Excellent Majesties. M DC XCII.
4 p. 29cm. fol.
Cut (royal arms) on t.-p. (Steele 118).
Calls for supplies necessary for the war against France.
Bound in Votes of the House of Commons, v.1, before Votes for 4 Nov 1692.
Wing W2390.

10377-5, 1914

B692 G934a Guerra, Juan, fl. 1690.
Arte De La Lengva Mexicana Segun la acostumbran hablar los Indios en todo el Obispado de Guadalaxara, parte del de Guadiana, y del de Mechoacan. Dispuesto, Por orden, y mandato de N. M. R. P. Fr. Ioseph De Alcaras, Predicador, Padre de la Santa Provincia de Zacatecas, y Ministro Provincial, de esta Santa Provincia de Santiago de Xalisco, y por el Reverendo, y Venerable Difinitorio de ella en Capitulo Intermedio. Dedicado A la Santa Provincia de Santiago de Xalisco. Por el R.P. Fr. Joan Gverra, Predicador, y Difinidor actual de dicha Provincia.
Con licencia, en Mexico, por la Viuda de Francisco Rodriguez Lupercio, en la puente de Palacio, año de 1692.
8 p.ℓ., 62 numb. ℓ., [2] p. 14cm. (15cm. in case) 8°
License dated (6th p.ℓ.) 17 Oct. 1692.
Preliminary matter includes poetry.
"Instrvccion Breve, para administrar los Sacramentos ..." (numb. ℓ. 49ᵛ-62ᵛ).
Imperfect: p.ℓ. 1-8, numb. ℓ. 1-14 wanting; available in facsim. There may have been another printed ℓ. at end; wanting in all recorded copies.
Sabin 29118; Medina (Mexico) 1518; Palau(2) 109789; Ugarte 187; Pilling 1611.

06430, 1884

D. Math C.31 Heads of Agreement Assented to by the United Ministers, formerly called, Presbyterian and Congregational.
[Boston, B. Green and J. Allen for Samuel Phillips, 1692]
12 p. 13cm. 12° (Issued as a part of Cotton Mather, Blessed Unions, Boston, 1692).
First pub. London, 1691.
Drawn up mainly by John Howe, Matthew Mead, and Increase Mather.
Holmes(C) 31n.

04337A, 1872

BA692 J91c Juana Inés de la Cruz, sister, 1651-1695.
Carta Athenagorica De La Madre Ivana Ynes De La Crvz Religiosa Professa De Velo, y Choro en el muy Religioso Conuento de S. Geronimo de la Ciudad de Mexico cabeça de la Nueua Espana. Que Imprime, Y Dedica A La Misma Sor Phylotea De La Crvz [pseud.] Su estudiosa aficionada en el Conuento de la Santissima Trinidad de la Puebla de los Angeles.
Con Licencia. En Mallorca. Por Miguel Capò Imp. Año 1692.
[46] p. 20.5cm. 4°
First pub. Puebla de los Angeles, 1690.
"... haze juizio de vn Sermon del Mandato, que predicó el Reuerendissimo P. Antonio de Vieyra ..." (p. [7]: i.e. Vieira's "Sermam Do Mandato Na Capella Real. Anno 1650" pub. in his Sermoens ... 7. parte, Lisboa, 1692, p. 333-374).
"Phylotea de la Cruz" is a pseudonym of Manuel Fernández de Santa Cruz y Sahagún.
Palau(2) 65267; Backer(8) 661.

71-255

DA692 K28a [Keith, George] 1639?-1716.
An Account of the Great Divisions, Amongst the Quakers, In Pensilvania, &c. As appears by their own Book, here following, Printed 1692. and lately came from thence, Intituled, viz. The Plea of the Innocent, against the False Judgment of the Guilty. Being a Vindication of George Keith, and his Friends...
London, Printed for, and are to be Sold, by John Gwillim, in Bishopsgate street, and Rich. Baldwin. in Warwick-lane, 1692.
15, 18-26 p. 19cm. 4°
First pub. under title: The plea of the innocent against the false judgment of the guilty [Philadelphia, 1692.]
Signed (p. 26): George Keith, Thomas Budd.
JCB(2)2:1434; Sabin 37178; Wing K136; Church 724; Smith(Friends) 2:25.

03682, before 1866

DA692 K28c [Keith, George] 1639?-1716.
The Christian Faith Of the People of God, called in Scorn, Quakers In Rhode-Island ... Vindicated From the Calumnies of Christian Lodowick, that formerly was of that Profession, but is lately fallen there-from. As also from the base Forgeries, and wicked Slanders of Cotton Mather ... To which is added, some Testimonies of our Antient Friends to the true Christ of God ...
Printed and Sold by William Bradford at Philadelphia in Pennsylvania, in the Year 1692.
16 p. 18cm. 4°

A reply to Christian Ludwig's <u>A Letter from the most ingenious Mr. Lodowick</u> [Boston? 1692] and to Cotton Mather's <u>Little flocks guarded against grievous wolves</u>, Boston, 1691.

"Here followeth some Testimonies Collected out of the Writings of our Antient Friends..." (p. 9-16) signed: Faithfully Collected...by Will. Bradford.

Evans 600; Wing K151; Sabin 37185; Hildeburn 42.

01990, 1851

DA692
K28s

[Keith, George] 1639?-1716.
Some Of The Fundamental Truths Of Christianity. Briefly hinted at, by way of Question and Answer. With a Postscript by the Author G.K. The 3d Edition.
[Philadelphia, William Bradford, 1692]
15, [1] p. 19cm. 4°
Caption title.
Abridgement of <u>Fundamental Truths of Christianity</u> (1st pub. London, 1688) with postscript added.
"Books lately Printed, and to be Sold by William Bradford in Philadelphia. 1692." last p.
Evans 604; Wing K213; Sabin 37217; Hildeburn 48.

4063, 1908

DA692
K28sr

[Keith, George] 1639?-1715.
Some Reasons and Causes Of The Late Seperation [sic] That hath come to pass at Philadelphia betwixt us, called by some the Seperate [sic] Meeting, ... With An Apology for the present Publication of these Things. ...
[Philadelphia, William Bradford, 1692]
36 p. 19.5cm. 4°
"An Apology for the present Publication of these Things" p. 2-8.
"An Account of our sincere Faith" p. 29-36.
Also issued with t.-p. reading (in place of "With an Apology for the present Publication of these Things"): With An Account of our Sincere Christian Faith.
In this copy one of the names listed on p. 19 (col. 3, line 6, "Simercy Adams") has been obliterated in a contemporary hand.
Wing K215; Evans 606; cf. Sabin 37219; cf. Hildeburn 49; cf. Smith (Friends) 2:25-26.

4813, 1908

DA692
K28t

Keith, George, 1639?-1716.
Truth and Innocency Defended Against Calumny and Defamation, In a late Report spread abroad concerning the Revolution Of Humane Souls, With a further Clearing of the Truth, by a plain Explication of my Sence, &c. By George Keith.
[Philadelphia, William Bradford, 1692]
20 p. 19cm. 4°
Caption title.
Evans 602; Wing K224; Sabin 37225; Hildeburn 52; Smith (Friends) 2:25; Church 725.

4061, 1908

E692
L462n
[R]

[Le Clercq, Chrétien] fl. 1641-1695.
Nouvelle Relation De La Gaspesie, Qui Contient Les Mœurs & la Religion des Sauvages Gaspesiens Porte-Croix, adorateurs du Soleil, & d'autres Peuples de l'Amerique Septentrionale, dit le Canada.
Imprimé à Paris, & se vend A Lyon, Chez Thomas Amaulry, ruë Merciere, au Mercure Galant. M. DC. XCII.
14 p. ℓ., 572, [4] p. 16cm. (17cm. in case) 12°
Dedication signed (13th p. ℓ.ᵛ) Chrestien Le Clercq.
Cut on t.-p.
Colophon (p. 572): De L'Imprimerie de Laurent Rondet.
"Achevé d'imprimer pour la premiere fois, le vingtiéme Avril 1691." (14th p. ℓ.ᵛ)
First pub. Paris, 1691. These are the same sheets with new t.-p., but "Table Des Chapitres" ([4] p. at end) is found in only some copies of the 1691 ed.
Examples of Micmac language: p. 158-164.
Cf. Paltsits, V.H., "Bibliographical description..." in Champlain Society edition, Toronto, 1910.
JCBAR 21:10; TPL 110n.

12913, 1920

E692
L651m

Lettre D'Un Marchand A Un De Ses Amis, Sur L'Epouvantable Tremblement de Terre, qui est arrivé au Port-Royal de la Jamaïque, Isle d'Angleterre, le 17. Juin 1692.
[Paris? 1692?]
4 p. 23cm. 4°
Caption title.

4124, 1908

B692
L732e

Lima y Escalada, Ambrosio de.
Espicilegio De la calidad, y vtilidades del trigo que comunmente llaman Blanquillo Con Repuesta á las razones, que los Protho-Medicos desta Corte alegaron contra èl. ... Escriviola D. Ambrosio De Lima, Y Escalada, Professor de Medicina.

[257]

Con licencia de los Superiores, en Mexico por los Herederos de la Viuda de Bernardo Calderon. Año de 1692.
4 p. l., 22 numb. l. 19.5cm. 4º
Approbation dated (4th p. l.ʳ) 26 Jan. 1692.
Palau(2)138398; Medina(Mexico)1523.

06620, 1900

F692
L978j
Luyts, Jan, 1655-1721.
Joannis Luyts, Philosophiæ Professoris, Introductio Ad Geographiam Novam Et Veterem; In Qua Necessaria hujus Scientiæ Prolegomena, intermixto usu Globi Terrestris, nec non Oceani & Regionum constitutio perspicuo ordine pertractantur. Adjiciuntur Suis locis Oceani, Terræ, & cujusque Regionis Tabulæ, item Chartæ LXV Sansonis, inter quas quædam hac forma antè ineditæ.
Trajecti ad Rhenum, Ex Officina Francisci Halma, Acad. Typogr. M. DC. XCII.
15 p. l., 764, [24] p. illus., 66 fold. maps. 4º
Title in red and black.
Cut (printer's device, incl. motto: Vivitur Ingenio) on t.-p.
Added t.-p., engraved: G. Hoet delin., J. Mulder fecit.
Dedication dated (7th p. l.) 13 Nov. 1692.
Pages 77-82 are cancels.
Preliminary matter includes commendatory poetry by Gerard de Vries, Lucas van de Poll, and A. Boschman.
Errata at end.
Sabin42743; Phillips(Atlases)511; Tiele703.

11637, 1918

BA692
-M385j
Martínez de Ripalda, Juan, 1646-1727.
Señor. Jvan Martinez de Ripalda, de la Compañia de Jesvs, Procurador General por las Provincias del Nuevo Reyno, y Quito: Dize, que aviendo presentado en vuestro Consejo de las Indias vn escrito con la nomina de los sugetos que en virtud de Reales Cedulas estàn concedidos à dichas dos Provincias, y sus Missiones, ...
[Madrid? ca. 1692]
6 numb. l. 30cm. fol.
Title from caption and beginning of text.
Cites document (numb. l. 4ʳ) dated 8 Febr. 1691.
Appeals order expelling non-Spanish Jesuits from the Indies.
Palau(2)155663.

14292, 1925 rev

D. Math
C.23
Mather, Cotton, 1663-1728.
Balsamum Vulnerarium ex Scriptura. The Cause and Cure Of a Wounded Spirit: in a Discourse Which Layes Open the Manifold and Amazing Wounds of a Troubled Conscience, and Pours the Balsame of Seasonable Councils and Comforts into those Terrible Wounds. Being Two Sermons, Preached at Boston, in the Month of December. 1691. By Cotton Mather. ...
Boston, Printed by Bartholomew Green, and John Allen, for Nicholas Buttolph, at the Corner of Gutteridges Coffee House. 1692.
2 p. l., 92 p. 13.5cm. 12º
Bound in contemporary calf.
Evans559; Holmes(C)23; WingM1082.

05948, before 1916

D. Math
C.31
Mather, Cotton, 1663-1728.
Blessed Unions. An Union With the Son of God by Faith, And an Union In the Church of God by Love, Importunately Pressed; in a Discourse Which makes Divers Offers for those Unions; Together with A Copy of those Articles, where-upon a most Happy Union, has been lately made between those two Eminent Parties in England, which have now Changed the Names of Presbyterians, and Congregationals, for that of United Brethren. By Cotton Mather. ...
Boston. Printed by B. Green, & J. Allen, for Samuel Phillips. 1692.
5 p. l., 86, 12 p. 13cm. 12º
Errata, p. 12 (2d count).
With, as issued, "Heads of Agreement Assented to by the United Ministers, formerly called, Presbyterian and Congregational" with separate paging and signature.
JCB(2)2:1435; Sabin46235; Evans621; Holmes(C)31; WingM1084.

04337, 1872

D. Math
C.235
Mather, Cotton, 1663-1728.
A Midnight Cry. An Essay For our Awakening out of that Sinful Sleep, To which we are at This Time too much disposed; And For our Discovering of what peculiar things there are in This Time, That are for our Awakening. In a Discourse given on a Day of Prayer, kept by the North-Church in Boston. 1692. By Cotton Mather. Now Published for the use of that Church, together with a Copy of Acknowledgments and Protestations made in pursuance of the Reformation, Whereto we are to be Awakened. ...
Boston, Printed by John Allen, for Samuel Phillips, and are to be Sold at his Shop, at the West-end of the Town-House. 1692.
71, [1] p. 13.5cm. 12º

D. Math Mather, Cotton, 1663-1728.
C.266-A¹ Ornaments for the Daughters of Zion. Or The Character and Happiness Of A Vertuous Woman: in A Discourse Which Directs The Female Sex how to Express, The Fear Of God, in every Age and State of their Life; and Obtain both Temporal and Eternal Blessedness. Written By Cotton Mather ...
Cambridge: Printed by S.[amuel] G.[reen] & B.[artholomew] G.[reen] for Samuel Phillips at Boston. 1692.
104 p., 1 ℓ. 13.5cm. 12°
Errata, final ℓ.
Also issued with imprint incorrectly dated 1691.
Bound in contemporary calf.
JCBAR30:27; Sabin46442: Evans624; Holmes(C)266-A¹; WingM1135; CP185.
15481, 1929

B692 Mexico (City)--Universidad.
-M611i Informe Qve La Real Vniversidad, Y Clavstro Pleno De Ella de la Ciudad de Mexico de esta Nueva-España. Haze A El Excellentissimo Señor Virrey de ella en conformidad de orden de su Excelencia de 3. de Iulio de este año 1692. Sobre Los Inconvenientes De La Bebida De El Pulque.
[Mexico, 1692]
1 p. ℓ., 17 numb. ℓ. 28.5cm. fol.
With names of 28 faculty members at end.

B692 ———Another copy. 29.5cm.
-M611i JCB(2)2:1438; Palau(2)119394; Medina
cop.2 (Mexico)1522; Sabin48501.
06433, before 1923
06434, before 1874

D692 Morton, Richard, 1637-1698.
M891p ΠΥΡΕΤΟΛΟΓΙΑ: Seu Exercitationes De Morbis Universalibus Acutis. Authore Richardo Morton, Med. D Regii Collegii Medicor. Lond. Socio & Censore. ...
Londini: Impensis Samuelis Smith, ad Insignia Principis in Cœmeterio Divi Pauli. CIↃ DC. XCII.

"A Catalogue of some other Books ... All by This Authour" (last p.).
"Acknowledgments and Protestations" (p. 71) dated: 10th day of the 2d Month.
Sabin46414; Evans622; Holmes(C)235; WingM1127.
05949, 1878

40 p. ℓ., 430, [18] p. front. (port.), 2 fold. tables. 19cm. 8°
"Ad Lectorem" dated (17th p. ℓ.ᵛ) 4 March 1691.
Errata, last page.
Preliminary matter includes commendatory poetry by John Bateman and Thomas Sutton.
Chapters 5-9 deal extensively with the use of cinchona.
Bound in contemporary vellum.
69-681 Title transliterated: Pyretologia

EA692 [Naudé, Philippe] 1654-1729.
N291h Histoire Abregée De La Naissance & du Progrez du Kouakerisme, Avec Celle de ses Dogmes.
A Cologne, Chez Pierre Marteau [i.e. Amsterdam]. 1692.
12 p. ℓ., 174, [5] p. 14cm. 12°
Cut (armillary sphere) on t.-p.
Bound in contemporary calf.
JCB(2)2:1440; Sabin66927; Smith(Anti-Quak)26.
03732, 1867

Z Peeters, Johannes, 1624-1677?
P375 L'Atlas En Abregé, Ou Nouvelle Description
1692 Du Monde, Tirée des meilleurs Auteurs de ce siecle, par Jaques Peeters.
A Anvers, Chez l'Auteur aux quatre Parties du Monde. M. DC. XCII. Avec Privilege du Roi.
3 p. ℓ., 82, [2] p. pl., 41 fold. maps. 18cm. 8°
Added t.-p., engr.: Atlas Par Jaques Peeters a Anvers ...
Cut on t.-p.
Added t.-p. and maps 1-12, 14-22, 30 signed by the engraver, Jacobus Harrewijn.
Privilege dated (at end) 12 Dec. 1691.
Imperfect: added t.-p. wanting; available in facsim.
Contemporary ms. annotations.
Bound in contemporary vellum
Phillips(Atlases)513; Tiele 849n.
Contents (maps):
[1] [La Mappe Monde...]
[2] [L'Europe]
[3] Asiæ.
[4] Africæ.
[5] Americæ.
[6] Les Pays Bas ou sont Remarquées Les Aqvisitions De La France Iusques à la Treve.
[7] Comitatus Flandriæ.
[8] Comitatus Artesiæ.

[9] Comitatus Hanoniæ.
[10] Namurci.
[11] Lutzenburgi...
[12] Limburgi Ducatus et Comitatus Valckenburgi Nová Descriptio...
[13] Ducatus Brabantiæ...
[14] Marchionatus S.I. Et Dom. Mechelini...
[15] Comitatus Hollandiæ...
[16] Comitatus Zelandiæ...
[17] Ultraiectini Dominii.
[18] Comitatus Zutphaniæ.
[19] Ducatus Geldriæ Et Comitatus Zutphaniæ.
[20] Over-Yssel...
[21] Dominium Groeningæ...
[22] Comittus Frisiæ...
[23] Espagne.
[24] La France Et ses Aequisitions [sic] Jusqu'à la Treue de 1684.
[25] Empire D Allemagne.
[26] Isles Britaniques ou sont Les Royaumes D'Angleterre D Escosse et D Irlande.
[27] Les Royaumes De Suede Et Norwege.
[28] Dane Marq Et Sud - Gothlande.
[29] L'Italie.
[30] Ducatus Saboudiæ Principatus Pedemontii Comitatus Nicæensis.
[31] Le Grand Royaume De Hongrie ou Partie Septentrionale De La Turquie En Europe. Divisée Par Grands Gouvernements, Suivant Ricant Anglois.
[32] Estats De La Couronne De Pologne.
[33] Grece Ou Partie Meridionale De La Turquie En Europe Diuisée en Grands Gouvernements Selon Ricaut Anglois.
[34] Rvssie Blanche ou Moscovie.
[35] Turquie En Asie.
[36] Perse.
[37] Grande Tartarie.
[38] Mogol.
[39A] Presqu Isle De L'Inde Deca Le Golfe Du Gange.
[39B] Presqu Isle De L Inde Delà Le Golfe De Gange.
[40] La Chine.
[41] Les Isles Philippines Molucques et de La Sonde. [Inset:] Les Isles Du Iapon.

13301, 1922

DA692
P412j
[Penn, William] 1644-1718.
Just Measures, In An Epistle, Of Peace & Love To Such Professors of Truth as are under any Dissatisfaction about the present Order practis'd in the Church of Christ. By a Lover of the Truth and Them, G. P. ...
London: Printed for Tho. Northcott, in George yard in Lumbard-street, 1692.
1 p.l., 21 p. 16cm. 8º.
Smith(Friends)2:305-306; WingP1310.

12516, 1920

bBB
P4716
1692
1
Peru(Viceroyalty)--Laws, statutes, etc., 1689-1705 (Portocarrero) 27 April 1692
Don Melchor Portocarrero Lasso de la Vega, Conde de la Monclova, ... Por Aver Hallado En Este Reyno, quando entre à gouernarle, gran confusion en la cobranza de Tassas, y entero de la Mita de Potosi, ...
[Lima, 1692]
[17] p. 30.5cm. fol.
Title from caption and beginning of text.
Regulations for the mita of Potosi.
Dated at end in Ciudad de los Reyes, 27 April 1692.
Signed in ms: Monclova.
Medina(Lima)644.

28202, 1938

bBB
P4716
1692
2
Peru(Viceroyalty)--Laws, statutes, etc., 1689-1705 (Portocarrero). 19 July 1692
El Exc.mo Señor Conde De La Monclova Uirrey Destos Reynos &c. En Despacho de 27. de Abril deste Año, refiere la tribulacion, en que halló a los Indios de las diez, y seis Prouincias sujetas a la Mita de Potosi, por los nuevos ordenes, que el Excelentissimo Señor Virrey Duque de la Palata su Antecessor dio ...
[Lima, 1692]
[4] p. 28.5cm. fol.
Title from beginning of text.
Dated at end in Ciudad de los Reyes, 19 July 1692.
Palau(2)122285; Medina(Lima)641.

69-541

E692
P958d
Les Principes De La Geographie Methodiquement expliquez, Pour donner une Idée generale de toutes les parties de l'Univers, & pour faciliter l'intelligence des Tables & des Cartes Geographiques. Avec Un Abregé Chronologique, Pour servir d'Introduction à l'Etude de l'Histoire. Suivant la Copie imprimée à Paris.
A Amsterdam, Chez Abraham Wolfgang, prés de la Bourse. 1692.
4 p.l., 352 p. 13.5cm. 12º
Bound in contemporary vellum.

68-221

CA692 S111s
Sá, Antonio de, 1620-1678.
Sermão Do Glorioso Sam Ioseph Esposo Da May De Deos, Que Pregou O M.R.P. Antonio De Saa Da Companhia de Jesu. ...
Em Coimbra. Com todas as licenças necessarias. Na officina de Joam Antunes Anno de 1692.
20 p. 19.5cm. 4°
First pub. Coimbra, 1675.
Palau(2)283209; Borba de Moraes 2:223; Backer 7:356.

69-189

B69 G643v 40
Salazar, Antonio de, fl. 1673-1698.
Villancicos, Qve Se Cantaron En Los Maytines De El Glorioso Principe de la Iglesia el Señor San Pedro, En la Santa Iglesia Cathedral Metropolitana de Mexico. ... Compuestos en Metro Musico Por el Maestro Antonio de Salazar, que lo es actual de Capilla de dicha Santa Iglesia.
En Mexico, por los Herederos de la Viuda de Bernardo Calderon Año de 1692.
[8] p. 20cm. 4°
Imprint at end.
Woodcut title vignette (St. Peter enthroned; inscribed at base: San Pedro.)
Bound, in contemporary vellum, as no. 40 with 42 other items.
Medina(Mexico)1530.

28940, 1941

HA692 S182r
Salvatore, Michele del.
Relatione Compendiosa, E Semplice Della Miracolosa Imagine della Beatissima Vergine. Di Copacavana Del Perv', La cui copia anco di gratie risplendente si riuerisce nella Chiesa di San Carlo di Torino de' MM. RR. PP. Agostiniani Scalzi. Composta dal Reuerendo Padre Michele Del Salvatore Scalzo Agostiniano già Lettore di Sacra Teologia Scuolastica, e Sacri Canoni. ...
In Torino MDCLXXXXII Per la Vedoua Colonna, e Fratelli Boetti. Con licenza de' Superiori.
1 p.l., 3-43 p. front. 17.5cm. 4°
License dated (p. 43) 23 Jan. 1692.
JCB(2)2:1441; Sabin 75876.

6442, before 1874

B692 S687h [R]
Solís y Rivadeneyra, Antonio de, 1610-1686.
Histoire De la Conquête du Mexique, Ou de la Nouvelle Espagne. Par Fernand Cortez. Traduite de l'Espagnol de Don Antoine De Solis, par l'Auteur du Triumvirat.
A La Haye, Chez Adrian Moetjens, Marchand Libraire prés la Cour, à la Librairie Françoise. M.DC.XCII.
2 v.: 18 p.l., 412,[15] p. 9 fold. plates, 2 fold. maps; 6 p.l., 378, [15] p. 3 fold. plates. 12°
Cut (Rahir marque 44) on title-pages; incl. motto "Amat Libraria Curam".
Transl. by S. de Broë, seigneur de Citry et de la Guette from Historia de la conquista de Mexico, Madrid, 1684. French translation 1st pub. Paris, 1691.
"Catalogue Des Livres qui se trouvent chez Adrian Moetjens." (v.1, p.l. 17^v-18^v).
JCB(2)2:1442; Sabin 86476; Medina(BHA)1773n; Palau(2)318671; Muller(1872)984; Arocena IV 2.9.

01621, 1847

D692 -S797t
State Tracts: Being a Farther Collection Of Several Choice Treatises Relating to the Government. From the Year 1660. to 1689. Now Published in a Body, to shew the Necessity, and clear the Legality of the Late Revolution, and Our present Happy Settlement, under the Auspicious Reign of Their Majesties, King William and Queen Mary.
London: Printed, and are to be Sold by Richard Baldwin near the Oxford-Arms in Warwick-Lane: MDCXCII.
4 p.l., 499 p. 32cm. fol.
Numerous errors in paging.
Bound in contemporary calf, rebacked, with binder's title: State tracts Vol. IV.
With this is bound: State tracts: being a collection of several treatises ... London, 1689.
Wing S5331; McAlpin 4:458.

831^1, 1905

CA679 V665s 7
Vieira, Antonio, 1608-1697.
Sermoens Do P. Antonio Vieyra da Companhia de Jesu, Prègador de Sua Magestade, Septima Parte.
Lisboa, Na Officina de Miguel Deslandes, Impressor de Sua Magestade. A custa de Antonio Leyte Pereira, Mercador de Livros. M.DC.LXXXXII. Com todas as licenças necessarias, & Privilegio Real.
6 p.l., 196, 199-558 p. 21cm. 4°

[261]

Cut (Jesuit trigram, floriated) on t.-p.
Permission (5th p. ℓ.ᵛ) dated 17 Oct. 1692.
Contains 15 sermons preached in Lisbon 1644, 1645, 1649, 1650, 1662, etc., Rome ca. 1670, etc., Bahia, Brazil, 1638, São Luiz, Brazil, 1654, etc., and in Odivellas, Portugal, and Pará, Brazil.
According to Leite there is a variant which has the table of contents at the end, rather than in the prelims. as here.
In this copy 3d-4th p. ℓ. are bound between p. 556-557 (as printed).
Bound in contemporary calf.
Rodrigues 2509; Backer 8:659; Leite 9:196; Innocencio 1:290.

68-345

BA692　Villavicencio, Diego Jaime Ricardo.
V727ℓ　Luz, Methodo, De Confesar Idolatras, Y Destierro De Idolatrias, Debajo Del Tratado Sigviente. Tratado De Avisos, Y Puntos Importantes, De La Abominable Seta de la Idolatria; para examinar por ellos al penitente en el fuero interior de la conciencia, y exterior judicial. Sacados no de los Libros; sino de la experiencia en las aberiguaciones con los Rabbies de ella. Por El Lic. Diego Jaymes Ricardo Villavicencio, Originario del Pueblo de Quechula, de la Provincia de Tepeaca, deste Obispado de la Puebla de los Angeles; Cura Beneficiado por su Magestad, Vicario, y Iuez Ecclesiastico del Partido de Santa Cruz Tlatlaccotepetl deste dicho Obispado, y assimismo Iuez Comissario en dicho Partido en causas de Fé cōtra Idolatrias, y otras supersticiones del demonio. . . .
Con licencia en la Puebla de los Angeles en la Imprenta de Diego Fernandez de Leon. Año de 1692.
2 pts. in 1 v.: 16 p. ℓ., 36, 40-131, 133-136 p. incl. front., coat of arms; 51, [2] p. 20.5cm. 4°
Paging 40-131 begins on a verso.
Preliminary matter includes letters from the bishops of Chiapa (dated 6th p. ℓ.ᵛ 16 Nov. 1692), Puebla, and Oaxaca.
Includes text in the Aztec language, pt. 2,
Imperfect: p. ℓ. 5-6 wanting; available in facsimile.
Bound in contemporary vellum.
Palau(2)123345; Medina(Puebla)153; Sabin 99693; Ugarte 427; Pilling 4038; Streit 1:720; Viñaza 232.

06044, before 1923

DA692　[Winthrop, John] 1588-1649, supposed author.
W792s　A Short Story Of the Rise, Reign, and Ruin of
[R]　the Antinomians, Familists, and Libertines That Infected the Churches Of New-England: And how they were Confuted by The Assembly of Ministers there: As also of the Magistrates proceedings in Court against them. Together with God's strange Remarkable Judgements from Heaven upon some of the Chief Fomenters of these Opinions; And the Lamentable Death of Mrs. Hutchison. Very fit for these Times; here being the same Errors amongst us, and Acted by the same Spirit. Published at the Instant Request of Sundry, by one that was an Eye and Ear-witness of the carriage of Matters there. . . .
London, Printed for Tho. Parkhurst, at the Bible and three Crowns at the lower end of Cheapside, near Mercer's Chappel. 1692.
9 p. ℓ., 6, 9-64 (i.e. 68) p. 21cm. 4°
Includes a preface, 2d-9th p. ℓ., by Thomas Weld.
First pub. without the preface, London, 1644 under title: Antinomians and familists condemned. Also pub. London, 1644, under title: A short story of the rise, reign, and ruin of the Antinomians . . . with the preface.
JCB(2)2:1443; Wing W1270; Sabin 104849.

01924, 1851

BA692　Ximénez Pantoja, Thomas, fl. 1700.
-X7p　Protesta A Favor De Sv Magestad, Svcessores En Sv Real Corona, Patronato, y Delegacion Apostolica en la America. Sobre El Oficio De Comissario General De Indias en el Orden de San Francisco, su jurisdiccion, y preeminencias; Contra Las Qve Pretende La Dignidad De Ministro General de dicho Orden: Hazela Por La Obligacion Del Pvesto El Lic. Don Thomas Ximenez Pantoja, Cauallero del Orden de Santiago, Fiscal en el Real, y Supremo Consejo de las Indias.
[Madrid? 1692]
1 p. ℓ., 167 p. 27cm. fol.
Cut (engr.: arms of the Casa de Contratación) at head of title.
Concerns a jurisdictional dispute between the Franciscan minister general, Marcos Zarçosa, and the Comisario General de Indias of the order, Julián Chumillas, associated with the beatification of Sebastián de Aparicio.
Medina records 2 variants at BHA 6990 and 8391.
In this copy there is a pasted cancel slip in marginal note on p. 83.
Palau(1)7:236; Medina(BHA)8462; Streit 2:2361.

69-645

1693

D693
-A172o
An Account Of Several Passages and Letters between his Excellency Benjamin Fletcher, Captain General and Governour in Chief of the Province of New-York, Province of Pennsilvania, Country of New-Castle, &c. Commissionated by their Majesties under the great Seal of England, to be their Lieut. and Commander in chief of the Militia, and of all the Forces by Sea and Land within their Majesties Collony of Connecticut, and of all the Forts and places of Strength within the same. And The present Administrators of the Laws in the Collony of Connecticut, in the Month of October, 1693.
A true Copy, Examined and allowed to be Printed, by M. Clarkson, Secretary. Printed and Sold by William Bradford, Printer to their Majesties, King William and Queen Mary, at the Bible in New-York, 1693.
8 p. 29cm. fol.
Caption title; imprint at end.
JCB(2)2:1449; Evans 674; Wing F1299; Sabin 53435; Eames(NY)27.

0554, 1846

BA693
A679s
Arellano, Diego de.
Sermon En La Solemne Fiesta, que el Santo Tribunal de la Inquisicion de esta Nueva-España haze à su Inclito Patron S. Pedro Martyr De Verona su Inquisidor, en el Real Convento de Santo Domingo de Mexico. ... Predicado Por el Reverendo Padre Fr. Diego de Arellano, Lector de Sagrada Theologia. ...
Con Licencia En Mexico Por Doña Maria de Benavides Viuda de Juan de Ribera. Año de 1693.
6 p.ℓ., 8 numb. ℓ. 20.5cm. 4º
License dated (6th p.ℓ.ᵛ) 27 May 1693.
Palau(2)15844; Medina(Mexico)1535.

1052, 1905

BA693
-A977c
Ayeta, Francisco de.
Crisol De La Verdad, Manifestada Por El R. P. Fr. Francisco De Ayeta, Religioso De La Orden Seraphica De N.P. San Francisco, Comissario General del Santo Oficio, Ex-Custodio, y Visitador dos vezes de las con-versiones de la Nueva Mexico, Padre de la Provincia del Santo Evangelio de Mexico, Procurador General en esta Corte de las Provincias de las Indias, en virtud de sus poderes. En Defensa De Dicha Sv Provincia. Sobre El Despojo, Y Seqvestro De Las 31. Doctrinas, de que la removiò el Reverendo Obispo D. Juan de Palafox, siendo Visitador del Reyno. ...
[Madrid? 1693?]
2 p.ℓ., 341 numb. ℓ., 1 ℓ. illus. 28.5cm. fol.
Errata, last leaf.
Some copies contain 2 additional p.ℓ. (dated 18 and 28 July 1693) which order the suppression of offensive passages on numb. ℓ. 324-325 and 341. In this copy those leaves have been removed and cancel leaves numbered 324 and 341 have been substituted. Facsims. available of the additional p.ℓ. and cancelled leaves.
Palau(2)20802; Medina(BHA)6240; Andrade 2260; Streit2:2289.

04161, 1870

D693
B356j
Bayard, Nicholas, 1644-1707.
A Journal Of The Late Actions Of The French at Canada. With The Manner of their being Repuls'd, by His Excellency, Benjamin Fletcher, Their Majesties Governour of New-York. Impartially Related by Coll. Nicholas Reyard [sic], and Lieutenant Coll. Charles Lodowick, who attended His Excellency, during the whole Expedition. To which is added, I. An Account of the present State and Strength of Canada, given by Two Dutch Men, who have been a long Time Prisoners there, and now made their Escape. II. The Examination of a French Prisoner. III. His Excellency Benjamin Fletcher's Speech to the Indians. IV. An Address from the Corporation of Albany, to His Excellency, Returning Thanks for His Excellency's early Assistance for their Relief. Licensed, Sept. 11th. 1693. Edward Cooke.
London, Printed for Richard Baldwin, in Warwick-Lane, 1693.
2 p.ℓ., 22 p. 20cm. 4º.
First pub. under (caption) title: <u>A Narrative Of an Attempt made by the French of Canada Upon The Mohaques Country.</u>
[New York, 1693]; cf. Adelaide R. Hasse's notes to the reprint of the American edition (New York, 1903) p. vii.
In addition to the sections mentioned on the t.-p., there are: "A Journal of the Actions in the Woods, between the French and Indians", signed: Peter Schyler [sic], Major [and 4 others] (p. 4-10); "The Answer of the Five

Nations, ..." to Fletcher's address, both given Feb. 25, 1692 (p. 16-18); "Proposals made by four of the chief Sachims of the Five Nations, to his Excellency Benjamin Fletcher...", Feb. 26, 1692 (p. 19-20). The journal (from Feb. 12 to 27, 1692) is signed: Nicholas Beyard, Col., Charles Lodwick, Lieut. Col. The address of the Corporation of Albany to Fletcher is signed: Peter Schuyler, Mayor [and 5 others].
In this copy there is a blank ℓ. at end.
JCB(2)2:1446; Sabin4035; WingB1458; Church727; Vail(Front.)267; cf. Harrisse(NF)171; cf. TPL113.

01925, 1866

C619
A949n
Bluteau, Raphael, 1638-1734.
Oraçoens Gratvlatorias Na Feliz Vinda Da Mvito Alta, E Mvito Poderosa Rainha Da Gram Bretanha, Compostas, E Recitadas Na Igreja da Divina Providencia à Nobreza de Portugal Nas Tres Ultimas Tardes Do Mez de Janeiro de 1693. Pelo P. D. Raphael Blvteav, Clerigo Regular Theatino da Divina Providencia, Doutor na Sagrada Theologia, & Prègador da Rainha Mãy de Inglaterra ...
Lisboa, Na Officina de Miguel Deslandes, Impressor de Sua Magestade. Com todas as licenças necessarias. Anno de 1693
4 p.ℓ., 44 p. 19.5cm. 4⁰
Cut on t.-p.
License dated (4th p.ℓ.ᵛ) 26 June 1693.
Bound as the 13th in a volume of 58 pamphlets, 1619-1702.

9354, 1913

D693
-B677g
Bohun, Edmund, 1645-1699.
A Geographical Dictionary Representing the Present and Antient Names and States Of All The Countries, Kingdoms, Provinces, Remarkable Cities, Universities, Ports, Towns, Mountains, Seas, Streights, Fountains, and Rivers of the whole World; Their Distances, Longitudes, and Latitudes, With A short Historical Account of the same, and a general Index of the Antient and Latin Names. ... Begun by Edmund Bohun, Esquire. Continued, Corrected, and Enlarged with great Additions throughout, and particularly with whatever in the Geographical Part of the Voluminous Morery and Le Clerk occurs observable, By Mr. Bernard. Together with all the Market-Towns, Corporations, and Rivers, in England, wanting in both the former Editions.
London: Printed for Charles Brome, at the Gun at the West End of S. Pauls. MDCXCIII.
4 p.ℓ., 232, 231-438, 431-437, [20] p.

30.5cm. fol.
Cut (world map in hemispheres) on t.-p.
First pub. London, 1688.
"A Reflection upon Le Grand Dictionaire Historique, &c. ... Of Lewis Morery, D.D. Printed at Utrecht 1692. with the Supplement of J. Le Clerc, D.D. in Four Tomes in Folio, French; And An Account of this Edition of the following Book" (2d-4th p.ℓ.ʳ) signed: J. A. Bernard.
Booksellers' advertisements, 4th p.ℓ.ʳ and last page; dated (4th p.ℓ.ʳ) 30 Dec. 1692.
Bound in contemporary calf.
WingB3454; Sabin6145.

62-02, 1961

BA693
B928o
Buendía, José, 1644-1727.
Oracion Fvnebre. Qve En Honras Del Immortal Valor De Los Soldado [sic] Espanoles [sic] Difuntos celebradas de orden de su Magestad en la Santa Iglesia Metropolitana de Lima el dia 15. de Noviembre de 1692. Dixo El M.R.P. M. Ioseph De Buendia de la Compañia de Iesvs. ...
Con Licencia De Los Svperiores En Lima Por Ioseph De Contreras. Año de 1693.
30 p.ℓ., 11 (i.e. 12) numb. ℓ. 19.5cm. 4⁰
License dated (22d p.ℓ.ʳ) 5 Apr. 1693.
Palau(2)36677; Medina(Lima)648; Backer2:339; Sabin57421.

10743, 1915

+Z
≡N442
1693
Cartes Marines A L'Usage Des Armées Du Roy De La Grande Bretagne. Faites sur les Memoires les plus nouveaux des plus experts Ingenieurs & Pilotes, & enrichies des porfils [sic] des plus fameux Ports de Mer & villes Maritimes de l'Europe. ... Gravées & recüeillies par le Sr. Romain De Hooge Commissaire de Sa Majesté.
A Amsterdam. Chez Pierre Mortier Libraire sur le Vygen Dam. M.DC.LXXXXIII. Avec Privilege de Nos Seigneurs les Estats de Hollande & West-Frise.
2 p.ℓ., 9 maps. 65.5cm. 1⁰
Continuation of Le Neptune François.
Title in red and black.
Cut (engr. ship vignette) on t.-p.; signed: J V Vianen f
Added t.-p., engr.: "Atlas Maritime ... Romanus de Hooghe ... auct. et inv. 1693. A Amsterdam Chez Pierre Mortier." There is an earlier version of the engraved t.-p. incl. the designation "Tom 2" (i.e. t. 2 of Le Neptune François).
Also issued with Dutch t.-p: Zee Atlas ..., Amsterdam, 1694.

Maps are double-page size, except for [2], [5], [6] which are single-page size, and [9] which is folded to double-page size.

In this copy all maps, the engr. t.-p., and the engr. vignette on printed t.-p. are colored.

In this copy the engr. t.-p. is bound after the maps.

Bound with Le Neptune François ... , Paris [i.e. Amsterdam] 1693, as the 2d of 3 sections.

Contents:

[1] "Carte Nouvelle des Costes De Hollande, Zéelande, Flandre, Picardie, & Normandie, depuis la Brille jusques à Dieppe, auec une Partie des costes D'Angleterre ... Par le S.r Romain De Hooge Commissaire du Roy. A Amsterdam Chez Pierre Mortier ..."

[2] "Carte Maritime des Environs de Dieppe ... Par le S.r R. De Hooge ... Amsterdam chez P. Mortier. ..."

[3] "Carte Nouvelle des Costes De Normandie Et De Bretagne ... Par le S.r Romain De Hooge ... À Amsterdam Chez Pierre Mortier ... 1693."

[4] "Carte Nouvelle des Costes de Bretagne ... Par le S.r Romain De Hooge ... à Amsterdam Chez Pierre Mortier ..."

[5] "Carte Maritime depuis la Riviére de Bourdeaux jusques à S.t Sebastien ... Par le S.r R. De Hooge ... à Amsterdam Chez P. Mortier ..."

[6] "Carte Marine des Environs de l'Isle D'Oleron ... Par le S.r Romain De Hooge ... À Amsterdam Chez P. Mortier. ... 1693."

[7] "Carte Nouvelle des Costes D'Angleterre depuis la Riviére de la Tamise jusques á Portland ... Par le S.r Romain De Hooge ... A Amsterdam Chez Pierre Mortier ... 1693."

[8] "Carte Maritime De L'Angleterre depuis les Sorlingues jusques à Portland ... Par le S.r Romain De Hooge ... à Amsterdam Chez Pierre Mortier ..."

[9] "Carte Nouvelle De La Mer Mediterranée ... par le S.r Romain De Hooge. A Amsterdam chez Pierre Mortier Auec Privilége 1694."

+Z ≡N442 1703A 1
——— Another copy. 65cm.
Contents as indicated above except that maps [1], [2], [4] and [8] are dated 1693.
In this copy only the maps are colored.
Bound with Le Neptune François ... , Paris [i.e. Amsterdam] 1703.

+Z ≡N442 1703B
——— Another copy. 63.5cm.
Contents as indicated above except maps [4] and [9] wanting.

In this copy only the maps are colored; the engr. t.-p. is bound after the maps.

Bound with Le Neptune François ... , Paris [i.e. Amsterdam] 1703, as the 2d of 3 sections.

See Chapin, H.M., "The French Neptune and its various editions," American book collector, II (1932), 16-19.

Koeman M.Mor 5; cf. Phillips(Atlases) 2835, 517; Scheepvaart Mus. 51; Muller (1872)1957*; cf. Tiele 791.

33014B, 33015-A, 1960
33117A, after 1900

B693
C327m
Cartilla Mayor, en Lengua Castellana, Latina, y Mexicana. Nuevamente Corregida, y Enmendada, y Reformada en esta vltima Impression. ...

Con Licencia, Y Privilegio. En Mexico en la Imprenta de la Viuda de Bernardo Calderon en la calle de San Agust n[sic] Y con prohibicion, que ninguna otra persona sino la dicha Viuda, en toda la Nueva-España pueda imprimir Cartillas, ni Doctrinas pena de ducientos pesos, y los moldes perdidos. Año de 1693.

[16] p. 18.5cm. 4º

Cut (Franciscan arms) on t.-p.
Imprint at end.

According to Icazbalceta (Apuntes) 97 (repeated by Medina (Mexico)1274; Viñaza 215; cf. Palau (2)2:46473, 48060; cf. Sabin48323) with this was issued [Castillo, Baltasar] Cathecismo cenca yn tech ... , Mexico [1683? i.e. 1693?]

JCBAR 10:79; Pilling 631.

6373, 1910 rev

BA693
C352c
[Castillo, Baltasar]
Cathecismo Cenca Yn Tech Moneqvi Qvimatizqve Yn Christianos Tlaneltocanime Ynicmomaquix. tizque

Con Licencia En Mexico: por la Viuda de Bernardo Calderon en la calle de S. Augustin [1683? i.e. 1693?].

[8] p. 19.5cm. 4º

Imprint at end.

"Oquimo nahuatlatolcuepili Padre F. Balthazar del Castillo, temachtiani, yhuan Ministro nican Altepetl S. Luis Obispo Vexotlan mani metztli 16 de Iulio de 1683 años. M.S.S. C.S.R.E." (p. [8]).

According to Icazbalceta (Apuntes) 97 (repeated by Medina (Mexico)1274; Viñaza 215; cf. Palau(2)46473, 48060; cf. Sabin 48323) this was issued as a part of an edition of the Cartilla mayor en lengua castellana, latina, y mexicana. The Library's copy was acquired with the Cartilla mayor ... , Mexico, 1693; such a

copy is also described by Pilling 631, 677a (the Murphy copy).
JCBAR 10:79; Pilling 677a.
6372, 1910   rev

BA693
C363m
Catholic Church--Liturgy and ritual.
Motivos Piadosos Para adelantar la devocion tierna de los Dolores de la SS. Virgen, esmerandose en el cordial afecto, culto, y verdadero, obsequio à N. Señora esclarecida Patrona, y querida Ama Señora Santa Ana Madre de la dignissima Madre de Dios, y Abuela verdadera del mejor Niño, mas agraciado, y Santo, que conocieron, y conocerán los sigloss [sic] y veneraron todos estados. El Dvlcissimo, Amabilissimo, Suavissimo, Piadosissimo Señor, y nuestro Señor, y Redemptor por nuestra suma dicha Jesvs. Qve Ofrece Para Desempeño suyo la Congregacion de N. Señora de los Dolores de el Colegio de S. Pedro, y S. Pablo de la Compañia de esta Ciudad. A devocion de algunas piadosas personas, y cō especialidad afectas de coraçon à la Gloriosa Sāta Ana, y esclarecido Consorte suyo San Joachin.
Con licencia, en Mexico por Doña Maria de Benavides en el Empedradillo. [ca. 1693]
7 p. l., 139 numb. l. incl. front. 14.5cm. 8°
Includes poetry.
Bound in contemporary vellum.
Palau(2)183589; Medina(Mexico)1941.
4929, 1908

BA693
=C363c
Catholic Church in Spain--Councils.
Collectio Maxima Conciliorum Omnium Hispaniæ, Et Novi Orbis, Epistolarumque Decretalium Celebriorum, Necnon Plurium Monumentorum Veterum Ad Illam Spectantium: Cum Notis Et Dissertationibus, Quibus Sacri Canones, Historia Ac Disciplina Ecclesiastica, Et Chronologia, Accurate Illustrantur. Tomus Primus [-Tomus Quartus]. Curâ & studio Josephi Saenz De Aguirre, Benedictinæ Congregationis Hispaniarum Magistri Generalis... Nunc S. R. E. Presbyteri Cardinalis, Tituli S. Balbinæ Protectoris Regni Siciliæ.
Romæ, M. DC. XCIII [-1694]. Typis Joannis Jacobi Komarek Bohemi apud S. Angelum Custodem. Superiorum Permissu.
4 v.: v. 1, 8 p. l., xvi, 750 p., 1 l. front.; v. 2, 4 p. l., ix-xxviii, 764 p. front.; v. 3, 2 p. l., v-xxviii, 692 p. front.; v. 4, 14 p. l., 767 p. front. 33.5cm. fol.
Cut on title-pages.
All vols. have same front.
Imprint varies v. 2 and 3: Romæ, M. DC. XCIV. Typis Jo: Jacobi Komarek Bohemi propè SS. Vincentium & Anastasium in Trivio. ...
Dated: v. 1 (p. viii) 4 May 1693, v. 2 (p. xvi) 16 Aug. 1694, v. 3 (p. x) 25 Oct. 1694, v. 4 (14th p. l.^{r}) 7 Nov. 1693.
Preliminary matter, v. 2 (p. ix-x) includes laudatory poetry by Juan Bautista Miro (in Greek and Latin in parallel columns).
Errata, v. 2, p. 763-764.

BA693
-C363c
cop. 2
——————Another copy. 31cm.
Vols. 1-2 only.
JCB(2)2:1445; Palau(2)284301; Medina(BHA) 1914; Sabin528; Streit 1:725.
69-278, 1968
06244, before 1882

DA693
C498n
Chauncy, Isaac, 1632-1712.
Neonomianism Unmask'd: Or, The Ancient Gospel Pleaded, Against the Other, Called, The New Law. Being The Continuation of the Second Part of the Theological Debate, occasioned by Mr. Dan. William's Book, Entituled, Gospel Truth Stated and Vindicated, &c. By Isaac Chauncy, M. A.
London, Printed for H. Barnard at the Bible in the Poultry, 1693.
1 p. l., 83-336 p. 20.5cm. 4° (Issued as a part of his Neonomianism unmask'd, pt. 2-3, London, 1693.)
A reply to: Williams, Daniel. Gospel-truth stated and vindicated. London, 1692.
Errata, p. 336.
With this is bound as issued his Neonomianism Unmask'd. Part III. [London, 1693.]
Wing C3754A; Sabin 12333; McAlpin 4:468.
4836, 1908

DA693
C498n
[Chauncy, Isaac] 1632-1712.
Neonomianism Unmask'd. Part III.
[London, Printed for H. Barnard at the Bible in the Poultry, 1693]
104 p. 20.5cm. 4° (Issued as a part of his Neonomianism Unmask'd, pt. 2-3, London, 1693.)
Caption title.
A reply to: Williams, Daniel. Gospel-truth stated and vindicated. London, 1692.
Errata, p. 104.
"A brief Reply to what Mr. Daniel Williams ..." (p. 100-102) signed: John Nesbit.
Bookseller's advertisement, p. 103-104.
Wing C3755; Sabin 12333; McAlpin 4:468.
4836A, 1908

D693 Child, Sir Josiah, bart., 1630-1699.
C536n   A New Discourse Of Trade, Wherein is Recommended several weighty Points relating to Companies of Merchants. The Act of Navigation. Naturalization of Strangers. And our Woollen Manufactures. The Ballance of Trade. And the Nature of Plantations, and their Consesequences [sic] in Relation to the Kingdom, are seriously Discussed. And some Proposals for erecting a Court of Merchants for determining Controversies, relating to Maritime Affairs, and for a Law for Transferrance of Bills of Debts, are humbly Offered. By Sir Josiah Child.
   London, Printed, and Sold by John Everingham, at the Star in Ludgate-Street, in the Year 1693.
   27 p.ℓ., 37, 208, 205-234 p. 16cm. 8°
   First pub. under title Brief observations concerning trade and interest of money, London, 1668.
   "Imprimator" (1st p.ℓ.ᵛ) dated: December 24. 1692.
   "A Small Treatise Against Usury." by Sir Thomas Culpeper (p. 205-230). First pub. London, 1641.
   A reply in part to Interest of money mistaken, 1st pub. London, 1668 and Thomas Manley, Usury at six percent examined, 1st pub. London, 1669.
   JCB(2)2:1447; Sabin12708n; WingC3860; Kress 1811.
04758, before 1882

H693 Coronelli, Vincenzo, 1650-1718.
C822e   Epitome Cosmografica, O Compendiosa Introduttione All' Astronomia, Geografia, & Idrografia, Per l'Uso, Dilucidatione, e Fabbrica Delle Sfere, Globi, Planisferj, Astrolabj, E Tavole Geografiche, E particolarmente degli stampati, e spiegati nelle Publiche Lettioni Dal P. Maestro Vincenzo Coronelli M.C. Cosmografo Della Serenissima Republica Di Venetia, e Lettore di Geografia in quella Università, per l' Accademia Cosmografica Degli Argonauti.
   Colonia, MDCLXXXXIII. Ad istanza di Andrea Poletti in Venetia. Con Privilegj.
   15 p.ℓ., 420, [16] p. incl. tables. 31 fold. plates, 6 fold. maps. 20.5cm. 8°
   Added t.-p., engr.
   "Opere ... dal Padre Coronelli": 12th p.ℓ.ᵛ-13th p.ℓ.ʳ
   "Dell' Eccellenza Inuenzione, e Progresso dell' Astronomia, Discorso Del Sig. Carlo Malavista...": p. [1-8] at end.
   Imperfect: 2 plates wanting; available in facsimile.
   Armao 99.
7088, 1910

DA693 Doolittle, Thomas, 1632?-1707
D691e   Earthquakes Explained And Practically Improved: Occasioned By the late Earthquake on Sept. 8. 1692. in London, many other parts in England, and beyond Sea. By Thomas Doolittle M. A. Jamaica's Miseries shew London's Mercies. Both Compared.
   London: Printed for John Salusbury at the Rising Sun over against the Royal Exchange in Cornhill. 1693.
   8 p.ℓ., 141, [142-144] p. 15.5cm. 8°
   Includes (p. 126-128) two letters from Port Royal. The first is dated 20 June, 1692. The second, dated June 28, 1692, was 1st pub. in A full account of the late dreadful earthquake at Port Royal, London, 1692.
   "Books printed for John Salusbury" (p. [142-144] at end).
   Bound in contemporary calf, rebacked.
   JCB(2)2:1448; WingD1882; Cundall(Jam.Supp.) 115; Sabin20607.
05937, before 1882

C585 The English Spira: Being A Fearful Example
E96t   Of An Apostate, Who had been a Preacher
16   many Years, and then Apostatized from his Religion; miserably Hanged himself, October the 13th. 1684. Giving An Account of his Dispair, and Divers Conferences had with him, by several Ministers and others of his Friends. Together With his Answer; and Papers Written by his own Hand. Left attested by Mr. T. Plant, Mr. H. Collings, Mr. B. Dennis. Mr. B. Keach.
   London: Printed for Tho. Fabian, at the Sign of the Bible in Cheap-side, near Bread-street End. MDCXCIII.
   1 p.ℓ., iv, 46 p. 20cm. 4°
   "Spira" refers to Francesco Spiera, apostate from Protestantism. "Apostate" is the Baptist preacher, John Child.
   First pub. under title: The Mischief of persecution, London, 1688. These are the same sheets with cancel t.-p.
   "Some Books Printed for Tho. Fabian ... 1688": p. 46.
   Bound as no. 16 of 19 items in vol. with binder's title: Tracts 1681-1701.
   McAlpin4:470; WingE3120.
11352-16, 1918 rev

B693 Fernández de Medrano, Sebastián, 1646-1705.
F363b   Breue Descripcion Del Mvndo, O Gvia Geographica De Medrano, Lo mas principal della en verso. ...
   Con Licencia Impressa en Cadiz por Christoual de Requena, Impressor, y Mercader de libros,

este año de 1693.
8 p.l., 120 p. 15cm. 8º
First pub. Brussels, 1688.
Abridged from his Breve descripción del mundo, Brussels, 1686. "De La Descripcion Del Mundo En General" (p. 7-24) versified by Manuel de Pellicer y Velasco.
Dedication (2d-3d p.l.) signed: Cadiz 20. de Agosto de 1693. ... Christoual de Requena.
Preliminary matter includes commendatory poetry by Nicolás de Oliver y Fullana and Manuel Pellicer y Velasco.
In this copy the t.-p. was mutilated to obscure a library stamp, without affecting text.

70-562

DA693
F598d
Fleming, Robert, 1630-1694.
A Discourse Of Earthquakes; As They are Supernatural and Premonitory Signs to a Nation; with a respect to what hath occurred in this Year 1692. And some special Reflections thereon. ... By R. Fleming, Minister of the Gospel at Rotterdam.
London: Printed for Thomas Parkhurst at the Three Bibles and Crown in Cheapside, and Jonathan Robinson at the Golden Lyon in St. Paul's Church-Yard, 1693.
4 p.l., 128 p. 17.5cm. 8º
Bound in contemporary calf, rebacked.
WingF1264.

13115, 1921

DA693
F992a
[R]
A Further Account Of The Tryals Of The New-England Witches. With The Observations Of a Person who was upon the Place several Days when the suspected Witches were first taken into Examination. To which is added, Cases of Conscience Concerning Witchcrafts and Evil Spirits Personating Men. Written at the Request of the Ministers of New-England. By Increase Mather, President of Harvard Colledge.
Licensed and Entred according to Order. London: Printed for J. Dunton, at the Raven in the Poultrey. 1693. Of whom may be had the Third Edition of Mr. Cotton Mather's First Account of the Tryals of the New-England Witches, Printed on the same size with this Last Account, that they may bind up together.
1 p.l., 10 p., 1 l., [2], 39, [40-48] p. 20cm. 4º
"A True Narrative of some Remarkable Passages relating to sundry Persons afflicted by Witchcraft at Salem Village in New-England, which happened from the 19th. of March to the 5th. of April, 1692. Collected by Deodat Lawson." (p. 1-9, 1st count). First pub. under title: A brief and true narrative of some remarkable passages... Boston, 1692.
"A Further Account of the Tryals of the New-England Witches, sent in a Letter from thence, to a Gentleman in London" (p. 9-10 1st count); probably also by Lawson.
With, as issued, Increase Mather. Cases of conscience, London, 1693, with special t.-p. and separate paging and signatures.
Bookseller's advertisement on verso of t.-p. and p. [45-48] at end.
JCB(2)2:1455; WingM1213; Sabin46687; Church 736; Holmes(I.)22B; Dexter(Cong.)2444.

01963, 1854 rev

D693
G133n
Gage, Thomas, 1603?-1656.
Thomas Gage Neue merckwürdige Reise-Beschreibung Nach Neu Spanien/ Was ihm daselbst seltsames begegnet/ und wie er durch die Provintz Nicaragua wider zurück nach der Havana gekehret: In welcher zu finden ist Ein ausführlicher Bericht von der Stadt Mexico, ... Ingleichen Eine vollkommene Beschreibung aller Länder und Provinzen/ welche die Spanier in gantz America besitzen; von ihrem Kirchen-und Policey-Regiment; ihrem Handel: wie auch von ihren und der Criollen, Mestifen, Mulaten, Indianer und Schwartzen/ Sitten und Lebens-Art. Deme allem zum Beschluss noch beygefüget ist Ein kurtzer Unterricht von der Poconchischen oder Pocomanischen Sprache. Aus dem Frantzöschen ins Deutsche übersetzt.
Leipzig/ Verlegts Johann Herbordt Kloss/ Buchhändl. Anno M. DC. XCIII.
3 p.l., 471 p. front. 20cm. 4º.
Title in red and black.
Transl. from: Nouvelle Relation, Contenant Les Voyages De Thomas Gage. 2 vols., Paris, 1676-1677, itself transl. from: A New Survey of the West-Indies, first pub. London, 1648, under title: The English-American his Travail by Sea and Land.
"Kurtzer Unterricht Die Indianische Sprache/ die man Poconchi oder Pocoman nennet/ ...": p. 457-471.
JCB(2)2:1450; Sabin26309; Palmer326; Streit 2:2293; Palau(2)96487; Pilling1368.

02579, 1851

BA693
G633p
Gómez de la Parra, José.
Panegyrica Oratio In Laudem Fidelissimi Illius magni servi Fundatoris Eximij Congregationis Oratorij De Urbe Divi Philippi Neri. Quam In Oratorio Civitatis Angelopolitanæ

Americæ Septentrionalis, ipsa die perillustris Patriarchæ, septimo Kalendas Jūnij, anni Domini MDCXCI recitavit D. D. Josephvs Gomes De La Parra. Olim Collega Et Rector Insignis Veteris Divæ Mariæ omnium Sanctorum Collegij in Imperiali Mexicana Metropoli, & in eius Regali Athæneo candida infula decoratus. Dein vallisolitana in Cathedrali Episcopatus Michoacanensis Canonicus Magistralis. Et pro nunc maioris huius Ecclesiæ Angelopolitanæ Capitularis. ...
Angelopoli: Ex Officina Plantiniana Didaci Fernandez de Leõ. anno 1693.
7 p.ℓ., 40 p. 20cm. 4º
Title and p.ℓ. 6ᵛ-7ᵛ in red and black.
Approbation dated (4th p.ℓ.ᵛ) 17 July 1693.
Preliminary matter includes poetry by Antonio Delgado.
Palau(2)104262; Medina(Puebla)161.

69-775

DB   Gt.Brit.--Parliament, 1692-1693--House of
-G7875   Commons.
1689
1   The Address of the House of Commons to His Majesty, touching the State of the Kingdom of Ireland.
London, Printed by Thomas Braddyll and Robert Everingham, and are to be sold at the Seven Stars in Ave-Mary-Lane. 1692[/3].
297-298 p. 29cm. 1/2º (Issued as a part of Gt.Brit.--Parliament, 1692-1693--House of Commons. Votes... , no. 99, London, 1692/3.)
Caption title; imprint at end.
Presented 9 Mar 1692[/3].
Bound in Votes of the House of Commons, v.1.

10376-4B, 1914 rev 3

DB   Gt.Brit.--Parliament, 1692-1693--House of
-G7875   Lords.
1689
1   The Address Of The Lords Spiritual & Temporal, In Parliament Assembled: Presented To His Majestʸ the 23d of this instant February 1692[/3]. With His Majesties Answer. ...
[London] In the Savoy: Printed by Edward Jones. M. DC. XCIII.
4 p. 29cm. fol.
Calls for the exclusion of foreigners from the service of England.
"His Majesties Answer" (p. 4) dated 24 Feb 1692[/3].
Bound in Votes of the House of Commons, v.1, before Votes for 23 Feb 1692/3.

DB   ———Another copy. Bound in Votes of the
-G7875   House of Commons, v.2, after Votes for 23 Feb
1689   1693/4.
2
10383-1, 1914
10383-3, 1914

DB   Gt.Brit.--Parliament, 1692-1693--House of
-G7875   Lords.
1689
1   The Address Of The Lords Spiritual and Temporal in Parliament Assembled. Presented to His Majesty the 9th of this Instant March, 1692[/3]. With His Majesties Gracious Answer. ...
[London] Printed by Edw. Jones in the Savoy, 169$\frac{2}{3}$.
3 p. 29cm. fol.
Caption title; imprint at end.
Concerns conditions in Ireland.
Order to print (p. 1) dated 10 Mar 1692[/3].
Bound in Votes of the House of Commons, v.1, before Votes for 9 Mar 1692/3.

10383-2, 1914

DB   Gt.Brit.--Sovereigns, etc., 1689-1694 (William
-G7875   and Mary)
1689
1   His Majesties Most Gracious Speech To both Houses of Parliament, On Tuesday the Fourteenth day of March, 169$\frac{2}{3}$.
London, Printed by Charles Bill and the Executrix of Thomas Newcomb, deceas'd; Printers to the King and Queens most Excellent Majesties. 169$\frac{2}{3}$.
4 p. 29cm. fol.
Cut (royal arms) on t.-p.
Message in anticipation of prorogation of Parliament.
Bound in Votes of the House of Commons, v.1, after Votes for 13 March 1692.
Wing W2395.

10377-6, 1914

bD693   Hudson's Bay Company.
H885c   The Case Of The Hudsons-Bay Company.
[London, 1693]
Broadside. 32 x 20cm. 1/2º
"...the Company have lain under such Difficulties [from the French] that they were obliged last Year [i.e. 1692] (to prevent the Trade being utterly lost to this Nation) to set forth an Expedition to recover their just Rights..." Because of the expenses of the expedition the Company petitions the House of Commons not to tax them on more than the original value of their stock [even though the stock had been trebled in 1690].

06793, before 1923

BA693   Huélamo, Melchor, d. 1621.
H887e   Epitome De Los Misterios De la Missa, compuesto por el Padre Fray Melchor Huelamo, Predicador de la Orden de Nuestro

Padre S. Francisco de la Provincia de Cartagena; impresso dos vezes en Cuenca con licencia del Real Consejo. Dase A Los Moldes Nvevamente Por direccion del Padre Predicador Fray Ioseph Gomes, Hijo de la Provincia de los Apostoles San Pedro, y San Pablo de Michoacan. ...
    Con licencia en Mexico, por Doña Maria de Benavides Viuda de Juan de Ribera. Año de 1693.
    4 p.ℓ., 28 numb. ℓ. 20cm. 4°
    Cut (crucifix) on t.-p.
    First pub. under title: <u>Espirituales discursos y predicables consideraciones ...</u> Cuenca, 1595.
    License dated (3d p.ℓ.ᵛ) 9 June 1693.
    Palau(2)116614; Medina(Mexico)1546.

69-799

BA693 J91s [R]
Juana Inéz de la Cruz, sister, 1651-1695.
    Segundo Tomo De Las Obras De Soror Juana Ines De La Crvz, Monja Professa En El Monasterio Del Señor San Geronimo De la Ciudad de Mexico. Añadido En Esta Segvnda Impression Por Sv Avtora.
    Año 1693. Con Licencias Necessarias. Impresso en Barcelona: Por Joseph Llopsis Y à su costa.
    4 p.ℓ., 467, [468-472] p. 20cm. 4°
    Cut on t.-p.
    First pub. Seville, 1692.
    In this copy the t.-p. is mutilated with slight loss of text; title completed from Henríquez Ureña.
    Palau(2)65224; Medina(BHA)1908; Henriquez Ureña 27; Sabin17735.

29672, 1945

DA693 K28c
Keith, George, 1639?-1716.
    The Christian Quaker: Or, George Keith's Eyes opened. Good News from Pensilvania. Containing a Testimony against that False and Absurd Opinion... By George Keith.
    Printed in Pensilvania, and Reprinted in London for Benjamin Keach; and are to be sold by him at his Horse-lie-down; and John Harris at the Harrow in the Poultrey, 1693. Price 2d.
    12 p. 21.5cm. 4°
    First pub. under title, <u>A Testimony against that false & absurd opinion</u> [Philadelphia, 1692]
    In imprint "for Benjamin Keach;" and "him at his Horse-lie-down" effaced in ms.
    JCB(2)2:1452; Wing K153; Sabin37186; Smith (Friends)2:26.

0553, 1846

DA693 K28h
[Keith, George] 1639?-1716.
    The Heresie and Hatred Which was falsly Charged upon the Innocent Justly returned upon the Guilty. Giving some brief and impartial Account of the most material Passages of a late Dispute in Writing, that hath passed at Philadelphia betwixt John Delavall and George Keith, with some intermixt Remarks and Observations on the whole.
    Printed and Sold by William Bradford at Philadelphia, Anno Dom. 1693.
    22 p., 1 ℓ. 19.5cm. 4°
    Signed (p. 22): George Keith.
    "The Printer's Advertisement." (last p.) signed: W.[illiam] B.[radford]
    Evans641; Wing K174; Sabin19367; Church729; Smith(Friends)2:27; Hildeburn62.

4062, 1918

DA693 K28m
Keith, George, 1639?-1714.
    More Divisions Amongst The Quakers: As appears by the following Books of their own Writing. Viz. I. The Christian Faith of New-England Quakers condemn'd by a Meeting of Pensilvanian Quakers. II. The false Judgment of a yearly Meeting of Quakers in Maryland, condemn'd by George Keith, Thomas Budd, &c. all Quakers. To which is added, A Discovery of this Mystery of Iniquity. By George Keith.
    First Printed beyond the Sea, and now Re-printed [London], and are to be Sold by Richard Baldwin near the Oxford-Arms in Warwick-Lane, 1693.
    1 p.ℓ., 22 p. 20.5cm. 4°
    <u>The Christian Faith of the People called Quakers</u>, 1st pub. Philadelphia, 1692. <u>False Judgments reprehended</u>, 1st pub. Philadelphia, 1692. <u>A Discovery of the Mystery of Iniquity</u> and Hypocrisie, 1st pub. Philadelphia, 1692.
    "Observation by another Hand." (p. 22) signed: 23 Nov. 1693. F.[rancis] B.[ugg]
    "Books lately published." p. 22.
    Wing K182; Sabin37202; Smith(Friends)2:28; Baer(Md.)149.

8093, 1911

DA693 K28n [F]
[Keith, George] 1639?-1716.
    New-England's Spirit of Persecution Transmitted To Pennsylvania, And the Pretended Quaker found Persecuting the True Christian-Quaker, In The Tryal Of Peter Boss, George Keith, Thomas Budd, and William Bradford, At the Sessions held at Philadelphia the Nineth, Tenth and Twelfth Days of December, 1692. Giving an Account of the most Arbitrary Procedure of that Court.
    [New York, William Bradford] Printed in the Year 1693.

    1 p. ℓ., 38 p. 18.5cm. 4º
    Evans642; Wing K186; Sabin37203; Hildeburn64; Smith(Friends)2:27; Eames(NY)1; Baer(Md.)150.
05866, 1898

DA693 [Keith, George] 1639?-1716.
K28t The Tryals Of Peter Boss, George Keith, Thomas Budd, and William Bradford, Quakers, For several Great Misdemeanors (As was pretended by their Adversaries) before A Court of Quakers: At the Sessions held at Philadelphia in Pensylvania, the Ninth, Tenth, and Twelfth Days of December, 1692. Giving also an Account of the most Arbitrary Procedure of that Court. ...
  Printed first Beyond-Sea, and now Reprinted in London, for Richard Baldwin in Warwick-lane. 1693.
   1 p. ℓ., 34 p. 20.5cm. 4º
   First pub. under title New-England's spirit of persecution transmitted to Pennsilvania, [New York, 1693]
   License dated (t.-p.) 19 Oct 1693.
   JCB(2)2:1459; Wing T2254; Sabin37226; Smith (Friends)2:27; Baer(Md.)151.
05869, before 1882

D. Math Mather, Cotton, 1663-1728.
C.454A.2 The Wonders of the Invisible World. Observations As well Historical as Theological, upon the Nature, the Number, and the Operations of the Devils. Accompany'd with, I. Some Accounts of the Grievous Molestations, by Dæmons and Witchcrafts ... By Cotton Mather.
[R]
  Boston Printed, and Sold by Benjamin Harris. 1693 [i.e. 1692].
   16 p. ℓ., 151, [1], 8, 17-32 p. 15cm. 8º
   Dated (p. 147) in Boston, 11 Oct. 1692; imprint post-dated (cf. Holmes(C.) p. 1258, 1266n. 35).
   Errata, p. [1] following p. 151.
   Preliminary matter (3d p. ℓ.ᵛ-4th p. ℓ.) signed by William Stoughton.
   Also issued with imprint: Boston Printed by Benj. Harris for Sam. Phillips. 1693.
   In this copy p. 23-24 and p. 83-84 are mutilated with slight loss of text.
   WingM1173; Holmes(C.)454A.2; Church733; cf. Evans657; cf. Sabin46603.
1172, 1905

D. Math Mather, Cotton, 1663-1728.
C.454B.1 The Wonders of the Invisible World: Being an Account of the Tryals Of Several VVitches, Lately Excuted [sic] in New-England: And of several remarkable Curiosities therein Occurring. ... By Cotton Mather. Published by the Special Command of his Excellency the Govenour [sic] of the Province of the Massachusetts-Bay in New-England.
[R]
  Printed first, at Bostun [sic] in New-England; and Reprinted at London, for John Dunton, at the Raven in the Poultry. 1693.
   4 p. ℓ., 5-16, 16, 33-80, 41-56, 89-98, [2] p. [ ]² A-K⁴ L-R² 21cm. 4º
   First pub. Boston, 1693 [i.e. 1692]
   "Imprimatur" (1st p. ℓ.ᵛ) dated 23 Dec. 1692.
   Half-title: The Tryals of Several VVitches, Lately Executed in New England ...
   Errata, p. 51 (2d count).
   Preliminary matter (4th p. ℓ.ʳ) signed by William Stoughton.
   Booksellers' advertisement, [2] p. at end.

D. Math ———Another copy. 21cm.
C.454B.1 Errata, p. 51 (2d count).
cop. 2 Imperfect: half-title and booksellers' advertisement wanting.
[R]

D. Math ———Variant. 21.5cm.
C.454B.2 In place of the errata on p. 51 (2d count) appears "Matter Omitted in the Trials ..."
[R]
   JCB(2)2:1453; WingM1174; Holmes(C.)454B; Sabin 46604; Church734.
05951, after 1891-1904
0551, 1846
6063, 1909

D. Math Mather, Cotton, 1663-1728.
C.454C The Wonders of the Invisible World: Being an Account of the Tryals Of Several Witches Lately Executed in New-England: And of several Remarkable Curiosities therein Occurring. By Cotton Mather. Published by the Special Command of his Excellency the Governour of the Province of the Massachusetts Bay in New-England. The Second Edition.
[R]
  Printed first, at Boston in New-England, and reprinted at London, for John Dunton, at the Raven in the Poultrey. 1693.
   24, 43-50, 41-56, 47-62 p. [A]² B-D² C-H⁴ 20cm. 4º
   First pub. Boston, 1693 [i.e. 1692]. This is an abridged version of the 1st London edition of 1693.
   "Imprimatur" (1st p. ℓ.ᵛ) dated 23 Dec. 1692.
   Half-title: The Tryals of Several Witches Lately Executed in New-England ...
   Preliminary matter (p. [7]) signed by William Stoughton.
   JCB(2)2:1454; WingM1175; Sabin46605; Holmes (C.)454C.
01968, 1850

DA693 L425f [R]	Mather, Increase, 1639-1723. 　Cases of Conscience Concerning Evil Spirits Personating Men; Witchcrafts, Infallible Proofs of Guilt in such as are Accused with that Crime. All Considered according to the Scriptures, History, Experience, and the Judgment of many Learned Men. By Increase Mather, President of Harvard Colledge at Cambridge, and Teacher of a Church at Boston in New England ... 　Printed at Boston, and Re-printed at London, for John Dunton, at the Raven in the Poultrey. 1693. 　2 p.ℓ., 39, [40-48] p. 20cm. 4° (Issued as a part of <u>A further account of the tryals of the New-England witches.</u> London, 1693.) 　First pub. Boston, 1693 (i.e. 1692). 　Bookseller's advertisement, p. [45-48]. 　JCB(2)2:1455; WingM1213; Sabin46687; Church 736; Holmes(I.)22B; Dexter(Cong.)2444. 01963A, 1854 rev		498 p. pl.; Jul., [1], 499-589 p. illus., fold. pl.; Aug., 1 p.ℓ., 593-692 p. pl.; Sept., 1 p.ℓ., 693-762 p. illus.; Oct., 1 p.ℓ., 763-854 p. pl.; Nov., 1 p.ℓ., 855-936 p. fold. pl.; Dec., 1 p.ℓ., p. 937-1012, [55] p. 17cm. 8° 　Edited by Wilhelm Ernst Tentzel. 　Each monthly part has a special t.-p. Title varies, Mar.-Nov. "... Sine censura & approbatione Auctoris." 　Cut on title-pages (Jan.-Jun., Aug.-Dec., armillary sphere; Jul., calligraphic device). 　Imprint varies, Mart.-Jun., Aug.-Nov.: In Verlegung Joh. Friedrich Gleditsch/Buchhl. 1693. 　Paging 499-589 begins on a verso. 　The last part includes general indexes. 　Bookseller's advertisements, p. 259-260, 337-338, 497-498, 690-692, 852-854. 　Errata, p. [53-55] at end. 　In this copy there are 2 blank ℓ. following p. 106 and 1 blank ℓ. following p. 182. 　Bound in contemporary vellum. 62-160　rev
D. Math I.60	Mather, Increase, 1639-1723. 　The Great Blessing, Of Primitive Counsellours. Discoursed in a Sermon, Preached in the Audience of the Governour, Council, and Representatives, of the Province of the Massachusets-Bay, in New England. May 31st. 1693. Being the Day for the Election of Counsellours, in that Province. By Increase Mather. President of Harvard Colledge in Cambridge, and Teacher of a Church at Boston, in New-England. ... 　Boston, Printed and Sold, by Benjamin Harris, Over-against the Old-Meeting-House. 1693. 　23, [1] p. 18cm. 4° 　"To The Inhabitants Of the Province of the Massachusets-Bay, In New-England." (p. 3-8), reprinted by W. H. Whitmore in <u>The Andros Tracts</u>, v.2, p. 301-311. 　"Advertisements" of books sold by Benjamin Harris, last p. 　JCB(2)2:1456; Sabin46689; Evans659; Holmes(I.) 60; WingM1215. 05889, 1878	Z M834 1693	Morden, Robert, d.1703. 　Geography Rectified: Or, A Description Of The World...Illustrated with Seventy eight Maps. The Third Edition, Enlarged. To which is added a Compleat Geographical Index to the Whole, Alphabetically digested. ... By Robert Morden. 　London: Printed for Robert Morden and Thomas Cockerill, at the Atlas in Cornhill, and at the Three Legs in the Poultrey, over-against the Stocks-Market. MDCXCIII. 　5 p.ℓ., 574,[2], 575-626,[74] p. illus. (engr.; 78 maps.) 20cm. 4° 　Title in red and black. 　Maps engr. in text, except "Tartaria in Europe", p. 88, which is pasted over "A New Description of Tartarie" which was printed there in error (as well as properly on p. 407). 　The section on America occupies p. 542-626. 　First pub. London, 1680. 　"Books Printed for, and Sold by Thomas Cockerill..." p. [73-74] at end. 　Bound in contemporary calf, rebacked. 　Sabin50535; WingM2621; Phillips(Atlases)4268; Baer(Md.)153. 11925, 1919
JC M736u 1693	Monatliche Unterredungen Einiger Guten Freunde Von Allerhand Büchern und andern annehmlichen Geschichten. Allen Liebhabern Der Curiositäten Zur Ergetzligkeit und Nachsinnen heraus gegeben. Januarius [-December] 1693. 　[Leipzig] in Verlegung Thomas Fritsch/1693. 　12 pts. in 1 v.: Jan., 1 p.ℓ., 160 (i.e. 106)p.; Febr., 1 p.ℓ., 107-182 p.; Mart., 1 p.ℓ., 183-260 p.; Apr., 1 p.ℓ., 261-338 p.; Mai., 1 p.ℓ., 339-414 p. pl.; Jun., 1 p.ℓ., 415-	DA693 M889s	Morton, Charles, 1627(ca.)-1698. 　The Spirit Of Man: Or, Some Meditations (by way of Essay) on the Sense of that Scripture. I Thes. 5.23. ... By Charles Morton, Minister of the Gospel at Charlstown in New-England. ...

Boston Printed by B. Harris, for Duncan Campbell, at the Dock-Head, over-against the Conduit. 1693.

4 p. ℓ., 100, [2] p. A⁴ B-D⁸ E⁴ F-H⁸ (-H8) 14.5cm. 8⁰

Preface signed (3d p. ℓ.ᵛ) Increase Mather, James Allen, Samuel Willard, John Baily, Cotton Mather.

Errata, verso of t.-p.

Bookseller's advertisement, [2] p. at end.

In this copy both halves of sheet E, 8⁰ half-sheet imposition, were bound up; duplicate leaves were partially excised (stubs visible) but p. 53-54 and p. 55-56 remain repeated.

In this copy t.-p. mutilated affecting imprint.

Bound in contemporary calf.

DA693　――― ――― Another copy. 15cm.
M889s　　Imperfect: 2d-3d p. ℓ., p. 7-10, 35-100,
cop.2　　[2] wanting.

Evans661; WingM2825; Sabin50994; Holmes (I.)76c; Holmes(C.)298.

31145, 1952
28524, 1940

+Z　Le Neptune François, Ou Atlas Nouveau
≡N442　Des Cartes Marines. Levées Et Gravées
1693　Par Ordre Exprés Du Roy. Pour L'Usage De Ses Armées De Mer ... Le tout fait sur les observations & l'experience des plus habiles Ingenieurs & Pilotes. Reveu & mis en ordre par les Sieurs Pene, Cassini & autres.

A Paris, Chez Hubert Jaillot aux deux Globes. [i.e. Amsterdam, Pierre Mortier] M.DC.LXXXXIII. Avec Privilege Du Roy.

2 p. ℓ., 6 p. plates, maps. 65.5cm. 1⁰

Of the various persons who participated in the composition of the Neptune François, according to the Catalogue général des livres ... du Département de la Marine et des Colonies Charles Pene "fut l'éditeur" and "Sauveur et de Chazelles doivent être regardés comme les auteurs".

First pub. Paris, Imprimerie Royale, 1693.

Continuations were published under titles: Cartes Marines ... Gravées & recüeillis par le Sr. Romain de Hooge and Suite Du Neptune François. With this copy of Le Neptune François are bound (as the 2d and 3d items) Cartes Marines, Amsterdam, 1693, and Suite, Amsterdam, 1700, which are described separately. Bound in contemporary calf, rebacked and covers papered over.

Preliminary matter captioned "Le Neptune François..." (p. 1-6) includes at end "Table Des Cartes &c. Contenues Dans Le Premier Volume Du Neptune François" and both a French privilege granted by Louis XIV to Charles Pene (dated 27 Dec. 1692) and a Dutch privilege granted by the Staten Generaal to Pierre Mortier (dated 17 June 1693). There is another printing of these prelims. which includes at end only the Dutch privilege and a "Table Des Cartes &c. ..." listing the contents of Le Neptune François as well as its continuations.

The "Table Des Cartes &c. ..." (p. 6) lists 3 ship plates and 29 maps. This copy contains in addition 1 scale plate, 16 ship plates, 11 flag plates, and 1 map (map [1]) which are not listed in the "Table Des Cartes &c. ...", for a total of 31 plates and 30 maps in this copy.

This copy also contains a printed table (pasted on the verso of the title-page) which lists the contents of Le Neptune François and its continuations. Caption: "Catalogue Des Cartes De Mer, Qui Sont Dans Le Neptune François, Qui se vendent à Amsterdam, chez Pierre Mortier... ." The table lists for Le Neptune François a twelfth flag plate "Pavillons de diverses Nations &c", which is not in this copy.

Two other issues are known with an imprint of Amsterdam, P. Mortier, 1693. One has Dutch preliminaries and was issued under title De Fransche Neptunus, and the other has English preliminaries and was issued under title The French Neptune.

See Chapin, H.M., "The French Neptune and its various editions," American book collector, II(1932), 16-19.

Koeman M. Mor 1; cf. Phillips(Atlases)517; Scheepvaart Mus. 51; Muller(1872)1957*; cf. Tiele 791.

Contents.

In this copy all plates and maps, the engraved title-page, and the engraved vignette on the printed t.-p. are colored.

Maps are double-page size, except for map [14] which is folded to that size.

preliminary matter:
[1] Engraved t.-p.; signed: Jan van Vianen fecit.
[2] Title-page, printed in red and black. With cut (engr. ship vignette) signed: J. V Vianen f
[3] Scale table: "I. Echelle pour trouver les Jours de la Semaine ..."
[4] Introductory text (p. 1-6).

ship plates:
[ ] "Vaisseau du premier rang portant pauillon d'Admiral. Jan van Vianen f."
[1] "Vaisseau Royal d'Angleterre. Konincklyke Schip van Engeland. a Amsterdam Chez Pierre Mortier Avec Privil. 1"
[2] "Coupe dun Amiral de. 104. pieces de Canon auec ses principales proportions et les noms des pieces du dedans. 2"
[3] "Vaisseau du troisième rang a la Voille.

TweeDecks Schip vande derde Rang. a Amsterdam Chez Pierre Mortier Avec Privil. 3"

[4] "Galiote a bombe. Bombardeer Galjoot. a Amsterdam Chez Pierre Mortier. Avec Privilege 4"

[5] "Bruslot a la Sonde Brander, leggende voor Anker. a Amsterdam Chez Pierre Mortier Avec Privil. 5"

[6] "Flute Vaisseau de charge a la Voile. Koopvaardy Fluydt. A Amsterdam Chez Pierre Mortier. Avec Privilege 6"

[7] "Polacre a la voille. Polacre Zeylende. A Amsterdam Chez Pierre Mortier Avec Privilege. 7"

[8] "Coupe Dvne Galere Auec Ses Proportions Door-Sneede Galey met syn Proportie. Quille Dvne Galere Sur le Chantier voet van een Galey op de Stapel. 8"

[9] "la Galere Reale a la sonde. Konincks Galley. A Amsterdam Chez Pierre Mortier. Avec Privilege 9"

[10] "Galere a la voille portant l'Estendart de chef d'Escadre, Zeylende Galley voerende d'Admiraals Vlag. a Amsterdam Chez Pierre Mortier Avec Privilege. 10"

[11] "La galere Patronne, a la rame. Roeyende Patroon Galley. A Amsterdam Chez Pierre Mortier Avec Privilege. 11"

[12] "Galeasse a la voile. Zeylende Galey. a Amsterdam Chez Pierre Mortier Avec Privilege 12"

[13] "Galeasse a la rame. Roeyende Galley. A Amsterdam Chez Pierre Mortier Avec Privil. 13"

[14] "Solemnité Du Bucentaure, Qui Se Celebre A Venise Le Jour De L'Ascension. Tome.1. Pag. 266. 14"

[15] "Saique batiment dont les Turcs se seruent en leuent pour leur trafic Saique daar de Turcke meede Negotieere in de Levant. a Amsterdam Chez Pierre Mortier Avec Privilege 15"

[16] "Brigantin donnant chasse a vne Felouque et prest a la border. Brigantin Attaqueerende een Sloep. a Amsterdam Chez Pierre Mortier Avec Privilege. 16"

[17] "Barque allant vent arriere. Barck Seylende voor de Windt. a Amsterdam Chez Pierre Mortier Avec Privilege. 17"

[18] "Tartane de Pesche Vissers Tartane. a Amsterdam Chez Pierre Mortier Avec Privil. 18"

flag plates:

[1] "Pavillons Avec L'Explication des Couleurs. &c. ... A Amsterdam Chez P. Mortier Avec Privil. 1"

[2] "Pavillons De France &c. ... A Amsterdam Chez P. Mortier Avec Privil. 2"

[3] "Pavillons D'Angleterre &c. ... 3"

[4] "Pavillons des Etats Generaux des Provinces Unies &c. ... A Amsterdam Chez P. Mortier Avec Privil. 4"

[5] "Pavillons des Colleges, et Villes, des Provinces Unies &c. ... A Amsterdam Chez P. Mortier Avec Privil. 5"

[6] "Pavillons D'Espagne &c. ... A Amsterdam Chez P. Mortier Avec Privil 6"

[7] "Autre Pavillons D'Espagne, et des Venesiens &c. ... A Amsterdam Chez P. Mortier Avec Privil 7"

[8] "Pavillon D'Italie &c. ... A Amsterdam Chez P. Mortier Avec Privil 8"

[9] "Pavillons de Danemarque, Suede, et Pologne. A Amsterdam Chez P. Mortier Avec Privil 9"

[10] "Pavillons de Brandebourg, Hambourg, Lubeek, Rostok &c. ... A Amsterdam Chez P. Mortier Avec Privil 10"

[11] "Pavillon du Grand Seign. de Moscovie et de Coerland ... 11"

maps:

[1] "Carte Generale De Toutes Les Costes Du Monde, Et Les Pays Nouvellement Decouvert, ... Principalement sur la Carte que Monsieur N. Witsen. à donnée au Public. A Amsterdam, Chez Pierre Mortier ..."

[2] "Carte Generale Des Costes De L'Europe Sur L'Ocean Comprises depuis Dronthem en Norvege Jusques au Destroit de Gibraltar Levée et Gravée par Ordre du Roy. à Paris 1693."

[3] "Carte De La Mer Báltique ... Levée et Gravée Par Ordre du Roy. a:Paris.1693."

[4] "Carte De La Mer De Dannemark Et Des Entrées Dans La Mer Baltique ..."

[5] "Carte Du Detroit Du Sond Contenant les Costes De L'Isle De Zélande ..."

[6] "Carte De La Mer D'Allemagne ... Faite Par Ordre du Roy. à Paris 1693."

[7] "Carte Des Entrées Du Suyder-Zee Et De L'Embs ... Levée et Gravée Par Ordre du Roy. a. Paris. 1693."

[8] "Carte Des Entrées De L'Escaut Et De La Meuse ..."

[9] "Carte De L'Entrée De La Tamise ..."

[10] "Carte De La Mer D'Ecosse ... "

[11] "Carte Generale des Costes D'Irlande, et des Costes Occidentales D'Angleterre avec une Partie de celles D'Ecosse. Levée et Gravée Par Ordre Exprez du Roy. A. Paris 1693."

[12] "Carte Particuliere Des Costes Occidentales D'Irlande ..."

[13] "Carte De La Manche. ... Reveue et

Corrigée Par le S.r Sanson. A Paris Chez Hubert Jaillot."
[14] "Carte Du Golfe De Gascogne Contenant les Costes de France et d'Espagne ..."
[15] "Carte Particuliere Des Costes Meridionales D'Angleterre ... Levée et Gravée Par Ordre du Roy. a. Paris. 1693."
[16] "Carte Particuliere Des Costes De Flandres, de Picardie Et De Normandie ... "
[17] "I. Carte Particuliere Des Costes De Normandie ..."
[18] "2.me Carte Particuliere des Costes de Normandie, Contenant les Costes du Cotentin ..."
[19] "1.re Carte Particuliere Des Costes De Bretagne ..."
[20] "2.me Carte Particuliere Des Costes De Bretagne ... Levee et Gravee Par Ordre du Roy. A. Paris 1693"
[21] "3.me Carte Particuliere Des Costes De Bretagne ..."
[22] "4.me Carte Particuliere Des Costes De Bretagne ..."
[23] "5.e Carte Particuliere Des Costes De Bretagne ... Levée et Gravée Par Ordre du Roy. A Paris. 1693."
[24] "6.me Carte Particuliere Des Costes De Bretagne ..."
[25] "7.me Carte Particuliere Des Costes De Bretagne ..."
[26] "8.eme Carte Particuliere Des Costes De Bretagne ..."
[27] "Carte Des Costes De Poitou D'Aunis et de Saintonge ..."
[28] "Carte Particuliere Des Costes De Guienne, de Gascogne en France Et De Guipuscoa en Espagne ... Levée et Gravée Par Ordre du Roy. A. Paris. 1693."
[29] "Carte Des Costes Septentrionales D'Espagne ..."
[30] "Carte Des Costes De Portugal et de Partie D'Espagne ... Levée et Gravée Par Ordre du Roy. A Paris 1693."

33014A, 1960

D696 -C737c
Payne, Henry Neville, fl. 1672-1710, supposed author.
A Coppy of the pretended Letter, whereupon the Inditement against Hendry [sic] Navilepaine [sic] is founded. The 3.d of December, 1692.
[Edinburgh? 1693?]
Broadside. 30.5 x 18.5cm. 1/2°
Bound in a volume of Scottish imprints and mss. as the 19th of 58 items.
Wing C6220.

7117, 1910

D696 -C737c
Payne, Henry Neville, fl. 1672-1710.
Navil Payn's Letter, And Some Other Letters That Concern the Subject of his Letter, With short Notes on them for the clearer Information of the Members of Parliament. In order to Navil Payn's Trial.
Edinburgh, Printed by George Mosman, According to Order, 1693.
10 p. 31.5cm. fol.
Caption title; imprint at end.
An advertisement (p. 1) mentions that "A fuller Account is intended" (Wing P890: 4° Edinburgh, 1693).
Imperfect: p. 9-10 wanting; available in facsim.
Bound in a volume of Scottish imprints and mss. as the 18th of 58 items.
Aldis 3309.

7116, 1910

D696 -C737c
Payne, Henry Neville, fl. 1672-1710.
To His Grace William Duke of Hamilton Their Majesties High Commissioner And the Honourable Estates of Parliament, Humbly Sheweth The Answers for Hendry [sic] Navilpayne [sic], To the Inditement raised at the Instance of Their Majesties Advocate, before the High Court of Parliament.
[Edinburgh, 1693]
4 p. 34.5cm. (31.5cm. in binding) fol.
Caption title.
Bound in a volume of Scottish imprints and mss. as the 22d of 58 items.

7120, 1910

E693 =P734d
Plumier, Charles, 1646-1704.
Description Des Plantes De L'Amerique. Avec Leurs Figures. Par le R.P. Charles Plumier, Religieux Minime.
A Paris, De L'Imprimerie Royale. M. DC. XCIII.
4 p.l., 94, [9] p. 108 plates. 42.5cm. fol.
Cut (royal arms) on t.-p.
Colophon: A Paris, De L'Imprimerie Royale. Par les soins de Jean Anisson, Directeur de ladite Imprimerie. M. DC. XCIII.
There are copies which have another state of the t.-p. with date misprinted: MDCCXIII.
In this copy the leaves bearing p. 47-48, 65-66 are cancels.
JCB(2)2:1458; Palau(2)229149; Sabin 63455; Hunt.Bot.Cat. 389; Pritzel 7213.

01926, 1854

E693 R253j
Raveneau de Lussan, ----b. 1663.
Journal Du Voyage Fait A La Mer De Sud, Avec Les Flibustiers De L'Amerique en 1684.

& années suivantes. Seconde Edition. Par le Sieur Raveneau De Lussan.
A Paris, Chez ◁La Veuve de Jean Bapt. Coignard, Imprimeur du Roy, & de l'Académie Françoise. Et Jean Baptiste Coignard, Fils, Imprimeur du Roy, & de l'Académie Françoise, ruë S. Jacques, à la Bible d'or. MDCLXXXXIII:
8 p. ℓ., 448 p., 2 ℓ. 17cm. 12º
Cut on t.-p., incl. motto : Alpha et Omega Principium et finis".
First pub. Paris, 1689.
"Achevé d'imprimer pour la premiere fois... le 22. Septembre 1689." (ℓ. 1 at end). These are probably a reissue of the sheets of the Paris, 1689, ed.
Testimonials for the author from le sieur de Cussy, governor of Saint Domingue (6th-8th p. ℓ.).
Bound in contemporary calf.
JCB(2)2:1460; Sabin67985.

03796, 1868

E693 Relation De ce qui s'est passé Dans Les Isles
R382d   De L'Amerique, Ou les Victoires remportées sur les Anglois par les Troupes du Roy, commandées par Mr. le Comte de Blenac. De la Martinique le 6. May 1693.
[Bordeaux, 1693]
4 p. 21.5cm. 4º
Caption title.
"Avec Permission de Monseigneur de Sourdis", at end.

30828, 1950

BA693 Rodrigo de la Cruz, 1637-1716.
-R696s   Discurso, Que Ha Parecido Adicionar A La Defensa Del Hermano Rodrigo de la Cruz, Prefecto General de la Compañia Bethleemitica: Sobre el Punto Principal del Passo de los Breves. En Exclvsion De La Ponderacion, Qve por el señor Fiscal se pudiere hazer, sobre el asserto Patronato Real de los Hospitales.
[Madrid, ca. 1693]
6+ p. 28cm. fol.
Caption title.
Imperfect: all after p. 6 wanting.
Bound in contemporary vellum with his Señor. El Hermano Rodrigo de la Cruz ... Que aviendo presentado ... dos Breves ... , Madrid, ca. 1693.

30880, 1951

BA693 Rodrigo de la Cruz, 1637-1716.
-R696s   Relacion De Los Hospitales, Qve Se han encargado, y fundado por los Hermanos de la Compañia Bethleemitica.
[Madrid, ca. 1693]
[4] p. 28cm. fol. (Issued as a part of his Señor. El Hermano Rodrigo de la Cruz ... Que aviendo presentado ... dos Breves ... , Madrid, ca. 1693.)
Caption title.

30879, 1951

BA693 Rodrigo de la Cruz, 1637-1716.
-R696s   Representacion Jvridica Por El Hermano Rodrigo de la Cruz, Prefecto General de la Compañia Bethleemitica. Con El Señor Fiscal Del Svpremo, y Real Consejo de las Indias. Sobre El pretenso passo de dos Breves Apostolicos, expedidos por la Santidad de Inocencio Vndezimo: El vno, en que se aprueban las Constituciones nuevamente formadas para el regimen de dicha Compañia, y observancia de sus Estatutos. Y el otro, en que se le nombrò por Prefecto General de dicha Compañia.
Con Licencia. En Madrid: Por Diego Martinez Abad, Impressor de Libros en la Calle de Atocha. Año M.DC.XCIII.
2 p. ℓ., 49 numb. ℓ., [9], [14] p. 28cm. fol.
Engraving (St. Francis Xavier) on t.-p.
Signed (numb. ℓ. 49ᵛ): Lic. Don Ioseph de Gurpegui. Lic. D. Ioseph de Castro y Araùjo.
License dated (2d p. ℓ.ʳ) 16 Nov. 1693.
In this copy there is a blank leaf at end.
Bound in contemporary vellum with his Señor. El Hermano Rodrigo de la Cruz ... Que aviendo presentado ... dos Breves ... , Madrid, ca.1693.
Palau(2)65325; Medina(BHA)1909; Sabin17738.

30881, 1951

BA693 Rodrigo de la Cruz, 1637-1716.
-R696s   Señor. El Hermano Rodrigo de la Cruz, puesto à los Reales pies de V. Mag. representa: Que aviendo presentado en el Real Consejo de las Indias dos Breves, expedidos por su Santidad ...
[Madrid, ca. 1693]
22 numb. ℓ., [4] p. 28cm. fol.
Title from caption and beginning of text.
Signed (numb. ℓ. 22ᵛ): Lic. D. Pedro Londaiz.
Concerns the official recognition of the Order of the Bethlehemites by the Council of the Indies.
With, as issued, his Relación de los hospitales [Madrid, ca. 1693]
With this are bound in contemporary vellum: his Discurso Que Ha Parecido Adicionar A La Defensa Del Hermano Rodrigo de la Cruz ... [Madrid, ca. 1693] and his Representacion Jvridica ... Madrid, 1693.
Palau(2)65324.

30878, 1951

BA693　Romero, Francisco, b. 1658 or 9.
R763ℓ　　Llanto Sagrado De La America Meridional,
[R]　Que busca aliuio en los Reales ojos de nuestro
Catholico, y siempre gran Monarcha Señor Don
Carlos Segvndo Rey De Las Españas, Y Em-
perador De Las Indias; Para Mayor Incremento
De La Militante Yglesia. Restablecimiento De
La Monarqvia. Y Nveva Dilatacion Del Imperio
Indiano. Presentale en el Supremo, y Real Con-
sejo de Indias; por mano del Reuerendissimo
Señor Padre Maestro Fray Pedro Matilla, del
Orden de Predicadores ... El Padre Fray Fran-
cisco Romero, Religioso del Orden Calçado de
N. P. S. Agustin; Missionario en el Perù, y hijo
de la mesma Prouincia ...
　En Milan, En el Real y Ducal Palacio, por
Marcos Antonio Pandulfo Malatesta Impressor
Regio y Camaral 1693.
　5 p. ℓ., 50 p. pl. (col., fold.) 25cm. 4°
　Dedication dated (3d p. ℓ.ᵛ) 28 Aug. 1692.
　In this copy there is a blank leaf at beginning
and at end.
　Bound in contemporary calf.
　Palau(2)277308; Medina(BHA)1912; Sabin73032;
Santiago Vela6:680-1:1; Streit2:2294.
15081, 1928

D693　St. Lo, George, d. 1718.
S145e　　England's Safety: Or, A Bridle To The French
King. Proposing A Sure Method for Encouraging
Navigation, and Raising Qualified Seamen for the
well Manning Their Majesties Fleet on any Occa-
sion, in a Months Time, without Impressing;
And a Competent Provision for all such as shall
be Wounded in Service against the Enemy... Also
An In-sight into the Advantages may be made by
the Herring and other Fisheries... Also En-
couragement for Commanders of Men of War,
Privatiers and Seamen... By Captain George
Sᵗ. Lo.
　London: Printed for W. Miller, at the
Gilded Acorn in St. Paul's Church-yard,
where Gentlemen and others may be furnish-
ed with Bound Books of most Sorts, Acts of
Parliament, Speeches, and other sorts of
Discourses, and State-Matters; as also Books
of Divinity, Church-Government, Humanity,
Sermons on most Occasions, &c. 1693.
　48 p. 20cm. 4°
　Added t.-p., illus.
　Bound in at end is "Books Printed for
Thomas Lee..." 2 p.
　WingS341; Sabin75324; Kress1823.
30013, 1947

B69　Salazar, Antonio de, fl. 1673-1698.
G643v　　Villancicos, Que Se Cantaron En Los Mayti-
20　nes de la Assumpcion De Nuestra Señora, En
La Santa Iglesia Cathedral de Mexico, ...
Compuestos en metro musico por Antonio De
Salazar Maestro de Capilla de dicha Santa
Iglesia.
　En Mexico por los Herederos de la Viuda de
Bernardo Calderon 1693.
　1 p. ℓ., [6] p. 20cm. 4°
　Woodcut title vignette (the Virgin surrounded
by angels)
　Bound, in contemporary vellum, as no. 20
with 42 other items.
28920, 1941

B69　Salazar, Antonio de, fl. 1673-1698.
G643v　　Villancicos, Que Se Cantaron En Los May-
41　tines Del Glorioso Principe de la Iglesia el
Señor San Pedro En la Santa Iglesia Cathedral
Metropolitana de Mexico. ... Compuestos
en Metro Musico por el Maestro Antonio de
Salazar, que lo es actual de Capilla de dicha
Santa Iglesia.
　Con licencia en Mexico, por los Herederos
de la Viuda de Bernardo Calderon, año de 1693.
　[8] p. 20cm. 4°
　Imprint at end.
　Woodcut title vignette (St. Peter enthroned;
inscribed at base: San Pedro.)
　Bound, in contemporary vellum, as no. 41
with 42 other items.
28941, 1941

B693　Sigüenza y Góngora, Carlos de, 1645-1700.
S579m　　Mercurio Volante Con La Noticia de la recu-
[R]　peracion de las Provincias Del Nvevo Mexico
Consegvida Por D. Diego De Vargas, Zapata,
Y Luxan Ponze De Leon, Governador y Capitan
General de aquel Reyno. Escriviola Por especial
orden de el Excelentissimo Señor Conde De Gal-
ve Virrey, Governador, Y Capitan General De
La Nueva-España, &c. Don Carlos De Sigvenza,
Y Gongora ...
　Con Licencia en Mexico: En La Imprenta De
Antuerpia de los Herederos de la Viuda de Ber-
nardo Calderon, año de 1693.
　1 p. ℓ., 18 numb. ℓ. 20.5cm. 4°
　Cut (winged horse) on t.-p.; incl. motto:
Sic Itvr Ad Astra.
　JCB(2)2:1461; Palau(2)312979; Medina(Mexico)
1551; Sabin80978; Wagner63.
02648, 1851

bBB　Spain--Sovereigns, etc., 1665-1700.
S7336　　(Charles II)　　13 Feb 1693.
1693　　El Rey. Por Quanto por la ley 8. titulo 11.
2　libro 1. de la Recopilacion de las Indias està

	dispuesto, y mandado, que los Prelados, Virreyes, Presidentes, y Governadores, guardando lo proveìdo por la ley 19. titulo 6. del mismo libro, ... [Madrid, 1693] 1 ℓ. 30.5cm. fol. Title from caption and beginning of text. At end: "... Para que los Virreyes, Presidentes, Obispos, y Fiscales de las Audiencias auisen de las vacantes Eclesiasticas de sus distritos." Dated in Madrid, 13 Feb 1693 (place, day, and month supplied in manuscript). Papel sellado dated 1693. With contemporary ms. annotations. With conjugate blank leaf which also bears contemporary ms. annotations. 28203, 1938 rev		Booksellers' advertisement, 1st p. ℓ.ᵛ. Bound in contemporary calf. WingT662.
		69-644	
		DA693 T866a	A True Account Of The Tryals, Examinations, Confessions, Condemnations, and Executions of divers Witches, At Salem, in New-England ... In a Letter to a Friend in London. Licensed according to Order. London, Printed for J. Conyers, in Holbourn. [1693] 8 p. 20cm. 4° Signed at end: Salem, 8th. Month, 1692. C.[otton] M.[ather] Not by Cotton Mather, but based chiefly on his Wonders of the invisible world. London, 1693 (cf. Holmes(C)p. 1133). JCB(2)2:1437; Sabin46563.
		0552, 1846	
bBB S7336 1693 1	Spain--Sovereigns, etc., 1665-1700 (Charles II). 31 Dec 1693 El Rey. Conde de la Moncloua Pariente, de mi Consejo de Guerra, y Iunta de Guerra de Indias, mi Virrey, Gouernador, y Capitan General de las Prouincias del Perù: El estado a que se halla reducida la Monarquia con la dilatada continuacion de la guerra, ... [Madrid, 1693] [2] p. 31.5cm. fol. Title from caption and beginning of text. Orders the reversion to the Treasury of one-third of the amount of salaries to be drawn from the Treasury in 1694. Dated in Madrid, 31 December 1693. With conjugate blank leaf bearing contemporary ms. annotations. Accompanied by 8 ℓ. with contemporary ms. annotations concerning a protest of officials of the Tribunal de la Santa Cruzada against this order. Papel sellado dated 1694-95. 28204, 1938	D693 T866ℓ	The Truest and Largest Account Of The Late Earthquake In Jamaica, June the 7th. 1692. Written by a Reverend Divine there to his Friend in London. With some Improvement thereof by another Hand. ... London, Printed for Tho. Parkhurst, at the Bible, and three Crowns at the lower End of Cheapside, near Mercers-Chappel. 1693. 4 p.ℓ., 26, [2] p. 21.5cm. 4° Preface signed: H. L. Letter (p. 1-13) dated: Jamaica. Withywood in the Parish of Vere. June 30th. 1692. "Books lately Printed for, and Sold by Thomas Parkhurst" (2p. at end); wanting, available in facsim. Also issued with imprint: London, Printed and are to be Sold by J. Buttler Bookseller at Worcester, 1693. JCB(2)2:1451; WingT3132; Sabin97172; Cundall (Jam.)250.
		03878, 1868	
D693 T287o	Temple, Sir William, bart., 1628-1699. Observations Upon The United Provinces Of The Netherlands. By Sir William Temple of Shene in the County of Surrey, Baronet, Ambassador at the Hague, and at Aix la-Chapelle, in the Year 1668. The Sixth Edition, Corrected and Augmented. London, Printed for Jacob Tonson, at the Judges-Head in Chancery-Lane, and Awnsham Churchil, at the Black-Swan in Pater-Noster Row. 1693. 8 p.ℓ., 279 p. 18cm. 8° First pub. London, 1673.	B693 V393a	Vázquez Gaztelu, Antonio. Arte De Lengua Mexicana Compvesto Por el Bachiller D. Antonio Vazquez Gastelu el Rey de Figueroa: Cathedratico de dicha lengua en los Reales Collegios de S. Pedro, y San Juan. Dase A La Estampa Segvnda Vez De orden del Illustrissimo Señor Doctor D. Manuel Fernandez de Santa Cruz, Obispo de la Puebla de los Angeles. Và añadido, y enmendado en esta segunda Impression. Con licencia en la Puebla de los Angeles, en

la Imprenta de Diego Fernandez de Leon, año de 1693. Impresso â su costa: hallarase en su Libreria en el portal de las flores.

2 p.ℓ., 50 numb. ℓ. 20cm. (22cm. in case) 4°

Cut (printer's device)on t.-p.
First pub. Puebla, 1689.
Bound in contemporary vellum. The endpapers of this copy are a fragment of Relación verdadera y sucinta de lo que ha obrado el Excmo. Señor Conde de Aguilar, General de la armada Real de España, en seguimiento de la de Francia, que bombardeó á Barcelona y á Alicante ..., Madrid, Sebastián Armendariz, 1691 (Palau(2)258970).
JCBAR40:25-29; Sabin26746; Medina(Puebla) 165; Ugarte410; Viñaza234; Streit 2, p. 73.

28596, 1940 rev

DA693
W695d
Willard, Samuel, 1640-1707.
The Doctrine Of The Covenant Of Redemption. Wherein is laid the Foundation of all our Hopes and Happiness. Briefly Opened and Improved. By Samuel Willard, Teacher of a Church in Boston. ...
Boston, Printed by Benj. Harris over-against the Old-Meeting-House. 1693.
4 p.ℓ., 165 p. 14.5cm. 8°
"To the Reader" (1st p.ℓ.ᵛ-4th p.ℓ.) signed by Increase Mather, 6 Feb. 1693.
Imperfect: bottom of title-page worn, affecting imprint; p. 159-165 wanting; available in facsim.
Bound in contemporary calf.
Evans684; WingW2274; Sabin104078; Holmes (I.)166.

10517, 1914

1694

D694
R665a
An Account Of Several Late Voyages & Discoveries To The South and North. Towards The Streights of Magellan, the South Seas, the vast Tracts of Land beyond Hollandia Nova, &c. Also Towards Nova Zembla, Greenland or Spitsberg, Groynland or Engrondland, &c. By Sir John Narborough, Captain Jasmen Tasman, Captain John Wood, and Frederick Marten of Hamburgh. To which are Annexed a Large Introduction and Supplement, Giving An Account of other Navigations to those Regions of the Globe. The Whole Illustrated with Charts and Figures.
London: Printed for Sam. Smith and Benj. Walford, Printers to the Royal Society, at the Prince's Arms in S. Paul's Churchyard, 1694.
xxix, [7], 196, 207 p. 19 plates (part fold.), 2 fold. maps, fold. table. 20.5cm. 8°
Title in red and black.
Edited by Sir Tancred Robinson, probably with the assistance of Sir Hans Sloane.
"To the Honourable Samuel Pepys" (p. iii-iv) signed: Samuel Smith, Benjamin Walford.
"The Bookseller's Preface, Or Introduction" (p. v-xxix) [by Tancred Robinson].
The Tasman and Martens accounts had previously been published. The Tasman account first appeared in Dirk Rembrantsz van Nierop's Eenige oefeningen in godlycke wiskonstige en natuerlyche dingen, Amsterdam, 1669-74. English translation first appeared in Philosophical collections, edited by Dr. Robert Hooke, no. 6, London, 1682. The Martens account is a translation of Gedenckwaerdige Reys Van Frederick Martens which appeared in De Noordsche Weereld, Hamburgh, 1675.
The Martens account has separate paging and signatures.
Booksellers' advertisement, p. 196 (1st count).
Bound in contemporary calf, rebacked.

D694
R665a
cop.2
———— ————Another copy. 20cm.
Imperfect: plate "Q" wanting.
Bound in contemporary calf.
JCB(2)2:1471; WingN154; Sabin72185; Chavanne 4.

05554, 1966
01927, 1854

E694
A238q
Les Admirables Qualitez Dv Kinkina, Confirmées Par Plusieurs Experiences, Et La Maniere De S'En servir dans toutes les fiévres, pour toute sorte d'âge, de sexe & de complexions. Seconde Edition.
A Paris, Chez Martin Jouvenel, Marchand Libraire, ruë de la Bouclerie, au bout du Pont S. Michel, à l'Image S. Augustin. M. DC. XCIV. Avec Approbation & Privilege du Roy.
12 p.ℓ., 164, [2], 4 p. 16cm. 12°
Cut (printer's monogram) on t.-p.
First pub. Paris, 1689; these are the same sheets with new t.-p.
Bookseller's advertisement, 4 p. at end.
"... Il y trouvera encore non seulement ce qu'en a dit & enseigné le Chevalier Talbot Anglois, mais aussi tout ce qu'il y a de meilleur dans Sebastien Bade...", 7th p.ℓ.
In this copy there is a blank leaf preceding the final 4 pages.
Bound in contemporary calf.

70-66

1694

BA694 A284t
Aguirre, Pedro Antonio de.
 Transito Gloriosissimo De N. Sṛ͞a La Santissima Virgen Maria Dixolo El R. P. Fr. Pedro Antonio de Agvirre de los Menores Descalços de N.S.P.S. Francisco Lector de Prima de Theologia en su Religiosissimo Convento de S. Diego de Mexico. Sacalo A Lvz, Y Sombra de la Cofradia de el Transito de N. Señora, que á titulo de suyo, lo celebrō en el Hospital de San Jvan De Dios de esta Corte el dia 22. de Agosto Dominica 12. post Pentec. de 1694. Sv Mas Officioso, Y Agradecido Reelecto Mayordomo Nicolas De Navarrete.
 Con licencia Impresso en Mexico en la Imprenta de Juan Joseph Guillena Carrascoso. [1694]
  10 p.ℓ., 8 numb. ℓ. 19.5cm. 4⁰
  License dated (8th p.ℓ.ᵛ) 30 Sept. 1694.
  Palau(2)3944; Medina(Mexico)1556.

1053, 1905

BA630 -M285s
[Alcedo Sotomayor, Carlos de]
 Por El Doctor Don Jvan De la Rea Zurbano, Cavallero del Orden de Alcantara, Oydor jubilado de la Real Audiencia de Quito. Sobre Que se dè por nullo todo lo que contra èl actuò Don Matheo Mata, Cavallero del Orden de Calatraua, Presidente de aquella Audiencia, en el juyzio de Visita. ...
  [Madrid? 1694]
  13 numb. ℓ. 28cm. fol.
  Caption title.
  Dated and signed at end: Hispal [i.e. Seville] die vigesima prima, Decembris anno 1694. Lic. D. Carlos de Alzedo Sotomayor.
  Bound as the 2d of 3 items with: Juan de Mañozca. Señor. El Licenciado Iuan de Mañozca Inquisidor Apostolico de la ciudad de Lima ... [Madrid? ca. 1630]
  Medina(BHA)1918.

5520, 1909

BA694 A473s
Alvarez de Toledo, Juan Bautista, Bp., 1655-1726.
 Sermon De La Dominica Sexagesima En La Eleccion Qve Hizo De Ministro Provincial la Santa Provincia del Santissimo Nombre de Jesvs de Guatemala el dia 13. de Febrero, y celebrò con accion de gracias, congregada el dia 14. en el Templo de N.P.S Domingo de Guatemala este año de 1694 Predicaba Fʳ Juan Baptista Alvarez De Toledo ...
 Con licencia Impresso en Mexico por Juan Joseph Guillena Carrascoso, en el Empedradillo Año de 1694.
  7 p.ℓ., 15 numb. ℓ., [5] p. 19.5cm. 4⁰
  License dated (4th p.ℓ.ᵛ) 17 Nov. 1694.
  Medina(Mexico)1558.

1054, 1905

EA694 A894h
[Aubin, Nicolas] b. ca. 1655.
 Histoire Des Diables De Loudun, Ou De la Possession des Religieuses Ursulines, Et de la condamnation & du suplice D'Urbain Grandier Curé de la même Ville.
 A Amsterdam, Chez Abraham Vvolfgang, Prés de la Bourse. 1694.
  1 p.ℓ., 189, 192-473 p. 14.5cm. 12⁰
  Cut on t.-p.
  First pub. Amsterdam, 1693.
  In this copy there is a blank leaf at front, following p. 94, and at end.
  Bound in contemporary calf.

69-595

BA694 A951s
Avendaño Suares de Sousa, Pedro de, b. ca. 1654.
 Sermon De N.S.S.P. y Señor San Pedro. Principe de la Iglesia. Predicado. En su Hospital Real de la Ciudad de los Angeles á 4. de Julio de 1694. En la fiesta Annual, que Celebra, su muy Illustre, y V. Congregacion Ecclesiastica: a cuyas expensas se dâ à la Estampa. Dixolo D. Pedro de Avendaño, Suarez de Soussa siendo Consultor actual, de dicha Congregacion ...
 Con Licencia En Mexico: en la Imprenta de Iuan Ioseph Gnillena [sic] Carrascoso Impresor, y mercader de libros en el Empedradillo, junto á las Cassas del Marquez del Valle Año de 1694.
  6 p.ℓ., 10 numb. ℓ. 19.5cm. 4⁰
  "Sentir" dated (6th p.ℓ.ᵛ) 18 Aug. 1694.
  Preliminary matter includes poetry.
  10th ℓ. numbered on verso.
  In this copy the last leaf is disintegrated; available in facsim.
  Palau(2)20149; Medina(Mexico)1559.

69-754

FA694 B424m
Bekker, Balthasar, 1634-1698.
 Le Monde Enchanté Ou Examen des communs sentimens touchant les Esprits, leur nature, leur pouvoir, leur administration, & leurs opérations. Et Touchant les éfets [sic] que les hommes sont capables de produire par leur communication & leur vertu, Divisé en quatre Parties Par Balthasar Bekker, Docteur en Théologie, & Pasteur à Amsterdam. Traduit du Hollandois.

A Amsterdam, Chez Pierre Rotterdam, Libraire sur le Vygendam. 1694.

68 p. ℓ., 387, [388-391] p. front. (port.) 14cm. (14.5cm. in case). 12⁰ (Issued as the 1st of 4 v., Amsterdam, 1694.)

Cut (P R monogram) on t.-p.

Transl. from: De Betoverde Weereld, Amsterdam, 1696; 1st pub. Leeuwarden, 1691.

Dedication dated (8th p. ℓ.ᵛ) 18 July 1693.

"Deze vertaling van het bekende boek van Bekker, dat in 1691 in het Holl. was verschenen ..., draagt voorin een 'Avis au lecteur: L' auteur ne reconnoit aucuns exemplaires pours les siens, en cette langue, que ceux qui sont imprimé à Amsterdam, par Pierre Rotterdam, & signés de sa main, comme ils le sont tous quatre.' Inderdaad zijn de opdrachten ... getekend door Bekker. Een nadruk, die ook het jaartal 1694 draagt, heeft die handtekening steeds gedrukt. Daar het portret van Bekker hier het onderschrift 'C. Mathey sculp.' heeft, neem ik aan dat dit een Parijse nadruk was, die net als de Amsterdamse met het adres van Pierre Rotterdam verscheen." (Eeghen, I.H. van. De Amsterdamse boekhandel, 1680-1725, v.4, p. 79)

This copy is apparently of the genuine Amsterdam issue. It has: initial letters measuring 2.3 x 2.3cm. (2d p. ℓ.), 2.2 x 2.2cm. (9th p. ℓ.), 1.5 x 1.5cm. (29th p. ℓ.), and 1.7 x 1.7cm. (p. 1); front. (port.) unsigned; "Epitre" signed in ms. (8th p. ℓ.ᵛ); errata leaf at end and uncorrected readings, e.g. p. 3, line 1: Lacteur; p. 374, line 32: leurs. In this copy front., t.-p., 7th-8th p. ℓ., and p. 385 to end supplied in photofacsimile.

Another copy at Brown University is apparently the Paris reprint. It has: initial letters measuring 1.7 x 1.7cm. (2d p. ℓ.), 1.3 x 1.3cm. (9th p. ℓ.), 1.7 x 1.7cm. (29th p. ℓ.), and 1.3 x 1.3cm. (p. 1); front. (port.) signed: C. Mathey sculp.; "Epitre" signed (8th p. ℓ.ᵛ) with a printed signature; no errata leaf and corrected readings, e.g. p. 3, line 1: Lecteur; p. 374, line 32: leur.

"A monsjeur Robert Calef de par l'auteur Bekker" in ms., front fly-leaf.

Bound in contemporary calf.

JCBAR38:34-38.

28136, 1938

B694 Bermejo y Roldán, Francisco, b. 1637.
V297m Discvrso De La Enfermedad Sarampion Experimentada En La Civdad de los Reyes del Perù. Por El Doc. D. Francisco, Bermejo, Y Roldan, Cathedratico de Prima en la facultad de Medicina, Prothomedico general de estos Reynos, y Medico de Camara del Excelentissimo Señor Conde de la Monclova, Uirrey, Governador, y Capitan General, de estos Reynos, &c. y del Excelentissimo è Ilustrissimo Señor Doctor Don Melchor de Liñan, y Cisneros Arçobispo de Lima del Consejo de su Magestad. ...

Con Licencia En Lima; Por Joseph De Contreras, y Alvarado, Año de 1694.

15 p. ℓ., 46, 45-48 p. pl. (coat of arms) 4⁰

Dated (p. 48) 11 Jan. 1694.

Preliminary matter includes poetry.

Bound with: Vargas Machuca, Francisco de. Medicos Discvrsos. Lima, 1694.

JCB(2)2:1462; Medina(Lima)655; Sabin72813.

03685, before 1866

C619 Bluteau, Raphael, 1638-1734.
A949n Porticus Trivmphalis, A Regali Palatio, Quà Meridiem spectat, In Tagum exporrecta, Ad publicam receptionem Augustissimæ Mariæ, Sophiæ, Elisabethæ, Portugalliæ Reginæ, Ulyssiponem ingredientis, Anno Domini M. DC. LXXXVII. Die 11. Augusti, Pictis, Inscriptisque Tabulis, Jussu Regis, Ornata A R. P. D. Raphaele Blvteavio, Clerico Regulari Theatino ...

Ulyssipone, Ex Typographia Michaelis Deslandes, Serenissimi Regis Typographi. Cum facultate Superiorum. Anno 1694.

68 p. 19.5cm. 4⁰

Includes (p. 52-68) "Inscriptiones Porticus Triumphalis. Svb Americæ effigie".

Bound as the 14th in a volume of 58 pamphlets, 1619-1702.

9355, 1913

D694 Bulkley, Thomas.
B934t To the Right Honourable William, Earl of Craven; John, Earl of Bath; John, Lord Berkley; George, Lord Cartret; Anthony, Lord Ashley; Sir John Colleton, Barronet: Being Proprietors of Carolina, and the Bahama Islands. Thomas Bulkley, a Free-holder, Inhabitant and Merchant of New Providence (one of the said Islands) Humbly presenteth the following Address, Viz.

[London? 1694?]

16 p. 21cm. 4⁰

Caption title.

Includes letters by Cadwallader Jones, Samuel Trott, and Peter Colleton.

WingB5408.

06043, before 1923

| DA697 B827b | Burnet, Gilbert, Bp. of Salisbury, 1643-1715.
Four Discourses Delivered to the Clergy Of The Diocess of Sarum, Concerning I. The Truth of the Christian Religion. II. The Divinity and Death of Christ. III. The Infallibility and Authority of the Church. IV. The Obligations to continue in the Communion of the Church. By the Right Reverend Father in God, Gilbert, Lord Bishop of Sarum.
London, Printed for Richard Chiswell, at the Rose and Crown in St. Paul's Church-yard. MDCXCIV.
1 p. ℓ., x, 110, [2] p. 22cm. 4°
Imprimatur (p. ℓ.^{v}) dated: Jan. 22. 169$\frac{3}{4}$.
Bookseller's advertisement at end.
Bound in mid-18th century half-calf with Bray, Thomas, <u>Bibliotheca parochialis</u>, London, 1697, as the 4th of 4 items.
WingB5793; McAlpin4:490. |

7621, 1911

| BA694 C352s | Castilla, Miguel de, 1652-1713.
Sermon De la Immaculada Concepcion de Maria Señora Nvestra. Predicado En el celebre, y devotissimo Santuario de la Soledad, y Dolores de la misma SS. Virgen en la Ciudad de Guadalaxara Año de 1693. Por el P. Migvel De Castilla Professo de la Compañia de Iesvs, Maestro de Theologia en el Colegio de la misma Ciudad, y Examinador synodal de el mismo Obispado. ...
Con Licencia: En Mexico, en la Imprenta nueva de Juan Joseph Guillena Carrascoso en el Empedradillo, junto las casas del Marquezado. [1694]
7 p. ℓ., 12 numb. ℓ. 20.5cm. 4°
"Parecer" dated (5th p. ℓ.^{r}) 22 Apr. 1694.
Palau(2)47994; Medina(Mexico)1561; Backer 2:848. |

69-798

| BA694 C352ℓ | Castillo, Baltasar.
Lvz, Y Gvia De Los Ministros Evangelicos. Para navegar por el mar proceloso deste mundo hasta llegar al puerto de la salvacion, y gozar eternamente de los thesoros de la gloria, y bienaventuranza. Dedicala El P. Fr. Balthasar Del Castillo Predicador, y Ministro, que fue de el Convento de S. Luis Obispo, y Pueblo de Uexotlan, ...
Con Licencia, En Mexico: por Juan Joseph Guillena, Carrascoso, Impressor, y Mercader de Libros, en el Empedradillo, junto las casas del Marques, Año de 1694.
5 p. ℓ., 11 numb. ℓ., [10] p., 3-16 numb. ℓ. 19cm. 4°
License dated (5th p. ℓ.^{r}) 4 March 1694. |

Text in Spanish followed by translation into Aztec.
Palau(2)48061; Medina(Mexico)1562; Sabin 11420; Pilling663; Viñaza235.

06059, before 1923

| DA694 C498d | Chauncy, Isaac, 1632-1712.
The Doctrine Which is according to Godliness Grounded upon the Holy Scriptures of Truth; and agreeable to the Doctrinal Part of the English Protestant Articles, and Confessions. To which is Annexed, A Brief Account of the Church-Order of the Gospel according to the Scriptures. ... By Isaac Chauncy, M.A.
London, Printed for the Author by H. Hills, and are to be Sold by Will. Marshal at the Sign of the Bible in Newgate-street, T. Fabin at the Bible in Cheapside, and H. Barnard, at the Bible in the Poultry. [1694?]
6 p. ℓ., 285, 296-352, [17] p. 14.5cm. 12°
Errata, 2d p. ℓ.^{r}.
Bound in contemporary calf.
WingC3749; Dexter(Cong.)2446. |

4237, 1908

| D694 C536n | Child, Sir Josiah, bart., 1630-1699.
A New Discourse Of Trade, Wherein is Recommended several weighty Points relating to Companies of Merchants. The Act of Navigation. Naturalization of Strangers. And our Woollen Manufactures. The Ballance of Trade. And the Nature of Plantations, and their Consequences in Relation to the Kingdom, are seriously Discussed. And some Proposals for erecting a Court of Merchants for determining Controversies, relating to Maritime Affairs, and for a Law for Transferrance of Bills of Debts, are humbly Offered. By Sir Josiah Child. The second Edition.
London Printed, and sold by Sam. Crouch, Tho. Horn, & Jos. Hindmarsh in Cornhill. 1694.
24 p. ℓ., 238 p. 17cm. 8°
First pub. under title <u>Brief observations concerning trade and interest of money</u>, London, 1690.
In this issue the t.-p. is a cancel. There is another issue of 1694 with the same imprint, but without an edition statement.
"A Small Treatise Against Usury" by Sir Thomas Culpeper (p. 217-236) 1st pub. London, 1641.
A reply in part to <u>Interest of money mistaken</u>, 1st pub. London, 1668, and Thomas Manly, <u>Usury at six percent examined</u>, 1st pub. London, 1669. |

F694 Clüver, Philipp, 1580-1622.
C649p   Philippi Cluverii Introductio In omnem Geographiam veterem æque ac novam olim studio & opera Johannis Bunonis, Gymnas. Lüneburg. Histor. P.P. & V.D.M. multis in locis emendata, memorabilibusq́ue aucta. Jam verò Tabulis Geographicis XLVI. amplius æri denuô incisis auctior nec non additamentis & annotationibus locupletata, locisq; in multis passim correctior curante Johanne Reiskio. Cum gratiâ & privilegio S. Cæsar. Majest. & Elect. Sax.
  Wolfenbüttelæ, sumptibus Hæredum Bunonianorum. Typis Caspari Johannis Bismarci, Anno M DC XCIV.
  16 p. ℓ., 608, [135] p. illus. (tables), 2 plates, port., 43 fold. maps, 3 tables (incl. 2 fold.) 22cm. 4º
  Title in red and black.
  Added t.-p., engr. by Herman Mosting.
  First pub. Leiden, 1624.
  Also issued with a variant, corrected index of [111] p.
  Dedication dated (4th p. ℓ.^{v}): ex Museo Wolffenbütt. VI. Kal. April. A. MDCXCIV.
  JCB(2)2:1463; Sabin13805.
06526, before 1882

DA694 The Concurrence & Unanimity Of the People Called
C744a Quakers; In Owning and Asserting the Principal Doctrines of the Christian Religion; Demonstrated in the Sermons or, Declarations, of several of their Publick Preachers, Namely Mr. Robert Barclay, Mr. George Whitehead, Mr. John Bowater, Mr. Charles Marshall, Mr. William Bingley, Mr. John Butcher, Mr. James Park, Mr. William Dewsberry, Mr. Francis Camfield, Mr. William Penn, Mr. Richard Ashby, Mr. Samuel Waldenfield, Mr. John Vaughton, and Mr. Francis Stamper. Exactly taken in Short-hand, as they were Delivered by them at their Meeting-Houses, in Grace-Church-street, Devonshire-House, St. Martins-le-Grand, St. John's-street, Wheeler-street, and Ratcliff, in and about London. And now Faithfully Transcribed and Published; With the Prayer at the end of each Sermon.
  London: Printed for Nath. Crouch, at the Bell in the Poultry, near Cheapside. 1694.
  2 p. ℓ., 79, 90-213, [1] p. 17cm. 8º
  Preface (1st p. ℓ.^{v}) signed: N.[athaniel] C.[rouch]
  Bookseller's advertisements, 1st p. ℓ.^{r} and last p.
  The 1st p. ℓ. and p. 213 are disintegrated with some loss of text; available in facsim.
  Bound in contemporary calf.
  WingC5715; Smith(Friends)2:556.
64-196

BA694 Corella, Jaime de, 1657-1699.
C797n   Noticia, Censura, Impugnacion, Y Explicacion De Las XXXI. Proposiciones Condenadas Por el Santissimo Padre Alexandro Papa VIII. Autor El R^{mo}. P. Fr. Jayme Corella, Ex-Lector de Theologia, Missionario Apostolico, y Predicador de su Magestad, Hijo de la Santa Provincia de Capuchinos de Navarra.
[R]
  En Madrid: Por Antonio Roman. Año de 1693. Y Por Su Original, Con Licencia, En Mexico: por la Viuda de Francisco Rodriguez Lupercio, en la Puente de Palacio. Año de 1694.
  3 p. ℓ., 48 p. 21cm. 4º
  Cut on t.-p.
  License dated (3d p. ℓ.^{v}) 8 Jan. 1694.
  Palau(2)61979; Medina(Mexico)1564.
69-755

BA694 Diaz, Diego.
D542s   Sermon Qve En la Solemne Profession de la Madre Maria Magdalena De La Soledad Predico El Padre Predicador Fray Diego Dias Predicador Conventual que fué del Convento de la Ciudad de los Angeles su Patria, Y Comendador actual por segunda ves del Convento, del Sagrado y Real Orden de Nuestra Señora de la Merced Redempcion de Cautivos de la Ciudad de Anteqvera Dixolo En el Monasterio de Señoras Religiosas de Nuestra Señora de la Concepcion Regina Coeli de dicha Ciudad Domingo de Septuagesima siete de Febrero del Año de 1694 Dedicalo Al Illustrissimo Señor Doctor Don Isidro Sariñana y Cuenca ... El Bachiller Antonio De Medina...
  Con Licencia En Mexico, Por la Viuda de Francisco Rodrigvez Lvpercio, En la Puente de Palacio. Año de 1694, [sic]
  12 p. ℓ., 10 numb. ℓ. 19.5cm. 4º
  License dated (5th p. ℓ.^{v}) 16 Oct. 1694.
  Preliminary matter includes poetry by Diego Gallegos.
  Palau(2)72108; Medina(Mexico)1565.
1055, 1905

[283]

D694 Dryden, John, 1631-1700.
D799 The Indian Emperour; Or, The Conquest Of Mexico By The Spaniards. Being the Sequel of The Indian Queen. By John Dryden, Esq; ...
London, Printed by T. Warren for Henry Herringman, and are to be Sold by R. Bentley, J. Tonson, F. Saunders, and T. Bennet, 1694.
4 p.ℓ., 55 p. 22cm. 4⁰.
First pub. London, 1667.
Macdonald(Dryden)69h; WingD2295.

10720, 1915

DA694 Ellwood, Thomas, 1639-1713.
E47e An Epistle To Friends. Briefly Commemorating the Gracious Dealings of the Lord with them; and warning them to beware of that Spirit of Contention and Division Which hath appeared of late in George Keith. And some few others that join with him, who have made a Breach and Separation from Friends in some Parts of America. By Thomas Ellwood. ...
London, Printed by T. Sowle at the Crooked-Billet in Holy-well-lane, Shoreditch, and near the Meeting-House in White-Hart-Court in Grace-Church-Street. 1694.
75 p. 16.5cm. (18.5cm. in case). 8⁰
Dated (p. 73): The 25th. of the 6th. Month 1694.
"Postscript" (p. 74-75) is a reply to [Robert Hannay] A true account of the proceedings, sence and advice ... , London, 1694.
Errata (p. 75).
Also issued with imprint "London, Printed and sold by T. Sowle ..."
WingE620; Sabin22350; Smith(Friends)1:565.

1817, 1906

DA694 Ellwood, Thomas, 1639-1713.
E47f A Further Discovery Of that Spirit of Contention & Division Which hath appeared of late in George Keith, &c. Being a Reply to Two Late Printed Pieces of his, the one Entituled, A Loving Epistle, &c. the other, A Seasonable Information, &c. Wherein his Cavils are Answered, ... By Thomas Ellwood. ...
London, Printed by T. Sowle at the Crooked-Billet in Holy-well-lane, Shoreditch, and near the Meeting-House in White-hart Court in Grace-Church-street. 1694.
128 p. 17cm. 8⁰
Keith's A loving epistle to all the moderate... , 1st pub. [London, 1694] and his Seasonable information and caveat, 1st pub. London, 1694.
Certificate (p. 127) dated: December the 10th. 1694.
Errata (p. 128).
WingE623; Sabin2 2351; Smith(Friends)1:565-566.

11480, 1918

BA694 Escalante, Thomas, d. 1708.
E74s Sermon Funebre, Que Predicò El P. Thomas De Escalante de la Compañia de Iesvs professo de quatro votos de ella. En las honrras de los Soldados difuntos Españoles, que de orden de su Magestad hizo celebrar en la Cassa Professa de la mesma Compañia de Jesus de Mexico el dia 15. de Febrero de este Año de 1694. El Ex.ᵐᵒ Señor D. Gaspar de Sandoval, Cerda, Silva, y Mendoza, Conde de Galve, Virrey ... A Quien Humilde le dedica su Autor.
Con licencia en Mexico: en la Imprenta de Iuan Ioseph Guillena Carroscoso. Año de 1694.
32 p.ℓ., 22, [34] p. 20cm. 4⁰
Dedication dated (19th p. ℓ.ʳ) 1 May 1694.
Dedication (2d-19th p. ℓ.) mentions the chief events in the administration of the viceroy since 1690.
With as issued: Mendez, Francisco. Fúnebres ecos, [Mexico, 1694]
Palau(2)80730; Medina(Mexico)1568; Sabin 22816; Wagner64; Backer3:425.

13060, 1921

BA694 Florencia, Francisco de, 1619-1695.
-F632i ... Historia De La Provincia De La Compañia De Jesvs. De Nveva-España, Dividida en ocho Libros ... Dispvesta Por el P. Francisco De Florencia de la misma Compañia, Qualificador de el S. Officio de la Inquisicion, y Prefecto de Estudios Mayores en el Colegio de S. Pedro, y S. Pablo de Mexico. Tomo Primero
Con Licencia En Mexico Por Ivan Ioseph Gvillena Carrascoso. Año De M. DC. XCIV.
11 p.ℓ., 140, 140-159, 156-409 p., 1 ℓ., [18] p. 29cm. fol.
At head of title IHS.
Title in red and black.
Paging 140-159, 156-409 begin on a verso.
Added t.-p., engraved: ... Mich. Guer. Soc Ies Inve. & Sculp. Mex.
No more published.
License dated (10th p. ℓ.ᵛ) 1 May 1694.
Errata at end.
Palau(2)92348; Medina(Mexico)1569; Sabin 24810; Backer3:799; Streit 2:2299.

06064, before 1874

DA694 Fox, George, 1624-1691.
-F791   A Journal Or Historical Account Of The Life,
1   Travels, Sufferings, Christian Experiences and La-
        bour of Love in the Work of the Ministry, Of That
        Ancient; Eminent and Faithful Servant of Jesus
        Christ, George Fox; Who departed this Life in great
        Peace with the Lord, the 13th of the 11th Month, 1690.
        The First Volume. ...
          London, Printed for Thomas Northcott, in George-
        Yard, in Lombard-Street. M DC XCIV.
          25 p. ℓ., xviii, 200, 201*-280* p., 281*-284*
        numb. ℓ., 285*-188* (i.e. 288*), 189-423,
        428-632, [16] p. A⁴(A1 + ²A-M²) a⁴ b² B-20⁴
        2P² 3A-4E⁴ 4F⁶ 5A-6B⁴ 6C-6G². 30cm. fol.
          The "second volume" is A collection of many
        select and Christian epistles ... , 1st pub.
        London, 1698.
          Preface (2d-25th p. ℓ.) is signed by William
        Penn and has imprint at end: London, Printed
        and Sold by T. Sowle, at the Crooked Billet in
        Holly-well-lane, Shoreditch, and near the
        Meeting-House in White-hart-court in Grace-
        church-street, 1694. This is the same text
        as A brief account of the rise and progress
        of the people called Quakers, 1st pub. London,
        1694.
          Includes "testimonies" of Margaret Fox, "of
        some of the author's relations", "from our
        second-days morning meeting in London, the
        26th of the 11th month, 1690", and by Thomas
        Ellwood (p. i-xvii).
          Errata, last page.
          In many copies the leaf bearing p. 309-310
        is a cancel (cf. Smith(Friends)1:691). This
        copy has the cancelland. In some copies the
        leaf bearing p. 441-442 may be a cancel.
          In this copy the title-leaf is remounted,
        slightly affecting text.
          Sabin25352; Smith(Friends)1:690, 2:312;
        WingF1854.
11466, 1918

D694   Franck, Richard, 1624?-1708.
F822n   Northern Memoirs, Calculated for the Merid-
        ian of Scotland. Wherein most or all of the
        Cities, Citadels, Sea-ports, Castles, Forts,
        Fortresses, Rivers and Rivulets are compen-
        diously described. Together with choice Collec-
        tions of Various Discoveries, Remarkable Obser-
        vations, ... To which is added, The Contempla-
        tive & Practical Angler, ... Writ in the Year
        1658, but not till now made publick, By Richard
        Franck, Philanthropus. ...
          London, Printed for the Author. To be sold by
        Henry Mortclock [sic] at the Phenix, in St. Paul's
        Church-yard. 1694.
          xxxix, 304 p. 17cm. (18cm. in case) 8⁰
          Preliminary matter includes poems by Franck,
        John Richards, Mercurius Hermon, John Slator,
        Richard Johnson.
          "Advertisement. Rabbi Moses...to be sold by
        the Author at his House..." (p. 304).
          Wing F2064.
30067, 1947

D694   Gage, Thomas, 1603?-1656.
G133n   Nouvelle Relation, Contenant Les Voyages De
        Thomas Gage dans la Nouvelle Espagne, ses
        diverses avantures, & son retour par la Pro-
        vince de Nicaragua jusques à la Havane. Avec
        La Description De La Ville De Mexique... En-
        semble Une Description exacte des Terres &
        Provinces que possedent les Espagnols en toute
        l'Amerique, de la forme de leur Gouvernement
        Ecclesiastique & Politique, de leur Commerce,
        de leurs Mœurs, & de celles des Crioles, des
        Metifs, des Mulatres, des Indiens, & des Negres.
        Tome II.
          A Amsterdam, Chez Paul Marret, Marchand
        Libraire dans le Beurs-straat. M. DC. XCIV.
          6 p. ℓ., 316 p. 5 fold. plates, fold. map.
        15.5cm. 12⁰
          Added t.-p., engr.: Voyage de Thomas
        Gage. Tome II.
          Transl. from: A New Survey of the West-
        Indies; 1st pub. London, 1648, under title:
        The English-American his Travail by sea and
        land; or, A new survey ...
          This transl., which has been attributed to
        Adrien Baillet, 1st pub. Paris, 1676. A
        section on the Pokonchi language has been
        omitted in this edition. An edition of Tome I
        was pub. Amsterdam, Paul Marret, 1695.
          There is another edition of Tome II, which
        also has imprint Amsterdam, Paul Marret,
        1694, but with 318 p. main paging.
          In this copy the "Table Des Chapitres"
        (2d-5th p. ℓ.) is misbound among the last few
        leaves (as printed).
          JCB(2)2:1478; cf. Streit 2:2301; cf. Sabin
        26304; cf. Palau(2)96485; cf. Leclerc(1867)
        603, (1878)221.
03687B, before 1866

DB   Gt.Brit.--Parliament, 1693-1694--House of
-G7875   Commons.
1689   Votes Of The House of Commons. Martis 7
2   die Nov. 1693 [-Mercurii 25 die Aprilis, 1694].
          London, Printed by John Leake, in Jewin-street;
        and are to be Sold by Randal Taylor, near
        Amen-Corner, 1694.
          404 p. 29cm. fol.
          Caption titles; imprint at end of each number.
          Issued in pts. numbered 1-138.

Imprint, no. 1: London, Printed by Thomas Braddyll and Robert Everingham, and are to be sold at the Seven Stars In Ave-Mary-Lane [1693].
Imprint of no. 2-41, 45, 51-52 dated 1693.
Bound in Votes of the House of Commons, v. 2.
10376-5, 1914

DB -G7875 1689 2
Gt. Brit. --Parliament, 1694-1695--House of Commons.
Votes Of The House of Commons, In the Sixth Session of this Present Parliament: Held at Westminster The 12th Day of November, in the Sixth Year of the Reign of King William and Queen Mary, Anno Domini, 1694.
London, Printed and Sold by John Leake, in Jewen-street; near Aldersgate-street, MDCXCIV [-1695].
1 p. ℓ., 78, 77-420 p. 29cm. fol.
Issued in pts. numbered 1-134 and dated 12 Nov 1694 - 3 May 1695, each of which has caption title and imprint at end.
Imprint of nos. 1-94 is the same as general t.-p.
Imprint of nos. 95-134: London, Printed for Thomas Cockerill at the Three Leggs in the Poultry, and Timothy Goodwin at the Queen's Head against St. Dunstan's Church in Fleet-street... Nos. 95-99 are dated 1694; nos. 100-134 are dated 1695.
Bound in Votes of the House of Commons, v. 2.
10376-6, 1914

DB -G7875 1689 2
Gt. Brit. --Parliament, 1694-1695--House of Commons.
Votes Of The House of Commons. Sabbati 29 die Decembris, 1694. The Address to the King.
London, Printed and Sold by John Leake in Jewin-street. 1694.
1 ℓ. 29cm. 1/2° (Issued as a part of Gt. Brit. --Parliament, 1694-1695--House of Commons. Votes..., no. 33, London, 1694.)
Caption title; imprint at end.
At head of title paged 77 and numbered as pt. 33, the same as the preceding leaf.
Occasioned by the queen's death. Presented 30 Dec 1694.
Bound in Votes of the House of Commons, v. 2.
10376-6A, 1914

D694 H838r
Houghton, Thomas.
Royal Institutions: Being Proposals for Articles To Establish and Confirm Laws, Liberties, & Customs Of Silver & Gold Mines, To All The King's Subjects, in such Parts of Africa, and America, which are Now (or Shall be) Annexed to, and Dependant on the Crown of England. With Rules, Laws, and Methods of Mining, and Getting of Precious Stones; The Working and Making of Salt-Petre; And also, The Digging and Getting of Lead, Tin, Copper, and Dutch-Silver-Oars [sic] ... By Thomas Houghton, of Lime-Street.
Licensed, Daniel Poplar. London, Printed for the Author, 1694.
6 p. ℓ., 126 p. 15cm. 12°
Bound in contemporary calf.
Wing H2935; Sabin 33164; Kress 1846.
69-144

DA694 J54s
Jennings, Samuel, d. 1708.
The State of the Case, Briefly but Impartially given betwixt the People called Quakers, In Pensilvania, &c. in America, who remain in Unity; And George Keith, With some few Seduced by him into a Separation from them. As also a Just Vindication of my Self from the Reproaches and Abuses of those Backsliders. By Samuel Jennings. ...
London, Printed and Sold by T. Sowle, near the Meeting-house in White-Hart-Court in Grace-Church-Street, and at the Crooked-Billet in Hollywell-Lane near Shoreditch. 1694.
3 p. ℓ., 80 p. 16.5cm. 8°
Certificate dated (p. 77): 4th. of the 10th. Month, 1693.
Wing J670; Sabin 36048; Smith(Friends) 2:10.
11481, 1918

BA694 J91i
Juan de la Anunciación, d. 1701.
La Inocencia Vindicada. Respvesta, Qve El Rmo. Padre Fray Jvan De La Anunciacion, ... al presente General del Orden de Descalços, y Descalças de N. S. del Carmen de la Primitiva Observancia. Dá A Vn Papel Contra El Libro De La Vida Interior del Ilustrissimo, Excelentissimo, y Venerable señor D. Jvan De Palafox Y Mendoza, ... Obispo de la Puebla de los Angeles, Arçobispo electo de Mexico, Virrey, Presidente, Governador, y Capitan General de la Nueva-España, ...
En Sevilla, por Lvcas Martin de Hermosilla. [1694]
17 p. ℓ., 222, [12] p. 21cm. 4°
A reply to Paolo Segneri's Parere del Padre Pablo Señeri sopra la vita interiore ..., itself a reply to Juan de Palafox y Mendoza's Vida Interior.
"Tassa" dated (16th p. ℓ.v) 28 July 1694.
Errata, 16th p. ℓ.

Bound in contemporary vellum.
Palau(2)13501; Medina(BHA)1919; Sabin 36796n.

11798, 1919

DA694
J92g
The Judgment Given forth by Twenty Eight Quakers Against George Keith, And his Friends, With Answers to the said Judgment, declaring those Twenty Eight Quakers to be No Christians. As Also, An Appeal (for which several were Imprisoned, &c.) by the said George Keith, &c. to the Yearly Meeting, Sept. 1692. With a Full Account of the said Yearly Meeting, Signed by Seventy Quakers. ...
Printed at Pensilvania; and now Re-printed at London, for Richard Baldwin, near the Oxford-Arms in Warwick-lane. 1694.
1 p.l., 22 p. 20cm. 4°
Contains "A true Copy of Three Judgments ... With Two Answers to the said Judgments" by Thomas Budd, (1st pub. [Philadelphia, William Bradford, 1692]), "An Appeal from the Twenty Eight Judges" by George Keith (1st pub. [Philadelphia, William Bradford, 1692]), and "From the Yearly Meeting at Burlington ... 1692."
"Books lately Published ... " (p. 22).
License dated (t.-p.): Octob. 28th, 1693.
Wing J1173; Sabin37200; Smith(Friends)2:28

1198, 1906

DA696
K28s
Keith, George, 1639?-1716.
Arraignment Of Worldly Philosophy, Or, The False Wisdom: Its being a great hinderance to the Christian Faith; And a great Enemy to the True Divine Wisdom. By George Keith. ...
London: Printed for R. Levis, MDCXCIV.
28 p. 21cm. 4°
In this copy Keith's name on t.-p. is mutilated.
Bound as the 11th in a vol. of 11 works by Keith.
JCB(2)2:1467; WingK143; Smith(Friends) 2:29.

04855, before 1874

DA694
K28c
[Keith, George] 1639?-1716.
The Causeless Ground of Surmises, Jealousies and unjust Offences removed, in a full clearing of faithful Friends, and a sober vindication of my Innocency, and the Friends concerned with me; in relation to the late Religious Differences and Breaches among some of the People called Quakers in America.

London, Printed for R. Levis, 1694.
16 p. 20cm. 4°
Caption title, imprint at end.
Signed (p. 16): George Keith.
WingK149; Sabin37182; Smith(Friends)2:29.

1195, 1906

DA694
K28t
Keith, George, 1639?-1716.
A Chronological Account Of The Several Ages of the VVorld From Adam To Christ. And from thence continued to the End of the World ...
[New York, William Bradford] Printed in the Year 1694.
32 p. 19cm. (21cm. in case) 4° (Issued as a part of his Truth advanced in the correction of many gross & hurtful errors, [New York] 1694.)
Wing K154; Evans691; Sabin37187; Church746; Eames(NY)36; Smith(Friends)2:29.

5236A, 1909

DA694
K28f
[Keith, George] 1639?-1716.
A Further Discovery Of the Spirit of Falshood & Persecution In Sam. Jennings, And his Party that joyned with him in Pensilvania; and some Abettors that cloak and defend him here in England: In Answer to his scandalous Book, called The State of the Case.
London: Printed for R. Levis, 1694.
52 p. 21.5cm. 4°
Caption title; imprint at end.
Signed (p. 52): George Keith.
A reply to Jennings's, The state of the case, London, 1694.
Wing K170; Sabin37196; Smith(Friends)2:28; Church744.

1816, 1906

DA694
K28s
Keith, George, 1639?-1716.
A Seasonable Information and Caveat Against a Scandalous Book of Thomas Elwood, Called, An Epistle to Friends, &c. By George Keith. ...
London: Printed for R. Levis, 1694.
1 p.l., 40, 39-40 p. 20cm. 4°
A reply to Thomas Ellwood, An epistle to Friends, London, 1694.
"It was desired by John Raunce, that these Lines should be herewith Printed." (last p.) signed: J.R. [a reply to Thomas Ellwood's A fair examination of a foul paper ... , London, 1693]
WingK203; Sabin37214; Smith(Friends)2:29; 2:472.

1196, 1906

DA694 Keith, George, 1639?-1716.
K28t   Truth Advanced In The Correction Of Many Gross & hurtful Errors; Wherein is occasionally opened & explained many great and peculiar Mysteries and Doctrines of the Christian Religion. By George Keith. Whereunto is added, A Chronological Treatise of the several Ages of the World: ...
[New York, William Bradford] Printed in the Year 1694.
5 p.ℓ., 175, 180-184, 32 p. 19cm. (21cm. in case). 4°
Errata, 5th p.ℓ.^{v}.
Title-page mutilated affecting 1st line.
With, as issued, his A chronological account of the several ages of the world, [New York] 1694, with special t.-p., separate paging and signatures.
Bound in contemporary calf.
Wing K223; Evans 691; Sabin 37224; Church 745; Eames(NY)36; Smith(Friends)2:29; Dexter 2449.

5236, 1909

B682   [Ledesma, Joseph de]
-L864p El Fiscal Del Consejo En Favor De La Regalia, Y Tribvnales Reales del Reyno de Navarra. Sobre El conocimiento de los Articulos de Immunidad Local, y vso de las fuerças de que han vsado por Costumbre, y possession immemorial en aquel Reyno.
En Madrid Año de 1694.
8 p.ℓ., 103 numb. ℓ., [1] ℓ. 28cm. fol.
Cut (royal arms) on t.-p.
Signed at end: Lic. D. Ioseph de Ledesma.
Ms. annotations, perhaps in hand of J. L. López y Martínez.
Bound as no. 13 in a vol. with binder's title: Luis Lopez Obras.
Palau(2)134187n; Leclerc(1878)1826.8(this copy).

14019, 1925

C585   Leeds, Peregrine Osborne, 2d duke of, 1658-1729.
E96t   A Journal Of The Brest-Expedition, By The Lord Marquiss Of Caermarthen.
17   London, Printed for Randal Taylor, near Amen-Corner. 1694.
46 p. fold. map. 20cm. 4°
Imperfect: fold. map wanting; available in facsim.
Bound as no. 17 of 19 items in a vol. with binder's title: Tracts 1681-1701.
Wing L917.

11352-17, 1918

D694   Locke, John, 1632-1704.
-L814e An Essay Concerning Humane Understanding. In Four Books. Written by John Locke, Gent. The Second Edition, with large Additions. ...
London, Printed for Awnsham and John Churchil, at the Black Swan in Pater-Noster-Row, and Samuel Manship, at the Shop in Cornhill, near the Royal Exchange, MDCXCIV.
20 p.ℓ., 407, [11] p. 32.5cm. fol.
Errata, 8th p.ℓ.^{v}
First pub. London, 1690.
Bound in contemporary calf, rebacked.
Wing L2740.

06001, before 1841

BA694 Lumbier, Raimundo, 17th cent.
L957d Destierro De Ignorancias Fragmento Aureo, Preciossimo [sic] de la juiciosa erudicion Moral del Doctissimo, y Religiosissimo P.M. Fr. Raymundo, Lumbier. Dalo A La Estampa Por Orden, Y Con Mandato de su Ilustrissima el Señor Arçobispo en obsequio de las Señoras Religiosas, alibio de sus PP. Capellanes, y consuelo de todos sus Confessores. El Padre Prefecto De La Purissima Y Su Illma. Concede 40. Dias de Indulgencia à qualquiera persona de los interesados en la materia por cada vez, que leyere algun Parrapho destos, con que todos 7. montan docientos, y ochenta dias de Indulgencia.
Con licencia en Nexico [sic]: En la imprenta de Juan Ioseph Guillena Carascoço [sic], año de 1694.
4 p.ℓ., 44, [2] p. 15cm. 8°
License dated (4th p.ℓ.^{r}) 30 July 1694.
Taken from: Fragmentos morales en prosecución a la Suma de Aranda. Saragossa, 1680-1683.
Palau(2)143974; Medina(Mexico)1572.

62-323

DA694 Makemie, Francis, 1658-1708.
M235a An Answer To George Keith's Libel. Against A Catechism Published, by Francis Makemie. To which is Added, by way of Postscript. A Brief Narrative of a Late Difference among the Quakers, begun at Philadelphia.
Boston, Printed, by Benjamin Harris, at the Sign of the Bible, over-against the Blew-Anchor. MDCXCIIII.
6 p.ℓ., 103 p. 15.5cm. 8°
"Imprimatur" (1st p.ℓ.^{v}) dated 31 Mar. 1694.
"Christian Reader" (2d-3d p.ℓ.) signed by Increase Mather, James Allen, Samuel Willard, John Baily, and Cotton Mather.
"A True Copy of George Keith's Paper, Delivered to Mr. George Layfield, At

D. Math Mather, Cotton, 1663-1728.
C.409D The Life and Death Of the Reverend Mr. John Eliot, Who was the First Preacher Of The Gospel To The Indians in America. With an Account of the Wonderful Success which the Gospel has had amongst the Heathen in that Part of the World: And of the many strange Customs of the Pagan Indians, In New-England. Written by Cotton Mather. ... The Third Edition carefully Corrected.
London: Printed for John Dunton, at the Raven in the Poultrey. MDCXCIV.
4 p.ℓ., 168, [4] p. 14cm. 12⁰
First pub. under title: The triumphs of reformed religion in America. The life of the renowned John Eliot, Boston, 1691.
"A Letter concerning the Success of the Gospel amongst the Indians in New-England. Written by Mr. Increase Mather..." (p. 94-99) is Cotton Mather's transl. of De Successu Evangelii, London, 1688.
"Books lately Printed for J. Dunton, at the Raven in the Poultrey." last 4 pages.
JCB(2)2:1468; Sabin46383; WingM1121; Holmes(C)409D.
03689, before 1866

D. Math Mather, Cotton, 1663-1728.
C.354 The Short History of New-England. A Recapitulation Of Wonderful Passages Which have Occurr'd, First in the Protections, and then in the Afflictions, of New-England. With A Representation Of Certain Matters calling for the Singular Attention of that Country. Made at Boston-Lecture, in the Audience of the Great and General Assembly of the Province of the Massachusett-Bay, June 7. 1694. By Cotton Mather. ...
Boston. Printed by B. Green, for Samuel Phillips, at the Brick Shop, at the West End of the Exchange, 1694.
67 p. 14cm. 8⁰
Errata, p. 67.
Imperfect: p. 11-12 wanting; available in facsim.
JCB(2)2:1469; Evans700; WingM1152; Sabin 46509; Holmes(C.)354.
03688, before 1866

Pocamok in Mary-Land." (p. 5-19)
Bookseller's advertisement, last p.
Evans693; WingM307; Sabin44077; Smith(Anti-Quak)282; Baer(Md.)160.
3718, 1907

D. Math Mather, Nathaniel, 1631-1697.
M.27A The Righteousness of God Through Faith Upon All without Difference who believe. In Two Sermons on Romans 3.22. By Nathaniel Mather, Preacher of the Gospel.
London, Printed for Nathaniel Hiller at the Princes-Arms in Leaden-Hall-Street, over against St. Mary Axe. 1694.
2 p.ℓ., 76 p. 19.5cm. 4⁰
"To the Reader" (2d p.ℓ.) dated: 14th of the 2d Month, 1694.
Errata, 2d p.ℓ.ᵛ
JCB(2)2:1470; WingM1265; Holmes(M)27A.
06183, 1875?

BA694 Mendez, Francisco, d. 1713.
E74s Fvnebres Ecos Con Que Responde A Las Vozes del llanto de sus Soldados difuntos, la piedad de nuestro Gran Monarcha Carlos II. por las lenguas de las luzes, que enciende en la sumptuosa pyra, que en obediencia à sus ordenes Erige El Exᵐᵒ. Señor D. Gaspar De Cerda, Sylva, Y Mendoza. Conde de Galve, ... Virrey, Governador, y Capitan General de esta Nueva-España, Presidente de su Real Chancilleria de Mexico. Por cuyo mandato los repite, y encomienda â la luz publica El P. Francisco Mendez de la Compañia de Iesus, que los dispuso.
[Mexico, 1694]
[34] p. 20cm. 4⁰ (Issued as a part of: Escalante, Thomas. Sermon fúnebre, Mexico, 1694.)
Includes poetry.
Palau(2)162908; Medina(Mexico)1603; Wagner 64n.
13060A, 1921

BA694 Miranda Villaizan, Antonio de, 1657-1713.
M672e Elogio Fvneral A la immortal memoria del Illᵐᵒ. Sr. Dr. D. Ivan De Santiago De Leon Garavito, De el Consejo de su Magestad, Obispo de Guadalaxara, Reyno de la Nueva-Galicia, en las Honras hechas por el Ilustrissimo Venerable Dean, y Cavildo de aquella Santa Iglesia Cathedral. Predicolo El Lic. D. Antonio De Miranda Villa Y San Capitular de la misma Iglesia, ... Sacalo A Lvz El Sargento Mayor D. Alexandro Brabo De Gamboa, Alguacil mayor proprietario de el Tribunal del S. Officio de la Inquisicion de la Nueva-España, en el Reyno de la Nueva-Galicia. Y Lo Dedica. Al Ilustrissimo Señor Doctor D. Manuel Fernandez de Santa Cruz, del Consejo de su Magestad, Obispo de la Puebla de los Angeles.
Con licencia Impresso en Mexico en la Impren-

tade [sic] Juan Joseph Guillena Carrascoso Año de 1694.
10 p.ℓ., 13 numb. ℓ. 20.5cm. 4°
Coat of arms of dedicatee, recto 2d p.ℓ.
License (recto 9th p.ℓ.) dated 30 Sept. 1694.
Dedication by Alexandro Brabo de Gamboa.
Palau(2)172303; Medina(Mexico)1574.

6549, 1910

JC
M736u
1694

Monatliche Unterredungen Einiger Guten Freunde Von Allerhand Büchern und andern annemlichen Geschichten. Allen Liebhabern Der Curiositäten Zur Ergetzligkeit und Nachsinnen heraus gegeben. Januarius [-December] 1694.
[Leipzig] In Joh. Friedrichs Gleditschens Buch-Laden verlegts J. Thomas Fritsch. 1694.
12 pts. in 1 v.: Jan., 86 p. pl.; Febr., 1 p.ℓ., 87-178 p. pl.; Mart., 1 p.ℓ., 181-256 p. pl.; Apr., 1 p.ℓ., 257-332 p. pl.; Mai., 1 p.ℓ., 333-408 p. pl.; Jun., 1 p.ℓ., 409-452, 455-510 p. pl.; Jul., 9 p.ℓ., 511-602 p. incl. pl. pl.; Aug., 1 p.ℓ., 599-682 p. pl.; Sept., 1 p.ℓ., 683-774 p. pl.; Oct., 1 p.ℓ., 775-850, 887-894 p. pl.; Nov., 1 p.ℓ., 895-968 p. 2 plates; Dec., 1 p.ℓ., 969-1012, [30] p. pl. 16.5cm. 8°
Edited by Wilhelm Ernst Tentzel.
Each monthly part has special t.-p.
Cut (armillary sphere) on title-pages.
Imprint varies, Febr.-Mart.: ... Johann Friedrich Gleditschens...; Apr.-Nov.: Verlegt von J. Thomas Fritschen/Buchhl. 1694; Dec.: Verlegt von J. Thomas Fritsch. 1694.
The last part includes general indexes.
Bookseller's advertisements, p. 177-178, 332, 680-682.
Includes special t.-p. (Jul., 2d p.ℓ.): Der Brandenburgische Pelican/In Stifftung der Neuen Friedrichs-Universität zu Halle/ Der gelehrten Welt vor Augen gestellet. Leipzig/ Bey Joh. Thomas Fritschen/Buchhl. 1694.
In this copy there is a blank ℓ. at end.
Bound in contemporary vellum.

62-161 rev

D694
M891p

Morton, Richard, 1637-1698.
ΠΥΡΕΤΟΛΟΓΙΑΣ, Pars Altera: Sive, Exercitatio De Febribus Inflammatoriis Universalibus. Authore Richardo Morton, Colleg. Med. Londin. Socio. ...
Londini: Impensis Sam. Smith & Benj. Walford, Regiæ Societatis Typographorum, ad Insignia Principis in Cœmeterio D. Pauli, 1694.

24 p.ℓ., 511, [16] p. front. (port.) 20cm. 8°
First pub. Bremen, 1693.
"Ad Lectorem" dated (5th p.ℓ.ᵛ) 20 May 1694.
Errata, 24th p.ℓ.ᵛ
Preliminary matter includes commendatory poetry by Simon Ford, Clopton Havers, Josh. Lasher, James Augustus Blondel, and Richard Morton.
Booksellers' advertisement, p. [15-16] at end.
Includes numerous references to cinchona.
His [Pyretologia]: Seu exercitaciones de morbis universalibus actutis pub. London, Samuel Smith, 1692.
Bound in contemporary calf.
WingM2833.

69-680   Title transliterated: Pyretologia

D700
M937m

Moxon, Joseph, 1627-1691.
Mechanick Exercises: Or, The Doctrine Of Handy-Works [v.1]. By Joseph Moxon, late Member of the Royal Society, and Hydrographer to King Charles II.
London, Printed and Sold by J. Moxon, 1694.
14 nos. in 1 v. 18 plates. 20.5cm. 4°
Contents:—Smithing.—Joinery.—House-carpentry.—Turning.
First pub. London, 1677-1680. Vol. 2 (printing) pub. London, 1683-1684.
In this copy: the general t.-p. is misbound in the part on turning; the part on smithing is wanting; the part on house-carpentry (only) has a special t.-p. (misbound before the part on joinery); the last 6 p. in the part on turning, an 8-page booksellers' advertisement at end, plates 4-7, 16 are wanting; there are 2 copies of plate 13.
Bound with his Mechanick exercises ... applied to the art of bricklayers-works, London, 1700.
Wing M3016.

67-403-2

D700
M937m

Moxon, Joseph, 1627-1691.
Mechanick Exercises: Or, The Doctrine Of Handy-Works. Applied to the Art of House-Carpentry. By Joseph Moxon, late Member of the Royal Society, and Hydrographer to King Charles II. The Second Edition with Additions.
London, Printed and Sold by J. Moxon, at the Atlas in Warwick-Lane, and at his Shop in Westminster-hall right against the Parliament Stairs, 1694.

67-403-2
        1 p. ℓ., 115-168 p. 8-11 plates. 20.5cm. 4° (Issued as a part of his Mechanick exercises [v.1], London, 1694.)
    First pub. London, 1678.
    Title-page misbound before his Mechanick exercises ... the art of joinery, [London, 1694]
    Bound with his Mechanick exercises ... applied to the art of bricklayers-works, London, 1700.
    Cf. Wing M3016.

D700 M937m [Moxon, Joseph] 1627-1691.
    Mechanick Exercises: Or, The Doctrine of Handy-Works. Applied to the Art of Turning.
    [London, J. Moxon, 1694]
    171-186, 179-180, 185-234 p. 12-18 plates. 20.5cm. 4° (Issued as a part of his Mechanick exercises [v.1], London, 1694.)
    Caption title.
    First pub. London, 1678-1680.
    Imperfect: pl. 16 and p. 203-208 wanting.
    This copy contains 2 copies of pl. 13.
    Bound with his Mechanick exercises ... applied to the art of bricklayers-works, London, 1700.
    Cf. Wing M3016.
67-403-2

D700 M937m [Moxon, Joseph] 1627-1691.
    Mechanick Exercises: Or, The Doctrine of Handy-Works. The Art of Joynery.
    [London, J. Moxon, 1694]
    59-114 p. plates. 20.5cm. 4° (Issued as a part of his Mechanick exercises [v.1], London, 1694.)
    Caption title.
    First pub. London, 1678.
    Imperfect: plates wanting.
    Bound with his Mechanick exercises ... applied to the art of bricklayers-works, London, 1700.
    Cf. Wing M3016.
67-403-2

BA694 N238s Narváez, Juan de, ca. 1650-1706.
    Sermon Qve En la Celebridad de la Translacion del Cuerpo del glorioso Apostol de la India S. Francisco Xavier En la Parrochia de la Sancta Vera-cruz de esta Ciudad Predico El D^{or}. Don Ivan De Narvaez Cathedratico Proprietario de Prima de Sagrada Escriptura, en esta Real Vniversidad. Prevendado desta Sancta Iglesia Metropolitana, y Examinador Sinodal de este Arçobispado. ...
    Con Licencia En Mexico: Por la Viuda de Franciso [sic] Rodriguez Lupercio. En Lapuente de Palacio. Año de 1694.
    8 p. ℓ., 8 numb. ℓ., [4] p. illus. (port.) 19.5cm. 4°
    License dated (8th p. ℓ.^{v}) 8 Oct. 1694.
    In this copy the t.-p. and the 3d p. ℓ. are mutilated with slight loss of text; t.-p. and 3d p. ℓ.^{v} available in facsim.
    Palau(2)187726; Medina(Mexico)1576.
1056, 1905

B694 P256d El Parnaso Del Real Colegio De San Martin Postrado A Los Pies Del Exc.^{mo} Senor Conde De La Monclova, Virrey, Gouernador, y Capitan General de estos Reynos &c. Le Consagra. Como A Su Esclarecido, Y Real Patron vna varia, hermosa, y florida selva de Poesias en aplauso de la heroyca obra del Muelle que en el Puerto del Callao à fabricado su Excelencia, que es la octava Marauilla. Siendo Rector De Dicho Colegio Real de San Martin, el Reverendo Padre Manuel de Herla Cathedratico, ...
    Con Licencia De Los Superiores. En Lima, en la Imprenta de Joseph de Contreras, y Avarado. Año de 1694.
    4 p. ℓ., [191] p. 20.5cm. 4°
    JCB(2)2:1464; Sabin 61151; Vargas Ugarte903; Medina(Lima)485.
03683, before 1866

B694 P494c [Petrei, Juan Francisco] 1641-1695.
    Causas Eficientes, Y Accidentales Del Fluxo, Y Refluxo Del Mar ... Explicanse Con Ilvstracion muchos discursos, que hizo Don Francisco de Seyxas y Lobera en su Teatro Naual, y se dà solucion à sus dificultades: ... Sv Avtor, El Capitan Don Pedro de Castro [pseud.].
    Con Licencia: En Madrid. En la Imprenta de Manuel Ruiz de Murga. Año de 1694.
    12 p. ℓ., 276, [7] p. illus. (diagrs.) 21.5cm. 4°
    "Tassa" dated (9th p. ℓ.) 5 Oct. 1694.
    Errata, 9th p. ℓ.
    Author's prologue, p. ℓ. 11^v - 12^v, includes poetry.
    Intended as an elucidation of the Theatro

naval hydrographico of Francisco de Seixas y Lovera, Madrid, 1688 (which Petrei had examined and approved for the Council of the Indies).
 Palau(2)224284; Navarrete2:540-541; Backer 6:63.

69-345

DA694
S431n
[R]

[Scottow, Joshua] 1618-1698.
 A Narrative Of The Planting of the Massachusets Colony Anno 1628. With the Lords Signal Presence the First Thirty Years. Also a Caution from New-Englands Apostle, the Great Cotton, How to Escape the Calamity, which might Befall them or their Posterity. And Confirmed by the Evangelist Norton With Prognosticks from the Famous Dr. Owen. Concerning the Fate of these Churches, and Animadversions upon the Anger of God, in sending of Evil Angels among us. Published by Old Planters, the Authors of the Old Mens Tears. ...
 Boston Printed and Sold by Benjamin Harris, at the sign of the Bible over against the Blew-Anchor. 1694.
 2 p.ℓ., 75, [1] p., 1 ℓ. 15cm. 8º
 Dedication signed (2d p.ℓ.^{v}) J.S.
 Errata, last two pages.
 "A Funeral Elegy, Upon the Death of ... John Cotton" by John Norton, p. 75, [1].
 Imperfect: last 2 ℓ. wanting; available in facsim; t.-p. repaired.
 JCB(2)2:1472; Evans709; WingS2099; Sabin 78434; Dexter(Cong.)2445.

02283, 1860

D694
S467p

Seller, John, fl. 1658-1698.
 Practical Navigation: Or, An Introduction to the Whole Art. Containing The Doctrine of Plain and Spherical Triangles, Plain Mercator, Great-Circle Sailing; and Astronomical Problems. The Use of divers Instruments; as also of the Plain-chart, Mercator's Chart, and both Globes. Sundry Useful Tables in Navigation: And a Table of 10000 Logarithms, and of the Logarithm-Sines, Tangents, and Secants. By John Seller, Hydrographer to the King. The Seventh Edition, carefully Corrected.
 London; Printed by J. D. for the Author at the Hermitage in Wapping, and Richard Mount at the Postern on Tower-Hill, 1694.
 4 p.ℓ., 348, 353-355,[1], [55], [92] p. incl. illus., tables. 8 diagrs. 20cm. 4º
 A Table Containing Ten Chiliads Of Logarithms ... ([55] p. at end) and A Triangular Canon Logarithmical ... ([92] p. at end) each has a special t.-p. with imprint "London; Printed by John Darby, for John Seller and Richard Mount, 1694" but have continuous signatures.
 First pub. London, 1669.
 Preface dated (2d p.ℓ.^{r}) 26 May 1694.
 Numerous errors in paging.
 Preliminary matter includes laudatory poetry by Nathaniel Friend (2d p.ℓ.^{v}-3d p.ℓ.^{r}).
 Booksellers' advertisements, 3d p.ℓ.^{r} and p. [356]; advertisement by John Colson, teacher of mathematical sciences, 4th p.ℓ.^{v}
 Imperfect: 2 plates wanting and p.ℓ. 1-3 disintegrated with some loss of text; available in facsimile.
 Wing S2483B.

29379, 1943 rev

DA604
B258s

Their Majesties Colony Of Connecticut in New-England Vindicated, From the Abuses Of a Pamphlet, Licensed and Printed at New-York 1694. Intituled, Some Seasonable Considerations for the Good People of Connecticut. By an Answer Thereunto. ...
 Boston in New-England. Printed by Bartholomew Green. Anno Dom. 1694.
 43 p. 18.5cm. 4º
 "To the Reader" signed: J.A., W.P.; thus sometimes attributed to John Allyn and William Pitkin.
 Order to print, by the Governor and Assistants of Connecticut Colony, dated in Hartford, 23 April 1694 (p. 2).
 A reply to Bulkeley, Gershom. Some seasonable considerations ... [New York, 1694]
 Bound in early 18th century calf as the 6th in a vol. of six 17th century works.
 Sabin15860; Evans686; WingT845.

690, 1905 rev

B694
V297m

Vargas Machuca, Francisco de.
 Medicos Discvrsos, Y Practica De Cvrar El Sarampion, Y El fatal morbo, que sobrevino en estado de convalecencia a los q̃ lo padecieron el año passado de 93. Y Methodo Facil De Remediar Algvnas enfermedades, que pueden acaecer en la Sierra con con [sic] la explicacion de la essencia, y causas de las Verrugas regionales, y patrias, y modo de curarlas. Ofrecidos ... Por Sv Avtor El Doct. D. Francisco De Vargas Machuca Presbytero, Medico de su Excelencia Ilustrissima, y el Tribunal de el Santo Oficio. Examinador en su facultad, y Regente que fue de la Cathedra de Prima de Medicina, y actual Cathedratico de el

Methodo, y Arte curativa de Galeno en esta Real Vniversidad de S. Marcos, y Medico de el Real Hospital de San Bartholome, &c.
Con Licencia De Los Svperiores En Lima, por Joseph de Contreras, y Alvarado Año de 1694.
12 p. l., 50, 55-60 numb. l. 19cm. 4°
Approbation dated (11th p. l.ᵛ) 16 Oct. 1694.
With this is bound: Bermejo y Roldán, Francisco. Discvrso De La Enfermedad ... Lima, 1694.
JCB(2)2:1473; Sabin98608; Vargas Ugarte895.

03684, before 1866

BA694 V297o
Vargas Machuca, Francisco de.
Oracion Panegyrica Al Glorioso Apostol S Bartholome Patron Del Hospital Real de Pobres Negros Horros enfermos, viejos, è impedidos fundado en esta Nobilissima Ciudad de los Reyes. En Ocasion, Qve Se Estrenaron Las Salas, y Claustro con las demas oficinas, que por ruyna del formidable Temblor del año passado de 87. reedificò el Sargento mayor Manuel Fernandez Davila ... Dixola. El Doc. D. Francisco Vargas Machvca Presbitero Cathedratico del Methodo de Galeno en la Real Vniuersidad de S. Marcos ...
Con Licencia De Todos Los Svperiores. En Lima: En la Imprenta de Ioseph de Contreras, y Alvarado. Año de 1694.
11 p. l., 29 p. 18.5cm. 4°
License dated (11th p. l.ᵛ) 6 May 1694.
Medina(Lima)664.

64-82

CA679 V665s 8
Vieira, Antonio, 1608-1697.
Xavier Dormindo, E Xavier Acordado: Dormindo, Em tres Oraçoens Panegyricas no Triduo da sua Festa, ... Acordado, Em doze Sermoens Panegyricos, Moraes, & Asceticos, os nove da sua Novena, o decimo da sua Canonizaçaõ, o undecimo do seu dia, o ultimo do seu Patrocinio, Author O Padre Antonio Vieyra Da Companhia de Jesu, Prègador de Sua Magestade. Oitava Parte.
Lisboa, Na Officina de Miguel Deslandes, Impressor de Sua Magestade. A custa de Antonio Leyte Pereira, Mercador de Livros.
M. DC. LXXXXIV. Com todas as licenças necessarias, & Privilegio Real.
12 p. l., 536 p. 20cm. 4° (His Sermoens, 8. parte)
Dedication (2d-7th p. l.) by Baltasar Duarte.
License dated (11th p. l.ᵛ) 9 June 1694.
According to Leite "Deste vol. de 1694 há duas impressões do mesmo ano."

Bound in contemporary calf.
Rodrigues2510; Backer8:659; Leite9:197, 8:201; Innocencio1:290.

68-344

bDA694 W592q
[Whitehead, George] 1636?-1723.
The Quakers Vindication Against Francis Bugg's Calumnies: In his Scandalous Pamphlet, stiled, Something in Answer to the Allegations of the Quakers (in their Printed Case, Presented to the House of Commons, December 1693.) But his second Edition, Stiled The Converted Quakers Answer. Together with Francis Bugg's own Vindication of the People called Quakers, since he left them and turned to the Church of England.
[London, 1694]
4 p. 30.5cm. fol.
Signed (p. 4): George Whitehead.
Caption title.
Docket title: The Quakers Vindication and Buggs Testimony > against < Bugg's Calumnies.
A reply to: Francis Bugg, Something in answer to the allegations of the Quakers. [London, 1693] and to his New Rome arraigned. The 2nd edition. London, 1694.
"To the Members of Parliament; And others to whom Bugg's said Pamphlet has been delivered" (p. 4) signed by 32 Quakers.
WingW1950; Smith(Friends)2:901.

8391, 1912

DA694 W695c
Willard, Samuel, 1640-1707.
The Character Of a Good Ruler. As it was Recommended in a Sermon Preached before his Excellency the Governour, and the Honourable Counsellors, and Assembly of the Representatives of the Province of Massachusetts-Bay in New-England. On May 30. 1694. Which was the Day for Election of Counsellors for that Province. By Samuel Willard, Teacher of a Church in Boston.
Boston Printed by Benjamin Harris, for Michael Perry, under the West-End of the Town-House. 1694.
3 p. l., 31 p. 15cm. 8°
Evans711; WingW2270; Sabin104071.

16852, 1936

1695

BA695 Argaiz y Vargas, Francisco Crisanto de,
A261d fl. 1694.
Las Dos Niñas De Los Ojos De Christo Sr. Nuestro, Y De Su Iglesia, En Cuya Metaphora El Br. Don Francisco Chrysanto De Argaiz, Y Vargas, Secretario, y discipulo de la Real Universidad de la Compañia de Jesvs de la Ciudad de Merida de Yucathan. Discurrio En Vn Sermon A las Reverendas Madres Sor Maria Manuela De Santa Rosa, y Sor Antonia De Santa Florencia. Primas hermañas [sic] suyas, è hijas del Sargento mayor Don Pedro Pardo de Lagos, y de Doña Maria de Argaiz Predicolo El dia que Professaron, que fué el de veinte y cinco de Noviembre de el Año de mil seiscientos y Noventa y quatro: dia de la Gloriosa Santa Catharina V. y M, en el Convento de Nuestra Señora de la Consolacion de Señoras Religiosas. Dedicalo Al Sanctissimo Mysterio de la Immaculada Concepcion de la Reyna de los Cielos, cuyo Orden se observa en aquel Santo Convento.
Con Licencia En Mexico, En la Imprenta de los Herederos de la Viuda de Bernardo Calderon, en la calle de S. Agustin. Año de 1695.
8 p.ℓ., 23 p. 19.5cm. 4°
Cut on t.-p.
License dated (verso 8th p.ℓ.) 7 Nov 1695.
Medina(Mexico)1581.

1057, 1905

BA695 Avendaño Suares de Sousa, Pedro de, b. ca.
A951s 1654.
Sermon Del Domingo De Ramos, Que en la Santa Iglesia Cathedral de la Puebla de los Angeles. Predicò D. Pedro De Avendaño, Suares De Sousa A 27. de Março de 1695. años. Sacalo A Luz El D.r Y M.o D. Miguel Gonzalez de Valdeoceras, Rector, que ha sido de la Real Vniversidad de Mexico. Y Lo Dedica Al General D. Diego Fernandez De Santillan Cavallero del Orden de Santiago, Governador, que ha sido de los Partidos de Teposcolula, y San Antonio Sochitepec.
Con licencia en Mexico, en la Imprenta de Juan Joseph Guillena Carrascoso Impressor, y Mercader de libros Año 1695.
4 p.ℓ., 10 numb. ℓ., [3] p. 19.5cm. 4°
License dated (verso 4th p.ℓ.) 20 July 1695.
Coat of arms of dedicatee, recto 2d p.ℓ.
Dedication, 2d p.ℓ., by Miguel González de Valdeosera.

Palau(2)20150; Andrade, V de P:1013; cf. Backer1:683-684; Medina(Mexico)1582.

1061, 1905

BA673 Ayeta, Francisco de.
-P434m Señor. Fray Francisco de Ayeta, Padre de la Provincia del Santo Evangelio de Mexico, y Procurador General de todas las de las Indias. Dize: Que deseando su Religion evitar todo genero de litigios con los Reverendos Obispos, por las malas consequencias, que de ellos nacen, reconociendo que las muchas, y repetidas, que se han experimentado de 55. años a esta parte han nacido del pleyto, que tiene desde el año de 40. con la Clerecia de la Puebla, sobre la remocion de 34. Doctrinas, que el muy Reverendo, y Venerable Don Iuan de Palafox, quitò à la Religion, hallandose Obispo de la Puebla, ...
[Madrid? 1695]
14 numb. ℓ. 31.5cm. fol.
Title from caption and beginning of text.
Bound as the 4th of 5 items with: Perea Quintanilla, Miguel de. Manfiesto a la reyna ... [Mexico? 1673?]

04155, 1870

BA695 [Ayeta, Francisco de]
-A977u Vltimo Recvrso De La Provincia De San Joseph De Yucathan; Destierro De Tinieblas, En Qve Ha Estado Sepvltada Sv Inocencia, Y Confvndidos Svs Meritos. Jvsticia Desagraviada, Y Hasta Aora No Defendida, Ni Debidamente Manifestada. Pleyto Con La Clerecia De Yvcathan. Sobre Diferentes Doctrinas, Qve Con Violentos Despojos, Vnos Con Mano De Jvsticia, Y Otros Sin Ella, Se Han Vsvrpado a Dicha Provincia.
[Madrid, 1695?]
2 p.ℓ., 200, 123, [1] numb. ℓ. 30cm. fol.
Signed (ℓ. 200^v): Fr. Francisco de Ayeta.
Reference (numb. ℓ. 66^r, 2d count) dated 1695.
Palau(2)20801; Medina(BHA)6241.

2048, 1906

F677 Berkel, Adriaan van, fl. 1670-1689.
B954c Amerikaansche Voyagien, Behelzende een Reis na Rio De Berbice, Gelegen op het vaste Land van Guiana, aande Wilde-kust van America, Mitsgaders een andere na de Colonie van Suriname, Gelegen in het Noorder Deel van het gemelde Landschap Guiana. Ondermengd met

alle de byzonderheden noopende de Zeden, Gewoonten, en Levenswijs der Inboorlingen, Boom- en Aardgewassen, Waaren en Koopmanschappen, en andere aanmerkelijke zaaken. Beschreven Door Adriaan van Berkel, Vercierd met kopere Plaaten.

Tot Amsterdam, By Johan Ten Hoorn, Boekverkooper tegen over het Oude Heeren Logement, inde Historischryver 1695.

4 p.ℓ., 139, [140-143] p. 2 fold. plates. 25.5cm. 4º

Cut on t.-p.

Added half title, engr.: Amerikaansche Voyagien Naar Rio De Berbice En Suriname. Signed: Caspar Luyken f.

Preliminary matter includes poetry signed: J. Schriek.

Bound with: Burg, P. van der. Curieuse beschrijving, Rotterdam, 1677.

JCB(2)2:1474; Sabin4874; Muller(1872)92 (this copy); Scheepvaart Mus.:280; Tiele95.

02521B, 1851

DA695
B582p
[R]

Bible--O.T.--Psalms--English--Paraphrases-- ca. 1695--Bay Psalm Book.

The Psalms Hymns And Spiritual Songs, Of The Old and New-Testament, Faithfully Translated into English Meetre [sic]. For the use, edification and Comfort of the Saints in publick and private; especially in New-England. ...

[Boston? John Allen and Vavasour Harris for Samuel Phillips? ca. 1695]

376, [6] p. 14cm. 12º

Bay Psalm Book; 1st pub. Cambridge, Mass., 1640.

Typographically very similar to the "8th edition", which has imprint: Boston, Printed by John Allen, and Vavasour Harris, for Samuel Phillips, at the Brick-Shop, near the Town-House. 1695.

Imperfect: lower half of t.-p. and p. 195-214 wanting.

Cf. WingB2594; cf. Evans714; cf. Holmes (M.)53-D.

31262, 1953

D695
B848e

Brewster, Sir Francis, fl. 1674-1702.

Essays On Trade And Navigation. In Five Parts. The First Part. By Sir Francis Brewster, K^t. Licensed, January 3. 169$\frac{4}{5}$.

London: Printed for Tho. Cockerill, at the Three Legs in the Poultrey, over-against the Stocks-Market. MDCXCV.

1 p.ℓ., xi p., 1 ℓ., 126, [2] p. 16.5cm. 8º

No more published.

Includes "Of the New-found-land Fishing" (p. 68-74) and many other references to America.

Bookseller's advertisement, p. [1-2] at end.

Bound in contemporary calf, rebacked. WingB4434; Sabin7778; Kress1867.

71-302

BA630
-M285s

Calderón, Pedro, 1637-1708.

Memorial Del Reverendissimo Padre Maestro Pedro Calderon, de la Compañia de Jesvs, Procurador General de la Provincia de Nuevo Reyno, y Quito, presentado en el Real, y Supremo Consejo de las Indias en 30. de Março de 1693. En Respvesta De Otro Impresso Del Reverendissimo Padre Maestro Fr. Ignacio de Quesada, del Orden de Santo Domingo, Procurador General de su Provincia de Santa Cathalina Martir de Quito. Dalo A La Estampa. Don Geronimo Lezcano, Y Sepvlbeda, Doctor en ambos Derechos.

Impresso con licencia en Colonia en la Oficina de Hermano Dehmen, año de 1695.

2 p.ℓ., 54 numb. ℓ. 28cm. fol.

Memorial concerning the disputes of the Jesuits and the Dominicans in Quito about academic degrees.

A reply to: Ignacio de Quesada. Memorial svmario en la cavsa del Real Collegio de San Fernando..., Madrid, 1692.

Errata, 2d p.ℓ.^{v}

Bound as the 3d of 3 items with: Juan de Mañozca. Señor. El Licenciado Iuan de Mañozca Inquisidor Apostolico de la ciudad de Lima... [Madrid? ca. 1630]

Palau(2)39736; Medina(BHA)1937; Sabin9886; Backer2:539; Streit2:2305.

5521, 1909

DA695
C178a

Cambridge, Mass.--Ministers' Association.

The Answer Of Several Ministers in and near Boston, To that Case of Conscience, Whether it is Lawful for a Man to Marry his Wives own Sister?

Boston in N.E. Printed and Sold by Bartholomew Green. 1695.

8 p. 14.5cm. (15.5cm. in case) 8º

Drawn up by Increase Mather as a report of the Cambridge Association of Ministers. Signed at end: Increase Mather [and others].

Evans729; WingM1182; Sabin46631; Holmes (I.)5A; Dexter(Cong.)2461; Brinley722(this copy).

66-224

BA695 Carrillo, José, fl. 1670-1695.
C317s   Sermon Panegyrico En La Solemnidad Principal, Que Celebra La Illustre Archi-Cofradia De La Cinta A Maria Santissima Señora Nuestra Con El Titulo de la Consolacion, Qve Predico El R. P. M. Fr. Joseph Carrillo Rector que ha sido del Colegio de San Pablo, Maestro por la Ordẽ y por la Real Universidad, en el Augusto Convento de Mexico, la Dóminica Infra octavam del gran P. y Doctor de la Iglesia San Augustin, dia señalado para dicha Fiesta, que al año de 95. fue treze Post Pentec. con la degollacion de San Juan Baptista, y patente el Santissimo Sacramento. Dalo A La Imprenta, A Repugnancia De su Autor, vn Sacerdote devoto de la Soberana Reyna, cuyo Patrocinio reproduce, siguiendo la Religiosa Idea, q̃ al declamarlo, se lo dedicô reverente.
    Con licencia en Mexico: por Iuan Ioseph Guillena Carrascoso Impresor, y Mercader de Libros. Año de 1695.
    6 p. ℓ., [1], 22 p. illus. 19.5cm. 4°
    Paging 1-22 begins on a verso.
    Ecclesiastical opinion and license dated (verso 4th p. ℓ.) 4 Mar 1695.
    Palau(2)45483; Medina(Mexico)1587; Santiago Vela 1:619.
1064, 1905

BA695 Castilla, Miguel de, 1652-1713.
C352ℓ   El Leon Mystico Oraçion Fvnebre, Y Elogio Panegyrico Del Illmo. y Rev^{mo}. Señor Dr. D. Jvan De Santiago De Leon Garavito De immortal memoria. Del Consejo de su Magestad Obispo de Guadalaxara, Reyno de la Nueva Galicia. Dixolo El Padre Migvel De Castilla Professo De la Compañia de Jesvs Cathedratico de Theologia en el Colegio de la misma Ciudad, ... En el sumptuoso Anniversario Cabo de Año, que á expensas, y cuidado del Lic. D. Pedro de Alcarazo Clerigo Presbytero Domiciliario de dicho Obispado, ... el dia 15. de Julio de 1695. Sacalo A Lvz El Lic. D. Juan Antonio Chipres Vidagaray, y Saraza, Presbytero, Honesta Persona del Tribunal del Santo Officio, ... Y Lo Dedica Al Señor D. Juan Martinez Gomez Dignissimo Canonigo de dicha Santa Iglesia, ...
    Con Licencia En Mexico, por Iuan Ioseph Guillena Carrascoso. [1695]
    9 p. ℓ., 13 numb. ℓ., [4] p. 19.5cm. 4°
    License dated (9th p. ℓ.) 22 Aug. 1695.
    Dedication (2d-5th p. ℓ.) by Juan Antonio Chipres Vidagaray y Saraza.
    Includes poetry [by Joseph de Arriola], p. 1-3, and [by Fernando Reinoso], p. 3-4.
    Palau(2)47996; Medina(Mexico)1589; Backer 2:848.
1065, 1905

BA695 Castro, José de, d. 1711.
C355v   Vida Del Siervo De Dios Fr. Jvan De Angulo, Y Miranda Español Indiano, Religioso Lego Del Orden de Menores de la Regular Observancia de la Provincia de los Zacatecas ... La Da A La Estampa El Doctor Don Jvan Ignacio de Castorena, y Vrzua Clerigo Presbitero. Escribela El M. R. P. M. Fr. Ioseph De Castro Zacatecano; Exlector de Sagrada Theologia, Notario Apostolico, Custodio que passò à Roma, y Chronista de la Santa Provincia de San Francisco de los Zacatecas:
    Con Licencia De Los Svperiores En Mexico, por Doña Maria de Benavides, Viuda de Iuan de Ribera. Año de 1695.
    16 p. ℓ., 26 numb. ℓ. illus. (incl. port.) 20cm. 4°
    License dated (13th p. ℓ.^r) 16 Aug. 1695.
    Preliminary matter includes poetry by Juan Ignacio de Castorena y Ursúa.
    Bound in contemporary vellum.
    Palau(2)48715; Medina(Mexico)1590; Streit 2:1590.
2990, 1907

D   [Charpentier, François] 1620-1702.
Scott   A Treatise Touching the East-Indian-Trade:
1   Or, A Discourse (Turned out of French into English) Concerning the Establishment of a French Company For the Commerce of the East--Indies. To which are Annexed the Articles, and Conditions, Whereupon the said Company For the Commerce of the East-Indies is Established.
    Edinburgh, Re-printed by the Heirs and Successors of Andrew Anderson, Printer to His most Excellent Majesty, Anno Dom. 1695.
    2 p. ℓ., 52 p. 20cm. 4°
    Transl. by Henry Brome from Discours d'un fidele sviet dv roy touchant l'establissement d'une compagnie françoise pour le commerce des Indes Occidentales, 1st pub. Paris, 1664. This transl. 1st pub. London, 1664.
    Reprinted to promote the Company of Scotland trading to Africa and the Indies. Preface (2d p. ℓ.) signed: By a True Lover of Trade.
    Wing C3716; Scott 1.
1438, 1906

BA695 Contreras y Pacheco, Miguel de, fl. 1673-1698.
C764s   Sermon De La Gloriosa Virgen, Y Martyr Santa Barbara Mistico Tres superiormente ajustado con sus virtudes, laureolas, y singularidad, por las voces de la Solfa, Que Declamô à onze de Diziembre en el Convento de Señor S.

Bernardo Abad, custodia de purezas consagradas, Parayso de angelicas perfecciones con el nombre de Maria en su Aparicion De Guadalupe El Br. Don Migvel De Contreras, Y Pacheco, ... Restituyelo de justicia à la famosa, grave, celebre Capilla de la Metropolitana Iglesia, vniversidad nobilissima, Santuario de cultos, Militante Empireo; y à su insigne Maestro Antonio De Salazar, que â crecidos gastos de la Octava añaden prorateado entre si el costoso de su Impression.
   Con licencia en Mexico por los Herederos de la Viuda de Bernardo Calderon. Ano de 1695.
   7 p. ℓ., 18 numb. ℓ. 20cm. 4⁰
   Licenses dated (verso 7th p. ℓ.) 9 June 1694.
   Palau(2)60822; Medina(Mexico)1591.

1063, 1905

DA695
C939g
   Croese, Gerard, 1642-1710.
   Gerardi Croesi Historia Quakeriana, Sive De vulgò dictis Quakeris, Ab ortu illorum usque ad recèns natum schisma, Libri III. In quibus præsertim agitur de ipsorum præcipuis antecessoribus, & dogmatis (ut & similibus placitis aliorum hoc tempore) factisque, ac casibus, memorabilibus.
   Amstelodami, Apud Henricum & Viduam Theodori Boom. 1695.
   8 p. ℓ., 581, [1] p. 16cm. 8⁰
   Title in red and black.
   Cut on t.-p.; includes motto "Tandem Fit Arbor Surculus" and initials "HDB" (similar to Bibliotheca belgica II 19 (Amsterdam) Boom 2).
   Errata, last page.
   Bound in contemporary vellum.
   Sabin17583; Smith(Friends)1:480; Baer(Md.)164.

67-216

D695
C952e
   [Crouch, Nathaniel] 1632?-1725?
   The English Hero: Or, Sir Francis Drake Reviv'd. Being a full Account of the Dangerous Voyages, Admirable Adventures, Notable Discoveries, and Magnanimous Atchievements of that Valiant and Renowned Commander ... Revised, Corrected, Inlarged, reduced into Chapters with Contents, and beautified with Pictures. By R. B. The fourth Edition Inlarged.
   Licensed and Entred. London, Printed for Nath. Crouch at the Bell in the Poultrey near Cheapside, 1695.
   2 p. ℓ., 174, [14] p. illus., front. (port.). 15cm. 12⁰
   First pub. London, 1687.
   Booksellers' advertisement, p. [3-14] at end.
   JCB(2)2:1475; WingC7322; Sabin9500.

03690, before 1866

BA695
D352o
   Delgado y Buenrostro, Antonio, fl. 1676-1696.
   Oracion Evangelica Del Milagroso Indice De La Providencia El Inclito Patriarca San Cayetano Que Hizo En la Iglesia de la Santa Veracruz, Oratorio del Glorioso San Felipe Neri de la Puebla de los Angeles año de 1694, Que Dedica Al Mvy Illvstre Señor Don Bartolomè Josef Antonio Ortiz de Casqueta, Cavallero del orden de Santiago, Marquès de Altamira, &c. El Licenciado Don Antonio Delgado y Buenrostro, ...
   Con licencia, Impresso en la Puebla de los Angeles, en la Imprenta de Diego Fernandez de Leon. Año de 1695.
   6 p. ℓ., 28 p. 20cm. 4⁰
   Engraved coat of arms of dedicatee (recto 2d p. ℓ.): Mich. Amat. excud.
   License dated (recto 6th p. ℓ.): 26 Jan 1695.
   Palau(2)4:70115; Medina(Puebla)170.

1066, 1905

BA695
D568g
   Diez de San Miguel y Solier, Nicolás Antonio, d. 1716.
   La Gran Fee Del Centurion Español: Sermon Moral, Que En La Capilla Del Santo Oficio de la Inquisicion desta Ciudad de los Reyes Lima, el primer Iueues de Quaresma Predico El Doct. D. Nicolas Antonio Diez De San Miguel, y Solier, Doctor en Sagrada Theologia por esta Real Vniversidad, Racionero entero desta S. Iglesia Metropolitana, Examinador Synodal deste Arçobispado, y Calificador del Santo Oficio, en 4. de Febrero de 1693 ...
   Con Licencia En Lima. Por Joseph De Contreras, Y Alvarado Impressor de su Magestad, y del S. Oficio. Año de 1695.
   27 p. ℓ., 12 numb. ℓ. plate (coat of arms). 19cm. 4⁰
   Dedication dated (20th p. ℓ.ᵛ) 30 Apr. 1695.
   Preliminary matter includes poetry, 25th p. ℓ. signed "F.M.L.A.", 26th-27th p. ℓ. signed "D.P.I.B."
   Sabin20136; Medina(Lima)665.

70-466

D695
D611o
   A Discourse Of The Duties on Merchandize, More Particularly of that on Sugars, Occasionally Offer'd, In Answer to a Pamphlet, Intituled, The Groans of the Plantations, &c. Exposing The Weakness of the said Pamphlet, ... By a Merchant.
   London, Printed in the Year, 1695.
   2 p. ℓ., 32 p. 22.5cm. 4⁰
   A reply to: Edward Littleton, <u>The groans of the plantations</u>, London, 1689.
   "The following Papers were Written in the

DA695 Ellwood, Thomas, 1639-1713.
E47t   Truth Defended: And The Friends thereof
       Cleared, From The False Charges, Foul Re-
       proaches, and Envious Cavils, cast upon It and
       Them, by George Keith, (An Apostate from
       them) In Two Books by him lately Published: The
       One being Called, A True Copy of a Paper given
       into the Yearly Meeting of the People called
       Quakers, &c. The Other, The Pretended Yearly
       Meeting of the Quakers, their Nameless Bull of
       Excommunication, &c. ... By Thomas Ellwood.
       ...
          London. Printed and Sold by T. Sowle, near
       the the [sic] Meeting-House in White-Hart-Court
       in Gracious Street. 1695.
          171 p. 17cm. 8°
          Keith's A True copy of a paper given into the
       Yearly Meeting, 1st pub. London, 1695; his
       The Pretended Yearly Meeting, 1st pub. London,
       1695.
          Dated (p. 160): The 12th of the 5th Month,
       1695.
          Errata, at end.
          In this copy t.-p. wanting; available in facsim.
       WingE629; Smith(Friends)1:566; McAlpin4:515.
8394, 1912

BA695 Espinosa Medrano, Juan de.
-E77n   La Nouena Marauilla Nvebamente Hallada
       En los Panegiricos Sagrados q'en varias Fes-
       tiuidades dixo el Sor Arcediano D^{or} D.
       Ivan De Espinosa Medrano primer Canonigo
       Magistral Tesorero Chantre y Finalmente
       Arcediano de la Cathedral del Cuzco en los
       Reynos del Piru. Presentolos Con Fineza
       Al Orden del gran Patriarca S^{to} Domingo el
       M^{o} Agustin Cortez de la Cruz Capellan Real
       de la gran Ciudad del Cuzco Dicipulo [sic]
       del Autor que los saca a luz y los imprime
       a su costa.
          Romæ Sup. Permissu Impresso en Vall^{d}·
       por Joseph de rueda Año de 1695 ...
          10 p.ℓ., 301, 302-331 p. 29cm. fol.
          Engraved t.-p., signed: B. Thiboust Sculp.
          "Svma De La Tassa" dated (5th p.ℓ.^{v}) 29
       Apr. 1695.
          Paging 302-331 begins on a recto.
          Errata, 5th p.ℓ.^{v}
          Palau(2)82811; Medina(BHA)1939; Zegarra
       140.
5514, 1909

          Year 1689 ..." ("Advertisement", 2d p.ℓ.^{v}).
       JCB(2)2:1477; WingD1604; Sabin20242; Kress
       1888.
05944, before 1866.

E695   [Foigny, Gabriel de] 1630?-1692.
F658v   Voyage De La Terre Australe Par M^{r}. Sadeur
       [pseud.]. Avec Ses Avantures dans la découverte
       de ce pays jusques icy inconnu & les particu-
       larités du séjour qu'il y fit pendant trente-
       cinq ans & son retour. Contenant Les Cou-
       tumes Et Les Moeurs Des Australiens ...
          A Lyon, Chez Jean-Bapt. & Nicolas De
       Ville, ruë Merciere, à la Science. M.DC.XCV.
          9 p.ℓ., 267 p. 14.5cm. 12°
          First pub. Vannes [i.e. Geneva] 1676, under
       title: La terre australe connue. The present
       ed., however, follows the text of the Paris,
       1692, ed. pub. under title: Les avantures de
       Jacques Sadeur.
          Bound in contemporary calf.
69-544

EB   France--Sovereigns, etc., 1643-1715 (Louis
-W&A   XIV).   30 May 1695
354.1   Arrest Du Conseil D'Estat Du Roy. Sa
       Majesté Y Estant. Du 30. May 1695. Qui Or-
       donne Qu'à commencer du mois de Juillet pro-
       chain, les Castors seront receus au Bureau des
       Fermes à Quebec, sur trois sortes & qualitez
       Et Regle le prix qu'en doivent payer Me Pierre
       Pointeau, ses Commis & Préposez, aux termes
       & en la maniere accoûtumée.
          [Paris, 1695]
          4 p. 26.5cm. (32cm. in case) 4°
          Caption title.
          Cf. Wroth & Annan354.
31741, 1955

EB   France--Sovereigns, etc., 1643-1715.
F8355   (Louis XIV).   12 Oct 1695
1695   Reglement Du Roy, Pour la Police & Dis-
1   cipline des Compagnies que Sa Majesté entre-
       tient dans les Isles Françoises de l'Amerique.
       Du 12. Octobre 1695.
          A Paris, Chez Estienne Michallet, premier
       Imprimeur du Roy, ruë S. Jacques, à l'Image
       S. Paul. M.DC.XCV.
          19 p. 25cm. 4°
          Cut (royal arms) on t.-p.
          Wroth&Annan357; Actes Royaux18614.
1456, 1906

DA695 Friends, Society of--Philadelphia Yearly
F911o   Meeting.
          Our Antient Testimony Renewed. Con-
       cerning our Lord and Saviour Jesus Christ,
       The Holy Scriptures, And The Resurrection.
       Occasioned at this time by several Unjust

Charges published against us, and our Truly Christian Profession, by some Late Adversaries, who have Unfairly and Untruly Misrepresented us. Given forth by a Meeting of Publick Friends, and Others, at Philadelphia in Pensylvania. ...
London, Printed and Sold by T. Sowle, in White-Hart-Court in Gracious-Street. 1695.
16 p. 17cm. 8°
In reply chiefly to George Keith.
Reprinted, with a special t.-p. bearing the same imprint, as a part of: Croese, Gerard. The general history of the Quakers, London, 1696.
Wing 0591; cf. Sabin 57908; Smith (Friends) 1:760.

8094, 1911

D695 G133n
Gage, Thomas, 1603?-1656.
Nouvelle Relation, Contenant Les Voyages De Thomas Gage dans la Nouvelle Espagne, ses diverses avantures; & son retour par la Province de Nicaragua, jusques à la Havane. Avec La Description De La Ville de Mexique... Ensemble Une Description exacte des Terres & Provinces que possedent les Espagnols en toute l'Amerique, de la forme de leur Gouvernement Ecclesiastique & Politique, de leur Commerce, de leurs Mœurs, & de celles des Criolles, des Metifs, des Mulatres, des Indiens, & des Negres. Tome I.
A Amsterdam, Chez Paul Marret, dans le Beurs-straat proche le Dam à la Renommée. M. DC. LXXXXV.
12 p.ℓ., 200, 178 p. 6 fold. plates, 3 fold. maps. 16.5cm. 12°
Added t.-p., engr.: Voyage De Thomas Gage Tome. I. P. Picard fec.
Transl. from: A New Survey of the West-Indies; 1st pub. London, 1648, under title: The English-American his Travail by sea and land; or, A new survey ...
This transl., which has been attributed to Adrien Baillet, 1st pub. Paris, 1676. A section on the Pokonchi language has been omitted in this edition.
Tome II was pub. (2 editions) with imprint Amsterdam, Paul Marret, 1694.
Bound in contemporary calf.

D695 G133n cop.2
—— ——Another copy. 15.5cm.
Imperfect: one plate wanting.
JCB(2)2:1478; cf. Streit 2:2301; Sabin 26304; Palau(2)96485; cf. Leclerc(1867)603; (1878)221.

04736, before 1874
03687A, before 1866

DB -G7875 1689 2
Gt.Brit.--Parliament, 1694-1695--House of Commons.
The Humble Representation Of The House of Commons To His Majesty.
London, Printed and Sold by John Leake, in Jewin-street, near Aldersgate street, MDC XCIV [i.e. 1695].
229-230 p. 29cm. 1/2° (Issued as a part of Gt.Brit.--Parliament, 1694-1695--House of Commons. Votes..., no. 85, London, 1694 [/5].)
Caption title; imprint at end.
Concerns irregularities of military finance, especially in a regiment commanded by Colonel Fardinando Hastings. Presented 4 Mar 1694/5.
Bound in Votes of the House of Commons, v. 2.

10376-6B, 1914 rev 3

DB -G7875 1689 2
Gt.Brit.--Parliament, 1694-1695--House of Lords.
The Humble Address Of the Right Honourable the Lords Spiritual & Temporal In Parliament Assembled, Presented to His Majesty The Seventh Day of March, 1694[/5]. And His Majesties Gracious Answer Thereunto.
London, Printed by Charles Bill and the Executrix of Thomas Newcomb, deceas'd, Printers to the Kings most Excellent Majesty. 1694[/5].
4 p. 29cm. fol.
Urges strengthening the navy.
Order to print dated 8 Mar 1694[/5].
Bound in Votes of the House of Commons, v.2, before Votes for 7 Mar 1694/5.

10383-4, 1914 rev 3

DB -G7875 1689 2
Gt.Brit.--Parliament, 1695-1696--House of Commons.
The Address of the House of Commons to the King.
London, Printed for Thomas Cockerill at the Three Leggs in the Poultry, and Timothy Goodwin at the Queen's-Head against St. Dunstan's Church in Fleet-street, MDC XCV.
1 ℓ. 29cm. 1/2° (Issued as no. 4 of Gt.Brit.--Parliament, 1695-1696--House of Commons. Votes..., London, 1695-1696.)
Caption title; imprint at end.
Address of thanks presented 28 Nov 1695 for prosecution of the war against France.
Bound in Votes of the House of Commons, v. 2.

10376-7A, 1914

DB -G7875 1689 2	Gt.Brit.--Parliament, 1695-1696--House of Commons. Votes Of The House of Commons, In The Parliament Began At Westminster The 22th [sic] Day of November, in the Seventh Year of the Reign of King William, Anno Domini, 1695. London, Printed for Thomas Cockerill at the Three Leggs in the Poultry, and Timothy Goodwin at the Queen's-Head against St. Dunstan's Church in Fleet-street, 1695[-1696]. 1 p.ℓ., 448 p. 29cm. fol. Issued in pts. numbered 1-128 and dated 23 Nov 1695 - 27 Apr 1696, each of which has caption title and imprint at end. Imprint of no. 102, 104, 106-128 dated 1696. Bound in Votes of the House of Commons, v.2. 10376-7, 1914	+Z ≡J25 1695	Jaillot, Charles Hubert Alexis, 1632-1712. Atlas François, Contenant Les Cartes Geographiques dans lesquelles sont tres exactement remarquez Les Empires, Monarchies, Royaumes et Estats De L'Europe, De L'Asie, De L'Afrique Et De L'Amérique: Avec Les Tables Et Cartes Particulieres, De France, De Flandre, D'Allemagne D'Espagne Et D'Italie. Dedié Au Roy, Par son tres-humble, tres-obeissant, tres-fidele Sujet et Serviteur AHubert Iaillot, Geographe ordinaire de sa Majesté. A Paris, Chéz le S.ʳ Iaillot, Geographe Du Roy, joignant les grands Augustins, aux deux Globes, avec Privilége, 1695. 3 v. double pl., col. maps. 54.4cm. fol. Contains maps dated 1674-1720. Engraved t.-p., signed: "Dieu Inuen. S.S." In this copy there is a contemporary ms. table of contents bound in at the beginning of each volume. Bound in contemporary calf. Phillips(Atlases)519, 520; Sabin35538. Contents, v.1. The maps are double-page size except for the following: 1, 5, 9, 13, 18, 21, 25bis, 29, 32, 40-42, 50, 53, 59-66, 76-78, 83, which are inlaid or mounted to that size; 11, 75, which are folded to that size, and 37, which is single-page size. Ms. table of contents. Plate: "La Sphere Artificielle Ou Armilaire Oblique ... A Paris Chez le S.ʳ de Fer dans l'Isle du Palais sur le quay de l'Orloge a la Sphere Royale. avec Privilege du Roy 1716." Engraved t.-p. Maps:
DB -G7875 1689 2	Gt.Brit.--Sovereigns, etc., 1694-1702 (William III). His Majesties Most Gracious Speech To both Houses of Parliament, On Friday the Third Day of May, 1695. London, Printed by Charles Bill and the Executrix of Thomas Newcomb, deceas'd, Printers to the Kings most Excellent Majesty. 1695. 4 p. 29cm. fol. Cut (royal arms) on t.-p. Message in anticipation of prorogation of Parliament. Bound in Votes of the House of Commons, v.2, after Votes for 3 May 1695. Wing W2402. 10377-7, 1914		
DB -G7875 1689 2	Gt.Brit.--Sovereigns, etc., 1694-1702 (William III). His Majesties Most Gracious Speech To both Houses of Parliament, On Saturday the Twenty third of November, 1695. London, Printed by Charles Bill and the Executrix of Thomas Newcomb, deceas'd, Printers to the Kings most Excellent Majesty. 1695. 4 p. 29cm. fol. Cut (royal arms) on t.-p. (Steele 130). Calls for supplies necessary for the war against France. Bound in Votes of the House of Commons, v.2, before general t.-p. for Gt.Brit.--Parliament, 1695-1696--House of Commons. Votes, London, 1695 [-1696] WingW2403. 10377-8, 1914	[1] [2] [3] [4] [5]	"Mappe-Monde Geo-Hydrographique ... Par le S.ʳ Sanson ... A Paris Chez H. Iaillot ... joignant les Grands Augustins, aux deux Globes Auec Privilége du Roy, pour vingt Ans. 169 " "Mappemonde a l'usage du Roy. Par Guillaume Delisle ... A Paris Chez Guillaume Delisle ... Sur le Quay de l'Horloge. Avec Privilege. 15.ᵉ Avril 1720." "Hemisphere Septentrional pour voir distinctement Les Terres Arctiques Par Guillaume Delisle ... AParis Chez l'Auteur sur le Quay de l'Horloge avec Privilege Juillet 1714." "Hemisphere Meridional pour voir plus distinctement Les Terres Australes Par Guillaume Del'Isle ... AParis chéz LAuteur sur le Quai de l'Horloge avec Privilege Juillet 1714." "L'Afrique ... Par G. De L'Isle ... A Paris, Chez l'Autheur Rue des Canettes prez de S.ᵗ Sulpice. Avec Privilege du Roy, pour 20. Ans 1700."

[6] "Carte De La Barbarie De La Nigritie Et De La Guinée Par Guillaume Del'Isle ... A Paris Chez l'Auteur sur le Quai de l'Horloge a l Aigle d'Or. avec Privilege Aout 1707."

[7] "Carte De L'Egypte De La Nubie De L'Abissinie &c. Par Guillaume Delisle ... A Paris Chez l'Auteur sur le Quai de l'Horloge a lAigle d'Or avec Privilege pour 20 ans Nov. 1707."

[8] "Carte Du Congo Et Du Pays Des Cafres Par G. Del'Isle ... A Paris Chez l'Auteur sur le Quai de l'Horloge. avec Privilege Janvier 1708."

[9] "L'Asie ... Par G. de l'Isle Geographe. A Paris Chéz l'Auteur Rue des Canettes préz de St Sulpice Auec Privilege du Roy pour 20. Ans 1700."

[10] "Carte De La Turquie De L'Arabie Et De La Perse ... Par G. De L'Isle ... A Paris, Chez l'Auteur sur le Quai de l'Horloge a l'Aigle d'Or Avec Privilege. 1701."

[11] "Carte Des Indes Et De La Chine ... Par Guillaume De L'Isle ... A Paris Chéz l'Auteur sur le Quai de l'Horloge. avec Privilege pour 20. ans. 1705."

[12] "Carte De Tartarie ... Par Guillaume Del'Isle ... A Paris Chez l'Auteur sur le Quai de l'Horloge á l'Aigle d Or avec Privilege 1706."

[13] "L'Amerique Septentrionale. ... Par G. De L'Isle ... A Paris. Chéz l'Autheur Rue des Canettes préz de St Sulpice Avec Privilege du Roy pour 20. ans. 1700."

[14] "Carte Du Canada Ou De La Nouvelle France ... Par Guillaume Del'Isle ... A Paris Chez l'Auteur sur la Quai de l'Horloge a lAigle d Or avec Privilege de sa Maj.^{te} pour 20. ans 1703. et se trouve a Amsterdam chez L. Renard Libraire prez de la Bourse"

[15] "Carte Du Mexique Et De La Floride ... Par Guillaume Del'Isle ... A Paris Chéz l'Auteur sur le Quai de l'Horloge Privilege du Roy po.^{r} 20. ans 1703"

[16] "Carte De La Louisiane Et Du Cours Du Mississipi ... Par Guill^{aume} Delisle ... A Paris Chez l'Auteur le Sr Delisle sur le Quay de l'Horloge avec Privilege du Roy Juin 1718."

[17] "Carte Des Antilles Françoises Et Des Isles Voisines ... Par Guillaume Del'isle ... A Paris Chez l'Auteur Sur le Quay de l'Horloge avec Privilége du Roy. Juillet 1717."

[18] "L'Amerique Meridionale ... Par G. De L'Isle Geographe. A Paris, Chéz l'Autheur, Rüe des Canettes préz de St Sulpice. Avec Privilege du Roy. pour 20. ans 1700."

[19] "Carte De La Terre Ferme Du Perou, Du Bresil Et Du Pays Des Amazones... Par Guillaume Del'Isle ... A Paris Chéz l'Auteur sur le Quai de l'Horloge a lAigle d'Or avec Privilege du Roy pour 20. ans 1703."

[20] "Carte Du Paraguay Du Chili Du Detroit De Magellan &c. ... Par Guillaume De L'Isle ... A Paris Chez l'Auteur sur le Quai de l'Horloge. avec Privilege du Roi pour 20 ans 1703."

[21] "L'Europe ... Par G. De L'Isle Geographe. A Paris, Chéz l'Auteur sur le Quai de l'Horloge a lAigle d'Or Avec Privilege du Roy pour 20. ans 1700."

[22] "Les Isles Britanniques ... Par G. De L'Isle ... A Paris Chéz l'Auteur sur le Quai de l'Horloge a l'Aigle d'Or Avec Privilege du Roy pour 20. ans. ... 1702."

[23] "Les Isles Brittanniques ... Par le Sr Sanson ... A Paris Chez H. Iaillot, joignant les grands Augustins, aux deux Globes, Avec Privilege du Roy pour vingt Ans. 1709."

[24] "Carte Des Royaumes D'Angleterre D'Ecosse Et D'Irlande ... Par ... C. Inselin ..."

[25.1] Part of the preceding. "A Paris Chez le Sr Jaillot Geographe, joignant les Grands Augustins, aux deux Globes, avec privil. du Roi 1715."

[25 bis] "The Natural Shape Of England ... By Philip Lea at the Atlas & Hercules in Cheapside London."

[26] "Carte Des Courones Du Nord ... Par ... Guillaume De l'Isle ... 1706. A Paris Chez l'Auteur sur le Quai de l'Horloge ... avec Privilege du Roy."

[27] Part of the preceding.

[28] "Carte Du Royaume De Danemarc Par Guill. Del'Isle ... avec Privilege Octob. 1710. ... A Paris chez LAuteur Sur le Quay de l Orloge."

[29] "Le Royaume De Danemark ... Par le Sr Sanson ... A Paris Chez H. Iaillot joignant les grands Augustins, aux 2. Globes Avec Privilege du Roy, pour vingt Ans. 169 "

[30] "Carte De Moscovie ... Par son tres humble et tres obeiss.^{t} Serviteur De l' Isle ... A Paris chez l'Auteur sur le Quai de l'Horloge avec Privilege 1706."

[31] Part of the preceding.

[32] "Estats De La Couronne De Pologne ... Par le Sr Sanson ... A Paris, Chez H. Iaillot joignant les grands Augustins, aux deux Globes Avec Privilege du Roy, pour vingt Ans 169 "

[33] "La Pologne ... Par Guillaume Del'Isle

[34] "... A Paris Chez l'Auteur sur le Quai de l Horloge a l Aigle dOr Avec Privilege du Roy"
[34] "Carte De La Hongrie ... Par Guillaume De l'Isle ... A Paris chez l'Auteur sur le Quai de l'Horloge avec Privilege du Roy pour 20 ans 1703."
[35] "Carte Particuliere De La Hongrie De La Transilvanie De La Croatie Et De La Sclavonie Par G. Del'isle ... a Paris chez l'auteur sur le Quai de l'Horloge avec Privil. 20 May 1717"
[36] "Carte De La Grece ... Par G. De L'Isle ... A Paris Chez l'Auteur Sur le Quai de l'Horloge avec Privilege Sept. 1707."
[37] "Le Cours Du Danube ... Par ... le P. Placide Augustin Déchaussé ... Avec Priv. de sa Maj^{te} pour 15. ans 1703."
[38] "Le Cours Du Danube Par le P. Placide Augustin Dechaussé ... A Paris chez Berey rüe St Iâque devant la fontaine St Severin a la Princesse de Savoye Avec Privil de sa Maj^{te} pour 15 ans"
[39] Part of the preceding.
[40] "Pontus Euxinus of Niewe en Naaukeurige Paskaart van de Zwarte Zee ... door N. Witsen, Cons: Amst. Apud L. Renard."
[41] "Estats De L'Empire Du Grand Seigneur Des Turcs ... Par le Sr Sanson ... A Paris, Chez H. Iaillot joignant les grands Augustins, aux deux Globes: Avec Privilege du Roy, pour vingt Ans, 1695"
[42] "L'Italie distingueé suivant l'estendüe de tous Les Estats, Royaumes, Republiques Duchés, Principautés, &c. ... Par le Sr Sanson ... A Paris Chez H. Iaillot joignant les grands Augustins, aux 2. Globes Avec Privilege du Roy, pour vingt Ans. 169 "
[43] "L'Italie ... Par G. De L'Isle Geographe A Paris Chez l'Auteur sur le Quai de l'Horloge, Avec Privilege du Roy. pour 20 ans. M.D.CC."
[44] "L'Italie Sur les Nouv. Observations Par Le S. Abbé Baudrand ... A Paris Chez I. Besson, Geog. du Roy, Sur le quay de l'Orloge du Palais a l'ancien Buits. Avec Priv. du Roy, pour 20. ans. 1701."
[45] "La Source Du Po, et les Passages de France en Piémont, Par le P. Placide Augustin Déc. ... A Paris Chez Berey graveur ruë St Jacques à la Princesse de Savoye 1704"
[46] "Le Cours du Po dans le Piemont et le Montferrat. Par le R. P. Placide Augustin Dèchaussé ... Avec Privilege du Roy pour 15. ans 1702."
[47] "Le Cours Du Po dans le Milanez. Par le P. Placide, Augustin Déchaussé ... 1703. A Paris chez Berey graveur rue St Jâque devant la Fontaine St Severin à la Princesse de Savoye. Avec Privilege du Roy pour 15. ans."
[48] "Le Cours du Po, dans le Duché de Mantoue. Par le P. Placide, Augustin Déchaussé ... 1703. Se Vend a Paris chez Berey Graveur rue St Jacques devant la Fontaine St Severin a la Princesse de Savoye Avec Privilege de S M pour 15 ans"
[49] "Le Cours du Po dans le Duché de Ferrare et les Etats de Venise. Par le P. Placide, Augustin Déchaussé ... Avec Privilege de sa Maj^{te} pour 15 ans. 1703. A Paris Chez Berey Graveur rue St Jâque devant la Fontaine St Severin a la Princesse de Savoye."
[50] "Les Duchés De Savoye, De Genevois, De Chablais; Les Comtés De Morienne, De Tarentaise et La Baronie De Faussigny ... A Paris Chez le Sr Iaillot, joignant les grands Augustins, aux deux Globes; Avec Privilege du Roy"
[51] "Carte Du Piemont et du Monferrat ... Par Guillaume De l'Isle ... A Paris Chez l'Auteur Sur le Quai de l'Horloge avec Privilege Avril 1707."
[52] "Partie Meridionale Du Piemont Et Du Monferrat Par Guillaume Del'Isle ... A Paris, Chéz l'Auteur sur le Quai de l'Horloge avec Privilege du Roy 1707"
[53] "Partie Du Duché De Milan, La Principauté De Piémont Le Montferrat; et La Republi^{que} De Genes ... A Paris, Chez H. Iaillot ... proche les Grands Augustins, aux 2. Globes Avec Privilege de S. Maj^{te}. 169 "
[54] "Le Duché De Milan ... Par ... AHubert Jaillot ... A Paris, Chez l'Auteur, joignant les grands Augustins, aux deux Globes, avec Privilege du Roy 1706"
[55] "Estat De La Seigneurie Et Republique De Venise ... A Paris, Chez l'Auteur le Sr Iaillot ... joignant les grands Augustins, aux deux Globes, Avec Privilege 1706"
[56] "Les Provinces Du Veronese, Du Vicentin Du Padouan, De Polesine De Rovigo et Du Dogado ou Duché a la République de Venise. ... A Paris Chez l'Auteur le Sr Iaillot ... joignant les grands Augustins, aux 2. Globes, Avec Privilege du Roy. 1705"

[57] "Les Duchez De Modene Et De Regio, Les Principautez De Carpi Et De Coreggio ... Par J.B. Liébaux ... A Paris chez l'Auteur, dessus le Petit Pont attenant le Petit Châtelet, au Planisfere Royal. Avec Privilege du Roy. 1703."

[58] "Etats De L'Eglise ... Par I.B. Nolin ... A Paris Chez l'Auteur sur le Quay de l'Enseigne de la Place des Victoires Vers le Pont-Neuf. ... Avec Privilege du Roi."

[59] "Patrimonio Di S. Pietro ... descritto da Giacomo Filippo Ameti Romano e dato in Luce da Domenico de Rossi erede di Gio. Giac.º de Rossi dalle sue Stampe in Roma alla Pace con Priuilegio del S.P. e licenza de Sup. l'Anno 1696. Parte Seconda Terrestra del Patrimonio di S. Pietro."

[60] Part of the preceding. "Parte Prima Terrestra del Patrimonio di S. Pietro."

[61] Part of the preceding. "Parte Seconda Maritima del Patrimonio di S. Pietro."

[62] Part of the preceding. "Parte Prima Maritima del Patrimonio di S. Pietro"

[63] "Il Lazio Con le sue piu Cospicue Strade Antiche, Moderne é principali Casali, e Tenute di esso. Descritto da Giacomo Filippo Ameti Romano e dato in Luce da Domenico de Rossi erede di Gio. Giac.º de Rossi dalle sue Stampe in Roma alla Pace con Pruilegio del Som Pontifice e Licenza de Sup. l'Anno 1693. Parte Prima Terrestre del Latio"

[64] Part of the preceding."Parte Seconda Terrestra del Latio, descritta da Giacomo Ameti, data in Luce da Domenico de Rossi l'Anno 1693. con Priuil. del Som. Pont e Lic.ª de Sup."

[65] Part of the preceding. "Parte Prima Maritima del Latio distinta con le sue strade Antiche e Moderne, descritta da Giacomo Ameti Romano, data in Luce da Domenico de Rossi erede di Gio. Giac.º de Rossi dalle sue stampe in Roma alla Pace con Priuil. del S.P. et lic.ª de Sup. l'Anno 1693."

[66] Part of the preceding. "Parte Seconda Maritima del Latio distinta con le sue strade Antiche e Moderne, descritta da Giac.º Ameti Romano data in Luce da Domenico de Rossi erede di Gio. Giac.º de Rossi dalle sue Stampe in Roma alla Pace con Priuil. del S.P. et licenza de Sup. l'An. 1693."

[67] "Le Royaume De Naples divisé en toutes ses Provinces ... Partie Septentrionale Du Royaume De Naples. Par le S.ʳ Iaillot ... A Paris, Chez l'Auteur, joignant les grands Augustins, aux 2. Globes; auec Priuilege 1703."

[68] Part of the preceding. "Partie Meridionale Du Royaume De Naples. Par le S.ʳ Iaillot ... A Paris, Chez l'Auteur joignant les grands Augustins, aux deux Globes, avec Privilege du Roy, 1706."

[69] "Carte De L'Isle Et Royaume De Sicile Par Guillaume De L'Isle ... A Paris chez l'Auteur Quay de l'Horloge avec Privilege Aout 1717."

[70] "L'Espagne ... Par G De L'Isle ... A Paris Chez l'Auteur sur le Quai de l'Horloge Avec Privilege du Roy pour 20. ans. 1701"

[71] Part of the following. "Partie Septentrionale Du Royaume De Portugal. ... Par le S.ʳ Iaillot ... A Paris, joignant les grands Augustins, aux deux Globes, avec privilege de sa Maj.ᵗᵉ"

[72] Part of the following. "Les Royaumes D'Aragon et De Navarre, Partie Des Deux Castilles et Du Royaume De Valence ... Par le S.ʳ Jaillot ... A Paris joignant les grands Augustins, aux deux Globes. avec Privilege desa Majesté"

[73] Part of the following. "Partie Meridionale Du Royaume De Portugal. ... A Paris, Chez le S.ʳ Iaillot ... joignant les grands Augustins, aux deux Globes, avec Privilége de sa Maj.ᵗᵉ 1711"

[74] "L'Espagne suivant l'étendue De Tous Ses Royaumes Et Principautés, Compris Sous Les Couronnes De Castille, D'Aragon: Et De Portugal. ... Le Royaume De Murcie, Partie Des Royaumes De Valence, De Castille Nouvelle, De Grenade &c. et L'Isle D'Yviça. Par le S.ʳ Jaillot ... A Paris, joignant les grands Augustins, aux 2. Globes, avec Privilége de sa Maj.ᵗᵉ"

[75] "Les Monts Pyrenées, Ou Sont Remarqués Les Passages De France En Espagne ... Par le S.ʳ Sanson ... A Paris Chez H. Iaillot, joignant les grands Augustins, aux deux Globes. Avec privilege du Roy pour vingt Ans. 1701."

[76] Part of the following.

[77] "Nova et Accurata Regni Aragoniæ cum Confinibus Descriptio Per Reverend. Adm. P. Magistrum Fratrem Joannem Seyra et Ferrer ... Anno 1715. ... Se Vende en Zaragoça"

[78] Part of the following. "Theatre De La Guerre D'Espagne. Par J. B. Bourguignon D'Anville ..."

[79] "Carte Du Royaume D'Aragon ...

Par ... Bourguignon D'Anville ...
M.DCC.XIX."
[80] Part of the following.
[81] "La Catalogue ... Par ... le P.
Placide, Augustin Dechaussé ...
A Paris Chez < M.elle Duval rüe
S.t Iacques pres la rüe de la
Parcheminerie Avec Privilege du
Roy. 1707."
[82] "Le Portugal ... Par ... le P.
Placide Augustin Desch.sé ... Avec
Privil. de Sa Majesté pour 15. ans.
A Paris Chez M.e Du Val, rue S.t
Jacques au Dauphin, vis à vis la
rue de la Parcheminerie."
[83] "Le Royaume De Galice ... Chez
I.B. Nolin ... sur le Quay de
l'Horloge du Palais a l'Enseigne de
la Place des Victoires ala desçente
du Pont Neuf Avec Privilege du Roy.
1704."
    Contents, v.2.
The maps are double-page size except for
the following: 4, 30, 31, 58-60, 68-73, which
are inlaid or mounted to that size; 2, 11, 12,
which are folded to that size.
    Ms. table of contents.
    Engraved t.-p.: same as in vol. 1.
    Maps:
[1] "Le Royaume De France distingué
suivant l'Estendüe de Toutes Ses Provinces Et Ses Acquisitions ... Par le S.t
Sanson ... A Paris Chez H. Iaillot,
joignant les grands Augustins, aux 2.
Globes Auec Priuilege du Roy, pour
Vingt Ans. 1713."
[2] "Le Royaume De France dressé sur
les memoires et nouvelles observations
de Messieurs de l'Acadamie Royalle
des Sciences ... A Paris Chez l'Auteur,
le S.t Iaillot ... joignant les grands
Augustins, and 2. Globes, avec privilége de sa Majesté, 1708."
[3] "Carte De France Dressée pour l'usage
du Roy; Par Guillaume Delisle ... A
Paris Chez l'Auteur sur le Quai de
l'Horloge Avec Privilége du Roy,
Avril 1721."
[4] "Carte D Artois Et Des Environs ...
Par Guillaume Del'Isle ... A Paris
Chez l Auteur sur le Quai de l'Horloge
avec Pr. Juill. 1711."
[5] "Partie Meridionale De Picardie ...
Par Guillaume Del'isle ... A Paris
Chez l'Auteur sur le Quai de l'Horloge
avec Privilege 11. Juill. 1712."
[6] "Carte De La Champagne Et Des Pays
Voisins ... Par Guillaume DelIsle ...
A Paris Chez l'Auteur sur le Quai de
l Horloge du Palais, Avec Privilege du
Roy 15 Mars 1713."
[7] "Partie Meridionale De Champagne.
Par Guillaume Del'Isle ... A Paris
chez l'Auteur sur le Quai de l'Horloge.
avec Privilege de sa Majesté Aoust.
1713."
[7 bis] " Evesché De Meaux ... Par ... A Hubert
Jaillot ... Partie Septentrionale De
L'Evesché De Meaux."
[8] "Partie Meridionale De L'Evesché De
Meaux. Levé ... Par M. Chevallier ...
A Paris Chez le S.r Iaillot Geographe du
Roy, joignant les grands Augustins,
aux 2. Globes, avec privilege desa
Majesté, 1701."
[9] "Carte De La Prevosté Et Vicomté De
Paris ... Par G. Delisle ... A Paris
Chez l'Auteur sur le Quay de l'Horloge
avec Privilege Avril 1711."
[10] "[La Banlieüe De Paris] Par N. de Fer
... a Paris Chez l'Auteur dans l'Isle
du Palais sur le Quay de l'Orloge a la
Sphere Royale, Avec Privilege du Roy
1717"
[11] "Carte Particuliere Du Canal De La
Riviere D'Eure Depuis Pontgoin,
Jusques A Versailles ... A Paris,
Chez le S.r Iaillot, Geographe Ordinaire
du Roy joignant les grands Augustins,
aux deux Globes Avec Privilége, 169 "
[12] Part of the preceding.
[13] Part of the following.
[14] "L'Archeveché De Paris ... A Paris
Chez le S.r de Fer ... dans l'Isle du
Palais sur le Quay de l'Orloge a la
Sphere Royale avec Priv. du Roy.
1708."
[15] Part of the preceding.
[16] Part of the preceding. "Avec Privilege du
Roy du 31. Decemb.r 1703. pour 15. ans..."
[17] "Carte Topographique Du Diocese De
Senlis ... Par Guillaume Del'Isle ...
A Paris Chez l'Auteur sur le Quay de
l'Horloge avec Privilege du 28 Aout
1709."
[18] "Carte Du Diocese De Beauvais ...
Par Guillaume Del Isle ... A Paris
Chez l'Auteur Sur le Quay de l'Horloge
avec Pr. Juin 1710. Se trouve a Beau-
vais chez Etienne Aleau Libraire rue
S Pierre"
[19] "Carte De Normandie ... Par Guillaume
DelIsle ... A Paris Chez l'Auteur Sur le
Quay de lHorloge avec Privilege du
Roy Decembre MDCCXVI."
[20] "Carte Particuliere Du Diocese de
Rouen Dressée Sur Les Lieux Par
M.r Fremont de Dieppe ... A Paris
Chez Berey Graveur ... rue S.t
Jacques à la Vieille Poste. Avec Privi-
lege du Roy 1715."
[21]-[25] Part of the preceding.
[26] Part of the following. "A Paris Chez N.
Langlois."

[27] "A Paris Chez N. Langlois Partie Septentrionale Du Diocese De Coutances."

[28] "Diocese De Coutances... Avec Privilege du Roi. 1689. ... A Paris chez I. Mariette rue S.t Iacques a la Victoire et aux Colonnes d'Hercules."

[29] "Partie Meridionale Du Diocese De Coutances. A Paris chez N. Langlois."

[30] "La Bretagne... Dedieé... Par... Hubert Iaillot... A Paris, joignant les Grands Augustins, aux deux Globes, Avec Privilége du Roy. 169 "

[31] "Carte De L'Evesché De Nantes Dediée... Par... G. de Lambilly Iesuite professeur d'hydrographie. ... A Paris, Chez le S.r Iaillot... joignant les grands Augustins, aux deux Globes, avec Privilege de Sa Majesté. 169 "

[32] "Carte Des Provinces Du Maine Et Du Perche... Par Guillaume Del'Isle... A Paris chez l'Auteur sur le Quai de l Horloge avec Privilege 25 Mai 1719."

[33] "Partie Superieure Occidentale De L'Evesché Du Mans."

[34] "L'Evesché Du Mans Dedié... Par... Hubert Jaillot... Partie Superieure Orientale De L'Evesché Du Mans."

[35] "Partie jnferieure Occidentale De L'Evesché Du Mans. ... A Paris, Chez le S.r Jaillot... joignant les grands Augustins, aux deux Globes avec Privilege desa Majesté 1706"

[36] "Partie inferieure Orientale Du L'Evesché Du Mans."

[37] "Carte Particuliere D'Anjou Et De Touraine ou de la Partie Meridionale De La Generalité De Tours Par Guillaume Delisle... A Paris Chez l'Auteur sur le Quay de l Horloge. Avec Priv. ce 27 May. 1720."

[38] "Carte De La Beauce Du Gatinois De La Sologne et Pays voisins compris dans la Generalité D Orleans Par Guillaume Delisle... A Paris chez l'Auteur le S.r Del'Isle sur le Quay de l'Horloge avec Privilege desa Majesté 6. Mars 1718."

[39] "Les Jonctions des deux grandes Rivieres de Loire et de Seine par le Nouveau Canal D'Orleans et celuy de Briare Mis au Iour par le S.r de Fer AParis dans l'Isle du Palais sur le Quay de l'Orloge a la Sphere Royale avec privilege du Roy. 1705." and "Description Du Canal De Briare... Description Du Nouveau Canal D'Orleans..."

[40] "La Province De Poitou Et Le Pays D'Aunis. ... A Paris, Chez l'Auteur, le S.r Iaillot... joignant les grands Augustins, aux. 2. Globes. Avec Privilege de Sa Majeste 1707."

[41] "La Province De Berry. La Generalité De Bourges... A Paris, Chéz l'Auteur le S.r Iaillot... joignant les grands Augustins, aux deux Globes, avec privilege de Sa Majesté, 1707."

[42] "La Generalité De Moulins... A Paris, Chez H. Iaillot joignant les grands Augustins aux 2. Globes. Auec Priuilege du Roy."

[43] "Les Provinces Et Gouvernemens Du Lionnois, Forez Et Beaujelois, De La Haute Et Basse Auvergne, Et Du Bourbonois. Nouvellement Dressez Par N. De Fer... A Paris Chez l'Auteur dans l'Isle du Palais sur le quay de l'Orloge a la Sphere Royale avec Privilege du Roy 1712."

[44] "La Province D'Auvergne Divisée En Haute Et Basse La Generalité De Riom... Avec privilege du Roy 1715... A Paris chez B. Jaillot sur le quay de l'Orloge ou des Morfondus entre la rue du Harlay et le pont neuf à l'Atlas françois et à present au bout du Pont neuf proche les grands Augustins aux 2 Globes"

[45] "La Generalité De Limoges... Par le Sieur. B. Iaillot... 1719. ... A Paris Chez le S.r Jaillot... joignant les grands Augustins, aux deux Globes, avec privilege du Roi."

[46] "Carte Du Bourdelois Du Perigord et des Provinces voisines Par G. Del'Isle... A Paris chez l'Auteur Quay de l'Horloge 1714."

[47] "Carte Du Bearn De La Bigorre De L'Armagnac Et Des Pays Voisins Par Guillaume Delisle... AParis Chez l'Auteur sur le Quai de l'Horloge avec Privilege.1712. 1. aout"

[48] "L'Eslection De Lomagne, Partie De Celles D'Armagnac De Riviere Verdun, De Montauban, De Cahors: Et Partie De La Generalité De Bordeaux. A Paris, Chez l'Auteur le S.r Iaillot... joignant les grands Augustins, aux 2. Globes, avec Privilége, 169 "

[49] "Les Eslections De Millau, De Rodez, De Villefranche, De Figeac, Partie De Celles De Cahors et De Montauban: les Frontieres Des Generalitéz De Limoges et De Riom. ... A Paris Chez le S.r Iaillot... joignant les grands Augustins, aux 2. Globes, avec Privilége, 1695"

[50] "Les Eslections De Comenge, D'Estarac, Partie De Celles De Riviere Verdun et D'Armagnac, Le Pays Des Quatre Vallées, Le Nebouzan et Le Comté De Foix. A Paris, Chez l'Auteur le S.r Iaillot... joignant les grands Augustins, aux deux Globes, Avec Privilege 1695."

[51] "Les Generalitez De Montauban et De Toulouse... Le Donazan. Le Pays De Sault, Le Fenouilledes, Les Corbieres-Partie De La Generalité De Montpellier. A Paris, Chez l'Autêur le Sr Iaillot... joignant les grands Augustins, aux deux Globes, avec Privilege 1701."

[52] "Le Diocese De Comminge... A Paris, Chez l'Auteur le Sr Iaillot... joignant les grands Augustins, aux 2. Globes avec Privilege 1700"

[53] "Gouvernement General De Languedoc..."

[54] Part of the preceding. "A Paris chez le Sr Jaillot... joignant les Grands Augustins Aux deux Globes. avec Privilege de sa Majesté 1721."

[55] Part of the following.

[56] "Le Canal Royal De Languedoc... A Paris Chez I. B. Nolin... Sur le Quay de l'Horloge du Palais a l'Enseigne de la Place des Victoires Vers le Pont Neuf Avec Privilege du Roy. en Janvier 1697. ..."

[57] Part of the preceding.

[58] "Diocese De Montauban Dedié... Par... E. G. Figuier Prêtre... A Paris, Chez J. Besson... sur le quay de l'Orloge du Palais au Mouton, prez le Pont-neuf. Avec Privilege du Roi po.~ 15. ans. 1707."

[59] "Le Diocese De Toulouse... A Paris, Chez le Sr Iaillot... joignant les grands Augustins, aux 2. Globes, avec Privilége 1695"

[60] "Diocese De Castres. décrit... Par... Hubert Iaillot... A Paris joignant les Grands Augustins, aux 2. Globes, Avec Privilége du Roy 1690"

[61] "Carte Du Diocese De Narbonne Dressée par Guillaume Lafont Bourgeois de Narbonne Rectifiée sur les Observations de l'Academie Royale des Sciences Par Guillaume Del'Isle... A Paris Chéz G. Del'Isle sur le Quai de l'Horloge avec Privilege 1704"

[62] "Carte Du Diocese De Beziers Dressée sur les lieux Par le S Gautier Ingenieur et Architecte de la Province de Languedoc, et Rectifiée sur les Observations de l'Academie R.^{le} des Sciěces Par G. Del'Isle... A Paris chez l'Auteur sur le Quai de l'Horloge a lAigle d'Or, avec Privil. p.^{r} 20. ans Mai 1708"

[63] "Le Diocese De Montpellier... A Paris, Chez l'Auteur le Sr Iaillot... joignant les grands Augustins, aux deux Globes, avec Privilége 1706"

[64] "Diocese De Nismes Dressé Nouvellement sur les Lieux par le Sr Gautier Architecte et Ingenieur de la Province de Languedoc... A Paris Chez I. B. Nolin... Sur le Quay de l'Horloge du Palais a l'Enseigne de la Place des Victoires vers le Pont Neuf Avec Privilege du Roy... l'An 1698."

[65] "Carte Du Diocese D'Uzès Dressée sur les Lieux Par Le Sr Gautier Ing.^{r} Archit. et Inspect.^{r} des Ponts et Chaussées de F.^{ce} Soumise aux dernieres Observations de M.^{rs} de l'Academie Royale des Sciences... Par... J. B. Nolin... A Paris Chez la Veuve du Sr Nolin... Sur la Quay de l'Horloge du Palais, à l'Enseig^{ne} de la Place des Victoires. ... On trouve aussi chez la V. Nolin le Languedoc, le Diocese de Nîmes, le Canal Royal et les Sevennes. Avec Privilege du Roi."

[66] "Carte De Provence et des Terres Adjacentes Par Guillau^{me} DelIsle... AParis Chez l'Auteur sur le Quay de l'Horloge avec Privilege Octobre 1715."

[67] "Le Dauphiné... A Paris Chez le Sr Jaillot... joignant les grands Augustins, aux deux Globes avec Privilege desa Majesté. 1710."

[68] Part of the following. "La Bresse, Le Bugey, Le Valromay, La Principauté De Dombes Et Le Viennois. Par le Sr Iaillot... A Paris Chez l'Auteur joignant les grands Augustins, aux deux Globes avec Privilege du Roy 169 "

[69] Part of the following. "Le Valentinois, Le Diois Et Les Baroñies, Dans Le Dauphiné, Le Comtat Venaiscin Et La Principauté D'Orange. A Paris Chez l'Auteur joignant les grands Augustins, aux deux Globes, avec Privilége du Roy, 169 ."

[70] Part of the following. "Les Duchés De Savoye, De Genevois, De Chablais; Les Comtés De Morienne, De Tarentaise et La Baronie De Faussigny. Le Balliage De Gex et La Seigneurie De Geneve. ... A Paris Chez le Sr Iaillot, joignant les grands Augustins, aux deux Globes; Avec Privilege du Roy, 169 ."

[71] Part of the following. "Partie Du Briançonnois, Du Graisivaudan, Du Gapençois Et L'Ambrunois Dans Le Daufiné. ... A Paris, Chez le Sr Iaillot... joignant les grands Augustins, aux deux Globes. Avec Privilége desa Majesté 169 "

[72] "Les Estats De Savoye Et De Piémont Le Dauphiné, La Bresse Partie Du Lionnois et De La Provence. &c. ... Le Duché D'Avost, La Seigneurie De

[73] Verceil, Le Marquisat D'Yvrée. &c. A Paris, Chez le S.ʳ Iaillot... joignant les grands Augustins, aux deux Globes, avec privilége de sa Majesté 169 "

[73] "La Principauté De Piémont, Les Marquisats De Saluce Et De Suze, Les Comtés De Nice Et D'Ast, Le Montferrat. &c. ... par... H. Iaillot... A Paris joignant les Grands Augustins, aux deux Globes Avec Privilége du Roy 169 "

[74] Part of the following. "Partie Septentrionale Du Duche De Bourgogne... A Paris Chez le S.ʳ Del'Isle sur le Quay de l'Horloge avec Privilege"

[75] "Carte Du Duché De Bourgogne Et Des Comtez En Dependans ... Par Guillaume Del'Isle de l'Academie R.ˡᵉ des Sciences. 1709. ... Partie Meridionale Du Duché De Bourgogne..."

[76] "La Franche Comté... Presenté... Par... Hubert Iaillot... a Paris joignant le gr' Augustins aux 2. Globes, avec Privilege 1695."

[77] Part of the preceding· "Partie Meridionale Du Comté De Bourgogne. A Paris, Chez l'Auteur le S.ʳ Iaillot... joignant les grands Augustins, aux deux Globes, avec Privilége 1695."

[78] "La Lorraine ... Par le S.ʳ Sanson... A Paris, Chez le S.ʳ Iaillot... ioignãt les Grands Augustins, aux deux Globes Avec Privilége du Roy 169."

[79] Part of the following. "1. Le Verdunois ... Par le S.ʳ Iaillot... 1704."

[80] "Les Estats, Du Duc De Lorraine... Par Hubert Jaillot... 1705 2. Le Pays Messin..."

[81] Part of the preceding. "3. Le Toulois... Par le S.ʳ Iaillot..."

[82] Part of the preceding. "4. Partie Meridionale Du Temporel De L'Evesché De Metz... Par le S.ʳ Iaillot... 1704 "

[83] Part of the preceding. "5. Partie Du Balliage De Vosge... Par le S.ʳ Iaillot ... 1704."

[84] Part of the preceding. "6. Les Prevotez ... A Paris, Chez le S.ʳ Iaillot... joignant les grands Augustins, aux deux Globes, avec privilége 1704"

[85] "L'Alsace Divisée En Ses Principales Parties ... Par le S.ʳ Sanson ... A Paris Chez le S.ʳ Iaillot... joignant les Grands Augustins, aux deux Globes Avec Privilege du Roy. 169 "

Contents, v. 3.
The maps are double-page size except for the following: 1, 9, 10, 23, 25, 27, 29-31, 50, 53, 56, 60, 65, which are inlaid or mounted to that size; 76-78, which are folded to that size; 22, 24, 26, 28 [imperfect], which are single-page size.

Ms. table of contents.
Maps:

[1] "L'Empire D'Allemagne... Par le S.ʳ Sanson... A Paris, Chez H. Iaillot, joignant les grands Augustins, aux deux Globes, Avec Privilege du Roy, pour vingt Ans. 169 "

[2] "L'Allemagne ... Par G. De L'Isle... A Paris Chez l'Auteur sur le Quai de l'Horloge avec Privilᵍᵉ pour 20 ans. 1701. ..."

[3] "Le Cercle De Westphalie ... Par le S.ʳ Sanson... A Paris, Chez le S.ʳ Iaillot... joignant les grands Augustins, aux deux Globes Avec Privilege du Roy, 1700."

[4] "Oost-Frise, ou Le Comté D'Embden ... Par le S.ʳ Sanson... A Paris, Chez H. Iaillot joignant les grands Augustins, aux deux Globes Avec Privilege du Roy, pour vingt Ans. 1709."

[5] "Basse Partie De LEvesché De Munster, Et Le Comté De Benthem. ... Par le S.ʳ Sanson... A Paris, Chez H. Iaillot, joignant les grands Augustins, aux deux Globes. Avec Privilege du Roy. 1700."

[6] "Haute Partie De L'Evesché De Munster ... Par le S.ʳ Sanson... A Paris, Chez H. Iaillot joignant les grands Augustins, aux deux Globes Avec Privilege du Roy, 1700."

[7] "Le Comté De La Marck, Les Seigneuries Des Abbayes De Werden, D'Essen, Et La Ville Imperiale De Dortmundt... Par le S.ʳ Sanson... A Paris, Chez Hubert Iaillot, joignant les grands Augustins, aux deux Globes. Auec Privilege du Roy 1700"

[8] "Le Duché De Westphalie ... Par le S.ʳ Sanson... A Paris, Chez H. Iaillot, joignant les grands Augustins, aux 2. Globes Auec Privilege du Roy. 1700."

[9] "Le Duché De Berg, Le Comté De Homberg, Les Seigneuries De Hardenberg, Et De Wildenborg. ... Par le S.ʳ Sanson... A Paris, Chez H. Iaillot, joignant les grands Augustins, aux deux Globes. Auec Privilege du Roy. 1674."

[10] "Le Cours De La Riviere Du Rhein ... Par le S.ʳ Sanson... A Paris, Chez H. Iaillott proche les Grands Augustins, aux deux Globes Avec Privilege du Roy, pour vingt Ans 169 "

[11] "Les Duchés, De Cleves, De Iuliers et De Limbourg ... A Paris Chez l'Auteur, le S. Iaillot... joignant les grands Augustins, aux deux Globes, auec Privilege"

[12] Part of the preceding. "Partie Meridionale De L'Archevesché Et Eslectorat De Cologne, Des Duchés De Iuliers Et De Berg, Le Duché De Limbourg,

[13] "La Basse Partie Du Cercle Du Haut Rhein... Par le Sr Sanson... A Paris Chez le Sr Iaillot... joignant les grands Augustins, aux 2. Globes Avec Privilege du Roy, pour vingt Ans. 1690"

[14] "Le Cercle Eslectoral Du Rhein... Par le Sr Sanson... A Paris, Chez le Sr Iaillot... joignant les grands Augustins aux deux Globes, Avec Privilege du Roy. 1690"

[15] Part of the following. "Parties Des Archevesches Et Eslectorats De Mayence, De Treves; Du Palatinat Et Eslectorat Du Rhein. &c. Par le Sr Iaillot... 1705. A Paris, Chez l'Auteur, joignant les grands Augustins, aux deux Globes, avec Privilege."

[16] "Les Archevesches et Eslectorats De Mayence et De Treves, Le Palatinat et Eslectorat Du Rhein, Le Duché De Wirtenberg. &c. ... L'Archevesche et Eslectorat De Mayence, Le Landgraviat De Hesse Darmstat, Le Territoire De Francfort, Les Comtés De Wertheim, D'Erpach, &c. Par le Sr Iaillot... A Paris, Chez l'Auteur joignant les grands Augustins, aux deux Globes, avec Privilege 1704."

[17] Part of the preceding. "Le Balliage De Deux Ponts, Partie De Celuy De Lictemberg, Les Seigneuries De Landstoul, De Hombourg, De Grevenstein; Partie Du Palatinat et De La Lorraine. A Paris, Chez l'Auteur, le Sr Iaillot... joignant les grands Augustins, aux deux Globes, avec Privilége 1705"

[18] Part of the preceding. "Partie Du Palatinat Du Rhein, Le Duché De Wirtenberg, Les Marquisats De Bade et De Durlac, Les Evesches De Worms et De Spire, et Le Comté Do Linange, Par le Sr Iaillot... A Paris, Chez l'Auteur, joignant les grands Augustins, aux deux Globes, avec Privilege de Sa Majesté 1695."

[19] "Le Cours Du Rhin depuis Worms, jusqua Bonne, Et Les Pays Adjacēs Par Guillaume Del'Isle... avec Privilege du Roy pour 20. ans. 1704."

[20] "Le Cours Du Rhin depuis Strasbourg jusqu'a Worms Et Les Pays Adjacens Par Guillaume Del'Isle... APariz chéz l'Auteur sur le Quai de lHrloge [sic] a la Courõ de Diamãs avec Priv se trouve a Amsterdam chez L. Renard prez de la Bourse"

[21] "Le Cours Du Rhin au dessus de Strasbourg, et les Païs adjacens. Par Guill. de l'Isle... A Paris chez l'Auteur sur le Quai de l'Horloge a lAigle dOr avec Privilege 1704. Se trouve a Amsterdam chez L. Renard Libraire préz de la Bourse"

[22] "Partie des Estats Des Cercles des quatre Electeurs et les Estats de Wetteravie et de Hesse Darmstatt ou sont les Environs des Villes"

[23] "Du Haut Rhin ou sont l'Archevesché et Electorat de Treves, Partie de Ceux de Mayence, et de Cologne de Treves de Montroyal de Coblens de Mayence et de Franckfort levé sur les lieux pend^t les guerres Par Henry Sengre... A Paris Chez le Sr Iaillot ... Avec Privilege du Roy 1695."

[24] "Estats entre la Nied la Sare et le Rhin ou sont la Lorraine Allemande l'Entrée en Alsace et en Lorraine par les Villes de Sarlouis de Hombourg"

[25] "Le Duché de Deux Ponts, les Comtés de Bitsche, de Spanheim et de Linange, Partie Du Palatinat Meridional de Landau et leurs Environs. Dressé sur les Memoires levés sur les lieux pendant les Guerres. Par Henry Sengre... A Paris, Chez le Sr Iaillot ... joignant les grands Augustins, aux deux Globes. Avec privilege du Roy 1695"

[26] "Les Frontieres de Lorraine ou sont Espinal St Diey, Luneville Marsal Vic les Sources des Rivieres de la Seille de la Sare de la Meurte et de la Moselle"

[27] "La Basse Alsace Divisée en Balliages et Seigneuries deça et dela le Rhin ou sont le Grand Balliag.^e D Haguenau, les Terres D'Hanau, de l'Evesch.^é de la Ville de Strasbourg et des Nobles les Montagnes noires Sep.^{les} l Ortnaw le Grand Marquisat de Bade et partie du Wirtenberg levé sur les lieux pendāt les guerres Par Henry Sengre ... se vend A Paris chez l'Autheur Faubourg St Germain a l'Hostel de Condé faut s'adresser au Suisse Avec Privilege du Roy 1695"

[28] "Les Frontieres De Lorraine et De La Comté De Bourgogne Partie des Montagnes de Vosges les Estats du Comté de Montbeliard"

[29] "La Haute Alsace Divisée en Balliages et Seigneuries tant deça que dela le Rhin ou sont le Suntgaw le Breisgaw les quatre Villes Forestieres les Montagnes Noires Meridionales et Partie de la Souabe et des Suisses levé sur les lieux pendāt les Guerres par Henry Sengre... A Paris Chez le Sr Iaillot... joignant les grands

Augustins aux deux Globes Avec Privilege du Roy 1695"

[30] "L'Alsace Divisée En Ses Principales Parties... La Basse Alsace, Partie De L'Ortnaw Et Le Marquisat De Bade et partie du Wirtenberg. A Paris, Chez le S. Iaillot... joignant les grands Augustins aux 2. Globes, avec privilege de sa Majesté 169 "

[31] Part of the preceding. "La Haute Alsace, Le Suntgaw, Partie De L'Ortnaw, Le Brisgaw Et Les Quatre Villes Forestieres. ... par... H. Iaillot... A Paris, Chez l'Auteur joignant les Grands Augustins, aux deux Globes avec Privilege du Roy 169 "

[32]-[35] [Cours d'uninghen jusqu'a constantz]

[36] "Carte De Suisse... Par Guillaume Del Isle... A Paris chez lAuteur sur le Quay de l Horloge avec Privilege Aout 1715"

[37] "Les Suisses Leurs Alliés Et Leurs Suiets Dedié ... Par... AH. Iaillot ... 1703 Partie Septentrionale Des Cantons De Berne Et De Fribourg, Les Cantons De Lucerne, De Soleurre, De Basle, La Seigneurie De L'Evesché De Basle. Le Comté De Baden, Les Balliages De Bremgarten, De Mellingen, De Granson, De Morat, Les Gouvernemens Libres, Le Comté De Neuchatel, &c. Par le Sr Iaillot... "

[38] Part of the preceding. "Les Cantons De Schafouse, De Zurich, De Schwytz, De Zug, De Underwald, De Glaris, D'Appenzel, Les Dix Droitures, L'Abbé Et La Ville De St Gal, Le Thurgow, Les Comtés De Rapperschwil, De Tockenburg, De Werdenberg, De Sargans, Les Balliages De Vitznach, De Gasteren, De Rheinthal, La Baronie D'Alt Sax &c. Par le Sr Iaillot ..."

[39] Part of the preceding. "Partie Meridionale Des Cantons De Berne Et De Fribourg, Le Valais, La Seigneurie De Geneve, Les Balliages D'Orbe Et De Schwarzenburg. ... A Paris, Chez L'Auteur le Sr Iaillot... joignant les grands Augustins, aux deux Globes, avec Privilege 1704."

[40] Part of the preceding. "Le Canton De Ury. Les Ligues Grise Et De La Maison-Dieu, La Valteline, Les Comtés De Chiavene Et De Bormio, Dans Les Grisons. Les Trois Balliages De Bellinzone, Les Quatre Gouvernements En Italie De Lugano, Locarno, Mendrisio et Valmadia. Les Sources des Rivieres du Rhein, du Rhône, du Tesin, de Russ, del' Aar, de l'Inn et de l'Adda ... Par le Sr Iaillot ... avec privilege 1701 "

[41] "Carte De La Souveraineté De Neuchatel Et Vallangin... Par... De Merveilleux"

[42] "Le Cercle De Souabe subdivisé en tous les Estats qui le composent ... Par le Sr Sanson ... A Paris, Chez H. Iaillot... joignant les Grands Augustins, aux 2. Globes avec Privilége du Roy po^r vingt ans. 1710"

[43] Part of the preceding. "Partie Septentrionale De La Souabe Par G. Del'Isle ... A Paris Chéz l'Auteur sur le Quai de l Horloge avec Privilege du Roy 1704 et se trouve a Amsterdam chez L. Renard Libraire prez de la Bourse"

[44] Part of the preceding. "Partie Meridionale De La Souabe. Par Guillaume Del'Isle ,.. Aparis Chez lAuteur sur le Quai de lHorloge a la Couro^e de Diamans avec privilege p. 20. ans. 1704. et se trouve a Amsterdam chez L. Renard Libraire prez de la Bourse"

[45] "Le Cours Du Danube, depuis sa Source jusques a Straubing, ou sont exactement distingués Les Estats qui sont dessus et aux environs. Par le Sr Iaillot... A Paris, joignant les grands Augustins, aux 2. Globes, avec Privilege de sa M^té 1705."

[46] "Le Cours Du Danube, depuis Straubing, Passaw, Lintz, jusques a Vienne, Par le Sr Iaillot... A Paris, joignant les grands Augustins, aux deux Globes, avec Privil. de sa Majesté 1705."

[47] "Le Cercle De Franconie subdivisé en tous les Estats qui le composent. Par le Sr Sanson... A Paris, Chez le Sr Iaillot... joignant les grands Augustins, aux deux Globes: Auec Privilege du Roy, pour vingt Ans. 1703."

[48] "Le Cercle De Baviere subdivisé en tous les Estats qui le composent Par le Sr Sanson... A Paris Chez le Sr Iaillot... joignãt les gr. Augustins, aux 2. Globes Avec Privilége du Roy. pour Vingt Ans. 1704."

[49] "Le Comté De Tirol, Les Eveschés De Trente et De Brixen, &c. ... Par... AHubert Iaillot... A Paris, Chez l'Auteur joignant les grands Augustins, aux 2. Globes, avec Privilege 1707."

[50] "Partie Du Cercle D'Austriche, ou sont Les Duchés De Stirie, De Carinthie, De Carniole et autres Estats, Hereditaires a la Maison d'Austriche Par le Sr Sanson... A Paris, Chez le Sr Iaillot... joignant les grands

[51] "Partie Du Cercle D'Austriche, sçavoir L'Archiduché D'Austriche Divisé En Haute Et Basse Par le S.ʳ Sanson... A Paris, Chez le S.ʳ Iaillot... joignant les grands Augustins, aux deux Globes, Avec Privilége du Roy. 1704"

[52] "Plan De La Ville De Vienne En Austriche et ses Environs   A Paris, Chez l'Autêur, le S.ʳ Iaillot... joignant les grands Augustins, aux deux Globes   Avec Privilege du Roy 1700"

[53] "Estats De La Couronne De Boheme qui comprennent Le Royaume De Boheme, Le Duché De Silesie, Les Marquisats De Moravie et De Lusace, subdivises en leurs principales parties. A Paris, Chez le S.ʳ Iaillot... joignant les grands Augustins, aux 2. Globes, Avec Privilege du Roy, 1695   Par le S.ʳ Sanson..."

[54] "Le Cercle De La Haute Saxe ou sont compris Le Duché et Eslectorat De Saxe Les Marquisats De Misnie, et De Lusace Le Landgraviat De Thuringe dans ce Cercle sont encor compris Le Brandebourg, et La Pomeranie qui ont chacune leur Carte separée Par le S Sanson... A Paris Chez le S.ʳ Iaillot... joignant les grāds Augustins, aux 2. Globes   Auec Privilége du Roy, pour vingt Ans, 1708."

[55] "Le Marquisat et Eslectorat De Brandebourg; qui fait partie du Cercle de la Haute Saxe divisé en ses principales Marches sçavoir Vieille, Moyenne, et Nouvelle, les Quartiers de Sternberg, Vckermarck, et le Comté de Rappin. A Paris Chez le S.ʳ Iaillot... joignant les grands Augustins, aux deux Globes, avec Privilége 1700   Par Le S.ʳ Sanson..."

[56] "Le Duché De Pomeranie compris sous le Cercle de la Haute Saxe divisé suivant qu'il est presentement partagé entre la Couronne de Suede et l'Eslecteur de Brandebourg... A Paris Chez le S.ʳ Iaillot... joignant les grands Augustins, aux 2. Globes, avec Privilege 1695   Par le S.ʳ Sanson..."

[57] "Le Cercle De La Basse Saxe subdivisé en tous Les Estats, et Principautés qui le composent Par le S.ʳ Sanson... A Paris Chez le S.ʳ Iaillot... joignant les grands Augustins, aux 2. Globes   Auec Privilége du Roy, pour Vingt Ans. 1708."

[58] "Les Dix-Sept Provinces Des Païs-Bas. ... Par... le P. Placide Augustin Déchaussé... A Paris. Chez La Veüve du S.ʳ Du Val... sur le Quay de l'Orloge, Au Grand Loüis d'Or   Avec Privilege du Roy. Pour quinze Ans. 1692."

[59] "Carte Des Provinces Unies Des Pays Bas... Par G. De L'Isle... A Paris Chez l'Auteur sur le Quai de l'Horloge... avec Privilege du Roy pour 20 ans 1702"

[60] "Provinces-Unies Des Pays-Bas avec leurs Acquisitions Dans La Flandre, Le Brabant, Le Limbourg Et Le Lyege Par le S.ʳ Sanson... A Paris, Chez H. Iaillot, proche les Grands Augustins, aux 2. Globes   Avec Privilege du Roy, pour Vingt Ans, 169 "

[61] "Partie Septentrionale Du Comté De Hollande... Par le S.ʳ Sanson... A Paris, Chez H. Iaillot, joignant les grands Augustins, aux deux Globes, Auec Privilege du Roy pour vingt Ans. 169 "

[62] "Partie Meridionale Du Comté De Hollande... Par le S.ʳ Sanson... A Paris, Chez H. Iaillot, joignant les grands Augustins, aux deux Globes. Auec Privilege du Roy 1700."

[63] "Le Comté De Zeelande... Par le S.ʳ Sanson... A Paris, Chez H. Iaillot joignant les grands Augustins, aux deux Globes. Avec Privilége du Roy. 1693"

[64] "La Seigneurie D'Vtrecht... Par le S.ʳ Sanson... A Paris, Chez H. Iaillot, joignant les grands Augustins, aux 2. Globes   Auec Privilege du Roy pour Vingt Ans. 1700."

[65] "La Veluwe, La Betuwe, et Le Comté De Zutphē, dans Le Duché De Gueldre... Par le S.ʳ Sanson... A Paris, Chez H. Iaillot, joignant les grands Augustins, aux deux Globes.   Auec Privilege du Roy. 1695"

[66] "La Seigneurie D'Over-Yssel, subdivisée en Trois Parties Sallant, Twente, et Drente... Par le S.ʳ Sanson... A Paris, Chez H. Iaillot, joignant les grands Augustins, aux deux Globes   Auec Privilege du Roy, pour Vingt Ans, 1700."

[67] "La Seignevrie D'Ovest-Frise ou Frise Occidentale; divisée en ses Trois Parties, subdivisées en leurs Iuridictions... Par le S.ʳ Sanson... A Paris, Chez H. Iaillot joignant les grands Augustins, aux 2. Globes. Auec Privilege du Roy, pour vingt Ans. 1709."

[68] "La Seigneurie De Groningue subdivisée en toutes ses Iuridictions. ... Par le S.ʳ Sanson... A Paris Chez H. Iaillot joignant les grands Augustins, aux deux Globes.   Auec Privilége du Roy, pour vingt Ans. 1700."

[69] "Les Provinces Des Pays-Bas Catho-

	liques distingueés suivant qu'elles sont presentement partageés, entre Le Roy De France Le Roy D'Espagne Et Les Estats Generaux Des Provinces Vnies Par le Sr Sanson ... A Paris, Chez H. Iaillot, proche les Grands Augustins, aux deux Globes: Avec Privilége du Roy, pour 20. Ans 169 "
[70]	"Carte Du Comté De Flandre ... Par Guillaume De L'Isle ... A Paris Chez l'Auteur sur le Quai de l'Horloge Avec Privilege, pour vingt ans M.DCCIIII"
[71]	"Le Comté De Flandres Divisé En Ses Chastellenies, Balliages, &c. Le Franc De Bruges et Le Pays De Waes ... Par ... Hubert Iaillot ... 1709 Partie Occidentale Du Comté De Flandre"
[72]	Part of the preceding. "Partie Orientale Du Comté De Flandre"
[73]	"Le Diocese De Tournay ... Par ... Bernard Cappelier ... A Paris Chez le Sr Iaillot ... joignant les grands Augustins, aux deux Globes. Avec Privilége de Sa Majesté 1709."
[74]	"Carte D Artois Et Des Environs ... Par Guillaume DeL'Isle ... A Paris Chez l Auteur sur le Quai de l Horloge avec Pr.^{e} Juill. 1711"
[75]	"Carte Des Comtéz de Hainaut de Namur et de Cambresis ... par Guillaume Del'Isle ... A Paris Chéz l'Auteur, sur le Quai de lHorloge avec Privilege du Roi. 1706"
[76]	"Carte Du Brabant ... Par Guillaume Del'Isle ... A Paris Chez l'Auteur sur le Quai de l'Horloge Avec Privilege du Roy 1705."
[77]	Part of the following. "Partie Septentrionale Du Duché De Brabant. ... par H. Iaillot ... 1705"
[78]	"Le Duché De Brabant Qui Comprend Les Quartiers De Louvain; Brusselles; Anvers Et Bosleduc Diviséz En Leurs Principales Iurisdictions La Seigneurie De Malines Et Le Marquisat Du Saint Empire. ... Par ... Hubert Iaillot ... Partie Meridionale Du Duché De Branbant. A Paris joignant les grands Augustins aux deux Globes. avec Privilege du Roy 1705"
[79]	"Le Duché De Luxembourg. diuisé en François, et Espagnol. ... Par le Sr Sanson ... A Paris Chez H. Iaillot, joignant les grands Augustins, aux 2. Globes. Auec Privilege du Roy. 1705"
[80]	Part of the following. "Le Comté De Namur, Partie De L'Evesché De Liege, Du Luxembourg, &c. Par le Sr Iaillot ... A Paris, Chez l'Auteur, joignant les grands Augustins, aux deux Globes 1705"
[81]	Part of the following.
[82]	Part of the following. "A Paris joignant les Grands Augustins, aux deux Globes, Avec Privilége du Roy. 1705"
[83]	"Le Duché De Luxembourg Divisé En Quartier Walon, Et Allemand dans chacun desquels sont diviséz Les Seigneuries, Prevostés Et Comtés. Le Duché De Bouillon; Le Comté De Namur Et Le Pays Entre Sambre Et Meuse. ... Par ... Hubert Iaillot ... Avec privilége de sa Majesté 1705"
13043-13045, 1921	

DA695 K28g	Keith, George, 1639?-1716. Gross Error and Hypocrisie Detected, In George Whitehead, And Some of his Brethren; As doth appear from the disingenuous and hypocritical Answer he and some others have given to some Queries sent to the last Yearly Meeting of the People call'd Quakers, in the Third Month, 1695...By George Keith. London, Printed for Walter Kettilby, at the Bishop's Head in St. Paul s Church-Yard, 1695. 9 p.ℓ., 23, [24-26] p. 20.5cm. 4° "A Postscript" (p. [24-26]) is a reply to Thomas Ellwood's Truth defended, London, 1695. "Their Answer, &c." (5th-6th p.ℓ.) dated: London, 3. Day 4. Month, call'd June, 1695. In this copy p.ℓ. 7-9 are misbound between p.ℓ. 1-2. WingK172; Sabin37198; Smith(Friends)2:30.
8392, 1912	

DA695 K28p	[Keith, George] 1639?-1716. The Pretended Yearly Meeting Of The Quakers, Their Nameless Bull Of Excommunication Given forth against George Keith, From a Party or Faction of Men that call themselves the Yearly Meeting ... With a brief Answer ... reproving the evil and wicked Practises of them in Pensilvania ... [London] Printed for R. Levis, 1695. 12 p. 20cm. 4° "At the Yearly Meeting in London, the 17. of the 3d. Month. 1695." (p. 2-3) signed: Benjamin Bealing. Signed at end: The 28th day of the 3d. Month, 1695. G. Keith. JCB(2)2:1479; Wing K193; Sabin37210; Smith (Friends)2:30.
04242, 1871	

DA695 K28t Keith, George, 1639?-1716.
　　The True Copy of a Paper Given in to the Yearly Meeting Of The People called Quakers, At their Meeting-Place in Grace-Church-street, London, 15 day of the 3d. Month 1695. By George Keith, which was read by him in the said Meeting, by their allowance. With a brief Narrative of the most material passages of Discourse betwixt George White-head, Charles Marshal, and George Keith, the said day, and the day following, betwixt George White-head, William Penn, and Francis Canfield on the one side, and George Keith on the other ... Together With a short List of some of the vile and gross Errors of George Whitehead, John Whitehead, William Penn...
　　London, Printed for R. Levis, 1695.
　　32 p. 20cm. 4º
　　Signed (p. 32): 26. Day of the 3d. Month, 1695. G. Keith.
　　Wing K220; Sabin 37222; Smith(Friends)2:29-30.
1197, 1906

bD695 K73a Know all Men by these presents, That [I Cornelis Joosten of the Citty of new yorke Carpenter am] Holden and firmly Bound unto [Coll: Abraham De Peyster of the Citty of new york merch^t.] in the Pænal Sum of [Sixty pounds ———] lawful Money of the Province of [new yorke] ...
　　[New York, William Bradford, ca. 1695]
　　Broadside. 29 x 19.5cm. 1/2º
　　Blank form completed in manuscript as indicated within brackets.
　　Title from beginning of text.
　　Dated 26 June 1695, with day, month, and last digit of year completed in ms.
　　Bristol 114.
29029, 1941

BA695 L473c Ledesma, Clemente de.
　　Compendio Del Despertador De Noticias De Los Santos Sacramentos, Que sacó à luz, y en este succinta (para los que se han de presentar de Confessores) dedicandole A Jesvs, Maria, Y Joseph. El M.R.P. Fray Clemente De Ledesma Ex-Lector de Phylosophia, y Theologia Moral, Predicador Iubilado, y Ministro Provincial de esta Provincia del Santo Evangelio de Mexico.
　　Con Licencia. En Mexico, por Doña Maria de Benavides. Viuda de Juan de Ribera. Año de 1695.
　　12 p.ℓ., 368, 32, [8] p. 15.5cm. 8º
　　License dated (11th p.ℓ.^{r}) 15 Aug. 1695.
　　Abridgment of his Dispertador de noticias de los Santos Sacramentos. Mexico, 1695.
　　JCB(2)2:1480; Palau(2)134130; Medina(Mexico) 1600; Sabin 39678.
06070, before 1874

BA695 L473d Ledesma, Clemente de.
　　Dispertador De Noticias De Los Santos Sacramentos. Primer Tomo. ... Su Autor El M.R.P. Fr. Clemente De Ledesma, Ex Lector de Phylosophia, y Theologia Moral, Predicador Iubilado: y Ministro Provincial de esta Provincia del Santo Evangelio de Mexico.
　　Con Licencia De Los Svperiores: En Mexico: por Doña Maria de Benavides: Viuda de Juan de Ribera. Año de 1695.
　　14 p.ℓ., 378, [5] p. incl. geneal. tables. 20cm. 4º
　　License dated (14th p.ℓ.^{v}) 9 Aug. 1694.
　　Continued by his Despertador de noticias teológicas morales ... segundo tomo, Mexico, 1698.
　　Bound in contemporary vellum.
　　Medina(Mexico)1599; Palau(2)134129.
70-50

E695 L545v Lemaire, Jacques Joseph, fl. 1682.
　　Les Voyages Du Sieur Le Maire Aux Isles Canaries, Cap-Verd, Senegal, Et Gambie. Sous Monsieur Dancourt, Directeur General de la Compagnie Roïale d'Affrique.
　　A Paris, Chez Jacques Collombat, ruë Saint Jacques, au Pelican. M. DC. XCV. Avec Privilege Du Roy.
　　6 p.ℓ., 205, [206-227] p. 5 plates, fold. map. 17cm. 12º
　　Cut (pelican; incl. motto "Hic Amor") on t.-p.
　　Edited by Barthélemy Saviard.
　　"Catalogue Des Livres nouveaux qui se vendent chez le même Libraire, ruë S. Jacques au Pelican" (5th-6th p.ℓ.)
　　"Relations Des Isles & environs des Rivieres de Bresalme, Gambie, Zamenée, S. Domingue, Geve & autres, &c." p. 181-205. ("... ils ne sont point du Sieur le Maire." cf. "Avis du Libraire au Lecteur," p. 180.)
　　"Achevé d'imprimer pour la premiere fois le premier May 1695." (p. [227]).
　　Bound in contemporary calf.
　　Leclerc(1878)638; Palau(2)134741.
69-15

FA695 L889b Loumans, Lodewijk, d. 1639.
　　Beatvs Dominicvs. Specvlum Peccatricis Animæ, Sive Orationes ad Deiparam quindecim per varios articulos vitæ S. Dominici, totidem contra vitia deprecantes virtutes. Ab Anonymo Authore Ord. Prædic. editæ. Opus sané aureum, in quo virtutũ omnium flammulæ, & exempla. Recensuit R.P. Ludovicus Loumans eiusdem Ord. Antuerpiensis. Ex-

pensis R.P.F. Antonij Ruyz Lozano Conventus S.P.N. Dominici Angelop. Viccarij.
    Antuerpiæ, apud Ioannem Cnobbarum, Typographum juratum, Anno 1635. Et iuxta eius exemplar, Mexicì ex typographia Viduæ Francisci Rodriguez Lupercio. 1695
    8 p.ℓ., 288 p. 10cm. 16º
    First pub. under title: Speculum peccatricis animæ. Antwerp, 1635.
    License dated (3d p.ℓ.ᵛ) 3 Nov. 1694.
    Dedication by Antonio Ruiz Lozano.
    Errata, 8th p.ℓ.ᵛ.
    Bound in contemporary vellum.
    Palau(2)142669; Medina(Mexico)1602.

4925, 1908

BA695
M337a
    Marín, Matías.
    Apologia Del Lic. Don Matias Marin, Cathedratico de Theologia. A Favor De Vnas Notas, Qve Consvltado En Roma El Reverendissimo Padre Pablo Señeri, de la Compañia de Jesvs, Predicador, Y Theologo De Sv Santidad, Y Examinador De Obispos Hizo Sobre La Vida Interior Escrita De El Ilvstrissimo Señor D. Jvan De Palafox. Respvesta Al Reverendissimo Padre Fray Jvan De La Anunciacion, General de Carmelitas Descalços à quien se dedica la Apologia.
    Con Licencia. En Valencia: por Iayme Bordaçal. Año de 1695.
    6 p.ℓ., 424 p. 20cm. 4º
    Also attributed to Juan Marín (cf. Backer).
    A reply to Juan de la Anunciación's La Inocencia Vindicada, first pub. Sevilla [1694], itself a reply to Paolo Segneri's Parere del Padre Pablo Señeri sopra la vita interiore..., first printed Milan, 1853-1855, itself a reply to Juan de Palafox y Mendoza's Vida Interior, first pub. Brussels, 1682.
    Errata, 4th p.ℓ.ᵛ.
    Imperfect: p. 373-380 wanting, p. 189-196 repeated.
    Bound in contemporary vellum.
    Palau(2)123092; Medina(BHA)1942; Backer 5:579.

5512, 1909

D. Math
C. 26
    Mather, Cotton, 1663-1728.
    Batteries upon the Kingdom of the Devil. Seasonable Discourses Upon Some Common, but Woful, Instances, Wherein Men Gratifie the Grand Enemy of their Salvation. By Mr. Cotton Mather ...
    London, Printed for Nath. Hiller, at the Princes-Armes in Leaden-Hall-Street, over-against St. Mary Axe. 1695.
    8 p.ℓ., 192 p. 16cm. 8º
    Edited by Nathaniel Mather.
    Dedication dated (4th p.ℓ.ᵛ) 15 Dec. 1693.
    Booksellers' advertisement, 8th p.ℓ.ᵛ.
    JCB(2)2:1482; WingM1083; Sabin46230; Holmes(C.)26; Holmes(M.)32A.

06185, before 1882

D. Math
C. 41A
    [Mather, Cotton] 1663-1728.
    Brontologia Sacra: The Voice Of The Glorious God In The Thunder: Explained and Applyed In a Sermon uttered by a Minister of the Gospel in a Lecture unto an Assembly of Christians abroad, ... Whereto are added Some Reflections formed on the Lords-Day following by the Voices of Thunders, upon the great things which the great God is now a doing in the World. A Discourse useful for all Men at all times, but especially intended for an Entertainment in the Hours of Thunder.
    London, Printed by John Astwood, 1695.
    2 p.ℓ., 38 p. 18cm. (19cm. in case) 8º
    In this copy there is a blank leaf at end.
    Imperfect: p. 9-10 wanting; available in facsim.
    WingM1086; Holmes(C.)41A; Sabin46243.

9109, 1913

D. Math
C. 97
    Mather, Cotton, 1663-1728.
    Durable Riches. Two Brief Discourses, Occasioned By the Impoverishing Blast of Heaven, which the Undertakings of Men, both by Sea and Land, have met withal. The One, handling, The true Cause of Loosing; The other, giving, The true Way of Thriving. By Cotton Mather. ...
    Boston, Printed by John Allen, for Vavasour Harris, and are to be Sold at his Shop over-against the Old Meeting House. 1695.
    [2], 33, 34, [2] p. 14.5cm. 12º
    "The True Way of Thriving" has separate paging, but continuous signatures.
    Booksellers' advertisement, at end.
    JCB(2)2:1483; Evans722; WingM1095; Holmes(C.)97; Sabin46290; McAlpin4:523; Brinley 1102 (this copy).

06186, 1878

D. Math
C. 188A
    Mather, Cotton, 1663-1728.
    Johannes in Eremo. Memoirs, Relating to the Lives, Of The Ever-Memorable, Mr. John Cotton, Who Dyed, 23.d. 10.m. 1652. Mr.

John Norton, Who Dyed, 5.d.2.m. 1663. Mr. John Wilson, Who Dyed, 7.d.6.m. 1667. Mr. John Davenport, Who Dyed, 15.d.1 m. 1670. Reverend and Renowned Ministers of the Gospel, All, in the more Immediate Service of One Church, in Boston; And Mr. Thomas Hooker, Who Dyed, 7.d.5.m. 1647. Pastor of the Church at Hartford; New-England. Written, by Cotton Mather. ...

[Boston] Printed for and Sold by Michael Perry, at his Shop, under the West End of the Town-House. 1695.

32, 80, 39, 46, 30, 45, [46-47] p. 14.5cm. 8°

Each part has separate paging and signatures, and caption title, except that the last part has also special t.-p.: Piscator Evangelicus. Or, The Life of Mr. Thomas Hooker. ... Printed in the year 1695.

"To the Reader" (p. 3-12, 1st count) signed: May. 16. 1695. Increase Mather.

Errata, verso of t.-p.

Booksellers' advertisement (books by Cotton Mather), p. [46-47] at end.

In this copy there is a blank leaf following p. 46, 4th count, and p. 30, 5th count.

JCB(2)2:1481; Evans724; WingM1117; Sabin 46371; Holmes(C.)188A; Holmes(I.)148.

0111, 1819

D.Math Mather, Cotton, 1663-1728.
C.188A   Piscator Evangelicus. Or, The Life of Mr. Thomas Hooker, The Renowned, Pastor of Hartford-Church, And Pillar of Connecticut-Colony, In New-England. Essay^{ed} by Cotton Mather. ...

[Boston] Printed in the Year 1695.

45, [46-47] p. 14.5cm. 8° (Issued as a part of his Johannes in Eremo. [Boston], 1695.)

Booksellers' advertisement (books by Cotton Mather), p. [46-47].

Evans727; WingM1141; Sabin46460; Holmes(C.)285; McAlpin4:523.

0111A, 1819

D.Math Mather, Cotton, 1663-1728.
C.352   Seven Select Lectures, Of Mr. Cotton Mather, of New-England, Or, Seasonable Discourses upon Some Common but Woful Distempers, wherein men gratify the Grand Enemy of their Salvation; And, upon, The Remedies of those Distempers. By a Singular Providence of God, Preserved from the Hands of the French, whereinto they were fallen, and now Published, by an English Gentleman who providentially litt upon them.

London, Printed for Nath. Hiller, at the Princes Arms, in Leaden-Hall-Street, over against St. Mary Axe. 1695. [i.e. Boston, by Bartholomew Green and John Allen for Joseph Wheeler, 1697?]

8 p.l., 192 p. 15cm. 8°

First pub. under title: Batteries upon the kingdom of the devil. London, 1695; these are the same sheets with new t.-p. printed in Boston, 1697? (cf. Holmes).

Edited by Nathaniel Mather.

Booksellers' advertisement, 8th p.l.^{v}.

Bound in contemporary calf, rebacked.

WingM1151; Sabin46505; Holmes(C.)352; Holmes(M.)32B.

8972, 1912

D.Math Mather, Increase, 1639-1723.
I.122A   Solemn Advice To Young Men, Not to Walk in the Wayes of their Heart, and in the Sight of their Eyes; but to Remember The Day Of Judgment: By Increase Mather, Præsident of Harvard Colledge in Cambridge, & Preacher of the Gospel at Boston, in New-England. ...

Boston in New-England, Printed by Bartholomew Green. Sold by Samuel Phillips, at the Brick Shop near the Old-Meeting-House. 1695.

111, [1] p. 14cm. 8°

Includes "The hatefull Evil Of Sin ... A Sermon", p. 65-111.

Booksellers' advertisement, last p.

Errata, at end.

In this copy "To The Young Generation, in New-England" (p. [3-4]) is dated in contemporary hand: Boston. August 28. 1694.

Bound in contemporary calf.

Evans728; WingM1252; Sabin46743; Holmes (I.)122A.

4972, 1908

DA695   Maule, Thomas, 1645-1724.
M449t   Truth held Forth And Maintained According to the Testimony of the holy Prophets, Christ and his Apostles recorded in the holy Scriptures. With some Account of the Judgements of the Lord lately inflicted upon New-England by Witch craft. To which is added, Something concerning the Fall of Adam ... by Thomas Maule.

[New York] Printed [by William Bradford] in the year 1695.

4 p.l., 260 p. 17.5cm. (19.5cm. in case) 4°

Dated at end: 4th. 1st. Mon. 1694.

For publishing this book Maule, a Quaker,

was arrested by the Massachusetts authorities, and copies were seized and publicly burned.

This copy contains numerous printing errors which are found press-corrected in other recorded copies.

Cf. Jones, M.B., "Thomas Maule," Essex Institute Historical Collections, LXXII (1936).

With this are bound in contemporary calf: his Nevv-England Persecutors mauld [New York, 1697], his An abstract of a letter to Cotton Mather [New York] 1701, and his For the service of truth against George Keith [Philadelphia] 1703.

Imperfect: p. ℓ. 1-4 wanting.

DA695 M449t cop. 2
———— Another copy. 18.5cm. 1st and 4th p. ℓ. disintegrated, affecting text.
Evans730; Sabin46935; WingM1354; Smith (Friends)2:167; Hildeburn(NY)4; Dexter(Cong.)2458.

3422, 1907
5236A, 1909

DA695 M469c [R]
Mayhew, Matthew, 1648-1710.
The Conquests and Triumphs Of Grace: Being A Brief Narrative of the Success which the Gospel hath had among the Indians of Martha's Vineyard (and the Places adjacent) in New-England. With Some Remarkable Curiosities, concerning the Numbers, the Customs, and the present Circumstances of the Indians on that Island. Further Explaining and Confirming the Account given of those Matters, by Mr. Cotton Mather, in the Life of the Renowned Mr. John Eliot. By Matthew Mayhew. Attested by the Reverend Mr. Nath. Mather, and others. Whereto is Added, An Account concerning the Present State of Christianity among the Indians, in other Parts of New-England: Expressed in the Letters of several Worthy Persons. best acquainted therewithal.

London, Printed for Nath. Hiller, at the Princes Arms in Leaden-hall-street, over against St. Mary Axe, 1695.

68 p., 1 ℓ. 15cm. 8°

First pub. under title: A brief narrative of the success... Boston, 1694.

Added to this edition are a preface by Nathaniel Mather dated "29th. of the 11th. Month, 169$\frac{4}{5}$" (p. 5-9) and a transl. of Increase Mather's De successu evangelii (p. 63-68, "A Letter Concerning The Success of the Gospel...") reprinted from the transl. in the Boston, 1691, edition of Cotton Mather's Triumphs of the reformed religion.

Bookseller's advertisement, last page.

JCB(2)2:1484; WingM1437; Sabin47152; Holmes (I.)128H; Holmes(M.)26.

0598, 1846

BA695 M611p
Mexico(City)--Universidad.
Panegyricos Fvnebres Del Illmo. Señor Doctor D. Jvan Cano Sandoval Obispo de la Santa Iglesia Cathedral de Yucatan del Consejo de su Magestad. En Svs Exeqvias Celebradas â 26. y 27. de Junio de 1695. por esta Real Vniversidad de Mexico. Y su Rector dos vezes actual El D^{or}. D. Manvel De Escalante Colombres, y Mendoza, ... que las saca à luz para ponerse con ellas á los pies De Carlos II. Maximo Rey De España Avgvsto Emperador De Las Indias N. S^r.

Con licencia en Mexico, por Juan Joseph Guillena Carrascoso Impresor y Mercader de Libros. Año de 1695.

20 p. ℓ., 12 numb. ℓ., [16] p. 19.5cm. 4°

License dated (recto 19th p. ℓ.) 28 Sept. 1695.

Royal coat of arms, recto 2d p. ℓ.

Includes: --Dedication by Manuel de Escalante Colombres y Mendoza.--Funebris Declamatio, by Carlos Bermúdez de Castro.-- Sermon En La Real Vniversidad De Mexico à las Honras de el Señor Obispo D. Juan Cano este año de 1695. à 27. de Junio, by Jerónimo de Colina.--Poetry by Martín de Olivas, Joseph de la Barrera Varaona, Alonso Ramírez de Vargas, and Thadeo de Rivera, and poem In Tumulum Ill^{mi}. Ac Rev^{mi}. Domini Doctor$\overline{\text{is}}$ D. Ioannis Cano De Sandoval, Episcopimeritissimi Yucatanensis. Epitaphivm.

Palau(2)80734; Medina(Mexico)1596.

1058, 1905

BA695 M645s
Millan de Poblete, Juan, d. 1709.
Sermon Qve A la solemne, annual, y titular fiesta del Gloriosissimo Principe de los Apostoles San Pedro, Que celebrò su Eclesiastica Congregacion en la Iglesia Collegio, y Hospital de la Santissima Trinidad de Mexico en la Dominica infraoctav$\overline{\text{a}}$ de su fiesta predicó El D.^{or} Don Jvan Millan De Poblete Prebendado de la Santa Iglesia Cathedral Metropolitana de la Ciudad de Mexico Corte Imperial de esta America Septemtrional [sic] en tres de Julio de 1695. Y Dedica Al Sor D.D. Manvel De Escalante, y Mendoza Cathedratico Jubilado de Prima de Canones en esta Real Vniversidad; segunda vez su actual Rector, ...

Con Lecencia [sic] En Mexico, por Iuan Ioseph Guillena Carrascoso. [1695]

8 p. ℓ., 10 numb. ℓ. 19.5cm. 4°

Coat of arms of dedicatee, recto 2d p. ℓ.

License dated (verso 8th p. ℓ.) 2 Aug 1695.

Palau(2)169712; Medina(Mexico)1604.

1062, 1905

DA695 P411a   Penington, John, 1655-1710.
An Apostate Exposed: Or, George Keith Contradicting himself and his Brother Bradford. Wherein Their Testimony to the Christian Faith of the People Called Quakers, is opposed to G. K's late Pamphlet, Stiled, Gross Error and Hypocrisie detected. By John Penington. ...
London, Printed and Sold by T. Sowle, near the Meeting-House in White-Hart-Court in Grace Church-street, 1695.
29 p. 16.5cm. 8º
A reply to George Keith's Gross error and hypocrisie detected, 1st pub. London, 1695.
"Postscript" (p. 24-29) a reply to Keith's A serious appeal to all the more sober, impartial and judicious people in New England, Philadelphia, 1692.
WingP1223; Sabin59663; Smith(Friends)2:362.

2343, 1906

DA695 P412b   Penn, William, 1644-1718.
A Brief Account Of The Rise and Progress Of the People called Quakers In Which their Fundamental Principle, Doctrines, Worship, Ministry and Discipline are Plainly Declared, ... By W. Penn.
London, Printed and Sold by T. Sowl' [sic], near the Meeting-house in VVhite-hart-court, in Gracious street. 1695.
5 p.ℓ., 158 p. 14.5cm. 12º.
First pub. as the preface to George Fox, Journal. London, 1694, under caption title: The Preface Being A Summary Account Of the Divers Dispensations of God To Men ...
Imperfect: edges of t.-p. worn, affecting imprint; 3d p.ℓ. wanting.
Smith(Friends)2:312.

30126, 1947

bBB P4716 1695 1   Peru(Viceroyalty)--Laws, statutes, etc., 1689-1705 (Portocarrero)   17 Jan 1695
Don Melchor Portocarrero Lasso de la Vega, Conde de la Monclova, ... Por aver dado forma su Magestad (que Dios guarde) a los Lutos, y Pompa funeral en Cedula de veinte y dos de Marzo de mil seiscientos, y noventa, y tres paraque precisamente se obserue, y cumpla: cuyo tenor es el siguiente. ...
[Lima, 1695]
[3] p. 31.5cm. fol.
Title from caption and beginning of text.
Dated in Lima, 17 Jan 1695.
Manuscript certification of true copy dated 23 Jan 1695. Manuscript certifications of the city of Huamanga dated 9 Mar 1695.
Papel sellado dated 1694, 1695.

28205, 1938

D695 P892p   Poyntz, John, fl. 1658-1695.
The Present Prospect Of The Famous and Fertile Island Of Tobago, To the Southward of The Island of Barbadoes. With A Description of the Scituation, Growth, Fertility and Manufacture of the said Island: Setting forth how that 100 ℓ. Stock in seven Years may be improved to 5000 ℓ. per Annum. To which is added Proposals for Encouragement of all those that are minded to settle there. By Captain John Poyntz. The Second Edition.
London, Printed by John Astwood for the Author, and sold by William Staresmore at the Half Moon and Seven Stars in Cornhill, and at the Marine Coffee-house in Birchin lane, 1695.
3 p.ℓ., 50 p. 20.5cm. 4º
First pub. London, 1683.
JCB(2)2:1486; WingP3131; Sabin64858.

01690, 1854

D -Scott 5b   Proposals For A Fond to Cary on A Plantation May 22. One Thousand six hundred and ninty five.
[Edinburgh? 1695]
3 p. 29.5cm. fol.
Caption title.
WingP3722; Scott 5b.

06034, 1905

+Z =P975 1695   Ptolemaeus, Claudius.
Claudii Ptolemaei Tabulae geographicae Orbis Terrarum Veteribus cogniti.
Franequeræ, Apud Leonardum Strik, Bibliopolam. Trajecti ad Rhenum, Apud Franciscum Halmam, Acad. Typograph. M.DC.XCV.
2 p.ℓ., 28 double-page maps. 42.5cm. fol.
Gerardus Mercator's maps to Ptolemaeus' Geographia (without descriptive text).
These maps 1st pub. Cologne, 1578; titles of the maps have been changed, and the plates have been otherwise reworked for this edition.
Engraved t.-p. (by Jan van Vianen); imprint on 2d p.ℓ.ᵛ
Sabin66498; Phillips(Atlases)518; Koeman Me5.
Contents:
[1] Vniversalis Tabvla Ivxta Ptolemæum.
[2] Tab. I. Africæ, in qua Mauritania Tingitana et Cæsariensis. ...
[3] Tab. II. Africæ, Complectens Africam Proprie dictam. ...
[4] Tab. III. Africæ, in qua Cyrenaica, Marmarica, ac Lybia Exterior. ...
[5] Appendix Tab. III. Africæ, Aegyptum Inferiorem Exhibens. ...
[6] Tab. IV. Africæ, in qua Libya Interior et Exterior. Æthiopia ...

[7] Tab. I. Asiæ, in qua Galatia, Cappadocia, Pontus, Bithynia, Asia Minor, Pamphylia, Lycia, ac Cilicia ...
[8] Tab. II. Asiæ, Sarmatiam Asiaticam repræsentans ...
[9] Tab. III. Asiæ, in qua Colchis, Iberia, Albania, ac Armenia Maior. ...
[10] Tab. IV. Asiæ, in qua Mesopotamia, Syria, Arabia Petrea, ac Deserta. ...
[11] Tab. V. Asiæ, Repræsentans Mediam, Hyrcaniam, Assyriam, Susianam, ac Persidem. ...
[12] Tab. VI. Asiæ, Arabiam Felicem, Carmaniam ac Sinum Persicum ...
[13] Tab. VII. Asiæ, exhibens Scythiam, intra Imaum Sogdianam, Bactrianam, Hircaniam, aliasq. Asiæ, Regiones ...
[14] Tab. VIII. Asiæ, Scythiam extra imaum, ac Sericam comprehendens ...
[15] Tab. IX. Asiæ, Continens Ariam, Paropanisum, Drangianam, Arachosiam, et Gedrosiam. ...
[16] Tab. X. Asiæ, Complectens Indiam intra Gangem. ...
[17] Tab. XI. Asiæ, comprehendens Indiam extra Gangem. ...
[18] Tab. XII. Asiæ, Taprobanam repræsentans. ...
[19] Tab. I. Europæ, Continens Albion, Britanniam, et Hiberniam. ...
[20] Tab. II. Europæ, Hispaniam ac Lusitaniam Complectens. ...
[21] Tab. III. Europæ, Galliam, Belgicam, ac Germaniæ, partem repræsentens. ...
[22] Tab. IV. Europæ, Germaniam et Galliam Belgicam exhibens. ...
[23] Tab. V. Europæ, in qua Rætia, Pannonia, Noricum, Liburnia, Dalmatia, Cum Italiæ parte. ...
[24] Tab. VI. Europæ, totam Italiam ob oculos ponens ...
[25] Tab. VII. Europæ, Complectens Sardiniam, Siciliam, ac Corsicæ, partem ...
[26] Tab. VIII. Europæ, in qua Sarmatia, Mæotis palus, ac Germaniæ, Daciæq pars. ...
[27] Tab. IX. Europæ, Continens Daciam, Misiam, Thraciam, ac Macedoniæ partem. ...
[28] Tab. X. Europæ, Macedoniam, Epirum ac Peloponnesum repræsentans ...

06910, 1884

BA695
R585s
Rio, Joseph del, fl. 1695.
Sermon De Gracias Por la justa eleccion, en que salió electo por Ministro Provincial de esta Santa Provincia de Santiago de Xalisco N.M.R.P. Fr. Joseph Azpilcueta Lector jubilado, y Padre Diffinidor habitual en ella. Predicado Por el R.P. Fr. Joseph Del Rio, Lector jubilado, Notario Apostolico y Publico, y Diffinidor actual. Ofrecelo Obsequioso A N. R.^{mo} P. Commissario General Fr. Juan Capistrano Lector Jubilado, Padre de la Santa Provincia de los Angeles, y Commissario General de todas las de la Nueva-España. A expensas del Alferes Nicolas Pisano.
Con licencia en Mexico en la Imprenta de Juan Joseph Guillena Carrascoso Impressor, y Mercader de libros. Año de 1695.
9 p. l., 9 numb. l., [3] p. 19.5cm. 4º
License dated (verso 7th p. l.) 17 July 1695.
Medina(Mexico)1620.

1059, 1905

B69
G643v
22
Salazar, Antonio de, fl. 1673-1698.
Villancicos Que Se Cantaron En La Santa Iglesia Cathedral Metropolitana de Mexico, en honor de Maria Sanctissima Madre de Dios, en su Assumpcion Triumphante ... Compuestos en metro musico; por Antonio de Salazar, Maestro de Capilla de dicha Sancta Iglesia.
Con licencia en Mexico, en la Imprenta de los Herederos de la Viuda de Bernardo Calderon. Año de 1695.
1 p. l., [6] p. 20cm. 4º
Imprint at end.
Woodcut title vignette (the Virgin surrounded by angels).
Bound, in contemporary vellum, as no. 22 with 42 other items.

28922, 1941

B69
G643v
42
Salazar, Antonio de, fl. 1673-1698.
Villancicos Qve Se Cantaron En La Santa Yglesia Metropolitana, de Mexico: En los Maytines del Glorioso Principe de la Yglesia El Señor San Pedro. ... Compuestos en metro musico por Antonio de Salazar Maestro de Capilla de dicha Santa Yglesia.
Con licencia en Mexico; por los Herederos de la Uiuda de Bernardo Calderon Año de 1695.
[8] p. 20cm. 4º
Imprint at end.
Woodcut title vignette (St. Peter enthroned; inscribed at base: San Pedro.)
Bound, in contemporary vellum, as no. 42 with 42 other items.

28942, 1941

BA696　Saldaña y Ortega, Antonio de.
S162o　　Oracion Evangelica del Principe, y Cabeza de la Iglesia nuestro esclarecido P. y Señor S. Pedro, Dixola D. Antonio De Saldana y Ortega, Lic$^{do.}$ en Sagrada Theologia. Natural de la Ciudad de los Angeles, Rector del Illustrissimo Collegio de San Bartholomé en la de Antequera, Valle de Oaxaca, Cathedratico de Visperas de Sagrada Theologia en el Seminario Real de Santa Cruz, Examinador Synodal del Obispado, y Qualificador del Santo Officio. En la Santa Iglesia Cathedral de dicha Ciudad de Antequera, presente el Ill$^{mo.}$ Señor Doctor D. Isidro Sariñana y Cuenca, Obispo de la dicha Iglesia su Sr. ...
　　Con Licencia, En la Puebla, en la Imprenta del Capitan Juan de Villa Real. en el Portal de las flores, Año de 1695. [i.e. 1696]
　　8 p.ℓ., 26 p. 20cm. 4°
　　License dated (8th p.ℓ.^{v}) 2 Jan. 1696.
　　Palau(2)287157; Medina(Puebla)177; Sabin 75612n.

69-777

BA695　Salduendo, Francisco Javier, 1659-1718.
S162s　　Los Siete Angeles Del Apocalypsis En Siete Sermones De Los Siete Miercoles de Quaresma, Qve Predico En La Iglesia Catedral De Lima, el R.P.M. Francisco Xavier Salduendo de la Compañia de Iesvs, Catedratico de Filososia, que fue en el Colegio Maximo de San Pablo. Y de Sagrada Theologia en la Real Vniversidad de la Plata. ...
　　Con Licencia De Los Svperiores. En Lima. A costa de Joseph de Contreras Impressor Real, y del Santo Oficio. Año de 1695.
　　15 p.ℓ., 510, [15] p. 20cm. 4°
　　Dedication dated (7th p.ℓ.^{v}) 1 Nov. 1695.
　　Errata, 14th p.ℓ.
　　In this copy there is a blank leaf following p. 510.
　　Palau(2)287213; Medina(Lima)676; Sabin 75621; Backer7:461.

5513, 1909

BA695　San Miguel, Isidoro de.
S196p　　Parayso Cvltivado De La Mas Senzilla Prvdencia Virtudes practicadas en la Inocentissima Vida Del V. Siervo De Dios, Y Portentoso Varon Fr. Sebastian De Aparicio, Religioso Lego de la Regular Obseruancia de Nuestro P.S. Francisco, Hijo de la Santa Prouincia de el Santo Euangelio de Mexico. ... Por Fray Ysidro De S. Migvel Hijo de la Santa Provincia de San Pedro de Alcantara de Menores Descalsos en el Reyno de Napoles.
　　En Napoles, M.DC.XCV. En la Stamperia de Iuan Vernuccio, y Nicolas Layno.
　　14 p.ℓ., 156, [26] p. front. (port.) 21cm. 4°
　　"Protesta" dated (13th p.ℓ.^{r}) 10 May 1695.
　　Errata, 14th p.ℓ.^{v}.
　　In this copy there is a blank leaf at end.
　　Imperfect: front. wanting.
　　JCB(2)2:1485; Palau(2)293100; Medina(BHA) 1947; Sabin76182.

06092, before 1874

B69　Santoyo, Felipe de.
G643v　　Villancicos, Que Se Cantaron En La Santa Iglesia Metropolitana de Mexico: En los Maytines de la Purissima Concepcion De Nuestra Señora; Este Año De 1695 Escrivelos Don Phelipe de Santoyo, ... Compuestos en Metro musico, por Antonio de Salazar, Maestro de Capilla de dicha Santa Iglesia.
　　Con licencia; En Mexico por los Hærederos de la Viuda de Bernardo Calderon; en la calle de San Augustin. Año de 1695,
　　[12] p. 20cm. 4°
　　Imprint at end.
　　Woodcut title Vignette (the Virgin standing on an inverted new moon)
　　Bound, in contemporary vellum, as no. 10 with 42 other items.
　　Medina(Mexico)1623.

28910, 1941

D　　Scotland--Laws, statutes, etc., 1694-1702
-Scott　　(William III).　　26 June 1695
2　　Act For a Company Tradeing to Affrica, and the Indies. June 26. 1695.
　　Edinburgh, Printed by the Heirs and Successors of Andrew Anderson, Printer to His most Excellent Majesty, 1695.
　　8 p. 30cm. fol.
　　Caption title; imprint at end.
　　Royal arms at head of title.
　　WingS1418; Sabin78198; Scott 2.

645, 1904

D　　Scotland--Laws, statutes, etc., 1694-1702
Scott　　(William III).　　26 June 1695
2c　　An Act Of Parliament, For Encourageing the Scots Affrican and Indian Company. Edinburgh, June 26. 1695.
　　[Edinburgh? 1695]
　　[7] p. 18.5cm. 4°
　　Caption title.

First pub. Edinburgh, 1695.
JCB(2)2:1476; WingS1127; Sabin78198; Scott 2c.
02469, 1851

D -Scott 2b
Scotland--Laws, statutes, etc., 1694-1702 (William III). 26 June 1695
An Act Of The Parliament Of Scotland For Erecting an East-India Company in That Kingdom.
Edinburgh, Printed by the Heirs and Successors of Andrew Anderson, Printer to his most Excellent Majesty, 1695. And Reprinted at London, for Sam. Manship at the Ship in Corn-hill, and Hugh Newman at the Grashopper in the Poultrey. [1695]
1 p.ℓ., 8 p. 30.5cm. fol.
Dated (p. 1): June 26. 1695.
First pub. Edinburgh, 1695.
WingS1145; Sabin18545; Scott2b.
29710, 1945

D Scott 3
Scotland--Laws, statutes, etc., 1694-1702 (William III). 26 June 1695
Literæ Patentes Seu Concessus, sub Magno Scotiæ Sigillo, Societati in Affricam & Indias Commercium Agenti. Per Actum Parliamenti ejusdem Regni.
Edinburgi: Excudebant Hæredes Andreæ Anderson Regis Typographi. In Usum Societatis prædictæ, 1695.
2 p.ℓ., 15 p. incl. front. (royal arms). 18.5cm. 8°
First pub. in English, Edinburgh, 1695, under title: Act for a company tradeing to Affrica ...
The act is dated (p. 15) in Edinburgh, 26 June 1695.
Certifications are dated (p. 15) 1 Oct. 1695.
WingL2540; Scott3.
762, 1905

DA691 W695m
[Sewall, Samuel] 1652-1730.
Mrs. Judith Hull, Of Boston, in N. E. Daughter of Mr. Edmund Quincey; late Wife of John Hull Esq. deceased.
[Boston, Printed by Bartholomew Green, 1695]
Broadside. 13 x 7.5cm. 8°
With epitaph in verse, 10 lines.
Mounted inside front cover of: Willard, Samuel. The Mourners Cordial Against Excessive Sorrow. Boston, 1691.

Evans738; Wing S2819; Sabin79442; Ford(Mass. Brds.)210.
6682-1, 1910

DA695 -S547p
Shepard, Thomas, 1605-1649.
The Parable Of The Ten Virgins Opened & Applied: Being the Substance of divers Sermons on Matth. 25. 1, ---13. Wherein, the Difference between the Sincere Christian and the most Refined Hypocrite, ... are clearly discovered, and practically Improved, By Thomas Shepard Late Worthy and Faithful Pastor of the Church of Christ at Cambridge in New-England. Now pubished [sic] from the Authors own Notes, at the desires of many, for the common Benefit of the Lords people, By Jonathan Mitchell Minister at Cambridge, Tho. Shepard, Son to the Reverend Author, now Minister at Charles-Town in New-England. ...
[London] Reprinted, and carefully Corrected in the Year, 1695.
4 p.ℓ., 198, 197-232, 190, [5] p. 27.5cm. fol.
First pub. London, 1660.
"To The Reader, And Especially to the Inhabitants of Cambridge In New-England" (2d-4th p.ℓ.) signed: Jonathan Mitchel.
"To the Reader" (verso 4th p.ℓ.) signed: William Greenhill, Edmund Calamy, John Jackson, Simon Ash, William Taylor. Decemb. 24. 1659.
"These Sermons preached by the Author, in a weekly Lecture, were begun in June 1636. and ended in May 1640." - cf. verso 3d p.ℓ.
Bound in contemporary calf.
Sabin80213; WingS3115.
4238, 1908

D696 -C737c
Some Account Of The Transactions Of Mr. William Paterson, In Relation to The Bank of England, And The Orphans Fund. In a Letter to a Friend.
London, Printed in the Year MDCXCV.
1 p.ℓ., 20 p. 31.5cm. fol.
Signed (at end): London, 3 July, 1695. J.S.
Imperfect: t.-p. partly disintegrated with loss of text; available in facsim.
Bound in a volume of Scottish imprints and mss. as the 17th of 58 items.
WingS89; Kress S1900.
7115, 1910

bD Scott 6
Some Considerations upon the late Act of the Parliament of Scotland, for Constituting an Indian Company. In a Letter to a Friend.

	London: Printed in the Year 1695. 4 p. 32.5cm. fol. Caption title; imprint at end. Dated at end 22 Nov. 1695. "... probably the composition of William Paterson ..." (Scott). Wing S4497; Scott 6; Kress S1901.
69-10	

B682 -L864p	Spain--Sovereigns, etc., 1665-1700 (Charles II) 24 Mar 1695 Carta Del Rey Nvestro Señor (que Dios guarde) al Illustrissimo señor Don Thoribio de Mior, Obispo de Pamplona, en que su Magestad le participa la resolucion que ha tomado en la controversia jurisdiccional de dicho señor Obispo, con los Ministros del Consejo, y Corte del Reyno de Navarra, sobre et conocimiento de la inmunidad Eclesiastica Local. [Madrid, 1695] [1] p. 28cm. fol. Caption title. Dated at end in Madrid, 24 March, 1695. Bound as no. 14 in a vol. with binder's title: Luis Lopez Obras.
14020, 1925	

BB -S7336 1695 1	Spain--Sovereigns, etc., 1665-1700 (Charles II) 25 April 1695 El Rey. Conde de Galve, ... Virrey, Governador, y Capitan General de las Provincias de Nueva España, ... ò à la persona, ò personas à cuyo cargo fuere su govierno: En despachos de 16. de Agosto de 1678. y 18. de Junio de 1682. dirigidos al Obispo de la Iglesia Catedral de la Ciudad de Guadalaxara, en la Nueva Galicia, le encarguè pusiesse se sequestro las Doctrinas de Antoyac, Teocuytlatlan, Sentipac, y Amaqueca, que estavan à cargo de la Religion de San Francisco, ... [Madrid, 1695] 40 numb. ℓ. 30cm. (31cm. in case) fol. Title from beginning of text. Compilation of 39 orders dated 25 Oct 1694 or 16 Mar 1695 (referring to orders dated 15 Oct 1595, 3 Dec 1686, 24 Sept 1688, 26 Mar 1689, or 25 Oct 1694, texts included) restoring to the Franciscans, at the instance of their Procurador General por las Indias (Francisco de Ayeta), missions which had been sequestered by the Bishop of Guadalajara (Juan de Santiago de León Garabito). Certifications dated in Madrid, 25 April 1695. Papel sellado dated 1695.
28206, 1938	

D695 -T413g1	Thesaurus Geographicus. A New Body of Geography: Or, A Compleat Description Of The Earth: Containing I. By way of Introduction, The General Doctrine of Geography. ... II. A Description of all the known Countries of the Earth ... Also Analytical Tables; whereby is shewn at a View, the Division of every Kingdom or State into Provinces and Counties, with their Divisions into Dioceses, Bailywicks, &c. and the chief Towns situated in each. III. The Principal Cities and most considerable Towns in the World ... IV. Maps of every Country of Europe, and General Ones of Asia, Africa and America ... Collected with great Care from the most approv'd Geographers and Modern Travellers and Discoveries, by several Hands. With an Alphabetical Table of all the Towns Names. London: Printed for Abel Swall and Tim. Child, at the Sign of the Unicorn at the West-end of St. Paul's Church. 1695. 4 p.ℓ., 44 p., 1 ℓ., [2], 42 p., 43-48 numb. ℓ., 49-178, 189-272, 231-404, 407-506, [12] p. illus. (incl. maps, plans, tables, diagrs.). 2 maps. 31.5cm. fol. [a]^2 b^2 B-N^2, 2A-2I^4 *2K^4 *2L^2 2K-2T^4 2U^6 2X-3G^4 3H^4(-3H3) 3I-3L^4 3M^2 3N-3U^4 3X^2 a-c^2 Errata, 4th p.ℓ.^{v} Booksellers' advertisements, p. 506, and p. [12] at end. In this issue line 29 of t.-p. reads "... Table of all the Towns Names". There is another issue, in which line 29 of t.-p. reads "... Table of the Names of Places", which has textual variations in preliminaries (t.-p. and preface, p.ℓ. 1-2), text (after p. 50, ^{2}G4^v, through p. 286, ^{2}2Q4^v), and index. In this copy there are contemporary ms. additions on the flyleaves and in the text. Bound in contemporary calf, rebacked. Wing T869; Phillips(Atlases)4269, 536n.
65-249	

D695 -T413g2	Thesaurus Geographicus. A New Body of Geography: Or, A Compleat Description Of The Earth: Containing I. By way of Introduction, The General Doctrine of Geography. ... II. A Description of all the known Countries of the Earth ... Also Analytical Tables; whereby is shewn at a View, the Division of every Kingdom or State into Provinces and Counties, with their Sub-divisions into Dioceses, Bailywicks &c. and the chief Towns situated in each. III. The Principal Cities and most considerable Towns in the World ... IV. Maps of every Country of Europe, and General Ones of Asia, Africa and America ... Collected with great Care from the most approv'd Geo-

graphers and Modern Travellers and Discoveries, by several Hands. With an Alphabetical Table of the Names of Places.

London: Printed for Abel Swall and Tim. Child, at the Sign of the Unicorn at the West-end of St. Paul's-Church. 1695.

4 p.ℓ., 44 p., 1 ℓ., [2], 42 p., 43-48 numb. ℓ., 49-50 p., 51-56 numb. ℓ., 57-144 p., 145-154 numb. ℓ., 155-234, 238 (i.e. 237)-[238], 239-506, [14] p. illus. (incl. maps, plans, tables, diagrs.). 2 maps. 31.5cm. fol. [a]^2 b^2 B-N^2, ^{2}A-Q^4 R^2 S-2H^4 I^6 2K-2P^4 2Q^2 2R-2T^4 2U^6 2X-3G^4 3H^4(-3H3) 3I-3L^4 3M^2 3N-3U^4 3X^2 a-d^2 (-d^2)

Numerous errors in paging.
Errata, 4th p.ℓ.^{v}
Booksellers' advertisements, p. 506, and p. [14] at end.
In this issue line 29 of t.-p. reads "... Table of the Names of Places". There is another issue, in which line 29 of t.-p. reads "... Table of all the Towns Names", which has textual variations in preliminaries (t.-p. and preface, p.ℓ. 1-2), text (after p. 50, ^{2}G4^v, through p. 286, ^{2}2Q2^v, and index.
Imperfect: separate map of the roads of England wanting; available in Library's copy of variant issue.
Bound in contemporary calf.
WingT869; Phillips(Atlases)4269, 536n.

9933, 1914

BA695 Vidal Figueroa, José, 1630-1702.
V649m Memorias Tiernas, Dispertador Afectuoso,
[R] Y Devociones Practicas Con Los Dolores De La Santissima Virgen, Sacadas De Varios Avthores. Dedicalas El Padre Joseph Vidal, De la Compañia de Jesus, Prefecto de la Congregacion de los Dolores, en el Colegio de S. Pedro, y S. Pablo de Mexico, à los Congregantes hijos recomendados de Christo desde la Cruz à su querida Madre la SS. Virgen de los Dolores.

En Amberez, Por Henrico Y Cornelio Verdussen. Año M.D.C.XCV.
12 p.ℓ., 395, [396-407] p. front., 2 plates. 16.5cm. 8°
Cut (monogram of Virgin Mary) on t.-p.
First pub. Mexico, 1686.
License dated (10th p.ℓ.^{v}) 20 Nov. 1694.
Includes poetry.
Bound in contemporary vellum.
Palau(1)7:174; Medina(BHA)1950; Backer 8:647; Peeters-Fontainas(1965)1374.

12124, 1919

1696

BA695 Torres Cano, Juan de.
T693s Sermon A La Pvblicacion Del Edicto De La Fee, Del Sancto Tribunal De La Inquissicion. Que se publicò En la Iglesia Parrochial de la Ciudad de Tehuacan en la Dominica Tercera de Quaresma, el dia seis de Março del año de 1695. Por Orden Del Br. Andres del Moral su Comissario en ella. Predicolo El Br. Don Iuan de Torres Cano Cura actual, Vicario, Iuez Eclesiastico, y Comissario subdelegado del Tribunal de la Santa Crvzada de dicha Ciudad, y Iuez de Diezmos de su Provincia...

Con licencia en Mexico: Por Iuan Ioseph Guillena Carrascoso en el empedradillo. Año de 1695.
7 p.ℓ., 11 numb. ℓ. illus. (coats of arms) 19.5cm. 4°
Licenses dated (7th p.ℓ.^{v}) 9 Aug. 1695.
Palau(2)336908; Medina(Mexico)1627.

1060, 1905

BA696 Avila, Juan de, fl. 1684.
A958h Los Hercules Seraphicos. Excellentissimos Señores Condes De Chinchon; Patronos de toda la Orden de S. Francisco. Sermon Que En El Convento De Victoria, en las Exequias, que todos los Capitulos Generales, la Orden de S. Francisco hazerlos acostumbra; concluyendo la funcion con la celebracion de sus Honras. Predicólo El M.R.P. Fr. Ivan De Avila, Predicador Iubilado, y General: Qualificador del Santo Officio en la Nueva España: Padre de la Provincia del Santo Evangelio de Mexico, y su Custodio al Capitulo General dicho. En 2. de Iunio de 1694. ...

Con Licencia En Mexico Por Doña Maria de Benavides, Viuda de Juan de Ribera en el Empedradillo. Año de 1696.
8 p.ℓ., 10 numb. ℓ. 20cm. 4°
First pub. Madrid, 1695.
License dated (7th p.ℓ.^{r}) 16 Feb. 1696.
Palau(2)20470; Medina(Mexico)1630.

1068, 1905

BA673
-P434m
Ayeta, Francisco de.
... Discurso Legal, Qve Propone El Padre Fr. Francisco Ayeta, Procurador General de la Orden de N.P.S. Francisco, de la Regular Observancia de todas las Provincias de los Reynos de las Indias, por la Provincia de Quito. En La Controversia, Qve Le Ha Movido El Doctor D. Sancho de Andrade y Figueroa, Obispo de dicha Provincia; y su Provisor el Doctor Don Pedro de Zumarraga. Sobre Pretender Le Toca El Derecho de nombrar Thenientes Coadjutores à los Curas Doctrineros ...
[Madrid? ca. 1696]
19 numb. ℓ. 31.5cm. fol.
At head of title: Jesvs, Maria, Y Joseph.
Signed at end: Fr. Francisco de Ayeta. Lic. D. Baltar de Azevedo.
Cites document (2d numb. ℓ.) dated 15 Jan. 1696.
Bound as the 2d of 5 items with: Perea Quintanilla, Miguel de, Manifiesto a la reyna ... [Mexico? 1673?].

04153, 1870

DA696
-B355r
Baxter, Richard, 1615-1691.
Reliquiæ Baxterianæ: Or, Mr. Richard Baxter's Narrative Of The most Memorable Passages Of His Life And Times. Faithfully Publish'd from his own Original Manuscript, By Matthew Sylvester...
London: Printed for T. Parkhurst, J. Robinson J. Lawrence, and J. Dunton. M DC XC VI.
14 p.ℓ., 448, 200, 132 p., 1 ℓ., 18, [8] p. front. (port.) 32cm. fol.
Errata: 14th p.ℓ.; erratum and binding directions: final ℓ.
"The Preface To The Reader" (3d-11th p.ℓ.) signed at end: London, May 13. 1696. M.S.
Pages 26-31 (2d count) incorrectly numbered: 34-39.
"...an Account of my Books and writings...": p. 106-124 (1st count).
Baxter's correspondence with John Eliot, John Endecott and John Norton: p. 290-298.
Appendices 1-9 (p. 1-132 at end) include replies to and defenses of Baxter's works.
With this is bound as issued: Sylvester, Matthew. Elisha's Cry After Elijah's God. London, 1696.
Bound in contemporary calf, rebacked.
WingB1370; Sabin4013; McAlpin4:535; Dexter (Cong.)2464.

12520, 1920

bDA696
B827pD
[R]
[Bray, Thomas] 1658-1730.
Proposals For the Incouragement and Promoting of Religion and Learning in the Foreign Plantations; And to Induce such of the Clergy of this Kingdom, as are Persons of Sobriety and Abilities, to accept of a Mission into those Parts.
[London, 1696]
4 p. 33.5cm. fol.
Caption title.
With the endorsement (p. 2) of the two archbishops and of 3 bishops.
Includes (p. 3-4) "The Present State Of The Protestant Religion In Mary-Land, Stands Thus"; signed: Thomas Laurence Secretary of Mary-Land.
Probably published in Oct. 1696. First pub. as early as Dec. 1695, [London] (without "The Present State...", which was added with this edition).
JCBAR34:12-16; Baer(Md.)163D, 165; cf. WingB4296.

16528, 1934

E696
-B853a
Briet, Philippe, 1601-1668.
Annales Mundi, Sive Chronicon Universale Secundum Optimas Chronologorum Epochas Ab Orbe Condito Ad Annum Christi, Millesimum Sexcentesimum Sexagesimum Perductum. Opera, & Studio Philippi Brietii, Abbavillæi Societatis Jesu Sacerdotis. In hac vero ultima Editione additum fuit supplementum usque ad Annum 1692. à Societatis Jesu, Sacerdote. Post Editionem Parisiensem Et Venetam Prima In Germania, A Plurimis Mendis Purgata. Cum Gratiâ & Privilegio Sacræ Cæsareæ Majestatis, Et facultate Superiorum. Augustæ Vindel. & Dilingæ, Sumptibus Joannis Caspari Bencard, Bibliopolæ. Anno M. DC. XCVI.
4 p.ℓ., 983, [984-1019] p. 33cm. fol.
Added t.-p., engr.: Leonh. Heckenauer Sc.
Title in red and black.
Cut on t.-p.
First pub. Paris, 1662-1663.
"Supplementum Ad Annales Et Chronicon Philippi Brietii Ab Anno 1663. Usque Ad Annum 1692", (p. [935]-983) by Casimir Freschot, 1st pub. Venice, 1692.
Backer2:159.

0191, 1825

BA696
C354a
Castorena y Ursúa, Juan Ignacio de, 1668-1733.
Abraham Academico En el Racional Iuicio de los Doctores Es la Uerdad de la Pureza la Doctrina de la Concepcion. Oracion Panegyrica Evangelica Con que la Real Augusta Pontificia Vniversidad Mexicana, Annualmente solemnisa el punto Immaculado de Maria Santissima en el primer instante de su Ser Purissimo. Predicola El vltimo dia de la

Octava, y fue el primer Sermon del El Doctor Don Ivan Ignacio De Castorena, Y Vrsva. Clerigo Presbitero ...
En Mexico: En la Imprenta de la Uiuda de Francisco Rodriguez Lupercio. En la puete de Palacio. Año 1696.
8 p.ℓ., 4 numb. ℓ., [12] p. illus. (coat of arms) 19.5cm. 4°
License dated (8th p. ℓ.^{v}) 26 Jan. 1696.
Palau(2)48491; Medina(Mexico)1632.

1069, 1905

BA696
C355s

Castro, José de, d. 1711.
Sermon Panegirico Moral, Qve En La Fiesta Annval, Qve acostumbra celebrar el Convento de Religiosos Predicadores de Santo Domingo de Zacatecas en el dia de su Santo Patriarcha. Predicò El M.R.P. Fr. Ioseph De Castro Ex-lector de Theologia, y Padre de la Provincia de N.P. San Francisco de dicha Ciudad. ...
Con Licencia En Mexico Por Doña Maria de Benavides, Viuda de Juan de Ribera en el Empedradillo. Año de 1696.
8 p.ℓ., 12 numb. ℓ. 19.5cm. 4°
License dated (7th p. ℓ.^{r}) 13 Feb. 1696.
Palau(2)48717; Medina(Mexico)1633.

1067, 1905

E687
D948v

Chavigny de La Bretonnière, François de, fl. 17th cent., supposed author.
La Religieuse Cavalier. Memoires Galands Par le Sieur de Chavigny.
A Brusselles, Chez George De Backer, Mar-chand Libraire, prés l'Hôtel du Prince de Berges. M.DC.LXXXXVI.
3 p.ℓ., 76 p. front. 14cm. 12°
Authorship has also been ascribed to Jean Barrin.
Cut on t.-p.
First pub. The Hague, 1682.
Bound, in contemporary calf, with: [Durand, of Dauphiné] Voyages d'un françois, The Hague, 1687.

1180-2, 1906

D696
-C737c

Church of Scotland--General Assembly--Commission.
Causes Of a Solemn National Fast and Humiliation, agreed upon by the Commission-ers of the late General Assembly, met at Edinburgh the 4. of June 1696: And presented to the Lords of His Majesties most Honourable Privy Council, To be read by the Ministers, in all the Churches at the Intimation of the said Fast.
[Edinburgh, 1696]
Broadside. 30.5 x 18cm. 1/2°
"The King's Majesty, being gone Abroad, and Engaged in a Dangerous War, and His Royal Person exposed to Danger, on whose Safety and Success under God, the Welfare of these Nations ..."
Bound in a volume of Scottish imprints and mss. as the 35th of 58 items.
Wing C4201E.

7130, 1910

D696
C611n

Clarke, Samuel, 1599-1683.
A New Description Of The World. Or A Compendious Treatise of the Empires, King-doms, States, Provinces, Countries, Islands, Cities and Towns of Europe, Asia, Africa and America ... By S. Clark. The Second Edition.
London, Printed for Hen. Rhodes at the Star the corner of Brides-lane, Fleet-Street, 1696.
3 p.ℓ., 218, [2] p. front. 15cm. 12°
First pub. London, 1689.
Booksellers' advertisement, 2 pages at end.
Wing C4554A; Baer(Md.)167.

10775, 1915

bD
Scott
22

Company of Scotland Trading to Africa and the Indies.
At Edinburgh, The 15 of June, 1696. The Council-General of the Company of Scotland, Trading to Africa and the Indies: Do Appoint and Ordain ...
[Edinburgh, 1696]
Broadside. 31 x 19.5cm. 1/2°
Wing C5592; Scott 22.

772, 1905

bD
Scott
23

Company of Scotland Trading to Africa and the Indies.
At Edinburgh, The 9.th Day of July, 1696. Whereas the Books of Subscription to the Company of Scotland Trading to Africa and the Indies ...
[Edinburgh, 1696]
Broadside. 32 x 19.5cm. 1/2°
Title from caption and beginning of text.
Declaration of the Court of Directors.
Followed by endorsement of the Council-General dated 3 Aug. 1696.

773, 1905   This copy closely trimmed at top, affecting 1st word.
WingC5593; Scott 23.

D696
-C737c   Company of Scotland Trading to Africa and the Indies.
The Company of Scotland, Trading to Africa and the Indies, Do hereby give Notice. That their Bookes of Subscription, will be opened at Edinburgh on Wednesday the 26 of this Instant February ...
[Edinburgh, 1696]
Broadside. 41.5 x 29.5cm. (fold. in binding 31.5cm.) 1°
Title from caption and beginning of text.
Includes texts of blank forms dated in Edinburgh 1696.
Bound in a volume of Scottish imprints and mss. as the 1st of 58 items.
7101, 1910

bD
Scott
16c   Company of Scotland Trading to Africa and the Indies.
Constitutions Agreed Upon By The Committee Of The Company of Scotland, Trading to Africa and the Indies. Edinburgh, 13 April 1696.
[Edinburgh, 1696]
Broadside. 37.5 x 31cm. 1°
WingC5593A.
10684, 1915

D
-Scott
18   Company of Scotland Trading to Africa and the Indies.
Constitutions Of The Company Of Scotland, Trading to Africa and the Indies.
[Edinburgh? G. Mosman? 1696]
3 p. 31cm. fol.
Caption title.
Dated at end: At Edinburgh, the Seventeenth of April. One Thousand Six Hundred Ninty [sic] and Six.
First pub. as broadside under title Constitutions agreed upon by the committee, dated 13 April, 1696.
JCB(2)2:1491; WingC5594; Sabin78208; Scott 18.
768, 1905

bD
Scott
15   Company of Scotland Trading to Africa and the Indies.
Edinburgh, March 24th 1696. At a Meeting of the Subscribers to the Company of Scotland, Trading to Africa and the Indies. The following Resolutions concluded upon.
[Edinburgh, 1696]
Broadside. 30 x 18cm. 1/2°
WingC5591; Scott 15.
766, 1905

bD
Scott
16a   Company of Scotland Trading to Africa and the Indies.
Edinburgh, April 3d. 1696. At a General Meeting of the Company of Scotland, Trading to Africa, and the Indies. My Lord Belhaven Chosen Præses.
[Edinburgh, 1696]
Broadside. 30 x 19cm. 1/2°
WingC5586; Scott 16a.
767, 1905

bD
Scott
17   Company of Scotland Trading to Africa and the Indies.
Edinburgh, The 17th, day of April, 1696. At a General Meeting of the Company of Scotland, Trading to Africa and the Indies. My Lord Tarbat Chosen Præses.
[Edinburgh, 1696]
Broadside. 30.5 x 19cm. 1/2°
WingC5587; Scott17.
769, 1905

bD
Scott
20   Company of Scotland Trading to Africa and the Indies.
Edinburgh the 12 of May 1696. At A General Meeting Of The Company Of Scotland, Trading to Africa and the Indies. The Viscount of Tarbat Chosen Præses.
[Edinburgh, 1696]
3 p. 31cm. fol.
WingC5588; Scott 20.
770, 1905

bD
Scott
21   Company of Scotland Trading to Africa and the Indies.
Edinburgh the 20 of May 1696. At A Court of Directors Of The Company Of Scotland, Trading to Africa and the Indies.

771, 1905
    [Edinburgh, 1696]
    Broadside. 31 x 18.5cm. 1/2⁰
    WingD256; Scott 21.

D   Company of Scotland Trading to Africa and
-Scott   the Indies.
19
    A List Of The Subscribers To The Company of Scotland, Trading to Africa and the Indies. Taken in Edinburgh &c. until the 21 of April inclusive 1696.
    [Edinburgh, 1696]
    12 p. 31.5cm. fol.
    Caption title.
    WingC5598; Sabin78226; Kress S1926. Scott 19.

646, 1905

D   Company of Scotland Trading to Africa
-Scott   and the Indies.
24
[R]   A Perfect List Of the several Persons Residenters in Scotland, Who have Subscribed as Adventurers In The Joynt-Stock Of The Company of Scotland Trading to Africa and the Indies. Together With the respective Sums which they have severally Subscribed in the Books of the said Company, Amounting in the Whole to the Sum of 400000 lib. Sterling.
    Edinburgh, Printed and Sold by the Heirs and Successors of Andrew Anderson, Printer to the King's most Excellent Majesty, Anno Dom. 1696.
    16 p. 35.5cm. fol.
    Cut (Company's arms) on t.-p.
    Bookseller's advertisement at end.
    WingC5599; Sabin18564; Scott24.

748, 1905

DA696   [Coole, Benjamin] d. 1717.
C774
    The Quakers Cleared from being Apostates: Or The Hammerer Defeated, And Proved an Imposter. Being an Answer to a Scurrilous Pamphlet, Falsly Intituled, William Penn and the Quakers either Apostates or Impostors; Subscribed Trepidantium Malleus. With a Postscript, Containing some Reflections on a Pamphlet, Intituled, The Spirit of Quakerism, and the Danger of their Divine Revelation, laid open. By B. C.
    London: Printed and Sold by T. Sowle, in White-Hart-Court in Gracious Street. 1696.
    95 p. 17.5cm. 8⁰.
    Postscript (p. 85-95) dated: London, September the 12th. 1696.
    Reply to [Samuel Young] William Penn And the Quakers. London, 1696. and [Henry Winder] The Spirit of Quakerism. London, 1696.
    Smith(Friends)1:450; Smith(Anti-Quak.)459; WingC6047.

11482, 1918

DA696   Croese, Gerard, 1642-1710.
C939g2
    The General History Of The Quakers: Containing The Lives, Tenents, Sufferings, Tryals, Speeches, and Letters Of all the most Eminent Quakers, Both Men and Women; From the first Rise of that Sect, down to this present Time. Collected from Manuscripts, &c. A Work never attempted before in English. Being Written Originally in Latin By Gerard Croese. To which is added, A Letter writ by George Keith, and sent by him to the Author of this Book: Containing a Vindication of himself, and several Remarks on this History.
    London, Printed for John Dunton, at the Raven in Jewen-street. 1696.
    8 p.ℓ., 189 p., 1 ℓ., 80, 85-196, 167-180 (i.e. 182), 213-276, 40 p. 18.5cm. 8⁰ A-N⁸ 2A-2R⁸ 3A⁸ 3B⁴ 3C⁸
    Transl. of Historia Quakeriana, Amsterdam, 1695, with additions.
    Includes at end: "An Appendix: Containing The True Copy of a Latine Letter Writ by George Keith, ... Translated out of his Latine Manuscript into English" (p. 1-24); "Something Added in Behalf of the People called Quakers, both with respect to the Historian, and also G. Keith" (p. 25-30); and (p. 31-40) with special t.-p., Our Antient Testimony Renewed. Concerning our Lord and Saviour Jesus Christ, The Holy Scriptures, And The Resurrection, Occasioned at this time by several Unjust Charges published against us, ... by G. Keith ... , Given forth by a Meeting of Publick Friends, and Others, at Philadelphia in Pensylvania, London, Printed and Sold by T. Sowle, in White-Hart-Court in Gracious-Street. 1695. Our antient testimony renewed 1st pub. London, 1695.
    Sabin17584; Smith(Friends)1:480-482, 1:760; WingC6965; McAlpin4:538; Baer(Md.) 169.

30503, 1949 rev

DA696   Croese, Gerard, 1642-1710.
C939g1
    Gerardi Croesi Historia Quakeriana, Sive De vulgo dictis Quakeris, Ab ortu illorum usque ad recens natum schisma, Libri III. In quibus

praesertim agitur de ipsorum praecipuis antecessoribus & dogmatis (ut & similibus placitis aliorum hoc tempore) factisque, ac casibus memorabilibus Editio Secunda Indice locupletior.
    Amstelodami, [Apud Henricum & Viduam Theordori Boom?] Anno M.DC.IVC.
      8 p.l., 580, [18] p. 16cm. 8°
      Title in red and black.
      Cut on t.-p.; includes motto "Tandem Fit Arbor Surculus" (similar to Bibliotheca belgica II 19 (Amsterdam) Boom 2, but without initials "H D B").
      First pub. Amsterdam, Apud Henricum & Viduam Theodori Boom, 1695.
      Bound in contemporary vellum.
      JCB(2)2:1490; Sabin17583; Smith(Friends) 1:480; Baer(Md.)170.
04957, before 1882 rev

D696   Dawson, Joseph, d. 1696, defendant.
-D272t   The Tryals Of Joseph Dawson, Edward Forseith, William May, > <William Bishop, James Lewis, and John Sparkes. For several Piracies and Robberies By them committed, In The Company of Every the Grand Pirate, near the Coasts of the East-Indies; and several other Places on the Seas. Giving an Account of their Villainous Robberies and Barbarities. At the Admiralty Sessions, begun at the Old-Baily on the 29th of October, 1696, and ended on the 6th. of November.
      London, Printed for John Everingham, Bookseller, at the Star in Ludgate-street, 1696.
      28 p. 32cm. fol.
      WingT2252.
68-51

DA696   Ellwood, Thomas, 1639-1713.
E47a   An Answer To George Keith's Narrative Of His Proceedings at Turners-Hall, On the 11th of the Month called June, 1696. Wherein His Charges against divers of the People called Quakers (Both in that, and in another Book of his, Called, Gross Error & Hypocrisie Detected) Are fairly Considered, Examined, and Refuted. By Thomas Ellwood.
      London: Printed and Sold by T. Sowle near, the Meeting-House in White-Hart-Court in Gracious-street 1696.
      232 p. 17.5cm. 8°
      Keith's An exact narrative of the proceedings at Turners-Hall, the 11th of the month, called June, 1696, 1st pub. London, 1696; his Gross error and hypocrisie detected, 1st pub. London, 1695.
      Bookseller's advertisement at end.
      Wing E613; McAlpin4:540; Smith(Friends)1:566.
6171, 1910

bDB   Gt.Brit.--Laws, statutes, etc., 1694-1702
G7863   (William III)
1696   Anno Regni Gulielmi III. Regis Angliæ, Scotiæ, Franciæ & Hiberniæ, Septimo & Octavo. At the Parliament begun at Westminster the Two and twentieth Day of November, Anno Dom. 1695. ...
      London, Printed by Charles Bill, and the Executrix of Thomas Newcomb deceas'd, Printers to the Kings most Excellent Majesty. MDCXCVI.
      1 p.l., 495-512 p. 6I-6N² 30.5cm. fol.
      (Issued as a part of its [session laws] London, 1696.)
      Cut (royal arms; Steele 132) on t.-p.
      Caption title, p. 495: ... An Act for Preventing Frauds, and Regulating Abuses in the Plantation Trade.
11274, 1917

DB   Gt.Brit.--Parliament, 1695-1696.
-G7875   The Humble Address Of the Right Honourable the Lords Spiritual & Temporal And Commons In Parliament Assembled, Presented to His Majesty On the Twenty-fourth of February, 1695[/6]. And His Majesties Most Gracious Answer Thereunto.
      London, Printed by Charles Bill and the Executrix of Thomas Newcomb, deceas'd, Printers to the Kings most Excellent Majesty. 1695[/6].
      4 p. 29cm. fol.
      Order to print (p. 2) dated 25 Feb 1695[/6].
      Testifies to Parliament's support on the occasion of the Barclay-Fenwick assassination plot.
      Bound in Votes of the House of Commons, v.2, before Votes for 24 Feb 1695/6.
10383-5, 1914 rev 3

DB   Gt.Brit.--Parliament, 1696-1697--House of
-G7875   Commons.
1689   The Humble Address of the House of Commons
3   to the King.
      London, Printed by John Leake for Timothy Goodwin, against St. Dunstan's Church in Fleet-street, and Thomas Cockerill at the Three

Leggs in the Poultry, 1696.
1 ℓ. 29cm. 1/2⁰ (Issued as no. 3 of Gt. Brit.--Parliament, 1696-1697--House of Commons. Votes... , London, 1696-1697.)
Caption title; imprint at end.
Testifies to Commons' support of the king in the war against France.
Presented 23 Oct 1696.
Bound in Votes of the House of Commons, v.3.
10376-8A, 1914

DB
-G7875
1689
3
Gt. Brit.--Parliament, 1696-1697--House of Commons.
Votes Of The House of Commons, In the Second Session of this Present Parliament Held At Westminster The 20ᵗʰ Day of October, in the Eighth Year of the Reign of King William III. Anno Domini, 1696.
London, Printed by John Leake for Timothy Goodwin, against St. Dunstan's Church in Fleet-street, and Thomas Cockerill at the Three Leggs in the Poultry, 1696 [-1697].
1 p.ℓ., 490 p. 29cm. fol.
Issued in pts. numbered 1-145 and dated 20 Oct 1696 - 16 Apr. 1697, each of which has caption title and imprint at end.
Imprint of no. 57-64, 66-80, 82-145 dated 1697.
Errata, p. 84, 250.
Bound in Votes of the House of Commons, v.3.
10376-8, 1914

DB
-G7875
1689
3
Gt. Brit.--Parliament, 1696-1697--House of Lords.
The Humble Address Of the Right Honourable the Lords Spiritual & Temporal In Parliament Assembled, Presented to His Majesty on Wednesday the Twenty Eighth day of October, 1696. And His Majesties Most Gracious Answer Thereunto.
London, Printed by Charles Bill and the Executrix of Thomas Newcomb, deceas'd; Printers to the Kings most Excellent Majesty. 1696.
4 p. 29cm. fol.
Order to print (p. 2) dated 28 Oct 1696.
Testifies to the Lords' support of the king in the war against France.
Bound in Votes of the House of Commons, v.3, after Votes for 28 Oct 1696.
10383-5.1, 1914

BA696
H674r
Hita, Alonso de.
El Regvlo Seraphico San Pedro Regalado. Promotor maravilloso en la Refforma de el Seraphico instituto, y fundador de los Conventos de Domus Dei de el Aguilera, y Scala Cœli de el Abroxo, primeros Santuarios de la Observancia de. España, en la Santa Provincia de la Concepcion. Sermon Que predicó el R. P. Fr. Alonso De Hita, Predicador jubilado, Custodio antes, y Diffinidor despues, de la Provincia del Santo Evangelio de Mexico, en su Convento principal, Domingo Infraoctavo de la Ascenssion; donde se dedicó Coratheral al Glorioso Santo; y en el pecho de su talla se colocó vna preciosa Reliquia de su Original, que es el Huesso principal del Cuello. ...
Con licencia: en Mexico, por la Viuda de Francisco Rodriguez Lupercio, en la puente de Palacio. Año de 1696. A Expensas De Vn Devoto De El Santo.
10 p.ℓ., 6, 8-12 numb. ℓ. incl. port. 19.5cm. 4⁰
License dated (5th p.ℓ.ᵛ) 11 July 1696.
Palau(2)115434; Medina(Mexico)1638.
1070, 1905

D
Scott
14
[Holland, John] d. 1722.
A Short Discourse On The Present Temper Of The Nation With Respect to the Indian and African Company; And of the Bank of Scotland. Also, Of Mr. Paterson's pretended Fund of Credit, By J.H.
Edinburgh, Printed by John Reid, and Sold by Mrs. Beiglie, in the Parliament Closs, in the Year MDCXCVI.
3 p.ℓ., 22 p. 19.5cm. 4⁰
Dedication (2d-3d p.ℓ.) signed: John Holland.
WingH2427; KressS1950; Scott14.
8781, 1912

DA696
K28a
Keith, George, 1639?-1716.
The Anti-Christs and Sadduces Detected Among a sort of Quakers: Or, Caleb Pusie of Pensilvania, and John Pennington; with his Brethren of the Second Days Meeting at London, called Quakers, Proved Antichrists and Sadduces, out of a Printed Book lately published by them, falsly called, A modest Account of the principal Differences in point of Doctrine, betwixt George Keith, and those of the People called Quakers in Pensilvania, &c.)... With some few Remarks on John Penningtons late Book, entitled, The People called Quakers cleared, &c. And Geo. Whitehead his Postscript, shewing some of their gross Perversions, Falsehoods, and Groundless Calumnies against G.K. And a Postscript ... By George Keith.
London, Printed for the Author, and are to be sold at his House at the Golden Ball over-against Red-Lyon-street in White-Chappel. [1696]

44 p. 20cm. 4º
Signed (at end): London, the 24th. of the Month called July, 1696. G.K.
Errata, p. 44.
A reply to Caleb Pusey, A modest account from Pensylvania of the principal differences in point of doctrine, London, 1696, and John Penington, The people called Quakers cleared, London, 1696. Includes (p. 41-44) "Advertisement" in reply to W. C.'s Mr. George Keith at Turner's Hall, London, 1696.
WingK138; Sabin37180; Smith(Friends) 2:31.

8095, 1911

DA696 Keith, George, 1639?-1716.
K28e   An Exact Narrative Of The Proceedings At Turners-Hall, The 11th of the Month called June, 1696. Together with the Disputes and Speeches There, Between G. Keith and other Quakers, Differing from Him in Some Religious Principles. The Whole Published and Revised, By George Keith. With an Appendix containing some New Passages to prove His Opponents guilty of Gross Errors and Self-Contradictions.
London, Printed for B. Aylmer at the Three Pigeons in Cornhill, and J. Dunton at the Raven in Jewen-street, 1696.
62 p., 1 ℓ. 21cm. 4º
In this copy p. 33-36 duplicated.
Errata, p. 62.
Booksellers' advertisements, leaf at end.
Bound as the 1st in a vol. of 7 works by Keith.
JCB(2)2:1495; WingK161; Sabin37191; Smith (Friends)2:32.

04788, before 1874

DA696 Keith, George, 1639?-1716.
K28s   A Sermon Preached at the Meeting of Protestant Dissenters, Called Quakers, In Turners-Hall London; On the 16th. of the Second Month, 1696. Being the Publick Day of Thanksgiving For the Deliverance of the King and Kingdom. By George Keith. To which is added a Testimony of Fidelity and Subjection to King William the III. from the aforesaid People on behalf of themselves and others of the same Perswasion with them.
London: Printed for B. Aylmer at the Three Pigeons in Cornhil, 1696.
31 p. 21cm. 4º
"Testimony" (p. 28-31) dated: The 26th of the Second Month, called April, 1696.

Bound as the 1st in a vol. of 11 works by Keith.
JCB(2)2:1497; WingK208; Smith(Friends) 2:31; McAlpin4:545.

04795, before 1874

DA696 [Kohlhans, Tobias Ludwig] fl. 1600-1700.
K79d   Dilucidationes quædam valde necessariæ in Gerardi Croesi Historiam Quakerianam Editæ a Philaletha.
Amstelodami. Typis impressæ pro Jacobo Claus, Bibliopola. MDCXCVI.
1 p. ℓ., 178, [2] p. 16cm. 8º
Cut on t.-p.
Errata, p. [1-2] at end.
A reply to Gerard Croese, Historia Quakeriana, 1st pub. Amsterdam, 1695.
William Sewel shared in the composition (cf. Hull, W.I., Willem Sewel of Amsterdam, p. 131-133).
In this copy there is a blank ℓ. at end.
Smith(Anti-Quak.)137.

05874, 1900

J696   [Leibniz, Gottfried Wilhelm, freiherr von]
L525g 1646-1716.
G.[odofredi] G.[uilielmi] L.[eibnitii] Relatio Ad Inclytam Societatem Leopoldinam Naturæ Curiosorum, De Novo Antidysenterico Americano Magnis Successibus Comprobato.
Hannov. Et Gvelpherpit. Sumptibus Gothofredi Freytagii, Anno 1696.
38 p. 17.5cm. 8º
Chiefly concerns ipecacuanha.
First appeared in Miscellanea curiosa of the Leopoldinisch-Carolinische Akademie der Naturforscher, ser. 3, v.3.
Waring526.

15076, 1928

DA696 [Leslie, Charles] 1650-1722.
L634s The Snake in the Grass. Or, Satan Transform'd into An Angel of Light. Discovering the Deep and Unsuspected Subtilty which is Couched under the Pretended Simplicity of many of the Principal Leaders of those People call'd Quakers. ...
London, Printed for Charles Brome, at the Gun at the West End of St. Paul's, 1696.
3 p. ℓ., cccxlii [i.e. ccclii] 271 p. 16.5cm. 8º
Errata, p. [ii]
Dated (p. 271): Feb. the 28th 169$\frac{4}{5}$.

Bound in contemporary calf.
Wing L1156; Sabin 40195; Smith(Anti-Quak)267.
6130, 1909

D
-Scott
12
A Letter From A Gentleman in the Country To His Friend at Edinburgh: Wherein it is clearly proved, That the Scottish African, and Indian Company, is Exactly Calculated for the Interest Of Scotland.
Edinburgh, Printed by George Mosman, in the Year 1696.
11 p. 31.5cm. fol.
Dated (p. 3): January 4. 1695/6.
Wing L1393; Kress 1977; Scott 12.
794, 1905

D
Scott
9a
A Letter From a Member of the Parliament of Scotland To his Friend at London, Concerning their late Act, for Establishing a Company of that Kingdom, Tradeing to Africa and the Indies.
Printed at London, and Re-printed at Edinburgh, by the Heirs and Successors of Andrew Anderson, Printer to the King's most Excellent Majesty, 1696.
19 p. 19.5cm. 4°
Caption title; imprint at end.
Signed (p. 18): Edinburgh, Novem. 14. 1695. ... Philonax Verax.
First pub. London, 1695.
JCB(2)2:1493; Wing L1413; Sabin 78220; Scott 9a.
02412, 1851

D
Scott
13
A Letter To A Member Of Parliament Concerning the Bank Of Scotland And the Lowering of Interest of Money.
Edinburgh, Printed by John Reid, and to be sold by Robert Allan, at his Shop, over foregainst the Court of Guard, 1696.
8 p. 20.5cm. 4°
Wing L1669; Scott 13.
747, 1905

DA696
L651g
A Letter To George Keith. Concerning his late Religious Differences with William Pen and his Party. By a moderate Churchman.
[London, 1696]
4 p. 21cm. 4°

Caption title.
A reply, in part, to Thomas Ellwood, Truth defended, London, 1695.
JCB(2)2:1496.
06036, before 1882

B682
-L864p
[R]
López y Martínez, Juan Luis, marqués del Risco, d. 1732.
Defensa Real, Y Sagrada. De La Jvrisdicion[sic] De Sv Santidad Cometida A Instancia De El Rey Nvestro Señor Al Jvez De El Breve Apostolico En El Principado De Catalvña, Y Condados De Rosellon, Y Cerdaña: Para El Conocimiento Privatibo Y Castigo De Los Delitos Atrozes De Los Ecclesiasticos. Por Don Ioan Lvis Lopez Fiscal De Sv Magestad En Sv S.S.R. Consejo De Los Reynos De La Corona De Aragon. Segvnda Impression Añadido [sic] En Mvchos Lvgares Con nuebos Breves Apostolicos, que se omitieron en la Primera, y vn Indice copioso de las cosas notables.
En Barcelona: Por Martin Gelabert Impressor. Año 1696. Vendense en la misma Imprenta delante la Retoria de Nuestra Señora del Pino.
9 p.ℓ., 187, [188-206]p. 28cm. fol.
"El Impressor A Los Lectores" (2d p.ℓ.) signed: Martin Gelabert Impressor.
Letter dated (p.[205]) 15 Dec. 1696.
Errata, p.[206].
Bound as no. 15 in a vol. with binder's title: Luis Lopez Obras.
Palau(2)141415; Medina(BHA)1960; Leclerc (1878)1826.9 (this copy).
14021, 1925

JA696
L973ℓ
[R]
Luther, Martin, 1483-1546.
Lutheri Catechismus/ Öfwersatt på American-Virginiske Språket.
Stockholm/ Tryckt vthi thet af Kongl. May:tt. privileg. Burchardi Tryckeri/af J. J. Genath/f. Anno M DC XCVI.
8 p.ℓ., 160 p. front. 17cm. 8°
Title in red and black.
Cut (royal arms) on t.-p.
Text in Delaware language and Swedish.
Transl. into Delaware language by Johan Campanius Holm.
German original first pub. under title: Der kleine Catechismus für die gemeine Pfarherr und Prediger...[Wittenberg] 1529.
"Vocabularium Barbaro-Virgineorum" (p. 133-154) has special t.-p.
"Vocabula Mahakuassica": p. 155-160.
In some copies a map is found; available in facsimile.
JCB(2)2:1498; Sabin 42726; Church 760; Pilling 571.
0555, 1846

[329]

E696 M379v [Martin, Claude] 1619-1696.
La Vie De La Venerable Mere Marie De L'Incarnation, Premiere Superieure Des Ursulines De La Nouvelle France. ...
A Paris, Chez Antoine Warin, ruë Saint Jacques, proche la Fontaine S. Severin, au Saint Scapulaire. M. DC. XCVI. Avec Approbation & Privilege.
18 p.l., 520, 523-757, [758-763] p. front. (port.) 25cm. 4º
"... composée par le R. P. Dom Claude Martin Religieux Benedictin de la Congregation saint Maur ..." (18th p.l.ᵛ).
Bookseller's advertisement, p. 757.
Errata, last page.
First pub. Paris, 1677; these are the same sheets (with uncorrected errata) and the same port., with a cancel t.-p.
Bound in contemporary calf.
Streit 2:2698.

961, 1905

BA696 M385o Martínez de la Parra, Juan, 1655-1701.
Oracion Fvnebre. En Las Annvales Honras, Qve Por Mandado, Y Reales expensas de Nuestro Catholico Rey, y Señor Carlos II. se celebraron en la Casa Professa de la Compañia de Jesvs de Mexico, por los Soldados, que han muerto en defensa de las Catholicas armas de España. Dijola El R. P. Jvan Martinez De la Parra de la mesma Compañia. Prefecto de la Illustre, y Venerable Congregacion del Salvador. En Presencia Del Illᵐᵒ. Y Exᵐᵒ. Señor Dr. D. Juan de Ortega Montañes dignissimo Obispo de Michoacan. Virrey, y Capitan General desta Nueva-España, y Presidente de la Real Audiencia de ella &c. Y Se La Offrece Su Mas Rendido Criado El Dr. D. Juan Joseph de Brizuela, Medico de Camara de su Exa.
En Mexico: Por Juan Joseph Guillena Carrascoso Impressor, y Mercader de libros en el Empedradillo. Año de 1696
8 p.l., 8 numb. l. 19cm. 4º
Dedication dated (4th p.l.ᵛ) 4 Dec. 1696.
Palau(2)155545; Medina(Mexico)1641; Backer5:635.

4926, 1908

D696 M414o Massachusetts Or The first Planters of New-England, The End and Manner of their coming thither, and Abode there: In several Epistles ...
Boston in New-England, Printed by B. Green, and J. Allen. Sold by Richard Wilkins, at his Shop near the Old-Meeting-House. 1696.
1 p.l., 56 p. 16.5cm. 8º
Said to have been printed at the suggestion of Joshua Scottow; also attributed to Thomas Dudley.
There are 3 variant issues of the title-page; in this variant there are 17 lines of quotations, and "thither" is divided.
Contents.—The Humble Request Of His Majesties Loyal Subjects, the Governour and the Company late gone for New-England ... [dated 7 Apr. 1630] (p. 1-5).—[Dudley, Thomas] To The Right Honourable, ... The Lady Bridget Countess of Lincoln. [dated 28 March 1631] (p. 7-27).—The Preface of the Reverend Mr. John Allin, of Dedham, and of Mr. Thomas Shepard of Cambridge in New-England, before their Defence of the Answer made into the Nine Questions. [dated 28 Nov. 1645] (p. 28-40).—[Cotton, John] In Domini Nortoni Librum, ad Lectorem Præfatio Apologetica. (p. 41-56).
"The Humble Request..." first pub. London, 1630.
"The Preface of... Allin... and... Shepard" is the 1st part of John Allin's and Thomas Shepard's A defence of the answer ..., 1st pub. London, 1645.
[Cotton, John] "In Domini Nortoni Librum ..." first appeared in John Norton's Responsio ad totam quæstionum syllogen à clarissimo viro Dom Guilielmo Apollonio..., London, 1648.
JCB(2)2:1494; WingS2098; Evans773; Church 761; Dexter(Cong.)2462; Sabin78431.

02750, 1859

D. Math C. 54 Mather, Cotton, 1663-1728.
The Christian Thank-Offering. A Brief Discourse On The Returns of Gratitude & Obedience Whereto Men are Obliged, by the Mercies Of God. Made On a Solemn Thanksgiving, kept in a Private Meeting of Christians, on the Occasion of some Deliverances. By Cotton Mather. ...
Boston, in N.E. Printed by B. Green, & J. Allen, for Michael Perry, at his Shop at the Town-House. 1696.
32 p. 14.5cm. 8º
Includes hymns (1st p.l.ᵛ and p. 32).
JCB(2)2:1499; Evans752; WingM1089; Holmes (C.)54; Sabin46255; Brinley1082(this copy).

06188, 1878

D. Math C. 390 Mather, Cotton, 1663-1728.
Things for a Distress'd People to think upon. Offered in the Sermon To the General Assembly

of the Province, of the Massachusetts-Bay, at the Anniversary Election. May, 27. 1696. Wherein, I. The Condition of the Future, as well as the Former Times, in which we are concerned, is Considered. II. A Narrative of the late Wonderful Deliverance, of the King, and the three Kingdoms, & all the English Dominions, is Endeavoured. III. A Relation, of no less than Seven Miracles, within this little while wrought by the Almighty Lord Jesus Christ, for the Confirmation of our Hopes, that some Glorious Works, for the welfare of His Church, are quickly to be done, is annexed. By Cotton Mather.
Boston in N E Printed by B Green, and J. Allen, for Duncan Campbel at his Shop over-against the Old-Meeting House. 1696.
1 p.ℓ., 86 p. 14cm. 8°
Evans755; WingM1158; Sabin46546; Holmes(C.)390.

3911, 1907

D.Math Mather, Increase, 1639-1723.
I.4   Angelographia, Or A Discourse Concerning the Nature and Power of the Holy Angels, and the Great Benefit which the True Fearers of God Receive by their Ministry: Delivered in several Sermons: To which is added, a Sermon concerning the Sin and Misery of the Fallen Angels: Also a Disquisition concerning Angelical-Apparitions. By Increase Mather, Præsident of Harvard Colledge, in Cambridge, and Preacher of the Gospel at Boston, in New-England. ...
Boston in N.E. Printed by B. Green & J. Allen, for Samuel Phillips at the Brick Shop. 1696.
8 p.ℓ., 132, 44 p. front. (port.) 15cm. 8°
"A Disquisition Concerning Angelical Apparitions" has special t.-p., separate paging, but continuous signatures.
Imperfect: portrait wanting; available in facsimile.
JCB(2)2:1501; Evans756; WingM1181; Sabin 46630; Holmes(I.)4.

06189, before 1866

D.Math Mather, Increase, 1639-1723.
I.128K Ein Brieff von dem Glücklichen Fortgang des Evangelii Bey den West-Indianern in Neu-Engeland An den berühmten Herrn Johann Leusden/Der H. Sprache Professor auff der hohen Schule zu Utrecht geschrieben von Crescentius Matherus, Diener des Worts Gottes bey den Bostoniensern und Rectore des Harvardinischen Collegii zu Cantabrig in Neu-Engeland Londen/druckts J.G. 1688. Zum andernmahl gedruckt und mit dem glücklichen Fortgang des Evangelii bey den Ost-Indianern vermehret Utrecht gedurckt [sic] bey W.B. 1693. ... Aus dem Lateinischen ins Hochteutsche übersetzet Von einem Bekenner der Warheit die nach der Gottseligkeit ist.
Halle/Gedruckt bey Christoph Salfelden/ 1696.
1 p.ℓ., [46] p. 18.5cm. 8°
Probably edited by Johannes Leusden, the addressee of the letters which comprise the text.
Includes in addition to Mather's letter: a preface by the translator (p. [3] - [14]); "Andere Schreiben von dem Glücklichen Fortgang des Evangelii bey den Ost-Indiern geschrieben theils von ... Hermann Specht ... in der Insul Ceylon theils von ... Adriano de Mey ... Rector des Malabarischen Collegii und von ... Franciscus Valentin ... in Amboin ..." (p. [31] - [43]); and a letter from Pierre Jurieu (p. [44] - [46]).
No copy is known of the edition of Utrecht, W.[ilhelm] B.[roedeleth], 1693, which (according to the t.-p.) this ed. was translated from. That ed. undoubtedly was pub. under the title De successu evangelii and included the reports from the East Indies and Jurieu's letter, as do Broedeleth's other editions, Utrecht 1697 and 1699.
Mather's letter 1st pub. London, 1688, under title: De successu evangelij. The East Indian reports and Jurieu's letter were undoubtedly 1st pub. in the Utrecht, 1693, ed.: one of the East Indian reports is dated 22 Jan. 1692 (p. [38] in this ed.) and all others are dated earlier.
JCB(2)2:1500; Sabin46643; Holmes(I.)128K.

02284, 1860

E733   [Meekeren, Johan van]
L166a   De Tovery Zonder Tovery, Blyspel.
Te Amsteldam, By de Erfgen: van J: Lescailje, op de Middeldam, op de hoek van de Vischmarkt, 1696. Met Privilegie.
3 p.ℓ., 88 p. 16cm. 8°
Cut (incl. motto "Perseveranter") on t.-p.
Privilege dated (3d p.ℓ.ᵛ) 28 Feb. 1696.
Dedication (2d p.ℓ.) signed: Johan van Meek'ren.
Bound, in contemporary calf, with: [Lafont, Joseph de] De Amerikaan. Amsterdam, 1733.

11898-3, 1919

BA696   [Miranda, Juan José de] d. 1700.
M672p   Practica De Asistir A Los Sentenciados â muerte. Y Lo que se observa con ellos

desde que los entran en la Capilla, hasta que se executa la sentencia, y se haze la Platica que se acostumbra en la horca. Por El P. Prefecto De La Congregacion de Nuestra Señora de los Dolores fundada con autoridad Apoctolica [sic] en el Collegio [sic] de San Pedro, y San Pablo de la Compañia de Jesvs.

En Mexico Por D. Iuan Ioseph Guillena Carrascoso Impresor, y Mercader de Libros. Año de 1696.

1 p.ℓ., 18, 18-29 numb. ℓ. 14.5cm. 8⁰

Erroneously attributed to José Vidal Figueroa. In this copy there is a blank leaf at end.

Bound in contemporary vellum.

Palau(2)172103; Medina(Mexico)1643; cf. Backer9:1247.

5324, 1909

DC M678ℓ 1695 22

Miscellaneous Letters, Giving an Account of the Works Of The Learned, Both at Home and Abroad. For the Month of December, 1695. With a Table of the Contents of this first Volume.

London; Printed for Henry Rhodes, at the Star at the Corner of Bride-Lane; and William Lindsey, at the Angel near Lincolns-Inn in Chancery-Lane. MDCXCVI. Where may be had Compleat Sets, or single ones to this time.

1 p.ℓ., 561-578, [16] p. 19.5cm. 4⁰

Running title: Numb. 22. December.

Includes a review of Two essays sent in a letter from Oxford to a nobleman in London, concerning some errors about the creation, general flood, and the peopling of the world. By L.P. London, 1695, and comments on its discussion of "Peopling and Planting the New World."

"Bibliographia: Or, A Catalogue of the Books, &c. printed here and beyond Sea; whereof an Account is given in this First Volume of the Miscellaneous Letters.": [16] p. at end.

Booksellers' advertisement at end.

Crane and Kaye 550.

8947

DA696 M678k

Mʳ. Keith No Presbyterian nor Quaker; But George the Apostate. Deduced from Proofs Both Clinched and Riveted. In a Second Letter To Himself. By the Author of the Former. ...

London Printed, and Sold by E. Whitlock, in Stationers Court, near Stationers-Hall. 1696.

20 p. 19cm. 4⁰

Signed (p.17, 20): W.C.

The first "letter to himself" was pub. London, 1696, under title: Mr. George Keith at Turner's-Hall ...

8393, 1912

E696 M688t

Mocquet, Jean, b. 1575.

Travels And Voyages Into Africa, Asia, and America, The East and West-Indies; Syria, Jerusalem, and the Holy-Land. Performed By Mʳ. John Mocquet, Keeper of the Cabinet of Rarities, to the King of France, in the Thuilleries. Divided into Six Books, and Enriched with Sculptures. Translated from the French, By Nathaniel Pullen, Gent.

London: Printed for William Newton, Bookseller, in Little-Britain; and Joseph Shelton; and William Chandler, Booksellers, at the Peacock in the Poultry, 1696.

16 p.ℓ., 224 p., 225-272 numb. ℓ., 273-352 p. incl. 8 woodcuts. 8⁰

Transl. from: Voyages En Afriqve, Asie, Indes Orientales & Occidentales, 1st pub. Paris, 1616.

JCB(2)2:1503; WingM2310; Sabin49794; McCoy (Hand-list)64.

02354, 1851

BA696 M967s

Muñoz de Castro, Pedro.

Sermon Del Glorioso Patriarcha San Joseph Predicado En su dia 19 de Marzo de este año de 1696 En la Feria segunda despues de la Dominica segunda de Quaresma, en la Iglesia del Hospital de Nuestra Señora de la Concepcion de esta ciudad de Mexico ... Su Author El Br. Pedro Mvñoz De Castro Presbytero de este Arçobispado.

Con licencia en Mexico en la Imprenta de Juan Joseph Guillena Carrascoso. Año de 1696.

7 p.ℓ., 11 (i.e. 9) numb. ℓ., 1 ℓ., 19.5cm. 4⁰

"Epistola" dated (7th p. ℓ.ᵛ) 24 June 1696.

Palau(2)185264; Medina(Mexico)1644.

69-753

DA696 P410s

[Penington, Edward] 1667-1701.

Some Brief Observations Upon George Keith's Earnest Expostulation, Contained In a Postscript to a late Book of his, Entituled, The Antichrists and Sadducees Detected, &c. Offered to the Perusal of such as the said Expostulation was Recommended to. By E P. ...

London: Printed and Sold by T. Sowle, in

White-Hart-Court in Gracious-Street. 1696.
24 p. 17.5cm. 8⁰
Signed: Edward Penington.
Keith's The Anti-Christs and sadduces detected, 1st pub. London 1696.
WingP1146; Sabin59657; Smith(Friends)2:364.

11483, 1918

DA696 Penington, John, 1655-1710.
P411p   The People Called Quakers Cleared By Geo, Keith, From The False Doctrines Charged upon them by G. Keith, and his Self-Contradictions laid open in the ensuing Citations out of his Books. By John Penington. ...
London: Printed and Sold by T. Sowle, in White-Hart-Court in Grace-Church-street, 1696.
54 p. 16.5cm. 8⁰
"Postscript" (p. 48-54) signed: London the 30th of the 4th Month. 1696. G. Whitehead.

DA696 ———— Another copy. 16cm.
P411p   In this copy there is a blank ℓ. at end.
cop. 2   Closely trimmed at top with some loss of text on t.-p.
WingP1229; Sabin59665; Smith(Friends)2:363; McAlpin 4:549.

11484, 1918
4396, 1908

B696   Pérez Landero Otañez y Castro, Pedro.
P438p   Practica De Visitas, Y Residencias Apropriada A los Reynos del Perù, y deducida de lo que en ellos se estila. Por Pedro Perez Landero Otañez, Y Castro, Natural de la Villa, y Corte de Madrid, Escriuano de su Magestad, y publico del numero de la Ciudad de los Reyes ... Y con affectuoso animo dirige A los Escriuanos, y Oficiales de dichos Reynos, que por su inexperiencia necessiten desta direccion.
En Napoles, por Nicolas Layno MDCXCVI. Con la licenzia de los Superiores.
8 p.ℓ., 272 p. 22cm. 4⁰
Cut on t.-p.
License dated (8th p.ℓ.^{r}) 9 May 1696.
Errata, 7th p.ℓ.^{v}
Bound in contemporary vellum.
Medina(BHA)1964; cf. Palau(2)221225-7.

5515, 1909

D70   [Price, Elizabeth]
-P769t   The True Countess of Banbury's Case, Relating to Her Marriage, Rightly Stated. In A Letter To The Lord Banbury.

London, Printed in the Year MDCXCVI
1 p.ℓ., 34 p. 30.5cm. fol.
Errata, 1st p.ℓ.^{v}
No. [6] in a volume with binder's title: Political tracts 1655-1702.
WingT2667.

9973-6, 1914

DA696 [Pusey, Caleb] 1650?-1727.
P987m   A Modest Account From Pensylvania, Of The Principal Differences In Point of Doctrine, Between George Keith, And those of the People Called Quakers, From whom he Separated: Shewing His great Declension, and Inconsistency with Himself Therein. Recommended to the Serious Consideration of Those who are Turned Aside, aud [sic] Joyned in his Schism. ...
London, Printed and Sold by T. Sowle in White-Hart-Court in Gracious-Street. 1696.
68 p. 16cm. 8⁰
Signed (p. 67): The 23d. 12th. Month, 1695. Caleb Pusey.
JCBAR 31:33; Wing P4248; Sabin66739; Smith (Friends) 2:438-439.

16007, 1931

BA696 Quesada y Sotomayor, Gregorio de, b. 1650.
Q5s   Sermon De La Pvrissima Concepcion De Maria Predicado En Sv Octavario este año de 1696. dia Septimo en que costeo la fiesta el Ilustre Tribunal del Consulado. Por El M.R. P. Fr. Gregorio De Qvessada, y Sotomayor del Orden Seraphico Lector Iubilado Calificador, y Consultor del Santo Oficio, Visitador General de las librerias, y Exdifinidor de esta Santa Provincia de los Doze Apostol [sic] de Lima. ...
Con licencia de los Superiores, En Lima en la Imprenta de Joseph de Contreras Impressor Real, y del S. Oficio. Año de 1696.
10 p.ℓ., 22 numb. ℓ. 20cm. 4⁰
License dated (8th p.ℓ.^{v}) 17 Apr. 1696.
Medina records several misprints on the t.-p., which are corrected in this copy.
Medina(Lima)682.

69-545

D696   Raleigh, Sir Walter, 1552?-1618, supposed
-R163s   author.
Select Observations Of the Incomparable Sir Walter Raleigh, Relating to Trade, Commerce, and Coin. As it was Presented to King James. Wherein is Proved; That Our Money, our Sea and Land Commodities, serve to Enrich and Strengthen

other Countries against Our Own. With other
Matters of the highest Moment for the Publick
Welfare.
London: Printed for J. S. and are to be Sold by
R. Baldwin, near Oxford-Arms-Inn in Warwick-
lane, MDCXCVI.
2 p.ℓ., 12 p. 31cm. fol.
Authorship has also been ascribed to John
Keymer (cf. Brushfield 267).
An enl. version of Observations touching
Trade & Commerce with the Hollander...
1st pub. London, 1653. "Some additional
Remarks and Observations Relating to Coin
and Trade." (p. 8-11).
Preface (2d p.ℓ.ʳ) signed: J.S.
WingR189; Sabin67599; Brushfield265.

30803, 1950

B69　Salazar, Antonio de, fl. 1673-1698.
G643v　　Villancicos, Que Se Cantaron En La Santa
12　Iglesia Metropolitana de Mexico: en los
Maytines de la Natividad De Maria Santissima
N. Señora, ... Compuestos en metro-Musico,
por Antonio De Salazar, Maestro de Capilla de
dicha Santa Yglesia.
Con licencia en Mexico; por los Hærederos
de la Viuda de Bernardo Calderon, en la calle
de San Augustin. Año de 1696.
[8] p. 20cm. 4º
Woodcut title vignette (statue of the Virgin
within an armorial border)
Bound, in contemporary vellum, as no. 12
with 42 other items.
Medina(Mexico)1653.

28912, 1941

B69　Salazar, Antonio de, fl. 1673-1698.
G643v　　Villancicos, Qve Se Cantaron En La Santa
23　Iglesia Metropolitana de Mexico: En honor
de Maria Santissima Madre de Dios, en su
Assumpcion Triumphante ... Compuestos
en Metro musico: por Antonio De Salazar,
Máestro de Capilla de dicha Sancta Iglesia
Año 1696.
Con liceneia [sic] en Mexico por los
Hærederos de la Viuda de Bernardo Calderon,
en la calle de San Aguustin, 1696, [sic]
[8] p. 20cm. 4º
Woodcut title vignette (the Virgin surrounded
by angels).
Bound, in contemporary vellum, as no. 23
with 42 other items.
Medina(Mexico)1652.

28923, 1941

D　Scotland--Laws, statutes, etc., 1694-1702
-Scott　(William III).
8　Act For A Company Trading To Affrica
and the Indies. June 26. 1695.
Edinburgh, Printed by the Heirs and Successors
of Andrew Anderson, Printer to His most Excellent
Majesty, Anno Dom. 1696.
7 p. 32cm. fol.
Cut (royal arms) on t.-p.: Steele 246.
First pub. Edinburgh, 1695.
WingS1419; Sabin18544; Scott 8.

06035, 1890-1900

DA696　Scripture Proof For Singing of Scripture Psalms,
S434p　Hymns and Spiritual Songs: Or, An Answer to
several Queries and Objections frequently made
use of to stumble and turn aside young Christians
from their Duty to God in Singing of Psalms.
Gathered out of the Scriptures of Truth. To which
is added The Testimony of some Learned Men, to
prove that Scripture-Psalms are intended by all
those three words, Psalms, Hymns and Songs, ...
By E. H. ...
London, Printed by John Astwood, and Sold by
Nath. Hiller at the Princes Arms and Leaden Hall
street, over against St. Mary Axe. 1696.
2 p.ℓ., 48 p. 16.5cm. 8º
Preface (2d p.ℓ.) signed by Nathanael Mather and
Isaac Chauncy.
WingH23.

68-507

J696　Sepp von Reinegg, Anton, 1655-1733.
S479r　RR. PP. Antonii Sepp, und Antonii Böhm/
Der Societät Jesu Priestern Teutscher
Nation, ... Reissbeschreibung wie dieselbe
aus Hispanien in Paraquariam kommen. Und
Kurtzer Bericht der denckwürdigsten Sachen
selbiger Landschafft/Volckern/und Arbeitung
der sich alldort befindenten PP Missionario-
rum. gezogen Aus denen durch R.P.Sepp,
Soc. Jes. mit aigener Hand geschriebenen
Briefen/zu mehrern Nutzen Von Gabriel
Sepp. von und zu Rechegg leiblichen Brudern
in Druck gegeben.
Mit Erlaubnus der Obern. Nürnberg/In
Verlegung Joh. Hoffmans 1696.
333 p. fold. ℓ. 13cm. 12º
First pub. Brixen, 1696.
"Pater Noster Et Ave Maria In Lingva
Paraqvariensi Hispanica Et Latina" [2] p.
(on fold. ℓ. inserted between p. 212-213).
JCB(2)2:1505; Sabin79162; Palmer388;
Streit2:2319.

03692, before 1866

DA696
S559a
A Short Account Of The Manifest Hand of God That hath Fallen upon Several Marshals and their Deputies, Who have made Great Spoil and Havock of the Goods of the People of God called Quakers, In The Island of Barbadoes, For their Testimony against Going or Sending to the Militia. With a Remarkable Account of some others of the Persecutors of the same People in the same Island. Together with an Abstract of their Sufferings.
London, Printed and Sold by T. Sowle, near the Meeting-house in White-hart-court in Graious-street. 1696.
23 p. fold. table. 19cm. 4°
Table dated: the 20th Day of the 4th Month, 1695.
JCB(2)2:1488; Wing S3540; Sabin3287; Smith (Friends)2:682.

05878, before 1882

D696
S634c
Sloane, Sir Hans, bart., 1660-1753.
Catalogus Plantarum Quæ In Insula Jamaica Sponte proveniunt, vel vulgò coluntur, cum earundem Synonymis & locis natalibus; adjectis aliis quibusdam Quæ In Insulis Maderæ, Barbados, Nieves, & Sancti Christophori nascuntur. Seu Prodromi Historiæ Naturalis Jamaicæ Pars Prima. Autore Hans Sloane, M.D. Coll. Reg. Med. Lond. nec non Soc. Reg. Lond. Soc.
Londini: Impensis D. Brown, ad Insigne Cygni & Bibliorum extra Portam vulgò dictam Temple-Bar. MDCXCVI.
6 p.ℓ., 232, [43] p. 17.5cm. 8°
No more published.
Imperfect: half-title wanting; available in facsimile.
JCB(2)2:1506; WingS3998; Sabin82166; Cundall(Jam.)415.

01928, 1854

D696
S727o
Southerne, Thomas, 1660-1746.
Oroonoko: A Tragedy As it is Acted at the Theatre-Royal, By His Majesty's Servants. Written by Tho. Southerne. ...
London: Printed for H. Playford in the Temple-Change. B. Tooke at the Middle-Temple-Gate. And S. Buckley at the Dolphin against St. Dunstan's Church in Fleetstreet. MDCXCVI.
4 p.ℓ., 84, [2] p. 21.5cm. 4°
Based on Aphra Behn's novel of the same title, 1st pub. London, 1688.
Epilogue (last leaf) by William Congreve.
Cf. Dodds, J.W. Thomas Southerne,
New Haven, 1933, p. 223.
JCB(2)2:1507; WingS4761; Sabin88519.

03693, 1866

DA696
-B355r
Sylvester, Matthew, 1636-1708.
Elisha's Cry After Elijah's God Consider'd and Apply'd, With Reference to the Decease of the late Reverend Mr. Richard Baxter. Who left this Life Decemb. 8th, 1691. And Preach'd in Part on Decemb. 18th, An. Eod. Being the Lord's-Day, At Rutland-House in Charter-house-Yard, London. By Matthew Sylvester...
London, Printed for T. Parkhurst, J. Robinson, J. Lawrence, and J. Dunton. 1696.
1 p.ℓ., 18 p. 32cm. fol. (Bound with as issued: Baxter, Richard. Reliquiæ Baxterianæ. London, 1696.)
WingS6330; McAlpin4:553.

12520A, 1920

E696
=T418r
Thévenot, Melchisédech, 1620?-1692.
Relations De Divers Voyages Curieux, Qui N'Ont Point Esté Publiées, Et qu'on a traduit ou tiré des Originaux des Voyageurs François, Espagnols, Allemands, Portugais, Anglois, Hollandois, Persans, Arabes & autres Orientaux, données au public par les soins de feu M. Melchisedec Thevenot. ... Nouvelle Edition, Augmentée de plusieurs Relations curieuses. Tome Premier. Contenant La I. Et II. Partie. [-Tome Second. Contenant La III. Et IV. Partie.]
A Paris, Chez Thomas Moette Libraire, ruë de la Bouclerie, à saint Alexis. M. DC. XCVI. Avec Privilege De Sa Majesté.
5 pts. illus., plates, maps. fol.
This is the 1696 issue of Thévenot's Relations. There is really only one edition of Thévenot's collection, issued in five parts between 1663 and 1696. Part 1 was first issued in 1663, part 2 in 1664, part 3 in 1666, part 4 during 1672-1674, and part 5 in 1696. During the course of publication the parts of the collection already published were reissued with new title-pages in 1664, 1666, 1672, 1683, and 1696. Some sheets were reprinted for these reissues.
The contents and arrangement of individual copies vary. The Library has six copies and some miscellaneous fragments (cop.1 in 1 vol., 36.5cm.; cop.2 in 1 vol., 41.5cm.; cop.3 in 3 vol., 36cm.; cop.4 in 3 vol., 35cm.; cop.5 in 4 vol., 35cm.; cop.6 in 2 vol., 36cm.). All copies but cop.5 are bound in contemporary calf.
The issues of 1663, 1664, and 1666 are entered in JCB(3)3 at p. 102, 121, and 148, respectively. For the issue of 1683 see this catalogue under that year.

JCB(2)2:936; Sabin95334; cf. JCB(2)2:935; (3)3: 102, 121, 148; cf. Sabin95333; cf. Camus: Thévenot; cf. Lenox:Thévenot; cf. Bibl. Lindesiana 8830-8840.

The 1696 issue consists of parts 1-5.
Contents:
(Locations in the Library's copies are indicated in the margin.)
(Due to reprintings which were made during the course of publication of the collection when required for the reissue of parts previously published and as a result of normal press variations, many variant states are observable in the pieces making up the collection. These are recorded in the Library's bibliographical files but are not specified here.)

t.1: cop. 5.1, 6.1; t.2: cop. 5.3, 6.2
There are two general title-pages, as above, in red and black, with cut on title-pages.

(1. partie)

cop.1 (2 cops.), 3.1, 4.1, 5.1, 5.2, fragments (2 cops.)
"Av Roy." [dedication to Louis XIV] [3] p. ã2·3.

cop.5.1, 5.4
"Catalogue Des Relations Et Des Voyages recueillis ou traduits par Melchisedec Thévenot." [2] p. [unsigned]
Imprint at end: A Paris, chez Thomas Moëtte, Libraire. 1696."
The paging of each relation is given. The last section, "Relations qui n'ont point encore paru", lists nine items.

cop.5.1, 6.1, fragments
[preliminaries, including variant of the preceding] 4 p. *2
"Advertissement. La reputation de Mr Thévenot...", p. [1-2].
"Catalogue Des Relations Et Des Voyages recueillis ou traduits par Melchisedec Thevenot", p. [3-4].
Imprint, p. [4]: A Paris, chez Thomas Moëtte, Libraire. 1696."
The "catalogue" does not give the paging of the relations. The section of "Relations qui n'ont point encore paru" lists eleven items. The contents of Thévenot's Recueil de voyages issued Paris, 1681, in 8º, and of his L'Art de nager, Paris, 1696, are also listed.
The copy among the fragments lacks p. [3-4].

cop.1, 2, 3.1, 4.1, 5.1, 6.1
"Avis, Sur le dessein, & sur l'ordre de ce Recueil." [6] p. ã^4(-ã1)
Includes, p. [6], "Table Des Relations De Cette Premiere Partie" in red and black.

cop.1, 2, 3.1, 4.1, 5.1, 6.1
"Description Des Pyramides D'Bgypte [sic], par Iean Greaues..." xxv, [xxvi-xxvii] p. incl. 2 plates. double pl. Δ^4-3 Δ^4 4Δ^2
Taken from: Greaves, John, Pyramidographia, London, 1646.
Includes (p. xxv) "Lettre du Sieur Tito-Liuio Burattini, contenant vne description des Momies d'Egypte, traduite de l'Italien."
In cop. 6.1 there are 2 copies of leaf 2 Δ 4.

cop.1, 2, 3.1, 4.1, 5.1, 6.1, fragments
[section] 52 p. fold. map. [signed with dagger: 1st-6th gatherings in 4s, 7th gathering in 2]
"Relation Des Cosaqves" [by Pierre Chevalier], p. 1-13. Also pub. as: Histoire de la guerre des Cosaques contre la Pologne..., Paris, 1663.
"Relation Des Tartares... Par Iean De Lvca...", p. [14]-23.
"Additions A La Relation Precedente... tirées des memoires du Sr de Beauplet[sic]", p. 24-30. Probably taken from: [Beauplan Guillaume Le Vasseur, sieur de] Description d'Ukraine, Rouen, 1660.
"Relation De La Colchide... Par Le P. Archange Lamberti...", p. 31-52. Transl. from: Relazione della Colchide, Rome 1653.
In cop. 5.1 there are 2 copies of fold. map. There is of this section among the fragments only the 3d leaf of the 4th gathering (2 cops.). In cop.1 the 3d leaf of the 4th gathering is wanting.

cop.1, 2, 3.1, 4.1, 5.1, 6.1
"Informatione Della Giorgia... Da Pietro Della Valle..." 26 p. incl. port. a-c^4 d1
Includes "Eloge De Sitti Maani Gioerida", p. [15-16], and "Nel Fvnerale Di Sitti Maani Gioerida sua consorte", p. 17-26.
Taken from: Valle, Pietro della, Viaggi, Rome, 1650.

cop.1, 2, 3.1, 4.1, 5.1, 6.1
[section] 17-40 p. c^4 d^4 (d1 + e2) f^2
"Avis, Sur la Nauigation d'Anthoine Ienkinson...", p. 17-18.
"Voyage D'Anthoine Ienkinson, Pour découurir le chemin du Cattay par la Tartarie...", p. 19-28. Taken from: Hakluyt, Richard, The principal navigations..., London, 1598-[1600]. Cordier 2070.
"Extrait Dv Voyage Des Hollandois, enuoyez és années 1656. & 1657. en qualité d'Ambassadeurs vers l'Empereur des Tartares... traduit du Manuscrit Hollandois", p. 29-28 (i.e. 32). Although taken by Thévenot from a ms., first pub. as: Nieuhof, Johan, Gezantschap der Neêrlandtsche Oost-Indische Compagnie..., Amsterdam, 1665. Thévenot pub. a longer version of this in the 3.ptie. under title: "Voyage des ambassadeurs...". Cordier 2346; Tiele 801n.
"Relation De La Prise De L'Isle Formosa par les Chinois...", p. 28 (i.e. 32)-40.
"... tirée du Manuscrit de M. de la Mauriniere..." (marginal note). Cordier 286.

cop.1, 2,   [section] 12, 80 p. illus., fold. map. 'A6'⁴
3.1, 4.1,   'B6'² **A-**B⁴ **D-**L⁴
5.1, 6.1
            "Relation De La Covr Dv Mogol, Par le Capitaine Havvkins", p. 1-7. Taken from: Purchas, Samuel, <u>Purchas his pilgrimes...</u>, London, 1625.
            "Discours Sur les Memoires de Thomas Rhoë", p. 7-12.
            "Memoires De Thomas Rhoe, Ambassadevr Dv Roy D'Angleterre Avpres Dv Mogol...", p. 1-80. Taken from: Purchas, Samuel, <u>Purchas his pilgrimes...</u>, London, 1625.
            In cop. 1 there are 2 copies of the fold. map; in cop. 5.1 there are 3 copies.

cop.1, 2,   "Voyage De Edovard Terri, Avx Indes
3.1, 4.1,   Orientales." 6, 30 p. illus. A-C⁴ D²
5.1, 6.1   Taken from: Purchas, Samuel, <u>Purchas his pilgrimes...</u>, London, 1625.
            "...on a joint icy la Carte qu'il a faite de l'Indostan..." (marginal note, p. 9). This refers to the map by Thomas Roe which is usually considered a part of the preceding section.

cop.1, 2,   [section] 24 p.incl. illus., 2 tables. ã⁴ẽ⁴ĩ⁴
3.1, 4.1,   "Description Des Animavx Et Des Plantes
5.1, 6.1,   Des Indes. Avec Vne Relation De L'Isle
frag-   Taprobane, tirée de la Topografie Chrestienne
ments   de Cosmas le Solitaire", p. 1-18. Pages 1-9 are the text in Greek (with p. 8 in red and black). Pages 10-18 are the text transl. into French. Title from caption, p. 10. Cordier 1922.
            "Abvlfeda Des Climas Alhend Et Allend... Avis sur les deux Tables suiuantes", p. 18-22. Probably taken from John Greaves' edition of Abū al-Fidā, <u>Chorasmiae et Mawaralnahrae</u>, London, 1650.
            "Description des Antiquitez de Persepolis...", p. 22-24.
            In cop. 5.1 there are 2 copies of leaf f1. There is of this section among the fragments a copy of leaf f4 only.

cop.1,   [Engraved double plate of Chaldean characters]
2.1, 3.1,   "Vera Delineatio Civitatis Bassorae..." [fold.
4.1, 5.1,   map]
6.1, frag-   Thévenot mentions these pieces in his "Avis
ments   sur le dessein... de ce recueil" (1.ptie.) in connection with a "Relation des Chrestiens de Bassora", which is found in the 5.ptie.
            There is among the fragments a copy of the fold. map only.

cop.1, 2,   [section] 35, [1] p. illus. 3*A⁴-3*D⁴ 3*E²
3.1, 4.1,   "Relation Des Royavmes De Golconda, Tan-
5.1, 6.1   nassery, Pegv, Arecan...par VVill. Methold", p. 1-15. Taken from: Purchas, Samuel, <u>Purchas his pilgrimes...</u>, London, 1625.
            "Iovrnal de Pierre VVill. Floris", p. 17-27. Taken from: Purchas, Samuel, <u>Purchas his pilgrimes...</u>, London, 1625.

            "Relation du Royaume de Siam, par Ioost Schuten...", p. 27-35. First pub. The Hague, 1638, under title: <u>Notitie vande situatie, regeeringe...des Coningrijks Siam</u>. Tiele 980n.
            The last page of this section in some copies is blank; some copies have an engraving entitled "Dronte..." printed on the last page; in some copies the engraving is on a slip pasted on the last page.
            In cop. 5.1 there are 3 copies of leaf 3*E2.

cop.1, 2,   [section] 56 p. illus., fold. map. 4A-4G⁴
3.1, 4.1,   "Relation Ov Iovrnal Dv Voyage De Bontekoe,
5.1, 6.1,   Avx Indes Orientales", p. 1-49. Transl. from:
frag-   <u>Journael ofte gedenckwaerdige beschrijvinghe</u>
ments   <u>van de Oost-Indische reyse...</u>, first pub. Hoorn, 1646. Cordier 2338.
            "La Terre Avstrale Descovverte Par Le Capitaine Pelsart", p. 50-56. Transl. from: <u>Ongeluckige voyagie...nae de Oost-Indien</u>, first recorded pub. Amsterdam, 1647. Tiele-Muller p. 268; cf. Tiele 850.
            In cop. 5.1 there are 2 copies of leaf 4G1 and there are 3 copies of leaf 4G4. In cop. 5.1 there are 2 copies of fold. map, and there is another copy in cop. 5.2. There is of this section among the fragments a copy of leaf 4G1 only.

cop.5.2   [section] 9, [10-11] p. [signed with paragraph mark: 1st gathering in 4, 2d gathering in 2]
            "Rovtier Povr La Navigation Des Indes Orientales...Par Aleixo Da Motta...", p. 1-9. Navarrete 1:8.
            "Privilege Dv Roy", p. [10-11]. Granted 1 June 1662.

                    (2.partie)
cop.1, 2,   [section] [3], [6] p. Θ⁴(-Θ1) [ ]²
3.2, 4.2,   "Advis Svr L'Ordre Des Pieces de la Seconde
5.2, 6.1   Partie", p. [1-2].
            "Extrait Dv Privilege Dv Roy" (granted 18 Feb. 1663), p. [3]. At end: "Acheué d'imprimer pour la premiere fois, le 25. Octobre 1664."
            "Relation De L'Estat Present Dv Commerce des Hollandois & des Portugais dans les Indes Orientales...", p. [1-3] 2d count. Cordier 2346.
            "Discovrs Svr Le Profit Et Svr Les auantages que la Compagnie Hollandoise des Indes Orientales pourroit tirer du Commerce du Iapon, si elle auoit la liberté de trafiquer à la Chine, Par Leonard Camps...", p. [4-6] 2d count. Includes (p. [6]) "Extraict D'Vne Lettre Dv Govvernevr General des Indes Orientales, aux Directeurs de la Compagnie, sur le sujet du Commerce du Iapon." Taken from: [Commelin, Izaäk] <u>Tweede deel van het begin ende voortgangh...</u> [Amsterdam] 1645.
            In cop. 5.2 a plate, "Batavia", has been in-

[337]

serted. Camus, p. 289, records an errata slip not found in any of the Library's copies.
Leaf Θ2 is wanting in cop. 2. Leaf Θ3 is wanting in cops. 3.2, 4.2.

cop. 1, 2, 3.2, 4.2, 5.2, 6.1 "Tres-Hvmble Remontrance Qve Francois Pelsart, principal facteur de la Compagnie Hollandoise des Indes Orientales, presente aux Directeurs de cette mesme Compagnie, sur le sujet de leur commerce en ces quartiers là..." 20 p. A-B⁴ C² [signatures are prefixed with a double dagger]
Tiele-Muller p. 268-269.

cop. 1, 2, 3.2, 4.2, 5.2, 6.1 "Rovtier Povr La Navigation Des Indes Orientales... Par Aleixo Da Motta... traduit d'vn Manuscrit Portugais." 60 p. 2 fold. maps. [signed with paragraph mark: 1st-6th gatherings in 4s, 7th gathering in 6].
Navarrete 1:8.
The first gathering was also issued as a part of the 1. ptie.
The two fold. maps (one depicting the coasts of Africa, Arabia, and India, the other depicting the East Indies, the Philippines, and parts of China and Japan) probably together constitute the "Carte portugaise de Carreira ou navigation des Indes orientales" to which Thévenot refers in the "Advis sur l'ordre des pieces de la seconde partie."
In cop. 2 the 2 fold. maps are colored, and there is an additional copy of the East Indies [etc.] map (uncolored). There is an additional copy of the East Indies [etc.] map in cop. 3.3; this map is wanting in cop. 4.2; and in cop. 5.2 there are 3 additional copies.

cop. 1, 2, 3.2, 4.2, 5.2, 6.1 "Memoires Dv Voyage Avx Indes Orientales Dv General Beavliev, Dressés Par Lvy-Mesme. ... imprimée sur l'original..." 128 p. incl. tables. 5 fold. plates.
Includes "Discovrs Svr Le Voyage Dv General Beavliev", p. 128.
The fold. plates (4 woodcut, 1 engr.) are coastal profiles.
In cop. 2 the woodcuts are colored. There are 2 copies of the woodcuts in cop. 3.2. The engr. pl. is wanting in cops. 2 and 6.1.

cop. 1, 2, 3.2, 4.2, 5.2, 6.1 [section] 40 p. A-E⁴ [signatures are prefixed with a paragraph mark]
"Relation Des Isles Philippines Faite Par L'Amirante D. Hieronimo De Bañvelos Y Carrillo", p. 1-7. Transl. from: Tratado del estado de las islas Filipinas y de sus conveniencias, Mexico, 1638.
"Relation Et Memorial De l'estat des Isles Philippines, & des Isles Moluques", p. 7-29. Transl. from: [Rios Coronel, Hernando de los] Memorial y relación..., Madrid, 1621. Palau(2)268536.
"Memoire Pour le Commerce des Isles Philipines...", p. 30-40. Transl. from: Grau y Monfalcón, Juan, Memorial informatorio..., Madrid, 1637. Palau(2)108813n. Retana 173.

cop. 1, 2, 3.2, 4.2, 5.2, 6.1 [section] 16 p. illus. *a-*b⁴ [signatures are prefixed with a section mark]
"Relation Des Isles Philipines, Faite par vn Religieux qui y a demeuré 18. ans", p. 1-13. "Cette Relation a esté traduite d'vn manuscrit Espagnol..." (marginal note).
"Relation De La Grande Isle De Mindanao...", p. 14-16. Includes "Lettre du Pere Marcello Francisco Mastrillo Iesuiste, dans laquelle il rend compte... de la conqueste de l'Isle de Mindanao...", p. 15-16. Palau (2)157617; Backer 5:716.
Taken from: Bobadilla, Diego de, ed., Relation de las gloriosas victorias..., Mexico, 1638.
In both versions of the "Catalogue des relations..." in the 1. ptie. the relations of the Philippine Islands are listed "avec une grande carte de la Chine, du Japon...". In some copies the East Indies [etc.] map which is found with the "Routier" of Aleixo da Mota (see above) is also bound with these relations of the Philippine Islands.
Retana 173.

cop. 1, 2, 3.2, 4.2, 5.2, 6.1 [section] 48 p. incl. illus., pl. []A-[]F⁴
"Relation De L'Empire Dv Iapon... que François Caron... fit... & purgée des fausses remarques & additions que Henry Hagenaer y auoit inserées...", p. 1-33. Transl. from: Rechte beschryving van het machtigh koninghrijck van Iappan..., The Hague, 1661. First pub. in: [Commelin, Izaäk] Tweede deel van het begin ende voortgangh... [Amsterdam] 1645, including annotations by Hagenaar, which Thévenot includes on p. 32-33. Thévenot also includes in his "Advis Svr La Relation..." (p. 1-2) answers to further inquiries which he posed to Caron.
"Recit De la persecution des Chrestiens du Iapon. par Reyr Gysbertz...", p. 34-47. First pub. Amsterdam, 1637, under title: De tyrannije ende wreedtheden der Jappanen, but probably taken by Thévenot from Commelin's collection (as above). Streit 5:1513n.
"Continuation du precedent recit... par Varen", p. 47-48. The original of this extract was first pub. Amsterdam, 1649, under title: Tractatus in quo agitur de Japoniorum religione.
Tiele 232n; Streit 5:1566n.

cop. 1, 2, 4.2, 5.2, 6.1 "Relation De la découuerte de la Terre d'Eso, au Nord du Iapon. Tradvite De L'Holandois." 4 p. fold. map. [unsigned]
Only the Library's copy 5.2 contains the map.

cop.1,2, [section] 30 p. 5 plates (incl. 3 fold.).
3.2, 4.2, (?)a-(?)D⁴ (-(?)D4)
5.2, 6.1,
frag-   "Briefve Relation De La Chine, Et De La
ments Notable Conversion des Personnes Royales
de cet Estat. Faicte par le tres-R.P.Michel
Boym de la Compagnie de Iesvs...", p. 1-14.
Transl. from: Breve relazione della China
..., first pub. Rome, 1652. Backer 2:72;
Streit 5:2224n; Cordier 819-820.
   "Flora Sinensis. Ov Traité Des Flervs [sic],
Des Frvits, Des Plantes, Et Des Animavx
particuliers à la Chine. Par le R.P.Michel
Boym Iesuiste", p. 15-30. Transl. from:
Flora Sinenses, Vienna, 1656. Backer 2:72;
Streit 5:2221n; Cordier 442.
   There is an additional colored set of the
plates in cop. 2. There is of this section
among the fragments an additional set of the
plates only.

(3. partie)
cop.1,2, [section] [8], 31-68, 27, [1] p. 12 plates
3.3, 4.3, (part fold.), fold. map. ã⁶(-ã 1,2; ã 3,
5.3, 6.2, 4 signed as ã 2, 3) [(?)D⁴] (?)E-(?)H⁴ (?)I²
frag-   ¼-[2²]⁴ 3²⁶
ments
   "Avis Svr Le Voyage Des Ambassadevrs
de la Compagnie Hollandoise...", p. [1-8].
"Errata" (p. [8]) covering "Voyage des
Ambassadeurs" and "Route des Hollandois..."
Includes "Extrait Dv Privilege Dv Roy"
(granted 8 June 1662) and statement "Achevé
d'imprimer pour la premiere fois le 25.
Octobre 1664" (p. [8]).
   "Voyage Des Ambassadevrs De La Compagnie
Hollandoise des Indes Orientales, enuoyés l'an
1656. en la Chine, vers l'Empereur des Tar-
tares, ... traduit d'vn Manuscrit Holandois",
p. 31-68. "Rovte Dv Voyage Des Holandois
A Pekin", p. 1-27. Although taken by
Thévenot from mss., first pub. as: Nieuhof,
Johan, Gezantschap der Neêrlandtsche Oost-
Indische Compagnie..., Amsterdam, 1665.
Thévenot pub. a shorter version of this in
the 1.ptie. under title: "Extrait du voyage
des Hollandois...". Includes, p. 67-68,
"Explication Des Figvres...". Tiele 801n;
Cordier 2346.
   "Grammaire De La Langve Des Tartares
Moguls ou Mogols, traduite d'vn Manuscrit
Arabe", p. [1] at end. "Le Manuscrit est
dans la Bibliotheque de M. Gaumin [i.e.
Gaulmin]" (marginal note). This is a
fragment of a Mongol grammar and is a
different work from the "Elementa Linguæ
Tartaricæ" found in the 5. ptie., which
treats the Manchu language. Cordier 2792.
   Some versions of the plates combine illus-
trations otherwise pub. in separate plates.
There are various numbers of plates in the
Library's copies and fragments.

   In cop. 2 there are 19 colored drawings
illustrating some of the same subjects as the
plates.
   There is another copy of the fold. map in
cop. 5.1; the fold. map is wanting in cops.
2 and 4.3. Leaf (?)I 2 and all ¼ gatherings
are wanting in cop. 2. There is of this section
among the fragments a set of the plates only.
   Also issued with special t.-p. under title:
Ambassade des Hollandois à la Chine...,
Paris, S. Mabre-Cramoisy, 1666.

cop.1,   "Description Geographiqve De L'Empire
3.3, 4.3, De La Chine, Par Le Pere Martin Martinivs,
5.3, 6.2 [S.] I. ..." 34, 33-60, 59-76, 73-216 p.
illus. (tables), fold. map. (A-(G⁴ ²(G⁴
(H-(2D⁴
   Reprinted from: Novus atlas sinensis
[French text], Amsterdam [1655] (v.6 of
the Blaeu Theatrum orbus terrarum).
Backer 5:650; Streit 5:2261n; Cordier 182.

cop.1,   "Rapport Qve Les Directevrs De La Com-
3.3, 4.3, pagnie Hollandoise des Indes Orientales ont
5.3, 6.2 fait à leurs Hautes Puissances, premierement
de bouche, & en suite deliuré par écrit, touchant l'estat des affaires dans les Indes
Orientales tel qu'il estoit lors que la Flotte
qui est depuis peu arriuée en ces Païs partit
de là..." 12 p. Σ A⁶
   Signed (p. 10) by Pieter van Dam, 22 Oct.
1664.
   In cop. 4.3 there are 2 copies of sheet
Σ A2·5.

(4. partie)
cop.5.4   The Library has a copy of the t.-p. for
t.1, issued Paris, Thomas Moette, 1696,
with a strip reading "IV. Partie." (taken
from the t.-p. for the 4.ptie. issued Paris,
André Cramoisy, 1672) pasted over the
section of the 1696 t.-p. reading "Tome
Premier. Contenant La I. Et II. Partie."

cop.5.4,   "Avis Svr La Svite Dv Recveil", [2] p.
frag-   [unsigned].
ments   Includes a passage attributed to "le Pere
[Alonso?] Oualle" and (at end) "Extrait Dv
Privilege Dv Roy" (granted 8 June 1662).

cop.1,   "L'Indien, Ov Portrait Av Natvrel Des
4.3, 5.4, Indiens, ... Par D. Iuan De Palafox..."
6.2,   14 p. *-2*⁴ (-2*4)
frag-   Transl. from a memorial known under
ments   title: [Virtudes del Indio, Madrid? ca. 1650]
(2 cops.) This and the following section were also
issued with special t.-p. under title: Voyage
du Sr. Acarette à Buenos-Ayres... et L'Indien
ou portrait au naturel..., Paris, A. Cramoisy,
1672, and Paris, G. Clousier, 1672.
   Palau(2)209716; Medina(BHA)7680n; Streit
2:2077.

cop.1,   "Relation Des Voyages Dv Sievr......[sic,
4.3, 5.4,   i.e. Acarete du Biscay] dans la riviere de la
6.2   Plate, & de là par terre au Perou..." 24 p.
                a-c^4

cop.1,   [section] 23 p. illus. (port.). A-C^4
4.3, 5.4,   "Voyage A La Chine Des PP. I. Grveber Et
6.2,   D'Orville" [by Lorenzo Magalotti], p. 1-19.
frag-   Includes comments by Thévenot, p. 19.
ments   "Ex Litteris Grueberi Kirchero inscriptis",
                p. 20-23.
                In cop. 5.4 there are 2 variants of gather-
             ing B. There are of this section among the
             fragments leaves B1, 3, 4 only.
                Also issued with special t.-p. under title:
             Voyage fait à la Chine en 1665... , Paris,
             G. Clousier, A. Cramoisy, 1673.
                Backer 3:149, 3:1885; Cordier 2903;
             Streit 5:2414.

cop.1,   [section] 23, [1] p. incl. pl. A-C^4
4.3, 5.4,   "Viaggio Del P. Giovanni Grveber, tor-
6.2   nando per terra da China in Europa" [by
             Lorenzo Magalotti], p. 1-18. This is the
             original of Thévenot's translation in the
             preceding section.
                "Autres Pieces..." (letters from Grueber),
             p. 18-23.
                "L'Alphabet des Chinois qui est ajoûté à
             cette Relation [i.e. the plate] vient du Pere
             Ruggieri Missionaire de la Chine..." (cf.
             Thévenot's comments in preceding section).
                In cop. 5.4 there are 2 variants of sheet
             C1·4.
                Backer 3:1885; Cordier 2903.

cop.1,   "Scientiæ Sinicæ Liber Inter Confvcii
4.3, 5.4,   Libros Secvndvs." 3-24 p. illus. A^4(-A1)
6.2   B-C^4
                Title from caption, p. 5.
                Transl. into Latin by Prospero Intorcetta.
                Includes (p. 19-24) partial translation into
             French by Thévenot.
                First pub. Goa [etc.], 1669 [etc.] (cf.
             Cordier).
                Also issued with special t.-p. under title:
             Sinarum scientia politico-moralis... , Paris,
             1672, and under title: La science des Chinois
             ... , Paris, G. Clousier, A. Cramoisy, 1672,
             and Paris, A. Cramoisy, 1673.
                Cordier 1388-1392; Backer 4:641; Streit 5,
             p. 850.

cop.1,   "Histoire De La Haute Ethiopie, Ecrite Svr
4.3, 5.4,   Les Lievx Par le R.P. Manoel D'Almeïda Iesuite,
6.2,   Extraite & traduite de la copie Portugaise du
frag-   R.P. Baltazar Tellez." 16 p. A-B^4
ments   Taken from: Historia geral de Ethiopa... ,
             Coimbra, 1660.
                In cop. 5.4 there are two variants of gather-
             ing B. There is of this section among the frag-
             ments a copy of gathering B only.

                This and the two following sections were also
             issued with special t.-p. under title: Histoire
             de la Haute Ethiopie... Relations de l'empire
             des Abyssins... , Paris, A. Cramoisy, 1674.
                Streit 16, p. 585.

cop.1,   "Remarqves Sur les Relations d'Ethiopie des
4.3, 5.4,   RR. PP. Ieronimo Lobo, & de [sic] Balthasar Tellez
6.2   Iesuites." 4 p. A^2
                Streit 16, p. 585.

cop.1,   "Relation Dv R. P. Ieronymo Lobo De
4.3, 5.4,   L'Empire Des Abyssins, Des Sources du Nil,
6.2   de la Licorne, &c." 16 p. illus., 2 fold.
             maps. A-B^4
                "... achevées d'estre imprimées pour la
             premiere fois le 11. Fevrier 1673." (p. 16).
                In cop. 5.4 there are: 2 copies of p. 1-16
             (exhibiting variants in leaves A1-4, B1-4),
             3 (variant) copies of fold. map "Carte d'Ethiopie
             ...", and 2 (variant) copies of fold. map
             "Entrées de quelques ports...". The copy of
             the latter map in cop. 1 is a further variant.
                Also issued with special t.-p. under title:
             Relations de l'empire des Abyssins... ,
             Paris, A. Cramoisy, 1673, and G. Clousier,
             A. Cramoisy, 1673.
                Streit 16, p. 585; Backer 4:1896.

cop.1   "Decovverte De Qvelqves Pays qui sont entre
4.3, 5.4,   l'Empire des Abyssins & la coste de Melinde."
6.2   8 p. Θ^4
                Concerns travels during 1613 and 1614 of
             Antonio Fernández, Jesuit missionary in
             Ethiopia.
                Streit 16, p. 585.

cop.1,   "Relation Du Voyage Du Sayd, Ou De La
4.3, 5.4,   Thebayde, Fait en 1668. par les PP. Protais
6.2   & Charles-François d'Orleans, Capucins
             Missionaires." 4 p. a^2
                Includes at end a covering letter "Du Caire
             le 6. Ianvier 1670" signed: F. Protais.
                Also issued with special t.-p., Paris, A.
             Cramoisy, 1673.
                Streit 16:4478n.

cop.1,   "Histoire Dv Mexiqve Par Figvres Expliqvées
5.4, 6.2   En Langve Mexicaine, Et depuis en langue
             Espagnole." 58 p. incl. 63 facsims. A-E^4
             F-K^2 (-K2)
                Title from caption, p. 47.
                Taken from: Purchas, Samuel, Purchas
             his pilgrimes... , London, 1625. Purchas'
             source was the manuscript "Codex Mendoza".
                In cop. 5.4 there are 2 (variant) copies of
             this section.
                This and the following section were also
             issued with special t.-p. under title: Histoire
             de l'empire mexicain... Relation du Mexique
             ... , Paris, A. Cramoisy [1673?] and Paris,
             T. Moette, 1696.

cop.1, 5.4, 6.2	"Relation Dv Mexiqve, Et De La Novvelle Espagne, Par Thomas Gages [sic], Traduite de l'Anglois." 40 p. *-3*^{4} 4*-7*^{2} An abridged transl. of: The English-American, his travail..., London, 1648. In cop. 5.4 there are 2 (variant) copies of this section. Palau(2)96490; Streit 2:2316.	cop.5.4, 6.2	"Voyage De La Tercere, Fait Par M. Le Commandevr De Chaste..." 18 p. A-B^4 C^2 (-C2)
		cop.5.4, 6.2	"Elementa Linguae Tartaricae." 1, 4-34 p. illus. A-H^2 This work by Ferdinand Verbiest has been erroneously ascribed to Jean François Gerbillon; it has also been mistakenly attributed to Philippe Couplet (cf. Cordier 4283). This concerns the Manchu language and is a different work from the "Grammaire de la langve des Tartares" found in the 3. ptie., which treats the Mongol language. Cordier 2752; Backer 2:1566, 3:1347, 8:583.
	(5. partie)		
cop.5.4, 6.2	"Voyage D'Abel Tasman. L'an M.DC.XLII." 4 p. A^2 Taken from: Nierop, Dirk Rembrantsz van, Eenige oefeningen in godlycke wiskonstige en natuerlycke dingen, v.2, Amsterdam, 1674.		
cop.5.4, 6.2	"Instrvction Des Vents Qvi Se rencontrent, & regnent plus frequemment entre les Païs bas & l'Isle de Iava." 12 p. A^4 B^2		
cop.5.4, 6.2	[section] 16 p. A-D^2 "Ambassade De S'Chahrok, Fils De Tamerlan, Et d'autres Princes ses voisins, A L'Empereur Du Khatai", p. 1-13. "Relatio Ablegationis Qvam Czarea Majestas Ad Catayensem Chamum Bogdi destinavit, ann. cIɔ.Iɔc.LIII.", p. 13-16.	cop.5.4, 6.2, fragments	"Dos Viages Del Adelantado Alvaro De Mendaña Con Intento De Poblar Las Islas De Salomon Y Descubrir La Parte Austral Incognita" 17 p. a-e^2(-e2) Title from type-facsimile reprint made for S. A. Sobolewski in 1848. Leaves a1·2 and c1·2 are wanting in all of the Library's copies, and leaf e1 is found only in cop. 5.4. These leaves are wanting in most copies (cf. JCB(2)2, p. 377-378). Palau(2)162851.
cop.5.4, 6.2	"Synopsis Chronologica Monarchiæ Sinicæ Ab Anno Post Diluvium CC.LXXV. Usque Ad Annum Christi M.DC.LXVI." 76 p. a-f^2 2f^2 g-s^2 "Sex Conditores Monarchiæ Sinicæ per annos D.LXXXVII", p. 1-19. Taken from: Martini, Martino, Sinicæ historiæ decas prima, first pub. Munich, 1658. "Historiæ Sinicæ Decas Secunda" (running title), p. 21-76. In copy 6.2 there are 2 (variant) copies of gathering d. Cordier 580; Backer 5:650.	cop.5.4, 6.2	[fragment] 17-48 p. 4*-11*^{2} Running title, p. 17: Asganii Sassonii. The fuller version of the "Catalogue des relations..." in the 1.ptie. lists this piece as "... Fragment servant à l'histoire de quelques Princes Orientaux." Additional fragments, p. 49-64, 77-80, wanting in the Library's copies, are found in a few other copies (cf. Camus: Thévenot p. 292 and Lenox: Thévenot 92). Although not listed in either version of the "Catalogue des relations..." in the 1.ptie., additional fragments, wanting in the Library's copies, are found in a few other copies. "Appendix ad Hist. Mogolum" (running title), 12 p. (cf. Camus: Thévenot p. 292 and Lenox: Thévenot p. 18). "Gramatica Linguæ Sinensis", 15 p. (cf. Lenox: Thévenot, p. 18). Cordier 1650.
cop.5.4, 6.2	"L'Asie De Barros, Ou L'Histoire Des Conqvestes Des Portvgais Avx Indes Orientales. Partie Premiere." 16 p. A-B^4 Covers through the year 1502. Abridged transl. of: Barros, João de, Asia [first decade], first pub. Lisbon, 1552.		
cop.5.4, 6.2	"Relation Des Chrestiens De S. Iean, faite par le Pere Ignace de Iesvs Carme Déchaux, Missionaire & Vicaire de la Maison de Sainte Marie des Remedes, à Bassora." [4] p. [unsigned] Abridged transl. of: Ignazio de Jesus, carmelite friar, Narratio originis, rituum et errorum christianorum Sancti Joannis..., Rome, 1652. Thévenot mentions this relation in his "Avis sur le dessein...de ce recueil" (1.ptie.) in connection with a plate of Chaldean characters and a map of Basra, which are found in the 1.ptie.		
		04807, 1849 03923, 1868	05132, 1884 05133, before 1884	04806, 1848 01929, 1854

BA696 T693s	Torres, Ignacio de. Seláh Mystico De La Iglesia Nuestro Esclarescido Padre, Y Senor San Pedro. Sermon Qve Predico Sv Dia En La Cathedral De La Puebla, El Doctor Ignacio De Torres, Cura Beneficiado de la Parochia de S. Sebastian en dicha Ciudad, Qualificador del Santo Officio de la Inquisision de esta Nueva España, y Juez Adjūto en la Causa de la Beatificacion de la V.

1696

69-776	Madre Maria de Jesvs. Año de 1696. ... [Puebla de los Angeles] Con licencia en la Imprenta del Capitan Iuan de Villa Real. [1696] 10 p. ℓ., 18 p. 19.5cm. 4° License dated (4th p. ℓ.ʳ) 28 Sept. 1696. Imperfect: 2d-3d p. ℓ. wanting; available in facsimile. Medina(Puebla)186.
CA679 V665s 11	Vieira, Antonio, 1608-1697. Sermoens Do P. Antonio Vieyra, da Companhia de Jesu, Prêgador de Sua Magestade. Undecima Parte ... Lisboa, Na Officina de Miguel Deslandes, Impressor de Sua Magestade. M.DC.LXXXXVI. Com todas as licenças necessarias, & Privilegio Real. 9 p. ℓ., 48, 69-168, 171-590, 23 p. plate (coat of arms). 20.5cm. 4° Cut (Jesuit trigram, floriated) on t.-p. Permission dated (8th p. ℓ.) 10 Dec. 1696. Errata, 9th p. ℓ. Contains 16 sermons preached in Bahia, Brazil, 1639, 1689, 1695, Lisbon, 1641, 1642 1649, 1655, Rome 1674, Odivellas, Portugal, 1651, etc Includes (23 p. at end) "Sermão do felicissimo nacimento da Serenissima Infanta Teresa Francisca Josepha; que por vir depois de impresso este Tomo, se acrecentou no fim delle." (cf. table of contents, 8th p. ℓ.ᵛ) According to Leite "Conhecem-se duas impressões, de 1696, deste volume." Rodrigues2513; Backer8:660; Leite9:198; Innocencio1:290.
68-340	
JA696 W419b	Weigel, Christoph, 1654-1725. Biblia Ectypa Minora, Veteris Testamenti Historias Sacras et res maximi momenti exhibentia, æri incisa et in Commodum Christianæ Iuventutis edita à Christophoro Weigelio, Augustæ [i.e. Augsburg], A.M.D.XCVI. [i.e. 1696] 1 p. ℓ., 152 p. of plates. front. 8cm. 32° Engraved throughout. Bound in contemporary vellum.
10952, 1916	
DA696 W724b	[Williams, John] Bp. of Chichester, 1636?-1709. A Brief Discourse Concerning the Lawfulness of Worshipping God By The Common-Prayer. Being in Answer To a Book, Entituled, A Brief Discourse concerning the Unlawfulness of the Common-Prayer Worship. Lately Printed in New-England, and Reprinted in London. In which, the Chief Things Objected Against the Liturgy, are considered. The Third Edition Corrected. ... London: Printed for Ri. Chiswell, at the Rose and Crown in St. Paul's Church-Yard, MDCXCVI. 2 p. ℓ., 36 p. 19.5cm. 4° First pub. London, 1693. A reply to Increase Mather's <u>A brief discourse concerning the unlawfulness of the common prayer worship</u>, [Cambridge, Mass., 1686] Imprimatur dated (verso t.-p.) Aug. 9, 1693. Sabin104256; Holmes(I.)p. 55, 537, Wing W2684.
10735, 1915	
DA696 Y76w	[Young, Samuel] fl. 1697. William Penn And the Quakers Either Impostors, or Apostates, Which they please: Proved from their avowed Principles, and contrary Practices. ... By Trepidantium Malleus [pseud.]. London: Printed for the Author, and are to be Sold by John Lawrence at the Angel in the Poultrey. 1696. 3 p. ℓ., 134 p. 14cm. 12° JCB(2)2:1504; Sabin106108; Smith(Anti-Quak.)459; WingY90.
04209, 1866-1882	

1697

BA697 A284s	Aguirre, Pedro Antonio de. San Pedro De Alcantara Celebrado Iman De La Seraphica Descalcez, y mas estrecha Observancia de los Religiosos Menores de N.S. P.S. Francisco, en su Convento de San Diego de Mexico en 19. de Octubre de 1696 años. ... Discvrrialo Fr. Pedro Antonio De Aguirre de los Menores Descalços de N.S.P.S. Francisco, Ex-Lector de Theologia, Calificador del Santo Officio, Definidor Actual, y Chronista de la Provincia de San Diego de Mexico. Con licencia impresso en Mexico en la Imprenta de Juan Joseph Guillena Carrascoso año de 1697.

[342]

15 p.ℓ., 32 p. 19.5cm. 4º
License dated (13th p.ℓ.ᵛ) 12 Sept. 1697.
Palau(2)3947; Medina(Mexico)1659.

12536, 1920

BA697 Avendaño Suares de Sousa, Pedro de, b. ca.
A951s 1654.
Sermon De La Esclarecida Virgen, Y Inclita Martyr De Christo Sᵗᵃ Barbara Que el dia 4. de Diziembre de este año de 1696 Predicó D. Pedro De Avendaño Suares De Sousa En la fiesta que su Illustrissima Congregacion celebra en el Convento de Señoras Religiosas de San Bernardo de esta Corte. Sacalo A Luz El Licᵈᵒ D. Mathias De Galves, y lo dedica Al Capitan D. Martin De Echagaray, Juez Contador por su Magestad de Menores, y Albaceasgos, á cuyas expensas se dà á la estampa.
Con licencia en Mexico en la Imprenta de Juan Joseph Guillena Carrascoso Año de 1697.
8 p.ℓ., 14 numb. ℓ. 20cm. 4º
Dedication, 2d-4th p.ℓ., signed: Mathias de Galves.
License dated (verso 8th p.ℓ.) 21 Jan 1697.
Imperfect: coat of arms on 2d p.ℓ. cut out, affecting text on verso.
Palau (2)20154; Medina(Mexico)1664.

1071, 1905

J697   Boecler, Johann Heinrich, 1611-1692.
B669j Jo. Henrici Boecleri De Rebus Seculi Post Christum Natum XVI. Liber Memorialis Cum Commentario: Recognitus, auctus, & ab innumeris, quibus scatebat, mendis repurgatus, Indicibusque necessariis instructus, operâ Jo. Burchardi Maji.
Kiloni, Sumtibus Joann. Sebast. Riechelii. Typis Joach. Reumanni. Anno MDCXCVII.
8 p.ℓ., 792, [111] p. 16cm. 8º
First pub. Strasbourg, 1685.
Errata, p. [110-111] at end.

69-821

DA697 Bray, Thomas, 1658-1730.
B827b Bibliotheca Parochialis: Or, A Scheme Of Such Theological Heads Both General and Particular, As Are More peculiarly Requisite to be well Studied by every Pastor of a Parish. Together with a Catalogue of Books Which may be Read upon each of those Points. Part. I. By Thomas Bray, D.D.
London, Printed by E.H. for Robert Clavel, at the Peacock in St. Paul's Church-Yard. MDCXCVII.

10 p.ℓ., 130 p. 22cm. 4º
No more published.
Errata, 10th p.ℓ.ᵛ.
"Proposals For the Incouragement and Promoting of Religion" (p. 121-124), 1st pub. [London, 1695]. "The Conclusion, Shewing the Present State of the Protestant Religion in Mary-Land" by Sir Thomas Lawrence (p. 126-130), 1st pub. in the [London, 1696] ed. of the Proposals.
In this copy there is a blank leaf at end.
Bound in mid-18th century half calf as the 1st of 4 items.
WingB4290; Sabin7474; Baer(Md.)175.

7618, 1911

DA697 Bray, Thomas, 1658-1730.
B827e An Essay Towards Promoting all Necessary and
[R]   Useful Knowledge, Both Divine and Human, In all the Parts of His Majesty's Dominions, Both at Home and Abroad. By Thomas Bray, D.D. ...
London, Printed by E. Holt for Robert Clavel, at the Peacock in St. Paul's Church-Yard, MDCXCVII.
4 p.ℓ., 22 p., [1] ℓ. 20.5cm. 4º
"The Catalogue of Books Design'd to lay the Foundation of Lending-Libraries To be fix'd in all the Market-Towns in England" (p. 17-22).
Bookseller's advertisement, last p.
JCB(2)2:1509; WingB4293; Sabin7476; McAlpin 4:558; Baer(Md.)176; Smith(Anti-Quak)85.

04014, before 1871

DA697   [Bray, Thomas] 1658-1730.
-B827pF Proposals For the Encouragement and Pro-
[R]   moting of Religion and Learning in the Foreign Plantations; and to induce such of the Clergy of this Kingdom, as are Persons of Sobriety and Abilities, to accept of a Mission into those Parts.
[London, 1697]
4 p. 33cm. fol.
Caption title.
With the endorsement (p. 2) of the two archbishops and of 4 bishops.
Includes (p. 3-4) "The Present State Of The The [sic] Protestant Religion In Mary-Land" (unsigned; by Sir Thomas Lawrence).
Probably published in Aug. 1697. First pub. as early as Dec. 1695, [London] (without "The Present State...", which was added in an edition pub. probably Oct. 1696, [London]).
JCBAR34:12-16; Baer(Md.)163F, 177; cf. Wing4296.

06030, before 1900

DA697　　[Bray, Thomas] 1658-1730.
-B827pG　　Proposals For the Encouragement and Pro-
[R]　　moting of Religion and Learning in the Foreign
Plantations; and to induce such of the Clergy
of this Kingdom, as are Persons of Sobriety and
Abilities, to accept of a Mission into those Parts.
[London, 1697]
4 p. 32.5cm. fol.
Caption title.
With the endorsement (p. 2) of the two arch-
bishops and of 5 bishops.
Includes (p. 3-4) "The Present State Of The
The [sic] Protestant Religion In Mary-Land"
(unsigned; by Sir Thomas Lawrence).
Probably published after Aug. 1697. First
pub. as early as Dec. 1695, [London] (without
"The Present State...", which was added in
an edition pub. probably Oct. 1695, [London]).
JCBAR35:47; Baer(Md.)163G, 178; cf. Wing
4296.
16770, 1935

DA697　　Bray, Thomas, 1658-1730.
B827s　　A Short Discourse Upon the Doctrine of our
Baptismal Covenant, Being An Exposition Upon
the Preliminary Questions and Answers Of Our
Church-Catechism. Proper to be read by all
Young Persons ... With Devotions ... By
Thomas Bray, D.D.
London, Printed by E. Holt, for Rob. Clavel
at the Peacock in St. Paul's Church-Yard, 1697.
16 p.ℓ., 160 p., 12 ℓ., 161-173, 172-174,
191-205 p., 1 ℓ., [6], 175-190, [7] p. A⁴a⁸b⁴
B-L⁸ (*)⁸ (+)⁴ M-O⁸ *⁴ P⁸ Q⁴ illus. (music).
16.5cm. 8°
"An Appendix ... Being A Method Of Family
Religion" (1 ℓ., [6], 175-190, [6] p. at end) has
separate t.-p.
Bookseller's advertisement, p. [7] at end.
WingB4297.
68-34

DA697　　Bugg, Francis, 1640-1724?
B931p　　A Brief History Of The Rise, Growth, and
Progress Of Quakerism; ... Containing Also,
A modest Correction of the General History of
the Quakers; wrot in Holland by Gerard Croese.
By Francis Bugg, Senior. ...
London, Printed Anno 1697.
7 p.ℓ., 196 p. 16.5cm. 8° (Issued as a
part of his The Picture Of Quakerism Drawn
to the Life, London, 1697.)
"A Short Map of Quakerism" p. 177-196,
signed: Francis Bugg. Sen. May 13. 1697.
"Books Wrote by Fra. Bugg. Sen." p. 196.
A reply to The general history of the Quakers,
by Gerard Croese, London, 1696.

In this copy there is a blank ℓ. at beginning.
Sabin9072; WingB5367; Smith(Friends)1:337;
McAlpin1:558.
30639A, 1950

DA697　　Bugg, Francis, 1640-1724?
B931p　　The Picture Of Quakerism Drawn to the Life.
In Two Parts. The First, Shewing the Vanity of
the Quakers ptetence [sic] of their being the one,
only Catholick Church of Christ; ... Also
shewing, That Legal Punishment is not Persecu-
tion, ... The Second, Containing, a brief History of the Rise, Growth, and Progress of
Quakerism; ... By Francis Bugg, Sen. ...
London, Printed for, and are to be sold by
W. Kettleby at the Bishop's-Head in St. Paul's
Church-yard, and W. Rogers at the Sun in
Fleet-street, 1697.
2 v. in 1: 8 p.ℓ., 123, [1] p.; 7 ℓ., 196 p.
double plate. 16.5cm. 8°
Errata: verso 8th p.ℓ.
Dedication signed (verso 5th p.ℓ.): May 3.
1697. Francis Bugg, Senior.
Plate, bound at front: a symbolic bird cage
containing names of prominent Quakers, re-
ferred to on p. 69-72 (1st count) of text.
"A Short Map of Quakerism" p. 177-196,
signed: Francis Bugg. Sen. May 13. 1697.
"Books Wrote by Fra. Bugg. Sen." p. 196.
With, as issued: A Brief History of The
Rise, ... Of Quakerism, with special t.-p.
and separate paging and signatures.
In this copy there is a blank ℓ. at beginning
of A Brief History ...
Sabin9072; Smith(Friends)1:337; McAlpin
4:559; WingB5381.
30639, 1950

B697　　Casas, Bartolomé de las, bp. of Chiapa, 1474-
C334d　　1566.
La Decouverte Des Indes Occidentales, Par
Les Espagnols. Ecrite par Dom Balthazar de
Las-Casas, Evêque de Chiapa. Dedié à Mon-
seigneur le Comte De Toulouse.
A Paris, Chez André Pralard, ruë Saint
Jacques, à l'Occasion. M. DC. XCVII. Avec
Privilege du Roi.
6 p.ℓ., 382, [2] p. illus. (coat of arms)
16cm. 12°
Cut on t.-p., signed: C.L.S. L'Aisne; incl.
motto: Inimicos Superabis Virtute.
Added t.-p., engr., signed: P. Giffart fili? fec.
Dedication (p.ℓ. 3-4ʳ) signed: Pralard.
"Achevé d'imprimer pour la premiere fois, le
10 Aoust 1697." (verso 6th p.ℓ.)
Translation by J.B. Morvan de Bellegarde based

on the nine tracts known under the title: Brevísima relación, pub. Seville, 1552.
 JCB(2)2:1510; Sabin11273; Palau(2)46966; Streit 1:733; Medina(BHA)v. 2, p. 472; Hanke(Las Casas) 559.
01931, 1854

BA697   Catholic Church--Liturgy and ritual--Ritual.
C363m   Manual De Administrar Los Santos Sacramentos à los Españoles, y Naturales de esta Provincia de Michuacan, conforme à la reforma de Paulo V. y Vrbano VIII. Compuesto Por el M.R.P. Fr. Angel Serra, Predicador, Ex Custodio de la Santa Provincia de los Apostoles S. Pedro, y S. Pablo de Michuacan, y Cura colado, que fue de la Doctrina del Pueblo de Charapan en la Sierra de Michuacan y Obispado de Valladolid, y actual Guardian, y Cura del Convento, y Doctrina de N.P.S. Francisco de la Ciudad de Queretaro, y Arçobispado de Mexico. ...
  Con Licencia De Los Superiores En Mexico por Doña Maria de Benavides Viuda de Iuan de Ribera, año de 1697.
  12 p.ℓ., 129 numb. ℓ., [8] p. 21.5cm. 4º
  Text in Latin, Spanish, and Tarascan language.
  License dated (5th p.ℓ.^{v}) 27 Apr. 1697.
  Imperfect: p.ℓ. 1-4, ℓ. 17 wanting; available in facsimile.
  Palau(2)309781; Medina(Mexico)1681; Sabin 79310; Pilling3571; Viñaza239; Ugarte396; Streit 2:2325.
06125, before 1902

BA697   Catholic Church--Liturgy and ritual--Ritual.
C363md   Manual De Administrar Los Santos Sacramentos de la Eucharistia, y Extremavncion, y oficiar los entierros, segun el vso, y observacion del Sagrario de la Santa Iglesia Metropolitana desta Ciudad de Mexico. Para el regimen, y vso de la Compañia, y Religion Betlemitica, para todos sus Convenventos [sic], y Hospitales, Qve Obseqvioso, Y Reverente ofrece, y dedica al Santo Nacimiento del Niño Dios El Br. Ioseph Dé Segura, Presbytero Domisiliario deste Arçobispado, Capellan del Convento de Nuestra Señora de Betlem, y Hospital de Convalecientes de S. Francisco Xavier desta Ciudad de Mexico. Año del Señor de 1697. Conforme à el Ritual de N. SS. P. Paulo V. Sugetandolo, como lo haze, à la correccion de N. S. M. Iglesia, Catholica Romana.
  Con licencia en Mexico por Doña Maria de Benavides, Viuda, Juan de Ribera, año de 1697.

  5 p.ℓ., 130, [3] p. incl. illus. 14.5cm. 8º
  "Parecer" (2d p.ℓ.^{r}) and license (3d p.ℓ.^{r}) dated 8 May 1697.
  Bound in contemporary vellum.
  Palau(2)306420; Medina(Mexico)1680.
11919, 1919

DA697   Chauncy, Isaac, 1632-1712.
C498d   The Divine Institution Of Congregational Churches, Ministry and Ordinances, ⟨As has bin Professed by those of that Persuasion⟩ Asserted and Proved from the Word of God. ... By Isaac Chauncy, M.A.
  London: Printed for Nathanael Hiller, at the Princes Arms in Leaden-Hall Street, over against St. Mary Ax, 1697.
  xii, 142 p. 17cm. 12º
  Errata, p. xii.
  In this copy there is a blank leaf at end.
  Bound in contemporary calf, rebacked.
  WingC3748; Dexter(Cong.)2473; McAlpin 4:560; Sabin12335n.
4239, 1908

F697   Clüver, Philipp, 1580-1622.
C649p   Philippi Cluverii Introductio In Universam Geographiam Tam veterem quam novam Tabulis Geographicis XLVI. ac Notis olim ornata à Johanne Bunone, Jam verò locupletata Additamentis & Annotationibus Joh. Frid. Hekelii & Joh. Reiskii. Cum privilegio Ordinum Holl. & Westfrisiæ.
  Venduntur Amstelædami, Apud Joannem Wolters, Bibliopolam op 't Water. MDCXCVII.
  12 p.ℓ., 368, 367-565, [61] p. illus. (tables), 3 plates, 43 fold. maps, 2 fold. tables. 23.5cm. 4º
  In this copy, imprint covered by label reading: Amstelædami, Typis Joannis Wolters. Londini, Prostant apud Sam. Smith & Benj. Walford, in Cœmeterio D. Pauli. MDCXCVII.
  Added t.-p., engr.
  Title in red and black.
  Cut (engr. bookseller's device) on t.-p. incl. motto: Aliis Inserviendo Consumor
  First pub. Leiden, 1624.
  Privilege dated (12th p.ℓ.^{r}) 1 Jan. 1693.
  In this copy there is a blank leaf at end.
  Bound in contemporary calf.

F697   ————Variant. 24cm.
C649p   Imperfect: 3 plates, 43 fold. maps
cop. 2   wanting.
  Bound in contemporary calf.
  Sabin13805; Muller(1872)366.
11575, 1918
M1575, 1914

DA699 [Crisp, Thomas] 17th cent.
M562a A Just and Lawful Tryal Of The Foxonian Chief Priests: By A Perfect Proceeding against Them. And They Condemn'd out of their own Ancient Testimonies. ...
London, Printed for the Author; and to be Sold by B. Aylmer against the Royal Exchange in Cornhil, 1697.
6 p.ℓ., 132 p. 16cm. 8°
Signed: Thomas Crispe.
Errata: verso 1st p.ℓ.
A reply to The Antient Testimony and Principle of the People, called Quakers [London?] 1696.
No. [7] in a volume of 7 pamphlets on Quakerism bound in contemporary vellum.
WingC6952; Smith(Friends)1:480; McAlpin 4:561.
M1592, 1914

D697   [Crouch, Nathaniel] 1632?-1725?
C952r Richardi Blome Englisches America, oder Kurtze doch deutliche Beschreibung aller derer jenigen Länder und Inseln so der Cron Engeland in West-Indien ietziger Zeit zuständig und unterthänig sind. durch eine hochberühmte Feder aus dem Englischen übersetzet und mit Kupffern gezieret.
Leipzig/Bey Johann Grossens Wittbe und Erben. Anno 1697.
36 p.ℓ., 744 p. 2 plates, 2 maps. 13cm. 12°
Transl. from: The English Empire in America, London, 1685, not, as implied by the t.-p., from Richard Blome's The Present State Of His Majesties Isles and Territories in America, London, 1687.
JCB(2)2:1508; Sabin5971; Palmer293; Baer (Md.)180.
03004, 1865

D697   Dampier, William, 1652-1715.
D166n1 A New Voyage Round The World. Describing particularly, The Isthmus of America, several Coasts and Islands in the West Indies, the Isles of Cape Verd, the Passage by Terra del Fuego, the South Sea Coasts of Chili, Peru, and Mexico; the Isle of Guam one of the Ladrones, Mindanao, and other Philippine and East-India Islands near Cambodia, China, Formosa, Luconia, Celebes, &c. New Holland, Sumatra, Nicobar Isles; the Cape of Good Hope, and Santa Hellena. Their Soil, Rivers, Harbours, Plants, Fruits, Animals, and Inhabitants. Their Customs, Religion Government, Trade, &c. By William Dampier. ...
[R]
London, Printed for James Knapton, at the Crown in St Pauls Church-yard. MDCXCVII.
5 p.ℓ., vi, 550, [4] p. incl. illus., map. 4 fold. maps. 19.5cm. 8°
Errata, p. [1] at end.
"Books sold by James Knapton..." p. [2-4] at end.
Bound in contemporary calf, rebacked.
JCBAR 50:50-60; WingD161; Sabin18374; Borba de Moraes 1:204.
30840, 1951

D697   Dampier, William, 1652-1715.
D166n2 A New Voyage Round The World. ... By William Dampier. ... The Second Edition Corrected.
[R]
London, Printed for James Knapton, at the Crown in St Paul's Church-yard. MDCXCVII.
5 p.ℓ., vi, 550, [4] p. incl. illus., map. 4 fold. maps. 19.5cm. 8°
First pub. London, the same year.
"Books sold by James Knapton..." p. [1-4] at end.
Manuscript annotations on inserted leaves.
Bound in contemporary calf, rebacked.
JCBAR 50:59-60; WingD162; Sabin18374; Borba de Moraes 1:204n.
30841, 1950

E697   Dernieres Decouvertes Dans L'Amerique Septen-
D436d1 trionale de M. De La Sale; Mises au jour par M. le Chevalier Tonti, Gouverneur du Fort Saint Loüis, aux Islinois.
A Paris Au Palais, Chez Jean Guignard, à l'entrée de la Grand' Salle, à l'image saint Jean. M.DC.LXXXXVII. Avec Privilege du Roy.
2 p.ℓ., 333, [334-354] p. 16.5cm. 12°
Authorship denied by Tonti.
Cut on t.-p.
"Achevé d'imprimer pour la premiere fois, le 21. Janvier 1697." (verso 2d p.ℓ.).
"Livres Nouveaux Imprimez, & qui se vendent chez le même Libraire." (p. [349-354]).
In this copy p. 3-4 disintegrated, affecting text.

E697   —— ——Another issue. 2 p.ℓ., 184, 185|186-
D436d2 -187|188, 189-333, [334-354] p. 16.5cm.
In this copy the leaves bearing p. 167-168, 171-172, 185-188 have been cancelled, suppressing passages referring to pearls. Cancel leaves for p. 167-168 and 171-172 have been substituted; the leaves bearing p. 185-188 are replaced by a single leaf numbered 185 and 186 on recto and 187 and 188 on verso.

DA697　Elys, Edmund, ca.1634-ca.1707.
E52g　　　George Keith His Saying, That the Light within
is not sufficient to Salvation without something
else: Prov'd To be contrary to the Foundation
of the Christian Religion. By Edmund Elys.
　　London, Printed and Sold by T. Sowle, next
Door to the Meeting-House in White-Hart-Court
in Gracious-Street, and at the Bible in Leaden-
Hall-Street near the Market, 1697.
　　3 p.　21cm.　4°
　　Caption title; imprint at end.
　　A reply in part to George Keith's A second
narrative... , London, 1697.
　　WingE675A; Smith(Friends)1:574.

05871, 1918

　　　　　　　Imperfect: p. [351-354] wanting.
　　　JCB(2) 2:1522; Sabin96172; Harrisse(NF)174;
Wagner67.

67-349
0809, 1846 rev

BA697　Esquerra, Matías de, d. 1720.
E77i　　　La Imperial Agvila Renovada Para La
Immortalidad de su nombre, en las fuentes
de las lagrimas que tributó a su muerte des-
pojo de su amor, y singular argumento de su
lealtad Esta Mexicana Corte Restitviendo Otra
Vez Sobre La movil fugacidad de su lago la
Aguila que durmió en el Señor parà que des-
canse en la lisonja pacifica de sus ondas pues
despierta á la eternidad La Reyna Nvestra
Señora D. Mariana De Austria cuias funebres
pompas Executó El Exmo Señor D. Juan De
Ortega Montañez Obispo de la Santa Iglesia de
Valladolid Virrey de esta Nueva España nom-
brando por Comissario de ellas Al Señor D.
Migvel Calderon De La Barca... Describelas
El Hermano Mathias De Esquerra estudiante
Theologo de la Compañia de Jesvs.
　　Con licencia impresso en Mexico en la Im-
prenta de Iuan Ioseph Guillena Carrascoso
año de 1697.
　　23 p.ℓ., 68 numb. ℓ., [1] p. 20cm.　4°
　　License dated (21st p.ℓ.^{v}) 12 Aug. 1697.
　　Dedication (2d-5th p.ℓ.) by Miguel Calderón
de la Barca.
　　"Sermon En Las Hourras De La Reyna
Nvestra Señora Doña Mariana De Austria
Qve Hizo El Reyno de la Nueva-España en la
Iglesia Cathedral Metropolitana de Mexico
dia 24 de Noviembre de 1696. Y Le Predicô
El D^{or} D. Joseph Vidal De Figueroa...":
numb. ℓ. 57-end.
　　Bound in contemporary vellum.
　　Palau(2)83126; Medina(Mexico)1669; Sabin
22919; Backer3:455.

62-341

EB　　　France--Sovereigns, etc., 1643-1715 (Louis XIV)
F8455　　　　　　　　　　　　　　　　15 Sept. 1696
1697　　　Contrat De Mariage De Monseigneur Le Duc De
1　　　Bourgogne Avec Madame La Princesse De Savoye.
　　A Paris, Chez Frederic Leonard, Imprimeur
ordinaire du Roy, ruë S. Jacques à l'Escu de
Venise. M. DC. XCVII. Avec Privilege Du Roy.
　　1 p.ℓ., 19-36 p. 26cm.　4° (Issued as a
part of Traité de suspension d'armes en Italie.
conclu à Vigevano le septiéme Octobre 1696,
Paris, 1697.)
　　Cut (royal arms) on t.-p.
　　Concluded in Turin, 15 Sept. 1696.
　　Ordinances dated (p. 36) 26 Nov. 1697.
　　Bound in contemporary vellum with Traité de
paix entre la France et la Savoye conclu à
Turin, Paris, 1697, as a part of the 2d of 6
items.

15111A, 1928

EB　　　France--Treaties, etc., 1643-1715 (Louis XIV)
F8455　　　　　　　　　　　　　　　　29 Aug. 1696
1697　　　Traité De Paix Entre La France Et La Savoye.
1　　　Conclu à Turin le 29. Aoust 1696.
　　A Paris, De l'Imprimerie de Frederic
Leonard, Imprimeur ordinaire du Roy.
M. DC. XCVII. Avec Privilege De Sa Majesté.
　　15, [1] p. 26cm.　4°
　　Cut (royal device) on t.-p.
　　Privilege dated (last p.) 10 Oct. 1696.
　　With this are bound, in contemporary vellum:
Traité de suspension d'armes en Italie. Conclu
à Vigevano le septiéme Octobre 1696, Paris,
1697; Contrat De Mariage De Monseigneur Le
Duc De Bourgogne Avec Madame LaPrincesse
De Savoye, Paris, 1697; Traité De Paix Entre
La France Et L'Espagne, Conclu à Ryswick le
20. Septembre 1697, Paris, 1697; Traité De
Paix Entre La France Et L'Angleterre. Conclu
à Rysvvick le 20. Septembre 1697, Paris, 1697;
Traitez De Paix Et De Commerce, Navigation
Et Marine, Entre La France Et Les Etats Generaux Des Provinces Unies Des Pays-Bas. Con-
clus à Rysvvick le 21. Septembre 1697, Paris,
1697; Traité De Paix Entre L'Empereur, La
France, Et L'Empire. Conclu à Rysvvick le
trentiéme Octobre 1697, Paris, 1697.

15110, 1928

EB　　　France--Treaties, etc., 1643-1715 (Louis XIV)
F8455　　　　　　　　　　　　　　　　7 Oct. 1696
1697　　　Traité De Suspension D'Armes En Italie.
1　　　Conclu à Vigevano le septiéme Octobre 1696.
　　A Paris, De l'Imprimerie de Frederic
Leonard, Imprimeur ordinaire du Roy.
M. DC. XCVII. Avec Privilege De Sa Majesté.
　　16 p., 1 ℓ., 19-36 p. 26cm.　4°
　　Cut (royal device) on t.-p.

Treaty between Leopold I, the German emperor, and Charles II, the king of Spain, on the one hand and Victor Amadeus, duke of Savoy, on the other regarding the conclusion of an armistice with Louis XIV. Text of treaty, acts of ratification by Leopold I and Charles II, and letters appointing plenipotentiaries for each of the signatories are embodied in Louis XIV's act of ratification.
    Ordinances dated (p. 36) 26 Nov. 1697.
    With, as issued, Contrat de Mariage de Monseigneur Le Duc De Bourgogne avec Madame La Princesse De Savoye, Paris, 1697, with special t.-p. but continuous paging and signatures.
    Bound in contemporary vellum with Traité de paix entre la France et la Savoye conclu à Turin, Paris, 1697, as the 2d of 6 items.

15111, 1928

C619
A949n

France--Treaties, etc., 1643-1715 (Louis XIV).
20 July 1697
    Proyecto De La Paz, Ofrecido Por Los Embaxadores Plenipotenciarios de Francia al Baron de Lelienroot, Embaxador Plenipotenciario, y Mediador de Suecia, en la Haya à veinte de Julio 1697. Traducido del Original Francès fielmente en Castellano.
    [Madrid, Antonio Bizarrón, 1697]
    8 p. 19.5cm. 4º
    Caption title.
    Proposals toward the Peace of Ryswick.
    An "extraordinary" of the Gaceta de Madrid.
    Bound as the 21st in a volume of 58 pamphlets, 1619-1702.
    Palau(2)239717.

9359, 1913

FB
F8159
1697
1

France--Treaties, etc., 1643-1715 (Louis XIV)
20 Sept. 1697
    Tractaet Van De Vreede, Gemaeckt/geslooten ende vast gesteldt tot Rijswijck in Hollandt/den 20. September/1697. Tusschen de Heeren Ambassadeurs en Plenipotentiarissen van Syne Majesteyt van Vranckryck, Ter eenre; En de Heeren Ambassadeurs en Plenipotentiarissen van de Staten Generael der Vereenighde Nederlanden. Ter andere zijde;
    In 'sGraven-Hage, By Paulus Scheltus, Ordinaris Drucker van de Hoogh Mog. Heeren Staten Generael der Vereenigde Nederlanden. Anno 1697. Met Privilegie.
    23, [1] p. 21.5cm. (22.5cm. in case) 4º
    Cut (coat of arms within border) on t.-p.
    Knuttel 14327; Davenport 84.

32786, 1960

EB
F8455
1697
1

France--Treaties, etc., 1643-1715 (Louis XIV)
20 Sept. 1697
    Traité De Paix Entre La France Et L'Angleterre. Conclu à Rysvvick le 20. Septembre 1697.
    A Paris, De l'Imprimerie de Frederic Leonard. Imprimeur ordinaire du Roy.
    M. DC. XCVII. Avec Privilege De Sa Majesté.
    16 p. 26cm. 4º
    Cut (royal device) on t.-p.
    Includes (p. 13-16) "Article Signé Avec Les Ministres De L'Empereur, Pour La Suspension D'Armes En Allemagne. A Rysvvick le vingtiéme Septembre 1697."
    Ratifications dated (p. 12, 16) 3 Oct. 1697.
    Bound in contemporary vellum with Traité de paix entre la France et la Savoye conclu à Turin, Paris, 1697, as the 4th of 6 items.
    Sabin 96534; Davenport 84.

15113, 1928

EB
F8455
1697
1

France--Treaties, etc., 1643-1715 (Louis XIV)
20 Sept. 1697
    Traité De Paix Entre La France Et L'Espagne, Conclu à Ryswick le 20. Septembre 1697.
    A Paris, Chez Frederic Leonard, Imprimeur Ordinaire du Roy, ruë Saint Jacques, à l'Ecu de Venize. M DC XCVII. Avec Privilege du Roy.
    16 p. 26cm. 4º
    Cut (royal device) on t.-p.
    Ratifications (p. 14, 16) dated 3 Oct. 1697.
    Bound in contemporary vellum with Traité de paix entre la France et la Savoye conclu à Turin, Paris, 1697, as the 3d of 6 items.

15112, 1928

EB
F8455
1697
1

France--Treaties, etc., 1643-1715 (Louis XIV)
21 Sept. 1697
    Traitez De Paix Et De Commerce, Navigation Et Marine, Entre La France Et Les Etats Generaux Des Provinces Unies Des Pays-Bas. Conclus à Rysvvick le 21. Septembre 1697.
    A Paris, De l'Imprimerie de Frederic Leonard, Imprimeur ordinaire du Roy.
    M. DC. XCVII. Avec Privilege De Sa Magesté.
    46 p. 26cm. 4º
    Cut (royal device) on t.-p.
    Ratifications dated (p. 15, 24, 43, 46) 3 Oct. 1697.
    In this copy there is a blank ℓ. at end.
    Bound in contemporary vellum with Traité de paix entre la France et la Savoye conclu à Turin, Paris, 1697, as the 5th of 6 items.

15114, 1928

D697　Gt. Brit. --Laws, statutes, etc.
G786a　　An Abstract Of all Such Acts Of
　　Parliament, Now in Force, As Relate to
　　the Admiralty And Navy of England.
　　　London: Printed by S. Bridge in Austin
　　Friers. MDCXCVII.
　　　6 p.ℓ., 94 p. 17cm. 8° A-N⁸
　　　Blank leaves integral to each gathering
　　(but not considered in the paging) serve as
　　interleaving. The 2d, 4th, 6th and 8th
　　leaves of gatherings B-N are blank, as are
　　A1, A8, and N7. In this copy only a stub
　　of N8 is present.
　　　Bound in contemporary calf.
30015, 1947

DB　Gt. Brit. --Parliament, 1697-1698--House of
-G7875　　Commons.
1689　　The Humble Address of the House of Commons
3　　to the King.
　　　London, Printed by John Leake for Timothy
　　Goodwin, against St. Dunstan's Church in
　　Fleetstreet, and Thomas Cockerill at the Corner
　　of Warwick-Lane, in Pater-Noster-Row, 1697.
　　　1 ℓ. 29cm. 1/2° (Issued as no. 4 of Gt. Brit.--
　　Parliament, 1697-1698--House of Commons.
　　Votes..., London, 1697-1698.)
　　　Caption title; imprint at end.
　　　Congratulations occasioned by the Peace of
　　Ryswick, ending the war with France.
　　　Presented 9 Dec 1697.
　　　Bound in Votes of the House of Commons, v.3.
10376-9A, 1914

DB　Gt. Brit. --Parliament, 1697-1698--House of
-G7875　　Commons.
1689　　Votes Of The House of Commons, In the Third
3　　Session of this Present Parliament Held At West-
　　minster The Third Day of December, in the
　　Ninth Year of the Reign of King William III.
　　Anno Domini, 1697[-1698].
　　　London, Printed by John Leake for Timothy
　　Goodwin, against St. Dunstan's Church in
　　Fleet-street, and Thomas Cockerill at the Corner of
　　Warwick-Lane, in Pater-Noster-Row, 1697.
　　　1 p.ℓ., 502 p. 29cm. fol.
　　　Issued in pts. numbered 1-174 and dated 3 Dec
　　1697 - 5 July 1698, each of which has caption title
　　and imprint at end.
　　　Imprint of no. 89-174 dated 1698.
　　　Errata, p. 84, 290.
　　　Bound in Votes of the House of Commons, v.3.
10376-9, 1914

DB　Gt. Brit. --Parliament, 1697-1698--House of
-G7875　　Lords.
1689　　The Humble Address Of the Right Honourable
3　　the Lords Spiritual & Temporal In Parliament
　　Assembled, Presented to His Majesty On Wed-
　　nesday the Eighth day of December, 1697. And
　　His Majesties Most Gracious Answer Thereunto.
　　　London, Printed by Charles Bill, and the Exec-
　　utrix of Thomas Newcomb deceas'd; Printers to
　　the Kings most Excellent Majesty. 1697.
　　　4 p. 29cm. fol.
　　　Order to print (p. 2) dated 13 Dec 1697.
　　　Congratulations occasioned by the Peace of
　　Ryswick, ending the war with France.
　　　Bound in Votes of the House of Commons, v.3,
　　before Votes for 9 Dec 1697.
10383-6, 1914

DB　Gt. Brit. --Sovereigns, etc., 1694-1702 (William
-G7875　　III).
1689　　His Majesties Most Gracious Speech To both
3　　Houses of Parliament, On Friday the Sixteenth
　　Day of April, 1697.
　　　London, Printed by Charles Bill, and the Exec-
　　utrix of Thomas Newcomb deceas'd; Printers to
　　the Kings most Excellent Majesty. 1697.
　　　4 p. 29cm. fol.
　　　Cut (royal arms) on t.-p.
　　　Message in anticipation of prorogation of
　　Parliament.
　　　Bound in Votes of the House of Commons, v.3,
　　after Votes for 16 Apr 1697.
　　　Wing W2410.
10377-9, 1914

DB　Gt. Brit. --Treaties, etc., 1694-1702 (William III).
-G7895　　Articles of Peace Between The Most Serene and
1697　　Mighty Prince William the Third, King of Great
1　　Britain, and the Most Serene and Mighty Prince
　　Lewis the Fourteenth, the Most Christian King,
　　Concluded in the Royal Palace at Ryswicke the
　　$\frac{10}{20}$. Day of September, 1697.
　　　By Command of Their Excellencies the Lords
　　Justices. London, Printed by Charles Bill and the
　　Executrix of Thomas Newcomb, deceas'd; Printers
　　to the Kings most Excellent Majesty. 1697.
　　　17 p. 31.5cm. fol.
　　　Cut (royal arms) on t.-p. (Steele 137).
　　　Sabin 2148; Wing W2309; Davenport 84.
933, 1905

D697 Hatton, Edward, b. 1664?
H366m The Merchant's Magazine: Or, Trades-Man's Treasury. ... The Second Edition. To which is Added in this Impression (besides many Additions in the former Work) Five whole Chapters ... Accommodated chiefly to the Practice of Merchants and Trades-men: But is likewise usefull for Schools, Bankers, Diversion of Gentlemen, Business of Mechanicks, and Officers of the King's Custom and Excise. By E. Hatton, Gent.
London, Printed by J. Heptinstall, for Chr. Coningsby, at the Golden Turk's Head against St. Dunstan's-Church in Fleetstreet, 1697.
8 p.ℓ., 172, [17], 194-258 p., 1 ℓ. illus. (tables), front. (port.), 9 plates. 21.5cm. 4°
First pub. London, 1695.
"America produceth chiefly, ..." (p. 220).
Errata, p. 258.
Booksellers' advertisement, last leaf.
Bound in contemporary calf, rebacked.
WingH1148.
12544, 1920

E697 Hennepin, Louis, ca. 1640-ca. 1705.
H515n Nouvelle Decouverte D'Un Tres Grand Pays Situé dans l'Amerique, Entre Le Nouveau Mexique, Et La Mer Glaciale, Avec les Cartes, & les Figures necessaires, & de plus l'Histoire Naturelle & Morale, & les avantages, qu'on en peut tirer par l'établissement des Colonies. Le Tout Dedie à Sa Majesté Britannique. Guillaume III. Par Le R. P. Louis Hennepin, Missionaire Recollect & Notaire Apostolique.
A Utrecht, Chez Guillaume Broedelet, Marchand Libraire. MDCXCVII.
36 p.ℓ., 506 (i.e. 516) p. 2 fold. plates, 2 fold. maps. 14.5cm. 12°
An amplification of his Description de la Louisiane, 1st pub. Paris, 1683 ("Les moeurs des sauvages" section, however, is omitted), but also with material appropriated from Chrétien LeClercq's Etablissement de la foy dans la Nouvelle France, Paris, 1691 (especially the account included therein of La Salle's discoveries, by Zénobe Membre).
Added t.-p., engr., signed: C. L[uyken] (closely trimmed at bottom, affecting imprint).
Includes 10 pages inserted after p. 312, each numbered 313*.
JCB(2)2:1513; Sabin31349; Harrisse(NF)175; Paltsits(Hennepin)lii; Church762; Streit 2:2773.
01933, 1849

EB Holy Roman Empire--Treaties, etc., 1658-
F8455 1705 (Leopold I). 30 Oct. 1697
1697 Traité De Paix Entre L'Empereur, La
1 France, Et L'Empire. Conclu à Rysvvick le trentiéme Octobre 1697.
A Paris, De l'Imprimerie de Frederic Leonard, Imprimeur ordinaire du Roy. M.DC.XCVII. Avec Privilege De Sa Majesté.
52 p. 26cm. 4°
Cut (royal device) on t.-p.
Treaty articles and letter appointing the emperor's plenipotentiaries in Latin and French in parallel columns.
Ordinances dated (p. 52) 26 Nov. 1697.
Bound in contemporary vellum with Traité de paix entre la France et la Savoye conclu à Turin, Paris, 1697, as the 6th of 6 items.
15115, 1928

DA696 Keith, George, 1639?-1716.
K28e A Second Narrative Of The Proceedings At Turners-Hall, The 29th of the Month called April, 1697. Giving an exact Account of all the Proofs G.K. brought out of the Quakers Books, and Read in that Meeting, to prove them Guilty, of the Four great Errors he had Charged them with, in his Printed Advertisements; as also the most Material Speeches he made on every Head, with Reference to the Authors of those Books, and more Particularly with Reference to G.W. T.E. W.P. J. Penington, and them of the Second-days Meeting, at Londn [sic]. By George Keith.
London, Printed for B. Aylmer at the Three Pigeons in Cornhill, 1697.
36 p. 21cm. 4°
Errata, p. 36.
Bound as the 2d in a vol. of 7 works by Keith.
JCB(2)2:1514; WingK204; Sabin37191; Smith (Friends)2:32.
04789, before 1874

DA697 [Leslie, Charles] 1650-1722.
L634d A Discourse Proving The Divine Institution Of Water-Baptism: Wherein The Quaker-Arguments Against it, Are Collected and Confuted. With as much as is Needful concerning The Lord's Supper. By the Author of, The Snake in the Grass. ...
London: Printed for C. Brome, at the Gun, at the West-End of St. Pauls. W. Keblewhite, at the White Swan, in St. Pauls Church-Yard. And H. Hindmarsh, at the Golden Ball, over-against the Royal Exchange, in Cornhill. M.DC.XC.VII.

[350]

DA697
L634s
67-330

[Leslie, Charles] 1650-1722.
    4 p.ℓ., 64 p. 21.5cm. 4⁰
Dated at end: July 17. 1696.
Erratum: 2d p.ℓ.ᵛ
Booksellers' advertisement: 2d p.ℓ.ᵛ
WingL1128; Smith(Anti-Quak)268; McAlpin4:567.

DA697
L634s
6172, 1910

[Leslie, Charles] 1650-1722.
    Satan Dis-Rob'd From his Disguise of Light: Or, The Quakers Last Shift to Cover their Monstrous Heresies, Laid Fully open. In A Reply To Thomas Ellwood's Answer (Published the End of Last Month) To George Keith's Narrative Of The Proceedings at Turners-Hall, June 11. 1696. Which also may serve for a Reply (as to the main Points of Doctrine) to Geo. Whitehead's Answer to The Snake in the Grass; to be published the End of next Month, if this prevent it not. By the Author of The Snake in the Grass. ...
    London: Printed for C. Brome at the Gun near the West End of St. Paul's; W. Keblewhite at the Swan in St. Paul's Church-Yard; and H. Hindmarsh at the Golden Ball over-against the Royal Exchange in Cornhil. 1697.
    2 p.ℓ., 48, 24 p. 24cm. 4⁰
Errata, 2d p.ℓ.ᵛ
"Some Gleanings, With Other further Improvements " (p. 1-24, 2d count); dated at end: Oct. 26. 1696.
Ellwood's An Answer to George Keith's narrative, 1st pub. London, 1696. Whitehead's An Antidote against the venome of the snake in the grass, 1st pub. London, 1697.
Wing L1149; cf. Smith(Anti-Quak)267-268.

DA697
L634sg

[Leslie, Charles] 1650-1722.
    Some Seasonable Reflections Upon The Quakers Solemn Protestation Against George Keith's Proceedings at Turner's Hall, 29. Apr. 1697. Which was by them Printed, and sent thither, as the Reasons of their not Appearing to Defend Themselves. Herein Annex'd Verbatim. By an Impartial Hand.
    London, Printed for Charles Brome, at the Gun at the west end of St. Pauls, 1697.
    1 p.ℓ., 14 p. 21cm. 4⁰
"A Solemn Protestation against George Keith's Advertisement ..." (p. 1-2).
Dated at end: May 8. 1697.
Also issued with variant reading in 7th line of t.-p.: "Against the Proceedings at" (compared with "Against George Keith's Proceedings at"

in this issue).
WingL1159; Smith(Anti-Quak.)462; Smith(Friends)2:44; Sabin37192.
6201, 1910

DA697
L634sp
11486, 1918

[Leslie, Charles] 1650-1722.
    Some Seasonable Reflections Upon The Quakers Solemn Protestation Against the Proceedings at Turner's-Hall, 29. Apr. 1697. Which was by them Printed, and sent thither, as the Reasons of their not Appearing to Defend Themselves. Herein Annex'd Verbatim. By an Impartial Hand.
    London, Printed for Charles Brome, at the Gun at the west end of St. Pauls, 1697.
    1 p.ℓ., 14 p. 21.5cm. 4⁰
"A Solemn Protestation against George Keith's Advertisement ..." (p. 1-2).
Dated at end: May 8. 1697.
Also issued with variant reading in 7th line of t.-p.: "Against George Keith's Proceedings at" (compared with "Against the Proceedings at" in this issue).
WingL1159; cf. Smith(Anti-Quak.)462; cf. Smith(Friends)2:44; cf. Sabin37192.

D. Math
C.103A
0556, 1846

Mather, Cotton, 1663-1728.
    Ecclesiastes. The Life Of The Reverend & Excellent, Jonathan Mitchel; A Pastor of the Church, And A Glory of the Colledge, In Cambridge, New-England. Written by Cotton Mather. ...
    Massachuset; Printed by B. Green and J. Allen. Sold at the Booksellers Shops in Boston. 1697.
    111, [1] p. 15.5cm. 8⁰
Dedication (p. 3-32) signed: May 7. 1697. Increase Mather.
Elegies (p. 108-111): one adapted from Richard Blackmore, another by Cotton Mather; epitaph (p. 111) signed F[rancis] D[rake].
Booksellers' advertisement, last p.
Also issued with errata, 5 lines, added to last p.
JCB(2)2:1515; Sabin46297; Evans790; Holmes(C.)103A; Holmes(I.)51A; WingM1099.

D. Math
C.228C

Mather, Cotton, 1663-1728.
    Memorable Providences, Relating to VVitchcrafts and Possessions: A Faithful Account of many Wonderful and Surprising Things, that have befallen several Bewitched and Possessed

Persons in New-England. Particularly, a Narrative of the marvellous Trouble and Relief, Experienced by a pious Family in Boston, very lately and sadly molested with Evil Spirits. Whereunto is added, A Discourse delivered unto a Congregation in Boston, on the Occasion of that Illustrious Providence. As also, A Discourse delivered unto the same Congregation; on the occasion of an horrible Self-Murder Committed in the Town. With an Appendix, in vindication of a Chapter in a late Book of Remarkable Providences, from the Calumnies of a Quaker at Pen-silvania. Written by Cotton Mather, Minister of the Gospel. And Recommended by the Ministers of Boston and Charleston.
 Printed at Boston in New-England, and Reprinted at Edinburgh by the Heirs and Successors of Andrew Anderson, Printer to his most Excellent Majesty, Anno Dom 1697.
 3 p.l., 102 p. 14.5cm. 8°
 "To the Reader" (p.l. 2^v-3) signed: Charles Morton. James Allen. Joshua Moody. Samuel Willard.
 The "Appendix" is a reply to George Keith's The Presbyterian and independent visible churches in New England, Philadelphia, 1689.
 JCB(2)2:1517; Sabin46408; Holmes(C)2286; WingM1124; Church765.

03829, 1868

D.Math [Mather, Cotton] 1663-1728.
C.279A   Pietas in Patriam: The Life Of His Excellency Sir William Phips, Knt. Late Captain General, and Governour in Chief of the Province of the Massachuset-Bay, New England. Containing the Memorable Changes Undergone, and Actions Performed by Him. Written by one intimately acquainted with Him. ...
 London: Printed by Sam. Bridge in Austin-Friers, for Nath. Hiller at the Princes-Arms in Leaden-Hall Street, over against St. Mary-Ax, 1697.
 6 p.l., 110, [8] p. 16cm. 12°
 Dated (p.l. 1^v, 4^v) 27 Apr. 1697.
 Dedication (p.l. 3-4) by Nathaniel Mather.
 Elegy "Upon The Death Of Sir William Phips, Knt. ..." p. [1-6] at end.
 Booksellers' advertisement, p. [7-8] at end.
 In this copy there is a blank leaf at end.
 JCB(2)2:1516; WingM1138; Sabin46455; Holmes(C.)279A; Holmes(M.)21A, 24A; Church766.

0808, 1846

DA695 [Maule, Thomas] 1645-1724.
M449t   Nevv-England Pesecutors [sic] Mauld VVith their own VVeapons. Giving some Account of the bloody Laws made at Boston against the Kings Subjects that dissented from their way of Worship. Together with a brief Account of the Imprisonment and Tryal of Thomas Maule of Salem, for publishing a Book, entituled, Truth held forth and maintained, &c. By Theo. Philathes [sic, i.e. Philalethes, pseud.]. ...
 [New York, William Bradford, 1697]
 3 p.l., 24, 27-62 p. 17.5cm. (19.5cm. in case) 4°
 An account of the persecutions in New England against Quakers and other dissenters, including the actions taken against Maule for publishing his Truth held forth [New York] 1695.
 In this copy there is a blank l. at beginning, which is the 4th l. of the gathering folded around.
 Other recorded copies have variant readings of the t.-p. including as the 4th word "Mauled" instead of "Mauld" and in the author's pseudonym "Tho." instead of "Theo."
 cf. Jones, M.B., "Thomas Maule," Essex Institute Historical Collections, LXXII (1936).
 Bound in contemporary calf with other of his works as the 2d of 4 items.
 Evans801; Sabin46934; WingM1353; Smith (Friends)2:167; Hildeburn(NY)5; Church767; Dexter2472.

3423, 1907

D696 A Memorial Given in to the Senate of the City of
-C737c Hamburgh in French, exactly Translated into English; Together with the Senate's Answer to the same.
 Edinburg, Printed in the Year 1697.
 2 p. 27.5cm. (31.5cm. in binding) fol.
 Caption title; imprint at end.
 Dated (p.2) in Hamburg, 7 Apr. 1697.
 Also pub. without the Senate's answer [Edinburgh? 1697?]
 The English diplomatic representatives in Hamburg protest the solicitation of subscriptions by the Company of Scotland Trading to Africa and the Indies.
 Bound in a volume of Scottish imprints and mss. as the 4th of 58 items.
 Cf. Scott 27.

7104, 1910

D696 A Memorial Given in to the Senate of the City of
-C737c Hamburgh in French faithfully Translated into English.

[Edinburgh? 1697?]
1 p. 29cm. (31.5cm. in binding) fol.
Dated in Hamburg, 7 Apr. 1697.
Also pub. with the Senate's answer, Edinburgh, 1697.
The English diplomatic representatives in Hamburg protest the solicitation of subscriptions by the Company of Scotland Trading to Africa and the Indies.
Laid in a volume of Scottish imprints and mss. as the 5th of 58 items.
Wing M1688; Kress 2037; Scott 27.

9141, 1913

BA697 Miranda, Juan José de, d. 1700.
M672e Explicacion De Los Passos de la Passion, que estan en el Altar del Santo Eccehomo en el Collegio de S. Pedro, y S. Pablo de la Compañia de Jesvs de esta Ciudad, con algunas devotas meditaciones. Sacalo A Lvz. El Br. D. Ivan Ioseph de Miranda, Prefecto de la Congregacion de N. Señora de los Dolores fundada con Authoridad Apostolica en dicho Collegio, y Capellan del Religioso Convento de San Lorenzo.
Con licencia en Mexico, por Doña Maria de Benavides. Año de 1697.
2 p.ℓ., 134 numb. ℓ., [1] ℓ. 14.5cm. 8°
Cut (Ecce Homo) on t.-p.
License dated (2d p.ℓ.ᵛ) 25 Nov. 1697.
Errata, last page.
Includes poetry.
Bound in contemporary vellum.
Palau(2)172104; Medina(Mexico)1672.

4927, 1908

BA685 Muñoz de Castro, Pedro.
F819i Exaltacion Magnifica De La Betlemitica Rosa De La Mejor Americana Jerico, Y Accion Gratulatoria Por su plausible Plantacion dichosa; nuevamente erigida en Religion sagrada por la Santidad del Sʳ. Inocencio XI. P.M. Que Celebrò en esta Nobilissima Ciudad de Mexico, el Venerable Dean, y Cabildo de esta S.Iglesia Metropolitana, y Sacratissimas Religiones ... Cuya dispossicion se encomendò à la idea del Bachiller Pedro Muñoz de Castro, Presbytero de este Arçobispado.
Con Licencia De Los Svperiores: En Mexico, por Doña Maria de Benavides, Viuda de Juan de Ribera en el Empedradillo año de 1697.
12 p.ℓ., 84 numb. ℓ. front. (port.) 20cm. 4°
License dated (12th p.ℓ.) 26 Aug. 1697.
Includes sermons by Juan de Narváes, Domingo de Sousa, Agustin de Vetancurt, Luis de Rivera, Juan de la Concepción, Nicolás Ramírez,

José de Porras, José Ignacio Rueda, and a pastoral letter by Francisco de Aguiar Seijas y Ulloa, Archbishop of Mexico.
Bound with: Franciscans. Instrvccion Y Doctrina De Novicios...Puebla, 1685.
Palau(2)185265; Medina(Mexico)1674; Sabin 51352.

05982, before 1923

E733   [Peys, Adriaan]˙fl. 1661-1699.
L166a Reinout In Het Betoverde Hof; Zynde het Gevolg van Armida. Met Konst- en Vliegwerken, verscheidene Sieraaden en Balletten.
Te Amsteldam, By de Erfg: van J: Lescailje, op de Middeldam, op de hoek van de Vischmarkt, 1697. Met Privilegie.
71 p. 16cm. 8°
Cut (incl. motto "Perseveranter") on t.-p.
Privilege dated (p. [4]) 8 Feb. 1697.
Bound, in contemporary calf, with: [Lafont, Joseph de] De Amerikaan. Amsterdam, 1733.

11898-4, 1919

B697   Quevedo y Villegas, Francisco Gómez de,
Q5f   1580-1645.
Fortune In Her Wits, Or, The Hour of all Men. Written In Spanish by the most Ingenious Don Francisco de Quivedo [sic] Villegas, Author of the Visions of Hell. Translated into English By Capt. John Stevens.
London, Printed for R. Sare at Gray's-Inn-Gate, F. Saunders in the New-Exchange, and Tho. Bennet in St. Paul's Church-Yard. 1697.
7 p.ℓ., 131 p. 18.5cm. 8°
Transl. from La fortuna con seso, 1st pub. Saragossa, 1650.
The 2d p.ℓ., which is the first ℓ. of the dedication (with caption "To Mark Arundell Esq;"), is a cancel in this issue. Also issued with the 2d p.ℓ. integral (with caption "To Sir Richard Bellings, knt.").
In this copy there is a blank ℓ. following the prelims.
Bound in contemporary calf, rebacked.
Wing Q188; Palau(2)244356.

70-343

BA697 Robles, Francisco de.
R666s Oracion Fvnebre, Qve Hizieron Sus Esclarecidas obras à la muerte de nuestra Serenissima Reyna Doña Mariana De Austria: En el dia, que obsequioso, triste, y agradecido celebrò las honras de su Cessarea Magestad, el Illustre, y Religioso Convento de N.P.S. Francisco de la Ciudad de Zacatecas, con asistencia del Clero,

1697

68-412
Religiones, y la Ciudad plena. Predicada Por el Padre Fray Francisco de Robles Lector de Sagrada Theologia, Examinador Synodal del Obispado de Guadalaxara, y Calificador del Santo Officio. ...
Con Licencia: En Mexico Por Juan Joseph Guillena Carrascoso Impressor, y Mercader de libros en el Empedradillo, año de 1697.
7 p.ℓ., 4, 4-7 numb. ℓ. 20.5cm. 4⁰
"Censura" dated (5th p.ℓ.ᵛ) 20 June 1697.
Medina(Mexico)1675; Palau(2)271149; Sabin72249.

BA697
S127b
1072, 1905
Saenz, José.
Brillante Trisagio, Que à todas luzes declara A Clara, Preclara Esposa de Jesu-Christo. Predicolo E. P. Lector Jubilado Fr Joseph Saenz, del Orden del Señor S Augustin en su Convento de la Puebla de los Angeles el dia 21. de Octubre del Año de 1696. ...
Con Licencia: En la Puebla, por los Herederos del Capitan Juan de Villa-Real, en el Portal de las flores. [1697]
10 p.ℓ., 8 numb. ℓ. 19cm. 4⁰
Dedication (2d-4th p.ℓ.) by Juan de Miranda.
License dated (10th p.ℓ.ᵛ) 5 May 1697.
In this copy upper outer corners of p.ℓ. 1-3 are missing with slight loss of text; available in facsimile.
Palau(2)284250; Medina(Puebla)184; Santiago Vela7:3-4; Sabin74853.

D
Scott
29c
Scotland--Laws, statutes, etc., 1694-1702 (William III).   26 June 1695
Lettres Patentes Ou Octroi Sous Le Grand Seau Du Royaume D'Ecosse, Pour La Compagnie Du Commerce de l'Afrique & des Indes. Etablie par Acte de Parlement dudit Royaume.
[Edinburgh?] Imprimé pour la Compagnie. M. DC. LXXXXVII.
10 p. 20.5cm. 4⁰
Cut (royal arms) on t.-p.
First pub. in English, Edinburgh, 1695, under title: Act for a Company trading to Affrica ... The act is dated (p. 8) in Edinburgh, 26 June 1695, and certifications are dated (p. 8) in Edinburgh, 1 Oct. 1695; a version in Latin pub. Edinburgh, 1695, under title: Literæ patentes seu concessus ... is likewise dated and certified.
Includes (p. 9-10, headed by the company's arms) "Constitutions De La Compagnie D'Ecosse ..." dated in Edinburgh, 17 Apr.

0560, 1846
1696, a transl. of Constitutions of the Company of Scotland, Trading to Africa and the Indies, [Edinburgh? 1696].
Imperfect: p. 9-10 wanting; available in facsim. This copy closely trimmed at bottom, affecting imprint and some text.
JCB(2)2:1512; Sabin78224; Scott 29c.

D696
-C737c
7131, 1910
Scotland--Privy Council.   15 Apr. 1697.
Act In favours of these of the Scots Nation in Konigsberg, for a Voluntar Collection. At Edinburgh, The fifteenth Day of April, 1697. Years.
Edinburgh, Printed by George Mosman, in the Year, 1697.
[4] p. 31.5cm. fol.
A collection of items promoting support for the Scots church in Königsberg.
Title from caption of the 1st item; imprint at end.
Also contains: "To the Venerable General Assembly of the Church of Scotland, ... The Humble and Earnest Request, of those of the Scots Nation resideing in Konigsberg in Prussia ..."(dated at Königsberg, 8 Feb. 1697).
—"Act Of the Provincial Synod of Lothian and Tweeddale, for a General Collection for the building of a Church, to the Scots Reformed Protestants, and others in the City of Konigsberg in Prussia..." (dated at Edinburgh, 5 May 1697).—Church of Scotland--General Assembly--Commission. "Act and Recommendation, Concerning a Collection, for helping to Build a Church in Konigsberg..." (dated in Edinburgh, 6 May 1697).
Bound in a volume of Scottish imprints and mss. as the 36th of 58 items.
Aldis3647.

J697
S479r
Sepp von Reinegg, Anton, 1655-1733.
RR. PP. Antonii Sepp, und Antonii Böhm/ Der Societät Jesu Priestern Teutscher Nation, ... Reissbeschreibung wie dieselbe aus Hispanien in Paraquariam kommen. Und Kurtzer Bericht der denckwürdigsten Sachen selbiger Landschafft/Völckern/und Arbeitung der sich alldort befindenten PP. Missionariorum, gezogen Aus denen durch R.P. Sepp, Soc. Jes. mit aigener Hand geschriebenen Briefen/zu mehrern Nutzen Von Gabriel Sepp, von und zu Rechegg, leiblichen Brudern in Druck gegeben.
Mit Erlaubnus der Obern. Nürnberg/In Verlegung Joh. Hoffmanns 1697.

[354]

333 p. 13.5cm. 12⁰
First pub. Brixen, 1696.
Mainly the same sheets as Nürnberg, 1696, ed.
JCB(2)2:1520; Sabin79164; Palmer388; Backer 7:1130; Streit2:2324.
0810, 1846

DA697 Sewall, Samuel, 1652-1730.
S513p Phænomena quædam Apocalyptica Ad Aspectum Novi Orbis configurata. Or, some few Lines towards a description of the New Heaven As it makes to those who stand upon the New Earth By Samuel Sewall sometime Fellow of Harvard Colledge at Cambridge in New-England. ...
Massachuset; Boston, Printed by Bartholomew Green, and John Allen, And are to be sold by Richard Wilkins, 1697.
4 p.ℓ., 60 p. 20cm. 4⁰
Dated (at end) 7 Oct. 1697.
JCB(2)2:1521; WingS2821; Evans813; Sabin79443; Church769; McAlpin4:572.
02918, 1861

C619 Spain--Treaties, etc., 1665-1700 (Charles II).
A949n   20 Sept. 1697
Capitulaciones De Las Pazes. Acordadas Entre España, Y Francia, Y Firmadas En El Castillo De Risvvick De La Provincia De Olanda, El Dia Veinte De Septiembre De Este Año De 1697. Por Los Señores D. Francisco Bernardo De Quirós, Y Conde De Tirlemon, Plenipotenciarios Por España; Y Los Señores Harlay, Conde De Creci, Y De Callieres, Por Francia.
Impressas en Madrid, Año de mil seiscientos y nouenta y siete.
3 p.ℓ., 3-16 p. 19.5cm. 4⁰
Colophon: Publicadas en Madrid el dia 10. de Noviembre de 1697. y impressas con las licencias de los Superiores. Por Antonio Bizarrón, Mercader de Libros, enfrente de San Felipe, donde se hallarán.
In this copy p. 15-16 misbound before p. 3.
Bound as the 17th in a volume of 58 pamphlets, 1619-1702.
Palau(2)43273.
9357, 1913

BB Spain--Treaties, etc., 1665-1700 (Charles II).
S7338   20 Sept.1697
1697 Capitulaçoens Das Pazes, Ajustadas Entre
1 Espanha, E França, & firmadas no Castello de Riswick da Provincia de Olanda, o dia 20. de Settembro deste anno dè 1697. Pelos Senhores Dom Francisco Bernardo de Quiros, & o Conde de Tirlemon Plenipotenciarios de Espanha, & os Senhores Herlay Conde de Crecy, & de Callieres, por França.
Em Lisboa Na Officina de Miguel Manescal, Impressor do Santo Officio. Anno de 1697.
20 p. 20cm. 4⁰
Cut on t.-p.
Davenport 84
Palau(2)43274n.
68-483

F697 Traktaat van Vrede, Geslooten op het Hof
T762v tot Ryswyk, in de Provintie van Hollant, den 20. September des Jaars 1697. Tusschen den Doorluchtichsten en Grootmachtichsten Vorst. William III. Koningh van Groot Brittanien, ter eenre, en den Doorluchtichsten en Grootmachtichsten Vorst Lodewyk de XIV. Koning van Vrankrijk en Navarre: ter andere zyde. Traktaat van Vrede, Tusschen de Kroonen van Vranckrijck en Spanjen, Gesloten en geteykent in het Hof tot Rijswijk den 20. September 1697. Traktaat van Vrede, Tusschen Haar Hoog. Mog. de Staten Generaal der Vereenigde Nederlanden ter eenre, en de Koningh van Vrankryk ter andere zijde. En het Tractaat van Commercie, Navigatie en Marine, Gesloten en geteykent in het Hof tot Rijswijk den 20. September 1697.
Tot Groningen, by Joannis Lens, in de Heerestraat. Gedruckt na de Copye van Haar Hoog. Mog. [1697] Met Privilegie.
[68] p. 18cm. 4⁰
Dutch text of each treaty 1st pub., separately, the Hague, 1697.
Announcement of exchanges of ratifications dated (p. [44, 68]) 15 Oct. 1697.
Bookseller's advertisement at end.
This copy closely trimmed with loss of last line of imprint.
62-127

DA697 Turner, William, 1653-1701.
=T954c A Compleat History Of the Most Remarkable Providences, Both Of Judgment and Mercy, Which have Hapned in this Present Age. Extracted From the Best Writers, the Author's own Observations, and the Numerous Relations sent him from divers Parts of the Three Kingdoms. To which is Added, Whatever is Curious in the Works of Nature and Art. The Whole Digested into One Volume, under Proper Heads; being a Work set on Foot Thirty Years ago, by the Reverend Mr. Pool, Author of the Synopsis Criticorum: And since Undertaken and Finish'd, By William Turner, M.A. Vicar of Walberton,

[355]

in Sussex, Recommended as useful to Ministers in Furnishing Topicks of Reproof and Exhortation, and to Private Christians for their Closets and Families. ...
London: Printed for John Dunton, at the Raven, in Jewen-Street. M DC XC VII.
3 pts. in 1 v.: pt.1, 3 p.ℓ., 26, [4], 140, 152, 144, [4], 145-172, 24; pt.2, 2 p.ℓ., 82; pt.3, 2 p.ℓ., 31, [1] p. 35cm. fol.
Pt.2 has special t.-p.: The Wonders of Nature. Part II. ...
Pt.3 has special t.-p.: The Curiosities of Art. Part III. ...
Contains various references to New England including extracts chiefly from works of Cotton Mather and Increase Mather.
Preliminary matter includes a poem by George Herbert.
Bookseller's advertisement, last two pages.
WingT3345; Sabin97495; McAlpin4:575.

70-35

B698 -V585t [R]
Vetancurt, Agustín de, 1620-1700.
Chronica De La Provincia Del Santo Evangelio De Mexico. Quarta parte del Teatro Mexicano de los successos Religiosos. Compuesta Por El Reverendo Padre Fray Augustin de Vetancur, Mexicano, hijo de la misma Provincia, Difinidor actual, Ex-Lector de Theologia, Predicador Iubilado General, y su Chronista Appostolico, Vicario, y Cura Ministro, por su Magestad, de la Iglesia Parrochial de San Ioseph de los Naturales de Mexico. ...
Con Licencia De Los Superiores. En Mexico, por Doña Maria de Benavides Viuda de Iuan de Ribera. Año de 1697.
6 p.ℓ., 136, [2] p. 1 ℓ., 156 p. 28.5cm. fol. (Issued as a part of his Teatro mexicano, Mexico, 1698.)
License dated (6th p.ℓ.v) 18 June 1696.
Errata, 6th p.ℓ.v.
"Menologio Franciscano De Los Varones Mas Señalados...": 1 ℓ., 156 p.
"Obras Del Autor": p.144, 2d count.
In this copy another copy of the last pt. of v.1, "Tratado de la ciudad de Mexico..." is bound at end.
JCB(2)2:1552; Palau(1)7:163; Medina(Mexico) 1684; Sabin99386; Wagner68; Streit 2:2326.

01939, 1854

BA697 V585o
Vetancurt, Agustín de, 1620-1700.
Oracion Funebre A Las Honras, Qve Hizo La Religion Seraphica A La muerte de la Augusta Señora Doña Mariana De Austria, nuestra Reyna, en el Convento de N.P.S. Francisco de Mexico. Año de mil seiscientos y noventa y seis. Dicha Por el Reverendo Padre Fr. Augustin de Vetancurt, Lector de Theologia, Predicador General Iubilado, Difinidor actual, Chronista Apostolico de la Provincia de el Santo Evangelio, Cura Ministro de la Iglesia Parrochial de el Señor S. Ioseph de los Naturales de Mexico. ...
Con Licencia en Mexico por Doña Maria de Benavides, Viuda de Juan de Ribera. Año de 1697.
7 p.ℓ., 7 numb. ℓ. 19.5cm. 4º
License dated (7th p.ℓ.v) 4 May 1697.
Errors in leaf-numbering.
Palau(1)7:163; Medina(Mexico)1685.

1073, 1905

F697 V984v
De Vryheyt Vertoont in den Staat der Vereenigde Nederlanden, Zijnde een Vertoogh van des zelfs maniere van Regeeringe, veelvoudige Middelen en Oorlogs-Lasten, Met de Autentyke Stukken, zo van de Munstersche als andere Vredens Tractaten, Unie en Verbonden voorsien.
In 'SGravenhage, By Engelbregt Boucquet, Boekverkooper in de Halstraat. MDC.XCVII.
4 p.ℓ., 400 p. 14cm. 12º
Cut on t.-p.
"Vande Collegien der Compagnien van beyde de Indien, door welcke nae het Oosten ende Westen gevaren wort" (p. 82-109).

71-234

DA697 W592a
[Whitehead, George] 1636?-1723.
An Antidote Against The Venome Of The Snake in the Grass: Or, the Book so stiled. And The Christian People Called Quakers Vindicated from its most gross Abuses and Calumnies. ... Unto which is Annex'd, A brief Examination of the Author's second Book, stil'd, Satan Dis-rob'd. Also, Some Notice taken of his Discourse for the Divine Institution of Water-Baptism. ...
London: Printed for Tho. Northcott, in George-yard in Lombard-street. 1697.
2 p.ℓ., xi, 268, [4] p. 17.5cm. 8º
Errata, 2d p.ℓ.v
Signed, p. 183: George Whitehead; p. 268: G.W.
A reply to The snake in the grass, London, 1696, Satan disrob'd from his disguise of light, London, 1697, and A discourse proving the divine institution of water baptism, London, 1697, all by Charles Leslie.

70-47	Wing W1889; Sabin 103655; Smith (Friends) 2:902; McAlpin 4:576.

D698
D246d
1
	Xenophon.
	   A Discourse Upon Improving The Revenue Of The State Of Athens. Written Originally in Greek by Xenophon. And made English from the Original, with some Historical Notes: By W. M. Esq;
	   London, Printed for J. Knapton, at the Crown in St. Paul's Church-Yard. 1697.
	   62, [2] p. 19.5cm. 8° (Issued as a part of [Charles Davenant] Discourses on the public revenues, v.1, London, 1698).
	   Transl. by Walter Moyle from Πόροι (De vectigalibus.)
	   Bookseller's advertisement, [2] p. at end.
	   Wing X18.

29013A, 1941	

DA697
Y76f
	[Young, Samuel] fl. 1697.
	   The Foxonian Quakers, Dunces Lyars and Slanderers, Proved out of George Fox's Journal, And other Scriblers; Particularly B. C. his Quakers no Apostates, or the Hammerer Defeated: Amanuensis, as is said, to G.C. (as he sometime wrote himself) Gulielmus Calamus, alias, William Penn. Also a Reply to W.C. (a Church-man, the Quakers Advocate) his Trepidantium Malleus Intrepidanter Malleatus, &c. ... By Trepidantium Malleus [pseud.].
	   London: Printed for W. Marshal at the Bible in Newgate-street, and J. Marshal at the Cible [sic] in Grace-church-street, near Cornhil, 1697
	   100, [6] p. 14cm. 12°
	   A reply to Benjamin Coole's The Quakers cleared from being apostate, London, 1696, and to Trepidantium malleus, intrepidanter malleatus ... by W.C., London, 1696.
	   "Books Printed for William Marshall ... and John Marshall ..." ([6] p. at end).

DA697
Y76w
	——— ———Another copy. 14cm.
	   In this copy the imprint reads correctly "at the Bible in Grace-church-street".
	   Bound in contemporary calf (rebacked) with, as issued, [his] William Penn and the Quakers, London, 1697, and [his] A reprimand for the author of a libel, London, 1697, as the 3d of 3 items.
	   In this copy there is a blank ℓ. at end.
	   JCB(2)2:1519; Sabin 106101; Smith(Anti-Quak.)459-460; Wing Y80.

04208, before 1882 11531-3, 1918 rev	

DA697
Y76w
	[Young, Samuel] fl. 1697.
	   A Reprimand For The Author of a Libel Entituled, George Keith An Apostate. Written by a Church-man. By Trepidantium Malleus [pseud.]. ...
	   London: Printed for John Marshal at the Bible in Grace-church-street, near Corn-hill, 1697. Price Four Pence.
	   60 p. 14cm. 12°
	   A reply to Mr. Keith no Presbyterian nor Quaker, London, 1696.
	   "Postscript" (p. 47-60) is a defence of [his] Vindiciae anti-Baxterianae, London, 1696.
	   Bound in contemporary calf (rebacked) with, as issued, [his] William Penn and the Quakers, London, 1697, and [his] The Foxonian Quakers ... , London, 1697, as the 2d of 3 items.
	   Sabin 106104; Smith(Anti-Quak.)460; Wing Y85.

11531-2 rev	

DA697
Y76w
	[Young, Samuel] fl. 1697.
	   William Penn And the Quakers Either Impostors, or Apostates, Which they please: Proved from their avowed Principles, and contrary Practices. ... By Trepidantium Malleus [pseud.].
	   London: Printed for W. Marshall, at the Bible in Newgate-street, and J. Marshall at the Bible in Grace-church-street. 1697.
	   3 p. ℓ., 134 p. 14cm. 12°
	   First pub. London, 1696. These are the same sheets with cancel t.-p.
	   Bound in contemporary calf, rebacked.
	   With this are bound, as issued: [his] A reprimand for the author of a libel ... , London, 1697, and [his] The Foxonian Quakers ... , London, 1697. "Books Printed for William Marshall ... and John Marshall ..." ([6] p. at end of The Foxonian Quakers ...) lists these three books together and notes: "This being the last the author designs on this Subject, those that are desirous, may have them ready Bound together."
	   Sabin 106108A; Wing Y91; cf. Smith(Anti-Quak.)459.

11531-1 rev	

1698

B698 V975a	Acarete du Biscay. An Account Of A Voyage Up The River de la Plata, And thence over Land to Peru. With Ob-

servations on the Inhabitants, as well Indians and Spaniards; the Cities, Commerce, Fertility, and Riches of that Part of America. By Mons. Acarete du Biscay.
 London: Printed for Samuel Buckley, at the Dolphin over against St. Dunstans Church in Fleetstreet. 1698.
 1 p.ℓ., 79 p. fold. map. 19cm. 8º (Issued as a part of Voyages And Discoveries in South-America. London, 1698.)
 First appeared in pt. 4 of Melchisédech Thévenot's Relations de divers Voyages, Paris, 1672.
 JCB(2)2:1523; Wing V746; Palau(2)2487; Sabin 152; Borba de Moraes 1:12; Backer 1:40; Streit 2:2328.
01932A, 1854

E698
A172o
[R]
An Account Of Monsieur de la Salle's Last Expedition and Discoveries In North America. Presented to the French King, And Published by the Chevalier Tonti, Governour of Fort St. Louis, in the Province of the Islinois. Made English from the Paris Original. Also The Adventures of the Sieur de Montauban, Captain of the French Buccaneers on the Coast of Guinea, in the Year 1695.
 London, Printed for J. Tonson at the Judge's Head, and S. Buckley at the Dolphin in Fleetstreet, and R. Knaplock, at the Angel and Grown [sic] in St. Paul's Church-Yard. 1698.
 1 p.ℓ., 211, 44 p. 17.5cm. 8º
 Transl. from Dernieres decouvertes dans l'Amerique septentrionale, Paris, 1697.
  Authorship denied by Tonti.
  Montauban's account has special t.-p., separate paging, but continuous signatures.
 JCB(2)2:1542; WingT1890; Sabin96171; Harrisse (NF)178; Wagner67a.
05721, 1881

B621
-S586a
Alcedo Sotomayor, Carlos de.
 Señor. Don Carlos de Alcedo Sotomayor, Cavallero del Orden de Santiago, Oydor de la Real Audiencia de Santa Fè, en el Nuevo Reyno de Granada, y Visitador General de la tierra dèl; puesto à los Reales Pies de V. Mag. Dize, que aviendo cursado sus estudios mayores en la Real Vniversidad de Valladolid ...
 [Madrid? ca. 1698]
 8 numb. ℓ. 28cm. fol.
 Title from caption and beginning of text. Concerns his services in Nueva Granada.
 Reference (numb. ℓ.4ᵛ) dated 24 Oct. 1697.
 Bound as the 3d of 3 items with: Silva, Juan de. Advertencias importantes, Madrid, 1621.
06888, 1888

DA682
P451f
Belcher, Joseph, 1669-1723.
 The Worst Enemy Conquered. A Brief Discourse On the Methods and Motives to pursue A Victory Over those Habits of Sin, Which War against the Soul. Delivered, on June 6th. 1698. the Day for Election of Officers, in the Artilery-Company, at Boston. By Mr. Joseph Belcher, Pastor of the Church in Dedham. ...
 Boston in New-England. Printed by Bartholomew Green, and John Allen. 1698.
 38 p. 15cm. (16cm. in case). 8º
 "Preface" (p. 3-4) signed: Cotton Mather.
 Imperfect: p. 3-4, 13-14 wanting; t.-p. mutilated; available in facsimile.
 In this copy there is a blank leaf at end.
 Bound with: Perkins, William. The Foundation of Christian Religion, Boston, 1682.
 WingB1783; Evans816; Sabin4398; Holmes(C.) 290-A.
13021-5, 1921

E698
B519a
[Bernard, Jacques] 1658-1718, ed.
 The Acts and Negotiations, Together with the Particular Articles at large, Of The General Peace, Concluded at Ryswick, By The Most Illustrious Confederates With The French King. To which is premised, The Negotiations and Articles of the Peace, concluded at Turin, between the same Prince and the Duke of Savoy. Translated from the Original Publish'd at the Hague.
 London: Printed for Robert Clavel at the Peacock, and Tim. Childe at the White Hart, at the West-end of St. Paul's Church-yard. 1698.
 6 p.ℓ., 223, 74-142 p. 2 fold. plans. 8º
 An abridged transl. of Actes et mémoires des négociations de la paix de Ryswick, The Hague, 1699 [i.e. 1697?]
 Booksellers' advertisement, 6th p.ℓ.ᵛ
 "The Acts And Negotiations Of The Treaty of Peace Held at the Palace of Ryswick" (p. [35]-142, 2d count) and "The Names and Qualities Of Their Excellencies The Ambassadors, Plenipotentiaries, Publick Ministers, Envoys; &c. That Assembled at the Congress Of The General Peace, At The Palace at Ryswick" (p. [125], 2d count - p. 142, 2d count) have special title-pages; "The Projects Of Peace ..." (p. [57]-101, 1st count) has half-title.
 Bound in contemporary calf.
 WingB1994.
69-279

DA698
B827a
Bray, Thomas, 1658-1730.
 Apostolick Charity, Its Nature and Excellence Consider'd. In A Discourse Upon Dan. 12.3. Preached at St. Pauls, Decemb. 19.

1697. at the Ordination of some Protestant Missionaries to be sent into the Plantations. To which is Prefixt, A General View of the English Colonies in America, with respect to Religion; In order to shew what Provision is wanting for the Propagation of Christianity in those Parts. By Thomas Bray, D.D.
    London, Printed by W. Downing, for William Hawes, at the Sign of the Rose in Ludgate-Street, 1698.
    6 p.l., 30 p., 1 l. 19cm. 4°
    Bookseller's advertisement (1 l. at end).
    This copy inscribed: "For the Lord Bishop of R...[ochester] from the Author T.B."
    WingB4285; cf. Sabin7473; Church770; Baer (Md.)182.
16676, 1934

B698 C334r   Casas, Bartolomé de las, bp. of Chiapa, 1474-1566.
    Relation Des Voyages Et Des Découvertes Que les Espagnols ont fait dans les Indes Occidentales; Ecrite par Dom B. de Las-Casas, Evêque de Chiapa. Avec la Relation curieuse des Voyages du Sieur de Montauban, Capitaine des Filbustiers, en Guinée l'an 1695.
    A Amsterdam, Chez J. Louis De Lorme Libraire sur le Rockin, à l'enseigne de la Liberté. M. DC XCVIII.
    6 p.l., 402,[2] p. incl. front. 17cm. 12°
    Title in red and black.
    Cut on t.-p.
    Colophons (p. [358] and 402): A Amsterdam, De l'Imprimerie de Daniel Boulesteys De La Contie, dans l'Eland-straat. M. D. XCVIII [sic].
    Dedication (3d p.l.) signed: Pralard.
    "Le Libraire De Hollande Aux Lecteurs." (5th-6th p.l.)
    The Las Casas section, transl. by J. B. Morvan de Bellevarde, is based on the nine tracts known under the title: Brevísma relación, pub. Seville, 1552. This transl. first pub. Paris, 1697, under title: La découverte des Indes occidentales.
    Montauban's Relation (p. 359-402) has special t.-p. but continuous paging and signatures.
    Bookseller's advertisement, [2] p. at end.
    In this copy there is a blank leaf following p. [358] and at end.
    Bound in contemporary calf.
    With this is bound, as issued, [Chèvremont, J.B. de] L'Art de voyager utilement, Amsterdam, 1698.
    JCB(2)2:1527; Sabin11274; Palau(2)46965n; Streit1:735; Medina(BHA)v.2, p. 472; Eeghen II 45; Hanke(Las Casas)560.
01936, 1854

BA698 C352e   Castilla, Miguel de, 1652-1713.
    Espejo De Exemplares Obispos Trasumpto Moderno De Los Antiguos Prel Ados [sic] De La Primitiva Yglesia Historiado, Y Discurrido En la ajustada Vida, y Heroycas Virtudes del Illustrissimo, y Reverendissimo Señor Doctor D. Joan De Santiago De Leon Garavito Obispo antes Electo de Puerto-Rico, y despues por mas de dies y ocho años de Guadalaxara. Escrivela El P. Miguel De Castilla, Cathedratico de Visperas de Sagrada Theologìa en el Collegio Maximo de S. Pedro, y S. Pablo de la Compañia de Jesus ... Y La Dedica A Maria SS. Madre de Dios siempre Virgen, ... en su devotissima Imagen, que se venera en el celebre Sanctuario de Zapopa.
    Con Licencia: En Mexico Por los Herederos de la Viuda de Bernardo Calderō. Año 1698
    6 p.l., 212, 214-297 p. 20.5cm. 4°
    Paging 214-297 begins on a recto.
    Includes his Leon Mystico, p. 229-259, 1st pub. Mexico [1695] and Antonio de Miranda Villaizan's Elogio funeral, p. 273-297, 1st pub. Mexico, 1694. Includes poetry by José de Arguiñano (p.l.4ᵛ-5), Miguel de Ortega (p.l. 5, p. 272), Bernardo de Riofrio (p. 269), José de Mora y Cuellar (p. 270), Felipe de Figueroa (p. 270-271), and Christval de Palma y Messa (p. 271).
    Palau(2)47997; Medina(Mexico)1690; Backer 2:848; Sabin11418
11801, 1919

D698 C443l [R]   [Chamberlayne, Richard] fl. 1682.
    Lithobolia: Or, The Stone-Throwing Devil. Being An Exact and True Account (by way of Journal) of the various Actions of Infernal Spirits, or (Devils Incarnate) Witches, or both; and the great Disturbance and Amazement they gave to George Waltons Family, at a place call'd Great Island in the Province of New-Hantshire [sic] in New-England ... By R.C. Esq; who was a Sojourner in the same Family the whole Time, and an Ocular Witness of these Diabolick Inventions. ...
    London, Printed, and are to be Sold by E. Whitlook [sic] near Stationers-Hall, 1698.
    3 p.l., 3-16 p. 21cm. 4°
    Preliminary matter includes poetry by the author addressed to R.F.
    JCB(2)2:1528; WingC1862; Sabin11786.
03704, before 1866

B698 C334r   [Chèvremont, Jean Baptiste de] 1640-1702.
    L'Art De Voyager Utilement. Suivant la Copie de Paris.
    A Amsterdam, Chez J. Louis De Lorme

Libraire sur le Rockin, à l'enseigne de la Liberté. M. DC. XCVIII.
2 p.l., 51, [1] p. 17cm. 12⁰
Cut on t.-p.
Colophon: A Amsterdam, De l'Imprimerie de Daniel Boulesteys De La Contie, dans l'Eland-straat. M. D. XCVIII [sic].
First pub. Paris, 1695, as the last part of La connoissance du monde.
Bound in contemporary calf.
Bound with, as issued, Casas, B. de las. Relation des voyages et des découvertes, Amsterdam, 1698.
JCB(2)2:1527; Eeghen II 46; cf. Sabin 11274.

01936-2, 1854

D696 Church of Scotland--Presbyteries--Dumfries.
-C737c Answers for the Presbytry of Dumfries, to a Calumnious Paper of Mr. Clanny's, Intituled a Supplication.
[Edinburgh, 1698]
[2] p. 31.5cm. fol.
Caption title
A reply to Hugh Clanny's Inquisitio nova, et inter Evangelicos hactenus inaudita ..., London, 1698.
This copy closely trimmed at bottom with slight loss of text.
Bound in a volume of Scottish imprints and mss. as the 56th of 58 items.
Wing A3468A.

7143, 1910

D698 [Clement, Simon] fl. 1695.
C626i The Interest of England, As it stands with Relation to the Trade of Ireland, Considered; The Arguments against the Bill, for Prohibiting the Exportation of Woollen Manufactures from Ireland to Forreign Parts, Fairly Discusst, And the Reasonableness and Necessity of Englands restraining her Colonies in all Matters of Trade, that may be prejudicial to her own Commerce, Clearly Demonstrated. With short Remarques on a Book, Entituled, Some Thoughts on the Bill depending before the Right Honourable the House of Lords, for Prohibiting the Exportation of the Woollen Manufactures of Ireland to Forreign Parts.
London, Printed by John Astwood, at his Printing-House behind St. Christophers-Church in Thread-needle-street, the backside of the Royal Exchange. 1698.
1 p.l., 23 p. 19.5cm. 4⁰
In part a reply to: Sir Richard Cox, Some thoughts on the bill ..., 1st pub. London, 1698.
Wing C4638A; Kress 2071.

32194, 1958

D696 Company of Scotland Trading to Africa and
-C737c the Indies.
To His Grace His Majesties High Commissioner, and the Right Honourable the Estates of Parliament. The humble Petition of The Council-General of the Company of Scotland Trading to Africa and the Indies.
[Edinburgh, 1698]
2 p. 31.5cm. fol.
Caption title.
Dated (at end) in Edinburgh, 22 June [i.e. July] 1698.
Protests "the English Ministers there [Hamburg] ... giving in a Memorial to the Senate of that City, Threatning both Senate and Inhabitants, with the King's outmost Displeasure, if they should Countenance, or Joyn with us in any Treaty of Trade, or Commerce ..." An English translation of the memorial was pub. as A memorial given in to the Senate of the City of Hamburgh ...
Bound in a volume of Scottish imprints and mss. as the 3d of 58 items.
Wing C5600; Scott 38.

7103, 1910

D698 Dampier, William, 1652-1715.
D166n A New Voyage Round The World. ... By
[R] William Dampier. ... The Third Edition Corrected.
London, Printed for James Knapton, at the Crown in St Paul's Church-yard. M DC XCVIII.
5 p.l., vi, 550, [4] p. incl. illus., map. 4 fold. maps. 19.5cm. 8⁰
First pub. London, 1697.
"Books sold by James Knapton..." p. [1-4] at end.
JCBAR 50:59-60; Wing D163; Sabin 18374; Borba de Moraes 1:204n.

30842, 1951

D698 Dampier, William, 1652-1715.
D166ni Nieuwe Reystogt Rondom De Werreld, ...
In 't Engelsch beschreeven door William Dampier, en daaruyt vertaald door W. Sewel. ...
In 's Gravenhage, By Abraham De Hondt, Boekverkooper op de Zaal van 't Hof/in de Fortuyn 1698 [-1704].
3 v.: v.1, 3 p.l., 6,184, 205-395, [396-406] p. illus., 7 plates (incl. 1 fold), 6 maps (incl. 3 fold.); v.2, 6 p.l., 284, 88, [8] p. 10 plates (incl. 2 fold.),

14 plates, double map. 21cm. 4°
The Dutch transl. of accounts of Dampier's voyages, 3 v. bound in 1.
First vol. transl. from: A new voyage round the world, 1st pub. London, 1697.
Tweede deel..., with t.-p. dated 1700, transl. from Voyages and descriptions, 1st pub. London, 1699. It includes Nieuwe reystogt en beschryving vande Land-engte van Amerika... door Lionel Wafer, with special t.-p. dated 1700 and separate paging and signatures, transl. from Wafer's A new voyage and description of the Isthmus of America, 1st pub. London, 1699.
Derde deel..., with t.-p. dated 1704, transl. from A voyage to New Holland, 1st pub. London, 1703.
Added title-pages, engr., v.1, 2; signed v.1: C. L.[uyken]; v.2: J.[oannes] Lamsvelt.
Cut on t.-p., v.1, 2.
Dedications, v.1, 3d p.ℓ., v.2, 3d p.ℓ., v.3, 2d p.ℓ. signed by Abraham de Hondt.
Errata: p. 395, v.1; last p., v.2.
In this copy there is a blank ℓ. at end of v.1, and the 3d p.ℓ., v.2, bearing dedication, is a cancel.
JCB(2)2:1529; Sabin18385; Tiele290.

03697, before 1866
03698, before 1866
03699, before 1866

D698 Dampier, William, 1652-1715.
D166no Nouveau Voyage Autour Du Monde, ... Par Guillaume Dampier. ... traduit de l'Anglois. Tome Premier [-Second].
A Amsterdam, Chez Paul Marret, Marchand Libraire dans le Beurs-straat à la Renommée. M. DC. XCVIII.
2 v. in 1: 6 p.ℓ., 315 p., 2 p.ℓ., [2], 317-616, [4] p. 7 plates (incl. 3 fold.), 5 maps (incl. 3 fold.). 15cm. 12°
Titles in red and black.
Both v. have the same added t.-p., engr., signed: J.V.D. Avele.
Transl. from A new voyage round the world, 1st pub. London, 1697.
Errata, p. [1] at end.
"Catalogue Des Livres Nouveaux De L'année 1698. qui se trouvent A Amsterdam. Chez Paul Marret" p. [2-4] at end.
In this copy in v.2 there is a blank ℓ. conjugate with the 1st p.ℓ. (added t.-p., engr.), and the next two leaves (2d p.ℓ., p. [1-2] are cancels.
JCB(2)2:1530; Sabin18381.

03700, before 1866

D698 [Davenant, Charles] 1656-1714.
D246d Discourses On The Publick Revenues, And On The Trade of England. In Two Parts. ... By the Author of The Essay on Ways and Means. ...
London: Printed for James Knapton, at the Crown in St. Paul's Church-yard. 1698.
2 v.: 8 p.ℓ., 279, [1], 62, [2] p. 3 fold. tables; 6 p.ℓ., 243 (i.e. 249), 254-434, 64 p. fold. table. 19.5cm. 8°
Pages are misnumbered in v.2, 243-244 for 242-243, 246-247 for 244-245, 249-250 for 246-247, 252 for 248, and 243 for 249.
With, as issued, (v.1) Xenophon, A Discourse upon improving the revenue of... Athens, and (v.2) [his] An Essay on the East-India-trade, each with special t.-p. and separate paging and signatures.
Includes (v.2, p. 259-261) William Penn's plan for a union of American colonies, submitted to the Lords Commissioners for Trade and Plantations, February, 1697.
Errata, v.1: p. [280]; v.2: p. 434.
Bookseller's advertisements: v.1, 1st p.ℓ.ᵛ, p. [280], [2] at end; v.2, p. 434.
Bound in contemporary calf.
JCBAR42:38-40; WingD306; Sabin18686; Kress 2074.

29013, 1941
29014, 1941

D698 [Davenant, Charles] 1656-1714.
D246d An Essay On The East-India-Trade. By The
2 Author Of The Essay on Ways and Means. Publish'd last Year, and now Reprinted.
London, Printed for J.[ames] K.[napton, 1698]
64 p. 19.5cm. 8° (Issued as a part of his, Discourses on the public revenues, v.2, London, 1698).
First pub. London, 1696.
WingD308.

29014A, 1941

E698 Dellon, Gabriel, b. ca. 1649.
D358v A Voyage To The East-Indies: Giving An Account of the Isles of Madagascar, and Mascareigne, of Suratte, the Coast of Malabar, of Goa, Gameron, Ormus, and the Coast of Brasil, with the Religion, Customs, Trade, &c. Of the Inhabitants, as also a Treatise, of the Distempers peculiar to the Eastern Countries. To which is Annexed an Abstract of Monsieur de Rennefort's History of the East-Indies, with his Propositions for the improvement of the East-India Company. Written Originally in French, By Mr. Dellon, M.D.
London, Printed for D. Browne, at the Black-Swan without Temple-Bar; A. Roper, at the

Black-Boy; and T. Leigh, at the Peacock, both in Fleet-Street, 1698.
  14 p.ℓ., 248, 43 p. 19.5cm. 8⁰.
  Dedication signed (4th p.ℓ.ᵛ) by the translator, J.[odocas] C.[rull]
  Transl. from Dellon's Relation d'un voyage fait aux Indes orientales, Paris, 1685, and Rennefort's Histoire des Indes orientales, Paris, 1688.
  Parts of Dellon's account, "An Account Of A Voyage To The East-Indies ... Part II" (p. [135]-219) and "A Treatise Of The Distempers Relating in Particular to the Eastern Countries ... By M.C.D.D.E.M." (p. [221]-248) each have special t.-p. but continuous paging and signatures.
  Rennefort's "A Supplement To ... Dellone's Relation ... Taken out of ... Rennefort's History" (43 p. at end) has special t.-p. and separate paging but continuous signatures.
  Wing D943; Borba de Moraes 1:216; Sabin 19447.

62-231

DA694 Fox, George, 1624-1691.
-F791   A Collection Of Many Select and Christian
2   Epistles, Letters and Testimonies. Written on sundry Occasions, by that Ancient, Eminent, Faithful Friend and Minister Of Christ Jesus, George Fox. The Second Volume. ...
  London, Printed and Sold by T. Sowle, in White-Hart-Court in Gracious-street, and at the Bible in Leaden-Hall-street, 1698.
  3 p.ℓ., 557, [14] p. 30cm. fol.
  "Errata": p. [1] at end.
  "An Epistle, By way of Preface" (2d-3d p.ℓ.); signed: London, 1698. George Whitehead.
  The "first volume" is A journal or historical account of ... George Fox, London, 1694.
  "Books Printed and Sold by T. Sowle ... 1699": p. [12-14] at end.
  Sabin 25347; Smith(Friends)1:691; Wing F1764. Baer(Md.)184.

11467, 1918

DA698 [Fox, George] 1624-1691.
F791   An Epistle To The Household Of The Seed Of Abraham, And To every Family in Particular, To Read and Practice. ...
  [London] Re-Printed in the Year 1698.
  1p.ℓ., 6p. 19cm. (20cm. in case) 4⁰
  Signed: G. F.
  First pub. London, 1682.
  cf. Smith(Friends)1:681; Wing F1813.

11440, 1918

EB   France--Sovereigns, etc., 1643-1715
S237   (Louis XIV).   Sept 1698
1716   Lettres Patentes. Pour L'Establissement De
1   La Compagnie Royale de Saint Domingue. Données à Versailles au mois de Septembre 1698.
  A Paris, Chez la Veuve Saugrain, & Pierre Prault, à l'entrée du Quay de Gesvres, du côté du Pont au Change, au Paradis. [1698]
  8 p. 24cm. 4⁰
  Caption title; imprint at end.
  Bound as no. [4] of 4 acts of French royal administration with binder's title: Status et reglemens St. Domingue. 1716.
  JCB(1)3:217; Wroth&Annan 382; Actes Royaux 19457.

06042, before 1870

BA698 Franciscans--Provincia de San Diego de
F819c   Mexico.
  Constitvciones De La Provincia De San Diego de Mexico de los Menores Descalços de la Mas Estrecha Observancia Regular de N.S.P.S. Francisco en esta Nueva-España, ... con las Constituciones Apostolicas pertenecientes á la Ereccion de dicha Provincia, ... y su Precedencia Seraphica respecto de la Chervbica Familia de N.P.S. Avgvstin, y demas Religiones Sagradas sus Immediatas ...
  Con licencia en Mexico: Por los Herederos de la Uiuda de Francisco Rodriguez Lupercio en la Puente de Palacio, año de 1698.
  18 p.ℓ., 263 numb. ℓ., [33] p. 20cm. 4⁰
  Title in red and black.
  License dated (10th p.ℓ.ᵛ) 31 May 1698.
  Errata, p. [33] at end.
  In this copy the margins of the 2d, 3d, 10th, 12th, and 13th p.ℓ. have been trimmed with loss of notes.
  Bound in contemporary vellum.
  Palau(2)59967; Medina(Mexico)1691; Sabin 76023; Streit 2:2344.

06640, 1898

E698 Froger, François, b. 1676.
F927r1   Relation D'Un Voyage Fait en 1695. 1696. & 1697. aux Côtes d'Afrique, Détroit de Magellan, Brezil, Cayenne & Isles Antilles, par une Escadre des Vaisseaux du Roy, commandée par M. De Gennes. Faite par le Sieur Froger Ingenieur Volontaire sur le Vaisseau le Faucon Anglois. ...
  Imprimée par les soins & aux frais du sieur De Fer, Geographe de Monseigneur le Dauphin. A Paris, Dans l'Isle du Palais, sur le Quay de

l'Horloge, à la Sphere Royale. Et Chez Michel Brunet, dans la grande Salle du Palais, au Mercure galant. M. DC. XCVIII. Avec Privilege Du Roy.
    7 p. ℓ., 219, [1] p. 17 plates (incl. 4 fold.), 12 maps (incl. 5 fold.). 18cm. 12°
    Added t.-p., engr.: Relation du Voyage de M.r De Gennes au detroit de Magellan par le S.r Froger. ...
    "Achevé d'imprimer pour la premiere fois le 9. Janvier 1698."(last p.)
    Colophon (last p.): De l'Imprimerie de Gilles Paulus-Du-Mesnil. 1698.
    Imperfect: fold. pl. at p. 14 wanting; available in facsim.
    JCB(2)2:1532; Sabin26001; Borba de Moraes2: 284.
01523, 1847

E698 F927r2   Froger, François, b. 1676.
    A Relation Of A Voyage Made in the Years 1695, 1696, 1697. on the Coasts of Africa, Streights of Magellan, Brasil, Cayenna, and the Antilles, by a Squadron of French Men of War, under the Command of M. de Gennes. By the Sieur Froger, Voluntier-Engineer on board the English Falcon. ...
    London, Printed for M. Gillyflower in Westminster-Hall; W. Freeman, M. Wotton in Fleetstreet; J. Walthoe in the Temple; and R. Parker in Cornhill. 1698.
    6 p. ℓ., 91, 96-173, [174-176] p. 10 plates (incl. 2 fold.), 4 maps (incl. 1 fold.) 19cm. 8°
    Added t.-p., engr.: A Iournal of a late Voyage of M.r de Gennes To the Straits of Magellan by le S.r. Froger.
    "Books Printed for M. Gillyflower, W. Freeman, M. Wotton, J. Walthoe, and R. Parker." (last p.)
    Transl. from: Relation d'un voyage, Paris, 1698.
    Bound in contemporary calf.
    JCB(2)2:1531; WingF2233; Sabin26004; Borba de Moraes1:285.
03701, before 1866

B698 -G249c   Gaspar de San Agustín, 1650-1724.
    Conquistas De Las Islas Philipinas: La Temporal, Por Las Armas Del Señor Don Phelipe Segundo El Prudente; Y La Espiritval, Por Los Religiosos Del Orden De Nuestro Padre San Augustin: Fvndacion, Y Progressos De Sv Provincia Del Santissimo Nombre De Jesus, Parte Primera. ... Escriviala El Padre Fray Gaspar De San Avgvstin, natural de Madrid, Procurador General de dicha Provincia del Santissimo Nombre de Jesus, Secretario, y Difinidor della, y Comissario del Santo Oficio.
    Con Privilegio: En Madrid: En la Imprenta de Manvel Rviz De Mvrga. Año de 1698.
    16 p. ℓ., 544, [7] p. fold. pl. 30cm. fol.
    Preliminary matter includes poetry.
    Errata, 10th p. ℓ.
    "Elogio" dated (15 p. ℓ.v) 24 May 1698.
    Covers the period 1511-1614. Material gathered for the second part was not pub. but formed the basis for a continuation prepared by Casmirio Díaz.
    Bound in contemporary vellum.
    Palau(2)289435; Streit5:980; Retana177; Medina(Filipinas)250; Sabin75996.
69-547

B69 G643v 2   González de la Sancha, Lorenzo Antonio.
    Villancicos, Que Se Cantaron En La Santa Iglesia Metropolitana de Mexico, en los Maytines De La Natividad De Maria SS. Nuestra Senora, ... Escribelos, el Br. D. Lorenço Antonio Gonzales de la Sancha. Compuestos en Metro-musico: por Antonio de Salazar, Maestro de Cpilla [sic] de dicha Santa Iglesia.
    Con Licencia: En Mexico: por los Herederos de la Viuda de Bernardo Calderon, en la calle de S. Agustin: Año 1698.
    [8] p. 20cm. 4°
    Woodcut title vignette (the Virgin kneeling atop a hill surrounded by a mandorla radiating light)
    Bound, in contemporary vellum, as no. 2 with 42 other items.
    Medina (Mexico) 1695.
28902, 1941

BA698 G643n   González de Quiroga, Diego, fl. 1694-1698.
    El Nvevo Apostol De Galicia El Venerable Padre Fr. Joseph De Carabantes, Religioso Capvchino, y Missionario Apostolico en la American, y Europa. Sv Vida, Virtvdes, Predicacion, Y Prodigios. ... Por El Lic. Don Diego Gonzalez de Quiroga, Juez Eclesiastico, Cura de Santa Eulalia, y Capellan mayor en el muy Religioso Convento de Franciscas Descalças de la Villa de Monforte de Lemus.
    Con Privilegio: En Madrid: En la Oficina de la Viuda de Melchor Alvarez. Año M.DC.XC.VIIJ.
    12 p. ℓ., 507, [508-532] p. pl. 21cm. 4°
    "Svma De La Tassa" dated (8th p. ℓ.v) 20 June 1698.

Errata, 8th p. ℓ.
JCB(2)2:1534; Palau(2)105767; Medina(BHA) 1984; Streit2:2335; Sabin67345.
02545, 1851

DB   Gt. Brit. --Parliament, 1697-1698--House of
-G7875   Commons.
1689   The Humble Address of the House of Commons
3   to the King.
              London, Printed by John Leake for Timothy Goodwin, against St. Dunstan's Church in Fleet-street, and Thomas Cockerill at the Corner of Warwick-Lane, in Pater-Noster-Row, 1698.
                490 (i.e. 491)-492 p. 29cm. 1/2º (Issued as no. 170 of Gt. Brit. --Parliament, 1697-1698--House of Commons. Votes..., London, 1697-1698.)
                Caption title; imprint at end.
                Address, p. 491, is a reply to William Molyneux's The case of Ireland's being bound by acts of Parliament in England stated, Dublin, 1698. Address, p. 492, calls for the suppression of the wool industry in Ireland and the encouragement of the linen industry.
                Presented 1 July 1698.
                Bound in Votes of the House of Commons, v. 3.
10376-9B, 1914

DB   Gt. Brit. --Parliament, 1697-1698--House of
-G7875   Lords.
1689   The Humble Address Of the Right Honourable
3   the Lords Spiritual & Temporal In Parliament Assembled, Presented to His Majesty. And His Majesties Most Gracious Answer Thereunto.
              London, Printed by Charles Bill, and the Executrix of Thomas Newcomb deceas'd; Printers to the Kings most Excellent Majesty. 1697[/8].
                4 p. 29cm. fol.
                Dated (p. 3) 16 Feb 1697[/8]; order to print (p. 2) dated 19 Feb 1697[/8].
                Calls for the exclusion of foreign manufactures.
                Bound in Votes of the House of Commons, v. 3, before Votes for 19 Feb 1697[/8].
10383-7, 1914 rev 2

DB   Gt. Brit. --Parliament, 1697-1698--House of
-G7875   Lords.
1689   The Humble Address Of the Right Honourable
3   the Lords Spiritual & Temporal In Parliament Assembled, Presented to His Majesty On Friday the Tenth Day of June, 1698. And His Majesties Most Gracious Answer Thereunto.
              London, Printed by Charles Bill, and the Executrix of Thomas Newcomb deceas'd; Printers to the Kings most Excellent Majesty. 1698.
                4 p. 29cm. fol.
                Order to print (p. 2) dated 10 June 1698.
                Calls for suppression of the wool industry in Ireland and the encouragement of the linen industry.
                Bound in Votes of the House of Commons, v. 3, before Votes for 10 June 1698.
10383-9, 1914

DB   Gt. Brit. --Parliament, 1698-1699--House of
-G7875   Commons.
1689   Votes Of The House of Commons, In The Parliament Began At Westminster The Sixth day of December, in the Tenth Year of the Reign of King William, Anno Domini 1698.
3   London, Printed for Edward Jones, and Timothy Goodwin. MDCXCVIII.[-1699].
                1 p. ℓ., 252 p. 29cm. fol.
                Issued in pts. numbered 1-113 and dated 9 Dec 1698 - 4 May 1699, each of which has caption title and (except for no. 1) imprint at end.
                Imprint of no. 82-113 dated 1699.
                Errata, p. 24.
                Bound in Votes of the House of Commons, v. 3.
10376-10, 1914

bD698   The Great Earthquake At Quito in Peru Which
G786e   destroyed a great Number of the Spainiards In The West Indies.
              [London? 1698?]
                Broadside. 29.5cm. x 17.5cm. 1/2º
                Caption title.
                Wing G1687.
06494, before 1902

B698   Grillet, Jean, 1624-1677.
V975a   A Journal Of The Travels Of John Grillet, And Francis Bechamel Into Guiana, In the Year, 1674. In Order to Discover the Great Lake of Parima, and the many Cities said to be situated on its Banks, and reputed the Richest in the World.
              London: Printed for Samuel Buckley. 1698.
                2 p. ℓ., 68 p. 19cm. 8º (Issued as a part of Voyages And Discoveries in South-America. London, 1698.)
                First appeared in vol. 2 of Cristóbal de Acuña's Relation De La Riviere Des Amazones, Paris, 1682.
                Includes "Notes Upon The Travels Of Father

John Grillet, And Father Francis Bechamel, ..." (p. 45-58) and "A Relation Of Guiana..." (p. 59-68).

JCB(2)2:1523; Wing V746; Palau(2)2487; Sabin 152; Borba de Moraes 1:12; Backer 1:40; Streit 2:2328.

01932B, 1854

E698 Hennepin, Louis, ca. 1640-ca. 1705.
H515a Aenmerckelycke Historische Reys-Beschryvinge Door verscheyde Landen veel grooter als die van geheel Europa onlanghs ontdeckt. ... Met Approbatie van Wilhelmus den III. Koningh Van Groot-Britanie. En aan deselve fijne Majesteyt opgedragen Door Lodewyck Hennepin, Missionaris Recollect, en Notaris Apostoliek.

Tot Utrecht, By Anthony Schouten. 1698.

16 p.ℓ., 242 (i.e. 142), [18] p. illus. (front.) 4 plates, fold. map. 19cm. 4°

Transl. from Nouveau voyage d'un pais plus grand que l'Europe, Utrecht, 1698.

Made up of material about LaSalle taken from Chrétien LeClercq's Etablissement de la foy dans la Nouvelle France, Paris, 1691, and the description of the Indians which had 1st appeared in his own Description de la Louisiane, Paris, 1683.

"Register Van eenige Historische Nederduytsche Boecken, dewelcke te bekomen sijn in de Winckel Van Anthoni Schouten." (p. [17-18] at end.)

Added title on front.: Reyse Door Nieuwe Ondekte Landen.

Imperfect: maps wanting; they are the same as those in the Library's copies of the Nouveau voyage, Utrecht, 1698.

JCB(2)2:1539; Sabin31358; Harrisse(NF)179; Muller(1872)909; Paltsits(Hennepin)lviii; Streit2:2778.

0812, 1846

E698 Hennepin, Louis, ca. 1640-ca. 1705.
H515nB A Continuation Of The New Discovery Of A Vast Country in America, Extending above Four Thousand Miles, Between New France and New Mexico; Giving an Account Of The Attempts of the Sieur De la Salle upon the Mines of St. Barbe, &c. The Taking of Quebec by the English; With the Advantages of a Shorter Cut to China and Japan. By L. Hennepin, now Resident in Holland. To which is added, Several New Discoveries in North-America, not publish'd in the French Edition.

London, Printed in the Year, 1698.

16 p.ℓ., 48, 45-178 p. 4 fold. plates, fold. map. 20cm. 8° (Issued as a part of his A new discovery, London, 1698 ["Bon-" edition]).

Inserted between his New discovery and the "added, Several New Discoveries" mentioned on the t.-p.

Transl. from Nouveau voyage d'un pais plus grand que l'Europe, Utrecht, 1698.

Another edition of this Continuation was issued London, 1698, as a part of the "Tonson" edition of his A new discovery.

JCB(2)2:1536; Sabin31371; WingH1450; Paltsits (Hennepin)lix; Church772; Harrisse(NF)181; Streit2:2780n.

05863A, before 1874

E698 Hennepin, Louis, ca. 1640-ca. 1705.
H515nT A Continuation, Of The New Discovery Of A
[R] Vast Country in America, Extending above Four Thousand Miles, Between New France and New Mexico; Giving an Account Of The Attempts of the Sieur De la Salle upon the Mines of St. Barbe, &c. The Taking of Quebec by the English; With the Advantages of a Shorter Cut to China and Japan. By L. Hennepin, now Resident in Holland. To which are added, Several New Discoveries in North-America, not publish'd in the French Edition.

London, Printed for M. Bentley, J. Tonson, H. Bonwick, T. Goodwin, and S. Manship. 1698.

16 p.ℓ., 228 p. 4 fold. plates, fold. map. 20cm. 8° (Issued as a part of his A New Discovery, London, 1698 ["Tonson" edition]).

A Continuation transl. from Nouveau voyage d'un pais plus grand que l'Europe, Utrecht, 1698.

The "added, Several New Discoveries" mentioned on the t.-p. are: Joliet's account of New France, p. 185-187; "An Account of M. La Salles Voyage to the River Mississipi. Directed to Count Frontenac, Governor of New-France", p. 188-195; "A Discovery of some New Countries and Nations in the Northern America. By Father Marquette", p. 196-223 (1st pub. as "Découverte de quelques pays et nations de l'Amerique septentrionale" in Melchisédech Thévenot's Recueil de voyages, Paris, 1681); and an account of La Salle's later discoveries and death, p. 224-228.

Bookseller's advertisement, last p.

Another edition of this Continuation was issued London, 1698, as a part of the "Bon-" edition of his A New Discovery.

This edition of the Continuation was also issued under title: A New Voyage Into The Northwest Parts Of America ... with imprint: London, Printed for Edw. Castle near Scotland-Yard Gate by Whitehall; and Sam. Buckley at the Dolphin over against St. Dunstan's Church in Fleetstreet, 1698.

JCB(2)2:1535; Sabin31370; WingH1451; Harrisse

[365]

1698

(NF)181; Paltsits(Hennepin)lxi; Church773; Streit 2:2780.
01935A, before 1854

E698　　Hennepin, Louis, ca. 1640-ca. 1705.
H515nr　　Neue Reise-Beschreibung Durch viele Länder/ weit grösser/als gantz Europa/Die neulichst zwischen Neu-Mexico und dem Eiss-Meer in America entdecket worden. ... In Frantzösischer Sprache beschrieben/und mit Genehmhaltung Sr. Königl. Majest. von Gross-Brittannien Wilhelm III. unterthänigst überreichet von R. P. Ludovico Hennepin, Missionario der Recollecten und Notario Apostol. Ins Teutsche übersetzet von M.J.G. Langen/Candid. Theol.
Bremen. In verlegung Phil. Gottfr. Saurmans/ 1698.
22 p.ℓ., 288 p. front., 4 fold. plates, fold. map. 13.5cm. 12º
Transl. from Nouveau voyage d'un pais plus grand que l'Europe, Utrecht, 1698.
Made up of material about LaSalle taken from Chrétien LeClercq's Etablissement de la foy dans la Nouvelle France, Paris, 1691, and the description of the Indians which had appeared in his own Description de la Louisiane, Paris, 1683.
Imperfect: front. wanting; available in facsim.
JCB(2)2:1540; Sabin31366; Harrisse(NF)180; Palmer336; Paltsits(Hennepin)lviii; Streit 2:2777.
03696, before 1866

E698　　Hennepin, Louis, ca. 1640-ca. 1705.
H515nB　　A New Discovery Of A Vast Country in America, Extending above Four Thousand Miles, Between New France and New Mexico. With A Description of the Great Lakes, Cataracts, Rivers, Plants, and Animals: Also, The Manners, Customs, and Languages, of the several Native Indians; And the Advantage of Commerce with those different Nations. With A Continuation: Giving an Account of the Attempts of the Sieur De la Salle upon the Mines of St. Barbe, &c. The Taking of Quebec by the English; With the Advantages of a Shorter Cut to China and Japan. Both Parts Illustrated with Maps and Figures, and Dedicated to His Majesty K. William. By L. Hennepin, now Resident in Holland. To which is added, Several New Discoveries in North-America, not publish'd in the French Edition.
London: Printed for M. Bentley, J. Tonson, H. Bonwick, T. Goodwin, and S. Manship. 1698.
12 p.ℓ., 299 ., 16 ℓ., 48, 45-178, [301]-355 p. incl. front. 6 fold. plates, 2 fold. maps.

20cm. 8º
The "Bon-" edition, so-called from 1st line ending of imprint. Another edition London, same year, is likewise known as the "Tonson" edition.
New discovery transl. from Nouvelle découverte d'un tres grand pays, Utrecht, 1697.
The "added, Several New Discoveries" mentioned on the t.-p. (with section title, p. [301], "An Account Of Several New Discoveries In North-America.") are: Joliet's account of New France, p. 303-306; "An Account Of M. la Salle's Voyage To The River Mississipi. Directed to Count Frontenac, Governour of New-France", p. 307-317; "A Discovery Of Some New Countries and Nations In The Northern-America. By Father Marquette", p. 318-349 (1st pub. as "Découverte de quelques pays et nations de l'Amerique septentrionale" in Melchisédech Thévenot's Receuil de voyages, Paris, 1681); and an account of LaSalle's later discoveries and death, p. 350-355.
Bookseller's advertisement, p. 355.
With, as issued, inserted between his New discovery and "added Several New Discoveries," his A continuation of the new discovery, London, 1698, with special t.-p., separate paging and signatures (transl. from Nouveau voyage d'un pais plus grand que l'Europe, Utrecht, 1698).
Bound in contemporary calf, rebacked.
JCB(2)2:1536; Sabin31371; WingH1450; Paltsits (Hennepin)lix; Church772; Harrisse(NF)181; Streit2:27804.
05863, before 1874

E698　　Hennepin, Louis, ca. 1640-ca. 1705.
H515nT　　A New Discovery Of A Vast Country in America, Extending above Four Thousand Miles, Be-
[R]　　tween New France and New Mexico; With A Description of the Great Lakes, Cataracts, Rivers, Plants, and Animals. Also, the Manners, Customs, and Languages of the several Native Indians; and the Advantage of Commerce with those different Nations. With A Continuation, Giving an Account of the Attempts of the Sieur De la Salle upon the Mines of St. Barbe, &c. The Taking of Quebec by the English; With the Advantages of a Shorter Cut to China and Japan. Both Parts Illustrated with Maps, and Figures, and Dedicated to His Majesty K. William. By L. Hennepin, now Resident in Holland. To which are added, Several New Discoveries in North-America, not publish'd in the French Edition.
London, Printed for M. Bentley, J. Tonson, H. Bonwick, T. Goodwin, and S. Manship. 1698.
12 p.ℓ., 243 p., 1 ℓ., [30], 228 p. incl. front. 6 fold. plates, 2 fold. maps. 20cm. 8º
The "Tonson" edition, so-called from 1st line ending of imprint. Another edition London, same

year, is likewise known as the "Bon-", edition.

New discovery transl. from Nouvelle découverte d'un tres grand pays, Utrecht, 1697.

With, as issued, his A continuation of the new discovery... to which are added several new discoveries, London, 1698, with special t.-p., separate paging and signatures.

Bookseller's advertisement, last page.

JCB(2)2:1535; Sabin31370; WingH1451; Harrisse (NF)181; Paltsits(Hennepin)lxi; Church773; Streit2:2780

01935, before 1854

E698 Hennepin, Louis, ca. 1640-ca. 1705.
H515n1   Nouveau Voyage d'un Pais plus grand que L'Europe Avec les reflections des entreprises du Sieur de la Salle, sur les Mines de St. Barbe, &c. Enrichi de la Carte, de figures expressives, des mœurs & manieres de vivre des Sauvages du Nord, & du Sud, de la prise de Quebec Ville Capitale de la Nouvelle France, par les Anglois, & des avantages qu'on peut retirer du chemin recourci de la Chine & du Japon, par le moien de tant de Vastes Contrées, & de Nouvelles Colonies. Avec approbation & dedié à sa Majesté Guillaume III. Roy de la grande Bretagne Par Le R. P. Louis Hennepin, Missionaire Recollect & Notaire Apostolique.

A Utrecht, Chez Antoine Schouten, Marchand Libraire. 1698.

35 p.ℓ., 389 p. 4 fold. plates, fold. map. 14.5cm. 12º

Title in red and black.

Made up of material about La Salle taken from Chrétien LeClercq's Etablissement de la foy dans la Nouvelle France, Paris, 1691, and the description of the Indians which had 1st appeared in his own Description de la Louisiane, Paris, 1683.

Also issued the same year only differing in imprint: A Utrecht, Chez Ernestus Voskuyl, Imprimeur...

In this copy there is a blank ℓ. following the preliminaries.

JCB(2)2:1537; Sabin31351; Harrisse(NF)177; Paltsits(Hennepin)lvi; cf. Church774n; Streit 2:2775.

01934, before 1854

E698 Hennepin, Louis, ca. 1640-ca. 1705.
H515n2   Nouveau Voyage d'un Pais plus grand que L'Europe Avec les reflections des entreprises du Sieur de la Salle, sur les Mines de St. Barbe, &c. Enrichi de la Carte, de figures expressives, des mœurs & manieres de vivre des Sauvages du Nord, & du Sud, de la prise de Quebec Ville Capitalle de la Nouvelle France, par les Anglois, & des avantages qu'on peut retirer du chemin recourci de la Chine & du Japon, par le moien de tant de Vastes Contrées, & de Nouvelles Colonies. Avec approbation & dedié à sa Majesté Guillaume III. Roy de la grande Bretagne Par Le R. P. Louis Hennepin, Missionaire Recollect & Notaire Apostolique.

A Utrecht, Chez Ernestus Voskuyl, Imprimeur 1698.

35 p.ℓ., 389 p. 4 fold. plates, fold. map. 15cm. 12º

Title in red and black.

Made up of material about La Salle taken from Chrétien LeClercq's Etablissement de la foy dans la Nouvelle France, Paris, 1691, and the description of the Indians which had 1st appeared in his own Description de la Louisiane, Paris, 1683.

Also issued the same year only differing in imprint: A Utrecht, Chez Antoine Schouten, Marchand Libraire...

Paltsits(Hennepin)lviii; Church774; Streit 2:2776.

04706, 1881

E698 Hennepin, Louis, ca. 1640-ca. 1705.
H515nd   Nouvelle Decouverte D'Un Tres Grand Pays Situé dans l'Amerique, Entre Le Nouveau Mexique, Et La Mer Glaciale, Avec les Cartes, & les Figures necessaires, & de plus l'Histoire Naturelle & Morale, & les avantages qu'on en peut tirer par l'établissem. des Colon. Le Tout Dedie à Sa Majesté Britannique. Guillaume III. Par Le R. P. Louis Hennepin, Missiouaire [sic] Recollect & Notaire Apostolique.

A Amsterdam, Chez Abraham van Someren, Marchand Libraire. MDCXCVIII.

36 p.ℓ., 506 (i.e. 516) p. 2 fold. plates, 2 fold. maps. 12º

First pub. Utrecht, 1697. This is a page-for-page reprint (except for division of the last few pages).

An amplification of his Description de la Louisiane, 1st pub. Paris, 1683 ("Les moeurs des sauvages" section, however, is omitted), but also with material appropriated from Chrétien Le Clercq's Etablissement de la foy dans La Nouvelle France, Paris, 1691 (especially the account included therein of LaSalle's discoveries, by Zénobe Membré).

Added t.-p., engr., signed C. L[uyken]

Includes 10 pages inserted after p. 312, each numbered 313*.

Imperfect: maps wanting; they are the same as those in the Library's copy of the Dutch transl. pub. Amsterdam, 1702, under title: Nieuw ontdekkinge...

1698   CATALOGUE OF THE JOHN CARTER BROWN LIBRARY

J698
H887j
   Hübner, Johann, 1668-1731.
   Johann Hübners/Rect. Gymn. Martisburg. Kurtze Fragen Aus der Neuen und Alten Geographie Auff Den Friedens-Schluss zu Ryswyck gegründet/Und Mit einer nützlichen Einleitung vor Die Anfänger/Auch Vollständigem Register vermehret. Achte Edition.
   Mit Röm. Käyserl. auch Königl. Pol. und Chur-Sächs. sonderbahrem Privilegio. [Leipzig?] Jm Jahr 1698. Verlegts Johann Friedrich Gleditsch.
   58 p.ℓ., 1003,[1004-1123] p. front. (fold. map). 14.5cm. 12º
   Title in red and black.
   First pub. Leipzig? ca. 1695.
   "Vorrede" dated (2d p.ℓ.ᵛ) 1 March 1698.
   Errata, p. [1123]
   Bound in contemporary vellum.

62-158

bD
Scott
127
   Information For Gaven Plummer Cashier to the Indian and African Company. Against John Lord Belhaven.
   [Edinburgh, 1698?]
   [2] p. 19.5cm. fol.
   Concerns expenses charged to the Darien Company by Lord Belhaven.
   Wing I164; Scott 127.

777, 1905

C698
-J62i
   João José de Santa Thereza, freire, b. 1658.
   Istoria Delle Gverre Del Regno Del Brasile Accadvte Tra La Corona Di Portogallo, E La Repvblica Di Olanda Composta, ... Dal P.F. Gio: Gioseppe di S. Teresa Carmelitano Scalzo. Parte Prima. [-Seconda.]
   Anno MDCXCVIII. In Roma, Nella Stamperia degl'Eredi del Corbelletti. Con Licenza De' Svperiori.
   2 pts. in 1 v.: 7 p.ℓ., 232, [16] p. front. (port.), 3 fold. pl., 12 fold. maps; 211, [20] p. front. (port.), 4 fold. pl., 4 fold. maps. 31cm. fol.
   Cut on each t.-p.
   Errata: pt. 2, last p.
   Added t.-p., engr. (pt. 1): Istoria del Regno del Brasile. Signed: Andreas Antonius Horatijs inu. et delin Benedictus Fariat sculpsit.
   Imprimatur dated (pt. 1, 6th p.ℓ.ʳ) 10 Sept. 1697.
   Imperfect: 2 fold. plates and fold. map wanting; available in facsim.
   JCB(2)2:1533; Sabin76793; Borba de Moraes 2: 230-231.

03695, before 1866

D698
J69c
   [Johnson, Samuel] 1649-1703
   A Confutation Of a late Pamphlet Intituled, A Letter Ballancing the Necessity of keeping a Land-Force in time of Peace, with the Dangers that may follow on it. The Second Edition Corrected.
   London, Printed for A. Baldwin, MDCXCVIII.
   2 p.ℓ., 35 p. 20cm. 4º.
   First pub. London, 1698.
   A reply to John Somers, A letter ballancing the necessity, London, 1697.
   WingJ825.

8915, 1912

DA698
K28a
   Keith, George, 1639?-1716.
   The Arguments Of The Quakers, More particularly, Of <George Whitehead. William Penn. Robert Barclay.><John Gratton. George Fox. Humphry Norton,> And my own, Against Baptism and the Supper Examined and Refuted. Also Some clear Proofs from Scripture; shewing that they are Institutions of Christ under the Gospel. With An Appendix, Containing some Observations upon some Passages, in a Book of W. Penn, called, A Caveat against Popery. And on some Passages of a Book of John Pennington, called, The Fig Leaf Covering Discovered. By George Keith. ...
   London, Printed for C. Brome at the Gun at the West-End of St. Paul's Church-yard. 1698.
   4 p.ℓ., 89, [90-112] p. 22.5cm. 4º
   A reply to various works by George Whitehead, William Penn, Robert Barclay, John Gratton, George Fox, Humphrey Norton, and in the appendix to William Penn's A seasonable caveat against popery, 1st pub. [London?] 1670, and to John Penington's The leaf covering discovered, 1st pub. London, 1697.
   Errata at end.
   In this copy p. [105-112] disintegrated with slight loss of text.
   With this are bound: his A Third Narrative Of The Proceedings At Turners-Hall, London, 1698, and his ... Fourth Narrative, Of His Proceedings At Turners-Hall, London, 1700.

JCB(2)2:1538; Sabin31350; Harrisse(NF) 176; Paltsits(Hennepin)liv; Streit2:2779.

04704, 1881

DA698 K28a cop.2 4894, 1908 05958	——Another copy. 21.5cm. WingK142; Smith(Friends)2:33; McAlpin 4:588.		p. 104 and 105. In this copy there is a blank leaf at end. Palau(2)130800; Medina(Mexico)1696.
		5516, 1909	

DA696 K28e   Keith, George, 1639?-1716.
A Third Narrative Of The Proceedings At Turners-Hall, The Twenty First Day of April 1698. Giving an exact Account of the Proofs brought by George Keith, out of the Quakers Printed Books, at the same Meeting ... Also W. Penn's Letter to George Keith ... By George Keith.
London, Printed for C. Brome at the Gun at the West-End of St. Paul's Church-yard. 1698.
2 p.ℓ., 68 p. 21cm. 4⁰
"A Copy of a Letter from William Penn to George Keith. Bristol, the 16th of the 2d Month, 1698" (p. 55 [i.e. 47]-48); 1st pub. in [Thomas Story] A Word to the well-inclin'd, London, 1698.
"A Letter from George Keith to William Penn, in Answer ..." (p. 48-53).
Errata, at end.
Attestation dated (2 p.ℓ.ᵛ) 28 May 1698.
Bound as the 3d in a vol. of 7 works by Keith.

DA698 K28a   ——Another copy. 22.5cm.
Bound as the 2d in a vol. of 3 works by Keith.
JCB(2)2:1541; WingK218; Sabin37191; Smith (Friends)2:32-33.
04790, before 1874
4895, 1908

BA698 L237d   Lampérez y Blázquez, Valentín.
Disciplina Vetvs Ecclesiastica A Sanctissimo D. N. D. Innocentio Div. Provid. Papa XII. Instavrata. In Bvlla Nouissime Expedita, Qvæ Incipit: Specvlatores Domvs Israel, Cvivs Scholiasticam Expositionem ... Exponit ... Dr. D. Valentinvs Lamperez Et Blazquez, Olim In Complutensi Theolog. Aragoniæ Insigni Collegio Alumnus, & Rector, nuncvero Almæ Metropolitanæ ac Patriarchal. Eccles. Hispal. Canonicus ...
Prinium [sic] Hispali prodijt apud Lucam Martinum; anno 1696. Nunc denuo iuxta eius prototypum, Mexici prælo tradita, Superiorum permissu, in Typographia Dñae Mariæ de Benavides Anno Dñi 1698.
16 p.ℓ., 322, [14] p., 1 ℓ. 21.5cm. 4⁰
First pub. Seville, 1696.
Preliminary matter includes text of the papal bull commented upon (11th-16th p.ℓ.).
Errata, last leaf.
In this copy p. 113-120 misbound between p. 104 and 105.
In this copy there is a blank leaf at end.
Palau(2)130800; Medina(Mexico)1696.

5516, 1909

DA693 L481c   Lee, Samuel, 1625-1691.
Contemplations On Mortality. Wherein The Terrors of Death are laid open, for a Warning to Sinners: And the Joyes of Communion with Christ for Comfort to Believers. By Samuel Lee. M. A. Sometime Fellow of Wadham Colledge. Oxon. ...
Boston in N. E. Reprinted by B. Green, and J. Allen, for Samuel Phillips, at the Brick Shop. 1698.
5 p.ℓ., 149 p., 14.5cm. 8⁰
First pub. London 1669.
Bound in contemporary calf.
Evans820; Sabin39793; WingL893.

31052, 1952

DA698 L634p   [Leslie, Charles] 1650-1722.
Primitive Heresie Revived, In The Faith and Practice Of the People Called Quakers: Wherein is shewn, in Seven Particulars, That the Principal and most Characteristick Errors of the Quakers, were Broached and Condemned, in the Days of the Apostles, and the first 150 Years after Christ. To which is Added, A Friendly Expostulation with William Penn, upon Account of his Primitive Christianity, lately Published.
London: Printed for C. Brome, at the Gun, at the West-End of St. Paul's. W. Keblewhite, at the Swan in St. Paul's Church-Yard. And H. Hindmarsh, at the Golden-Ball over-against the Royal Exchange. 1698.
2 p.ℓ., 32 p. 21.5cm. 4⁰
Errata, 2d p.ℓ.ᵛ
Text partly in Greek.
A reply, in part, to William Penn's Primitive Christianity, 1st pub. London, 1696.
WingL1140; Smith(Anti-Quak)270; McAlpin 4:589-90.

67-329

DA698 L634s   [Leslie, Charles] 1650-1722.
Satan Disrob'd from his Disguise of Light: Or, The Quakers Last Shift To Cover their Monstrous Heresies, Laid Fully Open. In A Reply To Thomas Ellwood's Answer (Published the End of Last Month) To George Keith's Narrative Of The Proceedings at Turners-Hall, June 11, 1696. Which Also may serve for a Reply (as to the main Points of Doctrine) to Geo. Whitehead's Answer

to The Snake in the Grass; to be Published the End of next Month, if this prevent it not. The Second Edition; with some Improvements. By the Author of, The Snake in the Grass. ...
London: Printed for C. Brome, at the Gun, near the West End of St. Paul's; W. Keblewhite, at the Swan, in St. Paul's Church-yard; and H. Hindmarsh, at the Golden-Ball, over-against the Royal-Exchange, in Cornhill, 1698.
6 p.ℓ., 100 p. 21.5cm. 4°
First pub. London, 1697.
Errata, 6th p.ℓ.ʳ.
"Some Gleanings: With Other further Improvements" (p. 68-99); dated at end: Octob. 26. 1696.
Ellwood's An Answer to George Keith's narrative, 1st pub. London, 1696. Whitehead's An Antidote against the venome of the snake in the grass, 1st pub. London, 1697.
Wing L1151; Smith(Anti-Quak)267-268.

11485, 1918

DA698
L634sn
[Leslie, Charles] 1650-1722.
The Snake in the Grass: Or, Satan Transform'd into An Angel of Light, Discovering The Deep and Unsuspected Subtilty which is Couched under the Pretended Simplicity, of many of the Principal Leaders of those People call'd Quakers. The Third Edition. ...
London, Printed for Charles Brome, at the Gun at the West-End of St. Paul's, 1698.
1 p.ℓ., xliv, [8], 168 p., 169-176 numb. ℓ., 177-336, 327-370, [10] p. front. 18.5cm. 8°
Includes revisions new to this ed. First pub. London, 1696.
"Advertisement" p. [1] at end; Leslie wants to buy or borrow various other anti-Quaker books which he cannot find among the booksellers.
Errata, p. [2] at end.
Bookseller's advertisement, p. [3-10] at end.
Bound in contemporary calf, rebacked.
Wing L1158; Sabin 40195; Smith(Anti-Quak.)267.

70-46

D698
L651f
[R]
A Letter From A Gentleman Of The City of New-York To Another, Concerning the Troubles which happen'd in That Province in the Time of the late Happy Revolution.
Printed and Sold by William Bradford at the Sign of the Bible in New-York, 1698.
24 p. 18cm. 4°
Concerns Leisler's Rebellion and contains the letter itself (p. 3-16; dated: New-York, December 31. 1697) and pertinent documents.
The pamphlet revives the case of the Anti-Leislerians, and its authorship was associated by the Earl of Bellomont, then Governor of New York, specifically with Nicholas Bayard. (cf. Documents relative to the colonial history of the state of New-York, v.4, p. 315).
JCB(2)2:1545; Wing L1397; Evans 823; Sabin 40295; Church 776; Hildeburn(NY)6.

0557, 1846

BA698
L729s
Lillo y la Barrera, Nicolás de, d. 1698.
Sermon En La Procession, Y Accion De Gracias Al Glorioso Apostol de la Yndia San Francisco Xavier, por el milagro, q̃ obrõ, dando repentina salud a la hermana Beatriz Rosa de San Francisco Xavier, Religiosa Carmelita Descalça, professa; Predicado en la Cathedral de Santiago, en la Infraoctava de la Concepcion, y fiesta que celebran los Señores Prevendados, en 13. de Diziembre de 1696. Por El M.R.P. Nicolas De Lillo, Y La Barrera de la Cõpañia de Iesus, Cathedratico antes de Artes, y Theologia en la Real Vniversidad, que está en el Colegio de Santiago de Chile, de dicha Compañia, y su perpetuo Canciller, y Decano. Sacalo A Lvz, El Doctor Don Ioachin de Morales Negrete, Cura de la Ciudad de Serena, de Chile, Vicario foraneo, y Iuez ordinario de todos los Curas de aquel partido, Comissario de la Santa Cruzada, y del Santo Oficio de la Inquisicion. ...
Con Licencia Impresso en Lima, por Ioseph de Contreras, y Alvarado, Impressor Real, y del Santo Oficio. Año de 1698.
13 p.ℓ., 10 numb. ℓ. 20cm. 4°
License dated (9th p.ℓ.ᵛ) 5 May 1698.
Preliminary matter includes poetry.
This copy closely trimmed at top with slight loss of text.
Medina(Lima)692; Backer 4:1836.

5517, 1909

D698
L814t
[Locke, John] 1632-1704.
Two Treatises Of Government: In the Former, The False Principles and Foundation Of Sir Robert Filmer, And His Followers, Are Detected and Overthrown. The Latter is an Essay Concerning The True Original, Extent, and End Of Civil-Government.
London: Printed for Awnsham and John Churchill, at the Black Swan in Pater-Noster-Row. 1698.
3 p.ℓ., 358 p. 20cm. 8°
First pub. London, 1690.
In part a reply to Robert Filmer, Patriarcha: or, the natural power of kings, 1st pub. London, 1680.
Errata, 3d. p.ℓ.ʳ.

D698
L945m

Ludlow, Edmund, 1617?-1692
  Memoirs Of Edmund Ludlow Esq; Lieutenant General of the Horse, Commander in Chief of the Forces in Ireland, One of the Council of State, and a Member of the Parliament which began on November 3, 1640. In Two [i.e. three] Volumes. ...
  Switzerland, Printed at Vivay [sic] in the Canton of Bern [i.e. London]. MDCXCVIII [-1699].
  3 v.: v.1, 1 p.ℓ., viii p., 1 ℓ., 430 p. port.; v.2, 1 p.ℓ., 435-878 p.; v.3, 4 p.ℓ., 159, 162-402, [56] p., 1 ℓ. 20cm. 8º
  Thought to have been edited by Isaac Littlebury, perhaps with the collaboration of John Toland on v.3.
  Imprint attributed is: London, John Darby.
  Vol. 2 has half-title page.
  With, as issued, his Memoirs ... the third and last part, Vevay [sic, i.e. London], 1699, with special t.-p., separate paging and signatures.
  Errata, v.1, ℓ. following p. viii; v.3, ℓ. at end.
  Preface, v.3, 2d-4th p.ℓ., dated in Bern, 26 Mar 1699.
  Imperfect: port. (v.1) wanting; v.1, p. 127-128 mutilated; available in facsim.
  WingL3460-3462.
68-352

CA698
M265c

Mamiani della Rovere, Lodovico Vincenzo, 1652-1730.
  Catecismo Da Doutrina Christãa Na Lingua Brasilica Da Nação Kiriri Composto Pelo P. Luis Vincencio Mamiani, Da Companhia de Jesus, Missionario da Provincia do Brasil.
  Lisboa, Na Officina de Miguel Deslandes, Impressor de Sua Magestade. Com todas as licenças necessarias. Anno de 1698.
  16 p.ℓ., 236 p. 14cm. 8º
  Cut (Jesuit monogram, floriated) on t.-p.
  Text in Kariri and Portuguese in parallel columns.
  License dated (14th p.ℓ.ᵛ) 3 July 1698.
  "Cantigas Na Lingua Kiriri Para cantarem os Meninos da Doutrina com a versaõ em versos Castelhanos do mesmo metro." 5thʳ-13thʳ p.ℓ.
  In this copy there is a blank leaf at end.
  Bound in contemporary vellum.
  Sabin44179; Backer5:453; Viñaza240; Borba de Moraes2:13; Innocencio5:334.
12137, 1919

In this copy the leaf bearing p. 39-40 is a cancel. Bound in contemporary calf.
  WingL2768.
456, 1904

BA698
M385m

Martínez de la Parra, Juan, 1655-1701.
  Memoria Agradecida A La Dedicacion Del nuevo sumptuoso retablo del Salvador del mundo, Que le consagró su Ilustrissima Congregacion en la Casa Professa de la Compañia de Jesus de Mexico. ... la dedica El R.P. Jvan Martinez De La Parra de la Compañia de Jesus. Prefecto Eclesiastico de la mesma Congregacion.
  Con licencia en Mexico por Doña Mar:a [sic] de Benavides, Viuda de Juan de Ribera. Año de 1698.
  8 p.ℓ., 7 numb. ℓ., 1 ℓ. 19.5cm. 4º
  Dedication dated (4th p.ℓ.ᵛ) 4 Apr. 1698.
  Medina(Mexico)1698; Backer5:636.
4928, 1908

D.Math
C.153A

Mather, Cotton, 1663-1728.
  A Good Man making a Good End. The Life and Death, of the Reverend Mr. John Baily, Comprised and Expressed In A Sermon, On the Day of his Funeral. Thursday. 16. d.10. m. 1697 By Cotton Mather. ...
  Boston in N. E. Printed by B. Green, and J. Allen, for Michael Perry, at his Shop, under the West End of the Town House. 1698.
  88 p. 14.5cm. 8º
  Errata, at end.
  In this copy p. 87-88 disintegrated with slight loss of text; available in facsimile.
  "... The Character of a Christian" p. 58-88.
  Evans828; WingM1111; Sabin46344; Holmes(C.)153A.
1257, 1906

D.Math
C.302

[Mather, Cotton] 1663-1728.
  [Present] from a farr Countrey, [To The] People of New England. I. A Great Voice from Heaven, to these Parts of the Earth: In an Excellent Letter Full Of Divine Rarities, Lately Written from a Terrible Prison in France ... II. The Golden Bells of the Great High Priest ... Or, Meditations upon the Methods of Grace ...
  Boston, Printed by B. Green, and J. Allen, for Michael Perry, at his Shop, under the West End of the Town-House. 1698.
  53, [1] p. 14.5cm. 8º
  Includes a translation by Nehemiah Walter of an account of the persecution of French Protestants by Elie Néau (p. [13]-21) with an introduction in French by Cotton Mather (p. 10-12).
  Holmes in reconstructing this book for his entry Holmes(C.)302 from this imperfect copy erred in thinking that a French version of Néau's account was also included.
  "A Brief Discourse, Made unto the Great

and General Assembly of the Province of the Massachusetts Bay, New England, 21 d. 8 m. 1697"; p. 22-53.
Erratum, p. 53.
Booksellers' advertisement (dated 1697), last page.
Imperfect: p. 1-22 wanting; available in facsim.
Words in title within brackets are reconstructed from facsimile of American Antiquarian Society copy, title-page of which is disintegrated.
Bound in contemporary sheep, rebacked with vellum.
Holmes(C.)302; Brinley 1120 (this copy).
06876, before 1911

D. Math   Mather, Increase, 1639-1723.
I. 25   David Serving His Generation. Or, A Sermon Shewing What is to be done in order to our so Serving our Generation, as that when we Dy, we shall Enter into a Blessed Rest. (Wherein Some account is given concerning many Eminent Ministers of Christ at London, as well as in N. E. lately gone to their Rest.) Occasioned by the Death, of the Reverend Mr. John Baily, Who Deceased at Boston in New-England. December 12th. 1697. By Increase Mather, President of Harvard Colledge. ...
Boston, Printed by B. Green, & J. Allen. 1698
39 p. 15cm. 8°
JCB(2)2:1543; Evans 831; Wing M1195; Sabin 46649; Holmes(I.)25.
03703, 1846?

D. Math   Mather, Nathaniel, 1631-1697.
M. 22A   A Discussion Of the Lawfulness of a Pastor's Acting as an Officer In Other Churches Besides that which he is specially Called to take the Oversight of. By the late Reverend Mr. Nathanael Mather.
London: Printed for Nath. Hiller at the Princes Arms in Leaden-Hall Street, over against St. Mary Ax, M DC XCVIII.
10 p.ℓ., 155, [1] p. 14cm. 12°
Booksellers' advertisement at end.
Bound in contemporary calf.
Wing M1263; Holmes(M.)22A; Sabin 46771; Dexter(Cong.)2484.
4573, 1908

BA698   Matías de San Juan Bautista, d. 1724.
M433c   Compendio De Las Maravillas De La Gracia. Discurrido en elogios de N.P.S. Francisco Por el R. P. Fray Mathias de S. Juan Bautista, Carmelita Descalzo, Lector de Philosophia, y Theologia, Prior que fue del Convento de la Ciudad de Valladolid, y actual del Convento de la Ciudad de Queretaro. En la solemnissima fiesta que celebrò este presente año de 1697. El muy Ilustre Convento, Parrochia, y Collegio de Nuestro Padre San Francisco de la Ciudad de Selaya. ...
Con Licencia De Los Superiores. En Mexico por Doña Maria de Benavides, Viuda de Juan de Ribera, En el Empedradillo Año de 1698.
11 p.ℓ., 13 numb. ℓ. 20.5cm. 4°
License dated (11th p.ℓ.ᵛ) 8 Jan. 1698.
Sabin 76134; Medina(Mexico)1713; Palau(2) 292578.
70-154

B698   [Meulen, Jean van der] 1642-ca. 1717.
-M597s   Señor. En virtud del caracter que V. M. se ha servido darme de Consejero Fiscal deste Supremo Almirantazgo ...
[Madrid, 1698]
[3] p. 29.5cm. fol.
Title from caption and beginning of text.
Signed: Bruselas 25. de Julio 1698. J. Vander Meulen.
Concerns commerce illegally conducted by the Dutch with Spanish territories in America.
69-542

B698   Montauban, ----de, 1650?-1700.
C334r   Relation Du Voyage Du Sieur De Montauban Capitaine Des Filbustiers en Guinée, en l'Année 1695. Avec une Description du Roïaume du Cap de Lopez, des mœurs, des coûtumes, de la & [sic] Religion du Païs.
A Amsterdam, Chez J. Louis De Lorme Libraire sur le Rockin. M. DC XCVIII.
1 p.ℓ., [3], 364-402, [2] p. 17cm. 12°
(Issued as a part of Casas, Bartolomé de las. Relation des voyages, Amsterdam, 1698.)
Cut on t.-p.
Colophon (p. 402): A Amsterdam, De l'Imprimerie de Daniel Boulesteys De La Contie, dans l'Eland-straat. M. D. XCVIII [sic].
"Lettre A Monsieur***." (p. [1-3]) signed: B**.
Bookseller's advertisement, [2] p. at end.
In this copy there is a blank leaf at end.
JCB(2)2:1527; Sabin 11274; Eeghen II45.
01936, 1854

E698 Montauban, ---- de, 1650?-1700.
A172o A Relation Of A Voyage Made by the Sieur de Montauban, Captain of the French Privateers, On The Coasts of Guinea, In the Year 1695. With A Description of the Kingdom of Cape de Lopez; and an Account of the Manners, Customs and Religion of the Natives of that Country.
London: Printed in the Year 1698.
44 p. 17.5cm. 8º (Issued as a part of An account of Monsieur de la Salle's last expedition, London, 1698.)
Transl. from: Relation du voyage du sieur de Montauban, Amsterdam, 1698. Another English transl. appeared London, the same year, issued as a part of Raveneau de Lussan, A journal of a voyage.
JCB(2)2:1542; WingT1890; Sabin96171.
05721A, 1881

BA698 Narvaez, Juan de, ca. 1650-1706.
N238s Sermon Fvnebre, Manifiesto Dolor De La Sancta Yglesia Metropolitana de Mexico, en las Exequias de el Illustrissimo, y Reverendissimo Señor Doctor, y Maestro Don Francisco De Agviar, Y Seixas su dignissimo Arçobispo, celebradas presente el Excellentissimo Señor D. Ioseph Sarmiento De Valladares, Conde de Moctezuma, Virrey Governador, y Capitan General de esta Nueva-España, la Real Audiencia, y todos los demas Tribunales de esta Corte. Predicado Por el D.or D. Juan de Narvaez Cathedratico Proprietario de Sagrada Escriptura en esta Real Vniversidad, Rector que ha sido en ella dos vezes, Racionero entero de esta Sancta Yglesia Metropolitana, Examinador Synodal, y Vicario Visitador de los Conventos de Regina Cœli, y Sancta Ynes. ...
Con licencia: en Mexico, por los Herederos de la Viuda de Francisco Rodriguez Lupercio, en la puente de Palacio. Año de 1698.
16 p.ℓ., 16 numb. ℓ. 20.5cm. 4º
"Parecer" dated (8th p.ℓ.r) 5 Oct. 1698.
Preliminary matter includes poetry by Pedro Ramírez, José López de Aviles, Pedro Muñoz de Castro, Nicolás Altamirano, and Miguel de Contreras Pacheco.
Palau(2)187727; Medina(Mexico)1703.
6550, 1910

D698 The New Atlas: Or, Travels and Voyages In Europe, Asia, Africa and America, Thro' the most Renowned Parts of the World ... Performed by an English Gentleman, in Nine Years Travel and Voyages, more exact than Ever.
London, Printed for J. Cleave in Chanchery-Lane near Serjeant's Inn, and A. Roper at the Black Boy in Fleet-street, 1698.
4 p.ℓ., 236 p. 18.5cm. 8º
Preface signed (4th p.ℓ.v) T. C.
Compiled from various works; chapters 22-25 (p. 193-236) concerning America are adapted from Thomas Gage's The English-American his travail by sea and land ... , 1st pub. London, 1648.
Bound in contemporary calf, rebacked.
WingC139; Sabin52454.
11648, 1918

DA698 Noyes, Nicholas, 1647-1717.
N952n New-Englands Duty and Interest, To be an Habitation of Justice, And Mountain of Holiness. Containing Doctrine, Caution & Comfort With Something relating to the Restaurations, Reformations and Benedictions, Promised to the Church and World in the latter dayes; With grounds of Hope, that America in General, & New-England in Particular, may have a Part therein. Preached to the General Assembly of the Province of the Massachusetts-Bay, at the Anniversary Election. May, 25. 1698. By Nicholas Noyes, Teacher of the Church at Salem.
Published by Order of Authority. Boston in New-England. Printed by Bartholomew Green, and John Allen. Printers to the Governour & Council. 1698.
6 p.ℓ., 99 p. 14cm. 8º
Dedication (2d-6th p.ℓ.) signed: Salem, June 20. 1698. John Higginson. ...
"Typographus Lectori" p. 89-99, an account of Grindall Rawson's and Samuel Danforth's "visiting the several Plantations of the Indians, within this Province" in 1698; signed at end in Boston, 12 July 1698.
In this copy outer margins p. 65-66 closely trimmed with slight loss of text.
Brinley 833 (this copy).

DA698 ---- ----Another copy. 16cm.
N952n Imperfect: p. 95-99 wanting; supplied in
cop.2 pen and ink facsim.
JCB(2)2:1546; Evans850; WingN1461; Sabin 56229; Church777; Dexter(Cong.)2483.
06155, before 1882
06156, after 1882

D696 Payne, Henry Neville, fl. 1672-1710.
-C737c Unto His Grace, The Earl Of Marchmont Lord High Commissioner Of Scotland And the Right Honourable Estates Of Parliament

The Petition of Henry Payne, Humbly Sheweth, That ...
   [Edinburgh, 1698]
   1 numb. ℓ. 31.5cm. fol.
   Title from caption and beginning of text.
   Bound in a volume of Scottish imprints and mss. as the 20th of 58 items.

7118, 1910

B698 P397i   Peña Montenegro, Alonso de la, bp., d. 1688.
   Itinerario Para Parochos De Indios, En Que Se Tratan Las Materias mas particulares, tocantes á ellos, para su buena Administracion: Compuesto Por El Ilustrissimo, Y Reverendissimo Señor Doctor Don Alonso De La Peña Montenegro, Obispo Del Obispado De San Francisco Del Quito, del Consejo de su Magestad, Colegial que fue del Colegio mayor de la Universidad de Santiago, &c. Nueva Edicion Purgada De Muchos Yerros.
   En Amberes. Por Henrico y Cornelio Verdussen. Año M.DC.XCVIII. Con Licencia.
   28 p.ℓ., 328, 325-697, [698-784] p. 20.5cm. 4°
   Title in red and black.
   Cut on t.-p., incl. motto: Concordiæ Frvctvs.
   Approbation dated (last p.) 28 Mar. 1698.
   First pub. Madrid, 1668.
   Bound in contemporary calf.
   JCB(2)2:1544; Medina(BHA)1986; Sabin59624; Palau(2)217534; Peeters-Fontainas(1965)672.

01940, 1861

D698 P412c   [Penn, William] 1644-1718.
   Caution Humbly Offer'd About Passing the Bill against Blasphemy.
   [London, 1698]
   7 p. 18.5cm. 4°.
   Caption title.
   Refers to a bill for "the more effectual suppressing blasphemy and profaneness" which was read for the first time in the House of Commons 7 Mar. 1697/8.
   Smith(Friends)2:317; WingP1264.

11519, 1918

DA698 P412d   Penn, William, 1644-1718.
   A Defence Of a Paper, Entituled, Gospel-Truths, Against the Exceptions Of The Bishop of Cork's Testimony. By W. Penn.
   London, Printed and Sold by T. Sowle, in White-Hart-Court, in Gracious-Street, and at the Bible in Leaden-Hall-Street, 1698.
   3 p.ℓ., 119 p. 16cm. 8°.
   "Preface" (2d-3d p.ℓ.) signed: Bristol, the 23d of the 7th Month, 1698. W. Penn.
   Includes the text of "Gospel-Truths" (p. 1-5), which is signed "Dublin, 4th of the 3d Month, 1698. William Penn [and three others]", and the reply ("Testimony") of Edward Wetenhall, bp. of Cork (p. 6-18), which is signed "Cork, July the 2d. 1698. Edw. Cork and Ross." Smith lists the form of these texts previous to this printing as: for "Gospel-Truths", a folio edition [n.p., 1698] (Friends 2:317); for Wetenhall's "Testimony", a ms. (Anti-Quaker 449).
   Bound in contemporary calf.
   Smith(Friends)2:317; Smith(Anti-Quaker) 449; McAlpin4:593; Sabin59691; WingP1273.

11517, 1918

DA698 P412q   [Penn, William] 1644-1718.
   The Quaker A Christian, Being An Answer To John Plimpton's Dis-Ingenuous Paper, Entituled, A Quaker No Christian. ...
   Dublin, Printed in the Year 1698.
   16 p. 20cm. 4°.
   Signed (p. 16): Subscribed the 18th of the Third Month, 1698. in behalf of our Selves and Friends, by William Penn. John Everet. Thomas Story.
   A reply to Plimpton's Quakerism. The Mystery of Iniquity Discovered. Dublin, 1698.
   Smith(Friends)2:317; WingP1346; Sabin59726.

11520, 1918

E698 P753r   Perrault, Charles, 1628-1703.
   Les Hommes Illustres Qui Ont Paru En France Pendant Ce Siecle. Augmenté des Eloges de Messieurs Arnauld & Pascal. Par Mr. Perrault, de l'Academie Françoise.
   [The Hague?] Suivant la copie imprimée A Paris. Chez Antoine Dezallier ruë Saint Jacques, 1698.
   6 p.ℓ., 25-240, [5] p. 16cm. 12°
   Cut (putto) on t.-p.
   First pub. Paris, 1696.
   In this copy there are 3 blank ℓ. at end.
   Bound in contemporary calf with: [Pointis, J.B. L.D.] Relation de l'expedition de Cathagene, Amsterdam, 1698.

10596, 1915

bBB P4716 1698 1   Peru(Viceroyalty)--Laws, statutes, etc., 1689-1705 (Portocarrero)   11 Nov 1698
   Don Melchor Portocarrero, Laso De La Vega Conde De La Monclova, ... Por quanto su Magestad, (que Dios guarde) con Despacho de veinte, y seis de Noviembre del año passado de

mil seiscientos noventa, y siete, me ha remitido los Tratados de la Paz General, q̃ se ha establecido entre los Dominios de su Real Corona, y la del Rey Christianissimo de Francia, y se ajustaron en Risvvit, Provincia de Olanda en veinte de Septiembre de dicho año, ... siendo lo mas principal de las Capitulaciones lo siguiente. ...
 [Lima, 1698]
 [3] p. 31.5 x 21.5cm. fol.
 Title from caption and beginning of text.
 Dated in Lima 11 Nov 1698.
 Signed in ms: Monclova.
 Manuscript certification of the city of Huamanga dated 10 Dec 1698.
 Papel sellado variously dated 1694-1699.
28207, 1938

DA698 Philadelphian Society.
P544u Ursachen und Gründe Welche hauptsächlich Anlass gegeben / Die Philadelphische Societät aufzurichten und zu befördern; So wol auch Aus denenselben ausgezogne / und in Heiliger Schrifft gegründete Propositiones. Und denn endlich Der zustand und Beschaffenheit dieser Societät: oder Die Gründe / worauf sie stehet / pro und contrà genauer betrachtet / und zu Abwendung aller Missverständnüssen öffentlich an Tag gegeben. Nunmehro Aus dem Englischen übergesetzt und zum Drucke befördert.
 Amsterdam in Jahre 1698.
 64 p. 16.5cm. 8º
 Cut on t.-p.
 English originals taken from its Theosophical transactions, London, 1697, and [Lee, Francis] The state of the Philadelphian Society, London, 1697.
 With special t.-p. for Propositiones, ausgezogen aus denen Ursachen... (p. 7) and for Der Philadelphischen Societät Zustand und Beschaffenheit ... (p. 17).
 Booksellers' advertisements, p. 16 and 64.
06167, before 1874

E698 Pointis, Jean Bernard Louis Desjean, baron de,
P753a 1645-1707.
 An Account Of the Taking of Carthagena By The French, In the Year 1697. Containing all the Particulars of that Expedition, from their first setting out, to their return into Brest. By Monsieur De Pointis, Commander in Chief. Illustrated with a large Copper Plate, Describing the Situation of Carthagena and Parts adjacent.
 London: Printed for Sam. Buckley, at the Dolphin over-against St. Dunstan's Church, in Fleet-Street. 1698.
 4 p.ℓ., 134, [2] p. fold. map. 19.5cm. 8º
 Transl. from Relation de l'expedition de Carthagene, Amsterdam, 1698.
 "Books Printed for Sam. Buckley..." ([2] p. at end).
 JCB(2)2:1547; Sabin63702; WingP2742; Cundall (WI)1995.
01945, 1854

E698 [Pointis, Jean Bernard Louis Desjean, baron de]
P753r 1645-1707.
 Relation De L'Expedition De Carthagene, Faite par les François en M.DC.XCVII.
 A Amsterdam, Chez les Héritiers D'Antoine Schelte. M.DC.XCVIII.
 4 p.ℓ., 143 p. 2 fold. maps. 16cm. 12º
 Cut (printer's device) on t.-p.; incl. motto: Qværendo.
 Erratum, 4th p.ℓ.ᵛ
 With this is bound in contemporary calf: Perrault, Charles. Les hommes illustres, [The Hague?], 1698.
 Sabin63700; Leclerc(1867)1187; Cundall (WI)1995.
10595, 1915

+Z Ptolemaeus, Claudius
=P975 Claudii Ptolemaei Tabulae geographicae
1698 Orbis Terrarum Veteribus cogniti.
 Trajecti ad Rhenum, Apud < Franciscum Halmam, Guiljelmum vande Water, > Bibliop. Et Franequeræ, Apud Leonardum Strick, Bibliop. MDCXCVIII.
 2 p.ℓ., 28 double-page maps. 40.5cm. fol.
 Engr. half-title, 1st p.ℓ., signed: J. V. Vianen fecit.
 Imprint from colophon, 2d p.ℓ.ᵛ
 Gerardus Mercator's maps to Ptolemaeus' Geographia (without descriptive text).
 These maps 1st pub. Cologne, 1578; maps printed from the same plates as used for the Franeker/Utrecht, 1695, edition.
 Sabin66498n; Phillips(Atlases)526; Koeman

Contents:
[1] Vniversalis Tabvla Ivxta Ptolemæum.
[2] Tab.I. Africæ, in qua Mauritania Tingitana et Cæsariensis. ...
[3] Tab.II. Africæ, Complectens Africam Proprie dictam. ...
[4] Tab.III. Africæ, in qua Cyrenaica, Marmarica, ac Lybia Exterior. ...
[5] Appendix Tab.III. Africæ, Ægyptum Inferiorem Exhibens. ...

1698

[6] Tab. IV. Africæ, in qua Libya Interior et Exterior. Æthiopia ...
[7] Tab. I. Asiæ, in qua Galatia, Cappadocia, Pontus, Bithynia, Asia Minor, Pamphylia, Lycia, ac Cilicia ...
[8] Tab. II. Asiæ, Sarmatiam Asiaticam repræsentans ...
[9] Tab. III. Asiæ, in qua Colchis, Iberia, Albania, ac Armenia Maior. ...
[10] Tab. IV. Asiæ, in qua Mesopotamia, Syria, Arabia Petrea, ac Deserta. ...
[11] Tab. V. Asiæ, Repræsentans Mediam, Hyrcaniam, Assyriam, Susianam, ac Persidem. ...
[12] Tab. VI. Asiæ, Arabiam Felicem, Carmaniam ac Sinum Persicum ...
[13] Tab. VII. Asiæ, exhibens Scythiam, intra Imaum Sogdianam, Bactrianam, Hircaniam, aliasq Asiæ Regiones ...
[14] Tab. VIII. Asiæ, Scythiam extra imaum, ac Sericam comprehendens ...
[15] Tab. IX. Asiæ, Continens Ariam, Paropanisum, Drangianam, Arachosiam, et Gedrosiam. ...
[16] Tab. X. Asiæ, Complectens Indiam intra Gangem. ...
[17] Tab. XI. Asiæ, comprehendens Indiam extra Gangem. ...
[18] Tab. XII. Asiæ, Taprobanam repræsentans. ...
[19] Tab. I. Europæ, Continens Albion, Britanniam, et Hiberniam. ...
[20] Tab. II. Europæ, Hispaniam ac Lusitaniam Complectens. ...
[21] Tab. III. Europæ, Galliam, Belgicam, ac Germaniæ, partem repræsentens. ...
[22] Tab. IV. Europæ, Germaniam et Galliam Belgicam exhibens. ...
[23] Tab. V. Europæ, in qua Rætia, Pannonia, Noricum, Liburnia, Dalmatia, Cum Italiæ parte. ...
[24] Tab. VI. Europæ, totam Italiam ob oculos ponens ...
[25] Tab. VII. Europæ, Complectens Sardiniam, Siciliam, ac Corsicæ, partem ...
[26] Tab. VIII. Europæ, in qua Sarmatia, Mæotis palus, ac Germaniæ, Daciæq pars. ...
[27] Tab. IX. Europæ, Continens Daciam, Misiam, Thraciam, ac Macedoniæ partem. ...
[28] Tab. X. Europæ, Macedoniam, Epirum ac Peloponnesum repræsentans ...

06912, between 1915 and 1917

BA698
R173v

Ramírez, José.
Via Lactea, Seu Vita Candidissima S. Philippi Nerii Presbyteri, cunctis olim cœlestem pandens viam: Nunc pulchrioribus Sacrorum Bibliorum stellulis, noviter Orbi illucescens SS. D. N. per Innocentio XI. P. O. M. Dictatum Opus, per Doct. Iosephum Ramirez, Valent. Metrop. Ecclesiæ, & S. Salvatoris Prebs. nec non vtriusque Parentis addictissimum filium. Denuo Progreditur. Vt Hunc Novum Orbem Illuminet, atque clarificet, transcripta [sic], ac prælo mandata, cura, solicitudine ac studio Doct. Ioannis De La Pedrosa, Presb. Præpositi Congregationis Oratorij eiusdem S. Philippi Mexicanæ. ...

Mexici: Ex Officina Dominæ Mariæ de Benavides. Anno 1698.
19 p. ℓ., 222, [12] p. front., pl. 20.5cm. 4°
First pub. Valencia, 1678.
License dated (16th p. ℓ.ʳ) 14 Oct. 1697.
Errata, p. [11-12] at end.
In this copy there is a blank leaf at beginning and at end.
Palau(2)216283, 246730-III; Medina(Mexico) 1705; Sabin59523, 67647.

11811, 1919

D699
H673o

Raveneau de Lussan, ——, b. 1663.
A Journal Of A Voyage Made Into The South Sea, By The Bucaniers or Freebooters Of America; From the Year 1684 to 1689. Written by the Sieur Raveneau de Lussan. To which is Added, The Voyage of the Sieur De Montauban, Captain of the Freebooters on the Coast of Guiney, in the Year 1695.

London: Printed for Tho. Newborough at the Golden Ball in St. Paul's Church-yard, John Nicholson at the King's Arms in Little Britain, and Benj. Tooke at the Temple-Gate near Temple-Bar. 1698.
2 p. ℓ., 204 p. 20cm. 8° (Issued as a part of The History of the bucaniers of America, London, 1699.)
Raveneau de Lussan's account transl. from: Journal du voyage fait à la mer de sud, 1st pub. Paris, 1689 (transl. probably from Paris editions of 1693 or 1699).
Montauban's account transl. from: Relation du voyage du sieur de Montauban, Amsterdam, 1698. Another English transl. issued London, 1698, as a part of An account of Monsieur de la Salle's last expedition.
WingR322; Sabin67986.

29757A, 1945

E698
R382d

Relation De Ce Qui S'est Fait A La Prise De Cartagene, Sçituée Aux Indes Espagnoles, Par L'Escadre Commandée Par Mr. De Pointis.
A Bruxelles, Chez Jean Fricx, Imp. & Mar-

[376]

chand Libraire. M. DC. XCVIII.
1 p.ℓ., 141 p. 16.5cm. 12⁰
Cut on t.-p.
Not the same as Pointis, J.B.L.D., Relation de l'expedition de Carthagene.
JCB(2)2:1548; Sabin63701; Leclerc(1878)1490.

03702, before 1866

E698
D358v
Rennefort, Urbain Souchu de, ca. 1630-ca. 1689.
A Supplement To The Sieur Dellone's Relation of his Voyage To The East-Indies. Taken out of the Sieur De Rennefort's History of the East-Indies. Containing A short Account of the Isle of St. Helens; Of the Isle of Teneriffe; Of the Isle of Ceylon; Of the Cape of Good-Hope; The Isle of Madagascar: And some other Matters, having a near Relation to the former Treatise.
London, Printed for A. Roper, at the Black-Boy, over against St. Dunstan's Church, Fleet-street, and D. Brown, at the Black-Swan and Bible, without Temple-Bar. 1698.
43 p. 19.5cm. 8⁰ (Issued as a part of Dellon's Voyage to the East-Indies, London, 1698).
Abridged transl. by Jodocus Crull from Histoire des Indes orientales, 1st pub. Paris, 1688.

62-231B

BA698
-S565c
Sicardo, José, 1643-1715.
Christiandad Del Japon, Y Dilatada Persecvcion Qve Padecio. Memorias Sacras, De Los Martyres De Las Ilvstres Religiones de Santo Domingo, San Francisco, Compañia de Jesvs; y crecido numero de Seglares: Y con especialidad, de los Religiosos del Orden de N.P.S. Augustin. Sv Avtor, El P.M. Fr. Joseph Sicardo, De Dicha Orden, Doctor en Theologia, por la Real Vniversidad de Mexico, Examinador Synodal, y Visitador del Obispado de Michoacan, Maestro de las Provincias de Castilla, y Mexico, Theologo, y Examinador del Tribunal de la Nunciatura de España, y Predicador de su Mag. ...
Año de 1698. Con Privilegio: En Madrid: Por Francisco Sanz, Impressor del Reyno, y Portero de Camara de su Magestad.
8 p.ℓ., 322, 321-448, [13] p. 28.5cm. fol.
"Tassa" dated (8th p.ℓ.ʳ) 14 June 1698.
Errata, 7th p.ℓ.ᵛ
Bound in contemporary vellum.
Palau(2)31 2228; Medina(BHA)1991; Sabin 80832; Streit 5:1616; Santiago Vela 7:497-498; Backer 11:1301; Retana 178.

69-48

bD698
S897o
A State of the Present Condition Of The Island of Barbadoes: With Some Reasons, Why there ought not to be any more Duties or Imposts laid on Sugars than what already are; shewing, that they pay full as much as thy [sic] can bear, and that they who make that Manufactory, pay more in proportion, than any other of His Majesty's Subjects. By a Merchant, Trading to the West-Indies.
London: Printed for Tho. Northcott in George-Yard in Lombart-street. [1698?]
4 p. 36.5cm. fol.
Caption title; imprint at end.
A reply to A Discourse of the duties on merchandize, London, 1695.

32340, 1959

DA698
S887w
[Story, Thomas] 1662-1742.
A Word to the Well-Inclin'd Of All Perswasions. Together with A Coppy of a Letter from William Penn to George Keith, upon his Arbitrary Summons and Unjust Proceedings, at Turners-Hall, against the People Called Quakers.
London, Printed and Sold by T. Sowle, next Door to the Meeting-House in White-Hart-Court in Gracious-Street, and at the Bible in Leaden-Hall-Street, near the Market, 1698.
8 p. 18.5cm. 4⁰
Caption title; imprint at end.
"A Word to the Well-Inclin'd ... Signed on the Behalf of those Concern'd, by T. Story" (p. 1-5) first pub. under title: Word to the wise, London, 1697.
"A Copy of a Letter from William Penn. Bristol, the 16th of the 2d Month, 1698" (p. 6-8).
Smith(Friends)2:636; 2:317; WingS7577; Sabin92330.

11518, 1918

D698
T456h
[R]
Thomas, Gabriel, fl. 1682-1698.
An Historical and Geographical Account Of The Province and Country Of Pensilvania; And Of West-New-Jersey In America. ... also a Touch upon George Keith's New Religion, in his second Change since he left the Quakers With a Map of both Countries. By Gabriel Thomas, who resided there about Fifteen Years.
London, Printed for, and Sold by A. Baldwin, at the Oxon Arms in Warwick-Lane 1698.
4 p.ℓ., 55 p., 6 ℓ., 34 p. fold. map. 16.5cm. 8⁰
With, as issued, his An Historical Description Of The Province and Country Of West-New-Jersey, London, 1698, with special t.-p. and separate

paging but continuous signatures.
Specimens of the Delaware language: p. 47, 1st count, and p. 8-13, 2d count.
In this copy there is a blank leaf at end; t.-p. closely trimmed at bottom, affecting imprint.
JCB(2)2:1550, 1551; WingT964; Sabin95395; Church778; Vail(Front.)280; Pilling3847, 3848; Smith(Friends)2:733; Baer(Md.)188.
0811, 1846

D698 T456h [R] Thomas, Gabriel, fl. 1682-1698.
An Historical Description Of The Province and Country Of West-New-Jersey In America. ... Never made Publick till now. By Gabriel Thomas.
London: Printed in the Year 1698.
6 p.ℓ., 34 p. 16.5cm. 8° (Issued as a part of his An historical and geographical account of the province and country of Pensilvania. London, 1698.)
Specimen of the Delaware language: p. 8-13.
In this copy there is a blank leaf at end.
JCB(2)2:1551; WingT964; Sabin95395; Church 778; Vail(Front.)280; Pilling3848; Smith(Friends) 2:733; Baer(Md.)188.
0811A, 1846

D698 T875s [Tryon, Thomas] 1634-1703.
Some General Considerations Offered, Relating to our present Trade. And intended For its Help and Improvement. By T. T. Merchant.
London, Printed for J. Harris, at the Harrow in Little-Britain, 1698.
2 p.ℓ., 26, [2] p. 21cm. 4°
Bookseller's advertisement, p. [1-2] at end.
Errata slip pasted at bottom of last page.
WingT63, T3195; Kress2101.
71-370

BA698 -V458c Venezuela (Diocese)--Synod, 1687.
Constituciones Synodales, del Obispado de Veneçuela, y Santiago de Leon de Caracas. Hechas En La Santa Iglesia Cathedral De Dicha Ciudad de Caracas, en el Año del Señor de 1687. Por El Ilvstrissimo, Y Reverendissimo señor Doctor Don Diego de Baños, y Sotomayor, Obispo del dicho Obispado, del Consejo de su Magestad, su Predicador, y Capellàn de Honor, &c. Y Aprobadas Por La Magestad del señor Rey Don Carlos Segundo. Año de 1698.
Con Licencia: Impressas en Madrid: En la Imprenta del Reyno, de Don Lucas Antonio de Bedmar, y Narvaez, en la Calle de los Preciados. [1698]
8 p.ℓ., 474 p. front. 31cm. fol.
Certificate at end dated in Madrid, 17 June 1698; place, day and month completed in ms.
Errata, 2d p.ℓ.
Imperfect: 3d-5th p.ℓ. wanting; available in facsim.
With this is bound an index in contemporary ms., [41] p. at end.
JCB(2)2:1524; Palau(2)23439, 60336; Medina (BHA) 7869; Sabin3221; Streit 2:2343.
01937, 1854

B698 V483r Verdadera Relacion, Y Cvrioso Romance, en que dà quenta, y declara las fatalidades q passò la Flota, desde la Vera, hasta que llegò à la Ciudad de Cadiz, y de los maravillosos milagros que obrò N. Señora del Rosario con el Almiranta, y Capitana por diferentes vezes, este año de 1698.
[Cadiz? 1698]
[4] p. 19.5cm. 4°
Caption title.
Poem in double columns.
Sabin98946.
13498, 1923

B698 -V585t [R] Vetancurt, Agustín de, 1620-1700.
Teatro Mexicano Descripcion Breve De Los Svcessos Exemplares, Historicos, Politicos, Militares, y Religiosos del nuevo mundo Occidental de las Indias, ... Dispvesto Por El R.P. Fr. Avgvstin De Vetancvrt, Mexicano, hijo de la misma Provincia, Difinidor actual, Ex-Lector de Theologia, Predicador Jubilado General, y su Chronista Apostolico, Vicario, y Cura Ministro, por su Magestad, de la Iglesia Parrochial de S. Joseph de los Naturales de Mexico.
Con Licencia De Los Svperiores. Ex Mexico por Doña Maria de Benavides Viuda de Iuan de Ribera. Año de 1698 [,1697].
2v.: 6 p.ℓ., 66, 168, [2], 56 p.; 6 p.ℓ., 136, [2] p., 1 ℓ., 156 p. 28.5cm. fol.
Vol. 2 issued under title: Chronica de la Provincia del Santo Evangelio de Mexico; quarta parte del Teatro Mexicano, Mexico, 1697.
License (same in both volumes) dated (v.1, 5th p.ℓ.ᵛ; v.2, 6th p.ℓ.ᵛ) 18 June 1696.
Errata, v.1: 5th p.ℓ.ᵛ, v.2: 6th p.ℓ.ᵛ.
Contents:--v.1--pte.1. Historia de los sucessos exemplares del nuevo mundo en la Nueva-España (p. 1-66),--pte 2. De los sucessos politicos (p. 1-100, 2d count).--

pte. 3. Sucesos militares (p.101-168, 2d count). --Tratado de la ciudad de Mexico; Tratado de la ciudad de la Puebla de los Angeles (p. 1-56, 3d count). --v. 2. --Chronica de la Provincia del Santo Evangelico de Mexico (p. 1-136, [2]). --Menologio Franciscano de los varones mas señalados (1 ℓ., p. 1-156, 2d count).
In this copy there is another copy of the Tratados bound into v. 2.
JCB(2)2:1552; Palau(1)7:163; Medina(Mexico) 1716, 1684; Sabin99388; Wagner70, 68.

01938, 1854
01939, 1854

B698 Victoria, Pedro Gobeo de, 1560?-1630?
V645j Joannis Bisselii è Societate Jesu, Argonauticon Americanorum, Sive Historiæ Periculorum Petri De Victoria Ac Sociorum Ejus. Libri XV. Gedani, Prostant apud Ægidium Janssonii à Waesberge. M. D. C. LXXXXVIII.
17 p. ℓ., 405, [406-420] p. front. (map). 13.5cm. 12°
Added t. -p., engraved.
Cut on t. -p.
Spanish original 1st pub. under title: Naufragio y peregrinacion de Pedro Gobeo de Vitoria, Seville, 1610.
This Latin transl., by Johannes Bissel, taken from German transl. pub. under title: Wunderbarliche und seltzame Raiss dess Iungen und Edlen Herrn Petri de Victoria, Ingolstadt, 1622.
Latin transl. 1st pub. Munich, 1647.
Translator's dedication dated (9th p. ℓ.^{v}): Monachii 3. Non. Maji [1647?].
"Le titre porte Dantzig, mais le nom de Janssonius a Waesberge prouve que le livre a été imprimé à Amsterdam" (Backer). But Gilles Janssonius van Waesberge fl. 1679-1706 as bookseller in Dantzig (Eeghen IV 153-154). Probably printed in Amsterdam for sale in Dantzig.
JCB(2)2:1525; Palau(2)102964; Medina(BHA) 1993; Sabin99444; Backer1:1515; Borba de Moraes1:94.

02315, 1851

B698 Voyages And Discoveries In South-America.
V975a The First up the River of Amazons to Quito in Peru, and back again to Brazil, perform'd at the Command of the King of Spain. By Christopher D'Acugna. The Second up the River of Plata, and thence by Land to the Mines of Potosi. By Mons. Acarete. The Third from Cayenne into Guiana, in search of the Lake of Parima, reputed the richest Place in the World. By M. Grillet and Bechamel. Done into English from the Originals, being the only Accounts of those Parts hitherto extant. The whole illustrated with Notes and Maps.
London, Printed for S. Buckley at the Dolphin over against St. Dunstan's Church in Fleetstreet. 1698.
viii, 176, 169-190 p., 1 ℓ., 79 p., 1 ℓ., [2], 68 p. 2 fold. maps. 19cm. 8°
An "Advertisement" (verso of t.-p.) reports the latest events in Cayenne.
Acuña's A Relation of the Great River of Amazons in South-America (p. 1-190, 1st count), an account of the expeditions under Pedro Teixeira, transl. from: Nuevo Descvbrimiento Del Gran Rio De Las Amazonas. Madrid, 1641. Enlarged by "A Computation of the Longitudes, Latitudes, and Distances of Places upon this Great River", (p. 183-190, 1st count.)
With, as issued, Acarete du Biscay's An Account Of A Voyage... and Jean Grillet's A Journal Of The Travels..., each with special t.-p. and separate pagings, but continuous signatures.
JCB(2)2:1523; WingV746; Palau(2)2487; Sabin 152; Borba de Moraes 1:12; Backer1:40; Streit 2:2328.

01932, 1854

D698 Waller, William, fl. 1698-1714.
W198e An Essay On The Value of the Mines, Late Of Sir Carbery Price. By William Waller, Gent. Steward of the said Mines. Writ for the private Satisfaction of all the Partners.
London: Printed in the Year, M DC XC VIII.
12 p. ℓ., 55 p. 2 fold. plans. 17.5cm. 8°
"A Description of the Mine of Potozi." (p. 10-14).
Bound in contemporary calf.
Wing W552A; Sabin101116; Kress2102.

32150, 1958

DA698 [Young, Samuel] fl. 1697.
Y76a An Apology For Congregational Divines: Against the charge of, 1. Crispianism, or Antinomianism. 2. Countenancing Incompetent Tradesmen, as Preachers. 3. Causeless Separation from the Publick Worship. Under which Head are Published Amicable Letters between the Author and a Conformist (a Man of Renown, known e[very]where to be such) about Liturgies and Ceremonies. By a Presbyterian. Also a Speech delivered at Turners-Hall, April 29. Where Mr. Keith, a Reformed Quaker, with the leave of the Lord Mayor and Bishop, required Mr. Penn, Mr. Elwood, &c. To Appear to An-

swer his Charge against them. By Trepidantium Malleus. ...
London, Printed for John Harris, at the Harrow in little Britain. 1698.
95, 95-190, 167-190 p. 15cm. 12º
WingY76; Sabin106097A; Dexter(Cong.)2486.

11492, 1918

1699

D699 A439a
Allison, Thomas, fl. 1697.
An Account Of A Voyage From Archangel In Russia, In the Year 1697. Of the Ship and Company Wintering near the North Cape in the Latitude of 71. ... By Tho. Allison, Commander of the Ship. Published at the Request of the Russia Company ...
London, Printed for D. Brown at the Black Swan and Bible without Temple-bar, and R. Parker at the Unicorn under the Royal Exchange. 1699.
8 p.ℓ., 96 (i.e. 112) p. 2 charts (incl. 1 fold.). 17cm. (19cm. in case) 8º
Errata, 8th p.ℓ.^{v}
Bound in contemporary sheep.
WingA1217; Chavanne1800.

70-469

DA699 M562a
An Answer To a Late Pamphlet, Called a Sober Dialogue, Between a Scotch Presbyterian a London Church-man, and a Real Quaker, scandalously reflecting on the Church of England, ... By a Friend to the Author of the Dialogue, called, a Sober Dialogue, between a Country Friend, a London Friend, and one of G. K.'s Friends.
London, Printed for Sam. Clark in George-yard in Lombard-street. 169$\frac{8}{9}$.
24 p. 16cm. 8º
A reply to A Sober Dialogue between a Scotch Presbyterian, a London Churchman, and a Real Quaker, London, 1699.
No. [4] in a volume of 7 pamphlets on Quakerism, bound in contemporary stained vellum.
WingA3305A; Smith(Anti-Quak)29.

M1589, 1914

BA699 -A977d
Ayeta, Francisco de.
... Discurso Legal, Qve Propone El Padre Fr. Francisco Ayeta, Procurador General de la Orden de N.P.S. Francisco, de la Regular Observancia de todas las Provincias de los Reinos de las Indias, por la Provincia de Quito. Fn [sic] La Controversia, Qve Le Ha Movido El Doctor D. Sancho de Andrade y Figueroa, Obispo de dicha Provincia; y su Provisor el Doctor D. Pedro de Zumarraga. Sobre Pretender Le Toca El Derecho de nombrar Thenientes Coadjutores à los Curas Doctrineros ...
[Madrid? ca. 1699]
28 numb. ℓ. 29cm. fol.
At head of title: Jesvs, Maria, Y Joseph.
Signed at end: Fr. Francisco de Ayeta.
Lic. D. Baltasar de Azevedo.
Includes (numb. ℓ. 26^v-28) document dated 4 Feb. 1699.
First pub. [Madrid? ca. 1696]; here with additions.
Palau(2)20799; Medina(BHA)7047.

68-276

DB =B228 1699 1
Barbados--Laws, statutes, etc.
The Laws Of Barbados, Collected In One Volume, By William Rawlin, of the Middle-Temple, London, Esquire. And Now Clerk of the Assembly Of The Said Island.
London, Printed for William Rawlin, Esq. in the Year MDCXCIX.
16 p.ℓ., 239 p. 39.5cm. fol.
Bound in contemporary calf.
WingB682B; Sabin3275; Cundall(WI)13.

7090, 1910

D699 B265j
[Baron, William] b. 1636.
A Just Defence Of The Royal Martyr K. Charles I. From the many false and malicious Aspersions in Ludlow's Memoirs, and some other virulent Libels of that Kind. ...
London, Printed for A. Roper at the Black-Boy, and R. Basset, both in Fleet-Street, and for W. Turner at Lincoln's-Inn back-Gate. 1699.
2 pts. in 1 v.: 8 p.ℓ., 199 p.; 1 p.ℓ., 88, 81-223 p. 19.5cm. 8º
Preface dated (v.1, 8th p.ℓ.^{v}) 6 Apr. 1699.
A reply to: Edmund Ludlow, Memoirs [London] 1698-1699.
Bound in contemporary calf, rebacked.
WingB897; McAlpin4:610.

551, 1904

DA699 B396b	Beckham, Edward, 1638-1714.
	    A Brief Discovery Of Some of the Blasphemous and Seditious Principles and Practices Of the People, Called Quakers: Taken out of their Most Noted and Approved Authors. Humbly Offered to the Consideration of the King, and both Houses of Parliament. By Edward Beekham D. D. and Rector of Gayten-Thorpe. Hen. Meriton, Rector of Oxborow. Lancaster Topcliffe, L.B. sometimes Sen. Fell. of Gon. & Caius Coll. Cambr. Norfolk.
	    London, Printed for John Harris at the Harrow in Little-Britain. M DC XC IX.
	        32 p. 22cm. 4°
	    The authors were referred to in the controversial literature as the "Norfolk clergymen."
	    Postscript (p. 27-32) signed: Feb. 18. 1698. Francis Bugg.
	        WingB1652; Smith(Anti-Quak)66; McAlpin4: 600.
	11468, 1918 rev
		D Scott 67a	[Belhaven, John Hamilton] 2d baron, 1656-1708.
			    A Defence Of The Scots Settlement At Darien. With An Answer to the Spanish Memorial against it. And Arguments to prove that it is the Interest of England to join with the Scots, and protect it. To which is added, A Description of the Country, and a particular Account of the Scots Colony.
			    Edinburgh, Printed in the Year M.DC.XC.IX.
			        4 p. ℓ., 86 p. A-F⁸. 18.5cm. 8°
			    Variously attributed to Belhaven, Andrew Fletcher, Archibald Foyer, and George Ridpath. W. C. Mackenzie, <u>Andrew Fletcher of Saltoun</u>, Edinburgh, 1935, p. 314-323, argues for Belhaven.
			    Dedication signed (4th p. ℓ.ᵛ): Philo-Caledon.
			    Errata, 1st p. ℓ.ᵛ.
			    "The chief Objections against the Legality of their Establishment, arise from the Memorial delivered in against it to the King, by the Ambassador Extraordinary of Spain, May 3. 1699. O.S. as follows:..." (p. 1-2).
			    First pub. the same year in 4°; also pub. the same year as 8° in half-sheets.
			    This is one of several variants pub. the same year in whole sheet 8° with the same page and signature collations. Its distinguishing points are reading of line 12 of t.-p., " Scots, and protect it.", and 2 rules above imprint.
			    In this copy there is a blank ℓ. at end.
			        JCB(2)2:1560; Scott67; cf. WingF1292; Sabin 18549; Kress 2117, S2106.
			0563, 1846

D Scott 67	[Belhaven, John Hamilton] 2d baron, 1656-1708.
	    A Defence Of The Scots Settlement At Darien. With An Answer to the Spanish Memorial against it. And Arguments to prove that it is the Interest of England to join with the Scots, and protect it. To which is added, A Description of the Country, and a particular Account of the Scots Colony.
	    Edinburgh, Printed in the Year M.DC.XC.IX.
	        4 p. ℓ., 86 p. A-M⁴. 20.5cm. (21.5cm. in case) 8°
	    Variously attributed to Belhaven, Andrew Fletcher, Archibald Foyer, and George Ridpath. W. C. Mackenzie, <u>Andrew Fletcher of Saltoun</u>, Edinburgh, 1935, p. 314-323, argues for Belhaven.
	    Dedication signed (4th p. ℓ.ᵛ):Philo-Caledon.
	    Errata, 1st p. ℓ.ᵛ.
	    "The chief Objections against the Legality of their Establishment, arise from the Memorial delivered in against it to the King, by the Ambassador Extraordinary of Spain, May 3. 1699. O.S. as follows:..." (p. 1-2).
	    First pub. the same year in 4°. Also pub. the same year as 8° in whole sheets.
	    In this copy H1 is a cancel, and there is a blank ℓ. at end.		

D Scott 67 cop.2	————Another copy. 18.5cm.
	    In this copy H1 is a cancel.
		D Scott 67b	[Belhaven, John Hamilton] 2d baron, 1656-1708.
			    A Defence Of The Scots Settlement At Darien. With An Answer to the Spanish Memorial against it. And Arguments to prove that it is the Interest of England to join with the Scots to protect it. To which is added, A Description of the Country, and a particular Account of the Scots Colony.
			    Edinburgh, Printed in the Year M.DC.XC.IX.
			        4 p. ℓ., 86 p. A-F⁸ 18.5cm. 8°
			    Variously attributed to Belhaven, Andrew Fletcher, Archibald Foyer, and George Ridpath. W. C. Mackenzie, <u>Andrew Fletcher of Saltoun</u>, Edinburgh, 1935, p. 314-323, argues for Belhaven.
			    Dedication signed (4th p. ℓ.ᵛ):Philo-Caledon.
			    Errata, 1st p. ℓ.ᵛ.
			    "The chief Objections against the Legality of their Establishment, arise from the Memorial delivered in against it to the King, by the Ambassador Extraordinary of Spain, May 3. 1699. O.S. as follows:..." (p. 1-2).
			    First pub. the same year in 4°; also pub. the same year as 8° in half-sheets.
			    This is one of several variants pub. the same year in whole sheet octavo with the same page and signature collations. Its distinguishing points are reading of line 12 of t.-p., "Scots to protect it.", and 1 rule above imprint.

D Scott 67 cop.3	————Another copy. 18cm.
	    In this copy H1 is a cancel.
	
	        JCB(2)2:1560; Scott67; cf. WingF1292; Sabin 18549; Kress 2117, S2106.
	7528, 1910
	06714, 1905
	06715, before 1915		

D
Scott
110
cop. 3
      In this copy there is a blank ℓ. at end.
      ———— Another copy. 17.5cm.
      Bound with [Ridpath, George] Scotland's grievances, [Edinburgh] 1700, as the 3d of 4 items.
      JCB(2)2:1560; cf. Scott 67; cf. Wing F1292; cf. Sabin 18549; cf. Kress 2117, S2106.
05210, before 1874
04751, before 1874

D
Scott
67a*
      [Belhaven, John Hamilton] 2d baron, 1656-1708.
      A Defence Of The Scots Settlement At Darien. With An Answer to the Spanish Memorial against it. And Arguments to prove that it is the Interest of England to join with the Scots, and protect it. To which is added, A Description of the Country, and a particular Account of the Scots Colony.
      Edinburgh, Printed in the Year M.DC.XC.IX.
      4 p. ℓ., 86 p. A-F⁸. 18.5cm. 8º
      Variously attributed to Belhaven, Andrew Fletcher, Archibald Foyer, and George Ridpath. W. C. Mackenzie, Andrew Fletcher of Saltoun, Edinburgh, 1935, p. 314-323, argues for Belhaven.
      Dedication signed (4th p. ℓ.ᵛ): Philo-Caledon.
      Errata, 1st p. ℓ.ᵛ.
      "The chief Objections against the Legality of their Establishment, arise from the Memorial delivered in against it to the King, by the Ambassador Extraordinary of Spain, May 3. 1699. O.S. as follows:..." (p. 1-2).
      First pub. the same year in 4º; also pub. the same year as 8º in half-sheets.
      This is one of several variants pub. the same year in whole sheet 8º with the same page and signature collations. Its distinguishing points are reading of line 12 of t.-p., "Scots, and protect it.", and 1 rule above imprint.
      JCB(2)2:1560; Scott 67; cf. Wing F1292; Sabin 18549; Kress 2117, S2106.
852, 1905

D
Scott
68
      [Belhaven, John Hamilton] 2d baron, 1656-1708.
      A Defence Of The Scots Settlement at Darien. With An Answer to the Spanish Memorial against it. And Arguments to prove, That it is the Interest of England to join with the Scots, and protect it. To which is added A Description of the Countrey, and a particular Account of the Scots Colony.
      [Edinburgh] Printed in the Year, M.DC.XC.IX.
      2 p. ℓ., 60 p. [A]² B⁴ C-P². 20cm. 4º
      Variously attributed to Belhaven, Andrew Fletcher, Archibald Foyer, and George Ridpath. W. C. Mackenzie, Andrew Fletcher of Saltoun, Edinburgh, 1935, p. 314-323, argues for Belhaven.
      Dedication signed (2d p. ℓ.ᵛ): Philo-Caledon.
      "The chief Objections against the Legality of their Establishment, arise from the Memorial delivered in against it to the King, by the Ambassador Extraordinary of Spain, May 3. 1699. O, S, as follows: ..." (p. 1-2).
      Also issued the same year in 8º.
      The entry in Scott giving same pagination with signatures as A² B-D⁴ E-P² is erroneous.
      In this copy the word "England" on the t.-p. is in italic capitals, D1 is correctly signed, and 2d p. ℓ.ᵛ, line 23, reads correctly: Therefore.

D
Scott
68
cop. 2
      ———— Variant. 19.5cm.
      In this copy the word "England" on the t.-p. is in roman capitals, D1 is missigned 'C', and 2d p. ℓ.ᵛ, line 23, reads: Thereforo [sic].
      JCB(2)2:1559; Scott 68; Wing F1292; Sabin 18549; cf. Kress 2117, S2106.
647, 1904
02457, 1851

D
Scott
61
      [Blackwell, Isaac]
      A Description Of The Province and Bay Of Darian: Giving an full Account of all it's Situation, Inhabitants, Way and Manner of Living and Religion, Solemnities, Ceremonies and Product; Being vastly rich with Gold Silver, and various other Commodities. By I.B. a Well-wisher to the Company who lived there Seventeen Years.
      Edinburgh, Printed by the Heirs and Successors of Andrew Anderson, Printer to the King's most Excellent Majesty, Anno Dom. 1699.
      2 p. ℓ., 16 p. 20cm. 4º
      Preface signed (2d p. ℓ.ʳ): Isaac Blackwell.
      JCB(2)2:1566; Wing B3091; Sabin 78214; Scott 61.
0562, before 1882

DA682
P451f
      Bond, Samson.
      The Sincere Milk of the Word, For The Children Of Barmuda. In A Short and Plain Catechism. By Mr. Sampson Bond, late Minister on that Island. ...
      Boston, Printed by B.[artholomew] Green, & J.[ohn] Allen. 1699.
      8 p. 15cm. (16cm. in case). 8º
      Caption title; imprint at end.
      Pages 1-2 mutilated, with some loss of text.
      Bound with: Perkins, William, The Foundation of Christian Religion, Boston, 1682.
      Wing B3587.
13021-7, 1921

DA699   Bray, Thomas, 1658-1730.
B827a   Apostolick Charity, Its Nature and Excellence Consider'd. In A Discourse Upon Dan. 12. 3. Preached at St. Paul's, at the Ordination of some Protestant Missionaries to be sent into the Plantations. To which is Prefixt, A General View of the English Colonies in America, with respect to Religion; in order to shew what Provision is wanting for the Propagation of Christianity in those Parts. Together with Proposals for the Promoting the same: And to induce such of the Clergy of this Kingdom, as are Persons of Sobriety and Abilities to accept of a Mission. And to which is subjoin'd The Author's Circular Letter lately sent to the Clergy there. By Thomas Bray, D.D.
          London, Printed for William Hawes, at the Sign of the Rose in Ludgate-Street, 1699.
          7 p. ℓ., [12], 30, [4] p., 1 ℓ. 20.5cm. 4°
          Apostolick Charity first pub. London, 1698, and another issue of those sheets was made London, 1699.
          These are the same sheets further reissued with additions: a dedication "To... Francis, Lord Guilford" (2d p. ℓ.), "Proposals For the Incouragement and Promotion of Religion ..." (p. [1-12]), and "A Circular Letter" (p. [1-4] at end) dated: London, June the 10. 1699.
          The "Proposals" were first pub. as early as Dec. 1695, [London].
          Bookseller's advertisement (last ℓ.).
          JCB(2)2:1553; WingB4286; Sabin7473; Baer (Md.)163 I, 190.
05983, before 1882

DA699   Bugg, Francis, 1640-1724?
M562a   Quakerism Expos'd To Publick Censure, By A Brief Narrative of the Proceedings between some of the Norfolk Clergy and the Quakers, at a late Conference at West-Dereham Church; ... Also, A Brief Answer to Four of the Quakers Books and Papers relating to the same. All Publish'd to prevent false Reports. By Francis Bugg. ...
          London, Printed for the Author: And are to be sold by J. Robinson at the Golden-Lion in St. Paul's Church-Yard. And H. Rhodes at the Star in Fleet-street. 1699.
          8 p. ℓ., 64 p. fold. pl. 16cm. 8°
          "Books wrote by Fr. Bugg, ..." p. 56.
          "Jezebel Withstood, And Her Daughter Anne Docwra, Publickly Reprov'd, For Her Lies and Lightness in Her Book, stiled, An Apostate Conscience. &c. By Francis Bugg." p. 57-64.
          Dated: Apr. 9th, 1699. A reply to Anne Docwra's An Apostate Conscience exposed, London, 1699. Bugg's Jezebel withstood was also issued separately [London, 1699], 16 p.

          "The Preface" signed, verso 8th p. ℓ.: Apr. 11. 1699. Fra. Bugg.
          Imperfect: plate "The Quakers Synod" wanting; available in facsimile.
          No. [2] in a volume of 7 pamphlets on Quakerism, bound in contemporary stained vellum.
          WingB5385; Smith(Friends)1:339.
M1587, 1914

D696   By the Honourable Sir William Beeston Kt.
-C737c   His Majesties Lieutenant Governour and Commander in chief, In, and over this his Island of Jamaica, and other the Territories depending thereon in America, and Vice-admiral of the same. A Proclamation
          Edinburgh, Re-Printed Exactly according to the Originals, Anno 1699.
          [3] p. 31.5cm. fol.
          Caption title; imprint at end.
          Contains 4 proclamations which provide that no assistance is to be given to the Scots settling at Darien: [1] by Sir William Beeston, Governor of Jamaica, dated 8 Apr. 1699; [2] by Ralph Grey, Governor of Barbados, dated 13 Apr. 1699; [3] by Richard Coote, earl of Bellomont as Governor of the Province of New York, dated in New York, 15 May 1699; [4] by Richard Coote, earl of Bellomont, as Governor of the Province of Massachusetts Bay and New York, dated in Boston. 3 June 1699.
          The text of each of Bellomont's proclamations includes its original imprint: "Printed by W. Bradford, Printer to the Kings most Excellent Majesty, in New-York. 1699" and "Boston, Printed by Bartholomew Green, and John Allen, Printers to His Excellency the Governor, and Council, 1699", respectively.
          Also issued with text of first two proclamations only (1 ℓ.) and also with a second proclamation by Ralph Grey, Governor of Barbados dated 5 Sept. 1699 on p. 4.
          Bound in a volume of Scottish imprints and mss. as the 6th [counted as items 6 and 7] of 58 items.
          WingB1695; Scott 57n.
7105, 1910

DA682   Cambridge, Mass.--Ministers' Association.
P451f   Thirty Important Cases, Resolved With Evidence of Scripture And Reason. <Mostly,> By several Pastors of Adjacent Churches, meeting in Cambridge, New-England.<With some other memorable matters.> Now Published for General Benefit.
          Boston in New England. Printed by Bartholomew Green, & John Allen Sold at the Book-sellers

Shops. 1699.
 78 p., 1 ℓ. 15cm. (16cm. in case). 8°
 "Advertisement" (p. 3-6) signed by the editor, Cotton Mather.
 "At A General Meeting of Ministers...Assembled at Boston, May 27. 1697.<The Following Instrument, was generally Signed...> Increase Mather [and others]" p. 77-78.
 Errata, last leaf.
 Title-page mutilated with some loss of text.
 Bound with: Perkins, William. The Foundation of Christian Religion, Boston, 1682.
 Evans878; WingM1160; Holmes(C.)394; Sabin46550.
13021-4, 1921

BA699 Carvajal y Ribera, Fernando de, Abp.
-C331s Señor: El Maestro Fr. Fernando de Carvajal y Ribera, Arçobispo de Santo Domingo, entrò por vltimos de Septiembre del año passado, en virtud de Decreto de su Magestad;...
 [Madrid? 1699?]
 7 p. 29cm. fol.
 Title from caption and beginning of text.
 Sets forth conditions in Santo Domingo in justification of the archbishop's leaving his see to go to Spain.
 JCB(2)2:1555; Medina(BHA)6335; Sabin 11177.
03705, before 1866

B699 Casas, Bartolomé de las, bp. of Chiapa, 1474-
C334a 1566.
 An Account Of the First Voyages and Discoveries Made by the Spaniards in America. Containing The most Exact Relation hitherto publish'd, of their unparallel'd Cruelties on the Indians, in the destruction of above Forty Millions of People. ... By Don Bartholomew de las Casas, Bishop of Chiapa, who was an Eye-witness of their Cruelties. ... To which is added, The Art of Travelling, shewing how a Man may dispose his Travels to the best advantage.
 London, Printed by J. Darby for D. Brown at the Black Swan and Bible without Temple-Bar, J. Harris at the Harrow in Little Britain, and Andr. Bell at the Cross-keys and Bible in Cornhil. M.DC.XC.IX.
 4 p.ℓ., 248, 40 p. 2 double plates. 19.5cm. 8°
 List of books "Newly publish'd" (verso 4th p.ℓ.).
 The Las Casas section is based on the nine tracts known under the title: Brevísima relación, pub. Seville, 1552. This transl. is taken from the French transl. pub. Paris, 1697, under title: La découverte des Indes occidentales or from an edition of that French transl. pub. Amsterdam, 1698, under title: Relation des voyages et des découvertes. The art of travelling [by J. B. de Chèvremont] is transl. from L'Art de voyager utilement, Amsterdam, 1698.
 Also issued London, 1699, under title: A relation of the first voyages and discoveries...

B699 ————Another copy. 19.5cm.
C334a In this copy are inserted plates from The
cop.2 World displayed, Philadelphia, 1795-1796.
 JCB(2)2:1556; WingC797; Sabin11289; Church780; Streit1:738; Medina(BHA)v.2, p. 475; Hanke(Las Casas)561.
1256, 1906
03706, before 1866

DA699 Church of England.
C561c A Collection Of Articles, Canons, Injunctions, &c. Together with several Acts of Parliament Concerning Ecclesiastical Matters; Some whereof are to be Read in Churches.
 London, Printed by Charles Bill, and the Executrix of Thomas Newcomb, deceas'd, Printers to the King's most Excellent Majesty. MDCXCIX.
 2 p.ℓ., 156, [3] p. 20cm. (21cm. in case) 8°
 Cut (royal arms; Steele 138) on t.-p.
 Drawn up to replace Anthony Sparrow's collection.
 Bound in contemporary calf.
 WingC4093; McAlpin4:604.
30893, 1951

D Church of Scotland--General Assembly--
Scott Commission.
66 Letter From The Commission Of The General Assembly Of The Church of Scotland To The Honourable Council and Inhabitants of the Scots Colony of Caledonia in America. Dated at Glasgow, July 21, 1699.
 Glasgow, Printed by Robert Sanders, One of His Majesties Printers 1699.
 1 p.ℓ., 16 p. 18.5cm. 4°
 Also pub. Edinburgh, the same year.
 This copy closely trimmed affecting marginal notes.
 WingC4231; Sabin18561; Scott66; McAlpin 4:611.
13019, 1920

D Church of Scotland--General Assembly--
Scott   Commission.
65   A Letter, From The Commission, Of The
General Assembly, Of The Church Of Scotland;
Met at Glasgow, July 21. 1699. To The Honour-
able Council, and Inhabitants, of the Scots
Colony of Caledonia, in America.
    Edinburgh, Printed by George Mosman, and
are to be sold at his Shop in the Parliament-
Closs, 1699.
    16 p. 19.5cm. 4º
    Also pub. Glasgow, the same year.
    Wing C4230; Sabin 78221; Scott 65.

743, 1905

DA699   The Church-Man And The Quaker Dialoguing:
C563q   With A Reply To An Answer to a late
Pamphlet, Called, A Sober Dialogue between
a Scotch Presbyterian, a London Church-Man,
and a Real Quaker. ...
    London Printed, and Sold by the Booksellers
of London and Westminster, 1699.
    30 p. 16.5cm. 8º
    A reply (p. 3-19) to George Keith, A serious
dialogue betwixt a church-man and a Quaker,
London, 1699, and (p. 20-30) to An Answer to
a late Pamphlet, London, 1699.
    Wing C3997; Smith(Friends)1:46; Smith(Anti-
Quak)29.

11498, 1918

bD   Company of Scotland Trading to Africa and
Scott   the Indies.
73   At a Council-General of the Company of Scotland,
Trading to Africa and the Indies, holden at Edin-
burgh the 18th day of October, 1699.
    [Edinburgh, 1699]
    Broadside. 30 x 19.5cm. 1/2º
    Concerns efforts to raise funds to maintain the
Company's credit (after the failure of the second
Darien expedition).
    Wing C5584; Scott 73.

774, 1905

bD   Company of Scotland Trading to Africa and
Scott   the Indies.
58   At a Court of Directors of the Company of
Scotland, Trading to Africa and the Indies.
Holden at Edinburgh the 18th of April 1699.
    [Edinburgh, 1699]
    Broadside. 31 x 19.5cm. 1/2º
    Concerns credits offered to encourage trade
to Darien.

    Also includes confirmation dated: 2d. Day of
May 1699.
    Wing C5585; Scott 58.

775, 1905

D   Company of Scotland Trading to Africa and
Scott   the Indies.
64b   Caledonia. The Declaration Of The Council
Constituted by the Indian and African Company
of Scotland; for the Government, and direction
of their Colonies, and Settlements in the Indies.
    Boston, Printed [by B. Green and J. Allen]
May, 15th. 1699.
    4 p. 19cm. 4º (Issued as a part of [Wil-
liam Paterson] An abstract of a letter, Boston,
1699.)
    Caption title; imprint at end.
    Dated (at end): New Edinburgh, December
28. 1698.
    Wing C5596; Scott 77b; Brinley 810(this copy);
Bristol 185.

06033A, 1878

bD   Company of Scotland Trading to Africa and
Scott   the Indies.
74   The Council-General of the Indian and African
Company's Petition to His Majesty.
    [Edinburgh? 1699]
    2 p. 30cm. fol.
    Caption title.
    "... Proclamations have been Issued out in
Your Majesty's Name, by your Governours in
all the American Plantations ... strictly for-
bidding all Your Majesty's Subjects, or Others
within these Plantations, to enter into any
Traffick or Commerce with the said [Darien]
Colony ..." (p. 1). The proclamations were
collected and reprinted Edinburgh, 1699, with
caption title beginning: By the Honourable Sir
William Beeston...
    Dated (p. 2) Edinburgh, 19 Oct. 1699, with
answer dated 2 Nov. 1699.
    Wing C5595; Scott 74.

06479, before 1906

BA699   Confraternity of the Blessed Sacrament.
-C748s   Sumario De Las Gracias, E Indvlgencias,
Qve Gozan los Esclavos Cofrades de la Es-
clavitud de el Santissimo Sacramento, Fvn-
dada Con Authoridad Apostolica, en la Iglesia
Parrochial de la Santa Vera-Cruz de esta
Ciudad de Mexico, en virtud de la Agregacion
à la Archi-Cofradia de la Minerva de la Santa
Ciudad de Roma, por la Santidad de N. M. S.

[385]

P. Inocencio XI. Para ganar estas Indulgencias han de tener la Bula de la Santa Cruzada de la vltima Predicacion.
Con licencia de los Superiores, y del señor Comissario General de la Santa Cruzada. En Mexico, por Doña Maria de Benavides. Año de 1699.
1 p. ℓ., [4] p. 30.5cm. fol.
Cut (angels with chalice) on t.-p.
Blanks in indulgence on p. [4] are completed in ms. with recipient's name (Joseph Anselmo) and a date (22 Apr. 1706). Signed in ms.: Br Joseph Matheo de Sifuentes Secre.º
Sabin93581

5166, 1909

bD Scott 83c
An Congratulatory Poem, On The safe Arrival of the Scots African and Indian Fleet in Caledonia, and their kind Reception by the Natives, with an Amicable advice to all concerned.
[Edinburgh? 1699?]
Broadside. 31 x 19 cm. 1/2º
Signed: R. A.
Scott 83c; Sabin78207.

06482, before 1900

DA699 C749c
Congregational Churches in Massachusetts--Boston Synod, 1680.
A Confession Of Faith Owned and consented unto by the Elders & Messengers of the Churches Assembled at Boston in New England, May 12. 1680. Being the Second Session of that Synod. ...
Boston. Re-printed by Bartholomew Green, and John Allen. 1699.
8 p. ℓ., 161, [162-165] p. 14.5cm. 8º
First pub. Boston, 1680. Text in English and Massachuset Indian dialect on alternate pages. Translation by Grindall Rawson perhaps with assistance of Samuel Treat.
Added t.-p.: Wunnamptamoe Sampooaonk Wussampoowontamun Nashpe moeuwehkomunga-nash ut New-England. Qushkenumun en Indiane Unnontowaonganit. Nashpe Grindal Rawson, &c. ... Mushauwomuk. Printeuun nashpe Bartholo-mew Green, kah John Allen. 1699.
"The Epistle Dedicatory." signed (recto 8th p. ℓ.): Brantrey, Nov. 4. 1699. G. Rawson.
Issued without the preface by Increase Mather.
Imperfect: English t.-p. (1st p. ℓ.) wanting; Indian t.-p. (2d p. ℓ.) mutilated affecting two words and border, completed in pen-and-ink facsimile; p. 159-160 mutilated; p. 161 to end wanting; available in facsimile.

DA699 C749c cop. 2
————Another copy. 14cm. (15cm. in case) Manuscript additions.
Imperfect: p. ℓ. 1-8, p. 1-12, 23-26, 33-36, 87-90, 135-138, 157 to end wanting or mutilated with text affected.
Sabin68013; Evans860; cf. Holmes(I.)p. 430; Pilling3203; WingC5793.

05101, 1884
05119, 1884

BA699 C957d
Cruz, Francisco Antonio de la.
Declamacion Funebre, Que en las Exequias, que consagrò à su amabilissimo Pastor, Ilus-trissimo, y Excelentissimo Señor Doctor D. Manvel Fernandez De Santa Crvz, el Colegio Real de S. Juan, y S. Pedro: Dixo En la Iglesia de la Santa Vera-Cruz, y Oratorio de N. P. San Phelipe Neri, el dia 28. de Febrero del Año de 1699. El Br. Francisco Antonio De Lacrvz, Cura Beneficiado por su Magestad, Vicario, y Juez Eclesiastico del Pueblo, y partido de San Francisco de Apango. ...
Con Licencia: En la Puebla, en la Imprenta de los Herederos del Capitan Juan de Villa-Real en el Portal de las flores. [1699]
10 p. ℓ., 8 p., 5-9 numb. ℓ., [2] p. 20.5cm. 4º
"Parecer" dated (10th p. ℓ.ʳ) 25 Oct. 1699.
Includes poems by Antonio Delgado y Buen-rostro ([2] p. at end).
Palau(2)65180; Medina(Puebla)197.

1074, 1905

D699 C977c
[Curson, Henry]
A Compendium Of The Laws and Government Ecclesiastical, Civil and Military, Of England, Scotland & Ireland, And Dominions, Plantations and Territories Thereunto belonging, With The Maritime Power thereof, And Jurisdiction of Courts Therein. Methodically Digested under their Proper Heads. By H.C. sometime of the Inner-Temple.
London, Printed by the Assigns of Rich. and Edw. Atkins, Esquires, for J. Walthoe, and are to be sold by John Deeve, at Bernard's-Inn-Gate in Holbourn. 1699.
8 p. ℓ., 642, [14] p. 16.5cm. 12º
Preface (3d p. ℓ.) signed: H. Curson.
With special title-pages dated 1699: "A Compendium Of The Laws and Government Of Scotland ..." p. [443], "A Compendium Of The Laws and Government Of Ireland ..." p. [461], "A Com-pendious Description Of The English Plantations ..." p. [489], "Addenda, Or, A Supplement..." p. [533].
Errata at end.
Booksellers' advertisement, 1st p. ℓ.ᵛ

In this copy the t.-p. is a cancel. Cancellandum t.-p., found in some of the other recorded copies, bears imprint: London... for J. Walthoe, and are to be sold at his Shop in the Middle-Temple Cloysters. 1699.
WingC7686; cf. Sabin15046; Baer(Md.)191.
9259, 1913

D699
D166n
1
[R]
Dampier, William, 1652-1715.
A New Voyage Round The World. ... By Captain William Dampier. ... The Fourth Edition Corrected.
London, Printed for James Knapton, at the Crown in St Pauls Church-yard. MDCXCIX.
5 p.l., vi, 550, [4] p. incl. illus., map. 4 fold. maps. 19.5cm. 8°
First pub. London, 1697.
Numbered "Vol. I." on t.-p. With this was issued in a separate vol. designated "Vol. II." on t.-p. his Voyages and descriptions, London, 1699.
"Books sold by James Knapton..." p. [1-4] at end.
This copy is bound in contemporary half leather, rebacked, as the 1st of a 3-vol. set also containing his Voyages and descriptions, 2d ed., London, 1700, and his A voyage to New Holland, London, 1703.
JCB(2)2:1557; Sabin18374; WingD164; Borba de Moraes 1:204n.
04760-1, before 1882
30843, 1951

D699
D166n
2
[R]
Dampier, William, 1652-1715.
Voyages and Description. ... In Three Parts, viz. 1. A Supplement of the Voyage round the World, Describing the Countreys of Tonquin, Achin, Malacca, &c. their Product, Inhabitants, Manners, Trade, Policy, &c. 2. Two Voyages to Campeachy; with a Description of the Coasts, Product, Inhabitants, Logwood-Cutting, Trade, &c. of Jucatan, Campeachy, New-Spain, &c. 3. A Discourse of Trade-Winds, Breezes, Storms, Seasons of the Year, Tides and Currents of the Torrid Zone throughout the World: With an Account of Natal in Africk, its Product, Negro's, &c. By Captain William Dampier. ... To which is Added, A General Index to both Volumes.
London, Printed for James Knapton, at the Crown in St Pauls Church-yard. MDCXCIX.
4 p.l., 184, 132 p., 2 l., 112, [76] p. 4 fold. maps. 19.5cm. 8°
Designated "Vol. II." on t.-p. With this was issued in a separate vol. designated "Vol. I." on t.-p. his A new voyage round the World, 4th ed., London, 1699.
Each pt. of this vol. and the index have separate paging and signatures, and pt.3 has special half-title.
Errata, p. [73-74] at end.
"Books sold by James Knapton..." p. [74-76] at end.
Bound in contemporary calf, rebacked.
JCBAR50:59-60; WingD165; Sabin18375; Borba de Moraes 1:204.
30843, 1951

D
Scott
70
The Defence Of The Scots Settlement At Darien, Answer'd, Paragraph by Paragraph. By Philo-Britan.
London, Printed, and Sold by the Booksellers of London and Westminster, 1699.
2 p.l., 6, 9-92 p. 18.5cm. 8°
A reply to [Belhaven, J.H., baron] A defence of the Scot's settlement at Darien, Edinburgh, 1699.
Includes the text of [Belhaven's] A defence, alternating paragraphs of "Defence" and "Answer".
Has been attributed to Walter Harris.
Includes half-title, 1st p.l.

D
Scott
70
cop.2
————Variant. 18.5cm.
In this copy page number 26 is misprinted for 34, 27 for 35, 30 for 38, and 31 for 39.
Imperfect: half-title wanting.
JCB(2)2:1561; Sabin18550; WingH881; Scott70; Kress S2115.
01947, 1854
787, 1905

DA699
E52v
Elys, Edmund, ca.1634-ca.1707.
A Vindication Of The Doctrine Concerning the Light Within, Against the Objections Of George Keith. In his Book, Entituled, The Deism of W. Penn, and his Brethren Expos'd. By Edmund Elys.
London, Printed and Sold by T. Sowle, in White-Hart-Court, in Gracious-Street, and at the Bible in Leaden-Hall-Street, 1699.
8 p. 20cm. 4°
Keith's The Deism of William Penn, 1st pub. London, 1699.
WingE698; Smith(Friends)1:574.
05872, 1918

D
[Ferguson, Robert] d. 1714.
A Just and Modest Vindication Of The Scots Design, For the having Established a Colony

at Darien. With A Brief Display, how much it is their Interest, to apply themselves to Trade, and particularly to that which is Foreign. ...
    [Edinburgh?] Printed in the Year, 1699.
    15 p. ℓ., 214 p. 18.5cm. 8°
    Also attributed to James Hodges.
    "To The Reader" (2d-15th p. ℓ.) is in part a reply to Walter Harris' A defence of the Scots abdicating Darien, 1st pub. [London?] 1700 [i.e. 1699?], and A defence of the Scots settlement at Darien answer'd, London, 1699.
    Bound with A choice collection of papers relating to state affairs, London, 1703.
    Wing F742; Sabin 32340; Scott 71; Kress 2116.

742, 1905

D
Scott
69

[Fletcher, Andrew] 1655-1716.
    A Short and Impartial View Of The Manner and Occasion Of The Scots Colony's Coming away from Darien. In A Letter to a Person of Quality. ...
    [Edinburgh] Printed [by James Watson] in the Year, M. DC. XC. IX.
    40 p. 22.5cm. 4°
    Signed at end: P. C. [i.e. Philo-Caledon]
    The printer is identified by a contemporary ms. annotation on the t.-p. of the Lenox copy, New York Public Library.
    JCB(2)1564; Wing F1297; Sabin 78233, 9753; Kress 2118; Scott 69.

01524, 1847

EB
-W&A
388

France--Laws, statutes, etc., 1643-1715
    (Louis XIV).   4 Mar 1699
    Ordonnance Du Roy, Portant Défenses De Transporter des especes d'Or & d'Argent dans l'Amérique. Du quatriéme de Mars 1699.
    A Paris, De L'Imprimerie Royale. M. DC. XCIX.
    4 p. 26cm. (32cm. in case) 4°
    Cut (royal arms) on t.-p.
    Wroth & Annan 388; Actes Royaux 19570.

12941, 1921

E699
F927r

Froger, François, b. 1676.
    Relation D'Un Voyage Fait en 1695. 1696. & 1697. Aux Cotes D'Afrique, Détroit de Magellan, Bresil, Cayenne Et Isles Antilles, Par une Escadre des Vaisseaux du Roi, commandée par M. De Gennes. Faite par le Sieur Froger Ingenieur Volontaire sur le Vaisseau le Faucon Anglois. ...
    A Amsterdam, Chez les Héritiers, D'Antoine Schelte. M. DC. XCIX.
    7 p. ℓ., 227 p. 16 plates (incl. 2 fold.), 12 maps (incl. 7 fold.) 16cm. 12°
    Cut (printer's device) on t.-p.; incl. motto Qværendo.
    Added t.-p., engr.: Relation du Voyage de M.r De Gennes au detroit de Magellan Par le S.r Froger ... signed: J. Lamsvelt.
    First pub. Paris, 1698.
    Bound in contemporary calf.
    JCB(2)2:1568; Sabin 26002; Borba de Moraes 1:285.

05722, before 1866

D699
G133n

Gage, Thomas, 1603?-1656.
    A New Survey of the West-Indies. Being A Journal of Three thousand and Three hundred Miles within the main Land of America: By Tho. Gage, the only Protestant that was ever known to have travel'd those Parts. Setting forth His Voyage from Spain to S. John de Ulhua; and thence to Xalapa, Tlaxcalla, the City of Angels, and Mexico: With a Description of that great City, ... Likewise His Journey thence through Guaxaca, Chiapa, Guatemala, ... With his Return through Nicaragua and Costa Rica, to Nicoya, Panama, Porto bello, Cartagena, and Havana. With An Account of the Spanish Navigation thither; their Government, Castles, Ports, Commodities, Religion, Priests and Friers, Negro's, Mulatto's, Mestiso's, Indians; and of their Feasts and Solemnities. With a Grammar, or some few Rudiments of the Indian Tongue, called Poconchi or Pocoman. The fourth Edition enlarg'd by the Author, with an accurate Map.
    London: Printed by M. Clark, for J. Nicolson at the Kings Arms in Little Britain and T. Newborough, at the Golden Ball in S. Paul's Church-Yard. 1699.
    4 p. ℓ., 384, 387-477, [18] p. fold. map. 19cm. 8°.
    "Some brief and short Rules for the better learning of the Indian tongue call'd Poconchi or Pocoman, commonly used about Guatemala ..." p. 465-467.
    First pub. under title: The English-American his Travail by Sea and Land. London, 1648. This ed. follows the revised ed., London, 1677.
    Bound in contemporary calf.
    In this copy there is a blank ℓ. at end.
    JCB(2)2:1570; Sabin 26301; Wing G115; Streit 2:2347; Palau(2)96481n; Pilling 1369.

02867, 1861

D699 Gage, Thomas, 1603?-1656.
G133nr   Nouvelle Relation, Contenant Les Voyages De Thomas Gage dans la Nouvelle Espagne, ses diverses avantures, & son retour par la Province de Nicaragua jusques à la Havane. Avec La Description De La Ville de Mexique... Ensemble Une Description exacte des Terres & Provinces que possedent les Espagnols en toute l'Amerique, de la forme de leur Commerce, de leurs Mœurs, & de celles des Criolles, des Metifs, des Mulatres des Indiens, & des Negres. Tome I. [-Tome II.] Troisiéme Edition Reveuë & Corrigée.
   A Amsterdam, Chez Paul Marret, dans le Beurs-straat proche le Dam à la Renommée. M. DC. XCIX.
   2 v.: 12 p.ℓ., 200, 176 p. 6 fold. plates, 3 fold. maps; 6 p.ℓ., 316, [3] p. 6 fold. plates, fold. map. 16cm. 12°.
   Each vol. has added t.-p., engr., with title: Voyage De Thomas Gage ...
   Cut (publisher's device) on t.-p., v.1.
   Transl. from: A New Survey of the West-Indies; first pub. London, 1648, under title: The English-American his Travail by Sea and Land; or, A new survey ...
   This transl., which has been attributed to Adrien Baillet, 1st pub. Paris, 1676. A section on the Pokonchi language has been omitted in this edition.
   Title-page of vol. 2 omits edition note and concludes: ... Chez Paul Marret, Marchand Libraire dans le Beurs-straat. M. DC. XCIX.
   "Catalogue Des Livres Nouveaux Qui se trouvent Chez Paul Marret...": vol. 2, last 3 p.
   JCB(2)2:1569; Sabin26305; Streit2:2346; Palau(2)96485n; Leclerc(1867)604.
01942A-B, 1854

EA699 [Gervaise, Nicolas] 1662 ca.-1729.
G385v   La Vie De Saint Martin Evêque De Tours, Avec L'Histoire De La Fondation de son Eglise, & ce qui s'y est passé de plus considerable jusqu'à present.
   A Tours, Chez Jean Barthe, Imprimeur de Messieurs du Chapitre de saint Martin, Grande-Rüe. Et Hugues Michel Duval Marchand Libraire, rüe de la Sellerie. M. DC. XCIX. Avec Privilege Du Roy. Et Approb.
   23 p.ℓ., 432 p., 1 ℓ., 433-454 p. illus. 25cm. 4°.
   Cut (monogram) on t.-p.
   Dedication signed (4th p.ℓ.^{r}) N. Gervaise.
   "Achevé d'imprimer pour la premiere fois le premier Juin 1699." (4th p.ℓ.^{v}).
   Errata, leaf following p. 432.
   "Lettre De Messire Jean-Baptiste de la Croix de saint Vallier, Evêque de Quebec ... ": p. 411-412.
32560, 1959

BA699 [González de Santalla, Tirso] 1624-1705.
-G643o   Oposición Hecha Al Progresso En Las Cavsas, y processos de la Beatificacion, y Canonizacion del V. S. de Dios el Ilustrissimo y Reverendissimo Señor Don Iuan de Palafox y Mendoza, Obispo que fue de la Puebla de los Angeles en la Nueva España, y despues de Osma en estos Reynos de Castilla. Y satisfacion à ella.
   [Rome? 1699?]
   20 numb. ℓ. 31cm. fol.
   Caption title.
   Consists of: A memorial to the Spanish king by Tirso González de Santalla; "Copia de carta circular, que el Reverendissimo Padre Tirso Gonçalez, General de la Compañia de Iesus escrivió à los Señores Prelados de España"; a memorial to Pope Innocent X by Juan de Palafox y Mendoza, dated in Puebla de los Angeles, 8 Jan. 1649; and a memorial by "Bernhardinus Peregrinus, Causæ Patronus", dated in Rome, 20 March 1699.
   Palau(2)201803, 209838; Medina(BHA)1997; Sabin57411.
69-540

bDB Gt.Brit.--Laws, statutes, etc., 1694-1702
G7863   (William III)
1699   Anno Decimo & Undecimo Gulielmi III.
2   Regis. An Act for Taking Off the Remaining Duties upon Glass Wares.
   [London, Charles Bill and the Executrix of Thomas Newcomb, 1699]
   281-283 p. 4B^2 31cm. fol. (Issued as a part of its [Session laws] London, 1699.)
   Caption title.
13084-2, 1921

bDB Gt.Brit.--Laws, statutes, etc., 1694-1702
G7863   (William III)
1699   Anno Regni Gulielmi III. Regis Angliæ,
1   Scotiæ, Franciæ & Hiberniæ, Decimo & Undecimo. At the Parliament begun at Westminster the Four and twentieth Day of August, Anno Dom. 1698. ... And from thence Continued by several Prorogations to the Sixth Day of December, 1698. ...
   London, Printed by Charles Bill, and the Executrix of Thomas Newcomb, deceas'd; Printers to the Kings most Excellent Majesty. MDC XCIX.
   1 p.ℓ., 335-364 p. 4P-4Y^2 31cm. fol. (Issued as a part of its [Session laws] London, 1699.)
   Cut (royal arms; Steele 133) on t.-p.
   Caption title, p. 335: ... An Act for Laying

further Duties upon Sweets, and for Lessening the Duties as well upon Vinegar, as upon certain Low Wines and Whale-Fins, and the Duties upon Brandy Imported, and for the more Easie Raising the Duties upon Leather, and for charging Cynders, and for permitting the Importation of Pearl Ashes, and for preventing Abuses in the Brewing of Beer and Ale, and Frauds in Importation of Tobacco.
    Arents 436.
13084-1, 1921

DB   Gt. Brit.--Parliament, 1698-1699--House of
-G7875   Commons.
1689   The Humble Address of the House of Commons
3   to the King.
    London: Printed for Edward Jones in the Savoy, and Timothy Goodwin at the Queen's-Head against St. Dunstan's Church in Fleetstreet, 1698[/9]. (Price 1 d.)
    1 ℓ. 29cm. 1/2⁰ (Issued as no. 38 of Gt. Brit.--Parliament, 1698-1699--House of Commons. Votes..., London, 1698-1699.)
    Caption title; imprint at end.
    At heading of title paged 87 and numbered as pt. 38.
    Occasioned by the king's speech expressing misgivings about reductions in the army.
    Presented 4 Feb 1698/9.
    Bound in Votes of the House of Commons, v. 3.
10376-10A, 1914 rev 3

DB   Gt. Brit.--Parliament, 1698-1699--House of
-G7875   Commons.
1689   The Humble Address of the House of Commons
3   to the King.
    London: Printed for Edward Jones in the Savoy, and Timothy Goodwin at the Queen's-Head against St. Dunstan's Church in Fleetstreet, 1698[/9]. (Price 1 d.)
    1 ℓ. 29cm. 1/2⁰ (Issued as no. 53 of Gt. Brit.--Parliament, 1698-1699--House of Commons. Votes..., London, 1698-1699.)
    Caption title; imprint at end.
    At head of title paged 119 and numbered as pt. 53.
    Calls for the expulsion of Catholics from London.
    Presented 21 Feb. 1698/99.
    Bound in Votes of the House of Commons, v. 3.
10376-10B, 1914

DB   Gt. Brit.--Parliament, 1698-1699--House of
-G7875   Commons.
1689   The Humble Address of the House of Commons
3   to the King; With His Majesty's Most Gracious Answer thereunto.
    London, Printed for Edw. Jones in the Savoy, and Tim. Goodwin against St. Dunstan's Church in Fleetstreet, 1699 (Price 1 d.)
    1 ℓ. 29cm. 1/2⁰ (Issued as [no. 82] of Gt. Brit.--Parliament, 1698-1699--House of Commons. Votes..., London, 1698-1699.)
    Caption title; imprint at end.
    Concerns the disbanding of the king's Dutch foot guards.
    Presented 24 Mar 1698/9.
    Bound in Votes of the House of Commons, v. 3.
10376-10C, 1914

DB   Gt. Brit.--Parliament, 1698-1699--House of
-G7875   Commons.
1689   The Humble Address of the House of Commons
3   to the King; With His Majesty's Most Gracious Answer thereunto.
    London: Printed for Edward Jones in the Savoy, and Timothy Goodwin at the Queen's-Head against St. Dunstan's Church in Fleetstreet, 1699. (Price 1 d.)
    1 ℓ. 29cm. 1/2⁰ (Issued as no. 91 of Gt. Brit.--Parliament, 1698-1699--House of Commons. Votes..., London, 1698-1699.)
    Caption title; imprint at end.
    At head of title paged 203 and numbered as pt. 91.
    Concerns financial irregularities in the navy.
    Presented 3 Apr 1699.
    Bound in Votes of the House of Commons, v. 3.
10376-10D, 1914

DB   Gt. Brit.--Parliament, 1698-1699--House of
G7875   Lords.
1699   The Humble Address Of The Lords Spiritual
1   and Temporal To His Majesty, In Relation to the Petition of Charles Desborow, Late Captain of His Majesty's Ship Mary Gally, Employ'd in the Expedition to Newfoundland, in the Year 1697, under the Command of Captain John Norris. And His Majesty's most Gracious Answer thereto.
    [London?] Printed for Charles Desborow, 1699.
    2 p. ℓ., 8 p. 19cm. 4⁰
    Includes "To the Right Honourable the Lords Spiritual and Temporal in Parliament Assembled. The humble Petition of Charles Desborow" (2d p. ℓ.).
    Dated 17 April 1699 (Address) and 21 April 1699 (Answer).
    Wing E2801; Sabin 19687.
11634, 1918

DB   Gt.Brit.--Parliament, 1698-1699--House of
-G7875   Lords.
1689   The Humble Address Of the Right Honourable
3   the Lords Spiritual & Temporal In Parliament
Assembled, Presented to His Majesty On Munday
the Sixth Day of February, 1698[/9]. And His
Majesties Most Gracious Answer Thereunto.
London, Printed by Charles Bill, and the Executrix of Thomas Newcomb deceas'd; Printers to
the Kings most Excellent Majesty. 1698[/9].
4 p. 29cm. fol.
Order to print (p. 2) dated 7 Feb 1698[/9].
Occasioned by the king's speech expressing mis-
givings about reductions in the size of the army.
Bound in Votes of the House of Commons, v.3,
before Votes for 6 Feb 1698/9.
10383-8, 1914 rev 2

DB   Gt.Brit.--Parliament, 1699-1700--House of
-G7875   Commons.
1689   The Humble Address of the House of Commons
3   to the King.
London: Printed for Edward Jones in the Savoy,
and Timothy Goodwin at the Queen's-Head against
St. Dunstan's Church in Fleetstreet. 1699.
(Price 1d.)
1 ℓ. 29cm. 1/2° (Issued as no. 9 of Gt.Brit.
--Parliament, 1699-1700--House of Commons.
Votes..., London, 1699-1700.)
Caption title; imprint at end.
At head of title paged 19 and numbered as pt. 9.
Seeks to improve relations between the king
and Parliament.
Presented 5 Dec 1699.
Bound in Votes of the House of Commons, v.3.
10376-11A, 1914

DB   Gt.Brit.--Parliament, 1699-1700--House of
-G7875   Commons.
1689   Votes Of The House of Commons, In The Par-
3   liament Began At Westminster The Sixteenth Day
of November, in the Eleventh Year of the Reign
of King William, Anno Domini 1699.
London, Printed for Edward Jones, and Timothy
Goodwin, MDCXCIX [-1700]. (Price 2d.)
1 p.ℓ., 204, 203-206 p. 29cm. fol.
Issued in pts. numbered 1-103 and dated
16 Nov 1699 - 11 Apr 1700, each of which has
caption title and imprint at end.
Imprint of no. 89-103 dated 1700.
Bound in Votes of the House of Commons, v.3.
10376-11, 1914

D699   Hack, William, fl. 1678-1700, ed.
H118c   A Collection Of Original Voyages: Containing
I. Capt. Cowley's Voyage round the Globe. II.
Captain Sharp's Journey over the Isthmus of
Darien, and Expedition into the South Seas,
Written by himself. III. Capt. Wood's Voyage
thro' the Streights of Magellan. IV. Mr.
Roberts's Adventures among the Corsairs of the
Levant; his Account of their Way of Living; De-
scription of the Archipelago Islands, Taking of
Scio, &c. ... Published by Capt William Hacke.
London, Printed for James Knapton, at the
Crown in St. Paul's Church-Yard. 1699.
8 p.ℓ., 45, 16, 33-100, 53, [54-56] p. illus., 3
plates (incl. 2 fold.), 3 fold. maps. 19cm. 8°
"Books Printed for J. Knapton..." p. [54-56]
at end.
JCB(2)2:1571; WingH168; Sabin29473; Scott82.
01944, 1854

bD   An Health To Caledonia, To the Tune of
Scott   Marin's Trumpet Air.
83b   [Edinburgh? 1699?]
Broadside. 32.5 x 20cm. 1/2°
Verse.
Scott 83b; Sabin78217.
04864, before 1900

E699   Hennepin, Louis, ca. 1640-ca. 1705.
H515nd   A Continuation Of The New Discovery Of A
Vast Country in America, Extending above Four
Thousand Miles, Between New France and New
Mexico; Giving an Account Of The Attempts of
the Sieur De la Salle upon the Mines of St. Barbe,
&c. The Taking of Quebec by the English; With
the Advantages of a Shorter Cut to China and
Japan. By L. Hennepin, now Resident in Holland.
To which are added, Several New Discoveries in
North America, not publish'd in the French
Edition.
London: Printed for H. Bonwick, at the Red
Lyon in St. Paul's Church-yard. 1699.
12 p.ℓ., 216 p. 4 fold. plates, fold. map.
19cm. 8° (Issued as a part of his A new dis-
covery, London, 1699.)
A Continuation transl. from Nouveau voyage
d'un pais plus grand que l'Europe, Utrecht, 1698.
The "added, Several New Discoveries" men-
tioned on the t.-p. are: Joliet's account of New
France, p. 174-176; "An Account of M. La Salles
Voyage to the River Mississipi. Directed to
Count Frontenac, Governor of New-France"
p. 176-184; "A Discovery of some New Countries
and Nations in the Northern-American. By Father
Marquette" p. 184-211 (1st pub. as "Découverte de

quelques pays et nations de l'Amerique septentrionale" in Melchisédech Thévenot's Recueil de voyages, Paris, 1681); and an account of La Salle's later discoveries and death, p. 212-216.

Bookseller's advertisement, last p.

This transl. 1st pub. London, 1698 ("Tonson" edition).

Sabin31372; WingH1452; Paltsits(Hennepin) lxiii; cf. Harrisse(NF)181.

06011A, before 1915

E699
H515ne
Hennepin, Louis, ca. 1640-ca. 1705.
Neue Entdeckung vieler sehr grossen Landschafften In America Zwischen Neu-Mexico und dem Eyss-Meer gelegen/welche bisshero denen Europäern noch unbekand gewesen/und an Grösse gantz Europa übertreffen . ... in Frantzösis. Sprache überreichet und beschrieben von R. P. Ludovy. Hennepin, Missionario Recollect. & Notario Apostol. Ins Teutsche übersetzet durch M. J. G. Langen C. Th. Mit Land-Charten und Kupffer-Figuren.

Bremen/In Verlegung Philip Gottfr. Saurmans/ Buchh. 1699.

23 p.ℓ., 382 p. 3 fold. plates, fold. map. 13cm. 12º

Title in red and black.

In this copy there is a blank ℓ. at end.

Transl. from Nouvelle decouverte d'un tres grand pays, 1st pub. Utrecht, 1697. An amplification of his Description de la Louisiane, 1st pub. Paris, 1683 ("Les moeurs des sauvages" section, however, is omitted), but also with material appropriated from Chrétien LeClercq's Etablissement de la foy dans la Nouvelle France, Paris, 1691 (especially the account included therein of La Salle's discoveries, by Zénobe Membré).

JCB(2)2:1572; Sabin31367; Palmer336; Paltsits (Hennepin)lvi.

05752, before 1866

E699
H515nd
Hennepin, Louis, ca. 1640-ca. 1705.
A New Discovery Of A Vast Country in America, Extending above Four Thousand Miles, Between New France & New Mexico; With A Deseription [sic] of the Great Lakes, Cataracts, Rivers, Plants, and Animals. Also, the Manners, Customs, and Languages of the several Native Indians; And the Advantage of Commerce with those different Nations. With A Continuation Giving an Account of the Attempts of the Sieur de la Salle upon the Mines of St. Barbe, &c. The Taking of Quebec by the English; With the Advantages of a shorter Cut to China and Japan. Both Illustrated with Maps, and Figures; and Dedicated to His Majesty King William. By L. Hennepin now Resident in Holland. To which are added, Several New Discoveries in North-America, not Publish'd In [sic] the French Edition.

London, Printed by for Henry Bonwicke, at the Red Lion in St. Paul's Church-Yard. 1699.

11 p.ℓ., 138, 155-170, 161-240, [24], 216 p. incl. front. 6 fold. plates, 2 fold. maps. 19cm. 8º

New discovery transl. from Nouvelle decouverte d'un tres grand pays, Utrecht, 1697.

With, as issued, his A continuation of the new discovery, London, 1699, with special t.-p., separate paging, but continuous signatures.

This transl. 1st pub. London, 1698 ("Tonson" edition).

Bookseller's advertisement, last p.

Sabin31372; WingH1452; Paltsits(Hennepin)lxiii; cf. Harrisse(NF)181.

06011, before 1915

E699
H515no
Hennepin, Louis, ca. 1640-ca. 1705.
Nieuwe Ontdekkinge Van een groot Land, gelegen in America, tusschen nieuw Mexico En De Ys-Zee. ... Door Lodewyk Hennepin, Missionaris Recollect en Notaris Apostoliek.

Tot Amsterdam, By Abraham van Someren, 1699.

13 p.ℓ., 220, [14] p. 2 fold. plates, 2 fold. maps. 20.5cm. 4º

Transl. from Nouvelle decouverte d'un tres grand pays, first pub. Utrecht, 1697. An amplification of his Description de la Louisiane, first pub. Paris, 1683 ("Les moeurs des sauvages" section, however, is omitted), but also with material appropriated from Chrétien LeClercq's Etablissement de la foy dans la Nouvelle France, Paris, 1691 (especially the account included therein of La Salle's discoveries, by Zénobe Membré).

Imperfect: maps (same as in Amsterdam, 1702, ed.) wanting.

Sabin31359; Harrisse(NF)183; Paltsits (Hennepin)lv.

06006, before 1902

E699
H515r
[Hennepin, Louis] ca. 1640-ca. 1705.
Relacion De Un Pais Que nuevamente se ha descubierto En La America Septentrional De Mas Estendido Que Es La Europa. Y que saca à luz en Castellano ... Don Sebastian Fernandez De Medrano, Director de la Academia Real y Militar de el Exercito de los Païses Bajos.

En Brusselas, En Casa de Lamberto Marchant, Mercader de Libros. M. DC. XCIX.

4 p.ℓ., 86 p. 2 plates, fold. map. 15.5cm.

12º
Cut on t.-p.
Abridged transl. of Nouvelle decouverte d'un tres grand pays. 1st pub. Utrecht, 1697.
An amplification of his Description de la Louisiane, 1st pub. Paris, 1683 ("Les moeurs des sauvages" section, however, is omitted), but also with material appropriated from Chrétien LeClercq's Etablissement de la foy dans la Nouvelle France, Paris, 1691 (especially the account included therein of La Salle's discoveries, by Zénobe Membré).
Preliminary matter includes poetry.
"Prologo" (3d-4th p.ℓ.) by the translator, Sebastián Fernández de Medrano.
JCB(2)2:1573; Sabin 31374; Medina(BHA)1995; Harrisse(NF)184; Paltsits(Hennepin)lv; Peeters-Fontainas(1965)588.
0891, 1846

D   The History Of Caledonia: Or, The Scots
Scott Colony In Darien In the West Indies. With
60   an Account of the Manners of the Inhabitants, and Riches of the Countrey. By a Gentleman lately Arriv'd.
London: Printed, and Sold by John Nutt, near Stationers-Hall. MDCXCIX.
54 p. 18.5cm. 8º
JCB(2)2:1563; Wing H2114; Sabin 18556; Scott 60.
01946, 1854

D699 The History Of The Bucaniers Of America; From
H673o their First Original down to this Time; Written in Several Languages; and now Collected into one Volume. ... The Whole newly Translated into English ...
London: Printed for Tho. Newborough at the Golden Ball in St. Paul's Church Yard, John Nicholson at the King's Arms in Little Britain, and Benj. Tooke at the Middle Temple Gate, Fleestreet [sic]. 1699.
2 p.ℓ., 180, 180, [12] p., 1 ℓ., [2], 204 p. illus. (incl. maps), 4 plates (incl. 2 fold.), 4 ports., 6 fold. maps. 20cm. 8º
Collection of 4 works (commonly entered under Exquemelin).
I. Account by Exquemelin; 1st pub. Amsterdam, 1678, under title: De Americaensche Zee-Roovers. This transl. 1st pub. London, Crooke, 1684, under title: Bucaniers Of America (editorial changes made for this ed.) and was transl. from the Spanish transl. 1st pub. Cologne, 1681, under title: Piratas De La America.
II. Account by Basil Ringrose; 1st pub. London, Crooke, 1685, under title: Bucaniers Of America.

The Second Volume (editorial changes made for ed.)
III. Account by Raveneau de Lussan; 1st pub. Paris, 1689, under title: Journal du voyage fait à la mer de sud.
IV. Account by Montauban; transl. from Relation du voyage du sieur de Montauban, Amsterdam, 1698.
III and IV issued with a special t.-p. (A journal of a voyage..., London, 1698) and separate paging and signatures.
Wing E3899; Sabin 23483.
29757, 1945

D   Information Concernant L'Affaire De Darien.
Scott [Paris? 1699?]
54   15 p. 21.5cm. 4º
JCB(2)2:1594; Sabin 18558; Scott 54; Kress S2120; Knuttel 15398.
0568, 1846

DA699 [Keith, George] 1639?-1716.
M562a An Abstract, By way of Index, of some very unsound, and some other Antichristian Passages, Collected out of G. Whitehead's and W. Penn's Books, plainly contradicting their late Creeds, one Signed by W. Penn at Dublin in Ireland, on which the B. of Cork hath made some seasonable Remarks, another Signed by G. W. called a few Positions of the sincere Belief, and Christian Doctrine of the people called Quakers, both Printed this present Year 1698.
London, Printed for the Author, and are to be Sold by B. Aylmer at the Three Pidgeons over against the Royal Exchange, Cornhill, and C. Brome at the Gun at the West-end of St. Pauls. 1699.
15 p. 16cm. 8º
Caption title: imprint at end.
A commentary on George Whitehead's A Few Positions of the Sincere Belief and Christian Doctrine..., 1st pub. London, 1698, and William Penn's [and others'] Gospel-Truths ..., 1st pub. [Dublin, 1698]; with extensive quotations.
Signed: Given forth by some Friends of Truth, belonging to the Meeting at Turner's-Hall, and some Friends in the Country in unity with them. London the 10th. 1698.
No. [6] in a volume of 7 pamphlets on Quakerism. Bound in contemporary stained vellum.
Wing W1886; Smith(Friends)2:34.
M1591, 1914

DA699 K28d	Keith, George, 1639?-1716. The Deism Of William Penn, And his Brethren, Destructive to the Christian Religion, Exposed, and plainly laid open. In The Examination and Refutation of his late reprinted Book, called, A Discourse of the General Rule of Faith and Practise, and Judge of Controversie. ... By George Keith. London, Printed for Brab. Aylmer at the Three Pigeons against the Royal Exchange in Cornhill, 1699. 4 p. ℓ., 152 p. 16cm. 8º Penn's <u>A Discourse of the general rule of faith and practice</u> 1st pub. London, 1674. Errata, 4th p.ℓ.v. Signed (p. 152): 28th of the First Month, 1699. G. K. Wing K156; Smith(Friends)2:36.	D699 -L651f 70-118	A Letter From A Gentleman in America, to his Friend in Scotland. Bolston [sic] November 8th. 1689 [sic, i.e. 1699]. [Edinburgh? 1699] Broadside. 30 x 17.5cm. (13cm. in binding). 1/2º Concerns the Scots Darien Colony.
6540, 1910			
DA699 M562a	[Keith, George] 1639?-1716. A Serious Dialogue Betwixt A Church-Man And A Quaker. London, Printed for Brab. Aylmer at the Three Pigeons against the Royal Exchange in Cornhil. 1699. 16 p. 16cm. 8º Signed: G. K. "Some Books lately Writ by G. Keith, and Sold by Brab. Aylmer..." p. [2]. "Advertisement" (of works by Keith) p. 16. No. [5] in a volume of 7 pamphlets on Quakerism bound in contemporary stained vellum. Wing K207; Smith(Friends)2:34.	D Scott 63 952, 1905	A Letter, giving A Description Of The Isthmus Of Darian: (Where the Scot's Colonie is settled;) From a Gentleman who lives there at present. With an Account of the Fertilness of the Soil, The Quality of the Air, The Manners of the Inhabitants, And the Nature of the Plants, and Animals. &c. And A particular Mapp of the Isthmus, and Entrance to the River of Darian. Edinburgh, Printed for John Mackie, in the Parliament-Close, and James Wardlaw on the North Side of the Street a little below the Cross, at the sign of the Bible. Price 7 Pence. M. DC. XC. IX. 24 p. 18.5cm. fold. map. 4º Wing L1549; Sabin78221; Scott 63.
M1590, 1914			
BA699 L473d	Ledesma, Clemente de. Despertador Republicano, Qve Por Las Letras Del A.B.C. Compendia El Segvndo Tomo de Noticias Theologicas Morales, y apunta, y despierta á los Republicanos de la general Republica de este mundo la obligacion que cada vno tiene en su estado, y en su oficio. ... Dedica El M. R. P. Fr. Clemente De Ledesma Ex Lector de Phylosofia, Predicador Jubilado, y Ex-Ministro Provincial, y Padre immediato de esta Provincia del Santo Evangelio. En Mexico por Doña Maria de Benavides. Año de 1699. 13 p. ℓ., 413, [414-420] p. 14.5cm. 8º License dated (13th p. ℓ.) 6 Febr. 1699. Abridgment of his <u>Despertador de noticias theológicas morales...Segundo tomo</u>, Mexico, 1698. Palau(2)134132; Medina(Mexico)1731.	BA699 L686b 12533, 1920 rev	Lezamis, José de. Breve Relacion De la Vida, y muerte del Illmo. y Rmo. Señor Doctor D. Francisco de Aguiar, y Seyxas, que está en la vida del Apostol Santiago el Mayor. Escrita Por El Ldo. Don Ioseph de Lezamis, Cura de la Santa Iglesia Cathedral de Mexico: y dada à la estampa à costa, y devocion del mismo Author. ... Con Licencia De Los Superiores En Mexico, por Doña Maria de Benavides. Año de 1699. [124] p. 20.5cm. 4º License dated (p. [120]) 9 Dec. 1698. Also issued as a part of his <u>Vida del apostol Santiago el mayor</u>, Mexico, 1699, the preliminary matter of which appears here on p. [112-124]. In this copy the first leaf appears to be a cancel. Palau(2)137582; Medina(Mexico)1732; Sabin 40909; Streit 2:2349.
69-779		BA699 L771s	Lisperguer y Solís, Matías, fl. 1687-1700. Sermon Panegirico En La Pvblicacion Solemne del Breue confirmatorio de la Religion Betleemitica Fecha En La Iglesia Catredal [sic] de Lima el Domingo quarto de Quaresma.

Predicolo El M.R.P.M. Fr. Mathias Lispergver y Solis Calificador de el Santo Oficio, Maestro en Artes, y Doctor Theologo en la Real Vniuersidad de S. Marcos. Catedratico (que fue) de Prima de Theologia en la Vniuersidad Pontificia de S. Ildefonso, Regente general de los Estudios, y Coronista de la Prouincia del Peru de el Orden de Nuestro P. S. Agustin. ...

Con Licencia De Los Superiores En Lima; por Joseph de Contreras, y Alvarado, Impressor Real del S. Oficio, y de la S. Cruzada. Año de 1699.

8 p.ℓ., [28] p. 20cm. 4°

Dedication and licenses dated (4th p.ℓ.^{r}, 8th p.ℓ.^{v}) 18 Dec. 1698.

Vargas Ugarte 949.

12529, 1920

D698
L945m
3

Ludlow, Edmund, 1617?-1692.
Memoirs Of Lieutenant General Ludlow. The Third and Last Part. With A Collection of Original Papers, serving to confirm and illustrate many important Passages of this and the preceding Volumes. To which is added, A Table to the whole Work.

Switzerland, Printed at Vevay [sic] in the Canton of Bern [i.e. London], 1699.

4 p.ℓ., 159, 162-402, [56] p., 1 ℓ. 20cm. 8°

(Issued as a part of his Memoirs, Vevey [i.e. London], 1698-99.)

Thought to have been edited by Isaac Littlebury, perhaps with the collaboration of John Toland.

Imprint attributed is: London, John Darby.

Errata, ℓ. at end.

Preface (2d-4th p.ℓ.) dated in Bern, 26 Mar. 1699.

Wing L3462.

68-352A

C699
M265a

Mamiani della Rovere, Lodovico Vincenzo, 1652-1730.
Arte De Grammatica Da Lingua Brasilica Da Naçam Kiriri Composta Pelo P. Luis Vincencio Mamiani, Da Companhia de Jesu, Missionario nas Aldeas da dita Naçáo.

Lisboa, Na Officina de Miguel Deslandes, Impressor de Sua Mag. Anno de 1699. Com todas as licenças necessarias.

8 p.ℓ., 124 p. illus. (table). 14cm. 8°

Cut (Jesuit trigram, floriated) on t.-p.

License dated (8th p.ℓ.^{r}) 3 July 1698.

Sabin 44178; Backer 5:454; Viñaza 243; Borba de Moraes 2:14; Innocencio 5:334.

12136, 1919

B699
=M333g

Mariana, Juan de, 1536-1624.
The General History Of Spain. From The first Peopling of it by Tubal, till the Death of King Ferdinand, Who United the Crowns of Castile and Aragon. With A Continuation To The Death of King Philip III. Written in Spanish, By the R.F.F. John de Mariana. To which are added, Two Supplements, The First By F. Ferdinand Camargo y Salcedo, the other by F. Basil Varen de Soto, bringing it down to the present Reign. The whole Translated from the Spanish By Capt John Stevens.

London: Printed for Richard Sare at Grays-Inn-Gate in Holbourn, Francis Saunders in the New-Exchange in the Strand, and Thomas Bennet at the Half-Moon in St. Paul's Church-Yard. 1699.

9 p.ℓ., 204 p., 205-216 (i.e. 217) numb. ℓ., 217-388, 401-563, 52, 57-95, [12] p. 35cm. fol.

First pub. in Latin under title Historiae de rebus Hispaniae, Toledo, 1592. Author's Spanish transl. 1st pub. Toledo, 1601, under title: Historia general de España. Text successively extended in the editions pub. during author's lifetime. Supplement by Camargo y Salcedo 1st pub. in Madrid, 1650, ed. Supplement by Varén de Soto 1st pub. in Madrid, [1670] ed., which probably also was source of Stevens' transl. (with some abridgment and rearrangement) into English.

Bound in contemporary calf.

Wing M599; Sabin 44553; Palau (2) 151712; Backer 5:555.

68-222

C619
A949n

Masa, Pedro de Chaves.
Llantos Funebres A La Sentida, Lamentable, Temprana, Exemplar Y Maravillosa Muerte De La Serenissima Señora Doña Maria Sophia Ysavel De Neoburg Reyna De Portugal ... Don Pedro De Chaves Masa, Su Autor Natural de la Ciudad de Truxillo.

Lisboa. Con las licencias necessarias. En la Imprenta de Bernardo Da Costa. Año 1699.

14 p. 19.5cm. 4°

Cut (royal arms of Portugal) on t.-p.

A group of poems.

This copy closely trimmed at top.

Bound as the 16th in a volume of 58 pamphlets, 1619-1702.

9356-2, 1913

DB
-M4143
1699
1

Massachusetts (Colony)--Laws, statutes, etc.
8 June 1692 - 31 May 1699
Acts And Laws, Of His Majesties Province of the Massachusetts-Bay, in New-England.

Boston. Printed by Bartholomew Green, and John Allen, (Printers to His Excellency the Governour and Council,) for, and Sold by Michael Perry at his Shop over against the Town-House, and Benjamin Eliot under the West-End of the Town-House. 1699.
158, [4] p. 30.5cm. fol.
Cut (royal arms) on t.-p.
"Re-printed, By Order Of His Excellency the Governour, Council and Assembly." (p. 2).
Contains session laws 8 June 1692 - 31 May 1699.
Imperfect: p. 1-4 wanting; available in facsim.
With this are bound session laws 31 May 1699 - 29 May 1706 which were issued as supplementary parts, Boston 1700-1706, and were paged 159-296 in continuation of this, except that An act passed by the ... fourth session [Boston, 1704] (p. 261-262) is wanting. Session laws 7 Aug 1706-October 1713 also were issued as supplementary parts, Boston 1706-1713, and were paged 297-406 in continuation of this, but those parts are wanting in this copy.
WingM949; Evans867; Sabin45566; Church781; Tower148.

R-S 2001-1, 1913

D.Math Mather, Cotton, 1663-1728.
C.121   The Faith of the Fathers. Or, The Articles of the True Religion, All of them Exhibited In the Express Words of the Old Testament. Partly, To Confirm those who do profess that Religion of God, and His Messiah. But Chiefly, To Engage the Jewish Nation, unto the Religion of their Patriarchs; ... By Cotton Mather. ...
Boston in New-England. Printed by B. Green, and J. Allen. 1699.
24 p. 16.5cm. 8°
JCB(2)2:1574; Evans874; WingM1108; Sabin 46316; Holmes(C.)121; Dexter(Cong.)2503; Brinley1113(this copy).

06346, 1878

D.Math Mather, Cotton, 1663-1728.
C.129   A Family Well-Ordered. Or An Essay To Render Parents and Children Happy in one another. Handling Two very Important Cases. I. What are the Duties to be done by Pious Parents, for the promoting of Piety in their Children. II. What are the Duties that must be paid by Children to their Parents, that they may obtain the Blessings of the Dutiful. By Cotton Mather. ...
Boston, Printed by B. Green, & J. Allen, for Michael Perry, at his Shop over-against the Town-House: & Benjamin Eliot, at his Shop under the West-End of the Town-House. 1699.
79, 5 p. 14cm. 12°
Paging 1-5 (2d count) begins on verso of p. 79.
"An Address, Ad Fratres in Eremo" 5 p. at end.
Bound in contemporary calf, rebacked.
Evans875; WingM1109; Sabin46324; Holmes (C.)129.

06347, after 1882

D.Math Mather, Increase, 1639-1723.
I.128E De Successu Evangelii Apud Indos Occidentales, In Novâ-Angliâ; Epistola. Ad Cl. Virum D. Johannem Leusdenum Linguæ Sanctæ in Ultrajectinâ Academiâ Professorem, Scripta, A Crescentio Mathero Apud Bostonienses V.D.M. nec non Collegii Harvardini quod est Cantabrigia Nov-Anglorum, Rectore. Londini, Typis J.G. 1688' Jam recusua, & successu Evangelii apud Indos Orientales aucta.
Ultrajecti, Apud Wilhelmum Broedeleth, Anno 1699.
16 p. 16cm. 8°
Probably edited by Johannes Leusden, the addressee of the letters which comprise the text.
Includes in addition to Mather's letter: De Successu Evangelii Apud Indos Orientales, Epistolæ Aliæ Conscriptæ Tum â D. Hermanno Specht, ... in Insula Ceilon. Tum etiam, â D. Adriano De Mey, ... Præfecto Collegii Malabarici; Et, â D. Francisco Valentino, ... in Amboina ... with special half-title but continuous paging ([9]-15) and signatures; and a letter from Pierre Jurieu (p. 15-16).
Mather's letter 1st pub. London, 1688, under title: De successu evangelij. The East Indian reports and Jurieu's letter were undoubtedly 1st pub. in another edition issued by Wilhelm Broedeleth in Utrecht, 1693, also under title: De successu evangelij: one of the East Indian reports is dated 22 Jan. 1692 (p. 13 in this ed.) and all others are dated earlier. The Utrecht, 1693 ed., however, is known only from a reference on the t.-p. of a German transl. issued Halle, 1696, under title: Ein Brieff von dem glücklichen Fortgang des Evangelii.
Sabin46750; Holmes(I.)128E.

05312, before 1898

DA682 Mather, Increase, 1639-1723.
P451f The Surest way to the Greatest Honour: Discoursed in a Sermon, Delivered In the Audience of His Excellency the Earl of Bellomont, Captain General and Governour in Chief, and of the Council, and Representatives of the General Assembly of the Province of the Massachusetts Bay, Covened at Boston in New-England, May 31st. 1699. Being the day for the Election of Counsellors in that Province. By Increase Mather.
Boston. Printed by Bartholomew Green, & John Allen, for Samuel Phillips, and are to be Sold at the Brick Shop near the Old. Meeting-House, 1699.
4 p. ℓ., 3-25, 28-42 p. 15cm. (16cm. in case). 8º
Dedication dated (4th p. ℓ.ᵛ) Boston, June 7, 1699.
Errata, p. 42.
Imperfect: p. ℓ. 1-4 and p. 1-20 wanting, p. 30-31 mutilated; available in facsim.
Bound with: Perkins, William. The Foundation of Christian Religion. Boston, 1682.
WingM1255; Evans880; Sabin46751; Holmes(I) 129.
13021-2, 1921

CA699 Mattos, Francisco de, 1636-1720.
M444s Sermam Do Grande Patriarcha S. Ignacio Que Pregou O Padre Mestre Francisco De Mattos da Companhia de Jesus, Reytor do Collegio do Rio de Janeiro, Na Igreja do mesmo Collegio, anno de 1697.
Lisboa, Na Officina de Antonio Pedrozo Galraõ. M. DC. XC. IX. Com todas as licenças necessarias.
38 p. 20cm. 4º
Cut (Jesuit trigram, floriated) on t.-p.
Includes commendatory verses by João Mendes da Silva, Miguel de Crasto Lara, and one anonymous, p. [3-5].
Borba de Moraes2:38; Backer5:743; Leite 1:363.
70-552

DA699 Meriton, John, 1666-1717.
M562a An Antidote Against the Venom of Quakerism, Or, Some Observations On a Little Pamphlet, Stiled, The Christianity of the People, Commonly Called Quakers. By John Meriton, A. M. Rector of Boughton in Norfolk. ...
London, Printed for the Author: And are to be sold by J. Robinson at the Golden-Lion in St. Paul's Church-Yard. And H. Rhodes at the Star in Fleet-street. 1699.
48 p. 16cm. 8º

A reply to George Whitehead's The Christianity of the people commonly called Quakers ..., London, 1690.
No. [1] in a volume of 7 pamphlets on Quakerism, bound in contemporary stained vellum.
WingM1816; Smith(Anti-Quak)289.
M1586, 1914

D699 Moxon, Joseph, 1627-1691.
M937t A Tutor to Astronomy and Geography. Or, an easie and speedy way to know the Use of both the Globes, Cœlestial and Terrestial. In Six Books. The ⟨1. Teaching the Rudiments of Astronomy and Geography, 2. 3. 4. 5. 6.⟩ Shewing by the Globes the Solution of ⟨Astronomical and Geographical Problems, Problems in Navigation, Astrological Problems, Gnomonical Problems, Trigonometrical Problems, ... With an Appendix shewing the use of the Ptolomaick Sphere. By Joseph Moxon. Whereunto is added the Antient Poetical Stories of the Stars; shewing Reasons why the several Shapes and Forms are Pictured on the Cœlestical Globe. As also a Discourse of the Antiquity, Progress and Augmentation of Astronomy. The Fifth Edition, Corrected and Enlarged. By Phillip Lea. ...
Globes, Sphers [sic], Maps, Mathematical Projections, Books and Instruments are made and Sold, By Phillip Lea, at the Atlas and Hercules in Cheapside, near the Corner of Friday street, London. [1699]
4 p. ℓ., 271, [272-280] p. incl. illus., front. (port.), tables. 20.5cm. 4º
A rev. and enl. of the 1st ed., London, 1659.
Fifth edition 1st pub. London, 1698. These are the same sheets with cancel t.-p.
Also issued with t.-p. bearing imprint: London, Printed for W. Hawes, 1699.
"... the Ancient Stories Of the several Stars and Constellations... Collected from Dr. Hood": p. 208-232.
"A Discourse Of the Antiquity, Progress and Augmentation Of Astronomy" by Pierre Gassendi: p. 233-271.
"A Catalogue of Globes, Celestial and Terrestrial, Spheres, Maps ... Made and Sold by J. Moxon": p. 272.
Bound in contemporary calf.
WingM3027.
29782, 1945

BA699 Narváez, Juan de, ca. 1650-1706.
N238s Sermon En La Solemnidad, Qve Se Consagrò á Christo S. N. Sacramentado, y à su Santissi-

ma Madre en su milagrosa Imagen de los Remedios por el feliz sucesso de la Flota en el viage de buelta à España. Qve Discvrrio En termino de quarenta horas, y predicò en esta S. Iglesia Metropolitana de Mexico el Sr Dr D. Jvan De Narvaes, Y Saabedra Racionero entero de dicha Santa Iglesia, Cathedratico de Prima de Sagrada Escriptura en la Real Vniversidad de esta Corte, Examinador Synodal de este Arçobispado, y Vicario Visitador de los Conventos de Regina Cœli, y S. Ynes. Sacale A Lvz El D^r y M^o D. Augustin De Cabañas Cura del Sagrario de esta S. Iglesia, Cathedratico Proprietario de Philosophia en esta Real Vniversidad, y Iuez del Colegio Seminario. ...
   Con licencia: en Mexico, por los Herederos de la Viuda de Francisco Rodriguez Lupercio en la puente de Palacio. Año de 1699.
   9 p. ℓ., 14 numb. ℓ. 19.5cm. 4°
   Approbation dated (9th p. ℓ.^{r}) 8 June 1699.
   Palau(2)187729; Medina(Mexico)1736.

13424, 1923

BA699 N238sq   Narváez, Juan de, ca. 1650-1706.
   Sermon Qve En La Opposicion A La Canongia Magistral de esta Santa Yglesia Cathedral Metropolitana de Mexico. Predico con termino de quarenta y ocho horas el Dr D. Ivan De Narvaes Saabedra Racionero entero de dicha Santa Yglesia, Cathedratico de Prima de Sagrada Escriptura, en la Real Universidad de esta Corte, Examinador Synodal deste Arçobispado, Vicario Visitador de los Conventos de N. Señora de Regina Cœli, y Santa Ynes. Dedicalo ... El D.D. Pedro Del Castillo, Y Vergara Cura Proprietario de la Parroquia de la Santa Vera-Cruz de esta Ciudad, Rector actual de la Real Vniversidad de ella, quien lo saca á luz.
   Con licencia: en Mexico, por los Herederos de la Viuda de Francisco Rodriguez Lupercio, en la puente de Palacio Año de 1699,
   8 p. ℓ., 14 numb. ℓ. 19.5cm. 4°
   Dedication dated (4th p. ℓ.^{r}) 13 June 1699.
   Palau(2)187728; Medina(Mexico)1737.

13425, 1923

bD Scott 88b   An Ode Made On The Welcome News Of The safe Arrival and Kind Reception Of The Scottish Collony At Darien in America.
   Edinburgh, Printed by James Watson in Craig's Closs 1699.
   [2] p. 32cm. fol.
   Caption title; imprint at end.
   Aldis3875; Sabin78228; Scott88b.

06227, before 1904

D Scott 64b   [Paterson, William] 1658-1719.
   An Abstract Of A Letter From a Person of Eminency and worth in Caledonia to a Friend at Boston in New-England.
   Boston, Printed [by B. Green and J. Allen] May, 15th. 1699.
   2, 4 p. 19cm. 4°
   Caption title; imprint at end.
   Signed (p. 2, 1st count): Fort St. Andrew. February, 18th. 1698, 9.
   First pub. Edinburgh, the same year.
   With, as issued: Company of Scotland Trading to Africa and the Indies. Caledonia; the declaration of the council, with caption title, separate paging and signature.
   JCB(2)2:1567; Evans892; Wing P708; Sabin78197; Scott 64b, c; Brinley810 (this copy).

06033, 1878

D699 P412a   [Penn, William] 1644-1718.
   An Account Of The Blessed End Of Gulielma Maria Penn, And Of Springet Penn, The Beloved Wife and Eldest Son of William Penn.
   [London?] Printed for the Benefit of his Family, Relations, and particular Friends, in Memory of them, and the Lord's Goodness to Them. [1699?]
   10, 18 p. 14cm. 8°.
   Signed (p. 18): William Penn.
   Smith(Friends)2:318; WingP1243.

04813, 1883-1890

DA699 P412c   Penn, William, 1644-1718.
   The Christian-Quaker And His Divine Testimony Stated and Vindicated, From Scripture, Reason and Authority. By W. Penn. ...
   London, Printed and Sold by T. Sowle, in White-Hart-Court in Gracious-Street, and at the Bible in Leaden-Hall-Street, near the Market, 1699.
   7 p. ℓ., 144, 149-254 p. 18cm. 8°
   Signed by Penn, 5th p. ℓ.^{v}, p. 202, 254.
   First pub. [London] 1674. Here material by George Whitehead found in earlier editions is omitted.
   With, as issued, [his] A Discourse Of The General Rule Of Faith and Practice [London] 1699, with special t.-p., but continuous paging and signatures.
   Smith notes another issue with an addition to the title and a "Postscript" at end.
   JCB(2)2:1575; Sabin59689n; Smith(Friends) 2:291-292; WingP1267.

04211, before 1882

DA699   [Penn, William] 1644-1718.
P412c   A Discourse Of The General Rule Of Faith
           and Practice, And Judge of Controversie. ...
           By the same Author. ...
              [London, T. Sowle] Printed in the Year, 1699.
              [203]-254 p. 18cm. 8⁰ (Issued as a part of
           his The Christian Quaker, London, 1699.)
              Signed (p. 254): William Penn.
              First pub. [London] 1674 with The Christian
           Quaker.
              Smith notes another issue (also a part of
           his The Christian Quaker, London, 1699) with
           a "Postscript" at end.
              Also issued with separate paging and sig-
           natures and with imprint: London, Printed
           and Sold by T. Sowle in White-Hart-Court...
           1699.
              Smith(Friends)2:292; WingP1277.
04211A, before 1882

bD   [Pennecuik, Alexander] 1652-1722.
Scott   Caledonia Triumphans: A Panegyrick To
84   the King.
              Edinburgh, Printed by the Heirs and Successors
           of Andrew Anderson, Printer to the Kin[g's] most
           Excellent Majesty, 1699.
              Broadside. 42 x 34cm. 1⁰
              Cut (arms of Darien Company) at head of title.
              Verse.
              Signed at end: By a Lover of Caledonia and
           the Muses.
              WingC285; Scott 84.
06230, before 1900

C619   Ponte, Ioaõ Baptista da, 1677-1741.
A949n   Queyxas Da Fermosura Contra As Tyran-
           nias Da Parca, Executadas Em O Coraçam
           De Portugal Por Meyo Da Morte De Sua
           Serenissima Rainha A Senhora D. Maria
           Sophia Isabel De Neoburg. Tiradas Do Soneto
           Oytenta E Tres Da Primeyra Parte das Rimas
           de Camões Por Joam Baptista Da Ponte.
              Lisboa. Na Officina de Manoel Lopes
           Ferreyra. M. DC. XC. IX. Com todas as
           licenças necessarias.
              1 p.ℓ., [8] p. 19.5cm. 4⁰
              Consists of a sonnet of Camões ("Que levas
           cruel Morte?..."), p. [1], with a verse gloss
           in 14 stanzas, p. [2-8].
              Bound as the 15th in a volume of 58 pamphlets,
           1619-1702.
9356-1, 1913

CB   Portugal--Conselho da Fazenda.
-P8539   Contrato Do Paço Da Madeira, Qve Se Fez
1699   No Concelho Da Fazenda com Francisco Pereira
1   Brandaõ, por seu Procurador Francisco Ferreira
           Soares, por tempo de tres annos.
              Lisboa, Na Officina de Migvel Deslandes, Im-
           pressor de Sua Magestade. M. DC. XCIX.
              12 p. 30cm. fol.
              Cut (royal arms) on t.-p.
              In part concerns commerce with Brazil
           (article XXI, p. 10).
              Registration dated (p. 12) 29 Jan. 1699.
69-182

E699   Raveneau de Lussan, ---- b. 1663.
R253j   Journal Du Voyage Fait A La Mer De Sud,
           Avec Les Flibustiers De L'Amerique. Par le
           Sieur Raveneau De Lussan.
              A Paris, Chez Jacques Le Febvre, Imprimeur-
           Libraire, ruë de la Harpe, au Soleil d'Or, vis-
           à-vis la ruë saint Severin, M. DC. XCIX. Avec
           Privilege Du Roy.
              9 p.ℓ., 448 p. 17cm. 12⁰
              Cut on t.-p., incl. motto: Ipsa Sibi Pretium
           Virtus Et Nescia Vinci.
              First pub. Paris, 1689.
              "Achevé d'imprimer pour la premiere fois,
           en vertu des presentes Lettres de Privilege,
           le 26, d'Octobre 1699." (verso 2d p.ℓ.)
              Testimonials for the author from le sieur
           de Cussy, governor of Saint Domingue, 7th-
           9th p.ℓ.
              A reissue of the sheets of the Paris, 1693,
           ed., which probably was a reissue of the
           sheets of the Paris, 1689, ed. In this ed.
           the 1st p.ℓ. and last two leaves of the 1693
           ed. have been cancelled and replaced by
           2 p.ℓ. and two new leaves at end.
              Issued as the 3d of a 3-vol. set with Ex-
           quemelin, A.O., Histoire des avanturiers
           flibustiers, Paris, 1699, 2 v. (cf. preface
           and privilege, 2d p.ℓ.)
              Bound in contemporary calf.
              Sabin67985, 23475n.
12910, 1920

bD   The Recruits for Caledonia Of the Rysing-
Scott   Sun, Their Farewell To Old Scotland.
87b   [Edinburgh? 1699]
              Broadside. 31 x 20cm. 1/2⁰
              Verse.
              Signed: By a Volunteer in this Expedition.
           In the Kyles of Bute September, 13. 1699.
              Sabin records this with imprint "Edinburgh:
           Printed by James Watson... 1699."
              Scott 87b; cf. Sabin78230.
06086, 1883, rev 3

[399]

E699　　　Relation Fidele De L'Expedition De Cartagene.
R382f　　　[Paris?] M. DC. XCIX.
　　　　　89 p. 16cm. 8º
　　　　　Probably written by or at the instance of Jean-Baptiste Ducasse, Governor of Saint Domingue and one of the chiefs of the expedition, in reply to the baron de Pointis' Relation de l'expedition, 1st pub. Amsterdam, 1698.
　　　　　In this copy there is a blank ℓ. at end.
　　　　　Bound in contemporary calf.
　　　　　JCB(2)2:1554; Sabin69286; Leclerc(1878) 1466.
01574, 1847 rev

D　　　　A Short Account from, And Description Of The Isthmus Of Darien, Where The Scots
Scott　　Collony Are Settled. With a Particular Map
62　　　of the Isthmus and Enterance to the River of Darien. According to our late News, and Mr. Dampier, and Mr. Wafer.
　　　　　Edinburgh, Printed [by James Watson]: And Sold by John Vallange, at his Shop on the Northside of the Street, a little above the Cross: And by James Wardlaw, at his Shop in the Parliament Closs. Price 7 Pence. 1699.
　　　　　2 p.ℓ., 19 p. illus., pl., fold. map. 19.5cm. 4º
　　　　　Taken in part from William Dampier's A new voyage round the world, 1st pub. London, 1697, and from Lionel Wafer's A new voyage and description of the Isthmus of America, 1st pub. London, 1699.
　　　　　Errata at end.
　　　　　In this copy the printer is identified in contemporary hand on the t.-p. as James Watson.
　　　　　JCB(2)2:1562; Wing S3531; Sabin78232; Scott 62; Aldis 3906.
0561, 1846

D699　　　Smith, John, 1580-1631.
S652s　　　The Sea-Man's Grammar and Dictionary, Explaining all the difficult Terms in Navigation: And The Practical Navigator and Gunner: In Two Parts. ... By Captain John Smith, Sometimes Governour of Virginia, and Admiral of New England. Now much Amplified and Enlarged, with variety of Experiments, since his Time, made by several Experienced Navigators and Gunners.
　　　　　London; Printed for Richard Mount, at the Postern on Tower-Hill, 1699.
　　　　　5 p.ℓ., 163 (i.e.171) p. illus. (tables, diagrs.), fold. pl., fold. table. 19cm. 4º
　　　　　[]¹ [A]⁴ B-H⁴ I⁴ (-I4) (k)² K⁴ (-K1) L-S⁴ T⁴ (±T3) U-Z².
　　　　　First pub. under title: An accidence or the path-way to experience, London, 1626. A rev. and enl. version of this 1st ed. was first pub. under title: A sea grammar, with the plaine exposition of Smiths Accidence ... , London, 1627. The enlargement consisted chiefly of material taken from a ms. compiled by Sir Henry Mainwaring which was 1st pub. in printed form London, 1644, under title: The sea-mans dictionary.
　　　　　A further enl. version with additions by "B.N." was first pub. under title: The sea-mans grammar and dictionary ... , London, 1691. The same setting of type was used for an edition of 1692 (except for the page nos. of signature U). These are the same sheets as the 1692 ed. with a new t.-p. and with the addition of a booksellers' advertisement.
　　　　　The alphabetical tables of Book I, "The Sea-Man's Grammar", and all of Book II, "Of Gunnery", (except for the first chapter) are by "B.N." (cf. "The Printer To The Reader", signed B.N., 3d p.ℓ., and Sabin).
　　　　　Booksellers' advertisement, 1st p.ℓ.ᵛ
　　　　　In this copy p. 63-66, (k)², and T3, paged 133-134, are cancels. Pages are misnumbered: p. 78 as 87, p. 96 as 86, and pages 137-171 as 129-144, 133-137, 130-131, 140, 153-163.
　　　　　JCB(2)2:1576; WingS4126; Sabin82843.
02435, 1851 rev

DA699　　A Sober Dialogue Between A Country Friend, a
M562a　　London Friend, and one of G. K's. Friends, Concerning The great Difference of Faith and Doctrin [sic] betwixt many of the Quakers, especially their Principal Teachers and him.
　　　　　London, Printed for the Author, And are to be Sold by B. Aylmer at the three Pidgeons over against the Royal-Exchange, Cornhil, 1699.
　　　　　16 p. 16cm. 8º
　　　　　Caption title: imprint at end.
　　　　　Occasioned by the Keithian schism.
　　　　　No. [3] in a volume of 7 pamphlets on Quakerism, bound in contemporary stained vellum.
　　　　　WingS4408; Smith(Friends)2:45; Sabin85662.
M1588, 1914

B699　　　Solís y Rivadeneyra, Antonio de, 1610-1686.
-S687i　　Istoria Della Conquista Del Messico Della
[R]　　　Popolazione, E De'Progressi Nell' America Settentrionale Conosciuta sotto nome di Nuova Spagna Scritta In Castigliano Da Don Antonio De Solis Segretario Di Sua Maesta'

Cattolica, E suo Primo Istoriografo dell' Indie, E Tradotta In Toscano Da Un' Accademico Della Crusca.

In Firenze, M.DC.IC. Nella Stamperia di S.[ua] A.[ltezza] S.[erenissima] per Gio: Filippo Cecchi. Con Lic. de'Sup.
16 p.ℓ., 763 p. illus., 3 ports. 27.5cm. 4°
Cut (printer's device) on t.-p.; incl. motto: Il Piv Bel Fior Ne Coglie.
Transl. by Filippo Corsini from Historia de la conquista de Mexico, Madrid, 1684.
Dedication (3d-4th p.ℓ.) signed: Gio: Filippo Cecchi.
License dated (16th p.ℓ.) 26 Aug. 1698.
Errata, p. 762.
Bound in contemporary calf.
JCB(2)2:1577; Sabin86486; Medina(BHA) 1773n; Palau(2)318688; Arocena IV 2.10.
03707, before 1866

BA699
S725s
Sousa, Domingo de, fl. 1663-1697.
Sermon En El Avto Publico De Feé, Que El Tribunal De El Santo Officio De Nueva-España, celebró el dia catorze de Junio de 1699. en el Real Convento de N.P.S. Domingo de Mexico Dixolo El M. Fr. Domingo De Soussa Qualificador del Santo Officio, Theologo, y Examinador Sinodal de la Nunciatura de España, Prior Provincial de la Provincia de Santiago de Predicadores de Nueva-España. ...
Con Licencia, En Mexico: Por los Herederos de la Viuda de Francisco Rodriguez Lupercio, en la puente de Palacio. Año de 1699.
12 p.ℓ., 8 numb. ℓ. 19.5cm. 4°
License dated (12th p.ℓ.ᵛ) 8 Aug. 1699.
In this copy 3d p.ℓ. mutilated; available in facsim.
Medina(Mexico)1753; Sabin88716.
06203, before 1902

D699
S727o
Southerne, Thomas, 1660-1746.
Oroonoko: A Tragedy, As it is Acted at the Theatre-Royal, By His Majesty's Servants. Written by Tho. Southerne. ... The Second Edition.
London: Printed for H. Playford in the Temple-Change. And B. Tooke at the Middle-Temple-Gate in Fleetstreet. M DC XC IX.
3 p.ℓ., 58 p. 22.5cm. 4°
Based on Aphra Behn's novel of the same title, 1st pub. London, 1688.
First pub. London, 1696.
Epilogue (3d p.ℓ.ᵛ) by William Congreve.
Cf. Dodds, J.W., Thomas Southerne, New Haven, 1933, p. 223.
JCB(2)2:1578; WingS4763; Sabin88521.
03708, before 1866

DA699
S932ℓ
Sowle, Tace, 1667-1746.
Books Printed and Sold by T. Sowle, in White-Hart-Court in Gracious-Street, and at the Bible in Leaden-Hall-Street, 1699.
[London, 1699]
[8] p. 16.5cm. 8°
Caption title.
John Crook, Truth's principles: 1st book listed. Josiah Child, A new discourse of trade: last book listed.
Lists a total of 33 books.
Bound with: [Stubbs, Henry] A light shining out of darkness, London, 1699.
Also issued in a version, [8] p., listing a total of 34 books.

DA699
S932ℓ
————Another copy. 19.5cm.
Bound with: Wyeth, Joseph. Anguis flagellatus, London, 1699.
68-160.1
05876.1

DA700
D553g
[R]
Sowle, Tace, 1667-1746.
Books Printed and Sold by T. Sowle, in White-Hart-Court in Gracious-Street, and at the Bible in Leaden-Hall-Street, 1699.
[London, 1699]
[8] p. 18.5cm. 8°
Caption title.
John Crook, Truth's principles: 1st book listed. Roger Hebden, A plain account of certain Christian experiences: last book listed.
Lists a total of 34 books.
Bound with: Dickinson, Jonathan, God's protecting providence, London, 1700.
Also issued in a version, [8] p., listing a total of 33 books.
16782-1, 1935

D699
S797o
The State of the Navy Consider'd In relation to the Victualling, Particularly in the Straits, and the West Indies. With Some Thoughts on the Mismanagements of the Admiralty for several Years past; and a Proposal to prevent the like for the future. Humbly offer'd to the Honourable House of Commons, by an English Sailor. The Second Edition.
London, Printed for A. Baldwin in Warwick-lane, 1699. Price 3d.
16 p. 19cm. (20cm. in case) 4°
First pub. London, 1699.
"A Catalogue of Books written against a Standing Army, and sold by A. Balwin [sic]." at end.
WingS5323; Sabin90621.
32329, 1959

DA682 P451f	Stone, Samuel, 1602-1663. A Short Catechism Drawn out of the Word Of God. By Samuel Stone, Minister of the Word at Hartford on Connecticot. Boston, Printed by Bartholomew Green, and John Allen, for William Gibbons. 1699. 12+ p. 15cm. (16cm. in case). 8° First pub. Boston, 1684. Imperfect: p. 1-12 only. Bound with: Perkins, William. The Foundation of Christian Religion, Boston, 1682. WingS5737; Sabin 92115.		"An Advertisement to the Reader." 2d p. ℓ.^{v} [by William Penn] Imperfect: t.-p. mutilated; available in facsim. With this is bound "Books Printed and Sold by T. Sowle ... 1699." ([8] p. listing 33 books). Bound in contemporary calf. WingS6058; Smith(Friends)1:36.
13021-8, 1921		68-160	
DA699 S932c	Stubbs, Henry, 1606?-1678. Conscience The Best Friend Upon Earth: or, The Happy Effects Of Keeping A Good Conscience. Very Useful for this Age. By Henry Stubbes, Minister of the Gospel. ... Boston, Reprinted by B. Green & J. Allen, for Nicholas Buttolph, and are to be Sold at his Shop at the corner of Gutteridg's Coffee-House. 1699. 10 p. ℓ., 64 p. 13cm. 12° First pub. London, 1677. Imperfect: p. ℓ. 1-2, 5 disintegrated; p. ℓ. 3-4, 9-10, p. 9-12, 21-24, 33-36, 45-48, 57-60 wanting. Title and imprint from Sabin and copy at New York Public Library. Sabin 93222; Bristol 201.	bD Scott 86b	Trade's Release: Or, Courage to the Scotch-Indian-Company. Being an Excellent New Ballad; To the Tune of, The Turks are all Confounded. [Edinburgh, 1699] Broadside. 38.5 x 30.5cm. fol. Sabin 96428; Scott 86b.
06877, before 1923		06228, 1883	
		BA699 T787o	Trejo, Antonio de. Oracion Evangelica del Pasmo de la Penitencia S. Pedro De Alcantara En Fiesta Qve Celebro En Sv Dia el Licenciado D. Antonio de Pereda Velazco, y Lazcano, Dignidad y Thezorero de la Sancta Iglesia Cathedral de Valladolid; quien affectuoso lo Dedica Al Illmo Y Exc^{mo} Señor Doctor D. Juan de Ortega Montañez, Obispo de Valladolid, del Consejo de su Magestad, Virrey, y Capitã General que fuê de esta Nueva España &c. Dixola El P. Fray Antonio de Trejo, Lector de Prima de Sagrada Theologia, y Guardian del Convento de San Buenaventura de dicha Ciudad de Valladolid ... Con Licencia, En la Puebla por los Herederos del Capitan Juan de Villa Real. [1699] 8 p. ℓ., 32 p. 20.5cm. 4° License (8th p. ℓ.^{v}) dated 29 Mar. 1699. Medina(Puebla)204.
DA699 S932ℓ	[Stubbs, Henry] 1632-1676. A Light Shining out of Darkness: Or, Occasional Queries Submitted To the Judgment of such as would Enquire into the True State of Things in our Times. The whole Work Revised by the Author, the Proofs Englished and Augmented, with sundry Material Discourses concerning the Ministry, Separation, Inspiration, Scriptures, Humane Learning, Oaths, Tithes, &c. With a Brief Apology for the Quakers, that they are not Inconsistent with Magistracy. By an Indifferent but Learned Hand. The Third Edition. London, Printed and Sold by T. Sowle, in White-Hart-Court in Gracious-Street, 1699. 2 p. ℓ., 230 (i.e. 258) p. 16.5cm. 8° First pub. London, 1659, probably based by Stubbs on material supplied by Sir Henry Vane. Vane undertook the 2d ed., London, 1659, which was revised and augmented with new material including that on Quakers. This 3d ed. undertaken by William Penn. "The Author's Preface To The Second Edition, in 1659." 2d p. ℓ. [by Henry Vane]	68-428	
		BA699 V433e [R]	Velasco, Alfonso Alberto de, 1635-1704. Exaltacion De La Divina Misericordia en la milagrosa renovacion de la Soberana Imagen De Christo Senor N. Crvcificado, Qve Se Venera En la Iglesia del Convento de San Ioseph de Carmelitas Descalzas de esta Ciudad de Mexico, Qve Consagra A La Madre De La Misericordia Maria Santissima de los Dolores El Doctor Alonso Alberto De Velasco, Cura mas antiguo desta Santa Iglesia Cathedral Metropolitana, Abogado de la Real Audiencia,

y de pressos del Santo Officio de la Inquisicion de esta Nueva España, y su Consultor, y del Colegio Seminario de dicha Santa Iglesia, Capellan del misma Convento. ...
  Con Licencia En Mexico: por Doña Maria de Benavides Viuda de Iuan de Ribera, en el Empedradillo. Año de 1699.
  8 p. ℓ., 67 numb. ℓ., [2] p. 20.5cm. 4º
  First pub. under title: <u>Renovacion por si misma de la soberana imagen de Christo Señor Nuestro crucificado</u> ... Mexico, 1688.
  License dated (8th p. ℓ.^{v}) 10 Dec. 1698.
  Errata, numb. ℓ. 67^v.
  Palau(1)7:137; Medina(Mexico)1754.

69-774

CA679
V665s
12
  Vieira, Antonio, 1608-1697.
  Sermoens Do P. Antonio Vieyra Da Companhia de Jesu, Prègador de Sua Magestade. Parte Duodecima...
  Lisboa, Na Officina de Miguel Deslandes, Impressor de Sua Magestade. Com todas as licenças necessarias. Anno de 1699. A' custa de Antonio Leyte Pereyra.
  10 p. ℓ., 441 p. 21.5cm. 4º
  Cut (Jesuit trigram) on t.-p.
  "Taxaō ..." dated (10th p. ℓ.) 14 Dec. 1699.
  Contains 16 sermons preached in Bahia, Brazil, 1633, 1635, Lisbon, 1642, 1644, 1645, 1646, 1669, Odivellas, Portugal, 1653, São Luiz, Brazil, 1653, 1657, Rome, 1672, etc.
  According to Leite "Deste tomo de 1699 conhecem-se duas impressões."
  In this copy p. ℓ. 5-6 are bound between p. 438-439 (as printed). In this copy there is a blank leaf at end.
  Bound in contemporary calf.
  Rodrigues2514; Backer8:660; Leite9:199; Innocencio1:290.

68-339

D699
W128n
[R]
  Wafer, Lionel, 1660?-1705?
  A New Voyage And Description Of The Isthmus of America, Giving an Account of the Author's Abode there, The Form and Make of the Country, the Coasts, Hills, Rivers, &c. Woods, Soil, Weather, &c. Trees, Fruit, Beasts, Birds, Fish, &c. The Indian Inhabitants, their Features, Complexion, &c. their Manners, Customs, Employments, Marriages, Feasts, Hunting, Computation, Language, &c. With Remarkable Occurrences in the South Sea, and elsewhere. By Lionel Wafer. Illustrated with several Copper-Plates.
  London: Printed for James Knapton, at the Crown in St. Paul's Church-yard, 1699.
  4 p. ℓ., 224, [16] p. 3 fold. plates, fold. map. 19.5cm. 8º
  Errata: 4th p. ℓ.^{v}
  "Of the Indian Inhabitants; their Manners, Customs, &c." (and brief vocabulary): p. 131-188.
  "Books sold by James Knapton": last leaf.
  Bound in contemporary calf, rebacked.
  JCB(2)2:1579; Sabin100940; Scott 81; Palau(1) 7:223; Field1617; WingW193.

01943, 1854

D699
-W258t
[R]
  [Ward, Edward] 1667-1731.
  A Trip To New-England. With A Character Of The Country and People, Both English and Indians.
  London, Printed in the Year, 1699.
  16 p. 32cm. fol.
  JCB(2)2:1580; Sabin101286; WingW764; Church 788.

03709, before 1866

DA682
P451f
  Willard, Samuel, 1640-1707.
  The Man of War. A Sermon Preached to the Artillery Company at Boston, on June 5. 1699. Being the Anniversary day for their Election Of Officers. By Samuel Willard, Teacher of a Church in Boston. ...
  Boston, Printed by B. Green, and J. Allen, for Benjamin Eliot, and are to be Sold at his Shop under the West End of the Town House. 1699.
  30 p., 1 ℓ. 15cm. (16cm. in case) 8º
  Booksellers' advertisement, last leaf.
  Bound with: Perkins, William. <u>The Foundation of Christian Religion</u>, Boston, 1682.
  WingW2284; Evans900; Sabin104093.

13021-3, 1921

DA699
W979a
  Wyeth, Joseph, 1663-1731.
  Anguis Flagellatus: Or, A Switch for the Snake. Being An Answer To the Third and Last Edition Of The Snake in the Grass. Wherein That Author's Injustice and Falshood, both in Quotation and Story, are Discover'd and Obviated. And the Truth Doctrinally Deliver'd by Us, Stated and Maintained in Opposition to his Misrepresentation and Perversion. By Joseph Wyeth. To which is added a Supplement, By George Whitehead. ...
  London, Printed and Sold by T. Sowle, in White-Hart-Court in Gracious-street, and at the Bible in Leaden-Hall-street, 1699.
  9 p. ℓ., 548 p. 19.5cm. 8º
  Errata, 9th p. ℓ.^{v}.

1699

A reply to [Charles Leslie's] Snake in the Grass, 3d ed., London, 1698, 1st pub. London, 1696.
    With this is bound "Books Printed and Sold by T. Sowle... 1699." ([8] p. listing 33 books).
    Bound in contemporary calf.
    Wing W3759; Sabin105650; Smith(Friends)2: 965-966; McAlpin4:621.

05876, after 1882

DA699
W979t
    [Wyeth, Joseph] 1663-1731.
    To all who are Advertised by G. Keith, of a Meeting intended to be held by him, at Turners-Hall, the 11th of the 11th Month, call'd January, 1699.
    London, Printed and Sold by T. Sowle, in White-Hart-Court, in Gracious-Street, 1699.
    4 p. 18.5cm. 4°
    Caption title; imprint at end.
    Signed: Joseph Wyeth.
    Wing W3762; Sabin105653; cf. Smith(Friends) 2:966.

11488, 1918

F699
Z34t
    Zanten, Laurens van.
    Treur-Tooneel Der Doorluchtige Vrouwen, Of Op en Ondergang Der Vorstinnen, En andere Beruchte Vrouwelijke Personagien ... Uit veele geloofwaardige Schrijvers, en verscheidene Taalen, met groote moeite by een versameld, Door Laurens van Zanten. Met curieuse Figuuren, (door J. Luyken gemaakt) verciert.
    t'Amsterdam, By Jan ten Hoorn, Boekverkooper, over 't Oude Heeren Logement, in de History-schryver, 1699.
    4 pts. in 1 v.: pt.1, 8 p.ℓ., 192 p. front., 3 plates; pt.2, 2 p.ℓ., 128 p. 3 plates; pt.3, 2 p.ℓ., 159 p. 3 plates; pt.4, 2 p.ℓ., 198 p. 3 plates. 23.5cm. 4°
    Title in red and black.
    Cut (monogram) on t.-p.
    Preliminary matter by Abraham van Zanten, Jan Claesz ten Hoorn (dated 1 Nov. 1699), and J. Verwey (poetry).
    Poetry at head of each chapter and side notes by Abraham Bogaert.
    "Treurige Geschiedenissen van Dona Dominica, Dochter van Don Pedro De Cardinas, Opperbevelhebber in de West-Indiën; En haar Gemaal Don Rodrigo De Cortez, En Anderen": pt.4, p. 84-91.
    In this copy part of the preliminary matter (poetry by J. Verwey) is repeated; there is a blank ℓ. at end.
    Imperfect: p. 121-124, 2d count, wanting.
    Bound in contemporary vellum.

12613, 1920

1700

bD
Scott
115
    The Address presented to His Majesty at Kensington the 11th. day of June 1700. by the Lord Ross, and the Lairds of Grubbet, Torwoodlie and Dollary, Commissioners appointed by the other Members of Parliament, who subscribed the same.
    [Edinburgh? 1700]
    Broadside. 36.5 x 30 cm. 1°
    "We do therefore ... Intreat, That Your Majesty will ... allow your Parliament to Meet ... for Redressing the Grievances of the Nation, Asserting its just Rights and Priviledges, as well at Home as Abroad, in its Colony of Caledonia ..."
    WingA555; Scott 115.

910, 1905 rev

DA701
B931n
    Atkinson, Christopher, fl. 1653-1655.
    Ishmael, And His Mother Cast out into the Wilderness Amongst the wild Beasts of the same Nature. Or, A Reply to a Book entitulled, The Scriptures proved to be the word of God, ... Given forth from the Spirit of the Lord in us that do suffer in the Goal of Norwich for the truths sake, which is persecuted and slandered by the Priests and Rulers of this City: Whose names in the flesh is, Christopher Atkinson, George Whitehead, James Lancaster, Thomas Simonds.
    London, Printed for Giles Calvert, at the Black Spread-Eagle, at the West end of Pauls, 1655 [i.e. London, R. Janeway, 1700].
    32 p. 16cm. 8° (Issued as pt. 2 of Francis Bugg, A modest defence, London, 1700.)
    A reply to Townsend, Sampson. The Scripture proved to be the word of God, London, 1654.
    Running title, p. 4-25: The Venemous Snake deeply wounded.
    Reprinted for Francis Bugg; includes, p. 27-32, in reply to the preceding: Bugg, Francis, "A Cutting Switch For the Wounded Snake."
    Smith(Friends)1:144.

16505A, 1934 rev

E700
B519r
[Bernard, Jacques] 1658-1718, ed.
Ryswykse Vrede-Handel, Bestaande in Autentike Acten, Memorien En Antwoorden, Dewelke in 't Keiserrijk, Sweeden, Savoyen, ende in de Nederlanden zijn voorgevallen; Mitsgaders alle de noodige Stukken en Documenten By de Heeren Ambassadeurs en Gevolmagtigden tot de generale Vrede, aan de Heeren Mediateurs tot Rijswijk, op het Koninglijk Huys Nieuwburg, overgegeven. Uyt het Fransch vertaalt.
In 's Gravenhaage, Gedrukt by <Gerrit Rammazeyn, Boekdrukker. En Meyndert Uytwerf, Boekverkooper. M.DCC.
19 p.l., 704, 162, [32] p. front., fold. table. 20.5cm. 4º
Cut on t.-p. Title in red and black.
Transl. from: <u>Actes et mémoires des négociations de la paix de Ryswick</u>, 1st pub. The Hague, 1699 [i.e. 1697?]

67-334

DA700
-B827ac
[R]
Bray, Thomas, 1658-1730.
The Acts Of Dr. Bray's Visitation. Held At Annopolis In Mary-Land, May 23, 24, 25. Anno 1700.
London, Printed by W. Downing in Bartholomew-Close near West-Smithfield, 1700.
1 p.l., 17 p. 31.5cm. fol.
"Proposals for the Propagation of the Christian Religion, and for the Reduction of the Quakers thereunto, in the Province of Pensylvania." p. 14.
The issue with single-rule above imprint: cf. Baer(Md.).
JCB(2)2:1582; Sabin 7472; Wing B4283; Baer (Md.)194B; Morgan C44.

04013, before 1871

DA700
B827a
Bray, Thomas, 1658-1730.
Apostolick Charity, Its Nature and Excellence Consider'd In A Discourse Upon Dan. 12. 3. Preached at St. Paul's, at the Ordination of some Protestant Missionaries to be sent into the Plantations. To which is Prefixt, A General View of the English Colonies in America, with respect to Religion; in order to shew what Provision is wanting for the Propagation of Christianity in those Parts. Together with Proposals for the Promoting the same: And to induce such of the Clergy of this Kingdom, as are Persons of Sobriety and Abilities to accept of a Mission. And to which is subjoin'd The Author's Circular Letter lately sent to the Clergy there. By Thomas Bray, D.D.

London, Printed by E. Holt for William Hawes, at the Sign of the Rose in Ludgate-Street, 1700.
1 p.l., 10, [8], 11-33 (i.e. 34) p. 20cm. 4º A⁴(-A1+[ ]²) B⁴(B1+[ ]⁴) C-D⁴ E².
<u>Apostolick Charity</u>, 1st pub. London, 1698.
"Proposals For the Encouragement and Promoting of Religion" ([8] p.); first pub. as early as Dec. 1695, [London].
"A Circular Letter", p. 31-33 (i.e. 34), dated: London, June the 10th, 1699.
In this copy there is a blank leaf at end.
Wing B4287; Sabin 7473; McAlpin 4:625; Baer(Md.)195A, 163J; Morgan C45.

04745, 1898

DA700
-B827c
[Bray, Thomas] 1658-1730.
A Circular Letter To the Clergy of Mary-Land, Subsequent to the late Visitation.
[London, 1700]
[6] p. 32cm. fol.
Caption title.
Signed (p. [5]): Thomas Bray.
Running title: Letter I.
"Cursus Catecheticus Americanus. Consisting of Books more particularly fitted for the Use of ... Catechumens." (p. [6]).
JCB(2)2:1583; Wing B4291; Sabin 7475; Baer (Md.)196.

04012, before 1871

DA700
-B827l
Bray, Thomas, 1658-1730.
A Letter From Dr. Bray, to such as have Contributed towards the Propagating Christian Knowledge in the Plantations.
[London, 1700]
3 p. 28.5cm. (30cm. in case) fol.
Caption title.
Although this has been ascribed to William Bradford's press in New York, prima facie it clearly is not an American imprint. Also it is clear from the text itself that it was prepared for Bray's sponsors in England upon his return there.
Sabin 7478; Baer(Md.)197; Evans 903; Smith (Anti-Quak)85; Morgan C46.

31744, 1955 rev

DA700
-B827m1
Bray, Thomas, 1658-1730.
A Memorial, Representing The Present State Of Religion, On The Continent Of North-America. By Thomas Bray, D.D.
London, Printed by William Downing, for

[405]

          the Author, 1700.
             12 (i.e. 15) p. 28cm. fol.
             First issue: cf. Baer(Md.).

DA700
-B827m3   ―― ―――Another issue.
            15 p. 31.5cm. fol.
            Third issue: cf. Baer(Md.).
            JCB(2)2:1584; WingB4294; Sabin7479; cf.
            Church789; Smith(Anti-Quak)85; Baer(Md)
            198; MorganC47.

04746
04011, before 1871

DA701   Bugg, Francis, 1640-1724?
B931n   A Modest Defence Of my Book, Entituled,
          Quakerism Expos'd: As Also, Of my Broad
          Sheet; with a Scheme of the Quakers Yearly
          Synod; and other Books, presented Anno
          1699. to the Parliament. And G. Whitehead's
          Inside Turn'd Outward, by Reprinting his
          Ancient Book Ishmael, &c. intirely; ... By
          Francis Bugg. ...
            London: Printed by R. Janeway, Jun. for the
          Author; and sold by J. Robinson, at the Golden
          Lion in St. Paul's Church-yard; H. Rhodes, at
          the Star at the Corner of Bride-Lane, Fleetstreet;
          Ch. Broome at the Gun in Ludgate-street; and J.
          Marshall at the Bible in Grace-Church-Street,
          1700.
            xxviii, 32, 32, 48, [4] p. A^8 a^4 b^2, B-C^8,
          ^{2}A-B^8, ^{3}B-D^8 E^2. 16cm. 8°
            Includes the following, designated as "parts":
          pt. 1. His, "George Whitehead Turn'd Topsie-
          Turvy" in reply to George Whitehead, Truth and
          innocency vindicated, London, 1699, and in de-
          fense of his, Quakerism expos'd, London, 1699,
          his, Some reasons humbly proposed to the lords,
          London, 1699, and Edward Beckham [and others]
          A brief discovery, London, 1699.
          pt. 2. Christopher Atkinson, George White-
          head [and others] "Ishmael and His Mother" and
          his, "A Cutting Switch." With special t.-p.,
          separate paging and signatures.
          pt. 3. His, "A Reply to a Book, Entituled,
          A Defence of an Apology," in reply to John Field,
          A defence of an apology, London, 1699.
            Errata, p. xxviii.
          "A Catalogue of Books wrote by Fran. Bugg"
          and list of Quaker books at Christ Church College,
          Oxford ([4] p. at end).
            Imperfect: last ℓ. wanting; available in facsim.
            Bound in contemporary calf, rebacked, as no. 5
          with 4 other works by Bugg, London, 1701.
            Smith(Friends)1:340; WingB5375; MorganC61.

16505, 1934 rev

DA700   Bugg, Francis, 1640-1724?
B931p   The Pilgrim's Progress, From Quakerism
          to Christianity: Containing, A farther Dis-
          covery of the Dangerous Growth of Quaker-
          ism, not only in Points of Doctrine, but also
          in their Politicks; respecting their Government
          within the Government, and opposite to it; to-
          gether with their Fund or Common Bank to
          support the same: With a Remedy proposed for
          this Malady; and, The Cure of Quakerism. To
          which is added an Appendix, Discovering A
          most Damnable Plot ... The Second Edition,
          Corrected and Enlarged. By a Servant of the
          Church, Fr. Bugg. ...
            London: Printed by R. Janeway, Jun. for the
          Author; and sold by J. Robinson, at the Golden
          Lion in St. Paul's Church-yard; and Ch. Brome,
          at the Gun in Ludgate-Street. 1700.
            lxiv, 224, 209-352, [2], 155-168(i.e. 368) p.
          (port.), fold. plate. 16.5cm. 8°
            First pub. London, 1698.
            Errata, p. lxiv.
          "A Collection Of Some Passages (Touching
          those call'd Quakers) Which were Writ ... by
          several that were, or still are, amongst that
          People ... " (p. [353]-168 (i.e. 368).
          "An Address" dated (p. [xii]): March $1\frac{699}{700}$.
          WingB5383; Smith(Friends)1:338; McAlpin
          4:626.

67-443

DA700   Bugg, Francis, 1640-1724?
B931w   William Penn, The Pretended Quaker, Dis-
          covered To hold a Correspondence With The
          Jesuite's at Rome. To which is Added, A
          Winding-Sheet For Ann Dockwra: By Francis
          Bugg.
            [London, 1700]
            16 p. 17.5cm. 8°
            Caption title.
            Dated at end: June 29. 1700.
            The second text a reply to Ann Docwra's The
          second part of an apostate-conscience exposed,
          London, 1700.
            Smith(Friends)1:340; WingB5399; MorganC62.

11532, 1918

D   Caledonia; Or, The Pedlar turn'd Merchant. A
Scott   Tragi-Comedy, As it was Acted by His Majesty's
128   Subjects Of Scotland, In The King of Spain's Prov-
          ince Of Darien.
            London: Printed, and sold by the Booksellers
          of London and Westminster. 1700.
            1 p. ℓ., 30 p. 20.5cm. 4°

A satire in verse.
JCB(2)2:1587; WingC282; Sabin9919; Scott128; Kress2207; MorganC71.

0565, 1846

DA700 Calef, Robert, 1648-1719.
C148m More Wonders Of The Invisible World: Or, The Wonders of the Invisible World, Display'd in Five Parts. Part I. An Account of the Sufferings of Margaret Rule, Written by the Reverend Mr. C.M. P.II. Several Letters to the Author, &c. And his Reply relating to Witchcraft. P.III. The Differences between the Inhabitants of Salem Village, and Mr. Parris their Minister, in New-England. P.IV. Letters of a Gentleman uninterested, Endeavouring to prove the received Opinions about Witchcraft to be Orthodox. With short Essays to their Answers. P.V. A short Historical Account of Matters of Fact in that Affair. To which is added, A Postscript relating to a Book intitled, The Life of Sir William Phips. Collected by Robert Calef, Merchant, of Boston in New-England.
Licensed and Entred [sic] according to Order. London: Printed for Nath. Hillar, at the Princes-Arms, in Leaden-Hall-street, over against St. Mary-Ax, and Joseph Collyer, at the Golden-Bible, on London-Bridge. 1700.
6 p.l., 156 p. 18cm. 4º
Preface (2d-4th p.l.) dated: Boston in New-England, Aug. 11. 1697.
"Another Brand Pluckt out of the Burning, Or, more Wonders of the Invisible World" (6th p.l.ᵛ-p.13) by Cotton Mather.
A reply in part to Cotton Mather, The wonders of the invisible world, 1st pub. Boston, 1692, and to Mather's Pietas in patriam; the life of Sir W. Phips, 1st pub. London, 1693.
JCB(2)2:1585; Sabin9926; WingC288; Holmes (C)15A; Morgan*C71a.

01951, before 1854

bBB Carlos II, King of Spain, 1661-1700.
C284 Copia De Las Clavsvlas del Testamento que
1700 otorgó el Rey nuestro señor Don Carlos Segundo
1 (que esté en gloria) tocantes á la formacion de la Junta de Govierno, en dos de Octubre de mil y setecientos.
[Madrid, 1700]
[3] p. 29.5cm. fol.
Caption title.
Certification of true copy dated in Madrid, 13 Nov 1700 (day of month blank, supplied in ms.)
Cf. Palau(2)44355-44362.

28208, 1938

bD Certain Propositions Relating to the Scots
Scott Plantation of Caledonia, and the National
106 Address for supporting thereof, breifly [sic] offered to Publick View, for removing of Mistakes and Prejudices.
Glasgow, Printed in the Year, 1700.
[2] p. 29cm. fol.
Caption title; imprint at end.
Refers to an address to the king presented 25 Mar. 1700 petitioning for a meeting of the Parliament of Scotland.
WingC1732; Scott 106; Sabin78205.

04748, before 1900

DA700 Chauncy, Isaac, 1632-1712.
C498a Alexipharmacon: Or, A Fresh Antidote Against Neonomian Bane and Poyson To The Protestant Religion. Being a Reply to the late Bishop of Worcester's Discourse of Christ's Satisfaction, in Answer to the Appeal of the late Mr. Steph. Lob. And also a Refutation of the Doctrine of Justification by Man's own Works of Obedience, delivered and defended by Mr. John Humphrey, and Mr. Sam. Clark, contrary to Scripture, and the Doctrine of the first Reformers from Popery. ... By Isaac Chauncy, M.A.
London: Printed for, and Sold by W. Marshall at the Bible in Newgate-Street, 1700.
4 p.l., 100, 176 p. 18cm. 8º
A reply to: Edward Stillingfleet, A discourse concerning the doctrine of Christ's satisfaction ... part II, London, 1700 (itself a reply to Stephen Lobb, An appeal to the Right Reverend Edward Lord Bishop of Worcester, London, 1698); to John Humfrey, The righteousness of God revealed, London, 1697; and to Samuel Clarke, Scripture-justification, London, 1698.
"The Doctrine Of Justification Explained and Vindicated": p. 1-176, 2d count.
Errata, p. 96, 1st count, and p. 176.
Booksellers' advertisement, 4th p.l.
Bound in contemporary calf.
WingC3744; McAlpin4:627; Sabin12335n; MorganC81.

4240, 1908

D Company of Scotland Trading to Africa and the
Scott Indies.
120 The Original Papers And Letters, Relating to the Scots Company, Trading to Africa and the Indies: From the Memorial given in against their taking Subscriptions at Hamburgh, by Sir Paul Ricaut, His Majesty's Resident there, to Their last Address sent up to His Majesty in December, 1699. Faithfully extracted from the Companies Books.

D Scott 110 cop.3
[Edinburgh?] Printed Anno 1700.
56 p. 19cm. 8°
The latest address to the king included here is one dated 19 Oct. 1699 with the king's answer dated 2 Nov. 1699 (p. 50-53; cf. Scott 74 for original). The last document included is the Company's petition to the Privy Council dated 20 Oct. 1699 (p. 54-56; cf. Scott 75 for original).

——— Another copy. 17.5cm.
Bound with [Ridpath, George] Scotland's grievances [Edinburgh] 1700, as the 4th of 4 items.
JCB(2)2:1593; Wing0434; Sabin 18563; Scott 120; Kress 2244; Morgan U119, U428.
01949, 1854
04752, before 1915

D Scott 113
Company of Scotland Trading to Africa and the Indies.
The Representation and Petition Of The Council-General Of The Indian and African Company To The Parliament
Edinburgh, Printed in the Year 1700.
19 p. 19cm. 8°
Dated at end in Edinburgh, 16 May 1700.
Caption (p. 3): "To His Grace His Majesty's High Commissioner, and the Right Honourable the Estates of Parliament. The humble Representation and Petition of the Council-General of the Company of Scotland, Trading to Africa and the Indies."
First pub. Edinburgh, the same year, under title same as caption given here.

D Scott 110 cop.3
——— Another copy. 17.5cm.
Bound with [Ridpath, George] Scotland's grievances [Edinburgh] 1700, as the 2d of 4 items.
JCB(2)2:1597; Sabin 18566; Wing C5599A; Scott 113; Kress S2187.
04754, before 1900
04750, before 1915

D Scott 124a
Company of Scotland Trading to Africa and the Indies.
Scotland's Right to Caledonia (Formerly called Darien) And the Legality of its Settlement, asserted in Three several Memorials presented to His Majesty in May 1699. By The Lord President of the Session and Lord Advocate, on behalf of the Company of Scotland, Trading to Africa and the Indies. ...
[Edinburgh] Printed in the Year, 1700.
1 p.ℓ., 34 p. 18.5cm. 8°
"Advertisement" of books "... proving the legality of the Settlement of Caledonia ... (p. 34).

D Scott 124b
——— Variant. 19cm.
The first text gathering is missigned "G", rather than "A."
JCB(2)2:1596; Wing C5599B; Scott 124; Sabin 78196; Kress 2264.
01950, 1854
7683, 1911

D Scott 121
Company of Scotland Trading to Africa and the Indies.
A Supplement Of Original Papers And Letters, Relating To the Scots Company Trading to Africa and the Indies.
[Edinburgh?] Anno Dom. 1700.
16 p. 18.5cm. 8°
The latest document included is dated (p. 16) 29 Jan. 1700.
A continuation of its The original papers and letters relating to the Scots Company Trading to Africa and the Indies [Edinburgh?] 1700.
Wing S6183, C5599D; Sabin 78238; Scott 121; Kress 2245.
04753, before 1900

D696 -C737c
Company of Scotland Trading to Africa and the Indies.
To His Grace His Majesty's High Commissioner, and the Right Honourable the Estates of Parliament. The humble Representation and Petition of the Council-General of the Company of Scotland, Trading to Africa and the Indies.
[Edinburgh? 1700]
4 p. 31.5cm. fol.
Caption title.
Dated (at end) in Edinburgh, 16 May 1700.
This copy is closely trimmed with slight loss of text.
Bound in a volume of Scottish imprints and mss. as the 9th of 58 items.
Wing C5602; Scott 112.
7107, 1910

bD Scott 118
Company of Scotland Trading to Africa and the Indies.
To His Grace, His Majesty's High Commissioner, and the Right Honourable the Estates of Parliament. The humble Representation and Petition of the Council-General of the Company of Scotland Trading to Africa and

776, 1905	the Indies. [Edinburgh, 1700] Broadside. 30 x 19.5cm. 1/2° "Signed at Edinburgh the 28th. day of October 1700". Supplements its petition dated 16 May 1700. Wing C5602; Scott 118.
DA700 C774h 11494, 1918	Coole, Benjamin, d. 1717. Honesty The Truest Policy, Shewing The Sophistry, Envy, and Perversion Of George Keith, In his Three Books, (viz) His Bristol Quakerism, Bristol Narrative and his Deism. By B. Coole. ... [Bristol? William Bonny?] Printed, for the Author, 1700. 1 p.ℓ., 166 (i.e. 128) p. 17.5cm. 8° Errata, last page. Dated, at end: Bristol, the 28th. of November 1700. Keith's The Deism of William Penn and his brethren, 1st pub. London, 1699; A Narrative of the proceedings of George Keith at Coopershall in the city of Bristol, 1st pub. London, 1700; Bristol Quakerism expos'd, 1st pub. London, 1700. Bound in contemporary calf, rebacked Wing C6046; Smith(Friends)1:449-450; Morgan C94.
D696 -C737c 7106, 1910	Coppy Of The Addres: Of a Great Number of the Members of the Parliament of Scotland, Presented to the King by my Lord Ross, and the other Commissioners with him at Kensingtoun, 11th of June, 1700. Edinburgh, Re-Printed by John Reid, 1700. Broadside. 30.5 x 18cm. 1/2° "We do therefore ... intreat that Your Majesty will ... allow Your Parliament to Meet ... for Redressing the Grievances of the Nation, Asserting it's just Rights and Priviledges, as well at Home as Abroad, in its Colony of Caledonia ..." First pub. under title The address presented to His Majesty at Kensington the 11th day of June. [Edinburgh? 1700] Bound in a volume of Scottish imprints and mss. as the 8th of 58 items. Wing C6201; Scott 116.
D700 D166v [R] 04760-2, before 1882	Dampier, William, 1652-1715. Voyages and Descriptions Vol. II. In Three Parts, viz. 1. A Supplement of the Voyage round the World ... 2. Two Voyages to Campeachy ... 3. A Discourse of Trade-Winds ... By Capt William Dampier. ... To which is Added, A General Index to both Volumes. The Second Edition. London, Printed for James Knapton, at the Crown in St Pauls Church-yard. MDCC. 4 p.ℓ., 184, 132 p., 2 ℓ., 112, [76] p. 4 fold. maps. 19.5cm. 8° First pub. London, 1699. The designation "Vol. II." on the t.-p. counts as "Vol. I." his A New voyage round the World, 1st pub. London, 1697. Each pt. and the index have separate paging and signatures, and pt. 3 has special half-title. "Books printed for, and sold by James Knapton ..." p. [73-76] at end. Bound in contemporary half leather, rebacked, as the 2d of a 3-vol. set also containing his A new voyage, 4th ed., London, 1699, and his A voyage to New Holland, London, 1703. Cf. JCB(2)2:1557; Wing D166; Sabin 18375.
D700 D246d 68-191	[Davenant, Charles] 1656-1714. A Discourse Upon Grants and Resumptions. Showing How our Ancestors Have Proceeded with such Ministers As have Procured to Themselves Grants Of The Crown-Revenue; And that the Forfeited Estates Ought to be Applied towards the Payment of the Publick Debts. By the Author of, The Essay on Ways and Means. ... London: Printed for James Knapton, at the Crown, in St. Paul's Church-yard. 1700. 8 p.ℓ., 167, 176-263, 272-345, 347 (i.e. 348)-448 p. 19cm. 8° Bookseller's advertisement, 8th p.ℓ.^{v}. Bound in contemporary calf. Wing D304; Kress 2215; Morgan C104.
D700 D314t	[Defoe, Daniel] 1661?-1731. The Two Great Questions Consider'd. I. What the French King will Do, with Respect to the Spanish Monarchy. II. What Measures the English ought to Take. London, Printed by R. T. for A. Baldwin, at the Oxford-Armes, in Warwick-lane. 1700. 2 p.ℓ., 28 p. 21cm. 4° This is one of several editions dated 1700, some partly in the same setting of type: cf.

[409]

70-173	Moore (Defoe). WingD850; Sabin97560; Moore(Defoe) 24n; BPL(Defoe)1205.

D
Scott
127b
 	
06061, before 1882
	[Denniston, Walter]
	Ad Amplissimos simul & Consultissimos Viros, Societatis Scoticanæ Ad Afros & Indos Negotiantium Rectores & Administratores Aequissimos, &c.
	   [Edinburgh, 1700]
	   8 p. 20.5cm. 4°
	   Caption title.
	   Verse.
	   Signed (p. 6): Gualterus Denneston.
	JCB(2)2:1599; WingD1047; Sabin78199; Scott 127b.

DA700
D553g
[R]
 	
16782, 1935
	Dickinson, Jonathan, 1663-1722.
	God's Protecting Providence, Man's Surest Help and Defence, In Times of the Greatest Difficulty, and most Eminent Danger. Evidenced In the Remarkable Deliverance of Robert Barrow, with divers other Persons, from the Devouring Waves of the Sea; amongst which they suffered Shipwrack: And also, From the cruel Devouring Jaws of the Inhumane Canibals of Florida. Faithfully Related by one of the Persons concerned therein, Jonathan Dickenson. ...
	   Printed in Philadelphia: Re-printed in London, and Sold by T. Sowle, in White-Hart-Court in Gracious-street, 1700.
	   5 p.ℓ., 85 p. 18.5cm. 8°
	   First pub. Philadelphia, 1699.
	   There was another edition London, the same year, with 89 p. main paging.
	   With this is bound "Books Printed and Sold by T. Sowle... 1699." ([8] p. listing 34 books).
	JCBAR36:17; WingD1390A; Sabin20015; Vail 285; Smith(Friends)1:529; Ayer-Captivities (Suppl.)43.

BA700
R337d
	Dominicans--Third Order.
	Regla De Los Hermanos De La Orden Tercera De La Milicia de N.S. Jesu Christo, y Penitencia que instituyò Santo Domingo, con vn breve Compendio de algunos de los Santos, y Siervos de Dios, que con su santa vida han ilustrado esta Tercera Orden. Dedicala Al Nuevo Reparador Del Orbe, gran Mayordomo de las Almas, y Apostol de la siempre Virgen Maria nuestra Señora el Glorioso Patriarcha Santo Domingo de Guzman, Sebastian Gonçalez de los Santos, Prior de la Tercera Orden de la Penitencia de Santo Domingo: sita en el Real Convento de San Pablo de la Ciudad de Sevilla.
	   En Sevilla, por Lvcas Martin De Hermosilla, Impressor, y Mercader de Libros. [ca.1700].
	   1 p.ℓ., 46 p. 14.5cm. 8°

05183, 1884	

D
Scott
126
 	
649, 1905
	[Donaldson, James] fl. 1688-1713.
	The Undoubted Art Of Thriving; Wherein is shewed, 1. That a Million L. Sterling Money, or more if need be may be raised for Propogating the Trade of the Nation, ... 2. How the Indian and African Company may Propogat their Trade, ... 3. How every one according to his quality, may Live Comfortably and Happily. ...
	   Edinburgh, Printed by John Reid, 1700.
	   4 p.ℓ., 135, [1] p. 14.5cm. 8°
	   Dedication (2d-4th p.ℓ.) signed: Ja. Donaldson.
	   Errata, p. [1] at end.
	   Bound in contemporary çalf, rebacked.
	WingD1856; Sabin20589; Kress2218; Scott 126; MorganC126.

D700
E18m
 	
69-304
	Echard, Laurence, 1670?-1730.
	A Most Compleat Compendium Of Geography, General and Special; Describing all the Empires, Kingdoms, and Dominions, In The Whole World. ... Together with an Appendix of General Rules for making a large Geography, with the great Uses of that Science. ... The Fifth Edition, Corrected and much Improved. By Laurence Echard, M.A. of Christ's College in Cambrige [sic].
	   London, Printed for J. Nicholson, at the King's-Arms in Little-Britain. [1700]
	   8 p.ℓ., 236, [12] p. 2 maps. 15.5cm. 12°
	   "America" p. 184-211.
	   Letter of recommendation from Edmund Bohun, 6th^V-8th p.ℓ.
	   Bookseller's advertisements, 1st p.ℓ.^{V}, 8th p.ℓ., p. [10-12] at end.
	   First pub. London, 1691.
	   Bound in contemporary calf.

D Scott 130	The Emblem of Our King, And of the Scots and English Parliaments: A Poem ... By a well Wisher to King and Parliaments. ...

	Edinburgh, Printed by John Reid 1700 8 p. 18.5cm. 4° Includes "Scotland's, or Affrica Companys second Address to the King" and "Scotland's, or African-Company's Third and last Address to His Majesty ...", p. 6-7, each an anagram on the word Ingratitude. Wing E702; Scott 130.
650, 1904	

D Scott 104
An Enquiry Into The Causes of the Miscarriage Of The Scots Colony at Darien. Or An Answer To A Libel Entituled A Defence of the Scots Abdicating Darien. Submitted to the Consideration of the Good People of England. ...
Glasgow. 1700.
4 p.ℓ., 112 p. A⁴ B-G⁸ H-I⁴. 19cm. 8°
A reply to [Harris, Walter] A defence of the Scots abdicating Darien [London?] 1700 [i.e. 1699?].
Attributed to George Ridpath.
Sabin records an edition of 1699.
This copy is figured * on B5 (under "his Majesty"), C3ᵛ, C7, D3ᵛ, D4ᵛ, E4ᵛ, and F3ᵛ.

D Scott 110 cop. 2
————— Another copy. 18cm.
Figured the same as the preceding.
Bound with [Ridpath, George] Scotland's grievances [Edinburgh] 1700.

D Scott 104 *
————— Variant. 19cm.
This copy is figured * on B5 (under "his") and pages are misnumbered as follows: p. 50 as 60, 51 as 61, 54 as 64, 55 as 65, 58 as 68, 59 as 69, 62 as 72, and 63 as 73.
JCB(2)2:1586; Sabin 78215; Wing I213; Scott 104; Kress 2220; Knuttel 14515.
04761, before 1915
0813, 1846
06481, 1846

B700 F363b
Fernández de Medrano, Sebastián, 1646-1705.
Breve Tratado De Geographia Divido [sic] En Tres Partes, Que la una contiene la Descripcion del Rio y Imperio de las Amazonas Americanas, con su Carta Geographica: La otra lo que poseen Franceses y Ingleses, &c. en el nuevo Mundo, y de la forma que se introducen en el: Y la tercera del Estado presente del Imperio del Gran Mogor y Reyno de Siam, y que faca à luz ... El General de Batalla Don Sebastian Fernandez De Medrano, Director de la Academia Real y Militar de el Exercito de los Payses-Baxos.
En Brusselas, En Casa de Lamberto Marchant, Mercader de Libros. 1700.
6 p.ℓ., 82 p. fold. map. 15.5cm. 12°
Dedication dated (4th p.ℓ.ʳ) 8 Febr. 1700.
Preliminary matter includes laudatory poetry signed by Chrysostomus de Monpleinchamp.
Imperfect: map wanting.
JCB(2)2:1618; Palau(2)89227; Sabin 47360; Borba de Moraes 1:260; Peeters Fontainas(1965)440.
03712, before 1866

DA700 F454w
Field, John, 1652-1723.
The Weakness Of George Keith's Reasons For Renouncing Quakerism, And Entering into Communion With The Church of England, &c. Manifested, and Replied to. By John Feild [sic]. ...
London, Printed and Sold by T. Sowle, in White-Hart-Court in Gracious-street, 1700.
22 p. 21cm. 4°
A reply to Mr. George Keith's reasons for renouncing Quakerism, London, 1700 (the authorship of which was denied by George Keith).
Wing F868; Smith(Friends)1:606.
11495, 1918

D Scott 107
[Fletcher, Andrew] 1655-1716.
Overtures Offered to the Parliament, In which this Proposition is Advanced, That a small Summ imposed on the Nation, for Reforming Our Standard, and for Repairing the Losses of the African and Indian Company, &c. ... will be of ten times more value to the Nation in General ... than the samen [sic] Summ will be, if Retained in each Particulars Hand.
Edinburgh, Printed by John Reid, in the Year M D CC.
3 p.ℓ., 7, 14 p. 19.5cm. 4°
"A Proposition For Remeding the Debasement of Coyne In Scotland": p. 1-7, 1st count.
"A Further Explication Of the Proposal relating to the Coyne": p. [1]-14, 2d count.
Wing F1296, F2557; Scott 107; Morgan C328.
753, 1905

D Scott 109
[Foyer, Archibald] supposed author.
Scotland's Present Duty: Or, A Call To The Nobility, Gentry, Ministry, and Commonality of this Land, to be duely affected with, and vigorously to act for, our Common Concern in Caledonia, as a Mean to Enlarge Christ's Kingdom, to Benefit our Selves, and do Good to all Protestant Churches.
[Edinburgh?] Printed in the Year, 1700.
28 p. 20.5cm. 4°
Signed (p. 27): Philo-Caledonius.
JCB(2)2:1595; Wing F2048; Sabin 18569; Scott 109.
0566, 1846

EB -W&A 397a	France--Sovereigns, etc., 1643-1715 (Louis XIV). 20 July 1700 Arrest Du Conseil D'Etat Du Roy, Qui Ordonne qu'en éxécution de l'Arrest du Conseil du 15. Septembre mil six cent quatre-vingt dix-neuf, les Officiers qui servent aux Isles Françoises de l'Amerique, seront payez sur le pied de quatre livres dix sols pour chacun cent pesant de sucre ... Du 20. Juillet 1700. [Paris, 1700] 3 p. 25cm. (32cm. in case) 4° Caption title. Reply to a petition by "Loüis Guigues, Fermier du Domaine d'Occident."		JCB(2)2:1602; Sabin26002; Borba de Moraes 1:285. 04762, before 1882

16530, 1934

EB F8355 1700 1	France--Sovereigns, etc., 1643-1715 (Louis XIV). 12 Nov. 1700 Copia De Carta Del Rey Christianissimo Luis Dezimoquarto à la Reyna nuestra Señora, y Señores del Govierno. Con Licencia: En Zaragoza: Por Pasqual Bueno, Impressor del Reyno, Año 1700. [4] p. 21cm. 4° Caption title; imprint at end. Concerns the death of Carlos II and the question of the Spanish succession. Dated (p. [3]) 12 Nov. 1700. Transl. from: Lettre du roy à la reine douairière d'Espagne et au conseil établi pour la régence de ce royaume ... Avignon, [1700]. There are numerous other Spanish translations published in the same year (cf. Palau (2) under Louis XIV and Luis XIV).	D Scott 122	A Full and Exact Collection Of All the Considerable Addresses, Memorials, Petitions, Answers, Proclamations, Declarations, Letters and other Publick Papers, Relating to the Company of Scotland Trading to Africa and the Indies, since the passing of the Act of Parliament, by which the said Company was established in June 1695, till November 1700. Together with a short Preface (including the Act it self) as also a Table of the whole Contents. ... [Edinburgh?] Printed in the Year 1700. 1 p.ℓ., x, 144, [8] p. 16.5cm. 8° "A Catalogue of the several Books and Pamphlets that have been hitherto Published, concerning the Indian and African Company of Scotland ..." p. [7-8] at end. This copy closely trimmed at top affecting some headlines. JCB(2)2:1591; WingC5597B; Scott 122; Sabin 18555; Kress2223.

68-27

01525, 1847

E700 F927r	Froger, François, b. 1676. Relation D'Un Voyage Fait en 1695. 1696. & 1697. aux Côtes d'Afrique, Détroit de Magellan, Brezil, Cayenne, & Isles Antilles, par une Escadre des Vaisseaux du Roy, commandée par Monsieur De Gennes. Faite par le Sieur Froger Ingenieur Volontaire sur le Vaisseau le Faucon Anglois. ... A Paris, Chez Nicolas Le Gras, au troisiéme Pilier de la grande Salle du Palais, à l'L couronnée. M.DCC. Avec Privilece [sic] Du Roy. 7 p.ℓ., 219, [1] p. 17 plates (incl. 4 fold.), 12 maps (incl. 5 fold.) 17cm. 12° Added t.-p., engr.: Relation du Voyage de Mr De Gennes au detroit de Magellan Par le Sr Froger. ... "Achevé d'imprimer pour la seconde fois le 18. Mars 1699." (last p.) First pub. Paris, 1698. Bound in contemporary calf.	D700 G133n	Gage, Thomas, 1603?-1656. Nieuwe ende seer naeuwkeurige Reyse Door de Spaensche West-Indien Van Thomas Gage; Met seer curieuse soo Land-kaerten als Historische Figueren vercierd ende met twee Registers voorsien. Overgeset door H. V. Q. Den Tweeden Druk. t'Amsterdam, By Willem De Coup, Willem Lamsvelt, Philip Verbeek en Johannes Lamsvelt, Boekverkoopers. Anno 1700. 10 p.ℓ., 168, 167-450, [67] p. 8 plates (incl. 2 fold.), 3 fold. maps. 20cm. 4° Cut on t.-p. Added t.-p., engraved: Nieuwe en seer Nauwkeurige Rejise... T'Amsterdam, By W. De Coup, W. Lamsveld, Ph. Verbeek en J. Lamsveld. 1700. J. Doesburgh, in. et fe. Dedication (3d-6th p.ℓ.) Signed: H. V. Quellenburgh. Transl., by Henrik van Quellenburgh, from A New Survey of the West-Indies, first pub. London, 1648, under title: The English-American his Travail by Sea and Land. Dutch transl. first pub. Utrecht, 1682. "Korte Onderwysinge, Om de Indiaansche Taale, welke men Poconchi ofte Pocoman noemt, te leeren" p. [439]-450. In this copy 2 plates are colored.

[412]

Imperfect: 3 maps wanting (same as in the Library's copy of Utrecht, 1682, ed.).
Bound in contemporary vellum.
JCB(2)2:1603; Sabin26311; Streit3:4; Palau(2) 96488; Cundall(W.I.)1978n; Muller(1872)611; Pilling1370.
03713, before 1866

DA700 G676o6
Gospel Order Revived, Being an Answer to a Book lately set forth by the Reverend Mr. Increase Mather, President of Harvard Colledge, &c. Entituled, The Order of the Gospel, &c. Dedicated to the Churches of Christ in New-England. By sundry Ministers of the Gospel in New-England. ...
[New York] Printed [by William Bradford] in the Year 1700.
6 p.ℓ., 40 p. 19.5cm. 4°
Collaboration on authorship has been ascribed at various times to Timothy Woodbridge, Benjamin Colman, Simon Bradstreet, and Ebenezer Pemberton. Thomas and William Brattle, Zechariah Tuthill, Solomon Stoddard, Solomon Southwick, and John Leverett were also associated with publication.
A reply to: Increase Mather, Order of the Gospel. Boston, 1700.
"Advertisement" (1st p.ℓ.ᵛ): 6 lines, ending "... so far for its Impression."
Errata slip pasted on verso of t.-p.

DA700 G676o7
————Variant. 19cm.
"Advertisement" (1st p.ℓ.ᵛ): 7 lines, ending "... printed with some Difficulty."
Errata slip pasted on verso of t.-p.
Evans966, 967; Sabin28052, 91945n; WingW3428; Church790; McAlpin4:630; Dexter(Cong.)2517; Holmes(C.)110n; Holmes (I.)84n; MorganC490.
6291, 1910
6437, 1910

DA700 G696b [R]
[Gould, Daniel] 1625-1716.
A brief narration of the sufferings of the People Called Quakers; who were put to death at Boston in New-England. Also An account from their own hands, of their Coming to Boston, and of their staying in their Iurisdiction after Banishment. With A Precious Epistle of William Robinson, to us his fellow-Prisoners, and other Epistles hereunto Annexed.
[Philadelphia, Reinier Jansen, 1700?]
38 p. 18.5cm. (21cm. in folder) 4°
Sabin notes: "Gould wrote his name on the copies circulated in England." In this copy the author's name appears in a contemporary hand on p. 28.
Caption title.
Evans gives imprint: [New York, William Bradford? 1700]. However, John Whiting, Truth and innocency defended, London, 1702, p. 81, refers to this book as Gould's "late Book, Printed in Pensilvania."
Includes accounts by William Robinson, Marmaduke Stevenson, William Ledra, and Mary Dyre.
Imperfect: partly disintegrated; p. 1-10, 15-16, 31-38 wanting; available in facsim.
Wing G1415; Evans911; Sabin28099; Smith (Friends)1:857.
30744, 1950

D70 -P769t
Gt.Brit.--Commissioners Appointed to Enquire into the Irish Forfeitures.
The Report Of The Commissioners Appointed By Parliament To Enquire into the Irish Forfeitures, Deliver'd to the Honᵇˡᵉ House of Commons the 15ᵗʰ of December, 1699. With Their Resolutions and Addresses To His Majesty Relating to those Forfeitures. As Also, His Majesty's Gracious Answers thereunto; And His most Gracious Speech to Both Houses of Parliament the 5ᵗʰ of January, 1690.
London, Printed for Edw. Jones in the Savoy, and Tim. Goodwin at the Queen's Head against St. Dunstan's Church in Fleetstreet, 1700.
32 p. 30.5cm. fol.
Order to print dated (p. 32) 9 Apr. 1700.
No. [7] in a volume with binder's title: Political tracts 1655-1702.
WingE2231; MorganC365.
9973-7, 1914

bDB G7863 1700 2
Gt.Brit.--Laws, statutes, etc., 1694-1702 (William III)
Anno Regni Gulielmi III. Regis Angliæ, Scotiæ, Franciæ & Hiberniæ, Undecimo & Duodecimo. At the Parliament begun at Westminster the Four and twentieth Day of August, Anno Dom. 1698. ... And from thence Continued by several Prorogations and Adjournments to the Sixteenth Day of November, 1699. ...
London, Printed by Charles Bill, and the Executrix of Thomas Newcomb, deceas'd, Printers to the Kings most Excellent Majesty 1700.
1 p.ℓ., 211-224 p. 3G-3K² 31cm. fol.
(Issued as a part of its [Session laws] London, 1700.)
Cut (royal arms; Steele 135) on t.-p.
Caption title, p. 211: ... An Act for the more effectual Suppression of Piracy.
13083, 1921

[413]

bDB G7863 1700 1

Gt. Brit. --Laws, statutes, etc., 1694-1702 (William III)
Anno Regni Gulielmi III. Regis Angliæ, Scotiæ, Franciæ & Hiberniæ, Undecimo & Duodecimo. At the Parliament begun at Westminster the Four and twentieth Day of August, Anno Dom. 1698. ... And from thence Continued by several Prorogations and Adjournments to the Sixteenth Day of November, 1699. ...
London, Printed by Charles Bill, and the Executrix of Thomas Newcomb, deceas'd, Printers to the Kings most Excellent Majesty 1700.
1 p. ℓ., 263-264 p. 3U² 31cm. fol. (Issued as a part of its [Session laws] London, 1700.)
Cut (royal arms; Steele 135) on t.-p.
Caption title, p. 263: ... An Act to Punish Governors of Plantations in this Kingdom; for Crimes by them Committed in the Plantations.

13082, 1921

bD Scott 48b

Gt. Brit. --Parliament, 1699-1700--House of Lords.   12 Feb. 1699 [i.e. 1700]
The Humble Address Of the Right Honourable the Lords Spiritual & Temporal In Parliament Assembled, Presented to His Majesty On Munday the Twelfth Day of February, 1699. And His Majesties Most Gracious Answer Thereunto.
London, Printed by Charles Bill and the Executrix of Thomas Newcomb, deceas'd, Printers to the Kings most Excellent Majesty. 1699 [i.e. 1700].
4 p. 29.5cm. fol.
Order to print (p. 2) dated 12 Feb. 1699.
"... this House came to this further Resolution, That the Settlement of the Scotch-Colony at Darien is Inconsistent with the good of the Plantation-Trade of this Kingdom. ..." (p. 4)
Sabin 78219; Scott 48b.

1183, 1906

D -Scott 104b

Gt. Brit. --Sovereigns, etc., 1694-1702 (William III).   29 Jan. 1699 (i.e. 1700)
By the King, A Proclamation. William R. Whereas We have been Informed, That a False, Scandalous and Traiterous Libel, Intituled, An Inquiry into the Causes of the Miscarriage of the Scotch-Colony at Darien, or, An Answer to a Libel, Intituled, A Defence of the Scots Abdicating Darien, has been Printed and Dispersed ...
London, Printed by Charles Bill, and the Executrix of Thomas Newcomb, deceas'd, Printers to the Kings most Excellent Majesty. 1699 [i.e. 1700].
Broadside. 37 x 30.5cm. (31.5cm. in binding) 1°
Cut (royal arms) at head of title (Steele 124).
Title from caption and beginning of text.
Dated 29 Jan. 1699 (i.e. 1700).
Wing W2447; Scott 104b; Steele E4271.

648, 1904

bD Scott 125

Gt. Brit. --Sovereigns, etc., 1694-1702 (William III).   25 July 1700.
Proclamation For Apprehending Captains Gavine Hamilton, Kenneth Mackenzie & Kenneth Urquhart.
Edinburgh, Printed by the Heirs and Successors of Andrew Anderson, Printers to the King's most Excellent Majesty, Anno Dom. 1700.
Broadside. 30.5 x 19cm. 1/2°
Dated (at end) 25 July 1700.
The persons mentioned "... were principal Instigators, Actors or Ring-leaders of the Tumult that hapned within our City of Edinburgh, on the Twentieth of June last, which proceeded to the unheard-of Outrages of burning and breaking up of Tolboth-doors, setting free the Prisoners specially Hugh Paterson and James Watson, accused before our Privy Council for Scandalous and seditious Pamphlets ...". James Watson was imprisoned in 1700 for printing [George Ridpath's] Scotland's Grievances, Relating to Darien ... [Edinburgh] 1700.
Wing W2462; Scott 125; Steele S3198.

908, 1905

D Scott 102

[Harris, Walter]
A Defence Of The Scots Abdicating Darien: Including An Answer To The Defence Of The Scots Settlement there. Authore Britanno sed Dunensi. ...
[London?] Printed in the Year, 1700 [i.e. 1699?].
10 p. ℓ., 60, 145-168 (i.e. 167) p. 20.5cm. (21.5cm. in case) 8°
Dedication (2d-10th p. ℓ.) signed: Phil. Scot.
Although dated 1700 on the t.-p., this probably was actually printed for issue in 1699 because it was replied to by [Robert Ferguson's] A just and modest vindication of the Scots design, [Edinburgh?] 1699.
Printed more than once with t.-p. dated 1700, partly from standing type and partly from reset type.

D Scott 102*	In this copy "Dunensi", line 13 of t.-p., is in italic type. A reply to [Belhaven, J.H.] A defence of the Scots settlement at Darien, Edinburgh, 1699. Also attributed to James Hodges ———Variant. 18.5cm. In this copy "Dunensi", line 13 of t.-p., is in roman type. JCB(2)2:1592; WingH2298; Sabin78209; Scott 102; Kress2226; Knuttel14514; MorganC206.

8782, 1912
04787, before 1875

D Scott 105	[Harris, Walter] A Short Vindication Of Phil. Scot's Defence Of The Scots Abdicating Darien: Being In Answer to the Challenge of the Author of the Defence of that Settlement, to prove the Spanish Title to Darien ... With A Prefatory Reply, to the False and Scurrilous Aspersions, of the New Author of, The Just and Modest Vindication, &c. And some Animadversions on the material Part of it, relating to the Title of Darien. ... London: Printed in the Year, 1700. 48 p. 18.5cm. 8° A defence of his A defence of the Scots abdicating Darien [London?] 1700 [i.e. 1699?], in further reply to [Belhaven, J. H.] baron, A defence of the Scots settlement at Darien, Edinburgh, 1699, and a reply to [Ferguson, R.] A Just and modest vindication, [Edinburgh?] 1699. "Postscript" (p. 48) identifies Ferguson as the author of A just and modest vindication. Also attributed to James Hodges. JCB(2)2:1588; WingH1600; Scott105; Kress2227; Sabin78234; MorganC377.

0567, 1846 rev

DA762 C932	Hebden, Roger, d.1695. A Plain Account Of Certain Christian Experiences Labours, Services and Sufferings, Of That Ancient Servant and Mininister [sic] of Christ, Roger Hebden Deceased ... London, Printed and Sold by T. Sowle, in White-Hart-Court in Gracious-street, 1700. 136p. 16cm. 8° Bound with Samuel Crisp, Two Letters, Philadelphia [1762] Smith(Friends)1:929; WingH1346A

735, 1905

D700 H673d	Historie Der Boecaniers, Of Vrybuyters Van America. Van haar eerste Beginzelen tot deze tegenwoordige tyd toe. ... t'Amsterdam, By Nicolaas Ten Hoorn, Boek-verkooper, over 't Oude Heeren Logemont, 1700. 4 p.ℓ., 219, 136, [6] p. 7 plates (incl. 1 fold.), fold. map. 20.5cm. 4° Cut on t.-p.; incl. motto: Ingenio Et Industria. Added t.-p., engr., signed: C. Huyberts. Collection of 4 works (commonly entered under Exquemelin). Transl. from The History of the bucaniers of America, London, 1699. I. Account by Exquemelin. This text derives from Dutch original (1st pub. Amsterdam, 1678, under title: De Americaensche Zee-Roovers), by way of a Spanish transl. (1st pub. Cologne, 1681, under title: Piratas De La America), which was the basis for an English transl. (1st pub. London, Crooke, 1684, under title: Bucaniers Of America). II. Account by Basil Ringrose; 1st pub. London, Crooke, 1685, under title Bucaniers Of America. The Second Volume. III. Account of Raveneau de Lussan; 1st pub. Paris, 1689, under title: Journal du voyage fait à la mer de sud. IV. Account by Montauban; 1st pub. Amsterdam, 1698, under title: Relation du voyage du sieur de Montauban. In this copy there is a blank ℓ. at end. JCB(2)2:1601; Sabin23469.

03711, before 1866

DA700 H784p	Hooker, Thomas, 1586-1647. The Poor Doubting Christian Drawn to Christ. Wherein the Main Lets and Hindrances, which keep Men from Coming to Christ, are discovered. With Special Helps to Recover God's Favour. By Thomas Hooker. The Twelfth Edition. London, Printed by R.J. for J. Robinson, A. and J. Churchill, J. Taylor, and J. Wyat. 1700. 167 p. 14cm. 12° First pub. London, 1629. Wing H2653; Sabin32845.

4574, 1908

DA700 H923ℓ	[Humfrey, John] 1621-1719. A Letter To George Keith, Concerning The Salvability of the Heathen. Together with A Testimony to the same Doctrine, as Long held, and not Newly taken up, out of several former Books of him that writ it. By his Respectful

Neighbour, J. H. ...
London Printed, and Sold by the Booksellers of London and Westminster, 1700.
36 p. 20.5cm. 4º
WingH3684; Smith(Anti-Quak.)241; Smith(Friends)2:49; Morgan*C216ª.

11496, 1918

DA700 H923p [Humfrey, John] 1621-1719.
A Paper To William Penn, At The Departure of that Gentleman to his Territory, for his Perusal, In Pensilvania. Wherein Two Points are proposed to him concerning the Quakers Religion ... By a Friend unknown. ...
London: Printed by T. M. for H. Mortlock at the Phænix in St. Paul's Church-yard, 1700.
2 p.l., 24 (i.e. 26)p., 1 l. 20.5cm. 4º
Errata, p. 24 (i.e. 26).
"Some Books Printed for Henry Mortlock..." (last p.).
WingH3698; Sabin58444; Smith(Anti-Quak.)241; Morgan C217.

8096, 1911

BA700 J91f [R] Juana Inés de la Cruz, sister, 1651-1695.
Fama, Y Obras Posthumas Del Fenix De Mexico, Decima Musa, Poetisa Americana, Sor Jvana Ines De La Crvz, Religiosa Professa En El Convento De San Geronimo De La Imperial Ciudad de Mexico ...
Con Privilegio, En Madrid: En la Imprenta de Manuel Ruiz De Murga, à la Calle de la Habada. Año de 1700.
71 p.l., 210, [5] p. port. 21cm. 4º
Title in red and black.
Edited by Juan Ignacio Castorena y Ursúa.
Forms v.3 of the author's works.
"Tassa" certificate dated (18th p.l.v) 25 Feb. 1700.
Errata, 18th p.l.r
Preliminary matter and p. 167 ff. consist chiefly of commendatory poetry by various authors.
Palau(2)65226; Medina(BHA)2013; Sabin36814.

32121, 1957

DA700 K28a Keith, George, 1639?-1716.
An Account Of The Quakers Politicks, Discovering some Material Passages as to their Government never before published; As Also Something Extracted from Several Letters Of Robert Bridgeman to George Keith, The Originals of all which I have by me, By George Keith.
London, Printed by W. Redmayne for Brab.
Aylmer at the Three Pidgeons in Cornhill, and Charles Brome at the Gun at the West-end of St. Paul's Church, 1700.
2 p.l., 39, [1] p. 20cm. 4º
Dated (p. 38) 7 June 1700.
Errata, (last p.).
Wing K137; Smith(Friends)2:38; Morgan C229.

63-283

DA696 K28e Keith, George, 1639?-1716.
George Keith's Fourth Narrative, Of His Proceedings At Turners-Hall. Divided into Three Parts: Detecting the Quakers Gross Errors ... read at three several Meetings, the 11th, the 18th, and 23d of Jan. 1699 ... More particularly discovering the Fallacious and Sophistical Defences of George Whitehead, Joseph Wyeth, and seven Quakers of Colchester ... By George Keith.
London: Printed for Brabazon Aylmer, at the Three Pigeons against the Royal Exchange in Cornhill, 1700.
4 p.l., 116, [4] p. 21cm. 4º
Includes an attestation of five ministers of the Church of England, 1st p.l.v
"Advertisement", 3d p.l., signed: London, 18th 10th Month, 1699/1700.
"A Catalogue of the Authors and Books of Quakers, quoted in this Narrative, and some "Books of their Opponents." (p. [1-2] at end).
Errata: p. [3-4] at end.
Bound as the 4th in a vol. of 7 works by Keith.

DA698 K28a ———— Another copy. 22.5cm.
Imperfect: 2d-3d p.l. wanting.
Bound as the 3d in a vol. of 3 works by Keith.
JCB(2)2:1606; WingK167; Sabin37191; Smith(Friends)2:35-6; McAlpin4:632; Morgan C234.

04791, before 1874
4896, 1908

DA700 K28m Keith, George, 1639?-1716.
Mr. George Keith's Account Of A National Church, And The Clergy, &c. Humbly Presented to the Bishop of London: With Some Queries Concerning the Sacrament.
London Printed, and Sold by the Booksellers of London and Westminster, 1700.
8 p. 20cm. 4º
Compiled from Keith's published works to discredit his conversion to the Anglican communion.
WingK135; Smith(Friends)2:47; Morgan C229.

8395, 1909

DA696　Keith, George, 1639?-1716.
K28e　　A Narrative Of the Proceedings of George Keith, At Coopers-Hall In The City of Bristol, The 14th Day of August, 1700. In Detecting the Errors of Benjamin Cool ... By George Keith.
　　London Printed for J. Gwillim, in Bishopsgate-Street, 1700.
　　31 p.　21cm.　4°
　　Bound as the 6th in a vol. of 7 works by Keith.
　　JCB(2)2:1605; cf. WingK185; Smith(Friends)2:37; cf. Morgan C231.
04793, before 1874

DA700　Keith, George, 1639?-1716.
K28q　　The Quakers Proved Apostats and Heathens. And A Specimen Of The Quakers Great Malice and Ignorance In their late Printed Epigram they have made or procured to be made against me both in Latin and English, and which their Printer Tacy Sowl doth publickly Sell, With some Observations of mine upon it. By George Keith.
　　London, Printed for Brabazon Aylmer at the Three Pidgeons in Cornhill, and Charles Brome at the Gun at the West-end of St. Paul's, 1700.
　　8 p.　21.5cm.　4°
　　Caption title; imprint at end.
　　A reply to In Georgium Keithum Caledonium apostatam epigramma [London] 1700 and (p. 7-8) to [John Field's] The Christianity of the people called Quakers, London, 1700.
　　WingK196; Smith(Friends)2:37.
9024, 1912

DA696　Keith, George, 1639?-1716.
K28s　　A Sermon Preach'd at the Parish-Church Of St. Helen's, London, May the 19th. 1700. By George Keith. Being his Third Sermon after Ordination.
　　London, Printed for J. Gwillim, against Crosby-Square in Bishopsgate-street, 1700.
　　31, [1] p.　21cm.　4°
　　"Advertisement. This is to give Notice, That a Printed Sheet, call'd, Mr. George Keith's Account of a National Church ... is a Quaker-Cheat, Writ and Publish'd altogether without my Consent or Knowledge ... G.K." (last p.).
　　Bound as the 4th in a vol. of 11 works by Keith.
　　JCB(2)2:1608; WingK211; Smith(Friends)2:37.
04798, before 1874

DA700　Keith, George, 1639?-1716.
K28st1　　A Sermon Preach'd at Turners-Hall, The 5th. of May, 1700. By George Keith. In which he gave an Account of his joyning in Communion with the Church of England. With some Additions and Enlargements made by Himself.
　　London: Printed by W. Bowyer, for Brab. Aylmer at the Three Pigeons in Cornhil, and Char. Brome at the Gun at the West-End of St. Paul's Church-yard. 1700.
　　32 p.　19.5cm.　4°
　　Half-title: Mr. Keith's Last Sermon At Turners-Hall ...
　　WingK209; Smith(Friends)2:36; McAlpin 4:633; Morgan C240.
8396, 1912

DA696　Keith, George, 1639?-1716.
K28s　　A Sermon Preach'd at Turners-Hall, The 5th. of May, 1700. By George Keith. In which he gave an Account of his joyning in Communion with the Church of England. With some Additions and Enlargements made by Himself. The Second Edition.
　　London: Printed by W. Bowyer, for Brab. Aylmer at the Three Pigeons in Cornhil, and Char. Brome at the Gun at the West-End of St. Paul's Church-yard. 1700.
　　32 p.　21cm.　4°
　　Half title: Mr. Keith's Last Sermon At Turners-Hall, May the 5th. 1700.
　　First pub. London, the same year. This ed. was reprinted from the same setting of type.
　　Bound as the 2d in a vol. of 11 works by Keith.
　　JCB(2)2:1609; WingK209A; Smith(Friends)2:36; cf. Morgan C240.
04796, before 1874

DA696　Keith, George, 1639?-1716.
K28s　　Two Sermons Preach'd at the Parish-Church Of St. George Botolph-Lane, London, May the 12th. 1700. By George Keith. Being his first Preaching after Ordination.
　　London, Printed by W. Bowyer, for Brab. Aylmer at the Three Pigeons in Cornhil; and Char. Brome at the Gun at the West-End of St. Paul's Church-yard. 1700.
　　31, [1] p.　21cm.　4°
　　"Books printed for Brab. Aylmer ... for Charles Brome ..." (last page).
　　Bound as the 3d in a vol. of 11 works by

DA700 K28t	Keith. JCB(2)2:1607; WingK226; Smith(Friends) 2:36; MorganC241. 04797, before 1874

DA700
K28t
Keith, George, 1639?-1716.
Two Sermons Preach'd at the Parish-Church Of St. George Botolph-Lane, London, May the 12th. 1700. By George Keith. Being his first Preaching after Ordination. The Second Edition.
London, Printed by W. Bowyer, for Brab. Aylmer at the Three Pigeons in Cornhil; and Char. Brome at the Gun at the West-End of St. Paul's Church-yard. 1700.
31, [1] p. 19.5cm. 4º
First pub. London, the same year. This ed. was reprinted from the same setting of type.
"Books Printed for Brab. Aylmer ... for Charles Brome ..." (last page).
WingK227; Smith(Friends)2:36; cf. Morgan C241.
8397, 1912

EA700
L516h
Le Gobien, Charles, 1653-1708.
Histoire Des Isles Marianes, Nouvellement converties à la Religion Chrestienne; & de la mort glorieuse des premiers Missionnaires qui y ont prêché la Foy. Par le Pere Charles Le Gobien, de la Compagnie de Jesus.
A Paris, Chez Nicolas Pepie, ruë S. Jacques, au grand Saint Basile, au dessus de la Fontaine de S. Severin. M.DCC. Avec Privilege Du Roy.
12 p.ℓ., 384, 383-433, [434-445] p. 2 fold. maps. 16cm. 12º
Cut on t.-p.
"Achevé d'imprimer pour la premiere fois, le 2. de janvier 1700." (p. [444]).
Errata, p. [445].
Bound in contemporary calf.
Backer3:1513; Streit21:348; Retana181.
71-296

DA700
L634d
[Leslie, Charles] 1650-1722.
A Defence Of A Book Intituled, The Snake in the Grass. In Reply To Several Answers put out to it by George Whithead, Joseph Wyeth, &c.
London, Printed by M. Bennet, for C. Brome at the Gun, W. Keblewhite at the Swan in St. Paul's Church-Yard. And Geo. Strahan at the Golden-Ball, over against the Royal-Exchange, in Cornhil. 1700.
8 p.ℓ., 184, 209 (i.e. 241), 93 p. 19.5cm. 8º
A reply in part to Joseph Wyeth, Anguis flagellatus, 1st pub. London, 1699, and to George Whitehead, An antidote against the snake in the grass, 1st pub. London, 1697.
Includes (93 p. at end) "A Collection Of Several Papers, Which Relate to the Fore-going Discourse."
Bound in contemporary calf, rebacked.
WingL1126; Sabin40196; Smith(Anti-Quak.) 269; McAlpin4:633-634, 514; MorganB206.
11505, 1918

D700
L651m
A Letter To A Member of Parliament In the Country, Concerning The Present Posture of Affairs in Christendom: First, In Defence of the Treaty Of Partition. Secondly, Shewing the great Prejudices that Europe in General, and England in Particular, are like to receive from the Acceptation of the late King of Spain's Will, contrary to the Obligations of the said Treaty. In Answer to A Letter from him upon that Subject.
London: Printed in the Year, 1700.
2 p.ℓ., 26 p. 22.5cm. (24cm. in case) 4º
Dated at end: London, Dec. I. 1700.
In this copy there is a blank leaf at end.
WingL1674; Kress2234; MorganC267.
67-426

D700
L651t
A Letter To S C.M. a Member of Parliament, From An Inhabitant of the Island of Barbadoes.
[London, ca. 1700]
8 p. 20.5cm. (21.5cm. in case) 4º
Caption title.
"Advetisement." [sic] p. 8, refers to an erratum "in a former Impression of this Sheet," corrected in this copy.
29858, 1946

D700
-R644m
Marius, John.
Advice Concerning Bills of Exchange. ... By John Marius, Publick Notary. ...
London: Printed for Tho. Horne, at the South-Entrance into the Royal-Exchange. MDCC.
67, [1] p. 33cm. fol. (Issued as a part of Roberts, Lewes, The merchants map of commerce, London, 1700.)
With, as issued (p. 35-67): Mun, Thomas, England's Benefit And Advantage By Forein-

71-7A	Trade, Plainly Demonstrated. ... By Tho. Mun, Merchant, London, 1700, which has a special t.-p. but continuous paging and signatures.
	    Marius' Advice 1st pub. London, 1651.
	    Mun's England's benefit 1st pub. London, 1664, under title England's treasure by forein trade ...
	    Bookseller's advertisement at end.
	    WingM608, cf. R1601.

DB
-M4143
1699
1
 	
R-S 2001-2, 1913
	Massachusetts (Colony)--Laws, statutes, etc.
	              31 May 1699 - 13 March 1700.
	    ... Acts and Laws, Passed by the Great and General Court or Assembly of the Province of the Massachusetts-Bay in New-England: Begun and Held at Boston, the Thirty-first of May, 1699. And continued by several Prorogations unto Wednesday the Thirteenth of March following, and then Sat.
	    [Boston, 1700]
	    159-176 p. 30.5cm. fol.
	    Caption title.
	    This is a supplement of Acts and Laws, of His Majesties province of the Massachusetts-Bay ... , Boston, 1699, and is bound with it and other supplements in order of paging.
	    A head-line and the enacting clause of the 1st act printed in this part are at the head of the title: Anno Regni Regis Gulielmi III. Duodecimo. Militia to be in a readiness.
	    WingM955; Evans917; Tower149.

DB
-M4143
1699
1
 	
R-S 2001-3, 1913
	Massachusetts (Colony)--Laws, statutes, etc.
	              29 May 1700
	    ... Acts and Laws, Passed by the Great & General Court or Assembly of His Majesties Province of the Massachusetts-Bay, in New-England: Begun and Held at Boston, on Wednesday the Twenty-ninth of May, 1700.
	    [Boston, 1700]
	    177-192 p. 30.5cm. fol.
	    Caption title.
	    This is a supplement of Acts and Laws, of His Majesties province of the Massachusetts-Bay ... , Boston, 1699, and is bound with it and other supplements in order of paging.
	    A head-line and the enacting clause of the 1st act printed in this part are at the head of the title: Anno Regni Regis Gulielmi III. Duodecimo. Jesuits & Popish Priests.
	    Cut (royal arms incl. motto: Semper Eadem) at head of title.
	    WingM955A; Evans918; Tower150.

D. Math
C.195A
 	
04861, 1878
	[Mather, Cotton] 1663-1728.
	    A Letter of Advice To The Churches Of The Non-conformists In The English Nation: Endeavouring their Satisfaction in that Point, Who are the True Church of England? ...
	    London, Printed, and Sold by A. Baldwin at the Oxford-Arms in Warwick-lane, 1700.
	    2 p.ℓ., 30, [2] p. 20cm. 4°
	    Signed (p. 30): Philalethes.
	    Booksellers' advertisement, 1st p.ℓ.^{v} and p. [1-2] at end.
	    JCB(2)2:1612; WingM1119; Sabin46377; Holmes(C.)195A; Dexter(Cong.)2527; Brinley 1151(this copy); Morgan C297.

D. Math
C.359B
 	
04860, 1878
	[Mather, Cotton] 1663-1728.
	    The Resolved Christian; Pursuing the Designs of Holiness and Happiness, In Ordering, First his own Heart and Life, and then his Family. With further Directions upon the Great Points, Of Spending our Time, & of Minding our End, And Of Behaving our selves well under all our Tryals. A Treatise that may be of use, to persons of all Conditions, and Especially to be Read in Families. ...
	    To be Sold by Nicholas Boone, at his Shop, over against the Old Meeting-house in Boston. 1700.
	    1 p.ℓ., 128 p. 14.5cm. 8°
	    First pub. under title: Small offers towards the service of the tabernacle. Boston, 1689; these are the same sheets without the dedication and with new t.-p.
	    JCB(2)2:1613; Evans933; WingM1146; Sabin 46486; Holmes(C.)359B; Brinley1213(this copy).

D. Math
C.403A
	[Mather, Cotton] 1663-1728.
	    A Token, for the Children of New-England. Or, Some Examples of Children, In whom the Fear of God was Remarkably Budding, before they Dyed; In Several Parts of New-England. Preserved and Published, for the Encouragement of Piety in other Children. And, Added as Supplement, unto the Excellent Janewayes Token for Children: Upon the Re-printing of it, in this Countrey.
	    Boston, in N.E. Printed by Timothy Green, for Benjamin Eliot, at his Shop, under the West-End of the Town House. 1700.
	    36 p. 13.5cm. 12° (Issued as a part of James Janeway's, A token for children, Boston, 1700.)
	    "Some Scriptural Hymns For Children",

p. 29-36.
This copy is without Janeway's A token for children.
Imperfect: p. 35-36 wanting; supplied in facsimile attached to Bib. Sheet.
JCB(2)2:1614; Evans914; WingM1162; Sabin 46555; Holmes(C.)403A; Brinley1250(this copy); MorganC295.
04859, 1878

D.Math C.439A
[Mather, Cotton] 1663-1728.
A Warning to the Flocks Against Wolves in Sheeps Cloathing. Or, A Faithful Advice, from several Ministers of the Gospel, in and near Boston, unto the Churches of New-England, relating to the Dangers that may arise from Impostors, Pretending to be Ministers. With A Brief History of some Impostors, Remarkably and Seasonably detected; Written, by One of the Ministers in Boston ...
Boston, Printed [by B. Green and J. Allen] for the Booksellers. 1700.
79, [1] p. 14.5cm. 8°
"Boston, 25d. 10m. 1699. A Letter, Containing a Remarkable History Of An Impostor" (p. 29-52) signed: Cotton Mather.
"A Faithful Advice, From Several Ministers of the Gospel ..." (p. 3-10) signed by 13 ministers and dated 28 Dec. 1699.
"Something to be known by all the Churches... At Boston-Lecture, 14. d. 10. m. 1699." (p. 54-79)
Booksellers' advertisement at end.
Imperfect: t.-p. wanting.
JCB(2)2:1610; WingM1165; Evans935; Sabin46587; Holmes(C.)439A; Dexter(Cong.)2524; MorganC296.
04858, before 1882

D.Math I.84A2
Mather, Increase, 1639-1723.
The Order of the Gospel, Professed and Practised by the Churches of Christ in New-England, Justified, by the Scripture, and by the Writings of many Learned men, both Ancient and Modern Divines; In Answer to several Questions, relating to Church Discipline By Increase Mather, President of Harvard Colledge in Cambridge, and Teacher of a Church at Boston in New England. ...
Boston, Printed by B. Green, & J. Allen, for Benjamin Eliot, at his Shop under the West End of the Town-House, 1700
143, [1] p. 14cm. 12°
Running title: The Order of the Churches in N. England Vindicated.
There is another issue with variant imprint: ... for Nicholas Buttolph, at his Shop at the Corner of Gutteridges Office-House ...

Dedication dated (p. 12); 1 m. 1700.
Errata, p. 143.
Bound in contemporary calf.
JCB(2)2:1615; WingM1235; Evans938; Sabin 46714n; Holmes(I.)84A2; Dexter(Cong.)2514; MorganC298.
03887, 1868

D.Math I.84B
Mather, Increase, 1639-1723.
The Order Of The Gospel, Professed and Practised by the Churches of Christ In New-England, Justified by the Scripture, and by the Writings of many Learned Men, both Ancient and Modern Divines. In Answer to several Questions relating to Church Discipline. By Increase Mather, President of Harvard-Colledge in Cambridge, and Teacher of a Church at Boston in New-England. ...
Printed at Boston in New-England, and Reprinted at London, and sold by A. Baldwin. 1700.
1 p.ℓ., vii, [1], 86 p. 16.5cm. 8°
Running title: The Order of the Churches in New-England Vindicated.
First pub. Boston, 1700.
Booksellers' advertisement, p. 85-86.
JCB(2)2:1616; WingM1236; Sabin46714n; Holmes(I.)84B; Dexter(Cong.)2514.
03714, before 1866

A700 M517p
Mela, Pomponius, fl. 43.
Pomponii Melæ Libri Tres De Situ Orbis Cum Observationibus Isaaci Vossii. Accedunt ejusdem Vossii observationum ad Pomponium Melam appendix & tres indices. Editio Secunda, In qua observationes textui subjectæ sunt, quæ in prima editione in fine operis apparebant.
Franekeræ, Apud Leonardum Strickium, Bibliopolam, MDCC.
8 p.ℓ., 419, [420-480], 70 p. pl., 7 diagrs. 19.5cm. 8°
Title in red and black.
Cut (device) on t.-p. incl. motto: Ne Extra Oleas
Added t.-p., engr.
Colophon: Franequeræ, Ex Officina Typographica Arnoldi Ielmeri. MDCC.
Dedication (3d p.ℓ.) signed: Leonardus Strik.
Errata, p. [480].
First printed Milan, 1471, with title: Cosmographia. Text edited by Vossius, 1st pub. The Hague, 1658.
With, as issued, Vossius, Isaac, ... Observationum ad Pomp. Melam Appendix with

D70
-P769t
[Melfort, John Drummond, 1st earl of] 1649-1714.
A Letter Directed to the Right Honourable The Earl of Perth, Governour To The Prince.
London, Printed by Charles Bill, and the Executrix of Thomas Newcomb, decead'd, Printers to the Kings most Excellent Majesty. 1700.
11 p. 30.5cm. fol.
Cut (royal arms) on t.-p.
Concerns activities of the Jacobite party in France. Intercepted in London and communicated to Parliament by the king.
No. [8] in a volume with binder's title: Political tracts 1655-1702.
Wing L1361; Morgan C262.

9973-8, 1914

half title, separate paging and signatures.
In this copy there is a blank leaf at end.
Bound in contemporary calf.

12968, 1921

D
Scott
5
Memorial To The Members of Parliament Of The Court Party.
[London, 1700]
6 p. 25.5cm. 4°
Caption title.
Concerns Scots' Darien colony.
Wing M1698; Scott 5.

752, 1905

Z
M834
1700
Morden, Robert, d. 1703.
Geography Rectified: Or, A Description Of The World...Illustrated with Seventy eight Maps. The Fourth Edition, Enlarged. To which is added a Complete Geographical Index to the Whole, Alphabetically digested...By Robert Morden.
London: Printed for R. Morden and T. Cockerill, and are to be sold by M. Fabian in Mercers-Chappel-Porch in Cheapside, and Ralph Smith at the Bible under the Exchange in Cornhill. MDCC.
5 p.l., 574, [2], 575-626, [72] p. illus. (engr.; 78 maps). 21cm. 4°
Title in red and black is a cancel.
Maps engr. in text except "Transilvania Moldavia Valachia Bvlgaria &c", p. 95, which is pasted over "The Maldives and Ceylon Islands", which was printed there in error (as well as properly on p. 448).
First pub. London, 1680.
Section on America occupies p. 542-626.
Bound in contemporary calf, rebacked.

Sabin 50535; Wing M2622; Phillips (Atlases) 3454.

11647, 1918

D700
M937m
[Moxon, James] fl. 1673-1705.
Mechanick Exercises: Or, The Doctrine Of Handy-Works. Applied to the Art of Bricklayers-Works.
London, Printed for, and Sold by J. Moxon, at the Atlas in Warwick-Lane, and at his Shop, at the Entrance of the West End of Cornhill, 1700.
1 p.l., 64 (i.e. 46) p. 3-8 plates (incl. pl. 8 fold.). 20.5cm. 4° (Issued as a part of Joseph Moxon's Mechanick exercises [v.1], London, 1700.)
The Mechanick exercises [v.1] (smithing, joinery, house-carpentry, turning) first pub. London, 1677-1680. This part on bricklaying was added in this edition.
This is usually included among the works of Joseph Moxon, but it more likely is by his son James.
Errata at end.
With this are bound parts of Joseph Moxon's Mechanick exercises [v.1], London, 1694.
Wing M3017.

67-403-1 rev

DA700
M942b
[Mucklow, William] 1631-1713.
A Bemoaning Letter Of An Ingenious Quaker, To a Friend of his. Wherein the Government Of The Quakers Among Themselves, (As hath been Exercised by George Fox, and others of their Ring-Leaders) is brought to Light. Wherein their Tyrannical and Persecuting Practices are Detected and Redargued. Also a Preface to the Reader, giving an account how the said Letter came to the hand of the Publisher. By G. I.
London, Printed for A. Baldwin in Warwick-Lane, 1700. (Price Stitcht 6d.)
45 p. 17cm. 8°
Preface, p. [3]-[8], signed: G. J.
Errata, p. [2].
First pub. under title: The spirit of the hat, London, 1673.
In this copy t.-p. is disintegrated with some effect on text; there is a blank l. at end.
Wing M3033; Smith (Friends) 2:190; Sabin 35327; cf. Morgan C308.

11452, 1918

BA70-
-N972m
[R]
Núñez de Roxas, Miguel, 1675 or 6-1731.
Memorial Informe Jvridico, Qve Presenta A Sv Magestad En Sv Real, Y Svpremo Con-

sejo De Las Indias Don Migvel Nvñez De Roxas, Cavallero del Orden de Santiago, A Favor De D. Migvel Nvñez De Sanabria, Sv Padre, Presidente de la Real Audiencia de Lima, y Capitan General, que fue, de los Reynos del Perù, y actual Oìdor Decano de la misma Audiencia. Sobre Que se declare no deberle preceder en el assiento, ni desposseerle de la dignidad de tal Decano en la Audiencia, y demàs actos, en que assistiere el Cuerpo de ella, D. Matheo de la Mata, Cavallero del Orden de Calatrava, y provisto al mismo Real, y Supremo Consejo, à quien su Magestad (que Dios guarde) se ha servido hazer merced de que buelva à servir la Plaza de Oìdor, que sirviò antes en aquella Audiencia.
[Madrid? 170-]
30 p. 29cm. fol.
Caption title.
Palau(2)197469; Medina(BHA)6681.

69-543

DA700 One Wonder more, Added to the Seven Wonders
P967w of the World. Verified in the Person of Mr. George Keith, once a Presbyterian, afterwards about Thirty Years a Quaker, then a Noun Substantive at Turners-Hall, and now an Itinerant Preacher (upon his Good Behaviour) in the Church of England: And all without Variation (as himself says) in Fundamentals. By a Protestant Dissenter.
[London? ca. 1700]
4 p. 20.5cm. 4°
Caption title.
Smith(Friends)2:48; Morgan C236.

8406, 1912 rev

BA700 Palafox y Mendoza, Juan de, Bp., 1600-1659.
P153c   Cartas Del V. Siervo De Dios D. Juan De Palafox Y Mendoza, Obispo De La Puebla De Los Angeles, Al R.mo P. Andres De Rada, Provincial de la Compañia de Jesus en Mexico, y de éste à su Excelencia Ilustrissima: Y Otros Documentos concernientes, que en parte de obsequio à la verdad, y justicia ofrece al Público D. Thomas Vasconsellos.
In Roma M.DCC. Appresso I. Fratelli Pagliarini. Con licenza de' Superiori.
117 p. 14cm. 8°
JCB(2)2:1620; Palau(2)209696; Medina(BHA) 2017; Sabin58286.

04863, before 1874

J700   Pastorius, Francis Daniel, 1651-1719.
P293u   Umständige Geographische Beschreibung
[R]   Der zu allerletzt erfundenen Provintz Pensylvaniæ, In denen End-Gräntzen Americæ In der West-Welt gelegen/Durch Franciscum Danielem Pastorium, J.V. Lic. und Friedens-Richtern daselbsten. Worbey angehencket sind einige notable Begebenheiten/und Bericht-Schreiben an dessen Herrn Vattern Melchiorem Adamum Pastorium, Und andere gute Freunde.
Franckfurt und Leipzig/Zu finden bey Andreas Otto. 1700.
6 p.l., 140 p. 16.5cm. 8°
Edited by Melchior Adam Pastorius.
Also issued with the preliminary leaves in a different setting of type.
Pages 80-81 contain various samples of Indian language.
"Zum Beschluss Folget des Eigen-Herrns und Ober-Haupts dieser Provintz selbst concepirte/ und an seine Freunde übersandte Beschreibung/ Deren Umstände notabel zu lesen sind" (p.[121]-140) is a slightly condensed reprint of: Penn, William, Beschreibung der in America neu-erfundenen Provinz Pensylvanien [Hamburg] 1684, the original texts of which were 1st pub. under titles: A letter from William Penn... to the Committee of the Free Society of Traders, London, 1683, and An abstract of a letter from Thomas Paskell, London, 1683.
JCB(2)2:1621; Sabin59028; Palmer370; Baer (Md.)208; Vail(Front.)287.

01592, 1847

bD700 The People of Scotland's Groans and Lamen-
P419s   table Complaints, Pour'd out before the High Court of Parliament [of Scotland].
[Edinburgh, 1700]
[2] p. 29cm. fol.
Caption title.
Hanson 12.

30499, 1949

DA700 The Portraiture Of Mr. George Keith The
P967p   Quaker, In Opposition to Mr. George Keith The Parson. Presented to the Hearers of his late Sermons. By a Protestant Dissenter. ...
London Printed, and Sold by the Booksellers of London and Westminster. 1700.
15 p. 21cm. 4°
Wing P3006; Smith(Friends)2:47; Morgan C237.

11499, 1918 rev

C619 A949n Primera Relacion Extraordinaria De La Salida Del Rey nuestro Señor Don Felipe Quinto, de Versallas para estos sus Reynos, y breves noticias de su Real Persona, assi propias, como adquiridas. Publicada Martes 21. de Diziembre de 1700.
Con Privilegio En Madrid: Por Antonio Bizarròn. [1700]
[4] p. 19.5cm. 4°
Caption title; imprint at end.
An "extraordinary" of the Gaceta de Madrid.
Bound as the 45th in a volume of 58 pamphlets, 1619-1702.
Palau(2)237445.

9361, 1913

D700 P957a The Printers Advertisement.
Boston, Printed by John Allen. 1700.
6 p. A⁴ 18.5cm. 4°
Caption title; imprint at end.
A reply to the "Advertisement" appearing on the 1st p.ℓ.ᵛ of Gospel order revived [New York], 1700, which claimed that the press in Boston was so much under the power of the Mathers that it was necessary to print that book in New York.
Contains: a denial by the Boston printer Bartholomew Green (dated 21 Dec. 1700); some remarks in support of Green which are thought to be by Cotton Mather (dated 24 Dec. 1700); and contrary depositions (dated 27 Dec. 1700) by Thomas Brattle, Zechariah Tuthill, and John Mico.
A4 is blank and present in this copy.
A supplement to this was issued, B² paged 7-10, captioned (p. 7) "The Deposition of Bartholomew Green, Printer" and with an imprint at end: Boston, Printed by Bartholomew Green, 1701. This supplement contains Green's deposition and a supporting deposition of John Allen and Timothy Green (both dated 4 Jan. 1700/01) and remarks "To the Candid Reader" by Green (dated 10 Jan. 1700/01).
Available in facsim.
WingP3504; Evans976; Sabin28506; Dexter (Cong.)2544; Church790n; Holmes(I.)84n.

6438, 1910

D Scott 108 A Proposal For Remeeding [sic] our Excessive Luxury.
[Edinburgh? 1700?]
4 p. 20.5cm. 4°
Caption title.
Evidently issued as a part of A Serious Advice To The African and Indian Company. [Edinburgh? 1700?]
WingP3697; Kress2251; Scott108n.

749A, 1905

F700 R134d Raei, Johannes de, d. 1702.
Dictionarium Geographicum Ofte Woorden-Boek Des Ganschen Aard-Ryks ... Toegepast op onse Hollandsche Land- en Zee-kaarten, waar in deselve op een gemakkelyke wyse sullen te vinden zyn. Nu voor de Tweedemaal, nevens een Kort Begryp der Geographie, in onse Neder-Duitsche taal in het ligt gebragt. Door Johannes De Raei De Jonge. En nu met eenige hondert benamingen vermeerdert; met byvoeging, hoe die eertyds van de Romeinen en Grieken benoemt zyn geweest.
t'Amsterdam, By Joan Ten Hoorn, Boekverkoper, over 't Oude Heere Logement, 1700.
4 p.ℓ., 22, [2], 623, [54] p. 23cm. 4°
Title in red and black.
Cut (monogram) on t.-p.
First pub. Amsterdam, 1680.
Enlarged by Steven Blankaart (cf. his "Aan Den Leeser", 4th p.ℓ.)
In this copy there is a blank leaf at end.
Bound in contemporary vellum.

12970, 1921

D700 R384u Remarks Upon a Late Pamphlet Intitul'd, The Two Great Questions Consider'd: I. What the French King will do with respect to the Spanish Monarchy. II. What Measures the English ought to take.
London, Printed in the Year 1700.
27 p. 21.5cm. 4°
A reply to Daniel Defoe's Two great questions consider'd. London, 1700.
WingR938; Sabin69516; BPL(Defoe)1206.

70-547

D Scott 110 [Ridpath, George] d. 1726.
Scotland's Grievances, Relating to Darien, &c. Humbly offered to the Consideration Of The Parliament. ...
[Edinburgh, James Watson] Printed, 1700.
3 p.ℓ., 54 p. 18cm. 8°
Errata, 1st p.ℓ.ᵛ
Imperfect: 1st p.ℓ. wanting.

D Scott 110 cop. 2 —— —— Another copy. 17.5cm.
With this is bound An Enquiry into the causes of the miscarriage of the Scots colony, Glasgow, 1700.

D Scott 110 cop. 3 —— —— Another copy. 17.5cm.
With this are bound: The representation and petition of the council-general of the Indian and African Company, Edinburgh, 1700; [Belhaven, J. H.] A defence of the Scots settlement at Darien, Edinburgh, 1699; and The original papers and letters relating

to the Scots Company Trading to Africa and the Indies [Edinburgh ?] 1700.
  JCB(2)2:1589, 1590; Sabin 18568; Wing R1464; Scott 110; Kress 2260; Morgan C368.

764, 1905
0814, 1846
04749, before 1915

D700 -R644m Roberts, Lewes, 1596-1640.
  The Merchants Map of Commerce: Wherein The Universal Manner and Matter Relating To Trade and Merchandize, Are fully Treated of ... By Lewis Roberts, Merchant. ... The Fourth Edition, carefully Corrected, and Enlarg'd. To which is Annexed, Advice concerning Bills of Exchange [by John Marius]; ... Together with ... England's Benefit and Advantage by Foreign Trade demonstrated: By Tho. Mun, of London, Merchant.
  London: Printed for Thomas Horne at the South Entrance of the Royal Exchange, in Cornhill. 1700.
  2 p.l., 176, 185-431, [15], 67, [1] p. 33cm. fol.
  Title in red and black.
  "Of America And The Provinces Thereof." p. 49 (i.e. 47)-62, 1st count.
  Bookseller's advertisement at end.
  With, as issued: Marius, John, Advice concerning bills of exchange, London, 1700, and Mun, Thomas, England's benefit and advantage by foreign-trade, London, 1700. Each of these has a special t.-p.; they are paged and signed together as a unit separate from the rest of the book.
  First pub., London, 1638. This is the same text as the 2d ed., London, 1671, with Marius and Mun's section appended.
  In this copy p. 189-192 are misbound between p. 186-187.
  Bound in contemporary calf, rebacked.
  Sabin 71909; Wing R1601; Kress 2261.

71-7

BA700 -R666c Robles, Antonio de.
  Consistencia De El Jvbileo Maximo De El Ano [sic] Santo, Y De La Suspension De Indulgencias dentro de el. Respuesta A las proposiciones de vn Anonymo, ... Por El Bachiller Don Antonio de Robles, Colegial, y Maestro de Ceremonias de el mismo Colegio, Colector de las limosnas de su Hospital, y Traductor de Breves Apostolicos.
  Con Licencia De Los Svperiores, En Mexico Por Doña Maria de Benavides: Viuda de Juan de Ribera en el Empedradillo. Año de 1700.
  5 p.l., 26 numb. l., [8] p. 30cm. fol.
  License dated (3d p.l.^{v}) 20 Apr. 1700.
  Part of a controversy concerning the suspension of indulgences during 1700, a jubilee year. The anonymous work to which this is a reply is entitled (cf. 5th p.l.^{r}): Alegato, y consulta en que se satisface haverse publicado la Absolucion general, no obstante el Iubileo del Año Santo en este año de 1700.
  Errata, at end.
  Palau(2)271124; Medina(Mexico)1778; Sabin 72247.

13959, 1925

BA700 R934o Ruiz Perea, Miguel.
  Oracion Panegyrica En la Solemnidad plausible, y Publicacion de la Santa Bulla, Deciala en la Santa Yglesia Metropolitana de Mexico en la Dominica primera de Adviento El Br Migvel Ruiz Perea Domiciliario de este Arçobispado, indigno Beneficiado por su Magestad Vicario in Capite, y Juez Ecclesiastico de la Doctrina del Real de Minas de Tzaqualpan, Ministro Mexicano. Otomi. Mazahua. Olmeco. Tepehua. Totonac, y Castellano. ...
  Con licencia, en Mexico: por los Herederos de la Viuda de Francisco Rodriguez Lupercio, en la puente de Palacio. Año de 1700.
  8 p.l., 12 numb. l. 20cm. 4º
  Licenses dated (6th p.l.^{r}, 8th p.l.^{v}) 9 Dec. 1699.
  The sermon is in Aztec language.
  Palau(2)282280; Medina(Mexico)1779; Sabin 74047.

04865, before 1900

bD Scott 130b Scotland's Lament For Their Misfortunes.
  [Edinburgh, 1700]
  Broadside. 32 x 19.5cm. 1/2º
  Verse.
  Refers to the misfortunes of the Darien Colony and the Edinburgh fire of 3 Feb. 1700.
  Scott 130b.

04868, 1883

D Scott 108 A Serious Advice To The African and Indian Company.
  [Edinburgh ? 1700 ?]
  [3]-12, 4 p. 20.5cm. 4º
  Caption title. Not recorded with a t.-p.

749, 1905

          With, evidently, as issued, A Proposal For Remeeding [sic] Our Excessive Luxury, p. 1-4, 2d count.
          WingS2603; Kress2266; Scott 108.

DA700
S485w
  A Serious Warning and Caution Unto George Keith, And to many Others. As Also, A Relation Of Some Expressions From George Keith, Concerning His Reasons which He then gave, for Opposing aud [sic] Exposing the Quakers, When at His Place at Turner's-Hall. The Intention of the Publication of which, and more that is in this Paper contain'd, is proposed for a Publick and General Good of All.
  London, Printed in the Year, 1700.
    15 p. 19cm. 8°
    Postscript dated (at end): Written in London, in the Seventh Month, 1700.
    A reply to Keith's A serious call to the Quakers, 1st pub. London, 1700.
    Title-page this copy mutilated affecting imprint.
    Wing S2620; Smith(Friends)2:46.

11477, 1918

D696
-C737c
  Seton, George.
    A Modest Vindication of Mr. Setons Address and Petition, To his Majesties High Commissioner, from the Cavils and Misconstructions of Anonymus.
    [Edinburgh? ca. 1700]
    4 p. 31.5cm. fol.
    Caption title.
    This copy disintegrated at former fold with slight loss of text.
    Bound in a volume of Scottish imprints and mss. as the 24th of 58 items.

7122, 1910

D
Scott
123b
  [Seton, Sir William] d. 1744.
    A Short Speech Prepared to be Spoken, By a Worthy Member In Parliament, Concerning the Present State Of The Nation. ...
    [Edinburgh] Printed in the Year 1700.
    16 p. 17.5cm. 8°
    Wing S2651; McAlpin4:639; Scott 123b; Morgan C384.

14211, 1925

BA700
S579o
  Sigüenza y Góngora, Carlos de, 1645-1700.
    Oriental Planeta Evangelico Epopeya Sacro-Panegyrica Al Apostol grande de las Indias S. Francisco Xavier. Escriviola El Dr. D. Carlos de Siguenza, y Gongora ... Diolo A La Estampa D. Gabriel Lopez De Siguenza, Y Lo Dedica Al Señor L^{do}.D. Antonio de Aunzibay, y Anaya, Canonigo de la Santa Iglesia Cathedral de esta Ciudad, Juez Provisor, y Vicario General de este Arçobispado.
    Con Licencia De Los Svperiores En Mexico por Doña Maria de Benavides, Año de 1700.
    6 p. ℓ., 24 p. 19.5cm. 4°
    Preliminary matter (poetry) by Andrés de los Reyes Villaverde, Bernardo de Villanueva, and Miguel Pérez de Gálvez.
    Dedication signed (5th p. ℓ.^{v}) 22 Oct. 1700.
    In this copy 2d p. ℓ. is misbound following 5th p. ℓ.
    Sabin 80979; Medina(Mexico)1783; Palau(2) 312983; Jones(1938)370 (this copy); cf. Wagner p. 298.

29389, 1943

D
Scott
110c
  Some Thoughts Concerning The Affairs of this Session Of Parliament, 1700. ...
    [Edinburgh?] Printed in the Year M.DCC.
    30 p. 16.5cm. 8°
    Wing S4626A; Scott 110c; Morgan C162.

63-284

BB
-S7336
1700
1
  Spain--Sovereigns, etc., 1700-1746 (Philip V)
                        [9 July 1700]
    El Rey. Muy Reverendos en Christo Padres, Arçobispos, y Reverendos Obispos de las Iglesias Metropolitanas, y Cathedrales de las Provincias de la Nueva España, Goatemala, Islas Filipinas, y de Barlovento, de mi Consejo ...
    [Madrid, 1700]
    [3] p. 34.5cm. fol.
    Title from caption and beginning of text.
    "... encargandoles zelen con grande aplicacion el contenido del Despacho de siete de Mayo de mil seiscientos y noventa y seis, sobre que no sean propuestos, ni presentados los Expulsos de las Religiones à Curatos, Beneficios, y Prebendas ..."
    Dated (at end in ms.) Madrid, 9 July 1700.
    Bound as the 1st in a volume of 7 miscellaneous items of Mexican interest.

65-290

DA700　Stoddard, Solomon, 1643-1729.
S869d　　The Doctrine Of Instituted Churches Explained and Proved From The Word Of God. By Solomon Stoddard, A.M. Minister of the Gospel in Northampton, New-England.
　　London: Printed for Ralph Smith, at the Bible under the Piazza of the Royal Exchange in Cornhil. 1700.
　　1 p.ℓ., 34 p. 21cm. 4°
　　A reply to: Increase Mather, The order of the gospel. Boston, 1700.
　　Wing S5708; Sabin 91945; Dexter(Cong.)2515; McAlpin 4:641; Morgan C424.
1528, 1906

+Z　　Suite Du Neptune Francois, Ou Atlas
≡N442　Nouveau Des Cartes Marines. Levées
1693　　Par Ordre Expres Des Roys De Portugal. Sous qui on a fait la Découverte de L'Afrique &c. Et données au Public par les soins de Feu Monsieur D'Ablancourt. ...
　　A Amsterdam, Chez Pierre Mortier, Libraire. M.D.CC. Avec Privilege De Nos Seigneurs Les Etats.
　　1 p.ℓ., 5 p. pl., 33 maps. 65.5cm. 1°
　　Cut (incl. Amsterdam coat-of-arms) on t.-p.
　　The African maps are based on material compiled by Jean Jacobé [also known as Nicolas] de Frémont d'Ablancourt.
　　"Description De Toutes Les Côtes De L'Afrique &c." (p. [1]-5) is an extract from Nicolas Perrot d'Ablancourt's translation of Luis del Mármol Carvajal's L'Afrique, Paris, 1667.
　　There is also an issue Amsterdam, Pieter Mortier, 1700, with preliminaries in Dutch and title: Vervolg van de Neptunus ...
　　Privilege (in Dutch) dated (p. 5) 17 June 1693.
　　Maps are double-page size, except [5], [10], [11], [12], [15], [17], [19], [24], [25], [29], [30], which are single-page size, and [2], which is folded to double-page size.
　　In this copy the plate and all maps are colored.
　　Bound with Le Neptune François ... Paris [i.e. Amsterdam] 1693, as the 3d of 3 sections.
　　　Contents:
[plate]"Boussole Des Vents..."
[1] "Carte Generale De L'Afrique ... A Amsterdam, Chez Pierre Mortier..."
[2] "Carte Des Costes De L'Afrique Sur la Mer Mediterranée ... A Amsterdam, Chez Pierre Mortier..."
[3] "Le De Troit De Gibraltar ... A Amsterdam Chez Pierre Mortier..."
[4] "Carte Des Costes De L'Afrique ou est compris une Partie de Guinée, Le Royaume De Benin, l'Isle de S!. Thomas ... A Amsterdam Chez Pierre Mortier..."
[5] "Carte Des Costes De L'Afrique Depuis Cap. de Lopo, Iusques à l'Isle Mazira ... A Amsterdam Chez Pierre Mortier..."
[6] "Carte Particuliere Des Costes De L'Afrique Qui comprend le Royaume De Maroc ... A Amsterdam Chez Pierre Mortier..."
[7] "Carte Particuliere Des Costes De L'Afrique Qui comprend le Royaume De Gualata ... A Amsterdam Chez Pierre Mortier..."
[8] "Carte Particuliere Des Costes De L'Afrique Qui comprend le Royaume De Cacheo le Province De Gelofo... A Amsterdam Chez Pierre Mortier..."
[9] "Carte Particuliere Des Costes De L'Afrique Qui comprend une Partie De La Guinée et Partie De Mina ... A Amsterdam Chez Pierre Mortier..."
[10] "Carte Des Costes De L'Afrique Depuis Cabo Corso Jusques à Omorro. ... A Amsterdam Chez Pierre Mortier..."
[11] "Carte Particuliere Des Costes De L'Afrique Qui comprend une Partie De Congo ... A Amsterdam Chez Pierre Mortier..."
[12] "Carte Particuliere Des Costes De L'Afrique Depuis Cabo Ledo Jusques au Cap De Bone Esperance. ... A Amsterdam Chez Pierre Mortier..."
[13] "Carte Particuliere Des Costes De Cap De Bone Esperance ... A Amsterdam Chez Pierre Mortier..."
[14] "Carte Particuliere Des Costes De L'Afrique Qui comprend le Pays De Cafres ... A Amsterdam Chez Pierre Mortier..."
[15] "Carte Particuliere Des Costes De L'Afrique Depuis C. Del Gado Jusques Rio Mocambo ... A Amsterdam Chez Pierre Mortier..."
[16] "Carte Particuliere De La Mer Rouge ... A Amsterdam Chez Pierre Mortier..."
[17] "Carte Des Principales Ports De Mer Bancs De Sable &c: Qui sont Dans la Mer Rouge ..."
[18] "Carte Particuliere De L'Isle Dauphine Ou Madagascar Et S!. Laurens ... A Amsterdam Chez Pierre Mortier..."
[19] "Carte Des Isles D'Açores ..."
[20] "Carte Des Costes De L'Asie Sur L'Ocean ... Amsterdam Chez Pierre Mortier..."
[21] "Carte Particuliere d'une Partie

D'Asie Ou Sont Les Isles D'Andemaon, Ceylan, Les Maldives ... A Amsterdam Chez Pierre Mortier ..."
[22] "Le Royaume De Siam Auec les Royaumes qui luy sont Tributaires, et les Isles de Sumatra, Andemaon ... A Amsterdam. Chez Pierre Mortier..."
[23] "Le Golfe De Mexique, et les Isles Voisine. ... A Amsterdam, Chez Pierre Mortier ..."
[24] "Ocean Atlantique, Ou Mer Du Nord... A Amsterdam, Chez Pierre Mortier..."
[25] "Carte De La Mer Meridional Contenant une partie des Costes de L'Afrique et de L'Amerique Meridionale ... A Amsterdam Chez Pierre Mortier ..."
[26] "Carte Nouvelle De L'Amerique Angloise ... A Amsterdam Chez Pierre Mortier ..."
[27] "Carte Particuliere De Virginie, Maryland, Pennsilvanie, La Nouvelle Iarsey, Orient et Occidentale ... A Amsterdam Chez P. Mortier. Avec Privilege ..."
[28] "Carte Particuliere De Isthmus, Ou Darien, Qui comprend le Golfe De Panama &c. Cartagene ... A Amsterdam Chez Pierre Mortier. ..."
[29] "Carte General De La Caroline. ... A Amsterdam Chez Pierre Mortier ..."
[30] "Carte Particuliere De La Caroline ... A Amsterdam Chez Pierre Mortier ..."
[31] "Mer De Sud, Ou Pacifique, Contenant L'Isle De Californe, les Costes de Mexique, Du Perou, Chili ... A Amsterdam, Chez Pierre Mortier ..."
[32] "Carte Particuliere De L'Amerique Septentrionale ... À Amsterdam, Chez Pierre Mortier ..."
[33] "Le Canada ou Partie De La Nouvelle France, Contenant La Terre De Labrador ..."

—————Another issue. 65cm.
In this copy the publisher's name on the title-page is covered by a label reading: George Gallet.
In this copy the plate and all maps are colored.
Contents is as indicated above except that a copy (uncolored) of the added, engr. t.-p. of Le Neptune François is bound at the beginning.
Bound in contemporary calf. This copy accompanies Le Neptune François, Paris [i.e. Amsterdam] 1703, and Cartes Marine, Amsterdam, 1693, which are bound together in a separate, like binding.
Laid into this copy is an engr. t.-p. (trimmed to 48.5 x 32 cm.): Plan De Plusieurs Bâtimens De Mer...

+Z
≡N442
1703B

—————Another copy. 63.5cm.
Contents as indicated above except as specified below.
In this copy maps nos. [31] and [33] have a variant imprint: A Amsterdam, Chez J. Cóvens et C. Mortier.
This copy contains an additional map (following no. [21]): Paskaert vande Caspise Zee.
Included in this copy (bound after the "Boussole Des Vents...") are 18 ship plates (which are sometimes bound as part of Le Neptune François):
ship plates:
[1] "Vaisseau Royal d'Angleterre. Koninckelyke Schip van Engeland. a Amsterdam Chez Pierre Mortier Avec Privil. 1"
[2] "Coupe dun Amiral de. 104. pieces de Canon auec ses principales proportions et les noms des pieces du dedans."
[3] "Vaisseau du troisiême rang a la Voille. Twee Decks Schip vande derde Rang. a Amsterdam Chez Pierre Mortier Avec Privil. 3"
[4] "Galiote a bombe. Bombardeer Galjoot. a Amsterdam Chez Pierre Mortier. Avec Privilege 4"
[5] "Bruslot a la Sonde Brander, leggende voor Anker. a Amsterdam Chez Pierre Mortier Avec Privil. 5"
[6] "Flute Vaisseau de charge a la Voile. A Amsterdam Chez Pierre Mortier. Avec Privilege "
[7] "Polacre a la voille. Polacre Zeylende. A Amsterdam Chez Pierre Mortier Avec Privilege. 7"
[8] "Coupe Dvne Galere Auec Ses Proportions Door-Sneede Galey met syn Proportie. Quille Dvne Galere Sur le Chantier voet van een Galey op de Stapel. 8"
[9] "la Galere Reale a la sonde. A Amsterdam Chez Pierre Mortier. Avec Privilege "
[10] "Galere a la voille portant l'Estendart de chef d'Escadre, Zeylende Galley voerende d'Admiraals Vlag. a Amsterdam Chez Pierre Mortier Avec Privilege. 10"
[11] "La galere Patronne, a la rame. Roeyende Patroon Galley. A Amsterdam Chez Pierre Mortier Avec Privilege. 11"
[12] "Galeasse a la voile. a Amsterdam Chez Pierre Mortier Avec Privilege"
[13] "Galeasse a la rame. A Amsterdam Chez Pierre Mortier Avec Privil. "
[14] "Solemnité Du Bucentaure, Qui Se Celebre A Venise Le Jour De L'Ascension. Tome.1. Pag. 266. 14"
[15] "Saique batiment dont les Turcs se

seruent en leuent pour leur trafic Saique daar de Turcke meede Negotieere in de Levant. a Amsterdam Chez Pierre Mortier Avec Privilege 15"

[16] "Brigantin donnant chasse a vne Felouque et prest a la border. Brigantin Attaqueerende een Sloep. a Amsterdam Chez Pierre Mortier Avec Privilege. 16"

[17] "Barque allant vent arriere. Barck Seylende voor de Windt. a Amsterdam Chez Pierre Mortier Avec Privilege. 17"

[18] "Tartane de Pesche Vissers Tartane. a Amsterdam Chez Pierre Mortier Avec Privil. 18"

In this copy the plates are not colored, but the maps are.

Bound with Le Neptune François... , Paris [i.e. Amsterdam] 1703, as the 3d of 3 sections.

See Chapin, H.M., "The French Neptune and its various editions," American book collector, II (1932), 16-19.

Koeman M. Mor 7; cf. Phillips(Atlases)517; Scheepvaart Mus. 51; Muller(1872)1958*; cf. Tiele 791.

33014C, 33015-2, 1960; 33118, after 1900

D700 Temple, Sir William, bart., 1628-1699.
T287b Brieven Van de Heer William Temple, Ridder, &c. Geschreven gedurende syne Ambassade in 's Gravenhage, Aan den Grave van Arlington, en den Ridder Jean Trevor, Geheimschrijvers van Staat, Onder de Regeering van Karel de Tweede, Waar in verscheide Geheimen die tot noch toe niet bekent waren, werden ontdekt. In 't Licht gegeven na de Origineelen, geschreven met de eygen Hand van den Auteur. Door M. D. Jones. Uyt het Engelsch overgeset.

In 's Gravenhage, By ⟨Meindert Uitwerf, En Engelbregt Boucquet, Boekverkoopers, 1700.

8 p.ℓ., 360 p. 17cm. 8⁰

Title in red and black.

Transl. from: Letters written by Sir W. Temple during his being Ambassador... , 1st pub. London, 1699.

Bound in contemporary vellum.

68-69

A700 Vossius, Isaac, 1618-1689.
M517p Isaaci Vossii Observationum Ad Pomp. Melam Appendix.
Franequeræ, Ex Officina Typographica Arnoldi Ielmeri. MDCC.

70 p. 19.5cm. 8⁰ (Issued as a part of: Mela, Pomponius. ... Libri tres de situ orbis, Franecker, 1700.)

Half title; imprint at end.

A reply to Jacobus Gronovius' notes in Pomponius Mela's ... Libri tres de situ orbis, Leiden, 1685.

First pub. London, 1686.

In this copy there is a blank ℓ. at end.

Bound in contemporary calf.

12968A, 1921

D70 The Voyages & Travels Of that Renowned Captain, Sir Francis Drake, Into The West-Indies, And Round about the World: Giving a perfect Relation of his strange Adventures, and many wonderful Discoveries, his Fight with the Spaniard, and many barbarous Nations; his taking St. Jago, St. Domingo, Carthagena, St. Augusta, and many other Places in the Golden Country of America, and other Parts of the World: His Description of Monsters, and Monstrous People. With many other remarkable Passages not before Extant: Contained in the History of his Life and Death; both pleasant and profitable to the Reader.

[London] Printed by C.[harles?] B.[rown?] for J.F. and sold by E.[benezer] Tracy, at the Three Bibles on London-bridge. [ca.1700]

24 p. 21.5cm. 4⁰

Cut (ship) on t.-p.

"Advertisement. A Most excellent Natural Balsam... is only to be had of E. Tracy": p. 24.

JCB(2)2:730; WingV747; Sabin20850.

02763, 1859

D698 Wafer, Lionel, 1660?-1705?
D166ni Nieuwe Reystogt En Beschryving Van De Landengte Van Amerika... Door Lionel Wafer, Uyt het Engelsch vertaald door W. Sewel.

In 's Gravenhage, By Abraham De Hondt, Boekverkooper op de Zaal van't Hof/in de Fortuyn 1700.

88 p. 4 plates (incl. 2 fold.), map. 21cm. 4⁰ (Issued as a part of Dampier, William. Tweede deel van William Dampiers reystogt rondom de Werreld, Hague, 1700.)

Cut on t.-p.

Transl. from A new voyage and description of the Isthmus of America, 1st pub. London, 1699.

JCB(2)2:1624; Sabin100943; cf. Tiele290.

03698A, before 1866

D700 -W257t	[Ward, Edward] 1667-1731. A Trip To Jamaica: With a True Character Of The People and Island. By the Author of Sot's Paradise. The Seventh Edition. Londod [sic], Printed and Sold by J. How, in the Ram-Head-Inn-Yard, in Fanchurch-Street, 1700. 16 p. 32cm. fol. Cut on t.-p. First pub. London, 1698. Advertisement of works by Edward Ward, verso of t.-p. Includes poetry. JCB(2)2:1625; WingW763; Sabin101285.	DA700 W695t	Willard, Samuel, 1640-1707. The Truly Blessed Man: Or, The way to be Happy here, And For Ever: Being the Substance of Divers Sermons Preached on, Psalm XXXII. By Samuel Willard, Teacher of a Church in Boston. N.E. ... Boston in N.E. Printed by B. Green, and J. Allen, for Michael Perry. 1700. 652, [3] p. 16.5cm. 8° Errata, p. 652 Bound in contemporary calf. Evans965; Sabin104109; WingW2298.
03710, before 1866		3038, 1907	
DA700 W695f	Willard, Samuel, 1640-1707. The Fountain Opened: Or, The Great Gospel Priviledge of having Christ exhibited to Sinfull Men. Wherein Also is proved that there shall be a National Calling of the Jevvs From Zech. XIII. I. By Samuel Willard, Teacher of a Church in Boston. ... Boston in New-England, Printed by B. Green, and J. Allen, for Samuel Sewall Junior. 1700. 2 p.ℓ., 208, [2] p. 14.5cm. 8° "Evangelical Perfection. Or How far the Gospel requires Believers to Aspire after being compleatly Perfect. As it was Delivered on a Lecture at Boston, on June 10th. 1694. By Samuel Willard, Teacher of a Church in Boston.": p. 167-208. Errata, last p. Bound in contemporary calf, rebacked. Evans960; WingW2277; Sabin104082; Morgan C478.	DA700 W979a	Wyeth, Joseph, 1663-1731. An Answer To A Letter From Dr. Bray, Directed to such as have contributed towards the Propagating Christian Knowledge In The Plantations. By Joseph Wyeth. London, Printed and Sold by T. Sowle, in White-Hart-Court in Gracious-street, 1700. 19 p. 18.5cm. 4° A reply to Thomas Bray's A letter from Dr. Bray, London, 1700. JCB(2)2:1626; WingW3759; Sabin105651; Smit (Friends)2:966; Baer(Md.)209B; MorganC492.
		04870, before 1882	
		B700 -X72p	[Ximénez Pantoja, Thomas] fl. 1700. Por Don Diego Rodillo De Arce Cavallero de la Orden de Santiago, Don Pedro de Estrada, y Antonio Farfan de los Godos, Iuezes Oficiales reales que fueron de las Reales caxas de la Ciudad de Cartagena. Con El Señor Fiscal Del Real Consejo De Las Indias. Sobre Que se admita la suplicacion que tienen interpuesta de la sentencia del Consejo, por la qual fueron condenados ... en priuacion de sus oficios. [Madrid? ca. 1700] 1 p.ℓ., [19] p. 29.5cm. fol. Cut (engr.) on t.-p.: El Santissimo Christo De S. Gines de Madrid. Con Privilegio. Signed at end: Lic. D. Tomás Ximinez Pantoja. Bound as the 1st of 4 items in a volume with binder's title: Asuntos del Virreinato de Nueva Granada.
16853, 1936			
DA700 W695p	Willard, Samuel, 1640-1707. The Peril Of The Times Displayed. Or The Danger of Mens taking up with a Form of Godliness, But Denying the Power of it. Being The Substance of several Sermons Preached: By Samuel Willard, Teacher of a Church in Boston. N.E. ... Boston, Printed by B. Green, & J. Allen. Sold by Benjamin Eliot. 1700. 168 p. 13cm. (14cm. in case). 12° "To The Reader" dated and signed (p. 12): Increase Mather... November, 1699. Bound in contemporary calf. Evans963; WingW2289; Sabin104098; Holmes (I.)168; Dexter(Cong.)2512; MorganC481.	5656, 1909	
		DA700 Y76s	[Young, Samuel] fl. 1697. A Censure Of Mr. Judas Tull His Lampoon. [London, John Marshall, 1700] 12 p. 15cm. (16cm. in case) 12° (Issued as
29910, 1946			

a part of his A confirmation of a late epistle, London, 1700).
Caption title.

11497-3, 1918

DA700 [Young, Samuel] fl. 1697.
Y76s A Confirmation of a late Epistle To Mr. George Keith, And The Reformed Quakers Against Plunging in Baptism, and for Effusion, commonly called Sprinkling. ... With an Epistle to a Lay Pedler in Philology, Oratory and Theology, Mr. Minge, about his Deceitful Title, and Epistle in a Book against me ... Also a Censure of Mr. Judas Tull his Lampoon. By Trepidantium Malleus.
London: Printed for John Marshall, at the Bible in Grace-Church-street. 1700.
1 p.ℓ., 12, 12 p. 15cm. (16cm. in case) 12°
In part a continuation of his A second friendly epistle to Mr. George Keith, London, 1700, and a reply in part to Thomas Minge's Gospel-baptism, London, 1700.
A Censure Of Mr. Judas Tull his Lampoon has caption title and separate paging and signatures.
Bound in contemporary calf as the 2d of 6 items by Young pub. London, 1700.
Wing Y77; Sabin 106098.

11497-2, 1918

DA700 [Young, Samuel] fl. 1697.
Y76s A Dialogue Between George Fox a Quaker, Geo. Keith a Quodlibitarian, Mr. M. an Anabaptist, Mr. L. an Episcoparian. With A Friendly address to them all, By Sam. Reconcilable. By Trepidantium Malleus.
London, Printed for John Marshal at the Bible in Grace-Church Street. 1700.
24 p. 15cm. (16cm. in case). 12°
"Mr. M." is probably Thomas Minge and "Mr. L." Charles Leslie.
Bound in contemporary calf as the 5th of 6 items by Young pub. London, 1700.
Wing Y78; Sabin 106099.

11497-6, 1918

DA700 [Young, Samuel] fl. 1697.
Y76s The Duckers Duck'd, and Duck'd, and Duck'd again, Head, and Ears, and all over; For Plunging, Scolding, and Defaming. Occasioned By a Message brought me by an Anabaptist. Thus, If you stop not the Press, Four Men will swear Sodomy against you. Humbly offered to the Consideration of Learned, Pious Anabaptists; who confess I have given their Cause of Plunging a dreadful Blow. With A Friendly Address to Mr. Philosensus ... With more Arguments against Plunging. By Trepidantium Malleus.
London, Printed for John Marshal at the Bible in Grace-church-street, 1700.
1 p.ℓ., 10 p. 15cm. (16cm. in case) 12°
Signed at end: Sam. Reconcileable.
In part a reply to A rod for T.M. or a letter to Sam. Reconcileable, by Philosensus. London, 1700.
Bound in contemporary calf as the 3d of 6 items by Young pub. London, 1700.
Wing Y79; Sabin 106100.

11497-4, 1918

DA700 [Young, Samuel] fl. 1697.
Y76s A Friendly Epistle To The Reverend Clergy, And Nonconforming Divines, who greatly approve of my late Epistle to Mr. George Kieth [sic] against Plunging, and for Sprinkling in Baptism. ... With A Censure of an Epistle to Mr. Keith, against mine to him, by a nameless Man, (or Men) ... By Trepidantium Malleus.
London: Printed for John Marshall at the Bible in Grace-Church Street. 1700.
1 p.ℓ., 22 p. 15cm. (16cm. in case). 12°
This copy closely trimmed at bottom, affecting imprint.
Bound in contemporary calf as the 4th of 6 items by Young pub. London, 1700.
Wing Y82; Sabin 106103; Morgan C496.

11497-5, 1918

DA700 [Young, Samuel] fl. 1697.
Y76s A Second Friendly Epistle To Mr. George Keith, And The Reformed Quakers. Who are now Convinc'd, That Water Baptism is an Ordinance of Christ, to continue to the End of the World. But are Enquiring about the Mode, and Form of Administration; Whether by Effusion or Plunging. ... Humbly offer'd to the Consideration of all the Baptized Congregations in England; and also of the Dipt Ones. By the Reformed Quakers old Friend, Trepidantium Malleus.
London: Printed for John Marshal, at the Bible in Grace-Church-Street. 1700.
36 p. 15cm. (16cm. in case). 12°
Signed at end: Sam. Reconcilable.
"Books Written by the Author of this Treatise; and Sold by John Marshal, at the Bible in Grace-Church Street."(p. 2).
In this copy outer margins p. 5-6, 11-12 closely trimmed with some loss of text.
Bound in contemporary calf as the 1st of 6

               items by Young pub. London, 1700.
                  WingY86; Sabin106105; Morgan C497.
11497-1, 1918

DA700   [Young, Samuel] fl. 1697.
Y76s   A Sober Reply To A Serious Enquiry. Or, An Answer to a Reformed Quaker, in Vindication of Himself, Mr. G. Keith and others, for their Conformity to the Church of England, against what I have written on that Subject. By Trepidantium Malleus.
           London, Printed, and sold by A. Baldwin, and John Marshal. 1700.
           12 p. 15cm. (16cm. in case). 12°
           A reply to <u>One of George Keith's friends serious enquiry</u>, by C.J., London, 1700.
           Bound in contemporary calf as the 6th of 6 items by Young pub. London, 1700.
           Wing Y88; Sabin106106.
11497-7, 1918

B700   Zárate, Agustín de, b. 1514.
Z36h   Histoire De La Decouverte Et De La Conquete Du Perou. Traduite de l'Espagnol D'Augustin De Zarate, Par S. D. C. Tome Premier [-Second].
           A Amsterdam, Chez J. Louis De Lorme, Libraire sur le Rockin, à la Liberté. M. DCC.
           2v.: 19 p. ℓ., 307 p. front., 13 plates (incl. 3 fold.), fold. map; 3 p. ℓ., 408 p. front. 15.5cm. 12°
           Titles in red and black.
           Cuts on title-pages (v.1, Rahir marque 58; v.2, a monogram).
           First pub. under title: <u>Historia del descubrimiento y conquista del Perú</u>, Antwerp, 1555. Transl. by S. de Broë, seigneur de Citry et de la Guette, probably from a ms. version of the text intermediate between the Antwerp, 1555 ed. and the Seville, 1577 ed. (cf. D.McMahon, "Some observations on... Zárate's <u>Historia</u>...", PBSA, xlix (1955), 95-111).
           Dedication dated (v.1, 1 th p. ℓ.^{r}) 30 March 1555.
           Errata, v.1, 19th p. ℓ.^{v}.
           Imperfect: fold. pl. wanting.

B700   —— ——Another copy. 16cm.
Z36h   Imperfect: 2 fold. plates wanting.
cop.2   Bound in contemporary calf.
           JCB(2)2:1627; Sabin106259; Medina(BHA) v.1, p. 413; Palau(1)7:250.
03018, 1865
02942, 1861

INDEX

Index entries refer to the year of imprint, not to a page number. The index has two kinds of entries:

1. The headings of the catalogue descriptions (reference is simply to an imprint year)
2. Additional entries derived from information within the catalogue descriptions (reference is to imprint year, followed by the heading of a catalogue description filed alphabetically within that year)

The index contains names of personal authors and corporate authors, uniform headings (such as Bible), and names of joint authors, editors, compilers, translators, and other contributors. All books by a particular author, personal or corporate, are listed in the index following the name of the author, but there is no separate index entry for titles of books entered in the body of the catalogue under a personal author if their author's name appears on the title-page. There are separate index entries for titles of books of unknown authorship, titles of books of known authorship issued pseudonymously or anonymously, and titles of books entered in the body of the catalogue under a corporate author or uniform heading.

A. B.: 1689, An Account of the Late Revolutions in New-England
A. B.: 1684, Exquemelin, Alexandre Olivier, The History Of The Bucaniers
A. B. C. Boek, 1689
A Don Juan Luis Lopez, 1692
A. L. See Lubin, Augustin
Aanmerkelijk Historisch-Verhaal Van De Inquisitie: 1688, Dellon, Gabriel
Aarent, Jacob. See Arentsz, Jacob
Abarca, Pedro, Los Reyes De Aragon, 1682
Abbeville, Pierre Duval d'. See Duval, Pierre
Aberdeen--University and King's College: 1675, Quakerism Canvassed
Ablancourt, Jean Jacobé de Frémont d'. See Frémont d'Ablancourt, Jean Jacobé de
Ablancourt, Nicolas Perrot d'. See Perrot d'Ablancourt, Nicolas
Abraham ben Mordecai Farissol. See Farissol, Abraham
Abraham in Arms: 1678, Nowell, Samuel
Abrahams, Jans. See Arentsz, Jacob
An Abstract, By way of Index: 1699, Keith, George
An Abstract Of A Letter: 1699, Paterson, William
An Abstract Of all Such Acts Of Parliament: 1697, Gt.Brit.--Laws, statutes, etc.
An Abstract, Or Abbreviation Of some Few of the Many (Later and Former) Testimonys, 1681
Abū al-Fidā: 1696, Thévenot, Melchisédech, Relations, 1.ptie.
Abulfeda. See Abū al-Fidā
Académie des Sciences, Paris: 1688, Picard, Jean

Acarete du Biscay
   An Account Of A Voyage Up The River de la Plata, 1698
   1691, Zani, Valerio, conte
   1696, Thévenot, Melchisédech, Relations, 4.ptie.
An Account Of Monsieur de la Salle's Last Expedition, 1698
An Account Of Several Late Voyages & Discoveries, 1694
An Account Of Several Passages, 1693
An Account Of The Blessed End Of Gulielma Maria Penn: 1699, Penn, William
An Account Of the Late Dreadful Earth-Quake, 1690
An Account of the Late Revolutions in New-England, 1689
An Account Of The Province Of Carolina: 1682, Wilson, Samuel
The Accuser of our Brethren Cast Down in Righteous Judgment: 1681, Whitehead, George
Acevedo, Francisco
   Villancicos, 1689
   1681, Santoyo, Felipe de
   1691, Sigüenza y Góngora, Carlos de
Act For a Company Tradeing to Affrica, and the Indies
   1695, Scotland--Laws, statutes, etc., 1694-1702 (William III)
   1696, Scotland--Laws, statutes, etc., 1694-1702 (William III)
An Act for Laying further Duties upon Sweets: 1699, Gt. Brit.--Laws, statutes, etc., 1694-1702 (William III), Anno Regni Gulielmi III...
An Act for Preventing Frauds: 1696, Gt.Brit.--Laws, statutes, etc., 1694-1702 (William III)

Index

An Act for Taking Off the Remaining Duties upon Glass Wares: 1699, Gt.Brit.--Laws, statutes, etc., 1694-1702 (William III), Anno Decimo & Undecimo Gulielmi III...
An Act for the more effectual Suppression of Piracy: 1700, Gt.Brit.--Laws, statutes, etc., 1694-1702 (William III), Anno Regni Gulielmi III...
Act in favours of these of the Scots Nation in Konigsberg: 1697, Scotland--Privy Council
An Act Of Parliament, For Encourageing the Scots Affrican and Indian Company: 1695, Scotland--Laws, statutes, etc., 1694-1702 (William III)
An Act Of The Parliament Of Scotland For Erecting an East-India Company: 1695, Scotland--Laws, statutes, etc., 1694-1702 (William III)
An Act to Punish Governors of Plantations in this Kingdom: 1700, Gt.Brit.--Laws, statutes, etc., 1694-1702 (William III), Anno Regni Gulielmi III...
Acts And Laws: 1699, Massachusetts (Colony)--Laws, statutes, etc.
The Acts and Negotiations: 1698, Bernard, Jacques
Acuña, Cristóbal de
   Relation De La Riviere Des Amazones, 1682
   1684, Rodriguez, Manuel, El Marañon, Y Amazonas
   1691, Zani, Valerio, conte
   1698, Voyages And Discoveries In South-America
Ad Amplissimos simul & Consultissimos Viros: 1700, Denniston, Walter
Adams, William
   God's Eye On The Contrite, 1685
   The Necessity Of The pouring out of the Spirit, 1679
   1682, Oakes, Urian
Addison, Lancelot, The Moores Baffled, 1681
The Address Of The House of Commons: 1692, Gt.Brit. --Parliament, 1692-1693--House of Commons (14 Nov. 1692)
The Address of the House of Commons: 1693, Gt.Brit. --Parliament, 1692-1693--House of Commons
The Address of the House of Commons: 1695, Gt.Brit. --Parliament, 1695-1696--House of Commons (28 Nov. 1695)
The Address Of The Lords...Presented to His Majesty the 9th of this Instant March, 1692[/3]: 1693, Gt.Brit.--Parliament, 1692-1693--House of Lords
The Address Of The Lords...Presented To His Majesty the 23d of this instant February 1692[/3]: 1693, Gt.Brit.--Parliament, 1692-1693--House of Lords
The Address presented to His Majesty, 1700
An Address To The Free-Men And Free-Holders: 1683, Bohun, Edmund
Les Admirables Qualitez Du Kinkina, 1689; 1694
Adriens, Jacob. See Arentsz, Jacob
An Advertisement Concerning the Province of East-New-Jersey, 1685
Advertisment Concerning East-New-Jersey, 1683
Advice to a Painter: 1679, Marvell, Andrew
Aerendt, Jacob. See Arentsz, Jacob
Affonseca e Payva, Sebastião. See Paiva, Sebastião da Fonseca e
Africanische Reissbeschreibung in die Landschaft Fetu: 1677, Müller, Wilhelm Johann

Aguiar Seijas y Ulloa, Francisco de, Abp.: 1697, Muñoz de Castro, Pedro
Aguilera, Francisco de, Sermon, 1689
Aguirre, Pedro Antonio de
   San Pedro de Alcantara, 1697
   Transito Gloriosissimo De N. S^ra La Santissima Virgen Maria, 1694
   1682, Medina, Baltasar de
Agurto y Loaysa, Joseph de
   Villancicos, 1676
   Villancicos, 1677
   Villancicos, 1681
   Villancicos, 1682
   Villancicos, 1684
   Villancicos, 1685
   Villancicos, 1686
   1685, Ramirez de Vargas, Alonso
   1686, Téllez Giron, Juan Alejo
   1688, Santillana, Gabriel de
Al Doctor Don Jvan Lvis Lopez, 1692
Alamandini, Fortunato: 1690, Cavazzi, Giovanni Antonio
Albany--Mayor, 1686-1694 (Peter Schuyler): 1693, Bayard, Nicholas
Albarez. See Alvarez
Alberti, Leone Battista: 1680, Fréart de Chambray, Roland
Alcaforado, Francisco. See Alcoforado, Francisco
Alcázar, Bartolomé: 1683, Vieira, Antonio, Qvinta Parte De Sermones
Alcedo Sotomayor, Carlos de
   Por El Doctor Don Jvan De la Rea Zurbano, 1694
   Señor ... , 1698
Alcoforado, Francisco, An Historical Relation, 1675
Alè, Francesco degli. See Allè, Francesco
Alejo Tellesgiron, Juan. See Téllez Giron, Juan Alejo
Alexander VI, Pope: 1678, Derby, Charles Stanley, 8th earl of
Alexander VIII, Pope: 1694, Corella, Jaime de
Alfaro Fernández de Córdova, Catalina: 1691, Juana Inés de la Cruz, sister, Poëmas
Een Algemeene Send-Brief aen de Vrienden der Waerheyt: 1675, Hendricks, Elizabeth, Quaker, Amsterdam
Allais, Denis Vairasse de. See Vairasse, Denis
Allè, Francesco: 1691, Zani, Valerio, conte
Allen, James
   New-Englands choicest Blessing, 1679
   Serious Advice, 1679
   1690, Mather, Cotton, The Principles of the Protestant Religion Maintained
   1691, Mather, Cotton, Late Memorable Providences
   1697, Mather, Cotton, Memorable Providences
Allin, John: 1696, Massachusetts Or The first Planters of New-England
Allison, Thomas, An Account Of A Voyage, 1699
Alloza, Juan de, Cielo Estrellado, 1691
Allyn, John: 1694, Their Majesties Colony Of Connecticut
Almeida, Manuel de
   1684, Recueil De Divers Voyages

1696, Thévenot, Melchisédech, Relations, 4.ptie.
An Alphabet Of Africa: 1687, Lea, Philip
An Alphabet of America: 1687, Lea, Philip
An Alphabet of Asia: 1687, Lea, Philip
An Alphabet of Europe: 1687, Lea, Philip
Altamirano, Nicolas: 1698, Narvaez, Juan de
Alvarez de Toledo, Domingo
 Copia De La Espantosa Carta, 1688
 Copy van een Brief, 1688
Alvarez de Toledo, Juan Bautista, Bp., Sermon De La Dominica Sexagesima, 1694
Alvarez Ossorio y Redin, Miguel
 Compañia Vniversal, 1690
 Discvrso Vniversal, 1686
 Extension Politica, 1686
 Medios Ciertos, 1690
 Señor ... , 1686
 Señor ... , 1687
 Zelador General, 1687
Alzedo Sotomayor, Carlos de. See Alcedo Sotomayor, Carlos de
Ambassade De S'Chahrok: 1696, Thévenot, Melchisédech, Relations, 5.ptie.
Amelot de La Houssaye, Abraham Nicolas, La Storia Del Governo Di Venezia, 1681
L'Amérique Angloise, Ou Description Des Isles: 1688, Blome, Richard
Ames, William
 Een Declaratie, 1675
 Een geklank uyt Sion, 1675
 Een Getuygenis, 1677
 Goeden raadt, 1678
Amman, Johann Jacob, Reiss in das Gelobte Land, 1678
Ampel en Breed Verhaal, 1692
Amy, Thomas: 1682, Carolina; Or A Description Of the Present State
Ana de la Cruz: 1679, Enríquez de Ribera, Payo, Abp., Viceroy of Mexico
Ander Theil Der Durchleuchtigen See-Helden: 1681, Bos, Lambert van den
Andosilla, Juan Carlos: 1682, Portugal--Treaties, etc., 1668-1706 (Pedro II)
Andrés de San Agustín, Dios Prodigioso, 1692
Andros Tracts
 1689, An Account of the Late Revolutions in New-England; Byfield, Nathaniel, An Account Of The Late Revolution In New-England (2 ed.); Mather Increase, A Brief Relation; Mather, Increase, New-England Vindicated; Some Considerations humbly Offered
 1690, New England's Faction Discovered; Palmer, John; A Vindication of Nevv-England
 1691, The Humble Address Of The Publicans; Mather, Increase, A Brief Account; Rawson, Edward; Stoughton, William
 1693, Mather, Increase, The Great Blessing
Anno Decimo & Undecimo Gulielmi III. Regis. An Act for Taking Off the Remaining Duties: 1699, Gt. Brit.--Laws, statutes, etc., 1694-1702 (William III)

Anno Regni Gulielmi III...[An Act for Laying further Duties upon Sweets]: 1699, Gt.Brit.--Laws, statutes, etc., 1694-1702 (William III)
Anno Regni Gulielmi III...[An Act for Preventing Frauds]: 1696, Gt.Brit.--Laws, statutes, etc., 1694-1702 (William III)
Anno Regni Gulielmi III...[An Act for the more effectual Suppression of Piracy]: 1700, Gt.Brit.--Laws, statutes, etc., 1694-1702 (William III)
Anno Regni Gulielmi III...[An Act to Punish Governors of Plantations]: 1700, Gt.Brit.--Laws, statutes, etc., 1694-1702 (William III)
Anno Regni Regis Gulielmi III. Acts and Laws: 1700, Massachusetts (Colony)--Laws, statutes, etc. (31 May 1699 - 13 March 1700)
Anno Regni Regis Gulielmi III...Acts and Laws: 1700, Massachusetts (Colony)--Laws, statutes, etc. (29 May 1700)
An Answer By An Anabaptist, 1688
The Answer Of Several Ministers in and near Boston: 1695, Cambridge, Mass.--Ministers' Association
An Answer To a Late Pamphlet, 1699
An Answer To several New Laws and Orders Made by the Rulers of Boston: 1678, Fox, George
Answers for the Presbytry of Dumfries: 1698, Church of Scotland--Presbyteries--Dumfries
An Antidote Against The Venome Of The Snake in the Grass: 1697, Whitehead, George
The Antithelemite: 1685, Maurice, Henry
Antonelli, Giovanni Batista: 1680, Gudenfridi, Giovanni Batista
Antonides van der Goes, Joannis: 1687, Brandt, Geeraert, Het Leven En Bedryf
Antonio de Santa Maria, Carmelite, España Trivnfante, 1682
Antwoort Op twee Vrágen: 1678, Fox, George
Anunciación, Juan de la. See Juan de la Anunciación
Anzi, Aurelio degli. See Zani, Valerio, conte
An Apology For Congregational Divines: 1698, Young, Samuel
An Apology For The Builder: 1689, Barbon, Nicholas
An Appeal from the Country to the City: 1679, Blount, Charles
Aranda Sidrón, Bartolomé de, Por Doña Ysabel, 1690
Aranzel De Los Jornales: 1687, Peru (Viceroyalty)--Laws, statutes, etc., 1681-1689 (Navarra y Rocafull)
Araujo, Antonio de, Catecismo Brasilico, 1686
Archicofradía de la Purísima Sangre de Nuestro Señor Jesu Cristo: 1686, Merlo, Nicolás
Ardagh, Edward, Bp. of. See Wetenhall, Edward, Bp. of Kilmore and Ardagh
Arellano, Diego de, Sermon En La Solemne Fiesta, 1693
Arenas, Pedro de, Vocabvlario Manual, 1683 (2 variants); 1690
Arentsz, Jacob: 1679, Spiegel Voor de Stad van Embden
Arequipa, Peru (Diocese)--Synod, 1684, Constitvciones Synodales, 1688
Argaiz, Gregorio de: 1678, López, Gregorio

Argaiz y Vargas, Francisco Crisanto de, Las Dos Niñas De Los Ojos De Christo Sr. Nuestro, 1695
Argote y Valdés, Juan de, Oracion Panegyrica, 1686
Argüello, Manuel de: 1691, Ramírez de Vargas, Alonso
Arguiñano, José de: 1698, Castilla, Miguel de
An Argument For Union: 1683, Tenison, Thomas, Abp. of Canterbury
Ari Thorgilsson Fróði, Schedæ, 1688
Arnauld, Antoine, Histoire De Dom Jean De Palafox, 1690 (2 variants)
Arrest Dv Conseil D'Estat Dv Roy...Portant Que faute par les Marchands Negocians: 1682, France--Sovereigns, etc., 1643-1715 (Louis XIV)
Arrest Du Conseil D'Estat Du Roy, Qui exempte de tous droits...: 1686, France--Sovereigns, etc., 1643-1715 (Louis XIV)
Arrest Du Conseil D'Estat Du Roy, Qui Ordonne que les Droits...: 1689, France--Sovereigns, etc., 1643-1715 (Louis XIV)
Arrest Dv Conseil D'Estat, Portant que conformément à L'Adivdication..., 1681
Arrest Du Conseil D'Estat...Pour Le Rétablissement De La Fabrique: 1685, France--Sovereigns, etc., 1643-1715 (Louis XIV) 8 Feb. 1685; 12 Apr. 1685
Arrest Du Conseil D'Estat: Qui Commet Les Sieurs Morel de Boistiroux...: 1684, France--Sovereigns, etc., 1643-1715 (Louis XIV)
Arrest Du Conseil D'Estat Du Roy...Qui ordonne Qu'à commencer du mois de Juillet...: 1695, France--Sovereigns, etc., 1643-1715 (Louis XIV) 30 May 1695
Arrest Du Conseil D'Etat Du Roy, Qui Ordonne qu'en éxécution...: 1700, France--Sovereigns, etc., 1643-1715 (Louis XIV) 20 July 1700
Arriola, Joseph de: 1695, Castilla, Miguel de
L'Art De Voyager Utilement: 1698, Chèvremont, Jean Baptiste de
The art of travelling: 1699, Casas, Bartolomé de las, Bp. of Chiapa
Articles Of Peace Between The Most Serene and Mighty Prince Charles II: 1677, Gt.Brit.--Treaties, etc., 1660-1685
Articles Of Peace Between The Most Serene and Mighty Prince William the Third: 1697, Gt.Brit.--Treaties, etc., 1694-1702 (William III)
The Articles, Settlement and Offices Of The Free Society Of Traders: 1682, Free Society of Traders in Pennsylvania
Articul-Brief Van de Generale Nederlandtsche Geoctroyeerde West-Indische Compagnie: 1675, Nederlandsche West-Indische Compagnie
Asenjo y Crespo, Ignacio de
 Exercicio Practico, 1682
 1682, Victoria Salazar, Diego de
Asganii Sassonii: 1696, Thévenot, Melchisédech, Relations, 5.ptie.
Ash, Thomas: 1682, Carolina; Or A Description Of the Present State
Assonica, Carlo: 1681, Passerone, Lodovico
At a Convention of the Representatives: 1689, Massachusetts (Colony)--Convention, 24 May 1689

At a Council-General of the Company of Scotland: 1699, Company of Scotland Trading to Africa and the Indies
At a Court of Directors of the Company of Scotland...: 1699, Company of Scotland Trading to Africa and the Indies
At Edinburgh, The 15 of June, 1696...: 1696, Company of Scotland Trading to Africa and the Indies
At Edinburgh, The 9th Day of July, 1696...: 1696, Company of Scotland Trading to Africa and the Indies
At the Court at Whitehall, The 20th of July, 1683...: 1683, Gt.Brit.--Sovereigns, etc., 1660-1685 (Charles II)
At the Court at Whitehall, This 26th day of March 1686...: 1686, Gt.Brit.--Sovereigns, etc., 1685-1688 (James II)
At the Town-House in Boston: 1689, Byfield, Nathaniel, An Account Of The Late Revolution In New-England (2 ed.)
Atkinson, Christopher, Ishmael, And His Mother, 1700
Atlas Maritime: 1693, Cartes Marines A L'Usage Des Armées...
Atondo y Antillón, Isidro. See Otondo y Antillón, Isidro
Aubin, Nicolas, Histoire Des Diables, 1694
Augustinus, Aurelius, Saint, Bp. of Hippo
 1684, María de la Antigua, madre
 1690, Dominicans
Ausführliche Beschreibung des theils bewohnt, theils unbewohnt, so gennannten Gröenlands: 1679, La Peyrère, Isaac de
Avtos De Las Conferencias De Los Comisarios: 1682, Portugal--Treaties, etc., 1668-1706 (Pedro II)
Avendaño Suares de Sousa, Pedro de
 Sermon De La Esclarecida Virgen, 1697
 Sermon De N.S.S.P. y Señor San Pedro, 1694
 Sermon Del Domingo De Ramos, 1695
 Sermon Qve En La Fiesta Titvlar..., 1688
Avila, Alonso de, Sermon, 1679
Avila, Juan de
 Amistad Geroglifica, 1684
 Coronado Non Plvs Vltra Franciscano, 1688
 Los Hercules Seraphicos, 1696
 Mariano Pentilitero, 1684
 Mercurio Panegyrico, 1690
 Pvreza Emblematica, 1686
 Sagrado Notariaco, 1688
 Sermon De El Glorioso Martyr S. Felipe De Iesvs, 1681
Ayerra y Santa Maria, Francisco de
 1683, Sigüenza y Góngora, Carlos de
 1684, Santoyo, Felipe de
 1691, Sigüenza y Góngora, Carlos de
Ayeta, Francisco de
 Crisol De La Verdad, 1693
 Defensa, 1689
 Discurso Legal, 1696; 1699
 Señor. Al mas modesto..., 1690
 Señor. Fray Francisco de Ayeta...Dize: Que deseando..., 1695

Señor. Fray Francisco de Ayeta...dize: Que estando... , 1688
Señor. Fray Francisco de Ayeta...dize: Que por decreto... , 1689
Señor. Fray Francisco De Ayeta...dize: Que por dos Reales Cedulas... , 1688
Vltimo Recvrso, 1695
1681, Sariñana y Cuenca, Isidro
1688, López de Cogolludo, Diego
1689, Yo Pedro de Arce y Andrade...
Ayres, Philip, The Voyages and Adventures, 1684
Aysma, Joannes, Spiegel Der Sibyllen, 1685
Azevedo, Baltasar de
1696, Ayeta, Francisco de
1699, Ayeta, Francisco de
Azevedo, Francisco de. See Acevedo, Francisco

B**: 1698, Montauban, ----de, Relation Du Voyage
B. C. See Coole, Benjamin
B. N.: 1699, Smith, John
B. T. See Tompson, Benjamin
B. W.: 1682, Rowlandson, Mary (White)
Bacon, Sir Francis, viscount St. Albans: 1682, Loddington, William
Bado, Sebastiano
1680, Gudenfridi, Giovanni Batista
1689, Les Admirables Qualitez Du Kinkina
1694, Les Admirables Qualitez Du Kinkina
Baerle, Kaspar van: 1690, Blaeu, Willem Janszoon
Baikov, Fedor Isakovich: 1681, Thévenot, Melchisédech
Bailey, John
Man's chief End, 1689
To my loving and Dearly Beloved Christian Friends, 1689
Baillet, Adrien
1676, Gage, Thomas, Nouvelle Relation
1694, Gage, Thomas, Nouvelle Relation
1695, Gage, Thomas, Nouvelle Relation
1699, Gage, Thomas, Nouvelle Relation
Baily, John. See Bailey, John
Baily, Lewis, Bp. of Bangor. See Bayly, Lewis, Bp. of Bangor
Ballesteros, Tomás de: 1685, Peru (Viceroyalty)--Laws, statutes, etc.
Bandello, Vincenzo: 1690, Dominicans
Baños y Sotomayor, Diego de, Bp.: 1698, Venezuela (Diocese)--Synod
Bañuelos y Carrillo, Jerónimo de: 1696, Thévenot, Melchisédech, Relations, 2.ptie.
Barba, Alvaro Alonso
Das Andere Buch von der Kunst der Metallen, 1676
Eines Spanischen Priesters und hocherfahrnen Naturkündigers Berg-Büchlein, 1676
Barbados--Governor, 1698-1701 (Grey): 1699, By the Honourable Sir William Beeston
Barbados--Laws, statutes, etc., The Laws Of Barbados, 1699
Barbon, Nicholas, An Apology, 1689

Barclay, Robert
An Apology For the True Christian Divinity, 1678; 1679
Epistola Amatoria, 1678
Theologiæ Verè Christianæ Apologia, 1676
1680, Rogers, William, The Third Part Of The Christian-Quaker
1688, Keith, George
Barlaeus, Caspar. See Baerle, Kaspar van
Barnard, John Augustine: 1693, Bohun, Edmund
Baron, William, A Just Defence, 1699
Barrera Varaona, Joseph de la
Sagrado Escvdo De Armas, 1692
1695, Mexico (City)--Universidad
Barrin, Jean: 1696, Chavigny De La Bretonnière, François de
Barrios, Miguel de
1681, Exquemelin, Alexandre Olivier, Piratas
1682, Exquemelin, Alexandre Olivier, Piratas (2 variants)
Barros, João de: 1696, Thévenot, Melchisédech, Relations, 5.ptie.
Bateman, John: 1692, Morton, Richard
Baxter, Richard
Faithful Souls, 1681
Mr. Baxter's Vindication Of The Church, 1682
Reliquiæ Baxterianæ, 1696
1691, Mather, Cotton, Late Memorable Providences
Bay Psalm Book
1688, Bible--O.T.--Psalms--English--Paraphrases--Bay Psalm Book
1695, Bible--O.T.--Psalms--English--Paraphrases--Bay Psalm Book
Bayard, Nicholas
A Journal Of The Late Actions, 1693
1698, A Letter From A Gentleman Of The City of New-York
Bayly, Lewis, Bp. of Bangor, Manitowompae... , 1685
Bayly, William, A Collection Of The Several Wrightings, 1676
Beale, John: 1680, Fréart de Chambray, Roland
Bealing, Benjamin: 1695, Keith, George, The Pretended Yearly Meeting
Beaufez, Jacques: 1676, Jarrige, Pierre
Beaulieu, Augustin: 1696, Thévenot, Melchisédech, Relations, 2.ptie.
Beaulieu, Huës O'Neil, sieur de. See O'Neil, Huës, sieur de Beaulieu
Beaumont, John
1682, VVeekly Memorials For The Ingenious
1683, VVeekly Memorials For The Ingenious
Beaumont, Simon Herbert van: 1676, Pertinente Beschrijvinge Van Guiana
Beauplan, Guillaume Le Vasseur, sieur de: 1696, Thévenot, Melchisédech, Relations, 1.ptie.
Beauplet, sieur de. See Beauplan, Guillaume Le Vasseur, sieur de
Becerra Tanco, Luis, Felicidad De Mexico, 1675; 1685
Béchamel, François
1682, Acuña, Cristóbal de
1698, Grillet, Jean

[437]

Beckham, Edward, A Brief Discovery Of Some of the Blasphemous and Seditious Principles, 1699
Becmann, Johann Christoph, Historia Orbis Terrarum, 1692
Beekham, Edward. See Beckham, Edward
Beer, Johann Christoph
    1681, Duval, Pierre
    1690, Duval, Pierre
Beeston, Sir William: 1699, By the Honourable Sir William Beeston
Behn, Aphra (Amis)
    The Widdow Ranter, 1690
    1696, Southerne, Thomas
    1699, Southerne, Thomas
Bekker, Balthasar
    De Betoverde Weereld, 1691
    Le Monde Enchanté, 1694
Belcher, Joseph, The Worst Enemy Conquered, 1698
Belhaven, John Hamilton, 2d baron
    A Defence Of The Scots Settlement at Darien, 1699 4º; 1699 8º (4 variants)
    1699, The Defence Of The Scots Settlement At Darien Answer'd
Belle, Pedro van: 1689, Pertinent en Waarachtig Verhaal
Bellegarde, Jean Baptiste Morvan de
    1697, Casas, Bartolomé de las, Bp. of Chiapa
    1698, Casas, Bartolomé de las, Bp. of Chiapa
Bellomont, Richard Coote, 1st earl of: 1699, By the Honourable Sir William Beeston
Belwood, Martin: 1677, Herbert, Sir Thomas
A Bemoaning Letter Of An Ingenious Quaker: 1700, Mucklow, William
Berart, Raimundo
    Relacion Con Insercion, 1685
    1686, Sandín, Alonso
Bergamori, Giuseppe Gaetano: 1691, Zani Valerio, conte
Berkel, Adriaan van, Amerikaansche Voyagien, 1695
Berkeley, Sir William: 1680, Godwin, Morgan
Bermejo y Roldán, Francisco, Discvrso De La Enfermedad, 1694
Bermuda Company
    Some of the By-Laws, 1677
    1676, Trott, Perient
Bermuda Islands--Council: 1676, Trott, Perient
A Bermudas Preacher Proved A Persecutor: 1683, Estlacke, Francis
Bermúdez de Castro, Carlos, Abp.: 1695, Mexico(City)--Universidad
Bernard, Jacques
    The Acts and Negotiations, 1698
    Ryswykse Vrede-Handel, 1700
Bernard, John. See Barnard, John Augustine
Bernard, Samuel: 1683, A Narrative Of Affairs
Beronius, Olaus: 1691, Spole, Anders
Beschreibung Der in America neu-erfundenen Provinz Pensylvanien: 1684, Penn, William
Bettendorf, João Filippe: 1687, Figueira, Luiz
Beughem, Cornelius à
    Bibliographia Historica, 1685
    Incunabula Typographiæ Notitiam exhibentia, 1688
Beyard, Nicholas. See Bayard, Nicholas

Bezerra Tanco, Luis. See Becerra Tanco, Luis
Bible--Massachuset--Eliot--1685, Mamusse... , 1685
Bible--O.T.--Ecclesiastes--English--Paraphrases--1685, A Paraphrase... , 1685
Bible--O.T.--Psalms--Dutch--1688: 1688, Bible--O.T.--Psalms--Hebrew--1688, Het Hebreus Psalmboeck
Bible--O.T.--Psalms--English--1688: 1688, Bible--O.T.--Psalms--Hebrew--1688, The Book of Psalmes
Bible--O.T.--Psalms--English--Paraphrases, The Whole Book of Psalms, 1677
Bible--O.T.--Psalms--English--Paraphrases--1688--Bay Psalm Book, The Psalms, Hymns, And Spiritual Songs, 1688
Bible--O.T.--Psalms--English--Paraphrases--ca.1695--Bay Psalm Book, The Psalms Hymns And Spiritual Songs, 1695
Bible--O.T.--Psalms--French--Paraphrases--1683: 1683, Church of England--Book of Common Prayer--French
Bible--O.T.--Psalms--Hebrew--1688
    Book of Psalmes, 1688
    Het Hebreus Psalmboeck, 1688
    Liber Psalmorum, 1688
Bible--O.T.--Psalms--Latin--1688: 1688, Bible--O.T.--Psalms--Hebrew--1688, Liber Psalmorum
Bible--O.T.--Song of Solomon--English--Paraphrases--1685, The Song of Solomon, 1685
Bible--N.T.--Massachuset--Eliot--1685, VVusku... , 1685
Biscay, Acarete du. See Acarete du Biscay
Bishop, William: 1696, Dawson, Joseph
Bissel, Johannes: 1698, Victoria, Pedro Gobeo de
Blackmore, Sir Richard: 1697, Mather, Cotton, Ecclesiastes
Blackwell, Isaac, A Description Of The Province And Bay Of Darian, 1699
Blackwell, John: 1688, A Model For Erecting a Bank
Blaeu, Willem Janszoon, Institutio Astronomica, 1690
Blankaart, Steven: 1700, Raei, Johannes de
Blégny, Nicolas de: 1687, Nigrisoli, Francesco Maria
Blome, Richard
    L'Amerique Angloise, 1688
    Cosmography And Geography, 1682
    A Description Of the Island of Jamaica, 1678
    A Geographical Description Of The World... The Second Part, 1680
    The present State Of Algiers, 1678
    The Present State Of His Majesties Isles, 1687
    1684, Carolina Described more fully then [sic] heretofore; Recueil De Divers Voyages
    1697, Crouch, Nathaniel
Blondel, James Augustus: 1694, Morton, Richard
Blount, Charles, An Appeal from the Country, 1679
Bluteau, Raphael
    Oraçoens Gratvlatorias, 1693
    Porticus Trivmphalis, 1694
Bobowski, Albert, afterwards Ali Bey, Tractatus, 1690
Bock, Johannes Christian: 1685, Kirchmayer Georg Kaspar
Bockenhoffer, Johann Joachim: 1677, Richshoffer, Ambrosius
Boecler, Johann Heinrich, De Rebus Seculi Post Christum Natum XVI, 1697

Index

Böhm, Anton
  1696, Sepp von Reinegg, Anton
  1697, Sepp von Reinegg, Anton
Bogaert, Abraham: 1699, Zanten, Laurens van
Bohun, Edmund
  An Address To The Free-Men, 1683
  A Geographical Dictionary, 1691; 1693
  The Second Part Of The Address, 1682
  The Third and Last Part Of The Address, 1683
  1700, Echard, Laurence
Boicoof, Saedor Iacovvits. See Baikov, Fedor Isakovich
Boim, Michał
  Briefve Relation De La Chine: 1696, Thévenot, Melchisédech, Relations, 2.ptie.
  Flora Sinensis: 1696, Thévenot, Melchisédech, Relations, 2.ptie.
Bond, Samson
  A Publick Tryal, 1682
  The Sincere Milk of the Word, 1699
Bonne-Maison, Alonso de
  1681, Exquemelin, Alexandre Olivier, Piratas
  1682, Exquemelin, Alexandre Olivier, Piratas (2 variants)
Bontekoe, Willem Ysbrandsz: 1696, Thévenot, Melchisédech, Relations, 1.ptie.
The Book Of Common Prayer, And Administration of the Sacraments: 1676, Church of England--Book of Common Prayer
The Book of Psalmes With the New England Translation: 1688, Bible--O.T.--Psalms--Hebrew--1688
Bos, Lambert van den
  Ander Theil Der Durchleuchtigen See-Helden, 1681
  Leben und Tapffere Thaten, 1681
  Leben und Thaten, 1681
  Leeven en Daaden, 1683
  Leeven en Daden, 1676
Boschman, A.: 1692, Luyts, Jan
Boston--Second Church: 1692, Mather Cotton, A Midnight Cry
Bourdelot, abbé. See Michon, Pierre
Boyle, Hon. Robert, General Heads For the Natural History, 1692
Boym, Michał. See Boim, Michał
Brabo de Gamboa, Alexandro: 1694, Miranda Villaizan, Antonio de
Bradford, William: 1693, Keith, George, The Heresie and Hatred
Bradstreet, Anne (Dudley), Several Poems, 1678
Bradstreet, Simon: 1700, Gospel Order Revived
Brady, Robert, An Historical Treatise Of Cities, 1690
Brandano, Alessandro, Historia Della Guerre, 1689
Brandaõ, Francisco Pereira. See Pereira Brandaõ, Francisco
Brandt, Geeraert
  Leben und Thaten, 1687
  Het Leven En Bedryf, 1687
  1678, De Nieuwe Hollantse Mercurius...Het Achentwintigste Deel
Brandt, Johannes
  1687, Brandt, Geeraert, Leben und Thaten; Brandt, Geeraert, Het Leven En Bedryf

Brandt, Kaspar
  1687, Brandt, Geeraert, Leben und Thaten; Brandt, Geeraert, Het Leven En Bedryf
Brattle, Thomas
  1700, Gospel Order Revived; The Printers Advertisement
Brattle, William: 1700, Gospel Order Revived
Bravo, Fernando, Oracion Evangelica Panegyrica, 1679
Bravo Davila y Cartagena, Juan, Oracion Panegyrica, 1684
Bray, Thomas
  The Acts Of Dr. Bray's Visitation, 1700
  Apostolick Charity, 1698; 1699; 1700
  Bibliotheca Parochialis, 1697
  A Circular Letter To the Clergy of Mary-Land, 1700
  An Essay Towards Promoting all Necessary and Useful Knowledge, 1697
  A Letter From Dr. Bray, 1700
  A Memorial, Representing The Present State Of Religion..., 1700
  Proposals For the Encouragement and Promoting of Religion, 1697 (2 variants)
  Proposals For the Incouragement and Promoting of Religion, 1696
  A Short Discourse Upon the Doctrine of our Baptismal Covenant, 1697
Breton, Raymond: 1681, Rochefort, Charles de, Histoire Naturelle Et Morale Des Iles Antilles
Breve De N. Santissimo Padre el Señor Vrbano VIII: 1690, Catholic Church--Pope, 1623-1644 (Urbanus VIII)
Breve Sanctissimi Domini Nostri Vrbani Papae VIII: 1690, Catholic Church--Pope, 1623-1644 (Urbanus VIII)
Brewster, Sir Francis, Essays On Trade And Navigation, 1695
Breynius, Jacobus: 1682, Mentzel, Christian
Bridgeman, Robert: 1700, Keith, George, An Account Of The Quakers Politicks
A Brief Account Concerning Several of the Agents: 1691, Mather, Increase
A Brief Account Of The Province Of East-Jersey, 1682
A Brief Account of the Province Of East-New-Jarsey, 1683
A Brief Account Of The Province of Pennsilvania: 1682, Penn, William
A Brief Advertisement, Concerning East-New-Jersey: 1685, Scot, George
A Brief and True Narration Of the Late VVars, 1675
  1676, A farther Brief and True Narration
A Brief Answer To A False and Foolish Libell: 1678, Penn, William
A Brief Discourse Concerning the Lawfulness of Worshipping God: 1696, Williams, John, Bp. of Chichester
A Brief History Of The Succession: 1689, Somers, John Somers, baron
A brief narration of the sufferings of the People Called Quakers: 1700, Gould, Daniel
A Brief Narrative And Deduction, 1679
A Brief Relation Of The State Of New England: 1689, Mather, Increase

Een Brief Van een Zeker Heer: 1689, Popple, Sir William
Brief, Van seeker Frans Heer, 1687
Briefve Deduction Par laquelle il est clairement monstré ...: 1676, Courland, James, Duke of
Briet, Philippe, Annales Mundi, 1696
Brigonci, Pietr' Antonio: 1686, Porcacchi, Tommaso
Brito Freire, Francisco de
  Nova Lusitania...Decada Primeira, 1675
  Viage Da Armada, 1675
Brizuela, Juan Joseph de. See Díaz Brizuela, José
Broë, S. de, seigneur de Citry et de La Guette
  1685, Histoire De La Conqueste De La Floride
  1691, Solís y Rivadeneyra, Antonio de, Histoire De La Conquête Du Mexique (2 variants)
  1692, Solís y Rivadeneyra, Antonio de, Histoire De La Conquête Du Mexique
  1700, Zárate, Agustín de
Broekhuizen, Gotfried van
  1681, Melton, Edward
  1682, Vairasse, Denis
Brome, Henry: 1695, Charpentier, François
Brontologia Sacra: 1695, Mather, Cotton
Brown, John, Quakerisme The Path-way to Paganisme, 1678
Brutus, Junius. See Blount, Charles
Buade, Louis de, comte de Frontenac. See Frontenac, Louis de Buade, comte de
Buckingham, George Villiers, 2d duke of, A Short Discourse, 1685
Budd, Thomas
  Good Order, 1685
  1694, The Judgment Given forth by Twenty Eight Quakers
Buena-Maison, Alonso de. See Bonne-Maison, Alonso de
Buendía, José
  Oracion Fvnebre, 1693
  Sudor, Y Lagrimas, 1676
  1688, Echave y Assu, Francisco de; Relaçam Do Exemplar Castigo; Relacion Del Exemplar Castigo
Bugg, Francis
  A Brief History Of The Rise, Growth, and Progress Of Quakerism, 1697
  A Modest Defence, 1700
  The Picture Of Quakerism, 1697
  The Pilgrim's Progress, 1700
  Quakerism Expos'd To Publick Censure, 1699
  William Penn, The Pretended Quaker, 1700
  1693, Keith, George, More Divisions Amongst The Quakers
  1699, Beckham, Edward
Bula De La Santidad De Inocencio XI: 1687, Catholic Church--Pope, 1676-1689 (Innocentius XI)
Bulkley, Edward: 1676, Wheeler, Thomas
Bulkley, Thomas, To the Right Honourable William, Earl of Craven, 1694
Buno, Johann
  1694, Clüver, Philipp
  1697, Clüver, Philipp

Burattini, Tito Livio: 1696, Thévenot, Melchisédech, Relations, 1.ptie.
Burchard, Johann: 1697, Boecler, Johann Heinrich
Burg, Pieter van der, Curieuse Beschrijving, 1677
Burnet, Gilbert, Bp. of Salisbury
  Four Discourses Delivered to the Clergy, 1694
  The History Of The Reformation, 1681
  1689, A Compleat Collection Of Papers, In Twelve Parts
Burnyeat, John
  The Truth Exalted, 1691
  1678, Fox, George, A New-England-Fire-Brand Quenched; Fox, George, A New England-Fire-Brand Quenched...The Second Part
  1679, Fox, George, A New-England-Fire-Brand Quenched
Burrough, Edward: 1680, Rogers, William, The First Part Of The Christian-Quaker
Burton, Richard. See Crouch, Nathaniel
Burton, Robert. See Crouch, Nathaniel
Bustos, Diego Joseph de: 1691, Sigüenza y Góngora, Carlos de
By the Honourable Sir William Beeston, 1699
By the King, A Proclamation For the most effectual Reducing...: 1688, Gt.Brit.--Sovereigns, etc., 1685-1688 (James II) 20 Jan. 1688
By the King, A Proclamation Prohibiting His Majesties Subjects...: 1688, Gt.Brit.--Sovereigns, etc., 1685-1688 (James II) 31 Mar. 1688
By the King, A Proclamation. William R. Whereas We have been Informed...: 1700, Gt.Brit.--Sovereigns, etc., 1694-1702 (William III) 29 Jan. 1699 [i.e. 1700]
Byfield, Nathaniel, An Account Of The Late Revolution In New-England, Edinburgh, 1689; London, 1689

C. B.: 1678, Bradstreet, Anne (Dudley)
C. D. See Dove, C.
C. L. C. See Le Clercq, Chrétien
Cabañas, Agustin de: 1699, Narváez, Juan de, Sermon En La Solemnidad
Caermarthen, Peregrine Osborne, marquis of. See Leeds, Peregrine Osborne, 2d duke of
Cæsar's Due Rendred unto Him: 1679, Fox, George
Calderón, Juan, España Illvstrada, 1682
Calderón, Pedro, Memorial, 1695
Calderón de la Barca, Miguel: 1697, Esquerra, Matías de
Calderón de la Barca, Pedro: 1682, Cubero Sebastián, Pedro
Calderon del Castillo, Antonio, Platica De El Archangel San Migvel, 1683
Calderwood, David, The Pastor, 1692
Caledonia; Or, The Pedlar turn'd Merchant, 1700
Caledonia, The Declaration Of The Council...: 1699, Company of Scotland Trading to Africa and the Indies
Caledonia Triumphans: 1699, Pennecuik, Alexander
Calef, Robert, More Wonders Of The Invisible World, 1700

Index

Calvert, Philip, A Letter From The Chancellour, 1682
Camacho Gayna, Juan: 1691, Juana Inés de la Cruz, sister, Poëmas
Camargo y Salgado, Fernando: 1699, Mariana, Juan de
Cambridge, Mass.--Ministers' Association
    The Answer Of Several Ministers, 1695
    Thirty Important Cases, 1699
Cambridge Platform, 1648: 1680, Congregational Churches in Massachusetts--Cambridge Synod, 1648
Camões, Luiz de: 1699, Ponte, Ioaõ Baptista da
Campanius Holm, Johan: 1696, Luther, Martin
Campen, Léonard: 1696, Thévenot, Melchisédech, Relations, 2.ptie.
Capell, Rudolf
    Norden/Oder Zu Wasser und Lande, 1678
    Vorstellungen Des Norden, 1675
Capitulaciones De Las Pazes: 1697, Spain--Treaties, etc., 1665-1700 (Charles II) 20 Sept. 1697
Capitulaçoens Das Pazes: 1697, Spain--Treaties, etc., 1665-1700 (Charles II) 20 Sept. 1697
Cardenas, Antonio de: 1682, Cubero Sebastián, Pedro
Care, George, A Reply To The Answer, 1685
Carew, George: 1679, A Brief Narrative And Deduction
Carew, Thomas, Hinc Illæ Lacrymæ, 1681
Carleton, Thomas: 1676, Howgill, Francis
Carli, Dionigi, Il Moro Trasportato, 1687
Carlos II, King of Spain
    Copia De Las Clavsvlas, 1700
    See also Spain--Laws, statutes, etc., 1665-1700 (Charles II); Spain--Sovereigns, etc., 1665-1700 (Charles II); Spain--Treaties, etc., 1665-1700 (Charles II)
Carlton, Thomas. See Carleton, Thomas
Carmarthen, Peregrine Osborne, marquis of. See Leeds, Peregrine Osborne, 2d duke of
Carolina--Charters: 1684, Carolina Described more fully then [sic] heretofore
Carolina--Constitution: 1684, Carolina Described more fully then [sic] heretofore
Carolina Described more fully then [sic] heretofore, 1684
Carolina; Or A Description Of the Present State, 1682
Caron, François: 1696, Thévenot, Melchisédech, Relations, 2.ptie.
Carrasco de Saavedra, Bernardo, Bp.: 1691, Santiago de Chile (Diocese)--Synod
Carrasco de Saavedra, Diego José, Sermon De La Pvrissima Concepcion, 1681
Carrillo, José, Sermon Panegyrico En La Solemnidad Principal, 1695
Carta Del Rey Nvestro Señor: 1695, Spain--Sovereigns, etc., 1665-1700 (Charles II) 24 Mar. 1695
Cartes Marines A L'Usage Des Armées Du Roy De La Grande Bretagne, 1693
Cartilla Mayor, En Lengua Castellana, 1691; 1693
Carvajal, Luis del Mármol. See Mármol Carvajal, Luis del
Carvajal y Ribera, Fernando de, Abp., Señor, 1699
Caryl, Joseph: 1682, Davenport, John

Casas, Bartolomé de las, Bp. of Chiapa
    An Account Of the First Voyages, 1699
    La Decouverte Des Occidentales, 1697
    Popery Truly Display'd, 1689
    Relation Des Voyages, 1698
Casas Zeinos, Diego de las: 1691, Ramírez de Vargas, Alonso
Casasola, Gregorio, Solemnidad Festiva, 1679
The Case Of John Wilmore: 1682, Wilmer, John
The Case Of Lay-Communion With The Church of England Considered: 1683, Williams, John, Bp. of Chichester
The Case Of The Hudsons-Bay Company: 1693, Hudson's Bay Company
The Case of the Lord Mayor, 1690
Cassini, Giovanni Domenico: 1693, Le Neptune François
Castañeda, Antonio de, Oracion Panegirica, 1680
Castellar, Baltasar de la Cueva, conde de, viceroy of Peru. See Cueva, Baltasar de la, conde de Castellar, viceroy of Peru
Castilla, Miguel de
    Espejo De Exemplares Obispos, 1698
    El Leon Mystico, 1695
    Sermon De La Immaculada Concepcion, 1694
Castillo, Baltasar
    Cathecismo Cenca, 1693
    Lvz, Y Gvia De Los Ministros Evangelicos, 1694
Castillo Marques, Diego del. See Castillomarques, Diego de
Castillo y Vergara, Pedro del: 1699, Narváez, Juan de, Sermon Qve En La Opposicion...
Castillomarques, Diego de: 1683, Medina, Baltasar de
Castorena y Ursúa, Juan Ignacio de
    Abraham Academico, 1696
    1695, Castro, José de
    1700, Juana Inés de la Cruz, sister
Castro, José de
    Sermon Panegirico Moral, 1696
    Vida Del Siervo De Dios Fr. Jvan De Angulo, 1695
Castro, Juan de, Fabrica De Lvz Sacada, 1692
Castro, Pedro de. See Petrei, Juan Francisco
Castro y Araùjo, José de: 1693, Rodrigo de la Cruz, Representacion Jvridica
Cathecismo Cenca: 1693, Castillo, Baltasar
Catholic Church--Liturgy and ritual, Motivos Piadosos, 1693
Catholic Church--Liturgy and ritual--Officium Beatissimae Virginis Mariae de Mercede Redemptionis Captivorum
    Officivm Beatissimæ Virginis, 1680
    Officivm B. Virginis, 1686
Catholic Church--Liturgy and ritual--Officium de Nomine Beatissimae Virginis Mariae, Die Dña infra Oct. Nativ. B. Maria Virginis, 1686
Catholic Church--Liturgy and ritual--Officium de Septem Doloribus Beatae Mariae Virginis, Officivm Septem Dolorvm, 1685
Catholic Church--Liturgy and ritual--Ritual, Manual De Administrar Los Santos Sacramentos à los Españoles, 1697

[441]

Index

Catholic Church--Liturgy and ritual--Ritual, Manual De Administrar Los Santos Sacramentos de la Eucharistia..., 1697
Catholic Church--Liturgy and ritual--Ritual, Manval De los Santos Sacramentos, 1690; 1691
Catholic Church--Liturgy and ritual--Special offices--Antoninus, Saint, Abp. of Florence, Die X. Maii..., 1685
Catholic Church--Liturgy and ritual--Special offices--Cajetanus, Saint, Die vij. Augusti..., 1685
Catholic Church--Liturgy and ritual--Special offices--Edward, the Confessor, King of England, Saint, Die xxij. Octobris..., 1683
Catholic Church--Liturgy and ritual--Special offices--Felipe de Jesús, Saint, Lectiones Tertii Nocturni Recitandæ, 1677
Catholic Church--Liturgy and ritual--Special offices--Fernando III, Saint
  Officivm In Festo B. Ferdinandi Tertij, 1677
  1685, Catholic Church--Liturgy and ritual--Special offices--Giovanni Gualberto, Saint
Catholic Church--Liturgy and ritual--Special offices--Francisco de Borja, Saint, Officivm S. Francisci Borgiæ, 1685
Catholic Church--Liturgy and ritual--Special offices--Gabriel, Archangel, Officium Sancti Gabrielis, 1685
Catholic Church--Liturgy and ritual--Special offices--Giovanni Gualberto, Saint, Die xij. Iulij..., 1685
Catholic Church--Liturgy and ritual--Special offices--Heinrich II, Saint: 1685, Catholic Church--Liturgy and ritual--Special offices--Giovanni Gualberto, Saint
Catholic Church--Liturgy and ritual--Special offices--Isidorus, Saint, patron of Madrid, Die 15. Maij..., 1685
Catholic Church--Liturgy and ritual--Special offices--Jean de Matha, Saint, Die viii. Februarii..., 1686
Catholic Church--Liturgy and ritual--Special offices--Liberata, Saint, Die xx. Iunij..., 1682
Catholic Church--Liturgy and ritual--Special offices--Margaret of Scotland, Saint, Officivm S. Margaritae, 1680
Catholic Church--Liturgy and ritual--Special offices--Patrick, Saint, Officivm, 1686
Catholic Church--Liturgy and ritual--Special offices--Rosa, of Lima, Saint
  Die xxx. August...Duplex Primae Classis, 1685
  Die xxx. Augusti...Omnia de Communi Virginam..., 1685
  1685, Catholic Church--Liturgy and ritual--Special offices--Cajetanus, Saint
Catholic Church--Pope, 1492-1503 (Alexander VI): 1678, Derby, Charles Stanley, 8th earl of
Catholic Church--Pope, 1623-1644 (Urbanus VIII)
  Breve De N. Santissimo Padre, 1690
  Breve Sanctissimi Domini Nostri, 1690

Catholic Church--Pope, 1670-1676 (Clemens X): 1689, Yo Pedro de Arce y Andrade...
Catholic Church--Pope, 1676-1689 (Innocentius XI)
  Bula, 1687
  1699, Confraternity of the Blessed Sacrament
Catholic Church--Pope, 1689-1691 (Alexander VIII): 1694, Corella, Jaime de
Catholic Church--Pope, 1691-1700 (Innocentius XII): 1698, Lampérez y Blázquez, Valentín
Catholic Church in Spain--Councils
  Collectio Maxima, 1693
  Notitia, 1686
Causas Eficientes: 1694, Petrei, Juan Francisco
The Causeless Ground of Surmises: 1694, Keith, George
Causes Of a Solemn National Fast: 1696, Church of Scotland--General Assembly--Commission
Caution Humbly Offer'd: 1698, Penn, William
Cavazzi, Giovanni Antonio, Istorica Descrittione, 1690
Cecchi, Giovanni Filippo: 1699, Solis y Rivadeneyra, Antonio de
Cellarius, Christoph, Geographia Antiqva iuxta & Nova, 1692
A Censure Of Mr. Judas Tull His Lampoon: 1700, Young, Samuel
Cerda Sandoval Silva y Mendoza, Gaspar de la, conde de Galve, viceroy of Mexico. See Galve, Gaspar de la Cerda Sandoval Silva y Mendoza, conde de, viceroy of Mexico
Cereceda, Juan Alonso de, Oracion Panegirica, Y Fvnebre, 1686
Certain Propositions Relating to the Scots Plantation, 1700
Chamberlayne, Peregrine Clifford: 1683, Dufour, Philippe Sylvestre
Chamberlayne, Richard, Lithobolia: Or, The Stone-Throwing Devil, 1698
Champion, Pierre: 1690, Arnauld, Antoine, Histoire De Dom Jean De Palafox (2 variants)
Charles II, King of Gt.Brit. See Gt.Brit.--Treaties, etc., 1660-1685 (Charles II)
Charonier, Gaspar Joseph, Clarissimo Et Excellentissimo Viro..., 1678
Charpentier, François, A Treatise..., 1695
The Charter Of Maryland
  1679, Maryland (Colony)--Charters
  1685, Maryland (Colony)--Charters
Chaste, Aimar de Clermont, seigneur de. See Clermont-Chatte, Aymard de
Chauncy, Isaac
  Alexipharmacon, 1700
  The Divine Institution, 1697
  The Doctrine Which is according to Godliness, 1694
  Neonomianism Unmask'd, 1692
  Neonomianism Unmask'd. Part III, 1693
  Neonomianism Unmask'd...The Continuation of the Second Part, 1693
  1696, Scripture Proof For Singing of Scripture Psalms
Chaves Masa, Pedro de. See Masa, Pedro de Chaves
Chavigny de La Bretonnière, François de, La Religieuse Cavalier, 1696

Index

Chazelles, Jean Mathieu de: 1693, Le Neptune François
Chevalier, Pierre: 1696, Thévenot, Melchisédech, Relations, 1.ptie.
Chèvremont, Jean Baptiste de
    L'Art De Voyager Utilement, 1698
    1699, Casas, Bartolomé de las, Bp. of Chiapa
Chevrières de Saint Vallier, Jean Baptiste de la Croix, Bp. of Quebec. See Saint Vallier, Jean Baptiste de la Croix Chevrières de, Bp. of Quebec
Cheyney, John: 1676, Penn, William
Child, John, The English Spira, 1693
Child, Sir Josiah, bart., A New Discourse Of Trade, 1693; 1694
Chipres Vidagaray y Saraza, Juan Antonio: 1695, Castilla, Miguel de
Chisini, Adriano: 1687, Carli, Dionigi
Chisini, Giuseppe: 1687, Carli, Dionigi
Church of Scotland--Presbyteries--Dumfries, Answers for the Presbytry of Dumfries, 1698
Church of Scotland--Synod of Lothian and Tweeddale: 1697, Scotland--Privy Council
A Circular Letter To the Clergy of Mary-Land: 1700, Bray, Thomas
Citry et de La Guette, S. de Broë, seigneur de. See Broë, S. de, seigneur de Citry et de La Guette
Claridge, Richard, A Defence Of The Present Government, 1689
Clarissimo Et Excellentissimo Viro, D. D. Joan. Bapt. Colbert: 1678, Charonier, Gaspar Joseph
Clarke, Samuel
    A New Description Of The World, 1689; 1696
    1684, Carolina Described More fully then [sic] heretofore
Claus, Jan
    1678, Fox, George, Spiegel Voor de Jóden
    1681, Penn, William, Eine Nachricht
Clemens X, Pope: 1689, Yo Pedro de Arce y Andrade...
Clement, Simon, The Interest of England, 1698
Clemente, Claudio, Tablas Chronologicas, 1689
Clermont-Chatte, Aymard de: 1696, Thévenot, Melchisédech, Relations, 5.ptie.
Cloche, Antonin: 1690, Dominicans
Clüver, Philipp
    Introductio In Omnem Geographiam, 1694
    Introductio in Universam Geographiam, 1697
Cobb, Alice: 1680, A Relation Of The Labour...
Codex Mendoza: 1696, Thévenot, Melchisédech, Relations, 4.ptie.
Cofradía de la Purísima Sangre de Nuestro Señor Jesucristo. See Archicofradía de la Purísima Sangre de Nuestro Señor Jesu Cristo
Coijmans, Balthasar: 1689, Pertinent en Waarachtig Verhaal
Colina, Jerónimo de: 1695, Mexico (City)--Universidad
Collectio Maxima Conciliorum Omnium Hispaniæ: 1693, Catholic Church in Spain--Councils
Collectio, Of Versamelinge, van eenige van de Tractaten..., 1680

A Collection Of Articles, Canons, Injunctions, &c.: 1699, Church of England
Crestien: 1691, Zani, Valerio, conte
Christelius, Bartholomaeus: 1683, Tanner, Mathias
Christendoms Saga: 1688, Kristnisaga
Christian V, King of Denmark: 1692, Denmark--Treaties, etc., 1670-1699 (Christian V)
Christliches Sendschreiben An Johannes III: 1678, Fox, George
The Church-Man And The Quaker Dialoguing, 1699
Church of England, A Collection Of Articles, Canons, Injunctions, &c., 1699
Church of England--Book of Common Prayer, The Book Of Common Prayer, 1676
Church of England--Book of Common Prayer--French, La Liturgie, 1683
Church of England--Liturgy and ritual, A Form Of Prayer, 1685
Church of Scotland--General Assembly--Commission
    Causes Of a Solemn National Fast, 1696
    A Letter, From The Commission, Of The General Assembly, Of The Church Of Scotland; Met at Glasgow, 1699
    Letter From the Commission Of The General Assembly Of The Church of Scotland To The Honourable Council, 1699
    1697, Scotland--Privy Council
Collection of papers relating to the present juncture of affairs in England, 1-12.
    1688, A Collection of Papers Relating to the Present Juncture of Affairs in England. Viz. 1. The Humble Petition...; A Second Collection...
    1689, A Compleat Collection Of Papers, In Twelve Parts; A Collection of Papers Relating to the Present Juncture of Affairs in England. Viz. 1. The Humble Petition...; A Second Collection...; A Third Collection...; A Fourth Collection...; A Fifth Collection...; A Sixth Collection...; A Seventh Collection...; The Eighth Collection...; A Ninth Collection...; A Tenth Collection...; Eleventh Collection...; The Twelfth and Last Collection...
Colleton, Peter: 1694, Bulkley, Thomas
Collins, John
    Salt And Fishery, 1682
    1677, Mitchel, Jonathan
Colman, Benjamin: 1700, Gospel Order Revived
Colmenero de Ledesma, Antonio: 1685, Dufour, Philippe Sylvestre, Tractatvs Novi; Dufour, Philippe Sylvestre, Traitez Nouveaux
Colombo, Fernando. See Colón, Fernando
Colomiès, Paul: 1686, Vossius, Isaac
Colón, Fernando
    Historie..., 1676; 1678; 1685
    La Vie De Cristofle Colomb, 1681
Colón de Portugal, Pedro Manuel, duque de Veragua, Señor..., 1691
Comber, Thomas
    Three Considerations, 1688

Comber, Thomas (continued)
  1689, A Seventh Collection of Papers Relating to Parliaments
Company for Propagation of the Gospel in New England and the Parts Adjacent in America, London: 1685, Bayly, Lewis, Bp. of Bangor
Company of Adventurers of London for the Plantation of the Summer Islands. See Bermuda Company
Company of Scotland Trading to Africa and the Indies
  At a Council-General of the Company of Scotland... , 1699
  At Edinburgh, The 15 of June, 1696... , 1696
  At Edinburgh, The 9th Day of July, 1696... , 1696
  Caledonia, The Declaration Of The Council... , 1699
  The Company of Scotland, Trading to Africa and the Indies... , 1696
  Constitutions Agreed Upon, 1696
  Constitutions Of The Company of Scotland, 1696
  The Council-General of the Indian and African Company's Petition... , 1699
  Edinburgh, April 3d. 1696... , 1696
  Edinburgh, March 24th 1696... , 1696
  Edinburgh, The 17th, day of April, 1696... , 1696
  Edinburgh the 12 of May 1696... , 1696
  Edinburgh the 20 of May 1696... , 1696
  A List Of The Subscribers To The Company of Scotland, 1696
  The Original Papers And Letters, 1700
  A Perfect List, 1696
  The Representation and Petition... , 1700
  Scotland's Right to Caledonia, 1700
  A Supplement Of Original Papers, 1700
  To His Grace His Majesties High Commissioner... The humble Petition of the Council-General, 1698
  To His Grace His Majesty's High Commissioner... The humble Representation and Petition of the Council-General [16 May], 1700
  To His Grace, His Majesty's High Commissioner... The humble Representation and Petition of the Council-General [28 October], 1700
The Company of Scotland, Trading to Africa and the Indies, Do hereby give Notice... : 1696, Company of Scotland Trading to Africa and the Indies
Compendio Della Vita, Virtù, e Miracoli Del B. Toribio Alfonso Mogrobeslo: 1681, Valladolid, Juan Francisco de
Compendio Historial, E Indice Chronologico Pervano: 1684, Rodríguez, Manuel
A Compendium Of The Laws: 1699, Curson, Henry
Competentia Ivrisdictionis Inter Reverendissimvm Ministrum Generalem: 1691, Salazar, Martín de
A Compleat Collection Of Papers, In Twelve Parts, 1689
The Compleat Library...August, 1692, 1692
The Compleat Library: Vol. II...December, 1692, 1692
A Complete Collection Of All The Lavvs Of Virginia: 1684, Virginia (Colony)--Laws, statutes, etc.
Compton, Henry, Bp. of London: 1690, To our Reverend...Ministers
Concepción, Juan de la. See Juan de la Concepción, fray

Concilia Limana, Constitvtiones Synodales: 1684, Lima (Ecclesiastical province)
The Concurrence & Unanimity Of the People Called Quakers, 1694
Conditien, De welcke by d'Ed. Mog. Heeren Staten van Hollandt... : 1675, Netherlands (United Provinces, 1581-1795)--Staten Generaal
Conferencia Cvriosa De La Assamblea Popvlar: 1687, Cortés Osorio, Juan
A Confession Of Faith Owned and consented unto by the Elders
  1680, Congregational Churches in Massachusetts--Boston Synod
  1699, Congregational Churches in Massachusetts--Boston Synod
A Confirmation of a late Epistle: 1700, Young, Samuel
Confraternity of the Blessed Sacrament, Sumario De Las Gracias, E Indvlgencias... , 1699
Confucius: 1696, Thévenot, Melchisédech, Relations, 4.ptie.
A Confutation Of a late Pamphlet: 1698, Johnson, Samuel
An Congratulatory Poem, On The safe Arrival of the Scots African and Indian Fleet, 1699
Congregational Churches in Massachusetts--Boston Synod, 1680
  A Confession of Faith, 1680; 1699
  1680, Mather, Increase, Returning unto God
Congregational Churches in Massachusetts--Cambridge Synod, 1648. A Platform Of Church-Discipline, 1680
Congreve, William
  1696, Southerne, Thomas
  1699, Southerne, Thomas
Connecticut (Colony)--General Assembly, 1693: 1693, An Account Of Several Passages
Connecticut (Colony)--Governor, 1689-1698 (Robert Treat): 1694, Their Majesties Colony Of Connecticut
Constitvciones De La Provincia De San Diego de Mexico de los Menores Descalços: 1698, Franciscans--Provincia de San Diego de Mexico
Constitvciones Synodales, del Obispado de Arequipa: 1688, Arequipa, Peru (Diocese)--Synod
Constituciones Synodales, del Obispado de Veneçuela: 1698, Venezuela (Diocese)--Synod
Constitutions Agreed Upon: 1696, Company of Scotland Trading to Africa and the Indies
Constitutions Of The Company Of Scotland: 1696, Company of Scotland Trading to Africa and the Indies
Consvlta Del Avditor General De La Gente De Mar: 1683, Peru (Viceroyalty)--Auditor General de la Gente de Mar y Guerra
Consvlta Qve Haze A Su Magestad... : 1689, Fernández de Santa Cruz y Sahagún, Manuel, Bp.
Conti, Stefano: 1687, Carli, Dionigi
A Continuation Of the State of New-England, 1676
The Continued Cry Of The Oppressed For Justice: 1675, Penn, William
Contrat De Mariage: 1697, France--Sovereigns, etc., 1643-1715 (Louis XIV)

Contrato Do Paço Da Madeira: 1699, Portugal--Conselho da Fazenda
Contreras Herrera, Juan de: 1682, Villegas, Manuel Juan
Contreras y Pacheco, Miguel de
  Sermon De La Gloriosa Virgen, 1695
  1698, Narvaez, Juan de
Conventie Tusschen den Koningh van Denemarcken ...: 1692, Denmark--Treaties, etc., 1670-1699 (Christian V)
Coole, Benjamin
  Honesty The Truest Policy, 1700
  The Quakers Cleared from being Apostates, 1696
Copia De Carta Del Rey Christianissimo: 1700, France--Sovereigns, etc., 1643-1715 (Louis XIV) 12 Nov. 1700
Copia De Carta Escrita A Vn Cavallero: 1691, Lopez, Francisco
Copia De Dos Cartas Escritas De Vn Missionero, 1682
Copia De Vna Carta, Escrita Al Padre Fray Alonso Sandin, 1684
Copia De Vna Carta, que escrivió vn Piloto del Patache, 1691
Copia van't Octroy, 1689
Coppy Of The Addres: Of a Great Number of the Members of the Parliament of Scotland, 1700
Corbet, John, Self-Imployment in Secret, 1684
Córdoba y Salinas, Diego de, Leben/Tugenden/vnnd Wunderwerck ..., 1676
Corella, Jaime de, Noticia, Censura, Impugnacion, Y Explicacion De Las XXXI. Proposiciones ..., 1694
Cork, Edward, Bp. of. See Wetenhall, Edward, Bp. of Kilmore and Ardagh
Coronelli, Vincenzo
  Atlante Veneto, 1691
  Epitome Cosmografica, 1693
Correa, Antonio
  Anillo De Salomon, 1682
  Fvnebre Panegyris, 1683
  Sylogismo Sacramental, 1683
Corsini, Filippo: 1699, Solís y Rivadeneyra, Antonio de
Cortés de la Cruz, Agustín: 1695, Espinosa Medrano, Juan de
Cortés Osorio, Juan, Conferencia Cvriosa, 1687
Cosmas Indicopleustes: 1696, Thévenot, Melchisédech, Relations, 1.ptie.
Cotolendi, Charles: 1681, Colón, Fernando
Cotton, John
  Nashauanittue Meninnunk ..., 1691
  1680, Congregational Churches in Massachusetts--Cambridge Synod
  1685, Bible--Massachuset--Eliot--1685
  1694, Scottow, Joshua
  1696, Massachusetts Or The first Planters of New-England
The Council-General of the Indian and African Company's Petition ...: 1699, Company of Scotland Trading to Africa and the Indies
The Country-Man's Companion: Or, A New Method Of Ordering Horses: 1684, Tryon, Thomas
Courland, James, Duke of, Briefve Deduction ..., 1676
Courtilz, Gatien de, sieur de Sandras, Histoire De La Guerre ..., 1689
Coutinho, Paschoal Ribeiro. See Ribeiro Coutinho, Paschoal
Cowley, William Ambrose: 1699, Hack, William
Cox, John: 1684, Ayres, Philip
Crawford, John: 1684, Carolina Described more fully then [sic] heretofore
Crestani, Antonio: 1687, Carli, Dionigi
Cripps, John
  1682, Ockanickon, Indian chief
  1683, Ockanickon, Indian chief
Crisp, Stephen
  Een Geklanck des Alarms, 1675
  Een naauw-keurigh ondersoek, 1675
  Noch een Ernstige Uermaeninge, 1678
  Een Sendt-Brief, 1676
  1678, Ames, William
  1680, Collectio, Of Versamelinge, van eenige van de Tractaten
  1687, Keith, George, The Benefit, Advantage, and Glory...
Crisp, Thomas, A Just and Lawful Tryal, 1697
Croese, Gerard
  The General History Of The Quakers, 1696
  Historia Quakeriana, 1695; 1696
Croissant, De Val. See Valcroissant, de Val.
Croix Chevrières de Saint Vallier, Jean Baptiste de la, Bp. of Quebec. See Saint Vallier, Jean Baptiste de la Croix Chevrières de, Bp. of Quebec
Crook, John: 1675, Green, Thomas
Crooke, William: 1681, Addison, Lancelot
Crouch, Nathaniel
  The English Empire, 1685
  The English Heroe, 1687; 1695
  Miracles Of Art and Nature, 1678
  Richardi Blome Englisches America, 1697
  1694, The Concurrence & Unanimity Of The People Called Quakers
Crull, Jodocus: 1698, Dellon, Gabriel; Rennefort, Urbain Souchu de
Cruz, Ana de la. See Ana de la Cruz
Cruz, Francisco Antonio de la, Declamacion Funebre, 1699
Cruz, Juana Inés de la. See Juana Inés de la Cruz, sister
Cruz, Rodrigo de la. See Rodrigo de la Cruz
Cruzado, Bartolomé: 1687, Valdés, Rodrigo de
Cruzado y Aragón, Francisco: 1687, Valdés, Rodrigo de
Cruzado y Ferrer, Esteban: 1687, Valdés, Rodrigo de
Cruzado y Ferrer, Francisco: 1687, Valdés, Rodrigo de
Cuadro, Francisco del. See Quadro, Francisco del

Cubero Sebastián, Pedro, Peregrinacion Del Mvndo, 1682
Cubillas Donyague, Francisco de. See Alcázar, Bartolomé
Cueva, Baltasar de la, conde de Castellar, viceroy of Peru: 1675, Rocha, Diego Andrés
Culpeper, Sir Thomas
    1693, Child, Sir Josiah, bart.
    1694, Child, Sir Josiah, bart.
Curieuse Beschrijving Van de Gelegentheid...: 1677, Burg, Pieter van der
Curson, Henry, A Compendium Of The Laws, 1699
Curwen, Alice: 1680, A Relation Of The Labour...
Curwen, Thomas: 1680, A Relation Of The Labour...
Cussy,   de, governor of Saint Domingue
    1690, Raveneau de Lussan, -----
    1693, Raveneau de Lussan, -----
    1699, Raveneau de Lussan, -----

D. D.: 1685, Verbiest, Ferdinand
D. P. I. B.: 1695, Diez de San Miguel y Solier, Nicolás Antonio
Daily Meditations: Or, Quotidian Preparations: 1682, Pain, Philip
Dampier, William
    A New Voyage Round The World, 1697; 1698; 1699
    A New Voyage Round The World...Second Edition Corrected, 1697
    Nieuwe Reystogt Rondom De Werreld, 1698
    Nouveau Voyage Autour Du Monde, 1698
    Voyages and Descriptions, 1699
    Voyages and Descriptions Vol.II, 1700
    1699, A Short Account from, And Description Of The Isthmus Of Darien
Dapper, Olfert, Description De L'Afrique, 1686
Dassié, F.
    L'Architecture Navale, 1677
    Description Generale Des Costes De L'Amerique, 1677
    Le Routier Des Indes Orientales, 1677
Davenant, Charles
    A Discourse Upon Grants and Resumptions, 1700
    Discourses On The Publick Revenues, 1698
    An Essay On The East-India-Trade, 1698
Davenport, John, The Saints Anchor-Hold, 1682
Dawson, Joseph, The Tryals Of Joseph Dawson, 1696
De Examine Symboli Politici: 1682, López y Martínez, Juan Luis, marqués del Risco
De La Theorie De La Manœuvre: 1689, Renau d'Eliçagaray, Bernard
Decima Relaçam Historica, 1686
Decima-Setima Relaçam Historica, 1686
Decission De La Real Avdiencia De Los Reyes: 1682, Peru (Viceroyalty)--Real Audiencia
Declaracion De La Guerra Por Su Magestad Britanica: 1689, Gt.Brit.--Sovereigns, etc., 1689-1694 (William and Mary) 7 May 1689
A Declaration From The Harmless & Innocent People of God: 1684, Fox, George (2 variants)
The Declaration Of The Reasons..., 1689

Decovverte De Qvelqves Pays qui sont entre l'Empire des Abyssins: 1696, Thévenot, Melchisédech, Relations, 4.ptie.
A Defence Of A Book: 1700, Leslie, Charles
A Defence Of The Duke of Buckingham, 1685
A Defence Of The Duke of Buckingham's Book Of Religion & Worship: 1685, Penn, William
A Defence Of The Present Government: 1689, Claridge, Richard
A Defence Of The Resolution Of This Case: 1684, Fowler, Edward, Bp. of Gloucester
A Defence Of The Scots Abdicating Darien: 1700, Harris, Walter
A Defence Of The Scots Settlement At Darien: 1699, Belhaven, John Hamilton, 2d baron 4º; 8º (4 variants)
The Defence Of The Scots Settlement At Darien Answer'd, 1699
Defensa De La Verdad: 1689, Ayeta, Francisco de
Defensa De Los Nvevos Christianos: 1690, Le Tellier, Michel
Defense Des Nouveaux Chrestiens: 1687, Le Tellier, Michel
Defoe, Daniel, The Two Great Questions Consider'd, 1700
Delavall, John
    1690, Keith, George, The Pretended Antidoe [sic]...
    1693, Keith, George, The Heresie and Hatred...
Delgado y Buenrostro, Antonio
    Accion De Gracias, 1679
    Oracion Evangelica, 1680; 1695
    1693, Gómez de la Parra, José
    1699, Cruz, Francisco Antonio de la
Dellon, Gabriel
    Aanmerkelijk Historisch-Verhaal..., 1688
    The History Of The Inquisition, 1688
    Relation De L'Inquisition, 1687; 1688 (2 editions)
    A Voyage To The East-Indies, 1698
A Demonstration To The Christians in Name: 1679, Fox, George
Denmark--Treaties, etc.
    1685, Gt.Brit.--Treaties, etc., 1660-1685 (Charles II)
    1686, Gt.Brit.--Treaties, etc., 1660-1685 (Charles II)
Denmark--Treaties, etc., 1670-1699 (Christian V), Conventie, 1692
Denniston, Walter, Ad Amplissimos simul & Consultissimos Viros, 1700
Denys, Nicolas, Geographische en Historische Beschrijving, 1688
La Deplorable Desolation, 1688
Derby, Charles Stanley, 8th earl of, The Jesuites Policy, 1678
Dernieres Decouvertes Dans L'Amerique Septentrionale, 1697
Desborow, Charles: 1699, Gt.Brit.--Parliament, 1698-1699--House of Lords (17 Apr. 1699)
Description des Antiquitez de Persepolis: 1696, Thévenot, Melchisédech, Relations, 1.ptie.

Index

A Description Of The Province and Bay Of Darian: 1699, Blackwell, Isaac
Desjean, Jean Bernard Louis, baron de Pointis. See Pointis, Jean Bernard Louis Desjean, baron de
Despachos, Y Cartas De Govierno: 1685, Peru (Viceroyalty)--Viceroy, 1681-1689 (Navarra y Rocafull)
The Devil Was and Is the Old Informer: 1683, Fox, George
A Dialogue Between An East-Indian Brackmanny Or Heathen-Philosopher..., 1683
A Dialogue Between George Fox a Quaker, Geo. Keith...: 1700, Young, Samuel
Diaz, Diego, Sermon Qve En la Solemne Profession..., 1694
Díaz Brizuela, José: 1696, Martínez de la Parra, Juan
Dick, William: 1684, Exquemelin, Alexandre Olivier, Bucaniers Of America
Dickinson, Jonathan, God's Protecting Providence, 1700
Die X. Maii. Officium In Festo S. Antonini Archiepiscopi Florentini: 1685, Catholic Church--Liturgy and ritual--Special offices--Antoninus, Saint, Abp. of Florence
Die Dña infra Oct. Nativ. B. Maria Virginis: 1686, Catholic Church--Liturgy and ritual--Officium de Nomine Beatissimae Virginis Mariae
Die xij. Iulij. In Festo S. Ioannis Gvalberti: 1685, Catholic Church--Liturgy and ritual--Special offices--Giovanni Gualberto, Saint
Die viii. Februarii In Festo S. Ioannis De Matha: 1686, Catholic Church--Liturgy and ritual--Special offices--Jean de Matha, Saint
Die 15. Maij. In Festo S. Isidori: 1685, Catholic Church--Liturgy and ritual--Special offices--Isidorus, Saint, Patron of Madrid
Die vij. Augusti. In Festo S. Caietani: 1685, Catholic Church--Liturgy and ritual--Special offices--Cajetanus, Saint
Die xxx. Augusti...Duplex Primae Classis: 1685, Catholic Church--Liturgy and ritual--Special offices--Rosa, of Lima, Saint
Die xxx. Augusti...Omnia de Communi Virginam: 1685, Catholic Church--Liturgy and ritual--Special offices--Rosa, of Lima, Saint
Die xx. Iunij. Officivm Sanctæ Liberatæ: 1682, Catholic Church--Liturgy and ritual--Special offices--Liberata, Saint
Die xxij. Octobris. Officivm S. Edvardi Confessoris: 1683, Catholic Church--Liturgy and ritual--Special offices--Edward, the Confessor, King of England, Saint
Diez de San Miguel y Solier, Nicolás Antonio, La Gran Fee Del Centurion Español, 1695
Digges, Leonard: 1685, Shakespeare, William
Dilucidationes quædam valde necessariæ: 1696, Kohlhans, Tobias Ludwig
Discours sur l'art de la navigation: 1681, Thévenot, Melchisédech
A Discourse Of The Duties on Merchandize, 1695
A Discourse Of The General Rule Of Faith and Practice: 1699, Penn, William

A Discourse Proving The Divine Institution: 1697, Leslie, Charles
A Discourse Upon Grants and Resumptions: 1700, Davenant, Charles
Discourses On The Publick Revenues: 1698, Davenant, Charles
Divine Immediate Revelation And Inspiration: 1684, Keith, George
Dockrey, Thomas: 1690, Some Testimonies Concerning the Life...
Doctrina Christiana, traducida de la Lengua Castellana
  1687, Ripalda, Gerónimo de
  1689, Ripalda, Gerónimo de
Dolben, Sir William: 1679, Scroggs, Sir William
Dom Pedro Por Graça De Deos, Principe De Portugal...: 1681, Portugal--Treaties, etc., 1668-1706 (Pedro II)
Dominguez Guerra del Corral, Gonzalo: 1684, Reyes, Gaspar de los
Dominicans, Regula S. Augustini, 1690
Dominicans--Third Order, Regla De Los Hermanos De La Orden Tercera, 1700
Don Gaspar de Sandoval, Cerda, Silva, y Mendoza Conde de Galve...Considerando su Magestad...: 1690, Mexico (Viceroyalty)--Laws, statutes, etc., 1688-1696 (Galve)
Don Gaspar de Sandoval, Cerda, Silva, y Mendoça Conde de Galve...Por quanto en cumplimiento...: 1689, Mexico (Viceroyalty)--Laws, statutes, etc., 1688-1696 (Galve) 12 Nov. 1689
Don Gaspar de Sandoval, Cerda, Silva, y Mendoça Conde de Galve...Por quanto Por la Ley primera...: 1689, Mexico (Viceroyalty)--Laws, statutes, etc., 1688-1696 (Galve) 1 Nov. 1689
Don Melchor De Navarra, y Rocafull...Duque de la Palata...Por quanto su Magestad...considerando...: 1683, Peru (Viceroyalty)--Laws, statutes, etc., 1681-1689 (Navarra y Rocafull)
Don Melchor de Nauarra y Rocafull...Duque de la Palata...Por quanto su Magestad...por su Real Cedula...: 1682, Peru (Viceroyalty)--Laws, statutes, etc., 1681-1689 (Navarra y Rocafull) 13 May 1682
Don Melchor de Nauarra y Rocafull...Duque de la Palata...Por quanto vno de los efectos...: 1682, Peru (Viceroyalty)--Laws, statutes, etc., 1681-1689 (Navarra y Rocafull) 13 May 1682
Don Melchor Portocarrero Lasso de la Vega...Por aver dado forma su Magestad...: 1695, Peru (Viceroyalty)--Laws, statutes, etc., 1689-1705 (Portocarrero)
Don Melchor Portocarrero Lasso de la Vega...Por Aver Hallado En Este Reyno...: 1692, Peru (Viceroyalty)--Laws, statutes, etc., 1689-1705 (Portocarrero) 27 Apr. 1692
Don Melchor Portocarrero, Laso De La Vega...Por quanto su Magestad...: 1698, Peru (Viceroyalty)--Laws, statutes, etc., 1689-1705 (Portocarrero)
Donaldson, James, The Undoubted Act Of Thriving, 1700
Donck, Adriaen van der: 1681, Melton, Edward

Index

Donneau de Vizé, Jean
   1678, Mercure Galant
   1690, Mercure Galant
Doolittle, Thomas, Earthquakes Explained, 1693
Dormer, Diego José: 1689, Clemente, Claudio
Dos Viages Del Adelantado Alvaro De Mendaña: 1696, Thévenot, Melchisédech, Relations, 5.ptie.
Douay, Anastase: 1691, Le Clercq, Chrétien, Etablissement De La Foy
Dove, C.: 1690, New-England's Faction Discovered
Drake, Francis: 1697, Mather, Cotton, Ecclesiastes
Drake, Sir Francis, bart.: 1683, The Voyages Of The Ever Renowned Sr. Francis Drake
Drummond, James, 4th earl of Perth. See Perth, James Drummond, 4th earl of
Drummond, John, 1st earl of Melfort. See Melfort, John Drummond, 1st earl of
Dryden, John
   The Indian Emperour, 1681; 1694
   1690, Behn, Aphra (Amis)
Duarte, Baltasar: 1694, Vieira, Antonio
Ducasse, Jean-Baptiste: 1699, Relation Fidele De L'Expedition De Cartagene
The Duckers Duck'd...: 1700, Young, Samuel
Dudley, Joseph: 1690, New-England's Faction Discovered
Dudley, Thomas: 1696, Massachusetts Or The first Planters of New-England
Dufour, Philippe Sylvestre
   Moral Instructions, 1683
   Tractatvs Novi, 1685
   Traitez Nouveaux, 1685
Durand,   of Dauphiné, Voyages, 1687
Durell, Jean: 1683, Church of England--Book of Common Prayer--French
Dutch East India Company. See Nederlandsche Oost-Indische Compagnie
Dutch West India Company. See Nederlandsche West-Indische Compagnie
Dutertre, Jean Baptiste: 1691, Zani, Valerio, conte
Duval, Pierre
   Geographiæ Universalis Pars Prior [-posterior], 1681
   Geographiæ Universalis Pars Prior, 1690
   Le Monde ou La Géographie Vniverselle, 1676
   1679, Pyrard, François
Dyck, Jochem van: 1678, Seer gedenckwaerdige Vojagien, Van Johan Sanderson
Dyer, Mary: 1700, Gould, Daniel

E. H.: 1696, Scripture Proof For Singing of Scripture Psalms
E. P. See Penington, Edward
E. R. See Rawson, Edward
E. W. See Wharton, Edward
Early Piety, Exemplified in The Life and Death...: 1689, Mather, Cotton
East India Company, Holland. See Nederlandsche Oost-Indische Compagnie

Ecclesia Gemens: 1677, Lee, Samuel
Echaburu y Alcaraz, José López: 1690, Le Tellier, Michel
Echard, Laurence, A Most Compleat Compendium, 1700
Echave y Assu, Francisco de, La Estrella De Lima, 1688
Edinburgh, April 3d. 1696...: 1696, Company of Scotland Trading to Africa and the Indies
Edinburgh, March 24th 1696...: 1696, Company of Scotland Trading to Africa and the Indies
Edinburgh, The 17th, day of April, 1696...: 1696, Company of Scotland Trading to Africa and the Indies
Edinburgh the 12 of May 1696...: 1696, Company of Scotland Trading to Africa and the Indies
Edinburgh the 20 of May 1696...: 1696, Company of Scotland Trading to Africa and the Indies
Edit Du Roy, Faisant défenses à toutes personnes: 1692, France--Laws, statutes, etc., 1643-1715 (Louis XIV)
Edit Du Roy, Portant revocation de la Compagnie des Indes Occidentales: 1675, France--Laws, statutes, etc., 1643-1715 (Louis XIV)
Eenige Annmerkingen voor den Philosopherenden Boer: 1676, Sonnemans, Arent
The Eighth Collection of Papers Relating to the Present Juncture of Affairs in England, 1689
The Elders Tenents in the Bay: 1676, Groome, Samuel
Elementa Linguæ Tartaricæ: 1696, Thévenot, Melchisédech, Relations, 5.ptie.
Eleventh Collection of Papers Relating to the Present Juncture of Affairs in England, 1689
Eliot, John
   The Harmony of the Gospels, 1678
   1685, Bayly, Lewis, Bp. of Bangor; Bible--Massachuset--Eliot
   1689, Shepard, Thomas
   1696, Baxter, Richard
Ellwood, Thomas
   An Answer To George Keith's Narrative, 1696
   An Epistle To Friends, 1694
   A Further Discovery, 1694
   Truth Defended, 1695
   1694, Fox, George
Elvas, Gentleman of, A Relation Of The Invasion..., 1686
Elys, Edmund
   George Keith His Saying..., 1697
   A Vindication Of The Doctrine..., 1699
The Emblem of Our King, 1700
Endecott, John: 1696, Baxter, Richard
Engeland Beroerd, 1689
Englands Great Interest in The Choice of this New Parliament: 1679, Penn, William
England's Present Interest Discover'd: 1675, Penn, William
The English Atlas, 1681
The English Empire In America: 1685, Crouch, Nathaniel

Index

The English Heroe
   1687, Crouch, Nathaniel
   1695, Crouch, Nathaniel
The English Spira: Being A Fearful Example Of An Apostate, 1693
An Enquiry Into The Causes..., 1700
Enríquez de Ribera, Payo, Abp., Viceroy of Mexico
   Tratado En Que Se Defienden Nueve Proposiciones, 1679
   See also Mexico (Viceroyalty)--Laws, statutes, etc., 1673-1680 (Enríquez de Ribera)
Episcopal Church in Scotland, Unto His Grace..., 1690
An Epistle, Containing A Salutation To All Faithful Friends, 1682
An Epistle of Love To Friends: 1680, Townsend, Theophila
An Epistle To All Christians: 1682, Fox, George
An Epistle To Friends: 1678, Fox, George
Escalante, Thomas
   Breve Noticia, 1679
   Sermon Funebre, 1694
Escalante Colombres y Mendoza, Manuel de, Bp.: 1695, Mexico (City)--Universidad
Escalona y Agüero, Gaspar de, Gazophilativm Regivm Pervbicvm, 1675
Escaray, Antonio de. See Ezcaray, Antonio de
Eschinardi, Francesco, De Impetv Tractatvs Dvplex, 1684
Escobar Salmeron y Castro, José de, Discvrso Cometologico, 1681
Espinosa, José: 1690, Octava Maravilla
Espinosa Medrano, Juan de, La Nouena Marauilla, 1695
Esquemeling, John. See Exquemelin, Alexandre Olivier
Esquerra, Matías de, La Imperial Agvila Renovada, 1697
An Essay On The East-India-Trade: 1698, Davenant, Charles
Estlacke, Francis, A Bermudas Preacher, 1683
Etablissement De La Foy Dans La Nouvelle France: 1691, Le Clercq, Chrétien
Evelino, Gaspar Juan, Especulacion Astrologica, 1682
Evelyn, John: 1680, Fréart de Chambray, Roland
Evelyn, Robert: 1681, An Abstract, Or Abbreviation...
Everot, John: 1698, Penn, William, The Quaker A Christian
An Exact Narrative Of The Tryals Of The Pyrats, 1675
An Exalted Diotrephes Reprehended, 1681
El Excmo. Señor Conde De La Monclova...En Despacho de 27. de Abril deste Año: 1692, Peru (Viceroyalty)--Laws, statutes, etc., 1689-1705 (Portocarrero) 19 July 1692
Exquemelin, Alexandre Olivier
   De Americaensche Zee-Roovers, 1678
   Bucaniers Of America, 1684 (2 variants)
   Histoire Des Avanturiers, 1686; 1688
   The History Of The Bucaniers, 1684
   Piratas De La America, 1681; 1682 (2 variants)
   1681, Melton, Edward

1691, Zani, Valerio, conte
1699, The History Of The Bucaniers; Raveneau de Lussan, -----
1700, Historie Der Boecaniers
Extension Politica, Y Economica: 1686, Alvarez Ossorio y Redín, Miguel
Extracten uyt het Register der Resolutien van de Hoogh Mog. Heeren Staten Generael, 1676
Extrait Dv Voyage Des Hollandois: 1696, Thévenot, Melchisédech, Relations, I.ptie.
Eyjólfsson, Einar: 1688, Jónsson, Arngrímur; Landnámabók
Ezcaray, Antonio de
   Deseos De Asertar..., 1683
   Hvmilde Desempeño, 1681
   Oracion Panegirica, 1683
   Sermon En El Entierro..., 1686
   Sermon Panegyrico, 1681

F. D. See Drake, Francis
F. M. L. A.: 1695, Diez de San Miguel y Solier, Nicolás Antonio
Fairfax, Thomas Fairfax, 3d baron: 1677, Herbert, Sir Thomas
Falckinburs, Henry Jacobs
   1682, Ockanickon, Indian chief
   1683, Ockanickon, Indian chief
Faria, Francisco de, The Information, 1680
Farissol, Abraham, Itinera Mundi, 1691
A farther Brief and True Narration, 1676
Favoravel declaração de El Rey de Inglaterra: 1687, Gt. Brit.--Sovereigns, etc., 1685-1688 (James II)
Febris China Chinæ Expvgnata: 1687, Nigrisoli, Francesco Maria
Fehr, Johannes Michael: 1682, Mentzel, Christian
Felipe IV, King of Spain
   1675, Escalona y Agüero, Gaspar de
   1681, Spain--Consejo de las Indias
Felipe V, King of Spain: 1700, Spain--Sovereigns, etc., 1700-1746 (Philip V)
Fell, Lydia (Erbury), A Testimony, 1676
Ferguson, Robert
   A Just and Modest Vindication, 1699
   1682, The Present State Of Carolina; A true Description Of Carolina
Fernández de Belo, Benito, Breve Aritmetica, 1675
Fernández de Leon, Diego: 1689, Vásquez Gaztelu, Antonio
Fernández de Medrano, Sebastián
   Breve Descripcion Del Mvndo, 1688 8°; 1688 12°; 1693
   Breve Tratado De Geographia, 1700
   1699, Hennepin, Louis, Relacion De Un País
Fernández de Mendoza, Francisco: 1682, Copia De Dos Cartas
Fernández de Piedrahita, Lucas, Historia General, 1688

Fernández de Santa Cruz y Sahagún Manuel, Bp.
  Consvlta, 1689
  1682, Asenjo y Crespo, Ignacio de
  1690, Juana Inés de la Cruz, sister
  1692, Villavicencio, Diego Jaime Ricardo
Fernández Navarrete, Domingo, Abp. of St. Domingo,
  Tratados Historicos, 1676
Ferro Machado, Juan, Señor..., 1688
Feuillet, Jean Baptiste: 1684, Lucchesini, Giovanni
  Lorenzo
Field, John
  The Weakness Of George Keith's Reasons, 1700
  1683, Taylor, John
A Fifth Collection of Papers, 1688
Figueira, Luiz, Arte De Grammatica, 1687
Figueroa, Diego de: 1688, Fernández de Piedrahita,
  Lucas
Figueroa, Felipe de: 1698, Castilla, Miguel de
El Fiscal Del Consejo En Favor De La Regalia: 1694,
  Ledesma, Joseph de
Fisher, Hallelujah: 1679, Fisher, Samuel, The Testi-
  mony Of Truth Exalted
Fisher, Samuel
  An Additional Appendix, 1679
  The Bishop..., 1679
  One Antidote More, 1679
  Rusticus ad academicos, 1679
  Supplementum Sublatum, 1679
  The Testimony Of Truth Exalted, 1679
  Velata Quædam Revelata, 1679
Fleming, Robert, A Discourse Of Earthquakes, 1693
Fletcher, Andrew
  Overtures Offered to the Parliament, 1700
  A Short and Impartial View, 1699
  1699, Belhaven, John Hamilton, 2d baron, A Defence
    Of The Scots Settlement at Darien 4º; 8º (4 var-
    iants)
Fletcher, Benjamin. See New York (Colony)--Gover-
  nor, 1692-1697 (Benjamin Fletcher)
Fletcher, Giles, Israel Redux, 1677
Flint, Josiah: 1679, Adams, William
Florencia, Francisco de
  La Casa Peregrina, 1689
  Descripcion Historica, Y Moral..., 1689
  La Estrella..., 1688
  Historia De La Provincia De La Compañia De Jesvs,
    1694
  La Milagrosa Invencion, 1685
  Relacion De La Exemplar y Religiosa vida..., 1684
  Sermon A La Festividad..., 1683
  Vida Admirable..., 1689
Florido, Sylvestre, Villancicos, 1682
Floris, Pieter: 1696, Thévenot, Melchisédech, Rela-
  tions, 1.ptie.
Foigny, Gabriel de, Voyage De La Terre Australe,
  1695
For The King And both Houses of Parliament: 1675,
  Hookes, Ellis
Forced Uniformity: 1675, Hutchinson, Thomas
Ford, Philip, A Vindication..., 1683
Ford, Simon: 1694, Morton, Richard

A Form Of Prayer: 1685, Church of England--Liturgy
  and ritual
Forseith, Edward: 1696, Dawson, Joseph
A Fourth Collection of Papers Relating to the Present
  Juncture of Affairs in England, 1689
Fowler, Edward, Bp. of Gloucester, A Defence Of The
  Resolution..., 1684
Fox, George, 1624-1691
  An Answer To several New Laws, 1678
  An Answer To The Speech..., 1688
  Antwoort Op twee Vrágen, 1678
  Cæsar's Due, 1679
  Cain Against Abel, 1675
  Christian Liberty Commended, 1675
  Christliches Sendschreiben, 1678
  A Collection Of Many Select and Christian Epistles,
    1698
  Concerning Persecution, 1682
  Concerning the Living God of Truth, 1680
  A Declaration..., 1684 (2 variants)
  A Demonstration To The Christians, 1679
  The Devil, 1683
  Eenige Vragen, 1678
  An Epistle To All Christians, 1682
  An Epistle To Friends, 1678
  An Epistle To the Household..., 1698
  An Exhortation, 1680
  For All The Bishops, 1675
  Een getuygenisse Aan alle Menschen, 1679
  A Journal Or Historical Account..., 1694
  The Man Christ Jesus, 1679
  A New-England-Fire-Brand Quenched, 1678; 1679
  A New-England-Fire-brand Quenched. The Second
    Part, 1678
  Primitive Ordination, 1675
  Een Sentbrief Aangaande Het Ware Vasten, 1678
  Something in Answer..., 1678; 1679; 1682
  Spiegel Voor de Jöden, 1678
  Spiritualis Necnon Divina Salutatio, 1690
  To All Kings, 1685
  To all that would Know the Way, 1675
  Traitte De la Revelation, 1681
  The True Christians, 1689
  Tythes, Offerings..., 1683
  A Vision, 1692
  1676, Groome, Samuel; Howgill, Francis
  1680, Townsend, Theophila
  1682, Loddington, William
  1688, The Life & Death, Travels And Sufferings...
  1690, Some Testimonies Concerning the Life...
  1691, Burnyeat, John
Fox, George, d. 1661, Een Eedele Salutatie, 1679
Fox, Margaret (Askew) Fell: 1694, Fox, George
Foxes And Firebrands: 1682, Nalson, John (2 variants)
The Foxonian Quakers: 1697, Young, Samuel
Foyer, Archibald
  Scotland's Present Duty, 1700
  1699, Belhaven, John Hamilton, 2d baron, A Defence
    Of The Scots Settlement at Darien 4º; 8º (4 var-
    iants)

[450]

Index

Fragment servant à l'histoire de quelques Princes Orientaux: 1696, Thévenot, Melchisédech, Relations, 5.ptie.
Fraichot, Casimir. See Freschot, Casimir
The Frame of the Government Of The Province of Pennsylvania: 1682, Penn, William
France--Laws, statutes, etc., 1643-1715 (Louis XIV)
    Edit Du Roy, 1675
    Edit Du Roy, 1692
    Ordonnance, 1681; 1682
    Ordonnance, 1699
France--Sovereigns, etc., 1643-1715 (Louis XIV)
    Arrest Dv Conseil D'Estat, 1681
    Arrest Dv Conseil D'Estat, 1682
    Arrest Du Conseil D'Estat, 1684
    Arrest Du Conseil D'Estat (8 Feb. 1685), 1685
    Arrest Du Conseil D'Estat (12 Apr. 1685), 1685
    Arrest Du Conseil D'Estat, 1686
    Arrest Du Conseil D'Estat, 1689
    Arrest Du Conseil D'Estat (30 May 1695), 1695
    Arrest Du Conseil D'Etat (20 July 1700), 1700
    Contrat De Mariage, 1697
    Copia De Carta Del Rey Christianissimo (12 Nov. 1700), 1700
    Lettres Patentes Pour L'Etablissement..., 1698
    Reglement Du Roy (12 Oct. 1695), 1695
France--Treaties, etc., 1643-1715 (Louis XIV)
    Proyecto De La Paz (20 July 1697), 1697
    Tractaet Van De Vreede (20 Sept. 1697), 1697
    Traité De Neutralité, 1687; 1689
    Traité De Paix Entre La France Et La Savoye (29 Aug. 1696), 1697
    Traité De Paix Entre La France Et L'Angleterre (20 Sept. 1697), 1697
    Traité De Paix Entre La France Et L'Espagne (20 Sept. 1697), 1697
    Traité De Suspension D'Armes En Italie (7 Oct. 1696), 1697
    Traitez De Paix Et De Commerce, Navigation Et Marine (21 Sept. 1697), 1697
    1685, Gt.Brit.--Treaties, etc., 1660-1685 (Charles II)
    1686, Gt.Brit.--Treaties, etc., 1660-1685 (Charles II); Gt.Brit.--Treaties, etc., 1685-1688 (James II), Tractatus Pacis; Gt.Brit.--Treaties, etc., 1685-1688 (James II), Treaty Of Peace
    1697, Gt.Brit.--Treaties, etc., 1694-1702 (William III); Holy Roman Empire--Treaties, etc., 1658-1705 (Leopold I); Spain--Treaties, etc., 1665-1700 (Charles II), Capitulaçoens Das Pazes; Traktaat van Vrede
Franciscans
    Instrvccion, Y Doctrina..., 1685
    Tabvla Geographica, 1680
Franciscans--Provincia de San Diego de Mexico, Constitvciones De La Provincia De San Diego de Mexico de los Menores Desçalcos, 1698
Francisci, Erasmus: 1681, Bos, Lambert van den, Leben und Tapffere Thaten...

Francisco Antonio de la Cruz. See Cruz, Francisco Antonio de la
Franck, Richard
    Northern Memoirs, 1694
    A Philosophical Treatise, 1687
Frasso, Pedro, De Regio Patronatv, 1677
Fréart de Chambray, Roland, The Whole Body Of Antient and Modern Architecture, 1680
Free Society of Traders in Pennsylvania, The Articles, Settlement and Offices, 1682
Freigius, Johann Thomas: 1675, Settle, Dionyse
Freire, Francisco de Brito. See Brito Freire, Francisco de
Frémont d'Ablancourt, Jean Jacobé de: 1700, Suite Du Neptune Francois
Frémont d'Ablancourt, Nicolas de. See Frémont d'Ablancourt, Jean Jacobé de
Freschot, Casimir
    1686, Hennepin, Louis
    1696, Briet, Philippe
Freyre, Antonio: 1681, Exquemelin, Alexandre Olivier
Friend, Nathaniel: 1694, Seller, John
Friendly Advice To The Gentlemen-Planters: 1684, Tryon, Thomas
A Friendly Epistle To The Reverend Clergy: 1700, Young, Samuel
Friends, Society of--London Yearly Meeting: 1695, Keith, George, The Pretended Yearly Meeting
Friends, Society of--Philadelphia Yearly Meeting
    Our Antient Testimony Renewed, 1695
    1696, Croese, Gerard, The General History Of The Quakers
Froger, François
    Relation D'Un Voyage, 1698; 1699; 1700
    A Relation Of A Voyage, 1698
Frontenac, Louis de Buade, comte de: 1691, Le Clercq, Chrétien, Etablissement De La Foy
Frontignières, ---de
    1686, Exquemelin, Alexandre Olivier
    1688, Exquemelin, Alexandre Olivier
Fuenlabrada, Nicolás de, Oracion Evangelica, 1681
A full Account of the Late Dreadful Earthquake, 1692
A Full and Exact Collection..., 1700
Funck, David, Der in Europa und America verehrliche Thron, 1691
Furer, Christopher: 1678, Seer gedenckwaerdige Vojagien...
Furly, Benjamin
    1675, Marshall, Charles; Penn, William, De Waarheyt Ontdekt
    1676, Sonnemans, Arent
    1680, Collectio, Of Versamelinge, van eenige van de Tractaten
    1681, Penn, William, Een kort Bericht...
    1684, Penn, William, Missive...; Penn, William, Recüeil...
A Further Account of East-New-Jarsey: 1683, Lockhart, George
A Further Account Of New Jersey, 1676
A Further Account Of the Province of Pennsylvania: 1685, Penn, William (2 variants)

Gt. Brit. --Sovereigns, etc., 1689-1694 (William and Mary) (continued)
  His Majesties Most Gracious Speech, 1690 (21 Mar. 1689/90)
  His Majesties Most Gracious Speech, 1690 (2 Oct. 1690)
  His Majesties Most Gracious Speech, 1692
  His Majesties Most Gracious Speech, 1693
  A Second Brief, 1690 (18 Feb. 1690)
  Their Majesties Declaration, 1689 (7 May 1689)
Gt. Brit. --Sovereigns, etc., 1694-1702 (William III)
  By the King, 1700 (29 Jan. 1699) [i.e. 1700]
  His Majesties Most Gracious Speech, 1695 (3 May 1695)
  His Majesties Most Gracious Speech, 1695 (23 Nov. 1695)
  His Majesties Most Gracious Speech, 1697
  Proclamation For Apprehending Captains Gavine Hamilton..., 1700 (25 July 1700)
Gt. Brit. --Treaties, etc., 1660-1685 (Charles II)
  Articles Of Peace, 1677
  Several Treaties, 1685; 1686
  1697, France--Treaties, etc., 1643-1715 (Louis XIV), Traité De Paix Entre La France Et L'Angleterre (20 Sept. 1697)
Gt. Brit. --Treaties, etc., 1685-1688 (James II)
  Tractatus Pacis, 1686
  Treaty Of Peace, 1686
  1687, France--Treaties, etc., 1643-1715 (Louis XIV) 16 Nov. 1686
  1689, France--Treaties, etc., 1643-1715 (Louis XIV) 16 Nov. 1686
Gt. Brit. --Treaties, etc., 1689-1694 (William and Mary):
  1692, Denmark--Treaties, etc., 1670-1699 (Christian V)
Gt. Brit. --Treaties, etc., 1694-1702 (William III)
  Articles Of Peace, 1697
  1697, Traktaat van Vrede
The Great Earthquake At Quito, 1698
Great Newes From The Barbadoes, 1676
Greaves, John: 1696, Thévenot, Melchisédech, Relations, 1.ptie.
Green, Bartholomew: 1700, The Printers Advertisement
Green, Thomas, Korte Antwoordt..., 1675
Greenhill, William: 1680, Shepard, Thomas
Grey, Ralph: 1699, By the Honourable Sir William Beeston
Grillet, Jean
  A Journal Of The Travels..., 1698
  1682, Acuña, Cristóbal de
Grímsson, Thorlákur: 1688, Landnámabók
The Groans of the Plantations: 1689, Littleton, Edward
Gronovius, Jacobus
  Dissertatio De Origine Romuli, 1684
  Responsio Ad Cavillationes Raphaelis Fabretti, 1684
Groome, Samuel, A Glass For The People, 1676
Grotius, Hugo, Nederlandtsche Jaerboeken, 1681
Guadalaxara, Nicolas: 1684, Florencia, Francisco de
Gualdo Priorato, Galeazzo, conte, Teatro Del Belgio, 1683
Guattini, Michele Angelo: 1687, Carli, Dionigi
Gudenfridi, Giovanni Batista, Replica Alla Risposta Dimostrativa, 1680

Guevara, Gaspar de: 1691, Sigüenza y Góngora, Carlos de
Guevara, Juan de
  1683, Sigüenza y Góngora, Carlos de
  1691, Sigüenza y Góngora, Carlos de
Guillet de Saint-George, Georges, Les Arts De L'Homme D'Epée, 1680
Gurpegui, José de: 1693, Rodrigo de la Cruz, Representacion Jvridica
Gusmão, Alexandre de
  Historia Do Predestinado Peregrino, 1685
  Sermão, 1686
Gutierrez Coronel, Juan: 1682, Villegas, Manuel Juan
Guy, Edward: 1676, Howgill, Francis
Guzmán y Córdova, Sebastián de: 1690, Sigüenza y Góngora, Carlos de
Gysbertz, Reyr. See Gijsbertz, Reyer

H. C. See Curson, Henry
H. L.: 1693, The Truest and Largest Account Of The Late Earthquake
H. S.: 1678, Bradstreet, Anne (Dudley)
H. V. Q. See Quellenburgh, Henrik van
Hack, William, A Collection Of Original Voyages, 1699
Hale, Sir Matthew, The Primitive Origination Of Mankind, 1677
Halley, Edmond: 1675, Seller, John
Hamilton, John. See Belhaven, John Hamilton, 2d baron
Hammond, Lawrence: 1691, To The King's Most Excellent Majesty. The Humble Address of divers of the Gentry
Hansen, Leonhard, Vita Mirabilis..., 1680
Hanson, Francis: 1683, Jamaica--Laws, statutes, etc.
Hanson, Samuel, The Case Of Samuel Hanson, 1684
Happel, Eberhard Werner
  Mundus Mirabilis Tripartitus, 1687
  Thesaurus Exoticorum, 1688
La Harangve Qve Le Roy De La Grand· Bretagne...: 1678, Gt. Brit.--Sovereigns, etc., 1660-1685 (Charles II) 28 Jan. 1678
Harford, Charles: 1681, An Exalted Diotrephes Reprehended
Harris, Benjamin, A Short But Just Account..., 1679
Harris, Walter
  A Defence Of The Scots Abdicating Darien, 1700
  A Short Vindication Of Phil. Scot's Defence, 1700
  1699, The Defence Of The Scots Settlement At Darien, Answer'd
Hartshorne, Richard: 1676, A Further Account Of New Jersey
Hatton, Edward, The Merchant's Magazine, 1697
Havers, Clopton: 1694, Morton, Richard
Hawkins, William: 1696, Thévenot, Melchisédech, Relations, 1.ptie.
Hayward, Nicholas: 1687, Durand, of Dauphiné
Hazart, Cornelius, Kirchen-Geschichte, 1684
An Health To Caledonia, 1699
Heath,   Dr.: 1692, Ampel en Breed Verhaal...;
  A Full Account of the Late Dreadful Earthquake
Hebden, Roger, A Plain Account..., 1700

Index

Fragment servant à l'histoire de quelques Princes Orientaux: 1696, Thévenot, Melchisédech, Relations, 5.ptie.
Fraichot, Casimir. See Freschot, Casimir
The Frame of the Government Of The Province of Pennsilvania: 1682, Penn, William
France--Laws, statutes, etc., 1643-1715 (Louis XIV)
   Edit Du Roy, 1675
   Edit Du Roy, 1692
   Ordonnance, 1681; 1682
   Ordonnance, 1699
France--Sovereigns, etc., 1643-1715 (Louis XIV)
   Arrest Dv Conseil D'Estat, 1681
   Arrest Dv Conseil D'Estat, 1682
   Arrest Du Conseil D'Estat, 1684
   Arrest Du Conseil D'Estat (8 Feb. 1685), 1685
   Arrest Du Conseil D'Estat (12 Apr. 1685), 1685
   Arrest Du Conseil D'Estat, 1686
   Arrest Du Conseil D'Estat, 1689
   Arrest Du Conseil D'Estat (30 May 1695), 1695
   Arrest Du Conseil D'Etat (20 July 1700), 1700
   Contrat De Mariage, 1697
   Copia De Carta Del Rey Christianissimo (12 Nov. 1700), 1700
   Lettres Patentes Pour L'Etablissement ... , 1698
   Reglement Du Roy (12 Oct. 1695), 1695
France--Treaties, etc., 1643-1715 (Louis XIV)
   Proyecto De La Paz (20 July 1697), 1697
   Tractaet Van De Vreede (20 Sept. 1697), 1697
   Traité De Neutralité, 1687; 1689
   Traité De Paix Entre La France Et La Savoye (29 Aug. 1696), 1697
   Traité De Paix Entre La France Et L'Angleterre (20 Sept. 1697), 1697
   Traité De Paix Entre La France Et L'Espagne (20 Sept. 1697), 1697
   Traité De Suspension D'Armes En Italie (7 Oct. 1696), 1697
   Traitez De Paix Et De Commerce, Navigation Et Marine (21 Sept. 1697), 1697
   1685, Gt.Brit.--Treaties, etc., 1660-1685 (Charles II)
   1686, Gt.Brit.--Treaties, etc., 1660-1685 (Charles II); Gt.Brit.--Treaties, etc., 1685-1688 (James II), Tractatus Pacis; Gt.Brit.--Treaties, etc., 1685-1688 (James II), Treaty Of Peace
   1697, Gt.Brit.--Treaties, etc., 1694-1702 (William III); Holy Roman Empire--Treaties, etc., 1658-1705 (Leopold I); Spain--Treaties, etc., 1665-1700 (Charles II), Capitulaçoens Das Pazes; Traktaat van Vrede
Franciscans
   Instrvccion, Y Doctrina ... , 1685
   Tabvla Geographica, 1680
Franciscans--Provincia de San Diego de Mexico, Constitvciones De La Provincia De San Diego de Mexico de los Menores Desçalcos, 1698
Francisci, Erasmus: 1681, Bos, Lambert van den, Leben und Tapffere Thaten ...

Francisco Antonio de la Cruz. See Cruz, Francisco Antonio de la
Franck, Richard
   Northern Memoirs, 1694
   A Philosophical Treatise, 1687
Frasso, Pedro, De Regio Patronatv, 1677
Fréart de Chambray, Roland, The Whole Body Of Antient and Modern Architecture, 1680
Free Society of Traders in Pennsylvania, The Articles, Settlement and Offices, 1682
Freigius, Johann Thomas: 1675, Settle, Dionyse
Freire, Francisco de Brito. See Brito Freire, Francisco de
Frémont d'Ablancourt, Jean Jacobé de: 1700, Suite Du Neptune Francois
Frémont d'Ablancourt, Nicolas de. See Frémont d'Ablancourt, Jean Jacobé de
Freschot, Casimir
   1686, Hennepin, Louis
   1696, Briet, Philippe
Freyre, Antonio: 1681, Exquemelin, Alexandre Olivier
Friend, Nathaniel: 1694, Seller, John
Friendly Advice To The Gentlemen-Planters: 1684, Tryon, Thomas
A Friendly Epistle To The Reverend Clergy: 1700, Young, Samuel
Friends, Society of--London Yearly Meeting: 1695, Keith, George, The Pretended Yearly Meeting
Friends, Society of--Philadelphia Yearly Meeting
   Our Antient Testimony Renewed, 1695
   1696, Croese, Gerard, The General History Of The Quakers
Froger, François
   Relation D'Un Voyage, 1698; 1699; 1700
   A Relation Of A Voyage, 1698
Frontenac, Louis de Buade, comte de: 1691, Le Clercq, Chrétien, Etablissement De La Foy
Frontignières, ---de
   1686, Exquemelin, Alexandre Olivier
   1688, Exquemelin, Alexandre Olivier
Fuenlabrada, Nicolás de, Oracion Evangelica, 1681
A full Account of the Late Dreadful Earthquake, 1692
A Full and Exact Collection... , 1700
Funck, David, Der in Europa und America verehrliche Thron, 1691
Furer, Christopher: 1678, Seer gedenckwaerdige Vojagien...
Furly, Benjamin
   1675, Marshall, Charles; Penn, William, De Waarheyt Ontdekt
   1676, Sonnemans, Arent
   1680, Collectio, Of Versamelinge, van eenige van de Tractaten
   1681, Penn, William, Een kort Bericht...
   1684, Penn, William, Missive... ; Penn, William, Recüeil...
A Further Account of East-New-Jarsey: 1683, Lockhart, George
A Further Account Of New Jersey, 1676
A Further Account Of the Province of Pennsylvania: 1685, Penn, William (2 variants)

A Further Account Of The Tryals Of The New-England Witches, 1693
A Further Discovery Of the Spirit of Falshood: 1694, Keith, George
A Further Explication Of the Proposal...: 1700, Fletcher, Andrew

G. C.   See Care, George
G. F.   See Fox, George
G. G. L.   See Leibniz, Gottfried Wilhelm, freiherr von
G. J.: 1700, Mucklow, William
G. K.   See Keith, George
G. W.: 1676, A Continuation Of the State of New-England
Gabriel de San Buenaventura.   See San Buenaventura, Gabriel de
Gaceta de Madrid
   1697, France--Treaties, etc., 1643-1715 (Louis XIV) 20 July 1697
   1700, Primera Relacion Extraordinaria
Gadbury, John, Ephemerides, 1680
Gage, Thomas
   Neue merckwürdige Reise-Beschreibung Nach Neu Spanien, 1693
   A New Survey of the West-Indies, 1677; 1699
   Nieuwe ende seer naeuwkeurige Reyse, 1682; 1700
   Nouvelle Relation..., 1676
   Nouvelle Relation...Tome I, 1695
   Nouvelle Relation...Tome II, 1694
   Nouvelle Relation...Tome I [-Tome II], 1699
   1678, Derby, Charles Stanley, 8th earl of
   1696, Thévenot, Melchisédech, Relations, 4.ptie.
   1698, The New Atlas
Gallegos, Diego: 1694, Diaz, Diego
Galve, Gaspar de la Cerda Sandoval Silva y Mendoza, conde de, viceroy of Mexico
   1694, Mendez, Francisco
   See also Mexico (Viceroyalty)--Laws, statutes, etc., 1688-1696 (Galve)
Galves, Mathias de: 1697, Avendaño Suares de Sousa, Pedro de
Gama, Antonio de
   1675, Becerra Tanco, Luis
   1685, Becerra Tanco, Luis
Gamboa, Alexandro Brabo de.   See Brabo de Gamboa, Alexandro
Garabito de León y Messía, Francisco: 1687, Valdés, Rodrigo de
García, Francisco
   Vida, y Martyrio..., 1683
   Vida, y Milagros..., 1683; 1685 (2 variants)
Garcilaso de la Vega, el Inca, The Royal Commentaries Of Peru, 1688
Gaspar de San Agustín, Conquistas De Las Islas Philipinas, 1698
Gassendi, Pierre
   1686, Moxon, Joseph
   1699, Moxon, Joseph
Gaztañeta y de Iturribálzaga, Antonio, Norte De La Navegacion, 1692
Gelabert, Martín: 1696, López y Martínez, Juan Luis, marqués del Risco
Gellie, Paul: 1675, Quakerism Canvassed
The General Laws And Liberties Of The Massachusets Colony: 1675, Massachusetts (Colony)--Laws, statutes, etc.
A General Testimony To the Everlasting Truth of God: 1677, Willsford, John
Il Genio Vagante: 1691, Zani, Valerio, conte
George Fox Digg'd out of his Burrovves: 1676, Williams, Roger
Gervaise, Nicolas, La Vie De Saint Martin Evêque De Tours, 1699
Giannettasio, Niccolò Partenio, Piscatoria et Nautica, 1685
Gijsbertz, Reyer: 1696, Thévenot, Melchisédech, Relations, 2.ptie.
Giovanni Antonio da Montecuccolo.   See Cavazzi, Giovanni Antonio
Giovanni da Lucca: 1696, Thévenot, Melchisédech, Relations, 1.ptie.
A Glass For the People of New-England: 1676, Groome, Samuel
Glover, Thomas: 1677, Royal Society of London
Gobeo de Victoria, Pedro.   See Victoria, Pedro Gobeo de
Godínez, Miguel, Practica De La Theologia Mystica, 1690
Godwin, Morgan
   The Negro's & Indians Advocate, 1680
   The Revival..., 1682
   A Supplement To The Negro's & Indian's Advocate, 1681
   Trade preferr'd before Religion, 1685
Gomberville, Marin Le Roy, sieur du Parc et de: 1682, Acuña, Cristóbal de
Gomes de la Parrá, José.   See Gómez de la Parra, José
Gómez, José: 1693, Huélamo, Melchor
Gómez de la Parra, José, Panegyrica Oratio, 1693
Gómez de Quevedo y Villegas, Francisco.   See Quevedo y Villegas, Francisco Gómez de
Gonzales de Olmeda, Balthasar, Sermon, 1680
González de Acuña, Antonio: 1684, Lucchesini, Giovanni Lorenzo
González de la Sancha, Lorenzo Antonio, Villancicos, 1690; 1698
González de Quiroga, Diego, El Nvevo Apostol De Galicia, 1698
González de Rosende, Antonio: 1690, Arnauld, Antoine, Histoire De Dom Jean De Palafox (2 variants)
González de Santalla, Tirso, Oposición Hecha Al Progresso En Las Cavsas..., 1699
González de Valdeosera, Miguel: 1695, Avendaño Suares de Sousa, Pedro de
Goos, Pieter, De Zee-Atlas, 1675
Gorazitu, Francisco de.   See Gorosito, Francisco de
Goris, Johannes: 1681, Grotius, Hugo
Gorosito, Francisco de, Sermon De N. Glorioss.mo Padre San Pedro Nolasco, 1687
Gorospe, Diego: 1690, Octava Maravilla

[452]

Index

Gorospe, Juan de: 1685, Navarro de San Antonio, Bartolomé

Gorospe e Irala, Juan: 1690, Octava Maravilla

Gorráez Vaumont y Navarra, Teovaldo: 1690, Aranda Sidrón, Bartolomé de

Gospel Order Revived, 1700

Gould, Daniel, A brief narration of the sufferings..., 1700

Grammaire De La Langve Des Tartares Moguls ou Mogols: 1696, Thévenot, Melchisédech, Relations, 3.ptie.

The Grand Pyrate: Or, the Life and Death of Capt. George Cusack, 1676

Grant of The Northern Neck in Virginia To Lord Culpepper: 1688, Gt.Brit.--Sovereigns, etc., 1685-1688 (James II) 27 Sept. 1688

Grau y Monfalcón, Juan: 1696, Thévenot, Melchisédech, Relations, 2.ptie.

Graves, Edward
   1679, A Brief Narrative And Deduction...
   1681, Rochefort, Charles de, Histoire Naturelle...

Gravesteyn, C.: 1675, Den Hollandtze Mercurius, 5. Deel

The Great and Popular Objection...: 1688, Penn, William

Gt.Brit.--Court of King's Bench: 1679, Scroggs, Sir William

Gt.Brit.--High Court of Admiralty: 1696, Dawson, Joseph

Gt.Brit.--Commissioners Appointed to Enquire into the Irish Forfeitures, The Report Of The Commissioners, 1700

Gt.Brit.--Laws, statutes, etc.
   An Abstract Of all Such Acts Of Parliament..., 1697
   1699, Church of England

Gt.Brit.--Laws, statutes, etc., 1694-1702 (William III)
   Anno Decimo & Undecimo Gulielmi III..., 1699
   Anno Regni Gulielmi III...[An Act for Laying further Duties upon Sweets], 1699
   Anno Regni Gulielmi III...[An Act for Preventing Frauds], 1696
   Anno Regni Gulielmi III...[An Act for the more effectual Suppression of Piracy], 1700
   Anno Regni Gulielmi III...[An Act to Punish Governors of Plantations], 1700

Gt.Brit.--Parliament--House of Commons, Votes, 1689

Gt.Brit.--Parliament, 1689-1690--House of Commons, Votes, 1689

Gt.Brit.--Parliament, 1689-1690--House of Commons--Speaker, The Speech..., 1689

Gt.Brit.--Parliament, 1690--House of Commons, Votes, 1690

Gt.Brit.--Parliament, 1690-1691--House of Commons, Votes, 1690 (8 Oct. 1690)

Gt.Brit.--Parliament, 1690-1691--House of Lords, Two Several Addresses, 1690

Gt.Brit.--Parliament, 1691-1692--House of Commons, Votes, 1691 (29 Oct. 1691)

Gt.Brit.--Parliament, 1692-1693--House of Commons
   The Address, 1692 (14 Nov. 1692)
   The Address, 1693
   Votes, 1692

Gt.Brit.--Parliament, 1692-1693--House of Lords
   The Address, 1693 (23 Feb. 1692/3)
   Address, 1693 (9 Mar. 1692/3)

Gt.Brit.--Parliament, 1693-1694--House of Commons, Votes, 1694

Gt.Brit.--Parliament, 1694-1695--House of Commons
   The Humble Representation, 1695
   Votes, 1694
   Votes, 1694 (29 Dec. 1694)

Gt.Brit.--Parliament, 1694-1695--House of Lords, The Humble Address, 1695

Gt.Brit.--Parliament, 1695-1696, The Humble Address, 1696

Gt.Brit.--Parliament, 1695-1696--House of Commons
   The Address, 1695 (28 Nov. 1695)
   Votes, 1695 (22 Nov. 1695)

Gt.Brit.--Parliament, 1696-1697--House of Commons
   The Humble Address, 1696 (23 Oct. 1696)
   Votes, 1696

Gt.Brit.--Parliament, 1696-1697--House of Lords, The Humble Address, 1696

Gt.Brit.--Parliament, 1697-1698--House of Commons
   The Humble Address, 1697 (9 Dec. 1697)
   The Humble Address, 1698
   Votes, 1697

Gt.Brit.--Parliament, 1697-1698--House of Lords
   The Humble Address, 1697
   The Humble Address, 1698 (16 Feb. 1698)
   The Humble Address, 1698 (10 June 1698)

Gt.Brit.--Parliament, 1698-1699--House of Commons
   The Humble Address, 1699 (4 Feb. 1699)
   The Humble Address, 1699 (21 Feb. 1699)
   The Humble Address, 1699 (24 Mar. 1699)
   The Humble Address, 1699 (3 Apr. 1699)
   Votes, 1698

Gt.Brit.--Parliament, 1698-1699--House of Lords
   The Humble Address, 1699 (6 Feb. 1699)
   The Humble Address, 1699 (17 Apr. 1699)

Gt.Brit.--Parliament, 1699-1700--House of Commons
   The Humble Address, 1699 (5 Dec. 1699)
   Votes, 1699

Gt.Brit.--Parliament, 1699-1700--House of Lords, The Humble Address, 1700

Gt.Brit.--Privy Council: 1686, Gt.Brit.--Sovereigns, etc., 1685-1688 (James II)

Gt.Brit.--Sovereigns, etc., 1660-1685 (Charles II)
   At the Court at Whitehall, 1683
   La Harangve, 1678 (28 Jan. 1678)
   His Majesties Gracious Speech, 1678 (28 Jan. 1678)

Gt.Brit.--Sovereigns, etc., 1685-1688 (James II)
   At the Court at Whitehall, 1686
   By the King, 1688 (20 Jan. 1688)
   By the King, 1688 (31 Mar. 1688)
   Favoravel declaraçaõ, 1687
   Grant of The Northern Neck, 1688 (27 Sept. 1688)

Gt.Brit.--Sovereigns, etc., 1689-1694 (William and Mary)
   Declaracion De La Guerra, 1689 (7 May 1689)
   His Majesties Most Gracious Speech, 1689 (19 Oct. 1689)
   His Majesties Most Gracious Speech, 1690 (27 Jan. 1689/90)

Gt. Brit.--Sovereigns, etc., 1689-1694 (William and Mary) (continued)
 His Majesties Most Gracious Speech, 1690 (21 Mar. 1689/90)
 His Majesties Most Gracious Speech, 1690 (2 Oct. 1690)
 His Majesties Most Gracious Speech, 1692
 His Majesties Most Gracious Speech, 1693
 A Second Brief, 1690 (18 Feb. 1690)
 Their Majesties Declaration, 1689 (7 May 1689)
Gt.Brit.--Sovereigns, etc., 1694-1702 (William III)
 By the King, 1700 (29 Jan. 1699) [i.e. 1700]
 His Majesties Most Gracious Speech, 1695 (3 May 1695)
 His Majesties Most Gracious Speech, 1695 (23 Nov. 1695)
 His Majesties Most Gracious Speech, 1697
 Proclamation For Apprehending Captains Gavine Hamilton... , 1700 (25 July 1700)
Gt. Brit.--Treaties, etc., 1660-1685 (Charles II)
 Articles Of Peace, 1677
 Several Treaties, 1685; 1686
 1697, France--Treaties, etc., 1643-1715 (Louis XIV), Traité De Paix Entre La France Et L'Angleterre (20 Sept. 1697)
Gt. Brit.--Treaties, etc., 1685-1688 (James II)
 Tractatus Pacis, 1686
 Treaty Of Peace, 1686
 1687, France--Treaties, etc., 1643-1715 (Louis XIV) 16 Nov. 1686
 1689, France--Treaties, etc., 1643-1715 (Louis XIV) 16 Nov. 1686
Gt.Brit.--Treaties, etc., 1689-1694 (William and Mary): 1692, Denmark--Treaties, etc., 1670-1699 (Christian V)
Gt.Brit.--Treaties, etc., 1694-1702 (William III)
 Articles Of Peace, 1697
 1697, Traktaat van Vrede
The Great Earthquake At Quito, 1698
Great Newes From The Barbadoes, 1676
Greaves, John: 1696, Thévenot, Melchisédech, Relations, 1.ptie.
Green, Bartholomew: 1700, The Printers Advertisement
Green, Thomas, Korte Antwoordt... , 1675
Greenhill, William: 1680, Shepard, Thomas
Grey, Ralph: 1699, By the Honourable Sir William Beeston
Grillet, Jean
 A Journal Of The Travels... , 1698
 1682, Acuña, Cristóbal de
Grímsson, Thorlákur: 1688, Landnámabók
The Groans of the Plantations: 1689, Littleton, Edward
Gronovius, Jacobus
 Dissertatio De Origine Romuli, 1684
 Responsio Ad Cavillationes Raphaelis Fabretti, 1684
Groome, Samuel, A Glass For The People, 1676
Grotius, Hugo, Nederlandtsche Jaerboeken, 1681
Guadalaxara, Nicolas: 1684, Florencia, Francisco de
Gualdo Priorato, Galeazzo, conte, Teatro Del Belgio, 1683
Guattini, Michele Angelo: 1687, Carli, Dionigi
Gudenfridi, Giovanni Batista, Replica Alla Risposta Dimostrativa, 1680

Guevara, Gaspar de: 1691, Sigüenza y Góngora, Carlos de
Guevara, Juan de
 1683, Sigüenza y Góngora, Carlos de
 1691, Sigüenza y Góngora, Carlos de
Guillet de Saint-George, Georges, Les Arts De L'Homme D'Epée, 1680
Gurpegui, José de: 1693, Rodrigo de la Cruz, Representacion Jvridica
Gusmão, Alexandre de
 Historia Do Predestinado Peregrino, 1685
 Sermão, 1686
Gutierrez Coronel, Juan: 1682, Villegas, Manuel Juan
Guy, Edward: 1676, Howgill, Francis
Guzmán y Córdova, Sebastián de: 1690, Sigüenza y Góngora, Carlos de
Gysbertz, Reyr. See Gijsbertz, Reyer

H. C. See Curson, Henry
H. L.: 1693, The Truest and Largest Account Of The Late Earthquake
H. S.: 1678, Bradstreet, Anne (Dudley)
H. V. Q. See Quellenburgh, Henrik van
Hack, William, A Collection Of Original Voyages, 1699
Hale, Sir Matthew, The Primitive Origination Of Mankind, 1677
Halley, Edmond: 1675, Seller, John
Hamilton, John. See Belhaven, John Hamilton, 2d baron
Hammond, Lawrence: 1691, To The King's Most Excellent Majesty. The Humble Address of divers of the Gentry
Hansen, Leonhard, Vita Mirabilis... , 1680
Hanson, Francis: 1683, Jamaica--Laws, statutes, etc.
Hanson, Samuel, The Case Of Samuel Hanson, 1684
Happel, Eberhard Werner
 Mundus Mirabilis Tripartitus, 1687
 Thesaurus Exoticorum, 1688
La Harangve Qve Le Roy De La Grand' Bretagne...: 1678, Gt.Brit.--Sovereigns, etc., 1660-1685 (Charles II) 28 Jan. 1678
Harford, Charles: 1681, An Exalted Diotrephes Reprehended
Harris, Benjamin, A Short But Just Account... , 1679
Harris, Walter
 A Defence Of The Scots Abdicating Darien, 1700
 A Short Vindication Of Phil. Scot's Defence, 1700
 1699, The Defence Of The Scots Settlement At Darien, Answer'd
Hartshorne, Richard: 1676, A Further Account Of New Jersey
Hatton, Edward, The Merchant's Magazine, 1697
Havers, Clopton: 1694, Morton, Richard
Hawkins, William: 1696, Thévenot, Melchisédech, Relations, 1.ptie.
Hayward, Nicholas: 1687, Durand,   of Dauphiné
Hazart, Cornelius, Kirchen-Geschichte, 1684
An Health To Caledonia, 1699
Heath,   Dr.: 1692, Ampel en Breed Verhaal... ; A Full Account of the Late Dreadful Earthquake
Hebden, Roger, A Plain Account... , 1700

[454]

Index

Het Hebreus Psalmboeck: 1688, Bible--O.T.--Psalms--Hebrew
Heckel, Johann Friedrich: 1697, Clüver, Philipp
Hedworth, Henry: 1675, Thompson, Thomas, The Quakers Quibbles; Thompson, Thomas, The Second Part Of The Quakers Quibbles; Tompson, Thomas, The Third Part Of The Quakers Quibbles
Heinsius, Nicolaas: 1687, Brandt, Geeraert, Het Leven En Bedryf...
Hendricks, Elizabeth, Quaker, Amsterdam
    Een Algemeene Send-Brief, 1675
    Een Brief Van toegenégentheyd, 1679
Hendricks, Pieter, Quaker, Amsterdam
    Noch een Goede, Getrouwe, en Ernstige Vermaninge, 1676
    Een tedere Groetenisse, 1678
    1679, Spiegel Voor de Stad van Embden
Hennepin, Louis
    Aenmerckelycke Historische Reys-Beschryvinge, 1698
    Beschreibung Der Landschafft Lovisiana, 1689
    Beschryving Van Louisania, 1688
    A Continuation, Of The New Discovery..., 1698 (2 variants); 1699
    Description De La Louisiane, 1683; 1684; 1688
    Descrizione Della Lvigiana, 1686
    Neue Entdeckung, 1699
    Neue Reise-Beschreibung, 1698
    A New Discovery, 1698 (2 variants); 1699
    Nieuwe Ontdekkinge, 1699
    Nouveau Voyage, 1698 (2 variants)
    Nouvelle Decouverte, 1697; 1698
    Relacion De Un Pais, 1699
    1691, Zani, Valerio, conte
Henrix, Elisabeth. See Hendricks, Elizabeth, Quaker, Amsterdam
Henrixsz, Pieter. See Hendricks, Pieter, Quaker, Amsterdam
Herbert, Charles: 1677, Herbert, Sir Thomas
Herbert, George: 1697, Turner, William
Herbert, Sir Thomas, Some Years Travels, 1677
The Heresie and Hatred Which was falsly Charged upon the Innocent: 1693, Keith, George
Herla, Manuel: 1694, El Parnaso Del Real Colegio De San Martin
Hernández de Mendoza, Francisco. See Fernández de Mendoza, Francisco
Herrera, Cipriano de: 1680, Nicoselli, Anastasio
Herries, Walter. See Harris, Walter
Hickeringill, Edmund
    The Black Non-Conformist, 1682
    The Black Non-Conformist...The Second Edition, 1682
    The Naked Truth. The Second Part, 1681
    A Vindication Of The Naked Truth, The Second Part, 1681
Hicks, Thomas
    Three Dialogues, 1679
    1683, Ford, Philip
Higgins, John: 1675, Marshall, Charles
Higginson, John
    Our Dying Saviour's Legacy, 1686
    1698, Noyes, Nicholas

His Majesties Gracious Speech To both Houses of Parliament: 1678, Gt.Brit.--Sovereigns, etc., 1660-1685 (Charles II)
His Majesties Most Gracious Speech To both Houses of Parliament. See Gt.Brit.--Sovereigns, etc., 1689-1694 (William and Mary); Gt.Brit.--Sovereigns, etc., 1694-1702 (William III)
Histoire Abregée De La Naissance...: 1692, Naudé, Philippe
Histoire Ameriqvaine, 1680
Histoire De Dom Jean De Palafox: 1690, Arnauld, Antoine (2 variants)
Histoire De La Conqueste De La Floride, 1685
Histoire De La Guerre De Hollande: 1689, Courtilz, Gatien de, sieur de Sandras
Histoire Des Diables De Loudun: 1694, Aubin, Nicolas
Histoire Dv Mexiqve Par Figvres Expliqvées En Langve Mexicaine: 1696, Thévenot, Melchisédech, Relations, 4.ptie.
Histoire Naturelle Et Morale Des Iles Antilles: 1681, Rochefort, Charles de
Historia General De Las Conqvistas: 1688, Fernández de Piedrahita, Lucas
Historia Navigationis Martini Forbisseri: 1675, Settle, Dionyse
Historia Orbis Terrarum, Geographica Et Civilis: 1692, Becmann, Johann Christoph
An Historical Account Of The Rise and Growth...: 1690, Thomas, Sir Dalby
Historie Der Boecaniers, Of Vrybuyters Van America, 1700
Historie Der Sevarambes: 1682, Vairasse, Denis
The History Of Caledonia, 1699
The History Of The Bucaniers Of America, 1699
Hita, Alonso de, El Regvlo Seraphico San Pedro Regalado, 1696
Hobbes, Thomas, Behemoth, 1679
Hodges, James
    1699, Ferguson, Robert
    1700, Harris, Walter, A Defence Of The Scots Abdicating Darien; Harris, Walter, A Short Vindication Of Phil. Scot's Defence
Hoffmann, Johann: 1686, Prospect Des ganzen Erdkreisses
Holland, Hugh: 1685, Shakespeare, William
Holland, John, A Short Discourse..., 1696
Hollandse Mercurius
    2. Deel, 1678
    5. Deel, 1675
    13. Deel, 1678
    14. Deel, 1679
    25. Deel, 1675
    26. Deel, 1676
    27. Deel, 1677
    29. Deel, 1679
    30. Deel, 1680
    31. Deel, 1681
    32. Deel, 1682
    33. Deel, 1683
    34. Deel, 1684
    35. Deel, 1685

Hollandse Mercurius (continued)
    36. Deel, 1686
    37. Deel, 1687
    38. Deel, 1688
    39. Deel, 1689
    40. Deel, 1690
    41. Deel, 1691
Hollandtze Mercurius. See Hollandse Mercurius
Hollantse Mercurius. See Hollandse Mercurius
Holloway, James, The Free and Voluntary Confession ..., 1684
Holme, Thomas: 1684, Penn, William, Missive...
The Holy Life Of Gregory Lopez: 1675, Losa, Francisco de
Holy Roman Empire--Treaties, etc., 1658-1705 (Leopold I)
    Traité De Paix, 1697
    1697, France--Treaties, etc., 1643-1715 (Louis XIV) 29 Aug. 1696; 7 Oct. 1696
Homwood, Nicholas, A Word Of Counsel, 1675
Hondt, Abraham de: 1698, Dampier, William, Nieuwe Reystogt Rondom De Werreld
Hood, Thomas
    1686, Moxon, Joseph
    1699, Moxon, Joseph
Hooghe, Romein de: 1693, Cartes Marines...
Hooke, William: 1682, Davenport, John
Hooker, Thomas: 1700, The Poor Doubting Christian
Hookes, Ellis
    For The King, 1675
    1676, Howgill, Francis
    1679, Fisher, Samuel, The Testimony Of Truth Exalted
Hoorn, Jan Claez ten
    1678, Exquemelin, Alexandre Olivier
    1699, Zanten, Laurens van
Hopkins, John: 1677, Bible--O.T.--Psalms--English--Paraphrases
Horn, Georg, Orbis Politicus Imperiorum, 1688
Hortensius, Martinus: 1690, Blaeu, Willem Janszoon
Houghton, Thomas, Royal Institutions, 1694
Howard, Luke: 1679, Fisher, Samuel, The Testimony Of Truth Exalted
Howgill, Francis, The Dawnings Of The Gospel-Day, 1676
Hubbard, William
    The Happiness of a People, 1676
    A Narrative Of The Troubles..., 1677
    The Present State Of New-England, 1677 (2 variants)
Huckens, Ester: 1676, A Further Account Of New Jersey
Hudson's Bay Company, The Case Of The Hudson's Bay Company, 1693
Hübner, Johann, Kurtze Fragen, 1698
Huélamo, Melchor, Epitome De Los Misterios De la Missa, 1693
Huet, Pierre Daniel, Bp., Traité De La Situation, 1691
The Humble Address Of the House of Commons
    1696, Gt.Brit.--Parliament, 1696-1697--House of Commons
    1697, Gt.Brit.--Parliament, 1697-1698--House of Commons
    1698, Gt.Brit.--Parliament, 1697-1698--House of Commons
    1699, Gt.Brit.--Parliament, 1698-1699--House of Commons (4 Feb. 1699; 21 Feb. 1699; 24 Mar. 1699; 3 Apr. 1699); Gt.Brit.--Parliament, 1699-1700--House of Commons (5 Dec. 1699)
The Humble Address Of the...Lords
    1695, Gt.Brit.--Parliament, 1694-1695--House of Lords
    1696, Gt.Brit.--Parliament, 1696-1697--House of Lords
    1697, Gt.Brit.--Parliament, 1697-1698--House of Lords
    1698, Gt.Brit.--Parliament, 1697-1698--House of Lords (16 Feb. 1698; 10 June 1698)
    1699, Gt.Brit.--Parliament, 1698-1699--House of Lords (6 Feb. 1699); Gt.Brit.--Parliament, 1698-1699--House of Lords (17 Apr. 1699)
    1700, Gt.Brit.--Parliament, 1699-1700--House of Lords
The Humble Address Of the...Lords...And Commons In Parliament: 1696, Gt.Brit.--Parliament, 1695-1696
The Humble Address Of The Publicans, 1691
The Humble Representation Of The House of Commons To His Majesty: 1695, Gt.Brit.--Parliament, 1694-1695--House of Commons
The Humble Request Of His Majesties Loyal Subjects: 1696, Massachusetts Or The first Planters of New-England
Humfrey, John
    A Letter To George Keith, 1700
    A Paper To William Penn, 1700
Humphreys, Humphrey, Bp. of Bangor: 1690, To our Reverend...Ministers...
Huser, Heinrich: 1678, Amman, Johann Jacob
Hutchinson, Richard, The Warr In New-England, 1677
Hutchinson, Thomas, Forced Uniformity, 1675
Hyde, Thomas
    1690, Bobowski, Albert, afterwards Ali Bey
    1691, Farissol, Abraham

I. B. See Blackwell, Isaac
I. D. L.: 1682, Nieuhof, Johan, Gedenkweerdige Brasiliaense Zee- en Lant-Reize
I. L. M. C. See Lange, Johann, medicinae candidatus
I. P. See Pennington, Isaac
Iarrige, Pierre. See Jarrige, Pierre
Ibáñez de Faria, Diego. See Ybáñez de Faria, Diego
Ibarra, Miguel de, Annvae Relectiones Ac Canonicæ Ivris Explicationes, 1675
Ignazio de Jesus, Carmelite friar: 1696, Thévenot, Melchisedech, Relations, 5.ptie.
In Tumulum...D. Ioannis Cano De Sandoval: 1695, Mexico (City)--Universidad
Informacion Ivridica: 1684, Peguero, Juan
Information Concernant L'Affaire De Darien, 1699
Information For Gaven Plummer, 1698
Informe Ivridico: 1682, Villegas, Manuel Juan

Index

Informe Qve La Real Vniversidad, Y Clavstro Pleno: 1692, Mexico (City)--Universidad
Innocentius XI, Pope. See Catholic Church--Pope, 1676-1689 (Innocentius XI)
Innocentius XII, Pope: 1698, Lampérez y Blázquez, Valentín
Instrvccion, Y Doctrina De Novicios: 1685, Franciscans
Instrvction Des Vents Qvi Se rencontrent...: 1696, Thévenot, Melchisédech, Relations, 5.ptie.
The Interest of England: 1698, Clement, Simon
The Interest Of The Nation, 1691
Isidoro de Jesus María, Maria Sanctissima Victoriosa, 1684
Isidoro de San Miguel. See San Miguel, Isidoro de
Ismā'īl Ibn' Alī ('Imād Al-Dīn Abū Al-Fieta), Prince of Hamāh. See Abū al-Fidā
Issaksz, Herman, Quaker, Vertoog Aan Den Baron de Kinski, 1680
Itinera Mundi: 1691, Farissol, Abraham

J. A.   See Allyn, John
J. A.   See Aysma, Joannes
J. B.   See Burnyeat, John
J. C.   See Claus, Jan
J. C.   See Crull, Jodocus
J. F. V.: 1683, López, Francisco
J. H.   See Holland, John
J. H.   See Humfrey, John
J. M.: 1689, Bailey, John, Man's chief End
J. M.: 1685, Shakespeare, William
J. M.   See Mitchel, Jonathan
J. M. S.: 1685, Shakespeare, William
J. R.   See Rounce, John
J. S.: 1696, Raleigh, Sir Walter
J. S.   See Scottow, Joshua
J. S.   See Sherman, John
J. S.: 1695, Some Account Of The Transactions Of Mr. William Paterson
J. T.   See Tyso, John
J. W.: 1682, A Letter From New-England
J. W.: 1684, Penn, William, Beschreibung...
J. W.   See Willsford, John
Jaillot, Charles Hubert Alexis, Atlas François, 1695
Jamaica--Governor, 1692-1702 (Beeston): 1699, By the Honourable Sir William Beeston
Jamaica--Laws, statutes, etc., The Laws Of Jamaica, 1683; 1684
James II, King of Gt.Brit.. See Gt.Brit.--Sovereigns, etc., 1685-1688 (James II); Gt.Brit.--Treaties, etc., 1685-1688 (James II)
Janeway, James, Mr. James Janeway's Legacy, 1675
Jansen, Reinier: 1679, Stephenson, Marmaduke
Jansz, Henrik, Quaker: 1680, Isaaksz, Herman, Quaker
Jarrige, Pierre, Les Iesvites Mis sur L'Echafavd, 1676
Jaymes Ricardo Villavicencio, Diego. See Villavicencio, Diego Jaime Ricardo

Jenkins, George: 1690, Behn, Aphra (Amis)
Jenkins, Sir Leoline: 1688, A Fifth Collection of Papers
Jenkinson, Anthony: 1696, Thévenot, Melchisédech, Relations, 1.ptie.
Jennings, Samuel, The State of the Case..., 1694
The Jesuites Policy To Suppress Monarchy: 1678, Derby, Charles Stanley, 8th earl of
Jesuits--Spain--Procurador General por las Provincias de Indias, Señor, Manuel Rodriguez..., 1682
Jesús, Ignazio de, Carmelite friar. See Ignazio de Jesús, Carmelite friar
Jesús María, Isidoro de. See Isidoro de Jesús María
Jezebel Withstood, And Her Daughter Anne Docwra, Publickly Reprov'd: 1699, Bugg, Francis
Jiménez Paniagua, Fernando: 1681, Spain--Laws, statutes, etc.
João da Madre de Deus, Abp.: 1686, Gusmão, Alexandre de
João José de Santa Thereza, freire, Istoria Delle Gverre..., 1698
Johnson, Marmaduke: 1682, Pain, Philip
Johnson, Samuel, A Confutation Of a late Pamphlet, 1698
Johnston, Arthur: 1677, Herbert, Sir Thomas
Jones, Cadwallader: 1694, Bulkley, Thomas
Jones, Charles: 1681, An Exalted Díotrephes Reprehended
Jones, D.: 1700, Temple, Sir William, bart.
Jones, Sir Thomas: 1679, Scroggs, Sir William
Jonson, Ben: 1685, Shakespeare, William
Jónsson, Arngrímur, Gronlandia Edur Grænlandz Saga, 1688
Josselyn, John, New-Englands Rarities Discovered, 1675
Journal des sçavans: 1683, VVeekly Memorials For The Ingenious
Juan de la Anunciación, La Inocencia Vindicada, 1694
Juan de la Concepción, fray: 1697, Muñoz de Castro, Pedro
Juan Francisco de Valladolid. See Valladolid, Juan Francisco de
Juana Inés de la Cruz, sister
   Carta Athenagorica, 1690
   Fama, Y Obras Posthumas, 1700
   Poëmas..., 1691
   Segundo Tomo De Las Obras, 1693
   Villancicos, Con Que Se Solemnizaron en la Santa Iglesia, 1691
   Villancicos Qve Se Cantaron En La Santa Iglesia, 1677
   1691, Sigüenza y Góngora, Carlos de
The Judgment Given forth by Twenty Eight Quakers, 1694
Jurieu, Pierre
   1696, Mather, Increase, Ein Brieff von dem Glücklichen Fortgang...
   1699, Mather, Increase, De Successu Evangelii
A Just and Lawful Tryal: 1697, Crisp, Thomas
A Just and Modest Vindication: 1699, Ferguson, Robert
A Just Defence: 1699, Baron, William
Just Measures, In An Epistle: 1692, Penn, William
Justel, Henri: 1684, Recueil De Divers Voyages

[457]

Kaheingh, Zacharias: 1682, Nieuhof, Johan, Zee en Lant-Reize
Keith, George
   An Abstract, By way of Index, 1699
   Account Of A National Church, 1700
   An Account Of The Quakers Politicks, 1700
   The Anti-Christs and Sadduces Detected, 1696
   The Arguments Of The Quakers, 1698
   Arraignment Of Worldly Philosophy, 1694
   The Benefit, Advantage, and Glory..., 1687
   The Causeless Ground, 1694
   The Christian Quaker, 1693
   A Chronological Account..., 1694
   Concerning Prayer, 1687
   The Deism Of William Penn, 1699
   Divine Immediate Revelation, 1684
   An Exact Narrative Of The Proceedings, 1696
   Fourth Narrative, Of His Proceedings, 1700
   The Fundamental Truths, 1688
   A Further Discovery, 1694
   Gross Error and Hypocrisie Detected, 1695
   The Heresie and Hatred, 1693
   Immediate Revelation, 1675; 1676
   More Divisions Amongst The Quakers, 1693
   A Narrative Of the Proceedings..., 1700
   New-England's Spirit of Persecution, 1693
   The Presbyterian and Independent Visible Churches, 1691
   The Pretended Antidoe [sic]..., 1690
   The Pretended Yearly Meeting, 1695
   The Quakers Proved Apostats, 1700
   The Rector Corrected, 1680
   A Seasonable Information, 1694
   A Second Narrative..., 1697
   A Serious Dialogue, 1699
   A Sermon Preach'd at the Parish-Church Of St. Helen's, 1700
   A Sermon Preach'd at Turners-Hall, 1700
   A Sermon Preach'd at Turners-Hall...The Second Edition, 1700
   A Sermon Preached at the Meeting of Protestant Dissenters, 1696
   A Third Narrative..., 1698
   The True Copy of a Paper, 1695
   Truth Advanced, 1694
   Truths Defence, 1682
   The Tryals Of Peter Boss, George Keith..., 1693
   Two Sermons Preach'd at the Parish-Church..., 1700
   Two Sermons Preach'd at the Parish-Church...The Second Edition, 1700
   The Way Cast up, 1677
   The Way To the City of God, 1678 (2 variants)
   1692, Fox, George
   1694, The Judgment Given forth by Twenty eight Quakers; Makemie, Francis
   1696, Croese, Gerard, The General History Of The Quakers
Ketting, P.: 1682, Nieuhof, Johan, Zee en Lant-Reize
Keymer, John: 1696, Raleigh, Sir Walter

Kick, Abraham: 1689, Mather Increase, A Brief Relation...
Kilmore, Edward, Bp. of. See Wetenhall, Edward, Bp. of Kilmore and Ardagh
Kino, Eusebio Francisco, Exposicion Astronomica De El Cometa, 1681
Kirchmayer, Georg Kaspar, De Atlantide ad Timæum, 1685
Knorz, Andreas: 1686, Prospect Des ganzen Erdkreisses
Know all Men by these presents, 1695
Kohlhans, Tobias Ludwig, Dilucidationes quædam valde necessariæ, 1696
Kort Berättelse om Wäst Indien, 1675
Een kort Bericht Van de Provintie ofte Landschap Penn-Sylvania, 1681
Kort En Opregt Verhaal..., 1683
Korte, Beknopte, en Nette Beschryving..., 1687
Kramer, Matthias: 1681, Bos, Lambert van den, Leben und Tapffere Thaten...
Kristnisaga, Christendoms Saga, 1688
Kurtze Erzehlung Von dem Anfange und Fortgange Der Schiffahrt, 1676
Ein kurtzer Discours von Der Schiff-Fahrt: 1676, Moxon, Joseph
Kuyper, Frans: 1676, Sonnemans, Arent

L. H. See Hammond, Lawrence
Labbé, Philippe: 1689, Clemente, Claudio
La Borde, sieur de: 1684, Recueil De Divers Voyages
La Croix Chevrières de Saint Vallier, Jean Baptiste de, Bp. of Quebec. See Saint Vallier, Jean Baptiste de la Croix Chevrières de, Bp. of Quebec
La Grue, Thomas: 1686, Ross, Alexander
La Guette, S. de Broë, seigneur de Citry et de. See Broë, S. de, seigneur de Citry et de La Guette
La Guilletière, sieur de. See Guillet de Saint-George, Georges
Lagúnez, Matías, Memorial, 1686
La Martinière, Pierre Martin de
   Herrn Martiniere Neue Reise, 1675
   De Noordsche Weereld, 1685
   Voyage Des Pays Septentrionavx, 1676
   1691, Zani, Valerio, conte
La Maurinière. See La Morinière, de
Lamberti, Arcangelo: 1696, Thévenot, Melchisédech, Relations, 1.ptie.
La Morinière, de: 1696, Thévenot, Melchisédech, Relations, 1.ptie.
Lampérez y Blázquez, Valentín, Disciplina Vetvs Ecclesiastica, 1698
Lancaster, James: 1700, Atkinson, Christopher
Landnámabók, Sagan Landnama, 1688
Lange, Johann, medicinae candidatus
   1675, La Martinière, Pierre Martin de
   1676, Barba, Alvaro Alonso, Das Andere Buch von der Kunst der Metallen; Barba, Alvaro Alonso, Eines Spanischen Priesters und hocherfahrnen Naturkündigers Berg-Büchlein

Index

Langen, Jean Georg: 1699, Hennepin, Louis, Neue Entdeckung
Langhorn, Thomas: 1676, Howgill, Francis
La Peyrère, Isaac de
   Ausführliche Beschreibung... , 1679
   Nauwkeurige Beschrijvingh... , 1678
   1691, Zani, Valerio, conte
Lara, Miguel de Crasto: 1699, Mattos, Francisco de
Lascari de Torres, Antonio, Sermon A La Celebridad ... , 1683
Lasher, Josh: 1694, Morton, Richard
Lasso de la Vega, Garcia, el Inca. See Garcilaso de la Vega, el Inca
Lawrence, Sir Thomas
   1696, Bray, Thomas, Proposals For the Incouragement and Promoting of Religion
   1697, Bray, Thomas, Bibliotheca Parochialis; Bray, Thomas, Proposals For the Incouragement and Promoting of Religion (2 variants)
The Laws Of Barbados: 1699, Barbados--Laws, statutes, etc.
The Laws Of Jamaica
   1683, Jamaica--Laws, statutes, etc.
   1684, Jamaica--Laws, statutes, etc.
Lawson, Deodat: 1693, A Further Account Of The Tryals Of The New-England Witches
Laythes, Thomas: 1690, Some Testimonies Concerning the Life...
Lazarte, Miguel de: 1684, Bravo Davila y Cartagena, Juan
Lea, Philip
   An Alphabet Of Africa, 1687
   An Alphabet of America, 1687
   An Alphabet of Asia, 1687
   An Alphabet of Europe, 1687
   1699, Moxon, Joseph
Leam, Bartholomeu de: 1686, Araujo, Antonio de
Leben und Tapffere Thaten der aller-berühmtesten See-Helden: 1681, Bos, Lambert van den
Leben und Thaten Der Durchläuchtigsten See-Helden: 1681, Bos, Lambert van den
Le Clercq, Chrétien
   Etablissement De La Foy, 1691
   Nouvelle Relation De La Gaspesie, 1691
   1697, Hennepin, Louis, Nouvelle Decouverte
   1698, Hennepin, Louis, Aenmerckelycke Historische Reys-Beschryvinge; Hennepin, Louis, Neue Reise-Beschreibung; Hennepin, Louis, Nouveau Voyage (2 variants); Hennepin, Louis, Nouvelle Decouverte
   1699, Hennepin, Louis, Neue Entdeckung; Hennepin, Louis, Nieuwe Ontdekkinge; Hennepin, Louis, Relacion De Un Pais
Lectiones Tertii Nocturni Recitandae In Festo Vnivs Martyris Non Pontificis: 1677, Catholic Church--Liturgy and ritual--Special offices--Felipe de Jesús, Saint
Leddra, William: 1700, Gould, Daniel
Ledesma, Clemente de
   Compendio Del Despertador De Noticias, 1695

   Despertador Republicano, 1699
   Dispertador De Noticias De Los Santos Sacramentos, 1695
   Vida Espiritval... , 1689
Ledesma, José, Silvos, 1683
Ledesma, Joseph de, El Fiscal Del Consejo, 1694
Ledra, William. See Leddra, William
Lee, Samuel
   [Chara Tez Pizeoz] The Joy of Faith, 1687
   Contemplations On Mortality, 1698
   Ecclesia Gemens, 1677
   [Eleothriambos] Or the Triumph of Mercy, 1677
   [Epeisagma] Or A Superaddition, 1677
   1677, Fletcher, Giles
Leeds, Peregrine Osborne, 2d duke of, A Journal Of The Brest-Expedition, 1694
Leeven en Daden Der Doorluchtighste Zee-Helden
   1675, Bos, Lambert van den
   1683, Bos, Lambert van den
Le Gobien, Charles, Histoire Des Isles Marianes, 1700
Leiba, Diego de
   Vida De El Venerable Padre Fr. Diego Romero, [Mexico] 1684; [Seville?] 1684
   Virtvdes, y Milagros... , 1687
Leibniz, Gottfried Wilhelm, freiherr von, Relatio Ad Inclytam Societatem Leopoldinam Naturae Curiosorum, 1696
Leiva, Diego de. See Leiba, Diego de
Lemaire, Jacques Joseph, Les Voyages Du Sieur Le Maire, 1695
Lemus, Diego de, Vida, Virtudes, Trabajos... , 1683
León, Antonio de, Bp.: 1688, Arequipa, Peru (Diocese)--Synod
León Pinelo, Antonio Rodríguez de: 1681, Spain--Laws, statutes, etc.
León y Becerra, Antonio de. See León, Antonio de, Bp.
Leopold I, Emperor of Germany
   Copia De La Promesa, 1685
   A Letter Written by the Emperor, 1689
   See also Holy Roman Empire--Treaties, etc., 1658-1705 (Leopold I)
Leopoldinisch-Carolinische deutsche Akademie der Naturforscher: 1696, Leibniz, Gottfried Wilhelm, freiherr von
Le Roux, Valentin: 1691, Le Clercq, Chrétien, Etablissement De La Foy
Leslie, Charles
   A Defence Of A Book, 1700
   A Discourse Proving The Divine Institution, 1697
   Primitive Heresie Revived, 1698
   Satan Dis-Rob'd From his Disguise, 1697; 1698
   The Snake in the Grass, 1696; 1698
   Some Seasonable Reflections Upon The Quakers Solemn Protestation Against George Keith's Proceedings, 1697
   Some Seasonable Reflections Upon The Quakers Solemn Protestation Against the Proceedings... , 1697
Leslie, John: 1675, Quakerism Canvassed

Index

Le Tellier, Michel
    Defensa De Los Nvevos Christianos, 1690
    Defense Des Nouveaux Chrestiens, 1687
A Letter Directed to the Right Honourable The Earl of Perth: 1700, Melfort, John Drummond, 1st earl of
A Letter From A Gentleman in America, 1699
A Letter From A Gentleman in the Country, 1696
A Letter From A Gentleman Of The City of New-York, 1698
A Letter From a Member of the Parliament of Scotland, 1696
A Letter From a Minister, 1688
A Letter from Jamaica, 1682
A Letter From New-England, 1682
A Letter, From The Commission, Of The General Assembly, Of The Church Of Scotland; Met at Glasgow, 1699
Letter From The Commission Of The General Assembly Of The Church of Scotland To The Honourable Council: 1699, Church of Scotland--General Assembly--Commission
A Letter, giving A Description Of The Isthmus Of Darian, 1699
A Letter of Advice To The Churches Of The Non-conformists: 1700, Mather, Cotton
A Letter To A Member of Parliament Concerning the Bank Of Scotland, 1696
A Letter To A Member of Parliament In the Country, 1700
A Letter To George Keith, 1696
A Letter To George Keith: 1700, Humfrey, John
A Letter To Mr Penn: With His Answer: 1688, Popple, Sir William (2 variants)
A Letter To S C. M., 1700
A Letter Written by the Emperor: 1689, Leopold I, Emperor of Germany
Lettres Patentes Ou Octroi...: 1697, Scotland--Laws, statutes, etc., 1694-1702 (William III)
Lettres Patentes. Pour L'Etablissement...: 1698, France--Sovereigns, etc., 1643-1715 (Louis XIV)
Leusden, Johannes
    1688, Bible--O.T.--Psalms--Hebrew--1688, The Book of Psalmes; Bible--O.T.--Psalms--Hebrew--1688, Het Hebreus Psalmboeck; Bible--O.T.--Psalms--Hebrew--1688, Liber Psalmorum
    1696, Mather, Increase, Ein Brieff von dem Glücklichen Fortgang...
    1699, Mather, Increase, De Successu Evangelii
Le Vasseur, Guillaume. See Beauplan, Guillaume Le Vasseur, sieur de
Leverett, John: 1700, Gospel Order Revived
Lewis, James: 1696, Dawson, Joseph
Leyba, Diego de. See Leiba, Diego de
Lezamis, José de, Breve Relacion de la Vida..., 1699
Lezcano y Sepulbeda, Gerónimo: 1695, Calderón, Pedro
Liber Psalmorum. Editus A Johanne Leusden: 1688, Bible--O.T.--Psalms--Hebrew
The Life & Death, Travels And Sufferings..., 1688
The Life Of St. Mary Magdalene Of Pazzi: 1687, Puccini, Vincenzio
The Life Of the Valiant & Learned Sir Walter Raleigh: 1677, Shirley, John

A Light Shining out of Darkness: 1699, Stubbs, Henry, 1632-1676
Ligon, Richard: 1684, Recueil De Divers Voyages
Lillo y la Barrera, Nicolás de, Sermon En La Procession, 1698
Lima--Colegio Real de San Martín: 1694, El Parnaso Del Real Colegio De San Martin
Lima (Ecclesiastical province), Concilia Limana, 1684
Lima y Escalada, Ambrosio de, Espicilegio De la calidad..., 1692
Liñan y Cisneros, Melchor, Abp., Ofensa, Y Defensa..., 1685
Linch, Sir Thomas. See Lynch, Sir Thomas
Lisperguer y Solís, Matías, Sermon Panegirico En La Pvblicacion Solemne..., 1699
A List Of The Subscribers To The Company of Scotland: 1696, Company of Scotland Trading to Africa and the Indies
Literæ Patentes Seu Concessus: 1695, Scotland--Laws, statutes, etc., 1694-1702 (William III) 26 June 1695
Lithobolia: Or, The Stone-Throwing Devil: 1698, Chamberlayne, Richard
Littlebury, Isaac: 1698, Ludlow, Edmund
Littleton, Edward, The Groans..., 1689
La Liturgie, C'est à dire, Le Formulaire des Prieres Publiques: 1683, Church of England--Book of Common Prayer--French
Llopis, José: 1691, Solís y Rivadeneyra, Antonio de, Historia De La Conqvista De Mexico
Lloyd, William, Bp. of Worcester: 1690, To our Reverend...Ministers
Loaysa y Agurto, Joseph de. See Agurto y Loaysa, Joseph de
Lobo, Jeronymo
    1684, Recueil De Divers Voyages
    1696, Thévenot, Melchisédech, Relations, 4.ptie.
Loccensius, Joannes: 1680, Thorsteins saga Vikingssonar
Locke, John
    An Essay Concerning Humane Understanding, 1694
    Two Treatises Of Government, 1698
Lockhart, George, A Further Account..., 1683
Loddington, William, Plantation Work, 1682
Lodwick, Charles: 1693, Bayard, Nicholas
Londaiz, Pedro: 1693, Rodrigo de la Cruz
London--Aldermen: 1690, The Case of the Lord Mayor
London--Corporation--Court of Common Council: 1690, To The Honourable The Knights
London--Lord Mayor: 1690, The Case of the Lord Mayor
London--Royal Society. See Royal Society of London
López, Francisco
    Copia De Carta, 1691
    Gemino Lvminari Toleto, 1685
    Noticias Del Sur, 1685
    Noticias Del Svr Continvadas, 1688
    Sermon En La Honoracion..., 1684
    Sermon Panegirico, 1683
    Vltimas Noticias Del Svr, 1688
    1682, López y Martínez, Juan Luis, marqués del Ris-

[460]

co, De Examine Symboli Politici
    1688, Relaçam Do Exemplar Castigo; Relacion Del Exemplar Castigo
López, Gregorio, Vida, Y Escritos..., 1678
López, Juan Luis. See López y Martínez, Juan Luis, marqués del Risco
López de Aguilar, Gregorio: 1691, Alloza, Juan de
López de Avilés, José: 1698, Narváez, Juan de
López de Cogolludo, Diego, Historia De Yucathan, 1688
López de Sigüenza, Gabriel: 1700, Sigüenza y Góngora, Carlos de
López Rosa, Duarte
    1681, Exquemelin, Alexandre Olivier, Piratas De La America
    1682, Exquemelin, Alexandre Olivier, Piratas De La America (2 variants)
López y Martínez, Juan Luis, marqués del Risco
    De Examine Symboli Politici, 1682
    Defensa Real, Y Sagrada..., 1696
    Discurso Ivridico, 1685
    Discvrso Legal, 1685
    Parecer Del Doctor Don Ivan Lvis Lopez, 1682
    Testimonio..., 1683
    1682, Peru (Viceroyalty)--Real Audiencia
    1683, López, Francisco; Peru (Viceroyalty)--Auditor General de la Gente de Mar y Guerra
Lorme, Jean Louis de: 1698, Casas, Bartolomé de las, Bp. of Chiapa
Losa, Francisco de, The Holy Life..., 1675
Louis XIV, King of France. See France--Laws, statutes, etc., 1643-1715 (Louis XIV); France--Sovereigns, etc., 1643-1715 (Louis XIV); France--Treaties, etc., 1643-1715 (Louis XIV)
Loumans, Lodewijk, Beatvs Dominicvs, 1695
Love, John, Geodæsia: Or, The Art Of Surveying, 1688
A Loving & Friendly Invitation: 1683, Taylor, John
Loza, Francisco de. See Losa, Francisco de
Lubin, Augustin: 1678, Scheffer, Johannes
Lucca, Giovanni da. See Giovanni da Lucca
Lucchesini, Giovanni Lorenzo, La Vie De Sainte Rose, 1684
Lucero, Lorenzo. See Luzero, Juan Lorenzo
Ludlow, Edmund
    Memoirs...In Two Volumes, 1698
    Memoirs...The Third and Last Part, 1699
Luís de la Presentación, brother: 1692, Andrés de San Agustín
Lumbier, Raimundo, Destierro De Ignorancias Fragmento Aureo, 1694
Luna y Arellano, Carlos de: 1690, Aranda Sidrón, Bartolomé de
Lussan, Raveneau de. See Raveneau de Lussan, -----
Luther, Martin, Catechismus, 1696
Luyts, Jan, Introductio Ad Geographiam, 1692
Lvz De Verdades Catholicas Y Explicacion De La Doctrina Christiana: 1691, Martínez de la Parra, Juan
Luzero, Juan Lorenzo: 1682, Copia De Dos Cartas Escritas De Vn Missionero
Luzuriaga, Juan de, Paranympho Celeste Historia, 1686; 1690
Lynch, Sir Thomas
    1683, A Narrative Of Affairs...
    1684, Jamaica--Laws, statutes, etc.
Lyttleton, Edward. See Littleton, Edward

M.C.D.D.E.M.: 1698, Dellon, Gabriel
El M. D. Fr. Payo De Ribera...Por Quanto en conformidad: 1677, Mexico (Viceroyalty)--Laws, statutes, etc., 1673-1680 (Enríquez de Ribera)
El M. D. Fr. Payo de Ribera...Por Quanto los dueños: 1677, Mexico (Viceroyalty)--Laws, statutes, etc., 1673-1680 (Enríquez de Ribera)
M. G. See Godwin, Morgan
M. J. See Johnson, Marmaduke
M. N. N.: 1679, Pyrard, François
M. S. See Sylvester, Matthew
Mabbe, James: 1685, Shakespeare, William
MacQuare, Robert
    1675, Rutherford, Samuel
    1678, Brown, John
Magalotti, Lorenzo
    Viaggio Del P. Giovanni Grveber: 1696, Thévenot, Melchisédech, Relations, 4.ptie.
    Voyage A La Chine: 1696, Thévenot, Melchisédech, Relations, 4.ptie.
Mainwaring, Sir Henry: 1699, Smith, John
Major, Johann Daniel, D. Johann-Daniel Majors See-Farth, 1683
Makemie, Francis, An Answer To George Keith's Libel, 1694
Malavista, Carlo: 1693, Coronelli, Vincenzo
Mallet, Alain Manesson
    Description De L'Univers, 1683
    Description De L'Univers...Tome Cinqvième, 1686
Mamiani della Rovere, Lodovico Vincenzo
    Arte De Grammatica Da Lingua Brasilica, 1699
    Catecismo Da Doutrina Christãa, 1698
Mamusse Wunneetupanatamwe...: 1685, Bible--Massachuset--Eliot
Manesson Mallet, Alain. See Mallet, Alain Manesson
Manitowompae Pomanta moonk...: 1685, Bayly, Lewis, Bp. of Bangor
Manso, Pedro: 1691, Ramírez de Vargas, Alonso
Manual De Administrar Los Santos Sacramentos à los Españoles, y Naturales: 1697, Catholic Church--Liturgy and ritual--Ritual
Manual De Administrar Los Santos Sacramentos de la Eucharistia, y Extremavncion: 1697, Catholic Church--Liturgy and ritual--Ritual
Manual de Los Santos Sacramentos Conforme Al Ritual De Pavlo V: 1691, Catholic Church--Liturgy and ritual--Ritual
Manval De los Santos Sacramentos en el Idioma de Michuacan: 1690, Catholic Church--Liturgy and ritual--Ritual
Manuel, Francisco. See Mello, Francisco Manuel de
Manwaring, Sir Henry. See Mainwaring, Sir Henry
Marchal, Charles. See Marshall, Charles
Marchetti, Pietro Maria: 1679, Ortelius, Abraham
María de la Antigua, madre, Estaciones De La Passion Del Señor, 1684

Mariana, Juan de, The General History Of Spain, 1699
Marie de l'Incarnation, mère
    L'Ecole Sainte, 1684
    Lettres, 1681
    Retraites, 1682
Marín, Juan: 1695, Marín, Matías
Marín, Matías, Apologia, 1695
Marín Falconi, Juan: 1684, Santoyo, Felipe de
Marius, John, Advice Concerning Bills, 1700
Mármol Carvajal, Luis del: 1700, Suite Du Neptune Francois
Marquette, Jacques
    1681, Thévenot, Melchisédech
    1689, Hennepin, Louis
Marradon, Bartolomeo: 1685, Dufour, Philippe Sylvestre, Tractatvs Novi; Dufour, Philippe Sylvestre, Traitez Nouveaux
Marshall, Charles, Een Boodschap Van Den Heere..., 1675
Martens, Friedrich
    Spitzbergische oder Groenlandische Reise Beschreibung, 1675
    Viaggio Di Spizberga O'Grolanda, 1680
    Viaggio Di Spizberga O'Gronlanda, 1680
    1685, La Martinière, Pierre Martin de
    1691, Zani, Valerio, conte
    1694, An Account Of Several Late Voyages & Discoveries
Martin, Claude
    La Vie De La Venerable Mere Marie De L'Incarnation, 1677; 1696
    1681, Marie de l'Incarnation, mère
    1682, Marie de l'Incarnation, mère
    1684, Marie de l'Incarnation, mère
Martindall, Anne: 1680, A Relation Of The Labour...
Martínez de Aibar, Ignacio: 1688, Fernández de Piedrahita, Lucas
Martínez de Araujo, Juan: 1690, Catholic Church--Liturgy and ritual--Ritual
Martínez de la Parra, Juan
    Lvz De Verdades Catholicas, 1691
    Memoria Agradecida, 1698
    Oracion Fvnebre, 1696
    Sermon Panegyrico, 1690
Martínez de la Puente, José, Compendio De Las Historias..., 1681
Martínez de Ripalda, Gerónimo. See Ripalda, Gerónimo de
Martínez de Ripalda, Juan, Señor. Jvan Martinez de Ripalda...Dize, que aviendo presentado, 1692
Martini, Martino: 1696, Thévenot, Melchisédech, Relations, 3.ptie.
Marvell, Andrew, Advice to a Painter, 1679
Mary II, Queen of Gt. Brit. See Gt. Brit.--Sovereigns, etc., 1689-1694 (William and Mary)
Maryland (Colony)--Charters, The Charter, 1679; 1685
Masa, Pedro de Chaves, Llantos Funebres, 1699
Mason, John: 1677, Mather, Increase, A Relation Of the Troubles

Massachusetts (Colony)--Convention, 24 May 1689, At a Convention..., 1689
Massachusetts (Colony)--Council, 1675
    1675, The Present State Of New-England (2 variants)
    1676, A farther Brief and True Narration; The Present State Of New-England
Massachusetts (Colony)--Governor, 1699-1700 (Richard Coote, 1st earl of Bellomont): 1699, By the Honourable Sir William Beeston
Massachusetts (Colony)--Laws, statutes, etc.
    Acts And Laws, 1699
    Anno Regni Regis Gulielmi III...Acts and Laws, 1700 (29 May 1700)
    Anno Regni Regis Gulielmi III. Acts and Laws, 1700 (31 May 1699 - 13 Mar. 1700)
    The General Laws And Liberties, 1675
Massachusetts Or The first Planters of New-England, 1696
Mastrilli, Marcello Francesco: 1696, Thévenot, Melchisédech, Relations, 2.ptie.
Mather, Cotton
    Balsamum Vulnerarium ex Scriptura, 1692
    Batteries upon the Kingdom of the Devil, 1695
    Blessed Union, 1692
    Brontologia Sacra, 1695
    The Call Of The Gospel, 1686
    The Christian Thank-Offering, 1696
    A Companion for Communicants, 1690
    Durable Riches, 1695
    Early Piety, 1689
    Ecclesiastes, 1697
    The Faith of the Fathers, 1699
    A Family Well-Ordered, 1699
    A Good Man making a Good End, 1698
    Johannes in Eremo, 1695
    Late Memorable Providences, 1691
    A Letter of Advice To The Churches Of The Non-conformists, 1700
    The Life and Death Of The Renown'd Mr. John Eliot, 1691
    The Life and Death Of the Reverend Mr. John Eliot, 1694
    Memorable Providences, 1689; 1697
    A Midnight Cry, 1692
    Ornaments for the Daughters of Zion, 1692
    Pietas in Patriam, 1697
    Piscator Evangelicus, 1695
    Present from a farr Countrey, 1698
    The Present State Of New-England, 1690
    The Principles of the Protestant Religion Maintained, 1690
    The Resolved Christian, 1700
    The Serviceable Man, 1690
    Seven Select Lectures, 1695
    Several Sermons, 1689
    The Short History of New-England, 1694
    Souldiers Counselled, 1689
    Speedy Repentance urged, 1690
    Things for a Distress'd People to think upon, 1696
    Things to be Look'd for, 1691

Index

A Token, for the Children of New-England, 1700
The Triumphs of the Reformed Religion, 1691
A Warning to the Flocks, 1700
The Way to Prosperity, 1690
The Wonderful Works of God, 1690
The Wonders of the Invisible World: Being an Account of the Tryals Of Several VVitches, 1693
The Wonders of the Invisible World: Being an Account of the Tryals Of Several Witches...The Second Edition, 1693
The Wonders of the Invisible World. Observations As well Historical as Theological, 1693
Work upon the Ark, 1689
1689, Byfield, Nathaniel, An Account Of The Late Revolution In New-England (2 ed.)
1690, A Vindication Of Nevv-England
1693, A True Account Of The Tryals, Examinations...
1697, Turner, William
1698, Belcher, Joseph
1699, Cambridge, Massachusetts--Ministers' Association
1700, Calef, Robert; The Printers Advertisement

Mather, Increase
   Angelographia, 1696
   A Brief Account..., 1691
   A Brief History Of The VVarr..., 1676 (2 variants)
   A Brief Relation..., 1689
   Ein Brieff von dem Glücklichen Fortgang..., 1696
   A Call from Heaven, 1679; 1685
   Cases of Conscience Concerning Evil Spirits, 1693
   David Serving His Generation, 1698
   De Successu Evangelij, 1688; 1699
   Diatriba De Signo Filii Hominis, 1682
   A Discourse Concerning the Danger..., 1679; 1685
   A Discourse Concerning the Subject of Baptisme, 1675
   The Divine Right, 1680
   The Doctrine Of Divine Providence, 1684
   An Earnest Exhortation, 1676
   An Essay For The Recording Of Illustrious Providences, 1684
   The First Principles, 1675
   The Great Blessing, 1693
   Heaven's Alarm, 1682
   An Historical Discourse..., 1677
   [Kometographia] Or A Discourse Concerning Comets, 1683
   The Mystery Of Christ, 1686 (2 variants)
   A Narrative Of the Miseries, 1688
   The Necessity Of Reformation, 1679
   New-England Vindicated, 1689
   The Order of the Gospel, Boston, 1700; London, 1700
   Practical Truths, 1682
   Pray for the Rising Generation, 1679; 1685
   A Relation Of The Troubles..., 1677
   Returning unto God, 1680
   A Sermon Occasioned by the Execution..., 1686
   A Sermon (Preached at the Lecture in Boston), 1685
   A Sermon Wherein is shewed..., 1682
   Solemn Advice To Young Men, 1695
   The Surest way to the Greatest Honour, 1699
   A Testimony Against several Prophane and Superstitious Customs, 1687
   The Wicked mans Portion, 1675
   1680, Congregational Churches in Massachusetts--Boston Synod
   1681, Willard, Samuel, Ne Sutor ultra Crepidam
   1683, Torrey, Samuel
   1684, Corbet, John
   1689, A Sixth Collection of Papers Relating to the Present Juncture of Affairs in England
   1690, A Vindication of Nevv-England
   1691, Mather, Cotton, The Life and Death...; Mather, Cotton, The Triumphs of the Reformed Religion; Rawson, Edward
   1693, Willard, Samuel, The Doctrine Of The Covenant
   1694, Mather, Cotton, The Life and Death...
   1695, Cambridge, Massachusetts--Ministers' Association; Mather, Cotton, Johannes in Eremo; Mayhew, Matthew
   1697, Mather, Cotton, Ecclesiastes; Turner, William
   1700, Willard, Samuel, The Peril Of The Times Displayed

Mather, Nathaniel
   A Discussion Of the Lawfulness..., 1698
   The Righteousness of God, 1694
   A Sermon Wherein Is Shewed..., 1684
   1683, Mather, Samuel
   1695, Mather, Cotton, Batteries upon the Kingdom of the Devil; Mather, Cotton, Seven Select Lectures; Mayhew, Matthew
   1696, Scripture Proof For Singing of Scripture Psalms
   1697, Mather, Cotton, Pietas in Patriam

Mather, Richard: 1680, Congregational Churches in Massachusetts--Cambridge Synod

Mather, Samuel
   The Figures Or Types, 1683
   1689, Mather, Cotton, Early Piety

Matías de San Juan Bautista
   Compendio De Las Maravillas De La Gracia, 1698
   1691, Ramírez de Vargas, Alonso

Matos Fragoso, Juan de: 1682, Cubero Sebastián, Pedro

Mattos, Francisco de, Sermam Do Grande Patriarcha S. Ignacio, 1699

Maule, Thomas
   Nevv-England Pesecutors [sic]..., 1697
   Truth held Forth, 1695

Maurice, Henry, The Antithelemite, 1685
May, William: 1696, Dawson, Joseph
Mayhew, Matthew, The Conquests and Triumphs Of Grace, 1695
Mead, Matthew: 1689, Mather, Cotton, Early Piety
The Measure Of The Earth: 1688, Picard, Jean
Mechanick Exercises...the Art of Bricklayers-Works: 1700, Moxon, James
Mechanick Exercises...The Art of Joynery: 1694, Moxon, Joseph
Mechanick Exercises...the Art of Turning: 1694, Moxon, Joseph

Med. Ferrariensis. See Nigrisoli, Francesco Maria
Medina, Antonio de: 1694, Diaz, Diego
Medina, Baltasar de
　Chronica De La Santa Provincia De San Diego, 1682
　Vida, Martyrio, Y Beatificacion..., 1683
Medina Picazo, Buenaventura: 1690, Aranda Sidrón, Bartolomé de
Meekeren, Johan van, De Tovery Zonder Tovery, 1696
Meese, Henry: 1682, Calvert, Philip
Mela, Pomponius, Libri Tres De Situ Orbis, 1700
Meléndez, Juan
　Tesoros Verdaderos, 1681
　1688, Fernández de Piedrahita, Lucas
Melfort, John Drummond, 1st earl of, A Letter Directed to the Right Honourable The Earl of Perth, 1700
Mello, Francisco Manuel de, Epanaphoras, 1676
Melton, Edward, Zeldzaame en Gedenkwaardige Zee- en Land-Reizen, 1681
Membré, Zénobe: 1691, Le Clercq, Chrétien, Etablissement De La Foy
Memoire Pour le Commerce des Isles Philipines: 1696, Thévenot, Melchisédech, Relations, 2.ptie.
Memoires Relating to the State Of The Royal Navy: 1690, Pepys, Samuel (2 variants)
A Memorial Given in to the Senate of the City of Hamburgh, 1697 (2 variants)
Memorial To The Members of Parliament, 1700
Mendez, Francisco, Fvnebres Ecos Con Que Responde A Las Vozes..., 1694
Méndez, Luis: 1691, Ramírez de Vargas, Alonso
Mendieta, Alonso de: 1676, Córdoba y Salinas, Diego de
Mendoza, Juan de
　Impression Mysteriosa, 1686
　Sermon De La Milagrosa Aparicion..., 1685
　Virtvd Jviziosa, 1686
Mendoza, Lorenzo de: 1685, Florencia, Francisco de
Mendoza Ayala, Juan de. See Mendoza, Juan de
Menocchio, Giovanni. See Giovanni da Lucca
Mentzel, Christian, Index Nominum Plantarum Universalis, 1682
Mercator, Gerardus
　1695, Ptolemaeus, Claudius
　1698, Ptolemaeus, Claudius
Mercure de France--Extraordinaire, n.18: 1678, Gt. Brit.--Sovereigns, etc., 1660-1685 (Charles II), La Harangve (28 Jan. 1678)
Mercure de France--Extraordinaire, n.19: 1678, Relation De La Prise Des Isles de Gorée
Mercure Galant, 1678; 1690
Meriton, Henry: 1699, Beckham, Edward
Meriton, John, An Antidote Against the Venom of Quakerism, 1699
Merlo, Nicolás, Espejo De Indvlgencias, 1686
Methold, William: 1696, Thévenot, Melchisédech, Relations, 1.ptie.
Meulen, Jean van der, Señor. En virtud del caracter..., 1698
Mexico (City)--Santa Catarina Mártir (Church): 1686, Merlo, Nicolás
Mexico (City)--Santa Vera Cruz (Church)--Archicofradía del Santísimo Sacramento: 1699, Confraternity of the Blessed Sacrament
Mexico (City)--Universidad
　Informe Qve La Real Vniversidad..., 1692
　Panegyricos Fvnebres, 1695
Mexico (Viceroyalty)--Laws, statutes, etc., 1673-1680 (Enríquez de Ribera)
　El M.D.Fr.Payo De Ribera...Por Quanto en conformidad..., 1677
　El M.D.Fr.Payo de Ribera...Por Quanto los dueños..., 1677
Mexico (Viceroyalty)--Laws, statutes, etc., 1688-1696 (Galve)
　Don Gaspar de Sandoval..., 1689 (1 Nov. 1689)
　Don Gaspar de Sandoval..., 1689 (12 Nov. 1689)
　Don Gaspar de Sandoval..., 1690
　Sirva esta, 1689 (12 Nov. 1689)
Mey, Adrianus de
　1696, Mather, Increase, Ein Brieff von dem Glücklichen Fortgang...
　1699, Mather, Increase, De Successu Evangelii
Michon, Pierre: 1675, Redi, Francesco, Epistola Ad Aliquas Oppositiones factas...
Mico, John: 1700, The Printers Advertisement
Middelen en motiven...: 1687, Muys van Holy, Nicolaas
Miege, Guy, A New Cosmography, 1682
Miguel, Vicente José: 1689, Clemente, Claudio
Millan de Poblete, Juan, Sermon Qve A la solemne, annual, y titular fiesta..., 1695
Milton, John: 1685, Shakespeare, William
Minot, Jacques, De La Nature, Et Des Causes De La Fièvre, 1691
Miracles Of Art and Nature: 1678, Crouch, Nathaniel
Miranda, Juan de: 1697, Sáenz, José
Miranda, Juan José de
　Explicacion De Los Passos de la Passion, 1697
　Practica De Asistir A Los Sentenciados à muerte, 1696
Miranda Villaizan, Antonio de
　Elogio Fvneral A la immortal memoria..., 1694
　1698, Castilla, Miguel de
Miro, Juan Bautista: 1693, Catholic Church in Spain--Councils
Miscellaneous Letters, Giving an Account of the Works Of The Learned... For the Month of December, 1695...first Volume, 1696
Mispilivar, Bernardo de, Sagrado Arbitrio, 1679
Mrs. Judith Hull: 1695, Sewall, Samuel
Mr. Keith No Presbyterian nor Quaker, 1696
Mitchel, Jonathan
　A Discourse Of The Glory..., 1677
　1695, Shepard, Thomas
Mocquet, Jean
　Travels And Voyages, 1696
　Wunderbare Jedoch Gründlich- und warhaffte Geschichte, 1688
A Model For Erecting a Bank, 1688
The Model Of The Government: 1685, Scot, George
A Modest Account From Pensylvania: 1696, Pusey, Caleb
Molina, Alonso de, Doctrina Christiana, 1675
Molloy, Charles, De Jure Maritimo, 1688

Monatliche Unterredungen Einiger Guten Freunde..., 1693
Monclova, Melchor Portocarrero Lasso de la Vega, conde de la. See Portocarrero Lasso de la Vega, Melchor, conde de la Monclova
Monginot, François de: 1687, Nigrisoli, Francesco Maria
Monpleinchamp, Chrysostomus de: 1700, Fernández de Medrano, Sebastián
Montalvo, Francisco Antonio de
    Breve Teatro, 1683
    El Sol Del Nvevo Mvndo, 1683
    Vida Admirable..., 1683
    1684, Lima (Ecclesiastical province)
Montanus, Arnoldus: 1681, Melton, Edward
Montauban, ---- de
    Relation Du Voyage, 1698
    A Relation Of A Voyage, 1698
    1698, Raveneau de Lussan, ----
    1699, The History Of The Bucaniers Of America
    1700, Historie Der Boecaniers, Of Vrybuyters Van America
Montecuccolo, Giovanni Antonio da. See Cavazzi, Giovanni Antonio
Montemayor y Córdova de Cuenca, Juan Francisco de
    Pastor Bonus, 1676
    1677, Spain--Laws, statutes, etc.
Montero y Aguila, Diego, Bp.: 1685, Liñán y Cisneros, Melchor, Abp.
Montoro, José
    Sermon, Qve En La Dedicacion De La Capilla..., 1685
    1689, Sariñana y Cuenca, Isidro
Moody, Joshua
    An Exhortation..., 1686
    A Practical Discourse..., 1685
    1690, Mather, Cotton, The Principles of the Protestant Religion Maintained
    1691, Mather, Cotton, Late Memorable Providences
    1697, Mather, Cotton, Late Memorable Providences
Moonen, Arnold: 1687, Brandt, Geeraert, Het Leven En Bedryf...
The Moores Baffled: 1681, Addison, Lancelot
Mora y Cuéllar, José de
    1683, Sigüenza y Góngora, Carlos de
    1698, Castilla, Miguel de
Moral Instructions Of A Father To His Son, 1683
Morale Pratique des Jesuites, t.4.: 1690, Arnauld, Antoine, Histoire De Dom Jean De Palafox (2 variants)
Morales Negrete, Joachim de: 1698, Lillo y la Barrera, Nicolás de
Morales Pastrana, Antonio: 1691, Sigüenza y Góngora, Carlos de
Mordecai Farissol, Abraham ben. See Farissol, Abraham
Morden, Robert
    Atlas Terrestris, 1690
    Geography Rectified, 1680; 1688; 1693; 1700
More, Caleb, shipmaster: 1677, Hutchinson, Richard
More, Nicholas, A Letter From Doctor More, 1687

Moro, Alessandro: 1675, Redi, Francesco, Epistola Ad Aliquas Oppositiones...
Morton, Charles
    The Spirit Of Man, 1693
    1690, A Vindication of Nevv-England
    1691, The Humble Address Of The Publicans; Mather, Cotton, Late Memorable Providences
    1697, Mather, Cotton, Memorable Providences
Morton, Richard
    [Pyretologia] Pars Altera, 1694
    [Pyretologia] Seu Exercitationes De Morbis Universalibus Acutis, 1692
Morvan de Bellegarde, Jean Baptiste. See Bellegarde, Jean Baptiste Morvan de
Mota, Aleixo da: 1696, Thévenot, Melchisédech, Relations, 1.ptie.; Thévenot, Melchisédech, Relations, 2.ptie.
Motivos Piadosos: 1693, Catholic Church--Liturgy and ritual
Motta, Aleixo da. See Mota, Aleixo da
Moxon, James, Mechanick Exercises...the Art of Bricklayers-Works, 1700
Moxon, Joseph
    Ein kurtzer Discours..., 1676
    Mechanick Exercises...[v.1], 1694
    Mechanick Exercises...the Art of House-Carpentry, 1694
    Mechanick Exercises...The Art of Joynery, 1694
    mechanick Exercises...the Art of Turning, 1694
    A Tutor To Astronomy, 1686; 1699
    1700, Moxon, James
Moyle, Walter: 1697, Xenophon
Mucklow, William, A Bemoaning Letter Of An Ingenious Quaker, 1700
Müller, Andreas. See Muller, Andreas, secretarius
Müller, Wilhelm Johann, Africanische Reissbeschreibung, 1677
Muhammad IV, Sultan of Turkey: 1688, Fox, George
Muller, Andreas, secretarius, Vervolg Van 't Verwerd Europa, 1688
Mun, Thomas: 1700, Marius, John
Muñoz de Castro, Pedro
    Descripcion De La Solemne Venida, 1685
    Exaltacion Magnifica De La Betlemitica Rosa, 1697
    Sermon Del Glorioso Patriarcha San Joseph, 1696
    1698, Narváez, Juan de
Murga, Francisco de: 1686, Avila Juan de
Mutio, Giovanni Battista: 1687, Carli, Dionigi
Muys van Holy, Nicolaas, Middelen en motiven..., 1687

N. C. See Crouch, Nathaniel
N. H.: 1678, Bradstreet, Anne (Dudley)
N. N.: 1676, Pertinente Beschrijvinge Van Guiana
N. S. See Saltonstall, Nathaniel
Een naauw-keurigh ondersoek: 1675, Crisp, Stephen
Eine Nachricht wegen der Landschaft Pennsilvania: 1681, Penn, William
Nader Informatie en Bericht..., 1686
Nader Informatie of Onderrechtinge...: 1686, Penn, William

Naironi, Antonio Fausto: 1685, Dufour, Philippe Sylvestre, Tractatvs Novi; Dufour, Philippe Sylvestre, Traitez Nouveaux
The Naked Truth. The Second Part: 1681, Hickeringill, Edmund
Nalson, John
   Foxes And Firebrands, 1682 (2 variants)
   Toleration and Liberty, 1685
Narbrough, Sir John: 1694, An Account Of Several Late Voyages & Discoveries
A Narrative Of Affairs..., 1683
A Narrative Of the Miseries of New-England: 1688, Mather, Increase
A Narrative Of The Planting of the Massachusets Colony: 1694, Scottow, Joshua
A Narrative Of The Proceedings Of Sir Edmond Androsse: 1691, Stoughton, William
Narváez, Juan de
   Sermon En La Solemnidad..., 1699
   Sermon Fvnebre, Manifiesto Dolor..., 1698
   Sermon Panegyrico, De El Dia Octavo..., 1691
   Sermon Qve En La Celebridad..., 1694
   Sermon Qve En La Oposicion..., 1699
   1691, Ramírez de Vargas, Alonso
   1697, Muñoz de Castro, Pedro
The Natural History Of Coffee, 1682
Naudé, Philippe, Histoire Abregée..., 1692
Nauwkeurige Beschrijvingh Van Groenland: 1678, La Payrère, Isaac de
Navarra y Rocafull, Melchor, duque de la Palata. See Peru (Viceroyalty)--Laws, statutes, etc., 1681-1689 (Navarra y Rocafull); Peru (Viceroyalty)--Viceroy, 1681-1689 (Navarra y Rocafull)
Navarrete, Nicolas de: 1694, Aguirre, Pedro Antonio de
Navarro de San Antonio, Bartolomé, Evangelico Panegiris, 1685
Navilepaine, Henry. See Payne, Henry Neville
Néau, Elie: 1698, Mather, Cotton, Present from a farr Countrey
The Necessity Of Reformation: 1679, Mather, Increase
Nederlandsche Oost-Indische Compagnie
   1676, Schouten, Wouter
   1696, Thévenot, Melchisédech, Relations, 3.ptie.
Nederlandsche West-Indische Compagnie, Articul-Brief, 1675
Negri, Francesco: 1691, Zani, Valerio, conte
Neonomianism Unmask'd. Part III: 1693, Chauncy, Isaac
Le Neptune François, Ou Atlas Nouveau Des Cartes Marines, 1693
   1693, Cartes Marines
   1700, Suite Du Neptune Francois
Nesbitt, John: 1693, Chauncy, Isaac, Neonomianism Unmask'd. Part III
Netherlands (United Provinces, 1581-1795)--Staten Generaal
   Conditien, 1675
   Extracten uyt het Register, 1675
   Octroy Ofte fondamentele Conditien, 1682
   Een Vertoogh van de considerabele Colonie, 1676
   1676, Pertinente Beschrijvinge Van Guiana
   1689, Copia van't Octroy
Netherlands (United Provinces, 1581-1795)--Treaties, etc.
   1685, Gt.Brit.--Treaties, etc., 1660-1685 (Charles II)
   1686, Gt.Brit.--Treaties, etc., 1660-1685 (Charles II)
   1692, Denmark--Treaties, etc., 1670-1699 (Christian V)
   1697, France--Treaties, etc., 1643-1715 (Louis XIV), Tractaet Van De Vreede (20 Sept. 1697); France--Treaties, etc., 1643-1715 (Louis XIV) 21 Sept. 1697; Traktaat van Vrede
Netherlands West Indies Company. See Nederlandsche West-Indische Compagnie
A New and Further Narrative Of the State of New-England, 1676
The New Atlas, 1698
Nevv-England Pesecutors [sic]...: 1697, Maule, Thomas
New-England Vindicated, From the Unjust Aspersions: 1689, Mather, Increase
New-England's Faction Discovered, 1690
New-England's Present Sufferings: 1675, Wharton, Edward
New-Englands Tears For Her Present Miseries: 1676, Tompson, Benjamin
New York (Colony)--Governor, 1692-1697 (Benjamin Fletcher): 1693, An Account Of Several Passages; Bayard, Nicholas
New York (Colony)--Governor, 1697-1701 (Richard Coote, 1st earl of Bellomont): 1699, By the Honourable Sir William Beeston
News From New-England, 1676
Nicolás de la Trinidad, Sermon A S. Antonio De Padua, 1691
Nicolson, William: 1681, The English Atlas
Nicoselli, Anastasio, Vita Del Beato Toribio Alfonso Mogrobesio, 1680
Nidelberg, Ambrosius: 1675, Kort Berättelse om Wäst Indien; Schouten, Joost
Nieremberg, Juan Euocbio: 1689, Clemente, Claudio
Nieuhof, Hendrik: 1682, Nieuhof, Johan, Gedenkwaerdige Zee en Lantreize
Nieuhof, Johan
   Gedenkwaerdige Zee en Lantreize, 1682
   Gedenkweerdige Brasiliaense Zee- en Lant-Reize, 1682
   Zee en Lant-Reize, 1682
   1685, Dufour, Philippe Sylvestre, Tractatvs Novi; Dufour, Philippe Sylvestre, Traitez Nouveaux
   1696, Thévenot, Melchisédech, Relations, 1.ptie.; Thévenot, Melchisédech, Relations, 3.ptie.
De nieuwe Hollantse Mercurius... Het Act-en-twintigste Deel, 1678
Nigrisoli, Francesco Maria, Febris China Chinæ Expvgnata, 1687
A Ninth Collection of Papers Relating to the Present Juncture of Affairs in England, 1689

Norfolk clergymen: 1699, Beckham, Edward
Noriega, José de, Sermon Panegirico, 1685
Noronha Freire, João de. See João José de Santa Thereza, freire
Norton, John
    1678, Bradstreet, Anne (Dudley)
    1694, Scottow, Joshua
    1696, Baxter, Richard
Notice Et Justification... , 1681
Noticia, E Ivstificaçam... , 1681
Noticias Del Sur: 1685, López, Francisco
Noticias Del Svr Continvadas: 1688, López, Francisco
Notitia Conciliorvm Hispaniae: 1686, Catholic Church in Spain--Councils
Nouvelle Relation de la Caroline, 1685
Nouvelles De L'Amerique, Ou Le Mercure Ameriquain, 1678
Nowell, Samuel, Abraham in Arms, 1678
Noyes, Nicholas, New-Englands Duty and Interest, 1698
Núñez de la Peña, Juan: 1691, Zani, Valerio, conte
Núñez de la Vega, Francisco, Bp.: 1692, Villavicencio, Diego Jaime Ricardo
Núñez de Miranda, Antonio
    Sermon De Santa Teresa De Iesvs, 1678
    1691, Ramírez de Vargas, Alonso
Núñez de Roxas, Miguel, Memorial Informe Jvridico, 1700
Nylandt, Petrus, Den Verstandigen Hovenier, 1677

Oakes, Urian
    The Soveraign Efficacy, 1682
    1680, Mather, Increase, The Divine Right
Ockanickon, Indian chief
    A True Account... , 1682; 1683
    1686, Budd, Thomas
Octava Maravilla, 1690
Octroy Ofte fondamentele Conditien: 1682, Netherlands (United Provinces, 1581-1795)--Staten Generaal
An Ode Made On The Welcome News... , 1699
Oexmelin, Alexandre Olivier. See Exquemelin, Alexandre Olivier
Officivm Beatissimæ Virginis Mariæ De Mercede Redemptionis Captivorum
    1680, Catholic Church--Liturgy and ritual--Officium Beatissimae Virginis Mariae de Mercede Redemptionis Captivorum
    1686, Catholic Church--Liturgy and ritual--Officium Beatissimae Virginis Mariae de Mercede Redemptionis Captivorum
Officivm In Festo B. Ferdinandi Tertij Regis Castellæ: 1677, Catholic Church--Liturgy and ritual--Special offices--Fernando III, Saint
Officivm S. Margaritæ Scotorvm Reginæ: 1680, Catholic Church--Liturgy and ritual--Special offices--Margaret of Scotland, Saint
Officivm S. Francisci Borgiæ: 1685, Catholic Church--Liturgy and ritual--Special offices--Francisco de Borja, Saint

Officium Sancti Gabrielis Archangeli: 1685, Catholic Church--Liturgy and ritual--Special offices--Gabriel, Archangel
Officivm. Sancti Patritij Hiberniæ Episcopi: 1686, Catholic Church--Liturgy and ritual--Special offices--Patrick, Saint
Officivm Septem Dolorvm B. Mariæ Virginis: 1685, Catholic Church--Liturgy and ritual--Officium de Septem Doloribus Beatae Mariae Virginis
Ogilby, John
    1683, Lockhart, George
    1684, Carolina Described more fully then [sic] heretofore
Old Planters. See Scottow, Joshua
Oldenburg, Henry: 1677, Royal Society of London
Olivares, José de, Oracion Panegyrica, 1683
Olivas, Martin de: 1695, Mexico (City)--Universidad
Oliver y Fullana, Nicolás de
    1688, Fernández de Medrano, Sebastián, Breve Descripcion Del Mvndo, 8°; 12°
    1693, Fernández de Medrano, Sebastián, Breve Descripcion Del Mvndo
Olmo, José Vicente del, Nveva Descripcion Del Orbe De La Tierra, 1681
One Wonder more, Added to the Seven Wonders of the World, 1700
O'Neil, Hues, sieur de Beaulieu: 1676, Gage, Thomas
Oposición Hecha Al Progresso...: 1699, González de Santalla, Tirso
Ordenanzas Del Consejo Real De Las Indias: 1681, Spain--Consejo de las Indias
Ordóñez de Ceballos, Pedro, Historia, Y Viage Del Mundo, 1691
Ordonnance De Louis XIV
    1681, France--Laws, statutes, etc., 1643-1715 (Louis XIV)
    1682, France--Laws, statutes, etc., 1643-1715 (Louis XIV)
Ordonnance Du Roy: 1699, France--Laws, statutes, etc., 1643-1715 (Louis XIV)
The Original Papers And Letters: 1700, Company of Scotland Trading to Africa and the Indies
Ortega, Miguel de: 1698, Castilla, Miguel de
Ortelius, Abraham, Theatro Del Mondo, 1679
Ortigas, Manuel: 1683, Ledesma, José
Ortiz, Francisco Antonio, Sermon Qve Predicó... , 1689
Ortiz, Lorenzo, Origen, Y Institvto De La Compañia De Iesvs, 1679
Ortiz de Salzedo, Francisco, Curia Eclesiastica, 1691
Ortiz de Zúñiga, Diego, Annales Eclesiasticos, 1677
Osborne, Peregrine Hyde, 2d duke of Leeds. See Leeds, Peregrine Osborne, 2d duke of
Osera y Estella, José Miguel, El Fisico Christiano, 1690
Osorio y Peralta, Diego, Principia Medicinæ, 1685
Otondo y Antillón, Isidro
    1685, Verbiest, Ferdinand
    1686, A Relation Of The Invasion...
Oudaan, Joachim: 1687, Brandt, Geeraert, Het Leven En Bedryf...

Our Antient Testimony Renewed: 1695, Friends, Society of--Philadelphia Yearly Meeting
Overton, John: 1687, Lea, Philip, An Alphabet Of Africa; Lea, Philip, An Alphabet of America; Lea, Philip, An Alphabet of Asia; Lea, Philip, An Alphabet of Europe
Overtures Offered to the Parliament: 1700, Fletcher, Andrew
Ovidius Naso, Publius: 1683, Tryon, Thomas
Owen, John: 1694, Scottow, Joshua

P. A.   See Ayres, Philip
P. C.   See Philo-Caledon
P. H.   See Hendricks, Pieter, Quaker, Amsterdam
P.P.V.S.
   1683, Kort En Opregt Verhaal...
   1684, De Seldsaame en Noit Gehoorde Wal-Vis-Vangst
P. V.D.B.   See Burg, Pieter van der
Pacheco de Silva, Francisco
   1687, Ripalda, Gerónimo de
   1689, Ripalda, Gerónimo de
Pain, Philip, Daily Meditations, 1682
Paine, Henry Neville.   See Payne, Henry Neville
Paiva, Sebastião da Fonseca e, Relaçam Da Feliz Chegada, 1687
Palafox y Mendoza, Juan de, Bp.
   Cartas Del V. Siervo De Dios, 1700
   Peregrinacion De Philotea, 1683
   Vida Interior, 1682; 1687; 1691
   1690, Arnauld, Antoine, Histoire De Dom Jean De Palafox (2 variants)
   1691, Zani, Valerio, conte
   1696, Thévenot, Melchisédech, Relations, 4.ptie.
   1699, González de Santalla, Tirso
Palata, Melchor de Navarra y Rocafull, duque de la. See Navarra y Rocafull, Melchor, duque de la Palata
Palavicino y Villarrasa, Francisco Javier, Sermon Panegyrico, 1691
Palma y Messa, Christval de: 1698, Castilla, Miguel de
Palmer, John, An Impartial Account..., 1690
Pane, Ramón, brother
   1676, Colón, Fernando
   1678, Colón, Fernando
   1681, Colón, Fernando
   1685, Colón, Fernando
Panegyricos Fvnebres Del Illmo. Señor Doctor D. Jvan Cano Sandoval: 1695, Mexico (City)--Universidad
A Paper To William Penn: 1700, Humfrey, John
Papin, Denis: 1692, Boyle, Hon. Robert
A Paraphrase Upon The Books Of Ecclesiastes: 1685, Bible--O.T.--Ecclesiastes--English--Paraphrases
Pardo y Aguiar, Diego: 1682, Vidal Figueroa, José
Paris--Académie des Sciences.   See Académie des Sciences, Paris
El Parnaso Del Real Colegio De San Martin, 1694
Parraga, Gabriel de: 1690, Le Tellier, Michel
Partenio, Niccolò Giannettasio.   See Giannettasio, Niccolò Partenio

Paschall, Thomas
   An Abstract of a Letter, 1683
   1684, Penn, William, Beschreibung...; Penn, William, Missive...; Penn, William, Recüeil...
   1700, Pastorius, Francis Daniel
Passerone, Lodovico, Gvida Geografica, 1681
The Pastor And The Prelate: 1692, Calderwood, David
Pastorius, Francis Daniel, Umständige Geographische Beschreibung, 1700
Pastorius, Melchior Adam: 1700, Pastorius, Francis Daniel
Paterson, William
   An Abstract Of A Letter, 1699
   1695, Some Considerations upon the late Act
Patrick, Simon, Bp. of Ely: 1685, Bible--O.T.--Ecclesiastes--English--Paraphrases; Bible--O.T.--Song of Solomon--English--Paraphrases
Payne, Henry Neville
   A Coppy of the pretended Letter, 1693
   Navil Payn's Letter, And Some Other Letters, 1693
   To His Grace William Duke of Hamilton, 1693
   Unto His Grace, The Earl Of Marchmont, 1698
Peake, Thomas: 1684, Carolina Described more fully then [sic] heretofore
Pederick, Roger: 1676, A Further Account Of New Jersey
Pedro II, King of Portugal.   See Portugal--Treaties, etc., 1668-1706 (Pedro II)
Pedroche, Cristóbal, Breve, Y Compendiosa Relacion..., 1684
Pedrosa, Juan de la: 1698, Ramírez, José
Peers, Richard: 1681, The English Atlas
Peeters, Johannes, L'Atlas En Abregé, 1692
Peguero, Juan, Informacion..., 1684
Pellicer y Velasco, Manuel de
   1688, Fernández de Medrano, Sebastián, Breve Descripcion Del Mvndo 8°; 12°
   1693, Fernández de Medrano, Sebastián, Breve Descripcion Del Mvndo
Pelsaert, Francisco: 1696, Thévenot, Melchisédech, Relations, 1.ptie.; Thévenot, Melchisédech, Relations, 2.ptie.
Pemberton, Ebenezer: 1700, Gospel Order Revived
Peña, Pedro de la, Signo Evcharistico, 1685
Peña Montenegro, Alonso de la, Bp., Itinerario Para Parochos De Indios, 1678; 1698
Pene, Charles: 1693, Le Neptune François
Penington, Edward, Some Brief Observations..., 1696
Penington, Isaac: 1680, Rogers, William, The Third Part Of The Christian-Quaker
Penington, John
   An Apostate Exposed, 1695
   The People Called Quakers, 1696
Penn, William
   An Account Of The Blessed End Of Gulielma Maria Penn, 1699
   An Address To Protestants, 1679
   Beschreibung Der...Provinz Pensylvanien, 1684
   A Brief Account Of The Province of Pennsilvania, 1682
   A Brief Account Of The Rise and Progress..., 1695
   A Brief Answer..., 1678

Index

A Brief Examination... , 1681
Caution Humbly Offer'd, 1698
The Christian-Quaker, 1699
The Continued Cry, 1675
A Defence Of a Paper, 1698
A Defence Of The Duke of Buckingham's Book, 1685
A Discourse Of The General Rule Of Faith and Practice, 1699
Englands Great Interest, 1679
England's Present Interest, 1675 (2 variants)
An Epistle, Containing A Salutation, 1682
The Frame of the Government, 1682
A Further Account... , 1685 (2 variants)
The Great and Popular Objection, 1688
Just Measures, 1692
Een kort Bericht... , 1681
A Letter...To...The Free Society of Traders', 1683
Missive...aan...de Vrye Societeyt der Handelaars, 1684
Eine Nachricht wegen der Landschaft Pennsilvania, 1681
Nader Informatie... , 1686
A Perswasive To Moderation, 1686
The Quaker A Christian, 1698
Reader, The Intention of this Map... , 1681
Recüeil...Concernant La Pensylvanie, 1684
The Skirmisher Defeated, 1676
Some Account... , 1681
The Speech Of William Penn To His Majesty, 1687
A Third Letter, 1687
Three Letters, 1688
To The Churches Of Jesus, 1677
A Treatise Of Oaths, 1675
Tweede Bericht... , 1686
De Waarheyt Ontdekt, 1675
1675, Thompson, Thomas, The Quakers Quibbles
1679, Fisher, Samuel, The Testimony Of Truth Exalted
1682, Loddington, William
1683, Ford, Philip
1685, A Defence Of The Duke of Buckingham; The Quakers Elegy
1687, More, Nicholas
1688, Popple, Sir William, A Letter To Mr. Penn (2 variants)
1689, Popple, Sir William, Een Brief Van een Zeker Heer...
1691, Burnyeat, John
1694, Fox, George
1698, Davenant, Charles, Discourses On The Publick Revenues; Keith, George, A Third Narrative... ; Story, Thomas
1699, Stubbs, Henry, 1632-1676
1700, Pastorius, Francis Daniel

Pennecuik, Alexander, Caledonia Triumphans, 1699
Pennington, Isaac: 1675, Marshall, Charles
Pennsylvania--Free Society of Traders. See Free Society of Traders in Pennsylvania
The Pensilvanian. See Penn, William
The People of Scotland's Groans, 1700
Pepys, Samuel, Memoires, 1690 (2 variants)

Peralta, Antonio de: 1691, Sigüenza y Góngora, Carlos de
Peregrino, Bernardino: 1699, González de Santalla, Tirso
Pereira, Francisco: 1686, Gusmão, Alexandre de
Pereira Brandaõ, Francisco: 1699, Portugal--Conselho da Fazenda
Pérez, Jacinto: 1690, Octava Maravilla
Pérez de Gálvez, Miguel: 1700, Sigüenza y Góngora, Carlos de
Pérez de Guzmán, Juan: 1684, Ayres, Philip
Pérez de Montora, José: 1691, Juana Inés de la Cruz, sister, Poëmas
Pérez Landero Otañez y Castro, Pedro, Practica De Visitas, 1696
Pérez y Turcios, Bernabé: 1689, Ledesma, Clemente de
A Perfect List: 1696, Company of Scotland Trading to Africa and the Indies
Peritsol, Abraham. See Farissol, Abraham
Perkins, William, The Foundation of Christian Religion, 1682
Perrault, Charles, Les Hommes Illustres, 1698
Perrot d'Ablancourt, Nicolas: 1700, Suite Du Neptune Francois
Person of honor. See Derby, Charles Stanley, 8th earl of
A Perswasive To Moderation To Church Dissenters: 1686, Penn, William
Perth, James Drummond, 4th earl of: 1700, Melfort, John Drummond, 1st earl of
Pertinent en Waarachtig Verhaal... , 1689
Pertinente Beschrijvinge Van Guiana, 1676
Peru (Viceroyalty)--Auditor General de la Gente de Mar y Guerra, Consvlta Del Avditor General, 1683
Peru (Viceroyalty)--Laws, statutes, etc.
Tomo Primero De Las Ordenanzas, 1685
1675, Escalona y Agüero, Gaspar de
Peru (Viceroyalty)--Laws, statutes, etc., 1681-1689 (Navarra y Rocafull)
Aranzel, 1687
Don Melchor De Navarra, y Rocafull...Por quanto su Magestad...considerando el desorden... , 1683
Don Melchor de Nauarra y Rocafull...Por quanto su Magestad...por su Real Cedula... , 1682 (13 May 1682)
Don Melchor de Nauarra y Rocafull...Por quanto vno de los efectos... , 1682 (13 May 1682)
1685, López y Martínez, Juan Luis, marqués del Risco, Discurso Ivridico
Peru (Viceroyalty)--Laws, statutes, etc., 1689-1705 (Portocarrero)
Don Melchor Portocarrero Lasso de la Vega...Por aver dado forma su Magestad... , 1695
Don Melchor Portocarrero Lasso de la Vega...Por Aver Hallado, 1692 (27 Apr. 1692)
Don Melchor Portocarrero, Laso De La Vega...Por quanto su Magestad... , 1698
El Excmo. Señor Conde De La Monclova...En Despacho, 1692 (19 July 1692)
Peru (Viceroyalty)--Real Audiencia, Decission De La Real Avdiencia, 1682

INDEX

Peru (Viceroyalty)--Real Audiencia--Alcalde del Crimen
    1682, López y Martínez, Juan Luis, marqués del Risco, Parecer Del Doctor Don Ivan Lvis Lopez
    1683, López y Martínez, Juan Luis, marqués del Risco, Testimonio De La Sentencia...
Peru (Viceroyalty)--Viceroy, 1681-1689 (Navarra y Rocafull), Despachos, Y Cartas, 1685
Petit, Pierre
    De Amazonibus Dissertatio, 1687
    De Natura & Moribus Anthropophagorum Dissertatio, 1688
Petiver, James
    1682, VVeekly Memorials For The Ingenious
    1683, VVeekly Memorials For The Ingenious
Petrei, Juan Francisco, Causas Eficientes, Y Accidentales..., 1694
Peys, Adriaan, Reinout In Het Betoverde Hof, 1697
Pfeiffer, August, Pansophia Mosaica, 1685
Phil. Scot. See Harris, Walter
Philadelphian Society, Ursachen und Gründe..., 1698
Philalethes. See Kohlhans, Tobias Ludwig
Philalethes: 1700, Mather, Cotton, A Letter of Advice To The Churches Of The Non-conformists
Philalethes. See Maule, Thomas
Philanglus. See Penn, William
Philanthropus: 1687, Franck, Richard
Philirenes. See Nalson, John
Philo-Britan: 1699, The Defence Of The Scots Settlement At Darien Answer'd
Philo-Caledon: 1699, Belhaven, John Hamilton, 2d baron, A Defence Of The Scots Settlement At Darien 4º; 8º (4 variants)
Philo-Caledon: 1699, Fletcher, Andrew
Philo-Caledonius: 1700, Foyer, Archibald
Philo-Dicaios: 1681, The Triumphs Of Justice
Philonax Verax: 1696, A Letter From a Member of the Parliament of Scotland
Philosophical Transactions: Giving Some Accompt...:
    1677, Royal Society of London
Philotheos Physiologus. See Tryon, Thomas
Phylotea de la Cruz. See Fernández de Santa Cruz y Sahagún, Manuel, Bp.
Picard, Jean, The Measure Of The Earth, 1688
Picazo de Hinojosa, Isabel: 1690, Aranda Sidrón, Bartolomé de
Pietas in Patriam: 1697, Mather, Cotton
Pinder, Richard: 1676, Howgill, Francis
Piratas De La America
    1681, Exquemelin, Alexandre Olivier
    1682, Exquemelin, Alexandre Olivier (2 variants)
Pithin, William: 1694, Their Majesties Colony Of Connecticut
Pitman, Henry, A Relation Of The Great Sufferings, 1689
Pitt, Moses: 1681, The English Atlas
Plan pour former un Establissement, 1686
Plant, Thomas: 1693, The English Spira
Plantagenet, Beauchamp: 1681, An Abstract, Or Abbreviation...
Plantation Work The Work Of This Generation: 1682, Loddington, William

A Platform Of Church-Discipline: 1680, Congregational Churches in Massachusetts--Cambridge Synod
Plaza, Simón: 1682, López y Martínez, Juan Luis, marqués del Risco, De Examine Symboli Politici
Plumier, Charles, Description Des Plantes, 1693
Plummer, Gavin: 1698, Information For Gaven Plummer
Poeme De Six Religievses Ursulines, 1682
Poincy, Louis de: 1681, Rochefort, Charles de, Histoire Naturelle
Pointis, Jean Bernard Louis Desjean, baron de
    An Account Of the Taking of Carthagena, 1698
    Relation De L'Expedition De Carthagene, 1698
Poll, Lucas van de: 1692, Luyts, Jan
Pompa funebre: 1691, Ramírez de Vargas, Alonso
Ponce de León, Nicolás, Historia De La Singvlar Vida..., 1686
Ponte, Ioaõ Baptista da, Queyxas Da Fermosura, 1699
Ponze de León, Nicolás. See Ponce de León, Nicolás
Poole, Matthew: 1697, Turner, William
Popple, Sir William
    Een Brief..., 1689
    A Letter To Mr. Penn, 1688 (2 variants)
Por Don Diego Rodillo De Arce: 1700, Ximénez Pantoja, Thomas
Por Doña Ysabel Picaso De Ynojosa: 1690, Aranda Sidrón, Bartolomé de
Por El Doctor Don Jvan De la Rea Zurbano: 1694, Alcedo Sotomayor, Carlos de
Por El Venerable Dean, Y Cavildo: 1688, Riofrío, Bernardo de
Porcacchi, Tommaso, L'Isole, 1686
Porras, José de: 1697, Muñoz de Castro, Pedro
Portillo, Nicolás: 1681, Santoyo, Felipe de
Portocarrero Lasso de la Vega, Melchor, conde de la Monclova. See Peru (Viceroyalty)--Laws, statutes, etc., 1689-1705 (Portocarrero)
The Portraiture Of Mr. George Keith, 1700
Portugal, Pedro Manuel Colón de. See Colón de Portugal, Pedro Manual, duque de Veragua
Portugal--Conselho da Fazenda, Contrato Do Paço Da Madeira, 1699
Portugal--Treaties, etc., 1668-1706 (Pedro II)
    Avtos De Las Conferencias, 1682
    Dom Pedro Por Graça De Deos..., 1681
Powle, Henry: 1689, Gt.Brit.--Parliament, 1689-1690--House of Commons--Speaker
Poyntz, John
    The Present Prospect, 1683; 1695
    1687, Blome, Richard
Pozuelo y Espinosa, Francisco, Compendio De Los Esquadrones Modernos, 1690
Practica De Asistir A Los Sentenciados â muerte: 1696, Miranda, Juan José de
The Practick Part Of the Office of A Justice of the Peace, 1681
Pralard, André
    1697, Casas, Bartolomé de las. Bp. of Chiapa
    1698, Casas, Bartolomé de las, Bp. of Chiapa
Pratt, Phinehas: 1677, Mather, Increase, A Relation Of the Troubles...

Index

Present from a farr Countrey: 1698, Mather, Cotton
The present State Of Algiers. In the Year, 1678: 1678, Blome, Richard
The Present State Of Carolina, 1682
The Present State Of His Majesties Isles: 1687, Blome, Richard
The Present State Of Jamaica, 1683
The Present State Of New-England, 1675 (2 variants); 1676
Presentación, Luis de la.   See Luis de la Presentación, brother
The Pretended Yearly Meeting Of The Quakers: 1695, Keith, George
Price, Elizabeth, The True Countess of Banbury's Case, 1696
Primera Relacion Extraordinaria, 1700
Primitive Heresie Revived: 1698, Leslie, Charles
Les Principes De La Geographie, 1692
The Principles of the Protestant Religion Maintained: 1690, Mather, Cotton
The Printers Advertisement, 1700
Proclamation For Apprehending Captains Gavine Hamilton... : 1700, Gt.Brit.--Sovereigns, etc., 1694-1702 (William III) 25 July 1700
A Proposal For Remeeding [sic] our Excessive Luxury, 1700
Proposals By The Proprietors Of East-Jersey, 1682
Proposals For A Fond, 1695
Proposals For the Encouragement and Promoting of Religion: 1697, Bray, Thomas (2 variants)
Proposals For the Incouragement and Promoting of Religion: 1696, Bray, Thomas
A Proposition For Remeding the Debasement... : 1700, Fletcher, Andrew
Prospect Des ganzen Erdkreisses, 1686
Protais, Capuchin missionary: 1696, Thévenot, Melchisédech, Relations, 4.ptie.
Protestant Dissenter: 1700, One Wonder more; The Portraiture Of Mr. George Keith
Proyecto De La Paz: 1697, France--Treaties, etc., 1643-1715 (Louis XIV) 20 July 1697
The Psalms, Hymns, And Spiritual Songs of the Old and New Testament
    1688, Bible--O.T.--Psalms--English--Paraphrases--Bay Psalm Book
    1695, Bible--O.T.--Psalms--English--Paraphrases--Bay Psalm Book
Ptolemaeus, Claudius, Tabulae geographicae, 1695; 1698
Puccini, Vincenzio, The Life... , 1687
Puebla de los Angeles--College of Saints Peter and John: 1690, Rendón de Soria, Diego
Pufendorf, Samuel, Freiherr von
    Introduction à L'Histoire, 1685
    Suite de L'Introduction, 1689
Pullen, Nathaniel: 1696, Mocquet, Jean
Purvis, John: 1684, Virginia (Colony)--Laws, statutes, etc.
Pusey, Caleb, A Modest Account From Pensylvania, 1696
Pyrard, François
    Voyage De François Pyrard, 1679
    1691, Zani, Valerio, conte

Quadro, Francisco del: 1687, Valdés, Rodrigo de
The Quaker A Christian: 1698, Penn, William
Quakerism Canvassed... , 1675
The Quakers Cleared... : 1696, Coole, Benjamin
The Quakers Elegy, 1685
The Quakers Quibbles: 1675, Thompson, Thomas
The Quakers Vindication... : 1694, Whitehead, George
Quellenburgh, Henrik van
    1688, Gage, Thomas
    1700, Gage, Thomas
Quesada y Sotomayor, Gregorio de, Sermon De La Pvrissima Concepcion, 1696
Quevedo y Villegas, Francisco Gómez de, Fortune In Her Wits, 1697
Quin, Walter: 1677, Herbert, Sir Thomas
Quirós, Pedro de, Sermones Varios, 1678
Quivedo Villegas, Francisco de.   See Quevedo y Villegas, Francisco Gómez de

R. A.: 1699, An Congratulatory Poem, On The safe Arrival of the Scots African and Indian Fleet
R. B.   See Barclay, Robert
R. B.   See Crouch, Nathaniel
R. C.   See Chamberlayne, Richard
R. F.   See Ferguson, Robert
R. M. Q.   See MacQuare, Robert
R. T.: 1680, A Relation Of The Labour...
R. W.   See Ware, Robert
R. W.   See Williams, Roger
Raei, Johannes de, Dictionarium Geographicum, 1700
Rahnen, Johann Rudolff.   See Rhanen, Johann Rudolff
Raleigh, Sir Walter
    The History Of The World, 1677
    Remains of Sr. Walter Raleigh, 1675
    Select Observations, 1696
    1682, Pain, Philip
Ramírez, José, Via Lactea, 1698
Ramírez, Nicolás: 1697, Muñoz de Castro, Pedro
Ramírez, Pedro: 1698, Narváez, Juan de
Ramírez de Arellano, José, Memorial, Y Discvrso Informativo... , 1687
Ramírez de Vargas, Alonso
    Sagrado Padron, 1691
    Villancicos, 1685
    1683, Sigüenza y Góngora, Carlos de
    1684, Santoyo, Felipe de
    1691, Sigüenza y Góngora, Carlos de
    1695, Mexico (City)--Universidad
Ramón, Juan: 1691, Sancho de Melgar, Estevan
Ramos, Alonso: 1691, Martínez de la Parra, Juan
Randolph, Edward: 1690, New-England's Faction Discovered
Raphael de Jesus, Castrioto Lvsitano, 1679
Rapp, Johann Heinrich: 1677, Richshoffer, Ambrosius
Rapport Qve Les Directevrs De La Compagnie Hollandoise des Indes Orientales... : 1696, Thévenot, Melchisédech, Relations, 3.ptie.
Raunce, John.   See Rounce, John
Rautenfels, Jacob: 1680, Martens, Friedrich, Viaggio Di Spizberga O'Grolanda; Martens, Friedrich, Viaggio Di Spizberga O'Gronlanda

Raveneau de Lussan, -----
   Journal Du Voyage, 1690; 1693; 1699
   A Journal Of A Voyage, 1698
   1699, The History Of The Bucaniers Of America
   1700, Historie Der Boecaniers, Of Vrybuyters Van America
Rawlin, William: 1699, Barbados--Laws, statutes, etc.
Rawson, Edward, The Revolution, 1691
Rawson, Grindall
   1689, Shepard, Thomas
   1691, Cotton, John
   1699, Congregational Churches in Massachusetts
Raynaud, Théophile: 1689, Clemente, Claudio
Reader, The Intention of this Map...: 1681, Penn, William
Reasons, why in this Juncture... , 1689
Recit De L'Estat Present...: 1681, Rochefort, Charles de
Reconcileable, Sam. See Young, Samuel
Recopilacion De Leyes...: 1681, Spain--Laws, statutes, etc.
The Recruits for Caledonia, 1699
Recueil De Divers Voyages, 1684
Recüeil De Diverses Pieces: 1684, Penn, William
Redi, Francesco
   Epistola Ad Aliquas Oppositiones factas in suas Observationes circa Viperas, 1675
   Experimenta circa res diversas naturales, 1675
   Observationes De Viperis, 1675
Reenhjelm, Jacob Isthmen: 1680, Thorsteins saga Vikingssonar
Regla De Los Hermanos De La Orden Tercera: 1700, Dominicans--Third Order
Reglement Du Roy, Pour la Police & Discipline des Compagnies: 1695, France--Sovereigns, etc., 1643-1715 (Louis XIV) 12 Oct. 1695
Regula S. Augustini Et Constitutiones FF. Ordinis Prædicatorum, 1690
Reinegg, Anton Sepp von. See Sepp von Reinegg, Anton
Reinegg, Gabriel Sepp von. See Sepp von Reinegg, Gabriel
Reinoso, Fernando: 1695, Castilla, Miguel de
Reinout In Het Betoverde Hof: 1697, Peys, Adriaan
Reiske, Johann
   1694, Clüver, Philipp
   1697, Clüver, Philipp
Relaçam Do Exemplar Castigo, 1688
Relaçam Verdadeira da ultima enfermidade, 1689
Relacion Con Insercion De Avtos...: 1685, Berart, Raimundo
Relacion De Un Pais: 1699, Hennepin, Louis
Relacion Del Exemplar Castigo, 1688
Relacion Verdadera, En Qve Se dà quenta del horrible Huracàn, 1680
Relación verdadera y sucinta...: 1693, Vázquez Gaztelu, Antonio
Relatio Ablegationis Qvam Czarea Majestas Ad Catayensem Chamum Bogdi destinavit: 1696, Thévenot, Melchisédech, Relations, 5.ptie.

Relatio Ad Inclytam Societatem Leopoldinam Naturæ Curiosorum: 1696, Leibniz, Gottfried Wilhelm, freiherr von
Relation De Ce Qui S'est Fait A La Prise De Cartagene, 1698
Relation De ce qui s'est passé Dans Les Isles De L'Amerique, 1693
Relation De Ce Qui S'Est Passé En Canada, 1691
Relation De La Bataille De Tabago, 1677
Relation De la découuerte de la Terre d'Eso: 1696, Thévenot, Melchisédech, Relations, 2.ptie.
Relation De La Grande Isle De Mindanao: 1696, Thévenot, Melchisédech, Relations, 2.ptie.
Relation de la Guiane: 1684, Recueil De Divers Voyages
Relation De La Levée Dv Siège De Quebec, 1691
Relation De La Prise De L'Isle Formosa par les Chinois: 1696, Thévenot, Melchisédech, Relations, 1.ptie.
Relation De La Prise Des Isles De Gorée, 1678
Relation De L'Estat Present Dv Commerce des Hollandois & des Portugais dans les Indes Orientales: 1696, Thévenot, Melchisédech, Relations, 2.ptie.
Relation De L'Expedition De Carthagene: 1698, Pointis, Jean Bernard Louis Desjean, baron de
Relation De L'Inquisition De Goa
   1687, Dellon, Gabriel
   1688, Dellon, Gabriel (2 ed.)
Relation Des Cosaqves: 1696, Thévenot, Melchisédech, Relations, 1.ptie.
Relation Des Isles Philipines, Faite par vn Religieux...: 1696, Thévenot, Melchisédech, Relations, 2.ptie.
Relation Des Voyages Dv Sievr---: 1696, Thévenot, Melchisédech, Relations, 4.ptie.
Relation du voyage fait sur costes d'Afrique: 1684, Recueil De Divers Voyages
Relation D'Un Grand Combat, 1687
Relation Et Memorial De l'estat des Isles Philipines: 1696, Thévenot, Melchisédech, Relations, 2.ptie.
Relation Fidele De L'Expedition De Cartagene, 1699
A Relation Of The Invasion... , 1686
A Relation Of The Labour... , 1680
Remarks Upon a Late Pamphlet, 1700
Remarks Upon The Petition and Petitioners... , 1690
Renau d'Eliçagaray, Bernard, De La Theorie... , 1689
Rendón de Soria, Diego, Vsque Quaque Extensa Lucis, 1690
Rennefort, Urbain Souchu de
   Histoire Des Indes Orientales, 1688
   A Supplement To The Sieur Dellone's Relation, 1698
Rentería, Martín de, Sermon, 1682
Replica Alla Risposta Dimostrativa: 1680, Gudenfridi, Giovanni Batista
A Reply To The Answer Of The Man of No Name: 1685, Care, George
The Report Of The Commissioners: 1700, Gt.Brit.--Commissioners Appointed to Enquire Into the Irish Forfeitures
The Representation and Petition...: 1700, Company of

Index

Scotland Trading to Africa and the Indies
A Reprimand For The Author of a Libel: 1697, Young, Samuel
Requena, Cristóbal de: 1693, Fernández de Medrano, Sebastián
The Resolved Christian: 1700, Mather, Cotton
Restaurand, Raymond: 1687, Nigrisoli, Francesco Maria
The Revival: Or Directions for a Sculpture: 1682, Godwin, Morgan
The Revolution In New England Justified: 1691, Rawson, Edward
El Rey. Conde de Galve, ...: 1695, Spain--Sovereigns, etc., 1665-1700 (Charles II) 25 Apr. 1695
El Rey. Conde de la Moncloua Pariente, ...: 1693, Spain--Sovereigns, etc., 1665-1700 (Charles II) 31 Dec. 1693
El Rey. Mvy Reuerendo in Christo Padre Arçobispo...: 1680, Spain--Sovereigns, etc., 1665-1700 (Charles II)
El Rey. Muy Reverendos en Christo Padres Arçobispos ...: 1700, Spain--Sovereigns, etc., 1700-1746 (Philip V)
El Rey Por quanto el Rey mi señor...: 1681, Spain--Sovereigns, etc., 1665-1700 (Charles II)
El Rey. Por Quanto por la ley...: 1693, Spain--Sovereigns, etc., 1665-1700 (Charles II) 13 Feb. 1693
Reyard, Nicholas. See Bayard, Nicholas
Reyes, Francisco de los, Sagrado Dvo, 1691
Reyes, Gaspar de los
    Sermon Al Glorioso San Francisco De Borja, 1688
    Sermon Del Gran Privado De Christo, 1689
    Sermon, Que predicó El P. Gaspar De Los Reyes, 1684
Reyes Villaverde, Andrés de los: 1700, Sigüenza y Góngora, Carlos de
Rhanen, Johann Rudolff: 1677, Simler, Johann Wilhelm
Rhodes, Alexandre de: 1685, Dufour, Philippe Sylvestre, Tractatvs Novi; Dufour, Philippe Sylvestre, Traitez Nouveaux
Rhoe, Thomas. See Roe, Thomas
Ribeiro Coutinho, Paschoal, Arco Triunfal Idea, 1687
Ribera, Diego de: 1680, Riofrío Bernardo de
Richardi Blome Englisches America: 1697, Crouch, Nathaniel
Richardson, Richard
    1675, Penn, William, A Treatise Of Oaths
    1683, Estlacke, Francis
Richshoffer, Ambrosius, Brassilianisch- und West Indianische Reisse Beschreibung, 1677
Ridpath, George
    Scotland's Grievances, Relating to Darien, 1700
    1699, Belhaven, John Hamilton, 2d baron, A Defence Of The Scots Settlement at Darien 4º; 8º (4 variants)
    1700, An Enquiry into The Causes...
Ringrose, Basil
    Bucaniers Of America, The Second Volume, 1685
    1699, The History Of The Bucaniers Of America

1700, Historie Der Boecaniers, Of Vrybuyters Van America
Rio, Joseph del, Sermon De Gracias, 1695
Riofrío, Bernardo de
    Centonicvm Virgilianvm Monimentvm, 1680
    Por El Venerable Dean... , 1688
    1698, Castilla, Miguel de
Ríos, Nicolas, marqués de los: 1684, Santoyo, Felipe de
Ríos Coronel, Hernando de los: 1696, Thévenot, Melchisédech, Relations, 2.ptie.
Ripalda, Gerónimo de, Doctrina Christiana, 1687; 1689
Risco, Juan Luis López y Martínez, marqués del. See López y Martínez, Juan Luis, marqués del Risco
Rivera, Luis de: 1697, Muñoz de Castro, Pedro
Rivera, Thadeo: 1695, Mexico (City)--Universidad
Roberts, -----: 1699, Hack, William
Roberts, Lewes, The Merchants Map, 1700
Robinson, Sir Tancred, An Account Of Several Late Voyages & Discoveries, 1694
Robinson, William: 1700, Gould, Daniel
Robles, Antonio de, Consistencia De El Jvbileo Maximo, 1700
Robles, Francisco de, Oracion Fvnebre, Qve Hizieron Sus Esclarecidas obras... , 1697
Robles, Juan de
    Sermon De La Pvrissima Concepcion, 1689
    Sermon Del Gloriossissimo Patriarcha, 1687
    Sermon Qve Predicó... , 1682
Rocha, Diego Andrés
    Carta Al Excmo. Señor. Don Baltasar De La Cueva, 1675
    Tratado Vnico, 1681
Rochefort, César de: 1681, Rochefort, Charles de, Histoire Naturelle
Rochefort, Charles de
    Histoire Naturelle, 1681
    Recit De L'Estat Present... , 1681
Rodrigo de la Cruz
    Discurso, Que Ha Parecido Adicionar A La Defensa ... , 1693
    Relacion De Los Hospitales, 1693
    Representacion Jvridica, 1693
    Señor... , 1693
Rodríguez, Manuel
    Compendio Historial, 1684
    El Marañon, Y Amazonas, 1684
    1682, Jesuits--Spain--Procurador General por las Provincias de Indias
Roe, Sir Thomas: 1696, Thévenot, Melchisédech, Relations, 1.ptie.
Roeloffs, Jan. See Werf, John Roeloffs vander
Rogers, John: 1678, Bradstreet, Anne (Dudley)
Rogers, William
    The Christian-Quaker, 1680
    The Fifth Part Of The Christian-Quaker, 1680
    The First Part Of The Christian-Quaker, 1680
    The Fourth Part Of The Christian-Quaker, 1680
    The Second-Part Of The Christian-Quaker, 1680
    The Third Part Of The Christian-Quaker, 1680

Index

Roggeveen, Arent
    Le Premier Tôme De La Tourbe Ardante, 1676
    Voorlooper Op 't Octroy, 1676
Roman, frà. See Pane, Ramón, brother
Romero, Diego, Meditaciones De La Passion, 1683
Romero, Francisco, Llanto Sagrado De La America Meridional, 1693
Ronquillo, Pedro, The Last Memorial, 1681
Rosales, Bartolomé: 1680, Riofrío, Bernardo de
Ross, Alexander, Les Religions Du Monde, 1686
Rounce, John: 1694, Keith, George, A Seasonable Information...
Rovte Dv Voyage Des Holandois: 1696, Thévenot, Melchisédech, Relations, 3.ptie.
Rouxel, Claude
    1685, Pufendorf, Samuel, Freiherr von
    1689, Pufendorf, Samuel, Freiherr von
Rowlandson, Joseph: 1682, Rowlandson, Mary (White)
Rowlandson, Mary (White), A True History... , 1682
Royal Society of London, Philosophical Transactions, 1677
Rudbeck, Olof: 1680, Thorsteins saga Vikingssonar
Rueda, José Ignacio: 1697, Muñoz de Castro, Pedro
Rueda, Juan de: 1691, Ramírez de Vargas, Alonso
Rugman, Jón: 1680, Thorsteins saga Vikingssonar
Ruiz Blanco, Matías
    Conversion De Piritv, 1690
    Manval Para Catekizar, 1683
    1683, Yangues, Manuel de
Ruiz de Torres, Juan: 1685, Montoro, José
Ruiz Lozano, Antonio: 1695, Loumans, Lodewijk
Ruiz Perea, Miguel, Oracion Panegyrica, 1700
Rutherford, Samuel
    Letters, 1675
    1677, Keith, George
Ruyz. See Ruiz
Rycaut, Sir Paul: 1688, Garcilaso de la Vega, el Inca
Ryswykse Vrede-Handel: 1700, Bernard, Jacques
Ryther, John
    Sea-Dangers, 1675
    1675, Janeway, James

S., Martha: 1676, A Further Account Of New Jersey
S. de V. See Vries, Simon de
S. G. See Groome, Samuel
S. L. See Lee, Samuel
S. N. See Nowell, Samuel
S. S. See Sewall, Samuel
S. von V. See Vries, Simon de
Sá, Antonio de
    Sermão Do Glorioso Sam Ioseph, 1692
    Sermão Dos Passos, 1689
Sadeur, Jacques. See Foigny, Gabriel de
Sadeur, James. See Foigny, Gabriel de
Sáenz, José, Brillante Trisagio, 1697
Sáenz de Aguirre, José, Cardinal
    1686, Catholic Church in Spain--Councils
    1693, Catholic Church in Spain--Councils
Sáenz de la Peña, Andrés
    1683, Lemus, Diego de
    1691, Catholic Church--Liturgy and ritual--Ritual

Sagan Landnama Vm fyrstu bygging Islands af Nordmønnum: 1688, Landnámabók
Saint-George, Georges Guillet de. See Guillet de Saint-George, Georges
St. Lo, George, England's Safety, 1693
Saint Vallier, Jean Baptiste de la Croix Chevrières de, Bp. of Quebec
    Estat Present De L'Eglise, 1688
    Relation Des Missions, 1688
    1699, Gervaise, Nicolas
Salazar, Antonio de
    Villancicos, Que Se Cantaron En La Sancta Igleia [sic] Cathedral De La Puebla de los Angeles, en los Maytines del Gloriosissimo Principe de la Iglesia... , 1683
    Villancicos...En La Santa Iglesia Cathedral Metropolitana de Mexico, en honor de Maria Sanctissima, 1695; 1696
    Villancicos...En La Santa Iglesia Metropolitana de Mexico: en los Maytines de la Natividad de Maria Santissima, 1696
    Villancicos...En La Santa Yglesia Metropolitana, de Mexico: En los Maytines Del Glorioso Principe de la Yglesia, 1695
    Villancicos...En Los Maytines De El Glorioso Principe de la Iglesia... , 1692
    Villancicos...En Los Maytines de la Assumpcion De Nuestra Señora, 1693
    Villancicos...En Los Maytines Del Glorioso Principe de la Iglesia, 1693
    1689, Acevedo, Francisco
    1690, González de la Sancha, Lorenzo Antonio
    1695, Santoyo, Felipe de
    1698, González de la Sancha, Lorenzo Antonio
Salazar, Martín de, Competentia Ivrisdictionis, 1691
Salazar y Bolea, Juan de: 1690, Godínez, Miguel
Salcedo, Juan de, Benedictine, Abbot of Valvanera: 1681, Sandoval, Prudencio de, Bp. of Pamplona
Saldaña y Ortega, Antonio de, Oracion Evangelica del Principe, y Cabeza de la Iglesia, 1695
Salduendo, Francisco Javier, Los Siete Angeles Del Apocalypsis, 1695
Salgado, José: 1690, Octava Maravilla
Saltonstall, Nathaniel
    1675, The Present State Of New-England (2 variants)
    1676, A Continuation Of the State of New-England; A New and Further Narrative Of the State of New-England; The Present State Of New-England
Salvatore, Michele del, Relatione Compendiosa, 1692
San Agustín, Andrés de. See Andrés de San Agustín
San Agustín, Gaspar de. See Gaspar de San Agustín
San Antonio, Bartolomé Navarro de. See Navarro de San Antonio, Bartolomé
San Buenaventura, Gabriel de, Arte De La Lengva Maya, 1684
San Juan Bautista, Matías de. See Matías de San Juan Bautista
San Miguel, Isidoro de, Parayso Cvltivado, 1695
Sánchez, Francisco, Informe, Y Parecer... , 1691
Sancho de Melgar, Estevan, Arte De La Lengva General ... , 1691

[474]

Sanderson, John: 1678, Seer gedenckwaerdige Vojagien ...
Sandín, Alonso
    Breve, Y Compendiosa Relacion, 1686
    Respvesta A Vna Relacion Sumaria, 1684
Sandoval, Prudencio de, Bp. of Pamplona, Historia de la Vida y Hechos Del Emperador Carlos V, 1681
Sandras, Gatien de Courtilz, sieur de. See Courtilz, Gatien de, sieur de Sandras
Sanson, Nicolas, 1600-1667
    L'Europe En Plusieurs Cartes, 1683
    1680, Blome, Richard
Sanson, Nicolas, 1626-1648: 1683, Sanson, Nicolas, 1600-1667
Santa Teresa, João José de. See João José de Santa Thereza, freire
Santiago de Chile (Diocese)--Synod, 1691, Synodo Diocesana, 1691
Santillana, Gabriel de, Villancicos, 1688
Santoyo, Felipe de
    Mistica Diana, 1684
    Panegyrica Dedicacion De El Templo, 1681
    Villancicos, 1695
Sariñana y Cuenca, Isidro
    Oracion Fvnebre, 1681
    Sermon De El Gloriosissimo Principe, 1683
    Sermon De N.S.P.S. Francisco, 1688
    Sermon Qve En las honras del V.P. Fr. Christoval Mvñoz, 1689
    1692, Villavicencio, Diego Jaime Ricardo
Satan Dis-Rob'd From his Disguise of Light
    1697, Leslie, Charles
    1698, Leslie, Charles
Sauveur, Joseph
    1689, Renau d'Eliçagaray, Bernard
    1693, Le Neptune François
Savage, Thomas, An Account Of The Late Action Of The New-Englanders, 1691
Savary, Jacques
    Le Parfait Negociant, 1679
    1691, Zani, Valerio, conte
Saviard, Barthélemy: 1695, Lemaire, Jacques Joseph
Savoy (Duchy)--Sovereigns, etc., 1675-1730 (Victor Amadeus II): 1697, France--Sovereigns, etc., 1643-1715 (Louis XIV)
Savoy (Duchy)--Treaties, etc.
    1685, Gt.Brit.--Treaties, etc., 1660-1685 (Charles II)
    1686, Gt.Brit.--Treaties, etc., 1660-1685 (Charles II)
    1697, France--Treaties, etc., 1643-1715 (Louis XIV) 7 Oct. 1696
Schedæ Ara Prestz Froda Vm Island: 1688, Ari Thorgilsson, Fródi
Scheffer, Johannes
    Histoire De La Laponie, 1678
    Lappland, 1675
    1691, Zani, Valerio, conte
Schelte, D.: 1687, Brandt, Geeraert, Het Leven En Bedryf...
Schoch, Johann Georg: 1688, Mocquet, Jean

Schouten, Joost
    Sanfärdig Beskrijffning/Om Konungarijket Siam, 1675
    1696, Thévenot, Melchisédech, Relations, 1.ptie.
Schouten, Wouter, Wouter Schoutens Oost-Indische Voyagie, 1676
Schuten, Joost. See Schouten, Joost
Schuyler, Peter: 1693, Bayard, Nicholas
Scot, George
    A Brief Advertisement, 1685
    The Model... , 1685
Scotland--Laws, statutes, etc., 1694-1702 (William III)
    Act For a Company Tradeing to Affrica, and the Indies, 1695; 1696
    An Act Of Parliament... , 1695
    An Act Of The Parliament Of Scotland, 1695
    Lettres Patentes Ou Octroi, 1697
    Literæ Patentes Seu Concessus, 1695
Scotland--Parliament: 1700, The Address presented to His Majesty; Coppy Of The Addres: Of a Great Number of the Members of the Parliament of Scotland
Scotland--Privy Council, Act In favours of these of the Scots Nation in Konigsberg, 1697
Scotland's Grievances, Relating to Darien: 1700, Ridpath, George
Scotland's Lament For Their Misfortunes, 1700
Scotland's Present Duty: 1700, Foyer, Archibald
Scotland's Right to Caledonia: 1700, Company of Scotland Trading to Africa and the Indies
Scottow, Joshua
    A Narrative Of The Planting of the Massachusets Colony, 1694
    1696, Massachusetts Or The first Planters of New-England
Scripture Proof For Singing of Scripture Psalms, 1696
Scroggs, Sir William, Speech In The Kings-Bench, 1679
Seaton, George. See Seton, George
A Second Brief for Irish Protestants: 1690, Gt.Brit.--Sovereigns, etc., 1689-1694 (William and Mary) 18 Feb. 1690
A Second Collection of Papers Relating to the Present Juncture of Affairs in England, 1688; 1689
A Second Friendly Epistle To Mr. George Keith: 1700, Young, Samuel
The Second Part Of Foxes And Firebrands: 1682, Ware, Robert (2 variants)
The Second Part Of The Address To The Free-Men: 1682, Bohun, Edmund
The Second Part Of The Quakers Quibbles: 1675, Thompson, Thomas
Sedeño, Gregorio, Descripciõ De Las Funerales Exequias, 1681
Seer gedenckwaerdige Vojagien, Van Johan Sanderson, 1678
Segura, José de: 1697, Catholic Church--Liturgy and ritual--Ritual, Manual De Administrar Los Santos Sacramentos de la Eucharistia, y Extremavncion
Segura, Melchor: 1680, Xaimes de Ribera, Juan
Seixas y Lovera, Francisco de
    Descripcion Geographica, 1690
    Theatro Naval Hydrographico, 1688
De Seldsaame en Noit Gehoorde Wal-Vis-Vangst, 1684

Index

Seller, John
   Atlas Maritimus, 1675
   Atlas Terrestris, 1676
   Practical Navigation, 1694
   1681, Penn, William, Reader, The Intention...
Señor. Al mas modesto, y prudente, nunca pudiera causar admiracion: 1690, Ayeta, Francisco de
Señor. En virtud del caracter...: 1698, Meulen, Jean van der
Señor, Manuel Rodriguez de la Compañia de Iesvs...: 1682, Jesuits--Spain--Procurador General por las Provincias de Indias
Señor mio. Manana Martes 10. del corriente..., 1680
Sepp von Reinegg, Anton, RR. PP. Antonii Sepp, und Antonii Böhm/Der Societät Jesu Priestern Teutscher Nation...Reissbeschreibung, 1696; 1697
Sepp von Reinegg, Gabriel
   1696, Sepp von Reinegg, Anton
   1697, Sepp von Reinegg, Anton
A Serious Advice To The African and Indian Company, 1700
A Serious Dialogue: 1699, Keith, George
A Serious Warning and Caution, 1700
Serra, Angel: 1697, Catholic Church--Liturgy and ritual--Ritual, Manual De Administrar Los Santos Sacramentos
Seton, George, A Modest Vindication, 1700
Seton, Sir William, A Short Speech, 1700
Settle, Dionyse, Historia Navigationis, 1675
A Seventh Collection of Papers Relating to Parliaments, 1689
A Seventh Collection of Papers Relating to the Present Juncture of Affairs in England, 1689
Several Poems: 1678, Bradstreet, Anne (Dudley)
Several Treaties Of Peace and Commerce
   1685, Gt.Brit.--Treaties, etc., 1660-1685 (Charles II)
   1686, Several Treaties Of Peace and Commerce
Sewall, Samuel
   Mrs. Judith Hull, 1695
   Phænomena quædam, 1697
   1691, Rawson, Edward
Sewel, Willem
   1686, Penn, William, Tweede Bericht...
   1689, Popple, Sir William
   1696, Kohlhans, Tobias Ludwig
   1698, Dampier, William, Nieuwe Reystogt Rondom De Werreld
   1700, Wafer, Lionel
Shakespeare, William, Comedies, Histories, And Tragedies, 1685
Sharp, Anthony: 1691, Burnyeat, John
Sharpe, Bartholomew: 1699, Hack, William
Shepard, Thomas, 1605-1649
   The Parable Of The Ten Virgins, 1695
   Sampwutteahae Quinnuppekompauaenin..., 1689
   The Sincere Convert, 1680
   1682, Perkins, William
   1696, Massachusetts Or The first Planters of New-England

Shepard, Thomas, 1635-1677: 1695, Shepard, Thomas, 1605-1649
Sherman, John
   1677, Hubbard, William, A Narrative Of The Troubles... (2 variants); Hubbard, William, The Present State Of New-England (2 variants)
   1682, Oakes, Urian
   1683, Mather, Increase
Shireff, Alexander: 1675, Quakerism Canvassed: Robin Barclay baffled in the defending of his Theses
Shirley, John
   The Life Of The Valiant & Learned Sir Walter Raleigh, 1677
   1677, Raleigh, Sir Walter
A Short Account from, And Description Of The Isthmus Of Darien, 1699
A Short Account Of The Manifest Hand of God, 1696
A Short Account Of The Present State Of New-England, 1690
A Short and Impartial View...: 1699, Fletcher, Andrew
A Short Discourse On The Present Temper Of The Nation: 1696, Holland, John
A short discourse shewing the great inconvenience...: 1689, Some Considerations humbly Offered
A Short Speech: 1700, Seton, Sir William
A Short Story Of The Rise, Reign, and Ruin of the Antinomians: 1692, Winthrop, John
A Short Vindication Of Phil. Scot's Defence: 1700, Harris, Walter
The Shorter Catechism Composed by the Reverend Assembly Of Divines: 1683, Westminster Assembly of Divines
Sicardo, José, Christiandad Del Japon, 1698
Siden, Thomas, captain. See Vairasse, Denis
Sigüenza, Gabriel. See López de Sigüenza, Gabriel
Sigüenza y Góngora, Carlos de
   Glorias De Queretaro, 1680
   Libra Astronomica, 1690
   Mercurio Volante Con La Noticia de la recuperacion..., 1693
   Oriental Planeta Evangelico Epopeya, 1700
   Parayso Occidental, 1684
   Theatro De Virtvdes Politicas, 1680
   Trivmpho Parthenico, 1683
   Trofeo De La Jvsticia Española, 1691
Silva, João Mendes da: 1699, Mattos, Francisco de
Silvos, Con Qve El Pastor Divino...: 1683, Ledesma, José
Simler, Johann Wilhelm, Vier Loblicher Statt Zürich verbürgerter Reissbeschreibungen, 1677
Simonds, Thomas: 1700, Atkinson, Christopher
Sirva esta de instruccion secreta: 1689, Mexico (Viceroyalty)--Laws, statutes, etc., 1688-1696 (Galve) 12 Nov. 1689
A Sixth Collection Of Papers Relating To the Present Juncture of Affairs, 1689
A Sixth Collection of Papers Relating to the Present Juncture of Affairs in England, 1689
Skene, Alexander: 1677, Keith, George
Skene, Lillias: 1679, Barclay, Robert

Index

Sloane, Sir Hans, bart.
　Catalogus Plantarum, 1696
　1694, An Account Of Several Late Voyages & Discoveries
Smids, Ludolf: 1689, Engeland Beroerd
Smith, John
　The Sea-Man's Grammar, 1699
　1678, Seer gedenckwaerdige Vojagien...
Smith, Samuel: 1694, An Account Of Several Late Voyages & Discoveries
Smith, Thomas: 1687, Puccini, Vincenzio
The Snake in the Grass
　1696, Leslie, Charles
　1698, Leslie, Charles
Snead, Richard: 1681, An Exalted Diotrephes Reprehended
Snellinx, Franciscus: 1675, Den Hollandtze Mercurius, 5. Deel
A Sober Dialogue Between A Country Friend... , 1699
A Sober Reply To A Serious Enquiry: 1700, Young, Samuel
Solís y Rivadeneyra, Antonio de
　Histoire De La Conquête Du Mexique, 1691 (2 variants); 1692
　Historia De La Conqvista De Mexico, 1684; 1691
　Istoria Della Conquista Del Messico, 1699
Solorzano Pereira, Juan de, Obras Posthvmas, 1676
Some Account Of The Province Of Pennsilvania: 1681, Penn, William
Some Account Of The Transactions Of Mr. William Paterson, 1695
Some Brief Observations Upon George Keith's Earnest Expostulation: 1696, Penington, Edward
Some Considerations humbly Offered, 1689
Some Considerations upon the late Act, 1695
Some General Considerations Offered: 1698, Tryon, Thomas
Some Letters And An Abstract, 1691
Some of the By-Laws made by the Governour: 1677, Bermuda Company
Some Seasonable Reflections Upon The Quakers Solemn Protestation Against George Keith's Proceedings: 1697, Leslie, Charles
Some Seasonable Reflections Upon The Quakers Solemn Protestation Against the Proceedings: 1697, Leslie, Charles
Some Testimonies Concerning the Life... , 1690
Some Thoughts Concerning The Affairs... , 1700
Some Years Travels: 1677, Herbert, Sir Thomas
Somers, John Somers, baron, A Brief History... , 1689
Somers, Nathan: 1682, The Present State Of Carolina; A true Description Of Carolina
Something in Answer to a Law: 1679, Fox, George
Something in Answer To A Letter: 1678, Fox, George
The Song of Solomon Paraphrased: 1685, Bible--O.T.--Song of Solomon--English--Paraphrases
Songhurst, John, An Epistle Of Love, 1681
Sonnemans, Arent, Eenige Annmerkingen... , 1676
Souchu de Rennefort, Urbain. See Rennefort, Urbain Souchu de

Sousa, Domingo de
　Sermon En El Avto Publico De Feé, 1699
　1697, Muñoz de Castro, Pedro
Soutermans, Mathias: 1684, Hazart, Cornelius
Southerne, Thomas, Oroonoko, 1696; 1699
Southwick, Solomon: 1700, Gospel Order Revived
Souza, Domingo de. See Sousa, Domingo de
Sowle, Tace, Books Printed and Sold by T. Sowle, 1699 (2 variants)
Spain--Consejo de las Indias
　Ordenanzas Del Consejo Real De Las Indias, 1681
　1677, Spain--Laws, statutes, etc.
Spain--Laws, statutes, etc.
　Recopilacion De Leyes, 1681
　Svmarios De La Recopilacion General, 1677
Spain--Laws, statutes, etc., 1621-1665 (Philip IV)
　1675, Escalona y Agüero, Gaspar de
　1681, Spain--Consejo de las Indias
Spain--Laws, statutes, etc., 1665-1700 (Charles II):
　1695, Peru (Viceroyalty)--Laws, statutes, etc., 1689-1705 (Portocarrero)
Spain--Sovereigns, etc., 1665-1700 (Charles II)
　Carta Del Rey Nvestro Señor, 1695 (24 Mar. 1695)
　El Rey. Conde de Galve... , 1695 (25 Apr. 1695)
　El Rey. Conde de la Moncloua Pariente... , 1693 (31 Dec. 1693)
　El Rey. Mvy Reuerendo in Christo Padre Arçobispo... , 1680
　El Rey Por quanto el Rey mi señor, 1681
　El Rey. Por Quanto por la ley 8. titulo 11 libro 1... , 1693 (13 Feb. 1693)
　1689, Yo Pedro de Arce y Andrade...
Spain--Sovereigns, etc., 1700-1746 (Philip V), El Rey. Muy Reverendos en Christo Padres, Arçobispos... , 1700
Spain--Treaties, etc., 1665-1700 (Charles II)
　Capitulaciones De Las Pazes, 1697 (20 Sept. 1697)
　Capitulaçoens Das Pazes, 1697 (20 Sept. 1697)
　1681, Portugal--Treaties, etc., 1668-1706 (Pedro II)
　1682, Portugal--Treaties, etc., 1668-1706 (Pedro II)
　1697, France--Treaties, etc., 1643-1715 (Louis XIV) 7 Oct. 1696; France--Treaties, etc., 1643-1715 (Louis XIV), Traité De Paix Entre La France Et L'Espagne (20 Sept. 1697); Traktaat van Vrede
　1698, Peru (Viceroyalty)--Laws, statutes, etc., 1689-1705 (Portocarrero) 11 Nov. 1698
Sparkes, John: 1696, Dawson, Joseph
Specht, Hermann
　1696, Mather, Increase, Ein Brieff von dem Glücklichen Fortgang...
　1699, Mather, Increase, De Successu Evangelii
The Speech Of the Right Honourable Henry Powle: 1689, Gt.Brit.--Parliament, 1689-1690--House of Commons--Speaker
Speed, John
　A Prospect Of The Most Famous Parts Of The World, 1676
　The Theatre of the Empire Of Great-Britain, 1676
Spencer, Thomas, secretary to Sir Timothy Thornhill, A True and Faithful Relation... , 1691

[477]

Spiegel Der Sibyllen: 1685, Aysma, Joannes
Spiegel Voor de Stad van Embden, 1679
Spörri, Felix Christian, Americanische Reissbeschreibung, 1677
Spole, Anders, Dissertatione Graduali Americam Noviter Detectam, 1691
Spon, Jacob
 1685, Dufour, Philippe Sylvestre, Tractatvs Novi; Dufour, Philippe Sylvestre, Traitez Nouveaux
 1687, Nigrisoli, Francesco Maria
Stanley, Charles, 8th earl of Derby. See Derby, Charles Stanley, 8th earl of
The State of the Navy, 1699
A State of the Present Condition Of The Island of Barbadoes, 1698
State Tracts: Being A Collection Of Several Treatises, 1689
State Tracts: Being a Farther Collection Of Several Choice Treatises, 1692
Steendam, Jacob: 1682, Nieuhof, Johan, Zee en Lant-Reize
Stephenson, Marmaduke, Een Roep, Van de Doot, tot het Leeven, 1679
Sternhold, Thomas: 1677, Bible--O.T.--Psalms--English--Paraphrases
Sterre, Dionysius van der, Zeer Aanmerkelijke Reysen, 1691
Stevens, John
 1697, Quevedo y Villegas, Francisco Gómez de
 1699, Mariana, Juan de
Stevenson, Marmaduke: 1700, Gould, Daniel
Stillingfleet, Edward, Bp. of Worcester
 The Unreasonableness of Separation, 1681
 1690, To our Reverend...Ministers
Stoddard, Solomon
 The Doctrine Of Instituted Churches, 1700
 1700, Gospel Order Revived
Stone, Samuel, A Short Catechism, 1699
Story, Thomas
 A Word to the Well-Inclin'd Of All Perswasions, 1698
 1698, Penn, William, The Quaker A Christian
Stoughton, William
 A Narrative Of The Proceedings..., 1691
 1693, Mather, Cotton, The Wonders of the Invisible World: Being an Account of the Tryals Of Several VVitches; Mather, Cotton, The Wonders of the Invisible World: Being an Account of the Tryals Of Several Witches...The Second Edition; Mather, Cotton, The Wonders of the Invisible World. Observations As well Historical as Theological
Strange News From Virginia, 1677
Stratford, Nicholas, Bp. of Chester: 1690, To our Reverend...Ministers
Strik, Leonard: 1700, Mela, Pomponius
Stubbs, Henry, 1606?-1678, Conscience The Best Friend, 1699
Stubbs, Henry, 1632-1676, A Light Shining out of Darkness, 1699
Sudor, Y Lagrimas De Maria Santissima: 1676, Buendía, José
Suite Du Neptune François, 1700

Sumario De Las Gracias, E Indvlgencias...: 1699, Confraternity of the Blessed Sacrament
Svmarios De La Recopilacion General De Las Leyes, Ordenanças: 1677, Spain--Laws, statutes, etc.
A Superaddition to the former Dissertation: 1677, Lee, Samuel
A Supplement Of Original Papers: 1700, Company of Scotland Trading to Africa and the Indies
A Supplement To The Negro's & Indian's Advocate: 1681, Godwin, Morgan
Sutton, Thomas: 1692, Morton, Richard
Swammerdam, Jan: 1681, Thévenot, Melchisédech
Sylva, Antonio da, Oraçam Funebre, 1691
Sylvester, Matthew
 Elisha's Cry, 1696
 1696, Baxter, Richard
Sylvestre Dufour, Philippe. See Dufour, Philippe Sylvestre
Symonds, Thomas. See Simonds, Thomas
Synodo Diocesana Con La Carta Pastoral: 1691, Santiago de Chile (Diocese)--Synod
Synopsis Chronologica Monarchiæ Sinicæ: 1696, Thévenot, Melchisédech, Relations, 5.ptie.

T. A. See Amy, Thomas
T. A. See Ash, Thomas
T. A. V.: 1675, Den Hollandtze Mercurius, 5. Deel
T. C.: 1698, The New Atlas
T. M.: 1682, A Letter from Jamaica
T. S. See Shepard, Thomas, 1605-1649
T. T. See Tryon, Thomas
Tabor, Sir Robert. See Talbor, Sir Robert
Tabvla Geographica Totius Seraphici Ordidinis: 1680, Franciscans
Talbor, Sir Robert
 1689, Les Admirables Qualitez Du Kinkina
 1694, Les Admirables Qualitez Du Kinkina
Tanner, Mathias
 Die Gesellschafft Jesu, 1683
 Societas Jesu, 1675
Tasman, Abel Janszoon
 1694, An Account Of Several Late Voyages
 1696, Thévenot, Melchisédech, Relations, 5.ptie.
Tauste, Francisco de, Arte, Y Bocabvlario, 1680
Taylor, John, A Loving & Friendly Invitation, 1683
Telles, Balthazar: 1684, Recueil De Divers Voyages
Téllez Giron, Juan Alejo, Villancicos, 1686
Temple, Sir William, bart.
 Brieven, 1700
 Observations Upon The United Provinces Of The Netherlands, 1693
Tenison, Thomas, Abp. of Canterbury, An Argument..., 1683
A Tenth Collection of Papers Relating to the Present Juncture of Affairs in England, 1689
Tentzel, Wilhelm Ernst: 1693, Monatliche Unterredungen Einiger Guten Freunde...
Terra Rossa, Vitale, Riflessioni Geografiche, 1686; 1687

[478]

Index

Terry, Edward: 1696, Thévenot, Melchisédech, Relations, 1.ptie.
Tertre, Jean Baptiste du. See Dutertre, Jean Baptiste
Tesoro Pervano, 1677
A Testimony and Warning: 1676, Fell, Lydia (Erbury)
Thatcher, Thomas: 1677, Wilson, John
Their Majesties Colony Of Connecticut in New-England Vindicated, 1694
Their Majesties Declaration Against the French King: 1689, Gt.Brit.--Sovereigns, etc., 1689-1694 (William and Mary) 7 May 1689
Thesaurus Geographicus, 1695 (2 variants)
Thévenot, Jean de, Voyages, 1684
Thévenot, Melchisédech
    Recueil De Voyages, 1681
    Relations De Divers Voayges [sic] Curieux, 1683
    Relations De Divers Voyages Curieux, 1696
The Third and Last Part Of The Address To The Free-Men: 1683, Bohun, Edmund
A Third Collection of Papers Relating to the Present Juncture of Affairs in England, 1689
A Third Letter From a Gentleman in the Country: 1687, Penn, William
Third Order of St. Dominic. See Dominicans--Third Order
The Third Part Of The Quakers Quibbles: 1675, Thompson, Thomas
Thirty Important Cases: 1699, Cambridge, Mass.--Ministers' Association
Thomas, Sir Dalby, An Historical Account..., 1690
Thomas, Gabriel
    An Historical and Geographical Account..., 1698
    An Historical Description..., 1698
Thompson, Thomas
    The Quakers Quibbles, 1675
    The Second Part Of The Quakers Quibbles, 1675
    The Third Part Of The Quakers Quibbles, 1675
Thorláksson, Thórdur: 1688, Ari Thorgilsson, Fródi; Jónsson, Arngrímur; Kristnisaga; Landnámabók
Thorsteins saga Vikingssonar, Thorstens Viikings-Sons Saga, 1680
Thorstens Viikings-Sons Saga På Gammal Göthska: 1680, Thorsteins saga Vikingssonar
Three Considerations proposed to Mr. William Pen: 1688, Comber, Thomas
Three Letters Of Thanks, 1683
Three Letters Tending to demostrate [sic]...: 1688, Penn, William
Thursday Lecture, Boston
    1682, Mather, Increase, Heaven's Alarm
    1685, Mather, Increase, A Sermon (Preached at the Lecture in Boston)...
    1686, Mather, Increase, A Sermon Occasioned by the Execution...
    1694, Mather, Cotton, The Short History of New-England
Tickell, Dorothy: 1690, Some Testimonies Concerning the Life...
Timberley, Henry: 1678, Seer gedenckwaerdige Vojagien...
To All Kings, Princes, Rulers: 1685, Fox, George

To all who are Advertised by G. Keith...: 1699, Wyeth Joseph
To His Grace His Majesties High Commissioner...The humble Petition Of The Council-General: 1698, Company of Scotland Trading to Africa and the Indies
To His Grace His Majesty's High Commissioner...The humble Representation and Petition of the Council-General [16 May 1700]: 1700, Company of Scotland Trading to Africa and the Indies
To His Grace, His Majesty's High Commissioner...The humble Representation and Petition of the Council-General [28 October 1700], 1700
To my Loving and Dearly Beloved Christian Friends: 1689, Bailey, John
To our Reverend...Ministers, 1690
To The Honourable The Knights..., 1690
To The King's Most Excellent Majesty. The Humble Address of divers of the Gentry, 1691
To The Parliament Of England, 1681
To the Right Reverend, and Reverend the Bishops, 1690
A Token, for the Children of New-England: 1700, Mather, Cotton
Toland, John: 1698, Ludlow, Edmund
Toleration And Liberty Of Conscience Considered: 1685, Nalson, John
Tomo Primero De Las Ordenanzas Del Peru: 1685, Peru (Viceroyalty)--Laws, statutes, etc.
Tompson, Benjamin
    New-Englands Tears, 1676
    1677, Hubbard, William, A Narrative Of The Troubles... (2 variants); Hubbard, William, The Present State Of New-England (2 variants)
Tompson, Thomas. See Thompson, Thomas
Tongeren, Barent van: 1679, Spiegel Voor de Stad van Embden
Tonti, Henri de
    1697, Dernieres Decouvertes Dans L'Amerique Septentrionale
    1698, An Account Of Monsieur de la Salle's Last Expedition
Topcliffe, Lancaster: 1699, Beckham, Edward
Toribio Alfonso Mogrovejo, Saint: 1684, Lima (Ecclesiastical province)
Torres, Ignacio de, Séláh Mystico, 1696
Torres, Tomás de: 1691, Copia De Vna Carta, que escrivió vn Piloto del Patache...
Torres Cano, Juan de, Sermon A La Pvblicacion..., 1695
Torrey, Samuel
    A Plea For the Life..., 1683
    1679, Adams, William
De Tovery Zonder Tovery: 1696, Meekeren, Johan van
Townsend, Theophila, An Epistle of Love, 1680
Tractaet Van De Vreede: 1697, France--Treaties, etc., 1643-1715 (Louis XIV) 20 Sept. 1697
Tractatvs Novi De Potv Caphé: 1685, Dufour, Philippe Sylvestre
Tractatus Pacis, Bonæ Correspondentiæ: 1686, Gt. Brit.--Treaties, etc., 1685-1688 (James II)
Trade's Release, 1699

[479]

Index

Traité De Neutralité, Conclv A Londres
    1687, France--Treaties, etc., 1643-1715 (Louis XIV)
    1689, France--Treaties, etc., 1643-1715 (Louis XIV)
Traité De Paix Entre La France Et La Savoye: 1697, France--Treaties, etc., 1643-1715 (Louis XIV) 29 Aug. 1696
Traité De Paix Entre La France Et L'Angleterre: 1697, France--Treaties, etc., 1643-1715 (Louis XIV) 20 Sept. 1697
Traité De Paix Entre La France Et L'Espagne: 1697, France--Treaties, etc., 1643-1715 (Louis XIV) 20 Sept. 1697
Traité De Paix Entre L'Empereur, La France...: 1697, Holy Roman Empire--Treaties, etc., 1658-1705 (Leopold I)
Traité De Suspension D'Armes En Italie: 1697, France--Treaties, etc., 1643-1715 (Louis XIV) 7 Oct. 1696
Traitez De Paix Et De Commerce, Navigation Et Marine: 1697, France--Treaties, etc., 1643-1715 (Louis XIV) 21 Sept. 1697
Traktaat van Vrede, 1697
Trapham, Thomas, A Discourse Of The State of Health..., 1679
Traslado De Vna Consvlta, 1687
Treat, Robert. See Connecticut (Colony)--Governor, 1689-1698 (Robert Treat)
Treat, Samuel: 1699, Congregational Churches in Massachusetts--Boston Synod
A Treatise Of Oaths: 1675, Penn, William
A Treatise Touching the East-Indian-Trade: 1695, Charpentier, François
Treaty Of Peace, Good Correspondence...: 1686, Gt.Brit.--Treaties, etc., 1685-1688 (James II)
Trejo, Antonio de, Oracion Evangelica, 1699
Trepidantium Malleus. See Young, Samuel
Trinidad, Nicolás de la. See Nicolás de la Trinidad
A Trip To Jamaica: 1700, Ward, Edward
A Trip To New-England: 1699, Ward, Edward
The Triumph of Mercy in the Chariot of Praise: 1677, Lee, Samuel
The Triumphs Of Justice, 1681
Trott, Perient, A True Relation of the just and unjust Proceedings..., 1676
Trott, Samuel: 1694, Bulkley, Thomas
A True Account Of the Most Considerable Occurrences, 1676
A True Account Of The Tryals, Examinations..., 1693
The True Christians Distinguished: 1689, Fox, George
The True Countess of Banbury's Case: 1696, Price, Elizabeth
A true Description Of Carolina, 1682
A True Relation of the just and unjust Proceedings of the Somer-Islands-Company: 1676, Trott, Perient
A True Relation Of the late Action, 1677
The Truest and Largest Account Of The Late Earthquake, 1693
Truths Defence: Or, the Pretended Examination...: 1682, Keith, George
The Tryals Of Peter Boss...: 1693, Keith, George

Tryon, Thomas
    The Country-Man's Companion, 1684
    A Dialogue, 1683
    Friendly Advice, 1684
    Some General Considerations Offered, 1698
Turkey--Treaties, etc.
    1685, Gt.Brit.--Treaties, etc., 1660-1685 (Charles II)
    1686, Gt.Brit.--Treaties, etc., 1660-1685 (Charles II)
Turner, Robert: 1685, Penn, William, A Further Account Of the Province of Pennsylvania (2 variants)
Turner, William, A Compleat History Of the Most Remarkable Providences, 1697
Tuthill, Zechariah: 1700, Gospel Order Revived; The Printers Advertisement
The Twelfth and Last Collection of Papers (Vol.1.) Relating to the Present Juncture of Affairs in England, 1689
The Two Great Questions Consider'd: 1700, Defoe, Daniel
Two Several Addresses From The House of Peers: 1690, Gt.Brit.--Parliament, 1690-1691--House of Lords
Two Treatises Of Government: 1698, Locke, John
Tyso, John
    1676, Groome, Samuel
    1683, Estlacke, Francis

Ulloa, Alfonso de
    1676, Colón, Fernando
    1678, Colón, Fernando
    1685, Colón, Fernando
Vltimas Noticias Del Svr. Y Felizes operaciones: 1688, López, Francisco
Vltimo Recvrso De La Provincia De San Joseph De Yucathan: 1695, Ayeta, Francisco de
The Undoubted Art Of Thriving: 1700, Donaldson, James
Unerhörter Christen-Verkauff, 1687
Unto His Grace William Duke of Hamilton...: 1690, Episcopal Church in Scotland
Urbanus VIII, Pope. See Catholic Church--Pope, 1623-1644 (Urbanus VIII)
Ursachen und Gründe...: 1698, Philadelphian Society

V. D. B. See Bos, Lambert van den
The Vain Prodigal Life, 1680
Vairasse, Denis, Historie Der Sevarambes, 1682
Valckenier, Pieter: 1688, Muller, Andreas, secretarius
Valcroissant, de: 1681, Rochefort, Charles de, Histoire Naturelle
Valdés, Rodrigo de, Poema Heroyco, 1687
Valente, Christovaõ: 1686, Araujo, Antonio de
Valentijn, François
    1696, Mather, Increase, Ein Brieff von dem Glücklichen Fortgang...
    1699, Mather, Increase, De Successu Evangelii
Valladolid, Juan Francisco de
    Compendio Della Vita..., 1681

1680, Nicoselli, Anastasio
Vallados, Matheo: 1691, Juana Inés de la Cruz, sister, Villancicos, Con Que Se Solemnizaron...
Valle, Gonzalo de
   Espejo De Varios Colores, 1676
   Palestra De Varios Sermones, 1676
Valle, José: 1690, Octava Maravilla
Valle, Pietro della: 1696, Thévenot, Melchisédech, Relations, 1.ptie.
Vanderwerf, John Roeloffs. See Werf, John Roeloffs vander
Vane, Sir Henry: 1699, Stubbs, Henry, 1632-1676
Vansleb, Johann Michael. See Wansleben, Johann Michael
Varen, Bernhard
   1682, Blome, Richard
   1696, Thévenot, Melchisédech, Relations, 2.ptie.
Varén de Soto, Basilio: 1699, Mariana, Juan de
Vargas Machuca, Francisco de
   Medicos Discvrsos, Y Practica De Cvrar El Sarampion, 1694
   Oracion Panegyrica Al Glorioso Apostol S Bartholome, 1694
Varona y Loaiza, Gerónimo: 1683, Montalvo, Francisco Antonio de, Vida Admirable...
Vasconsellos, Tomás: 1700, Palafox y Mendoza, Juan de, Bp.
Vásquez de Medina, Juan: 1690, Aranda Sidrón, Bartolomé de
Vázquez Gaztelu, Antonio, Arte De Lengva Mexicana, 1689; 1693
Veedor, José: 1685, Franciscans
Vega, José de la, Oracion Espiritual A Sor Maria Francisca, 1691
Veiras, Denis. See Vairasse, Denis
Velasco, Alfonso Alberto de, Exaltacion De La Divina Misericordia, 1699
Velasco, Tomás de, Breviloqvio Moral Practico, 1681
Vélez de Guevara, Juan, Octavas A La Aparicion..., 1679
Venezuela (Diocese)--Synod, 1687, Constituciones Synodales, 1698
Veragua, Pedro Manuel Colón de Portugal, duque de. See Colón de Portugal, Pedro Manuel, duque de Veragua
Verart, Raimundo. See Berart, Raimundo
Verbiest, Ferdinand
   Voyages De L'Empereur, 1685
   1686, A Relation Of The Invasion...
   1696, Thévenot, Melchisédech, Relations, 5.ptie.
Verdadera Relacion, Y Cvrioso Romance..., 1698
Verdussen, Jérôme: 1681, Sandoval, Prudencio de, Bp. of Pamplona
Verelius, Olof: 1680, Thorsteins saga Vikingssonar
Vergara, Miguel de: 1691, Palafox y Mendoza, Juan de, Bp.
Vertoog Aan Den Baron de Kinski: 1680, Isaaksz, Herman, Quaker
Een Vertoogh van de considerabele Colonie: 1676, Netherlands (United Provinces, 1581-1795)--Staten Generaal

Vervolg Van 't Verwerd Europa: 1688, Muller, Andreas, secretarius
Verwey, J.: 1699, Zanten, Laurens van
Vetancurt, Agustín de
   Chronica De La Provincia Del Santo Evangelio De Mexico. Quarta parte del Teatro Mexicano, 1697
   Oracion Funebre A Las Honras..., 1697
   Teatro Mexicano, 1698
   1697, Muñoz de Castro, Pedro
Viaggio Del P. Giovanni Grveber: 1696, Thévenot, Melchisédech, Relations, 4.ptie.
Vickris, Richard: 1681, An Exalted Diotrephes Reprehended
Victoria, Pedro Gobeo de, Joannis Bisselii è Societate Jesu, Argonauticon Americanorum, 1698
Victoria Salazar, Diego de
   Sermon De La Gloriosa Virgen, 1682
   1690, Octava Maravilla
Vida Admirable, Y Mverte dichosa...: 1689, Florencia, Francisco de
Vidal Figueroa, José
   Memorias Tiernas, 1695
   Vida Exemplar..., 1682
   1691, Ramírez de Vargas, Alonso
   1696, Miranda, Juan José de
   1697, Esquerra, Matías de
Vídálin, Arngrímur Jónsson. See Jónsson, Arngrímur
La Vie De La Venerable Mere Marie De L'Incarnation
   1677, Martin, Claude
   1696, Martin, Claude
La Vie De Saint Martin Evêque De Tours: 1699, Gervaise, Nicolas
La Vie De Sainte Rose De Ste Marie: 1684, Lucchesini, Giovanni Lorenzo
Vieira, Antonio
   Maria Rosa Mystica...I. Parte, 1686
   Maria Rosa Mystica...II. Parte, 1688
   Palavra De Deos Empenhada, 1690
   Qvinta Parte De Sermones, 1683
   Sermoens...Primeyra Parte, 1679
   Sermoens...Segvnda Parte, 1682
   Sermoens...Terceira Parte, 1683
   Sermoens...Quarta Parte, 1685
   Sermoens...Qvinta Parte, 1689
   Sermoens...Sexta Parte, 1690
   Sermoens...Septima Parte, 1692
   Sermoens...Undecima Parte, 1696
   Sermoens...Parte Duodecima, 1699
   Xavier Dormindo, E. Xavier Acordada...Oitava Parte, 1694
Villalobos, Juan de, Manifiesto Que A Sv Magestad..., 1682
Villancicos A Los Maytines..., 1687
Villancicos, Que se cantaron en la Santa Iglesia Metropolitana...: 1685, Ramírez de Vargas, Alonso
Villanueva, Bernardo de: 1700, Sigüenza y Góngora, Carlos de
Villavicencio, Diego Jaime Ricardo, Luz, Methodo, De Confesar Idolatras 1692
Villegas, Manuel Juan, Informe Ivridico, 1682

Villiers, George, 2d duke of Buckingham: See Buckingham, George Villiers, 2d duke of
A Vindication of Nevv-England, 1690
A Vindication Of The Naked Truth. The Second Part: 1681, Hickeringill, Edmund
A Vindication of William Penn: 1683, Ford, Philip
Virginia (Colony)--Laws, statutes, etc., A Complete Collection, 1684
A Vision Concerning The Mischievous Seperation [sic] ...: 1692, Fox, George
Visscher, Nicolaes, Atlas Minor, 1690
Vitoria, Pedro Gobeo de. See Victoria, Pedro Gobeo de
Vittorio Amedeo I, King of Sardinia: 1697, France--Sovereigns, etc., 1643-1715 (Louis XIV); France--Treaties, etc., 1643-1715 (Louis XIV) 7 Oct. 1696
Vizé, Jean Donneau de. See Donneau de Vizé, Jean
Vollenhove, Joannes: 1687, Brandt, Geeraert, Het Leven En Bedryf...
Vossius, Isaac
    Observationum Ad Pomp. Melam Appendix, 1686; 1700
    1700, Mela, Pomponius
Votes of the House of Commons. See Gt. Brit.--Parliament--House of Commons
Voyage A La Chine: 1696, Thévenot, Melchisédech, Relations, 4.ptie.
Voyage De La Terre Australe: 1695, Foigny, Gabriel de
Voyage Des Ambassadevrs De La Compagnie Hollandoise des Indes Orientales: 1696, Thévenot, Melchisédech, Relations, 3.ptie.
The Voyages and Adventures Of Capt. Barth. Sharp: 1684, Ayres, Philip
Voyages And Discoveries In South-America, 1698
The Voyages & Travels Of that Renowned Captain, Sir Francis Drake, 1700
Voyages De L'Empereur De La Chine: 1685, Verbiest, Ferdinand
Voyages D'Un Francois: 1687, Durand, of Dauphiné
The Voyages Of The Ever Renowned Sr. Francis Drake, 1683
Vries, Gerard de: 1692, Luyts, Jan
Vries, Simon de
    Curieuse Aenmerckingen..., 1682
    Wonderen..., 1687
    1678, La Peyrère, Isaac de
    1679, La Peyrère, Isaac de
    1685, La Martinière, Pierre Martin de
De Vryheyt Vertoont in den Staat der Vereenige Nederlanden, 1697

W. B. See Berkeley, Sir William
W. B. See Bradford, William
W. C.: 1696, Mr. Keith No Presbyterian nor Quaker
W. D. See Dick, William
W. L. See Loddington, William
W. M. See Moyle, Walter

W. P. See Penn, William
W. P. See Pithin, William
W. P.: 1685, The Quakers Elegy
W. S. See Sewel, Willem
Wade, Robert: 1676, A Further Account Of New Jersey
Wafer, Lionel
    A New Voyage, 1699
    Nieuwe Reystogt, 1700
    1699, A Short Account from, And Description Of The Isthmus Of Darien
Wagner, Johann Christoph
    Cometa Disparens, 1681
    Gründlicher und warhaffter Bericht..., 1681
Waldenfels, Christoph Philippus von, Selectæ Antiquitatis Libri XII, 1677
Walford, Benjamin: 1694, An Account Of Several Late Voyages & Discoveries
Waller, Richard: 1688, Picard, Jean
Waller, William, An Essay On The Value of the Mines, 1698
Walter, Nehemiah: 1698, Mather, Cotton, Present from a farr Countrey
Wansleben, Johann Michael: 1681, Melton, Edward
Ward, Edward
    A Trip To Jamaica, 1700
    A Trip To New-England, 1699
Ward, Nathaniel: 1678, Bradstreet, Anne (Dudley)
Ware, Robert
    The Second Part Of Foxes And Fire-brands, 1682 (2 variants)
    1682, Nalson, John, Foxes And Fire-brands (2 variants)
A Warning to the Flocks: 1700, Mather, Cotton
The Warr In New-England Visibly ended: 1677, Hutchinson, Richard
Watson, John: 1691, Burnyeat, John
Webb, Robert: 1686, Nader Informatie en Bericht
VVeekly Memorials For The Ingenious, 1682; 1683
Weigel, Christoph, Biblia Ectypa Minora, 1696
Weld, Thomas: 1692, Winthrop, John
Werf, John Roeloffs vander: 1679, Spiegel Voor de Stad van Embden
Werndle, Johann Georg von: 1676, Córdoba y Salinas, Diego de
Westminster Assembly of Divines, The Shorter Catechism, 1683
Wetenhall, Edward, Bp. of Kilmore and Ardagh: 1698, Penn, William, A Defence Of a Paper
Wharton, Edward, New-England's Present Sufferings, 1675
Wharton, Henry: 1688, Dellon, Gabriel, The History Of The Inquisition
Wharton, Richard: 1676, The Grand Pyrate
Wheeler, Thomas, A Thankefull Remembrance Of Gods Mercy, 1676
Whicker, John: 1689, Pitman, Henry
Whitehead, George
    The Accuser of our Brethren, 1681
    An Antidote Against The Venome Of The Snake in the Grass, 1697

Index

The Quakers Vindication, 1694
1675, Thompson, Thomas, The Second Part Of The Quakers Quibbles; Thompson, Thomas, The Third Part Of The Quakers Quibbles
1696, Penington, John
1698, Fox, George, A Collection Of Many Select and Christian Epistles
1699, Wyeth, Joseph, Anguis Flagellatus
1700, Atkinson, Christopher
Whitehead, John: 1679, Stephenson, Marmaduke
The Whole Body Of Antient and Modern Architecture: 1680, Fréart de Chambray, Roland
The Whole Book of Psalms; Collected into English Metre By Thomas Sternhold: 1677, Bible--O.T.--Psalms--English--Paraphrases
Wilhelmi, Johannes Gerlach: 1682, Mentzel, Christian
Wilkinson, William, commander of ship "Henry and William", Systema Africanum, 1690
Wilkinson, William, of Bermudas: 1683, Estlacke, Francis
Willard, Samuel
    The Character Of a Good Ruler, 1694
    The Doctrine Of The Covenant Of Redemption, 1693
    The Fountain Opened, 1700
    The Man of War, 1699
    Mercy Magnified, 1684
    The Mourners Cordial, 1691
    Ne Sutor ultra Crepidam, 1681
    The Peril Of The Times Displayed, 1700
    The Truly Blessed Man, 1700
    1686, Higginson, John
    1690, Mather, Cotton, The Principles of the Protestant Religion Maintained
    1691, Mather, Cotton, Late Memorable Providences
    1697, Mather, Cotton, Memorable Providences
William III, King of Gt.Brit. See Gt.Brit.--Laws, statutes, etc., 1694-1702 (William III); Gt.Brit.--Sovereigns, etc., 1689-1694 (William and Mary); Gt.Brit.--Sovereigns, etc., 1694-1702 (William III); Gt.Brit.--Treaties, etc., 1689-1694 (William and Mary); Gt.Brit.--Treaties, etc., 1694-1702 (William III); Scotland--Laws, statutes, etc., 1694-1702 (William III)
William, Paul: 1680, The Vain Prodigal Life...
William Penn And the Quakers
    1696, Young, Samuel
    1697, Young, Samuel
Williams, John, Bp. of Chichester
    A Brief Discourse Concerning the Lawfulness of Worshipping God, 1696
    The Case of Lay-Communion, 1683
Williams, Roger, George Fox Digg'd out of his Burrovves, 1676
Williams, Roger, mariner, To the King's Most Excellent Majesty, 1681
Willsford, John, A General Testimony..., 1677
Wilmer, John, The Case Of John Wilmore, 1682
Wilsford, John. See Willsford, John
Wilson, John, A Seasonable VVatch-VVord, 1677

Wilson, Samuel
    An Account Of The Province..., 1682
    1684, Carolina Described more fully then [sic] heretofore
Winthrop, John, A Short Story..., 1692
Wolley, Richard: 1692, The Compleat Library...August, 1692; The Compleat Library: Vol.II...December, 1692
Wood, Capt. John
    1694, An Account Of Several Late Voyages & Discoveries
    1699, Hack, William
Woodbridge, Benjamin: 1678, Bradstreet, Anne (Dudley)
Woodbridge, John: 1678, Bradstreet, Anne (Dudley)
Woodbridge, Timothy: 1700, Gospel Order Revived
Woolley, Richard. See Wolley, Richard
A Word to the Well-Inclin'd: 1698, Story, Thomas
VVusku Wuttestamentum...: 1685, Bible--N.T.--Massachuset--Eliot
Wyche, Sir Peter: 1684, Recueil De Divers Voyages
Wyeth, Joseph
    Anguis Flagellatus, 1699
    An Answer To A Letter, 1700
    To all who are Advertised by G. Keith..., 1699

Xaimes de Ribera, Juan
    Hazer De Si Mismo Espejo Sermon, 1689; Sermon, 1680
Xarque, Francisco, Insignes Missioneros, 1687
Xenophon, A Discourse Upon Improving The Revenue, 1697
Ximénez, Francisco: 1679, Escalante, Thomas
Ximénez Pantoja, Thomas
    Por Don Diego Rodillo De Arce, 1700
    Protesta A Favor De Sv Magestad, 1692

Yangues, Manuel de
    Principios, Y Reglas..., 1683
    1690, Ruiz Blanco, Matías
Ybáñez de Faria, Diego, D. D. Didacus Covarruvias A Leiva, 1688
Yo Pedro de Arce y Andrade..., 1689
Young, Samuel
    An Apology For Congregational Divines, 1698
    A Censure Of Mr. Judas Tull His Lampoon, 1700
    A Confirmation of a late Epistle, 1700
    A Dialogue Between George Fox a Quaker, Geo. Keith..., 1700
    The Duckers Duck'd..., 1700
    The Foxonian Quakers, 1697
    A Friendly Epistle To The Reverend Clergy, 1700
    A Reprimand For The Author of a Libel, 1697
    A Second Friendly Epistle To Mr. George Keith, 1700
    A Sober Reply To A Serious Enquiry, 1700
    William Penn And the Quakers, 1696; 1697

Zamboni, Giovanni: 1680, Gudenfridi, Giovanni Batista
Zani, Valerio, conte, Il Genio Vagante, 1691
Zanten, Abraham van: 1699, Zanten, Laurens van
Zanten, Laurens van, Treur-Tooneel Der Doorluchtige Vrouwen, 1699
Zapata, Francisco Xavier: 1691, Sigüenza y Góngora, Carlos de

Zaragoza, Joseph
    Esphera En Comvn Celeste, 1675
    Fabrica, Y Vso... , 1675
Zárate, Agustín de, Histoire De La Decouverte Et De La Conquete Du Perou, 1700
Zeller, Johann Jakob: 1678, Amman, Johann Jacob
Zepeda, Pedro: 1690, Octava Maravilla
Zur-Eich, Hans Jacob. See Müller, Wilhelm Johann